D0181249

Greek Islands

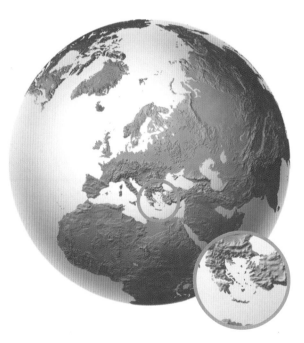

Korina Miller
Michael Stamatios Clark, Chris Deliso,
Des Hannigan, Victoria Kyriakopoulos

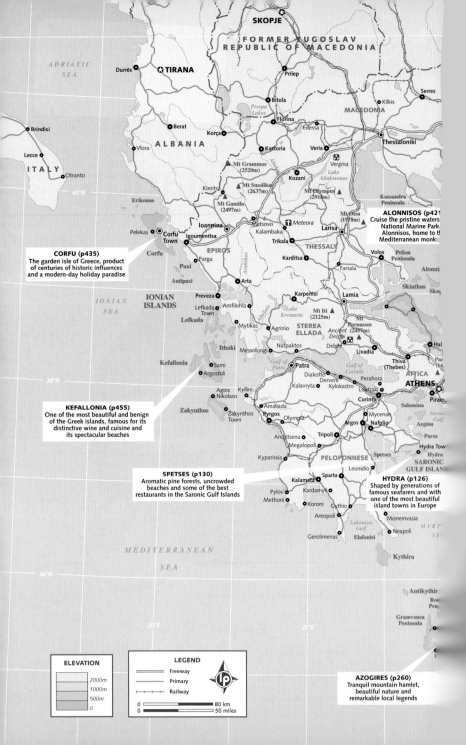

SKOPJE

FORMER YUGOSLAV
REPUBLIC OF MACEDONIA

ADRIATIC
SEA

Durrës ○ TIRANA
Prilep ○

Serres ○

Bitola ○
Kilkis ○

Prespa
Lakes
MACEDONIA

Florina ○
Thessaloniki ○

Berat ○
Edessa ○

Korça ○
Veria ○

ALBANIA

Vlora ○
Kastoria ○
Vergina

Brindisi ○
Lecce ○
Mt Grammos
(2520m) ▲
Kozani ○

ITALY
Otranto ○
Konitsa ○
Mt Smolikas
(2637m) ▲
Mt Olympus
(2918m) ▲

40°N
Erikousa
Mt Gamila
(2497m) ▲
Kassandra
Peninsula

Pelekas ○ Corfu
Town ○
Ioannina ○
Metsovo ○
Meteora
Mt Ossa
(1978m) ▲

ALONNISOS (p421)
Cruise the pristine waters
National Marine Park
Alonnisos, home to th
Mediterranean monk

Igoumenitsa ○
Kalambaka ○
Larisa ○

Corfu
EPIROS
Trikala ○
THESSALY

CORFU (p435)
The garden isle of Greece, product
of centuries of historic influences
and a modern-day holiday paradise
Paxi ○
Parga ○
Karditsa ○
Volos ○
Pelion
Peninsula

Antipaxi ○
Farsala ○
Alonni

IONIAN
SEA
IONIAN
ISLANDS
Preveza ○
Arta ○
Karpenisi ○
Lamia ○
Skiathos
Sko

Lefkada
Town ○
Amfilohia ○
Lake
Kremasta
Mt Iti ▲
(2125m)

Lefkada
Mytikas ○
Agrinio ○
STEREA
ELLADA
Mt
Parnassos
(2457m) ▲
Hal

Ithaki
Messolongi ○
Nafpaktos ○
Ancient
Delphi
Delphi ○
Thiva
(Thebes) ○
AR

Kefallonia ○ Sami
Gulf of
Patra
Patra ○
Gulf of
Corinth
Livadia ○
ATTIC
ATHENS ○

○ Argostoli
Diakofto ○
Derveni ○
Perahora ○
Piraeu

38°N
Agios
Nikolaos ○
Kyllini ○
Kalavryta ○
Xylokastro ○
Loutraki ○
Salamina
Saro
Gulf

Zakynthos
Amaliada ○
Corinth ○
Aegina

KEFALLONIA (p455)
One of the most beautiful and benign
of the Greek islands, famous for its
distinctive wine and cuisine and
its spectacular beaches
Zakynthos
Town ○
Pyrgos ○
Olympia ○
Mycenae
Nafplio ○
Poros

Andritsena ○
Argos ○
Hydra Tow ○
Hydra
SARONIC
GULF ISLAN

Megalopoli ○
Tripoli ○
Spetses
PELOPONNESE
Leonidio ○

Kyparissia ○

SPETSES (p130)
Aromatic pine forests, uncrowded
beaches and some of the best
restaurants in the Saronic Gulf Islands
Kalamata ○
Sparta ○

HYDRA (p126)
Shaped by generations of
famous seafarers and with
one of the most beautiful
island towns in Europe

Pylos ○
Kardamyli ○
Methoni ○
Koroni ○
Gythio ○
Monemvasia ○

Areopoli ○
Neapoli ○
MYRT
SE

Lakonian
Gulf
Gerolimenas ○
Elafonisi ○

MEDITERRANEAN
SEA
Kythira ○

36°N

Antikythir
Ro
Pen

Gramvousa
Peninsula ○

20°E
22°E

AZOGIRES (p260)
Tranquil mountain hamlet,
beautiful nature and
remarkable local legends

ELEVATION
2000m
1000m
500m
0

LEGEND
━━━ Freeway
━━━ Primary
┣━┫ Railway

0 ___ 80 km
0 ___ 50 miles

CHIOS (p366)
Intriguing architecture, hospitable locals and great eco-adventures

IKARIA (p349)
Laid-back with some of the Aegean's best beaches, plus vivacious traditional festivals

MYKONOS (p148)
Cycladic style, fashion and fun make for an irresistible mix in the dazzling light of the Aegean

KOS (p317)
The beaches you've been dreaming of – endless, sun-kissed and lapped by azure waters

NISYROS (p313)
A path descends into the volcanic crater, where the earth bubbles and steams around you

SANTORINI (p189)
World-famous destination where a sophisticated life-style and Greek culture merge with spectacular landscapes

KARPATHOS (p294)
Olympos clings to the mountain's edge and is home to an utterly unique culture that dates back to the Doric age

KNOSSOS (p231)
Restored Minoan palace that attests to one of antiquity's greatest civilisations

On the Road

KORINA MILLER
Coordinating Author

Not surprisingly, I discover it's rather windy next to this mill set in the sea. But from here I can see the sun setting on the beautiful, colourful buildings of Agia Marina (p333), with the castle perched high on the hill above. And thankfully, I'm only a few precarious steps away from one of Leros' most atmospheric restaurants, where I can dine on fresh fish next to the lapping waves.

MICHAEL STAMATIOS CLARK

Walking and biking is the only way to go in Skopelos Town (see p417), especially around the harbour. And I never worried about leaving the bike unlocked. Besides, who had a lock? No kickstand, either – just lean it against the nearest waterfront wall, and it was always there – island living at its best.

CHRIS DELISO They seldom come more iconic than Georgios the elder. With a long beard and an unbreakable olive-wood cane, this black-clad elder descended on me in Rethymno's bus station, bearing 700 years of Cretan history and an ever so slight whiff of Crete's famous firewater, *raki*. Fifteen minutes later the history lesson was over and the other waiting tourists, like all of Crete's would-be past invaders, had left the scene.

DES HANNIGAN Always find time for an acropolis; but not just your common or garden Athenian pile of old rocks. This is the Mycenaean acropolis of Koukounaries (p164) near Naousa, on Paros. Unbeatable viewpoint, enough old stones to stir the imagination, and rarely anyone else there. Don't all rush.

VICTORIA KYRIAKOPOULOS Where did you say that bar was? Getting the low-down on new bars, restaurants and the latest hotspots in Athens (p87) is serious business involving serious research and leg work. Walking around exploring Athens is always full of surprises and rewards, with new places to discover all the time.

For full author biographies see p539.

Greek Islands Highlights

With so many gorgeous islands scattered throughout a dazzling blue sea, you may feel like a kid in a candy shop – unable to choose which ones to try. Fortunately, we've done the legwork for you, having island hopped our way throughout the region in search of its ultimate offerings. Here are our authors' top finds. Share yours at lonelyplanet.com/greece.

JOHN ELK I

1 CORFU TOWN

The story of Corfu Town (p437) is written across the handsome facades of its buildings. This is a place of human scale, yet a place that crams into its small compass a remarkable lexicon of international architecture. A stroll through this most engaging of Greek towns takes you from decaying Byzantine fortresses to the neoclassical palaces of the 19th-century British Protectorate, to Parisian-style arcades, Orthodox church towers and the narrow, sun-dappled canyons of the Venetian Old Town; all of it the legacy of the Mediterranean's tumultuous history.

Des Hannigan

HYDRA HEIGHTS

Hydra (p126) is the diva of the Saronic Gulf Islands. Its beautiful harbour town is a mix of elegant buildings and historic attractions, overlaid by a seductive veneer of fashion and celebrity, all of which draw devotees in their thousands. However, beyond the madding, and sometimes maddening crowds, the only way is up, steeply at times, onto the island's high ground to the venerable monasteries of Moni Profitis Ilias and Moni Agias Efpraxias (see p129). Keep going and you'll find the remote, serene Hydra that locals inherit each winter.

Des Hannigan

2

3 ANAFI

The island of Anafi (p200) lies a mere 15km to the east of glitzy Santorini (Thira). It's only an hour away, if you get the ferry schedules right and if the island has not moved overnight. So ephemeral does it look through the Aegean haze. This is nostalgic Greece, certainly, and a popular tourist island in summer; but Anafi, with its rugged landscape and authentic local life and culture, holds on to its integrity and is very still and very quiet, more often than not.

Des Hannigan

4 LESVOS

Massive Lesvos (Mytilini; p378) is tremendously varied. Rolling olive groves and cool pine forests in the hilly east and centre become arid plains in the west, which is where also stands one of the world's few petrified forests (see p386) to be found outside the USA. The coasts are ringed by beaches – many hardly touched by tourism. Lesvos' capital, lively Mytilini Town (p380), is energised by a large student population, as attested by its busy cafes and bars. Fine local ouzo and wine, magisterial Byzantine churches, and the odd medieval castle town seal the deal.

Chris Deliso

FOURNI ISLANDS

For long sunsets and some of the Aegean's best seafood, head to the untroubled isles of Fourni (p356) – a former pirate's lair nestled between Ikaria and Samos. This tranquil, escapist archipelago has few cars, and fewer cares. Rest anywhere from a remote beach tent to romantic luxury digs in the islands' pretty fishing-port capital, Fourni Korseon.

Chris Deliso

PREVELI BEACH, CRETE

Bisected by a river spilling from a gorge into the sea, and flanked by cliffs and a sublime monastery, Preveli Beach (p242) is one of Greece's most celebrated stretches of sand. It's well worth the ten-minute walk downhill to luxuriate in Preveli's warm southcoast waters and soak up the sun.

Chris Deliso

MAGARACA | DREAMSTIME.CO

7 SPINALONGA ISLAND, CRETE

Set dramatically on its own, long-uninhabited island in the northeast of Crete, the former Venetian castle of Spinalonga (p268) has a remarkable number of legends concealed in its warrens of ruined chambers, tunnel passages and steep ramparts overlooking the sea. This singular place held out for decades against the Turks, even after the rest of Crete had fallen, and in the 20th century became Europe's last leper colony for a time. More of Spinalonga's fascinating history is revealed when you explore its hidden corners, candlelit churches, cisterns and watchtowers. In summer, cheap excursion boats from Agios Nikolaos, Elounda and Plaka visit Spinalonga regularly.

Chris Deliso

CATRIONA BASS / ALAM

8 NATIONAL MARINE PARK OF ALONNISOS

Greece is home to one of the Mediterranean's national marine parks (p423), whose crystal blue waters – considered the most pristine in Greece – offer sanctuary to the endangered Mediterranean monk seal. Small excursion boats explore the marine park and drop anchor at several inviting harbours around Alonnisos and several islets to the northeast.

Michael Stamatios Clark

SKYROS – POTTER'S PARADISE

Skyros (p426) is home to a vibrant artistic community, and island ceramics are among the most handsome in Greece, dating back to the days when passing pirates traded pottery and other pilfered treasures for local goods. The arrangement caught on and eventually Skyrians began their own pottery tradition. Skyros Town, Magazia, and Atsitsa have open studios where visitors can check out this legacy of larceny (see p430).

Michael Stamatios Clark

MICHAEL STAMATIOS CLARK

RHODES

After losing yourself within the medieval walls of Rhodes Old Town (p280), hop in a car and venture out across the island. The south coast has well-discovered sandy beaches while the north is wild, windswept and dotted with crumbling castles that offer some of the best sunset views in the Aegean. You'll likely have the ruins to yourself, with the waves crashing far below. Magical.

Korina Miller

GEORGE TSAFOS

11 PATMOS

Visiting the atmospheric Monastery of St John the Theologian (p341) is an awe-inspiring experience. Crowning Patmos' Old Town and protected by giant heavy walls, the inside is filled with wafting incense, chanting priests and elaborate decor. Few sights capture the spirit of a place so well. On Patmos, artists and the spiritually inclined linger and a sense of peace flows free.

Korina Miller

12 LEROS

Arriving in Agia Marina shows little Leros (p333) in its best light. Colourful 19th-century buildings line the lively harbour where locals linger over coffee and fishing boats bob in the sea. Leros is a friendly, slow-paced kind of place with cool restaurants, unusual sights and a small but spirited nightlife. Getting there is easy. Leaving is not.

Korina Miller

Contents

Regional Map Contents

Northeastern
Aegean Islands
p348

Athens & the
Mainland Ports
p78

Ionian
Islands
p434

Evia &
the Sporades
p406

Saronic Gulf
Islands
p118

Dodecanese
p275

Cyclades
p135

Crete
pp220–1

Destination Greek Islands

Whether you've seen them in the movies, read about them in a travel magazine or simply heard a friend gush on about them after returning from holiday, the Greek islands are likely to have flirted with your imagination. On this archipelago of over 1400 islands and islets, you'll soon discover that the islands don't disappoint. It's here that the days melt from one to the next, filled with big blue skies and endless miles of aquamarine coastline with some of Europe's cleanest beaches. Soak up the majestic beauty of Santorini or head for the pulsing nightlife of Mykonos or the adrenaline-rushing possibilities of many of the islands' mountainous interiors. Wander through lush wildflowers in spring or laze on isolated sandy coves in summer with the warm sea lapping at your feet.

Island life gets under your skin. You'll quickly become acquainted with the melancholy throb of *rembetika* (Greek blues songs), the tang of homemade tzatziki, and the ability of the historic locations to kindle equal doses of awe and recognition. Many travellers simply settle down and never go home.

While ancient sites might take the limelight in many tourist itineraries, the Greeks certainly aren't stuck in the past. Sure, it's easy to find remote, traditional villages with brilliant white buildings and roaming donkeys and goats, but the shepherd is likely to be talking on his mobile phone and making a date for the local, trendy cafe. Athens has a firm grip on style and a sophistication to rival any European capital; the Greek modern art scene is fresh and vibrant; and the political scene is passionate. It's a nation that welcomes, and even insists upon, change – as seen from the internet cafes found on the smallest islands to modern, impressive museums popping up around the nation. There are few cultures that embrace the past so fondly while simultaneously welcoming the future with open arms.

Like everywhere, it's not always smooth sailing in Greece. And while the islands may feel like a long way from Athens, national controversies and events find their way to the otherwise languid isles. Like elsewhere throughout Greece, issues are debated and handled with strong will, as is evident in the heated conversations at the local *kafeneio* (coffee house). The past three decades of increased wealth and improved living standards have gone hand and hand with rising unemployment, growing public debt and a credit crunch that's left many Greeks disillusioned and angry. The government's proposals of reforms in pensions and labour, plans for privatisation and alleged corruption have recently incited many Greeks to take to the street in massive strikes and protests. On many of the islands these problems are exacerbated by foreign investment that hikes up property prices, fragmented infrastructures, a lack of water resources and seasonal isolation.

Since the early '70s, battles between youth and the police have been a mainstay of Greek society, as students protest against authoritarianism. Increases in youth unemployment and downward mobility have added fuel to the youth movement. In December 2008 a 15-year-old boy was shot by the Athenian police in the student neighbourhood of Exarhia in Athens after an alleged exchange between youths and police. News of the shooting quickly spread (largely via texting, Facebook and Twitter) and hundreds of youths took to the streets in a social uprising that spread to Crete, Samos and Corfu and lasted for days, putting considerable political pressure upon the government.

FAST FACTS

Population: 11,260,000

Percentage of women: 50%

Life expectancy: 80 years

Inhabitants per square kilometre: 87

Tourists: 18.8 million annually

GDP: US$345 billion

Per capita income: US$32,005

Inflation: 1.57%

Unemployment: 9.3%

External debt: US$92.19 billion

The colossal bushfires of 2007 had little impact on the islands, but sparked greater distrust in the government and authorities for the way in which they were (or weren't) dealt with. Greeks are, in general, becoming increasingly aware of environmental degradation, with calls for bans on sprawling development and more opportunities to recycle. Climate change, diminished water supplies and the rising of sea levels are very real concerns to islanders and today you'll find student groups, environmental charities and locals teamed up with expats working to protect the environment. But the debate is often tangled in the mixed interests of locals versus developers or backdoor deals with local government.

On a more global front, many of the islands have become truly multicultural in recent years and the pros and cons of this are another hot topic of conversation. Once an emigrant country, with thousands of Greeks moving from the islands to North America and Australia, and later a popular refuge for expats, Greece now sees a huge influx of returning emigrants alongside new arrivals such as economic migrants and refugees from Afghanistan, Iraq and Africa who cross the border from Turkey. As islands like Samos struggle to house boatloads of migrants, there is mounting criticism from the international community on the poor conditions and treatment of refugees and immigrants in Greece. With the lowest acceptance rate in Europe for asylum requests (only 379 out of 20,000 were accepted in 2008), many illegal immigrants and refugees simply disappear into Greece's informal economy or attempt to cross into other European countries. Others linger on the islands in shanty towns and deportation centres.

All of this would have once been discussed in a haze of smoke at the local *kafeneio*, but in July 2009 Greece brought in antismoking laws similar to those across Europe, meaning all public places should be smoke-free. Greeks are some of the heaviest smokers in Europe and it will be interesting to see how well this law is enforced, particularly in the small villages, remote islands and party hubs. It seems likely that the majority will continue to rule.

Despite these passionate debates and controversy, the islands are essentially laid back. Lounge at the cafe over an endless coffee, stroll along the seafront, park yourself on the beach and take your time over meals and you'll fit right in. Greeks know how to enjoy life and are renowned as some of the most hospitable people on the globe. Their generosity and warmth is as genuine as the soft sand between your toes and the warmth of the Aegean sun.

Getting Started

It's easy to find what you're after on the Greek islands – whether that's one island to stay put on, a dozen to hop between, a plush retreat to check-in to or somewhere to pitch a tent. How much advance planning you need to do depends on how much time you have and where you're headed. If you're on a tight schedule and want to visit remote isles, some pre-planning is advisable. If you're simply after relaxation and adventure and aren't short of time, packing your bag and buying your plane ticket may be all the preparation necessary.

WHEN TO GO

Spring and autumn are the best times to visit the Greek islands, specifically May, June, September and October. Most of the islands' tourist infrastructures go into hibernation from the end of October until mid-April; in some places you'll be hard-pressed to find a hotel or restaurant open, while bus and ferry services are either drastically reduced or cancelled. Some of the smaller islands close completely as islanders head off to alternative homes on the mainland for a few months.

The cobwebs are dusted off in time for Orthodox Easter (usually around April; see p23), when the first tourists start to arrive. Conditions are perfect between Easter and mid-June: the weather is pleasantly warm in most places; beaches and ancient sites are relatively uncrowded; public transport operates at close to full schedules; and there's a bigger variety of accommodation options to choose from.

Mid-June to the end of August is high season, when everything is in full swing and the majority of festivals take place. Most beaches and sites are swarming and in some places, accommodation is booked solid. It's also very hot – in July and August the mercury can soar to 40°C (over 100°F) in the shade just about anywhere in the country. The high season starts to wind down in September and conditions are ideal once more until the end of October. By November the endless blue skies of summer have disappeared and it's wet and surprisingly cold with snow commonly falling in the mountains of Evia and Crete.

See Climate Charts (p479) for more information.

COSTS & MONEY

Prices have rocketed since the adoption of the euro in 2002 and, although they appear to be levelling off, the Greek islands are no longer the cheap destination they once were. While tiny hole-in-the-wall restaurants continue to deliver hearty meals for low prices, eating out anywhere more upmarket has become a pricey venture. Accommodation has also sky rocketed, making many of the budget options not really worth the price and many midrange options appearing much more appealing for only a few extra euros.

A rock-bottom daily budget for a solo traveller is about €50. This would mean buses, staying in youth hostels or camping, and only occasionally eating in restaurants or taking ferries. Allow €100 per day if you want your own room and plan to eat out, travel about and see the sights. If you're after comfortable rooms and restaurants all the way, you will need closer to €150 per day. These budgets are for individuals travelling in the high season (July/August). Couples sharing a room can get by on less.

Your money will go much further if you travel during the quieter months of May to June and September to October when accommodation is a lot cheaper. You will also be able to negotiate better deals if you stay a few

HOW MUCH?

Local telephone call €0.30 per minute

Minimum taxi fare €4

Single Greek coffee €2

City bus ticket €1

Greek salad €6

days. Families can achieve considerable savings by looking for self-catering apartments and shopping for food at supermarkets and local produce markets. Travelling by boat can also save money as children under five board for free and you can save a night's accommodation.

Prices quoted throughout this book are for the high season of mid-June to late August.

TRAVELLING RESPONSIBLY

As with many popular European destinations, the Greek islands' environment is pushed to the limit each year by the massive influx of tourists. While the bigger picture can seem rather overwhelming to an individual tourist (see p70), there are a number of things you can do that can help lessen your impact without compromising your holiday.

The first thing to consider is how you will travel to Greece. While short vacations don't always offer the luxury of avoiding the carbon footprints involved in flying, reaching Greece from the rest of Europe by train and/or boat is a viable option for those with a little more time (see also p490 and p491). The experience of long-distance train travel can also be a highlight of your trip.

Next consider when you're going to travel. Visiting Greece on the shoulder seasons – early spring or autumn – means the weather is more bearable and puts less pressure on precious resources like food and water. You'll also find few crowds and cheaper prices.

Once you're there, how you get around can make a difference to the environment. Not everyone (in fact, very few of us!) have the gumption and stamina to tackle the hilly, hot terrain on bicycle, but you can opt for local buses rather than rented cars, or for fast, fuel-economic ferries rather than slow petrol-guzzlers or planes. We've got all of the info you need to tackle the local transport (p496 and p501).

Water scarcity is a serious problem throughout the islands; a number are without their own source. It's impractical to avoid buying bottled water entirely – in fact, in many areas, it's the safest bet unless you are able to boil it or carry a purifying pump. If local water is not safe to drink, choose bottled water that has travelled the least distance so as to lessen the carbon footprint of transporting it. You can also cut down on water use by not requesting hotels to wash your towels daily and by taking quick showers.

DON'T LEAVE HOME WITHOUT...

Bags feel twice as heavy in the heat. Clothes also dry super fast under the Greek sun, so don't take more than you really need.

- A few novels or a deck of cards to wile away the hours spent riding ferries.
- A shady hat, sunglasses and sun block – indispensable in Greece's hot climate.
- An inflatable neck pillow and eye shades for overnight ferry journeys.
- Lonely Planet's *Greek phrasebook* – talk like the locals.
- CDs – life-saving if you rent a car in a remote area.
- A bathing suit in your day pack – for those unexpected coves and beaches.
- Sturdy, nonslip shoes – many sights, historic towns and villages have slippery, rocky paths.
- A penchant for octopus – it's on nearly every island menu.
- Insect repellent – to ward off mosquitoes and sand fleas.

GREEN CHOICES

Green doesn't have to mean composting toilets and a holiday without showers. Here are excellent ways to enjoy your vacation and do your bit for the earth at the same time.

- Milia (Crete; p260) – mountaintop ecolodges
- National Marine Park of Alonnisos (Evia & the Sporades; p423) – pristine preserve of the Mediterranean monk seal
- Tilos (Dodecanese; p309) – for rare birds
- Octopus Sea Trips (Cyclades; p166) – ecofriendly family activities

- Hydra (Saronic Gulf Islands; p126) – car- and scooter-free
- Masticulture Ecotourism Activities (North-eastern Aegean islands; p373) – traditional cultivation of mastic trees, olive trees and grapevines
- feel ingreece (Evia & the Sporades; p429) – catch a glimpse of wild ponies

BIG NIGHTS OUT

Put on your dancing shoes. The islands aren't known for their party scenes for nothing.

- Mykonos (Cyclades; p154) – glittering nightlife where tourists, celebrities and backpackers mingle on the dance floor
- Rhodes Town (Dodecanese; p285) – atmospheric, chic (and very well-stocked) bars
- Agios Nikolaos (Crete; p267) – vibrant night-life drawing revellers from far and wide

- Santorini (Cyclades; p196) – locally made wine and classy (if expensive) bars
- Corfu (Ionian islands; p443) – where the cool crowds party (very) late
- Kos (Dodecanese; p322) – bar hopping with backpacker party scene
- Iraklio (Crete; p229) – hang-out with hip locals in stylish bars and clubs

SUBLIME SEA VIEWS

Sometimes the islands are all about lazing on the beaches.

- Banana Beach (Kos; p324)
- Moni Island beach (Perdika, Aegina; p122)
- Porto Katsiki (Lefkada; p454)
- Elafonisi (Crete; p260)
- Mikri Vigla (Naxos; p173)

- Seychelles Beach (Ikaria; p354)
- Agios Gordios (Corfu; p445)
- Pori (Koufonisia; p179)
- Kambos Beach (Patmos; p341)
- Livadaki Beach (Samos; p361)

'Organic' and 'green' are increasingly popular buzzwords in Greece. The rise in agrotourism means more options for staying in local, environmentally-friendly places (p476). You'll also find increasing options for recycling and for buying organic food, and for guided activities like hiking (p71) and cycling (p73). As much of Greek cuisine is based on local produce, restaurant proprietors are catching on to the movement and advertising their dishes as locally grown and, in many cases, organic. Shops are also selling local, organic herbs, honey, soap and other wares as souvenirs, making it possible to support the local economy and the environment in one go. You'll find all of these greener options in our GreenDex (p555).

TRAVEL LITERATURE

Travel writers can be a great source of inspiration for those planning to follow in their footsteps.

Captain Corelli's Mandolin (Louis de Bernières; 1995) Made into a Hollywood movie, this is the original story of life on Kefallonia during WWII.

Falling for Icarus: A Journey Among the Cretans (Rory MacLean; 2004) The author journeys to Crete to live out his dream of constructing and flying his own plane and entwines his tale with history, myths and portrayals of village life.

It's All Greek to Me! (John Mole; 2004) The humorous and much-acclaimed account of an English family converting a stone ruin into a home on Evia, including their outlandish attempts to 'fit in'.

My Family and Other Animals (Gerald Durrell; 1977) The classic, witty story of a childhood spent on Corfu, told by a now-famous naturalist and conservationist. Not surprisingly, flora and fauna find their way into the pages.

Patmos: A Place of Healing the Soul (Peter France; 2003) A poignant tale of an expat's search for a better life and spiritual living in the Greek islands.

The Bellstone: The Greek sponge Divers of the Aegean (Michael Kalafatas; 2003) An intriguing family history woven into a novel about sponge divers on Kalymnos.

The Dark Labyrinth (Lawrence Durrell; 1962) A peek into Cretan life and landscape that's steeped in mystery and wit.

The Island (Victoria Hislop; 2007) A dark tale of family secrets and life on the Spinalonga island leper colony.

The Magus (John Fowles; 1965) Full of intrigue, this hefty, classic novel was inspired by Fowles' time on Spetses.

INTERNET RESOURCES

There are a huge number of websites providing information about Greece and its islands.

Greek National Tourist Organisation (GNTO; www.gnto.gr) For concise tourist information.

Greece On-line (www.greece-on-line.gr) An interactive map that lets you pinpoint things like beaches, museums, ski resorts or airports.

Greek Travel Pages (www.gtp.gr) One-stop site with access to ferry schedules, accommodation listings and destination details.

Lonely Planet (www.lonelyplanet.com) Get the latest updates and ask questions before you go or dispense advice when you get back.

Ministry of Culture (www.culture.gr) Details of events, sights, galleries, monuments and museums.

Travel Guide to Greece (www.greektravel.com) Matt Barrett's comprehensive site to travelling in Greece.

Events Calendar

The islands host an endless array of festivals and events and attending one can easily be a highlight of your trip. Atmospheric and jubilant, they're often seen as an excuse for a good party. Below are some of the main events; there are also countless religious festivals that towns and entire islands celebrate with great gusto. Check locally and look in the destination chapters for more information.

JANUARY

**FEAST OF AGIOS
VASILIOS (ST BASIL)**   1 Jan
A church ceremony followed by the exchanging of gifts, singing, dancing and feasting; the *vasilopita* (golden glazed cake for New Year's Eve) is cut and the person who gets the slice containing a coin will supposedly have a lucky year.

**EPIPHANY
(BLESSING OF THE WATERS)**   6 Jan
The day of Christ's baptism by St John is celebrated throughout Greece. Seas, lakes and rivers are blessed with the largest ceremony at Piraeus (p91).

FEBRUARY

CARNIVAL SEASON   3 weeks before Lent
Prior to the fasting of Lent, carnival season has many regional variations, but fancy dress, feasting, traditional dancing and general merrymaking prevail in most instances. The most bizarre is on Skyros (p429).

**CLEAN MONDAY
(SHROVE MONDAY)**   Mon before Ash Wed
On the first day of Lent (a day that is referred to as Kathara Deftera), people take to the hills throughout Greece to have picnics and fly kites.

MARCH

INDEPENDENCE DAY   25 Mar
The anniversary of the hoisting of the Greek flag by independence supporters is celebrated with parades and dancing throughout Greece. This act of revolt marked the start of the War of Independence.

APRIL

ORTHODOX EASTER   40 days after the start of Lent
The Lenten fast ends on Easter Sunday with the cracking of red-dyed Easter eggs, feasting and dancing. This is the most important festival in the Greek Orthodox religion. The Monastery of St John the Theologian in Patmos (p337) is a great place to witness it.

**FEAST OF AGIOS GEORGIOS
(ST GEORGE)**   23 Apr or 1st Tue Following Easter
The feast day of St George, Greece's patron saint and patron saint of shepherds, is celebrated with dancing, feasting and much merriment.

MAY

MAY DAY   1 May
This day is marked by a mass exodus from towns to the country. During picnics, wildflowers are gathered and made into wreaths to decorate homes.

JUNE

NAVY WEEK   early Jun
Celebrating their long relationship with the sea, fishing villages and ports on many islands host historical re-enactments and parties.

FEAST OF ST JOHN THE BAPTIST   24 Jun
This widely celebrated holiday sees Greeks making bonfires from the wreaths made on May Day.

WHAT'S IN A NAME?

Religious festivals flood the Greek calendar. In fact, according to tradition, every day of the year is dedicated to a saint or a martyr. Christian Greeks are more likely to celebrate the day for the saint they are named after than their birthday. On a person's name day, greet them with *'Hronia polla'* (good wishes and prosperity) and, if you go to visit or meet them while out, take a small gift. Islands and towns also celebrate the day of their patron saint with church services in historic chapels, feasting and often some dancing.

ROCKWAVE FESTIVAL   end of Jun
With major international artists (like Moby, The Killers and Mötley Crüe) and massive crowds, this event (p84) is held on a huge parkland on the edge of Athens. See www.rockwavefestival.gr for more.

HELLENIC FESTIVAL   Jun-Aug
The most prominent Greek summer festival features music, dance and drama staged at the Odeon of Herodes Atticus (p81) in Athens and the world famous Theatre of Epidavros, near Nafplio in the Peloponnese.

JULY

FOLEGANDROS FESTIVAL   Late Jul
This week-long festival (p204) features music and feasting at a range of locations around the island's beautiful old *hora* (old town).

WINE & CULTURE FESTIVAL   early Jul-end Aug
Held at Evia's coastal town of Karystos, this festival (p411) includes theatre, traditional dancing, music and visual art exhibits. It ends with a sampling of every local wine imaginable.

SPEED WORLD CUP   Jul or Aug
Kitesurfers from around the world hit Karpathos (p298) for its excellent surfing conditions and big prize money. Event dates change annually; check www.speedworldcup.com for more details.

AUGUST

AUGUST MOON FESTIVAL   Full moon
The full moon is celebrated with musical performances at historical venues like the Acropolis (p79) in Athens and other sites around the country. Check local papers for details.

FEAST OF THE ASSUMPTION   15 Aug
Assumption Day is celebrated with family reunions; the whole population is seemingly on the move on either side of the big day. Thousands make a pilgrimage to Tinos (p141) to its miracle-working icon of Panagia Evangelistria.

SEPTEMBER

GENNISIS TIS PANAGIAS   8 Sep
The birthday of the Virgin Mary is celebrated throughout Greece with religious services and feasting.

EXALTATION OF THE CROSS   14 Sep
Celebrated throughout Greece with processions and hymns.

OCTOBER

OHI (NO) DAY   28 Oct
Metaxas' refusal to allow Mussolini's troops free passage through Greece in WWII is commemorated with remembrance services, military parades, folk dancing and feasting.

DECEMBER

CHRISTMAS DAY   25 Dec
Christmas is celebrated with religious services and feasting plus added 'Western' features, such as Christmas trees, decorations and presents.

CRACKIN' HOLIDAY

Forget Christmas or birthdays. In Greece, the biggest day of the year is Easter when communities joyously celebrate Jesus' Resurrection. The festival begins on the evening of Good Friday with the *perifora epitafiou,* when a shrouded bier (representing Christ's funeral bier) is carried through the streets in a moving candle-lit procession. One of the most impressive of these processions climbs Lykavittos Hill (p83) in Athens to the Chapel of Agios Georgios. If you visit churches early in the morning on Good Friday, you'll often see the bier being decorated with countless flowers.

Resurrection Mass starts at 11pm on Saturday night. At midnight, packed churches are plunged into darkness to symbolise Christ's passing through the underworld. The ceremony of the lighting of candles that follows is the most significant moment in the Orthodox year, for it symbolises the Resurrection. The ceremony ends with candle-lit processions through the streets and fireworks representing the sound of the boulder rolling away from in front of Jesus' tomb. The Lenten fast ends on Easter Sunday with the cracking of red-dyed Easter eggs, symbolising the blood of Christ and new life – taken together this represents the new life given through Christ's resurrection on the cross. An outdoor feast of roast lamb takes places in the afternoon, followed by Greek dancing. The day's greeting is '*Hristos anesti*' (Christ is risen), to which the reply is '*Alithos anesti*' (truly He is risen).

Itineraries
ISLAND HOPPING

ONE WEEK TO SPARE
One Week / Piraeus to Spetses

You don't need to travel far from Athens to sample island life. Hop on a local ferry from **Piraeus** (p91) to **Aegina** (p118), the Athenians' island playground. See the striking Temple of Aphaia and dine on fresh fish in the busy harbour. Detour to minuscule and cosy **Angistri** (p122) for a lazy day of swimming, then head south for the mainland-hugging island of **Poros** (p123) to try waterskiing across turquoise waters. Next visit classy **Hydra** (p126), an artists' and ecofriendly hang-out with a beautiful yacht-filled harbour and streets filled with pedestrians and donkeys (but nary a car). A final hop takes you across to the languid island of **Spetses** (p130), encircled by a serpentine road that guides you to quiet, pine-shaded beaches. Watch the sun go down from a seaside taverna, enjoy the island's refined nightlife and then hop on a fast ferry back to Piraeus.

This relaxed, 130km-long trip is easily done on a quick week's getaway from work. All islands are a short hop from Athens, are well connected, and offer cushy options for accommodation and dining.

THE CYCLADES   Two Weeks / Syros to Serifos

From Athens, head to **Syros** (p143) where you can easily spend a couple of days exploring **Ermoupolis** (p145), a graceful capital that was once the busiest and largest port in the Aegean. The next port of call is **Mykonos** (p148), from where you can make the short excursion across to the island of **Delos** (p157) with its impressive antiquities. You can recover on **Naxos** (p168), the greenest and most fertile of the Cyclades with some good beaches and great walks.

If time permits, take a detour for a couple of days to either **Koufonisia** (p179) or **Schinousa** (p178), an island outback that's decidedly low-key. Otherwise head straight on to spectacular **Santorini** (Thira; p189). Its white cubic, clifftop houses defy gravity, while sunsets from the village of Oia are perhaps the best in the Aegean Sea. Divers can check out the activities of the new volcano that is developing underwater.

The journey back north starts with friendly **Folegandros** (p202), followed by **Milos** (p206), an island that is often overlooked despite its superb beaches and unique Christian catacombs. The final port of call before returning to Athens is **Serifos** (p212), home to arguably the finest of all the Cycladic capitals.

For a classic Greek island-hopping holiday, take on this 580km-loop from Athens. You'll encounter some of the most arche-typically Aegean islands that match glitter and splen-dour with coyness and history.

IONIAN EXPERIENCE
Two Weeks / Corfu to Zakynthos

Start with a few days on **Corfu** (p435), exploring the sights of the old town and savouring the island's distinctive cuisine. Include a day trip over to the west-coast resort of **Paleokastritsa** (p445), lingering long enough to enjoy the sunset. Next up is tiny **Paxi** (p446), where visitors can explore a lost world of ancient, gnarled olive groves and derelict farmhouses.

With no ferry connections south, hop back on a boat to Corfu or Igoumenitsa to make your way south to **Lefkada** (p450). The beaches of the west coast are the finest in the Ionians, while the southern **Vasiliki Bay** (p453) is renowned as a prime windsurfing spot. It's also the departure point for ferries to **Kefallonia** (p455), which arrive at the charming port of **Fiskardo** (p461), the only Kefallonian town not devastated by the great earthquake of 1953. Hop across from Fiskardo to **Ithaki** (p462) and spend a couple of days exploring the homeland of Homer's 'Odyssey' before returning to Kefallonia.

Call in at the stunning west-coast village of **Assos** (p460) and magic beach of **Myrtos** (p272) on the journey south to Kefallonia's lively capital, **Argostoli** (p457). Here you'll find connections to **Zakynthos** (p464) – via the ports of Pesada (Kefallonia) and Agios Nikolaos (Zakynthos). Known to the Venetians as the 'Flower of the Orient', the island's capital, **Zakynthos Town** (p466), boasts some fine examples of Venetian and neoclassical architecture.

Done the Aegean and want to see the west? This 355km-long north–south route shows off the best of the Ionians and their Italian-influenced culture. Mix Captain Corelli and Odysseus on this fascinating island-hopping adventure.

THE EASTERN ISLAND RUN   Three Weeks / Rhodes to Alexandroupoli

Spend a few days on **Rhodes** (p274), exploring the old city and visiting the **Acropolis of Lindos** (p288). If you have time, take a day trip to **Symi** (p305) to enjoy its picturesque harbour and the ornate **Moni Taxiarhou Mihail Panormiti** (p309). Next, set sail for the remote-feeling **Tilos** (p309), a great place for walkers and birdlovers.

The next stop is lush **Nisyros** (p313), where you can explore the moon-like volcanic landscape. You'll need to call briefly at **Kos** (p317) to pick up a ferry onward to **Patmos** (p337), with its lovely beaches and beautiful monastery dedicated to St John who penned his *Book of Revelations* here. From Patmos, it's a short hop to **Samos** (p357), where you can hike through lush forests and laze on idyllic beaches, before continuing to **Chios** (p366) and the fabulous villages of the island's south.

The next stop is **Lesvos** (Mytilini; p378), birthplace of the poet Sappho and producer of some of Greece's finest olive oil and ouzo. From here hop to Limnos and quickly on to **Agio Efstratios** (p393) for volcanic sand beaches. Head back to Limnos (p389), from where you can jump on a boat to the vibrant city of Thessaloniki (p94) or Athens (p76).

The final leg is to the Thracian port of **Alexandroupoli** (p107), where travellers will find several good transport connections to Athens and Thessaloniki.

Start this 735km-long trip in the busy resort island of Rhodes and work your way northwards through languid coastal islands, with wildlife, lush scenery, amazing sights and divine beaches. You could spend three weeks or three months.

THE GRAND TOUR
One Month / Athens to Kythira

From **Athens** (p76), head first to spectacular **Santorini** (Thira; p189), whose capital **Fira** (p191) perches precariously atop the sheer walls of a volcanic caldera created by one of the greatest eruptions ever recorded. Next visit fertile **Naxos** (p168), famous for its crops and fine wines, followed by party island **Mykonos** (p148), favoured by backpackers and socialites alike. Be sure to take a day trip to visit the temples and sanctuaries of sacred **Delos** (p157) before moving on to laid-back **Ikaria** (p349) – where Icarus crash-landed after he flew too close to the sun.

Next up is **Samos** (p357), where the unspoiled villages of the interior offer lots of opportunities for walkers. **Kos** (p317) need be no more than a stopover en route to **Rhodes Town** (p278), the amazing fortress city built by the Knights of St John.

The journey west from Rhodes offers the possibilities of stops at either **Karpathos** (p294) or **Kasos** (p301) on the way to the Cretan port of **Sitia** (p269). Travel along Crete's northern coast to **Iraklio** (p222) and **Knossos** (p231), the ancient capital of Minoan Crete, before moving west to the pretty twin ports of **Rethymno** (p235) and **Hania** (p245) with their harbourside restaurants and buzzing bars. Leave Crete via the northwestern port of **Kissamos** (p262) to **Kythira** (p470). From Kythira, there's a choice of catching a ferry or flight back to Athens, or travelling back through the Peloponnese.

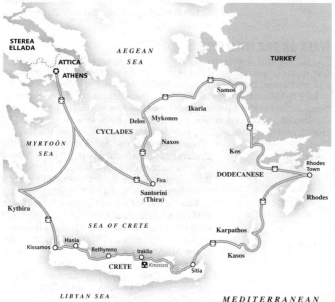

With time on your hands and the Aegean as your horizon, get into some serious island hopping on this 1350km-long voyage around the periphery of Greece's world of water and rock. Making use of scheduled ferries, this is a good trip if you want variety and the odd challenge.

TAILORED TRIPS

ISLAND HOPPING WITH KIDS

Travelling through the islands with children is a joy. While few islands have sights catering exclusively to kids, an endless supply of boat rides, beaches and ruined castles to explore will ignite most children's imaginations.

Rhodes (p274), in particular, is very child-friendly, with an **aquarium** (p282), plenty of castles, a **Bee Museum** (p290), **Petaloudes** (Valley of the Butterflies; p290) and some of the best playgrounds in Greece.

Walking down into the steaming volcano on **Nisyros** (p313) will excite most children (and their parents!). **Kos** (p317) offers flat terrain that's safe for cycling and easily accessible sandy beaches.

Head to **Alonnisos** (p423) for a boat trip to the National Marine Park of Alonnisos, where kids can count dolphins from a classic Greek boat. There's family canoeing on **Kefallonia** (p457), while **Zakynthos** has glass-bottomed boat trips from Cape Skinari to caves and Shipwreck Beach (p468).

Braver kids will love the **cable car** (p191) from Fira on Santorini and a boat trip to the hot springs on the volcanic island of **Nea Kameni** (p200).

Kid's imaginations can run wild in the **Palace of Knossos** (p231) on Crete. Iraklio's **Cretaquarium** (p231) has sharks, octopi and tropical oddities for kids to ponder, and its fantastic **Natural History Museum** (p226) is also a favourite haunt for children.

WALK ON THE WILD SIDE

The islands offer wonderful opportunities for walkers. The best time to go is in spring (especially April and May) when the weather is pleasantly warm and wildflowers transform the countryside into a riot of colour.

Batsi (p137), on Andros, is an ideal base for exploring the countryside along ancient cobbled paths. **Naxos** (p168) has a mountainous interior, with the **Tragaea** (p174) region being a particular favourite with walkers. The coastal resorts of **Samos** (p357) may be a tour-group fave, but the interior

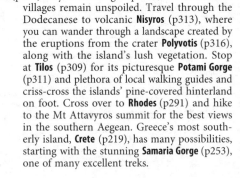

villages remain unspoiled. Travel through the Dodecanese to volcanic **Nisyros** (p313), where you can wander through a landscape created by the eruptions from the crater **Polyvotis** (p316), along with the island's lush vegetation. Stop at **Tilos** (p309) for its picturesque **Potami Gorge** (p311) and plethora of local walking guides and criss-cross the islands' pine-covered hinterland on foot. Cross over to **Rhodes** (p291) and hike to the Mt Attavyros summit for the best views in the southern Aegean. Greece's most southerly island, **Crete** (p219), has many possibilities, starting with the stunning **Samaria Gorge** (p253), one of many excellent treks.

History

Over the centuries, the Greek islands have been the stepping stones between North Africa, Asia Minor and Europe. The islands' close proximity to other strong ancient civilisations, such as the Persian, Roman, Egyptian and Phoenician, helped establish strong cultural references and artistic exchange, economic endeavours and, often, political upheaval. Though the Greek nation is still challenged by geopolitical issues due to its Mediterranean location, it continues to celebrate the legacies of many significant historical influences.

Greece Before History, by Priscilla Murray and Curtis Neil Runnels, is a good introduction to Greece's earliest days.

ANCIENT CIVILISATIONS

Around 3000 BC, settlers from Phoenicia introduced the processing of bronze into Greece, which helped forge two remarkable ancient civilisations: the Cycladic and the Minoan.

Cycladic Civilisation

The Cycladic civilisation – centred on the islands of the Cyclades – comprised a cluster of small island communities that relied primarily on Neolithic farming methods and fishing. However, their society developed a sophisticated artistic temperament.

Scholars divide the Cycladic civilisation into three periods: Early (3000–2000 BC), Middle (2000–1500 BC) and Late (1500–1100 BC).

The most striking legacy of this civilisation is the carving of the statuettes from Parian marble – the famous Cycladic figurines. The statuettes depicted images of the Great Mother (a pagan goddess). Other remains include bronze and obsidian tools and weapons, gold jewellery, and stone and clay vases and pots. Cycladic sculptors are also renowned for their impressive, life-sized *kouroi* (marble statues), carved during the Archaic period.

The Cycladic people were also accomplished sailors who developed prosperous maritime trade links with Crete, continental Greece, Asia Minor (the west of present-day Turkey), Europe and North Africa.

Minoan Civilisation

The Minoans – named after King Minos, the mythical ruler of Crete – were the first advanced civilisation to emerge in Europe, drawing their inspiration from two great Middle Eastern civilisations: the Mesopotamian and the Egyptian.

Most archaeologists split the Minoan civilisation into three phases: Early (3000–2100 BC), Middle (2100–1500 BC) and Late (1500–1100 BC).

The Minoan civilisation reached its peak during the Middle period; around 2000 BC the large palace complexes of Knossos, Phaistos, Malia and Zakros were built, marking a sharp break from Neolithic village life. Evidence uncovered in these grand palaces on Crete indicates a sophisticated society, splendid architecture and wonderful detailed frescoes. It had highly developed

TIMELINE

3000–1100 BC	1700–1550 BC	1500–1200 BC
The discovery of how to blend copper and tin into a strong alloy gives rise to the Bronze Age. Trade gains traction and increased prosperity sees the flourishing of the Cycladic and Minoan – and later, the Mycenaean – civilisations.	The island of Santorini (Thira) erupts with a cataclysmic explosion, one of the largest volcanic events in recorded history, causing a Mediterranean-wide tsunami that scholars suggest contributed to the destruction of Minoan civilisation.	The rigid and authoritarian Mycenaean culture from the Peloponnesian mainland usurps much of the Cretan and Cycladic cultures. Goldsmithing is a predominant feature of Mycenaean life.

agriculture, an extensive irrigation system and advanced hydraulic sewerage systems (that included the use of ventilation shafts).

In pre-classical times, the Ionians were the Hellenic people who inhabited Attica and parts of Asia Minor. These people colonised the islands that later became known as the Ionian Islands.

The advent of bronze enabled the Minoans to build great boats, which helped them establish a powerful *thalassocracy* (prosperous maritime trade). They used tremendous skill to produce fine pottery and metalwork of great beauty, and exported their wares throughout Greece, Asia Minor, Europe and North Africa.

Scholars are still debating the sequence of events that led to the ultimate demise of the Minoans. Scientific evidence suggests the civilisation was weakened by a massive tsunami and ash fallout attributed to the eruption of a cataclysmic volcano on Santorini (Thira) around 1500 BC. Some argue a second powerful quake a century later decimated the society.

The decline of the Minoan civilisation coincided with the rise of the first great civilisation on the Greek mainland, the Mycenaean (1900–1100 BC), which reached its peak between 1500 and 1200 BC. Its own collapse is often attributed to Dorian incursion (see Geometric Age, below); however, this was a period of major upheaval throughout the eastern Mediterranean, and scholars are considering whether natural disasters are responsible.

GEOMETRIC AGE

The Dorians worshipped male gods instead of fertility goddesses and adopted the Mycenaean gods of Poseidon, Zeus and Apollo, paving the way for the later Greek religious pantheon.

The warrior-like Dorians filtered through from northern Greece, later fanning out to occupy much of the mainland, seizing control of the Mycenaean kingdoms and enslaving the inhabitants. The Dorians also spread their tentacles into the Greek islands, founding the cities of Kamiros, Ialysos and Lindos on Rhodes in about 1000 BC, while Ionians fleeing to the Cyclades from the Peloponnese established a religious sanctuary on Delos.

The Dorians also brought iron with them and developed a new style of pottery, decorated with striking geometric designs – although art historians are still divided on whether these were merely refinements of the sophisticated oriental forms and designs perfected by Ionians in Attica.

ARCHAIC AGE

Greek is Europe's oldest written language, and second only to Chinese in the world. It is traceable back to the Linear B script of the Minoans and Mycenaens. For more on Linear B script, try www.ancientscripts.com/linearb.html.

During the so-called Archaic age, from around 800 to 650 BC, Greek culture developed rapidly; many of the advancements in literature, sculpture, theatre, architecture and intellectual endeavour began; this revival overlapped with the golden age (opposite).

By about 800 BC Greece had begun to settle into a new social and political structure. The Dorians had developed into a class of landholding aristocrats and Greece had been divided into a series of independent city-states. Led by Athens and Corinth (which took over Corfu in 734 BC), the city-states created a Magna Graeca (Greater Greece) with southern Italy as an important component.

800–700 BC	800–650 BC	594 BC
Homer's classic work, the 'Iliad', relates in poetic epithet a mythical episode of the Trojan War. Its sequel, the 'Odyssey', recounts the epic adventures of Odysseus and his companions in their journey home from the Trojan War.	Independent city-states begin to emerge in the so-called Archaic Age as the Dorians mature and develop. The Greek alphabet emerges from the Phoenician script.	Solon, a ruling aristocrat in Athens, introduces rules of fair play to his citizenry. His radical rule-changing – in effect creating human and political rights – is credited as being the first step to real democracy.

GOLDEN AGE

During Greece's archetypal golden age, from the 6th to 4th centuries BC, many of the city-states enjoyed increased economic reform, political prosperity and greater cultural creativity. Athens' rapid growth as a major city-state meant heavy reliance on food imports from the Black Sea; and Persia's imperial expansions threatened coastal trade routes across Asia Minor. Athens' support for a rebellion in the Persian colonies of Asia Minor sparked the Persian Wars.

In 477 BC Athens founded the Delian League, the naval alliance that was based on Delos and was formed to liberate the city-states still occupied by Persia, and to defend against further Persian attack. The alliance included many of the Aegean islands and some of the Ionian city-states in Asia Minor. Swearing allegiance to Athens and making an annual contribution to the treasury of ships (later just money) were mandatory.

When Pericles became leader of Athens in 461 BC, he moved the treasury from Delos to the Acropolis. He used the treasury's funds to construct new buildings and grander temples on the Acropolis to replace those destroyed by the Persians (see p79).

With the Aegean Sea safely under its wing, Athens looked westwards for more booty. One of the major triggers of the first Peloponnesian War (431–421 BC) that pitted Athens and Sparta as opponents was the Corcyra incident, in which Athens supported Corcyra (present-day Corfu) in a row with Corinth, its mother city. Athens finally surrendered to Sparta after a drawn-out series of pitched battles.

FOREIGN RULE
Roman Era

While Alexander the Great was forging his vast empire in the east, the Romans had been expanding theirs to the west. By 146 BC the mainland became the Graeco-Roman province of Achaea. Crete fell in 67 BC, and the southern city of Gortyn became capital of the Roman province of Cyrenaica, which included a large chunk of North Africa. Rhodes held out until AD 70. As the Romans revered Greek culture, Athens retained its status as a centre of learning. During a succession of Roman emperors, namely Augustus, Nero and Hadrian, Greece experienced a period of relative peace, known as the Pax Romana, which was to last for almost 300 years. Indeed, the Romans adopted most aspects of Hellenistic culture, spreading its unifying traditions throughout their empire.

Byzantine Empire & the Crusades

The Pax Romana began to crumble in AD 250 when the Goths invaded Greece, the first of a succession of invaders spurred on by the 'great migrations' of the Visigoths and then the Ostrogoths from the middle Balkans.

Admired and feared, the Spartan soldiers were held in mythic awe by their fellow Greeks for their ferocious and self-sacrificing martial supremacy; living (and very often dying) by the motto 'return with your shield or on it'.

In *The Peloponnesian War*, Thucydides sets out a historical narrative of the quarrels and warfare between Athens and Sparta.

The Romans were the first to refer to the Hellenes as Greeks, derived from the word *graikos* – the name of a prehistoric tribe.

5th century BC	477 BC	461–432 BC
The Histories, written by Herodotus, chronicles the conflicts between the ancient Greek city-states and Persia. The work is considered to be the first narrative of historical events ever written.	Seeking security while building a de facto empire, the Athenians establish a political and military alliance called the Delian League. Many city-states and islands join the new club.	New Athenian leader Pericles (d 429 BC) shifts power from Delos to Athens, and uses the treasury wealth of the Delian League to fund massive works, including the construction of the magnificent Parthenon, an enduring legacy.

In AD 324 the Roman Emperor Constantine I, a Christian convert, transferred the capital of the empire from Rome to Byzantium, a city on the western shore of the Bosphorus, which was renamed Constantinople (present-day İstanbul). While Rome went into terminal decline, the eastern capital began to grow in wealth and strength as a Christian state. In the ensuing centuries, Byzantine Greece faced continued pressure from Venetians, Franks, Normans, Slavs, Persians and Arabs; the Persians captured Rhodes in 620, but were replaced by the Saracens (Arabs) in 653. The Arabs also captured Crete in 824. Other islands in the Aegean remained under Byzantine control.

The Byzantine Empire began to fracture when the renegade Frankish leaders of the Fourth Crusade decided that Constantinople presented richer pickings than Jerusalem. Constantinople was sacked in 1204 and much of the Byzantine Empire was partitioned into fiefdoms ruled by self-styled 'Latin' (mostly Frankish or western-Germanic) princes. The Venetians, meanwhile, had also secured a foothold in Greece. Over the next few centuries they took over key mainland ports, the Cyclades, and Crete in 1210, and became the most powerful traders in the Mediterranean.

Despite this sorry state of affairs, Byzantium clung on. In 1259 the Byzantine emperor Michael VIII Palaeologos recaptured the Peloponnese and made the city of Mystras his headquarters. Many eminent Byzantine artists, architects, intellectuals and philosophers converged on the city for a final burst of Byzantine creativity. Michael VIII managed to reclaim Constantinople in 1261, but by this time Byzantium was a shadow of its former self.

Ottoman Rule

On 29 May 1453 Constantinople fell under Turkish Ottoman rule (referred to by Greeks as *turkokratia*). Once more Greece became a battleground, this time fought over by the Turks and Venetians. Eventually, with the exception

The Venetian Empire by Jan Morris vividly describes the imperial influence of the Venetians across the Greek islands. This very readable account includes the social, cultural and architectural legacies still evident today.

ALEXANDER THE GREAT

Stepping into the role of king in 336 BC, 20-year-old Alexander the Great wasted no time in gathering the troops and winning a few bloody battles with the Persians. Alexander then marched through Syria, Palestine and Egypt – where he was proclaimed pharaoh and founded the city of Alexandria. He continued his reign east into parts of what are now Uzbekistan, Afghanistan and northern India.

After Alexander's untimely death in 323 BC at the age of 33, his generals swooped like vultures on the empire and carved it up into independent kingdoms. The Dodecanese became part of the kingdom of Ptolemy I of Egypt, while the remainder of the Aegean islands became part of the League of Islands ruled by the Antigonids of Macedon.

334–323 BC	AD 250–324	1204
Alexander the Great sets out to conquer the known world. Thebes is the first victim, followed by the Persians, the Egyptians and finally the peoples of today's central Asia. He dies in 323 BC.	The AD 250 invasion of Greece by the Goths signals the decline of Pax Romana, and in 324 the capital of the empire is moved to Constantinople. Christianity gains traction and by 394 is declared the official religion.	Marauding Frankish crusaders sack Constantinople. Trading religious fervour for self-interest, the Crusaders strike a blow that sets Constantinople on the road to a slow demise.

of the Ionian Islands (where the Venetians retained control), Greece became part of the Ottoman Empire.

Ottoman power reached its zenith under Sultan Süleyman the Magnificent (r 1520–66). His successor, Selim the Sot, added Cyprus to their dominions in 1570, but his death in 1574 marked an end to serious territorial expansion. Although they captured Crete in 1669 after a 25-year campaign, the ineffectual sultans that followed in the late 16th and 17th centuries triggered the empire's steady decline.

Venice expelled the Turks from the Peloponnese in a three-year campaign (1684–87) that saw Venetian troops advance as far as Athens. During this campaign Venetian artillery struck gunpowder stored inside the ruins of the Acropolis and badly damaged the Parthenon.

The Ottomans restored rule in 1715, but never regained their former authority. By the end of the 18th century Turkish officials, aristocrats and influential Greeks had emerged as self-governing cliques who often ruled over the provincial Greek peasants. But there also existed an ever-increasing group of Greeks, including many intellectual expatriates, who aspired to emancipation.

The web portal www
.ancientgreece.com
is great for all things
ancient and Greek.

INDEPENDENCE

In 1814 the first Greek independence party, the Filiki Eteria (Friendly Society), was founded. The underground organisation's message spread quickly. On 25 March 1821 the Greeks launched the War of Independence. Uprisings broke out almost simultaneously across most of Greece and the occupied islands. The fighting was savage and atrocities were committed on both sides; in the

---

A FEMALE FORCE

Greek women have played a strong role in Greek resistance movements throughout history and Laskarina Bouboulina (1771–1825), a celebrated seafarer, is one such woman. She became a member of Filiki Eteria (Friendly Society), a major organisation striving for independence against Ottoman rule. Originally from Hydra, she settled in Spetses, from where she commissioned the construction of and commanded – as admiral – several warships that were used in significant naval blockades (the most famous vessel being the *Agamemnon*). She helped maintain the crews of her ships and a small army of soldiers, and supplied the revolutionaries with food, weapons and ammunition, using her ships for transportation. Her role in maritime operations significantly helped the independence movement. However, political factionism within the government led to her postwar arrest and subsequent exile to Spetses, where she died.

Distinguished as a national heroine, streets across Greece bear her name and her image appeared commemoratively on the (now-disused) one-drachma coin. Moreover, her great-granddaughter, Lela Karagiannis, also fought with the resistance in WWII. There are statues dedicated to both women in Spetses Town; and Bouboulina's home is now a private museum (see p132).

1453	1821	1827–33
Greece becomes a dominion of the Ottoman Turks after they seize control of Constantinople (modern-day İstanbul), sounding the death knell for the Byzantine Empire.	The 25th of March signals the beginning of the War of Independence on the mainland. Greece celebrates this date as its national day of Independence.	Ioannis Kapodistrias is appointed prime minister of a fledgling government, but discontent ensues and Kapodistrias is assassinated. In 1833 Prince Otto of Bavaria (King Otto) becomes modern Greece's first monarch.

Peloponnese 12,000 Turkish inhabitants were killed after the capture of the city of Tripolitsa (present-day Tripoli), while the Turks retaliated with massacres in Asia Minor, most notoriously on the island of Chios.

The campaign escalated, and within a year the Greeks had won vital ground, and they proclaimed independence on 13 January 1822 at Epidavros. Meanwhile, regional wrangling twice escalated into civil war (1824 and 1825). The Ottomans took advantage and by 1827 the Turks (with Egyptian reinforcements) had regained control. The Western powers intervened and a combined Russian, French and British naval fleet sunk the Turkish-Egyptian fleet in the Battle of Navarino in October 1827. Sultan Mahmud II defied the odds and proclaimed a holy war, prompting Russia to send troops into the Balkans to engage the Ottoman army. Fighting continued until 1829 when, with Russian troops at the gates of Constantinople, the sultan accepted Greek independence with the Treaty of Adrianople (independence was formally recognised in 1830).

THE MODERN GREEK NATION

In April 1827 Greece elected Corfiot Ioannis Kapodistrias as the first president of the republic. But his tenure was not to last – Kapodistrias was assassinated in 1831. The London Convention of 1832 established Greece as a kingdom and 17-year-old Bavarian Prince Otto became King of Greece in 1833. The new kingdom consisted of the Peloponnese, Sterea Ellada, the Cyclades and the Sporades. By 1862, however, Otto had been ousted in a bloodless coup.

The Great Idea

Greece's foreign policy (dubbed the 'Great Idea') was to assert sovereignty over its dispersed Greek populations, particularly those under Ottoman rule in Asia Minor. Set against the background of the Crimean conflict, British and French interests were nervous at the prospect of a Greek alliance with Russia against the Ottomans.

British influence in the Ionian Islands had begun in 1815 (following a spell of political ping-pong between the Venetians, Russians and French). The British did improve the islands' infrastructure and many locals adopted British customs (such as afternoon tea and cricket). But, Greek independence put pressure on Britain to give sovereignty to the Greek nation, and in 1864 the British left. Meanwhile, Britain simultaneously eased onto the Greek throne the young Danish Prince William, crowned King George I in 1863, whose reign lasted 50 years.

In 1881 Greece acquired Thessaly and part of Epiros as a result of a Russo-Turkish war. But Greece failed miserably when it tried to attack Turkey in the north in an effort to reach *enosis* (union) with Crete (who had persistently agitated for liberation from the Ottomans). Timely diplomatic intervention by the great powers prevented the Turkish army from taking Athens.

Eugène Delacroix' oil canvas *The Massacre at Chios* (1824) was inspired by the events in Asia Minor during Greece's War of Independence in 1821. The painting hangs in the Louvre Museum in Paris.

The poet Lord Byron was one of a large group of philhellenic volunteers who played an active role in fanning the independence cause. Byron's war effort was cut short when he died in 1824.

1862–64	1914	1919–23
The British return to Greece the Ionian Islands (a British protectorate since 1815). A new constitution in 1864 establishes the power of democratically elected representatives.	The outbreak of WWI sees Greece initially neutral but eventually siding with the Western Allies against Germany and Turkey on the promise of land in Asia Minor.	Greece embarks on the 'Great Idea' campaign to unite the former Hellenic areas of Asia Minor. The bid fails and leads to a population exchange between Greece and Turkey in 1923, often referred to as the Asia Minor catastrophe.

Crete was placed under international administration, but the government of the island was gradually handed over to Greeks, and in 1905 the president of the Cretan assembly, Eleftherios Venizelos, announced Crete's union with Greece (although this was not recognised by international law until 1913). Venizelos went on to become prime minister of Greece in 1910 and was the country's leading politician for the next two decades.

The outcome of the Balkan Wars of 1912 and 1913 was the Treaty of Bucharest (August 1913), which greatly expanded Greek territory (and with it its fertile agricultural resources). Its borders now took in the southern part of Macedonia (which included Thessaloniki, the vital cultural centre strategically positioned on the Balkan trade routes), part of Thrace, another chunk of Epiros and the Northeastern Aegean Islands; the treaty also recognised the union with Crete.

WWI & Smyrna

As the Great War dragged on, the Allies (Britain, France and Russia) put increasing pressure on neutral Greece to join forces with them against Germany and Turkey, promising concessions in Asia Minor in return. Greek troops served with distinction on the Allied side, but when the war ended in 1918 the promised land in Asia Minor was not forthcoming. Venizelos then led a diplomatic campaign to further the 'Great Idea' and sent troops to Smyrna (present-day İzmir) in May 1919. With a seemingly viable hold in Asia Minor, by September 1921 Greece had advanced as far as Ankara. However, the Turkish forces, commanded by Mustafa Kemal (later to become Atatürk), halted the offensive. The Greek army retreated but Smyrna fell in 1922, and tens of thousands of its Greek inhabitants were killed.

The outcome of these hostilities was the Treaty of Lausanne in July 1923, whereby Turkey recovered eastern Thrace and the islands of Imvros and Tenedos, while the Italians kept the Dodecanese (which they had temporarily acquired in 1912 and would hold until 1947).

The treaty also called for a population exchange between Greece and Turkey to prevent any future disputes. Almost 1.5 million Greeks left Turkey and almost 400,000 Turks left Greece. The exchange put a tremendous strain on the Greek economy and caused great bitterness and hardship for the individuals concerned. Many Greeks abandoned a privileged life in Asia Minor for one of extreme poverty in emerging urban shanty towns in Athens and Thessaloniki.

WWII & the Civil War

In November 1935 King George II installed the right-wing General Ioannis Metaxas as prime minister, who assumed dictatorial powers under the pretext of preventing a communist-inspired republican coup. Metaxas'

Prince Philip, the Duke of Edinburgh, was part of the Greek royal family – born in Corfu as Prince Philip of Greece and Denmark in 1921. Former king of Greece Constantine is Prince William's godfather and Prince Charles' third cousin.

Inside Hitler's Greece: The Experience of Occupation, 1941–44, by Mark Mazower, is an intimate and comprehensive account of Greece under Nazi occupation and the rise of the resistance movement.

1924–35	1940	1941–44
Greece is proclaimed a republic and King George II leaves the country. The Great Depression counters the nation's return to stability. Monarchists and parliamentarians under Prime Minister Venizelos tussle for control of the country.	The 28th of October marks the day when Greeks shouted 'No!' to the Italian Fascists who demanded surrender without a fight. Officially referred to as 'No-Day', though many Greeks use language that is rather more colourful for this day.	Germany invades and occupies Greece. Monarchists, republicans and communists form resistance groups that, despite infighting, drive out the Germans after three years.

grandiose vision was to create a utopian Third Greek Civilisation, based on its glorious ancient and Byzantine past, but what he actually created was more like a Greek version of the Third Reich. He exiled or imprisoned opponents, banned trade unions and the recently established Kommounistiko Komma Elladas (KKE, the Greek Communist Party), imposed press censorship, and created a secret police force and fascist-style youth movement. But Metaxas is best known for his reply of *ohi* (no) to Mussolini's ultimatum to allow Italians passage through Greece at the beginning of WWII. (The Italians invaded anyway, but the Greeks drove them back into Albania.)

Despite Allied help, when German troops invaded Greece on 6 April 1941 the whole country was rapidly overrun, including Crete, which the Germans used as an air and naval base to attack British forces in the eastern Mediterranean. The civilian population suffered appallingly during the occupation, many dying of starvation. The Nazis rounded up more than half the Jewish population and transported them to death camps. Numerous resistance movements sprang up, eventually polarising into royalist and communist factions. These groups fought one another with as much venom as they fought the Germans, often with devastating results for the civilian Greek population.

The Germans began to retreat from Greece in October 1944, but the communist and monarchist resistance groups continued to fight one another. A bloody civil war resulted, lasting until 1949. The civil war left Greece in chaos, politically frayed and economically shattered. More Greeks had been killed in three years of bitter civil war than in WWII, and a quarter of a million people were homeless. The sense of despair triggered a mass exodus. Almost a million Greeks headed off in search of a better life elsewhere, primarily to countries such as Australia, Canada and the US. Villages – whole islands even – were abandoned as people gambled on a new start abroad.

The Cyprus Issue

Since the 1930s Greek Cypriots (four-fifths of the island's population) had desired union with Greece, while Turkey had maintained its claim to the island ever since it became a British protectorate in 1878 (it became a British crown colony in 1925). Greece was in favour of a union, a notion strongly opposed by Britain and the US on strategic grounds. In 1959 after extensive negotiations, Britain, Greece and Turkey agreed on a compromise solution whereby Cyprus would become an independent republic, with Greek Cypriot Archbishop Makarios as president and a Turk, Faisal Kükük, as vice president. But in reality this did little to appease either side: right-wing Greek Cypriots rallied against the British, while Turkish Cypriots clamoured for partition of the island.

1944–49	1967–74	1973
The end of WWII sees Greece descend into civil war, pitching monarchists against communists. The monarchy is restored in 1946; however, the civil war takes its toll and many Greeks migrate in search of a better life.	Right- and left-wing factions continue to bicker, provoking in April 1967 a right-wing military coup d'état by army generals who establish a junta. They impose martial law and abolish many civil rights.	On 17 November tanks ram the gates of the Athens Polytechnio (Technical University) and troops storm the school buildings in a bid to quash a student uprising against the junta. More than 20 students die.

Colonels, Monarchs & Democracy

Back in Greece, Georgios Papandreou came to power in February 1964. He had founded the Centre Union (EK) and wasted no time in implementing a series of radical changes: he freed political prisoners and allowed exiles to come back to Greece, reduced income tax and the defence budget, and increased spending on social services and education. The political right in Greece was rattled by Papandreou's tolerance of the left, and a group of army colonels, led by Georgios Papadopoulos and Stylianos Patakos, staged a coup on 21 April 1967. They established a military junta with Papadopoulos as prime minister.

The colonels declared martial law, banned political parties and trade unions, imposed censorship, and imprisoned, tortured and exiled thousands of dissidents. In June 1972 Papadopoulos declared Greece a republic and appointed himself president.

For an insight into the 1967 colonels' coup read Andreas Papandreou's account in *Democracy at Gunpoint*.

On 17 November 1973 tanks stormed a building at the Athens Polytechnio (Technical University) to quell a student occupation calling for an uprising against the US-backed junta. While the number of casualties is still in dispute (more than 20 students were reportedly killed and hundreds injured), the act spelt the death knell for the junta.

Shortly after, the head of the military security police, Dimitrios Ioannidis, deposed Papadopoulos. In July 1974 Ioannidis tried to impose unity with Cyprus by attempting to topple the Makarios government in Cyprus. However, Makarios got wind of an assassination attempt and escaped. Consequently, mainland Turkey sent in troops until they occupied northern Cyprus, partitioning the country and displacing almost 200,000 Greek Cypriots who fled their homes for the safety of the south (reportedly more than 1500 Cypriots remain missing).

The junta dictatorship collapsed. Konstandinos Karamanlis was summoned from Paris to take office and his New Democracy (ND) party won a large majority at the November elections in 1974 against the newly formed Panhellenic Socialist Union (PASOK), led by Andreas Papandreou (son of Georgios). A plebiscite voted 69% against the restoration of the monarchy and the ban on communist parties was lifted.

The 1980s &1990s

In October 1981 Andreas Papandreou's PASOK party was elected as Greece's first socialist government, ruling for almost two decades (except for 1990–93). PASOK promised ambitious social reform, to close the US air bases and to withdraw from NATO. US military presence was reduced, but unemployment was high and reforms in education and welfare were limited. Women's issues fared better: the dowry system was abolished, abortion legalised, and civil marriage and divorce were implemented. But, by 1990, significant policy wrangling and economic

1974	1981	1981–90
A botched plan to unite Cyprus with Greece prompts the invasion of Cyprus by Turkish troops and results in the fall of the military junta. This acts as a catalyst for the restoration of parliamentary democracy in Greece.	Greece joins the EU, effectively removing protective trade barriers and opening up the Greek economy to the wider world for the first time. The economy grows smartly.	Greece acquires its first elected socialist government (PASOK) under the leadership of Andreas Papandreou. The honeymoon lasts nine years. The conservatives ultimately reassume power.

upheaval wore thin with the electorate and it returned to office the ND, led by Konstandinos Mitsotakis.

Intent on redressing the country's economic problems, the government imposed a wage freeze for civil servants and steep increases in public-utility costs and basic services. By late 1992 corruption allegations were being levelled against the government and many Mitsotakis supporters abandoned ship; the ND lost its parliamentary majority and an early election in October returned Andreas Papandreou's PASOK party.

Papandreou stepped down in early 1996 due to ill health and he died on 26 June. His departure produced a dramatic change of direction for PASOK, with the party abandoning Papandreou's left-leaning politics and electing economist and lawyer Costas Simitis as the new prime minister (who won a comfortable majority at the October 1996 polls).

The 21st Century

'The new millennium has seen billions of euros poured into large-scale infra-structure projects'

Simitis' government focused almost exclusively on the push for further integration with Europe (this meant, in general terms, more tax reform and austerity measures), and by 2004 PASOK's popularity was in decline. Greece changed course when the ND party won at the polls in March 2004, with Konstandinos Karamanlis as prime minister.

The new millennium has seen living standards increase and billions of euros poured into large-scale infrastructure projects across Greece, including the redevelopment of Athens – spurred on largely by its hosting of the 2004 Olympic Games. However, rising unemployment, ballooning public debt, slowing inflation and the squeezing of consumer credit have taken their toll. The conservatives scraped through the September 2007 election, amid widely held criticism of its handling of the emergency response to that summer's severe bushfires that caused widespread destruction throughout Greece. (The criticism reignited when large tracts of forest north of Athens burned in August 2009.)

Over recent years a series of massive general strikes have highlighted mounting electoral discontent. Hundreds of thousands of people have protested against proposed radical labour and pension reforms and privatisation plans that analysts claim will help curb public debt. The backlash against the government reached boiling point in December 2008, when urban rioting broke out across the country, led by youths in Athens outraged by the fatal shooting by police of a 15-year-old boy following an alleged exchange between police and a group of teenagers. Concern is growing over political tangles in an ongoing investigation regarding alleged corruption among state executives (on both sides of the political fence) in connection with the Siemens Hellas group. This follows another controversy that involved land-swap deals between a monastery and the government, which some commentators believe to have gone heavily in the monastery's favour, at the expense of taxpayers.

1999	2008	2009
Turkey and Greece experience powerful earthquakes within weeks of each other that result in hundreds of deaths. The two nations respond to each disaster by pledging mutual aid and support, initiating a warming of diplomatic relations.	Police shoot and kill a 15-year-old boy in Athens following an alleged exchange between police and youths. This sparks a series of urban riots nationwide.	PASOK secures the vote in the European Parliamentary elections in June. George Papakonstadinou heads the Greek contingency, represented by 22 members of the European Parliament (MEPs).

A general election held in October 2009, midway through Karamanlis' term, saw PASOK take back the reins in a landslide win against the conservatives.

Relations with Turkey these days are more neighbourly. Greece supports Turkey's steps towards EU-ascension, and is urging joint action between the two nations to manage illegal immigration across Greece's borders. But Greece has expressed rumblings of concern since Turkey declared its intention to explore for oil and gas in the eastern Aegean, sparking a diplomatic headache.

2009	2009	2009
On 20 June, the much-acclaimed new Acropolis Museum holds its official inauguration. A public-relations campaign still rages for the repatriation of the Parthenon Marbles from the British Museum.	Greece raises concerns when Turkey declares its intention to explore for oil and gas off the coasts of Kastellorizo and Cyprus. Diplomatic tension mounts when locals spot Turkish jets flying low over several Greek islands in the eastern Aegean.	Konstandinos Karamanlis calls for an early general election. Socialist PASOK, under Georgios Papandreou, wins the October election with a landslide result against the conservatives.

The Culture

REGIONAL IDENTITY

In a country where regional identities remain deep-rooted, it is not surprising that Greek islanders often identify with their island first (as Cretans, Ithacans or Kastellorizians etc) and as Greeks second. Even those who have left the islands to live on the mainland, or moved to bigger islands or abroad, invariably maintain a strong connection to their ancestral island. One of the first questions Greeks will ask a stranger is what part of Greece they come from. It is an important part of their identity and sense of community, with even the remotest island villages coming alive during summer, Easter, elections and other excuses for family reunions and homecomings.

With the Greek islands sprawling from the shores of Turkey to Italy, the regional distinctions and characteristics are apparent across the seven island groups. Individual histories and topography have influenced island customs and traditions, from their cuisine to architecture, music and dance, down to the characteristics of their people and the produce that gave them livelihoods.

In the Ionians, Corfu escaped Turkish rule and has a more Italian, French and British influence, and its people retain an aristocratic air. The Cretans are renowned for their independent (bordering on lawless) streak and hospitality, and have perhaps the most enduring and distinctive folk culture and traditions, as well as their own cosmopolitan dialect. Mykonos' stylised island image is a far cry from traditional customs in villages such as Olymbos in far eastern Karpathos, where many women still wear traditional dress, including headscarves and goatskin boots. Sifnos is renowned for its unique pottery tradition; on Chios the mastic tree has spawned its own industry; while Kalymnos' sponge-diving industry shaped the island's identity as much as fishing and agriculture have forged those of others.

'In its fast-tracked quest for modernity, Greek society is facing a massive generational and technological divide'

While foreign invasions now take the form of tourists, these have nonetheless changed the fortunes and nature of many islands. Beneath the friendly and laid-back veneer of island life, the islands today are also dealing with the rapid social and economic changes that have swept the country in the past 30 years.

In its fast-tracked quest for modernity, Greek society is facing a massive generational and technological divide, widening urban-rural disparities and all the while delicately balancing cultural and religious mores. The culture clash is most stark on the islands where many people continue to live in a time warp of traditional island life outside the bustling tourist resorts.

Greek islanders have by necessity been relatively autonomous, but they share a common history spanning centuries with the mainland, along with the peculiar traits of the Greek psyche.

Years of hardship and isolation have made islanders stoic and resourceful, generous yet shrewd and suspicious. Like most Greeks they are fiercely independent, patriotic and proud of their heritage. They pride themselves on their *filotimo* (dignity and sense of honour) and their *filoxenia* (hospitality, welcome) and have an undeniable zest for life, with a work-to-live attitude.

Personal freedom and democratic rights are almost sacrosanct and there is residual mistrust of authority and disrespect for the state. Rules and regulations are routinely ignored or seen as a challenge. Patronage and nepotism are rife, an enduring by-product of having to rely on personal networks to survive (though graft and corruption are its more extreme form).

Greeks are forthright and argumentative and few subjects are off limits, from your private life and why you don't have children to how much you paid for your house or shoes.

While some Greeks like to flaunt their newfound wealth with top-brand clothing and flashy cars and are prone to displays of excess, as if making up for lost time, others continue to live frugal and traditional agrarian lives.

Stereotypes about Greek men being mummy's boys are not totally unfounded, while AIDS and the sexual liberation of Greek women has virtually killed off the cliché Greek lover and the *kamaki* (a fishing trident, referring to the practice of fishing for foreign women) of the islands, á la *Shirley Valentine* (p54).

LIFESTYLE

Island life is completely seasonal. From May to September the islands kick into summer mode, with visitors far outnumbering the local population. Traditional agrarian life on many islands has been replaced by tourism-related pursuits, though they often coexist, with families running hotels and beach tavernas in summer and engaging in agricultural or business pursuits in the winter.

Winter can be especially tough for the people living on isolated smaller islands with short tourism seasons, especially those without airports. On larger islands such as Crete and Corfu there is a winter population shift from the beach resorts back to mountain villages and larger towns with schools and infrastructure, while on some islands people move back to Athens after the season.

Overall, the lifestyle of the average Greek has changed beyond all recognition in the last 50 years. Tourism has brought prosperity to many islands, while better transport, technology, telecommunication and infrastructure has made life a lot easier and far less isolated.

However, the sharp rise in the cost of living since the arrival of the euro and the recent economic downturn has left many Greeks feeling the financial pinch, relying on credit and curtailing holidays and eating out (though Greeks still spend a higher percentage of their income on restaurants and holidays than their EU counterparts).

Island life has a more laid-back and relaxed pace than the mainland, revolving largely around the tourism industries. The majority of people are self-employed and run family businesses. Most island stores and businesses close during the heat of the day and reopen in the evenings after the siesta until around 11pm, which is when locals generally head out to dinner.

Regardless of the long working hours, Greeks are inherently social animals and enjoy a rich communal life. Shopkeepers will sit outside their stores chatting to each other until a customer walks in, and in villages you will see people sitting outside their homes watching the goings on. In the evenings the seafront promenades and town squares are bustling with people of all ages, and at night the sophisticated bars and clubs are always lively.

PEOPLE & SOCIETY
Population

Greece's population exceeded 11.2 million in 2009, with nearly a third of the population (3.4 million) living in the Greater Athens area. Less than 15% live on the islands, the most populous being Crete, Evia and Corfu.

Regional development, decentralisation and the improved lot of many rural communities have largely stemmed the tide of people moving to Athens, especially in growth areas such as Iraklio in Crete, but many islands

First published in 1885, James Theodore Bent's *The Cyclades, or Life Among the Insular Greeks,* is a classic account of the islands, while John Freely's more recent *The Cyclades* is rich on history and insight.

Greeks are among the world's biggest mobile phone users, with more than 11.9 million mobile phones connected, more than the estimated population of 11.2 million.

still lose their young people to the mainland or bigger islands for work and educational opportunities.

Greece has an ageing population and a declining birth rate, with large families a thing of the past. The main population growth has been the flood of migrants since 1991, with about 1.5 million migrants estimated to be living in Greece, many of them illegal or of indeterminate status.

Greece's remote islands have seen an increase in new arrivals (such as economic migrants, as well as asylum seekers). It's reported that these increases are causing major social problems, especially on smaller islands unable to cope with the number of arrivals, which can exceed their resident population.

Family Life

Greek society remains dominated by the family. Extended family plays an important role, with grandparents often looking after grandchildren while parents work or socialise. Many working Athenians send their children to their grandparents on the islands for the summer.

It's still uncommon for young people to move out of home before marrying, unless they leave to study or work, which is inevitable on most islands where employment and education opportunities are limited. While this is slowly changing among professionals and people marrying later, low wages are also keeping young Greeks at home.

The majority of businesses are small, family-run enterprises. Parents strive to provide homes for their children when they get married, often building apartments for each child above their own (thus the number of unfinished buildings you see).

Greeks attach great importance to education, determined to provide their children the opportunities they lacked. English and other languages are widely spoken, while Greece has the highest number of students per capita studying at universities abroad, though many of these students end up overeducated and underemployed.

Multiculturalism

Greece has been a largely homogenous society since independence. The disparate *xenoi* (foreigners) living in its midst were mostly the odd Hellenophile, and foreign women married to locals as a result of summer romances, especially on the islands.

But with the influx of economic migrants over the past 15 years, the islands are teeming with foreign labourers, who have become an economic necessity in the agriculture, construction and tourism sectors, doing the hard and menial labour Greeks no longer want to do.

Migration and multiculturalism are posing major challenges for both the community and the state, which were ill-prepared for dealing with the sudden wave of migrants. Economic migrants exist on the social fringe, but as they seek Greek citizenship and try to integrate into mainstream society, community tolerance and notions of Greek identity are also being tested.

Albanians, who make up roughly two-thirds of the migrant population, remain stigmatised, though the Greeks' initial xenophobic reaction has waned. Mixed marriages are becoming increasingly common, particularly in rural communities and islands where foreign brides (most from Eastern Europe) fill the void left by Greek women leaving to study or work in the cities.

Media

Greece has a disproportionate number of newspapers and TV stations given its size – more than 20 national dailies (and more than 10 sports dailies) and seven national broadcasters. While coverage of island issues is

Greeks are the EU's biggest smokers: 37.6% of people over 15 are heavy smokers, and women smoke as much as men. In 2009 smoking bans were optimistically extended to restaurants, bars and nightclubs.

ISLAND HOMECOMINGS

The twang of Australian accents echoing around the tiny harbour of Kastellorizo every summer has become a curious feature of the island. A large part of the island's population emigrated to Australia in the late 1920s, but their descendants (and a few of the oldies) return annually to what at times can seem like the furthermost Aussie outpost.

A similar phenomenon occurs on most islands, which see an annual procession of Greeks returning from the USA, Australia, Canada and other reaches of the Greek diaspora. Strong sentimental connections endure and many expat Greeks are involved in the political and cultural life of their ancestral islands, often retiring in Greece. A growing stream of young second- and third-generation Greeks are also repatriating.

More than five million people of Greek descent are said to be living in 140 countries around the world, having emigrated at various tumultuous times.

---

patchy, many islands have their own newspapers and radio stations, and some have small local TV stations.

Newspapers, like most Greeks, are openly partisan and represent the gamut of political views. Commercial TV news is highly sensationalist and dominated by domestic news and scandals.

The country's media owners have an extremely influential role in shaping public opinion, with media ownership spread around half a dozen major players. The often contentious entangled relationship between media owners, journalists, big business and the government is what the Greeks have coined *diaplekomena* (intertwined).

Religion & Identity

The Orthodox faith is the official religion of Greece and a key element of Greek identity and culture. While younger people aren't necessarily devout, nor attend church regularly, they observe the rituals and consider their faith part of their identity.

During foreign occupations the church was the principal upholder of Greek culture, language and traditions. Under Ottoman rule, religion was one of the most important criteria in defining a Greek. The church still exerts significant social, political and economic influence.

The Greek year is centred on the saints' days and festivals of the church calendar. Namedays (celebrating your namesake saint) are celebrated more than birthdays, and baptisms are an important rite. Most people are named after a saint, as are boats, suburbs and train stations.

You will notice taxi drivers, motorcyclists and people on public transport making the sign of the cross when they pass a church, and many Greeks will go to a church when they have a problem to light a candle or leave a *tama* (votive offering) to the relevant saint. The roadside iconostases (tiny chapels) you see on country roads are either shrines to people who died in road accidents or dedications to saints.

While religious freedom is part of the constitution, the only other officially recognised religions in Greece are Judaism and Islam.

There are more than 50,000 Roman Catholics, mostly of Genoese or Frankish origin living in the Cyclades, especially on Syros, where they make up 40% of the population. A small Jewish community lives in Rhodes (dating back to the Roman era).

If you wish to look around a church or monastery, you should always dress appropriately. Women should wear skirts that reach below the knees, men should wear long trousers, and arms (and cleavage) should be covered.

Greeks have their own distinctive body language – 'yes' is a swing of the head and 'no' is a curt raising of the head (or eyebrows), often accompanied by a 'ts' click of the tongue sound.

THE BIG SPLIT

Greece was one of the first places in Europe where Christianity emerged, with St Paul reputedly first preaching the gospel in AD 49 in the Macedonian town of Philippi. After Constantine the Great officially recognised Christianity in AD 313, he transferred the capital of the Roman Empire to Byzantium (today's İstanbul) in AD 330.

By the 8th century differences of opinion and increasing rivalry emerged between the pope in Rome and the patriarch of the Hellenised Eastern Roman Empire. One dispute was over the wording of the Creed, which stated that the Holy Spirit proceeds 'from the Father', but Rome added 'and the Son'. Other points of difference included Rome decreeing priests had to be celibate, while Orthodox priests could marry before becoming ordained, and the Orthodox Church forbidding wine and oil during Lent. Another big rift was the Western church using the Gregorian calendar and the Eastern church using the Julian calendar.

Their differences became irreconcilable, and in the great schism of 1054 the pope and the patriarch went their separate ways as the Orthodox Church (Orthodoxy means 'right belief') and Roman Catholic Church.

Orthodox Easter is often held at different times to the Western churches because of a continuing dispute about the calendars and complex formulas involving the full-moon cycles and dates of the Jewish Passover – it falls on the first Sunday after the first full moon after the vernal equinox (21 March on the Julian calendar), after the Jewish Passover. Every few years they coincide.

Women in Greece

Greek women have a curious place in Greek society and the male-female dynamic throws up some interesting paradoxes. Despite the machismo, it is very much a matriarchal society. Men love to give the impression that they rule the roost but, in reality, it's often the women who run the show, both at home and in family businesses.

Despite sexual liberation, education and greater participation in the workforce, 'mother' and 'sex object' are still the dominant role models and stereotypes, which Greek women often play on with gusto.

Old attitudes towards the 'proper role' for women have changed dramatically since the 1980s, when dowry laws were abolished, legal equality of the sexes established and divorce made easier.

While there are many benefits for mothers in the public sector, Greek women generally do it tough in the male-dominated workplace. They are significantly under-represented, often earn less than men and struggle to even find the corporate ladder.

In conservative provincial towns and villages, many women maintain traditional roles, though women's agricultural cooperatives play a leading role in regional economies and in the preservation of cultural heritage. Things are far more liberal for women living in bigger towns.

On the domestic front, Greek women (at least the older generation) are famously house-proud and hone their culinary skills. It's still relatively rare for men to be involved in housework or cooking and boys are generally waited on hand and foot. While girls are involved in domestic chores from an early age, these days they are more likely to be found in a gym or beauty salon than in the kitchen.

In 2009 Lesbians from the island of Lesvos lost a bid in the Greek courts to stop the world's lesbians monopolising the term, which stems from the island's famous poet (and lesbian icon) Sappho.

ARTS
Architecture

The advanced Minoan palace complexes in Crete, including the famous palace at Knossos (p231), are among the earliest examples of ancient Greek architecture, along with the Akrotiri site (p199) on Santorini.

The Mycenaeans later built citadels on a compact, orderly plan, fortified by strong walls, while the next great architectural advance came with the monumental stone temples built in the Archaic and classical periods, characterised by the Doric, Ionic and Corinthian orders of columns.

The most famous Doric temple in Greece is the Parthenon (p79), but the Temple of Aphaia (p121) on Aegina and the small Doric temple of Isis (the most prominent remaining structure of the Shrine to the Egyptian Gods; p159) on Delos, near Mykonos, are also fine examples.

Theatre design was another hallmark of the classical period, with stone theatres built into hills providing excellent acoustics. On the islands you will find the marble theatre at Delos (p159), the ancient theatre at Eretria (p408) on Evia, the Hellenistic theatre of Samothraki (p397), and theatres in Thassos, Rhodes, Crete, Santorini and Milos.

During the Byzantine period, churches usually featured a central dome supported by four arches on piers and flanked by vaults, with smaller domes at the four corners and three apses to the east. The external brickwork, which alternated with stone, was sometimes set in patterns. Fortified Byzantine monasteries include the imposing monastery of St John (p341) on Patmos.

The Venetians left the greatest architectural legacies (see the boxed text, p48), while little architecture of the Ottoman period survives. After the War of Independence, buildings took on the neoclassical style that had been dominant in Western European architecture.

Architectural sensibilities took a back seat for most of the tumultuous 20th century, when many neoclassical buildings were destroyed in the untamed modernisation and sudden population expansion that took place in the 1920s and the post-boom in the '50s, '60s and '70s, during which most of the ugly concrete apartment blocks that characterise modern Athens (and most Greek towns) were built.

While there are some modern buildings of architectural note, it is only in recent times that modern architecture has come to the fore.

The World of the Ancient Greeks (2002), by archaeologists John Camp and Elizabeth Fisher, is a broad and in-depth look at how the Greeks have left their imprint on politics, philosophy, theatre, art, medicine and architecture.

Theatre

Drama in Greece can be dated back to the contests staged at the Ancient Theatre of Dionysos in Athens during the 6th century BC for the annual Dionysia festival. During one of these competitions, Thespis left the ensemble and took centre stage for a solo performance. This is regarded as the first true dramatic performance – thus the term 'thespian'.

The so-called 'father of tragedy' was Aeschylus (c 525–456 BC), whose best-known work is the Oresteia trilogy. Sophocles (c 496–406 BC), regarded as the greatest tragedian, is thought to have written over 100 plays, of which only seven survive, including *Antigone*, *Electra* and his most famous play, *Oedipus Rex*.

Euripides (c 485–406 BC) was more popular than Aeschylus and Sophocles because his plots were considered more exciting. His most famous works are *Medea, Andromache, Orestes* and *Bacchae*.

Aristophanes (c 427–387 BC) wrote often ribald comedies dealing with topical issues, ridiculing Athenians who resorted to litigation over trivialities in *The Wasps* and poking fun at their gullibility in *The Birds*.

You can see plays by ancient Greek playwrights at the Athens Festival (p83), the ancient theatre at Epidavros and festivals around the country.

The most distinguished modern Greek playwrights are Giorgos Skourtis, Pavlos Matessis and the father of postwar drama, Iakovos Kambanellis.

ISLAND STYLE

Stark white chapels juxtaposed against stunning blue Aegean skies and cubed houses with bright-blue shutters are the most iconic and enchanting images of Greek island architecture. The distinctive blue-and-white Cycladic style was pragmatic more than aesthetic. Apart from reflecting the scarcity of construction materials, the labyrinthine narrow alleys with flat-roofed houses huddled together were designed to protect against the elements – strong winds and pirates – and the whitewashed walls reflected the sun's heat.

Mykonos is a superb example, with its unique asymmetrical buildings, exemplified by the church of Panagia Paraportiani (p152). On Santorini, the islanders protected themselves by building their cubed villages on the cliff tops, extending their homes into the rock, which provided insulation in winter and cooling in summer. A lack of water meant there were no gardens, just a few bright pots of hardy geraniums and bougainvillea. Blue-domed island chapels were built in this distinctive Cycladic style. One of the best-preserved Cycladic settlements is Hora (p183), on Amorgos.

Beyond the Cycladic style, Greek island architecture reflects an island's wealth, and turbulent and colourful history, giving each island a unique style.

Remnants of Ottoman times are evident in Rhodes and in the evocative Cretan port towns of Hania (p245) and Rethymno (p235), where you will see old mosques and minarets, Turkish-style wooden balconies attached to Venetian mansions and *hammams* (Turkish baths) incorporated into hotels and restaurants.

The Venetian legacy of massive fortifications, grand squares, fountains and mansions is evident in Corfu Town (p437), now on Unesco's World Heritage list, but Mykonos also has its famous Little Venice (p293).

Gracious stone and white mansions dominate Hydra's stunning amphitheatrical port (p126), while the capital of Symi (p305) in the Dodecanese is a protected settlement of pastel- and ochre-coloured neoclassical mansions. Rhodes' Old Town (p278), one of the largest inhabited medieval settlements in Europe, is also World Heritage–listed.

Literature

The first, and greatest, ancient Greek writer was Homer, author of the 'Iliad' and the 'Odyssey', which tell the story of the Trojan War and the subsequent wanderings of Odysseus.

Herodotus (5th century BC) was the author of the first historical work about Western civilisation. His highly subjective account of the Persian Wars, however, led some to regard him as the 'father of lies' as well as the 'father of history'. The historian Thucydides (5th century BC) was more objective, but took a high moral stance in his account of the Peloponnesian Wars.

Pindar (c 518–438 BC) is regarded as the pre-eminent lyric poet of ancient Greece. He was commissioned to recite his odes at the Olympic Games. The greatest writers of love poetry were Sappho (6th century BC) and Alcaeus (5th century BC), both of whom lived on Lesvos. Sappho's poetic descriptions of her affections for women gave rise to the term 'lesbian'.

Zakynthos-born Dionysios Solomos (1798–1857) and Andreas Kalvos (1796–1869) are regarded as the first modern Greek poets. Solomos' work was heavily nationalistic, and his *Hymn to Freedom* became the Greek national anthem.

The best-known 20th-century poets are Nobel prize–winners George Seferis (1900–71) and Odysseas Elytis (1911–96), while Stratis Myrivilis (1892–1969) is considered one of the great prose writers.

The most celebrated novelist of the early 20th century is Crete's Nikos Kazantzakis (1883–1957), whose widely translated novels are full of drama and larger-than-life characters, such as the magnificent Alexis Zorbas of

Not your usual tale of idyllic island life, Vangelis Hatziyannidis' *Four Walls* – a compelling mystery of entangled lives, imprisonment, jealousy and the secret to making honey – was shortlisted for a British foreign literature award.

Zorba the Greek and the tortured Michalis of *Freedom and Death,* two of his finest works.

Leading contemporary Greek writers include Thanassis Valtinos, Ziranna Ziteli, Ersi Sotiropoulou and playwright Kostas Mourselas. Two award-winning writers from Crete are Rhea Galanaki and Ioanna Karystiani.

While not enough literature is translated into English, look out for Apostolos Doxiadis' *Uncle Petros and Goldbach's Conjecture,* Petros Markaris' excellent detective novels *The Late Night News* and *Zone Defence,* and the popular children's books by criminologist-cum–children's author Eugene Trivizas.

Young writers making inroads into foreign markets include Vangelis Hatziyannidis, Alexis Stamatis with *Bar Flaubert* (2000), and Panos Karnezis *(The Birthday Party, The Maze).*

Fine Arts

PAINTING

Apart from drawings on vases, the few existing examples of early Greek painting are the famous frescoes unearthed on Santorini and now mostly housed in the National Archaeological Museum (p81) in Athens. Stylistically they are similar to the paintings of Minoan Crete found at Knossos.

Greek painting came into its own during the Byzantine period, when churches were usually decorated with frescoes on a dark blue background with a bust of Christ in the dome, the four Gospel writers in the pendentives supporting the dome and the Virgin and Child in the apse. They also featured scenes from the life of Christ and figures of the saints. In the later centuries the scenes in churches and icons involved more detailed narratives.

With the fall of Constantinople in 1453 many Byzantine artists fled to Crete, while many Cretan artists studied in Italy, where the Renaissance was in full bloom. The result was the Cretan School of icon painting that combined technical brilliance and dramatic richness. In Iraklio alone there were over 200 painters working from the mid-16th to mid-17th centuries who were equally at ease in Venetian and Byzantine styles, and the technique spread through monasteries throughout Greece. The finest exponent of the Cretan school was Michail Damaskinos, whose work is in Iraklio's Museum of Religious Art (p226).

The Cretan School was a formative influence for arguably Greece's most famous artist, Cretan-born El Greco (meaning 'The Greek' in Spanish; his real name was Dominikos Theotokopoulos), who became one of the great Renaissance painters in Spain.

With little artistic output under Ottoman rule, modern Greek painting per se began after Independence, when painting became more secular, with representations of the War of Independence a common theme among major 19th-century painters such as Dionysios Tsokos, Theodoros Vryzakis, Nikiforos Lytras and Nicholas Gyzis.

From the first decades of the 20th century artists such as Konstantinos Parthenis drew on their heritage and assimilated various developments in modern art, a trend that continues among the new generation of artists.

Significant artists of the '30s generation were cubist Nikos Hadjikyriakos-Ghikas and surrealists Nikos Engonopoulos, Yiannis Tsarouchis and Panayiotis Tetsis.

Other leading artists include Yannis Moralis, Giorgos Zongolopoulos (with his trademark umbrella sculptures), Dimitris Mytaras, Yannis Tsoclis, abstract artist Yannis Gaitis, Christos Caras and Alekos Fassianos.

Acclaimed writer Stratis Myrivilis' classic novel *The Mermaid Madonna* is set on his native Lesvos; a harsh yet poignant portrayal of life in a fishing village during the Greek expulsion from Anatolia.

Ioanna Karystiani's *The Jasmine Isle* is an epic story set on Andros, delving into the lives of men of the sea and the women they leave behind.

Modern Greek painting has attracted serious sums at leading art auctions, with Lytras' *The Naughty Grandchild* setting a record for a Greek artist when it sold for more than one million euros in London in 2006.

Athens has a burgeoning contemporary arts scene, with a host of galleries around Psyrri, Kolonaki and Metaxourghio. The National Art Gallery (p81) has the most extensive collections of 20th-century art.

SCULPTURE

The extraordinary sculptures of ancient Greece hold pride of place in the collections of the great museums of the world, revered for their beauty and form.

Prehistoric Greek sculpture has been discovered only recently, most notably the remarkable figurines produced in the Cyclades from the high-quality marble of Paros and Naxos in the middle of the 3rd millennium BC. Their primitive and powerful forms have inspired many artists since.

Greek Art and Archaeology, by John Griffiths Pedley, is a super introduction to the development of Greek art and civilisation.

Displaying an obvious debt to Egyptian sculpture, the marble sculptures of the Archaic period are precursors of the famed Greek sculpture of the classical period. They began to represent figures that for the first time were true to nature, rather than flat and stylised. Seeking to master the depiction of both the naked body and of drapery, sculptors focused on *kouroi* (figures of naked youths), with their set symmetrical stance and enigmatic smiles. These can be admired at the National Archaeological Museum (p81) in Athens.

The quest for total naturalism continued in the Hellenistic period; works of this period were animated, almost theatrical, in contrast to their serene Archaic and classical predecessors. These were revered by later artists such as Michelangelo, who was at the forefront of the rediscovery of Greek works in the Renaissance. The end of the Hellenistic age signalled the decline of Greek sculpture's pre-eminent position in the art form. The torch was handed to the Romans, who proved worthy successors.

Two of the foremost modern sculptors, Dimitrios Filippotis and Yannoulis Halepas, were from Tinos, where marble sculpture tradition endures today. The biggest collection of contemporary Greek and international sculpture can be seen at the **National Sculpture Gallery** (off Map p78; ☎ 210 770 9855; Army Park, Katehaki; adult/concession €6/3; ☾ 9am-3pm Mon & Wed-Sat, 10am-3pm Sun) in Athens.

POTTERY

The painted terracotta pots of ancient Greece, excavated after being buried throughout Greece over millennia, have enabled us to appreciate in small measure the tradition of ancient pictorial art.

One of the most ancient arts, vases were first built with coils and wads of clay, but the art of throwing on the wheel was introduced in about 2000 BC and was then practised with great skill by Minoan and Mycenaean artists.

Minoan pottery is often characterised by a high centre of gravity and beak-like spouts, with flowing designs of spiral or marine and plant motifs. The Archaeological Museum of Iraklio (p225) has a wealth of Minoan pots.

Mycenaean pottery shapes include a long-stemmed goblet and a globular vase with handles resembling a pair of stirrups. Decorative motifs are similar to those on Minoan pottery but are less fluid.

The 10th century BC saw the introduction of the Protogeometric style, with its substantial pots decorated with blackish-brown horizontal lines around the circumference, hatched triangles and compass-drawn concentric circles. This was followed by the new vase shape and more crowded decoration of the Geometric period. By the early 8th century BC figures were introduced, marking the introduction of the most fundamental ele-

---

SUMMER ARTS

As the Athens arts scene winds down for the summer, many exhibitions by local and international artists are held on the islands. One of the big annual arts events is held on Andros at the **Museum of Contemporary Art** (p138), which also has a permanent exhibition of Andriot sculptor Michael Tombros and the Goulandris' private collection.

In Hydra artist Dimitris Antonitsis curates the annual Hydra School Project at the island's primary school, while major exhibitions are run by the **Rethymnon Centre for Contemporary Art** (☎ 28310 52530; www.rca.gr; Himaras 5, Rethymno; admission free except for special exhibitions; ✆ 9am-1pm & 7-10pm Tue-Fri, 11am-3pm Sat) in Crete.

The **Rhodes Modern Greek Art Museum** (admission €3) is a major gallery spread across three historic buildings: the main permanent collection of 20th-century Greek art is in the **New Art Gallery** (☎ 22410 43780; Nestoridio Melathron Bldg, Haritou Sq; ✆ 8am-2pm & 5-8pm Tue-Sat); the **Municipal Gallery of Rhodes** (☎ 22410 23766; Plateia Symis 2, Old Town) has the most extensive collection of 20th-century Greek art after the National Art Gallery in Athens, and there is a **Modern Art Centre** (Sokratous 179, Old Town; ✆ 8am-2pm Tue-Sat).

---

ment in the later tradition of classical art – the representation of gods, men and animals.

Reproductions of these styles are found at souvenir shops throughout the country. Some contemporary ceramicists are still making pots using ancient firing and painting techniques. Minoan-style pottery is made in Crete, while the island of Sifnos continues its distinctive pottery tradition.

Music

Greece's strong and enduring musical tradition dates back at least to the 2000 BC Cycladic figurines found holding musical instruments resembling harps and flutes. These days most people associate Greek music with the distinctive sound of the six- or eight-stringed bouzouki, a long-necked lute-like instrument, which is a relative newcomer to the scene. Other traditional instruments include the *baglamas*, a baby version of the bouzouki used in *rembetika* (known as the Greek blues), and the *tzouras*, which is halfway between the two.

The strident sound of the Cretan *lyra* (lyre), the staccato rap of the *toumberleki* (lap drum), the *mandolino* (mandolin) and the *gaïda* (bagpipe) share many characteristics with instruments all over the Middle East.

Every region in Greece has its own musical tradition. *Nisiotika*, the up-beat music of the islands, is far lighter than the grounded and somewhat melancholy *dimotika* of the mainland. The powerful music of Crete is represented in the world-music scene as a genre in its own right. It remains the most dynamic traditional music, with a popular local following and regular performances and new recordings by folk artists.

Folk music can be heard in open-air festivals *(paniyiria)* around Greece during summer.

Byzantine music is mostly heard in Greek churches these days, though Byzantine hymns are performed by choirs in concerts in Greece and abroad and the music has influenced folk music.

Greek music today encompasses a range of styles, from traditional folk music to the modern pop *tsifteteli* (bellydance derivative) hybrid beats played in Greek clubs. The urban *rembetika* music that emerged in the 1920s is still popular and played in clubs around Greece, as is *laïka* (urban folk music), which emerged in the '50s and '60s with the popular Stelios Kazantzidis and Grigoris Bithikotsis.

The memorable opening-credits track from the 1994 film *Pulp Fiction* was based on surf guitar legend Dirk Dale's 1960s version of 'Misirlou' – originally recorded by a Greek *rembetika* band around 1930.

Entehni (artistic) music was first introduced by the outstanding composers Mikis Theodorakis and Manos Hatzidakis, who used traditional instruments such as the bouzouki in more symphonic arrangements. They also brought poetry to the masses by making hits using lyrics from Greece's great poets. Cretan Yiannis Markopoulos continued this new wave by introducing rural folk music and traditional instruments, such as the *lyra*, *santouri*, violin and *kanonaki* into the mainstream and bringing folk performers like Crete's legendary Nikos Xylouris to the fore. During the junta years, Theodorakis' and Markopoulos' music became a form of political expression and protest. Theodorakis is one of Greece's most prolific composers, though, somewhat to his dismay, he is best known for the classic 'Zorba' tune.

Comparatively few Greek performers have made it big on the international scene – 1970s icons Nana Mouskouri and kaftan-wearing Demis Roussos remain the best known.

Greek music veteran George Dalaras has covered the gamut of Greek music and collaborated with Latin and Balkan artists, as well as Sting, while Dionysis Savopoulos is known as the Dylan of Greece. Distinguished women of Greek music include Haris Alexiou, Glykeria, Dimitra Galani and Eleftheria Arvanitaki.

Stand-out new-generation artists include Cypriot-born 'modern troubadour' Alkinoos Ioannides, with his rocky folk-inspired songs and ballads, as well as singer-songwriters Thanasis Papakonstantinou, Dimitris Zervoudakis and Miltiadis Pashalidis.

For a comprehensive run-down of arts and cultural events and exhibitions around Greece check out www.elculture.gr.

Greece's answer to Madonna is Anna Vissi, while the youth vote was firmly with pop idol Mihalis Hatziyiannis and Greek-Swedish singer Elena Paparizou, who claimed Greece's first-ever Eurovision Song Contest win in 2005 (a feat heart-throb Sakis Rouvas failed to repeat in his two attempts). The big *laïka* performers include Yiannis Ploutarhos and Antonis Remos, while siren Despina Vandi has broken into the US dance charts.

Contemporary Greek music can include elements of traditional folk music, folk rock, heavy metal, rap and electronic dance music. Vocal artist Savina Yannatou and folk-jazz fusion artists Kristi Stasinopoulou and Mode Plagal are making a mark on the world-music scene. Other notable musicians include Cretan-influenced band Haïnides, Achilleas Persidis and pop-rock band Raining Pleasure.

During summer you can see Greece's leading acts in outdoor concerts on the bigger islands and around the country. The popular nightclubs known as *bouzoukia* are glitzy, expensive, cabaret-style venues where the bouzouki reigns supreme. Musical taste can sometimes take a back seat in second-rate clubs referred to as *skyladika* (dog houses) – apparently because the crooning singers resemble a whining dog.

For a nation without a strong Western classical tradition, Greece has spawned a surprisingly formidable list of soloists and conductors, many of whom lived abroad.

Sopranos Elena Kelessidi and Irini Tsirakidou are following in the footsteps of original opera diva Maria Callas. Greece's best-known conductor was composer Dimitris Mitropoulos, who led the New York Philharmonic in the 1950s, while Loukas Karytinos is Greece's leading conductor. Greece's most distinguished composers include Stavros Xarhakos and the late Yannis Xenakis. Mezzo-soprano Agnes Baltsa and acclaimed pianist Dimitris Sgouros are internationally known, while Greece's answer to Andrea Bocelli is tenor Mario Frangoulis.

Composer Vangelis Papathanasiou is best known for film scores, including Oscar-winner *Chariots of Fire*. Stamatis Spanoudakis wrote the excellent soundtrack to *Brides,* while Evanthia Remboutsika and Eleni Karaindrou have written award-winning film scores.

Dance

Dancing has been part of social life in Greece since the dawn of Hellenism. Some of today's folk dances derive from the ritual dances performed in ancient Greek temples. The *syrtos* (traditional Greek dance) is depicted on ancient vases and there are references to dances in Homer's works. Many folk dances are performed in a circular formation; in ancient times, dancers formed a circle in order to seal themselves off from evil influences or would dance around an altar, tree, figure or object. Dancing was also part of military education, while under occupation it was a way for men to keep fit under the noses of their enemies.

Regional dance styles often reflect the climate or disposition of the participants and dance is a way of expressing sorrow and joy.

The islands, with their bright and cheery atmosphere, give rise to light, springy dances such as the *ballos* and the *syrtos,* while the graceful and most widely known Kalamatianos, originally from Kalamata, reflects years of proud Peloponnese tradition. In Crete they dance a graceful and slow *syrtos,* the fast and triumphant *maleviziotiko* and the dynamic *pentozali,* which has a slow and fast version, in which the leader impresses with high kicks and leaps.

The so-called 'Zorba dance', or *syrtaki,* is a stylised dance for two or three men or women with arms linked on each other's shoulders, though the modern variation is danced in a long circle with an ever-quickening beat.

The often spectacular solo male *zeïmbekiko,* with its whirling, meditative improvisations, has its roots in *rembetika,* where it was originally danced while drunk or high on hashish. Women have their own sensuous *tsifteteli,* a svelte, sinewy show of femininity evolved from the Middle Eastern belly dance.

The best place to see traditional dancing is at local festivals around the country and at the Dora Stratou Dance Theatre in Athens (p87).

Contemporary dance in Greece is gaining prominence, with leading local dance troupes taking their place among the international line-up at the prestigious Kalamata International Dance Festival and the Athens International Dance Festival (p84). Acclaimed choreographer Dimitris Papaioannou was the creative director of the Athens 2004 opening and closing ceremonies.

The *syrtaki* dance, immortalised by Anthony Quinn in the final scene in *Zorba the Greek,* was in fact a dance he improvised, as he had hurt his leg the day before the shoot and could not perform the traditional steps and leaps originally planned.

Cinema & TV

Greek cinema took off after the end of the civil war and peaked in the 1950s and early '60s, when domestic audiences flocked to a flurry of comedies, melodramas and musicals being produced by the big Greek studios. Since those heydays Greece's film industry has largely been in the doldrums – Greece has not had a major international hit since *Zorba the Greek* made its debut in the '50s.

The demise of the studios with the advent of TV and inadequate funding was compounded by the slow-moving cerebral style of the 'new Greek cinema' of the '70s and '80s, which was generally too avant-garde to have mass appeal. The leader of this school is award-winning 'auteur' director Theodoros Angelopoulos, who received the 1998 Golden Palm award at the Cannes Film Festival for *Eternity and a Day.*

A shift in cinematic style in the 1990s achieved moderate domestic commercial successes with lighter social satires and a more contemporary style and pace, but beyond the festival circuit few have made an impact outside Greece. Two major mainstream films that gained international cinematic releases – the first in many years – were Tasos Boulmetis' *A Touch of Spice*

ON LOCATION

You've seen the movie but where in Greece was it shot?

Big Blue (1988) Memorable black and white opening scenes of unspoilt Amorgos.

Bourne Identity (2002) The final scenes were shot at the Sea Satin restaurant in Little Venice, Mykonos.

Captain Corelli's Mandolin (2001) Shot largely in the port of Sami, Kefallonia.

For Your Eyes Only (1981) James Bond explores Corfu's beaches, hotels and even the Turkish fort in Corfu Town.

Lara Croft Tomb Raider (2001) Lara Croft went diving off Santorini.

Mamma Mia (2008) The mystical island bopping away to Abba was Skopelos.

Mediterraneo (1991) Italian soldiers are garrisoned on tiny Kastellorizo in the Dodecanese.

My Life in Ruins (2009) Nia Vardalos led her tour bus around Athens and the Peloponnese.

Never on a Sunday (1960) Greece's big star Melina Mercouri received an Oscar nomination for her role as a prostitute in Piraeus.

Pascali's Island (1988) Ben Kingsley plays a Turkish spy on Symi during the dying days of Ottoman occupation.

Shirley Valentine (1989) The classic foreign woman's Greek island romance fantasy was in Mykonos.

Summer Lovers (1982) Darryl Hannah and Peter Gallagher got raunchy on Santorini, Mykonos and Crete.

Zorba the Greek (1964) Where else but Crete? The famous beach dance scene was at Stavros, near Hania.

(*Politiki Kouzina*; 2003) and Pantelis Voulgaris' 2004 hit *Brides (Nyfes)*, which was executively produced by Martin Scorsese. Perakis' chauvinistic but fun 2005 comedy *Sirens in the Aegean* was a big local hit.

The latest wave of filmmakers is attracting international attention with films that present a grittier, up-close and candid look at contemporary Greek life, a shift from the idealised and romanticised views from the past. Directors to watch include Konstantinos Giannaris, whose provocative documentary-style films like *From the Edge of the City* and *Hostage* seem to split audiences and critics alike.

Writer-Director Yorgos Lanthimos won the new talent (Un Certain Regard) section at Cannes in 2009 for his drama *Dog Tooth (Kynodonta)*, the major prize at the festival for Greece in a decade.

Another internationally known veteran Greek director is Paris-based Costa-Gavras, who won an Oscar in 1969 for *Z*. His recent films include *Amen* (2003) and *Eden is West* (2009).

Greek TV offers a jumble of local programs from histrionic comedy series, talk shows and soap operas to Greek versions of reality TV game shows and star-producing talent shows, though there have also been some excellent dramas of late tackling social themes such as immigration, single mothers and life in rural Greece.

SPORT

Football (soccer) remains the most popular spectator sport in Greece, followed by basketball and volleyball. For a brief time after Greece's astounding football victory in the 2004 European Cup, Greece was the reigning European champion in both football and basketball (2005 winners). This followed the resounding success of the Athens 2004 homecoming Olympic Games, but little of international note has since happened in the sporting arena.

Football's first division is dominated by the big-glamour clubs of the league: Olympiakos of Piraeus and Panathinaikos of Athens, with their rivalry occasionally interrupted by AEK Athens and PAOK from Thessaloniki.

Greek football teams have attracted some top international players in recent years, but hooliganism and violence at football matches has affected attendance at games. Greece normally fields two teams in the European

Champions League, but remains in the shadow of Europe's football heavyweights.

Greece is, however, one of the powerhouses of European basketball. Panathinaikos, Olympiakos and AEK also dominate Greek basketball. Panathinaikos won their fifth Euroleague title in 2009.

No islands are large enough or have a big enough permanent population to field a team in national sports leagues, with the exception of Crete. Corfu is home to the Greek Cricket Federation, the only place in Greece where they play cricket (a quirky legacy of the British), though recent immigrants have introduced the game to the capital.

Food & Drink

Long lunches at a rickety table by the beach or alfresco dining on balmy summer nights have long been highlights of the Greek island experience. The ambience may help you to forgive the indifferent offerings at many tourist-trap tavernas, but travellers who seek out traditional Greek cooking are amply rewarded. Exploring traditional cuisine on the busier islands still requires venturing beyond the 'tourist' trail: heading to the mountain villages for fresh local meat, seeking out local cheese and wine, or sampling the day's catch in a tiny fishing village. But the Greek culinary scene has become increasingly diverse. A new breed of contemporary Greek tavernas and upscale restaurants have seen the current generation of Greek chefs reinventing Greek cuisine, refining traditional recipes and bringing regional produce and local gourmet delights to the fore. Greek wine has likewise experienced a renaissance, with winemakers using local grape varieties to producing some unique fine wines.

The Glorious Foods of Greece, by award-winning food writer Diane Kochilas, is a superb and passionate regional exploration of Greek cuisine, its history and culture.

Traditional Greek cuisine derives from rustic provincial cooking, which brings out the flavours of the Mediterranean. It is generally unfussy and is steeped in tradition, reflecting a versatility and resourcefulness that evolved from years of subsistence living during hard times, and drawing from the produce and influences of each region. The cuisine of the Greek islands, spread across the seas from Italy to Turkey, is heavily influenced by their history and topography. Arid landscapes and the limited availability of local produce on many islands meant making the most of the fruits of the sea and whatever grew wild, from capers to artichokes.

Although you'll find the familiar Greek staples on most island taverna menus, regional variations and specialities abound, along with subtle accents from Asia Minor and Italy.

Despite the proliferation of trendy Greek eateries, the casual taverna is still the mainstay of the Greek islands, and some of the best meals will be in family-run places where simple home-style food is cooked with produce from the owner's garden or livestock. In the big cities and on larger and more cosmopolitan islands, you will also find international-style restaurants and ethnic cuisine.

THE GREEK KITCHEN

Traditional Greek cuisine epitomises the healthy Mediterranean diet, which is lean on meat and big on vegetables, pulses and legumes. Plentiful consumption of fruit, bread, wheat and cereals, fish, wild greens and red wine also contributed to the nutritional benefits identified in scientific studies into the Greek diet. Meat has, however, become a more prominent part of the modern Greek diet, especially locally reared lamb, kid goat and pork (most beef is imported). Grilled meat is popular when dining out and meat is now often added to vegetable stews.

More than 75% of Greece's entire annual production of oil is good enough to be labelled extra virgin. Compare that to 50% for Italy and 30% for Spain.

Greece has some exceptional produce that makes simple meals remarkable, not least the abundance of fresh fruit and vegetables. Simple, pure and intense flavours dominate – olive oil, garlic, lemon, pungent wild oregano, mint, dill and fennel.

Olive oil, the elixir of Greece, is a vital ingredient and the key to making salads, vegetables and legumes tastier (these largely vegetarian dishes are called 'ladera' because olive oil is used in cooking and often added afterwards). Extra-virgin olive oil is produced commercially and in family-run groves across the country. The majority of Greek olive oil

---

SAY CHEESE

Greeks are the world's biggest per capita consumers of cheese, eating something like 25kg per capita annually – more than the French and Italians. Widely used in both savoury and sweet dishes, cheese is also a virtually mandatory accompaniment to any meal.

Greece probably produces as many different types of cheese as there are villages, with infinite variations in taste. Several Greek cheeses have gained appellation of origin status. Most are made from the milk of the nation's 16 million goats and sheep and many artisan cheesemakers still use traditional methods.

Feta, the national cheese made from sheep's and/or goat's milk, was the first Greek product to gain the same protected status as Parma ham and champagne – only feta made in Greece can be called feta, an EU ruling that will eventually apply worldwide.

The islands have contributed their own distinctive delights to the Greek cheese map.

Graviera, a nutty, mild Gruyère-like sheep's-milk cheese is a speciality of Naxos and Crete, where it is often aged in special mountain caves and stone huts (called *mitata*).

Anthotyro, a low-fat soft unsalted whey cheese similar to *myzithra* (a ricotta-like cheese, often dried and hardened and grated over pastas) and the hardened sour *xinomyzithra* are also specialities of Crete.

Ladotyri, a hard golden cheese from Lesvos, is preserved in olive oil, in Samos *tourloumotyri* is aged in goatskins, while in Kos, Nisyros and Sifnos, *krasotyri* is aged in wine. Other island cheeses include *mastelo* from Chios and the soft *chloro* of Santorini.

Tinos, Syros, Naxos and Corfu produce cow's milk cheese, a tradition from the Venetians.

---

is produced in the southern Peloponnese and the islands of Crete, Lesvos and Corfu.

Each region has its variation of meat and fish dishes and *pites* (pies), the most common being the *tyropita* (cheese pie) and *spanakopita* (spinach pie).

Bread is a mandatory feature of every meal, the most popular being the white crusty *horiatiko* (village) loaf.

Greece's tangy, thick-strained sheep's milk yoghurt is exceptionally flavourful and ideal for breakfast or dessert with thick aromatic thyme honey, walnuts and fruit.

DINING OUT

Eating out is an integral part of Greek social life. Meals are rowdy affairs and people still prefer the relaxed taverna style of dining, normally sharing a range of dishes. This is why meat and fish are often sold by the kilo, not per portion.

The key to picking a restaurant is to find places where locals are eating, rather than overpriced 'tourist' tavernas (touts and big illuminated photos and signs are usually a giveaway). Try to adapt to local eating times – a restaurant that was empty at 7pm might be heaving at 11pm (see also Habits & Customs, p62). Don't be fooled by super-extensive menus, you may well be better off at a nondescript place with only a handful of fresh dishes. Solo diners remain a curiosity but are looked after. Most island tavernas are family run and open all day, but upmarket restaurants often open for dinner only.

By law, all eating establishments must display a written menu with prices.

Foods of the Greek Islands by Aglaïa Kremezi explores the history, culture and cuisine of the islands and presents classic and new recipes from her travels and from New York's Molyvos restaurant.

Mezedhes & Starters

Sharing a range of mezedhes (appetisers) is a great way to sample various dishes, and it is quite acceptable to make a full meal of these or combine with a main. You can also order a *pikilia* (mixed mezedhes plate).

Common mezedhes include dips, such as *taramasalata* (fish-roe), *tzatziki* (yoghurt, cucumber and garlic), *melitzanosalata* (aubergine), *keftedhes* (meatballs), *loukaniko* (sausage) and *saganaki* (skillet-fried cheese).

Vegetarians will appreciate rice-filled dolmadhes (in vine leaves), deep-fried zucchini or aubergine slices, tasty *yigantes* (lima beans in tomato and herb sauce) and tongue-twisting *kolokythokeftedhes* (zucchini fritters).

You will often see locally caught *ohtapodi* (octopus) hung out to dry ready to be grilled as a mezes (appetiser; it is also commonly pickled). Other typical seafood mezedhes are *lakerda* (cured fish), mussel or prawn *saganaki* (with tomato sauce and cheese) and crispy fried calamari or *maridha* (whitebait). *Gavros* (white anchovies) are delicious marinated or grilled.

Soup is not normally eaten as a starter, but can be an economical and hearty meal with bread. On the islands, you'll most likely find a *psarosoupa* (fish soup) with vegetables. *Kakavia*, a bouillabaisse-style speciality laden with various fish and seafood, is made to order.

The main summer salad is the ubiquitous Greek salad (*horiatiki*, translated as 'village salad'), with tomato, cucumber, onion, feta and olives (occasionally purslane or capers in the Cyclades). Other seasonal salads include lettuce, cabbage and *roka* (rocket), while *horta* (wild or cultivated greens) make a great warm salad, and *pantzaria* (beetroot) are divine with garlic, vinegar and oil.

Most Greeks can't go past a plate of *patates tiganites*, hand-cut potatoes cooked in olive oil (though frozen potatoes are taking over).

Mains

Most tavernas have a selection of one-pot stews, casseroles and ready-cooked oven-baked meals *(mayirefta)* and food cooked to order *(tis oras)*, such as grilled meats. *Mayirefta* are usually prepared early in the day and left to cool, which enhances the flavour (they're often better served lukewarm, though many places microwave them).

A summer favourite is *yemista* (tomatoes and seasonal vegetables stuffed with rice and herbs), while almost every taverna will have *mousakas* (layers of eggplant, minced meat and potatoes topped with cheese sauce and baked). Other popular dishes include hearty *youvetsi*, meat baked in a tomato sauce

The healthy Mediterranean diet has become a victim of changing lifestyles and the rise of fast-food/junk-food culture, with Greeks recording the highest obesity rates in the EU.

WHERE TO EAT & DRINK

The most common Greek eatery is the taverna; a basic and casual, family-run (and child-friendly) place where the waiter usually arrives with bread and cutlery in a basket. The taverna has barrel wine, paper tablecloths and standard menus. Other eateries include the following.

bar-restaurant – a more recent urban concept, they become incredibly loud after 11pm

estiatorio – a restaurant, where you pay more for essentially the same dishes as in a taverna or *mayireio* (below), but with a nicer setting and formal service; these days it also refers to an upmarket restaurant that serves international cuisine

kafeneio – a traditional coffee house that serves Greek coffee and spirits (in villages it may also serve food); they remain largely the domain of men

mayireio – specialises in traditional home-style one-pot dishes and oven-baked meals (known as *mayirefta*)

mezedhopoleio – offers lots of small plates of mezedhes (appetisers)

ouzerie – traditionally serves tiny plates of mezedhes with each round of ouzo; the Cretan equivalent is a *rakadhiko* (serving *raki*)

psarotaverna – taverna that specialises in fish and seafood

psistaria – taverna that specialises in char-grilled or spit-roasted meat (sometimes may be called a *hasapotaverna*)

zaharoplasteio – a cross between a patisserie and a cafe (though some only cater for takeaway and gifts)

FISHY BUSINESS

One of the most memorable culinary treats in Greece is a simply char-grilled whole fish, freshly plucked from the sea by local fishermen and ideally eaten by the seaside. These days fish is a bit of a luxury, largely as a result of overfishing, and there's certainly not enough fish caught locally to cater to millions of tourists each summer. The fish on your plate may well be from Senegal or a local fish farm, but some places charge the same regardless.

On the islands, many tavernas will not have fish if their local fishermen didn't catch any. Most places will state if the fish and seafood is frozen, though sometimes only on the Greek menu (indicated by the abbreviated 'kat' or an asterisk). Smaller fish are often a safer bet – the odder the sizes, the more chance that they are local and fresh.

Fish is usually sold by weight and it is customary to go into the kitchen and choose the fish yourself (go for firm flesh and glistening eyes). Check the weight (raw) so you know what to expect on the bill as the price for fresh fish can start at around €50 per kilo.

The choice fish for grilling are *tsipoura* (gilthead sea bream), *lavraki* (sea bass) and *fangri* (bream), served with a *ladholemono* (lemon and oil) dressing; while smaller fish, such as the *barbouni* (red mullet), is delicious fried. See the glossary (p65) for other common fish names.

with *kritharaki* (rice-shaped pasta), and mince- and rice-filled cabbage rolls filled with *avgolemono* (egg and lemon) sauce.

Ladhera are a particular type of *mayirefta*, often vegetable dishes such as beans and okra, cooked in plenty of olive oil.

Lamb is often baked with potatoes, lemon and oregano, while beef and chicken are cooked in tomato-based stews *(kokkinisto)*. Rabbit and beef are made into a sweet *stifadho* (braised with onions and tomato), while *kokoras* (cockerel) *kokkinisto* is served with *hilopites* (flat egg pasta).

Tasty charcoal-grilled meats – most commonly *païdakia* (lamb cutlets) and *brizoles* (pork chops) – are often ordered by the kilo. Restaurants tend to serve souvlaki – cubes of grilled meat on a skewer, rather than *gyros* (meat slithers cooked on a vertical rotisserie; usually eaten with pitta bread).

Fish is normally cooked with minimum fuss, usually grilled (see also Fishy Business, above) or baked *plaki* – baked with tomato, potatoes and herbs.

Seafood dishes include octopus in wine with macaroni, grilled or stewed *soupies* (cuttlefish), squid stuffed with cheese and herbs or rice, and fried salted cod served with *skordalia* (a lethal garlic and potato purée).

> Lamb *kleftiko* (stolen) originates from the days when brigands or stock thieves cooked their bounty in sealed containers underground. Nowadays the dish is cooked in baking paper, retaining the juices.

Sweet Treats

After a meal, Greeks traditionally serve fruit rather than dessert, so peruse local bakeries and *zaharoplasteia* (patisseries) for sweet specialities.

Syros makes delicious *loukoumia* ('Grecian delight'; gummy squares usually flavoured with rosewater) and *halvadopites* (nougat-like confectionery). The Cyclades are known for *amygdalota* (almond confectionery), particularly the marzipan-style sweets made on Andros. Zakynthos specialities include the *pasteli* (made from sesame seeds and almonds) and nougat-like *mandolato*.

Traditional sweets include baklava, *kataïfi* (nut-filled angel-hair pastry), fluffy *loukoumadhes* (ball-shaped doughnuts served with honey and cinnamon), *rizogalo* (rice pudding) and *galaktoboureko* (syrupy custard slice also commonly served with crushed walnuts). Look out for semi-sweet *myzithra*-cheese pies such as Crete's *lihnarakia* and Santorini's *melitinia*, made with *myzithra*, yoghurt and honey.

Fruit preserves (syrupy sweets served on a tiny plate eaten with a spoon, commonly referred to as *glika koutaliou*, ie spoon sweets), traditionally a welcome offering to guests, are also delicious on yoghurt or ice cream.

ISLAND SPECIALITIES

While there are staple Greek dishes you will find throughout the islands, each island group – and sometimes each island – has its own specialities and subtle variations.

The cuisine of the Ionian Islands, which were never under Turkish rule, has a distinct Italian influence, as seen in Corfu's spicy braised beef or rooster *pastitsada,* served with pasta and in a red sauce, and *sofrito* – a braised veal with garlic and wine sauce – is cooked in Corfu and across the Ionians. In Zakynthos, grilled *pancetta* (pork spare ribs) is popular.

The arid landscape, dry climate and isolation of the Cyclades meant many islanders relied on beans and pulses as the foundation of their winter diet and foraged for wild greens and herbs. Sifnos' famous *revythadha* (chickpea stew) is made in a specially shaped clay pot, slow-cooked overnight, while *revythokeftedhes* (chickpea fritters) are another speciality. Santorini is renowned for its tasty *fava* (yellow split-pea) purée, usually topped with finely chopped onion and lemon juice. See also Island Gourmet Trails (p62) for more information on regional cuisine.

In Folegandros you will come across *matsata*, a pasta dish with rabbit or chicken in red sauce. Before imports became feasible, the drier islands were limited to hardy sheep and goats for their meat and cheese.

The sea remains the other major food source and it's recommended to seek out tavernas run by local fishing families. Spaghetti with lobster is a decadent island speciality, particularly in the Cyclades. *Ahinosalata* (fresh sea urchin–egg salad) gives you a powerful taste of the sea.

The preservation of food using various methods was integral to survival during the winter. Isolated islands, such as Symi, are renowned for their sun-dried preserved fish and seafood. Cured fish, such as *kolios* (mackerel), is a popular mezes, while the sun-dried fish dish *liokafto* is a speciality of Folegandros. You'll also find some excellent cured meats, such as the vinegar-cured pork *apaki* in Crete, spicy wine-marinated and smoked *louza* (pork) in Tinos, and rare goat *pastourmas* in Ikaria and Karpathos. Mykonos is known for its sausages, while Lesvos is renowned for fresh or salted sardines and *gavros*.

Barley or wholemeal *paximadhia* (hard rusks), double-baked to keep for years, are moistened with water and topped with tomato and olive oil (and feta or *myzithra* cheese) in the Cretan *dakos*.

> Acclaimed London chef Theodore Kyriakou sails in search of recipes for *A Culinary Voyage Around the Greek Islands*, a delectable sequel to *The Real Greek at Home* and *Real Greek Food*.

> In *Prospero's Kitchen*, Diana Farr Louis and June Marinos present rare and traditional recipes from the Ionian Islands.

TRAVEL YOUR TASTE BUDS

Look out for the following specialities on your island travels.

ahinosalata – sea urchin eggs with lemon juice; various islands

amygdalota – almond sweets; Andros and Mykonos

anthi – zucchini flowers stuffed with rice and herbs; Crete

astakomakaronada – decadent lobster spaghetti; common in the Cyclades, available throughout the islands

dakos – rusks topped with tomato, olive oil and *myzithra* (a ricotta-like whey cheese); Crete

domatokeftedhes – tasty tomato fritters; Santorini

fava – yellow split-pea purée; Santorini

hohlioi bourbouristoi – Crete's famous snail dish

kopanisti – spicy creamy cheese; Mykonos

loukoumi – Syros' renowned 'Grecian delight' (aka Turkish delight); also available throughout Greece

mastiha – mastic-flavoured *ypovryhio* or 'submarine' sugar confectionary from Chios, served on a spoon dipped in a glass of water or try the chilled liqueur

raki – you're unlikely to leave Crete without tasting the local firewater

Samos dessert wine – prized sweet wine from the local Muscat grape

soumada – nonalcoholic almond drink; Cyclades

Crete produces the richest bounty and has the most distinctive island cuisine. You'll find spiky wild artichokes, and herb-rich dishes such as *soupies* with wild fennel, or wild greens with rabbit and the local delicacy, *hohlioi* (snails). Lamb or goat is often cooked *tsigariasto* (sautéed) or *ofto* (grilled upright around hot coals), or stewed with *stamnagathi* (wild mountain greens) or artichokes. The Cretan *boureki* (a cheese, zucchini and potato bake) is a favourite, while *kalitsounia* are the tasty local version of the *pita* (filled with *myzithra* or wild greens, the former are also eaten with honey). Festive occasions invariably involve spit-roasted and boiled lamb, the stock of which is used to make the divine *pilafi*, commonly known as *gamopilafo* (wedding rice).

Chios' claim to fame is mastic, the aromatic resin from the mastic trees that grow almost exclusively on the island. Most people associate it with chewing gum, or *mastiha* (the sticky white fondant sweet served in a glass of water, called *ypovryhio* or 'submarine'), but it is also used to flavour pastries and other foods (as well as for medicinal purposes and skin products).

Vefa's Kitchen is a weighty 750-page bible of Greek cooking from TV cooking matron Vefa Alexiadou, with 650 recipes, including some from leading Greek chefs around the globe.

Quick Eats

Souvlaki is the favourite fast food of Greece, both the *gyros* and skewered versions wrapped in pitta bread, with tomato, onion and lashings of *tzatziki*. Most souvlaki meat is pork.

Tyropites (cheese pies) and *spanakopites* (spinach pies) and other variations can be found in bakeries, hole-in-the-wall stores and fast-food chains. You'll also come across street vendors selling the *koulouri* (round, sesame-covered pretzel-like bread) and other seasonal snacks, such as grilled corn, nuts and chestnuts.

There is no shortage of Western-style *fastfoudadhika* (fast-food joints) in major towns on the islands.

VEGETARIANS & VEGANS

A legacy of lean times and the Orthodox faith's fasting traditions mean vegetables feature prominently in the Greek kitchen, making it easier and tastier to go vegetarian in Greece.

Ladhera are the mainstay of religious fasts. Look for popular vegetarian dishes, such as *fasolakia yiahni* (green bean stew), *bamies* (stuffed okra) and *briam* (oven-baked vegetable casserole). Artichokes and aubergines are also widely used, while vine leaf or cabbage dolmadhes and *anthoi* (stuffed zucchini flowers) are a staple. Beans and pulses are widely used, and you will often find dishes such as *yigantes* on the menu. Of the wild greens, *vlita* (amaranth) are the sweetest, but other common varieties include wild radish, dandelion, stinging nettle and sorrel.

There are more than 300 edible *horta* (wild and cultivated greens) in Greece, though identifying the full range of edible greens is a dying art. Rare and difficult to find mountain greens fetch high prices.

FEASTS & CELEBRATIONS

Food plays an integral part in Greek religious and cultural celebrations, with every morsel laced with symbolism. The Lenten fast before Easter involves special dishes without meat or dairy products – or even oil if you go strictly by the book. Come the Resurrection Mass, though, the celebrations begin with a supper that includes a bowl of *mayiritsa* (offal soup), while the highlight of the Easter Sunday feast is spit-roasted or baked lamb.

Red-dyed boiled eggs are part of the Easter festivities, for both cracking and decorating the *tsoureki*, a brioche-style bread flavoured with *mahlepi* (mahaleb cherry kernels).

Easter sweets include *koulourakia* (biscuits), *melomakarona* (honey biscuits) and *kourabiedes* (almond shortcake biscuits).

With as many anecdotes as recipes, Emma Tennant's *Corfu Banquet: A Seasonal Memoir with Recipes* is a delightfully evocative book.

ISLAND GOURMET TRAILS Victoria Kyriakopoulos

Greece's culinary delights have been increasingly coming to the fore, with modern restaurants placing more emphasis on regional cuisine and produce and moving beyond the familiar staples. On the islands, you can still find traditional cooking and local specialities if you venture beyond the tourist-trap tavernas.

Island cuisine evolved from people making the most of local conditions. Santorini's volcanic soil is renowned for producing unique wines (see p198), but it also reaps intensely flavoured cherry tomatoes, made into tangy *domatokeftedhes* (tomato fritters). Its famous *fava* is made into a delicious creamy purée, while Santorini has its own white eggplant. The Cyclades' plump wild capers are the best in Greece.

Preserving the islands' culinary heritage is becoming a challenge. With the easy availability of produce today, few people were still growing fava beans and cherry tomatoes and even fewer on the Cyclades were rearing sheep and goats for producing cheese (see the boxed text, p57). Places like Santorini's Selene restaurant promote local cuisine on the menu and owner Yiorgos Hatziyannakis also runs summer cooking seminars (see opposite).

'We try to keep them going because no one wants to be a farmer or shepherd these days. They have five rooms (for rent) in summer and they're fine', says Hatziyannakis.

Crete is tapping into its potential as a gourmet tourism destination, with traditional cooking making a comeback and evolving, helped along by agrotourism ventures, agricultural cooperatives and programs, such as **Concred** (www.concred.gr), which accredits restaurants serving authentic Cretan cuisine.

'We use only Cretan ingredients and traditional dishes, though sometimes we change the combinations and method', explains Katerina Xekalou, who presides over the elegant restaurant Avli (p239) in Rethymno, one of the finest restaurants in Greece.

Mushrooms and *apaki* (cured pork) were never used in the same dish but it works beautifully, while Avli's signature dish of goat with thyme and honey evolved from her grandmother dipping boiled goat in honey.

'It's Cretan food with a twist. You don't have to replicate the past for it to be authentic.'

The New Year's *vasilopita* (golden-glazed cake) is baked with a lucky coin in the mix, giving the recipient good luck for the year.

HABITS & CUSTOMS

Hospitality is a key element of Greek culture, from the glass of water when you arrive at a cafe or restaurant to the customary complimentary fruit at the end of the meal.

Dining is a drawn-out ritual, so if you are eating with locals pace yourself and don't gorge on the mezedhes, because there will be more to come. Greeks generally order way too much, and notoriously overcater at home, as they would rather throw it out (or give it away) than not have enough.

Though you will find Western-style breakfasts and omelettes, breakfast is not a big Greek tradition (more often coffee and cigarettes or a *tyropita* on the run).

The people of Crete probably eat more snails than the French, and Cretan snails are even exported to France. You'll see groups out in force after rain.

Changes in working hours are affecting traditional meal patterns; however, lunch still largely remains the big meal of the day and does not start until after 2pm. Most Greeks wouldn't think of eating dinner before the sun goes down, which coincides with shop closing hours, so restaurants don't fill up until after 10pm. Cafes do a roaring trade after the siesta, between 6pm and 8pm.

The pace of service in tavernas can be slow by Western standards, but they are not in a rush to get you out of there either. Once you have your meals they are likely to leave you alone and often not clear the table until you ask for the bill.

Greeks don't traditionally drink coffee after a meal and many tavernas don't offer it.

EATING WITH KIDS

Greece is very child-friendly and families will feel comfortable at a taverna and *psistaria* (taverna that specialises in char-grilled meat) where no-one is too fussed if children play between the tables. You will see families dining out late at night and packs of children playing outside while their parents indulge in a long dinner. Kid's menus are not common, but most places will accommodate requests. For more information on travelling with children, see also p479).

COOKING COURSES

Several cooking courses and food tours are held on the islands.

Santorini's acclaimed **Selene** (www.selene.gr) restaurant runs one-day courses focusing on island specialities and wine.

Aglaïa Kremezi and her friends open their kitchens and gardens on Kea for five-day hands-on **cooking workshops** (www.keartisanal.com).

Award-winning Greek-American food writer Diane Kochilas runs the **Glorious Greek Kitchen** (www.gloriousgreekkitchen.com) summer cooking course on her ancestral island Ikaria.

Crete's Culinary Sanctuaries (www.cookingincrete.com) combines cooking classes, farm tours, hiking and cultural excursions around the island.

DRINKS
Wine

The Greeks invented wine, with the wine god Dionysos tramping the vintage even before the Bronze Age, yet until recently Greek wine was not associated all that favourably with the distinctive retsina (pine-resinated white wine) introduced to the world in the 1960s. In the past 20 years a renaissance in the Greek wine industry has seen a new generation of progressive, internationally trained winemakers reinventing Greek wine. Indigenous grape varieties are being revived and brought to the fore, with some exquisite results.

Island vineyards produce some distinctive local wines from unique and rare grape varieties, including *robola* in Kefallonia and *assyrtiko*, *athiri* and *aidani* in the Cyclades, especially on Paros and Santorini (see also p198). Wine tourism is popular in Santorini, where the volcanic soil produces unique wines; the vines here are trained into a circle to protect the grapes from wind and the cellars are underground because of the heat. Crete's massive wine industry (producing about 20% of Greek wine) has become savvier and produces fine local varieties, including the white *vilana* and *thrapsathiri* grapes and the reds, *liatiko*, *kotsifali* and *mandilari*. Other Greek varieties include the white *moschofilero*, *roditis* and *savatiano*, and red *xinomavro and agiorgitiko*. A rose *agiorgitiko* is the perfect summer wine. Greek wines are produced in relatively small quantities, however, and many are boutique wines (and priced accordingly). Greek island sweet wines include muscats from Samos, Limnos and Rhodes, and Santorini's Vinsanto (yes, the Greeks invented it).

For the largest collection of Greek recipes online try www.greek-recipe.com, www.gourmed.com or check out Diane Kochilas' Greek Food TV segments on YouTube.

The Illustrated Greek Wine Book by Nico Manessis is the definitive guide, tracing the history of Greek wine and profiling leading Greek winemakers and wine regions. Also check out www.greekwine.gr.

DOS & DON'TS

- Do ask what the local speciality is and be adventurous.
- Do ask to look in the pots in the kitchen to select your meal.
- Don't insist on paying if you are invited out – it insults your host.
- Don't refuse a coffee or drink – it's offered as a gesture of hospitality and goodwill.

As for retsina, nowadays it has taken on an almost folkloric significance with foreigners, some of whom confuse it with barrel wine (which is non-resinated). It goes well with strongly flavoured food, especially seafood, but it's an acquired taste.

Spirits

Apart from ouzo, Greece's main firewater is *tsipouro*, a highly potent distilled spirit produced from grape skins left over from winemaking. A similar but smoother variation called *raki* or *tsikoudia* is drunk in copious amounts in Crete.

Look out for sweet liquors like Kumquat from Corfu, Mastiha from Chios (best served chilled) and citrus-flavoured Kitro from Naxos.

Greek brandies tend to be sweet and flowery in the nose. The dominant brandy is Metaxa.

Beer

The most common beer is locally brewed Dutch lagers Amstel and Heineken, though you can find a range of other European beers. Major Greek brands include Mythos and Alfa.

A number of excellent smaller boutique breweries have sprouted in recent years. Look out for Vergina, the organic Piraïki beer and Hillas, while Craft beer is widely available in draught form.

The only island with its own beer is Crete, where the Rethymniaki brewery produces a selection of blonde and dark lagers that are making inroads throughout Greece.

Corfu produces a unique nonalcoholic ginger beer called Tsitsibira.

Hot Beverages

A legacy of Ottoman rule, Greek coffee is traditionally brewed in a special copper *briki* (pot) – usually on a hot sand apparatus called a *hovoli* – and served in a small cup, where the grounds sink to the bottom (don't drink them). It is best drunk *metrio* (medium, with one sugar). Greek coffee is, however, struggling to maintain its place as the national drink against the ubiquitous frappé, the iced instant coffee concoction that you see everyone drinking. Espresso also comes in refreshing chilled form (*freddo*).

THE ART OF OUZO

Ouzo is Greece's most famous but misunderstood tipple. While it can be drunk as an apéritif, for most Greeks ouzo has come to embody a way of socialising – best enjoyed during a lazy, extended summer afternoon of seafood mezedhes (appetisers) by the seaside.

There are more than 360 brands of ouzo but Greece's best ouzo is produced on the island of Lesvos (Mytilini), particularly the top brand Plomari, named after the region where it is widely made.

Made from distilled grapes in a similar way to grappa or *raki* (Cretan firewater), ouzo is also distilled with residuals from fruit, grains and potatoes and flavoured with spices, primarily aniseed, giving it that liquorice flavour.

Ouzo is meant to be sipped slowly and ritually to cleanse the palate between tastes (it also cuts through the oiliness of some foods). It is usually served in small bottles or *karafakia* (carafes) with water and a bowl of ice cubes, and is commonly drunk on the rocks, diluted with water (it turns a cloudy white). In some regions they prefer it straight or just with icy water (and claim ice crystallises the sugar and alcohol and makes you drunk quicker). Whatever the case, mixing it with cola is a foreign abomination.

These days more ouzo is drunk in Germany than Greece, where Johnnie Walker dominates and the trendy young things are downing mojitos.

Herbal tea is quite popular, especially camomile tea and aromatic *tsai tou vounou* (mountain tea), which is nutritious and delicious. Crete's native Diktamo (Cretan dittany) is known for its healing properties, and the island's other reputedly medicinal warm tipple (found in many parts of Greece) is *rakomelo* – raki, honey and cloves.

EAT YOUR WORDS

Get behind the cuisine scene by getting to know the language. For pronunciation guidelines, see p529.

For comprehensive articles about Greek cuisine and ingredients, including a downloadable glossy magazine with recipes, check out www .kerasma.gr.

Food Glossary

STAPLES

αλάτι	a-*la*-ti	salt
αυγά	a-*vgha*	eggs
βούτυρο	*vu*-ti-ro	butter
γάλα	*gha*-la	milk
ελαιόλαδο	e-le-*o*-la-dho	olive oil
ελιές	e-*lyes*	olives
ζάχαρη	*za*-ha-ri	sugar
μέλι	*me*-li	honey
ξύδι	*ksi*-dhi	vinegar
πιπέρι	pi-*pe*-ri	pepper
τυρί	ti-*ri*	cheese
ψωμί	pso-*mi*	bread

MEAT, FISH & SEAFOOD

αρνί	ar-*ni*	lamb
αστακός	a-sta-*kos*	lobster
βοδινό	vo-dhi-*no*	beef
γαρίδες	gha-*ri*-dhes	prawns
ζαμπόν	zam-*bon*	ham
καλαμάρι	ka-la-*ma*-ri	squid
κατσικάκι	ka-tsi-*ka*-ki	kid (goat)
κέφαλος	*ke*-fa-los	grey mullet
κολιός	ko-li-*os*	mackerel
κοτόπουλο	ko-*to*-pu-lo	chicken
κουνέλι	ku-*ne*-li	rabbit
λαγός	la-*ghos*	hare
μαρίδα	ma-*ri*-dha	whitebait
μοσχάρι	mos-*ha*-ri	veal
μπαρμπούνια	bar-*bu*-nya	red mullet
μύδια	*mi*-di-a	mussels
ξιφίας	ksi-fi-as	swordfish
ροφός	ro-*fos*	blackfish
σαρδέλες	sar-*dhe*-les	sardines
σουπιά	su-*pia*	cuttlefish
σφυρίδα	sfi-*ri*-da	grouper
φαγρί/λιθρίνι/μελανούρι	fa-*ghri*/li-*thri*-ni/me-la-*nu*-ri	bream
χταπόδι	okh-ta-*po*-dhi	octopus
χοιρινό	hyi-ri-*no*	pork

FRUIT & VEGETABLES

αγγινάρα	ang-gi-*na*-ra	artichoke
αρακάς	a-ra-*kas*	peas
βλήτα	*vli*-ta	greens, seasonal/amaranth

καρότο	ka·*ro*·to	carrot
κεράσι	ke·*ra*·si	cherry
κρεμμύδια	kre·*mi*·dhi·a	onion
λάχανο	*la*·ha·no	cabbage
λεμόνι	le·*mo*·ni	lemon
μελιτζάνα	me·li·*dza*·na	aubergine
μήλο	*mi*·lo	apple
ντομάτα	do·*ma*·ta	tomato
πατάτες	pa·*ta*·tes	potatoes
πιπεριές	pi·per·*yes*	peppers/capsicum
πορτοκάλι	por·to·*ka*·li	orange
ροδάκινο	ro·*dha*·ki·no	peach
σκόρδο	*skor*·dho	garlic
σπανάκι	spa·*na*·ki	spinach
σπαράγγι	spa·*rang*·gi	asparagus
σταφύλια	sta·*fi*·li·a	grapes
φράουλα	*fra*·u·la	strawberry
(άγρια) χόρτα	(*a*·ghri·a) *hor*·ta	greens, seasonal (wild)

DRINKS

καφές	ka·*fes*	coffee
κρασί (κόκκινο/άσπρο)	kra·*si* (*ko*·ki·no/*a*·spro)	wine (red/white)
μπύρα	*bi*·ra	beer
νερό	ne·*ro*	water
τσάι	*tsa*·i	tea

Environment

THE LAND

Think Greece and you're likely to picture a land awash with rugged mountains, indigo water and innumerable islands. These dominating features of the Greek landscape were shaped by submerging seas, volcanic explosions and mineral-rich terrain.

No matter where you go in Greece, it's impossible to be much more than 100km from the sea. The country is made up of a mainland peninsula and around 1400 islands, of which 169 are inhabited. The islands contribute only a small percentage of the nation's total landmass of 131,900 sq km, but fill 400,000 sq km of territorial waters.

The majority of the islands are spread across the shallow waters of the Aegean Sea between Greece and Turkey. These are divided into four main groups: the Cyclades, the Dodecanese, the islands of the Northeastern Aegean and the Sporades. The two largest Aegean islands, Crete and Evia, are independent of the island groups.

The other island groups are the Saronic Gulf Islands, which lie between Athens and the Peloponnese, and the Ionians, in the Ionian Sea between Greece and southern Italy, while Kythira stands alone below the southeastern tip of the Peloponnese.

Like the mainland, most of the island terrain is extremely rugged. Crete has half a dozen peaks over 2000m, the highest of which is Mt Ida at 2456m. Evia, Karpathos, Kefallonia and Samothraki all boast peaks of more than 1500m. The islands' mountainous terrain, dry climate and poor soil leave farmers at a loss. There are several exceptions, such as Naxos and Crete, both of which are famous for the quality of their produce, and verdant Samothraki and Nisyros.

The Greek Orthodox Church is the second largest landowner in Greece.

Greece is the most seismically active country in Europe, with more than half of the continent's volcanic activity.

WILDLIFE
Animals

Greece's relationship with its fauna has not been a happy one. Hunting of wild animals is a popular activity with Greeks as a means of providing food. Despite signs forbidding hunting, Greek hunters often shoot freely at any potential game, including rare and endangered species.

You're unlikely to encounter much in the way of wildlife on most of the islands. The exception is on larger islands like Crete and Evia, where squirrels,

---

EARTHQUAKES – ISLAND TREMBLERS

The Greek islands lie in one of the most seismically active regions in the world, and unpredictable tremblers regularly shake, rattle and roll the tenants of this vast watery archipelago. Almost 3000 years ago a chain of massive volcanic eruptions and earthquakes all but destroyed Santorini (see Santorini's Unsettling Past, p290) and helped to reshape the landscape of the region. To check out Greece's explosive past, visit the craters of Santorini (p189) and Nisyros (p313).

More than 20,000 quakes have been recorded in Greece in the last 40 years. Recent accounts across the islands include the 1953 quake that razed many of Zakynthos' neoclassical buildings, and the massive 1956 quake in Santorini that killed scores of people and destroyed many homes. In August 2003 an earthquake measuring 6.4 hit Lefkada and quakes were also recorded in the Ionians in 2006 and 2007, giving more than a few islanders the jitters. Fortunately, most quakes are very minor in nature – detectable only by sensitive seismic monitoring equipment stationed throughout the country.

Bird lovers should head to
www.ornithologiki.gr for
articles, links and heaps
of info on the habitats
and environmental pro-
tection of their feathered
friends.

rabbits, hares, foxes and weasels are all fairly common. Lizards are in abundance and there is hardly a dry-stone wall without one of these curious creatures clambering around. In spring and summer you may spot snakes on roads and pathways. Fortunately the majority are harmless, though the adder and less common viper and coral snake are poisonous (see also p527).

Birdwatchers have a field day on the islands as Greece is on many north–south migratory paths. Not surprisingly, seabirds are also a major feature. Assorted gulls, petrels, shearwaters and shags are common throughout the Aegean. The islands are also home to a rich variety of birds of prey, particularly the mountains of larger islands like Crete and Evia. They include the spectacular griffon vulture and several species of eagle, as well as peregrine falcons, harriers and hawks.

Lesvos (p378) draws a regular following of birders from all of Europe who come to spot some of the over 279 recorded species that stop here annually. About 350 pairs (60% of the world's population) of the rare Eleonora's falcon nest on the island of Piperi (p426) in the Sporades and on Tilos (p309), which is also home to the very rare Bonelli's eagle and the shy, cormorant-like Mediterranean shag.

ENDANGERED SPECIES
The golden jackal is a strong candidate for Greece's most misunderstood mammal. Although its diet is 50% vegetarian (and the other 50% is made up of carrion, reptiles and small mammals), it has traditionally shouldered much of the blame for attacks on stock and has been hunted by farmers as a preventative measure. Near the brink of extinction, it was declared a protected species in 1990 and now survives only in small areas of Central Greece and on the island of Samos (p357).

Between 1974 and 1980
more than 4000 jackals
were hunted and killed
in Greece.

The Cretan wild goat, the *kri-kri,* only survives in the wild in the Samaria Gorge area (p253) and on the tiny islet of Kri Kri, off Agios Nikolaos (p264) on Crete.

Endangered Marine Life
Claiming top position for Europe's most endangered marine mammal, the monk seal *(Monachus monachus)* ekes out an extremely precarious existence in Greece. Approximately 200 to 250 monk seals, about 90% of Europe's

---

RESPONSIBLE TRAVEL

Visitors should travel responsibly at all times. Please follow these common-sense rules.

- Take care with your beach umbrella – you may be disturbing turtle eggs.
- Don't disturb nesting birds – they may be endangered.
- Don't toss garbage into the sea from ferry boats.
- Take all refuse with you when vacating a beach.
- Use water sparingly in your hotel room – it is a costly commodity on an island.
- Do not discard items that could start a fire (cigarette butts, glass bottles etc) – forest fires are an annual torment.
- Stick to footpaths wherever possible.
- Do not pick flowers or wilfully damage tree bark or roots – some of the species you see are protected.
- Respect landowners' property and do not trespass.
- Take care when walking near cliffs – they can be dangerously slippery and quick to crumble.

minuscule population, are found in both the Ionian and Aegean Seas. Small colonies also live on the island of Alonnisos (p421) and there have been reported sightings on Tilos (p309). Pervasive habitat encroachment is the main culprit for its diminished numbers.

The waters around Zakynthos (p464) are home to the last large sea turtle colony in Europe, that of the endangered loggerhead turtle (*Caretta caretta*; see the boxed text, p469). The loggerhead also nests in smaller numbers on Crete. Greece's turtles have many hazards to dodge – fishing nets, boat propellers, rubbish, sun-loungers and beach umbrellas. It doesn't help that the turtles' nesting time coincides with the European summer holiday season.

Overfishing has severely impacted Greece's dolphin populations. Once spotted during almost any ferry trip, a number of the species are now considered vulnerable, while the number of common dolphins (*Delphinus delphis*) has dropped from 150 to 15 in the past decade. The main threats to dolphins are a diminished food supply and entanglement in fishing nets. In the early 1990s the striped dolphin also fell victim to an infection called morbillivirus, which killed several thousand in the Mediterranean Sea.

Plants

Greece is endowed with a variety of flora unrivalled elsewhere in Europe. The wildflowers are spectacular, with over 6000 species, including 100 varieties of orchids. They continue to thrive because most of the land is inadequate for intensive agriculture and has therefore escaped the ravages of chemical fertilisers.

The Lefka Ori mountains of Crete (p256) gets more than its fair share of wildflowers, with trees beginning to blossom as early as the end of February and flowers appearing in March. Common species include anemones, white cyclamens, irises, lilies, poppies, gladioli, tulips and countless varieties of daisy. Look out for the blue-and-orange Cretan iris (*Iris cretica*), one of 120 wildflowers unique to Crete. Others are the pink Cretan ebony, the white-flowered symphyandra and the white-flowered *Cyclamen cretica*. Other rare species found on the islands include the *Rhododendron luteum*, a yellow azalea that grows only on Lesvos (Mytilini; p378).

Spectacular plants include the coastal giant reed – you may get lost among high, dense groves on your way to a beach – as well as the giant fennel, which grows to 3m, and the tall yellow-horned poppy, both of which grow by the sea. The white-flowered sea squill grows on hills above the coast while the perfumed sea daffodil grows along southern coasts, particularly on Crete and Corfu. The conspicuous snake's-head fritillary (*Fritillaria graeca*) has pink flowers shaped like snakes' heads, and the markings on the petals resemble a chequerboard – the Latin word *fritillus* means dice box.

While the forests that once covered ancient Greece have been decimated by thousands of years of clearing for grazing, boat-building and housing, and more recently by forest fires (see Environmental Issues, p70), you will undoubtedly encounter the Cyprus plane (*Platanus orientalis insularis*), which thrives wherever there is ample water. Australian eucalypts were widely used in tree-planting programs from the 1920s onwards, particularly on Crete.

Herbs grow wild throughout much of Greece and you'll see locals out picking fresh herbs for their kitchen. Locally grown herbs are also increasingly sold as souvenirs and are generally organic.

NATIONAL PARKS

National Parks were first established in Greece in 1938 with the creation of Mount Olympus National Park, followed quickly by the establishment of Parnassos National Park. There are now 10 parks and two marine parks that

On beaches frequented by large numbers of tourists, turtles return to breed only to find the sand packed so hard that they're unable to dig into it to make a nest.

Loggerhead hatchlings use the journey from the nest to the sea in order to build their strength. Helping the baby turtles to the sea can actually lower their chances of survival.

For details and pictures of the thousands of mountain flowers you may stumble across in Greece, check out www .greekmountainflora.info.

aim to protect the unique flora and fauna of Greece. The only national parks on the islands are the Samaria Gorge (p253) on Crete and the Tilos Park on Tilos (p309). Facilities for visitors are often basic but, chances are, you'll hardly notice as you'll be so gobsmacked by the surroundings. Abundant walking trails are not always maintained and the clutch of simple refuges offer only basic facilities.

There are marine parks off the coast of Alonnisos (p423) in the Sporades, and at the Bay of Laganas (p468) on Zakynthos in the Ionians.

ENVIRONMENTAL ISSUES

Greece is belatedly becoming environmentally conscious. Global awareness, a greater sensitivity on the part of younger generations and sheer financial inducements from funding bodies are shifting Greece's devil-may-care attitude of yesteryear to a growing awareness that the environmental rape and pillage of a land cannot go on forever.

Nevertheless, general environmental awareness remains at a low level, especially where litter is concerned. The problem is particularly bad in rural areas, where roadsides are strewn with soft-drink cans and plastic packaging hurled from passing cars. On smaller islands there's the added dilemma of how to dispose of collected rubbish.

Long-standing problems such as deforestation and soil erosion date back thousands of years. Live cultivation and goats have been the main culprits, while firewood gathering, shipbuilding, housing and industry have all taken their toll.

Forest fires are a major problem, with many thousands of hectares destroyed annually, often in some of the most picturesque areas of Greece. The increasing scale of recent fires is blamed on rising Mediterranean temperatures and high winds. The fires of 2000 were particularly bad on Samos, while the disastrous mainland fires of 2007 affected only the island of Evia. Many locals argue that the government continues to be ill-prepared to deal with the annual fires and that it remains slow to react.

In its vast amounts of sea territory, Greece's marine life leads a precarious existence. In many respects, tourism has been the cause of much of the demise of the Greek seas, as well as the motivation for cleaning it up. Legislation aimed at preventing water pollution has been noticeably effective at keeping the quality of Greece's seawater at a respectable level of salinity. The country's bathing water quality is now rated as number two in Europe by the European Commission.

Global warming is playing havoc with the Greek thermometer and it's believed that by the end of the century, the average temperature in Athens will rise by 8°C, while some 56,000 hectares of coastal land will be flooded. Islands at greatest risk include Corfu, Crete and Rhodes. It's predicted that a simultaneous decline in rainfall will mean a severe shortage of water throughout the country.

Herbs in Cooking is an illustrative book by Maria and Nikos Psilakis that can be used as both an identification guide and a cookbook for Greek dishes seasoned with local herbs.

www.cleanupgreece.org .gr promotes programs and events aimed at building awareness of the protection of Greece's environment.

The current advance of global warming means that 0.4% of Greece's land mass is predicted to be submerged by water before the end of the century.

Greek Islands Outdoors

The Greek islands are ideal for relaxing and soaking up culture, but if you're after something a little more energetic, you'll feel like a kid in a candy shop. From kitesurfing and waterskiing to scaling precipitous rocks, hiking through hidden gorges and cycling along coastal trails, the islands have something for everyone who wants to get out and explore.

HIKING

The Greek islands are a paradise for hikers, offering an extraordinary variety of landscapes ranging from remote coastal paths to dramatic mountain gorges.

Spring (April to May) is the best time. Walkers will find the countryside green and fresh from the winter rains, and carpeted with the spectacular array of wildflowers for which the islands are justly famous. Autumn (September to October) is another good time, but July and August, when the temperatures are constantly up around 40°C, are not much fun at all. Whatever time of year you opt to set out, you'll need to come equipped with a good pair of walking boots to handle the rough, rocky terrain, a wide-brimmed hat, a water bottle and a high UV-factor sunscreen.

For details of hikes on Crete for all abilities, along with articles, interviews, photos and directories, check out www.climbincrete.com.

HIKING ON THE GREEK ISLANDS

Island Group	Destination	Skill Level	Description
Crete	Samaria Gorge (p253)	easy-medium	One of Europe's most popular hikes with 500m vertical walls, countless wildflowers and endangered wildlife (impassable from mid Oct–mid Apr)
Crete	Zakros & Kato Zakros (p270)	easy-medium	Passing through the mysterious Valley of the Dead, this trail leads to a remote Minoan palace site
Cyclades	Tragaea, Naxos (p174)	easy-medium	A broad central plain of olive groves, unspoiled villages and plenty of trails
Cyclades	Filoti, Naxos (p174)	medium-difficult	A strenuous climb to the Cave of Zeus (a natural cavern on the slopes of Mt Zeus)
Dodecanese	Tilos (p309)	easy-medium	Countless traditional trails along dramatic clifftops and down to isolated beaches; a bird-lover's paradise
Dodecanese	Nisyros (p313)	easy-medium	A lush volcanic island with hikes that lead into the hissing craters of Mt Polyvotis
Evia	Steni (p408)	medium-difficult	Day hikes and more serious trekking opportunities up Mt Dirfys, Evia's highest mountain
Ionians	Paxi (p446)	easy	Paths along ancient olive groves and snaking dry-stone walls; perfect for escaping the crowds
Ionians	Ithaki (p462)	easy-medium	Mythology fans can hike between sites linked to the Trojan War–hero Odysseus
Northeastern Aegean Islands	Samos (p364)	easy-medium	Explore the quiet interior with mountain villages and the forested northern slopes of Mt Ampelos
Saronic Gulf Islands	Hydra (p126)	easy	A vehicle-free island with a well-maintained network of paths to beaches and monasteries
Sporades	Alonnisos (p421)	easy	A network of established trails that lead to pristine beaches
Sporades	Skopelos (p417)	easy	Well-maintained trails through pine forests, olive groves, orchards and vineyards

Some of the most popular hikes are detailed in this book, but there are possibilities just about everywhere. While the most popular routes are well walked and maintained, the **EOS** (Greek Alpine Club; ☎ 210 321 2429; Plateia Kapnikareas 2, Athens) is grossly underfunded and consequently many of the lesser-known paths are overgrown and inadequately marked. You'll find EOS branches on, Crete (Mountaineering & Skiing Club of Iraklio; p228) and Evia (Halkida Alpine Club; p408).

On small islands it's fun to discover pathways for yourself, and you are unlikely to get hopelessly lost as settlements or roads are never far away. You will encounter a variety of paths: *kalderimia* are cobbled or flagstone mule paths that have linked settlements since Byzantine times, and other paths include *monopatia* or shepherd's trails that link settlements with sheepfolds or link remote settlements via rough unmarked trails. Be aware that shepherd or animal trails can be very steep and difficult to manoeuvre.

If you're going to be venturing off the beaten track, a good map is essential. Unfortunately, most of the tourist maps sold around the islands are completely inadequate. The best hiking maps for the islands are produced by Anavasi (see p484 for details), a company based in Athens.

See the boxed text, p71, for details of some of the best hiking possibilities around the islands.

Organised Hikes

You'll encounter companies running organised walks on almost all of the islands popular with hikers. The largest company is **Trekking Hellas** (Map p78; ☎ 210 331 0323; www.trekking.gr; Rethymnou 12, Exarhia, Athens), which offers a variety of hikes on the islands, such as an eight-day hike (€900) through the Lefka Ori (White Mountains) of Crete or a nine-day island-hopping walk (€1250) through the Cyclades. If you're travelling alone and want to hit the trails, you could join a group to make the experience more enjoyable and infinitely safer.

DIVING & SNORKELLING

Snorkelling can be enjoyed just about anywhere along the coast of Greece and equipment is cheaply available. Especially good spots to don your fins are

Tourists' increasing interest in hiking in Greece has led to the salvation and restoration of many ancient cobbled footpaths that might otherwise have been destroyed to make room for new roads.

The sheer rugged cliffs and gnarled mountainsides of Kalymnos (p331) have made it a paradise for rock climbers who are after some adrenaline-pumping scaling of vertical rock.

DIVING INTO HISTORY

In the last few years, Greek dive laws have relaxed to allow divers to visit many more underwater locations. While most divers and dive companies are heralding this as a positive move, historians and archaeologists are increasingly alarmed and calling for a return to the law prior to 2007, which strictly limited diving to a handful of areas. Their reason? The looting of underwater archaeological sites.

Greece's underwater world holds a wealth of historic discoveries. Over the centuries, a great many statues on land were melted down to make weapons and coins. Consequently, many of the largest ancient statues you'll see in Greek museums have been salvaged from the watery depths in the past century. The sea is now the country's largest archaeological site left. Approximately 100 known underwater sites are protected; however, historians claim there are likely to be thousands more yet to be discovered. Greece's ocean bed is a graveyard to countless shipwrecks dating all the way back to Classical times, which are considered both fascinating dive sites and archaeological hotbeds.

Despite a law dating back to 1932 that asserts that all found artefacts belong to the state (see also Customs, p480), divers are said to be surfacing with sculptures, jewellery, warrior helmets and more. Meanwhile, archaeologists claim that the removal of even the most seemingly mundane objects can affect and eventually destroy sites.

The moral for divers? Don't become another masked and finned pirate. Look but don't touch.

THE ISLANDS BY BIKE

While it's possible to hire a bike for a day, many people are choosing cycling as their main form of transport. Bicycles usually travel for free on the ferries so there is no extra outlay, nor do you have to pony-up valuable cash to hire motorised wheels when you arrive. You can be last onto the ferry and first off – free to pedal off to the nearest beach or to look for accommodation.

Most islands aren't exactly flat but a bike with a good set of gears should tackle most inclines with ease. While virtually any island will lend itself to some kind of cycling activity, Kos (p317), in the Dodecanese, is perhaps the best equipped and most cyclist friendly. Bicycle-hire outfits are everywhere and a bicycle is almost de rigueur for many visitors. Groups of cyclists can be encountered all over the flat and winding lanes of the north coast of Kos.

Islands don't have the frenzied traffic of the mainland; however, motorists are also notoriously fast and not always travelling in the expected lane; extra caution on corners and narrow roads is well warranted. In remote locations, be sure to carry repair and first-aid kits with you. In July and August, most cyclists break between noon and 4pm to avoid sunstroke and dehydration. For lots of information and routes, also see Anthony Campbell's site at www.acampbell.ukfsn .org/cycling/greece.

There are an increasing number of tour companies specialising in cycling holidays. **Cycle Greece** (www.cyclegreece.gr) runs road and mountain-bike tours across most of Greece for various skill levels, and **Hooked on Cycling** (http://www.hookedoncycling.co.uk/Greece/greece.html) offers boat and bike trips through the islands.

Monastiri (p164) on Paros; Paleokastritsa (p445) on Corfu; Ammoöpi (p298) in southern Karpathos; Xirokambos bay (p336) on Leros; and anywhere off the coast of Kastellorizo (Megisti; p303). Many dive schools also use their boats to take groups of snorkellers to prime spots.

Greek law insists that diving be done under the supervision of a diving school in order to protect the many antiquities in the depths of the Mediterranean. Traditionally, the number of dive sites were severely limited; however, the laws have recently relaxed and many more sites have opened up, with dive schools flourishing. You'll find schools on Corfu (p447), Crete (p238), Evia (p407), Hydra (p127), Leros (p336), Milos (p207), Mykonos (p156), Paros (p166), Rhodes (p283), Santorini (p199) and Skiathos (p416).

The **Professional Association of Diving Instructors** (PADI; www.padi.com) has lots of useful information, including a list of all PADI-approved dive centres in Greece.

For a comprehensive list of dive centres and sites in Greece, along with links and articles, visit www.diving-greece.net.

WINDSURFING

Windsurfing is a very popular water sport in Greece. Hrysi Akti (p166) on Paros, and Vasiliki (p453) on Lefkada vie for the position of the best windsurfing beach. According to some, Vasiliki is one of the best places in the world to learn the sport.

There are numerous other prime locations around the islands, including Afiartis Bay (p298) on Karpathos; Ormos Korthiou (p139) on Andros; Kalafatis Beach (p156) on Mykonos; Agios Georgios (p173) on Naxos; Milopotas beach (p186) on Ios; Cape Prasonisi (p292) in southern Rhodes; around Tingaki (p323) on Kos; Kokkari (p364) on Samos; around Skala Sotira (p401) on Thasos; and Koukounaries Beach (p415) on Skiathos.

You'll find sailboards for hire almost everywhere. Hire charges range from €10 to €25, depending on the gear and the location. If you are a novice, most places that rent equipment also give lessons. Sailboards can be imported freely from other EU countries, but importing boards from other destinations, such as Australia and the USA, is subject to regulations. Theoretically, importers

The islands of Naxos and Paros receive the strongest *meltemi* (northeasterly wind) in July and August, making for ideal windsurfing conditions.

need a Greek national residing in Greece to guarantee that the board will be taken out again. Contact the **Hellenic Windsurfing Association** (Map p82; ☎ 210 323 3696; Filellinon 4, Syntagma, Athens) for more information.

KITESURFING

Also known as kiteboarding, this action water sport has taken off big in Greece and you'll find beaches festooned with athletic surfers. The **Greek Wakeboard & Kiteboarding Association** (☎ 6944517963; www.gwa.gr) has details of popular locales in Greece for this growing action sport. Each summer, Karpathos hosts an international kitesurfing competition (see p294).

WATERSKIING

There are three islands with water-ski centres: Kythira (p470), Paros (p159) and Skiathos (p412).

Given the relatively calm and flat waters of most island locations and the generally warm waters of the Mediterranean, waterskiing can be a very pleasant activity. August can be a tricky month, when the *meltemi* (northeasterly wind) can make conditions difficult in the central Aegean. Poros (p123), near Athens, is a particularly well-organised locale, with an organisation, **Passage** (☎ 22980 42540; www.passage.gr; Neorion Bay), hosting a popular school and slalom centre.

YACHTING

Yachting is an amazing way to see the Greek islands. Nothing beats the experience of sailing the open sea, and the freedom of being able to visit remote and uninhabited islands.

The free EOT booklet *Sailing the Greek Seas,* although long over-due for an update, contains lots of information about weather conditions, weather bulletins, entry and exit regulations, entry and exit ports and guidebooks for yachties. You can pick up the booklet at any Greek National Tourist Organisation (GNTO/EOT) office either abroad or in Greece (see p487 for locations). **Hellenic Yachting Server** (www .yachting.gr) has general information on sailing around the islands and lots of links, including information on chartering yachts.

The sailing season lasts from April until October, although the most popular time is between July and September. Unfortunately, it also happens to be the time of year when the *meltemi* is at its strongest. This isn't an issue in the Ionian Sea, where the main summer wind is the *maistros,* a light to moderate northwesterly that rises in the afternoon and usually dies away at sunset.

If your budget won't cover buying a yacht, there are several other options open to you. You can hire a bare boat (a yacht without a crew) if two crew members have a sailing certificate. Prices start at €1000 per week for a 28-footer that will sleep six. It will cost an extra €850 per week to hire a skipper.

Individuals can check out week-long island cruises offered by **Ghiolman Yachts & Travel** (Map p78; ☎ 210 325 5000; www.ghiolman.com; 8 Propileon, Acropoli, Athens), operating weekly from early May to the end of September. **Trekking Hellas** (Map p78; ☎ 210 331 0323; www.trekking.gr; Rethymnou 12, Exarhia, Athens) also offers a range of yachting and sailing holidays around the Cyclades and the Ionians by caïque or by yacht. For more information, see also Cruising (p497).

Kitesurfing dates back to 13th-century China, when it was used as a simple means of transport. Learn basic skills to extreme tricks, as well as tips on safety, locations and gear, at www.kitesurfing now.com.

For a look at the history of flotillas and the impact of yachting on the Greek islands, pick up a copy of *From the Deck of Your Own Yacht* (2009) by Mike Jakeways. The author has spent the past 20 years sailing the Greek seas.

Athens & the Mainland Ports

Athens deserves much more than a brief dalliance enroute to Greek island adventures. The magnificent Parthenon temple, perched atop the sacred rock of the Acropolis, rises majestically over a city with a glorious and tumultuous history, where precious antiquities fill world-class museums and dot street corners.

But beyond its rich cultural heritage, contemporary Athens is also one of Europe's liveliest capitals, with an enviable cafe lifestyle, bustling street life, alfresco dining culture, great shopping and burgeoning contemporary arts scene. Come nightfall, an extraordinary choice of lively bars creates an almost festive atmosphere year-round in the city's ever-changing hotspots. Summer festivals and glamorous beach clubs give way to eclectic winter live-music venues and pulsating nightclubs.

Post-Olympic Athens is undeniably more polished and urbane, with a modern metro and efficient public transport, and host of trendy restaurants, galleries, refurbished hotels, revamped shopping precincts and unique cultural offerings.

Beyond the capital, many island travellers will connect via Greece's other diverse mainland ports, from the graceful northern city of Thessaloniki, busy Patra in the south to the small town of Volos on the east coast, renowned for its bustling portside ouzeries.

But old Athens is never far away – with its anarchic energy and architectural hotchpotch of neoclassical elegance, Byzantine grace, modern concrete jungle and semi-gentrified neighbourhoods, albeit with their own ramshackle charm. It is a restless city in a constant state of flux, with a new multicultural face and its fair share of big-city shortcomings. At times exhilarating, exasperating, surprising and confronting, Athens is an intriguing city to explore.

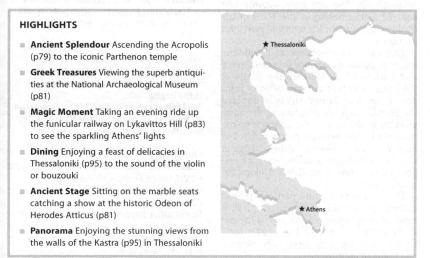

HIGHLIGHTS

- **Ancient Splendour** Ascending the Acropolis (p79) to the iconic Parthenon temple
- **Greek Treasures** Viewing the superb antiquities at the National Archaeological Museum (p81)
- **Magic Moment** Taking an evening ride up the funicular railway on Lykavittos Hill (p83) to see the sparkling Athens' lights
- **Dining** Enjoying a feast of delicacies in Thessaloniki (p95) to the sound of the violin or bouzouki
- **Ancient Stage** Sitting on the marble seats catching a show at the historic Odeon of Herodes Atticus (p81)
- **Panorama** Enjoying the stunning views from the walls of the Kastra (p95) in Thessaloniki

★ Thessaloniki

★ Athens

ATHENS ΑΘΗΝΑ

pop 3.7 million

HISTORY

The early history of Athens is so interwoven with mythology that it's hard to disentangle fact from fiction.

Occupied since Neolithic times, the Acropolis was an excellent vantage point and the steep slopes formed natural defences on three sides. By 1400 BC the Acropolis was a powerful Mycenaean city. Its power peaked during the so-called golden age of Athens in the 5th century BC, following the defeat of the Persians at the Battle of Salamis. The city fell into decline after its defeat by Sparta in the long-running Peloponnesian War, but rallied again in Roman times when it became a seat of learning. The Roman emperors, particularly Hadrian, graced Athens with many grand buildings.

After the Roman Empire split into east and west, the power shifted to Byzantium (modern day İstanbul) and Athens fell into obscurity. By the end of Ottoman rule, Athens was little more than a dilapidated village (the area now known as Plaka).

In 1834, the newly crowned King Otto transferred his court from Nafplio in the Peloponnese and made Athens the capital of independent Greece. The city was rebuilt along neoclassical lines, with large squares, tree-lined boulevards and imposing public buildings. The city grew steadily and enjoyed a brief heyday as the 'Paris of the Mediterranean' in the late 19th and early 20th centuries.

This came to an abrupt end with the forced population exchange between Greece and Turkey, which followed the Treaty of Lausanne in 1923. The huge influx of refugees from Asia Minor virtually doubled the population overnight, forcing the hasty erection of the first of the concrete apartment blocks that dominate the city today. The belated advent of Greece's industrial age in the 1950s brought another wave of migration, this time of rural folk looking for employment.

The city's infrastructure, particularly road and transport, could not keep pace with such rapid and unplanned growth, and by the end of the 1980s the city had developed a sorry reputation as one of the most traffic-clogged and polluted in Europe.

The 1990s appear to have been a turning point in the city's development. Jolted into action by the failed bid to stage the 1996 Olympics, authorities embarked on an ambitious program to prepare the city for the 21st century, including the extension of the metro network and the new airport.

The city's successful staging of the 2004 Olympics left a lasting legacy and the economic growth is reflected across the city. Athens today is a radically different city – it's a more attractive, cleaner, greener and efficient capital, though it is still a work in progress.

ORIENTATION

Although Athens is a sprawling city, nearly everything of interest to short-term visitors lies within a small area of the city's historic and commercial centre. The city's two major landmarks, the Acropolis and Lykavittos Hill, can be seen from just about everywhere in this area.

Plaka, the old Ottoman quarter that was all that existed when Athens was declared the capital of independent Greece, nestles on the northeastern slope of the Acropolis. It may be touristy, but it's the most attractive and historic part of Athens and the majority of visitors make it their base.

INFORMATION
Bookshops

Anavasi (Map p82; ☎ 210 321 8104; www.anavasi .gr; Stoa Arsakiou, Panepistimio) Travel bookshop with extensive range of Greece maps, walking and activity guides.

Eleftheroudakis Plaka (Map p82; ☎ 210 322 9388; Nikis 20); Syntagma (Map p82; ☎ 210 331 4180; Panepistimiou 17) The seven-floor Panepistimiou store is the biggest bookshop in Athens, with a level dedicated to English-language books.

Road Editions (Map p78; ☎ 210 361 3242; www.road .gr; Solonos 71, Exarhia) A wide range of travel literature and all the Road Editions maps.

Emergency

Athens Central Police Station (Off Map p78; ☎ 210 770 5711/17; Leoforos Alexandras 173, Ambelokipi)

ELPA Road Assistance (☎ 10400)

Police (☎ 100)

Tourist police (Map p78; ☎ 24hr 171, 210 920 0724; Veïkou 43-45, Koukaki; ☼ 8am-10pm)

Visitor Emergency Assistance (☎ 112) Toll-free 24-hour service in English.

Internet Access

Most hotels have internet access and increasingly are installing wi-fi. There are free wi-fi hot spots at Syntagma, Thisio, Gazi, Plateia Kotzia and the Port of Piraeus. Internet cafes charge €2 to €4 per hour.

Bits & Bytes Internet Café (Map p82; ☎ 210 382 2545; Kapnikareas 19, Monastiraki; per hr €2.50; ✆ 24hr)

Cyberzone (Map p78; ☎ 210 520 3939; Satovrianidou 7, Omonia; per hr €2; ✆ 24hr) Cheaper rates of €1.50 per hour apply between midnight and 8am.

Ivis Internet (Map p82; Mitropoleos 3, Syntagma; per hr €3; ✆ 24hr)

Internet Resources

www.breathtakingathens.gr Official visitor site of the Athens Tourism and Economic Development Agency, with handy what's on listings.

www.culture.gr Ministry of Culture guide to museums, archaeological sites and cultural events.

www.elculture.gr Informative bilingual arts and culture guide, including theatre, music and cinema listings.

Laundry

Laundromat (Map p78; ☎ 210 923 5811; Veïkou 3A, Makrygianni; wash per 10kg €5, dry €2; ✆ 8am-10pm).

Left Luggage

Many hotels will store luggage free for guests. You'll find left-luggage facilities at the airport and the metro stations at Omonia, Monastiraki and Piraeus.

Pacific Travel Luggage Storage (Map p82; ☎ 210 324 1007; Nikis 26, Syntagma; per day €2; ✆ 8am-8pm Mon-Sat)

Medical Services

Ambulance/First-Aid Advice (☎ 166)

Duty Doctors & Hospitals (☎ 1434 in Greek) Published in the *Kathimerini* English-language supplement in the daily *International Herald Tribune*.

Pharmacies (☎ 1434 in Greek) Check pharmacy windows for notice of nearest duty pharmacy. There is a 24-hour pharmacy at the airport.

SOS Doctors (☎ 1016, 210 821 1888; ✆ 24hr) Pay service with English-speaking doctors.

Money

Most major banks have branches around Syntagma and there are ATMs all over the city. Standard bank opening hours are 8am to 2.30pm Monday to Thursday and 8am to 2pm on Friday, though some private banks open certain branches until 8pm weekdays and on Saturdays.

Alpha Bank (Map p82; ☎ 210 324 1039 Panepistimiou 3; ✆ 8am-8pm Mon-Fri, 10am-4.30pm Sat)

Eurochange Monastiraki (Map p82; ☎ 210 322 2657; Areos 1); Omonia (Map p78; ☎ 210 552 2314; Kotopoulou 1); Syntagma (Map p82; ☎ 210 331 2462; Karageorgi Servias 2; ✆ 9am-9pm) Exchanges travellers cheques and arranges money transfers.

National Bank of Greece (Map p82; ☎ 210 334 0500; cnr Karageorgi Servias & Stadiou, Syntagma) Has a 24-hour automatic exchange machine.

Post

Athens Central post office (Map p78; www.elta.gr; Eolou 100, Omonia; ✆ 7.30am-8pm Mon-Fri, 7.30am-2pm Sat) Unless specified otherwise, all poste restante is sent here.

Parcel post office (Map p82; Nikis 33, Syntagma; ✆ 7.30am-2pm Mon-Fri) Parcels weighing over 2kg must be taken here, unwrapped, for inspection.

Syntagma post office (Map p82; Plateia Syntagmaos, Syntagma; ✆ 7.30am-8pm Mon-Fri, 7.30am-2pm Sat)

Telephone

Public phones all over Athens allow international calls. Phone cards are available at kiosks.

Toilets

Public toilets are relatively scarce in Athens and keep inconsistent hours. There are 24-hour portable, self-cleaning pay toilets (€0.50) around the city centre.

Tourist Information

EOT (Greek National Tourist Organisation; www.gnto.gr) Airport (☎ 210 353 0445-7; Arrivals Hall; ✆ 9am-7pm Mon-Fri, 10am-4pm Sat & Sun); Syntagma (Map p82; ☎ 210 331 0392; Leoforos Vasilissis Amalias 26a; ✆ 9am-7pm Mon-Fri, 10am-4pm Sat & Sun) Has a handy free map of Athens and public transport information.

DANGERS & ANNOYANCES

Athens has its fair share of the problems found in all major cities, but is one of Europe's safest capitals. Violent street crime remains rare, though travellers should be alert to the traps listed here. The streets northwest and southwest of Omonia have become markedly seedier, with the increasing presence of prostitutes, junkies and mostly illegal immigrants, and should be avoided at night.

Watch for pickpockets on the metro system, particularly the Piraeus–Kifisia line, and the crowded streets around Omonia, Athinas and the Monastiraki flea market.

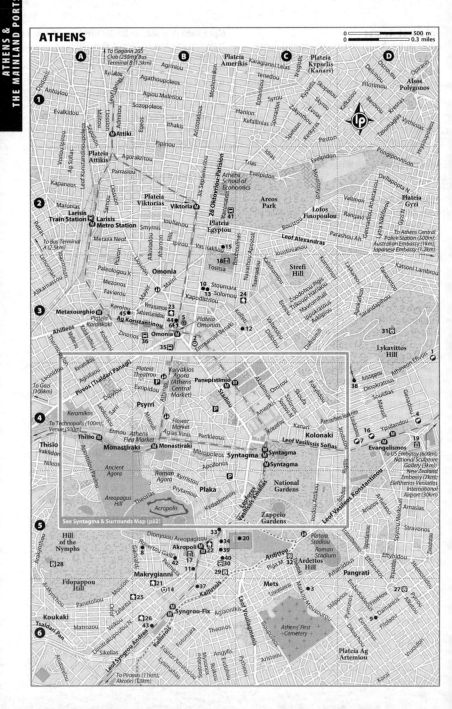

ATHENS

INFORMATION		
Albanian Embassy	1	D3
Athens Central Post Office	2	B3
Athens Centre	3	C6
Canadian Embassy	4	D4
Cyberzone	5	B3
Eurochange	6	B3
German Embassy	7	D4
Ghiolman Yachts & Travel	8	B5
Greek Youth Hostel Organisation	9	D6
Hellenic Society for the Study & Protection of the Monk Seal	10	B3
Laundromat	11	B5
Panhellenic Camping Association	12	C3
Sea Turtle Protection Society of Greece	13	B3
Tourist Police	14	B6
Trekking Hellas	15	B2
UK Embassy	16	D4
SIGHTS & ACTIVITIES		
Acropolis Museum	17	B5
National Archaeological Museum	18	B3
National Art Gallery	19	D4
Temple of Olympian Zeus	20	C5
SLEEPING		
Art Gallery Hotel	21	B6
Athens Backpackers	22	B5
Athens Easy Access Hostel	23	B3
Hotel Exarchion	24	C3
Hotel Tony	25	B6
Marble House Pension	26	B6
ENTERTAINMENT		
Alavastro Café	27	D6
Dora Stratou Dance Company	28	A5
Granazi	29	B5
Lamda Club	30	B5
Lykavittos Theatre	31	D3
Vitrine	32	C5
TRANSPORT		
Avis	33	B5
Budget	34	B5
Bus 049 to Piraeus	35	B3
Bus 051 to Bus Terminal A	36	B3
Europcar	37	B6
Funicular Railway	38	D4
Hertz	39	B5
Kosmos	40	B5
Mavromateon Bus Terminal	41	B2
Motorent	42	B5
Olympic Air	43	B6
Olympic Air	44	B3
OSE	45	A3

Lonely Planet continues to hear from readers who have been taken in by one of the various bar scams that operate around central Athens. The scam runs something like this: friendly Greek approaches male traveller and reveals that he, too, is from out of town, or has a cousin in Australia etc. Why don't they go to this great bar and have a beer? They order a drink and before they know it women appear, more drinks are ordered and the conman disappears, leaving the traveller to pay an exorbitant bill. The smiles disappear and the atmosphere often turns threatening. Other bars don't bother with the acting. They target intoxicated males with talk of sex and present them with outrageous bills.

Some bars and clubs serve what are locally known as *'bombes'*, adulterated drinks that have been diluted with cheap illegal imports or methanol-based spirit substitutes, that can leave you feeling worse for wear the next day.

SIGHTS

The Acropolis

The **Acropolis** (Map p80; ☎ 210 321 0219; adult/concession €12/6; ⏲ 8.30am-8pm Apr-Oct, 8am-5pm Nov-Mar; ♿) is the most important ancient site in the Western world. Crowned by the Parthenon, it stands sentinel over Athens, visible from almost everywhere within the city. Most of the monuments of Pentelic marble that grace the sacred hill were commissioned by Pericles during the golden age of Athens in the 5th century BC. The Persians had destroyed an earlier temple complex on the eve of the Battle of Salamis.

The entrance to the Acropolis is through the **Beulé Gate**, a Roman arch that was added in the 3rd century AD. Beyond this is the **Propylaia**, which was the ancient entrance. It was damaged by Venetian bombardment in the 17th century, but has been restored. To the south of the Propylaia is the small **Temple of Athena Nike**.

Built on the highest part of the Acropolis, the iconic **Parthenon** is the monument that epitomises the glory of ancient Greece. It was completed in 438 BC and is unsurpassed in grace and harmony. Its lines were ingeniously curved to counteract optical illusions. The base curves upwards slightly towards the ends, and the columns become narrower towards the top, with the overall effect of making it look straight.

Above the columns are the remains of a Doric frieze, which was partly destroyed by the Venetian shelling. The best surviving pieces are the controversial Parthenon Marbles carted off to Britain by Lord Thomas Elgin in 1801. The Parthenon, dedicated to Athena, contained an 11m-tall, gold-and-ivory statue of the goddess completed in 438 BC by Pheidias of Athens (only the statue's foundations survive today).

To the north is the **Erechtheion** with its distinctive Caryatids, the six maidens who support its southern portico. These are plaster casts. The originals (except for one removed by Lord Elgin) are in the Acropolis Museum (p81).

The Acropolis can also be reached from the entry at its southern foothills via the **Theatre of Dionysos**, originally constructed in the

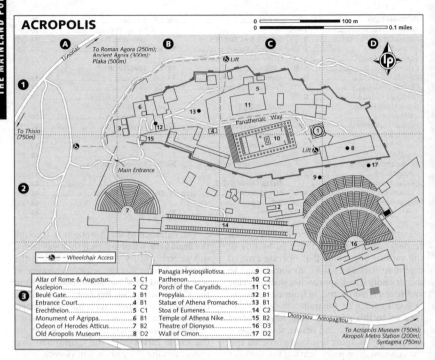

ACROPOLIS

Altar of Rome & Augustus..........1 C1	Panagia Hrysospiliotissa.............9 C2
Asclepion...............................2 C2	Parthenon...............................10 C2
Beulé Gate..............................3 B1	Porch of the Caryatids..............11 C1
Entrance Court..........................4 B1	Propylaia................................12 B1
Erechtheion............................5 C1	Statue of Athena Promachos.......13 B1
Monument of Agrippa................6 B1	Stoa of Eumenes........................14 C2
Odeon of Herodes Atticus..........7 B2	Temple of Athena Nike.............15 B2
Old Acropolis Museum...............8 D2	Theatre of Dionysos.................16 D3
	Wall of Cimon.........................17 D2

6th century BC to host the festival of the Great Dionysia. During the 5th century the theatre was the stage for the plays of the great Greek playwrights, such as Euripides, Sophocles and Aristophanes. It was reconstructed in the 4th century with a 17,000-seat capacity and some of the VIP seats at the front survive, including the grant throne reserved for the Priest of Dionysos.

The Acropolis admission includes entry to other sites (see the boxed text, opposite).

Ancient Agora

The **agora** (market; Map p82; ☎ 210 321 0185; Adrianou; adult/concession €4/2, free with Acropolis pass; 🕒 8.30am-8pm Apr-Oct, 8am-5.30pm Nov-Mar) was the marketplace – and focal point – of civic life. The main monuments are the **Temple of Hephaestus**, the 11th-century **Church of the Holy Apostles** and the **Stoa of Attalos**, which houses the museum.

Roman Agora

The Romans built an **agora** (market; Map p82; ☎ 210 324 5220; cnr Pelopida & Eolou; adult/concession €2/1, free with Acropolis pass; 🕒 8.30am-8pm Apr-Oct, 8am-5.30pm

Nov-May) east of the Ancient Agora. Visit the Tower of the Winds, built in the 1st century BC by the Syrian astronomer Andronicus; this ingenious construction functioned as a sundial, weather vane, water clock and compass.

Changing of the Guard

Every hour, on the hour, catch the colourful changing of the guard ceremony in front of the Tomb of the Unknown Soldier in the forecourt of the **parliament** (Map p82; Syntagma). On Sundays at 11am, a platoon of traditionally dressed *evzones* (guards) marches down Leoforos Vasilissis Sofias, accompanied by a band.

Keramikos

The city's cemetery from the 12th century BC to Roman times was the **Keramikos** (Map p82; ☎ 210 346 3552; Ermou 148, Keramikos; adult/concession €2/1 incl museum; 🕒 8.30am-8pm Apr-Oct, 8am-5.30pm Nov-Mar). It was discovered in 1861 during the construction of Pireos, the street that leads to Piraeus. It is one of the most green and tranquil of Athens' ancient sites.

MORE FOR YOUR MONEY

The €12 admission charge to the Acropolis buys a collective ticket that gives entry to all the other significant ancient sites in Athens: the Ancient Agora, the Roman Agora, the Keramikos, the Temple of Olympian Zeus and the Theatre of Dionysos. The ticket is valid for 48 hours, otherwise individual site fees apply.

If you're only in town for three days, it's worth getting the new €15 transport ticket, which allows unlimited travel on all public transport, including airport services and the Athens Sightseeing bus for three days.

Temple of Olympian Zeus

This is the largest **temple** (Map p78; ☎ 210 922 6330; adult/concession €2/1; ☽ 8.30am-8pm Apr-Oct, 8am-5.30pm Nov-Mar) in Greece and sits just east of the Acropolis. It took over 700 years to build – construction was begun in the 6th century BC by Peisistratos, but was abandoned for lack of funds. Various other leaders had stabs at completing the temple, but it was left to Hadrian to complete the work in AD 131.

The temple is impressive for the sheer size of its 104 Corinthian columns (17m high with a base diameter of 1.7m), of which 15 remain – the fallen column was blown down in a gale in 1852. Hadrian put a colossal statue of Zeus in the cella and, in typically immodest fashion, placed an equally large one of himself next to it.

Odeon of Herodes Atticus

On the southern foothills of the Acropolis is the stunning **Odeon of Herodes Atticus** (Map p82), one of the oldest theatres still in use. Built in 161 by wealthy Roman Herodes Atticus in memory of his wife Regilla, it was excavated in 1857–58 and restored between 1950 and 1961. Performances of drama, music and dance are held here during the Athens Festival (p83). It is only open to the public during performances.

Museums & Galleries

One of the world's great museums, the **National Archaeological Museum** (Map p78; ☎ 210 821 7717; www.namuseum.gr; 28 Oktovriou-Patision 44; adult/concession €7/3; ☽ 1.30-8pm Mon, 8.30am-8pm Tue-Sun Apr-Oct, 8.30am-3pm Nov-Mar) houses the finest collection of Greek antiquities. Treasures include exquisite sculptures, pottery, jewellery, frescoes and artefacts found throughout Greece, dating from the Neolithic era to the Bronze Age, Cycladic, Minoan, Myceanean and Classical periods.

Housed in an imposing 19th-century neoclassical building, the museum has been totally overhauled since it was damaged in the 1999 earthquake. The final galleries opened in 2009, bringing to light previously unseen collections. The exhibits are displayed largely thematically and are beautifully presented.

With 10,000 sq metres of exhibition space, it could take several visits to appreciate the museum's vast holdings, but it is possible to see the highlights in half a day.

The crowd-pullers are the magnificent, exquisitely detailed gold artefacts from Mycenae and the spectacular Minoan frescoes from Santorini (Thira).

The new **Acropolis Museum** (Map p78; ☎ 210 900 0901; www.theacropolismuseum.gr; Dionysiou Areopagitou 15, Akropoli; admission €5; ☽ 8am-8pm Tues-Sun; ⴕ) showcases the surviving treasures of the Acropolis. At the entrance to the imposing modernist building you can see the ruins of an ancient Athenian neighbourhood uncovered during excavations.

The 1st-floor Archaic gallery is a veritable forest of statues, including stunning examples of 6th-century *kore* (maidens). But the crowning glory is the top-floor Parthenon Gallery, built in alignment with the temple itself, which houses the Parthenon sculptures, metopes and the 160m frieze, which for the first time in more than 200 years can be seen as one narrative about the Panathenaic procession, with stark white-plaster replicas of the missing pieces held by the British Museum.

The **Benaki Museum** (Map p82; ☎ 210 367 1000; www.benaki.gr; Koumbari 1, cnr Leoforos Vasilissis Sofias, Kolonaki; adult/concession €6/3, free Thu; ☽ 9am-5pm Mon, Wed, Fri & Sat, 9am-midnight Thu, 9am-3pm Sun) is arguably Greece's finest private museum, housing the collection of Antonis Benakis, accumulated during 35 years of avid collecting throughout Europe and Asia. The collection includes ancient sculpture, Bronze Age finds from Mycenae and Thessaly, early works by El Greco and a stunning collection of Greek regional costumes.

The **Goulandris Museum of Cycladic & Ancient Greek Art** (Map p82; ☎ 210 722 8321; www.cycladic.gr; cnr Leoforos Vasilissis Sofias & Neofytou Douka, Kolonaki;

SYNTAGMA & SURROUNDS

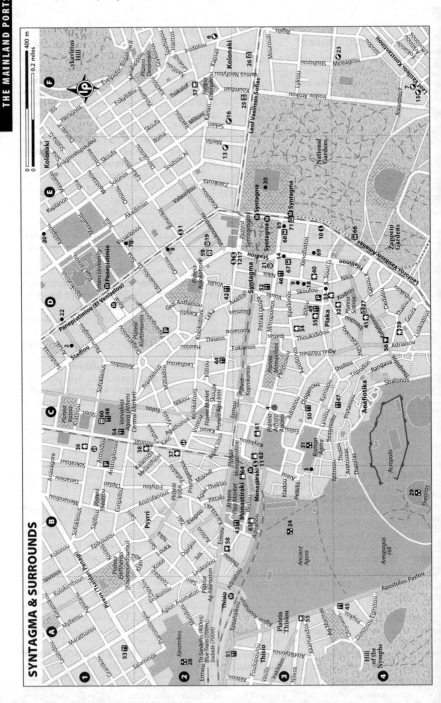

adult/concession €7/3.50; ☺ 10am-5pm Mon, Wed, Fri & Sat, 10am-8pm Thu, 11am-5pm Sun; ♿) houses the show-piece Cycladic collection, dating from 3000 BC to 2000 BC, which includes the marble figurines with folded arms that inspired many 20th-century artists with their simplicity and purity of form.

The emphasis in the **National Art Gallery** (Map p78; ☎ 210 723 5857; Leoforos Vasileos Konstantinou 50, Hilton; adult/concession €6/5; ☺ 9am-3pm & 6-9pm Mon & Wed, 9am-3pm Tue & Thu-Sat, 10am-2pm Sun) is on 19th- and 20th-century Greek painting, with a few works by European masters, including Picasso and El Greco.

Lykavittos Hill

This striking rocky landmark (277m high) rises out of a sea of concrete to offer the finest views in Athens. On clear days there are panoramic views of the city, the Attic basin, the surrounding mountains, and the islands of Salamis and Aegina. A fairly steep path leads to the summit from the top of Loukianou. Alternatively, you can take the **funicular railway** (Map p78; ☎ 210 721 0701; return €6; ☺ 9am-3am, half-hourly), referred to commonly as the 'teleferik' *(télépherique)*, from the top of Ploutarhou. On

the summit is the little **Chapel of Agios Giorgios**, along with a cafe and upmarket restaurant.

The open-air **Lykavittos Theatre** (Map p78), northeast of the summit, is used for concerts in summer.

FESTIVALS & EVENTS
Athens Festival

The annual **Athens Festival** is the city's most important cultural event, running from mid-June to late September. Major shows are held in the stunning setting of Odeon of Herodes Atticus (Map p82), one of the world's most historic venues, with the floodlit Acropolis as a backdrop. A diverse program of international standing ranges from ancient theatre and classical music to contemporary dance. Events are also held in various theatres and venues around the city.

Tickets can be bought online, by phone or at the **Hellenic Festival box office** (Map p82; ☎ 210 327 2000; www.greekfestival.gr; Arcade, Panepistimiou 39, Syntagma; ☺ 8.30am-4pm Mon-Fri, 9am-2pm Sat). Tickets go on sale three weeks before a performance. There are student discounts for most performances on production of an International Student Identity Card (ISIC; see p481).

Other Festivals & Events

Athens' jam-packed summer festival season features top international and local artists. Many free events are held at the **Technopolis** (Off Map p78; ☎ 210 346 7322; Gazi), the former Gasworks complex turned cultural centre. Major festivals include June's **Rockwave Festival** (☎ 210 882 0426; www.rockwavefestival.gr), the **European Jazz Festival** (May/June) and the **International Dance Festival** in July.

For information on what's on in Athens, check out the www.elculture.gr and www.breathtakingathens.gr websites.

SLEEPING
Budget
HOSTELS

Athens Easy Access Hostel (Map p78; ☎ 210 524 3211; www.athenseasyaccess.com; Satovrianidou 26, Omonia; dm €14-18, d/tr/q €25/23/18, incl breakfast; ✱ 🖳 ☎) Right behind Plateia Omonias (Omonia Sq), this friendly backpacker hotel has been newly renovated with a smart fit-out, and a range of doubles and dorm accommodation. The breakfast room becomes a popular happy-hour bar with cheap beer and meals. There's free wi-fi, an internet centre and laundry.

Athens Backpackers (Map p78; ☎ 210 922 4044; www.backpackers.gr; Makri 12, Makrygianni; dm incl breakfast €17-25; ✱ 🖳) The popular rooftop bar with cheap drinks and Acropolis views is a major drawcard of this modern and friendly Australian-run backpacker favourite, right near the Acropolis metro. There's a barbecue in the courtyard, a well-stocked kitchen, and a busy social scene with film nights and bar crawls. The six-bed dorms with private bathrooms and lockers have bedding but towels cost €2.

Student & Travellers' Inn (Map p82; ☎ 210 324 4808; www.studenttravellersinn.com; Kydathineon 16, Plaka; dm €18, d/tr without bathroom €65/81, s/d/tr with bathroom €55/65/90; ✱ 🖳) Its location in the heart of Plaka makes this long-established hostel popular with visitors of all ages. It's a friendly place with a pleasant shady courtyard with large-screen TV, free wi-fi and a helpful travel service. There's a mix of dorms and basic rooms, some with private bathroom and air-conditioning, though shared bathrooms are run-down and complaints about cleanliness common.

HOTELS
Plaka & Syntagma

Adonis Hotel (Map p82; ☎ 210 324 9737; www.hotel-adonis.gr; Kodrou 3, Plaka; s/d incl breakfast €60/85; ✱ 🖳)

This comfortable, if bland, pension on a quiet pedestrian street in Plaka is a decent budget base if you're out sightseeing all day. The rooms are basic and clean and come with TV, though the bathrooms are small. There are great views of the Acropolis from the 4th-floor rooms, and from the rooftop bar where breakfast is served. The hotel doesn't accept credit-card payments.

Hotel Phaedra (Map p82; ☎ 210 323 8461; www.hotelphaedra.com; Herefondos 16, Plaka; s €65, d €65-80, tr €95; ✱ 🖳) Many of the rooms at this small family-run hotel have balconies overlooking a church or the Acropolis. The hotel had an Olympics makeover and is tastefully furnished, though room sizes vary from small to snug. Some rooms have private bathrooms across the hall. A great rooftop terrace, friendly staff and location make this one of the better deals in Plaka.

Makrygianni & Koukaki

Marble House Pension (Map p78; ☎ 210 923 4058, 210 922 8294; www.marblehouse.gr; Zini 35a, Koukaki; d/tr without bathroom €40/53, s/d/tr with bathroom €35/45/59; ✱) This pension in a quiet cul-de-sac is one of Athens' best-value budget hotels, though it is a fair walk from the tourist drag (but close to the metro). Rooms have been artfully updated, with wrought-iron beds and furniture. All rooms have a fridge and ceiling fan and some have air-con (€9 extra). Breakfast costs an extra €5.

Hotel Tony (Map p78; ☎ 210 923 0561; www.hoteltony.gr; Zaharitsa 26, Koukaki; s/d/tr €45/65/75; ✱ ☎) This clean, well-maintained pension has been upgraded, with all but one of the rooms having private bathrooms. Air-con costs €9 extra and hot water can be patchy. All have fridge, TV and air-con. Tony also has roomy, well-equipped studio apartments nearby, which are similarly priced and excellent for families or for longer stays.

Omonia & Surrounds

Hotel Exarchion (Map p78; ☎ 210 380 0731; www.exarchion.com; Themistokleous 55, Exarhia; s/d/tr incl breakfast €50/65/80; ✱ 🖳) Right in the heart of bohemian Exarhia, this characterless but comfortable 1960s high-rise hotel offers reasonably priced accommodation, with updated, well-equipped rooms. There's a rooftop cafe-bar and plenty of dining and entertainment options at your doorstep. It's a 10-minute walk from Omonia metro station.

Midrange

PLAKA & SYNTAGMA

Acropolis House Pension (Map p82; ☎ 210 322 2344; www.acropolishouse.gr; Kodrou 6-8, Plaka; d €59-65, s/d/tr incl breakfast €72.50/87/113.50; ✖ ⚛) This atmospheric family-run pension is in a beautifully preserved, 19th-century house, which retains many original features and has lovely painted walls. There are discounts for stays of three days or more. Some rooms have bathrooms across the hall.

Niki Hotel (Map p82; ☎ 210 322 0913; www.nikihotel.gr; Nikis 27, Syntagma; s/d/q incl buffet breakfast €110/117/240; ✖ ▣) This small hotel bordering Plaka has undergone one of the more stylish makeovers in the area, with contemporary design and furnishings. The rooms are well appointed and there is a two-level suite for families, with balconies offering Acropolis views.

Central Hotel (Map p82; ☎ 210 323 4357; www.centralhotel.gr; Apollonos 21, Plaka; s/d/tr incl buffet breakfast from €111/136/185; ✖ ▣) This stylish hotel has been tastefully decorated in light, contemporary tones. It has comfortable rooms with all the mod cons and decent bathrooms. There is a lovely roof terrace with Acropolis views, which has a small Jacuzzi and sun lounges. Central is in a handy location between Syntagma and Plaka.

MONASTIRAKI

Hotel Attalos (Map p82; ☎ 210 321 2801; www.attaloshotel.com; Athinas 29, Monastiraki; s/d/tr €76/94/110; ✖ ▣ ⚛) Though decor has never been its strong point, this nonetheless comfortable and reliable budget hotel had an Olympic makeover. It's very central and close to the metro but its best feature remains the rooftop bar that offers wonderful views of the Acropolis by night, and the rooms at the back with Acropolis views from the balconies. There's free internet.

Hotel Cecil (Map p82; ☎ 210 321 7909; www.cecil.gr; Athinas 39, Monastiraki; s/d/tr incl breakfast €80/115/150; ✖ ⚛) This charming old hotel on busy Athinas has beautiful high, moulded ceilings, polished timber floors and an original cage-style lift. The simple rooms are tastefully furnished, but don't have fridges. Two connecting rooms with a shared bathroom are ideal for families or friends.

MAKRYGIANNI & KOUKAKI

Art Gallery Hotel (Map p78; ☎ 210 923 8376; www.artgalleryhotel.gr; Erehthiou 5, Koukaki; s/d/tr/q €70/100/120/140;

✖ ⚛) This charming, family-run place is full of personal touches and works by an artist who once had her studio upstairs. Some rooms are a little small but all have been refurbished. Original '60s furniture has been retained in the communal areas. You can have a generous breakfast (€7) on the balcony with Acropolis views. There are a few cheaper rooms with shared bathrooms. Wi-fi is free.

OMONIA & SURROUNDS

our pick Fresh Hotel (Map p82; ☎ 210 524 8511; www.freshhotel.gr; Sofokleous 26, cnr Klisthenous, Omonia; s/d/ste incl buffet breakfast from €115/130/350; ✖ ⚛ ☑) The first of the hip hotels to open in the gritty Omonia area, this is a cool place as long as you're happy to ignore the working girls hovering in the streets below after hours. Once inside the candy-coloured reception, the seediness gives way to chic design and brightly coloured rooms and suites with all the mod cons. The fantastic rooftop – with pool, bar and restaurant with Acropolis views – couldn't be further from the world below.

Top End

There are some lovely luxury hotels in Athens, but the upper end of the market is generally outrageously priced, though you can find the odd low-season discount.

Electra Palace (Map p82; ☎ 210 337 0000; www.electrahotels.gr; Navarhou Nikodimou 18, Plaka; d/ste incl breakfast from €220/560; Ⓟ ✖ ▣ ☑) One for the romantics, you can have breakfast under the Acropolis on your balcony in the front rooms (from €325) and dinner on the rooftop restaurant at Plaka's smartest hotel. Completely refurbished in classic style, the rooms are well appointed and there is an indoor swimming pool and gym as well as a rooftop pool with Acropolis views.

EATING

For most people, Plaka is the place to be. It's hard to beat the atmosphere of an afternoon coffee break in its cobbled streets or dining out beneath the floodlit Acropolis.

Budget

PLAKA

Paradosiako (Map p82; ☎ 210 321 4121; Voulis 44a; mains €4-10) For great traditional fare, try this inconspicuous, no-frills taverna on the periphery of Plaka, with a few tables on the footpath. There's a basic menu, but daily specials include fresh and delicious seafood. Get there early before the locals arrive.

Platanos (Map p82; ☎ 210 321 8734; Diogenous 4; mains €6.20-12.50; ☻ noon-4.30pm & 6.30pm-midnight Mon-Sat) This age-old Plaka taverna with an antiquated, badly translated menu is in a pleasant village-style square away from the main tourist drag. There are tables under a giant plane tree and reliable home-style fare, such as chicken with okra. No credit cards.

Vizantino (Map p82; ☎ 210 322 7368; Kydathineon 18; specials €5-9.50) Also recommended, despite the touts, is this place, which is touristy in the extreme, but the best of the restaurants around Plateia Filomousou Eterias.

SYNTAGMA

ourpick Filema (Map p82; ☎ 210 325 0222; Romvis 16; mezedhes €4.50-12) This popular *mezedhopoleio* (restaurant specialising in mezedhes) has two shopfronts and fills tables on both sides of this narrow street, which is a busy commercial area by day, but a peaceful spot when the shops close. It has a great range of mezedhes, such as the plump *keftedhes* or grilled sardines.

Lena's Bio (Map p82; ☎ 210 324 1360; Nikis 11; salads €6-10; ☻ 8am-6pm Mon-Fri, 8am-4pm Sat) For a wholesome option, this has a delicious range of organic meals, snacks and juices – if you can snag a table.

OMONIA

The streets around the colourful and bustling **Varvakios Agora** (Athens Central Market; Map p82; Athinas; ☻ Mon-Sat) are a sensory delight. One of the market's tavernas, **Papandreou** (☎ 213 008 2297; Aristogitonos 1; mains €7-10; ☻ 24hr) is an Athenian institution, turning out huge quantities of tasty, traditional fare. The clientele ranges from hungry market workers to late-night revellers in search of a bowl of hangover-busting *patsas* (tripe soup).

Midrange
PLAKA & SYNTAGMA

Tzitzikas & Mermingas (Map p82; ☎ 210 324 7607; Mitropoleos 12-14, Syntagma; mezedhes €5.90-9.90) This bright, cheery, modern *mezedhopoleio* isn't in the most atmospheric of locations, but it dishes out a great range of delicious and creative mezedhes. There are shelves lined with Greek products and the theme extends playfully to the toilets.

Palia Taverna tou Psara (Map p82; ☎ 210 321 8734; Erehtheos 16, Plaka; seafood dishes €11.50-26) Hidden away from the main hustle and bustle of Plaka, this taverna is a cut above the rest, which is why it fills the tables on the street, the terrace and the place next door. There is a choice of mezedhes, but it is known as the best seafood tavern in Plaka (top fresh fish €62 per kilogram).

AKROPOLI & THISIO

Filistron (Map p82; ☎ 210 346 7554; Apostolou Pavlou 23, Thisio; mezedhes €7.50-15; ☻ Tue-Sun) It's wise to book a prized table on the rooftop terrace of this excellent *mezedhopoleio*, which enjoys breathtaking Acropolis and Lykavittos views. Specialising in regional cuisine, there's a great range of tasty mezedhes – try the grilled vegetables with haloumi or the Mytilini onions stuffed with rice and mince – and an extensive Greek wine list.

To Steki tou Ilia (Map p82; ☎ 210 345 8052; Eptahalkou 5, Thisio; chops per portion/kg €9/30; ☻ 8pm-late) You'll often see people waiting for a table at this *psistaria* (taverna that specialises in char-grilled or spit-roasted meat), famous for its tasty grilled lamb chops. With tables on the quiet pedestrian strip opposite the church, it's a no-frills place with barrel wine and simple offerings of dips, chips and salads. Those not keen on lamb should know that there are pork chops, too.

GAZI

ourpick Café Avyssinia (Map p82; ☎ 210 321 7407; Kynetou 7, Monastiraki; mezedhes €4.50-16.50; ☻ noon-1am Tue-Sat, noon-7pm Sun) Hidden away in the grungy Flea Market, this bohemian *mezedhopoleio* gets top marks for atmosphere, food and friendly service. It specialises in regional Greek cuisine, from warm fava to eggplants baked with tomato and cheese, and has a great selection of spirits, such as ouzo, *raki* and *tsipouro*. There is often acoustic live music, and fantastic Acropolis views upstairs.

Sardelles (Off Map p82; ☎ 210 347 8050; Persefonis 15, Gazi; fish dishes €9-15.50) This modern fish taverna specialises in simply cooked seafood. It's a friendly place with tables outside opposite the illuminated gasworks, excellent service and nice touches such as the fishmonger paper tablecloths and souvenir pots of basil. Try the grilled *thrapsalo* (squid) and excellent *taramasalata* (purée of potatoe and fish roe). Meat eaters should venture next door to Butcher Shop.

Top End

Varoulko (Map p82; ☎ 210 522 8400; Pireos 80, Gazi; mains €20-35; ☻ dinner from 8pm Mon-Sat) For a magical

Athens dining experience, you can't beat the winning combination of Acropolis views from the superb rooftop terrace and delicious seafood by Lefteris Lazarou, the only Greek Michelin-rated chef. The service is faultless and the wine list enviable. Reservations essential.

DRINKING
Cafes
Athens' myriad of packed cafes prompts many a visitor to wonder if anyone ever works in this city (and why it has Europe's most expensive coffee – between €3.50 and €5). Locals cheekily suggest the charge includes chair hire, as people can 'sit' on a coffee for hours at a time.

Athinaion Politeia (Map p82; Akamandos 1, Thisio) There are great views from the tables outside this neoclassical building on the pedestrian promenade.

Da Capo (Map p82; Tsakalof 1, Kolonaki) Has excellent coffee in a prime people-watching spot, if you can find a table.

Bars
For more bars than you could possibly crawl through, follow the crowds to Gazi and Psyrri.

Brettos (Map p82; Kydathineon 41, Plaka) This is a delightful old bar and distillery, with a stunning wall of colourful bottles and barrels. You can sample shots of Brettos' homemade ouzo, brandy and other tipples.

James Joyce (Map p82; ☎ 210 323 5055; Astingos 12, Monastiraki; mains €9-14) This Irish pub, with free-flowing Guinness, decent pub food and live music, also has plenty of travellers and expats.

Gay & Lesbian Venues
The greatest concentration of gay bars is around Gazi and Makrygianni.

Start the night in Gazi at **Blue Train** (Off Map p82; ☎ 210 346 0677; www.bluetrain.gr; Leoforos Konstantinoupoleos, Gazi) along the railway line. **Sodade** (Off Map p82; ☎ 210 346 8657; www.sodade .gr; Triptolemou 10, Gazi) attracts a young clubbing crowd.

Other popular spots include the long-running **Granazi** (Map p78; ☎ 210 924 4185; Lembesi 20, Makrygianni) and the **Lamda Club** (Map p78; ☎ 210 922 4202; Lembesi 15, Makrygianni).

Most places open at 11pm, but the crowd arrives after midnight.

ENTERTAINMENT
For English-language entertainment guides and listings try the daily English-language *Kathimerini* (www.ekathimerini.com) supplement in the *International Herald Tribune*, *Athens News* or *Athens Plus*. You can also check out www.elculture.gr for events and concerts around town.

Greek Folk Dancing
Dora Stratou Dance Theatre (Map p78; ☎ 210 921 4650; www.grdance.org; Filopappou Hill; adult/concession €15/10; ☺ performances 9.30pm Tue-Sat, 8.15pm Sun May-Sep) Every summer the Dora Stratou company performs folk dances from all over Greece at its open-air theatre on the western side of Filopappou Hill.

The theatre is signposted from the western end of Dionysiou Areopagitou. Take trolley-bus 22 from Syntagma and get off at Agios Ioannis.

Live Music
Athens has a healthy rock music scene and is on most European touring schedules. In summer, check festival programs, as you may be able to see your favourite band perform in open-air theatres around town.

Gagarin 205 Club (Off Map p78; www.gagarin205 .gr; Liosion 205) Primarily a rock venue, gigs are mostly on Friday and Saturday nights and feature leading rock and underground music bands. Tickets are available from **Ticket House** (Map p82; ☎ 210 360 8366; www.tickethouse.gr; Panepistimiou 42, Syntagma).

Alavastro Café (Map p78; ☎ 210 756 0102; Damareos 78, Pangrati) A casual and intimate venue featuring an eclectic mix of modern jazz, ethnic and *entehno* Greek music.

Stoa Athanaton (Map p82; ☎ 210 321 4362; Sofokleous 19, Omonia; ☺ 3-6pm & midnight-6am Mon-Sat Oct-May) This almost legendary *rembetika* (blues) club, above the central meat market, has a respected band of musicians – often starting from mid-afternoon. Access is by a lift in the arcade.

Nightclubs
Admission to most venues ranges from €10 to €15. The price often includes one free drink. Expect to pay about €5 for a beer and €8 for spirits. Clubs don't start to get busy until around midnight.

our pick **Venue** (Off Map p78; ☎ 210 341 1410; www .venue-club.com; Pireos 130, Rouf; admission €10-15; ☺ midnight-late Fri & Sat) Arguably the city's biggest dance club puts on the biggest dance parties with the world's biggest DJs at this new venue with a three-stage dance floor and energetic crowd.

Akrotiri (Off Map p78; ☎ 210 985 9147; Vasileos Georgiou B 5, Agios Kosmas; ☼ 10pm-5am) One of the city's top beach clubs, this massive venue has a capacity for 3000, with bars, restaurant and lounges over different levels. It hosts great party nights with top resident and visiting DJs, and pool parties during the day.

Vitrine (Map p78; ☎ 210 924 2444; Markou Mousourou 1, Mets; ☼ 10pm-late) A favourite central nightspot, the name of this venue may keep changing but the superb Acropolis and city views from the top never do.

SHOPPING
Flea Markets
Athens' traditional Monastiraki Flea Market (Map p82) has a festive atmosphere. The permanent antique, furniture and collectables stores have plenty to sift through and are open all week, while the streets around the station and Adrianou fill with vendors selling jewellery, handicrafts and bric-a-brac.

The big Sunday Flea Market (Map p82) takes place at the end of Ermou, towards Gazi, where traders peddle their stuff from the crack of dawn. You can find some bargains, interesting collectables and kitsch delights among the junk. Don't be shy – haggle. It winds up around 2pm.

Traditional Handicrafts & Souvenirs
Melissinos Art (Map p82; ☎ 210 321 9247; www .melissinos-art.com; Agias Theklas 2, Psyrri; ☼ 10am-8pm Mon-Sat, 10am-6pm Sun) Artist Pantelis Melissinos continues the sandal-making tradition of his famous poet/sandal-maker father Stavros, whose past customers include the Beatles, Rudolph Nureyev, Sophia Loren and Jackie Onassis. It's the best place for authentic handmade leather sandals based on ancient Greek styles (€25 to €29).

Centre of Hellenic Tradition (Map p82; ☎ 210 321 3023; Pandrosou 36, Plaka; ☼ 10am-7.30pm) Upstairs from the arcade are great examples of traditional ceramics, sculptures and handicrafts from around Greece. There is also a great *ouzerie* (ouzo bar) and a gallery on the 1st floor.

GETTING THERE & AWAY
Air
Eleftherios Venizelos International Airport (Off Map p78; ☎ 210 353 0000; www.aia.gr) is at Spata, 27km east of Athens.

The state-of-the-art airport, named in honour of the country's leading 20th-century politician, has all the standard facilities, great shopping and a transit hotel. If you have time to kill, it is worth visiting the small archaeological museum on the 1st floor above the check-in hall. The airport website has real-time flight information.

The majority of domestic flights are operated by **Olympic Air** (www.olympicairlines.com; Makrygianni Map p78; ☎ 801 144 444, 210 926 9111; Leoforos Syngrou 96, Makrygianni; Omonia Map p78; ☎ 210 926 7218; Kotopoulou 1, Omonia; Syntagma Map p82; ☎ 210 926 4444; Filellinon 15, Syntagma), which takes bookings online.

Aegean Airlines (☎ reservations 801 112 0000, 210 626 1000; www.aegeanair.com) competes with Olympic Air on the most popular domestic routes. Aegean has the best earlybird specials and bookings can be made online. Aegean has daily flights to Thessaloniki, Iraklio, Rhodes, Mykonos, Santorini and Hania, as well as several flights weekly to key destinations around Greece. There's an office in **Syntagma** (Map p82; ☎ 210 331 5522; Othonos 15).

See Getting Around (p90) for public transport to/from the airport. For international flights to/from Athens, see p490.

For information about flights to the Greek islands, see Island Hopping (p509).

Boat
Most ferry, hydrofoil and high-speed catamaran services to the islands leave from Athens' massive port at Piraeus (p93). Piraeus is the busiest port in Greece, with a bewildering array of departures and destinations, including daily services to all the island groups, except the Ionians and the Sporades. The departure points for ferry destinations are shown on Map p92.

For more information see also Island Hopping (p505).

Bus
There are two main intercity (IC) **KTEL** (www .ktel.org) bus terminals in Athens.

Bus Terminal A (Off Map p78; ☎ 210 512 4910; Kifisou 100), about 7km northwest of Plateia Omonias, has regular departures to the Peloponnese, the Ionian Islands, and western and northern Greece. City bus 051 (Map p78) runs between the terminal and the junction of Zinonos and Menandrou, near Omonia, every 15 minutes from 5am to midnight.

KEY BUS DEPARTURES FROM ATHENS

Bus Terminal A

Destination	Duration	Fare	Frequency
Corfu*	9½hr	€47.50	3 daily
Igoumenitsa	7½hr	€40.40	4 daily
Lefkada	5½hr	€30.50	4 daily
Patra	3hr	€17.00	half-hourly
Zakynthos*	6hr	€30.70	4 daily

*includes ferry ticket

Bus Terminal B

Destination	Duration	Fare	Frequency
Agios Konstantinos	2½hr	€14.70	hourly
Volos	4½hr	€24.70	12 daily

Mavromateon Terminal

Destination	Duration	Fare	Frequency
Lavrio port	1¼hr	€5.20	half-hourly
Rafina port	1hr	€2.20	half-hourly

Bus Terminal B (Off Map p78; ☎ 210 831 7181; Liosion 260, Kato Patisia) is about 5km north of Plateia Omonias, off Liosion, and has departures to central Greece and Evia. The terminal entrance is one block east from Lioson on Agiou Dimitriou Oplon (head right down Gousiou to the end of the street). From the city centre take bus 024 from outside the main gate of the National Gardens (Map p82) and get off Praktoria KTEL stop.

Buses for Rafina and Lavrio depart from the **Mavromateon Terminal** (Map p78; ☎ 210 880 8000; cnr Leoforos Alexandras & 28 Oktovriou-Patision, Pedion Areos), 250m north of the National Archaeological Museum.

For information on international bus services, see p493.

Car & Motorcycle

The upgraded National Rd 1 (Ethniki Odos) is the main route north. It starts at Nea Kifisia. Take Vasilissis Sofias from Syntagma or the Ymittos ring road via Kaisariani to the new toll motorway Attiki Odos, which services the airport. National Rd 8 begins beyond Dafni and goes to the Peloponnese and northwestern Greece. Take Agiou Konstantinou from Omonia.

The top end of Leoforos Syngrou, near the Temple of Olympian Zeus, is lined with car-hire firms. Local companies tend to offer better deals than the multinationals. The average price you can expect to pay for a small car for a day is €50, less for three or more days.

Athens Airport Car Rentals (☎ 210 965 2590; www .athensairport-car-rentals.com; Spata)
Avis (Map p78; ☎ 210 322 4951; Leoforos Vasilissis Amalias 48, Makrygianni)
Budget (Map p78; ☎ 210 921 4771; Leoforos Syngrou 8, Makrygianni)
Europcar (Map p78; ☎ 210 924 8810; Leoforos Syngrou 43, Makrygianni)
Hertz (Map p78; ☎ 210 922 0102; Leoforos Syngrou 12, Makrygianni)
Kosmos (Map p78; ☎ 210 923 4695; www.kosmos -carrental.com; Leoforos Syngrou 9, Makrygianni)

You can hire mopeds and motorcycles if you have the appropriate licence and the confidence to take on the traffic. **Motorent** (Map p78; ☎ 210 923 4939; www.motorent.gr; Rovertou Galli 1, Makrygianni) has machines from 50cc to 250cc. High-season prices for a 50cc scooter start at €16 per day.

Train

Intercity trains to central and northern Greece depart from the central **Larisis train station** (Map p78), about 1km northeastwest of Plateia Omonias (metro Line 2).

For the Peloponnese, take the suburban rail to Kiato and change for other OSE services there. A new rail hub (SKA) is going to be located about 20km north of the city.

OSE (☎ 1110; www.ose.gr; ☽ 24hr; Omonia Map p78; ☎ 210 529 7005; Karolou 1, Omonia; ☽ 8am-3pm Mon-Fri; Syntagma Map p82; ☎ 210 362 4405; Sina 6, Syntagma;

8am-3pm Mon-Sat) handles advance bookings. See p493 for international trains.

GETTING AROUND
To/From the Airport
BUS

Express bus services operate between the airport and the city, and between the airport and Piraeus. Bus X95 runs between the airport and Syntagma 24 hours (every 30 minutes). The journey takes about an hour, depending on traffic. The Syntagma bus stop is on Othonos St.

Bus X93 goes to the Terminal B bus station, while bus X94 services Ethniki Amyna metro station. Bus X96 to Plateia Karaïskaki in Piraeus runs 24 hours (about every 20 minutes).

Tickets for airport buses cost €3.20 and are valid for one trip only, and are not valid for other forms of public transport.

Additionally, KTEL runs express buses from the airport to the port of Rafina (€2.20) roughly every one hour and 40 minutes, and to the port of Lavrio (€5.20, change at Markopoulo) roughly every two hours.

METRO & SUBURBAN RAIL

The metro is the best way to travel between the airport and central Athens. It is not express, so you can pick it up at any station along Line 3. Just check that it is the airport train (displayed on the train and platform screen). Otherwise you can take any train to the Doukissis Plakentias metro station, where you can connect to the airport train.

Trains run every 30 minutes, leaving Monastiraki between 5.50am and midnight and the airport between 5.30am and 11.30pm.

Full adult fares cost €6/10 for one way/return (return is only valid for 48 hours). Note that the fare for two or more passengers works out at €5 each, so purchase tickets together (same applies to suburban rail). The airport ticket is valid for all forms of public transport for 90 minutes. If you are still in transit before the 90 minutes is up, revalidate your ticket on the final mode of transport to show you are still on the same journey.

From the airport, you can also take the suburban rail to Nerantziotissa, and change to line 2 on the ISAP Line or to Doukissis Plakentias metro station. Trains to the airport run from 6am to midnight, while trains from the airport to Athens run from 5.30am to 11.30pm. The trip takes 38 minutes and trains run every 15 minutes from Nerantziotissa. The suburban rail has the same pricing as the metro, but the return ticket is valid for a month.

The suburban rail also goes from the airport to Piraeus (change trains at Neratziotissa) and Kiato in the Peloponnese (via Corinth).

TAXI

Taking a taxi to or from the airport is a relatively easy business as long as the basic ground rules are understood and adhered to. Check that the meter is set to the correct tariff (day or night). In addition to the fare, you will be required to pay a €3.40 surcharge on trips *from* the airport, a €2.70 toll for using the toll road connecting the airport to the city plus €0.35 for each piece of luggage over 10kg. In case of a dispute, take the taxi driver's permit number and car registration number, and report the details to the tourist police. Drivers can and will be prosecuted for overcharging.

The trip from the airport to the city centre – via the much faster Ymyttos ring road and the Katehaki exit – should take between 40 and 55 minutes depending on traffic. Taxis to Piraeus will take longer and cost more as drivers may prefer to take the longer, but less congested, southern loop route via Vari and Glyfada. Expect to pay about €25 to €30 from the airport to the city, and €30 to Piraeus

Around Athens

Athens has an extensive and inexpensive integrated public transport network of buses, metro, trolleybuses and tram.

Athens Urban Transport Organisation (OASA; ☎ 185; www.oasa.gr; Metsovou 15, Exarhia/Mouseio; 6.30am-11.30pm Mon-Fri, 7.30am-10.30pm Sat & Sun) can assist with most inquiries. Transport maps can be downloaded from its website and are available at the airport and train stations.

A €1 ticket can be used on the entire Athens transport network, including the suburban rail (except airport services) and is valid for 90 minutes. There is also a daily €3 ticket and a weekly €10 ticket with the same restrictions on airport travel.

A new €15 tourist ticket, valid for three days, allows unlimited travel on all public transport, including airport services and the Athens Sightseeing bus.

Children under six travel free; people under 18 and over 65 travel at half-fare.

Plain-clothed inspectors make spot checks. The penalty for travelling without a validated ticket is 60 times the ticket price.

BUS & TROLLEYBUS

Buses and electric trolleybuses operate every 15 minutes from 5am until midnight.

Buses run 24 hours between the city centre and Piraeus – every 20 minutes from 6am until midnight – and hourly at other times.

Tickets for buses and trolleybuses (€1) can be purchased at a transport kiosk or at most *periptera* (kiosks) and validated on board.

METRO

The expanding and efficient **metro** (www .ametro.gr) has transformed travel around central Athens, making it quick and easy to get around. The stations are an attraction in their own right, displaying contemporary art and finds from the excavation works. Trains and stations can be stifling in summer as limited (or no) air-conditioning was installed. All have wheelchair access. Tickets must be validated at the machines at platform entrances. Trains operate between 5am and just after midnight. They run every three minutes during peak periods, dropping to every 10 minutes at other times.

Line 1 (Green)

The Kifisia–Piraeus line has transfer stations at Omonia and Attiki for Line 2; Monastiraki is the transfer station for Line 3. Nerantziotissa connects with the suburban rail. The hourly all-night bus service (bus 500) follows this route, with bus stops located outside the train stations.

Line 2 (Red)

Line 2 runs from Agios Antonios in the northwest to Agios Dimitrios in the southeast (check the boards so you don't confuse your saints). Attiki and Omonia connect with Line 1, while Syntagma connects with Line 3.

Line 3 (Blue)

Line 3 runs northeast from Egaleo to Doukissis Plakentias, with the airport train continuing from there. Syntagma is the transfer station for Line 2.

TAXI

Hailing one of Athens' yellow taxis often involves standing on the pavement and shouting your destination. If a taxi is going your way, the driver may stop even if there are passengers inside. The fare is not shared: each person is charged the fare on the meter (note where it is at when you get in).

Make sure the meter is switched on when you get in. The flag fall is €1.05, with a €0.95 surcharge from ports, train and bus stations, and a €3.40 surcharge from the airport. After that, the day rate (tariff 1 on the meter) is €0.60 per kilometre. The night tariff (tariff 2 on the meter) increases to €1.05 per kilometre between midnight and 5am. Baggage is charged at a rate of €0.35 per item over 10kg. The minimum fare is €2.80. Most short trips around central Athens should cost around €4.

TRAM

Athens' **tram** (www.tramsa.gr) makes for a scenic coastal journey to Faliro and Voula, via Glyfada, but it is not the fastest means of transport. The tram operates from 5am to 1am Monday to Thursday, then 24 hours from Friday night to Sunday (services reduce to every 40 minutes), servicing revellers travelling to the city's seaside clubs. The trip from Syntagma to Faliro (SEF) takes about 45 minutes, while Syntagma to Voula takes around one hour. The central terminus (Map p82) is on Amalias, opposite the National Gardens. There are ticket vending machines on platforms.

A tram extension to Piraeus was expected to be completed by the time you read this.

THE MAINLAND PORTS

This section provides information on the major mainland port towns with ferry connections to the different island groups. You may find they are worth a visit in their own right or make an interesting pit-stop. Most ferries leave from Greece's biggest port, Piraeus, about 10km south of Athens. There are two smaller ports in Attica, and major ports at Patras and Thessaloniki. Other port towns on the mainland service specific island groups.

PIRAEUS ΠΕΙΡΑΙΑΣ
pop 175,697

Apart from being the major port for Athens, Piraeus is Greece's main port and the biggest in the Mediterranean, with more than 20 million passengers annually. It's the hub of the Aegean ferry network, centre for Greece's maritime import-export and transit trade and base for its large merchant navy. While Piraeus was once a separate city, nowadays it virtually melds imperceptibly into the expanded urban sprawl of Athens.

lonelyplanet.com

PIRAEUS

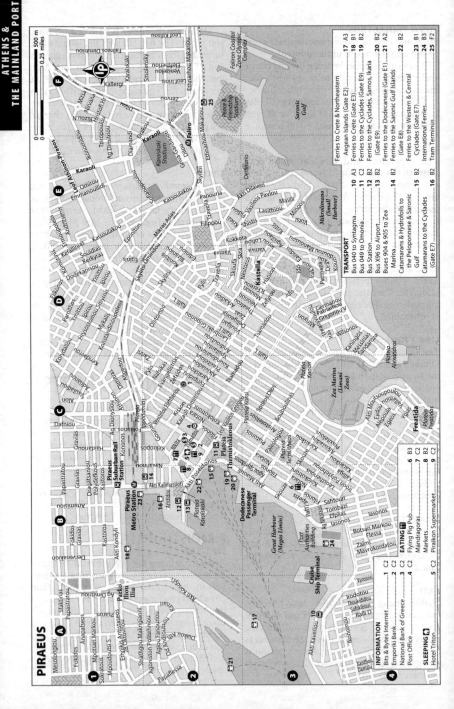

History

The histories of Athens and Piraeus are inextricably linked. Themistocles transferred his Athenian fleet from the exposed port of Phaleron (modern Faliro) to the security of Piraeus at the start of the 5th century BC.

Piraeus was a flourishing commercial centre during the classical age but, by Roman times, it had been overtaken by Rhodes, Delos and Alexandria. During medieval and Turkish times Piraeus shrank to a tiny fishing village and by the time Greece became independent it was home to fewer than 20 people.

Piraeus' resurgence began in 1834 when Athens became the capital of independent Greece. By the start of the 20th century, Piraeus had superseded Syros as Greece's principal port.

Orientation

Piraeus is 10km southwest of Athens. The largest of its three harbours is the Kentriko Limani (Main Harbour), on the western side of the Piraeus peninsula, which is the departure point for all ferry, hydrofoil and catamaran services. Limani Zeas (Zea Marina) and the picturesque Mikrolimano (Small Harbour), on the eastern side, are for private yachts.

The metro and suburban train lines from Athens terminate at the northeastern corner of the Main Harbour.

Information

Bits & Bytes Internet (☎ 210 412 1615; Iroön Polytehniou 2; per hr €3; ☼ 8am-10pm)
Emporiki Bank (cnr Antistaseos & Makras Stoas) Has a 24-hour ATM.
National Bank of Greece (cnr Antistaseos & Tsamadou) Near the Emporiki Bank.
Post office (cnr Tsamadou & Filonos; ☼ 7.30am-8pm Mon-Fri, 7.30am-2pm Sat)

Sleeping

Many hotels around the Great Harbour are shabby and aimed more towards accommodating sailors and clandestine liaisons than tourists, with the better hotels geared for the business market. Don't attempt to sleep out – Piraeus is probably one of the most dangerous places in Greece to do so.

Hotel Triton (☎ 210 417 3457; www.htriton.gr; Tsamadou 8; s/d/tr incl breakfast €55/70/80; ☐ ✷) Has a refurbished executive-style rooms, some overlooking the colourful market square.

WHICH PORT?

The following list details the ports serving each island group:

- Crete – Piraeus, Thessaloniki, Gythio, Kythira
- Cyclades – Piraeus, Rafina, Thessaloniki, Lavrio
- Dodecanese – Piraeus, Thessaloniki, Alexandroupoli
- Evia & the Sporades – Rafina (Evia only), Agios Konstantinos, Thessaloniki, Volos
- Ionians – Patra, Igoumenitsa, Kyllini, Piraeus (Kythira only), Gythio (Kythira and Antikythira only), Neapoli (Kythira only)
- Northeastern Aegean Islands – Piraeus, Thessaloniki, Kavala, Alexandroupoli
- Saronic Gulf Islands – Piraeus, Porto Heli, Ermioni, Galatas

---

Eating

The waterfront around the Great Harbour is lined with cafes, restaurants and fast-food places, but the better restaurants are in the backstreets and the smaller harbours.

Flying Pig Pub (☎ 210 429 5344; Filonos 31; ☼ 9am-1am) Run by a friendly Greek-Australian, the Pig is a popular bar with a large range of beers. It also serves decent food, including a generous English breakfast.

You can stock up on supplies in the area just inland from Akti Poseidonos. The **markets** (☼ 6am-4pm Mon-Fri) are on Dimosthenous.
Piraikon supermarket (☎ 210 417 5764; Ippokratous 1; ☼ 8am-8pm Mon-Fri, 8am-4pm Sat) is opposite the markets, or try the gourmet deli **Mandragoras** (☎ 210 417 2961; Gounari 14).

Getting There & Away
BOAT

Piraeus has a bewildering array of departures and destinations, including daily ferry services to all the island groups except the Ionians and Sporades. Hydrofoil and catamaran services from Piraeus serve the Saronic Gulf Islands and the Cyclades. The port is massive and a free bus between the ferry terminal gates and passenger terminals runs regularly from the metro station. The departure points for ferry destinations are shown on the Piraeus map. For details of all the destinations that can be reached from Piraeus, see Island Hopping (p510).

BUS
Buses 040 and 049 run 24 hours between Piraeus and central Athens, every 20 minutes from 6am until midnight and then hourly. Bus 040 runs between Akti Xaveriou in Piraeus and Filellinon in Athens. Bus 049 runs between Plateia Themistokleous in Piraeus and Omonia in Athens. The X96 Piraeus–Athens Airport Express buses leave from the southwestern corner of Plateia Karaïskaki.

METRO & SUBURBAN RAIL
The metro is the fastest and easiest way of getting from the Great Harbour to central Athens (see p91). The station is at the northern end of Akti Kalimassioti. Travellers should take extra care of valuables on the metro; the section between Piraeus and Monastiraki is notorious for pickpockets.

The Piraeus train station is the terminus of the suburban rail network. Suburban trains run from the airport to Piraeus (change trains at Neratziotissa).

RAFINA ΡΑΦΗΝΑ
pop 11,909
Tucked into Attica's east coast, Rafina is Athens' main fishing port and second-most important port for passenger ferries. It is much smaller and less confusing than Piraeus – and fares are about 20% cheaper, but it's an hour by bus to get there. The **port police** (☎ 22940 22300) occupies a kiosk near the quay, which is lined with fish restaurants and ticket agents. The main square, Plateia Plastira, is at the top of the ramp leading to the port.

Getting There & Away
There are daily ferry and catamaran services to the Cyclades from Rafina, including Tinos, Mykonos, Andros and Paros. There are also daily ferries to the port of Marmari on the island of Evia. For details, see Island Hopping (p510). There are frequent buses between the Mavromateon terminal in Athens and Rafina (€2.20, one hour) between 5.45am and 10.30pm.

LAVRIO ΛΑΥΡΙΟ
pop 8558
An industrial town on the east coast of Attica, 60km southeast of Athens, Lavrio is the departure point for ferries to the islands of Kea

and Kythnos, and for high-season catamaran services to the western Cyclades. In antiquity, it was an important mining town. Lavrio has many fish tavernas and *ouzeries*, as well as a great fish market.

Getting There & Away
Catamaran services operate from Lavrio between mid-June and September, with daily departures (except Wednesday) to Kea, Kythnos, Syros and Mykonos. For details see Island Hopping (p510). The ticket office at Lavrio is opposite the quay; the **Lavrio Port Authority** (☎ 22920 25249) has ferry information. Buses to Lavrio run hourly, departing from the Mavromateon terminal in Athens (€5.20, 1½ hours).

THESSALONIKI ΘΕΣΣΑΛΟΝΙΚΗ
pop 363,987
Greece's second-largest city, Thessaloniki (thess-ah-lo-*nee*-kih) neither lies in the shadow of, or tries to emulate, the capital. It is a sophisticated, hip city with its own distinct character and cultural delights. Thessaloniki sits at the top of the Thermaic Gulf. The oldest part of the city is the Turkish quarter, with streets circling the Byzantine fortress on the slopes of Mt Hortiatis.

Orientation
Thessaloniki is laid out on a grid stretching back from Leoforos Nikis, which runs from the port in the west to the Lefkos Pyrgos (White Tower) in the east. The two main squares, both abutting the waterfront, are Plateia Eleftherias, which doubles as a local bus terminal, and Plateia Aristotelous. The other main streets of Mitropoleos, Tsimiski, Ermou and Egnatia run parallel to Leoforos Nikis. Egnatia is the main thoroughfare, running east from Plateia Dimokratias. Kastra, the old Turkish quarter, is north of Plateia Dimokratias.

Information
Bianca Laundrette (Panagias Dexias 3; per 6kg load €7; ☯ 8am-8.30pm Tue, Thu & Fri, 8am-3pm Mon, Wed & Sat).
First-Aid Centre (☎ 2310 530 530; Navarhou Koundourioti 10)
Ippokration (☎ 2310 837 921; Papanastasiou 50) Largest public hospital; 2km east of the city centre.
National Bank of Greece (Tsimiski 11) Opens at the weekend for currency exchange.
Office of Tourism Directorate (☎ 2310 221 100; Tsimiski 136; tour-the@otenet.gr; ☯ 8am-8pm Mon-Fri, 8am-2pm Sat) Located in a grand building near the White

Tower, with friendly and well-informed staff providing assistance in English and German.

Port police (☎ 2310 531 504)

Post office Aristotelous (Aristotelous 26; ☺ 7.30am-8pm Mon-Fri, 7.30am-2.15pm Sat, 9am-1.30pm Sun); Koundouriotou (Koundouriotou 6; ☺ 7.30am-2pm)

Tourist police (☎ 2310 554 871; 5th fl, Dodekanisou 4; ☺ 7.30am-11pm)

Travel Bookstore Traveller (☎ 2310 275 215; www .traveler.gr, in Greek; Proxenou Koromila 41) Hole-in-the-wall shop selling maps and travel guides.

Web (☎ 2310 237 031; S Gonata 4, Plateia Navarino; per hr €2.40; ☺ 24hr) Big, central and well-equipped, but often packed with loud teenage gamers.

Sights

The **Archaeological Museum** (☎ 2310 830 538; Manoli Andronikou 6; adult/student €6/free; ☺ 8.30am-8pm) showcases prehistoric, ancient Macedonian and Hellenistic finds, including a well-preserved **Petralona hoard** – a collection of axes and chisels, and some filigree gold wreaths and jewellery from burial sites all over Macedonia.

The snazzy **Museum of Byzantine Culture** (☎ 2310 868 570; www.mbp.gr; Leoforos Stratou 2; admission €4; ☺ 8am-8pm Tue-Sun, 1.30-8pm Mon) features a running wall placard text explaining over 3000 Byzantine objects, including frescoes, mosaics, embroidery, ceramics, inscriptions and icons from the early Christian period to the Fall of Constantinople (1453).

The imposing **Arch of Galerius**, at the eastern end of Egnatia, is the finest of the city's Roman monuments. Featuring sculpted soldiers in combat, it was erected in AD 303 to celebrate a victory over the Persians. The nearby **Rotunda** (☎ 2310 218 720; Plateia Agiou Georgiou; admission free; ☺ 8am-5pm Tue-Sun) was built as a mausoleum for Galerius, but never fulfilled this function; Constantine the Great transformed it into a church.

The 15th-century **White Tower** (☎ 2310 267 832; Plateia Lefkos Pyrgos; adult €2; ☺ 8am-7pm Tue-Sun, 12.30-7pm Mon) is both the city's symbol and most prominent landmark. In 1826, insubordinate janissaries were massacred there and it became known as the 'bloody tower'. After independence it was whitewashed to expunge this grisly past. You can climb to the top via a wide circular stairway – the views are impressive. The tower's new interactive **museum** presents the city's history through several levels of cool multimedia displays.

In the northeast of the city, the atmospheric Turkish quarter of **Kastra**, with its narrow steep streets flanked by timber-framed houses and tiny, whitewashed dwellings with shutters, is all that is left of 19th-century Thessaloniki. The original ramparts of Kastra were built by Theodosius (379–475), but were rebuilt in the 14th century. From Kastra there are stunning views of modern Thessaloniki and the Thermaic Gulf.

Take bus 22 or 23 from Plateia Eleftherias, or walk north along Agias Sofias, which becomes Vlatadon then Dimadou Vlatadou after Athinas, and turn right into Eptapyrgiou at the top.

Sleeping

Hotel Pella (☎ 2310 555 550; Ionos Dragoumi 63; s/d €40/50) A larger, port-area hotel, the Pella is less noisy than Egnatia hotels and has clean, well-maintained rooms and friendly staff.

Hotel Aegeon (☎ 2310 522 921; www.aegeonhotel. gr; Egnatia 19 14; s/d €45/60; ☒ ☎) Recently renovated, this place in a historic building on Egnatia is surprisingly good value. The decent, clean rooms have low-key decor, bathroom and most mod cons. It's a five- to 10-minute walk to the train station.

Tourist Hotel (☎ 2310 270 501; www.touristhotel.gr; Mitropoleos 21; s/d/tr incl breakfast €55/70/90; ☒ ▯) This classic place (built 1925) has an old-school gated lift and ornate chandeliers. The clean, well-kept rooms have soundproof windows.

Le Palace Hotel (☎ 2310 257 400; www.lepalace .gr; Tsimiski 23; s/d incl breakfast €85/100; ☒ ☎) At night gaze down from your little balcony at twinkling Tsimiski roaring by below (there's soundproofing). Le Palace has spacious, modern rooms with all mod cons.

Eating

To Etsi (☎ 2310 222 469; Nikoforos Fokas 2; grills €2.50-4) This bawdily decorated, iconic eatery near the White Tower offers refreshingly light souvlaki and *soutzoukakia* (meat rissoles) with vegetable dips in Cypriot-style pitta bread. Look for the neon sign.

Ouzou Melathron (☎ 2310 275 016; Karypi 21; mezedhes from €4.50, mains €6-11) This sidestreet *ouzerie* near Plateia Aristotelou is a bit touristy but still popular with locals. Occupy yourself with ouzo and mezedhes, then dig into heartier fare such as lamb in sweet wine sauce.

Panellinion (☎ 2310 567 220; Salaminos 1; mains €6-10) This friendly taverna has traditional Ladadika decor, with its wooden floors and walls lined with olive-oil bottles and tins of produce. Panellinion's varied choices include a world of

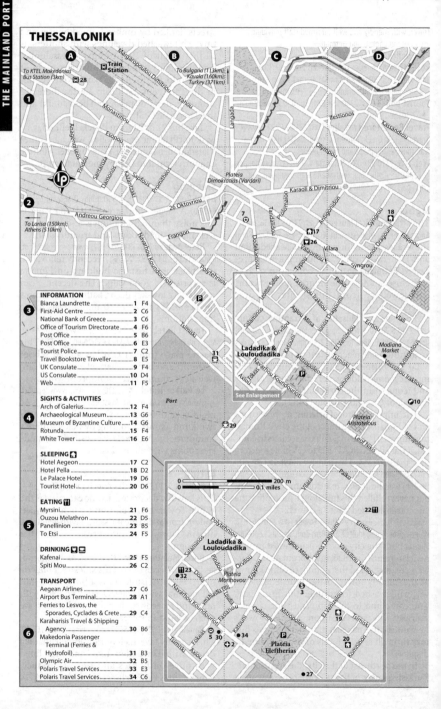

THESSALONIKI

To KTEL Makedonias
Bus Station (3km)

Train
Station

To Bulgaria (113km);
Kavala (160km);
Turkey (371km)

To Larisa (150km);
Athens (510km)

Plateia
Dimokratias (Vardari)

Ladadika &
Louloudadika

See Enlargement

Port

Modiano
Market

Plateia
Aristotelous

INFORMATION
Bianca Laundrette **1** F4
First-Aid Centre **2** C6
National Bank of Greece **3** C6
Office of Tourism Directorate **4** F6
Post Office **5** B6
Post Office **6** E3
Tourist Police **7** C2
Travel Bookstore Traveller............**8** E5
UK Consulate **9** F4
US Consulate **10** D4
Web **11** F5

SIGHTS & ACTIVITIES
Arch of Galerius **12** F4
Archaeological Museum................**13** G6
Museum of Byzantine Culture **14** G6
Rotunda **15** F4
White Tower **16** E6

SLEEPING
Hotel Aegeon **17** C2
Hotel Pella **18** D2
Le Palace Hotel **19** D6
Tourist Hotel **20** D6

EATING
Myrsini..**21** F6
Ouzou Melathron **22** D5
Panellinion **23** B5
To Etsi **24** F5

DRINKING
Kafenai..**25** F5
Spiti Mou.......................................**26** C2

TRANSPORT
Aegean Airlines **27** C6
Airport Bus Terminal......................**28** A1
Ferries to Lesvos, the
   Sporades, Cyclades & Crete.......**29** C4
Karaharisis Travel & Shipping
   Agency.......................................**30** B6
Makedonia Passenger
   Terminal (Ferries &
   Hydrofoil)...................................**31** B3
Olympic Air....................................**32** B5
Polaris Travel Services...................**33** E3
Polaris Travel Services...................**34** C6

Ladadika &
Louloudadika

0 ———————— 200 m
0 ———————— 0.1 miles

Plateia
Morihovou

Plateía
Eleftherias

Platía
Eleftherias

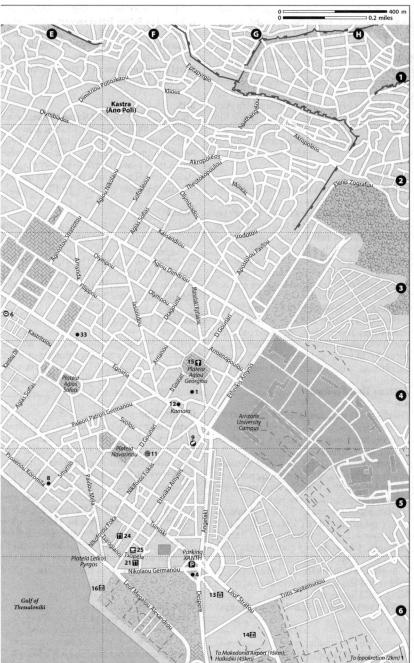

ouzos and cheeses to delicious seafood mezedehes; only organic vegetables are used.

our pick **Myrsini** (☎ 2310 228 300; Tsopela 2; mains €7-10) The only sad thing about Myrsini is that it's usually closed in July and August. Hearty portions of authentic and delicious Cretan dishes are served here, from *dakos* (rusks) topped with tomato, Cretan olive oil and soft cheese and flavourful *horta* (wild greens) to roast rabbit, pork and – crucially – *myzithropitakia* (flaky filo triangles with sweet *myzithra* cheese). Decor is simple, with worn wood floors and traditional accoutrements enhanced by Greek music.

Drinking

Spiti Mou (cnr Valaoritou & Leontos Sofou; ☽ 1pm-late; ⊚) A new bar upstairs in a lofty old building in the Syngrou district, 'My House' (as the name means in Greek) was opened after its young owners realised their parties were becoming too big to fail. The relaxed feel is enhanced by eclectic music, well-worn decor and big couches spread out on a chequered floor. There's live music on Sundays and occasional costume parties.

Kafenai (☎ 2310 220 310; cnr Ethnikis Amynis & Tsopela; ☽ 9am-2am) This new *kafeneio* (coffee house) impressively revives the spirit of old Salonica. With 1950s-style Greek decor, high ceilings supported by columns and low-key jazz, no wonder the place attracts local artists and musicians.

Getting There & Away

AIR

Thessaloniki's **Makedonia Airport** (☎ 2310 473 212; www.thessalonikiairport.gr) is 16km southeast of town. It serves numerous destinations throughout Europe and Greece.

Olympic Air (☎ 2310 368 666; www.olympicairlines.com; Navarhou Koundourioti 1-3) is near the port, and **Aegean Airlines** (☎ 2310 280 050; www.aegeanair.com; Venizelou 2) is on Plateia Eleftherias.

Olympic Air operates over 15 domestic routes, mostly to Athens and islands including Limnos, Lesvos, Corfu, Iraklio, Hania, Mykonos, Chios, Skyros and Samos. Some flights are via intermediate airports.

Aegean Airlines has 12 daily flights to Athens and less frequent services to Mytilini, Rhodes and Santorini.

For island flights, see Island Hopping (p524).

BOAT

Thessaloniki is a major ferry and hydrofoil hub; see Island Hopping (p525).

Many port-area travel agencies sell tickets. Try **Polaris Travel Services** (polaris@otenet.gr; Agias Sofias ☎ 2310 278 613; Egnatia 81, Agias Sofias; ☽ 8am-8.30pm; Port ☎ 2310 548 655; Navarhou Koundourioti 19, Port; ☽ 8am-8.30pm) or **Karaharisis Travel & Shipping Agency** (☎ 2310 524 544; Navarhou Koundourioti 8; ☽ 8am-8.30pm).

BUS

Thessaloniki's main **KTEL Makedonias bus station** (☎ 2310 595 408; Monastiriou 319), situated 3km west of the city centre, has departures to Athens Alexandroupoli and Kavala. Athens buses also depart from a small terminal opposite the train station. Local bus 1 travels between the bus station and the train station every 10 minutes.

TRAIN

Ten regular trains daily serve Athens (€28, 6¾ hours), while three daily travel to Alexandroupoli (€10, six hours) and 11 daily to Larisa (€10, two hours) with connections to Volos (€14, 4½ hours). The Athens intercity is more expensive (IC/ICE €36/48), but not significantly faster (5½ hours).

GYTHIO ΓΥΘΕΙΟ
pop 4489

Gythio (*yee*-thih-o), once the port of ancient Sparta, is now an attractive fishing port at the head of the Lakonian Gulf. It is a convenient departure point for the island of Kythira, and Kissamos on Crete.

Orientation

Gythio is easy to get around. Most restaurants and cafes are along the seafront on Akti Vasileos Pavlou. The bus station is at the northeastern end, next to the small triangular park known as the Perivolaki. Behind this is the main square, Plateia Panagiotou Venetzanaki.

The square at the southwestern end of Akti Vasileos Pavlou is Plateia Mavromihali, hub of the old quarter of Marathonisi. The ferry quay is opposite this square. Beyond it the waterfront road becomes Kranais, which leads south to the road to Areopoli. A causeway leads out to Marathonisi Islet at the southern edge of town.

Information

EOT (☎ /fax 27330 24484; Vasileos Georgiou 20; ☽ 8am-2.30pm Mon-Fri) This is the information equivalent of Monty Python's famous cheese-free cheese shop: remarkably information free, even by EOT's lamentable standards.

Hassanakos Bookstore (☎ 27330 22064; Akti Vasileos Pavlou 39) Also stocks international newspapers.
Internet Jolly Cafe (cnr Dirou & Grigoraki; per hr €2.50) One block from the bus station.
Police (☎ 27330 22100; Akti Vasileos Pavlou)
Post office (cnr Ermou & Arheou Theatrou; ☼ 7.30am-2pm Mon-Fri)

Sights
Pine-shaded **Marathonisi Island** is linked to the mainland by a causeway at the southern edge of town. According to mythology, it was here that Paris (prince of Troy) and Helen (wife of Menelaus) consummated the affair that kicked off the Trojan Wars. The 18th-century Tzanetakis Grigorakis tower houses a small **Museum of Mani History** (☎ 27330 24484; adult/concession €2/1; ☼ 8am-2.30pm) that relates Maniot history through the eyes of European travellers who visited the region between the 15th and 19th centuries. The architecturally minded will find an absorbing collection upstairs of plans of Maniot towers and castles.

Sleeping & Eating
Saga Pension (☎ 27330 23220; Kranais; d €50; 😾) This is a good-value comfortable place with balconies. It's 150m from the port, overlooking Marathonisi Islet.
Matina's (☎ 27330 22518; d/tr €60/65) A clean and comfortable abode in a great location in a house-cum-hotel, right in the heart of town. Owner Matina speaks no English but is welcoming.
Taverna Petakou (☎ 27330 22889; mains €3-7) This no-frills local favourite has the day's menu written down in an exercise book in Greek. It may include a hearty fish soup, which comes with a large chunk of bread on the side. It's beside the stadium on Xanthaki.
Taverna O Potis (☎ 27330 23245; mains €6.50-16; ☼ closed Thu) This ship-shape place has a spotless kitchen and generous helpings that locals flock aboard for. The house red is a bit like a massive ocean swell, but it's well worth the walk to the far end of the promenade, opposite Maronisi Islet.
Saga Restaurant (☎ 27330 23220; Kranais; mains €9-15, fish per kilogram €45-70) This upmarket restaurant is downstairs at Saga Pension.

Getting There & Away
LANE Lines has one weekly summer ferry to Crete via Kythira and Antikythira. For more, see Island Hopping (p510), or check the ever-chang-

ing schedule with **Rozakis Travel** (☎ 27330 22207; rosakigy@otenet.gr), on the waterfront at Pavlou 5.
The **KTEL Lakonias bus station** (☎ 27330 22228; cnr Vasileos Georgiou & Evrikleos), northwest along the waterfront in Jande Cafe, has buses to Athens (€21.40, 4½ hours, six daily) via Sparta (€3.90, one hour).

PORTS TO THE SARONIC GULF ISLANDS
There are connections to the Saronic Gulf Islands from several ports around the Argolis Peninsula of the eastern Peloponnese. The small resort of **Porto Heli**, at the southwestern tip of the peninsula, has daily hydrofoils to Spetses and Hydra, while nearby **Ermioni** has services to Hydra. **Galatas**, on the east coast, is a stone's throw from Poros. Small boats shuttle back and forth on the five-minute journey across the Poros Strait from 6am to 10pm. For details, see Island Hopping (p508).
All three ports can be reached by bus from **Nafplio**, the main town/transport hub of the Argolis. There are two buses daily weekdays from Nafplio to Galatas (€7.40, two hours), but travelling to Ermioni and Porto Heli from Nafplio involves changing to local buses at Kranidi (€1.40, two hours, two to three daily, except Sunday). There are hourly buses to Nafplio (€12, 2½ hours) from Terminal A in Athens.

PORTS TO THE CYCLADES
For information on getting to/from the Cyclades, see the mainland ports of Piraeus (p91), Rafina (p94) and Lavrio (p94).

PORTS TO THE IONIANS
Patra Πάτρα
pop 167,600
Named after King Patreas, who ruled the Peloponnese prefecture of Achaïa in about 1100 BC, Patra is Greece's third-largest city and the principal port for boats travelling to and from Italy and the Ionian Islands. It's not wildly exciting, but it is a cosmopolitan city with a vibrant cafe and clubbing scene (helped by the presence of Patra's 40,000 university students), some interesting sites, good shopping, and a busy arts and culture community. Patra has a history stretching back 3000 years. The city was destroyed during the War of Independence and rebuilt on a modern grid plan of wide, arcaded streets, large squares and ornate neoclassical buildings. The impressive Rio-Andirio suspen-

sion bridge links the city with western continental Greece.

ORIENTATION

Patra's grid system means easy walking. The waterfront is known as Iroön Polytehniou at the northeastern end, Othonos Amalias in the middle and Akti Dimeon to the south. Customs is at the Iroön Polytehniou end, and the main bus and train stations are on Othonos Amalias. Most of the agencies selling ferry tickets are on Iroön Polytehniou and Othonos Amalias.

INFORMATION

First-Aid Centre (☎ 2610 277 386; cnr Karolou & Agiou Dionysiou; ☽ 8am-8pm)

Info Center (☎ 2610 461 740/1; www.infocenterpatras .gr; Othonos Amalias 6; ☽ 8am-10pm) This well-organised and helpful municipal tourist information office is stocked with maps, brochures and information on transport and hotels. There's free 20-minute internet access and free bike hire.

National Bank of Greece (Plateia Trion Symachon; ☽ 8am-2.30pm Mon-Thu, 8am-2pm Fri) Opposite the train station.

Netp@rk (Gerokostopoulou 36a; per hr €2; ☽ 24hr)

Newsstand (☎ 2610 273 092; Agiou Andrea 77) International newspapers and magazines and a small selection of novels.

Plazanet@Internet (Gerokostopoulou 28; per hr €2.10; ☽ 9am-midnight)

Post office (cnr Zaïmi & Mezonos; ☽ 7.30am-8pm Mon-Fri, 7.30am-2pm Sat & Sun)

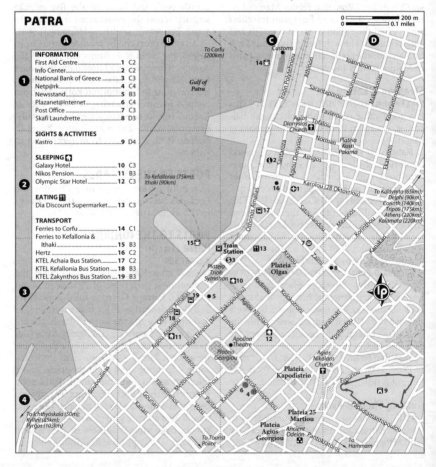

PATRA

0 — 200 m
0 — 0.1 miles

To Corfu (200km)

Customs

Gulf of Patra

To Kefallonia (75km); Ithaki (90km)

Iroön Polytehniou

Athinon

Ioanninon

Sarantaporou

Mourouzi

Makedonias

Konstantinoupoleos

Favierou

Agios Dionysios Church

Tofalou

Norman

Plateia Kosti Palama

Ekaterinis

Santaroza

Agiou Dionysiou

Astigos

Karolou (28 Oktovriou)

Sxoiniandou

Mezonos

Korinthou

Kanakari

To Kalavryta (65km); Delphi (90km); Corinth (140km); Tripoli (175km); Athens (220km); Kalamata (220km)

Othonos Amalias

Train Station

Plateia Trion Symahon

Radinou

Plateia Olgas

Aratou

Zaïmi

Kolokotroni

Karaiskaki

Ypsilandou

Othonos Amalias

Agiou Andreou

Riga Fereou (Michalakopoulou)

Ermou

Agiou Nikolaou

Patreos

Apollon Theatre

Plateia Georgiou

Agios Nikolaos Church

Bouboulinas

Gounari

Kanari

Filopimenos

Mezonos

Korinthou

Kanakari

Pantanassa

Vatsi

Gerokostopoulou

Plateia Kapodistrio

Plateia 25 Martiou

Plateia Agios Georgiou

Ancient Odeion

Pantokratoros

Figourou

Papadiamantopoulou

To Hammam

To Ichthyóskala (50m); Kyllini (85km); Pyrgos (103km)

To Tourist Police

Skafi Laundrette (☎ 2610 620 119; Zaïmi 49; per load €8; ☽ 9am-2.30pm Mon-Sat, 5.30-8.30pm Tue, Thu & Fri) Will wash and dry a load.

Tourist police (☎ 2610 695 191; 4th fl, Gounari 52 & Ypsilandou; ☽ 7.30am-9pm)

Train Station (left-luggage lockers per 8hr €2, per 24hr €3; ☽ 5am-3am) Has large lockers.

www.infocenterpatras.gr An excellent website for information on the city.

SIGHTS & ACTIVITIES

The city's wonderful old **Kastro** (Fortress; admission free; ☽ 8am-3pm Tue-Sun) stands on the site of the Acropolis of Ancient Patrai. The structure is of Frankish origin, remodelled many times over the centuries by the Byzantines, Venetians and Turks. It was in use as a defensive position until WWII and remains in good condition. Set in an attractive park, it's reached by climbing the steps at the end of Agiou Nikolaou.

The **Hammam** (☎ 2610 274 267; Boukaouri 29; ☽ 9am-9pm Mon-Sat) is a privately run venture, but you can scrub up here as the ancient Turks (AD 1500) did before you.

FESTIVALS & EVENTS

Patra's citizens party hard during the annual **Patra Carnival** (www.carnivalpatras.gr), which begins in mid-January leading up to a wild weekend of costume parades, colourful floats and celebrations in late February or early March.

The **Summer Festival** (www.infocenterpatras. gr) runs from June to August and features a range of music and other acts with visiting international performers.

SLEEPING & EATING

Nikos Pension (☎ 2610 623 757; cnr Patreos & Agiou Andreou; s/d with shared bathroom €23/33, with private bathroom €28/38; ✄) Don't judge this centrally located, '60s-style place by its flaking shutters. Inside, Nikos runs a tight ship with clean rooms across several floors and a pleasant roof terrace.

Olympic Star Hotel (☎ 2610 622 939; www.olympic star.gr; Agiou Nikolaou 46; s/d incl breakfast €65/90; ✄ 🖳) Popular with the business traveller, this modern place has a slight try-hard business feel, but with a solid performance. Its contemporary rooms feature hydro showers and personal flat-screened computers. Reduced prices without breakfast.

Galaxy Hotel (☎ 2610 275 981; www.galaxyhotel .com.gr; Agiou Nikolaou 9; s/d/tr incl breakfast €68/88/108; ✄ 🖭) This orange and brown, black and grey (think contemporary retro) joint does some good marketing – even the carpet bears its name in a contemporary design. Although its makeover in the mid-noughties has worn off a bit, it's still reasonably sleek. Its efficient service ensures its popularity with business travellers.

Ichthyóskala (☎ 2610 333 778; fish per kg €50-60) This unpretentious place offers few trimmings, save for a lemon wedge or two. But that's all you need to enhance fresh fish eaten alfresco. It's about 1km from central Patra.

Dia Discount supermarket (Agiou Andreou 29) Ideally located for travellers planning to buy provisions and keep moving.

GETTING THERE & AWAY

Boat

Patra is the departure point for ferry services to Kefallonia, Ithaki and Corfu. For details, see Island Hopping (p506). See p494 for services to Italy.

Bus

The main **KTEL Achaia bus station** (☎ 2610 623 886; Othonos Amalias) has buses to Athens (€17, three hours, every half-hour) via Corinth Isthmus (€11.30, 1½ hours). There are also buses to Thessaloniki (€40, seven hours, four daily) and Kalamata (€20, four hours, two daily).

Buses to the Ionian Islands of Lefkada (€14.50, two weekly, three hours) and Kefallonia leave from the **KTEL Kefallonia bus station** (☎ 2610 274 938, 2610 277 854; cnr Othonos Amalias & Gerokostopoulou). Services to Kefallonia travel by ferry to Poros (€16.50, three hours) and continue by road to Argostoli (€21, one hour).

Four daily buses to Zakynthos (including ferry; €15, 3½ hours, three on Sunday) leave from the **KTEL Zakynthos bus station** (☎ 2610 220 129; Othonos Amalias 48). Conveniently, they also travel via the port of Kyllini (€6.80, 1¼ hours). Note: the schedules change seasonally.

Train

For Athens, there are at least seven trains daily from Patra to Kiato, where you change for the *proastiako* (the smart suburban rail) to Athens. Five are normal trains (€3.70, 2½ hours) and two are Intercity (IC; express) services (€6.90, 2½ hours). Note: on arrival in Athens you can use your ticket for 1½ hours on the metro, but to do this you *must* validate the ticket or you will be fined.

Igoumenitsa Ηγουμενίτσα
pop 9104
Opposite the island of Corfu, the busy, characterless port town of Igoumenitsa (ih-goo-meh-*nit*-sah) is the main port of northwest Greece. Few travellers hang around any longer than it takes to buy a ferry ticket.

ORIENTATION
Ferries for Italy and Corfu leave from three adjacent but separate quays on the Ethnikis Andistasis waterfront. Ferries for Ancona and Venice (in Italy) depart from the new, southern port; those for Brindisi and Bari (in Italy) use the old port by the shipping offices; and ferries for Corfu (Kerkyra) and Paxi go from just north of the new port. The bus station is on Kyprou, two blocks behind the waterfront.

SLEEPING & EATING
Hotel Aktaion (☎ /fax 26650 22707; Agion Apostolon 17; s/d €40/50) and **Jolly Hotel** (☎ 26650 23971; jollyigm @otenet.gr; Ethnikis Andistasis 44; s/d incl breakfast €55/65; 🖳) are both waterfront C-class hotels with uninspiring yet quiet rooms; the latter offers better services.

Alekos (☎ 26650 23708; Ethnikis Andistasis 84; mains €4.50-7) Popular with the locals, the humble Alekos serves *mayirefta* (ready-cooked meals) and grilled meat.

GETTING THERE & AWAY
Igoumenitsa is a major ferry hub for Piraeus, Corfu and Italy. Hydrofoils to/from Corfu and Paxi usually run in summer. For details on ferries and hydrofoils from Igoumenitsa, see Island Hopping (p513). Book tickets at portside agencies or through the ferry companies. The **bus station** (☎ 26650 22309; Kyprou 29) has buses to Athens (€32.60, eight hours, five daily) and Thessaloniki (€30.20, eight hours, one daily).

Kyllini Κυλλήνη
The tiny port of Kyllini (kih-*lee*-nih), which sits about 78km southwest of Patra, warrants a mention only as the jumping-off point for ferries to Kefallonia and Zakynthos. Most people pass through Kyllini on buses from Patra that board the ferries plying the Ionian Sea.

GETTING THERE & AWAY
Boats travel to Zakynthos, Poros and Argostoli on Kefallonia. For details see Island Hopping (p506).

There are three to seven buses daily to Kyllini (€6.80, 1¼ hours) from the Zakynthos bus station in Patra (some have connecting ferries), five from the KTEL Kefallonia bus station and five from the KTEL Zakynthos bus station. Note: there are no buses from Kyllini to Patra. You can, however, catch buses from Lethena, 16km from Kyllini. A **taxi** (☎ 69735 35678) to Lethena costs €13, and to Patra €60.

PORTS TO KYTHIRA
Dangling off the southeastern tip of the Peloponnese, Kythira is the odd island out. It belongs in theory to the Ionian Island group, but in practice is administered from Athens. The best access is from the ports of Gythio and Neapoli.

Neapoli Νεάπολη
pop 2727
Lying close to the tip of the eastern finger of the Peloponnese, Neapoli (neh-*ah*-po-lih) is a fairly uninspiring town, in spite of its location on a huge horseshoe bay. Most travellers come to Neapoli to catch a ferry to the island of Kythira, which is clearly visible across the bay.

The western flank of the bay is formed by the small island of **Elafonisi**, renowned for its white beaches, visiting loggerhead turtle and sun-loving nudists. Regular ferries make the 10-minute trip (per person/car €1/10) from a small port several kilometres west of Neapoli.

SLEEPING & EATING
Hotel Aivali (☎ 27340 22287; Akti Voion 164; s/d €50/60; 🞄 🛜) This small family hotel is ideally located right on the seafront, close to the ferry dock for Kythira.

There are numerous lively *ouzeries* along the waterfront, serving the local speciality: delicious grilled octopus.

GETTING THERE & AWAY
There are daily ferries from Neapoli to Diakofti on Kythira. Tickets are sold at **Vatika Bay Shipping Agency** (☎ 27340 24004), 350m before the small bridge. (Leave plenty of time to find the place and buy the ticket.)

KTEL (☎ 27340 23222) has buses from Neapoli to Athens (€33, three hours, three daily) via Sparta (€12.80).

PORTS TO THE SPORADES
Agios Konstantinos
Άγιος Κωνσταντίνος
pop 2657

The closest port serving the Sporades for travellers from Athens is Agios Konstantinos, 175km northwest of the capital.

SLEEPING & EATING

With judicious use of buses from Athens, you will not need to stay overnight. If you do stay, try the well-managed **Hotel Amfitryon** (☎ 22350 31702; fax 22350 32604; Eivoilou 10; s/d incl breakfast €45/65; P 🅿️ 🏋️ 🛜) between the port and central square.

Several tavernas keep company with the ferry ticket offices, including the reliable **Taverna Kaltsas** (☎ 22350 33323; mains €5-9.50).

GETTING THERE & AWAY

Agios Konstantinos is a gateway to the northern Sporades isles of Skiathos, Skopelos and Alonnisos. For details see Island Hopping (p508).

There are hourly buses (starting from 6.15am) between Agios Konstantinos **bus station** (☎ 22350 32223) next to the Galaxias supermarket, about 200m south of the ferry landing, and Athens Terminal B bus station (€14.20, 2½ hours).

Volos Βόλος
pop 85,394

A bustling city on the northern shores of the Pagasitic Gulf, Volos is the port for ferry and hydrofoil services to the Sporades. The town has an inviting boardwalk lined with tavernas, *ouzeries*, small hotels, churches and cafes, and a lively student population.

According to mythology, Volos was ancient Iolkos, from where Jason and the Argonauts set sail on their quest for the Golden Fleece.

ORIENTATION

Volos is laid out on an easy grid system stretching inland parallel to the waterfront street of Argonafton, which is where most services for travellers are to be found. The main square, Plateia Riga Fereou, is at the northwestern end of Argonafton.

INFORMATION

Post office (cnr Dimitriados & Agiou Nikolaou; 🕒 7.30am-8pm)

Tourist police (☎ 24210 76987; 28 Octovriou 179) Locals also refer to the street name for 28 Octovriou as Alexandras.

Volos Information Centre & Hotels' Association of Magnesia (☎ 24210 30940; www.travel-pelion.gr; cnr Grigoriou Lambraki & Sekeri; 🕒 8am-8pm; P 🖥️) Gives out town maps, bus and ferry schedules and information about hotels, and has free internet.

Web (☎ 24210 30260; Iasonos 41; per hr €3; 🕒 24hr) Many waterfront cafe-bars have free wi-fi.

SLEEPING & EATING

Hotel Roussas (☎ 24210 21732; fax 24210 22987; Iatrou Tzanou 1; s/d from €29/35; 🏋️ 🛜) This small and friendly no-frills waterfront hotel has simple and spotless tile-floored rooms with balcony, though street-side rooms will catch weekend traffic noise.

Hotel Aegli (☎ 24210 24471; www.aegli.gr; Argonafton 24; s/d incl breakfast €60/80; 🏋️ 🛜) Art deco touches extend from a swanky and breezy lobby to stylish and spacious rooms. Best of all, the Aegli is 100m from the port, and surrounded by waterfront cafes and tavernas.

Kyklos Tsipouradiko (☎ 24210 20872; Mikrasiaton 85; mezedhes €1.50-6) Flagstone floors and wood-beamed ceilings lend plenty of atmosphere to this popular university hang-out. Go for the house favourite, potatoes baked in a wood-fired oven.

Kerasia Tsipouradiko (Cherry Tree; ☎ 24210 27920; Papakiriazi 40; mezedhes €2-4) Like most traditional *tsipouradika* (northern *ouzeries*), Kerasia Tsipouradiko is open from 9am to 6pm. A typical round of *tsipouro* and mezedhes plate is about €3.50. The basic rule: don't expect a drink without a plate!

VOLOS OUZERIES

If you transit the busy port of Volos on your way to or from the Sporades, be sure to linger for dinner at one of the town's famous *ouzeries*, reputedly the best in Greece. An *ouzerie* (strictly speaking called a *tsipouradhiko* here) is an informal restaurant where you eat from small plates of mezedhes – or appetisers. Best enjoyed with a group of friends, you nibble on anchovies, olives, cheese, spicy dips, octopus, fried zucchini and other dishes, and wash it down with a few stiff carafes of *tsipouro*, a distilled spirit that's similar to ouzo but is a bit stronger – taken neat or with water. You dine and imbibe until you are full. '*Stin iyia sas!*'

VOLOS

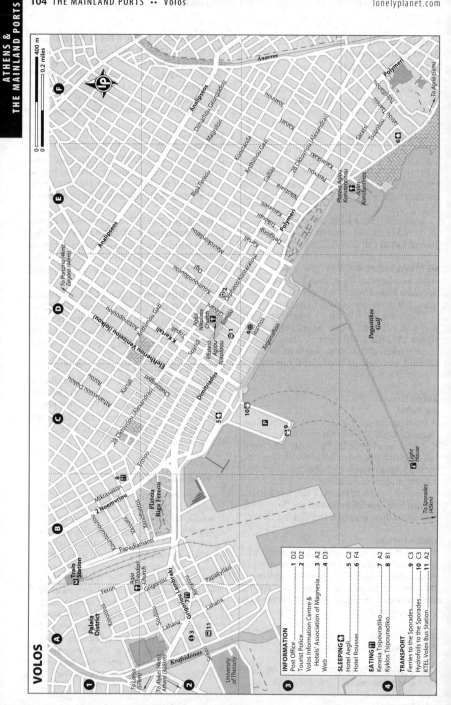

GETTING THERE & AWAY
Boat
Volos is a gateway to the northern Sporades isles of Skiathos, Skopelos and Alonnisos. For details, see Island Hopping (p525).

Bus
From the **KTEL Volos bus station** (☎ 24210 33254; cnr Zachou & Almyrou) there are 11 buses daily to Athens (€24.70, 4½ hours) and nine buses to Thessaloniki (€16.60, 2½ hours).

Train
Trains run to Athens (IC €28.20, five hours, two daily; normal €12.80, six hours, six daily) and Thessaloniki (IC €21.60, two hours, three daily; normal €12.90, three hours, three daily), both via Larisa.

PORTS TO THE NORTHEASTERN AEGEAN
Kavala Καβάλα
pop 60,802
Kavala, one of Greece's most attractive port towns, spills gently down the foothills of Mt Symvolon to a large palm-lined harbour. The old quarter of Panagia nestles under a big Byzantine fortress. Kavala is an important ferry hub, with sea connections to the northeast Aegean, the Dodecanese and Attica.

ORIENTATION
Kavala's focal point is Plateia Eleftherias, which has the tourist information. The main thoroughfares, Eleftheriou Venizelou and Erythrou Stavrou, run west from here parallel with the waterfront (Ethnikis Andistasis). The old quarter, Panagia, stands at the harbour's southeastern side, above Plateia Eleftherias. The bus station occupies the corner of Hrysostomou Kavalas and Filikis Eterias, near the Thasos hydrofoil quay. Public toilets stand near the hydrofoil departure point.

INFORMATION
Banks that are ATM-equipped line Eleftheriou Venizelou.
Cybernet (☎ 25102 30102; Erythrou Stavrou 64; per hr €2; 🕑 6am-4am)
Post office (cnr Hrysostomou Kavalas & Erythrou Stavrou)
Tourist information (☎ 25102 31011; detaktic@otenet .gr; Plateia Eleftherias; 🕑 8am-9pm Mon-Fri) Helpful, English- and German-speaking staff provide maps, plus transport and events information and hotel booking assistance.
Tourist police (☎ 25102 22246; Omonias 119)

SIGHTS
If you've got time to spare, explore the streets of **Panagia**, the old Turkish quarter surrounding the massive Byzantine fortress on the promontory south of Plateia Eleftherias.

The pastel-hued houses in the narrow, tangled streets of the Panagia quarter are less dilapidated than those of Thessaloniki's Kastra and the area is less commercialised than Athens' Plaka. The most conspicuous building is the **Imaret** (☎ 25102 20151; www.imaret .gr; Poulidou 6), a huge structure with 18 domes, which overlooks the harbour from Poulidou; formerly a hostel for Islamic theology students, it is now an exclusive hotel.

The **Archaeological Museum** (☎ 25102 22335; Erythrou Stavrou 17; admission €2; 🕑 8am-3pm Tue-Sun), on Ethnikis Andistasis' western end, houses well-displayed finds from ancient Amphipolis, an Athenian colony west of Kavala that operated gold mines on nearby Mt Pangaeum.

The **Municipal Museum of Kavala** (☎ 25102 22706; Filippou 4; admission free; 🕑 8am-2pm Mon-Sat) displays contemporary Greek art.

SLEEPING & EATING
Giorgos Alvanos Rooms (☎ 25102 21781; Anthemiou 35; s/d €20/30) Kavala's best budget option has simple rooms with shared bathrooms in a 300-year-old house up in Panagia. Rooms have refrigerators and sea views. It's a steep walk uphill to get here, so call in advance.

Galaxy Hotel (☎ 25102 24521; Eleftheriou Venizelou 27; s/d €40/50; 🖭) Opposite the tourist information centre, the Galaxy is showing the ravages of time, offering ordinary, old-style rooms and indifferent service, though it is central. Some rooms have port view.

Limonidis Bougatsa (☎ 25108 32526; cnr Ionos Dragoumi & Megas Alexandrou; bougatsa €3.20; 🕑 6am-2pm) Behind the tourist information centre, this canopied outdoor place is excellent for breakfast and espresso.

Psarotaverna Panos Zafira (☎ 25102 27978; cnr Plateia Karaoli & Dimitriou; fish €9-15; 🕑 10am-1am) Since 1965, this friendly place on the eastern waterfront has been serving fresh fish dishes, along with regular taverna fare.

Poulidou in Panagia has good tavernas, while lively cafe-bars are on the western waterfront.

GETTING THERE & AWAY
AIR
Kavala shares Alexander the Great Airport, near Hrysoupoli (29km), with Xanthi. **Olympic**

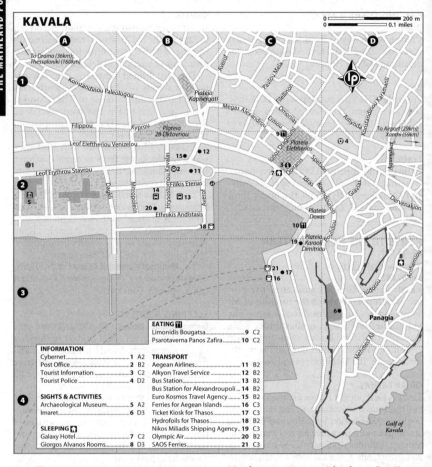

KAVALA

INFORMATION
Cybernet..........................1	A2
Post Office.......................2	B2
Tourist Information 3	C2
Tourist Police 4	D2

SIGHTS & ACTIVITIES
Archaeological Museum....5	A2
Imaret............................6	D3

SLEEPING
Galaxy Hotel...................7	C2
Giorgos Alvanos Rooms....8	D3

EATING
Limonidis Bougatsa.....................9	C2
Psarotaverna Panos Zafira...........10	C2

TRANSPORT
Aegean Airlines........................11	B2
Alkyon Travel Service 12	B2
Bus Station..............................13	B2
Bus Station for Alexandroupoli ...14	B2
Euro Kosmos Travel Agency........15	B2
Ferries for Aegean Islands..........16	C3
Ticket Kiosk for Thasos..............17	C3
Hydrofoils for Thasos................18	B2
Nikos Miliadis Shipping Agency...19	C3
Olympic Air.............................20	B2
SAOS Ferries............................21	C3

Air (☎ 25102 23622; www.olympicairlines.com; Ethnikis Andistasis 8) has two daily flights to Athens (€76); **Aegean Airlines** (☎ 25210 2900; Erythrou Stavrou 1) has one daily flight to Athens (€66). The few island flights all go via Athens.

Boat

There are ferries from Kavala to Skala Prinou on Thasos, and an hourly service in summer from the small port of Keramoti, 46km east of Kavala, to Thasos town (Limenas; p399). For information on boats from Kavala to the Northeast Aegean Islands, see Island Hopping (p515).

Ferry tickets for Thasos are sold on the eastern waterfront's **ticket kiosk** (☎ 25930 24001; www.thassos-ferries.gr). For ferry tickets to the

Northeastern Aegean Islands try **Euro Kosmos Travel Agency** (☎ 25102 21960; www.eurokosmos .gr; Erithrou Stavrou 1), near the bus station, **Nikos Miliadis Shipping Agency** (☎ 25102 26147; Karaoli-Dimitriou 36) or **Alkyon Travel Service** (☎ 25102 31096; alkyon-trv@ticketcom.gr; Eleftheriou Venizelou 37).

In Kavala, hydrofoils berth at the port's western side, by the port police kiosk, which posts hydrofoil and ferry schedules. Buy tickets upon boarding.

Bus

The **bus station** (☎ 25102 22294; cnr Filikis Eterias & Hrysostomou Kavalas) has departures to Athens (€52, 8¾ hours, two daily), Keramoti (€4.20, one hour, hourly) and Thessaloniki (€13.30, 2¼ hours, 15 daily).

Buses for Alexandroupoli (€10.95, two hours, seven daily) depart from the **bus station** (Hrysostomou 1) outside the 7-Eleven Snack Bar and opposite the KTEL office. Get tickets and information inside.

Alexandroupoli Αλεξανδρούπολη
pop 49,176

The capital of the prefecture of Evros, Alexandroupoli (ah-lex-an-*droo*-po-lih) is a modern town with a lively student atmosphere, supplemented by a population of young soldiers. Most travellers come here in transit heading east to Turkey, or to catch ferries to Samothraki, or the Dodecanese. The maritime ambience of this town, and its year-round activity, make it a pleasant stopover. The town was named Alexandroupoli (Alexander's City) in honour of King Alexander and has been part of the Greek state since 1920. There are few sights, except for the still-operating 19th-century lighthouse parked conspicuously on the main promenade. Crowds flock here on warm summer evenings to stroll and to relax in the many cafes and restaurants that stretch westwards from the port.

ORIENTATION
The town is laid out roughly on a grid system, with the main streets running east–west, parallel with the waterfront, where the lively evening *volta* (promenade) takes place. Karaoli Dimitriou is at the eastern end of the waterfront, with Megalou Alexandrou at the western end. The main squares are Plateia Eleftherias and Plateia Polytehniou, both just one block north of Karaoli Dimitriou. Alexandroupoli's train station is on the waterfront south of Plateia Eleftherias, beside the local bus station, 100m east of the port, where boats leave for Samothraki. The main bus station (Eleftheriou Venizelou 36) is five blocks inland.

INFORMATION
ATM-equipped banks line Leoforos Dimokratias.

Internet Station Meganet (☎ 25510 33639; cnr Dikastirion & Psaron; per hr €2.40; ☻ 24hr)

Kassapidis Exchange (☎ 25510 80910; Leoforos Dimokratias 209; ☻ 8am-9.30pm Mon-Sat, 10am-2pm Sun) Changes 87 currencies, including Balkan ones; does Western Union money transfers.

Municipal Tourist Office (☎ 25510 64184; Leoforos Dimokratias 306; ☻ 7.30am-3pm) The helpful staff provide maps, plus accommodation and transport information.

Port police (☎ 25512 26468; cnr Megalou Alexandrou & Markou Botsari)

Post office (cnr Nikiforou Foka & Megalou Alexandrou)

Tourist police (☎ 25510 37424; Karaïskaki 6)

SIGHTS
The **Ethnological Museum of Thrace** (☎ 25510 36663; www.emthrace.com; 14 Maiou 63; admission €3; ☻ 10am-2pm Tue-Sun & 6-9pm Tue-Sat) faithfully displays Thracian traditional customs, with a superb collection of traditional artefacts and tools.

The excellent **Ecclesiastical Art Museum of Alexandroupoli** (☎ 25510 26359; Plateia Agiou Nikolaou; admission €3; ☻ 9am-2pm Tue-Fri, 10am-2pm Sat) is one of the best in the country, with a priceless collection of icons and ecclesiastical ornaments brought to Greek Thrace by refugees from Asia Minor. It is in the grounds of the Cathedral of Agios Nikolaos.

SLEEPING & EATING
Camping Alexandroupoli (☎ 25510 26055; Leoforos Makris; camp sites per adult/tent €5/4.50) This large camp site (2km west) is clean, well run and with good facilities. Take local bus 7 from Plateia Eleftherias.

Hotel Alex (☎ 25510 26302; Leoforos Dimokratias 294; s/d/tr €35/40/50; ☒) Up on the main road, this decent budget option has good rooms, though cramped, and the necessary amenities. Ask for a back room to minimise noise.

Hotel Bao Bab (☎ 25510 34823; www.baobobhotel.gr; Alexandroupoli-Komotini highway; s/d/tr €40/60/70; P ☒ ☐) Just 1km west of town, this lavish waterfront hotel has large, comfortable rooms. There's decent swimming on the sandy, shallow beach and an excellent restaurant and lounge bar, making it the area's best-value hotel.

Hotel Marianna (☎ 25510 81456; fax 25510 81455; Malgaron 11; s/d €45/60) This friendly central hotel with small, clean rooms and a colourful breakfast area is run by the hospitable and multilingual Georgios Hrysohoidis and his Italian wife, Patricia.

Nea Klimataria (☎ 25510 26288; Plateia Polytehniou; mains €5-8) This heavy-duty, popular place is not setting records, but it does have tasty prepared dishes, good roast chicken and big salads.

our pick Psarotaverna tis Kyra Dimitras (☎ 25510 34434; cnr Kountouriotі & Dikastirion; fish €6-11) Venerable old Kyra Dimitra is still running the show at this seafood restaurant, in the family since 1915. Choose from the daily catch, set out on ice at the front; *tsipoura* (sea bream) is tasty and only €20 per kilo, while a plateful of

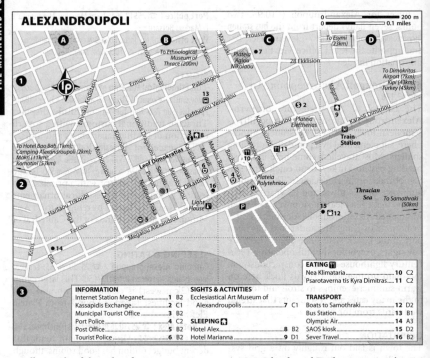

ALEXANDROUPOLI

INFORMATION	
Internet Station Meganet.................1	B2
Kassapidis Exchange........................2	C1
Municipal Tourist Office 3	B2
Port Police 4	C2
Post Office 5	B2
Tourist Police 6	B2

SIGHTS & ACTIVITIES	
Ecclesiastical Art Museum of	
Alexandroupolis 7	C1

SLEEPING	
Hotel Alex.......................................8	B2
Hotel Marianna 9	D1

EATING	
Nea Klimataria...............................10	C2
Psarotaverna tis Kyra Dimitras.....11	C2

TRANSPORT	
Boats to Samothraki.......................12	D2
Bus Station 13	B1
Olympic Air 14	A3
SAOS kiosk 15	D2
Sever Travel 16	B2

small crunchy fish makes for a scrumptious lunch.

GETTING THERE & AWAY

Alexandroupoli's Dimokritos Airport is 7km east of town near Loutra.

Olympic Air (☎ 25510 26361; www.olympicairlines .com; cnr Ellis & Koletti) is central; **Aegean Airlines** (☎ 25510 89150; www.aegeanair.com) is at the airport. Both offer four daily flights to/from Athens (€75, 55 minutes). For information on flights from Alexandroupoli to the islands, see Island Hopping p508).

Boat

Alexandroupoli is a major ferry port for Samothraki; however, at the time of writing, the longstanding ferry line to the Northeast

Aegean Islands and Dodecanese wasn't running. For information on ferries and hydrofoils from Alexandroupoli to Samothraki, see Island Hopping (p508). Get tickets from the portside SAOS kiosk, or from travel agencies such as **Sever Travel** (☎ 25510 22555; sever1@otenet .gr; Megalou Alexandrou 24).

Bus

From the **bus station** (☎ 25510 26479; Eleftheriou Venizelou 36) there is a daily bus service to Athens (€61, 10 hours) and buses to Thessaloniki (€26.50, 3¾ hours, nine daily) via Xanthi and Kavala.

Train

From the **train station** (☎ 25510 26395) six daily trains serve Thessaloniki (€9, seven hours); one continues to Athens (€49, 14 hours).

ISLAND TEMPTATIONS

The Greek Islands are more than you imagined. Whatever initially drew you to them – sun-drenched beaches or towering ruins – you'll be amazed by how much more the islands have to offer. Picture steaming volcanoes and exotic wildlife; world-class kitesurfing and hiking through verdant forests; view-laden castles and colourful ports. With endless awe-inspiring options, the islands can be as exhilarating or as laid-back as you want. The only tricky part will be convincing yourself to go home.

CHRIS CHRISTO

Natural Wonders

The Greek Islands are undeniably gorgeous and it shouldn't be too surprising that they're laden with natural treasures. Delve into the interiors for breath-taking forests, unexpected wildlife and volcanic moonscapes. Or explore the coasts for magnificent sea-hewn landscapes, inspiring marine life and the beaches you've always dreamt of.

GEORGE TSAFOS

PAUL BIGLAND

Author Tip

It's worth paying that little bit extra for a room with a view, seeking out a restaurant over the seaside or finding a spot on deck during a ferry journey. The islands' beauty washes over you in these tranquil moments – it's then that the colours and serenity are most poignant.

❶ Elafonisi

Unquestionably one of Greece's most stunning beaches, the white- and pink-sand Elafonisi (p260) is as close as the Med gets to tropical, with overlapping sandspits creating warm, shallow lagoons. The beach gets packed in summer, but out of high season it's tranquil.

❷ Paxi

Paxi (p446) is famed for its wooded and peaceful interior, but on its western coast lie spectacular cliffs, sea caves, rock arches and offshore pinnacles, all rising from a sea of exquisite blue.

❸ Skyros

Skyros (p426) is home to the unique, and endangered, Skyrian pony, a small-bodied horse that has roamed wild since ancient times. Visitors can glimpse the horses in natural habitats, and even join local efforts to protect this rare breed.

❹ Nisyros

Be mesmerised in the centre of Nisyros' volcano (p316) as it hisses and steams around you. Arrive early and you'll have the caldera to yourself. Beyond the caldera's rim, the verdant mountainside is blanketed in wildflowers and greenery as it tumbles to the sea.

❺ Spetses

The wealthy philanthropist Sotirios Anargyrios planted forests of Aleppo pine on Spetses (p130) as a gift to his native island. Many of these forests have survived the onslaught of time and devastating forest fires and continue to give the island its particular beauty.

❻ Milos

The famous volcanic island of Santorini may boast the most spectacular volcanic landscapes, but Milos (p206) has more accessible, and at times more surreal, volcanic legacies, such as the bone-white rock features of Sarakiniko (p209).

Island Activities

You may have planned to spend your entire holiday lazing on the beach, but when you catch sight of the windsurfers zipping past or hear talk of the mysterious gorges and rugged peaks, the only way to satisfy your curiosity is to get up and get active.

JOHN ELK III

① Samothraki

The mountainous interior and woodland waterfalls of Samothraki (p394) make for excellent trekking opportunities. This chilled-out island all by itself in the northeastern Aegean, two hours south of Alexandroupoli, attracts a young, alternative crowd and is a great place for swimming and camping on secluded beaches.

② Hydra

Dolphins feed and frolic in the deeper Saronic Gulf. The Kallianos Diving Center (p127) is on the island of Kapari, between Hydra and the mainland. Join them for organised diving-with-dolphins trips, as well as other outings and courses at all levels.

③ Samaria Gorge

On an island built for outdoor action, the Samaria Gorge (p253) – said to be Europe's longest – stands out for its stunning location in Crete's Lefka Ori (White Mountains). The 16km-long (six-hour) hike down to the sea passes rugged cliffs, abandoned settlements and rocky streams.

④ Amorgos

Amorgos (p181) is an island that demands adventure. Its mountainous interior offers exhilarating walks, while the rocky buttresses above Aegiali and the towering coastal cliffs are catching the attention of rock climbers.

⑤ Karpathos

Rated as one of the top kitesurfing locations on the globe, Afiartis Bay (p298) draws an international crowd for its waves, as well as for being one of the best places for beginners. Just up the road is some of the clearest water for snorkelling in the whole of the Aegean.

Island Architecture

An eclectic array of colourful buildings awaits you, attesting to the vibrant mix of cultures that have influenced the islands. Cosy yourself up inside a 17th-century captain's house, drink coffee on a Venetian portside or explore towering relics from long ago.

NEIL SETCHFIELD

GEORGE TSAFOS

Author Tip

Look down. Greek buildings are often flattered with intricately decorated floors. In ancient Greece, frescoes adorned floors and on many islands the art of *hohlakia* (pebble mosaic flooring) continues to flourish, with thousands of black and white stones laid in mesmerising patterns.

❶ Rhodes Old Town

Get lost in Rhodes Old Town (p280). Not only is it easily done within the labyrinth of cobbled twists and turns but it will be a highlight of your Greek adventure. Narrow alleys with stone arches open onto lively *plateies* (squares). Traditional shops, atmospheric bars, and gourmet dining await within this picturesque, walled town.

❷ Chios

Chios is wonderfully varied. The central Kampos region (p370) is filled with flowers and fruit trees and has lovely old mansions, while Pyrgi's (p372) eclectic and geometric patterned grey-and-white work defines its traditional houses. Mesta (p372), a masterpiece of medieval defensive architecture, is a completely enclosed 14th-century castle town.

❸ Palace of Knossos

Let your imagination run wild in the home of the mythical Minotaur kept by King Minos. Partially restored, the Minoan Palace of Knossos (p231) tantalises the senses with vibrant frescoes and mighty columns.

❹ Halki

Built during the 17th century, sea captains' houses are grand and beautiful, with views out to sea for the family to watch for the return of the ship. Book yourself into one of these restored houses on Halki (p292) and experience the life of locals from days of yore.

❺ Corfu

Corfu's main town (p437) is the architectural jewel of the Ionian Islands. Occupied in its time by the Corinthians, Byzantines, Venetians, French, Russians and English, the town now boasts an eclectic mix of building styles influenced by each period.

❻ Hania

The former Venetian port town of Hania (p245) is one of Greece's most evocative cities. Its gorgeous Old Town bursts with colourful, restored houses that are set on winding stone lanes. Towering Venetian and Ottoman defensive and religious architecture attests to the city's fascinating history.

Unwind

There are few places that encourage you to relax as well as the Greek Islands. Linger over a sunset, spend an entire day lounging on an isolated beach, or chill out with the locals at small village *plateies*. It's all about unwinding into the pace of island life and soaking up the tranquillity.

Author Tip

Settle down on a beachside sun lounge with some Greek chill-out music or a novel set on the islands. It's a great way to relax and embrace the local scene all in one go.

❶ Crete's Southern Coast

Not only those on yoga retreats gravitate to the quietude of Agios Pavlos and Triopetra (p243), overlapping beaches along Crete's southern coast, backed by reddish cliffs. With but a few tavernas and rooms, these isolated beaches are ideal for unwinding far from the masses.

❷ Poros

Beyond the attractive port town and the tiny island of Sferia, lies Poros' forested hinterland of Kalavria (p123) where you can escape into quieter corners and catch glimpses of the mountainous Peloponnese of the mainland.

❸ Psara

Practically unknown, Psara (p375), a tiny speck in the sea two hours west of Chios, makes an ideal place to peace out. Nothing much happens here, but it has pristine, far-flung beaches, plenty of good walking opportunities and a likeable port village.

❹ Kymi

Though it's only 4km from the port of Paralia Kymis on Evia, the quaint hillside town of Kymi (p408) sees few tourists. Join the regulars who gather daily for coffee at the town *plateia* (square), and you're sure to be asked how on earth you found them.

Saronic Gulf Islands
Νησιά του Σαρωνικού

The Saronic Gulf Islands offer a fast track to the Greek island dream.

They may lack the romantic image of the hazy Cyclades or the far-flung Dodecanese, yet the main islands of the group have enough allure to satisfy anyone's expectations and they all have facilities aplenty. There is a reassuring sense of accessibility about the Saronics and collectively the islands seem to merge the best of Greece's mainland attractions with all that is the best of island life. Yet the islands are also remarkably distinctive. You can ring the changes as you island-hop between classical heritage, resort beaches, stylish architecture, a sense of island escapism and top-class Greek cuisine.

The most accessible islands, Aegina and Angistri, are just under an hour by ferry from Piraeus. Aegina is almost an Athenian suburb, yet this lively bustling place has more than its fair share of cultural sights. Twenty minutes to the east of Aegina lies pine-clad Angistri, a typical holiday island but one with reassuring corners of tranquility, even in high season.

Further south is Poros, only a few hundred metres across the water from the Peloponnese and with several decent beaches and a peaceful forested hinterland. Next comes the Saronic showpiece, Hydra, where a tiered jigsaw of pastel-hued houses rises from a harbourside that is always frothing with fashionable life. Deepest south of all is pine-scented Spetses, only minutes away from the mainland yet entirely part of the Aegean Island world.

HIGHLIGHTS

- **Glorious Past** Exploring Aegina's ancient history at the Temple of Aphaia (p121)
- **Good Food Guide** Being spoiled for choice among Spetses Town's top restaurants (p132)
- **Dolphin Divas** Diving near Hydra on a nonintrusive dolphin safari (p127)
- **Slow Tourism** Exploring the peaceful interiors of Poros (p123), Hydra (p126) and Spetses (p130)
- **Museum Musing** Enjoying some of the best small museums in Greece on Hydra (p127) and Spetses (p132)

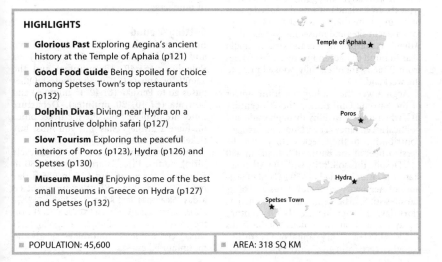

- POPULATION: 45,600
- AREA: 318 SQ KM

AEGINA ΑΙΓΙΝΑ

pop 13,500

Beyond its bustling port, Aegina (*eh*-yi-nah) has the seductive, easygoing character of a typical Greek island but with the added bonus of having more than its fair share of prestigious ancient sites and museums. Weekending Athenians sharpen the mix and visitors should bear in mind that, even in winter, fast ferries from Piraeus are often fully booked prior to the weekend.

Aegina was the leading maritime power of the Saronic Gulf during the 7th century BC, when it grew wealthy through trade and political ascendancy. The island made a major contribution to the Greek victory over the Persian fleet at the Battle of Salamis in 480 BC. Despite this solidarity with the Athenian state, the latter invaded in 459 BC out of jealousy of Aegina's wealth and status and of its liaison with Sparta. Aegina never regained its glory days although in the early 19th century it played a bold part in the defeat of the Turks and was the temporary capital of a partly liberated Greece from 1827 to 1829.

Today the island plays a more mundane role as Athens' island suburb and Greece's main producer of pistachio nuts. Past glory lingers, however, not least at the splendid ruin of the 5th-century Temple of Aphaia. There are modest beaches too and an enjoyable taverna and nightlife scene.

Getting There & Away

Aegina's main port is Aegina Town, which has links to Piraeus, Angistri, Poros and Methana, in the Peloponnese. There are no direct ferries from Aegina and Angistri to Hydra and Spetses or to mainland Ermioni and Porto Heli. For these destinations you need to connect with fast ferries at Piraeus or Poros. The smaller Aegina ports of Agia Marina and Souvala have links with Piraeus in the high season only. You should always check details close to the date of your planned trip. For details see Island Hopping (p507).

A local small ferry, the distinctive blue and yellow *Agistri Express*, which is owned by the Angistri community, makes several trips daily to and from Aegina to Angistri's main port of Skala (€5, 20 minutes) and then on to neighbouring Mylos (€5.20, 25 minutes). It leaves from midway along the Aegina harbour front and timetables are displayed there.

Another option between Aegina and Angistri is the **water taxi service** (☎ 22970 91387, 6972229720). It costs €40 one way, regardless of numbers.

Getting Around

Buses run frequently between Aegina Town and Agia Marina (€1.70, 30 minutes) via Paleohora (€1.40, 15 minutes) and the Temple of Aphaia (€1.70, 25 minutes). Other buses go to Perdika (€1.40, 15 minutes) and Souvala (€1.40, 20 minutes). Departure times are displayed outside the ticket office on Plateia Ethnegersias and you must buy tickets at the booth.

There are numerous car and motorcycle hiring outfits. Prices start at around €30 to €40 a day for a car and €15 to €25 a day for a 50cc machine. Bicycles are about €8 a day. **Sklavenas Rent A Car** Aegina Town (☎ 22970 22892; Kazantzaki 5); Agia Marina (☎ 22970 32871), on the road towards the Temple of Apollo, hires cars, jeeps, scooters, motorbikes, quads and mountain bikes.

AEGINA TOWN
pop 7410

Aegina Town replicates some of the vibrancy of downtown Athens with its gritty charm and decidedly Greek edge. The town is the capital and main port of the island, and its long harbour front buzzes with life. The two-lane harbour-front road is a bit of a speedway, so take care when crossing.

The waterside promenade that runs the length of the harbour makes for a pleasant open stroll, but canopied cafes overwhelm its inland counterpart. Narrow lanes strike inland from the harbour front, across parallel streets that are crammed with shops of every kind. A few 19th-century neoclassical buildings survive and Ancient Greece is represented by the impressive ruins of the Temple of Apollo just to the north of the ferry quays.

Orientation

The large outer quay, with its little church of St Nikolaos, is where the bigger ferries dock. The smaller inner quay is where hydrofoils dock. Crossing the road from the end of either quay and then bearing left leads to Plateia Ethnegersias where the bus terminal and post office are located. This road then continues past the Temple of Apollo, where it becomes single-lane, and on towards the north coast. Turning right from the end of the quays leads along the busy harbour front for about 500m to the Church of Panagytsa and then on to Perdika or Agia Marina.

SARONIC GULF ISLANDS

Information

Aegina does not have an official tourist office, but you can find some useful information at www.aegina greece.com.

There is a line of ferry ticket offices at the exit to the main quay and an information board listing accommodation options with a telephone handset for direct contact.

Alpha Bank and the Bank of Piraeus are located opposite the end of the hydrofoil quay. The National Bank of Greece is about 300m to the right of the ferry quays. All the banks have ATMs.

Kalezis Bookshop (☎ 22970 25956; ☾ from May) Midway along the harbour front; has a selection of foreign newspapers and books.

Perla Laundry (☎ 22970 23497; Mitropoleos 23; 7am-1.30pm & 5-9pm; 2kg wash & dry/wash only €5/3) Also does pick up and delivery.

Port police (☎ 22970 22328) At the entrance to the ferry quays.

Post office (Plateia Ethnegersias; ☾ 7.30am-2pm Mon-Fri)

Tourist police (☎ 22970 27777; Leonardou Lada) A short distance up a lane opposite the hydrofoil dock.

Sights

The intriguing remains of the **Temple of Apollo** (☎ 22970 22637; adult/concession €3/2; ☾ 8.30am-3pm Tue-Sun) stand on the hill of Coloni, northwest of the port. The ruined walls, pavements, cisterns and broken pillars in honey-coloured stone are lorded over by a solitary surviving column, all that's left of a 5th-century-BC temple that was once part of an ancient acropolis. Just below is the informative **Sanctuary Museum** (☾ 8.30am-3pm Tue-Sun), where you buy tickets and which displays artefacts from the temple. Information is in Greek, English and German.

Festivals & Events

Fistiki means pistachio nut and the three-day **Aegina Fistiki Fest** (www.aeginafistikifest.gr) was inaugurated in 2009 to promote Aegina's famous pistachio through events such as live-music concerts, visual-arts events, trade fairs and culinary contests. It is hoped to stage the festival in mid September each year, at the end of the pistachio harvesting period.

Sleeping

Aegina has a reasonable selection of hotels and rooms, but it's advisable to book ahead, especially at weekends. Some of the more basic hotels are not the best value and can be overpriced.

Marianna Studios (☎ 22970 25650, 6945869465; www.aeginarooms.com/mariannastudios; 16-18 Kiverniou St; s/d/tr €35/40/45; 🖧) These simple, very basic rooms are an excellent budget option. The tiny entrance hides a sizeable courtyard and some rooms overlook a quiet, leafy garden. The welcome is very friendly.

Electra Domatia (☎ 22970 26715, 6938726441; www.aegina-electra.gr; Leonardou Lada 25; s/d €45/50; 🖧). There are no scenic views from this small pension, but rooms are impeccable and comfy and are in a quiet corner of town. It outclasses nearby hotels by a long way. Head up Leonardou Lada, opposite the ferry quays.

Aeginitiko Archontiko (☎ 22970 24968; www.aeginitikoarchontiko.gr; cnr Ag Nikolaou & Thomaiados; s/d/tr/ste €60/70/80/120; 🖧) This old Aegina mansion retains period features that hark back to the glory days of 19th-century Greece's first years of independence. The splendid breakfast costs about €10 per person.

our pick **Rastoni** (☎ 22970 27039; www.rastoni.gr; Metriti 31; s/d/tr €85/80/110; 🅿 🖧 🖳 🛜) Each of the spacious rooms at this handsome boutique hotel has individual decor reflecting Asian and African themes. There's a lovely garden with views to the Temple of Apollo. The hotel is in a quiet area a few minutes walking distance from the harbour front. There are discounts for several days' stay. Breakfast is €5.

Eating

The inland side of the harbour front is packed with cafes and restaurants. They make for lazy world-watching, but are not particularly good value, unless you hit the local unvarnished *ouzeries* (a place serving ouzo and light snacks) scattered throughout. Local pistachio nuts are on sale everywhere, priced from €6 for 500g.

Babis (☎ 22970 23594; mains €5-12) Located at the far end of the harbour front, the cool, stylish decor of this inventive restaurant complements its creative cuisine, which includes its resilient signature dish, chicken with pistachio and unsalted *anthotyro* (dry white cheese).

Tsias (☎ 22970 23529; Dimokratias 47; mains €6-7.50) Street-side Greek eating at its best. Try shrimps with tomatoes and feta, or crab salad for under €5, followed by pork fillet. There are also simple fish dishes for under €10.

Mezedopoleio to Steki (☎ 22970 23910; Pan Irioti 45; dishes €6-12) Tucked in behind the noisy mid-harbour fish market is this vibrant place.

Together with its immediate neighbour, I Agora, it's always packed with people tucking into hell-fired octopus or sardines, plus other classic mezedhes.

Drinking & Entertainment

Music bars and cafes along the harbour front have luxurious seating in competing colours.

Heaven (☎ 22970 28872; Dimokratias) Soft sofas and upbeat decor feature in this popular music bar–cafe.

Yes! (☎ 22970 28306; Dimokratias) Easy-listening daytime sounds and sharper spins from local and visiting DJs at night give Yes! its edge for a younger crowd.

Avli (☎ 22970 26438; Pan Irioti 17) Avli mixes '60s and Latin music and plays Greek sounds when Athenian weekenders hit town.

AROUND AEGINA
Temple of Aphaia

The impressive **Temple of Aphaia** (☎ 22970 32398; adult/concession/under 18yr €4/2/free; ⏰ 8am-7.30pm Apr-Oct, 8.30am-5pm Nov-Mar) celebrates a local deity of pre-Hellenic times and is the major ancient site of the Saronic Gulf Islands. It was built in 480 BC, soon after the Battle of Salamis.

The temple's pediments were decorated with splendid Trojan War sculptures, most of which were robbed in the 19th century and now decorate Munich's Glyptothek. The remains of the temple stand proudly on a pine-covered hill with far-reaching views over the Saronic Gulf. There are interpretive panels in Greek and English.

Aphaia is 10km east of Aegina Town. Buses to Agia Marina stop at the site (€1.70, 20 minutes). A taxi from Aegina Town costs about €12 one way. If relying on buses it should be remembered that there might be several hours between services. It can be a hot hill top.

Paleohora Παλαιοχώρα

This enchanting site has had several of its old churches and chapels renovated recently and is a haven of peace. The ancient town of Paleohora was Aegina's capital from the 9th century and throughout the medieval period and was abandoned finally only during the 1820s. Over 30 surviving churches and chapels punctuate the rocky heights of the original citadel, and several have been carefully refurbished in recent years. Many are open to visitors and are linked by a network of

FLYING FREE

Yiannis Poulopoulos, the director of the **Hellenic Wildlife Hospital** (EKPAZ; see p122) on Aegina is larger than life. He needs boundless energy to maintain his lifelong commitment to wounded wild animals, which began when he was a veterinary student and nurtured injured small birds in his student flat. Yiannis has never stopped caring for wild creatures. Now he devotes virtually every waking hour to the wildlife hospital in the rugged hills of central Aegina. Here, Yiannis and his many devoted colleagues and volunteer helpers have had many successes, not least the release of rehabilitated eagles into the wilds of Crete and northern Greece.

At the EKPAZ base there are scores of creatures, many of them protected species and most of them the victims of humankind's desire to hunt and kill with guns. 'Why do they shoot such magnificent beings?' is Yiannis' eternal question.

Here you see the rarest of creatures – Eleonora's falcons (down to single figures in some countries), their wings half shot away; imperial eagles, Egyptian vultures, white storks, herons and waders, with smashed legs, some even blinded, disabled griffon vultures grumping and gossiping in one compound. These are all Yiannis' 'chickens'. 'They are all family,' he says. 'We are all one, surely.'

It is illegal to shoot protected species, but education, persuasion and example are probably the only ways, albeit painfully slow, to stop the destruction of wild creatures for sport. The brutal fact is that to point a gun at birds such as eagles, vultures, storks and swans means an inevitable cheap triumph for the shooter. Such slow, stately creatures do not twist and turn. Once fixed in the sights they are easy meat for just about anyone who can squeeze a trigger. As Yiannis drolly puts it: 'To shoot a wild bird is no achievement, no triumph. Perhaps they should try video games instead.'

Until they do, Yiannis Poulopoulos and his small army of colleagues and volunteers will continue their work in the hills of Aegina.

paths. The site is 6.5km east of Aegina Town near the enormous modern church of **Moni Agiou Nektariou**. Buses from Aegina Town to Agia Marina stop at the turn-off to Paleohora (€1.40, 10 minutes). A taxi is €8 one way.

Christos Capralos Museum

From 1963 until 1993, the acclaimed sculptor Christos Capralos (1909–93) lived and worked on Aegina during the summer months. Today, many of his works are on display at the **Christos Capralos Museum** (☎ 22970 22001; Livadi; admission €2; ⏰ 9am-2.30pm & 5-8pm Tue-Sun Jun-Oct, 10am-4pm Fri-Sun Nov-May) in his one-time home and studio on the coast near Livadi, 1.5km north of Aegina Town. At first glance the monumental works, especially those in eucalyptus wood, may seem harsh and discomfiting, but their fluidity and power are exhilarating. The *Crucifixion Tableau* is superb. In a separate gallery is the 40m-long *Pindus Frieze*, a powerful memorial to the Battle of Pindus, in which the Greek Army beat back an Italian advance in WWII.

Hellenic Wildlife Hospital

The oldest and largest wildlife rehabilitation centre in Greece and Southern Europe, the **Hellenic Wildlife Hospital** (Elliniko Kentro Perithalpsis Agrion Zoön; ☎ 22970 28607, 6973318845; www.ekpaz .gr; ⏰ 10am-7pm) each year treats and cares for anything from 3000 to 4500 wounded and disabled wild animals (see boxed text, p121). You can visit the hospital, which lies amidst rugged hills about 10km southeast of Aegina Town and 1km east of Pahia Rahi on the road to Mt Oros. Admission is free, but donations are appreciated. It is best to phone ahead to ask if a visit is possible. If you want a more hands-on commitment, the centre welcomes volunteers for whom accommodation is supplied. Potential volunteers should be aware that the work is hard and unglamorous, albeit hugely rewarding.

Perdika Πέρδικα

The fishing village of Perdika lies about 9km south of town on the southern tip of the west coast. Perdika's harbour inlet is very shallow and swimming is not much fun. Instead, catch one of the regular caïques (€4) from the harbour to the little island of Moni, a few minutes away. Moni is a nature reserve and has a magic tree-lined beach and summertime cafe.

There are a couple of hotels and a few rooms in Perdika. **Villa Rodanthos** (☎ 22970 61400; www

.villarodanthos.gr; s/d €45/65; 🞔 🖵) is a gem of a place, not least because of its charming owner. Each room has its own colourful decor and is equipped with a kitchen. It is about 100m along the right-hand branch road that starts opposite the bus stop at the edge of town.

Tavernas line the raised harbour-front terrace and dish up Greek staples for about €6 to €10. It all buzzes with life in summer and the tavernas mix it with some swaggering late-night music bars. A smart newcomer is Muzik, the ideal place for Perdika sunsets and relaxing sounds.

Buses run every couple of hours to Perdika from Aegina Town (€1.40, 30 minutes). A taxi is €10 one way.

Beaches

Beaches are not Aegina's strongest points. The east-coast town of **Agia Marina** is the island's main package resort. It has a shallow-water beach that is ideal for families, but it's backed by a fairly crowded main drag and it gets very busy in summer.

There are a couple of sandy beaches by the roadside between Aegina Town and Perdika, such as the pleasant **Marathonas** where the taverna **Ammos** (☎ 22970 28160; Marathonas; mains €5.50-12) offers excellent local dishes with an international flair.

ANGISTRI ΑΓΚΙΣΤΡΙ

pop 700

Angistri lies a few kilometres off the west coast of Aegina and offers a rewarding day trip or a worthwhile longer escape from the mainstream; better so out of high season.

The port of **Skala** is a resort village crammed with small hotels and apartment blocks, tavernas and cafes. Its beach, the best on the island, all but disappears beneath sun loungers and grilling flesh in July and August; but life, in general, still ticks along gently. Angistri's other port of **Mylos** (Megalochori) has a more appealing traditional character.

Orientation & Information

There is a board on Skala's ferry quay that lists accommodation options, with phone numbers. A right turn from the quay leads to the small harbour beach and then along a paved walkway to a church on a low headland. Beyond here lies the long, but narrow, main beach. A kilometre further west takes you to Mylos, with rooms and tavernas, but no beach. Turning left from the quay at Skala takes you south in about half an hour to the pebbly and clothing-optional **Halikadha Beach**.

There is a branch of Emboriki Bank with ATM in Skala's main street.

Sleeping & Eating

Angistri has many sleeping places, but booking ahead is advised, especially in August and at summer weekends.

Alkyoni Inn (☎ 22970 91378; www.alkyoni.com; s/d/tr €40/50/60; ☷) The welcoming Alkyoni Inn is a 10-minute stroll southeast of the ferry quay. Its seafront rooms and apartments have great views. Other rooms back onto the road. The Alkyoni has a popular taverna (mains €4.50 to €12) with well-prepared fish and meat dishes at reasonable prices.

our pick **Rosy's Little Village** (☎ 22970 91610; www.rosyslittlevillage.com; s/d/tr €50/70/90; ☷ ☷) A complex of Cubist-style buildings that step gently down to the sea, a short way to the east of Skala's ferry quay. Rosy's is full of light and colour. Free sunbeds and free mountain bikes enhance things even more and there's a weekly picnic and a live-music evening in summer. Breakfasts are €6.50 and there's a restaurant serving lunch and dinner with emphasis on organic sources. Mains are about €6.50 to €10. Check the website for information on various cultural courses that are available.

Two good local tavernas are **Gialos** (☎ 6977787785), just outside Skala on the Mylos road, and **Kafeses** (☎ 22970 91357), overlooking Mylos harbour. Both offer local specialities. In Skala, **Pizzeria Avli** (☎ 22970 91573) has above-ordinary pizzas.

Getting There & Away

Angistri is well-served by ferries, especially in summer, with several fast hydrofoils running each day to Angistri from Piraeus via Aegina and a car ferry running several days a week from Piraeus via Aegina. For details see Island Hopping (p509). The local ferry, Agistri Express, runs to and from Aegina several times a day (see p118).

The **water taxi service** (☎ 22970 91387, 6972229720) costs €40 one way between Aegina and Angistri, regardless of numbers.

Getting Around

Several buses a day run from 6.30am to about 9pm during the summer months from Skala and Mylos to the little village of Limenaria and to Dhragonera Beach. It's worth hiring a moped (€15) or sturdy mountain bike (€10) to explore the island's coastline road. Good hire outfits are **Kostas Bike Hire** (☎ 22970 91021; Skala) and **Takis Rent A Bike & Bicycles** (☎ 22970 91001; Mylos).

You can also follow tracks from Metohi overland through cool pine forest to reach the west-coast beach of Dhragonera. Take a compass with you; the tracks divide often and route finding can be frustrating.

POROS ΠΟΡΟΣ

pop 4500

Poros is a popular holiday island, yet it has a refreshing sense of remoteness in its sparsely populated and forested interior. The island is separated from the mountainous Peloponnese by a narrow sea channel, and the picturesque surroundings make the main settlement of Poros Town seem more like a lakeside resort in the Swiss Alps than a Greek island port. The mainland town of Galatas lies on the opposite shore.

Poros is in fact made up of two 'almost' islands: tiny Sferia, which is occupied mainly by the town of Poros, and the much larger and mainly forested Kalavria, which has the island's beaches and its larger seasonal hotels scattered along its southern shore. An isthmus, cut by a narrow canal and spanned by a road bridge, connects the two islands.

Getting There & Away

There are numerous daily ferries from Piraeus to Poros in summer and about four daily in winter. Fast ferries continue south to Hydra, Spetses, Ermioni and Porto Heli. Conventional ferries connect Aegina to Poros and on to Methana on the mainland. For details see Island Hopping (p520).

Caïques shuttle constantly between Poros and Galatas (€0.80, five minutes) on the mainland. They leave from the quay opposite Plateia Iroön in Poros Town. Hydrofoils dock about 50m north of here and car ferries to Galatas leave from the dock several hundred metres north again, on the road to Kalavria.

Getting Around

A bus operates May to October every half hour from 7am until midnight on a route that starts near the main ferry dock on Plateia Iroön in Poros Town. It crosses to Kalavria and goes east along the south coast as far as Moni Zoödohou Pigis (€1.50, 10 minutes), then turns around and heads west as far as Neorion Beach (€1.50, 15 minutes).

Some of the caïques operating between Poros and Galatas switch to ferrying tourists to beaches during summer. Operators stand on the harbour front and call out destinations.

There are several places on the road to Kalavria offering bikes for hire, both motorised and pedal-powered. Bikes start at €8 per day, and mopeds and scooters are €15 to €20.

POROS TOWN
pop 4102

Poros Town is a pleasant place where whitewashed houses with red-tiled roofs look out across the narrow channel towards the shapely mountains of the Peloponnese. Fast ferries and sizeable conventional ferries glide through the channel to dock on the harbour front, and smaller vessels scurry to and fro between the island and the mainland town of Galatas. Behind the harbour front a rocky bluff rises steeply to a crowning clock tower.

The town is also a useful base from which to explore the ancient sites of the adjacent Peloponnese.

Orientation

The main ferry dock is at the western end of the town's long harbour front.

Across the road from the main ferry dock is the small triangular-shaped 'square' of Plateia Iroön. To either side of the *plateia* the road is lined with cafes, tavernas and tourist shops. The island bus leaves from next to the kiosk at the eastern end of Plateia Iroön. Steps lead up from the inner corner of the *plateia* to the attractive lanes and squares of the upper town and to the clock tower and cathedral. A short distance south of Plateia Iroön is Plateia Karamis, set back from the harbour-front road and boasting a small war memorial.

A left turn from the dock leads north along the extended harbour front and on to the Kalavria road.

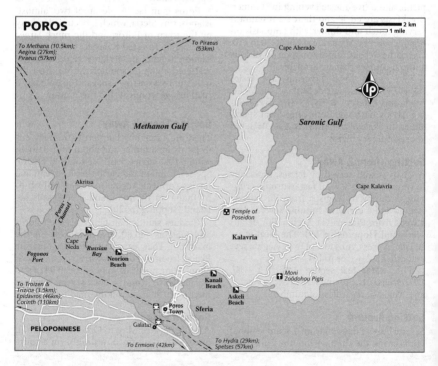

POROS

Information

Poros doesn't have a tourist office, but you can find useful information at www.poros.gr.

Alpha Bank (Plateia Iroön) Has an ATM.

Bank Emporiki (Plateia Iroön) Has an ATM.

Family Tours (☎ 22980 25900; www.familytours.gr) On the harbour front. Sells ferry tickets and arranges accommodation, car hire, tours and cruises.

Marinos Tours (☎ 22980 23423; www.marinostours.gr) On the harbour front. Arranges hydrofoil tickets and other services.

National Bank of Greece (Papadopoulou) About 100m north of Plateia Iroön; has an ATM.

Post office (☎ 22980 22274; Tombazi; ☺ 7.30am-2pm Mon-Fri) Next to Seven Brothers Hotel.

Suzi's Laundrette Service (Papadopoulou; 5kg wash & dry €12; ☺ 8am-2pm & 6-9pm Mon-Sat May-Oct, 9am-2pm Mon-Sat Nov-Apr) Next to the National Bank of Greece.

Tourist police (☎ 22980 22462/22256; Dimosthenous 10) Behind the Poros high school.

Sleeping

Georgia Mellou Rooms (☎ 22980 22309, 6937850705; Plateia Georgiou; s/d/tr €35/45/55; ⌗) Tucked away at the heart of the old town, next to the cathedral and high above the harbour front, these simple, old-fashioned rooms are a decent budget option. The owner is charming and there are great views from the west-side rooms.

Seven Brothers Hotel (☎ 22980 23412; www.7brothers.gr; Plateia Iroön; s/d/tr €55/65/75; ⌗ ▯) Conveniently close to the hydrofoil dock, this modern hotel has bright, comfy rooms with small balconies and tea- and coffee-making facilities.

Hotel Manessi (☎ 22980 22273/25857; www .manessi.com; Paralia; s/d €70/80; ⌗ ☍) Well-placed at the mid-point of the harbour front, the recently renovated Manessi is a central option. The business-style rooms are comfy and immaculate.

Eating

There's not much haute cuisine on Poros, but there are traditional tavernas with character to match the cooking.

Taverna Karavolos (☎ 22980 26158; mains €5-7.80; ☺ 7pm-late) Karavolos means 'big snail' in Greek and snails are a speciality of the house here, served in a thick tomato sauce (€6). Classic Greek meat dishes and some fish dishes are also on the oft-changing menu. Head north from the cathedral for about 100m, then go left and down broad steps towards the harbour.

Taverna Rota (☎ 22980 25627; Plateia Iroön; mains €5-15) Located on the edge of Plateia Iroön, this longstanding, family-run taverna dishes up breakfast (€4.50 to €7), traditional dishes, a range of salads, pasta and pizzas. The fish soup (€6) is excellent and they make their own flavoursome bread. The mixed seafood platter for two costs €25.

Dimitris Family Taverna (☎ 22980 23709; mains €4.50-20) The owners of this cheerful, family-run place have a butcher's business. Cuts of pork, lamb and chicken are of the finest quality, yet vegetarians can still mix and match a selection of nonmeat dishes. To get here, head north from the cathedral for 20m, turn right and then left for 100m.

AROUND POROS

Poros has several good beaches. **Kanali Beach**, on Kalavria 1km east of the bridge, is pebbly. **Askeli Beach** is about 500m to the east and has a long sandy stretch. The **Hotel New Aegli** (☎ 22980 22372/23200; www.newaegli.com; s/d/st €70/80/120; ⌗ ☍ ▯) is a decent resort-style hotel on Askeli Beach, with all the expected amenities, and even weekend Greek music and dancing. **Neorion Beach**, 3km west of the bridge, has water skiing and banana-boat and air-chair rides. The best beach is at **Russian Bay**, 1.5km past Neorion.

The 18th-century **Moni Zoödohou Pigis**, on Kalavria, has a beautiful gilded iconostasis from Asia Minor. The monastery is well signposted, 4km east of Poros Town.

From the road below the monastery you can head inland to the 6th-century **Temple of Poseidon**. There's very little left of this temple, but the walk is worthwhile and there are superb views of the Saronic Gulf and the Peloponnese. From the ruins you can continue along the road and go back to the bridge onto Sferia. It's about 6km in total.

PELOPONNESIAN MAINLAND

The Peloponnesian mainland opposite Poros can be explored conveniently from the island, with caïques running constantly between Poros and Galatas (see Getting There & Away, p123).

The ruins of ancient **Troizen**, legendary birthplace of Theseus, lie in the hills near the modern village of Trizina, 7.5km west of Galatas. There are buses to Trizina (€1.40, 15 minutes) from Galatas, leaving a walk of about 1.5km to the site.

SARONIC GULF ISLANDS

The inspiring ancient theatre of **Epidavros** (in the Argolis region) can be reached from Galatas. Your own transport is the most convenient way of getting there. Otherwise a couple of buses depart daily from Galatas (€8, two hours) and can drop you off at the ancient site, but you should check the return times and ongoing connections.

HYDRA ΥΔΡΑ

pop 2900

Hydra (*ee*-dhr-ah) is still the catwalk queen of the Saronics. Details matter here, such as the absence of ugly overhead power lines from the town and of cars and scooters from the streets. The island has long attracted throngs of tourists, cruise passengers and yacht crews, and the occasional celebrity on their way to hidden holiday homes among the tiers of picturesque buildings that rise above the harbour. Beyond the town, there are corners of lovely wilderness, accessible to those willing to hike – usually uphill.

Inflated prices sometimes go with the Hydra experience, but there are affordable gems among the sleeping and eating options and there are serene corners outside the harbour area and the main tributary streets.

History

Hydra experienced the light hand of an overstretched Ottoman Empire. Consequently the island prospered mightily after enterprising Greeks from the Peloponnese settled here to escape the more repressive Turkish regime of the mainland. Hydra was ever barren and waterless, so the new settlers began building boats and took to the thin line between maritime commerce and piracy with enthusiasm. By the 19th century, Hydra was a maritime power, earning itself the ambivalent sobriquet of 'Little England'. Wealthy shipping merchants built most of the town's grand old mansions and Hydra supplied 130 ships for a blockade of the Turks during the Greek War of Independence. The island bred such leaders as Georgios Koundouriotis, who was president of Greece's national assembly from 1822 to 1827, and Admiral Andreas Miaoulis, who commanded the Greek fleet. Streets and squares all over Greece are named after these two champions.

Getting There & Away

At the time of writing only fast ferries linked Hydra with Poros, Piraeus and Spetses, and Ermioni and Porto Heli on the mainland. For details see Island Hopping (p513). You can buy tickets from **Idreoniki Travel** (☎ 22980 54007; www.hydreoniki.gr), opposite the ferry dock.

Getting Around

In summer, there are caïques from Hydra Town to the island's beaches. There are also **water taxis** (☎ 22980 53690), which will take you anywhere you like; examples are Kamini (€11) and Vlyhos (€15).

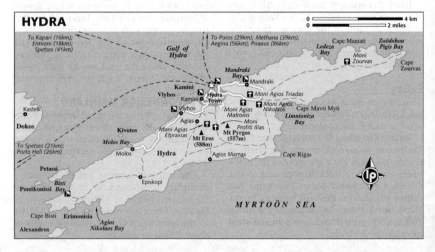

HYDRA

0 — 4 km
0 — 2 miles

To Kapari (16km); Ermioni (18km); Spetses (41km)

Gulf of Hydra

To Poros (29km); Methana (39km); Aegina (56km); Piraeus (86km)

Cape Maniati

Ledeza Bay

Zoödohou Pigis Bay

Moni Zourvas

Cape Zourvas

Mandraki Bay

Mandraki

Kamini

Vlyhos

Kamini

Hydra Town

Moni Agios Triadas

Kastelli

Vlyhos

Moni Agios Nikolaos

Cape Mavri Myti

Moni Agias Matronis

Agios

Moni Agias Efpraxias

Moni Profiti Ilias

Dokos

Kivotos

Limnioniza Bay

To Spetses (21km); Porto Heli (26km)

Molos Bay

Mt Eros (588m)

Mt Pyrgos (557m)

Molos

Hydra

Agios Mamas

Cape Rigas

Petassi

Bisti

Episkopi

Pontikonissi Bay

MYRTOÖN SEA

Cape Bisti   Erimonisia

Agios Nikolaos Bay

Alexandros

The donkey owners clustered around the port charge around €16 to transport your bags to your hotel.

HYDRA TOWN
pop 2526

Hydra Town's red-roofed houses with their pastel-painted walls form a pretty amphitheatre behind the harbour, where the cobbled quayside is a colourful throng of ambling pedestrians, mules and donkeys. The mules and donkeys are the main means of heavy transport; they load the air with a reassuring bouquet of genuine earthiness. Fast ferries with imperious beaked bows glide frequently through the harbour gaps and smart yachts come and go alongside the quay in an absolute froth of bad rope management. Behind the harbour, steep steps and alleyways paved with multicoloured stone lead ever upwards to the rock-studded slopes of old Hydra. The harbour front and the streets leading inland are crammed with cafes and craft and souvenir shops.

Information

There is no tourist office on Hydra but a useful website is www.hydradirect.com.

There is an ATM at Saitis Tours on the harbour front. The **post office** (✆ 7.30am-2pm Mon-Fri) is opposite the fish market on a small side street that runs between the Bank Emporiki and the National Bank of Greece, both of which have ATMs. The **tourist police** (☎ 22980 52205; Votsi; ✆ mid-May–Sep) can be found sharing an office with the regular police.

You can check email at the **Flamingo Internet Café** (☎ 22980 53485; Tombazi; per 30min €3; ✆ 8.30am-late).

There are loos of last resort alongside the fish market.

Sights & Activities

Hydra's star cultural attraction is the handsome **Lazaros Koundouriotis Historical Mansion** (☎ 22980 52421; nhmuseum@tee.gr; adult/concession €4/2; ✆ 9am-4pm Tue-Sun), an ochre-coloured building sitting high above the harbour. It was the home of one of the major players in the Greek independence struggle and is a fine example of late-18th-century traditional architecture. The main reception rooms of the 2nd floor have been restored to their full. The mansion is quite a steep hike up steps from the southwest corner of the harbour.

On the eastern arm of the harbour is the **Historical Archives Museum of Hydra** (☎ 22980 52355; www.iamy.gr; adult/child €5/3; ✆ 9am-4pm & 7.30-9.30pm Jul-Oct, 9am-4pm Nov-Jun). It houses a collection of portraits and naval oddments, with an emphasis on the island's role in the War of Independence.

The **Ecclesiastical Museum** (☎ 22980 54071; admission €2; ✆ 10am-5pm Tue-Sun Apr-Oct) is housed in the peaceful complex of the Monastery of the Assumption of the Virgin Mary on the harbour front. It contains a collection of icons and assorted religious paraphernalia.

Kallianos Diving Center (☎ 27540 31095; www .kallianosdivingcenter.gr) is based at the private island of Kapari. Activities include a two-dive outing for €80 with full equipment supplied, or €125 with instructor. There's a monthly diving-with-dolphins trip starting at €200, with a 50% refund if the dolphins don't turn up. PADI courses are also available. The centre does pick-up and return to Hydra, and non-divers can also take the trip to Kapari (€15).

Festivals & Events

Hydriots celebrate their contribution to the War of Independence in late June by staging an exuberant mock battle in Hydra harbour during the **Miaoulia Festival**, held in honour of Admiral Miaoulis. Much carousing, feasting and fireworks accompany it. **Easter** is also celebrated in colourful fashion.

Sleeping

Accommodation in Hydra is of a generally high standard. You pay accordingly, but there are also some very reasonably priced places of quality. The prices shown are for high season, which in Hydra means weekends as well as July and August. Most owners will meet you at the harbour if pre-arranged and will organise luggage transfer.

BUDGET & MIDRANGE

Pension Erofili (☎ /fax 22980 54049; www.pensionerofili .gr; Tombazi; s/d/tr €45/55/65; ✷) Tucked away in the inner town, these pleasant, unassuming rooms are a decent budget deal for Hydra. The young family owners add a friendly sparkle. It also has a large studio room with private kitchen. During July and August you can get breakfast for €7.

Bahia (☎ 22980 52257, 6977462852; Oikonomou; s/d €55/60; ✷) These decent rooms are above a clothes and jewellery shop called Alexander. They have cooking facilities.

Glaros (☎ 22980 53679, 6940748446; s/d €50/60; ✖) These simple, well-kept rooms are in a very convenient position down an alleyway just back from the harbour front.

Pension Loulos (☎ 22980 52411/6972699381; s/d/tr €50/60/70; ✖) A grand old house brimming with seagoing history and tradition. Loulos' eponymous owner was a noted sea captain and his rooms have old-fashioned charm, but with every amenity including tea- and coffee-making facilities. Most have glorious views. The roof terrace is sunset heaven. The

pension is a few minutes inland on the slopes above Tombazi.

our pick Nereids (☎ 22980 52875; www.nereids -hydra.com; Tombazi; s/d €60/65; ✖ 🛜). These lovely rooms represent exceptional value and quality. They are spacious, peaceful and have beautiful decor and open views to Hydra's rocky heights. Nereids is a few minutes' walk up Tombazi from the harbour, but it's worth it.

Pension Alkionides (☎ 22980 54055; www .alkionidespension.com; off Oikonomou; d/tr €60/75, ste €100-120; ✖) The Alkionides is in a peaceful cul-de-sac and has a pretty courtyard. Rooms are smart, though some are quite small, and they have tea- and coffee-making facilities.

TOP END

Hotel Leto (☎ 22980 53385; www.letohydra.gr; off Miaouli; s €123-137, d €160-180, tr €197-220; ✖ 🖥 🛜 ⚹) Stylish, modernist decor, spacious rooms and a relaxing atmosphere make Leto one of Hydra's classiest hotels. The price ranges depend on such variables as room size, balconies and floor location. There's one fully equipped room for disabled use. Buffet breakfast is included and there's a fitness studio, sauna and bar.

Angelica Hotel (☎ 22980 53202; www.angelica.gr; Miaouli; s €130-160, d €150-180, tr €220; ✖ 🛜) An attractive boutique hotel in a quiet location, the Angelica has comfortable, luxurious rooms, all individually themed and named after Greek gods. There's a minipool and Jacuzzi and relaxing public areas.

Hotel Orloff (☎ 22980 52564; www.orloff.gr; Rafalia; s/d incl breakfast €160/200; ✖ 🛜) There's a marvellous sense of historic Hydra without stuffiness at this beautiful, old mansion. A Russian admiral of the 18th century gave his name to the original house. The comfortable rooms have elegant furnishings and there's a lovely garden in which buffet breakfast is served. It's family-run and the welcome is warm.

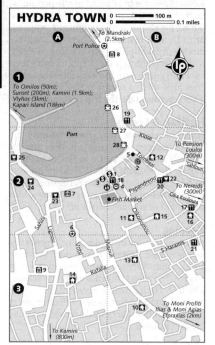

HYDRA TOWN
0 — 100 m
0 — 0.1 miles

Eating

You'll pay extra for basic coffee at some of the harbour-front cafes, but lively people-watching comes with it.

Creperie Mikro Café (☎ 22980 52335; Oikonomou; meals €3-7.20; ☒ 10am-1am) A handy budget option, just inland from the harbour, this little place offers sandwiches and hamburgers as well as crepes.

Isalos Café (☎ 22980 53845; snacks €3.50-7) A good bet right by the ferry dock, Isalos offers decent snacks and drinks at reasonable prices.

ourpick Taverna Gitoniko (Manolis & Christina; ☎ 22980 53615; Spilios Haramis; mains €4-9) Greek atmosphere with Greek courtesy is the tone at this long-established place that is better known by the first names of its owners, a sure sign of continuity and family tradition. Classic Greek favourites, such as zucchini balls, spinach pies and dolmadhes are tops, as is the local lamb. The family was in the process of building a new taverna on Tombazi, which should be open by the time you read this.

Paradosiako (☎ 22980 54155; Tombazi; mains €7-15) This little streetside *mezedhopoleio* (restaurant specialising in mezedhes) is traditional Greek personified. Classic pies come in cheese, beef, shrimp and vegie varieties and favourite mezedhes are plentiful. A bottle of decent wine starts at about €12, but the house wine at €7 is just fine.

Bratsera (☎ 22980 52794; Tombazi; mains €9-20; ☒ 1-4pm & 8-11pm Apr-Oct) The in-house restaurant by the pool of the Bratsera Hotel makes imaginative use of fresh local ingredients and sources the best cuts of meat. There's even fresh salmon when available. The wine list is equally selective.

Sunset (☎ 22980 52067; mains €9-22) Famed by name alone for its splendid location a short distance to the west of the harbour, the Sunset throws in live Greek music in summer to accompany such longstanding favourite starters as mackerel salad. Local fish are well prepared with mains such as grilled sea bream marinated in herbs, and meat and pasta dishes are also done with flair.

There's a supermarket, fruit shop and fish market just inland, mid-harbour side. O Fournos is an aroma-rich bakery next to the Pirate club across the alleyway.

Drinking & Entertainment

Hydra's harbour front revs up at night, when daytime cafes become hot music bars. Most bars are at the far end of the harbour, where places like **Pirate** (☎ 22980 52711) and **Saronikos** (☎ 22980 52589) keep going until dawn. Most play lounge sounds by day; at night Pirate plays rock, while Saronikos goes more for Greek pop.

Notionally closing in the 'early hours', the definitely red-hot **Red** (☎ 6974421398) has been known to keep things rocking for days at a time. It plays exuberant Greek sounds but also whatever suits the crowd.

A few blocks inland from the harbour front the more chilled **Amalour** (☎ 6977461357; Tombazi) does a lively line in cocktails and smoothies to a Latin rhythm. About 100m beyond the western edge of the harbour is the waterside **Omilos** (☎ 22980 53800), a chic daytime cafe and night-time dance venue.

AROUND HYDRA

Hydra's stony, arid interior, now with some regenerating pine woods, makes a robust but peaceful contrast to the clamour of the quayside.

An unbeatable Hydra experience is the long haul up to **Moni Profiti Ilias**, but you need to be fit and willing. Starting up Mialou from the harbour, it's a tough hour or more through relentless zigzags and pine trees. Just follow your nose and the occasional timely sign. You can visit the **Moni Agias Efpraxias** just before reaching Profiti Ilias itself. The latter is a wonderful complex of central church within a rectangular walled compound. Inside are beautiful icons and serenity; it's worth the hike.

Other paths lead to **Mt Eros** (588m), the island's highest point, and also along the island spine to east and west, but you need advanced route-finding skills or reliable walking directions from knowledgeable locals. A useful map for walkers is the *Hydra* map in the Anavasi Central Aegean series (www.mount ains.gr).

Hydra's shortcoming – or blessing – is its lack of appealing beaches to draw the crowds. There are a few strands all the same. **Kamini**, about a 1.5km walk along the coastal path from the port, has rocks and a very small pebble beach. **Vlyhos**, a 1.5km walk further on from Kamini, is an attractive village offering a slightly larger pebble beach, two tavernas and a ruined 19th-century stone bridge.

A path leads east from the port to the reasonable pebble beach at **Mandraki**, 2.5km away. **Bisti Bay**, 8km away on the south-western side of the island, has a decent pebble beach.

SARONIC GULF ISLANDS

SPETSES ΣΠΕΤΣΕΣ

pop 4000

Spetses is only a few kilometres across the sea from the mainland Peloponnese, but there is a stronger sense of island Greece here than in other Saronic Gulf destinations. The novelist John Fowles used the island as the setting for his powerful book *The Magus* (1965). His portrayal of lascivious heat and pine-scented seduction probably sent many a northern European hotfooting it to the beautiful south on their first Greek-island idyll.

Long before Fowles' day, Spetses, like Hydra, grew wealthy from shipbuilding. Island captains busted the British blockade during the Napoleonic Wars and refitted their ships to join the Greek fleet during the War of Independence. In the process they immortalised one local woman, albeit from a Hydriot family, the formidable Laskarina Bouboulina, ship's commander and fearless fighter (see p132).

The island's forests of Aleppo pine, a legacy of the far-sighted and wealthy philanthropist Sotirios Anargyrios, have been devastated by fires several times in the past 20 years. Many trees survive, however, and burnt areas are slowly recovering. Anargyrios was born on Spetses in 1848 and emigrated to the USA, returning in 1914 as a very rich man. He bought two-thirds of the then largely barren island and planted the pines that stand today. Anargyrios also financed the Spetses road network and commissioned many of Spetses Town's grand buildings.

Getting There & Away

At the time of writing only fast ferries linked Spetses with Hydra, Poros and Piraeus, and Ermioni and Porto Heli on the mainland. For details see Island Hopping (p524).

Ferry tickets can be bought at **Bardakos Tours** (☎ 22980 73141; Dapia Harbour) and at **Mimoza Travel** (☎ 22980 75170), a few metres to the left of the ferry quay.

In summer, there are caïques from the harbour to Kosta on the mainland (€4 per person). The larger car ferry, Katerina Star, costs €1 per person.

Getting Around

Spetses has two bus routes that start over the Easter period, then continue, depending on demand, until the end of May. From June to September there are three or four buses daily. The routes are from Plateia Agiou Mama in Spetses Town to Agii Anargyri (€3, 40 minutes), travelling via Agia Marina and Xylokeriza. All departure times are displayed on a board by the bus stop. There are also hourly buses in summer (every two hours in winter) to Ligoneri (€1.40). They leave from in front of the Hotel Possidonion, the monumental old building (being renovated at the time of writing) on the seafront just to the northwest of Dapia Harbour.

Only locally owned vehicles are allowed on Spetses. There are not too many of these, although the number is increasing. Hundreds of noisy scooters and motorbikes more than make up for it. There are motorbike-hire shops everywhere; rental is around €16 to €25 per day.

For quieter pedal power, there are sturdy bikes for hire (€6 per day) to suit all ages, including baby seats, from the excellent **Bike Center** (☎ 22980 74143; 9.30am-9.30pm) behind the fish market.

Water taxis (☎ 22980 72072; Dapia Harbour) leave from the quay opposite the Bardakos Tours office. Fares are displayed on a board. One-way fares are €16 to the Old Harbour, €30 to Agia Marina, €63 to Agii Anargyri, €45 to mainland Porto Heli, and €20 to Kosta. A round trip of the island costs €80. Fares are per trip, not per person. Add 50% to the price from midnight to 6am.

SPETSES TOWN

pop 3550

Spetses Town lies on the northeast coast of the island. It straggles a lengthy waterfront and its houses rise steeply from behind the main Dapia Harbour.

There's evidence of an early Helladic settlement near the Old Harbour (Palio Limani) and at Dapia. Roman and Byzantine remains have been found in the area behind Moni Agios Nikolaos, halfway between the two.

From the 10th century Spetses is thought to have been uninhabited for almost 600 years, until the arrival of Albanian refugees fleeing the fighting between Turks and Venetians in the 16th century.

The Dapia district has a few impressive *arhontika* (old mansions). The main part of town is given over to chic tourist shops and cafes. There are some rich ironies, not least the

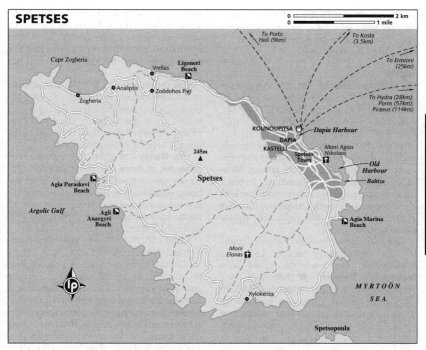

SPETSES

To Porto Heli (9km)
To Kosta (3.5km)
To Ermioni (25km)
To Hydra (28km); Poros (57km); Piraeus (114km)

Cape Zogheria
Vrellas
Ligoneri Beach
Analipsis
Zogheria
Zoödohos Pigi
KOUNOUPITSA
DAPIA — Dapia Harbour
KASTELLI
Spetses Town
Moni Agios Nikolaos
245m
Spetses
Old Harbour
Baltiza
Agia Paraskevi Beach
Argolic Gulf
Agii Anargyri Beach
Agia Marina Beach
Moni Elonas
MYRTOÖN SEA
Xylokeriza
Spetsopoula

juxtaposition of the cheerfully whiffy fish market with fashion shops selling such fragrant lines as Danoff, Clink, Zulu and Trussardi.

The town is awash with noisy motorbikes, scooters and quad bikes. Take great care at sharp corners.

A kilometre or so along the eastern harbour front takes you to the attractive Old Harbour (Palio Limani), the Church of Agios Nikolaos, and Baltiza yacht anchorage and boatbuilding area.

Orientation

At Dapia Harbour the quay serves both ferries and hydrofoils. A left turn at the end of the quay, facing in, leads east through Plateia Limenarhiou and along the harbour-front road of Sotiriou Anargyriou, past the town beach and Plateia Agiou Mama. Beyond here, the seafront road continues to the Old Harbour and on to Baltiza.

From the inner left-hand corner of Plateia Limenarhiou a narrow lane leads left to Plateia Orologiou (Clocktower Sq), which is enclosed by cafes, tavernas and shops and is overlooked by its namesake clock tower.

The narrow 'Main Street' climbs directly inland from the back of Plateia Limenarhiou.

From the north side of the harbour a road leads through the harbour-front Kounoupitsa area to become the road that runs northwest to Ligoneri.

Information

There is no tourist office on Spetses. A useful website is www.spetses direct.com.

Alpha Bank at Dapia Harbour has an ATM and there are others outside Alasia Travel on the waterfront and the Bank of Piraeus at the entrance to Plateia Orologiou. There are ATMs just up to the right along the harbour terrace.

The **port police** (☎ 22980 72245), **tourist police** (☎ 22980 73100; ☿ mid-May–Sep) and OTE (telephone office) all share the same building just beyond the Dapia Harbour upper terrace.

1800 Net Café (☎ 22980 29498; near Hotel Possidonion; per hr €3; ☿ 9am-midnight; ☎) Wi-fi is free to customers.

Mimoza Travel (☎ 22980 75170; mimoza-kent@aig .forthnet.gr) On the harbour front just past Plateia Limenarhiou; can help with accommodation and other services.

Newsagent (☎ 22980 73028; Main St) Impressive selection of newspapers and magazines in numerous languages.
Post office (☣ 7.30am-2pm Mon-Fri) On the street running behind the seafront hotels.

Sights

The **Spetses museum** (☎ 22980 72994; adult/concession €3/2; ☣ 8.30am-2.30pm Tue-Sun) is housed in the old mansion of Hatzigiannis Mexis (1754–1844), a shipowner who became the island's first governor. The collections on view are not extensive, but are fascinating. They include traditional costumes, folkloric items and portraits of the island's founding fathers. Most have Greek and English annotations. To reach the museum, go straight up from the top left-hand corner of Plateia Orologiou, turn left at the junction and then right, then follow the signposts.

The mansion of Spetses' famous daughter, the 19th-century seagoer Laskarina Bouboulina, has been converted into **Bouboulina's Museum** (☎ 22980 72416; www.bouboulinamuseum-spetses.gr; adult/concession/child €5/3/1; ☣ 10am-9pm Mar-Oct). Times may vary. Entry is via a 40-minute guided tour, which run every 45 minutes. Billboards around town advertise the starting times of tours and in which language. To reach the museum, turn left at the end of the line of cafes on the Dapia Harbour terrace.

There's an impressive **statue** of Bouboulina on the harbour front opposite the Hotel Possidonion. For more details about Bouboulina, see A Female Force (p35).

The **Old Harbour** (Palio Limani), which is about a 1.5km stroll from Dapia, is usually filled with a jumble of commercial vessels. A bit further on is **Baltiza**, a sheltered inlet crammed with all types of craft, from half-built caïques to working fishing boats, minor-league private cruisers and yachts.

Sleeping

Spetses has a decent mix of sleeping options and most places offer discounts outside August.

Klimis Hotel (☎ 22980 72334; klimishotel@hol.gr; s/d/tr €40/65/80; ☒) Serviceable rooms at this standard waterfront hotel are as cheap as you'll get in Spetses. The ground floor sports a cafe-bar and patisserie.

Hotel Kamelia (☎ 6939095513; s/d €50/55; ☣ Apr-Sep; ☒) These fresh, airy rooms are good value. The hotel is tucked away from the busy sea-front. Head along the lane to the right of the kiosk in Plateia Agiou Mama for 100m, then bear right before a little bridge. In another 100m or so, go right along a narrow lane to a quiet square, where the Kamelia lies drenched in bougainvillea.

Villa Christina Hotel (☎ 22980 72218; www.villachristinahotel.com; s/d/tr incl breakfast €50/70/85; ☒) Located about 200m uphill on the main road inland from the harbour, these well-kept rooms are tucked away from the worst traffic noise. There's a lovely garden area.

Villa Marina (☎ 22980 72646; www.villamarinaspetses.com; off Plateia Agiou Mama; s/d €60/75; ☒) Under new ownership, this handy hotel was being refurbished at the time of writing. It's just to the right of Plateia Agiou Mama. All rooms have refrigerators and there is a well-equipped communal kitchen downstairs.

Kastro (☎ 22980 75319; www.kastro-margarita.com; s/d/tr/apt incl breakfast €90/100/120/200; ☒ ☒) These studios and apartments are in a choice position close to the centre, yet within a private and quiet complex. Decor and furnishings combine traditional style with modern amenities and there are attractive public areas. There are discounts in low season. Head west along the harbour front for several hundred metres and Kastro is along a short lane to the left.

Nissia (☎ 22980 75000; www.nissia.gr; studio incl breakfast €270-365; ☣ Apr-Oct; ☒ ☐ ☎ ☒) Nissia is an exclusive oasis of peace and quiet in stylish surroundings. Studios are arranged around a spacious courtyard, complete with swimming pool and soothing greenery. It's about 300m northwest of Dapia Harbour. The hotel has a restaurant (mains €8 to €26).

Eating

Cockatoo (☎ 22980 74085; mains €1.50-7; ☣ noon-midnight) At this budget base, you can get a souvlaki for €2, a Greek salad for €5 or a takeaway chicken for €12. Head left from the top of Plateia Limenarhiou, and then right.

Taverna O Lazaros (☎ 22980 72600; mains €5-9) A hike of about 400m up Main St from the harbour sharpens your appetite for Greek standards at this very local taverna where the goat in lemon sauce is still the favourite and the house retsina complements it all. Open evenings only.

our pick Akrogialia (☎ 22980 74749; Kounoupitsa; mains €9-17; ☣ 9am-midnight) This excellent restaurant is on the Kounoupitsa harbour front and matches its great food with friendly service and

---

PEDAL POWER

Spetses' circular coast road can be enjoyed astride motorbike or scooter, but it cries out for a cycle – an antidote to all that fine Greek food. The road is satisfyingly sinuous and scenic and the circuit hugs the coast for 26km. Which way to go is definitely arguable. Locals advise anticlockwise to get some hefty climbs behind you, but going clockwise leaves some well-earned freewheeling at the end of the trip. Why not do it twice, both ways, and get really fit and virtuous? You can bounce off all of the island's beaches on the way.

The interior of the island is crisscrossed with quieter roads and woodland tracks and you can veer off for some more strenuous uphill off-roading into the lovely wooded hills of the island. (But take a decent map and compass with you.)

Bike Center (☎ 22980 74143; 9.30am-9.30pm) behind the fish market hires out bikes for €6 per day.

---

a bright setting. There are tasty options such as oven-baked *melitzana rolos* (eggplant with cream cheese and walnuts). Fish is by the kilo but you can enjoy a terrific fish risotto for €17 or settle for a choice steak; all accompanied by a thoughtful and classy selection of Greek wines. Breakfast, coffee and lunch are also available.

To Nero tis Agapis (☎ 22980 74009; Kounoupitsa; mains €12-19) The sweetly named 'Water of Life' is a sister restaurant to Tarsanas (below) but offers meat as well as fish dishes. The crayfish tagliatelle is worth every bite, as is the *zarzuela* (fish stew). Meat-eaters can settle for pork fillet in a cream sauce, and there's a selection of creative salads. It's located about 1km northwest of Dapia Harbour.

Tarsanas (☎ 22980 74490; Old Harbour; mains €17-26) A hugely popular *psarotaverna* (fish taverna), this family-run place deals almost exclusively in fish dishes using fresh local fish when available. It can be pricey, but the fish soup at €6 alone is a delight and other starters such as anchovies marinated with lemon start at about €4.50. For mains try the Tarsanas special: a seafood *saganaki* (fried cheese) for €17.

Self-caterers will find everything they need at **Kritikos Supermarket** (☎ 22980 74361; Kentriki Agora), next to the fish market on the harbour front. The entrance is along a covered passageway. There's also a fruit and vegetable shop next to the newsagents in Main St.

Drinking & Entertainment

Bar Spetsa (☎ 22980 74131; 8pm-late) One of life's great little bars, this Spetses institu-

tion never loses its integrity and its easygoing atmosphere. The music is guaranteed to stir memories for just about everyone with a soul. The bar is 50m beyond Plateia Agiou Mama on the road to the right of the kiosk.

Balconi Wine Bar (☎ 22980 72594; Sotiriou Anargyriou; 10.30am-3am May-Oct, 7pm-3am Nov-Apr) Paying stylish homage to cocktails, wine and well-sourced whisky, this smart place next to the seafront Stelios Hotel features classical music by day and subtle jazz riffs by night.

Music and dance venues are concentrated at the Old Harbour–Baltiza area and include Fortezza and Mourayo, which play Greek pop, Tsitsiano for traditional Greek and the big dance venue Baltiza, which may have a cover charge.

AROUND SPETSES

Spetses' coastline is speckled with numerous coves with small, pine-shaded beaches. The beach at **Ligoneri**, about 2.5km west of town, is easily reached by bus. The long, pebbly **Agia Paraskevi** and the sandier **Agii Anargyri** on the southwest coast have good, albeit crowded, beaches; both have water sports of every description. **Agia Marina**, about 2km southeast of Spetses Town, is a small resort with a beach that gets crowded.

A surfaced road skirts the entire coastline, so a scooter is the ideal way to explore the island. Or for a healthy alternative take a bicycle (see boxed text, above).

Cyclades Κυκλάδες

The Cyclades (kih-*klah*-dhez) lie at the deep blue heart of the Aegean and are so named because they form a *kyklos* (circle) around the island of Delos, the most compelling ancient site in the Aegean. The circle is not entirely symmetrical, but the symbolism is what matters. During archaic times Delos was the sacred equivalent of the Vatican and commercially was the treasure house, or Wall Street, of the Greek world.

Today, the Cyclades are the symbol of what dream islands should be: white cubist houses, golden beaches, olive groves, pine forests, herb-strewn mountain slopes and terraced valleys. Throw in a dash of hedonism and a vivid culture, and the Greek island dream can become reality.

Other realities are more down to earth, at least for native islanders, who have often struggled for a living through centuries of deprivation. Beneath the tourism gloss, many still raise livestock and grow food on reluctant soil, or chase a diminishing supply of fish from seas that are regularly rough and dangerous. Winters are often grey, bleak and unforgiving.

The Cyclades range from big fertile Naxos, with its craggy mountains and landlocked valleys, to the tiny outliers of Donousa and Koufinissi, where the sea dominates, with attitude, on every side. The beaches of Mykonos and Ios are awash with sun-lounger society and raucous diversions; their main towns seethe with commercialism. Iconic islands such as Santorini are world destinations for the fashion conscious and the cruise-ship aficionado. Other islands, such as Andros, Amorgos and Sifnos, have kept tourism to a more sedate scale, while tiny retreats such as Iraklia and Anafi are remote jewels in the Cycladean circle.

HIGHLIGHTS

- **Ancient Glories** Exploring the wonderful archaeological sites of Delos (p157) and Ancient Thira (p198)
- **Cycladic Cuisine** Being spoiled for choice by modern Greek cuisine on Mykonos (p148) and Paros (p159)
- **Off Track** Veering off to the remoter islands of the Little Cyclades (p176) and Anafi (p200)
- **Night Play** Partying until dawn on Mykonos (p148) and Ios (p185)
- **Sunset Serenade** Viewing spectacular sunsets from Fira and Oia on Santorini (p189)
- **High Life** Hiking through the mountains of Naxos (p168) and Andros (p136)

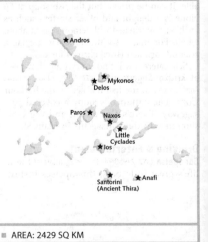

- POPULATION: 109,814
- AREA: 2429 SQ KM

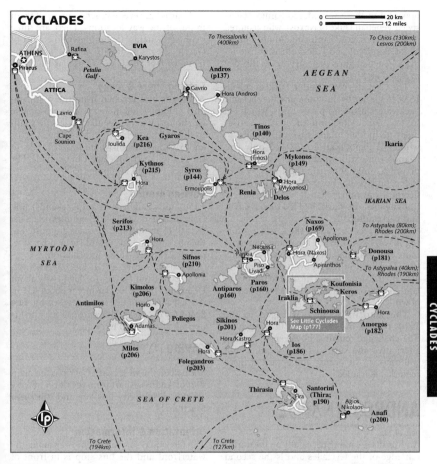

CYCLADES

History

The Cyclades are said to have been inhabited since at least 7000 BC. Around 3000 BC there emerged a cohesive Cycladic civilisation that was bound together by seagoing commerce and exchange. During the Early Cycladic period (3000–2000 BC) the tiny but distinctive Cycladic marble figurines, mainly stylised representations of the naked female form, were sculpted.

In the Middle Cycladic period (2000–1500 BC) many of the islands were occupied by the Minoans – at Akrotiri, on Santorini, a Minoan town has been excavated. At the beginning of the Late Cycladic period (1500–1100 BC) the archipelago came under the influence of

the Mycenaeans, who were followed by the Dorians in the 8th century BC.

By the middle of the 5th century BC the islands were members of a fully fledged Athenian empire. In the Hellenistic era (323–146 BC) they were controlled by Egypt's Ptolemaic dynasties and then by the Macedonians. In 146 BC the islands became a Roman province and lucrative trade links were established with many parts of the Mediterranean.

The division of the Roman Empire in AD 395 resulted in the Cyclades being ruled from Byzantium (Constantinople), but after the fall of Byzantium in 1204, they came under a Venetian governance that doled out the islands to opportunistic aristocrats. The most powerful of these was Marco Sanudo (self-styled Venetian Duke of Naxos), who acquired Naxos, Paros, Ios, Santorini, Anafi, Sifnos, Milos, Amorgos and Folegandros, introducing a Venetian gloss that survives to this day in island architecture.

The Cyclades came under Turkish rule in 1537. Neglected by the Ottomans, they became backwaters prone to pirate raids, which led to frequent relocation of coastal settlements to hidden inland sites and, finally, to wholesale depopulation. In 1563 only five islands were still inhabited. The Cyclades played a minimal part in the Greek War of Independence, but became havens for people fleeing from other islands where insurrections against the Turks had led to massacres and persecution.

Italian forces occupied the Cyclades during WWII. After the war the islands emerged more economically deprived than ever. Many islanders lived in deep poverty; many more gave up the struggle and headed to the mainland, or to America and Australia, in search of work.

The tourism boom that began in the 1970s revived the fortunes of the Cyclades. The challenge remains, however, of finding alternative and sustainable economies that will not mar the beauty and appeal of these remarkable islands.

ANDROS ΑΝΔΡΟΣ

pop 10,112

Andros sits dreaming peacefully on the northern edge of the Cyclades and is the second largest of the group, after Naxos. It makes for a rewarding escape for those who want a less tourist-oriented world.

Satisfyingly remote in places, Andros is a mix of bare mountains and green valleys where tall cypresses, like green tapers, rise above smaller trees. Neoclassical mansions and Venetian tower-houses contrast with the rough unpainted stonework of farm buildings and patterned dovecotes. Handsome stone walls, made up of large slabs with smaller boulders packed between them, lock the sometimes friable hill slopes in place. A network of footpaths, many of them stepped and cobbled, is also maintained, and the island has a fascinating archaeological and cultural heritage.

Andros has several beaches, many of them in out-of-the way locations. There are three main settlements: the unpretentious port of Gavrio, the resort of Batsi and the handsome main town of Hora, known also as Andros.

Getting There & Away

Andros is best reached from the mainland port of Rafina, 66km away and a reasonable two hours by ferry. Regular ferries run south to the neighbouring islands of Tinos, Syros and Mykonos, from where onward links to the rest of the archipelago can be made. For details see Island Hopping (p509).

Getting Around

Nine buses daily (fewer on weekends) link Gavrio and Hora (€3.80, 55 minutes) via Batsi (€2.10, 15 minutes). Schedules are posted at the bus stops in Gavrio and Hora; otherwise, call ☎ 22820 22316 for information.

A **taxi** (☎ Gavrio 22820 71171, Batsi 22820 41081, Hora 22820 22171) from Gavrio to Batsi costs about €8 and to Hora, €30. Car hire is about €35 in August and about €25 in the low season. **Euro Rent A Car** (☎ 22820 72440; www.rentacareuro.com) is opposite the Gavrio ferry quay.

GAVRIO ΓΑΥΡΙΟ
pop 798

Located on the west coast, Gavrio is the main port of Andros. Apart from the flurry of ferry arrivals, it is pretty low key and can seem touch drab.

Orientation & Information

The ferry quay is situated midway along the waterfront and the bus stop is in front of it. The post office is 150m to the left as you leave the ferry quay. There's an ATM outside Kyklades Travel and there's a bank with ATM on the middle of the waterfront.

Kyklades Travel (☎ 22820 72363; lasia@otenet .gr) A helpful office opposite the ferry quay with another office about 50m to the right next to the Agricultural Bank of Greece. They sell ferry tickets and can arrange accommodation.

Port police (☎ 22820 71213) Located on the waterfront.

Sleeping & Eating

Andros Camping (☎ 22820 71444; www.campingandros .gr; adult/child/tent €6.50/3/3; P 🚉) Located about 400m behind the harbour front, this pleasant camping site is shaded by trees. You can rent a small tent for €6 or a large one for €10.

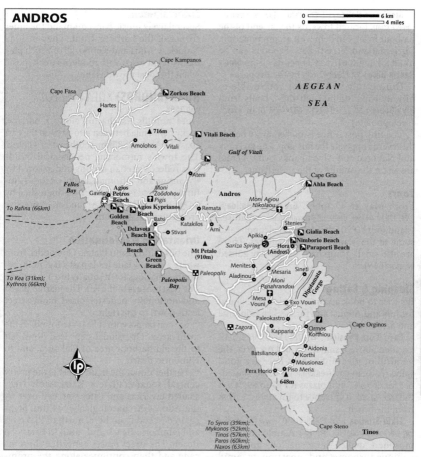

ANDROS

Cape Kampanos

Cape Fasa

Hartes

Zorkos Beach

AEGEAN

SEA

▲716m
Amolohos Vitali

Vitali Beach

Gulf of Vitali

Ateni

Cape Gria

Ahla Beach

Fellos Bay
Gavrio Agios Petros Beach

Moni Zoödohou Pigis

Andros

Moni Agiou Nikolaou

To Rafina (66km)

Golden Beach

Agios Kyprianos Beach
Batsi

Remata

Katakilos Arni

Stenies

Gialia Beach

Delavoia Beach

Stivari

Apikia

Sariza Spring

Hora (Andros)

Nimborio Beach
Paraporti Beach

Anerousa Beach

Green Beach

▲ Mt Petalo (910m)

To Kea (31km); Kythnos (66km)

Menites

Mesaria

Sineti

Paleopolis Bay

Paleopolis

Aladinou

Moni Panahrandou

Dipotamata Gorge

Mesa Vouni

Exo Vouni

Paleokastro

Zagora

Kapparia

Ormos Korthiou

Cape Orginos

Batsilianos

Korthi
Mousionas

Aidonia

Pera Horio Piso Meria

648m

To Syros (39km); Mykonos (52km); Tinos (57km); Paros (60km); Naxos (63km)

Cape Steno

Tinos

0 —— 6 km
0 —— 4 miles

CYCLADES

Ostria Studios (☎ 22820 71551; www.ostria
-studios.gr; s/d/apt €60/70/85; P ⌨ 🖳) Rooms at
this well-located place, located about 300m
along the Batsi road, are getting a bit worn,
but they are spacious, have cooking facilities
and stand in a pleasant terraced complex.

To Konaki (☎ 22820 71733; mains €5-14) Located
about 50m to the left of the ferry quay, To
Konaki has a healthy selection of fish, meat
and vegetarian dishes with a local flavour.
The cod in garlic sauce is a speciality.

Sails (☎ 22820 71333; mains €7-22) An excellent
ouzerie (place that serves ouzo and light
snacks) and *psarotaverna* (fish tavern), Sails
usually has some good locally caught fish.
You'll pay about €22 for a decent-sized sea

bream. There are chicken and pork dishes
as well.

BATSI ΜΠΑΤΣΙ
pop 971

Easy-going yet upbeat, Batsi is the island's
main resort. It has a small yacht marina that
brings a bit of seaborne colour in summer.
The resort lies 7km south of Gavrio on the
inner curve of a handsome bay. A sandy
beach on the north side merges eventually
with a harbour front promenade backed by a
colourful swath of cafes, tavernas and shops.
There's a dusty car park across the road from
the beach and a smaller one at the far end of
the harbour front.

Greek Sun Holidays (☎ 22820 41198; www.andros
-greece.com), located towards the far end of the
harbour front, can help with accommodation,
car rental and ferry tickets. Scooters can be
hired for about €16 to €24 per day from **Dino's
Rent-a-Bike** (☎ 22820 42169), by the car park.

During July and August you're able to
hire well-maintained self-drive boats from
Riva Boats (☎ 22820 24412, 6974460330) in Hora
(see opposite).

The tiny post office is tucked away beside
the taverna opposite the bus stop. The taxi rank
and National and Alpha banks (with ATMs)
are all on the middle of the waterfront.

Tours

From May to October, **Greek Sun Holidays**
(☎ 22820 41198; greeksun@travelling.gr) organises
island tours (€20) that take in Paleopolis and
some of the island's loveliest villages. There
are also small-group half- or full-day guided
walks (€18).

Sleeping & Eating

It's wise to book accommodation well ahead
for July and August and for weekends in June
and September.

Cavo D'ora Pension (☎ 22820 41766; s/d €25/45)
Located above a snack bar and pizzeria, the
handful of pleasant rooms here are good
value. You can get breakfast for €5.50, mezedhes for €6 to €7 and pizzas for €7 to €9. It's at
the tree-shaded entrance to town, just across
from the beach.

Likio Studios (☎ 22820 41050; www.likiostudios
.gr; s/d/apt €64/80/130; P ☼) A welcoming atmosphere makes these spacious and well-
equipped rooms and apartments amid
a peaceful flower-filled garden a great
choice. It is about 150m inland from Dino's
Rent-a-Bike.

Oti Kalo (☎ 22820 41287; mains €5-9) The name
means 'everything good', and it's no idle
boast. Specialising in the Andros speciality,
froutalia (spicy sausage and potato omelette),
while other mains include meat and fish as
well as pasta.

Stamatis Taverna (☎ 22820 41283; mains €6.50-16)
A well-run taverna on the terrace above the
harbour, offering a great choice of starters
such as *pikandiko* (feta, tomato, green pepper, oregano and spices cooked in a pot). For
€7 you can enjoy a fish or vegetable soup and
they have a fine touch with local dishes also.

Entertainment

Several lively music bars command the inner
corner of the harbour front. They include
Nameless, Aqua and Kimbo, all of which play
mainstream disco with modern Greek music
when the local crowd is in.

HORA (ANDROS) ΧΩΡΑ (ΑΝΔΡΟΣ)
pop 1508

Hora unfolds its charms along a narrow,
rocky peninsula between two bays on the east
coast of Andros, 35km southeast of Gavrio.
The town's numerous neoclassical buildings reflect Venetian origins underscored by
Byzantine and Ottoman accents. Hora's cultural pedigree is even more distinguished by
its Museum of Modern Art and an impressive
archaeological museum.

Orientation & Information

The bus station is on Plateia Goulandri, from
where a narrow lane leads past a taxi rank, beside the spacious town square, to a T-junction.
The post office is to the left. The marble-paved
and notionally pedestrianised main street
leads down to the right.

Several banks with ATMs are found on the
main street. Occasional steps lead down left
to the old harbour area of Plakoura, and to
Nimborio Beach.

Further down the main street is the pretty
central square, Plateia Kaïri, with tree-
shaded tavernas and cafes watched over by
the Andros Archaeological Museum. Steps
again descend from here, north to Plakoura
and Nimborio Beach and south to Paraporti
Beach. The street passes beneath a short arcade and then continues along the promontory, bends left, then right and ends at
Plateia Riva – a big, airy square with crumbling balustrades and a giant bronze statue
of a sailor.

Sights & Activities

Hora has two outstanding museums; both
were donated to the state by Basil and Elise
Goulandris, of the wealthy ship-owning
Andriot family. The **Andros Archaeological
Museum** (☎ 22820 23664; Plateia Kaïri; adult/child/student
€3/2/free; ☼ 8.30am-3pm Tue-Sun) contains impres-
sive finds from the settlements of Zagora and
Paleopolis (9th to 8th century BC) on Andros'
east coast, as well as items of the Roman,
Byzantine and early Christian periods. They

include a spellbinding marble copy of the 4th-century bronze **Hermes of Andros** by Praxiteles.

The **Museum of Contemporary Art** (☎ 22820 22444; www.moca-andros.gr; adult/student €6/3 Jun-Sep, €3/1.50 Oct-May; ☷ 10am-2pm & 6-8pm Wed-Sat & Mon, 10am-2pm Sun Jun-Sep, 10am-2pm Sat-Mon Oct-May) has earned Andros a reputation in the international art world. The main gallery features the work of prominent Greek artists, but each year during the summer months the gallery stages an exhibition of works by one of the world's great artists. To date there have been exhibitions featuring original works by Picasso, Matisse, Braque, Toulouse-Lautrec and Miro, a remarkable achievement for a modest Greek island. To reach the gallery, head down the steps from Plateia Kaïri towards the old harbour.

The huge **bronze statue** of a sailor that stands in Plateia Riva celebrates Hora's great seagoing traditions, although it looks more Russian triumphalist than Andriot in its scale and style. The ruins of a **Venetian fortress** stand on an island that is linked to the tip of the headland by the worn remnants of a steeply arched bridge.

A great option is to hire a self-drive boat and head out to some of the west and north coasts' glorious beaches, most of which are difficult to reach by road. **Riva Boats** (☎ 22820 24412, 6974460330; Nimborio) has superb 4.5m Norwegian-built open boats with 20HP outboards, life raft and anchor, and even a mobile phone. Hire per boat for a minimum of one day is about €90 and no licence is necessary. Riva can also arrange by phone for boats to be hired from Batsi.

Scooters and motorbikes can be hired from Riva Boats and through Karaoulanis Rooms (see below) for €15 to €18 per day.

Sleeping & Eating

Karaoulanis Rooms (☎ 22820 24412, 6974460330; www.androsrooms.gr; d/apt €50/100) This tall, old house is right down by the harbour and has bright and pleasant rooms. There are good discount prices in low season. Greek, English and French are spoken by family members. Check here also for scooter and boat hire.

Karaoulanis Studios-Apartments (☎ 22820 24412, 6974460330; www.androsrooms.gr; d €50-60, apt €100) In 2009 the same family opened stylish new apartments on the outskirts of Hora that command splendid views across the wooded slopes to the south of town.

Alcioni Inn (☎ 22820 24522, 6973403934; alcioni@ hellastourism.gr; Nimborio; d €70-80) These comfortable self-catering rooms are in the midst of the main Nimborio beachfront, below and to the north of Hora.

Niki (☎ /fax 22820 29155; xenonaw.nik@g.mail.com; s/d/tr €70/90/100; ☒) Open-beamed ceilings and wooden galleries enhance the traditional style and modernised facilities of this handsome old house on Hora's main street. There's a ground-floor cafe with a large veranda where you can relax and get breakfast for about €8.

Ermis (☎ 22820 22233; Plateia Kaïri) A pleasant little cafe and pastry shop on Plateia Kaïri.

Nonna's (☎ 22820 23577; Plakoura; mains €5-10) Authentic mezedhes and main dishes of fresh fish from the family's own boat are the order of the day at this popular little taverna at the old harbour. Sea bream, monkfish and red mullet are just a few of the fish dishes available. Vegetarians have a decent choice too, from salads to zucchini pie.

Palinorio (☎ 22820 22881; Nimborio; mains €5.50-8.50; ☷ 11am-2am) Fish is priced by the kilo at this long-established and reliable restaurant on the waterfront at the edge of Nimborio Beach. Lobster dishes are especially well prepared. Traditional Greek dishes and pasta dishes are also available.

AROUND ANDROS

Between Gavrio and Paleopolis Bay are several pleasant beaches, including **Agios Kyprianos**, where there's a little church with a taverna close by; **Delavoia**, one half of which is naturist, **Anerousa** and **Green**.

Paleopolis, 7km south of Batsi on the coast road, is the site of Ancient Andros, where the Hermes of Andros was found. The small but intriguing **Archaeological Museum of Paleopolis** (☎ 22829 41985; admission free; ☷ 8.30am-3pm Tue-Sun) displays and interprets finds from the area.

If you have transport, a worthwhile trip is to head down the west coast of the island before turning northeast at Batsilianos through a charming landscape of fields and cypresses to reach **Ormos Korthiou**, a bayside village that lacks only a decent beach to give it full resort status. Head north from here along a lovely coastal road that climbs and turns through raw hills and wooded valleys for 20km to reach Hora.

CYCLADES

From Hora you can continue north on a lovely scenic route through the high hills of central Andros before descending through switchbacks to Batsi.

TINOS ΤΗΝΟΣ

pop 8614

Hora, the port of Tinos, is a focus of Orthodox devotion that climaxes, with fervour, during festivals at the imposing Church of Panagia Evangelistria, home to the sacred icon of the Megalochari, the Holy Virgin. The icon is one of Greece's most famous and is said to have been found in 1822 on land where the church now stands. Healing powers were accorded to the icon, thus leading to mass pilgrimage and a commercial future for Tinos. Religion still takes centre stage in Hora, although the town rattles and hums around it all like a typical island port should.

Beyond all this, Tinos survives as an island of great natural beauty. Its landscape of rugged hills is dotted with over 40 villages that protrude like marble outcrops from the brindled slopes. Scattered across the countryside are countless ornate dovecotes, legacy of Venetian influence. There is a strong artistic tradition on Tinos, not least in the sculptors' village of Pyrgos in the north of the island where the island's marble quarries are located.

Getting There & Away

Tinos is well served by ferries and there are regular connections to the mainland ports of Rafina and Piraeus as well as to the neighbouring islands of Syros and Andros and south to Mykonos and beyond. For details see Island Hopping (p525).

There are two ferry departure quays in Hora, known locally as 'ports'. The Outer Port is the main dock for conventional and larger fast ferries. It is about 300m to the north of the main harbour. The Middle Port, where smaller, fast ferries dock, is at the north end of the town's main harbour. When you buy a ferry ticket it's essential to check which of these two ports your ferry is leaving from. Allow at least 20 minutes to walk from the centre of Hora to the Outer Port.

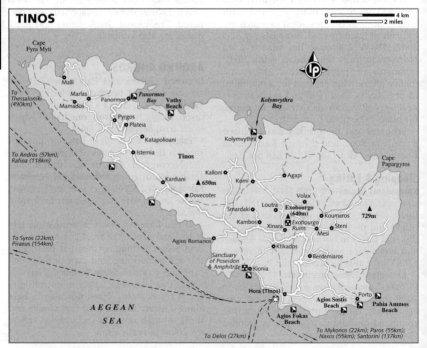

Getting Around

From June to September there are frequent buses from Hora (Tinos) to Porto and Kionia (€1.40, 10 minutes) and several daily to Panormos (€4, one hour) via Kambos (€1.40, 15 minutes) and Pyrgos (€3.30, 50 minutes). Buses leave from the bus station on the Hora harbour front opposite the bus ticket office, which is next to the Poseidon Hotel. You buy tickets on the bus.

Motorcycles (per day €15 to €20) and cars (minimum per weekday €44; on weekends €60) can be hired from a number of outfits along the waterfront at Hora. Rates drop out of season. **Vidalis Rent a Car & Bike** (☎ 22830 25670; Trion Ierarhon 2) is a reliable firm.

HORA (TINOS) ΧΩΡΑ (ΤΗΝΟΣ)
pop 4934

Hora, also known as Tinos, is the island's capital and port. The harbour front is lined with cafes and hotels and the narrow streets behind are full of restaurants and tavernas. The streets leading up to the Church of Panagia Evangelistria are lined with shops and stalls crammed with souvenirs and religious ware.

Orientation & Information

There are two ferry departure quays, the locations of which visitors definitely need to know (see opposite).

The uphill street of Leoforos Megaloharis, straight ahead from the middle of the main waterfront, is the route pilgrims take to the church. The narrower shopping street of Evangelistria, also leading to the church, is to its right.

The post office is at the southeastern end of the harbour front, just past the bus station, and the National Bank of Greece (with ATM) is 50m left of Hotel Posidonion.

Malliaris Travel (☎ 22830 24241; fax 22830 24243; malliaris@thn.forthnet.gr; Paralia) On the waterfront near Hotel Posidonion; sells ferry tickets.

Port police (☎ 22830 22348; Kionion) Just up from Windmills Travel.

Symposion (☎ 22830 24368; Evangelistria 13) A pleasant cafe-restaurant with internet access (€3 for 30 minutes).

Windmills Travel & Tourism (☎ 22830 23398; www.windmillstravel.com; Kionion 2) Just across the way from the Outer Port ferry quay, Windmills is very helpful, and staff can arrange accommodation, car hire and much more.

Sights

The neoclassical **Church of Panagia Evangelistria** (Church of the Annunciation; ☾ 8am-8pm) is built of marble from the island's Panormos quarries. The complex lies within a pleasant courtyard flanked by cool arcades. Inside the main building, the acclaimed icon of the Holy Virgin is draped with gold, silver, jewels and pearls, and is surrounded by gifts from suppliants. A hanging garden of chandeliers and lampholders fills the roof space.

Set into the surface of the street on one side of Leoforos Megaloharis is a rubberised strip, complete with side lights. This is used by pilgrims, who may be seen at any time of year heading for the church on their hands and knees, pushing long candles before them. The final approach is up carpeted steps.

Within the church complex, several **museums** house religious artefacts, icons and secular artworks.

The small **archaeological museum** (☎ 22830 22670; Leoforos Megaloharis; admission €2; ☾ 8am-3pm Tue-Sun), on the right-hand side of the street as you descend from the church, has a collection that includes impressive clay *pithoi* (Minoan storage jars), grave reliefs and sculptures.

Sleeping

Hora should be avoided on 25 March (Annunciation), 15 August (Feast of the Assumption) and 15 November (Advent). If not booked into a hotel months ahead, you'll have to join the roofless devotees who sleep on the streets at these times.

BUDGET

Camping Tinos (☎ 22830 22344; www.camping.gr/tinos; camp sites per adult/child/tent €7/4/4, bungalows with/without bathroom €28/20) A well-equipped site with good facilities. South of the town near Agios Fokas, it's about a five-minute walk from the Middle Port. A minibus meets ferries.

Nikoleta (☎ 22830 24719; nikoleta@thn.forthnet.gr; Kapodistriou 11; s/d without air-con €25/30, s/d with air-con €40/50, ste €55; 🅿) Some distance inland from the south end of town, but its spotless, uncluttered rooms are exceptional value and come with a charming welcome. There is a lovely garden area.

Faros (☎ 22830 22712, 6932800525; s/d/tr €35/50/80; 🅿) This is a handy place for the Outer Port ferry quay. The rooms are colourful and quirky, but some are rather small. The small outside courtyard is filled with leafy colour.

CYCLADES

MIDRANGE

Oceanis (☎ 22830 22452; oceanis@mail.gr; Akti G Drosou; s/d/tr €35/50/70; 🔀) Rooms are not overly large at this modern, well-run hotel, but they are clean and well equipped. It even has some genuine, if very small, single rooms. There's a lift to all floors. Breakfast costs €5.

Hotel Posidonion (☎ 22830 23123; www.poseidonio .gr; Paralia 4; s/d/tr €60/70/85; 🔀) A convenient midwaterfront position makes this long-established hotel with decent, comfortable rooms a popular choice. Communal lounges overlooking the harbour front are a pleasant feature.

Altana Hotel (☎ 22830 25102; www.altanahotel.gr; s/d €85/100, ste €145-195; P 🔀 🖳 🛜) Located about 700m to the north of town, this charming boutique hotel has a modernist Cycladean style, all snowy white walls and cool interiors incorporating distinctive Tinian motifs. Altana is an ideal base from which to explore the island, and its young family owners are courteous and friendly. Full breakfast is included.

Eating

Malamatenia (☎ 22830 24240; G Gagou; mains €6.50-12) A local favourite, Malamatenia is just up from To Koutouki and has specialities such as shrimps in a wine and tomato sauce with feta cheese, and *youvetsi*, beef in tomato sauce cooked in a clay pot, with pasta.

To Koutouki tis Elenis (☎ 22830 24857; G Gagou 5; mains €7-18) This cosy little place on the narrow lane that veers off from the bottom of Evangelistria has such worthwhile dishes as chicken in lemon sauce, fresh cuttlefish and fish soup.

Pallada Taverna (☎ 22830 23516; Plateia Palladas; mains €7.50-11) Excellent Greek dishes are on offer here with some particularly fine items such as fresh squid stuffed with rice, and zucchini balls with anise and cheese. Local wines from the barrel are persuasive and the house retsina is more than fine.

Metaxy Mas (☎ 22830 25945; Plateia Palladas; mains €8-20) Modern Mediterranean cuisine is the rule at this stylish restaurant where starters such as Tinian artichokes, aubergine soufflé and *louza* (local smoked ham) smooth the way to mains of chicken, pork and veal or specialities such as cuttlefish with spinach.

our pick Symposion (☎ 22830 24368; Evangelistria 13; mains €9-18) A pretty staircase leads to this elegant cafe-restaurant. It does breakfasts (€4 to €13), crêpes and sandwiches (€3.50 to €8.50), as well as pasta dishes, mixed plates, and main dishes such as grilled sea bass with piquant local greens.

Drinking & Entertainment

Café Piazza (☎ 22830 23483) A busy, gossipy place at the inner end of the line of cafe-bars on the Tinos harbour front. It has a deep terrace and a cosy inside area.

Koursaros (☎ 22830 23963; ⏱ 8am-3am) This long-established bar spins an engaging mix of rock, funk and jazz. It's at the far end of the line of harbour-front cafe-bars.

In the back lanes opposite the Middle Port there's a clutch of music and dance bars such as Village Club, Volto and Sibylla, glowing with candy-coloured light and churning out clubby standards and Greek pop as a counterbalance to all that sacred song.

AROUND TINOS

Outside Hora's conspicuous religiosity and down-to-earth commercialism, the countryside of Tinos is a revelation in itself, a glorious mix of wild hill tops crowned with crags, unspoiled villages, fine beaches and fascinating architecture that includes picturesque dovecotes.

At **Porto**, 6km east of Hora, there's a pleasant, uncrowded beach facing Mykonos, while about a kilometre further on is the even lovelier **Pahia Ammos Beach**.

Kionia, 3km northwest of Hora, has several small beaches. Near the largest are the scant remains of the 4th-century-BC **Sanctuary of Poseidon & Amphitrite**, a once enormous complex that drew pilgrims in much the same way as the present Church of Panagia Evangelistria does today.

About 12km north of Hora on the north coast is **Kolymvythra Bay**, where there are two sandy beaches, the smaller with sun loungers, umbrellas and a seasonal cafe; the larger backed by reed beds.

On the north coast, 28km northwest of Hora, is the seaside village of **Panormos**, from where the distinctive green marble, quarried in nearby **Marlas**, was once exported. The waterfront at Panormos is lined with tavernas.

Pyrgos, on the way to Panormos, is a handsome village where even the cemetery is a feast of carved marble. Many of the houses have attractive fanlights. During the late 19th and early 20th centuries Pyrgos was the centre of a remarkable tradition of sculpture sustained by the supply of excellent local marble.

Just across the road from the car park at the entrance to Pyrgos is the **Museum House of Yannoulis Halepas** (adult/child €5/2.50; 10.30am-2.30pm & 5-8pm Apr–mid-Oct). It's a fascinating place, where the sculptor's humble rooms and workshop, with their striated plaster walls and slate floors, have been preserved. An adjoining gallery has splendid examples of the work of local sculptors. Outstanding are *Girl on a Rock* by Georgios Vamvakis; *Hamlet* by Loukas Doukas; and a copy of the superb *Fisherman* sculpture by Dimitrios Filippolis.

About 6km directly north of Hora is the tiny village of **Volax**, a scribble of white houses at the heart of an amphitheatre of low hills studded with thousands of dark-coloured boulders. Behind the doorways, Volax really is old Greece. There's a small **folklore museum** (ask at the nearest house for the key), an attractive Catholic chapel and a small outdoor theatre. There are a couple of tavernas, including the recommended **Rokos** (22830 41989; mains €6-9), serving reliable Greek favourites.

The ruins of the Venetian fortress of **Exobourgo** lie 2km south of Volax, on top of a mighty 640m rock outcrop.

SYROS ΣΥΡΟΣ

pop 20,220

Syros is an authentic merging of traditional and modern Greece. It is one of the smallest islands of the Cyclades (its outline bears a quirky resemblance to the British mainland), yet it has the highest population and is the legal and administrative centre of the entire archipelago; the ferry hub of the northern islands; and home to Ermoupolis, the largest and handsomest of all Cycladic towns. If you break the lightest of laws anywhere in the Cyclades, you may end up at court in Syros. Go under your own steam instead and discover one of the most endearing islands in the Aegean, with several attractive beaches, great eating options and the best of everyday Greek life.

History

Excavations of an Early Cycladic fortified settlement and burial ground at Kastri in the island's northeast date from the Neolithic period (2800–2300 BC).

During the medieval period Syros had an overwhelmingly Roman Catholic population. Capuchin monks and Jesuits settled on the island during the 17th and 18th centuries, and such was the Catholic influence that France was called upon by Syros to help it during Turkish rule. Later Turkish influence was benevolent and minimal and Syros busied itself with shipping and commerce.

During the War of Independence thousands of refugees from islands ravaged by the Turks fled to Syros. They brought with them an infusion of Greek Orthodoxy and a fresh commercial drive that made Syros the commercial, naval and cultural centre of Greece during the 19th century. This position was lost to Piraeus in the 20th century. The island's industrial mainstay of shipbuilding has declined, but Syros still has textile manufacturing, a thriving horticultural sector, a sizable administrative and service sector and a small but healthy tourism industry. There is still a local Catholic population.

Getting There & Away

With Syros being of such administrative and social importance there are ferry connections to the mainland ports of Piraeus and Rafina, to neighbouring islands and even to such far-flung destinations as Folegandros. For details see Island Hopping (p524).

Getting Around

About nine buses per day run a circular route from Ermoupolis to Galissas (€1.40, 20 minutes), Vari (€1.40, 30 minutes) and Kini (€1.70, 35 minutes). They leave Ermoupolis every half-hour from June to September and every hour the rest of the year, with alternating clockwise and anticlockwise routes. All of these buses will eventually get you to where you want to go, but it's always worth checking which route is quickest.

There is a bus from Ermoupolis bus station to Ano Syros at 10.30am every morning except Sunday (€1.30, 15 minutes). Taxis (22810 86222) charge €4 to Ano Syros from the port.

A free bus runs along the length of the entire harbour front between car parking at the north and south ends of town about every half-hour from around 7am until late evening. It does not run after 2pm Saturday or on Sunday.

Cars can be hired per day from about €40 and scooters per day from €15 at numerous hire outlets on the waterfront.

SYROS

0 — 2 km
0 — 1 mile

To Andros (57km); Rafina (63km);
Kythnos (74km); Kea (76km)

To Thessaloniki
(460km)

Cape Trimeson

Cape
Diapori

*AEGEAN
SEA*

Grammata
Beach

Kampos

Lia Beach

Kastri

Aetos
Beach

431m

To Tinos (22km);
Mykonos (35km);
Ikaria (75km);
Samos (150km)

Varvarousa

Mytikas

*AEGEAN
SEA*

Delfini
Beach

Pirgos
(440m)

Agios
Georgios

Kini
Beach

Kini

Ano Syros

Vrodado
Ermoupolis

Syros

Danakos

Mt Volakas
(312m)

Lazareto

To Paros (48km);
Naxos (55km);
Ios (102km);
Milos (115km);
Santorini (135km)

Cape
Katakefalos

*Galissas
Bay*
Armeos Beach

Galissas

Pagos

Ano
Manno

Manna

Mesaria

Parakopi

Vissa

Azolimnos
Beach

Finikas
Beach

Finikas

Adiata

Hrousa

Atelio

*Finikas
Bay*
Posidonia
Beach

Posidonia

Mt Axachas
(319m)

Vari

Angathopes
Beach

Vari
Beach

Shinonisi

*Vari
Bay*

Nisi

Strongylo

Megas
Gialos

Megas Gialos
Beach

Cape Viglostasi

To Lavrio (102km); Piraeus
(154km); Crete (244km)

CYCLADES

ERMOUPOLIS ΕΡΜΟΥΠΟΛΗ
pop 13,000

Ermoupolis grew out of the refugee town that sprang up during the Greek War of Independence. The refugees were Greek Orthodox and, after some early antagonism, lived in harmony with the original Catholic majority. In 1826 the town was named formally after Hermes, the god of commerce. Ermoupolis is a lively and likeable place, full of paved stairways, restored neoclassical mansions and handsome public buildings, and has a busy shopping scene.

The Catholic settlement of Ano Syros and the Greek Orthodox settlement of Vrodado lie to the northwest and northeast and both spill down from high hill tops, with even taller hills rising behind.

Orientation

The main ferry quay is at the southwestern end of the port. The bus station is on the waterfront, just along from the main ferry quay.

To reach the central square, Plateia Miaouli, walk northeast from the ferry quay for about 200m, and then turn left into El Venizelou for another 100m. There are three sets of public toilets: at the eastern end of the port, off Antiparou and on Akti Papagou near the ferry quay.

Information

There is an information booth run by the Syros Hotels' Association on the waterfront, about 100m northeast of the main ferry quay; opening times are not guaranteed. The website www.syros.com has a reasonable amount of information.

Alpha Bank (El Venizelou) Has an ATM.

Enjoy Your Holidays (☎ 22810 87070; Akti Papagou 2) Opposite the bus station. Sells ferry tickets and can advise on accommodation.

Eurobank (Akti Ethnikis Andistasis) Has an ATM.

Hospital (☎ 22810 96500; Papandreou)

InSpot (☎ 22810 85330; Akti Papagou; internet per hr €3.40; ☺ 24hr) Fast connections but often monopolised by game fans.

Piraeus Bank (Akti Petrou Ralli) Has an ATM.

Police station (☎ 22810 82610; Plateia Vardaka) Beside the Apollon Theatre.

Port police (☎ 22810 82690/88888; Plateia Laïkis Kyriarchias) On the eastern side of the port.

Post office (Protopapadaki) Western Union money transfer.

Teamwork Holidays (☎ 28810 83400; www.teamwork.gr; Akti Papagou 18) Just across from the main ferry quay. Sells ferry tickets and can arrange accommodation, excursions and car hire.

Sights

The great square of **Plateia Miaouli** is the finest urban space in the Cyclades and is worthy of Athens. Once the sea reached as far as here, but today the square is well inland and is flanked by palm trees and lined along its south side by cafes and bars. The north side of the square is dominated by the dignified neoclassical **town hall**. The small **archaeological museum** (☎ 22810 88487; Benaki; admission €3; ☺ 8.30am-3pm Tue-Sun) at the rear, founded in 1834 and one of the oldest in Greece, houses a tiny collection of ceramic and marble vases, grave stelae and some very fine Cycladic figurines.

The **Industrial Museum of Ermoupolis** (☎ 22810 84764; Papandreos; adult/concession €2.50/1.50, free Wed; ☺ 10am-2pm & 6-9pm Thu-Sun, 10am-2pm Mon & Wed Apr-Sep, 10am-2pm & 5.30-7.30pm Mon, Wed, Sat & Sun, 10-2pm Fri Oct-Mar) is about a kilometre from the centre of town. It celebrates Syros' industrial and shipbuilding traditions and occupies old factory buildings. There are over 300 items on display.

Ano Syros, originally a medieval settlement, has narrow alleyways and whitewashed houses. It is a fascinating place to wander around and has views of neighbouring islands. Be wise and catch the bus up to the settlement. From the bus terminus, head into the steeply rising alleyways and search out the finest of the Catholic churches, the 13th-century **Agios Georgios** cathedral, with its star-fretted barrel roof and baroque capitals. Follow your nose down from the church, past stunning viewpoints to reach the main street.

Activities

Cyclades Sailing (☎ 22810 82501; csail@otenet.gr) can organise yachting charters, as can **Nomikos Sailing** (☎ 22810 88527); call direct or book through Teamwork Holidays (left).

You can also book a day **coach trip** (adult/child €20/7) around the island on Tuesday, Thursday and Saturday through Teamwork Holidays.

Sleeping

Ermoupolis has a reasonably broad selection of rooms, with most budget options clustered above the waterfront near where the ferry docks. Most places are open all year.

CYCLADES

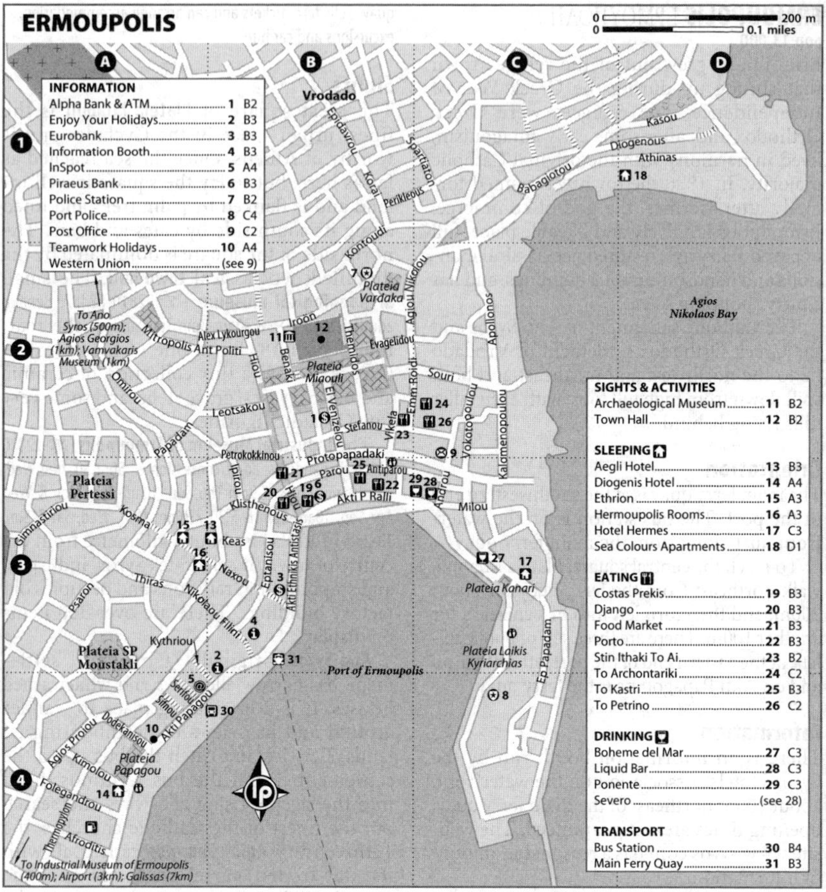
ERMOUPOLIS
0 200 m
0 0.1 miles
INFORMATION
Alpha Bank & ATM 1 B2
Enjoy Your Holidays 2 B3
Eurobank 3 B3
Information Booth 4 B3
InSpot 5 A4
Piraeus Bank 6 B3
Police Station 7 B2
Port Police 8 C4
Post Office 9 C2
Teamwork Holidays 10 A4
Western Union (see 9)
SIGHTS & ACTIVITIES
Archaeological Museum 11 B2
Town Hall 12 B2
SLEEPING
Aegli Hotel 13 B3
Diogenis Hotel 14 A4
Ethrion 15 A3
Hermoupolis Rooms 16 A3
Hotel Hermes 17 C3
Sea Colours Apartments 18 D1
EATING
Costas Prekis 19 B3
Django 20 B3
Food Market 21 B3
Porto 22 B3
Stin Ithaki To Ai 23 B2
To Archontariki 24 C2
To Kastri 25 B3
To Petrino 26 C2
DRINKING
Boheme del Mar 27 C3
Liquid Bar 28 C3
Ponente 29 C3
Severo (see 28)
TRANSPORT
Bus Station 30 B4
Main Ferry Quay 31 B3
Vrodado
Agios Nikolaos Bay
Port of Ermoupolis
Plateia Vardaka
Plateia Miaouli
Plateia Pertessi
Plateia SP Moustakli
Plateia Papagou
Plateia Kanari
Plateia Laikis Kyriarchias
To Ano Syros (500m); Agios Georgios (1km); Vamvakaris Museum (1km)
To Industrial Museum of Ermoupolis (400m); Airport (3km); Galissas (7km)

Hermoupolis Rooms (☎ 22810 87475; Naxou; s/d/tr €35/50/70; ❄) Clean, well-kept rooms tucked away in narrow Naxou, a short climb up from the waterfront. Front rooms open on to tiny, bougainvillea-cloaked balconies.

Ethrion (☎ 22810 89066; www.ethrion.gr; Kosma 24; s €50, d €60-75; ❄ 💻 📶) Close to the harbour front and centre of town yet in a quiet area, Ethrion has comfortable rooms, several having balconies with views over the town. The price range indicates rooms with or without balconies and sea views.

Diogenis Hotel (☎ 22810 86301-5; www.diogenishotel.gr; s/d €73/99; ❄ 📶) Business-class quality is the rule at this well-run, child-friendly waterfront hotel. Breakfast is an extra €10, but is filling. There's a pleasant cafe on the ground floor.

Aegli Hotel (☎ 22810 79279; hotegli@otenet.gr; Klisthenous 14; s/d/tr incl breakfast €83/105/130; ❄ 💻 📶) Located in a quiet side street, yet very close to the centre, this attractive hotel has an air of exclusivity. Rooms are comfortable, and upper-floor balconies at the front have great views over the port. There's a roof garden.

Also recommended:

Hotel Hermes (☎ 22810 83011; fax 22810 87412; Plateia Kanari; s/d/tr incl buffet breakfast €65/100/120; ❄ 📶) The Hermes is a long-established hotel in a fine position on the eastern side of the waterfront.

Sea Colours Apartments (☎ 22810 81181/83400; Athinas; s/d €50/66, apt €72; ❄) These pleasant apartments overlook Agios Nikolaos Bay at the north end of town.

Eating

Standard restaurants and cafes throng the waterfront, especially along Akti Petrou Ralli and on the southern edge of Plateia Miaouli. In quieter corners, however, there are several fine tavernas and restaurants.

Django (☎ 22810 82801; Hiou; snacks from €2.50) This useful little streetside crêperie and snack bar is right at the heart of bustling Hiou and is up and running in the mornings before most cafes. It dishes out sandwiches and hot and cold drinks as well, and has voluptuous tubs of some seriously wicked ice cream.

To Kastri (☎ 22810 83140; Antiparou 13; mains €5-6; ♥ 9am-5pm) Sentiment should never influence the stomach, but this unique eating place deserves support, and the food's great anyway. It's run by an association of local women who cook up a storm of traditional island dishes. They sell an attractive cookery book (with Greek and English editions).

Porto (☎ 22810 81178; Akti Petrou Ralli 48; mains €5-8) The place with the brightly painted tables and chairs midwaterfront, Porto is a classic little *ouzerie* offering a range of seafood dishes including crab and tuna salads, mussels and shrimps. Snails figure also and the pumpkin pie is rich. They do pork and veal dishes as well.

To Petrino (☎ 22810 87427; Stefanou 9; mains €5-17) Swaths of bougainvillea bedeck the pleasant little enclave of Stefanou, and at its heart is the popular To Petrino serving dishes such as small pork chops with mustard sauce, and squid stuffed with feta.

Stin Ithaki to Ai (☎ 22810 82060; Stefanou 1; mains €5.50-8) Try the *flogeres* (pie stuffed with cheese and ham) or main dishes such as *tsoukalaki* (veal baked in a pot with mushrooms and potatoes and a light cheese sauce).

To Archontariki (☎ 22810 81744; Emm Roidi 8; mains €6-18) Classic Greek dishes go well with a fine selection of regional wines, including Santorini vintages, at this long-established restaurant. Starters, such as spinach with mushrooms and leek pie, lead on to inventive mains of veal with plums or prawn tails in ouzo.

The best place to buy fresh produce is at the small but well-stocked morning **food market** (Hiou; ♥ 7am-1pm).

Also on Hiou is **Costas Prekis** (☎ 22810 87556; Hiou 4) a shop with a fine selection of traditional products, including snails, capers, local cheeses, sauces, pasta, jams, dried figs and liqueurs.

ELEFTHERIA *Des Hannigan*

There is a distinctive type of young, modern Greek. Confident, wise, stylish, focused, thoughtful, fearless. And just a little bit scary. They have attitude, in the best sense of the word. On Syros there is Eleftheria Thymianou. She does not let me off with anything. 'That's a great name,' I say. 'Eleftheria equals "freedom". What do they call you for short?' I get the full weight of Greek history in my face. 'No one shortens my name,' she says. 'That name means something…'

Entertainment

Music bars are clustered along the waterfront on Akti Petrou Ralli. They play mostly lounge music by day and a mix of house, funk and modern Greek music by night. They draw a great local crowd and rock into the early hours.

Heading up the young scene is **Boheme del Mar** (☎ 22810 83354), with the also lively **Liquid Bar** (☎ 22810 82284) about 60m to the northwest. Next door to Liquid is **Severo** (☎ 22810 88243), which has a great racy atmosphere and good DJs, while new kid on the block **Ponente** (☎ 6944918748) is a very chilled lounge with all the right sounds.

GALISSAS ΓΑΛΗΣΣΑΣ
pop 120

When Ermoupolis becomes too metro for you, head west on a short bus ride to Galissas, a small resort with one of the best beaches on Syros, several bars and restaurants and some great places to stay. The main bus stop is at an intersection behind the beach.

Sleeping

Two Hearts Camping (☎ 22810 42052; www.twohearts -camping.com; camp sites per adult/child/tent €8/4/4) Set in a pistachio orchard about 400m from the village and beach, this popular camping ground has good facilities. It also rents a range of fixed accommodation from wooden 'tents' to bungalows from €12 to €20 per person. A minibus meets ferries in high season.

Oasis (☎ 22810 42357, 6948274933; freri_stefania@ hotmail.com; s/d/studios €30/45/55; ♀ ☎) A genuine 'oasis', this lovely little farm has bright and airy rooms, and the welcome is charming. It's about 400m back from the village, set amid olive trees and vines. Follow signs from the main bus stop intersection in the village.

CYCLADES

Hotel Benois (☎ 22810 42833; www.benois.gr; s/
d/tr incl breakfast €70/90/110, apt €150; ✖ ☐ ☎ ☎)
A well-run hotel, the Benois has pleasant,
spick-and-span rooms. It's close to the beach
at the northern entrance to the village.

Eating & Drinking

Socrates (☎ 22810 43284; mains €4.50-9) Eat beneath a leafy canopy on the garden terrace
at this well-run place with traditional dishes
including *youvetsi* (choice pieces of lamb in
a tomato sauce, baked with pasta).

Iliovasilema (☎ 22810 43325; mains €5-12) A good
local eatery where fish such as black bream
is by the kilo, but where there are reasonably
priced seafood starters and fish soup.

Savvas (☎ 22810 42998; mains €6-10) Next door
to Iliovasilema, Savvas is distinguished by
locally sourced ingredients and authentic
Syran cuisine; signature dishes include pork
in honey and aniseed.

Also recommended is the Green Dollars
Bar on the beach road, for daytime snacks
and music while you drink. Rock and reggae
are favourites from 10am to 4am.

AROUND SYROS

The beaches south of Galissas all have domatia (rooms, usually in a private home) and
some have hotels. Some beaches are narrow,
roadside strips of dullish sand, but they're
not too busy. They include **Finikas**, **Posidonia**
and **Angathopes**. Back on the main road and
on the south coast proper, the town of **Megas
Gialos** has a couple of roadside beaches.

The pleasant **Vari Bay**, further east,
has a sandy beach with some development, including a couple of hotels and a
beachfront taverna.

Kini Beach, out on its own on the west
coast, north of Galissas, has a long stretch
of beach and is developing into a popular
resort with standard modern hotels, apartments, cafes and tavernas.

MYKONOS ΜΥΚΟΝΟΣ

pop 9660

Mykonos is the great glamour island of the
Cyclades and happily flaunts its camp and
fashionable reputation with style. Beneath
the gloss and glitter, however, this is a
charming and hugely entertaining place
where the sometimes frantic mix of good-
time holidaymakers, cruise-ship crowds, pos-
turing fashionistas and preening celebrities
is magically subdued by the cubist charms of
Mykonos town, a traditional Cycladic maze.
Local people have had 40 years to get a grip
on tourism and have not lost their Greek
identity in doing so.

Be prepared, however, for the oiled-
up lounger lifestyle of the island's packed
main beaches, the jostling street scenes and
the relentless, yet sometimes forlorn, partying.
That said, there's still a handful of off-track
beaches worth fighting for. Plus, the stylish
bars, restaurants and shops have great appeal, and you can still find a quieter pulse
amid the labyrinthine old town. Add to all
this the archaeological splendour of the
nearby island of Delos, and Mykonos really
does live up to its reputation as a fabulous
destination.

Getting There & Away

Mykonos is well served by air connections to
Athens, Thessaloniki and Santorini. There
are also direct Easyjet flights to London from
about May to mid September.

With Mykonos being such a major tourist
destination, ferry connections to the mainland
ports of Piraeus and Rafina are very good,
as are connections to neighbouring islands.
Links south to that other popular destination, Santorini, and to points between are also
excellent.

Mykonos has two ferry quays: the Old Port,
400m north of town, where some conventional ferries and smaller fast ferries dock,
and the New Port, 2km north of town, where
the bigger fast ferries and some conventional
ferries dock. There is no hard-and-fast rule,
and when buying outgoing tickets you should
always double-check which quay your ferry
leaves from.

For further details see Island Hopping
(p518).

Getting Around

TO/FROM THE AIRPORT

Buses from the southern bus station serve
Mykonos' airport (€1.40), which is 3km
southeast of the town centre. Make sure you
arrange an airport transfer with your accommodation (expect to pay around €6) or take
a **taxi** (☎ 22890 22400, airport 22890 23700).

BOAT

Caïque (little boat) services leave Hora
(Mykonos) for Super Paradise, Agrari and Elia

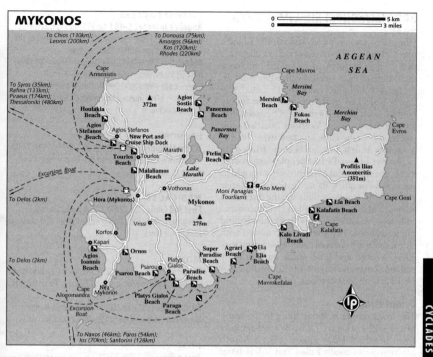

MYKONOS

0 — 5 km
0 — 3 miles

To Chios (130km);
Lesvos (200km)

To Donousa (75km);
Amorgos (96km);
Kos (120km);
Rhodes (220km)

*AEGEAN
SEA*

Cape
Armenistis

Cape Mavros

To Syros (35km);
Rafina (133km);
Piraeus (174km);
Thessaloniki (480km)

*Mersini
Bay*

Houlakia
Beach

372m

Agios
Sostis
Beach

Mersini
Beach

Panormos
Beach

Fokos
Beach

*Merchias
Bay*

Agios
Stefanos
Beach

Agios Stefanos
New Port and
Cruise Ship Dock

*Panormos
Bay*

Cape
Evros

Marathi

Tourlos
Beach

Tourlos

Ftelia
Beach

*Profitis Ilias
Anomeritis
(351m)*

Excursion Boat

Malaliamos
Beach

*Lake
Marathi*

Ano Mera

To Delos (2km)

Vothonas

*Moni Panagias
Tourlianis*

Mykonos

Lia Beach

Kalafatis Beach

Cape Goni

Hora (Mykonos)

275m

Cape
Kalafatis

Vrissi

Korfos

Kalo Livadi
Beach

Kapari

To Delos (2km)

Ornos

Super
Paradise
Beach

Agrari
Beach

Elia

Elia
Beach

Agios
Ioannis
Beach

Psarou

Platys
Gialos

Paradise
Beach

Psarou Beach

*Cape
Mavrokefalas*

Nea
Mykonos

Cape
Alogomandra

Platys Gialos
Beach

Paraga
Beach

Excursion
Boat

To Naxos (46km); Paros (54km);
Ios (70km); Santorini (128km)

CYCLADES

Beaches (June to September only) and from Platys Gialos to Paradise (€7), Super Paradise (€8), Agrari (€7) and Elia (€7) Beaches.

BUS

The Mykonos bus network (☎ 22890 26797; www .ktelmykonos.gr) has two main bus stations and a pick-up point at the New Port. The **northern bus station** (Remezzo) is behind the OTE office and has frequent departures to Agios Stefanos via Tourlos (€1.40), and services to Ano Mera, (€1.40), Elia Beach (€1.70) and Kalafatis Beach (€1.90). Trips range from 20 minutes to 40 minutes. There are buses daily to Kalo Livadi Beach (€1.50). Buses for the New Port, Tourlos and Agios Stefanos stop at the Old Port. The **southern bus station** (Fabrika Sq [Plateia Yialos]) serves Agios Ioannis Beach (€1.40), Ornos, (€1.40), Platys Gialos (€1.40), Paraga (€1.40) and Paradise Beach (€1.40). Trips range from 15 minutes to 40 minutes.

Bus tickets are sold at machines, street kiosks, minimarkets and tourist shops. You must buy a ticket before boarding (buy return tickets if required), validate the ticket on the bus and hang on to it. From 12.15am to 6am all prices are €1.70.

CAR & MOTORCYCLE

For cars, expect to pay (depending on model) from about €45 per day, plus insurances, in high season; €35 in low season. For scooters it starts at €20 to €40 (ATVs) in high season; €15 to €30 in low season. Reliable hire agencies are the Mykonos Accommodation Centre (p150) and **OK Rent A Car** (☎ 22890 23761; Agio Stefanos). There are several car- and motorcycle-hire firms around the southern bus station in Hora.

TAXI

If you're after a **taxi** (☎ 22400 23700/22400), you'll find them at Hora's Taxi Sq (Plateia Manto Mavrogenous) and by the bus stations and ports. The minimum fare is €3, but there's a charge of €0.30 for each item of luggage. Fares from Hora to beaches: Agios Stefanos €8.50, Ornos €8, Platys Gialos €8.70, Paradise €9, Kalafatis €14.70 and Elia €14.70. Add €1.50 for phone booking.

HORA (MYKONOS) ΧΩΡΑ (ΜΥΚΟΝΟΣ)
pop 6467

Hora (also known as Mykonos), the island's port and capital, is a warren of narrow alleyways that wriggle between white-walled buildings, their stone surfaces webbed with white paint. In the heart of the Little Venice area (Venetia), tiny flower-bedecked churches jostle with trendy boutiques, and there's a deluge of bougainvillea around every corner. Without question, you will soon pass the same junction twice. It's entertaining at first, but can become frustrating as throngs of equally lost people, fast moving locals and disdainful Mykonos veterans add to the stress. For quick-fix navigation, familiarise yourself with main junctions and the three main streets of Matogianni, Enoplon Dynameon and Mitropoleos, which form a horseshoe behind the waterfront. The streets are crowded with chic fashion salons, cool galleries, jangling jewellers, languid and loud music bars, brightly painted houses and torrents of crimson flowers – plus a catwalk cast of thousands.

Orientation

The town proper is about 400m to the south of the Old Port ferry quay, beyond the tiny town beach. A busy square, Plateia Manto Mavrogenous (usually called Taxi Sq), is 100m beyond the beach and on the edge of Hora. East of Taxi Sq, the busy waterfront leads towards the Little Venice neighbourhood and the town's iconic hill-top row of windmills. South of Taxi Sq and the waterfront, the busy streets of Matogianni, Zouganelli and Mavrogenous lead into the heart of Hora.

The northern bus station is 200m south of the Old Port ferry quay, on the way into town. The southern bus station is on Fabrika Sq, on the southern edge of town. The quay from where boats leave for Delos is at the western end of the waterfront.

Information

BOOKSHOPS
International Press (☎ 22890 23316; Kambani 5) Numerous international newspapers, although editions are a day late. Also a wide range of magazines and books.

EMERGENCY
Police station (☎ 22890 22716) On the road to the airport.
Port police (☎ 22890 22218; Akti Kambani) Midway along the waterfront.
Tourist police (☎ 22890 22482) At the airport.

INTERNET ACCESS
Angelo's Internet Café (☎ 22890 79138; Xenias; per hr €4; ⏰ 10am-midnight) On the road between the windmills and the southern bus station.
Bolero Bar (☎ 6936322484; Malamatenias; 📶) Free internet for customers. Consoles and wi-fi.
Stairs Café (☎ 22890 26904; Plateia Manto Mavrogenous; 📶) Free internet for customers until 10.30pm. Consoles and wi-fi.

LAUNDRY
White Mykonos (☎ 22890 27600, 6977352531; Xenias; ⏰ 9.30am-2pm & 5-9pm Mon-Fri) Machine wash and dry up to 5kg €10.

MEDICAL SERVICES
First Aid Clinic (☎ 22890 22274; Agiou Ioannou)
Hospital (☎ 22890 23994) Located about 1km along the road to Ano Mera.

MONEY
Several banks by the Old Port quay have ATMs. Eurobank has ATMs at Taxi Sq and Fabrika Sq.
Eurochange (☎ /fax 22890 27024; Plateia Manto Mavrogenous) Money exchange office in Taxi Sq.

POST
Post office (☎ 22890 22238; Laka) In the southern part of town.

TOURIST INFORMATION
Tourist Information Office (☎ 22890 25250; www .mykonos.gr; Plateia Karaoli Dimitriou; ⏰ 9am-9pm Jul & Aug, 10am-5pm Easter-Jun, Sep & Oct) This office is run by the municipality and was launched in 2007.

TRAVEL AGENCIES
Delia Travel (☎ 22890 22322; travel@delia.gr; Akti Kambani) Halfway along the inner waterfront. Sells ferry tickets and tickets for Delos. It's also the French Consulate.
Mykonos Accommodation Centre (☎ 22890 23408; www.mykonos-accommodation.com; 1st fl, Enoplon Dynameon 10) Well organised and very helpful for a range of information. Can also arrange midrange, top-end and gay-friendly accommodation.
Sea & Sky (☎ 22890 22853; Akti Kambani) Information and ferry tickets.
Windmills Travel (☎ 22890 26555; www. windmillstravel.com; Xenias) By the southern bus station on Fabrika Sq, this is another helpful office for all types of information, including gay-related. Also sells ferry tickets.

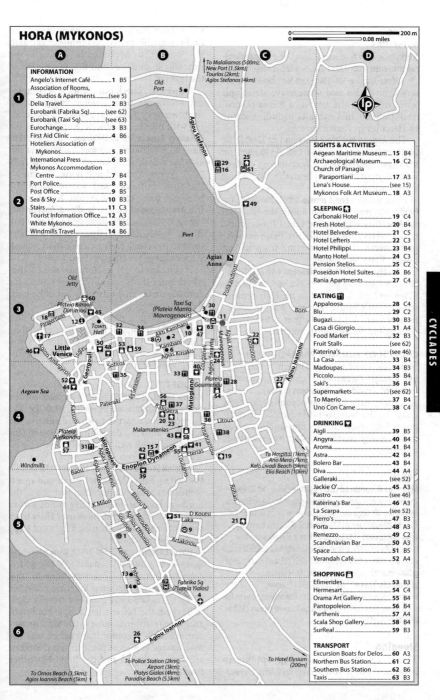

HORA (MYKONOS)

0   200 m
0   0.08 miles

INFORMATION
Angelo's Internet Café	**1** B5
Association of Rooms, Studios & Apartments	(see 5)
Delia Travel	**2** B3
Eurobank (Fabrika Sq)	(see 62)
Eurobank (Taxi Sq)	(see 63)
Eurochange	**3** B3
First Aid Clinic	**4** B6
Hoteliers Association of Mykonos	**5** B1
International Press	**6** B3
Mykonos Accommodation Centre	**7** B4
Port Police	**8** B3
Post Office	**9** B5
Sea & Sky	**10** B3
Stairs	**11** C3
Tourist Information Office	**12** A3
White Mykonos	**13** B5
Windmills Travel	**14** B6

SIGHTS & ACTIVITIES
Aegean Maritime Museum	**15** B4
Archaeological Museum	**16** C2
Church of Panagia Paraportiani	**17** A3
Lena's House	(see 15)
Mykonos Folk Art Museum	**18** A3

SLEEPING
Carbonaki Hotel	**19** C4
Fresh Hotel	**20** B4
Hotel Belvedere	**21** C5
Hotel Lefteris	**22** C3
Hotel Philippi	**23** B4
Manto Hotel	**24** C3
Pension Stelios	**25** C2
Poseidon Hotel Suites	**26** B6
Rania Apartments	**27** C4

EATING
Appaloosa	**28** C4
Blu	**29** C2
Bugazi	**30** B3
Casa di Giorgio	**31** A4
Food Market	**32** B3
Fruit Stalls	(see 62)
Katerina's	(see 46)
La Casa	**33** B4
Madoupas	**34** B3
Piccolo	**35** B4
Saki's	**36** B4
Supermarkets	(see 62)
To Maerio	**37** B4
Uno Con Carne	**38** C4

DRINKING
Aigli	**39** B5
Angyra	**40** B4
Aroma	**41** B4
Astra	**42** B4
Bolero Bar	**43** B4
Diva	**44** A4
Galleraki	(see 52)
Jackie O'	**45** A3
Kastro	(see 46)
Katerina's Bar	**46** A3
La Scarpa	(see 52)
Pierro's	**47** B3
Porta	**48** A3
Remezzo	**49** C2
Scandinavian Bar	**50** A3
Space	**51** B5
Verandah Café	**52** A4

SHOPPING
Efimerides	**53** B3
Hermesart	**54** C4
Orama Art Gallery	**55** B4
Pantopoleion	**56** B3
Parthenis	**57** A4
Scala Shop Gallery	**58** B4
SurReal	**59** B3

TRANSPORT
Excursion Boats for Delos	**60** A3
Northern Bus Station	**61** C2
Southern Bus Station	**62** B6
Taxis	**63** B3

CYCLADES

To Malaliamos (500m);
New Port (1.5km);
Tourlos (2km);
Agios Stefanos (4km)

Old Port

Old Jetty

Plateia Karaoli Dimitriou

Paraportiani

Town Hall

Little Venice

Aegean Sea

Windmills

Plateia Aletfkandra

Port

Agias Anna

Taxi Sq (Plateia Manto Mavrogenous)

Akti Kambani

Kambani

Agias Kiriakis

Plateia Goumenou

Matogianni

Malamatenias

Enoplon Dynameon

D.Koutsi

Laka

Fabrika Sq (Plateia Yialos)

To Hospital (1km);
Ano Mera (7km);
Kalo Livadi Beach (9km);
Elia Beach (10km)

To Hotel Elysium (200m)

Agiou Ioannou

To Ornos Beach (3.5km);
Agios Ioannis Beach (5km)

To Police Station (2km);
Airport (3km);
Platys Gialos (4km);
Paradise Beach (5.5km)

Sights

MUSEUMS

Mykonos has five museums. The **archaeological museum** (☎ 22890 22325; adult/concession €2/1; ☺ 8.30am-3pm Tue-Sat, 10am-3pm Sun) houses pottery from Delos and some grave stelae and jewellery from the island of Renia (Delos' necropolis). Chief exhibits include a statue of Hercules in Parian marble.

The **Aegean Maritime Museum** (☎ 22890 22700; Tria Pigadia; adult/concession €4/1.50; ☺ 10.30am-1pm & 6.30-9pm Apr-Oct) has a fascinating collection of nautical paraphernalia, including ships' models.

Next door, **Lena's House** (☎ 22890 22390; Tria Pigadia; admission €2; ☺ 6.30-9.30pm Mon-Sat, 7-9pm Sun Apr-Oct) is a charming late-19th-century, middle-class Mykonian house (with furnishings intact). It takes its name from its last owner, Lena Skrivanou.

The **Mykonos Folk Art Museum** (☎ 6932178330; Paraportianis; admission free; ☺ 5.30-8.30pm Mon-Sat, 6.30-8.30pm Sun Apr-Oct), housed in an 18th-century sea captain's house, features a large collection of furnishings and other artefacts, including old musical instruments.

CHURCH OF PANAGIA PARAPORTIANI

Mykonos' most famous church is the rock-like **Panagia Paraportiani** (admission free, donations appreciated; ☺ variable, usually open mornings). A rugged, rocky little building beyond Delos ferry quay on the way to Little Venice, it comprises four small chapels plus another on an upper storey that is reached by an outside staircase.

Tours

Mykonos Accommodation Centre (MAC; ☎ 22890 23408; www.mykonos-accommodation.com; 1st fl, Enoplon Dynameon 10) Organises guided tours to Delos (return €15, 30 minutes; see p157). The MAC also runs tours to Tinos (adult/child €58/38), as well as a Mykonos bus tour (adult/child €33/22), island cruise (adult/child €58/33) and a wine and culture tour (adult/child €29/21), and can arrange private charter, including gay-only, boat cruises.

Windmills Travel (☎ 22890 23877; www.windmillstravel.com; Plateia Yialos) The booking agent for snorkelling (€25 for 30 minutes) and island cruises (€50 to €60, four weekly).

Sleeping

There are scores of sleeping options in Mykonos, but if you arrive without a reservation between July and September and you find reasonably priced accommodation, grab it – 'budget' in Mykonos is relative to the generally high prices and this is reflected in the listings.

Otherwise, check out the local accommodation organisations – when you get off at the town ferry quay, you will see a low building with numbered offices. Number 1 is the **Hoteliers Association of Mykonos** (☎ 22890 24540; www.mha.gr; Old Port; ☺ 8am-4pm). The association also has a desk at Mykonos Airport (☎ 22890 25770; ☺ 9am-10pm) and will book a room on the spot, but does not accept telephone bookings prior to your arrival. Number 2 is the **Association of Rooms, Studios & Apartments** (☎ 22890 24860; fax 22890 26860; ☺ 9am-5pm Apr-Oct). If you choose domatia from the owners who meet ferries check their exact location and ask if they charge for transport (some do).

If you plan to stay in Hora and want somewhere quiet, think carefully before settling for domatia on the main streets – bar noise until dawn is inevitable.

Some places only advertise doubles, but single occupancy may be negotiable. During late July and early August some hotels will only accept a minimum of three-night stays.

BUDGET

Manto Hotel (☎ 22890 22330; www.manto-mykonos.gr; Agias Anna; s/d/tr incl breakfast €75/100/125; ✖) Buried in the heart of town and close to the action, Manto is a decent budget option (for Mykonos), with well-kept rooms and a pleasant breakfast room.

Pension Stelios (☎ 22890 24641, 6944273556; s/d/tr €90/100/130) Fairly basic but clean and quiet, Stelios has a hillside location just above the northern bus station about five minutes from Taxi Sq. There are great views over Hora from some of the small balconies. Flights of steps lead to the pension.

Hotel Lefteris (☎ 22890 27117; www.lefterishotel.gr; Apollonos 9; s/d €90/115, studios €190-240; ✖) A colourful entranceway sets the tone for this welcoming international meeting place for all ages. Tucked away from the crowds, close to Taxi Sq, the Lefteris has simple but bright and comfy rooms, most with fans or air-con. There is a communal kitchen and the roof terrace is a great place to relax. Studios are well equipped and the hotel has other rooms nearby.

MIDRANGE

Hotel Philippi (☎ 22890 22294; chriko@otenet.gr; Kalogera 25; s/d €90/125; ✷ ☎) A pleasant garden full of trees, flowers and shrubs makes this a good choice in the heart of Hora. There's an appealing ambience in the bright, clean rooms that open onto a railed veranda overlooking the garden. Rooms have tea- and coffee-making facilities.

Rania Apartments (☎ 22890 28272/3; www.rania-mykonos.gr; Leondiou Boni 2; s €105, d €135-195, tr €210-220, q €255-285, apt €365; ✷ ☎) A great location high above the harbour means a bit of an uphill walk from town, but the apartments are easily accessed from Agiou Ioannou, the 'ring road'. In a lovely garden setting, the accommodation is charming and well appointed. Facilities include hot plate and coffeemaker.

Poseidon Hotel-Suites (☎ 22890 22437; www.poseidonhotelmykonos.gr; Agiou Ioannou; s €110-141, d 130-166, tr/ste 186/319; ℗ ✷ ☎ ✷) One of the best locations in Mykonos, the Poseidon is located overlooking the sea and is within a few minutes' walk along the shore to Windmill Hill. Standard rooms are more than adequate and the newer suites are plush and overlook the attractive pool area.

our pick Carbonaki Hotel (☎ 22890 24124/22461; www.carbonaki.gr; 23 Panahrantou St; s/d/tr/q €120/160/200/240; ✷ ☎) This family-run boutique hotel, right on the edge of central Mykonos, has a delightful ambience and charming owners. Rooms are comfortable and bright and there are relaxing public balconies dotted round the pleasant central courtyards. A Jacuzzi and small sauna were being added at time of research. Breakfast is €10.

Fresh Hotel (☎ 22890 24670; www.mariashotel-mykonos.com; Kalogera 31; s/d incl breakfast €130/170; ✷ ▯ ☎) Previously Mario's Hotel, the gay-friendly Fresh is located right in the heart of town and is handy for all the action. There's a pleasant central garden, an attractive breakfast room and bar, and a Jacuzzi. Rooms have wooden floors and furnishings are a pleasant mix of old and new.

TOP END

Hotel Elysium (☎ 22890 23952; www.elysiumhotel.com; s €260-340, d €310-400, tr €480-560; ☺ Apr-Oct; ℗ ✷ ▯ ✷) Located high above the main town in the School of Fine Arts area, this stylish gay hotel (although nongays are also welcome) has cool decor and good-sized comfortable rooms. There are plenty of special trimmings, including personal computers in suites and deluxe rooms, and a spa and massage service.

Hotel Belvedere (☎ 22890 25122; www.belvederehotel.com; Rohari; d €280-2000; ℗ ✷ ▯ ☎ ✷) It's all billowing drapes and white linen amid the modernist landscape and furnishings of this leading Mykonos hotel. The Belvedere has had a major refurbishment in recent years. Jacuzzis, massage therapy, a fitness studio, and music and movie facilities seal the deal. Within the complex is the Matsuhisa Restaurant, under the aegis of the noted Japanese chef, Nobu Matsuhisa; and the Belvedere Restaurant, recently renovated and with a menu created by the equally noted Australian-Greek chef, George Calombaris.

Eating

High prices don't necessarily reflect high quality in many Mykonos eateries. There are, however, excellent good-value restaurants of all kinds.

BUDGET

Piccolo (☎ 22890 22208; Drakopoulou 18; snacks €3.90-7.80) There are no linen-draped tables at this little food outlet, but the food is first class and ranges from crisp salads to a great selection of sandwich fillings that include Mykonian prosciutto, *manouri* (soft cheese), smoked local ham, smoked eel and crab.

Madoupas (☎ 22890 22224; mains €7-12) Walk into Madoupas of a Sunday morning and all of local Mykonos is there. This is the place for morning coffee or for big helpings of good Greek standards for as little as €7. The evening menu has a broader choice.

There's also a cluster of cheap fast-food outlets and crêperies around town:

Bugazi (☎ 22890 24066; snacks €4.60-6.70) Good selection of crêpes, just off the edge of Taxi Sq.

Saki's (☎ 22890 24848; Agion Saranta) A popular place with locals, Saki's dishes out kebabs and souvlaki for €2.50, and other budget fillers for €5 to €7.

There are supermarkets and fruit stalls, particularly around the southern bus station area, and there's a food and fish market on the waterfront where Mykonos' famous pelicans hang out.

MIDRANGE & TOP END

La Casa (☎ 22890 24994; Matogianni 8; mains €9.90-18.90) The classic La Casa has a strong Greek basis with Italian, Arabic and Lebanese influences. Starters of smoked cheeses with mushrooms and inventive salads – including a Mykonian special with *louza* (local smoked ham), local prosciutto cheeses and rocket – lead on to mains such as pork fillet with mustard, *pleurotus* mushrooms and tarragon.

our pick **Katerina's** (☎ 22890 23084; Agion Anargyron; mains €11-25) The famous Katerina's Bar, whose eponymous matriarch was celebrated in the 1950s as Greece's first female boat skipper at age 18, has now branched out with its own small restaurant. There's a thoughtful and creative menu of crisp salads and starters such as prawn *saganaki* (skillet-fried) or wild Porcini mushrooms. Mains include fresh sea bass or mixed seafood plate for two (€50) or vegetarian options. The balcony view is to die for, of course, as is the 'Chocolate from Heaven' sweet.

Blu (☎ 22890 22955; mains €12-24) Just along from the Old Port on the way into town, this stylish place has an attractive terrace with a great view of the harbour. A subtle menu includes such starters as sautéed mushrooms in sweet wine and cumin sauce, and mains of veal fillet in Marsala wine with dark rice. Fish is by the kilo and the wine list is well chosen. The adjoining Blu-Blu cafe has internet.

To Maereio (☎ 22890 28825; Kalogera 16; dishes €14-21) A small, but selective menu of Mykonian favourites keeps this cosy little place popular. The mainly meat and poultry dishes can be preceded by salad mixes that include apple and pear, yoghurt and a balsamic vinegar sauce.

Uno Con Carne (☎ 6944479712; Panachra; mains €19-98) Recently opened as Mykonos' major place for meateaters, this big, stylish space knows how to prepare the best steaks, from prime Chateaubriand and South American Pichana 'Black Angus' to Tyson T-bone and mouth-melting 'proper' hamburger. Starters of scampi tartare or gazpacho prepare for the main feast and you can cool the palate later with sorbet or ice cream. Lamb and chicken dishes also feature.

Also recommended:

Appaloosa (☎ 22890 27086; Mavrogenous 1, Plateia Goumeniou; mains €8.50-29) International cuisine with Mexican and Indonesian influences. A hot line in tequila and cocktails goes with cool music.

Casa di Giorgio (☎ 6932561998; Mitropoleos; mains €12-22) A good range of pizzas and pastas, as well as meat and seafood dishes, served on a big terrace.

Drinking

Hora's Little Venice quarter is not exactly the Grand Canal, but it does offer the Mediterranean at your feet as well as rosy sunsets, windmill views, glowing candles and a swath of colourful bars. The music meanders through smooth soul and easy listening, but can ear crunch you at times with shattering decibel rivalries.

A good spot is **Galleraki** (☎ 22890 27188), which turns out superb cocktails. Nearby, it's the sunset view at **Verandah Café** (☎ 22890 27400), while **La Scarpa** (☎ 22890 23294) lets you lean back from the sea on its cosy cushions. Further north, **Katerina's Bar** (☎ 22890 23084; Agion Anargyron) has a cool balcony and eases you into the evening's action with relaxing sounds.

Deeper into town, the relentlessly stylish **Aroma** (☎ 22890 27148; Enoplon Dynameon; ⏰ breakfast-late) sits on a strategic corner, providing the evening catwalk view. It's open for breakfast and coffee as well. Just across the way, down an alleyway is **Bolero Bar** (☎ 6936322484; Malamatenias) a longstanding favourite, frequented in its time by such stellar celebs as Keith Richards.

Further down Enoplon Dynameon is **Astra** (☎ 22890 24767), where the decor is modernist Mykonos at its best, and where some of Athens' top DJs feed the ambience with rock, funk, house and drum'n'bass. Just across from Astra, cocktail-cool **Aigli** (☎ 22890 27265) has another useful terrace for people watching. Matogianni has a couple of music bars, including **Angyra** (☎ 22890 24273), which sticks with easy listening and mainstream.

Scandinavian Bar (☎ 22890 22669; Ioanni Voinovich 9) is mainstream mayhem with ground-floor bars and a space upstairs for close-quarters moving to retro dance hits.

For big action into the dawn, **Space** (☎ 22890 24100; Laka) is the place. The night builds superbly through a mix of techno, house and progressive, and the bar-top dancing fires up the late-night action. **Remezzo** (☎ 22890 24100; Polykandrioti) is run by the Space team but features lounge and dance for a more relaxing scene. Entry is around €20 to each of the clubs.

GAY BARS

Mykonos is one of the world's great gay-friendly destinations. Gay life is less overt here, but Hora has many gay-centric clubs and hang-outs from where the late-night crowds spill out onto the streets.

Kastro (☎ 22890 23072; Agion Anargyron) With a leaning towards stylish classical sounds, this is a good place to start the night on cocktails as the sun sets on Little Venice.

Jackie O' (☎ 22890 79167; www.jackieomykonos .com; Plateia Karaoli Dimitriou) Hottest gay bar in Mykonos in 2009, Jacki O' seems set to hold centre stage for some time yet. Straight-friendly and with a fabulous vibe revved up by fabulous shows.

Diva (☎ 22890 27271; K Georgouli) A great up-beat atmosphere makes this a Mykonos favourite with a mixed crowd and a loyal lesbian core.

Porta (☎ 22890 27807; Ioanni Voinovich) Head downstairs into Porta's cruisey ambi-ence where things get crowded and cosy towards midnight.

Pierro's (☎ 22890 22177; Agias Kiriakis) Long-standing last stop for the nightwatch, where things round off with a backdrop of heavy-beat house and superbly over-the-top drag action in upstairs Ikaros. Can take over the outdoors, also.

Shopping

Style and art venues vie for attention through-out Hora's streets and include authentic Lacoste, Dolce & Gabbana, Naf Naf, Diesel and Body Shop. Clothes hanging apart, there are some stand-out venues worth seeking out.

Scala Shop Gallery (☎ 22890 26992; www .scalagallery.gr; Matogianni 48) Scala is one of the more stylish galleries of Mykonos. It stages changing displays of fine art and also sells contemporary jewellery and ceramics. The owner, Dimitris Rousounelos, is an ac-complished writer on Mykonos traditions. His book, *Tastes of Sacrifice*, on sale at the gallery, gives a trenchant and evocative view of Mykonian life beyond the gloss of fashionable tourism.

Parthenis (☎ 22890 23089; Plateia Alefkandra) Featuring the distinctive couture – in black-and-white only – of Athens de-signer and long-time Mykonos resident Dimitris Parthenis.

Hermesart (☎ 22890 24652; Plateia Goumenio) There's some quirky and appealing art at this small gallery, with smaller pieces at affordable prices.

Orama Art Gallery (☎ 22890 26339; Fournakia) Just off Enoplon Dynameon, Orama shows the highly original work of Louis Orosko and Dorlies Schapitz.

Pantopoleion (☎ 22890 22078; Kalogera 24) A genuine all-organic grocery with products covering just about every need from fresh fruit and vegetables, cheese, pasta and bread to herbal cosmetics and even organic cleaning products and books on all things organic.

For original gift ideas try **Efimerides** (☎ 22890 79180; Drakopoulou 4) with its selec-tion of objets d'art, while opposite is **SurReal** (☎ 22890 28323; Drakopoulou 1), which specialises in leaflike leatherware.

AROUND MYKONOS
Beaches

Mykonos has a good number of beaches and most have golden sand in attractive loca-tions. They're not big enough, though, that you'll escape from the crowds, and they're extremely popular and busy, especially from June onwards. Don't expect seclu-sion, although there can be a distinct sense of *exclusion* as various cliques commandeer the sun loungers, while segregation zones of style and sheer snobbery dominate at some locations.

You need to be a party person for the likes of Paradise and Super Paradise. It can all get very claustrophobic, but it's heaven for the gregarious. Most beaches have a varied clien-tele, and attitudes to toplessness and nudity also vary, but what's accepted at each beach is obvious when you get there.

An excellent guide to island beaches and their specific or mixed clientele can be found on the beaches link of www.mykonos-acc ommodation.com.

The nearest beaches to Hora (Mykonos), which are also the island's least glamorous beaches, are **Malaliamos**; the tiny and crowded **Tourlos**, 2km to the north; and **Agios Stefanos**, 4km. About 3.5km south of Hora is the packed and noisy **Ornos**, from where you can hop onto boats for other beaches. Just west is **Agios Ioannis**. The sizable package-holiday resort of **Platys Gialos** is 4km from Hora on the southwest coast. All of the above beaches are family orientated.

Platys Gialos is the caïque jumping-off point for the glitzier beaches to the east, such as Paradise and Super Paradise.

CYCLADES

Approximately a kilometre south of Platys Gialos you'll find the pleasant **Paraga Beach**, which has a small gay section. About 2km east of here is the famous **Paradise**, which is not a recognised gay beach, but has a lively younger scene. **Super Paradise** (aka **Plintri** or **Super P**) has a fully gay section. Mixed and gay-friendly **Elia** is the last caïque stop, and a few minutes' walk from here is the small and pleasant **Agrari**. Nudity is fairly commonplace on all of these beaches.

North-coast beaches can be exposed to the *meltemi* (northeasterly wind), but **Panormos** and **Agios Sostis** are fairly sheltered and becoming more popular. Both have a mix of gay and nongay devotees.

For out-of-the-way beaching you need to head for the likes of **Lia** on the southeast coast, or the smaller **Fokos** and **Mersini** on the east coast, but you'll need tough wheels and undercarriage to get there.

ACTIVITIES

Dive Adventures (☎ 22890 26539; www.diveadventures .gr; Paradise Beach) offers a full range of diving courses with multilingual instructors. Two introductory dives cost €130; snorkelling costs €30. There are various dive packages starting with a five-dive deal for €225 and PADI certification courses are available.

On a great location at Kalafatis Beach, **Planet Windsailing** (☎ 22890 72345; www.pezi-huber. com) has a one-hour or one-day windsurfing for €26 or €60, respectively, or a three-hour beginner's course for €75.

Also at Kalafatis, the **Kalafati Dive Center** (☎ 22890 71677; www.mykonos-diving.com) has the full range of diving courses including a 10-boat-dive deal with tank and weights for €290 and with full gear for €390. A single boat dive with tank and weights costs €45, or with all equipment €60. A 'discover scuba diving' session is €45. There's a 10% discount for prepaid bookings.

SLEEPING

Mykonos Camping (☎ 22890 24578; www.mycamp.gr; camp sites per adult/child/tent €10/5/5, bungalows per person €15-30, apt €180-235) This budget option is by the pleasant Paraga Beach (a 10-minute walk from Platys Gialos). Total peace and privacy cannot be guaranteed but facilities are reasonable and there are also bungalows and apartments that sleep two to six people.

Twins Apartments (☎ 22890 26241; www.twins-mykonos. com; d/tr/q €130/145/160; 🖳) Located close to Ornos beach, these bright, spacious apartments are ideal for families and have cooking facilities.

Princess of Mykonos (☎ 22890 23806; www.princess ofmykonos.gr; s €200, d €220-280, tr €245-320 incl breakfast; 🅿 🖳 🖳 🖳) Sea-view rooms are the most expensive at this swish hotel, which merges traditional island style with Art Deco touches. The hotel is above the often busy Agios Stefanos beach.

EATING

our pick **Christos** (☎ 22890 26850; Agios Ioannis Beach; mains €6-18) Fisherman, chef and sculptor Christos runs his beachside eatery with unassuming style. It's right on the 'Shirley Valentine' shoreline, but Christos really is authentic Mykonos, where the best fish and seafood, not least unbeatable *astakos* (crawfish or spiny lobster), is prepared with skill.

Tasos Trattoria (☎ 22890 23002; Paraga Beach; mains €9-19) Central to Paraga Beach, this popular taverna does terrific fish, chicken, pork and veal dishes and a great mix of vegie options.

ENTERTAINMENT

Cavo Paradiso (☎ 22890 27205; www.cavoparadiso.gr) When dawn gleams just over the horizon, hard-core bar-hopper s move from Hora (Mykonos) to Cavo Paradiso, the megaclub that's been blasting at Paradise Beach since 1993 and has featured top international DJs ever since, including house legends David Morales and Louie Vega.

Ano Mera Ανω Μέρα
pop 1310

The village of Ano Mera, 7km east of Hora, is the island's only inland settlement and is worth a passing visit as an antidote to Hora and the beaches. It's a fairly unassuming place with a big central square flanked on three sides by tavernas offering standard fare. There's a big car park adjoining the main square.

The 6th-century **Moni Panagias Tourlianis** (☎ 22890 71249; ⏱ 9am-1pm & 2-7.30pm) has a fine, multistage, marble bell tower with elegant carvings and 16th-century icons painted by members of the Cretan School, but pride of place goes to an exquisite wooden iconostasis carved in Florence in the late 1700s.

DELOS ΔΗΛΟΣ

The Cyclades fulfil their collective name (*kyklos*) by encircling the sacred island of **Delos** (☎ 22890 22259; museum & sites adult/concession €5/3; ☒ 8.30am-3pm Tue-Sun), but Mykonos clutches the island jealously to its heart. Delos has no permanent population and is a soothing contrast to the relentless liveliness of modern Mykonos, although in high summer you share it all with fellow visitors. The island is one of the most important archaeological sites in Greece and the most important in the Cyclades. It lies a few kilometres off the west coast of Mykonos.

Delos still hides its secrets and every now and then fresh discoveries are made. In recent years a gold workshop was uncovered alongside the Street of the Lions.

History

Delos won early acclaim as the mythical birthplace of the twins Apollo and Artemis and was first inhabited in the 3rd millennium BC. From the 8th century BC it became a shrine to Apollo, and the oldest temples on the island date from this era. The dominant Athenians had full control of Delos – and thus the Aegean – by the 5th century BC.

In 478 BC Athens established an alliance known as the Delian League, which kept its treasury on Delos. A cynical decree ensured that no one could be born or die on Delos, thus strengthening Athens' control over the island by expelling the native population.

Delos reached the height of its power in Hellenistic times, becoming one of the three most important religious centres in Greece and a flourishing centre of commerce. Many of its inhabitants were wealthy merchants, mariners and bankers from as far away as Egypt and Syria. They built temples to their homeland gods, but Apollo remained the principal deity.

The Romans made Delos a free port in 167 BC. This brought even greater prosperity, due largely to a lucrative slave market that sold up to 10,000 people a day. During the following century, as ancient religions lost relevance and trade routes shifted, Delos began a long, painful decline. By the 3rd century AD there was only a small Christian settlement on the island, and in the following centuries the ancient site was looted of many of its antiquities. It was not until the Renaissance that its antiquarian value was recognised.

Getting There & Away

Boats for Delos (return €15, 30 minutes) leave Hora (Mykonos) about six times a day from about 9am in high season with the last outward boat about 12.50pm. Departure and return times are posted on the ticket kiosk at the entrance to the Old Jetty at the south end of the harbour. There are fewer boats outside July and August. There are no boats on Monday when the site is closed. Boats return from the island between 11am and 3pm. When buying tickets establish which boat is available for your return, especially later in the day. In Hora (Mykonos), **Delia Travel** (☎ 22890 22322; travel@delia.gr; Akti Kambani) and the **Mykonos Accommodation Centre** (☎ 22890 23408; www.mykonos-accommodation.com; 1st fl, Enoplon Dynameon 10) sell tickets. You pay an entrance fee of €3 at a kiosk on the island.

The Mykonos Accommodation Centre organises guided tours to Delos at 10am every day except Monday, between May and September (adult/child €40/31, three hours). They include boat transfers from and to the Old Jetty, and admission to the site and museum. Tours are in English, French, German and Italian, and in Spanish and Russian on request.

A boat departs for Delos from Platys Gialos on Mykonos' (€14, 30 minutes) at 10.15am daily.

ANCIENT DELOS

The quay where excursion boats dock is south of the tranquil Sacred Harbour. Many of the most significant finds from Delos are in the National Archaeological Museum (p81) in Athens, but the site **museum** still has an interesting collection, including the lions from the Terrace of the Lions (those on the terrace itself are plaster-cast replicas).

Overnight stays on Delos are forbidden and boat schedules allow a maximum of about six or seven hours there. Bring water and food, as the cafeteria's offerings are poor value for money. Wear a hat and sensible shoes.

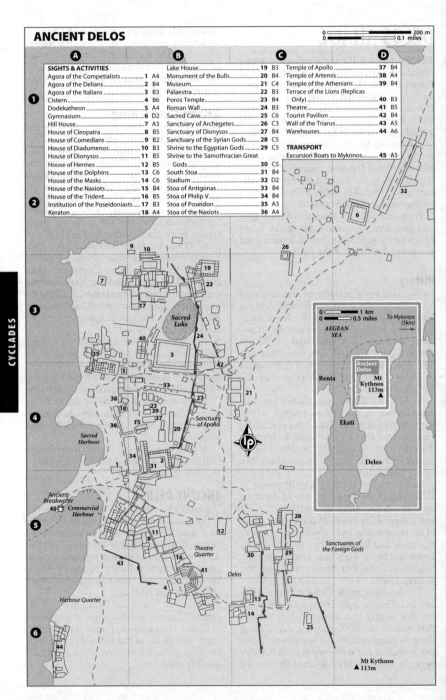

ANCIENT DELOS

SIGHTS & ACTIVITIES
Agora of the Competialists	**1** A4
Agora of the Delians	**2** B4
Agora of the Italians	**3** B3
Cistern	**4** B6
Dodekatheon	**5** A4
Gymnasium	**6** D2
Hill House	**7** A3
House of Cleopatra	**8** B5
House of Comedians	**9** B2
House of Diadumenos	**10** B3
House of Dionysos	**11** B5
House of Hermes	**12** B5
House of the Dolphins	**13** C6
House of the Masks	**14** C6
House of the Naxiots	**15** B4
House of the Trident	**16** B5
Institution of the Poseidoniasts	**17** B3
Keraton	**18** A4
Lake House	**19** B3
Monument of the Bulls	**20** B4
Museum	**21** C4
Palaestra	**22** B3
Poros Temple	**23** B4
Roman Wall	**24** B3
Sacred Cave	**25** C6
Sanctuary of Archegetes	**26** C3
Sanctuary of Dionysos	**27** B4
Sanctuary of the Syrian Gods	**28** C5
Shrine to the Egyptian Gods	**29** C5
Shrine to the Samothracian Great Gods	**30** C5
South Stoa	**31** B4
Stadium	**32** D2
Stoa of Antigonas	**33** B4
Stoa of Philip V	**34** B4
Stoa of Poseidon	**35** A3
Stoa of the Naxiots	**36** A4
Temple of Apollo	**37** B4
Temple of Artemis	**38** A4
Temple of the Athenians	**39** B4
Terrace of the Lions (Replicas Only)	**40** B3
Theatre	**41** B5
Tourist Pavilion	**42** B4
Wall of the Triarus	**43** A5
Warehouses	**44** A6

TRANSPORT
Excursion Boats to Mykonos	**45** A5

Exploring the Site

The following is an outline of some significant archaeological remains on the site. For further details, a guidebook from the ticket office is advisable, or take a guided tour.

The rock-encrusted **Mt Kythnos** (113m) rises elegantly to the southeast of the harbour. It's worth the steep climb, even in the heat; on clear days there are terrific views of the surrounding islands from its summit.

The path to Mt Kythnos is reached by walking through the **Theatre Quarter**, where Delos' wealthiest inhabitants once built their houses. These houses surrounded peristyle courtyards, with colourful mosaics (a status symbol) being the most striking feature of each house.

The most lavish dwellings were the **House of Dionysos**, named after the mosaic depicting the wine god riding a panther, and the **House of Cleopatra**, where headless statues of the owners were found. The **House of the Trident** was one of the grandest. The **House of the Masks**, probably an actors' hostelry, has another mosaic of Dionysos resplendent astride a panther. The **House of the Dolphins** has another exceptional mosaic.

The **theatre** dates from 300 BC and had a large **cistern**, the remains of which can be seen. It supplied much of the town with water. The houses of the wealthy had their own cisterns – essential as Delos was almost as parched and barren then as it is today.

Descending from Mt Kythnos, explore the **Sanctuaries of the Foreign Gods**. Here, at the **Shrine to the Samothracian Great Gods**, the Kabeiroi (the twins Dardanos and Aeton) were worshipped. At the **Sanctuary of the Syrian Gods** there are the remains of a theatre where an audience watched ritual orgies. There is also the **Shrine to the Egyptian Gods**, where Egyptian deities including Serapis and Isis were worshipped.

The **Sanctuary of Apollo**, to the northeast of the harbour, is the site of the much-photographed **Terrace of the Lions**. These proud beasts, carved from marble, were offerings from the people of Naxos, presented to Delos in the 7th century BC to guard the sacred area. To the northeast is the **Sacred Lake** (dry since it was drained in 1925 to prevent malarial mosquitoes breeding) where, according to legend, Leto gave birth to Apollo and Artemis.

PAROS ΠΑΡΟΣ

pop 13,000

Paros has a friendly, welcoming face. Its rolling hills are less formidable than the genuine mountains of neighbouring Naxos, and their slopes rise smoothly to the central high point of Mt Profitis Ilias (770m). White marble made Paros prosperous from the Early Cycladic period onwards – most famously, the *Venus de Milo* was carved from Parian marble, as was Napoleon's tomb.

Busy Parikia is the main town and port. The other major settlement, Naousa, on the north coast, is a lively resort with a still-active fishing harbour. On the east coast is the engaging little port and low-key resort of Piso Livadi, while deep at the heart of Paros is the peaceful mountain village of Lefkes.

The smaller island of Antiparos, 1km southwest of Paros, is easily reached by car ferry or excursion boat.

Getting There & Away

Paros is the main ferry hub for onward travel to other islands in the Aegean. It is thus well served by regular ferries from Piraeus and by connections to and from most of the other islands of the eastern Cyclades, and also Thessaloniki, Crete and the Dodecanese. For details see Island Hopping (p519).

Getting Around

BOAT

Water taxis leave from the quay for beaches around Parikia. Tickets range from €8 to €15 and are available on board.

BUS

About 12 buses daily link Parikia and Naousa (€1.40) directly, and there are seven buses daily from Parikia to Naousa via Dryos, Hrysi Akti, Marpissa, Marmara, Prodromos, Lefkes, Kostos and Marathi. There are 10 buses to Pounta (for Antiparos; €1.40) and six to Aliki (via the airport; €1.40).

CAR, MOTORCYCLE & BICYCLE

There are rental outlets along the waterfront in Parikia and all around the island. A good outfit is **Acropolis** (☎ 22840 21830). Minimum hire per day in August for a car is about €45; for a motorbike it's €20.

CYCLADES

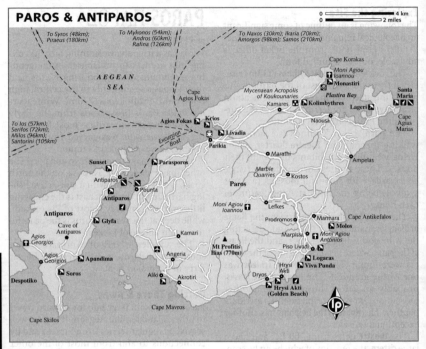

PAROS & ANTIPAROS

0 — 4 km
0 — 2 miles

To Syros (48km);
Piraeus (180km)

To Mykonos (54km);
Andros (60km);
Rafina (126km)

To Naxos (30km); Ikaria (70km);
Amorgos (98km); Samos (210km)

AEGEAN
SEA

Cape Korakas

Moni Agiou
Ioannou

Monastiri

Santa
Maria

Cape
Agios Fokas

Mycenaean Acropolis
of Koukounaries

Plastira Bay

Kamares   Kolimbythres

Lageri

Cape
Agias
Marias

To Ios (57km);
Serifos (72km);
Milos (96km);
Santorini (105km)

Agios Fokas   Krios

Livadia

Naousa

Excursion
Boat

Parikia

Marathi

Ampelas

Sunset

Parasporos

Marble
Quarries

Kostos

Antiparos

Pounta

Paros

Antiparos

Moni Agiou
Ioannou

Lefkes

Prodromos

Marmara

Cape Antikefalos

Antiparos

Glyfa

Kamari

Molos

Cave of
Antiparos

Marpissa

Moni Agiou
Antoniou

Agios
Georgios

Angeria

Mt Profitis
Ilias (770m)

Piso Livadi

Agios
Georgios

Apandima

Logaras

Soros

Aliki

Akrotiri

Dryos

Hrysi
Akti

Viva Punda

Despotiko

Hrysi Akti
(Golden Beach)

Cape Skilos

Cape Mavros

TAXI

Taxis (☎ 22840 21500) gather beside the roundabout in Parikia. Fixed fares: airport €12, Naousa €10, Pounta €8, Lefkes €10 and Piso Livadi €13. Add €1 if going from the port. There are extra charges of €2 if you book ahead more than 20 minutes beforehand, €3 if less than 20 minutes. Each piece of luggage is charged €0.30.

PARIKIA ΠΑΡΟΙΚΙΑ
pop 4522

Parikia is a lively, colourful place full of the comings and goings of a typical island port but enhanced by a labyrinthine old town, 13th-century Venetian *kastro* (fort) and a long, straggling waterfront crammed with tavernas, bars and cafes.

Orientation

The busy hub of Parikia is the windmill roundabout, where you come off the ferry quay. The large main square, Plateia Mavrogenous, refurbished in 2007–08, is straight ahead from the windmill. The busy road to the left (east) leads along the water-

front to the beach at Livadia. The road to the right (south) follows the waterfront past a long line of cafes and tavernas and on towards Pounta (for Antiparos) and the south of the island.

Agora (Market St) is the main commercial thoroughfare running southwest from Plateia Mavrogenous through the narrow and pedestrianised streets of the old town and up into the area known as Kastro, where the Venetian *kastro* once stood.

The bus station is 50m to the right of the quay (looking inland) and the post office is 400m to the left.

A free, green by nature, green in colour bus – powered by electricity – runs around Parikia at regular intervals from early morning until late evening all year; a laudable energy-saving strategy by the local authority, it is reportedly well-used by locals at all times.

Information
BOOKSHOPS

Newsstand (Ekatondapylianis) A great selection of newspapers, magazines and books in all languages.

EMERGENCY

Police station (☎ 22840 23333; Plateia Mavrogenous)
Port police (☎ 22840 21240) Back from the northern waterfront, near the post office.

INTERNET ACCESS

Wired Café (☎ 22840 22003; Agora; per hr €3.50; 🕙 10.30am-2pm & 6-11pm Mon-Sat, 6-11pm Sun) Reliable internet access in a relaxed atmosphere. Also has webcam and connections for laptop computers, and digital-picture transfer.

INTERNET RESOURCES

Parosweb (www.parosweb.com)

LAUNDRY

Ostria Laundry (☎ 22840 21969, 6949079176; per wash & dry per 5kg around €12; 🕙 9am-9pm Mon-Sat, 10am-2pm Sun Jun-Sep, 9am-2pm & 5.30-8.30pm Oct-May) The average load is ready in one hour at this efficient place.

MEDICAL SERVICES

Health Centre (☎ 22840 22500; Prombona; 🕙 9am-1.30pm Mon-Fri) Also has a dentist.

MONEY

The following banks all have ATMs.
Alpha Bank (Ekantondapylianis)
Commercial Bank of Greece (Plateia Mavrogenous)
Eurobank (Ekantondapylianis)
National Bank of Greece (Plateia Mavrogenous)

POST

Post office (☎ 22840 21236) Located 400m east of the ferry quay.

TOURIST INFORMATION

In high season, kiosks on the quay give out information on domatia and hotels (see Rooms Association, right).

TRAVEL AGENCIES

Santorineos Travel Services (☎ 22840 24245) On the waterfront, just to the southwest of the windmill roundabout. Sells ferry tickets and can advise on accommodation and tours, and has a luggage store (€1 per hour). Other services include bureau de change, FedEx (dispatch only) and MoneyGram (international money transfers).

Sights

The **Panagia Ekatondapyliani** (☎ 22840 21243; Plateia Ekatondapyliani; 🕙 7.30am-9.30pm Easter-Sep, 8am-1pm & 4-9pm Oct-Easter), which dates from AD 326, is one of the most splendid churches in the Cyclades. The building is three distinct churches: Agios

Nikolaos, the largest, with superb columns of Parian marble and a carved iconostasis, is in the east of the compound; the others are the Church of Our Lady and the Baptistery. The name translates as Our Lady of the Hundred Gates, but this is a wishful rounding-up of a still-impressive number of doorways. The **Byzantine Museum** (admission €1.50; 🕙 9.30am-2pm & 6-9pm), within the compound, has a collection of icons and other artefacts.

Next to a school and behind the Panagia Ekatondapyliani, the **Archaeological Museum** (☎ 22840 21231; admission €2; 🕙 8.30am-2.45pm Tue-Sun) is a cool escape from the heat and hustle of town. It harbours some marvellous pieces, including a 5th-century Nike on the point of alighting and a 6th-century Gorgon also barely in touch with the sullen earth. Earlier examples of splendid pottery include the bosky *Fat Lady of Saliagos*, while a major exhibit is a fragment slab of the 4th-century **Parian Chronicle**, which lists the most outstanding artistic achievements of ancient Greece. It was discovered in the 17th century and, rather typically, two other slabs ended up in the Ashmolean Museum, in Oxford, England.

North along the waterfront there is a fenced **ancient cemetery** dating from the 7th century BC; it was excavated in 1983. Roman graves, burial pots and sarcophagi are floodlit at night.

The **Frankish kastro** was built by Marco Sanudo, Duke of Naxos, in AD 1260, on the remains of a temple to Athena. Not much of the *kastro* remains, save for a large wall that is a jigsaw of unpainted column bases and dressed blocks.

Tours

Santorineos Travel Services (☎ 22840 24245) can book bus tours of Paros (€32), boat trips to Mykonos and Delos (€40), and boats to Santorini (including a bus tour of the island, €55).

Sleeping

In August the **Rooms Association** (☎ 22840 22722, after hrs 22840 22220), located on the quay, has information on domatia; otherwise, owners meet ferries. The **Hotel Association** (☎ 22840 51207) has information about hotels on Paros and Antiparos. All camping grounds have minibuses that meet ferries.

BUDGET

Koula Camping (☎ 22840 22801; www.campingkoula.gr; camp sites per adult/child/tent €8/3/4; 🕙 Apr-Oct; P 🛜)

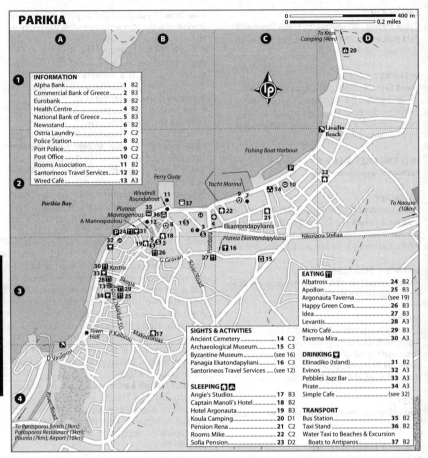

PARIKIA

0 — 400 m
0 — 0.2 miles

INFORMATION
Alpha Bank	1	B2
Commercial Bank of Greece	2	B3
Eurobank	3	B2
Health Centre	4	B2
National Bank of Greece	5	B3
Newsstand	6	B2
Ostria Laundry	7	C2
Police Station	8	C2
Port Police	9	C2
Post Office	10	C2
Rooms Association	11	B2
Santorineos Travel Services	12	B2
Wired Café	13	A3

SIGHTS & ACTIVITIES
Ancient Cemetery	14	C2
Archaeological Museum	15	C3
Byzantine Museum	(see 16)	
Panagia Ekatondapyliani	16	C3
Santorineos Travel Services	(see 12)	

SLEEPING
Angie's Studios	17	B3
Captain Manoli's Hotel	18	B2
Hotel Argonauta	19	B3
Koula Camping	20	D1
Pension Rena	21	C2
Rooms Mike	22	C2
Sofia Pension	23	D2

EATING
Albatross	24	B2
Apollon	25	B3
Argonauta Taverna	(see 19)	
Happy Green Cows	26	B3
Idea	27	B3
Levantis	28	C2
Micro Café	29	B3
Taverna Mira	30	A3

DRINKING
Ellinadiko (Island)	31	B2
Evinos	32	A3
Pebbles Jazz Bar	33	A3
Pirate	34	A3
Simple Cafe	(see 32)	

TRANSPORT
Bus Station	35	B2
Taxi Stand	36	B2
Water Taxi to Beaches & Excursion Boats to Antiparos	37	B2

Koula is a pleasant, shaded little site behind the beach at the north end of the Parikia waterfront and only minutes from the centre. Two-person bungalow tents are €20; three-person €25.

Krios Camping (☎ 22840 21705; www.krios-camping. gr; camp sites per adult/child/tent €8/4/3; ☻ Jun-Sep; ⓅⒹ🛜🚌) This site is on the north shore of Parikia Bay about 4km from the port, but there's a water taxi across the bay to Parikia every 10 minutes for €4 per person (return). You can rent bungalow tents for €25. There's an on-site restaurant (dishes from €4 to €8).

Pension Rena (☎ 22840 22220; www.cycladesnet. gr/rena; s/d/tr €35/45/55; 🚫🛜) One of the best choices in town, these immaculate rooms are excellent value, and there's a friendly welcome. The rooms are in a quiet but handy location just back from the waterfront. Air-con is €5 extra. The owners also have good apartments to rent in Naousa.

Rooms Mike (☎ 22840 22856; www.roomsmike .com; s/d/tr €35/45/60; 🚫) A long-standing favourite in sight of the ferry quay, you'll never be short of chat and advice at Mike's place. There's a shared kitchen and a roof terrace. Mike also has well-maintained and well-equipped studios (€55) elsewhere in town. Enquire for details. Credit cards are accepted.

Captain Manoli's Hotel (☎ 22840 21244; www .paroswelcome.com; s/d/tr €50/60/72; 🚫) Hidden away at the centre of town are these decent rooms that are clean and brightly decorated. Check prices for July and August when there is a minimum-stay requirement.

MIDRANGE

our pick **Sofia Pension** (☎ 22840 22085; www.sofia pension-paros.com; s/d/tr €65/75/90; P 🏴 💻 🛜) Set in a garden full of greenery and flowers lovingly tended, this delightful place has immaculate rooms with individual decor. The owners are charming. Breakfast is available for €8.

Hotel Argonauta (☎ 22840 21440; www.argonauta .gr; Plateia Mavrogenous; s/d/tr €65/85/95; 🏴 🛜) A long-established, family-run hotel with a central location overlooking Plateia Mavrogenous, the Argonauta has a welcoming atmosphere and has been recently refurbished. The furnishings have attractive traditional touches and the rooms are spotless and comfy and have double-glazing.

Angie's Studios (☎ 22840 23909/6977; www.angies -studios.gr; Makedonias; d/tr €80/90; ☀ Apr-Oct; P 🏴) A garden glowing with bougainvillea surrounds these handsome studios. They are in a very quiet area that's about a level 500m from the ferry dock. The studios are big and extremely well kept and each has its own kitchen. There are generous discounts in the low season.

Eating

Micro Café (☎ 22840 24674; Agora; snacks €4-5) This great gathering spot for locals and visitors alike is bright and cheerful and lies at the heart of Kastro. It does breakfasts for €4, as well as coffee and snacks, sandwiches, fresh fruit and vegetarian juices. There are drinks and music into the early hours.

Parasporos Restaurant (☎ 6947183732; Parasporos Beach; mains €5-10) The owner of Micro Café also runs this restaurant on Parosporos Beach, 2km south of town. The emphasis at both venues is on vegetarian food.

Albatross (☎ 22840 21848; D Vasiliou; mains €5-15) Albatross is a local favourite not least because of its excellent fish dishes. The fisherman's salad for €15 is a sure bet, or savour cuttle-fish with spinach in an unfussy setting on the waterfront.

Taverna Mira (☎ 22840 22592; mains €5.80-10.80) One of the best eateries along Parikia's fairly relentless southern strip of cafes, bars and tavernas, Mira's is known for its *arni lemonato* (lamb in lemon sauce) and *kleftiko* (lamb baked in a clay pot with feta cheese and wine). Vegetarians also have a good choice of combinations.

Idea (☎ 22840 21038; mains €7-9.50) For a peaceful alternative to the often traffic-logged waterfront, this relaxed cafe-bar is opposite Panagia Ekatondapyliani and shares some of its tranquillity. It does crêpes, omelettes and heftier dishes such as pork cooked in beer and honey with rice. Breakfasts are €5 to €8.

our pick **Levantis** (☎ 22840 23613; Kastro; dishes €9-15) A courtyard garden setting enhances dining at this long-established restaurant at the heart of the Kastro area. There is a truly splendid cuisine with imaginative starters such as fennel and pear salad with mixed greens, croutons and Parmesan shavings, while mains include honey-spiced lamb with apples, prunes and almonds. Lovely desserts, such as honey and almond truffles covered in bitter cocoa, round things off with a flourish. Excellent house wine is underpinned with a good choice of Greek vintages.

Happy Green Cows (☎ 22840 24691; dishes €12-23; ☀ 7pm-midnight) Camp decor and upbeat service goes with the quirky name (inspired by a surreal dream, apparently) of this little eatery that is a vegetarian's delight. It's a touch pricey, but worth it for the often saucily named dishes. Dishes include sweetcorn croquettes in a lemon and yoghurt sauce or marinated artichokes in olive oil with fresh herbs topped with Parmesan cheese.

Also recommended:

Argonauta Taverna (☎ 22840 23303; mains €4.50-9) Attached to the hotel of the same name and offering sturdy Greek standards.

Apollon (☎ 22840 21875; Agora; mains €9-24) A long-established restaurant in Kastro.

Drinking

our pick **Pebbles Jazz Bar** (☎ 22840 22283; 🛜) Heading down through Kastro in the late evening you'd think Pebbles' sunset backdrop was a vast painting. Perched above the seafront, this chilled place has lounge music by day and jazz in the evenings, with a classical climax for the sunset and occasional live performers during July and August. Pebbles has an adjacent *mezedhopoleio* (restaurant specialising in mezedhes) open from 9am to 1am, with breakfast from €4.50 to €7 and a great selection of mezedhes for €7 to €8, as well as omelettes and salads.

Pirate (☎ 6974315991) Ultracool corner of Parikia, Pirate is an ideal refuge, lulled by hazy jazz and blues beats to combat all that brilliant Cycladean light. It's just off the far end of Market St beyond Micro Café.

OFF THE BEATEN TRACK

Athens may think it has the acropolis *par excellence*, but Paros has its own little Mycenaean acropolis at **Koukounaries** near Naousa, where you won't mix it with too many fellow admirers. This is a grand site atop a gnarly little hill of boisterous sandstone boulders and buttresses, smoothed over and frozen into Dalí-esque shapes. Over 35,000 pieces of broken pottery have been found at the site. Signs point the way from the main Naousa road to parking at the base of the hill, but fade thereafter. Be warned: good footwear and careful footwork are essential to negotiate the initial rocky slabs, which are water-polished in places. At the top of the slabs you bear right towards a distinctive curved pillar just below the skyline. Follow your nose thereafter to the top of the hill and the scattered roots of buildings, unadorned and simple. The views are classic.

Ellinadiko (☎ 22840 25046) Also known as 'Island', this popular local bar with foot-stomping Greek music and late-night dancing is in an alleyway between Plateia Mavrogenous and the seafront.

There are more bars along the southern waterfront, including the popular **Evinos** (☎ 22840 23026) and **Salon D'Or** (☎ 22840 22176).

NAOUSA ΝΑΟΥΣΑ
pop 2865

Fast stealing some of the glitz and glamour of Mykonos, Naousa has transformed itself from a quiet fishing village into a popular tourist resort. Located on the shores of the large Plastira Bay on the north coast of Paros, there are good beaches nearby, and the town has several excellent restaurants and a growing number of stylish beach-side cafes and bars. Behind the waterfront is a maze of narrow whitewashed streets, peppered with fish and flower motifs and with a mix of smart boutiques and souvenir shops.

Orientation & Information

The bus from Parikia terminates some way up from the main square just in from the waterfront, where a dried-up riverbed serves as a road leading south and inland. The main street of Naousa lies on the left of the riverbed. If arriving by car, be warned: parking in certain areas is banned from June to September. Signs may not be clear, but the €35 fines are painfully so. There's parking by the harbour and along the sides of the riverbed road, with a larger car park at the top end of the riverbed road.

Naousa Information (☎ 22840 52158; ☼ 10am-midnight Jul & Aug, 11am-1pm & 6-10pm mid-Jun–Jul) can find you accommodation and is based in a booth by the main square.

The post office is a tedious uphill walk from the main square. There are several banks with ATMs around the main square.

For internet access, try **Jamnet3** (☎ 22840 52203; per hr €2.50; ☼ 10am-1am), just by the entrance to the main square.

Sights & Activities

Naousa's **Byzantine museum** (admission €1.80; ☼ 10am-1pm & 6-9pm Aug) is housed in the blue-domed church, about 200m uphill from the central square on the main road to Parikia. A small **folklore museum** (☎ 22840 52284; admission €1.80; ☼ 9am-1pm & 6-9pm), which focuses on regional costumes, can be reached by heading inland from the main square to another blue-domed church. Turn right behind the church.

The best beaches in the area are **Kolymbythres** and **Monastiri**, which has some good snorkelling and a clubbing venue. Low-key **Lageri** is also worth seeking out. **Santa Maria**, on the other side of the eastern headland, is good for windsurfing. They can all be reached by road, but caïques go from Naousa to each of them during July and August.

Kokou Riding Centre (☎ 22840 51818; www.kokou.gr) has morning (€45), evening (€30) and one-hour (€25) horse rides, and can arrange pick-up from Naousa's main square for a small charge. The rides explore the surrounding countryside and coast.

Sleeping

There are two camping grounds, both with minibuses that meet ferries. Visit the Naousa Information booth (see left) for help with finding accommodation.

Surfing Beach (☎ 22840 52491; fax 22840 51937; info@surfbeach.gr; camp sites per adult/child/tent €7.50/3.60/4) A fairly large site, but with reasonable facilities and a good location at

Santa Maria. The site has a windsurfing and waterskiing school.

Young Inn (☎ 6976415232; www.young-inn.com; dm €9-20, d & tr €66; P ✘ ▣) This well-run place caters for a young, international clientele and organises events and outings. Scooter hire can be arranged. Breakfasts start at €3. It's located to the east of the harbour, behind Naousa's cathedral.

Hotel Stella (☎ 22840 51317; www.hotelstella.gr; s/d €55/75 ✘ ▣) Deep in the heart of the old town and within a leafy, colourful garden, the Stella has decent rooms and good facilities. It's best reached by heading up the main street, turning left at the National Bank, going beneath an archway and then turning right and up past a small church.

Hotel Galini (☎ 22840 53382; www.hotelgaliniparos.com; s/d/tr €60/70/85; ✘ ☎) Opposite the blue-domed local church (Byzantine museum), on the main road into town from Parikia, this little hotel has comfortable, recently updated rooms. Be certain that this is our recommended hotel. There is a similarly named establishment elsewhere in town.

our pick **Katerina's Rooms** (☎ 22840 51642; www.katerinastudios.gr; s/d/tr/studio €60/75/90/120; ✘) Unbeatable views make these immaculate rooms (complete with tea- and coffee-making facilities) an excellent choice. You need to hike uphill a touch, but it's all worth it.

Sunset Studios and Apartments (☎ 22840 51733; www.paros.biz; d/tr €85/102, apt €180-216; P ✘ ☎) Tucked away on the hill above the centre of Naousa and a few minutes stroll from the harbour are these peaceful rooms and apartments enhanced by a leafy garden and a warm welcome.

Eating & Drinking

Moshonas (☎ 22840 51623; dishes €4.50-9) An unbeatable location right at the edge of the harbour makes this family-run *ouzerie* and fish restaurant a favourite with locals and visitors alike. Fish is by the kilo but there are mains fish dishes at reasonable prices and you'll likely see the family's own caïques tie up and deliver the fresh octopus that will soon be on your plate.

Glafkos (☎ 22840 52100; mains €6-12) There's a great take on seafood at this beachside eatery, with subtle dishes such as shrimps and *manouri*, and scallops in a cream sauce.

Perivolaria (☎ 22840 51598; dishes €7-19) Reliable Greek and international cuisine, pastas and wood-fired pizzas are the style at this long-established restaurant where there's a lovely garden setting. Try the *pastourmali* (pastrami and cheese pie, a mix of meat, tomatoes, feta and *manouri*). Perivolaria is reached along the river road from the main square.

Christos (☎ 22840 51442; dishes €10-29; ☯ 7pm-1am Apr-Oct) A leafy canopy of vines adds style to the lovely courtyard dining area of Christos, which is enhanced even more by the paintings that line the walls. The food matches the attentive service and is modern Mediterranean with flair, all backed by a superb wine list. Head up the main street and it's on the left after about 50m.

Beyond the harbour, there's a beachfront line of cafes and music bars with cool lounge decor worthy of Mykonos. Places like **Fotis** (☎ 6938735017) and **Briki** (☎ 22840 52652) spill out onto little beaches and play a mix of classical strands by day and jazzier, funkier sounds by night.

AROUND PAROS

Lefkes Λεύκες
pop 494

Lovely Lefkes clings to a natural amphitheatre amid hills whose summits are dotted with old windmills. Siesta is taken seriously here and the village has a general air of serenity. It lies 9km southeast of Parikia, high among the hills, and was capital of Paros during the Middle Ages. The village's main attractions are its pristine alleyways and buildings. The **Cathedral of Agia Triada** is an impressive building, shaded by olive trees.

From the central square, a signpost points to a well-preserved Byzantine path, which leads (in 3km) to the village of **Prodromos**. At the edge of the village, keep left at a junction (signposted) with a wider track. Sections of the route retain their original paving.

Down on the southeast coast is the attractive harbour and low-key resort of **Piso Livadi**, where there is a pleasant beach. **Perantinos Travel & Tourism** (☎ 22840 41135; perantin@otenet.gr) can arrange accommodation, car hire and boat trips to other islands, and also arranges money exchange. There is an ATM next to Perantinos.

Beaches

There is a fair scattering of beaches around the island's coastline, including a good one at **Krios**, accessible by water taxi (return €4) from

CYCLADES

Parikia. Paros' top beach, **Hrysi Akti** (Golden Beach), on the southeast coast, is hardly spectacular, but it has good sand and several tavernas, and is popular with windsurfers.

There is a decent enough beach at **Aliki** on the south coast.

SIGHTS & ACTIVITIES

The straits between Paros and Antiparos are especially suited to windsurfing and the spectacular sport of kiteboarding – effectively windsurfing in midair.

Down the coast at Pounta, **Eurodivers Club** (☎ 22840 92071; www.eurodivers.gr) has an impressive range of diving courses and dives for all levels and interests. A PADI open-water certification course costs €410, all inclusive.

Paros Kite Pro Center (☎ 22840 92229; www.paroskite-procenter.com), well run by the same team as Eurodivers Club, has a range of courses. These include an introductory one-hour kiteboarding session for €45, while more intensive courses start at €190 for four to six hours.

At Golden Beach, **Aegean Diving College** (☎ 22840 43347, 6932289649; www.aegeandiving.gr) offers a range of dives of archaeological and ecological interest led by scientists and experienced professional divers. A 'discover scuba' dive costs €80, and PADI open-water certification is €450.

Octopus Sea Trips (☎ 6932757123; www.octopuseatrips.com), based at Golden Beach and affiliated with Aegean Diving College, runs marine environmental courses and activities with snorkelling and diving for families and children.

Fanatic Fun Centre (☎ 6938307671; www.fanatic-paros.com; Hrysi Akti) runs catamaran sailing, waterskiing and windsurfing. One-hour windsurfing instruction costs €23 and a two-hour kiteboarding course is €75.

SLEEPING & EATING

Piso Livadi, which has a sunny magic of its own, has a number of modern rooms and apartments and a few decent tavernas.

ourpick Anna's Studios (☎ 22840 41320; www.annasinn.com; Piso Livadi; s/d/tr/ste/apt €43/57/65/65/95; ✗ ☲) Anna's bright and spacious studios, just inland from the harbour, are unbeatable value, right down to the exquisite decorative embroidery pieces by Anna's mother. The family also has well-kept rooms right on the harbour front, but without the seclusion of the studios. There are tea- and coffee-making facilities.

Halaris Taverna (☎ 22840 43257; mains €5-9) Right on the Piso Livadi waterfront, Halaris is one of the best tavernas on Paros and specialises in fresh fish from the family's boat as well as traditional meat and vegetable dishes. A fish plate costs €10. The cod croquettes, shrimp pies and tomato croquettes are peerless. Add in the local wine and cheerful service and it doesn't get better than this.

Thea (☎ 22840 91220, 6945751015; Pounta; dishes €9-18) The location of this great restaurant, near the Antiparos ferry quay at Pounta, may be unassuming but the views across the channel are marvellous. There are rich aromas of old Greece and Asia Minor in the air, and the food is superb. Mains include Cappadocian lamb with apricots, and beef with quinces, rice and plums. There are over 400 different vintages kept in a wine room–cum-bar, which even has a glass floor with bottles nestling beneath your feet. The music collection is every bit as fine.

ENTERTAINMENT

Punda Beach Club (☎ 22840 41717; www.pundabeach.gr; Viva Punda) For the ultragregarious this all-day clubbing venue, on the east coast south of Piso Livadi, is the place to head for. It's a huge complex with swimming pools, bars, restaurants, a gym, live music shows and a relentlessly crowded beach scene.

ANTIPAROS
ΑΝΤΙΠΑΡΟΣ

pop 1037

Change down several gears for Antiparos, a laid-back and lovely island, which is rightly proud of its distinctiveness and independence from Paros; you forget this at your peril in front of local people. The main village and port (also called Antiparos) is a relaxed place. There's a touristy gloss round the waterfront and main streets, but the village runs deep inland to quiet squares and alleyways that give way suddenly to open fields.

ORIENTATION & INFORMATION

Go right from the ferry quay along the waterfront. The main street, Agora, heads inland just by the Anargyros Restaurant. Halfway up the main street are an Emporiki Bank and

CYCLADES

National Bank of Greece, next to each other and both with ATMs. The post office is also here. The central square is reached by turning left at the top of the main street and then right, behind Smiles Cafe.

To reach the *kastro*, another Venetian creation, go under the stone arch that leads north off the central square.

The rest of the island runs to the south of the main settlement through quiet countryside. There are several decent beaches, especially at Glyfa and Soros on the east coast.

Nautica Café (☎ 22840 61323; internet per hr €2; 🖳 🛜) is a busy waterfront cafe with internet access and free wi-fi for customers.

There are several tour and travel agencies, including **Cave Travel** (☎ 22840 61376) and **Oliaris Tours** (☎ 22840 61231; oliaros@par.forthnet.gr). **Blue Island Divers** (☎ 22840 61493; www.blueisland-divers.gr) can also arrange accommodation and car hire.

SIGHTS & ACTIVITIES
Despite previous looting of stalactites and stalagmites, the **Cave of Antiparos** (admission €3.50; 🕐 10.45am-3.45pm summer) is still awe-inspiring. It is 8km south of the port. Follow the coast road south until you reach a signed turn-off into the hills. From the port there are hourly buses to the cave (one way €5), and there are cave tours every hour.

On the main pedestrian thoroughfare of town, with a gear and clothes shop attached, is the helpful **Blue Island Divers** (☎ 22840 61493; www.blueisland-divers.gr) which has a wide range of dive options. The owners have a great knowledge of the Antiparos scene. Accommodation and car rental can also be arranged. A four-day PADI open-water course is €350 and an advanced course is €270. A 'discover scuba diving' day session is €50. Trips can be tailored to suit individual wishes.

TOURS
MS Thiella (☎ 22840 61028) runs tours around the island daily, stopping at several beaches. The price (adult/child €45/25) covers barbecue and drinks; you can book at local travel agencies.

SLEEPING
Camping Antiparos (☎ 22840 61221; camp sites per adult/child/tent €6/4/4) This pleasant beachside camping ground is planted with bamboo 'compartments' and cedars and is 1.5km north of the port. It has a minimarket, bar

and restaurant. A site bus picks up from the port.

Anarghyros (☎ 22840 61204; mak@par.forthnet.gr; s/d €40/55; 🌣) There's good value at this well-kept, family-run hotel on the waterfront, where rooms are a decent size and come with tea- and coffee-making facilities. Attached to the hotel is a decent restaurant offering standard Greek dishes from €5 to €9.

Hotel Mantalena (☎ 22840 61206; www.hotelmantalena. gr; s/d/tr €50/65/75; 🌣 🖳 🛜) The Mantalena has bright, clean rooms and is located a short distance to the north of the main harbour quay. There's a pleasant terrace and the building is set back from the harbour road. You get a decent breakfast for €6.

EATING & DRINKING
The waterfront and main street of Antiparos have several cafes and tavernas serving Greek staples and fish dishes. You'll also find supermarkets and a bakery in the main street.

Yannis Place (☎ 22840 61469; mains €5-8) Halfway up the main street is this bright place with a little streetside terrace, ideal for people watching. Breakfast is €6 to €8, and it does omelettes, toasties, crêpes and pastas, as well as smoothies and ice cream for post-midday, and cocktails for the evening gear change.

Maki's (☎ 22840 61616; dishes €5.50-12) Seafood is the speciality at this harbour-front taverna. It's generally excellent, from the prawn souvlaki with calamari to lobster (by the kilo when available).

Yam Bar Restaurant and Cocktail Bar (dishes €6-9; 🕐 8pm-4am mid-Jun–mid-Sep) You can enjoy salads and cold plates of chicken or pasta at this relaxing spot with views of the sea. Sounds are a general mix that includes Latin, house and occasional jazz. It's signposted left off the top end of Market St.

Soul Sugar is along to the right from the top of the main street. It plays funk, disco and house into the small hours, and serves great cocktails.

GETTING THERE & AWAY
In summer, frequent excursion boats depart for Antiparos from Parikia. There is also a half-hourly car ferry that runs from Pounta on the west coast of Paros to Antiparos (one way €1, per scooter €1.80, per car €6, 10 minutes); the first ferry departs from Pounta about 7.15am and the last boat returning to Pounta leaves Antiparos at about 12.30am.

GETTING AROUND

The only bus service on Antiparos runs, in summer, to the cave in the centre of the island (see p167; €5). The bus continues to Soros and Agios Georgios.

Cars, scooters and bicycles can be hired from **Aggelos** (☎ 22840 61626/61027), the first office as you come from the ferry quay. Cars start at €42 per day in high season, scooters are €15 per day and bicycles are €5 per day.

NAXOS ΝΑΞΟΣ

pop 18,188

It was on Naxos that an ungrateful Theseus is said to have abandoned Ariadne after she helped him escape the Cretan labyrinth. In keeping with even mythic soap opera, she didn't pine long, and was soon entwined with Dionysos, the god of wine and ecstasy and the island's favourite deity. Naxian wine has long been considered a fine antidote for a broken heart.

The island was a cultural centre of classical Greece and of Byzantium. Venetian and Frankish influences have also left their mark.

Naxos is more fertile than most of the other islands and produces olives, grapes, figs, citrus fruit, corn and potatoes. Mt Zeus (1004m; also known as Mt Zas or Zefs) is the Cyclades' highest peak and is the central focus of the island's mountainous interior, in which you find enchanting villages such as Halki and Apiranthos. There are numerous fine beaches and the island is a great place to explore on foot, as many old paths between villages, churches and other sights still survive. There are walking guides and maps available from local bookshops.

Getting There & Away

Like Paros, Naxos is something of a ferry hub of the Cyclades, with a similar number of conventional and fast ferries making regular calls to and from Piraeus, and weekly links to and from the mainland ports of Thessaloniki and Lavrio and eastward to the Dodecanese. There is a daily flight to and from Athens. There are daily connections to the other main Cycladic islands in summer. For details see Island Hopping (p518).

Getting Around

TO/FROM THE AIRPORT

The airport is 3km south of Hora. There is no shuttle bus, but buses to Agios Prokopios Beach and Agia Anna pass close by. A taxi costs €12 to €15 depending on the time of day and if booked.

BUS

Frequent buses run from Hora to Agia Anna (€1.80). Five buses daily serve Filoti (€2) via Halki (€1.80); four serve Apiranthos (€3) via Filoti and Halki; and at least three serve Apollonas (€5), Pyrgaki (€2.50) and Melanes (€1.80). There are less frequent departures to other villages.

Buses leave from the end of the ferry quay in Hora; timetables are posted outside the **bus information office** (☎ 22850 22291; www.naxos destinations.com), diagonally left and across the road from the bus stop. You have to buy tickets from the office.

CAR & MOTORCYCLE

August rates for hire cars range from about €45 to €55 per day, and motorcycles from about €18. **Rental Center** (☎ 22850 23395; Plateia Evripeou) is a good bet.

HORA (NAXOS) ΧΩΡΑ (ΝΑΞΟΣ)

pop 6533

Busy Hora, on the west coast of Naxos, is the island's port and capital. It's a large town, divided into two historic neighbourhoods – Bourgos, where the Greeks lived, and the hill-top Kastro, where the Venetian Catholics lived.

Orientation

The ferry quay is at the northern end of the waterfront, with the bus station at its inland end. The broad waterfront, Protopapadaki, known universally as Paralia, leads off to the south from the ferry quay and is lined with cafes, tavernas and shops on its inland side. Behind Paralia, narrow alleyways twist and turn beneath archways as they seem to vanish into the old town area of Bourgos and climb into the Kastro.

A northerly turn at the end of the ferry quay leads to a causeway over to Palatia Islet and the unfinished **Temple of Apollo**, Naxos' most famous landmark, known as the Portara. There is not much else to see at

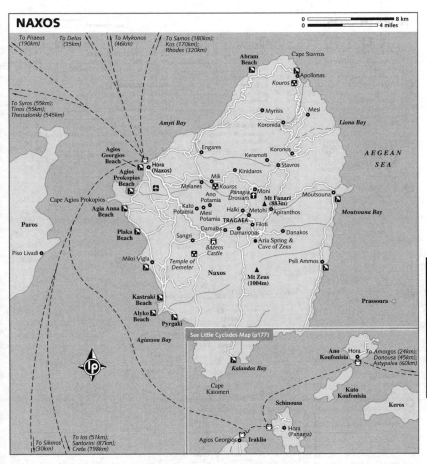

NAXOS

the temple other than the two columns and their crowning lintel surrounded by fallen masonry, but it makes for a romantic spot, especially at sunset.

There are a few swimming spots along the waterfront promenade below the temple. Southwest of the town is the pleasant, but busy, beach of Agios Georgios.

Information
BOOKSHOPS
Zoom (☎ 22850 23675; Paralia) A large, well-stocked newsagent and bookshop that has most international newspapers the day after publication.

EMERGENCY
Police station (☎ 22850 22100; Paparrigopoulou) Southeast of Plateia Protodikiou.

Port police (☎ 22850 22300) Just south of the quay.

INTERNET ACCESS
Grotta Tours (☎ 22850 25782; Paralia; per hr €3)
Rental Center (☎ 22850 23395; Plateia Evripeou; per hr €3)
Zas Travel (☎ 22850 23330; fax 22850 23419; Paralia; per hr €4)

LAUNDRY
To Ariston (☎ 22850 26750; 5kg wash & dry €10; 8am-2pm & 5.30-9pm Mon, Tue, Thu & Fri, 8am-2pm Wed & Sat)

MEDICAL SERVICES
Hospital (☎ 22853 60500; Prantouna) New hospital opened in 2009.

HORA (NAXOS)

0 — 200 m
0 — 0.1 miles

INFORMATION	
Agricultural Bank of Greece	1 C4
Alpha Bank	2 B5
Bus Information Office	3 B3
Grotta Tours	4 B3
Hospital	5 D5
Information Booth	6 B3
National Bank of Greece	7 C4
Naxos Tours	8 C4

OTE	9 B5
Port Police	10 B3
Post Office	11 B6
Rental Center	12 C5
To Ariston	13 C5
Town Hall	14 B6
Zas Travel	15 B3
Zoom	16 C4

SIGHTS & ACTIVITIES
Archaeological Museum	17 C4
Della Rocca-Barozzi Venetian Museum	18 C3

Mitropolis Museum	19 C3
Naos Silver Gallery	20 C4
Roman Catholic Cathedral	21 C4

SLEEPING
Chateau Zevgoli	22 C3
Despina's Rooms	23 C3
Hotel Anixis	24 C3
Hotel Glaros	25 B6
Hotel Grotta	26 D2
Pension Irene I	27 D5
Pension Irene II	28 D6
Pension Sofi	29 C3

EATING
Bakery	(see 16)
East West Asian Restaurant	30 C6
Irini's	31 B3
Lucullus	32 B3
Meltemi	33 B6
Meze 2	34 B3
O Apostolis	35 C3
Picasso Mexican Bistro	36 C6
Vidalis Supermarket	37 D3
Zoom Minimarket	38 C4

DRINKING
Jam	39 C5
Jazz-Blues Café	40 B3
On the Rocks	41 C5

ENTERTAINMENT
Abyss	42 C3
Cine Astra	43 D6
Della Rocca-Barozzi Venetian Museum	(see 18)
Ocean	44 B5

SHOPPING
Antico Veneziano	(see 17)
Kiriakos Tziblakis	45 C5
Naksia	46 C5
Takis' Shop	47 B3

TRANSPORT
Bus Station	48 B3
Ferries to Mykonos, Paros, Piraeus, Ios & Santorini	49 B3
Ferry to Little Cyclades & Amorgos	50 B4

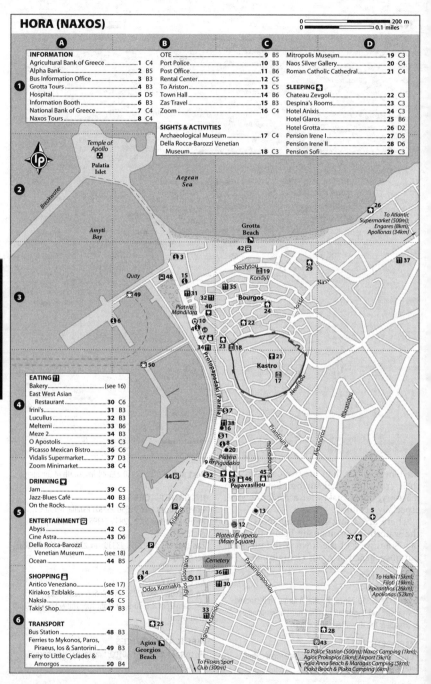

MONEY

All the following banks have ATMs:

Agricultural Bank of Greece (Paralia)

Alpha Bank (cnr Paralia & Papavasiliou)

National Bank of Greece (Paralia)

POST

Post office (Agios Giorgiou) Go past the OTE, across Papavasiliou, and left at the forked road.

TELEPHONE

OTE (telecommunications office; Paralia) Has several phone kiosks in an alleyway.

TRAVEL AGENCIES

There is no official tourist information office on Naxos. Travel agencies can deal with most queries. Naxos Tours and Zas Travel both sell ferry tickets and organise accommodation, tours and rental cars.

Grotta Tours (☎ 22850 25782; Paralia)

Naxos Tours (☎ 22850 22095; www.naxostours.net; Paralia)

Zas Travel (☎ 22850 23330; zas-travel@nax.forthnet .gr; Paralia)

Sights

To see the Bourgos area, head into the winding backstreets behind the northern end of Paralia. The most alluring part of Hora is the residential **Kastro**. Marco Sanudo made the town the capital of his duchy in 1207, and several Venetian mansions survive. Take a stroll around the Kastro during siesta to experience its hushed, timeless atmosphere.

A short distance behind the northern end of the waterfront are several churches and chapels, and the **Mitropolis Museum** (☎ 22850 24151; Kondyli; admission free; ☽ 8.30am-3pm). The museum features fragments of a Mycenaean city of the 13th to 11th centuries BC that was abandoned because of the threat of flooding by the sea. It's a haunting place where glass panels underfoot reveal ancient foundations and larger areas of excavated buildings.

The **archaeological museum** (☎ 22850 22725; admission €3; ☽ 8.30am-3pm Tue-Sun) is in the Kastro, housed in the former Jesuit school where novelist Nikos Kazantzakis was briefly a pupil. The contents include Hellenistic and Roman terracotta figurines and some early Cycladic figurines.

Close by, the **Della Rocca-Barozzi Venetian Museum** (☎ 22850 22387; guided tours adult/student €5/3; ☽ 10am-3pm & 7-10pm end May–mid-Sep), a handsome old tower house of the 13th century, is within the Kastro ramparts (by the northwest gate). There are changing art exhibitions in the vaults. Tours are multilingual. The museum also runs tours (adult/student €15/10) of the Kastro at 11am Tuesday to Sunday; tours last just over two hours. Evening concerts and other events are staged in the grounds of the museum (see p173). The **Roman Catholic cathedral** (☽ 6.30pm-8.30pm), also in the Kastro, is worth visiting too.

Activities

Flisvos Sport Club (☎ 22850 24308; www.flisvos-sportclub. com; Agios Georgios) has a range of windsurfing options, starting with a beginner's course of six hours for €150, or a five-hour Hobie Cat sailing course for €95. The club also organises walking trips and hires out mountain bikes at a per-week rate of €60.

Naxos Horse Riding (☎ 6948809142) organises daily horse rides (10am to 1pm and 5pm to 8pm) inland and on beaches (per person €48). You can book a ride up until 6pm the day before and can arrange pick-up and return, to and from the stables. Beginners, young children and advanced riders are catered for. Bookings can also be made at the **Naos Silver Gallery** (☎ 22850 24130; Pigadakia).

Tours

There are frequent excursion boats to Mykonos (adult/child €45/23), Delos (€45) Santorini (adult/child €55/30), Paros and Naousa (adult/child €20/10) and Iraklia and Koufonissi (adult/child €40/20); book through travel agents (see left).

Sleeping

Hora has plenty of good accommodation options. If you settle for an offer at the port from a persistent accommodation hawker, establish with certainty the true distance of the rooms from the centre of town. In high season there may be booths on the quay dispensing information about hotels and domatia.

BUDGET

Despina's Rooms (☎ 22850 22356; fax 22850 22179; Kastro; s/d €40/50; ☒) These decent rooms are tucked away in the Kastro and some have sea views. Rooms on the roof terrace are popular despite their small size. There's a communal kitchen.

CYCLADES

Hotel Anixis (☎ 22850 22932; www.hotel-anixis.gr; s/d/tr €50/60/75; ✉ ☎) Tucked away in a quiet location in Kastro, this pleasant hotel, in a garden setting, has bright and well-kept rooms and there are great views to the sea. Breakfast is €5.

Pension Irene I (☎ 22850 23169; www.irene pension-naxos.com; s/d €50/60; ✉ ☎) This long-standing favourite is a bit of a hike from the ferry dock but is in a quiet side street and has clean, comfortable rooms.

There are several camping grounds near Hora, and all have good facilities. Minibuses meet the ferries. The sites are all handy to good beaches and there's an approximate price per person of €9.

Camping Maragas (☎ 22850 24552; www.maragas camping.gr) At Agia Anna Beach, south of Hora.

Naxos Camping (☎ 22850 23500; www.naxos -camping.gr; ✿) About 1km south of Agios Georgios Beach. The camping ground closest to town.

Plaka Camping (☎ 22850 42700; www.plakacamping .gr; ▢) At Plaka Beach, 6km south of town.

MIDRANGE

Pension Irene II (☎ 22850 23169; www.irenepension -naxos.com; s/d €60/70; ✉ ▢ ☎ ✿) Bright, clean rooms and a swimming pool have made this well-run place popular with a younger set.

Pension Sofi (☎ 22850 25593; www.pensionsofi.gr; s/d/tr €65/70/90; ✉) Hospitality is the rule at this family-run place. It's just a short distance inland from the port and is framed by one of the biggest bougainvilleas you're likely to see. Rooms are clean and well equipped and include cooking facilities.

Hotel Glaros (☎ 22850 23101; www.hotelglaros .com; Agios Georgios; s incl breakfast €65, d incl break-fast €85-95; ✉ ▢ ☎) The attractive decor of Hotel Glaros captures the colours of sea and sky. Service is efficient and thoughtful and the rooms are bright and clean. The hotel is only a few steps away from the beach. The owners also have attractive studios nearby (€65 to €100).

our pick Hotel Grotta (☎ 22850 22215; www.hotel grotta.gr; Grotta; s/d incl breakfast €70/85; Ⓟ ✉ ▢ ☎) Located on high ground to the east of the ferry quay, this fine modern hotel has comfortable and immaculate rooms, great sea views from the front, spacious public areas and a Jacuzzi. It's made even better by the cheerful, attentive atmosphere.

Chateau Zevgoli (☎ 22850 26123; www.apollon hotel-naxos.gr; Kastro; s/d/ste €75/90/120; ✉ ☎) Tucked away at the heart of Kastro is this long-established hotel. It has a leafy garden setting to go with the traditional Naxian style of rooms and furnishings.

Eating

Naxian cuisine cherishes such local specialities as *kefalotyri* (a hard cheese made from sheep's milk), honey, *kitron* (a liqueur made from the leaves of the citron tree – see p174), *raki* (Greek firewater, smoother than *tsipouro*, Greece's main firewater), ouzo and fine white wine.

Meze 2 (☎ 22850 26401; Paralia; mains €3-9) The emphasis at this popular *mezedhopoleio* is on fish, and even the local fishermen eat here. Superb seafood is prepared and served by family members in an atmosphere that is never less than sociable. There is another Meze at Plaka Beach.

Meltemi (☎ 22850 22654; Komiakis; mains €5.50-14) Top dishes at this family-run taverna are lamb flavoured with fresh lemon juice and oregano, and *exohiko*, tender pieces of baked meat with Gruyere cheese and vegetables. They also do three-course fixed menus for €10 to €12.50, all served with courtesy and good humour on a leafy terrace that makes up for an otherwise dull street scene.

O Apostolis (☎ 22850 26777; Old Market; mains €5.50-17) Right at the heart of the labyrinthine Old Market area of Bourgos, Apostolis serves up rewarding dishes such as mussels in garlic butter and parsley, and *bekri mezes*, a popular Cretan dish of casseroled beef. The *kleftiko*, lamb wrapped in filo pastry with sautéed vegetables and feta cheese is particularly good.

Irini's (☎ 22850 26780; Paralia; mains €6-9.50) The real deal at this pleasant taverna is the terrific selection of dishes such as codfish croquettes and shrimp *saganaki* – from which you can construct a very satisfying meal.

Lucullus (☎ 22850 22569; Old Market St; mains €6.50-18) One hundred years' service and still going strong, this famous restaurant has starters such as mushroom pie, while mains include *lemonato*, tender veal in a fresh lemon juice and white wine sauce. The fisherman's pasta mixes shrimps, tomatoes, garlic and dill.

Also recommended:

East West Asian Restaurant (☎ 22850 24641; Odos Ko-miakis; dishes €5.60-13) Thai, Chinese and Indian favourites.

Picasso Mexican Bistro (☎ 22850 25408; Agiou Arseniou; dishes €5.25-12.75; ⏰ 7pm-late) The fajitas at this great Tex-Mex place are world class. Also at Picasso on the Beach, Plaka Beach.

Near the Zoom newsagent and bookshop is the town's best bakery. Next door is the Zoom Minimarket. The cheapest supermarkets are Atlantic and Vidalis, both a little way out of town on the ring road.

Drinking

The seafront Paralia has a good mix of music cafe-bars interspersed with shops and offices, all ideal for people watching.

our pick **On the Rocks** (☎ 22850 29224; Pigadakia; 🖳 🛜) The place to go for character and cocktails. Enjoy Havana cigars or a *sheesha* (water pipe) with a wide selection of flavours from apple to mango, peach or pistachio. Or go for Cuban-style daiquiris or tequila. It all goes with sounds that vary between funk, house and electronic. Occasional live performances and karaoke stir the mix.

Jazz-Blues Café (☎ 22850 22006; Old Market St) A cosy little evening and late-night cafe-bar that plays what it says it does, just where the narrow, almost tunneled alleyways start to wriggle up into Kastro.

Jam (Pigadakia) A huge playlist with rock and standard favourites is the background to this long-established music bar. There's a matching list of cocktails.

Entertainment

CINEMAS

Cine Astra (☎ 22850 25381; Andreas Papandreou; adult/child €8/5) About a five-minute walk from the main square, it shows newly released mainstream films and has a bar. Sessions are at 9pm and 11pm.

NIGHTCLUBS

Abyss (Grotta; admission €12; 🕙 11.30pm-3am May–mid-Sep, 11.30pm-late Fri & Sat mid-Sep–Apr) Previously known as Super Island, this place has had something of a makeover inside and out, but plays much the same sounds with house and modern Greek at the fore.

Ocean (☎ 22850 26766; Seafront; admission €12; 🕙 11.30pm-3am May–mid-Sep, 11.30pm-late Fri & Sat mid-Sep–Apr) A sizeable space features house and some modern Greek music, and runs special nights with guest DJs.

SUNSET CONCERTS

Della Rocca-Barozzi Venetian Museum (☎ 22850 22387; Kastro; events admission €15-20; 🕙 8pm Wed-Sun Apr-Oct) Special evening cultural events are held at the museum, and comprise traditional music and dance concerts, and classical and contemporary music recitals. Prices depend on seat position.

Shopping

Takis' Shop (☎ 22850 23045; Plateia Mandilara) Among the splendid wines here are such fine names as Lazaridis from northern Greece, Tslepos from the Peloponnese and Manousakis from Crete – all masterful vintages. You can also find Vallindras *kitron* (see p174) and ouzo here. Incorporated is Takis' jewellery shop, where fine individual pieces from some of Greece's most famous designers often reflect ancient designs and the imagery of the sea.

Kiriakos Tziblakis (☎ 22859 22230; Papavasiliou) A fascinating cavelike place crammed with traditional produce and goods, from pots and brushes to herbs, spices, wine, *raki* and olive oil.

Naksia (☎ 22850 23660; Plateia Pigadakia) For a remarkable collection of candles try this colourful shop tucked away in a cul-de-sac off the Plateia.

Antico Veneziano (☎ 22850 26206; Kastro) Deep within Kastro is this upmarket antique store and gallery that makes for a fascinating visit.

AROUND NAXOS
Beaches

Conveniently located just south of the town's waterfront is **Agios Georgios**, Naxos' town beach. It's backed by hotels and tavernas at the town end and can get very crowded, but it runs for some way to the south and its shallow waters mean the beach is safe for youngsters.

The next beach south of Agios Georgios is **Agios Prokopios**, in a sheltered bay to the south of the headland of Cape Mougkri. It merges with **Agia Anna**, a stretch of shining white sand, quite narrow but long enough to feel uncrowded towards its southern end. Development is fairly solid at Prokopios and the northern end of Agia Anna.

Sandy beaches continue down as far as **Pyrgaki** and include **Plaka**, **Kastraki** and **Alyko**.

One of the best of the southern beaches is **Mikri Vigla** – its name translates as 'little lookout', a watching place for pirates, and is a reference to the headland, all golden granite slabs and boulders, that divides the beach into two. The settlement here is a little scattered and is punctuated by half-finished buildings in places, but there's a sense of escapism and open space.

CYCLADES

Near the beach at Ágios Prokopios is **Villa Adriana** (☎ 22850 42804; www.adrianahotel.com; s/d/tr/apt €75/85/90/120; P ✖ ☎ ☑), a well-appointed hotel with excellent service and bright, comfortable rooms.

A great 'away from it all' option is **Oasis Studios** (☎ 22850 75494; www.oasisnaxos.gr; d/tr/apt €87/100/116; P ✖ ☎ ☑) at Mikri Vigla, 20km south of Hora. It is close to the beach and has lovely big rooms with kitchens. The owner and staff are very helpful and there's an outside terrace with a swimming pool and bar that encourages sociability.

The beachside **Taverna Liofago** (☎ 22850 75214, 6937137737; dishes €4.50-9) has a dreamy beach location. It has been in business for decades and favours a variety of dishes with special Naxian flavour. The *keftedhakia* (meatballs) are a speciality.

South of Mikri Vigla, at Kastraki, is one of the best restaurants on the island, **Axiotissa** (☎ 22850 75107), noted for its sourcing of organic food and for its traditional dishes with added Anatolian flair.

Tragaea Τραγαία

The Tragaea region is a vast plain of olive groves and unspoilt villages, couched beneath the central mountains.

MT ZEUS

Filoti, on the slopes of **Mt Zeus** (1004m), is the region's largest village. It has an ATM booth just down from the main bus stop. On the outskirts of the village (coming from Hora), an asphalt road leads off right to the isolated hamlets of **Damarionas** and **Damalas**.

From Filoti, you can also reach the **Cave of Zeus (Zas)**, a large, natural cavern at the foot of a cliff on the slopes of Mt Zeus. There's a junction signposted Aria Spring and Zas Cave, about 800m south of Filoti. If travelling by bus, ask to be dropped off here. The side road ends in 1.2km. From the road-end parking, follow a walled path past the **Aria Spring & Cave of Zeus**, a fountain and picnic area, and on to a rough track uphill to reach the cave. The path leads on from here steeply to the summit of Zas. It's quite a stiff hike of about 3km. A good way to return to Filoti, taking another 4km, is to follow the path that leads north from the summit. This is not a mere stroll, so be fit and come equipped with good footwear, water and sunscreen. A longer, but less strenuous, route up Mt Zeus starts from the little chapel

of Aghia Marina on the road to Danakos. Ask to be let off the Apiranthos bus at the Danakos junction about 6km beyond Filoti.

HALKI ΛΛΚΕΙΟ

One of Naxos' finest experiences is a visit to the historic village of Halki, which lies at the heart of the Tragaea, about 20 minutes' drive from Naxos town. Halki is a vivid reflection of historic Naxos and is full of the handsome facades of old villas and tower houses, legacy of a rich past as the one-time centre of Naxian commerce.

The main road skirts Halki. There is some roadside parking but you may find more at the schoolyard at the north end of the village and on a piece of rough ground just beyond the school. Lanes lead off the main road to the beautiful little square at the heart of the village.

Since the late 19th century Halki has had strong connections with the production of **kitron**, a unique liqueur. The citron (*Citrus medica*) was introduced to the Mediterranean area in about 300 BC and thrived on Naxos for centuries. The fruit is barely edible in its raw state, but its rind is very flavoursome when preserved in syrup as a *glika koutaliou* (spoon sweet). *Kitroraki*, a *raki*, can be distilled from grape skins and citron leaves, and by the late 19th century the preserved fruit and a sweet version of *kitroraki*, known as *kitron*, were being exported in large amounts from Naxos.

The **Vallindras Distillery** (☎ 22850 31220; ☉ 10am-11pm Jul-Aug, 10am-6pm May-Jun & Sep-Oct) in Halki's main square, distils *kitron* the old-fashioned way. There are free tours of the old distillery's atmospheric rooms, which still contain ancient jars and copper stills. *Kitron* tastings round off the trip and a selection of the distillery's products are on sale. To arrange a tour during the period November to April you need to phone ☎ 22850 22534 or ☎ 6942551161.

Another Halki institution is the world-class ceramics shop **L'Olivier** and its nearby gallery (see boxed text, opposite).

There are sleeping possibilities in Halki and Filoti, but you are best to ask around locally.

Near the L'Olivier gallery is the fascinating shop **Era** (☎ 22859 31009; eraproducts@mail .gr) where marmalade, jam and spoon desserts are made using the best ingredients.

ART OF THE AEGEAN: L'OLIVIER, NAXOS *Des Hannigan*

The first time I walked into **L'Olivier** (☎ 22850 32829; www.fish-olive-creations.com; Halki), a ceramics gallery and shop in the little village of Halki on Naxos, it was late evening, early summer. The velvety dusk of the Tragaea, the mountain basin of Naxos, had settled like a veil on Halki's little village square. Young owls hooted from marble ledges on the facades of old Naxian mansions. Inside L'Olivier it was as if a sunset glow lingered. Even the artificial lighting was subtly deployed. Everywhere I looked were pieces of stoneware ceramics and jewellery that took my breath away.

Each piece of work reflected the ancient Mediterranean themes of fish and olive that are at the heart of the work of Naxian potter Katharina Bolesch and her partner, artist and craftsman Alexander Reichardt. Three-dimensional ceramic olives framed the edges of shining plates or tumbled down the side of elegant jugs and bowls. Grapes too, hung in little ceramic bunches. Painted shoals of fish darted across platters and swam around bowls and dishes. Silver and ceramic fish jewellery extended the theme. Those first impressions have never faded. Each time I walk into L'Olivier now, the world lights up.

Katharina Bolesch was partly brought up on Naxos and is rooted in the island's landscape and culture. Alex Reichardt is entirely of the Mediterranean. His life among the islands and his long experience as a diver inspire his painted fish motifs, his silver and ceramic fish jewellery, and his work in wood and marble. These two outstanding artists are based in a tiny Cycladean village, yet their fame is international and their work has been exhibited in such major galleries and museums as the Academy of Athens, the Goulandris Natural History Museum, Greece's Cretaquarium, the UN Headquarters in New York and the Design Museum of Helsinki.

President of the Goulandris Natural History Museum, Mrs Niki Goulandris, is a longstanding patron. She speaks enthusiastically of the work of Bolesch and Reichardt and places it within the traditions of classical Greek and Cycladic art while recognising its modern context. 'Their work represents boldness and commitment to tradition,' she says. 'Their motifs are emphatically the symbols of the Greek land and sea.'

In spite of such a high profile, the work of Bolesch and Reichardt remains entirely accessible and affordable. L'Olivier is a cornucopia of beautiful yet functional work that includes jewellery, tiles and dishes, large jugs and bowls of luminous beauty, fine artefacts in olive wood, and olive products such as oil and soap.

In 2006 Bolesch and Reichardt opened a separate gallery and workshop just around the corner from their shop. Here they stage exhibitions by accomplished artists in a building that has been designed with great style and that fits perfectly amid Halki's traditional Naxian facades and the serene beauty of the Tragaea. (Poor-quality imitations of Katharina Bolesch's work are sold elsewhere on Naxos, so be warned.)

In Halki's central square, **Yianni's Taverna** (☎ 22850 31214; dishes €5.50-7.50) is noted for its good local meat dishes and fresh salads with *myzithra* (sheep's-milk cheese). Do not miss **Glikia Zoi** (Sweet Life; ☎ 22850 31602), directly opposite the L'Olivier gallery. Here Christina Falierou works her magic in a traditional cafe setting, making delicious cakes and sweets to go with coffee or drinks. Also of interest is **Penelope** (☎ 6979299951), a shop where you'll find some splendid handwoven textiles and embroidery work.

Halki is spreading its cultural wings even further with the inception of an annual music, arts and literary festival, the **Axia Festival** (Aug/Sep), which will feature international musicians, artists and writers. The festival is nonprofit and is organised by the L'Olivier gallery.

An alternative scenic route from Hora to Halki is along the road that passes **Ano Potamia**. It's here that you'll find **Taverna Pigi** (☎ 22850 32292; mains €5-22), known for good local cooking, enjoyed with the serene music of the gurgling spring that the taverna is named after.

Panagia Drosiani Παναγία Δροσιανή

The **Panagia Drosiani** (☉ 10am-7pm May–mid-Oct) just below **Moni**, 2.5km north of Halki, is one of the oldest and most revered churches in Greece. It has a warren of cavelike chapels, and several of the frescoes date back to the 7th century. Donations are appreciated.

CYCLADES

Sangri Σαγκρί

The handsome towerlike building of **Bazeos Castle** (☎ 22850 31402; ⏰ 10am-5pm & 6-9pm) stands prominently in the landscape about 2km east of the village of Sangri. The castle was built in its original form as the Monastery of Timios Stavros (True Cross) during the 17th century, but monks abandoned the site in the early 19th century. It was later bought by the Bazeos family, whose modern descendants have refurbished the building and its late-medieval rooms with great skill and imagination. The castle now functions as a cultural centre and stages art exhibitions and the annual **Naxos Festival** during July and August, when concerts, plays and literary readings are held. The price of admission to these varies.

About 1.5km south of Sangri is the impressive **Temple of Demeter** (Dimitra's Temple; ☎ 22850 22725; ⏰ 8.30am-3pm Tue-Sun). The ruins and reconstructions are not large, but they are historically fascinating. There is a site **museum** with some fine reconstructions of temple features. Signs point the way from Sangri.

Apiranthos Απείρανθος

Apiranthos is an atmospheric mountain village of unadorned stone houses, marble-paved streets and alleyways that scramble up the slopes of Mt Fanari (883m). Its inhabitants are descendants of refugees who fled Crete to escape Turkish repression; they retain a strong individuality and a rich dialect, and the village has always been noted for its spirited politics and populism. There is an impressive trio of museums.

On the main road, to the right of the start of the village's main street, is the **museum of natural history** (admission €3; ⏰ 8.30am-2pm Tue-Sun). The **geology museum** (admission €3; ⏰ 8.30am-2pm Tue-Sun) and the **archaeology museum** (admission free; ⏰ 8.30am-2pm Tue-Sun) are part-way along the main street. The latter has a marvellous collection of small Cycladian artefacts. The museums are notionally open from 7pm to 10pm in summer, but all the opening times stated here are 'flexible', in keeping with an admirable local spirit of independence.

There are a number of tavernas and *kafeneia* (coffee houses) in the village.

There is parking at the entrance to Apiranthos, on the main Hora–Apollonas road.

Moutsouna Μουτσούνα
pop 74

The road from Apiranthos to Moutsouna descends in an exhilarating series of S-bends through spectacular mountain scenery. Formerly a busy port that shipped out the emery mined in the region, Moutsouna is now a quiet place, although there is some development. Seven kilometres south of the village is a good beach at **Psili Ammos**.

There are a few pensions and tavernas, mainly in Moutsouna, but some are scattered along the coast road.

Apollonas Απόλλωνας
pop 107

Tavernas line the waterfront adjoining a reasonable beach at Apollonas, on the north coast, but the main attraction here is a giant 7th-century-BC **kouros** (male statue of the Archaic period), which lies in an ancient quarry in the hillside above the village. It is signposted to the left as you approach Apollonas on the main inland road from Hora. This 10.5m statue may have been abandoned before being finished, because weaknesses in the stone caused cracking. Apollonas has several domatia and tavernas.

With your own transport you can return to Hora via the west-coast road, passing through wild and sparsely populated country with awe-inspiring sea views. Several tracks branch down to secluded beaches, such as **Abram**.

LITTLE CYCLADES
ΜΙΚΡΕΣ ΚΥΚΛΑΔΕΣ

Step off the already slow-paced world of the larger Cycladic islands and head, with time to spare, for the chain of small islands between Naxos and Amorgos. Only four – Donousa, Ano Koufonisia, Iraklia and Schinousa – have permanent populations. All were densely populated in antiquity, as shown by the large number of ancient graves found on the islands. During the Middle Ages, only wild goats and even wilder pirates inhabited the islands. Post Independence, intrepid souls from Naxos and Amorgos recolonised. Now, the islands welcome growing numbers of independent-minded tourists.

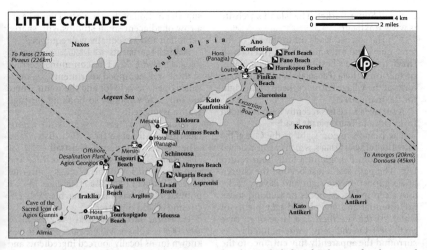

LITTLE CYCLADES

0 ————— 4 km
0 ————— 2 miles

CYCLADES

Donousa is the northernmost of the group and the furthest from Naxos. The others are clustered near the southeast coast of Naxos. Each has a public telephone and post agency and there are ATMs on all islands except Iraklia, although you should still bring a decent amount of ready cash with you.

Getting There & Away

There are daily connections to and from Naxos to the Little Cyclades but services can be disrupted when sea conditions are poor; make sure you have plenty of time before committing yourself – these islands are not meant for last-minute visits or for one-night tick lists. In recent years the big Blue Star car ferries have established a regular schedule from Piraeus via Naxos to all of the Little Cyclades islands and on to Amorgos and Astypalea and back.

The sturdy little ferry **Express Skopelitis** (☎ 22850 71256/519; Katapola, Amorgos) runs from Naxos (daily in summer, four days a week in winter) to the Little Cyclades and Amorgos. It's a defining Cycladic experience but bad weather can blow the schedule. Most seating is open deck so, when it's windy, brace yourself for some real rocking and rolling. In rough weather you'll know what's coming when the crew starts dishing out the *see-through* sick bags. If you're on deck, work out exactly which side of the boat is protected from wind and sea on each section between islands and stay there, or that bracing sea air may become a bracing Aegean Sea deluge. Regardless of sea conditions, locals, the crew and this writer

head straight below for the comfy saloon and bar where they become engulfed in cigarette smoke and gossip. The choice is yours…

For details see Island Hopping (Iraklia p514, Schinousa p522, Koufonisia p516 and Donousa p512).

IRAKLIA HPAKΛEIA

pop 115

Iraklia (ir-a-*klee*-a) is only 19 sq km in area, a little Aegean gem dozing in the sun. Dump the party gear and spurn the nightlife, the 'sightseeing' and the dreary souvenirs. Instead, brace yourself for a serene and quiet life and Iraklia will not disappoint. Only in July and August will you have to share the idyll with like-minded others.

The island now has the distinction of having the first offshore **desalination plant** in Greece. *And* it's driven by solar panels and windpower. You pass it as you enter the harbour. Raise a cheer for sustainability.

The port and main village of Iraklia is Agios Georgios. It has an attractive cove-like harbour, complete with a sandy beach. Turn right at the end of the ferry quay, and then go up left for a well-supplied general store, Perigiali Supermarket. Further uphill is a smaller store and *kafeneio* (coffee house) called Melissa's, which is also the ferry ticket office, postal agency and perennial gossip shop. There are card phones outside Perigiali Supermarket and Melissa's and there is an ATM just up from the harbour. A medical centre is located next to

Perigiali Supermarket. The island's website is www.iraklia.gr.

A surfaced road leads off to the left of the ferry quay, and after about 1km you'll reach **Livadi**, the island's best beach. A steep 2.5km further on is **Hora (Panagia)**. Where the road forks at the village entrance, keep to the right for the main street.

A surfaced road has recently been extended from Hora to **Tourkopigado Beach**.

The island's major 'sight' is the **Cave of the Sacred Icon of Agios Giannis**, which can be reached on foot from Panagia in a four-hour return trip. The path starts just beyond the church at a signpost on the right and is very rocky and steep in places; boots or walking shoes are essential and you should take plenty of water. At the site there is a large open cave on the left. On the right, white-painted rocks surround the apparently tiny entrance to the main sequence of caves. A torch is useful and the initial scramble along a low-roofed tunnel is worth it, leading as it does to caves full of stalactites and stalagmites. On 28 August, the eve of the death of John the Baptist, crowds of local people assemble at the cave and crawl inside to hold a candle-lit service.

Beyond the cave the path leads to the beach at **Alimia**, which is also served by boat from Agios Georgios in summer, offering a shortcut to the cave.

During July and August, a local boat ferries people to island beaches and also runs day trips to nearby Schinousa. Enquire at Perigiali Supermarket.

Sleeping & Eating

Domatia and tavernas are concentrated in and around Agios Georgios, although a few open on the beach at Livadi in summer. Domatia owners meet the boats, but in high season it's advisable to book.

Anna's Place (☎ 22850 71145; s €40, d €50-70, tr €85; ⊠) Located on high ground above the port, these lovely, airy rooms have stylish furnishings and the front balconies have sweeping views. There's a big communal kitchen and outside eating area.

Agnadema/Dimitri's (☎/fax 22850 71484, 6978048789; studio/d €40/50; ⊠) There's a great choice at this peaceful, family-owned property on the hillside above Agios Georgios harbour. Agnadema's rooms are big, bright and immaculate. Agnadema means 'great view', an understatement considering the superb position of the property. Dimitri's are a row of adjacent small studios with shared verandah and are equally well equipped.

Maistrali Apartments (☎ 2285071807; nickmaistrali @in.gr; d/tr €40/60; ⊠) The communal terrace at these well-equipped apartments has unrivalled open views to Ios and the south. There are only a few rooms, so booking for high season is advised.

There are a few tavernas in Agios Georgios. All serve fresh fish dishes and other Greek standards. **Maïstrali** (☎ 22850 71807; dishes €3.80-7) has a pleasant terrace and also has rooms and fairly creaky internet access. **Perigiali** (☎ 22850 71118; dishes €4-7), a popular place, has a large marble table encircling an old pine tree.

In Hora, **Taverna to Steki** (☎ 22850 71579; dishes €4-8) is a classic village eatery and is well known for its locally sourced ingredients and traditional food.

SCHINOUSA ΣΧΙΝΟΥΣΑ
pop 206

Schinousa (skih-*noo*-sah) lies a mere 2km across the sea from Iraklia and is similar in nature – slow-paced and endearing. It has a number of beaches, although not all are attractive, and down-to-earth Hora (Panagia) on the breezy crest of the island has sweeping views of the sea.

Ferries dock at the fishing harbour of Mersini. Hora is a hot 1km uphill (domatia owners are always around to meet ferries with transport).

Paralos Travel (☎ 22850 71160; fax 22850 71957) is halfway along the main street. It sells ferry tickets and also doubles as the post office. **Grispos Travel** (☎ 22850 29329), at the far end of the village, sells ferry tickets.

There's a public telephone in the main square and an ATM next to Deli restaurant. A reasonably useful website is www.schinousa.gr.

On the way down to Tsigouri beach is a little **folk museum** that features a reconstructed bread oven. Opening hours go with the flow of island life.

Dirt tracks lead from Hora to beaches around the coast. The nearest are **Tsigouri** and **Livadi**, both uncrowded outside August. Haul a little further to decent beaches at **Almyros** and **Aligaria**. With the exception of Tsigouri, there are no shops or tavernas at the beaches, so take food and water.

Sleeping

There are a few rooms down at Mersini, but if you want to see the rest of the island you're much better off staying in Hora.

Anna Domatia (☎ 22850 71161; Hora; s/d/tr €40/45/50; ✖) Well-kept, good-sized rooms, just behind the main street on the west side of the village, make Anna's a good-value choice. For an extra €5 you can get a room with a kitchen.

Iliovasilema (☎ 22850 71948; iliovasilema@schinousa .gr; Hora; s €45, d €55-60, tr €60-65; ✖ 🖦) Ideally located on the western outskirts of the village, looking south over the island, this bright, clean place has good-sized rooms and most of the balconies have fine views.

Galini (☎ 22850 71983, 21046 29448; s/d/tr €50/50/60) Most rooms at this well-positioned pension have fabulous views. It stands right at the far end of town in its own grounds. Rooms are bright and clean and pleasantly quaint. There's no air conditioning, but there are sturdy ceiling fans.

Eating

Akbar (☎ 22850 72001; dishes €3-6.50) A colourful little cafe in the main street, Akbar has mezes and fresh salads, as well as breakfast for about €7.

Loza (☎ 22850 71864; dishes €4.50-9.50) Just opposite Akbar and a local rendezvous for breakfasts (€7.50) as well as salads and pizzas. It's also a bakery and makes pastries, including baklava and walnut pie.

our pick **Deli Restaurant and Sweet Bar** (☎ 22850 74278; mains €7.50-9) The outstanding Deli is run by the same creative team that once ran Margarita's down the road. Excellent Greek cuisine, with a strong local basis, features starters such as millefeuille eggplant with fresh tomatoes and local soft cheese, or fava beans with onions and olive oil. Mains include chicken with herbs and lemon, and small pieces of local pork with peppers in a wine sauce. Vegetarians can enjoy a plate of the day. They also do breakfast for €6. The upper floor houses the restaurant, the ground floor is a very cool cafe-bar and downstairs there's a sweet section. The wine list is trim but excellent with some fine Macedonian vintages.

KOUFONISIA ΚΟΥΦΟΝΗΣΙΑ

pop 366

The islands of **Ano Koufonisia** and **Kato Koufinisia** face each other across blue waters. It's Ano Koufonisia that's populated. Its excellent beaches make it one of the most visited islands of the Little Cyclades, and modernisation has taken hold. New hotels and studios are springing up, and a marina with capacity for 50 yachts is due to be completed 'any time now'. Koufinisia's substantial fishing fleet still sustains a thriving local community outside the summer season.

A caïque ride away, Kato Koufonisia has some beautiful beaches and a lovely church. Archaeological digs on **Keros**, the rocky, bull-backed mountain of an island that looms over Koufonisia to the south, have uncovered over 100 Early Cycladic figurines, including the famous harpist and flautist now on display in Athens' National Archaeological Museum (p81). Important finds in recent years seem to confirm that Keros was a Cycladian site of major importance.

Orientation & Information

Koufinisia's only settlement spreads out behind the ferry quay. On one side of the quay is the planned yacht marina; on the other side is a wide bay filled with moored fishing boats. A large beach of flat, hard sand gives a great sense of space to the waterfront. Its inner edge is used as a road and everyone uses it as a football pitch. The older part of town, the *hora*, sprawls along a low hill above the harbour and is one long main street, often strewn with fallen leaves of bougainvillea.

There are a couple of supermarkets along the road that leads inland from the beach to link with the main street, and there's a ticket agency halfway along the main street. The post office is along the first road that leads sharply left as you reach the road leading inland. There is an ATM outside the post office.

Sights

BEACHES

An easy walk along the sandy coast road to the east of the port leads in a couple of kilometres to **Finikas**, **Harakopou** and **Fano** beaches. All tend to become swamped with grilling bodies in July and August and nudity becomes more overt the further you go.

Beyond Fano a path leads to several rocky swimming places, then continues to the great bay at **Pori**, where a long crescent of sand slides effortlessly into the ultimate Greek-island-dream sea. Pori can also be reached by an inland road from Hora.

Tours

Koufonissia Tours (☎ 22850 71671; www.koufonissiatours
.gr), based at Villa Ostria hotel (see below), organises caïque trips to Keros, Kato Koufonisia
and to other islands of the Little Cyclades.
Bike hire is also available.

Sleeping

Independent camping is not permitted on
Koufonisia. There is a good selection of domatia and hotels, and Koufonissia Tours organises accommodation on the island.

Lefteris Rooms (☎ 22850 71458; d/tr €40/45) Right
behind the town beach and above Lefteris
restaurant are these simple but colourful
rooms, with the ones at the back being the
most peaceful.

Anna's Rooms (☎ 22850 71061, 6974527838; s/d/tr/q
€50/60/70/80; 🔀) In a quiet location at Loutro
on the west side of the port, these big, bright
rooms are a great choice and the welcome is
charming. Rooms overlook the old harbour
and are set amid colourful gardens. Each
room has tea- and coffee-making facilities.

Ermis (☎ 22850 71693; fax 22850 74214; s/d €55/70;
🔀) In a quiet, leafy location behind the post
office, these spacious rooms have attractive
decor and generous balconies at the front.

ourpick Alkyonides Studios (☎ 22850 74170; www
.alkionides.gr; d/tr/q incl breakfast €70/75/80) Taking the
high ground on Koufinisia are these well-
located studios above Loutro's little harbour.
The name 'Alkyonides' is proudly displayed
on an old boat, just one of a few eccentric
touches. The spacious, bright rooms have fans
rather than air conditioning, a plus as far as
some are concerned. Breakfast is included (the
egg layers are just down the road). Don't be
put off by the rocky road approach or the odd
abandoned car. A path leads down to Loutro
in a few minutes.

Villa Ostria (☎ 22850 71671; www.koufonissiatours.gr;
s/d/tr incl breakfast €70/85/90; 🔀 🛜) A stylish, small
hotel, Villa Ostria stands on the high ground
above the beach and has a charming garden
area. Rooms are smart and comfortable and
have fridges.

Eating

Kalamia Café (☎ 22850 74444; snacks €3-5.50; 🖥 🛜) A
great gathering point and net-browsing venue.
Link-up is free to customers and there's a
bar-top screen if you don't have your own
kit. They do a range of breakfast fare from
€3.50 to €6.

Karnagio (☎ 22850 71694; mains €4-10) Don't miss
this little *ouzerie* at Loutro where the tables
skirt the harbour. It operates out of a tiny
building. Prawn *saganaki* and seafood platters
at €10 for small, €20 for large, go well with
the ambience.

Lefteris (☎ 22850 71458; dishes €4.50-8) Lefteris
dishes up reasonably priced Greek standards
to huge numbers of visitors in high summer.
Its vast terrace looks out over the town beach
and it's open for breakfast and lunch also.

Capetan Nikolas (☎ 22850 71690; mains €4.50-11)
One of the best seafood places on the islands,
this happy, family-run restaurant overlooks
the little harbour at Loutro. Shrimp salad for
€6.50 is a good bet while locally caught fish,
such as red mullet and sea bream, are a speciality and are priced by the kilo.

Drinking

Scholeio (☎ 22850 71837; ⏰ 6pm-3.30am) A little
island bar and crêperie that goes well with
the island's laid-back ambience. Scholeio
does a great line in cocktails and other
drinks, and plays jazz, blues, rock and other
choice sounds. It's right at the western end
of the village's main street above Loutro.
The owners are accomplished photographers
and often have exhibitions of their work
on show.

Sorokos (☎ 22850 71704; ⏰ 4pm-3am) Drinks
and snacks and hot sounds that range from
early-hours lounge music to harder vibes at
night make this a popular hangout beyond
the town beach.

DONOUSA ΔΟΝΟΥΣΑ
pop 110

Donousa is the out-on-a-limb island where
you stop bothering about which day it might
be. In late July and August the island can
be swamped by holidaymaking Greeks and
sun-seeking north Europeans, but out of
season be prepared to linger – and be rewarded for it.

Agios Stavros is Donousa's main settlement
and port, a cluster of functional buildings
round a handsome church, overlooking a
small bay. Little has changed here over the
years, but water shortage – on an island that
was once always well supplied – has resulted
in recent pipe-laying to houses from a new
storage tank for imported water. New surfaced walkways have been a welcome side-
effect. The town also has a good **beach**, which

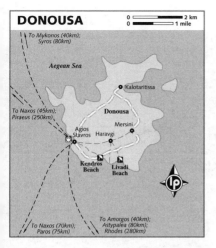

DONOUSA

0 — 2 km
0 — 1 mile

To Mykonos (40km);
Syros (80km)

Aegean Sea

Kalotaritissa

To Naxos (45km);
Piraeus (250km)

Donousa

Mersini

Agios
Stavros   Haravgi

Kendros
Beach   Livadi
Beach

To Naxos (70km);
Paros (75km)

To Amorgos (40km);
Astypalea (80km);
Rhodes (280km)

also serves as a thoroughfare for infrequent vehicles and foot traffic to a clutch of homes, rental rooms and a taverna across the bay.

Roussos Travel (☎ 22850 51648) on the waterfront is the ticket agency for the local ferry *Express Skopelitis*.

Sigalis Travel (☎ 22850 51570, 6942269219) in the To Iliovasilema restaurant complex (see right) sells tickets for Blue Star ferries.

There is an ATM outside Roussos Travel (it's sometimes hidden behind a blue shutter for protection from blown sand). But be sure to bring sufficient cash in high season. There is a public telephone up a steep hill above the waterfront; it's hidden behind a tree. You can get telecards at the souvenir shop just up from the quay-end of the beach.

There is a **medical centre** (☎ 22850 51506) and postal agency just below the church.

Kendros, situated 1.25km to the southeast of Agios Stavros, along a rather ugly bulldozed track, is a sandy and secluded beach with a seasonal taverna. **Livadi**, a dusty 1km hike further east, sees even fewer visitors. Both Kendros and Livadi are popular with naturists. Bulldozed, unsurfaced roads have marred Donousa in places, but there are still paths and tracks that lead into the hills to timeless little hamlets such as **Mersini**.

Sleeping & Eating

Most rooms on the island are fairly basic but are well kept, clean and in good locations. You should book ahead for stays in July and August, and even early September.

Prasinos Studios (☎ 22850 51579; d €40-60, apt €80) In a lofty position on the high ground on the far side of the beach, this pleasant complex has a mix of well-kept rooms.

To Iliovasilema (☎ 22850 51570; d/tr/studios €45/50/55; 🖳) Reasonable rooms, some with kitchens, overlook the beach. There's a popular restaurant with a fine terrace and a good selection of food (dishes €4.50 to €20).

Capetan Giorgis (☎ 22850 51867; mains €4.50-9) Sturdy traditional food is on the menu at the Capetan's, where the terrace, just above the harbour, has good views across the bay.

There are a couple of food shops that have a reasonable selection of goods in July and August.

The hub of village life is Kafeneio To Kyma by the quay, where things liven up late into the night in summer.

AMORGOS ΑΜΟΡΓΟΣ

pop 1873

Amorgos (ah-mor-ghoss) lies well to the southeast of the main Cycladic group; this lovely island rises from the sea in a long dragon's back of craggy mountains that is 30km from tip to toe and 822m at its highest point. The island's southeast coast is unrelentingly steep and boasts an extraordinary monastery embedded in a huge cliff. The northern half of the opposite coast is equally spectacular, but relents a little at the narrow inlet where the main port and town of Katapola lies.

Amorgos' other port town, Aegiali, lies at the island's northern end and is more appealing as a resort. It has a good beach and is encircled by rugged mountains. The enchanting Hora (also known as Amorgos) nestles high in the mountains above Katapola.

There's plenty of scope for beaching, but Amorgos is much more about archaeology and the outdoor world – there's great walking, scuba diving and a burgeoning rock-climbing scene, although currently the latter is for the very experienced rather than the passing thrillseeker.

CYCLADES

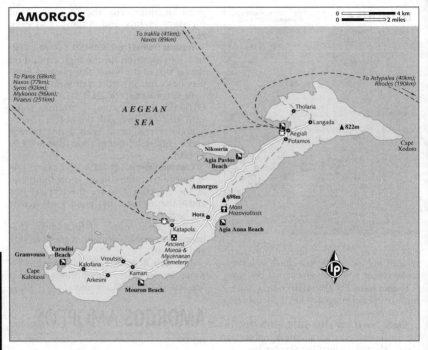

AMORGOS

To Iraklia (41km);
Naxos (89km);

To Paros (68km);
Naxos (77km);
Syros (92km);
Mykonos (96km);
Piraeus (251km)

To Astypalea (40km);
Rhodes (190km)

AEGEAN SEA

Tholaria
Langada
▲822m
Aegiali
Potamos
Cape Xodoto

Nikouria
Agia Pavlos Beach

Amorgos
▲698m
Moni Hozoviotissis
Hora
Katapola
Agia Anna Beach

Ancient Minoa & Mycenaean Cemetery

Paradisi Beach
Gramvousa
Vroutsis
Kalofana
Cape Kalotassi
Kamari
Arkesini
Mouron Beach

CYCLADES

Getting There & Away

Connections between Amorgos and Naxos are very good with the small ferry, *Express Skopelitis*, running each day and connecting the Little Cyclades and Amorgos. The big Blue Star ferries also run to and from Piraeus and continue to Astypalea and to Rhodes while other ferries link from Piraeus via Folegandros and Santorini. For details see Island Hopping (p508).

Getting Around

Regular buses go from Katapola to Hora (€1.40, 15 minutes), Moni Hozoviotissis (€1.60, 15 minutes) and Agia Anna Beach (€1.50, 20 minutes), and less-frequent services go to Aegiali (€2.40, 30 minutes). However, there are fewer services on weekends. There are also buses from Aegiali to the picturesque village of Langada. Schedules are posted on bus windscreens.

Cars and motorcycles are available for hire from the travel agencies **N Synodinos** (☎ 22850 71201; synodinos@nax.forthnet.gr; Katapola) and **Aegialis Tours** (☎ 22850 73107; fax 22850 73394; www.amorgos-aegialis.com; Aegiali).

KATAPOLA ΚΑΤΑΠΟΛΑ
pop 130

The island's principal port, Katapola, straggles round the curving shoreline of a dramatic bay in the most verdant part of the island. The fascinating and extensive remains of the ancient city of **Minoa**, as well as a **Mycenaean cemetery**, lie above the port and can be reached by a steep, surfaced road. Amorgos has also yielded many Cycladic finds; the largest figurine in the National Archaeological Museum (p81) in Athens was found in the vicinity of Katapola.

Orientation & Information

Boats dock right on the waterfront. The bus station is to the left along the main waterfront, on the eastern shore of the bay.

A bank (with ATM) is midwaterfront and there's an ATM next to N Synodinos. There is a postal agency next to the Hotel Minoa on the central square.

Hotel Minoa (☎ 22850 71480; ⏰ 9am-2pm & 7-10pm; internet per hr €5)

N Synodinos (☎ 22850 71201; synodinos@nax.forth net.gr) Sells ferry tickets and has money exchange and car hire (per day in high season €45).
Port police (☎ 22850 71259) On the central square.

Sleeping & Eating

Domatia owners usually meet ferries and are among the most restrained and polite in the Cyclades.

Diosmarini (☎ 22850 71636; www.diosmarini.com; d/tr/apt €50/70/100) On the northern shores of the bay and about 1km from the ferry quay, Diosmarini is a good option away from the main port. It has big rooms in a handsome and modern Cycladic-style building. There are airy views from most balconies.

Pension Sofia (☎ 22850 71494; www.pensionsofia.gr; d/tr €55/80; ⚡) The charming, family-run Sofia stands amid gardens and little meadows in a quiet area of town. Rooms are fresh and colourful. The same family has well-equipped studios and apartments elsewhere in the area (€120 to €150).

Eleni's Rooms (☎ 22850 71628; roomseleni@gmail .com; s/d/tr €60/65/75) An unbeatable position to the west of the ferry quay makes these unfussy but bright and airy rooms an excellent choice. The rooms rise through several levels and offer unbeatable views. You can even hop down in seconds for a morning swim at an adjoining beach.

Mouragio (☎ 22850 71011; dishes €4.50-9) Down to earth and nearly always packed by mid-evening, Mouragio specialises in seafood. It's on the main waterfront near the ferry quay. Shellfish are by the kilo but reasonable dishes include fish soup.

Elichryson (☎ 22850 71517; dishes €5-8.50; ⏱ 8am-10pm) Ideal for breakfast (€3.50 to €8), the pleasant Elichryson cafe is just back from the main waterfront.

Vitsentzos (☎ 22850 71518; dishes €5.50-9) A fine traditional restaurant with exposed stonework and a varnished wooden floor in its interior, Vitsentzos also has a leisurely terrace overlooking the bay. Food is classic Greek with modern influences. Seafood is by the kilo.

Drinking

Moon Bar (☎ 22850 71598) On the northern waterfront, this is the place to reflect on all that is well with the world with reassuring views to the sea and great background sounds that range from classical through blues, rock and funk into the early hours. Breakfasts are €5.

Le Grand Bleu (☎ 22850 71633) Still keeping alive the spirit of the iconic film *The Big Blue*, this popular bar plays rock, reggae and modern Greek music on the northern waterfront.

HORA ΧΩΡΑ
pop 416

The old capital of Hora sparkles like a snow-drift across its rocky ridge. It stands 400m above sea level and is capped by a 13th-century *kastro* atop a prominent rock pinnacle. Old windmills stand like sentinels on surrounding cliffs. There's a distinct veneer of sophistication, not least in the handful of trendy bars and shops that enhance Hora's appeal without eroding its timelessness.

The bus stop is on a small square at the edge of town. The post office is on the main square, reached by a pedestrian lane from the bus stop. The island's **police station** (☎ 22850 71210) is halfway along the main street.

Hora's **archaeology museum** (⏱ 9am-1pm & 6-8.30pm Tue-Sun) is on the main pedestrian thoroughfare, near Café Bar Zygós.

Sleeping & Eating

Hora has a handful of pleasant pensions.

Pension Ilias (☎ 22850 71277; s/d/tr/apt €45/55/65/80) Tucked away amid a jumble of traditional houses just down from the bus stop is this unpretentious, family-run place with decent rooms.

View To Big Blue (☎ 22850 71814, 6932248867; s/d €50/70) At the top end of the village is this attractive place in its own little garden. Rooms are very bright and comfy.

Café Bar Zygós (☎ 22850 71155; snacks €3-8; ⏱ 8am-3am) Right at the cool, colourful heart of Hora, Zygos is open for breakfast, sandwiches, baguettes, salads and cold plates as well as coffee, cakes, candied fruit and ice cream – all to lounge sounds by day, and dance music with cocktails at night. A speciality is a selection of distinctive mushroom dishes.

Keep heading up the winding main street to reach **Tsagaradiko** (☎ 6937281226; dishes €3-8), a great little *ouzerie* with tables on a lovely small square.

MONI HOZOVIOTISSIS ΜΟΝΗ ΧΟΖΟΒΙΩΤΙΣΣΗΣ

Amorgos is defined by this iconic **monastery** (⏱ 8am-1pm & 5-7pm), a dazzling white building embedded in an awesome cliff face high above the sea. It lies on the precipitous east coast below Hora. The monastery contains a miraculous icon that was found in the sea below the cliff. It got there (allegedly unaided) from Asia Minor, Cyprus or Jerusalem – depending on which legend you're told. A few monks still live here and short tours, which usually end with a pleasant chat with one of the monks, take place sporadically, usually when a reasonable number of visitors have gathered at the door of the monastery. The tour is free but donations are appreciated.

Out of respect, modest dress is essential: long trousers for men; a long skirt or dress for women, who should also cover their shoulders. Wraps are no longer available at the entrance, so make sure you are prepared.

AEGIALI ΑΙΓΙΑΛΗ
pop 232

Aegiali is Amorgos' second port and has more of a resort style, not least because of the fine sweep of sand that lines the inner edge of the bay on which the village stands. Steep slopes and impressive crags lie above the main village.

Efficient **Amorgos Travel** (☎ 22850 73401; www.amorgostravel.gr), above the central supermarket on the waterfront, can help with a host of travel needs including ferry tickets, accommodation and island tours. Check it out for diving and walking possibilities also. Long-established **Aegialis Tours** (☎ 22850 73107; www.aegialistours.com) sells ferry tickets, and can organise accommodation, tours and vehicle hire.

There's a postal agency about 100m uphill from Aegialis Tours.

Tours

Ask at travel agencies about a daily bus outing (€25) around the island that leaves at 9.30am and returns at 4.30pm, with stops at Agia Pavlos, Moni Hozoviotissis and Hora. Boat trips around the island (€30) and to the Little Cyclades (€40) can also be arranged.

Sleeping

As is the case in Katapola, domatia owners meet the ferries.

Aegiali Camping (☎ 22850 73500; www.aegiali camping.gr; camp sites per adult/child/tent €5.50/2.70/3.50) Good facilities and a pleasantly shaded location on the road behind the beach makes this camping ground an attractive proposition. You can rent a tent for €6.30.

Pension Askas (☎ 22850 73333; www.askas pension.gr; d €60-70, tr €65-75; ▨ 🖛) Next to Aegiali Camping is this decent pension in a garden setting, with clean, attractive rooms.

Lakki Village (☎ 22850 73505; www.lakkivillage.gr; s/d/tr incl breakfast €85/95/105, apt incl breakfast €110-145; ▨ 🖳 🖳) This attractive, well-kept complex ambles inland from the beachfront through lovely gardens and water features. Rooms are in Cycladic-style buildings and have colourful traditional furnishings. Top-priced apartments sleep four people.

Eating

Restaurant Lakki (☎ 22850 73253; mains €3.50-8) A beach and garden setting makes the restaurant of Lakki Village a relaxing place to enjoy well-prepared Greek dishes.

To Koralli (☎ 22850 73217; dishes €4-12.50) Up a flight of steps at the eastern end of the waterfront, To Koralli has an airy view that goes with excellent Greek cuisine. Treat yourself to a platter of shrimps, octopus and squid, and small fish or meat dishes such as veal with eggplant, cheese, tomatoes and peppers.

Askas Taverna (☎ 22850 73333; mains €4.50-7) Adjoining Aegiali Camping and Pension Askas, this taverna offers good helpings of Greek standards. They stage *rembetika* (Greek blues) music evenings four times a week in July and August.

our pick **To Limani** (☎ 22850 73269; dishes €4.50-9) Traditional fare prepared with home-grown produce makes Limani a popular place. Local dishes include baked goat and, for fish lovers, fish soup, while vegetarians can enjoy fava beans with stuffed eggplant. For dessert the home-made orange pie is superb. There's a hugely popular Thai food night every Friday except during August. The owners also have beautiful rooms, studios and apartments (from €80 to €115) high above the bay in the village of Potamos.

AROUND AMORGOS

On the east coast, south of Moni Hozoviotissis, is **Agia Anna Beach**, the nearest beach to both Katapola and Hora. Don't get excited; the car park is bigger than any of the little pebbly beaches strung out along the rocky shoreline, and all the beaches fill up quickly. Next to the car park on the cliff-top there's a small cantina selling food and drinks.

CYCLADES

The lovely villages of **Langada** and **Tholaria** nestle amid the craggy slopes above Aegiali. The views from both are worth the trip alone. The two are linked to each other, and to Aegiali, by a signposted circular path that takes about four hours (Greek time). Regular buses run between the villages and Aegiali.

In Langada the **Pagali Hotel** (☎ 22850 73310; www.pagalihotel-amorgos.com; d/ste €75/95; ⚡ 🎧) is tucked away in the lower village and has superb views. The spacious rooms and studios are fronted by an almost Alpine-like terrace, where there's a long, narrow pitch of earth used for the nightly game of *bales*, the Amorgan version of *boules*, played with balls roughly carved out of olive wood. The hotel is a good contact point for alternative holidays that include experiencing the owners' organic farm, yoga and meditation sessions, art workshops, walking and rock climbing on the neighbouring crags.

The adjoining **Nico's Taverna** (☎ 22850 73310; mains €6-8) is run by the same family that owns the Pagali Hotel. Nico's makes a strong play for sustainability, with organic ingredients from the family's own farm, including olive oil, home-made wine and cheeses. Vegetarians should be in their element, but local goat dishes are also superb.

Special-Interest-Holidays (SP.IN; ☎ 6939820828; www.amorgos.dial.pipex.com), based at Langada, organises walking holidays with very experienced and knowledgeable guides.

IOS ΙΟΣ

pop 1900

Ios is slowly shedding its image as the party capital of the Cyclades. It has always been as traditional in landscape and cultural terms as any other island in the group, and Greek life goes on sturdily beyond the wall-to-wall bars and nightclubs of Hora and the beach scene. The opening of the recently excavated Bronze Age site of Skarkos (see p186) has enhanced the island's appeal and there is evidence that families and older holidaymakers are heading for Ios in increasing numbers. There's still hard partying, though, and you need some stamina to survive the late-night action in the centre of Hora.

Getting There & Away

Ios lies conveniently on the Mikonos–Santorini ferry axis and has regular connections with Pireaus. For details see Island Hopping (p514).

Getting Around

In summer crowded buses run between Ormos, Hora and Mylopotas Beach about every 15 minutes (€1.40). From June to August private excursion buses go to Manganari Beach (one way €3) and Agia Theodoti Beach (one way €2.50). Buses leave at 11am and return at 4.30pm.

Caïques travelling from Ormos to Manganari cost €12 per person for a return trip (departing 11am daily). Ormos and Hora both have car and motorcycle hire that can be booked through the Plakiotis Travel Agency (p186) and Acteon Travel (below).

HORA, ORMOS & MYLOPOTAS
ΧΩΡΑ, ΟΡΜΟΣ & ΜΥΛΟΠΟΤΑΣ

Ios has three population centres, all very close together on the west coast: the port, Ormos; the capital, Hora (also known as the 'village'; population 1656), 2km inland by road from the port; and Mylopotas (population 73), the beach 2km downhill from Hora.

Orientation

The bus terminal in Ormos is straight ahead from the ferry quay on Plateia Emirou. If you don't mind the heat, it's possible to walk from the port to Hora by heading up left from Plateia Emirou, then right up a stepped path after about 100m. It's about 1.2km.

In Hora the main landmark is the big cathedral opposite the bus stop, on the other side of the dusty car park and play area. Plateia Valeta is the central square.

There are public toilets uphill behind the main square.

The road straight ahead from the bus stop leads to Mylopotas Beach.

Information

There's an ATM right by the information kiosks at the ferry quay. In Hora, the National Bank of Greece, behind the church, and the Commercial Bank, nearby, both have ATMs.

The post office in Hora is a block behind the main road (town-hall side).

Acteon Travel (☎ 22860 91343; www.acteon.gr) On the square near the quay, and in Hora and Mylopotas. Internet is €4 per hour.

CYCLADES

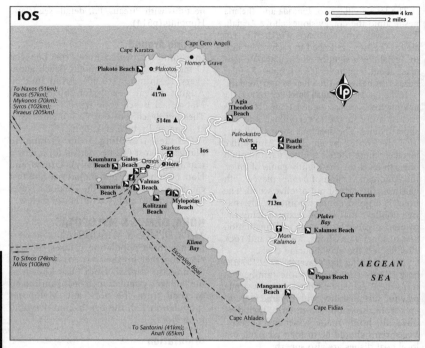

IOS

To Naxos (51km);
Paros (57km);
Mykonos (70km);
Syros (102km);
Piraeus (205km)

Cape Karatza

Cape Gero Angeli

Homer's Grave

Plakoto Beach   Plakotos

417m

Agia
Theodoti
Beach

514m

Paleokastro
Ruins   Psathi
             Beach

Skarkos   Ios

Koumbara   Gialos
Beach   Beach   Ormos
                     Hora

Tsamaria   Valmas
Beach   Beach

Kolitzani   Mylopotas
Beach   Beach

To Sifnos (74km);
Milos (100km)

713m   Cape Pountas

Plakes
Bay
         Kalamos Beach

Klima
Bay

Moni
Kalamou

AEGEAN
SEA

Papas Beach

Manganari
Beach

To Santorini (41km);
Anafi (65km)

Cape Ahlades

Cape Fidias

0 ___ 4 km
0 ___ 2 miles

CYCLADES

Doubleclick Internet (☎ 22860 92155; Hora; per hr €4) A well-equipped place with good connection.

Hospital (☎ 22860 91227) On the way to Gialos, 250m northwest of the quay; there are several doctors in Hora.

Plakiotis Travel Agency (☎ 22860 91221; plaktr2@otenet.gr) On the Ormos waterfront.

Port police (☎ 22860 91264) At the southern end of the Ormos waterfront, just before Ios Camping.

Sights

Hora is a lovely Cycladic village with a labyrinth of narrow lanes and cubist houses. It's at its most charming during daylight hours when the bars are shut and it recaptures the atmosphere of other island towns.

Ios can rightly celebrate a cultural triumph in its award-winning archaeological site of **Skarkos** (the Snail). This early-to-late Bronze Age settlement crowns a low hill in the plain just to the north of Hora. The site was not yet open to the public at the time of writing but was scheduled to open midsummer 2009. There is likely to be an entrance fee. Walled terraces surrounding the settlement have been restored and the low ruins of several Cycladic-style buildings of the period are exposed. A visitor centre is part of the development. The site lies on the lower ground to the north of Hora.

Finds from Skarkos are displayed at the excellent **archaeological museum** (Hora; admission €2, EU students free; 🕑 8.30am-3pm Tue-Sun) in the town hall by the bus stop in Hora. There are also exhibits from island excavations in general.

At the time of writing a remarkable **art gallery** was under construction on the summit of the highest hill behind Hora. It's being built to house the works of the radical artist Yiannis Gaitis, who had a house on Ios, and his wife, the sculptor Gabriella Simosi. The works of other artists will also be exhibited. The building comprises several huge gallery spaces worthy of European capitals. Fingers crossed it will be completed soon.

Activities

Banana rides (€12), canoe hire (per hour €15) and mountain-bike hire (per day €15) are all available at **Yialos Watersports** (☎ 22860 92463, 6944926625; ralfburgstahler@hotmail.com; Gialos Beach). You can also hire windsurfing equipment (per half-day €30) or take a tube ride (€14 to €17).

HOMER'S GRAVE RIDDLE

Homer is said to have died on the island of Ios because of the distress brought on by his inability to solve a riddle posed by fishermen that 'what they caught they discarded and what they could not catch, they kept'. Ios has long laid claim to being the site of 'Homer's Grave' although Homer would have puzzled himself to death over why a major surfaced road (for Ios) should now wind its way through empty hills for 12km to end a few hundred metres from his – alleged – last resting place, a rather forlorn little mausoleum that looks decidedly post-Homeric. The views are worth it, however. Sikinos, Naxos, Iraklia and Schinousa make for a nicely balanced crescent of islands across the sea. Homer would have appreciated the symmetry (if not the fishermen's fleas…).

Mylopotas Water Sports Center (☎ 22860 91622; www.ios-sports.gr; Mylopotas) has snorkelling and windsurfing gear, pedal boats (per hour €15) and canoes (single/double per hour €15/20) for hire. Waterskiing (per 15 minutes €30), banana rides (€12 to €15) and sailing (per hour/day €25/70) are also available. Beach volleyball and soccer rental is from €3 to €15. There is also a speedboat taxi available for hire.

New Dive Diving Centre (☎ 22860 92340; www.ios-sports.gr; Mylopotas) runs a PADI 'discover scuba diving' session (€65), plus more intensive PADI courses from €290 to €795. Speciality courses range from deep diving to underwater photography, fish identification and underwater navigation (€250 to €350). There are also daily diving and snorkelling trips, with shore dives (from €25).

Windsurfing (per hour/day €15/40) is on offer at **Meltemi Water Sports** (☎ 22860 91680; www.meltemiwatersports.com; Mylopotas) at the beach opposite Far Out Camping. Laser sailboats (per hour/day €30/65) are also available for hire, as are canoes and pedalos. Tube rides cost from €15 to €30. Meltemi runs a similar scene at Manganari Beach and has a water taxi from Mylopotas to other beaches.

Sleeping

ORMOS

The port has several good sleeping options, reasonable eating places, a couple of handy beaches and regular bus connections to Hora and other beaches.

Ios Camping (☎ 22860 92035; fax 22860 92101; camp sites per person €8; 🏊) Tucked away on the west side of Ormos, this site has good facilities, including a restaurant in high season. Head all the way round the waterfront.

Golden Sun Hotel (☎ 22860 91110; www.iosgoldensun.com; s/d/tr incl breakfast €70/80/90; 🅿 ❌ 🖥) The road from Gialos to Hora may not seem ideal sleeping territory, but this pleasant family-run hotel is located just up from the port and lies well down from the road. It overlooks open fields towards the sea. The good-sized rooms are well cared for.

Hotel Poseidon (☎ 22860 91091; www.poseidonhotelios.gr; s/d/tr €71/88/112; ❌ 🏊) A very pleasant family-run hotel that lifts you high above the bustle and noise of the port, the Poseidon has terrific views from its front balconies. A flight of steps leads up to the hotel where rooms are immaculate and well equipped and there's a pleasant swimming pool.

GIALOS BEACH

Hotel Helena (☎ 22860 91276; www.hotelhelena.gr; s/d/tr/apt €50/70/90/120; ❌ 🖥 🛜 🏊) Set a short way back from the midpoint of the beach is this quiet and well-run place. It has a cool patio, kindly owners and bright, clean rooms.

To Corali (☎ 22860 91272; www.coralihotel.com; d/tr incl breakfast €95/105, apt €120; 🅿 ❌ 🖥 🛜) These sparkling rooms are in a good position right opposite the beach and are attached to the restaurant of the same name. There's a colourful garden at the rear and the owners create a happy atmosphere.

HORA

Francesco's (☎ 22860 91223; www.francescos.net; dm €15, s €40-45, d €50-60; 🖥) Long established and very well run, the famous Francesco's has clean dormitories and rooms, and is in an enviable position with great views of the bay. It's away from the centre but is a lively meeting place for the younger international set. There's a busy bar and terrace and a big aprés-beach Jacuzzi. Francescos is reached by going up right from the cathedral for about 30m and then going left along Odos Scholarhiou for a couple of hundred metres.

Skala Hotel (☎ 22860 92027; skalahtl@otenet.gr; d/tr €85/100, apt €90-160; ❌ 🖥 🏊) A short hike uphill from the centre of town takes you well above the action zone to this well-situated hotel with great views over Hora. Good-sized rooms are bright and half of them have kitchenettes. Guests also have access to the pool and Jacuzzi.

MYLOPOTAS

Purple Pig Stars Camping & Bungalows (☎ 22860 91302; www.purplepigstars.com; camp sites per person €9, dm/d €20/45; 🖳) This pleasant camping ground is right at the entrance to the beach and has a relaxing tempo while being close to the action. It's shaded by trees.

Far Out Camping, Village Hotel & Beach Club (☎ 22860 91468; www.faroutclub.com; camp sites per adult/child €12/6, bungalows €12-22, studio €90; 🖳 🖳) There's plenty of action here, backed by wall-to-wall facilities. Meltemi Water Sports (see p187) is just across the road, and a diving centre has been established in recent years. There's a bar, restaurant and four swimming pools. The 'bungalows' range from small tent-sized affairs to neat little 'roundhouses' with double and single beds. The studios are in a separate location and have all mod cons.

Paradise Rooms (☎ 22860 91621; parios11@otenet.gr; s/d €55/65; 🖳) The family-run rooms here are about halfway along the beachfront, and the beautiful garden is looked after with love and skill. Breakfast costs €3 to €4.

our pick Hotel Nissos Ios (☎ 22860 91610; www .nissosios-hotel.com; s/d/tr €60/75/90; 🖳 🖳) This excellent place has bright and fresh rooms, and wall murals add a colourful touch. Each room has tea- and coffee-making facilities. The welcome is good-natured, and the beach is just across the road. There's an outdoor Jacuzzi. In front of the hotel is the Bamboo Restaurant & Pizzeria (opposite).

Paradise Apartments (☎ 22860 91621; apt €90-140; 🖳 🖳) These apartments are located a short distance away from Paradise Rooms, and are run by a member of the same family. They're located in a secluded setting and have a lovely pool and big patio. At both Paradise accommodations, guests can get a 50% reduction at Mylopotas Water Sports Center (p187).

Eating

ORMOS

Peri Anemon (☎ 22860 92501; mains €5-10) A pleasant little cafe-taverna in the square next to Akteon Travel on the Ormos harbourfront, where you can get snacks and Greek standards.

GIALOS BEACH

To Corali (☎ 22860 91272; dishes €5-9) Mouthwatering wood-fired pizzas are list-toppers at this well-run eatery that's right by the beach and in front of the hotel of the same name. You can sit out at tables on the beach. It does pastas and salads as well, and it's a great spot for coffee, drinks and ice cream.

HORA

Porky's (☎ 22860 91143; snacks €2-4.50) Fuel up with toasties, salads, crêpes and hamburgers at this relentless Ios survivor, just off the main square.

Ali Baba's (☎ 22860 91558; dishes €7-12) Another great Ios favourite. this is the place for Thai dishes, including *pad thai* (thin rice noodles stir-fried with dried shrimp, bean sprouts, tofu and egg) cooked by authentic Thai chefs. The service is very upbeat and there's a garden courtyard. It's on the same street as the Emporiki bank.

Lord Byron (☎ 22860 92125; dishes €7-14) Near the main square, this long-standing favourite is relaxing and intimate, and the food is a great fusion of Greek and Italian. Dishes range from shrimp cooked in a tomato sauce with feta and ouzo, to penne with a wild mushroom and cream sauce – and it all comes in generous helpings.

Pomodoro (☎ 22860 91387; dishes €8-14) Spread over two floors, Pomodoro is just off the main square above Disco 69. There's a fabulous roof garden with panoramic views. Big helpings are the order of the day and authentic wood-fired pizzas are just part of its excellent, modern Italian and Mediterranean menu.

our pick Pithari (☎ 22860 92440; mains €9-17) A longstanding local favourite located alongside the cathedral, Pithari has an excellent menu of traditional Greek cuisine given a modern twist. Shrimps flambé vie with filo pastry pies of feta cheese with honey and sesame seeds. They also do lunch, with pastas and other well-sourced local dishes.

There are also *gyros* (meat slivers cooked on a vertical rotisserie; usually eaten with pitta bread) stands where you can get a cheap bite.

MYLOPOTAS

Harmony (☎ 22860 91613; dishes €4-12) Few places take chill-out to the honed level of this great bar. Hammocks, deckchairs and discerning sounds set the pace and kids are well looked after here. It's just along the northern arm of

Mylopotas beach. There's live music too, and Tex-Mex food is the main attraction.

Drakos Taverna (☎ 22860 91281; dishes €4.50-9) Enjoy reasonably priced fish dishes (although some species are by the kilogram) at this popular taverna that overlooks the sea at the southern end of the beach.

Bamboo Restaurant & Pizzeria (☎ 22860 91648; dishes €6.50-8.50) Run by a member of the same family that operates Hotel Nissos Ios (opposite), this pleasant place does a good line in traditional *mousakas* and pizzas, plus a range of other Greek dishes. Breakfasts are €4.50 to €7.50.

Entertainment

Nightlife on Ios is a blitz. No one signs up for an early night in Hora's tiny main square, where it gets so crowded by midnight that you won't be able to fall down, even if you want to. Be young and carefree – but (women especially) also be careful. For a marginally quieter life there are some less full-on venues around.

Slammer Bar (☎ 22860 92119; Main Sq, Hora) Hammers out house, rock and Latin, as well as multiple tequila shots; head-banging in every sense.

Superfly (☎ 22860 92259; Main Sq, Hora) Plays funky house tunes.

Disco 69 (☎ 22860 91064; Main Sq, Hora) Hardcore drinking – and hard-core T-shirts – to a background of disco and current hits.

Other central venues are Blue Note, Flames Bar, Red Bull and Liquid.

Outside the centre of Hora are equally popular bars and some bigger dance clubs.

Ios Club (☎ 22860 91410) Head here for a cocktail and watch the sun set to classical, Latin and jazz music from a great terrace with sweeping views. It's along the pathway by Sweet Irish Dream.

Orange Bar (☎ 22860 91814) A more easy-paced music bar playing rock, indie and Brit-pop just outside the war zone.

Scorpion's is a late-night dance-to-trance and progressive venue with laser shows. A great favourite is Kandi featuring top Norwegian guest DJs, while Aftershock goes for sensation with raunchy dancers and house, trance and Greek hits.

AROUND IOS

Travellers are lured to Ios by its nightlife, but also by its beaches. Vying with Mylopotas as one of the best is **Manganari**, a long swath of fine white sand on the south coast, reached by bus or by caïque in summer (see Getting Around, p185).

From Ormos, it's a 10-minute walk past the little church of Agia Irini for **Valmas Beach**. A 1.3km walk northwest of Ormos, **Koumbara** is the official clothes-optional beach. **Tsamaria**, nearby, is nice and sheltered when it's windy elsewhere.

Agia Theodoti, **Psathi** and **Kalamos Beaches**, all on the northeast coast, are more remote. Psathi is a good windsurfing venue.

On Cape Gero Angeli, near Plakoto Beach at the northernmost tip of the island and 12km from Hora, is the alleged site of **Homer's Grave** (see boxed text, p187).

Moni Kalamou, on the way to Manganari and Kalamos Beaches, stages a huge **religious festival** in late August and a **festival of music and dance** in September.

SANTORINI (THIRA)
ΣΑΝΤΟΡΙΝΗ (ΘΗΡΑ)

pop 13,670

Santorini will take your breath away. Even the most jaded traveller succumbs to the spectacle of this surreal landscape, relic of what was probably the biggest eruption in recorded history. You do share the experience with hordes of other visitors, but the island somehow manages to cope with it all.

The caldera and its vast curtain of multicoloured cliffs is truly awesome. If you want to experience the full dramatic impact it's worth arriving by a slower ferry with open decks, rather than by enclosed catamaran or hydrofoil.

Santorini is famous for its spectacular sunsets. The village of Oia on the northern tip of the island is a hugely popular sunset-viewing site because there is an uninterrupted view of the sun as it finally sinks below the horizon.

Santorini is not all about the caldera, however. The east side of the island has black-sand beaches at popular resorts such as Kamari and Perissa and although the famous archaeological site of Akrotiri is closed for the forseeable future, Ancient Thira above Kamari is a major site.

The island's main port, Athinios, stands on a cramped shelf of land at the base of Sphinxlike cliffs and is a scene of marvellous chaos that always seems to work itself out when ferries arrive. Buses (and taxis) meet all ferries and then cart passengers through an ever-rising series of S-bends to the capital, Fira, which fringes the edge of the cliffs like a snowy cornice.

History

Minor eruptions have been the norm in Greece's earthquake record, but Santorini has bucked the trend – with attitude – throughout history. Eruptions here were genuinely earth-shattering, and so wrenching that they changed the shape of the island several times.

Dorians, Venetians and Turks occupied Santorini, as they did all other Cycladic islands, but its most influential early inhabitants were Minoans. They came from Crete some time between 2000 BC and 1600 BC, and the settlement at Akrotiri (p199) dates from the peak years of their great civilisation.

The island was circular then and was called Strongili (Round One). Thousands of years ago a colossal volcanic eruption caused the centre of Strongili to sink, leaving a caldera with towering cliffs along the east side – now one of the world's most dramatic sights. The latest theory, based on carbon dating of olive-oil samples from Akrotiri, places the event 10 years either side of 1613 BC.

Santorini was recolonised during the 3rd century BC but for the next 2000 years sporadic volcanic activity created further physical changes that included the formation of the volcanic islands of Palia and Nea Kameni at the centre of the caldera. As recently as 1956 a major earthquake devastated Oia and Fira, yet by the 1970s the islanders had embraced tourism as tourists embraced the island and today Santorini is a world destination of truly spectacular appeal.

Getting There & Away

There are several flights a day to and from Athens, Thessaloniki, Crete, Mykonos and Rhodes. There are also a good number of ferries a day to and from Piraeus and to and from many of Santorini's neighbouring islands. There are daily ferries to Crete and about four ferries a week go to Rhodes and Kos in the Dodecanese. For details see Island Hopping (p522).

SANTORINI'S UNSETTLING PAST

Santorini's volcanic landscape became partly dormant around 3000 BC and, soon after, the first human settlers arrived to take advantage of the fertile soil of the post-volcanic landscape. Between 2000 BC and 1600 BC it was occupied by the Minoans and, from evidence found at Akrotiri (see p199), they seemed to have fashioned a highly sophisticated culture.

About 1613 BC a chain of earthquakes and eruptions culminated in one of the largest explosions in the history of the Earth. Thirty cubic kilometres of magma spewed forth and a column of ash 36km high jetted into the atmosphere. The centre of the island collapsed, producing a caldera that the sea quickly filled. The eruption also generated huge tsunamis that travelled with dangerous force and devastating effect all the way to Crete and Israel.

After the Big One, Santorini settled down for a time and was even recolonised. In 236 BC volcanic activity separated Thirasia from the main island. In 197 BC the islet now known as Palia Kameni appeared in the caldera. The south coast of Santorini collapsed in 1570, taking the ancient port of Eleusis with it. An eruption in 1707 created Nea Kameni Islet next to Palia Kameni.

In recent history a major earthquake measuring 7.8 on the Richter scale savaged the island in 1956, killing scores of people and destroying most of the houses in Fira and Oia. Today's renaissance is remarkable; the resilience and insouciance of locals even more so. Sophisticated monitoring devices are said to be capable of reasonably early warnings of any potential volcanic activity in the future.

Getting Around

TO/FROM THE AIRPORT

There are frequent bus connections in summer between Fira's bus station and the airport, located southwest of Monolithos Beach. Enthusiastic hotel and domatia staff meet flights, and some also return guests to the airport. A taxi to the airport costs €12.

BUS

In summer buses leave Fira every half-hour for Oia (€1.40), Monolithos (€1.40), Kamari (€1.40) and Perissa (€2). There are less-frequent buses to Exo Gonia (€1.40), Perivolos (€2) and Vlyhada (€2.20). In summer the last regular bus to Fira from Oia leaves at 11.00pm.

Buses leave Fira, Kamari and Perissa for the port of Athinios (€2, 30 minutes) an hour and a half before most ferry departures. Buses for Fira meet all ferries, even late at night. It is wise to check port departures well in advance.

CABLE CAR & DONKEY

A **cable car** (☎ 22860 22977; M Nomikou; ⏱ every 20min 7am-10pm, to 9pm winter) hums smoothly between Fira and the small port below, known as Fira Skala, from where volcanic island cruises leave. One-way cable car tickets cost €4 per adult, and €2 per child; luggage is €2. You can make a more leisurely, and aromatic, upward trip by donkey (€5).

CAR & MOTORCYCLE

A car is the best way to explore the island during high season, when buses are intolerably overcrowded and you're lucky to get on one at all. Be very patient and cautious when driving – the narrow roads, especially in Fira, can be a nightmare. Note that Oia has no petrol station, the nearest being just outside Fira.

Two very good local hire outfits are **Damigos Rent a Car** (☎ 22860 22048, 6979968192) and, for scooters, **Zerbakis** (☎ 22860 33329, 6944531992).

TAXI

Fira's **taxi stand** (☎ 22860 23951/2555) is in Dekigala just round the corner from the bus station. A taxi from the port of Athinios to Fira costs €12, and a trip from Fira to Oia is also €12. Both cost €13 if you book ahead. If you miss the last bus from Oia to Fira, three or four people can bargain for a shared taxi for about €12. A taxi to Kamari is €10, to Perissa €15 and to Ancient Thira €22 one way.

FIRA ΦΗΡΑ

pop 2113

A multitude of fellow admirers cannot diminish the impact of Fira's stupendous landscape. Views from the edge of the caldera over the multicoloured cliffs are breathtaking, and at night the caldera edge is a frozen cascade of lights that eclipses the displays of the gold shops in the streets behind.

Orientation

The busy heart of Fira is Plateia Theotokopoulou (Central Sq). It's a fairly crowded, chaotic place; the main road, 25 Martiou, intersects the square as part of a one-way system that just manages to keep the nonstop traffic flow going. The bus station is on Mitropoleos, 150m south of Plateia Theotokopoulou. Between 25 Martiou and the caldera is the essence of Fira, a network of pedestrianised alleyways, the main ones running parallel to 25 Martiou. Erythrou Stavrou is the main commercial thoroughfare.

A block west of Erythrou Stavrou is Ypapantis, whose southern section is known also as Gold St because of its many jewellers. It runs along the edge of the caldera and has superb panoramic views until the shops intrude. Below the edge of the caldera is the paved walkway of Agiou Mina, which heads north and merges eventually with the clifftop walkway that continues north past the pretty villages of Firostefani and Imerovigli. Keep going and you'll reach Oia; but it's a long, hot 8km.

Information

Fira doesn't have an EOT (Greek National Tourist Organisation) or tourist police. It's best to seek out the smaller travel agents in the town, where you'll receive helpful service.

Toilets are north of Plateia Theotokopoulou near the port police building. You may need to brace yourself (they're of squat vintage). Bring your own paper – but not to read.

BOOKSHOPS

Books & Style (☎ 22860 24510; Dekigala) An excellent range of books in various languages. There's a great selection of volumes on Greece as well as travel guides, children's books and novels.

EMERGENCY

Hospital (☎ 22860 22237) On the road to Kamari. A new hospital at Karterados was under construction at the time of writing.
Police station (☎ 22860 22649; Karterados) About 2km from Fira.
Port police (☎ 22860 22239; 25 Martiou) North of the square.

INTERNET ACCESS

PC World (☎ 22860 25551; Plateia Theotokopoulou; per hr €1.90; ☺ 9am-9pm) A good range of services.

LAUNDRY

AD the Laundry Station (☎ 22860 23533; average load wash & dry €10; ☺ 9am-9pm)

MONEY

There are numerous ATMs scattered around town.
Alpha Bank (Plateia Theotokopoulou) Represents American Express and has an ATM.
National Bank of Greece (Dekigala) South of Plateia Theotokopoulou, on the caldera side of the road. Has an ATM.

POST

Post office (Dekigala)

TRAVEL AGENCIES

Aegean Pearl (☎ 22860 22170; www.aptravel.gr; Danezi) An excellent, helpful agency that sells all travel tickets and can help with accommodation, car hire and excursions.
Pelican Tours & Travel (☎ 22860 22220; fax 22860 22570; Plateia Theotokopoulou) Sells ferry tickets and can book accommodation and excursions.

Sights & Activities

MUSEUMS

Near the bus station, the **Museum of Prehistoric Thera** (☎ 22860 23217; Mitropoleos; admission €3; ☺ 8.30am-8pm Tue-Sun Apr-Sep, 8.30am-3pm Tue-Sun Oct-Mar) houses extraordinary finds that were excavated from Akrotiri (where, to date, only 5% of the area has been excavated). Most impressive is the glowing gold ibex figurine, measuring around 10cm in length and dating from the 17th century BC.

The **Archaeological Museum** (☎ 22860 22217; M Nomikou; adult/EU student/non-EU student €3/free/2; ☺ 8.30am-3pm Tue-Sun), near the cable-car station, houses finds from Akrotiri and Ancient Thira, some Cycladic figurines, and Hellenistic and Roman sculptures.

Megaron Gyzi Museum (☎ 22860 22244; Agiou Ioannou; adult/student €3.50/2; ☺ 10.30am-1pm & 5-8pm Mon-Sat, 10.30am-4.30pm Sun May-Oct) has local memorabilia, including fascinating photographs of Fira before and immediately after the 1956 earthquake.

Petros M Nomikos Conference Centre (☎ 22860 23016; adult/child €4/free; ☺ 10am-7pm May-Oct) The centre is run by the Thera Foundation (www.therafoundation.org) and hosts major conferences but also stages the fascinating Wall Paintings of Thera exhibition, a collection of three-dimensional life-size reproductions of the finest Akrotiri wall paintings. There's

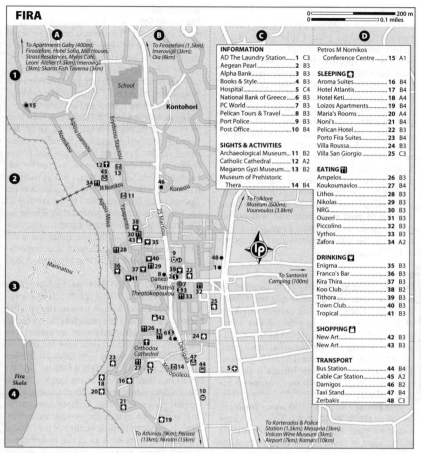

FIRA

0 — 200 m
0 — 0.1 miles

INFORMATION	
AD The Laundry Station	**1** C3
Aegean Pearl	**2** B3
Alpha Bank	**3** B3
Books & Style	**4** B3
Hospital	**5** C4
National Bank of Greece	**6** B3
PC World	**7** B3
Pelican Tours & Travel	**8** B3
Port Police	**9** B3
Post Office	**10** B4

SIGHTS & ACTIVITIES	
Archaeological Museum	**11** B2
Catholic Cathedral	**12** A2
Megaron Gyzi Museum	**13** B2
Museum of Prehistoric Thera	**14** B4

Petros M Nomikos Conference Centre	**15** A1

SLEEPING	
Aroma Suites	**16** B4
Hotel Atlantis	**17** B4
Hotel Keti	**18** A4
Loizos Apartments	**19** B4
Maria's Rooms	**20** A4
Noni's	**21** B3
Pelican Hotel	**22** B3
Porto Fira Suites	**23** B4
Villa Roussa	**24** B3
Villa San Giorgio	**25** C3

EATING	
Ampelos	**26** B3
Koukoumavlos	**27** B4
Lithos	**28** B3
Nikolas	**29** B3
NRG	**30** B3
Ouzeri	**31** B3
Piccolino	**32** B3
Vythos	**33** B3
Zafora	**34** A2

DRINKING	
Enigma	**35** B3
Franco's Bar	**36** B3
Kira Thira	**37** B3
Koo Club	**38** B2
Tithora	**39** B3
Town Club	**40** B3
Tropical	**41** B3

SHOPPING	
New Art	**42** B3
New Art	**43** B3

TRANSPORT	
Bus Station	**44** B4
Cable Car Station	**45** A2
Damigos	**46** B2
Taxi Stand	**47** B4
Zerbakis	**48** C3

also a photographic exhibition of excavations at Akrotiri.

Located on the eastern tip of the island, the **Folklore Museum of Santorini** (☎ 22860 22792; adult/child €3/free; ⏰ 10am-2pm & 6-8pm Apr-Oct) houses an intriguing collection that casts light on Santorini's traditions and history. The museum is in a lovely setting and a major feature is an ancient *canava*, a sizeable cave excavated from the volcanic earth.

Tours

Tour companies operate various trips to and fro across the caldera. A tour to the volcanic island of Nea Kameni is €13, to the volcano and hot springs (including swimming) of Palia Kameni, €18, full-day boat tours to the volcanic islets Thirassia and Oia, €25, sunset boat tour €35 and a bus tour including wine tasting €25. Book at travel agencies.

The *Bella Aurora*, an exact copy of an 18th-century schooner, scoots around the caldera every afternoon on a sunset buffet dinner tour (€45, from May to October), stopping for sightseeing on Nea Kameni and for ouzo on Thirasia. Most travel agencies sell tickets.

Courses

If you fancy a professional photography course based on Santorini, contact **Greek Island Workshops** (www.glennsteiner.com). It's run by top professional Glenn Steiner.

Sleeping

Few of Fira's sleeping options are cheap, and even budget places hike their prices in July and August. Domatia touts at the port reach impressive heights of hysteria in their bids for attention. Some claim their rooms are in town, when they're actually a long way out; ask to see a map showing the exact location. If you're looking for a caldera view, expect to pay at least double the prices of elsewhere. Many hotels in Fira, especially on the caldera rim, cannot be reached by vehicle. If you have heavy luggage, this is worth remembering, especially as there may be several flights of steps leading to and from your accommodation. Most budget and midrange places offer free transfer to port or airport and will porter your luggage to and from your accommodation. Some top-end places may charge up to €15 for transfers.

BUDGET

Santorini Camping (☎ 22860 22944; www.santorini camping.gr; camp sites per adult/child/tent €10/6/5; 🅿 🖳 🖭) Located on the eastern outskirts of town, this camping ground has some shade and decent facilities. There's a self-service restaurant, minimarket and pool. It's 400m east of Plateia Theotokopoulou. There are two-person bungalows also with air-con (€70), with one equipped for disabled use.

Villa Roussa (☎ 22860 23220; www.villaroussa.gr; Dekigala; s/d €55/75; 🅿 🖭 🖭 🖭) You don't have a caldera view but this small hotel is right at the heart of town and is hard to beat for value with its bright and immaculate rooms. It even has a swimming pool.

Villa San Giorgio (☎ 22860 23516; www.sangiorgio villa.gr; s/d/tr €60/70/85; 🖭 🖭) Not a scenic location but very close to the centre of Fira and an excellent option with its decent rooms and friendly owners.

Hotel Sofia (☎ 22860 22802; Firostefani; s/d €60/75; 🖭 🖭) These fresh, comfy rooms at the heart of Firostefani are a pleasant alternative to the bustle of Fira. Fira's centre is about 1.5km south, along a lovely caldera-edge walkway. Breakfast is €8.

Maria's Rooms (☎ 22860 25143, 6973254461; Agiou Mina; d €70; 🖭) A handful of charming rooms open onto a shared terrace that has unbeatable caldera and sunset views. Rooms are small but immaculate, and blissfully peaceful.

MIDRANGE

Apartments Gaby (☎ 22860 22057; Nomikou; d €65-95, tr €110, apt €120; 🖭) The rooms on the series of roof terraces at this excellent place guarantee sunset views, and there's a quiet and reassuring local feel that transcends Fira's surface gloss. Gaby is just beyond the Petros M Nomikos Conference Centre on the caldera-edge path where it reaches Firostefani.

Loizos Apartments (☎ 22860 24046; www.loizos .gr; s €75, d €85-95, tr/apt €110/140; 🅿 🖭 🖳 🖭 🖭) Recently refurbished and with friendly, professional service, Loizos is one of the best places in Fira. It's in a quiet cul-de-sac, yet has the advantage of vehicular access and is only minutes from the centre of town and the caldera edge. Rooms range from standard to deluxe and all are bright, clean and comfortable. Those on the front upper floor have a panoramic view towards Kamari and the sea. Breakfast is €7. The same owners have cheaper accommodation (single/double €55/65) at Messaria, 2.5km southeast of Fira.

Hotel Keti (☎ 22860 22324; www.hotelketi.gr; Agiou Mina; d €90-120, tr/ste €117/140; 🖭 🖭) Recently refurbished, Hotel Keti is one of the smaller 'sunset view' hotels in a peaceful caldera niche. Its attractive traditional rooms are carved into the cliffs. Half of the rooms have Jacuzzis.

our pick **Aroma Suites** (☎ 22860 24112; www .aromasuites.gr; Agiou Mina; s €120, d €140-160; 🖭 🖭) In an excellent location at the quieter end of the caldera edge, and more accessible than similar places, this boutique hotel has charming service to match its overall ambience. Stylish, modern facilities enhance traditional caldera interiors, such as in the honeymoon suite: a classic Fira cave chamber, complete with Jacuzzi.

Also recommended:

Pelican Hotel (☎ 22860 23113; www.pelican.gr; Danezi; s/d/tr incl breakfast €70/80/100; 🖭 🖳 🖭) There's no caldera view, but rooms are comfy and well appointed at this longstanding hotel only metres from the centre of town.

Nonis (☎ 22860 24112; s/d €120/140) Run by the owners of Aroma Suites, Noni's has similar rooms with terrace Jacuzzi and superb caldera views.

TOP END

Hotel Atlantis (☎ 22860 22232; www.atlantishotel .gr; Mitropoleos; s/d incl breakfast €195-300; 🅿 🖭 🖭) The Atlantis is a handsome old building that overlooks the southern end of Ypapantis with dignity. It's full of cool, relaxing lounges and terraces, and the bright and airy bedrooms in the front have caldera views. The price range indicates views and window or balcony options.

Mill Houses (☎ 22860 27117; www.millhouses.gr; Firostefani; ste incl breakfast €210-410; ❌ 🅡 🖳) Located on the side of the caldera at Firostefani, these superb studios and suites are full of light and Cycladic colour. The creative decor and stylish furnishings go with first-class facilities and service. A sunset view is inevitable.

Porto Fira Suites (☎ 22860 22849; www.portofira.gr; Agiou Mina; 2-/3-/4-person ste incl breakfast €274/336/376; ❌ 🅡 🛜) This top-rated Fira hotel merges tradition with luxury and modern conveniences. Rooms are individually furnished and have huge stone-based beds and Jacuzzis. There's a cafe-bar and restaurant and breakfasts are lush affairs.

Strass Residences (☎ 22860 33765; www.thestrass. com; Firostefani; ste incl breakfast €280-420; ❌ 🅡) They even manage palm trees round the pool at this exclusive little enclave of three luxury studios, all in glorious white. It feels as if the rest of the world is miles away, but Fira is just down the road.

Eating

Tourist-trap eateries, often with overpriced, indifferent food, are still an unfortunate feature of summertime Fira. In some places singles, and even families with young children, may find themselves unwelcome in the face of pushy owners desperate to keep tables full and their turnover brisk. However, there are excellent exceptions.

BUDGET

There are numerous fast-food outlets and cafes in Fira. Plateia Theotokopoulou has a few cafe-bars where the terraces are great for seeing all human life pass by.

Vythos (☎ 22860 22285) A local favourite, located at the start of the *plateia*.

Mylos Café (☎ 22860 25640; Firostefani; 🖳 🛜) On the caldera edge in Firostefani, this stylish and relaxing venue is located in a converted windmill and is the ideal place for relaxing drinks and light snacks. It has a unique circular internet area (per hour €3.50) on the top floor and the cafe is a wi-fi hotspot.

Piccolino (☎ 22860 22595; Danezi; snacks €1-2.30) A snack bar and takeaway that dishes out a terrific range of sandwiches, wraps and other snacks, as well as hot and cold drinks.

NRG (☎ 22860 24997; Erythrou Stavrou; dishes €2.20-6.20) Still one of the best places to stop for a snack at the heart of Fira, this popular little crêperie offers crêpes, sandwiches, tortillas and an ever-popular Indian curry (€5), as well a range of ice cream, coffee and smoothies.

Nikolas (☎ 22860 24550; Erythrou Stavrou; dishes €6-9) The traditional Nikolas just keeps on flying the flag for the village taverna, at the heart of Fira. No-nonsense service dishes out grilled calamari, cuttlefish in a wine sauce and beef stew with onions.

Ouzeri (☎ 6945849921; Fabrika Shopping Centre; dishes €6.50-13.50) Fish dishes are especially good at this central *mezedhopoleio* and include prawn *saganaki* and a seafood platter of mixed fish. Starters such as artichoke *saganaki* ring the changes, as do meat dishes that include *youvetsi* (veal in tomato sauce with pasta) and pork fillet in a mustard sauce. Vegetarians can enjoy Dakos salads and a variety of nonmeat starters.

You'll also find several *gyros* stands in and around Fira's main square.

MIDRANGE

Lithos (☎ 22860 24421; Agiou Mina; mains €7-19.50) Amid a swath of eateries on the caldera edge, Lithos stands out for its well-prepared dishes and attentive service. Choose from persuasive starters such as fava with cheese and cherry tomatoes. Salads are crisp and fresh and mains cover poultry, meat, fish and shellfish dishes.

Zafora (☎ 22860 23203; cnr Nomikou & M Nomikou; mains €8.50-22.50) Sturdy Greek classics come with stunning caldera views at this big restaurant near the cable-car station. The pork tenderloin marinated in red wine, ginger, honey and soy sauce is a favourite and there are fish dishes, pasta and crêpes also on offer and breakfasts at €4.50 to €8.50.

Ampelos (☎ 22860 25554; Fabrika Shopping Centre; mains €10-26) There's plenty of space in this central Fira restaurant with its 2nd-floor terrace with a view. Try the grilled shrimp in a red pepper sauce with rice or the mussels *saganaki* or settle for a selection of such starters as stuffed mushrooms with dill, garlic and parsley in white wine and the speciality pie of green onion, dill, pine nuts and Parmesan cheese. There's a pleasing house wine or excellent Santorini and mainland reds and whites for up to €50 or so a bottle.

CYCLADES

our pick Koukoumavlos (☎ 22860 23807; mains €25-35) Discreet in location and outstanding for cuisine, the terrace of this fine restaurant has good views, while the interior has retained the vaulted style of its original Fira mansion. An uncrowded menu lists such certainties as lobster and monkfish terrine, or Santorini fava and smoked trout and salmon in a mandarin sauce with roasted almonds. Meat dishes are equally subtle and the wine list likewise. Look for the wooden doorway down to the right of the Hotel Atlantis.

Drinking

Drinks prices can be cranked up in Fira, even for beer, never mind the stellar cocktail prices. You're often paying for the view, so don't glaze over too early.

Kira Thira (☎ 22860 22770; Erythrou Stavrou) This bar is comfortable with itself; unsurprisingly as it's the oldest bar in Fira and one of the best. Smooth jazz, ethnic sounds and occasional live music fill out the background beneath the barrel roof.

Tropical (☎ 22860 23089; Marinatou) Nicely perched just before the caldera edge Tropical draws a vibrant crowd with its seductive mix of rock, soul and occasional jazz, plus unbeatable balcony views that are still there into the early hours.

Franco's Bar (☎ 22860 24428; Marinatou) Check your cuffs for this deeply stylish and ultimate sunset venue where music means classical sounds only. Expensive cocktails match the sheer elegance and impeccable musical taste.

Entertainment

After midnight Erythrou Stavrou fires up the clubbing caldera of Fira.

Koo Club (☎ 22860 22025; Erythrou Stavrou) Several bars with variable moods rise through the levels here. Sounds are soft house, trance and Greek hits, and you're never alone.

Town Club (☎ 22860 22820; Erythrou Stavrou) Still clinging defiantly to stylish kitsch, Town Club has faux-Classical facades, in lilac, to go with its gleaming whiteout interior. Modern Greek music and mainstream are just right for this upbeat place.

Tithora (☎ 22860 23519; off Danezi) Fira's big rock venue 'underneath the arches', where you can bliss out to big sounds.

Enigma (☎ 22860 22466; Erythrou Stavrou) A full-on dance venue when it gets going, this is the catwalk clientele's favourite spot amid coolness and floaty drapes. House and mainstream hits fit the style.

Shopping

So much shopping, so little time for the flood of cruise-ship passengers who forage happily through Fira's glitzy retail zones. You can get everything from Armani and Versace to Timberland and Reef – at rather glitzy prices, too.

Fira's jewellery and gold shops are legion. The merchandise gleams and sparkles, though prices may dull the gleam in your eye.

New Art (☎ 22860 23770; Erythrou Stavrou & Fabrika Shopping Centre) Forget the standard painted-on T-shirts. If you want quality to take back home, the subtle colours and motifs of designer Werner Hampel's Ts have real style.

Leoni Atelier (☎ 22860 23770; Firostefani) For art lovers, the studio and gallery of the internationally acclaimed artist, Leoni Schmiedel, is a worthwhile visit. Here, the artist creates her nuanced and multilayered collages that are inspired by Santorini's geology, natural elements and intense colours. The studio is reached by heading north past the windmill in Firostefani and then by following signs to the left.

AROUND SANTORINI
Oia Οία
pop 763

The village of Oia (*ee*-ah), known locally as Pano Meria, reflects the renaissance of Santorini after the devastating earthquake of 1956. Restoration work and upmarket tourism have transformed Oia into one of the loveliest villages in the Cyclades. Efforts are under way to introduce schemes that will ease the serious overcrowding; the price Oia pays in high summer for its attractiveness. Built on a steep slope of the caldera, many of its dwellings nestle in niches hewn into the volcanic rock. Oia, believe it or not, gets more sunset time than Fira, and its narrow passageways get very crowded in the evenings.

ORIENTATION & INFORMATION

From the bus terminal, head left and uphill to reach the rather stark central square and the main street, Nikolaou Nomikou, which skirts the caldera.

CYCLADES

Atlantis Books (☎ 22860 72346; www.atlantisbooks
.org; Nikolaou Nomikou) A fascinating and well-stocked
little bookshop run with flair and enthusiasm by an
international group of young people. Cultural events are
sometimes staged here.

ATMs On Main St, outside Karvounis Tours, and also by the
bus terminus.

Karvounis Tours (☎ 22860 71290; www.idogreece
.com; Nikolaou Nomikou) For obtaining information, booking hotels, renting cars and bikes, and making international calls. It's also a wedding specialist.

SIGHTS & ACTIVITIES

The **maritime museum** (☎ 22860 71156; adult/stu-
dent €3/1.50; ☯ 10am-2pm & 5-8pm Wed-Mon) is located along a narrow lane that leads off right
from Nikolaou Nomikou. It's housed in an
old mansion and has endearing displays on
Santorini's maritime history.

Ammoudi, a tiny port with good tavernas and
colourful fishing boats, lies 300 steps below
Oia at the base of blood-red cliffs. It can also
be reached by road. In summer, boats and
tours go from Ammoudi to Thirasia daily;
check with travel agencies in Fira (p192) for
departure times.

SLEEPING

Oia Youth Hostel (☎ 22860 71465; www.santorinihostel
.gr; dm incl breakfast €17; ☯ May–mid-Oct; ▯) One of
the cleanest and best-run hostels you'll hope
to find. It has better facilities than some hotels.
There's a small bar and a lovely rooftop terrace with great views. Internet is €2 per hour.
To find the hostel, keep straight on from the
bus terminus for about 100m.

Chelidonia (☎ 22860 71287; www.chelidonia.com;
Nikolaou Nomikou; studios €155, apt €170-205, ste €220-230;
▤ ▯) Traditional cliffside dwellings that have
been in the owner's family for generations
offer a grand mix of old and new at Chelidonia.
Buried beneath the rubble of the 1956 earthquake, the rooms have been lovingly restored.
Modern facilities are nicely balanced by the
occasional fine piece of traditional furniture
and each unit has a kitchenette. Some places
are reached by several flights of steps.

Perivolas (☎ 22860 71308; www.perivolas.gr; ste
€505-1590; ▤ ▯ ▨ ▣ ▧) Ultimate caldera-
edge accommodation at over-the-edge prices.
This is one of Greece's most renowned hotels, however, and features beautiful rooms
with vaulted ceilings, individual terraces and
kitchenettes. Breakfast, of rare quality, is included. There's a Wellness Studio, bar and

restaurant and the infinity pool has graced
the cover of *Condé Nast Traveller* magazine.
You know where you're at…

EATING & DRINKING

Thomas Grill (☎ 22860 71769; €7-15) Tucked into
the alleyway that leads up from the bus terminus, this Oia institution serves down-to-earth
Greek favourites, including its noted signature
dish, stuffed pork.

218 degrees (☎ 22860 71801; dishes €8-15) Opened
in 2009 and little sister to Oia's top restaurant,
1800, a great caldera-edge location at this stylish place enhances such dishes as steamed
mussels with ouzo, fresh tomatoes and herbs.
It's open all day for breakfast, lunch, coffee
and drinks.

Nectar (☎ 22860 71504; €8-18) Quality cuisine, creative salads and main dishes such
as chicken with figs, plus some seriously
fine wines, ensure a rewarding meal at this
bright eatery.

Skala (☎ 22860 71362; Nikolaou Nomikou; dishes €8-19)
Watch life pass up and down to Ammouda
from the high ground of Skala's lovely terrace. Subtle international touches enhance the
traditional Greek dishes here, such as rabbit
stifadho (sweet stew cooked with tomato and
onions) and chicken fillet stuffed with mushrooms. The mezes are special. Try the cheese
pies with added onion and pine nuts.

Ambrosia (☎ 22860 71504; www.ambrosia-nectar.com;
mains €24-31) A top Oia restaurant, Ambrosia
presents a swath of handsome dishes from
starters of Santorini fava purée with grilled
octopus and caramelised onions to lobster
veloute, sautéed crawfish and cream of sea
urchin, or millefeuille of veal fillet layered
and roasted with tomatoes and goat's cheese
and smoked aubergine purée. The wine list
matches it all.

Megalahori Μεγαλωχωρί
pop 457

Signposts on the main road to Perissa and
Akrotiri indicate the 'traditional settlement'
of Megalohori village amid what at first seems
a fairly dull landscape. Turn off, however, to
parking at the entrance to the village and then
descend gently on foot into an older Santorini,
passing unvarnished old houses and beneath a
church belltower that straddles the street. At
the heart of Megalahori are a pleasant little
square and a handsome church with a little
pebble-surfaced enclave and war memorial.

SANTORINI WINES

Santorini's lauded wines are its crisp, clear dry whites, such as the delectable Assyrtico, and the amber-coloured, unfortified dessert wine Vinsanto. Most local vineyards hold tastings and tours.

A worthwhile visit is to **Santo Wines** (☎ 22860 22596; www.santowines.gr; Pyrgos) where you can sample a range of wines and browse a shop full of choice vintages as well as local products including fava, tomatoes, capers and preserves.

One of the most entertaining venues is the **Volcan Wine Museum** (☎ 22860 31322; www.volcan wines.gr; admission €5; ☉ noon-8pm), housed in a traditional *canava* (winery) on the way to Kamari. It has interesting displays, including a 17th-century wooden winepress. Admission includes an audio guide and three wine tastings. On Friday night from May to October there's a festival night (€48), which includes a visit to the museum, three tastings, free buffet, free wine, live music and traditional costume dances, and even plate breaking.

There's also the Art Space gallery-winery outside Kamari – see below.

The following wineries should be contacted before visiting:

Boutari (☎ 22860 81011; www.boutari.gr; Megalohori)

Canava Roussos (☎ 22860 31278; www.canavaroussos.gr; Mesa Gonia)

Hatzidakis (☎ 22860 32552; www.hatzidakiswines.gr; Pyrgos Kallistis)

Sigalas (☎ 22860 71644; www.sigalas-wine.com; Oia)

There are a few cafes and tavernas and the signposted **Gavalas Winery** is worth a visit for its traditional ambience.

Kamari Καμάρι
pop 1351

Kamari is 10km from Fira and is Santorini's best-developed resort. It has a long beach of black sand, with the rugged limestone cliffs of Cape Mesa Vouno framing its southern end with the ancient site of Ancient Thira on its summit. The beachfront road is dense with restaurants and bars. Things get very busy in high season. Other less appealing but quieter beaches lie to the north at **Monolithos**.

Lisos Tours (☎ 22860 33765; lisostours@san.forthnet .gr) is especially helpful and has an office on the main road into Kamari, and another just inland from the centre of the beach. It sells ferry tickets and can organise accommodation and car hire. All kinds of tours can be arranged and there's internet access and a bureau de change.

The unmissable gallery **Art Space** (☎ 22860 32774; Exo Gonia) is just outside Kamari. It is located in **Argyro's Canava**, one of the oldest wineries on the island. The atmospheric old wine caverns are hung with superb artworks while sculptures transform lost corners and niches. The collection is curated by the owner and features some of Greece's finest modern artists. Winemaking is still in the owner's blood, and part of the complex is given over to producing some stellar vintages. A tasting of Vinsanto greatly enhances the whole experience.

SLEEPING

Anna's Rooms (☎ 22860 22765; s/d €25/35) Unbeatable budget deals can be had at these straightforward rooms. One group of rooms is behind Lisos Tours at the back of town; the other is behind Lisos Tours in the village.

Hotel Matina (☎ 22860 31491; www.hotel-matina .com; s/d/tr/ste incl breakfast €108/116/144/192; ✹ ☐ ☎) A very well-run independent hotel, the Matina has spacious, brightly decorated rooms and is set back from the road in quiet grounds.

ourpick Aegean View Hotel (☎ 22860 32790; www.aegeanview-santorini.com; studio/apt €130/150; P ✹ ☐ ☎ ☎) Tucked below the limestone cliffs high above Kamari, this outstanding hotel has spacious studios and apartments superbly laid out and with first-class facilities, including small kitchen areas. There's a lift to some rooms.

EATING

Amalthia (☎ 22860 32780; dishes €3.50-12) A long-established local favourite, Amalthia is a couple of blocks inland at the southern end of town, and there's a lovely garden area and a terrace with barbecue. There are well-prepared Greek dishes (the lamb is particularly good) and a range of pastas.

Mistral (☎ 22860 32108; mains €5.50-14) Seafood is what this classic *psarotaverna* is all about. Fish plates for two are about €30 and the likes of bream and red mullet are by the kilo.

our pick **Mario No 1** (☎ 22860 32000; Agia Paraskevi, Monolithos; dishes €6.50-12) Right on the beach at Monolithos, near the airport, is this outstanding restaurant, one of Santorini's best. Fish is by the kilo and you can select shellfish from a display. There's a great list of mezedhes such as mussels' *saganaki* or sweet red peppers stuffed with feta, garlic, tomato and parsley. Meat dishes include roast lamb with rosemary and proper *mousaka*.

Ancient Thira Αρχαία Θήρα

First settled by the Dorians in the 9th century BC, **Ancient Thira** (admission €4; ☾ 8am-2.30pm Tue-Sun) consists of Hellenistic, Roman and Byzantine ruins and is an atmospheric and rewarding site to visit. The ruins include temples, houses with mosaics, an *agora* (market), a theatre and a gymnasium. There are splendid views from the site. With the current closure of Ancient Akrotiri, this site more than makes up for it.

From March to October **Ancient Thira Tours** (☎ 22860 32474; Kamari) runs a bus every hour from 9am until 2pm, except on Monday, from Kamari to the site. If driving, take the surfaced but narrow, winding road from Kamari for just over 1km. From Perissa, on the other side of the mountain, a hot hike up a dusty path on sometimes rocky, difficult ground takes over an hour to the site.

Ancient Akrotiri Αρχαίο Ακρωτήρι

Excavations at **Akrotiri** (☎ 22860 81366), the Minoan outpost that was buried during the catastrophic eruption of 1650 BC, began in 1967 and have uncovered an ancient city beneath the volcanic ash. Buildings, some three storeys high, date back to the late 16th century BC. Outstanding finds are the stunning frescoes and ceramics, many of which are now on display at the Museum of Prehistoric Thera (p192) in Fira.

At the time of writing the site was closed indefinitely, pending ongoing negotiations over remedial construction work – one visitor was killed and several others injured when a section of the roof collapsed during the summer of 2005. You may find that there is a degree of confusion locally about whether or not the site is open. Check the 'archaeological sites' section of www.culture.gr and check thoroughly on arrival at Santorini before making a bus or taxi journey to what may still be a closed site. You can experience some of the rich value of the site at the archaeological museum (p192) and the Petros M Nomikos Conference Centre (p192) both in Fira.

Beaches

At times Santorini's black-sand beaches become so hot that a sun lounger or mat is essential. The best beaches are on the east and south coasts.

One of the main beaches is the long stretch at **Perissa**, a popular destination in summer. **Perivolos** and **Agios Georgios**, further south, are more relaxed. **Red Beach**, near Ancient Akrotiri, has high red cliffs and smooth, hand-sized pebbles submerged under clear water. **Vlyhada**, also on the south coast, is a pleasant venue. On the north coast near Oia, **Paradise** and **Pori** are both worth a stop.

Based at Perissa and **Akrotiri Beach** is the **Santorini Dive Centre** (☎ 22860 83190; www.divecenter .gr), offering a good range of courses including 'discover scuba diving' for €55, half-day snorkelling for €40 and an open-water diving course for €380.

SLEEPING & EATING

The main concentration of rooms can be found in and around Perissa.

Youth Hostel Anna (☎ 22860 82182; www.hostel world.com; dm €12-15, d €25; ☾ May-Sep; P ☒ 🖳) A well-managed and popular hostel, Anna's is on the busy roadside at the entrance to Perissa and about five minutes from the beach. The private rooms are in a separate building. You can book excursions and boat tickets here, there's money exchange, and credit cards are accepted. A minibus picks up guests from the ferry port.

Stelio's Place (☎ 22860 81860; www.steliosplace .com; d/tr/q €70/90/120; ☾ year-round; P ☒ 🛜 🖳) In a great position set back from the main drag but barely a minute from the beach, and with immaculate, well-appointed rooms, Stelio's is great value. Prices can drop below half in the low season.

Hotel Drossos (☎ 22860 81639; www.familydrossos .gr; s/d/tr incl breakfast €102/112/153; P ☒ 🖳 🛜 🖳) Behind the simple facade of this fine hotel lies a lovely complex of rooms and studios with stylish decor and furnishings.

CYCLADES

There's reliable Greek food on offer at **God's Garden** (☎ 22860 83027; dishes €4.50-11), a decent taverna with fish dishes starting at about €6.

Most beaches have a range of tavernas and cafes.

THIRASIA & VOLCANIC ISLETS
ΘΗΡΑΣΙΑ & ΗΦΑΙΣΤΕΙΑΚΕΣ ΝΗΣΙΔΕΣ

Unspoilt Thirasia (pop 158) was separated from Santorini by an eruption in 236 BC. The cliff-top *hora,* **Manolas**, has tavernas and domatia. It's an attractive place, noticeably more relaxed and reflective than Fira could ever be.

The unpopulated islets of **Palia Kameni** and **Nea Kameni** are still volcanically active and can be visited on various boat excursions from Fira Skala and Athinios (see Tours, p193). A day's excursion taking in Nea Kameni, the **hot springs** on Palia Kameni, Thirasia and Oia is about €28.

ANAFI ΑΝΑΦΗ

pop 272

Anafi is the escape clause of Santorini, an island perched on a distant horizon somewhere between yesterday's dream and a modern-day holiday delight; a slow-paced traditional lifestyle and striking Cycladic landscapes are the marks of this endearing island. There are few other visitors outside high summer, although Anafi is growing in popularity.

Orientation & Information

The island's small port is **Agios Nikolaos**. From here, the main village, **Hora**, is a 10-minute bus ride up a winding road, or a 1km hike up a less winding but steep walkway. In summer a bus runs every two hours from about 9am to 11pm and usually meets boats. Hora's main pedestrian thoroughfare leads uphill from the first bus stop and has most of the domatia, restaurants and minimarkets.

There is an ATM in a small kiosk just past a public telephone halfway along the harbour front, on the left.

There is a postal agency that opens occasionally, next to Panorama at the entrance to Hora.

You can buy ferry tickets at the **travel agency** (☎ 22860 61408) in Hora's main street next to Roussou minimarket or at a small office on the harbour front before ferries are due.

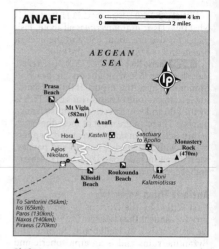

Sights

There are several lovely **beaches** near Agios Nikolaos. Palm-lined **Klissidi**, a 1.5km walk to the port, is the closest and most popular.

Anafi's main sight is the monastery of **Moni Kalamiotissas**, 9km by road from Hora or reached by a more appealing 6km walk along a path. It's in the extreme east of the island, near the meagre remains of a **sanctuary to Apollo** and below the summit of the 470m **Monastery Rock**, the highest rock formation in the Mediterranean Sea, outstripping even Gibraltar. The walk to the monastery is a rewarding expedition but it's a fairly tough trip in places and is a day's outing there and back. There is also a ruined Venetian *kastro* at **Kastelli**, east of Hora.

Sleeping

Domatia owners prefer long stays in high season, so if you're only staying one night you should take whatever you can get, or book ahead.

Apollon Village Hotel (☎ 22860 28739; www.apollon villa.gr; s/d/tr €48/65/75, studios €58-75; apt €70-125; ♨ 🖘) Rising in tiers above Klissidi Beach, these lovely individual rooms and studios, each named after an Olympian god and with glorious views, are outstanding value. Breakfast is €8 and the Blue Cafe-Bar is a cool stylish adjunct to the hotel with home-made sweets and pastries on offer.

Margarita's Rooms (☎ 22860 61237; anafi1@hotmail .com; s/d €50/60) Right by the beach and next to

Margarita's Café, these pleasant little rooms hark back to the beach life of quieter times.

Many of the rooms in Hora have good views across Anafi's rolling hills to the sea and to the great summit of Monastery Rock. The following recommended options are open all year and all charge about €45 for a double room:

Panorama (☎ 22860 61292)

Paradise (☎ 22860 61243)

Villa Gallini (☎ 22869 61279) In a particularly good location.

Eating

There are several tavernas in Hora, all of which are in the main street.

Liotrivi (☎ 22860 61209; mains €4-9) Great fish dishes (by the kilo), with the catch supplied from the family's boat; just about everything else, from eggs to vegetables and honey, comes from their garden.

Armenaki (☎ 22860 61234; mains €5-6.50) Good Greek traditional food at this great taverna is enhanced by an airy terrace and the pleasure of live bouzouki music on summer evenings.

Margarita's (☎ 22860 61237; Klissidi; mains €6-10.50) A sunny little terrace overlooking the bay at Klissidi makes for enjoyable eating here. Pork with mushrooms in a lemon sauce is a good option. Breakfasts are €2.50 to €5.

Getting There & Away

Anafi may be out on a limb and you can still face a challenge getting there out of season, but in summer the island has reasonable connections to Piraeus, Santorini, Sikinos, Folegandros, Naxos, Paros and even Syros. For details see Island Hopping (p509).

Getting Around

A small bus takes passengers from the port up to Hora. Caïques serve various beaches and nearby islands.

SIKINOS ΣΙΚΙΝΟΣ

pop 238

Lonely Sikinos (*see*-kee-noss) is another attractive escape from the clamour of Ios and Santorini, yet this lovely island is not much smaller than Santorini. It has a mainly empty landscape of terraced hills that sweep down to the sea. The main clusters of habitation are the port of **Alopronia**, and the linked inland villages of **Hora** and **Kastro**. The latter are reached by a 3.4km winding road that leads up from the port. There's a post office at the entrance to Kastro, and a National Bank of Greece ATM in the central square of Kastro. The medical centre is next door to the ATM. Ferry tickets can be bought in advance at **Koundouris Travel** (☎ 22860 51168, 6936621946). There is a petrol station outside Alopronia on the road to Kastro. You can hire scooters here for about €15 to €20.

Sights

Kastro, so named from an original Venetian fortress of the 13th century of which little physical sign remains, is a charming place, with winding alleyways between brilliant white houses. At its heart is the main square with a central war memorial surrounded by peaceful old buildings, one with ornate stone window-frames and sills long since white-washed over. On one side is the **church of Pantanassa**. On the northern side of Kastro, the land falls sharply to the sea and the shells of old windmills punctuate the cliff edge. A flight of whitewashed steps leads up to the once-fortified church of **Moni Zoödohou Pigis** above the town.

To the west of Kastro, above steeply terraced fields and reached by an equally steep flight of steps, is the reclusive **Hora**, where numerous derelict houses are being renovated.

CYCLADES

From the saddle between Kastro and Hora, a surfaced road leads southwest to **Moni Episkopis** (admission free; ⊙ 6.30pm-8.30pm). The remains here are believed to be those of a 3rd-century-AD Roman mausoleum that was transformed into a church in the 7th century and then became the monastery Moni Episkopis 10 centuries later. From here you can climb to a little **church** and **ancient ruins** perched on a precipice to the south, from where the views are spectacular.

Caïques (about €6) run to good beaches at **Agios Georgios**, **Malta** – with ancient ruins on the hill above – and **Karra**. **Katergo**, a swimming place with interesting rocks, and **Agios Nikolaos Beach** are both within easy walking distance of Alopronia.

At the time of writing, a surfaced road was being laid to Agios Georgios and surrounding beaches. It is expected that buses will run to these beaches from Alopronia in summer.

Sleeping & Eating

There are several accommodation options at the port, but Hora is a more worthwhile place to stay.

Persephone's Rooms (☎ 22860 51229; Kastro; s/d/tr €40/60/70) Decent studio-type rooms on the outskirts of Kastro make for a good base on the island.

Lucas Rooms (☎ 22860 51076; www.diakopes.gr; Alopronia; d/studios €55/85; ✱) Two good locations are on offer here and rooms are decent and clean; one set of rooms is on the hillside, 500m uphill from the port. The studios are on the far side of the bay from the ferry quay and have great views.

Kastro Studios (☎ 22860 51026/51283; Kastro; r €80; ✱) There are only two places here but they are very new and quietly luxurious and have great views. They have cooking facilities.

Porto Sikinos (☎ 22860 51220; www.portosikinos.gr; Alopronia; s/d/tr incl breakfast €90/110/125; ✱) Just up from the quay, the attractive rooms here rise in a series of terraces and have great balcony views. There's also a bar and restaurant.

Rock (☎ 22860 51186; Alopronia; dishes €2.60-8) High above the ferry quay is this seasonal cafe and pizza place, where you can also chill into the early hours (sometimes to live music). There are rooms here as well, with doubles priced at €40 to €60.

To Steki tou Garbi (Kastro; dishes €4-8) A good traditional grillhouse just around the corner from Koundouris Travel in Kastro.

To Iliovasilema (☎ 22860 51173; Kastro; mains €4.50-8) Outstanding views enhance a stop at this seasonal place, which dishes up standards as well as pizzas and pasta.

Lucas (☎ 22860 51076; Alopronia; dishes €6-13) Down at the port, this is the favourite taverna, offering Greek standards without frills and fish by the kilo.

Kastro Bar (☎ 22860 51026; Kastro) You'll find this little bar on the way to Moni Zoödohou Pigis. Coffee, drinks and ice cream are the mainstay and Greek music the style. Open morning until late.

There's a minimarket next to Lucas in Alopronia and another in Kastro.

Getting There & Around

For details of ferry services from Sikinos see Island Hopping (p523).

The local bus meets all ferry arrivals and runs between Alopronia and Hora/Kastro (€1.40, 20 minutes) every half-hour in August, but less frequently at other times of the year. A timetable is sometimes posted near the minimarket. It's wise to be in good time at the departure point.

FOLEGANDROS
ΦΟΛΕΓΑΝΔΡΟΣ

pop 662

Folegandros (fo-*leh*-gan-dross) sits elegantly on the southern edge of the Cycladics, a rocky ridge, barely 12km in length and just under 4km at its widest point. Much of the land is over 200m in height, the highest point being Agios Eleftherios at 414m.

The remoteness and ruggedness of Folegandros made it a place of exile for political prisoners from Roman times to the 20th century, and as late as the military dictatorship of 1967–74, yet today it is cherished by devotees of its beauty and character.

The capital is the concealed, cliff-top Hora, one of the most appealing villages in the Cyclades. Boats dock at the little harbour of Karavostasis, on the east coast. The only other settlement is Ano Meria, 4km northwest of Hora. There are several good beaches, but be prepared for strenuous walking to reach some of them.

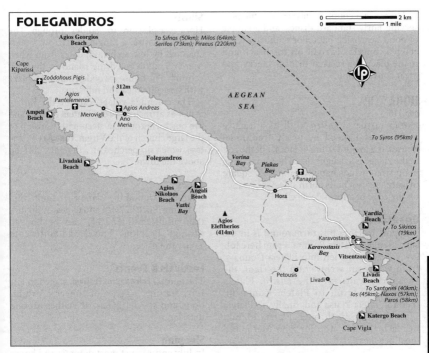

FOLEGANDROS

CYCLADES

Getting There & Away

Once poorly served by ferries, Folegandros at least in summer has good connections with Piraeus through the western Cyclades route. It even has connections to Santorini and as far as Amorgos during the summer. For details see Island Hopping (p513).

Getting Around

The local bus meets all ferry arrivals and takes passengers to Hora (€1.40). From Hora there are buses to the port one hour before all ferry departures. Buses from Hora run hourly in summer to Ano Meria (€0.80) and divert to Angali Beach. The bus stop for Ano Meria is located on the western edge of Hora.

There is a **taxi service** (☎ 22860 41048, 6944693957) on Folegandros.

You can hire cars for about €40 per day, and motorbikes from about €15 per day, from a number of outlets.

In summer, small boats ply regularly between beaches.

KARAVOSTASIS ΚΑΡΑΒΟΣΤΑΣΙΣ
pop 55

Folegandros' port is a sunny little place serviced by a sprinkling of domatia and tavernas, and with a pleasant pebble beach. Within a kilometre north and south of Karavostasis lies a series of other beaches, all enjoyable and easily reached by short walks. In high season, boats leave Karavostasis for beaches further afield.

Sleeping & Eating

Aeolos Beach Hotel (☎ 22860 41205; s/d/studios €50/55/80) Just across from the beach, this handy hotel has a pretty garden and clean straightforward rooms.

Vrahos (☎ 22860 41450; www.hotel-vrahos.gr; s incl breakfast €73, d incl breakfast €91-123, studios & apt €97-182; 🏖 💻 🛜) In a great location at the far end of the beach, Vrahos rises through a series of terraces, and the front balconies have great views of the bay. Rooms have cool decor and there's an outdoor Jacuzzi, a bar and a breakfast area. Breakfast is €12.50.

There are a couple of tavernas at the port serving fairly standard dishes, and a couple of good beachside bars. For enduring character, Evangelos is right on the beach and is the place for relaxed drinks, snacks and great conversation.

HORA ΧΩPA

pop 316

Hora's medieval *kastro,* with its attractive main street flanked by lovely traditional houses, is a major feature of Hora, but the rest of the village is a delight also. The meandering main street winds happily from leafy square to leafy square. On its north side, Hora stands on the edge of a formidable cliff.

Orientation

The port to Hora bus turnaround is in the square called Plateia Pounta. From here follow a road to the left into Plateia Dounavi, from where an archway on the right, the Paraporti, leads into the *kastro.* Plateia Dounavi leads on to Plateia Kontarini, then to Plateia Piatsa and, finally, to Plateia Maraki. Keep on through Plateia Maraki to reach the bus stop for Ano Meria and most beaches.

Information

Folegandros does not have an official tourism office. A good source of information is www.folegandrosisland.com.

There's no bank, but there is an ATM on the far side of Plateia Dounavi, next to the community offices. The post office is on the port road, 200m downhill from the bus turnaround.

Travel agencies can exchange travellers cheques.

Diaplous Travel (☎ 22860 41158; www.diaploustravel .gr; Plateia Pounta) Helpful and efficient agency – sells ferry tickets, exchanges money and arranges accommodation, car and bike hire and boat excursions. Internet access per 15 minutes costs €1.

Maraki Travel (☎ 22860 41273; fax 22860 41149; Plateia Dounavi; ⏲ 10.30am-noon & 5-9pm) Sells ferry tickets and exchanges money.

Medical Centre (☎ 22860 41222; Plateia Pounta)

Police station (☎ 22860 41249) Straight on from Plateia Maraki.

Sottovento Tourism Office (☎ 22860 41444; www .folegandrosisland.com) On Plateia Pounta; doubles as the Italian consulate and is very helpful on all tourism matters, including accommodation, international and domestic flights and boat trips.

Sights

Hora is a pleasure to wander through. The medieval **kastro**, a tangle of narrow streets spanned by low archways, dates from when Marco Sanudo ruled the island in the 13th century. The houses' wooden balconies blaze with bougainvillea and hibiscus.

The extended village, outside the *kastro,* is just as attractive. From Plateia Pounta and the bus turnaround, a steep path leads up to the large church of the Virgin, **Panagia** (⏲ 6pm-8pm), which sits perched on a dramatic cliff top above the town.

Tours

Boat trips around the island (per adult/child including lunch €27/10) and to nearby Sikinos (per adult/child €22/11) can be booked through Diaplous Travel and Sottovento Tourism Office.

Festivals & Events

The annual **Folegandros Festival**, staged in late July, features a series of concerts, exhibitions and special meals, at venues around the island.

Sleeping

In July and August most domatia and hotels will be full, so book well in advance.

Evgenia (☎ 22860 41006; www.evgeniafol@yahoo .gr; s/d €60/70 ste €80-120; ☒) These clean and well-kept rooms and studios are right at the entrance to Hora.

Pounta Accommodation (☎ 22860 41063; apt €80-90) Located about 1km from Hora, these are proper Folegandrian houses rather than studios or apartments and have great character within a superb setting.

Aegeo (☎ 22860 41468; aegeofol@hol.gr; s/d/tr €85/90/115; ☒ ☐ ☎) Located on the outskirts of town, Aegeo captures the classic Cycladean style with its central courtyard area, all white and blue and draped with crimson bougainvillea. Rooms are immaculate and bright.

Hotel Polikandia (☎ 22860 41322; www.polikandia -folegandros.gr; s €85, d €95-120, ste €200; ☒ ☎ ☒) A major makeover has transformed this always decent place into a colourful boutique hotel with lovely rooms encircling a gleaming pool. Decor and facilities are of high quality. It's just before the bus turnaround. Breakfast is €10. Bikes are offered free.

Anemomylos Apartments (☎ 22860 41309; www .anemomilosapartments.com; d €150-200; ☒ ☐ ☒ ☒)

A prime position on top of a cliff ensures awesome views from the seaward-facing rooms of this stylish complex and from its terraces. Rooms are elegant and fine antiques add to the ambience. Anemomylos is just up from the bus turnaround. One unit is equipped for use by those with disabilities.

Eating

Melissa (☎ 22860 41067; Plateia Kontarini; mains €5-9) Good food is matched by charming owners. The island speciality of *matsata* (handmade pasta) with meat of your choice is always worthwhile, as is the fish soup. Vegetarians will relish the stuffed cabbage. It also does good breakfasts.

Zefiros (☎ 22860 41556; dishes €5.50-9.50) A great *ouzerie* and *mezedhopoleio* with a challenging selection of ouzo varieties. There are mezedhes plates for two at €20, as well as mixed small plates, and dishes such as lamb in vine leaves and shrimp *saganaki*. Keep left beyond Plateia Kontarini.

our pick **Pounta** (☎ 22860 41063; Plateia Pounta; dishes €6-13) In Pounta's garden setting there's an inescapable sense of an older Greece, and the courteous service underlines this. The traditional food is excellent, from breakfasts starting at €4.50, to evening meals of rabbit *stifadho* or artichoke casserole. It's all served on lovely crockery made by one of the owners, Lisbet Giouri; you can buy examples of her work.

Eva's Garden (☎ 22860 41110; mains €8-24) Opened in the past couple of years, Eva's brings an added flair to Folegandros cuisine. Starters include fava-bean purée with onion and parsley, while mains feature pork fillet in smoked cheese sauce or grilled marinated shrimps in a lime sauce with basmati rice. The wine list goes well with it all and includes Argiros vintages from Santorini. Keep right beyond Plateia Kontarini.

Also recommended:

Piatsa Restaurant (☎ 22860 41274; dishes €3-9.50)

Chic (☎ 22860 41515; dishes €4-9.50).

Drinking & Entertainment

Folegandros has some stylish cafe-bars such as **Caffé de Viaggiatori** (☎ 22860 41444), next door to Sottovento Tourism Office and offering Italian wines and finger food. Deeper into Hora is **To Mikro** (☎ 22860 41550), a good place for coffee, crêpes and cakes by day and cocktails at night.

At Hora's very own 'West End' is a clutch of colourful music bars starting with **Greco Café-Bar** (☎ 22860 41456), with a great mix of sounds from a stock of over 1000 CDs, all against a backdrop of vivid murals. Next door are **Avli Club** (☎ 22860 41100) for early evening lounge music and later rock, disco, Latin and Greek; and **Kolpo** (☎ 22860 41570) for reggae, world music and soul, and a hammock garden with scenic views.

A Folegandros local drink is *rakomelo* – heated *raki* with honey and cloves. One of the best bars to enjoy it and get into the spirit of things is Astarti, next to the Melissa taverna on Plateia Kontarini.

AROUND FOLEGANDROS
Ano Meria Άνω Μεριά
pop 291

The settlement of Ano Meria is a scattered community of small farms and dwellings that stretches for several kilometres. This is traditional island life where tourism makes no intrusive mark and life happily wanders off sideways.

The **folklore museum** (admission €1.50; ☼ 5pm-8pm) is on the eastern outskirts of the village. Ask the bus driver to drop you off nearby.

There are several very traditional tavernas in Ano Meria, including **I Synantisi** (☎ 22860 41208; dishes €4-8) and **Mimi's** (☎ 22860 41377; dishes €4). Things may get a touch fraught at busy periods.

Beaches

For **Livadi Beach**, 1.2km southeast of Karavostasis, follow the signs for Camping Livadi. Further round the coast on the southeastern tip of the island is **Katergo Beach**, best reached by boat from Karavostasis.

The sandy and pebbled **Angali** beach, on the coast opposite to Hora, is a popular spot, now with a surfaced road to it and a bus turnaround. There are some rooms here and two reasonable tavernas.

About 750m over the hill, by footpath, west of Angali is **Agios Nikolaos**, a nudist beach. **Livadaki** beach is over 2km further west again. It is reached by another 1.5km hike from the bus stop near the church of Agios Andreas at Ano Meria. Boats connect these west-coast beaches in high season. **Agios Georgios** is north of Ano Meria and requires another demanding walk. Have tough footwear, sun protection and, because most beaches have no shops or tavernas, make sure you take food and water.

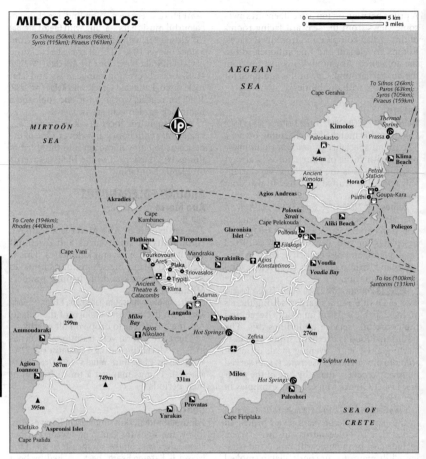

MILOS & KIMOLOS

To Sifnos (50km); Paros (96km); Syros (115km); Piraeus (161km)

AEGEAN
SEA

Cape Gerahia

MIRTOÖN
SEA

To Sifnos (26km); Paros (63km); Syros (105km); Piraeus (159km)

Thermal Spring

Kimolos

Paleokastro

Prassa

364m

Klima Beach

Ancient Kimolos

Petrol Station

Hora

Akradies

Agios Andreas

Psathi

Goupa-Kara

To Crete (194km); Rhodes (440km)

Cape Kambanes

Glaronisia Islet

Polonia Strait

Cape Pelekouda

Aliki Beach

Poliegos

Plathiena

Firopotamos

Pollonia

Cape Vani

Fourkovouni

Areti

Mandrakia

Sarakiniko

Agios Konstantinos

Filakopi

Voudia

Plaka

Triovasalos

Trypiti

Voudia Bay

Ancient Theatre & Catacombs

Klima

Adamas

To Ios (100km); Santorini (131km)

Langada

Milos Bay

Papikinou

299m

Agios Nikolaos

Hot Springs

Zefiria

276m

Ammoudaraki

Agiou Ioannou

387m

749m

331m

Milos

Hot Springs

Sulphur Mine

Paleohori

395m

Provatas

Yarakas

Cape Firiplaka

SEA OF CRETE

Kleftiko   Aspronisi Islet

Cape Psalida

0 ——— 5 km
0 ——— 3 miles

In July and August, weather permitting, excursion boats make separate trips from Karavostasis to Katergo, Angali and Agios Nikolaos and from Angali to Livadaki beach.

MILOS ΜΗΛΟΣ

pop 4771

Milos (*mee*-loss) has a dramatic coastal landscape with colourful and surreal rock formations that reflect the island's volcanic origins. It also has hot springs, the most beaches of any Cycladic island and some compelling ancient sites.

The island has a fascinating history of mineral extraction dating from the Neolithic period when obsidian was an important material and was even exported to the Minoan world of Crete. Over the years sulphur and kaolin have been mined and today Milos is the biggest bentonite and perlite production and processing centre in the EU.

Filakopi, an ancient Minoan city in the island's northeast, was one of the earliest settlements in the Cyclades. During the Peloponnesian Wars, Milos was the only Cycladic island not to join the Athenian alliance. It paid dearly in 416 BC, when avenging Athenians massacred the adult males and enslaved the women and children.

The island's most celebrated export, the beautiful *Venus de Milo* (a 4th-century-BC statue of Aphrodite, found in an olive grove in 1820) is far away in the Louvre (allegedly having lost its arms on the way to Paris in the 19th century).

Getting There & Away

There are two flights weekly between Milos and Athens. These are often quite heavily booked ahead. Milos is on the same western-Cyclades ferry routes as its northern neighbour Serifos. For details see Island Hopping (p518).

Getting Around

There are no buses to the airport (south of Papikinou), so you'll need to take a **taxi** (☎ 22870 22219) for €7.65, plus €0.30 per piece of luggage, from Adamas. A taxi from Adamas to Plaka is €6.50; add €1 for evening trips. **Taxi Andriotis** (☎ 6942590951) is a friendly service.

Buses leave Adamas for Plaka and Trypiti every hour or so. Buses run to Pollonia (four daily), Paleohori (three daily), Provatas (three daily) and Achivadolimni (Milos) Camping (right), east of Adamas (three daily). All fares are €1.40.

Cars, motorcycles and mopeds can also be hired from places along the waterfront. A helpful outfit is **Giourgas Rent a Car** (☎ 22870 22352, 6937757066; giourgas@otenet.gr), reached by heading east from the ferry quay, going inland from where the waterfront road crosses a dry river bed and then turning right after several hundred metres.

ADAMAS ΑΔΑΜΑΣ

pop 1391

Plaka is the capital of Milos and the most appealing of all the settlements, but the pleasant, lively port of Adamas has most of the accommodation, shops and general services, plus a diverting waterfront scene.

Orientation

For the town centre, turn right from the arrival quay. The central square, with the bus stop, taxi rank and outdoor cafes, is at the end of this stretch of waterfront, where the road curves inland. Just past the square is a road to the right that skirts the town beach.

Information

ATMs can be found along the main harbour front and in the main square. The post office is along the main road, 50m from the main square, on the right.

Internet Info (☎ 22870 23218; per 30min €1.50; ☉ 9am-midnight) Located in the main street, just inland and on the right.

Municipal Tourist Office (☎ 22870 22445; www .milos-island.gr; ☉ 8am-midnight mid-Jun–mid-Sep) Opposite the quay.

Police station (☎ 22870 21378) On the main square, next to the bus stop.

Port police (☎ 22870 22100) On the waterfront.

Terry's Travel Services (☎ 22870 22640; www .terrysmilostravel.com) Knowledgeable and helpful service goes with a great love of the island here. Help with accommodation, car hire, kayaking and sailing trips, diving and much more. Head left from the ferry quay, and, just past the bend in the road, go right up a lane.

Sights & Activities

The **Milos Mining Museum** (☎ 22870 22481; www .milosminingmuseum.gr; adult/concession €3/1.50; ☉ 9am-2pm & 6-9pm Jul–mid-Sep, 8.30am-2.30pm Tue-Sat mid-Sep–Jun) is a must for mining enthusiasts; in fact, it's a must for everyone. It's about 600m east of the ferry quay.

Dive courses are offered by **Milos Diving Center** (☎ 22870 41296; www.milosdiving.gr), based at Pollonia. It's a member of the International Association for Handicapped Divers.

Kayak Milos (☎ 22870 23597; www.seakayakgreece .com) organises day trips for €60 per person, including picnic lunch. Longer expeditions and week-long packages are also available.

Tours

Around Milos Cruise (☎ 6944375799; tours €25; ☉ May-Sep) Cruise on the wooden-hulled Captain Yiangos departing daily at 9am, stopping at beaches around the island and pausing at Kimolos for lunch. Return is about 6pm. Buy tickets on the waterfront.

Festivals & Events

The **Milos Festival**, a well-orchestrated event, is held in early July and features traditional dancing, cooking and jazz.

Sleeping

In summer, lists of available domatia are given out at the tourist office on the quay, but good options are thin on the ground – call ahead.

Achivadolimni (Milos) Camping (☎ 22870 31410; www.miloscamping.gr; Arhiva-dolimni; camp sites per adult/child/tent €7/4/4, bungalows €60-125; ☉ 😞) This camping ground has excellent facilities, including a restaurant, a bar and bike rental.

CYCLADES

It's 4.5km east of Adamas; to get here, follow the signs along the waterfront from the central square or take the bus (see Getting Around, p207).

Hotel Delfini (☎ 22870 22001; fax 22870 22294; s/d €45/65; ☼ Apr–Oct; ✷) A pleasant, comfortable hotel with good rooms and facilities. Neighbouring hotels have rather stolen the view, but there's a lovely terrace and a warm ambience. It's to the west of the ferry quay and is tucked in behind the Lagada Beach Hotel.

Terry's Rooms (☎ 22870 22640; teristur@otenet .gr; d €50, apt €100-120; ✷) A great option, these homely rooms are in a quiet location above the harbour and are a nice mix of traditional and modern. Follow directions for Terry's Travel Services (see p207).

Studios Helios (☎ 22870 22258; fax 22870 23974; heaton.theologitis@utanet.at; apt €90-100; ☼ mid-May–mid-Oct; ✷) In an unbeatable location, high above the port, are these stylish, beautifully furnished apartments for two or four people.

Portiani Hotel (☎ 22870 22940; www.portianimilos .com; s/d incl breakfast €110/135; P ✷) Right next to the square and busy waterfront, these well-appointed rooms manage to feel secluded. The upper balconies have great views. There's a lift to the upper floors. The buffet breakfast features local products.

Eating

I Milos (☎ 22870 22210; dishes €3.50-9) This likeable place is at the far end of the main square's line of waterfront cafes and tavernas. Breakfasts are €4.10 to €6.20. Lunch dishes include pizzas and pastas.

Taverna Barko (☎ 22870 22660; dishes €4.50-12) A classic *mezedhopoleio*. On the road to Plaka, near the outskirts of town, Barko serves local dishes such as Milos cheese pie and octopus in wine, as well as pastas.

Flisvos (☎ 22870 22275; dishes €5-9) Fish is by the kilogram at this busy waterfront taverna, to the east of the ferry quay. It serves good charcoal-grilled Greek specialities, salads are crisp and fresh, and the cheese and mushroom pies are mouth-melting.

Entertainment

Halfway up the first staircase along from the ferry quay are a couple of popular music bars including Ilori and Vipera Lebetina, playing disco, pop and Greek music during July and August.

Akri (☎ 22870 22064) Further uphill, opposite Villa Helios, Akri is in a beautiful location with a fine terrace overlooking the port. Music favours ethnic, funk and easy listening.

PLAKA & TRYPITI ΠΛΑΚΑ & ΤΡΥΠΗΤΗ

Plaka (population 877), 5km uphill from Adamas, is a typical Cycladic town with white houses and labyrinthine lanes. It merges with the settlement of Trypiti (population 489) to the south and rises above a sprawl of converging settlements, yet has a distinctive and engaging character.

Plaka is built on the site of Ancient Milos, which was destroyed by the Athenians and rebuilt by the Romans.

Sights & Activities

The **archaeology museum** (☎ 22870 21629; admission €3; ☼ 8.30am-3pm Tue-Sun) is in Plaka, just downhill from the bus turnaround. It's in a handsome old building and contains some riveting exhibits, including a plaster cast of *Venus de Milo* that was made by Louvre craftsmen – as a sort of *Venus de Mea Culpa*, perhaps, considering the French 'appropriated' the original. Best of all is a perky little herd of tiny bull figurines from the Late Cycladic period.

The **Milos Folk & Arts Museum** (☎ 22870 21292; ☼ 10am-2pm & 6-9pm Tue-Sat, 10am-2pm Sun & Mon) has fascinating exhibits, including traditional costumes, woven goods and embroidery. It's signposted from the bus turnaround in Plaka.

At the bus turnaround, go east for the path that climbs to the **Frankish Kastro**, built on the ancient acropolis and offering panoramic views of most of the island. The 13th-century church, **Thalassitras**, is inside the walls.

There are some Roman ruins near Trypiti, including Greece's only Christian **catacombs** (☎ 22870 21625; admission free; ☼ 8am-7pm Tue-Sun). The site was closed for some time but has been skilfully renovated and was due to be open by 2010. Stay on the bus towards Trypiti and get off at a T-junction by a big signpost indicating the way. Follow the road down for about 500m to where a track (signed) goes off to the right. This leads to the rather forlorn, but somehow thrilling, spot where a farmer found the *Venus de Milo* in 1820; you can't miss the huge sign. A short way further along the track is the well-preserved **ancient theatre**, which hosts the **Milos Festival** every July. Back on the surfaced road, head downhill to reach the 1st-century catacombs.

Sleeping & Eating

All of the following places are located in Plaka.

Betty's Rooms (☎ 22870 21538; d €70) Forget Santorini; these rooms in a family house are at the bottom end of Plaka and have fantastic views.

Archondoula Karamitsou Studios (☎ 22870 23820; www.archondoula-studios.gr; ste €75-130) More great views are enjoyed at these traditional rooms, which are full of local craftwork and island antiques. Prices drop substantially outside August.

Windmill of Karamitsos (☎ 6945568086; kali-opekavalierou@yahoo.gr; r €170) A fascinating and unique sleeping experience can be had at this converted windmill that has a separate cooking and eating annexe. It's in a peaceful position on a hill top, of course, with great views.

ourpick Archondoula (☎ 22870 21384; dishes €5-15) All the family is involved at this great *mezedhopoleio*. The food is classic traditional across a range of favourites from fresh salads to beef with honey sauce and shrimps with cream sauce. It's just along the main street from the bus turnaround in Plaka.

Utopia Café (☎ 22870 23678) One of the best viewpoints in the Cyclades can be enjoyed from the cool terrace of Utopia, down the narrow alley opposite Archondoula.

AROUND MILOS

The village of **Klima**, below Trypiti and the catacombs, was the port of ancient Milos. It's a picturesque fishing village with a lovely little harbour. Whitewashed buildings, with coloured doors and balconies, have boathouses on the ground floor and living quarters above.

Plathiena is a fine sandy beach below Plaka, to the north. On the way to Plathiena you can visit the fishing villages of **Areti** and **Fourkovouni**.

At **Sarakiniko** are snow-white rock formations and natural terraces. **Pollonia**, on the north coast, is a fishing village-cum-resort with a beach and domatia. The boat to Kimolos departs here.

The beaches of **Provatas** and **Paleohori**, on the south coast, are long and sandy, and Paleohori has **hot springs**.

KIMOLOS ΚΙΜΩΛΟΣ

pop 769

Kimolos (Map p444) feels like a genuine step back in time. Perched off the northeast tip of Milos, it receives a steady trickle of visitors, especially day-trippers arriving from Pollonia. The boat docks at the port of **Psathi**, from where it's 1.5km to the pretty capital of **Hora**. The medieval **kastro**, embedded at the heart of Hora, is a mazelike joy. Albeit in ruins, there are surviving walls and restoration work is ongoing.

There's an ATM by the town hall in Hora.

Beaches can be reached by caïque from Psathi. At the centre of the island is the 364m-high cliff on which sits the fortress of **Paleokastro**.

There are domatia, tavernas, cafes and bars enough in Hora and Psathi. Domatia owners meet ferries. Expect to pay single/double rates of about €35/50.

The taverna **To Kyma** (☎ 22870 51001; dishes €5-12), on the beach at Psathi, is fine for Greek-standard meals.

There is one petrol station on Kimolos; it's about 200 metres to the north of Psathi.

Getting There & Away

Kimilos shares much the same regular ferry schedules as Milos. For details see Island Hopping (p516). A car ferry goes daily to and from Pollonia on Milos, departing from Kimolos at 8am, 10am, 1.15pm, 5.30pm and 10pm (€2, 20 minutes).

SIFNOS ΣΙΦΝΟΣ

pop 2900

Sifnos (*see-fnoss*) captivates the visitor with its hidden charms. It seems a barren place of heavy hills as you approach by sea, until the port of Kamares appears, as if by magic. Beyond the port and between the flanking slopes of rugged mountains lies an abundant landscape of terraced olive groves and almond trees, of oleanders and juniper and aromatic herbs covering the softer hillsides. The main settlement of Apollonia and the scenic village of Kastro have great appeal, and plenty of unspoiled paths link the island villages. Walking on Sifnos is particularly satisfying. The Anavasi map series *Topo 25/10.25 Aegean Cyclades/Sifnos* is useful for footpath details.

SIFNOS

0 ——— 4 km
0 ——— 2 miles

To Serifos (24km);
Kythnos (63km);
Paros (74km);
Piraeus (146km)

AEGEAN SEA

Cape Heronisos

Heronisos

Agios Dimos

476m

Kamares Bay
Kamares

Sifnos

Ano Petali • Artemonas

Apollonia • Kastro
Katavati • Kato Petali • Seralia
680m ▲ • Exambelas

To Milos (50km);
Santorini (105km)

Moni Profiti Ilia

Moni Hrysopigis • Faros
Fasolou Beach
Hrysopigis Beach

Vathy • Platys Gialos

Vathy Bay

201m ▲

Platys Gialos Bay

Cape Kondou

Kitriani

During the Archaic period (from about the 8th century BC) the island was very wealthy because of its gold and silver resources, but by the 5th century BC the mines were exhausted and Sifnos' fortunes were reversed. The island has a tradition of pottery making, basket weaving and cooking.

Getting There & Away

Sifnos is on the Piraeus–western-Cyclades ferry route and has good summer connections south to Serifos, Milos and Folegandros and with Santorini and Amorgos. For details see Island Hopping (p522).

Getting Around

Frequent buses link the island's main town, Apollonia, with Kamares (€1.20), with some services continuing on to Artemonas (€1.20), Kastro (€1.20), Vathy (€1.70), Faros (€1.30) and Platys Gialos (€1.70).

Taxis (☎ 22840 31347) hover around the port and Apollonia's main square. Fares from Kamares are €6 to Apollonia, €8 to Platys Gialos and €9 to Vathy. Cars can be hired from **Stavros Hotel** (☎ 22840 31641) in Kamares,

and from **Apollo Rent a Car** (☎ 22840 32237) in Apollonia, for €30 to €55.

KAMARES ΚΑΜΑΡΕΣ
pop 186

The port of Kamares (kah-*mah*-rez) always seems to have a holiday atmosphere, not least because of its large beach and the narrow, bustling beachside road with its waterfront cafes and tavernas and colourful mix of shops. The bus stop is by the tamarisk trees just past the inland end of the ferry quay.

Information

There are toilets near the tourist office, plus an ATM booth.

Municipal tourist office (☎ 22840 31977/31975; www.sifnos.gr) Opposite the bus stop is this very helpful and well-organised office. Opening times vary depending on boat arrivals. It sells ferry tickets and can find accommodation anywhere on the island. There's luggage storage (per item €1) and you can buy useful information sheets about the island as well as bus and boat timetables.

Sleeping & Eating

Domatia owners rarely meet boats and in high season it's best to book ahead.

Camping Makis (☎ 22840 32366, 6945946339; www.makiscamping.gr; camp sites per adult/child/tent €7/4/4, r from €55; ☉ Apr-Nov; ℗ ✖ ☎) This pleasant camping ground is just behind the beach. It has an outdoor cafe, a barbecue area, minimarket, a laundry, shaded sites and friendly owners.

Simeon (☎ 22840 31652; studios_simeon@hotmail.com; s/d/tr €50/70/80, apt €100-140; ☉ Apr-Oct; ✖ ☎) From their little balconies, the small front rooms have stunning views down across the port and along the beach to soaring mountains beyond. Other rooms are not so blessed, but are bigger. You get here by going up steepish steps from the waterfront.

Stavros Hotel (☎ 22840 31641/33383; www.sifnostravel.com; s/d/tr €55/70/75; ✖) Main street's Stavros has bright and comfy rooms of good size. Attached to the hotel is an information office that can arrange car hire and has a book exchange. The same family owns Hotel Kamari (☎ 22840 33383) on the outskirts of Kamares, on the road to Apollonia – rooms here are €40/50/55 per single/double/triple.

Hotel Afroditi (☎ 22840 31704; www.hotel-afroditi.gr; s/d/tr incl breakfast €70/91/114; ℗ ✖ ☎) The welcoming, family-run Afroditi is across the road from the beach. Rooms are a decent size and have been renovated recently. The breakfast is a definite plus. There are sea views to the front and mountain views to the rear.

Café Stavros (☎ 22840 33500; snacks €4-6) Overlooking the water halfway along the main street is this relaxing place, ideal for people watching. It does good breakfasts for about €5.

0 Symos (☎ 22840 32353; dishes €4-8) Among a choice of waterfront tavernas, this popular place uses locally sourced ingredients in such appealing dishes as linguini and shrimps in saffron (€12) and *revythia* (chickpea) soup.

Another good eatery is the family-run **Posidonia** (☎ 22840 32362; dishes €3-8), where you can get breakfast for €6.

APOLLONIA ΑΠΟΛΛΩΝΙΑ
pop 1054

The 'capital' of Sifnos is situated on the edge of a plateau 5km uphill from the port.

The stop for buses to and from Kamares is on Apollonia's busy central square, where the post office and Museum of Popular Art are located. Because of congestion, all other buses pick up passengers about 50m further on, at a T-junction where the road to the right goes to Vathy and Platys Gialos and the road to the left goes to Artemonas and Kastro. Constant traffic seems to be the norm, but step away from the main road onto the pedestrian street behind the museum and Apollonia is transformed.

There is free parking at the big car park at the entrance to the village.

There is an ATM by the bus stop and at the Alpha Bank. The Piraeus Bank and National Bank of Greece (both with ATMs) are just around the corner from the Kamares stop on the road to Artemonas; the police station is another 50m beyond.

Internet Café 8 (☎ 22840 33734; per hr €4; ☯ 9am-1am) is about 150m along the road to Platys Gialos. The **bookshop** (☎ 22840 33523), just down from the bus stop, has newspapers and a good selection of books in various languages.

The quirky **Museum of Popular Art** (☎ 22840 31341; admission €1; ☯ 10am-2pm & 7.30-11.30pm Tue-Sun) on the central square contains a splendid confusion of old costumes, pots, textiles and photographs that could keep you going for hours.

Sleeping & Eating

Mrs Dina Rooms (☎ 22840 31125, 6945513318; s/d/tr/q €50/60/70/80; ☒) Laughter and flowers charac-

terise this pleasant little complex of rooms, located a couple of hundred metres along the road south towards Vathy and Platys Gialos. The rooms are well above the road and have views towards Kastro.

Gerontios Rooms (☎ 22840 31473; s/d/tr €50/60/70; ☒) There's another floral welcome here, high above the village centre with wide views to Kastro. From the post office head uphill and take the lane to the right of a small cafe.

Hotel Artemon (☎ 22840 31303; Artemonas; s/d/tr €55/70/84; P ☒ ☞) In Artemonas, 2km uphill from Apollonia, is this old-style but very reasonable hotel that has enough rooms to make it a possible best bet in August if you're not booking ahead. Front rooms overlook the main road.

Veranda (☎ 22840 33969; snacks from €4; ☞) A cool corner in Apollonia, with wi-fi for customers, Veranda is next to the T-junction bus stop. Knotted white drapes dangle streetside from the eponymous veranda. It does breakfasts (€3.50 to €10), sandwiches and baguettes, ice cream and sweets and you can while the night away with drinks and lounge sounds.

Lempesis (☎ 22840 31303; Artemonas; mains €5.50-9) Part of the Hotel Artemon and run by the exuberant chef-owner, Artemon is a local favourite, not least for terrific baked meats and dishes like *revythia* soup, *exohiko* (lamb in pastry with cheese) and goat kid in lemon sauce. The house wine is very good indeed.

To Liotrivi (☎ 22840 31246; Artemonas; mains €6-9) Located in the pleasant square of Artemonas, this one-time olive press serves traditional Sifniot meat dishes such as rabbit with onions, while vegetarians can enjoy artichokes with potatoes, or *briam*, stewed vegetables.

Apostoli to Koutouki (☎ 22840 31186; dishes €8.50-12.50) Signature dishes such as beef baked in a clay pot with tomatoes, aubergine, cheese and wine complement fish dishes which are by the kilo at this long-established place on Apollonia's pedestrianised main street.

AROUND SIFNOS

Not to be missed is the walled cliff-top village of **Kastro**, 3km from Apollonia. The former capital, it is a magical place of buttressed alleyways and whitewashed houses. It has a small **archaeological museum** (☎ 22840 31022; admission free; ☯ 8.30am-3pm Tue-Sun).

Buses go to Kastro from Apollonia but you can walk there, mainly on old paved pathways. The start of the path is 20m to the right (Vathy

CYCLADES

road) from the T-junction in Apollonia. Go right down some steps and then through a tunnel beneath the road. A pleasant path circumnavigates Kastro and is especially scenic on its northern side. Midway round the northern side, above the glittering sea, is the charming little art workshop of **Maximos** (Panagiotis Fanariotis; ☎ 22840 33692), whose speciality is handmade jewellery in original gold and silver motifs. Prices for these lovely pieces start at about €6 and are far below the usual price charged for work of such high quality. There is also accommodation here (see below).

Platys Gialos, 6km south of Apollonia, has a big, generous beach, entirely backed by tavernas, domatia and shops. The bus terminates at the beach's southwestern end. The **Chrisopigi Travel Agency** (☎ 22840 71523; www.sifnoschrisopigi.gr) is a useful agency in Platys Gialos that sells ferry tickets, hires cars, books excursions and can find accommodation. **Vathy**, on the west coast, is an easy-going little village within the curved horns of an almost circular bay. **Faros** is a cosy little fishing hamlet with a couple of nice beaches nearby, including the little beach of **Fasolou**, reached up steps and over the headland from the bus stop.

Sleeping & Eating
KASTRO
Maximos (☎ 22840 33692; r €50) A tiny terrace with unbeatable sea views comes with this quirky little room beside Maximos' workshop, located on the northern side of Kastro.

Rafeletou Apartments (☎ 22840 31161, 69324 74001; d €60-77, tr €70-90, apt €105-120) For an authentic Kastro experience, these family-run apartments at the heart of the village are ideal.

our pick **To Astro** (☎ 22840 31476; mains €5-9; ☽ mid-Apr–Oct) Kastro's genuine 'star', as the name translates, certainly lives up to its appellation. Lovingly run by the owner-cook, it has tasty island dishes including eggplant and meatballs, octopus with olives, and lamb in traditional Sifniot style.

PLATYS GIALOS ΠΛΑΤΥΣ ΓΙΑΛΟΣ
Although there are plenty of sleeping places here, many cater for package tourists.

Angeliki Rooms (☎ 22840 71288; d/tr €55/70) A beachfront venue with pleasant rooms, near the quieter south end of the beach and just back from the bus terminus.

Hotel Efrosini (☎ 22840 71353; www.hotel-efrosini .gr; s/d/tr incl breakfast €65/95/117; ☒ ☜) Right on the beach, this bright and well-kept hotel is one of the best on the Platys Gialos strip. The small balconies overlook a leafy courtyard.

Ariadne Restaurant (☎ 22840 71277; mains €6-16) You can tell from the well-kept and well-presented seating area that some care goes into this fine eatery. The lamb in red-wine sauce with herbs is a speciality. Fish is by the kilo, but you can settle for a seafood risotto for €16 or fish soup for €15.

VATHY ΒΑΘΥ
Areti Studios (☎ 22840 71191; d/apt €60/100; ℗ ☒) Just in from the beach and amidst olive groves and a lovely garden, rooms here are clean and bright and some have cooking facilities. If you are driving, the approach is down a rough and at times very narrow track that goes off left just before the main road ends.

Vathy has a fair choice of beachfront tavernas, such as Oceanida and Manolis, offering reliable Greek dishes.

SERIFOS ΣΕΡΙΦΟΣ

pop 1414
Serifos (seh-ri-fohs) has a raw and rugged beauty that is softened by green folds in its rocky hills. The traditional *hora* is a dramatic scribble of white houses that crowns a high and rocky peak, 2km to the north of the port of Livadi. It catches your eye the minute the port comes in sight.

In Greek mythology, Serifos is where Perseus grew up and where the Cyclops were said to live. The island, in real time, was brutally exploited for iron ore during the 19th and 20th centuries and the rough remains of the industry survive (see boxed text, opposite).

There is some fine walking on Serifos and the Anavasi map series *Topo 25/10.26 Aegean Cyclades/Serifos* is useful.

Getting There & Away
Like Sifnos, Serifos is on the Piraeus–western-Cyclades route and has good summer connections south to Sifnos, Milos and Folegandros and even with Santorini and Amorgos. For details see Island Hopping (p522).

Getting Around

There are frequent buses between Livadi and Hora (€1.40, 15 minutes); a timetable is posted at the bus stop by the yacht quay. A taxi to Hora costs €6. Vehicles can be hired from Krinas Travel in Livadi.

LIVADI ΛΙΒΑΔΙ

pop 537

The port town of Serifos is a fairly low-key place where, in spite of growing popularity, there's still a reassuring feeling that the modern world has not entirely taken over. Just over the headland that rises from the ferry quay lies the fine, tamarisk-fringed beach at **Livadakia**. A walk further south over the next headland, **Karavi Beach** is the unofficial clothes-optional beach.

Information

A useful website is www.e-serifos.com.

There is an Alpha Bank (with ATM) located on the waterfront and an ATM under the bakery sign opposite the yacht quay.

The post office is midway along the road that runs inland from opposite the bus stop and then bends sharply right.

Krinas Travel (☎ 22810 51488; www.serifos-travel.com) Just where the ferry quay joins the waterfront road, this helpful agency sells ferry tickets and organises car (per day €45) and scooter (per day €20) hire. It also has internet access at €2 per half-hour and a book exchange.

Port police (☎ 22810 51470) Up steps just beside Krinas Travel.

Sleeping & Eating

The best accommodation is on and behind Livadakia Beach, a few minutes hike from the quay. Most owners pick up at the port by arrangement.

Coralli Camping (☎ 22810 51500; www.coralli.gr; camp sites per adult/child/tent €7/3/6, bungalows s/d

€30/60; P 🛜 🖼) In a great location just back from Livadaki Beach, this well-equipped camping ground is shaded by tall eucalypts. Bungalows have mountain or sea views. There's also a restaurant and a minimarket. A minibus meets all ferries.

Marieta Rooms (☎ 22810 51399; kamatso@otenet.gr; r/apt €45/90; 🖼) The rooms at this modest place are small but bright and perfectly formed. Everything fits with ease and so will you. The apartment is, in turn, spacious. The rooms have a hot plate and welcome ceiling fans complement the air conditioning.

Medusa (☎ 22810 51128; rodolfosstamatakis@yahoo.gr; s/d/tr €55/65/70; P 🖼) A great outlook is just one advantage of this immaculate place that stands above a lovely garden and has views of nearby Lividakia Bay and distant Sifnos. Rooms are big and comfy and each has a little hot plate and coffee-making facilities.

HARD TIMES

The Greek islands we love today were often desperate places in a less-favoured age. On Serifos, where industrial mining for iron ore began in the mid-19th century under draconian management, hundreds – some claim thousands – of miners are said to have died because of appalling working conditions. In 1916 the miners went on strike for better conditions and wages. Militia were dispatched to the island. The militia opened fire, killing four of the strikers; the miners and their wives, and even their children, responded with some fury, killing several of the militia. Working conditions improved slightly after this, but the miners' dream of a workers' co-operative came to naught. The mines were finally abandoned in the 1960s. A memorial to the four miners who died stands at Megalo Livadi in the southwest of the island.

CYCLADES

Alexandros-Vassilia (☎ 22810 51119; fax 22810 51903; d/tr/apt €80/96/125; 🔀) A rose-fragrant garden right on the beach makes this place a happy choice. Rooms are a good size and are clean and well equipped (apartments have cooking facilities). The garden taverna does sturdy Greek staples for €6 to €15 and toothsome dishes such as shrimps with pasta.

Yacht Club Serifos (☎ 22810 51888; breakfast €3.30-10.50, snacks & sandwiches €3.50-5.80; 🕙 7am-3am) Popular and always with a happy buzz, this waterfront cafe-bar plays lounge music by day and mainstream, rock, disco and funk late into the night.

Anemos Café (☎ 22810 51783; dishes €4-6) Views of the distant Hora from a sunny balcony overlooking the harbour make for a relaxed stop at this cafe at the inner end of the ferry dock. It's open early until late and does breakfast for about €7.

There are numerous tavernas along the waterfront.

Some recommended options:

Passaggio (☎ 22810 52212; mains €5.50-16) Traditional cuisine with international touches.

Stamatis (☎ 22810 51309; mains €5-11) A long-established taverna with decent food and good helpings.

Entertainment

Metalleio (☎ 22810 51755; 🕙 9pm-late) Tucked away on the road beyond the waterfront, Metalleio doubles as a decent restaurant and a very cool music venue featuring an eclectic array of sounds from around the world, including jazz, funk, Afro, Asian groove and Latin. The restaurant features mainly poultry and meat dishes (mains €5 to €12.50).

There are several music bars in the central waterfront area such as Shark and Edem that play mainly Greek sounds.

HORA ΧΩΡΑ

The *hora* of Serifos spills across the summit of a rocky hill above Livadi and is one of the most striking of the Cycladic capitals. Ancient steps lead up from Livadi, though they are fragmented by the snaking road that links the two. You can walk up, but in the heat of summer, going up by bus and then walking back down is wiser. There's a post office just up from the bus turnaround.

Just up from Hora's bus terminus, steps climb into the maze of Hora proper and lead to the charming main square, watched over by the imposing neoclassical town hall. From the square, narrow alleys and more steps lead ever upwards to the remnants of the ruined 15th-century **Venetian kastro**. Low walls enclose the highest part of the *kastro*, from where the views are spectacular. A small church occupies part of the summit.

Hora has a small **archaeological museum** (☎ 22810 51138; admission free; 🕙 8.30am-3pm Tue-Sun) displaying fragments of mainly Hellenic and Roman sculpture excavated from the *kastro*. Exhibits are sparse and the museum tiny, but it is a pleasure to visit. Panels in Greek and English spell out fascinating details, including the legend of Perseus.

There is a pleasant **walk** on a fine cobbled pathway that starts just above the archaeological museum and leads up the mountain to the little church of **Agios Georgios**. The views are superb.

Sleeping & Eating

I Apanemia (☎ 22810 51517, 6971891106; s/d €40/50; 🔀) You'll find excellent value at this good-natured, family-run place. The decent, well-equipped rooms (tea- and coffee-making facilities included) have front balcony views down towards the distant sea and side views towards Hora.

Karavomylos (☎ 22810 51261; dishes €4.50-14) Near the bus terminus, this is a local favourite offering mezedhes and local dishes. It does breakfast also (€3 to €9) and there's music in the bar and occasional live sessions of Greek traditional music, including *rembetika*. The famous *rakomelo*, a *raki* and honey drink, adds to the pleasure.

ourpick Stou Stratou (☎ 22810 52566; plates €5-18) The tradition of the *mezedhopoleio* is alive and well at this cafe-bar in the pretty main square. There are tasty mezedhes (€3 to €5) and choices such as a vegetarian plate or a mixed plate of Cretan smoked pork, ham, cheese, salami, stuffed vine leaves, feta, potato, tomatoes and egg, which will keep two people more than happy. Also available are breakfasts, ice creams, home-made cakes and cocktails. The menu is more like a little book and features the work of famous artists as well as excerpts from a number of writers.

AROUND SERIFOS

About 1.5 kilometres north of Livadi along a surfaced road is **Psili Ammos Beach**. A path from Hora heads north for about 4km to the pretty village of **Kendarhos** (aka Kallitsos), from where you can continue by a very windy road for another 3km to the 17th-century fortified **Moni Taxiarhon**, which has impressive 18th-century frescoes. The walk from the town to the monastery takes about two hours. You will need to take food and water, as there are no facilities in Kendarhos.

KYTHNOS ΚΥΘΝΟΣ

pop 1700

Kythnos is not high on the must-see list of foreign holidaymakers, but is a favourite of mainland Greeks and something of a weekend destination for 'gin palace' motorcruises also. Yet this is a Greek island of rare character, in spite of its rather dull port, and it has an easygoing lifestyle. The capital, Hora, is an endearing place and the very traditional village of Dryopida is rewarding.

Getting There & Away

Kythnos has reasonable connections with daily ferries to and from Piraeus and several ferries a week to Lavrio. Onward connections to islands to the south are fairly regular in summer. For details see Island Hopping (p517).

Getting Around

There are regular buses in high summer from Merihas to Dryopida (€1.40), continuing to Kanala (€2.50) or Hora (€1.40). Less regular services run to Loutra (€2.50). The buses supposedly meet the ferries, but usually they leave from the turn-off to Hora in Merihas. During term-time the only buses tend to be school buses.

Taxis (☎ 22810 32883, 6944 271609) are a better bet, except at siesta time. Hora is €8 and Dryopida €6.

A **taxi-boat** (☎ 6944906568) runs to and from local beaches in summer.

MERIHAS ΜΕΡΙΧΑΣ
pop 289

Merihas (*meh-*ree-hass) does not have a lot going for it other than a bit of waterfront life and a slightly grubby beach. But it's a reasonable base and has most of the island's accommodation options. There are better beaches within walking distance north of the quay (turn left facing inland) at **Episkopi** and **Apokrousi**.

Information

There's an Emboriki bank (with ATM) on the road above the Merihas waterfront, and an ATM just past the flight of steps as you come from the ferry quay.

Larentzakis Travel Agency (☎ 22810 32104, 6944906568) Sells ferry tickets, arranges accommodation and hires cars starting at about €35 a day in August. Scooters start at €20. They also run a taxi boat to beaches (price depending on numbers). It's up the flight of steps near Ostria Taverna that leads to the main road.

Port police (☎ 22810 32290) On the waterfront.

Thermia Travel (☎ 22810 32345) Attached to a neat little wine and food store, this is the place for efficient ferry ticketing and other tourism services.

Sleeping & Eating

Domatia owners usually meet boats and there are a number of signs along the waterfront advertising rooms. A lot of places block-book during the high season and there is some reluctance towards one-night stopovers. You should definitely book ahead for July and August.

Panayiota Larentzaki Rooms (☎ 22810 32268; s/d/tr €45/50/60; ❄) Serviceable, if a touch weary, these

KYTHNOS

0 ——— 4 km
0 ——— 2 miles

To Syros (74km);
Tinos (81km);
Mykonos (98km)

Cape Kefalos

AEGEAN
SEA

To Kea (Tzia)
(39km);
Lavrio
(48km)

297m

Loutra ○ Thermal Baths

Kythnos

308m

Fikiado Beach ○ Apokrousi Beach

Episkopi Beach

To Piraeus
(96km)

Hora (Kythnos)

Merihas

Dryopida

Cape Tzoulis

Kataphyki Cave

302m

Flambouria Beach

To Kimolos (41km);
Serifos (52km);
Sifnos (63km);
Milos (85km);
Santorini (155km)

Kanala ○

Dimitrios Beach

Cape Berou

CYCLADES

rooms are a few metres up the road by the bridge. Cheerful Mrs P will probably find you first, as you wander uncertainly past her cafe.

Anna Gouma Rooms (☎ 22810 32105, 6949777884; s/d €50/60; ❄) These pleasant, good-sized rooms are right across the bay from the ferry quay, and are away from the hubbub.

Studios Maria Gonidi (☎ 22810 32324; s/d/tr €50/60/70; ❄) Over on the far side of the bay with lofty views, these are a top choice. Spacious, sparkling rooms have full self-catering facilities. During July and August there's little chance of securing short stays, however. Greek only spoken.

Café Vegera (☎ 22810 32636; snacks €4-6) Kythnos style jumps several scales at this cafe-bar that has a lovely waterside veranda. It beats Mykonos' Little Venice, and is without the hype and megahigh decibel count. Breakfast in the sun is €4 to €8.

Taverna to Kandouni (☎ 22810 32220; mains €6-14) On the southern bend of the waterfront, Kandouni is a popular family-run taverna specialising in grilled meat dishes.

Ostria (☎ 22810 32263; mains €6-15) Just along from the ferry quay, Ostria is the place for fish, with fish soup or a portion of anchovies as favourites. Seafood is generally by the kilo and they do meat dishes also.

AROUND KYTHNOS

The capital, **Hora** (also known as Kythnos or Messaria), is steadily taking on a distinctive charm, underpinned by its inherent Greek character. Small, colourful cafes and shops are growing in number. The long straggling main street, its surface decorated with painted motifs, makes for a pleasant stroll. The post office and the island's **police station** (☎ 22810 31201) are at the entrance to town coming from Merihas.

The resort of **Loutra** is 3km north of Hora on a windy bay and hangs on to its status through its surviving **thermal baths**.

From Hora there is a pleasant 5km-long walk south to **Dryopida**, a picturesque town of red-tiled roofs and winding streets clustered steeply on either side of a ravine. It is home to a remarkable cave called **Kataphyki** that extends for 600m. Much work has been carried out to make the cave accessible, but there was no access at the time of writing due to technical problems, although these may be resolved soon. You're best to cover the 5km back by road to Merihas by bus or taxi.

There are good beaches at **Flambouria** about 2.5km south of Merihas, and near **Kanala** on the southeast coast.

Sleeping & Eating

There are plenty of rooms and apartments in Loutra although they tend to be block-booked for stays of more than two days. In Dryopida some private houses let rooms in summer. Ask at shops and tavernas.

Filoxenia (☎ 22810 31644; www.filoxenia-kythnos.gr; d/tr/q €65/75/90; Ⓟ ❄) One of the best bets in Hora, these attractive studios are just at the entrance to the main village and overlook a garden. Rooms are immaculate and have good facilities and there's a charming welcome.

There are several decent tavernas in Hora including Koursaros, To Steki and Mezzeria.

KEA (TZIA) KEA (TZIA)

pop 2417

Kea is the most northerly island of the Cyclades and, being the island closest to Attica, attracts more mainland locals than foreign visitors. It

KEA (TZIA)

is an island that wears its many charms quietly. Between its bare hills, green valleys are filled with orchards, olive groves and almond and oak trees. The main settlements on the island are the port of Korissia, and the attractive capital, Ioulida, about 5km inland. There are several fine beaches and some excellent signposted footpaths. Local people use the name Tzia for their island.

Getting There & Away

The island's main connection to the mainland is through the port of Lavrio in southern Attica; there are no ferries from Piraeus to Kea. Connections onwards to other Cycladic islands are few. Boats are usually packed on Fridays and you should avoid the Sunday night ferry to Lavrio, unless you enjoy controlled rioting. If you plan a Sunday departure, make sure you get your ticket before Friday – and brace yourself for a bit of a mosh pit. For details see Island Hopping (p516).

Getting Around

In July and August there are, in theory, regular buses from Korissia to the villages of Vourkari, Otzias, Ioulida and Piosses although there may be irregularities in the schedules. A **taxi** (☎ 22880 21021/228) may be a better bet, to Ioulida (€6) especially. A taxi to Otzias is €5 and to Piosses, €20.

For motorcycle and car rental expect to pay, per day, €17 for a scooter and from €45 for a car. Try **Lion Cars** (☎ 22880 21898) located mid harbour front.

KORISSIA ΚΟΡΗΣΣΙΑ
pop 555
The port of Korissia (koh-ree-*see*-ah) is a fairly bland place, but there are enough tavernas and cafes to pass the time. The north-facing beach tends to catch the wind.

Information
There are ATMs on the waterfront and the Piraeus Bank, facing the beach, has an ATM. There is a small ferry ticket office next to the car-hire agency on the waterfront.

Internet Café (☎ 22880 22635; per hr €4; ☷ 10am-2.30pm & 5.30pm-midnight Mon-Fri, 10am-midnight Fri-Sun) Located just up an alleyway midway along the waterfront.

Tourist information office (☎ 22880 21500) The official tourist office, opposite the ferry quay, has lists of domatia in Greek, but not much more.

Sleeping & Eating
Domatia owners don't meet ferries. It's wise to book in high season and at weekends.

United Europe (☎ 22880 21362; uekeastudios@yahoo.gr; s/d/tr €40/60/70; ☷) Big, airy self-catering rooms make this quiet place an excellent option. All of the rooms are well kept and some have been refurbished in recent years. It's about 200m along the river road behind the beach.

Hotel Karthea (☎ 22880 21204; fax 22880 21417; s/d €65/85) Architectural blandness from a lost age defines the Karthea, but rooms are clean and comfortable and those at the rear overlook a quiet garden area. There's no lift to the several floors. In 1974, the deposed colonels of the Greek junta were said to have been imprisoned in the then newly opened hotel. You sleep with history…

Porto Kea Suites (☎ 22880 22870; www.portokea-suites.com; d €159, ste €197-338; ☷ ☷ ☷ ☷) Korissia's top option, these rooms and suites are luxurious and their decor features white-painted stone walls and bright, stylish fittings. They all have small kitchen areas and there's an outside pool, a cafe and a restaurant.

Red Tractor Farm (☎ 22880 21346; www.redtractorfarm.com; d €90, studios €120-150; ☷ ☷ ☷) Tucked away in the handsome hills of Kea alongside the owners' olive grove and vineyard is this lovely complex of buildings. The farm has received EU backing for its ecotourism achievements. Organic products are a feature and there are various seminars and activities.

Steki tou Strogili (☎ 22880 21025; 6976401015; mains €7-13) Popular with locals and in a pleasant setting above the main quay and next to the church, Strogili has a decent menu of traditional Greek favourites. Its selection of salads features a special version that includes chicken.

There are several tavernas along the waterfront, all dishing up fairly standard fare for about €5 to €11, with **Akri** (☎ 22880 21196) being one of the best.

Kea has more supermarkets than most islands. On Friday nights they get very busy as the weekender influx stocks up.

Drinking
There are traditional bars and cafes along the waterfront but for a more modern upbeat scene try Jamaica for mostly rock, or next door the bigger **Echo Club** (☎ 6947004625) goes for Greek sounds.

CYCLADES

A ROSE BY ANY OTHER NAME

Piosses (or Pisses as once enunciated) has grown self-conscious of its unfortunate English slang connotations and is struggling to rechristen itself as Piosses. The Greek is, technically, Pioses. The form Piosses is now used on signposts and even the camping site uses this form. We see no reason why we should not help them with their semantic makeover!

IOULIDA ΙΟΥΛΙΔΑ
pop 700

Ioulida (ee-oo-*lee*-tha) is Kea's gem and has a distinctly cosmo feel at weekends. It's a pretty scramble of narrow alleyways and rising lanes that lies along the rim of a natural amphitheatre among the hills. It was once a substantial settlement of ancient Greece, but few relics remain and even the **Venetian kastro** has been incorporated into private houses. The houses have red-tiled roofs like those of Dryopida on Kythnos.

The bus turnaround is on a square just at the edge of town. Other than taxis and delivery vehicles there is no parking here. Cars should park in the car park, which is located below the square. From the car park follow steps up to a T-junction and turn right for the bus turnaround, from where an archway leads into the village. Beyond the archway, turn right and uphill along the main street and into the more interesting heart of Ioulida proper. The post office is partway up on the right.

There's a bank in the turnaround square but with no ATM. There's an ATM in the square by the town hall, halfway up the main street of Ioulida.

Sights

Ioulida's **archaeological museum** (☎ 22880 22079; adult/child €3/2; ☼ 8.30am-3pm Tue-Sun) is just before the post office on the main thoroughfare. It houses some intriguing artefacts, including some superb terracotta figurines, mostly from Agia Irini (right).

The famed **Kea Lion**, chiselled from slate in the 6th century BC, lies on the hillside beyond the last of the houses. Head uphill from the museum and keep going until abreast of the Kea Lion across a shallow valley. The path

then curves round past a cemetery and the lion, with its Mona Lisa smile, is ahead and is reached through a gate and down some steps. Continuing beyond the lion, the path leads in a few minutes to a big drinking fountain behind a huge plane tree. From just beyond here, a splendid path branches left and leads to the road just above Otzias in just over 3km. It's then 3km, unfortunately by road, to Korissia.

Sleeping & Eating

There are a few domatia in Ioulida, and several decent tavernas. Ask about rooms at tavernas.

Recommended eateries with good Greek dishes from about €4.50 to €9 (with lamb and fresh fish costing more):

Estiatorio I Piatsa (☎ 22880 22195) Just inside the archway.

Kalofagadon (☎ 22880 22118) On the main square.

AROUND KEA

The beach road from Korissia leads past **Gialiskari Beach** for 2.5km to where the waterfront quay at tiny **Vourkari** is lined with yachts and cafes. The **Marina Keas Gallery** (☎ 22880 21458) is set back midwaterfront among the cafes and restaurants; it stages changing exhibitions of world-class art works over the summer.

Just across the bay from Vourkari are the truncated remains of the Minoan site of **Agia Irini**, which lie rather forlornly behind rusting wire fences. Excavations during the 20th century indicated that there had been a settlement here since 3200 BC and that it functioned for over 2000 years.

The road continues for another 3km to a fine sandy beach at **Otzias**. A surfaced road with rugged coastal views continues beyond here for another 5km to the 18th-century **Moni Panagias Kastrianis** (☎ 22880 24348).

Piosses is the island's best beach and is 8km southwest of Ioulida. A daily bus runs from and to Korissia in summer although hours are awkward. Piosses has a long and sandy beach that is backed by a verdant valley of orchards and olive groves, with rugged hills rising above. There's an extremely well-kept campsite here, **Piosses Camping** (☎ 22880 31302/4; fax 22880 31303; adult/child/tent €6/3/6; ☼ May-Sep) with a shop and cafe on site.

Crete Κρήτη

Crete is in many respects the culmination of the Greek experience. Its hospitable, spirited people maintain a proud sense of separateness, evident in everything from their haunting, violin-driven traditional music to their hearty, homegrown food and drink.

Everything about Crete is larger than life. Millions upon millions of olive trees produce some of the finest olive oil in Greece – and arguably, in the world – while the island is the mythical birthplace of Zeus himself, and site of the legendary Minoan civilisation; the much-visited Palace of Knossos is its most striking reminder. And, with their pretty pastel houses set on narrow stone lanes, the ancient Venetian ports of Hania and Rethymno are among Greece's most evocative towns. All in all, Crete bursts with the relics of millennia of culture, stretching from the prehistoric through Minoan, Byzantine, Venetian and Ottoman eras. Most visitors hang around the north-coast resorts, so it's easy to escape the crowds by heading for the south coast's numerous deserted beaches and inland rugged terrain trodden only by goats. Spectacular mountain ranges are dotted with thousands of caves and sliced by dramatic gorges that spill into the sea.

The northern coast features Crete's urban areas, and most of its package-tour resorts. Head south for off-the-beaten-track outdoors activities and pristine, peaceful beaches. The rugged interior, intermittently made up of mountains, agricultural plains and plateaus, hosts some of Crete's most authentic and down-to-earth villages, where you'll get a warm welcome from black-clad elders; such humble places often have the best (and cheapest) locally produced olive oil, honey, *raki* (Cretan firewater) and other superlative Cretan products.

HIGHLIGHTS

- **Time Out** Wandering the beautiful back lanes of Hania's Venetian Old Town (p245)
- **Minoan Magnificence** Visiting the grand, reconstructed Minoan palace at Knossos (p231)
- **Sylvan Idylls** Experiencing the haunted woodlands waterfalls and hermits' caves of offbeat Azogires village (p260)
- **Soldiering On** Taking the six-hour hike through Europe's longest gorge, Samaria (p253)
- **Back in Time** Exploring the ruined Venetian fortress of Spinalonga (p268), occupying its own islet in Crete's northeast
- **Beach Bliss** Swimming under a full moon at the south coast's remote Agios Pavlos and Triopetra beaches (p243)
- **Livin' Large** Kicking back amid the olive groves, beaches and big winds of lively Plakias (p241)

- POPULATION: 540,045
- AREA: 8335 SQ KM

CRETE

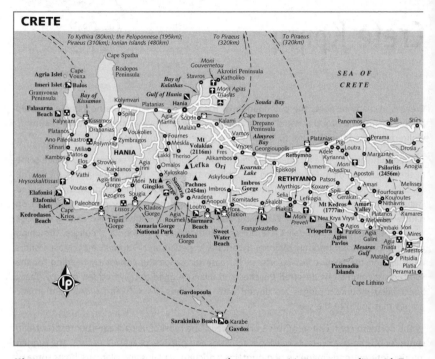

CRETE

History

Although it's been inhabited since Neolithic times (7000–3000 BC), Crete is most famous for its advanced Minoan civilisation. Traces of this still enigmatic society were only uncovered in the early 20th century, when British archaeologist Sir Arthur Evans discovered and then restored the palace at Knossos. Since no one knew what to call this lost race, Sir Arthur made an adjective of the mythical King Minos, the legendary former ruler of Knossos – and so emerged the name 'Minoans'.

Their actual name notwithstanding, we do know that the Minoans migrated to Crete in the 3rd millennium BC. These mysterious people were expert in metallurgy, making unprecedented artistic, engineering and cultural achievements during the Protopalatial period (3400–2100 BC); their most famous palaces (at Knossos, Phaestos, Malia and Zakros) were built then. Artistically, the frescoes discovered at Knossos have a naturalism lacking in contemporary Cycladic figurines, ancient Egyptian artwork and later Archaic sculpture. The Minoans also began producing their exquisite Kamares pottery and silverware, and became a maritime power, trading with Egypt and Asia Minor.

Around 1700 BC, however, an earthquake destroyed the great palace complexes. Undeterred, the Minoans built bigger and better ones over the ruins, while settling more widely across Crete. Around 1450 BC, when the Minoan civilisation was in the ascendant, the palaces were mysteriously destroyed again, probably by a giant tsunami triggered by the massive volcanic eruption on Santorini (Thira). Knossos, the only palace saved, was finally burned down around 1400 BC.

Archaeological evidence shows that the Minoans lingered on for a few centuries in small, isolated settlements before disappearing as mysteriously as they had come. They were followed by the Mycenaeans, and the Dorians (around 1100 BC). By the 5th century BC, at the acme of classical Greek civilisation, Crete was divided into city-states. However, the island did not benefit particularly from the cultural glories of mainland Greece, and was bypassed by Persian invaders and the Macedonian conqueror Alexander the Great.

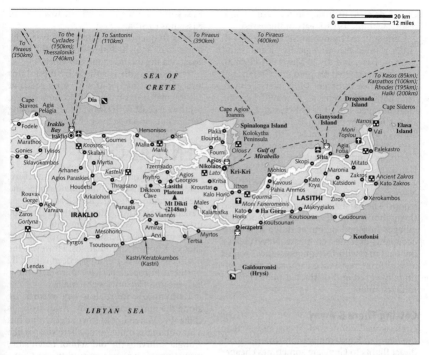

By 67 BC Crete had become the Roman province of Cyrenaica, with south-central Gortyna its capital; this province also included large chunks of North Africa. With the empire's division in AD 395 Crete, along with most of the Balkan Peninsula, fell under the jurisdiction of Greek-speaking Constantinople – the emerging Byzantine Empire. Things went more or less fine until AD 824, when Arabs appropriated the island, making it an emirate. Relatively little is known about this period.

In AD 961, however, the great Byzantine general and ill-fated emperor Nikiforas Fokas (AD 912–69) won the island back in the so-called 'expedition to Crete'. Fokas led approximately 300 ships and 50,000 men, taking the island following a nine-month siege of Iraklio (then called El Khandak by the Arabs). Crete flourished under Byzantine rule, but with the infamous Fourth Crusade of 1204 – when the Christian countries of the Latin West targeted Byzantium, instead of the Arabs – the maritime power of Venice received Crete as part of its 'payment' for supplying the Crusaders' fleet.

The Venetian period lasted until 1669, when Iraklio (then called Candia) became the last domino to fall after a 21-year Ottoman siege. Much of Crete's most impressive surviving architecture dates from this period, which also marked modern Crete's cultural peak (see the boxed text, p227). Turkish rule brought new administrative organisation, Islamic culture and Muslim settlers. Cretan resistance was strongest in the mountain strongholds, such as rugged Skafia in the southwest; here in 1770 the dashing Ioannis Daskalogiannis led the first notable rebellion. This and subsequent revolts were put down brutally, and it was only with the Ottoman Empire's disintegration in the late 19th century that Europe's great powers expedited Crete's sovereign aspirations.

Thus in 1898, with Russian and French consent, Crete became a British protectorate. However, the banner under which future Greek prime minister Eleftherios Venizelos and other Cretan rebels were fighting was *Enosis i Thanatos* (Unity or Death) – unity with Greece, not mere independence from Turkey. Yet it would take the Greek army's stunning successes in the Balkan Wars (1912–13) to turn

Crete's de facto inclusion in the country into reality, with the 1913 Treaty of Bucharest.

Crete suffered tremendously during WWII. Hitler wanted the strategically placed island as an air base, and on 20 May 1941 German parachutists started dropping in. Cretans put up resistance but were soon overwhelmed. The Battle of Crete, as it would become known, raged for 10 days between German and Allied troops from Britain, Australia, New Zealand and Greece. For two whole days the battle hung in the balance until the Germans captured Maleme airfield, near Hania. The Allied forces fought a valiant rearguard action, however, enabling the British Navy to evacuate 18,000 of the 32,000 Allied troops. The harsh German occupation lasted throughout WWII, with many mountain villages bombed or burnt down and their occupants executed en masse. Nevertheless, the Cretans (with foreign assistance) waged a significant resistance campaign that continually vexed and distracted their German military rulers.

Getting There & Away

Crete is well connected by air and boat to the mainland and, remarkably, international direct flights to Crete are sometimes cheaper than flying to the island from elsewhere in Greece – even from Greek carriers themselves. Aegean Airlines has direct scheduled flights from Iraklio to Milan, Rome and other European cities, while Olympic serves even more airports abroad.

If coming from a Western European country, it may be possible to score a cheap seat on a charter flight operating for package tourists without actually having to buy the rest of the package (accommodation, food, etc). However, you'll have to check with a travel agency in such a country to see if it's feasible.

European budget airlines are also starting to serve Crete in summer months. Iraklio, Sitia, Hania, Rethymno and Kissamos have ferry ports. The first three have airports also; Iraklio's being the largest. For more comprehensive information, see Island Hopping (p505).

Getting Around

A north-coast national highway runs from Kissamos in the west to Agios Nikolaos in the east, with an extension to Sitia planned.

Buses link the major northern towns from Kissamos to Sitia.

Less frequent buses operate between the north coast's towns and resorts and the south coast, via the inland mountain villages.

The wild south is spliced by mountains and gorges – many parts have no roads at all. Regular boats connect Paleohora on the southwest coast with Hora Sfakion, including settlements and beaches between them.

CENTRAL CRETE

Central Crete comprises the Iraklio prefecture, named after the island's burgeoning capital, and the Rethymno prefecture, named after its lovely Venetian port town. Along with its dynamic urban life and Venetian remnants, Iraklio's major attractions include the nearby Minoan sites of Knossos and Phaestos. However, the north coast east of Iraklio has been ruined by northern-European package tourism, particularly around Hersonisos and Malia.

Rethymno's more low-key resorts lie along the north coast nearby. Aside from its charming Venetian old town, Rethymno has a mountainous hinterland, where villages like Anogia cultivate the old-school machismo, moustaches and rugs of traditional Crete. The largely unspoilt southern coast boasts great beaches and the likeable, relaxed resort of Plakias.

IRAKLIO ΗΡΑΚΛΕΙΟ
pop 130,920

Iraklio (ee-*rah*-klee-oh), also called Heraklion, is Greece's fifth-largest city and the centre of Crete's economic and administrative life. It's a somewhat hectic place, full of the sounds of motorbikes throttling in unison at traffic lights while airplanes constantly thrust off into the sky in summer, over a long waterfront lined with the remnants of Venetian arsenals, fortresses and shrines.

Indeed, Iraklio does have some notable historic structures, though its traditional neighbourhoods suffered major bomb damage during WWII, robbing it of an architectural legacy comparable to that of Hania or Rethymno. Nevertheless, Iraklio is lively, with excellent eating, drinking and shopping. The best places lie off the interconnected pedestrianised stretches of the centre, where ongoing renovations continue to beautify things.

Iraklio hosts several worthwhile museums and, just south, the reconstructed Minoan palace at Knossos, one of Greece's most significant and most visited ancient sites. To the east of town, the Cretaquarium (p231) and an adjoining water park will keep kids happy. Further inland beyond Knossos, the Iraklio prefecture includes pretty traditional villages like Arhanes (p234). Full of olive trees and vineyards, this bucolic region is where Crete's best wines are produced.

History
Although Iraklio had always been populated, it didn't become the capital until AD 824, when Arabs arrived. Naming the city El Khandak (after its surrounding moat), the Arabs reputedly made it the Eastern Med's slave-trade capital. When the Byzantines recovered Crete in AD 961, they Hellenicised the name as 'Khandakos'. The Venetians added an Italian twist, calling the city Candia.

Venice used Crete, and its well-defended capital, to expand its maritime commercial empire. The fortifications it built were sufficiently strong to keep the Ottomans at bay for 21 years, even after the rest of Crete was lost; the Venetians finally surrendered Candia in 1669.

When Turkish control over Crete ended in 1898, Hania became the capital, and Candia was renamed Iraklio. However, because of its location, Iraklio became a hub of commerce and in 1971 once again became Crete's administrative centre.

Orientation
Iraklio is a work in progress, meaning some unfinished projects (like a lengthy pedestrian mall along the waterfront) may be completed soon. There are two main squares: Plateia Venizelou, also called Lion Sq after its famous landmark, Morosini Fountain, is most central, while the sprawling Plateia Eleftherias overlooks the harbour.

Many appealing sights are nestled around the pleasing, pedestrianised arc of Morosini Fountain down Handakos, and around Dedalou and Korai – the hub of Iraklio's lively cafe scene. The ferry port is 500m east of the old port. Iraklio's airport is 5km east of the centre.

From the bus station and port look towards the Hotel Megaron's parking lot; a concealed stone stairway here doubles back and up, accessing Epimenidou and the centre.

CRETE ONLINE

For information online, see www.interkriti .org, www.infocrete.com and www.explore crete.com.

Information
BOOKSHOPS
Planet International Bookshop (☎ 2810 289605; Handakos 73) Literature, history and travel books, including many recommended in this guide.

Road Editions (☎ 2810 344610; Handakos 29) Specialist travel bookshop with numerous maps, travel books and Lonely Planet guidebooks.

Vivliopoleion Filippos Athousakis (☎ 2810 229286; Epimenidou; ☺ 8.30am-2.30pm & 5-9pm) Opposite Lato Boutique Hotel; sells books on Crete, plus Lonely Planet and other travel guides.

EMERGENCY
Tourist police (☎ 2810 397111; Halikarnassos; ☺ 7am-10pm) No longer centrally located; now housed east with other police services in the new main station, (Astynomiko Megaron) in the Halikarnassos suburb, near the airport.

INTERNET ACCESS
In Spot Internet Cafe (☎ 2810 300225; Koraï 6; per hr €2.40, midnight-noon per hr €1.20; ☺ 24hr)

INTERNET RESOURCES
www.heraklion-city.gr Official municipal website with useful information, such as phone numbers, opening hours and coming events.

LAUNDRY
Sweaty Iraklio is full of laundromats. Most charge €6 for wash and dry, and offer dry cleaning.

Inter Laundry (☎ 2810 343660; Mirabelou 25; ☺ 9am-9pm)

Laundry Perfect (☎ 2810 220969; cnr Malikouti 32 & Idomeneos; ☺ 9am-9pm Mon-Sat)

Laundry Washsalon (☎ 2810 280858; Handakos 18) Also offers left-luggage storage (per day €3).

Wash Center Laundry (☎ 2810 242766; Epimenidou 38; per load €7; ☺ 8am-9pm)

LEFT LUGGAGE
Bus Station A Left Luggage Office (☎ 2810 246538; per day €2; ☺ 6.30am-8pm)

Iraklio Airport Luggage Service (☎ 2810 397349; per day €2.50-5; ☺ 24hr) Near the airport's local bus stop.

CRETE

IRAKLIO

0 _____ 200 m
0 _____ 0.1 miles

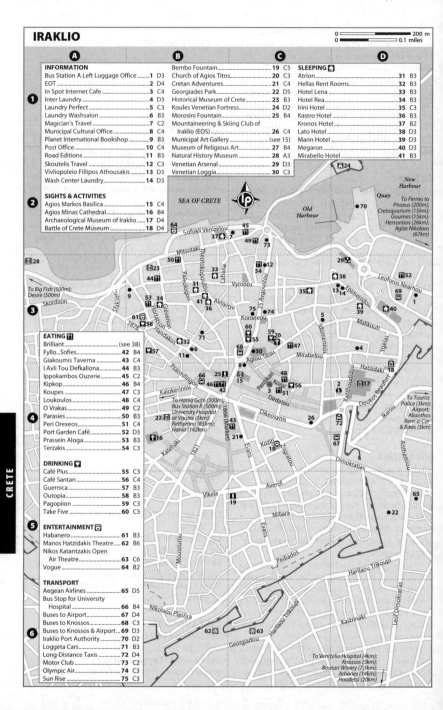

A

INFORMATION
Bus Station A Left Luggage Office	**1** D3
EOT	**2** D4
In Spot Internet Cafe	**3** C4
Inter Laundry	**4** D3
Laundry Perfect	**5** C3
Laundry Washsalon	**6** B3
Magician's Travel	**7** C2
Municipal Cultural Office	**8** C4
Planet International Bookshop	**9** B3
Post Office	**10** C4
Road Editions	**11** B3
Skoutelis Travel	**12** C3
Vivliopoleio Fillipos Athousakis	**13** D3
Wash Center Laundry	**14** D3

SIGHTS & ACTIVITIES
Agios Markos Basilica	**15** C4
Agios Minas Cathedral	**16** B4
Archaeological Museum of Iraklio	**17** D4
Battle of Crete Museum	**18** D4

B

Bembo Fountain	**19** C5
Church of Agios Titos	**20** C3
Cretan Adventures	**21** C4
Georgiades Park	**22** D5
Historical Museum of Crete	**23** B3
Koules Venetian Fortress	**24** D2
Morosini Fountain	**25** B4
Mountaineering & Skiing Club of Iraklio (EOS)	**26** C4
Municipal Art Gallery	(see 15)
Museum of Religious Art	**27** B4
Natural History Museum	**28** A3
Venetian Arsenal	**29** D3
Venetian Loggia	**30** C3

C

SLEEPING
Atrion	**31** B3
Hellas Rent Rooms	**32** B3
Hotel Lena	**33** B3
Hotel Rea	**34** B3
Irini Hotel	**35** C3
Kastro Hotel	**36** B3
Kronos Hotel	**37** B2
Lato Hotel	**38** D3
Marin Hotel	**39** D3
Megaron	**40** D3
Mirabello Hotel	**41** B3

D

EATING
Brilliant	(see 38)
Fyllo...Sofies	**42** B4
Giakoumis Taverna	**43** C4
I Avli Tou Defkaliona	**44** B3
Ippokambos Ouzerie	**45** C2
Kipkop	**46** B4
Koupes	**47** C3
Loukoulos	**48** C4
O Vrakas	**49** C2
Parasies	**50** B3
Peri Orexeos	**51** C4
Port Garden Café	**52** D3
Prassein Aloga	**53** B3
Terzakis	**54** C3

DRINKING
Café Plus	**55** C3
Café Santan	**56** C4
Guernica	**57** B3
Outopia	**58** B3
Pagopiion	**59** C3
Take Five	**60** C3

ENTERTAINMENT
Habanero	**61** B3
Manos Hatzidakis Theatre	**62** B6
Nikos Katantzakis Open Air Theatre	**63** C6
Vogue	**64** B2

TRANSPORT
Aegean Airlines	**65** D5
Bus Stop for University Hospital	**66** B4
Buses to Airport	**67** D4
Buses to Knossos	**68** C3
Buses to Knossos & Airport	**69** D3
Iraklio Port Authority	**70** D2
Loggeta Cars	**71** B3
Long-Distance Taxis	**72** D4
Motor Club	**73** C2
Olympic Air	**74** C3
Sun Rise	**75** C3

SEA OF CRETE

New Harbour

Old Harbour

To Ferries to Piraeus (200m);
Cretaquarium (15km);
Gournes (15km);
Hersonisos (26km);
Agios Nikolaos (67km)

To Big Fish (500m);
Desire (500m)

To Hania Gate (300m);
Bus Station B (500m);
University Hospital
at Voutes (5km);
Rethymno (85km);
Hania (142km)

To Tourist
Police (3km);
Airport;
Alianthos
Rent-a-Car
& Bikes (5km)

To Venizelio Hospital (4km);
Knossos (5km);
Boutari Winery (7.5km);
Arhanes (14km);
Houdetsi (20km)

CRETE

MEDICAL SERVICES

Iraklio's two hospitals are far from the centre and work alternate days – call first to find out where to go.

Venizelio Hospital (☎ 2810 368000) On the road to Knossos, 4km south of Iraklio.

University Hospital (☎ 2810 392111) At Voutes, 5km south of Iraklio (bus 11, ticket price €1.50), this is the best-equipped medical facility.

MONEY

Banks and ATMs line 25 Avgoustou, and are widespread throughout the centre.

POST

Post office (☎ 2810 234468; Plateia Daskalogianni; ☺ 7.30am-8pm Mon-Fri, 7.30am-2pm Sat)

TOURIST INFORMATION

EOT (Greek National Tourist Organisation; ☎ 2810 246299; Xanthoudidou 1; ☺ 8.30am-8.30pm Apr-Oct, 8.30am-3pm Nov-Mar) Opposite the archaeological museum.

TRAVEL AGENCIES

Magician's Travel (☎ 2810 301471; operation@ driveongreece.gr; Mitsotaki 1B) This helpful, patient travel agency near the waterfront can arrange and inform about all ferry and plane tickets.

Skoutelis Travel (☎ 2810 280808; www.skoutelis travel.gr; 25 Avgoustou 24) Airline and ferry bookings, excursions, accommodation help and car hire can all be arranged here.

Sights

ARCHAEOLOGICAL MUSEUM OF IRAKLIO

The outstanding Minoan collection makes Iraklio's **archaeological museum** (☎ 2810 279000; Xanthoudidou 2; admission €4, incl Knossos €10; ☺ 8am-8pm Tue-Sun, 8am-1pm Mon Apr-Oct, 8am-3pm Tue-Sun, noon-3pm Mon late Oct-early Apr) second only to Athens' National Archaeological Museum. A €21-million restoration was unfinished at the time of writing (temporary entrance on Hatzidakis), meaning that a temporary exhibition of 400 (out of 15,000 total) artefacts is now exhibited, covering Neolithic until Roman times. Fear not, however – the collection's most valuable Minoan masterpieces are all displayed.

This treasure trove includes pottery, jewellery, figurines and sarcophagi, plus some famous frescoes. The most exciting Minoan finds come from the sites of Knossos, Phaestos, Malia, Zakros and Agia Triada.

The superlative Knossos frescoes include the **Procession fresco**, the **Griffin Fresco** (from the Throne Room), the **Dolphin Fresco** (from the Queen's Room) and the amazing **Bull-leaping Fresco**, which depicts a seemingly double-jointed acrobat somersaulting on the back of a charging bull.

Other frescoes include the lovely, restored **Prince of the Lilies**, along with two frescoes for the New Palace period – the priestess archaeologists have dubbed **La Parisienne**, and the **Saffron Gatherer**.

Also from Knossos are **Linear A and B tablets** (the latter have been translated as household or business accounts), an ivory statue of a **bull leaper**, and some exquisite **gold seals**.

From the Middle Minoan period, the most striking piece is the 20cm black-stone **Bull's Head**, a libation vessel. The bull's fine head of curls sprouts golden horns, and features extremely lifelike painted crystal eyes. Other fascinating contemporaneous exhibits include the tiny, glazed colour reliefs of Minoan houses from Knossos, called the **town mosaic**. Finds from a Knossos shrine include fine figurines of a bare-breasted **snake goddess**.

Among the treasures of Minoan jewellery is the beautiful **gold bee pendant** from Malia, depicting two bees dropping honey into a comb.

From Phaestos, the most prized find is the fascinating **Phaestos Disk**, a 16cm circular clay tablet inscribed with (still undeciphered) pictographic symbols.

Also displayed is the elaborate **Kamares pottery**, named after the sacred cave of Kamares where it was discovered; a superbly decorated vase from Phaestos with white sculpted flowers is here, too.

Finds from Zakros include the gorgeous **crystal rhyton** vase, discovered in over 300 fragments and painstakingly repaired, along with vessels decorated with floral and marine designs.

The most famous of Minoan sarcophagi, and one of Minoan art's greatest achievements, is the **sarcophagus of Agia Triada**, painted with floral and abstract designs and ritual scenes. Other significant Agia Triada finds include the **Harvester Vase**, of which only the top part remains, depicting young farm workers returning from olive picking. Another, the **Boxer Vase** shows Minoans indulging in two of their favourite pastimes – wrestling and bull-grappling. The **Chieftain Cup** depicts a more cryptic scene: a chief holding a staff and three men carrying animal skins.

CRETE

Finds from Minoan cemeteries include two small clay models of groups of figures, found in a *tholos* (tomb shaped like a beehive). One depicts four male dancers in a circle, arms around one another's shoulders, possibly participants in a funerary ritual. The other shows two groups of three figures in a room flanked by two columns, with two large seated figures being offered libations by a smaller figure. Whether the large figures represent gods or departed mortals is unclear.

More insight into the inscrutable lifestyle of the Minoans can be gleaned from another exhibit, the elaborate **gaming board** decorated with ivory, crystal, glass, gold and silver, from Knossos' New Palace period.

HISTORICAL MUSEUM OF CRETE

The engrossing **Historical Museum** (☎ 2810 283219; www.historical-museum.gr; Sofokli Venizelou; admission €5; ☺ 9am-5pm Mon-Sat summer, 9am-3pm Mon-Sat winter) contains exhibits from Crete's Byzantine, Venetian and Turkish periods, displaying plans, charts, photographs, ceramics and maps. The 1st floor houses the only El Greco paintings in Crete – *View of Mt Sinai and the Monastery of St Catherine* (1570) and the tiny *Baptism of Christ*. Other rooms contain 13th- and 14th-century fresco fragments, coins, jewellery, liturgical ornaments and vestments, plus medieval pottery.

Highlights upstairs include the reconstructed **library of author Nikos Kazantzakis**, a **Battle of Crete** section and an outstanding **folklore collection**.

NATURAL HISTORY MUSEUM

Established by the University of Crete, the child-friendly **Natural History Museum** (☎ 2810 282740; www.nhmc.uoc.gr; Leoforos Venizelou; admission €3, adult accompanying child free; ☺ 10am-7pm Tue-Sun), in a restored former electricity building on the waterfront, has interactive appeal with a discovery centre for kids, complete with labs and excavation projects. Apart from the broader evolution of humankind, it explores the flora and fauna of Crete, the island's ecosystem and habitats, and its caves, coastline and mountains, plus Minoan life.

OTHER ATTRACTIONS

Iraklio burst out of its **city walls** long ago, but these massive fortifications, with seven bastions and four gates, still dwarf the concrete 20th-century structures around them.

Venetians built the defences between 1462 and 1562. You can follow them around the heart of the city for views of Iraklio's neighbourhoods, though it's not a particularly scenic trip.

The 16th-century **Koules Venetian fortress** (Iraklio Harbour; admission €2; ☺ 9am-6pm Tue-Sun), at the end of the Old Harbour's jetty, was called Rocca al Mare under the Venetians. It stopped the Turks for 22 years and then became a Turkish prison for Cretan rebels. The impressive exterior features reliefs of the Lion of St Mark. The interior has 26 overly restored rooms and good views from the top. The ground-level rooms are used as art galleries, while music and theatrical events are held in the upper level.

The long, vaulted arcades of the **Venetian Arsenal** are opposite the fortress.

Several other notable Venetian structures survive. Most famous is the **Morosini Fountain** (Lion Fountain) on Plateia Venizelou, which spurts water from four lions' jaws into eight ornate marble troughs. Built in 1629, the fountain was commissioned by Francesco Morosini, then governor of Crete. Its centrepiece marble statue of Poseidon with his trident was destroyed during the Turkish occupation. Opposite is the three-aisled, 13th-century **Agios Markos Basilica**. Frequently reconstructed, it's now the **Municipal Art Gallery** (☎ 2810 399228; 25 Avgoustou; admission free; ☺ 9am-1.30pm & 6-9pm Mon-Fri, 9am-1pm Sat). A little north is the attractively reconstructed 17th-century **Venetian Loggia**. A Venetian version of a gentleman's club where aristocrats came to drink and gossip, it's now the Town Hall.

The delightful **Bembo Fountain**, at the southern end of 1866, was built by the Venetians in the 16th century. The ornate hexagonal edifice adjacent was a pump house added by the Turks, and is now a *kafeneio* (coffee house).

The **Museum of Religious Art** (☎ 2810 288825; Monis Odigitrias; admission €2; ☺ 9.30am-7.30pm Mon-Sat Apr-Oct, 9.30am-3.30pm Nov-Mar) is in the former Church of Agia Ekaterini beside **Agios Minas Cathedral**. Its impressive collection of icons, frescoes and elaborate ecclesiastical vestments include six icons by Mihail Damaskinos, mentor of El Greco.

The **Church of Agios Titos** (Agiou Titou) was constructed after the Byzantine reconquest of Crete in AD 961, was converted to a Catholic church by Venetians, and then became an Ottoman mosque. It has been rebuilt twice

RENAISSANCE MEN OF VENETIAN CRETE

While many people have heard of a certain Cretan painter nicknamed El Greco, most visitors would be surprised to learn just how significant Cretan scholars and humanists were to the Italian Renaissance, and to early modern thought in general.

When the Turks conquered Constantinople in 1453, many Byzantine scholars took refuge in Venetian-held Crete, bringing with them priceless manuscripts and knowledge. The island became a way-station for intellectuals and ideas – at precisely the moment when a hunger for learning ancient Greek and Latin texts in the original was growing in Italy and other Western European countries. Indeed, wealthy Italian noblemen such as that great Florentine, Cosimo de' Medici, were funding whole Platonic 'academies', where aspiring scholars sat enraptured at the feet of learned Greek émigrés.

Further, the simultaneous invention of the printing press meant that ancient texts suddenly could be made widely available. And a Cretan typesetter and calligrapher, **Markos Mousouros** (1470–1517), designed the typeface in which Europeans would read many of the first printed Ancient Greek texts. His employer, Aldus Manutius, a Venetian publisher who revolutionised and popularised the study of Ancient Greek philosophy and literature, used the typeface based on Mousouros' own handwriting to print his editions of the Greek classics.

According to Dr George Karamanolis, professor of ancient philosophy at Crete's University of Rethymno, 'Cretan scholars and humanists played a considerable role in transmitting Greek texts and learning to Renaissance Italy'. The unique mixed culture on the Venetian-administered island, he says, meant that, 'cultural activity and scholarly life in Crete was quite similar to intellectual currents in Western Europe. Whole academies flourished, like the Accademia degli Stravaganti in Candia, while fiery contests of rhetorical oratory took place.'

One significant reason for the high level of Crete's intellectual life was the excellent education provided by the Catholic Venetians. Promising Cretan students were educated under church supervision, and this aided their travels. Dr Karamanolis, a noted expert on the subject, cites some of these prominent Cretans. **Maximos Margounios** (1549–1602), for example, was educated in Sitia by the learned Catholic bishop there, Gaspare Viviano. He later studied in Padua and finally lived in Venice, where he wrote on philosophy, rhetoric and theology, translating ancient and Byzantine texts. Margounios, who would have close collaboration with leading humanists in Italy, Germany and even England, was commended in a contemporaneous Venetian document as being 'very expert in Greek and Latin, with few equals in all Greece in erudition.'

According to Dr Karamanolis, Margounios 'retained close ties with humanist circles in his native Crete, and played an important role in assisting the projects of several European thinkers. Margounios' humanist peers considered his commentaries on philosophical texts by Aristotle and Porphyry very valuable.'

Another Cretan, **Frangiskos Portos** (1511–81), was a distinguished professor in the University of Geneva, 'appointed by Calvin himself'. The most beloved Cretan Renaissance man of all, however, was a poet. Over the four centuries of Venetian rule there was a unique and mutually influential fusion of Greek and Italian literature in Crete, at the same time as similar literary innovations elsewhere in Europe.

Vitsentzos Kornaros (1553–1617), a contemporary of Shakespeare, is today considered the father of Cretan poetry and one of Greece's greatest poets. Born into a Venetian-Cretan aristocratic family near Sitia, Kornaros penned Crete's national epic poem – the 'Erotokritos', a ballad dealing with traditional themes such as love, courage, bravery and friendship. A massive work, at 10,012 rhyming verses, the 'Erotokritos' was composed in the Cretan dialect, and in the traditional Byzantine dekapentasyllabic (15-syllable) verse style. It was meant to be sung as a *mantinadha* – Crete's traditional song style both then and now. Until quite recently, one could encounter elderly village women reciting the entire poem by heart while doing their work.

Today, Crete's Renaissance men are still obscure to all but specialists (and some proud Cretans). Yet their contributions, says Dr Karamanolis, enriched and expedited the progression of Western European thought tremendously. 'Without these Cretan humanists,' he attests, 'the Renaissance as we know it could not have unfolded as it did – we do owe them a debt of gratitude.'

CRETE

after being destroyed by fire and then an earthquake.

The **Battle of Crete Museum** (☎ 2810 346554; cnr Doukos Beaufort & Hatzidaki; admission free; ⏲ 8am-3pm) chronicles this historic battle.

Activities

Cretan Adventures (☎ 2810 332772; www.cretanadventures.gr; 1st fl, Evans 10) is a well-regarded company run by two intrepid brothers, who organise hiking and trekking tours, mountain biking, plus specialist and extreme activities.

The **Mountaineering & Skiing Club of Iraklio** (EOS; ☎ 2810 227609; www.interkriti.org/orivatikos/orivat.html; Dikeosynis 53; ⏲ 8.30pm-10.30pm) arranges weekend mountain climbing, cross-country walking and skiing excursions around Crete.

Iraklio for Children

Iraklio is surprisingly entertaining for kids. Aside from the lions spitting water, big buildings and motorcycles, there's the stuffed animals and interactive displays of the **Natural History Museum** (p226), plus the massive **Cretaquarium** (p231).

When the kids get museumed out, the waterfront **Port Garden Café** (☎ 2810 242411; Paraliaki Leoforo; ☎ 7am-late) opposite the Megaron Hotel has indoor and shady outdoor play areas, including jumping castles and swings. Kids can also run around in **Georgiades Park**, which has a shady cafe.

CRETE

Festivals & Events

Iraklio's Summer Arts Festival happens at the **Nikos Kazantzakis Open Air Theatre** (☎ 2810 242977; Jesus Bastion; ⏲ box office 9am-2.30pm & 6.30-9.30pm), near the moat of the Venetian walls, the nearby Manos Hatzidakis theatre and at the Koules fortress (p226). Check www.heraklion-city.gr for the program or consult the **Municipal Cultural Office** (☎ 2810 399211; Androgeiou 2; ⏲ 8am-4pm) behind the Youth Centre cafe.

Sleeping

While the majority of Iraklio's larger and more established hotels operate year-round, most of the smaller, budget places close in the low season.

BUDGET

Hellas Rent Rooms (☎ 2810 288851; Handakos 24; dm/d/tr without bathroom €12/30/42; ⏲ Apr-Nov; 🛜) Iraklio's de facto youth hostel is a relaxed place with a reception area and rooftop bar three flights up. The rooms are somewhat stuffy, but have fans, wash basin and balconies. The shared bathrooms are basic but clean. Breakfast (€3) is available on the upstairs bar terrace.

Mirabello Hotel (☎ 2810 285052; www.mirabello-hotel.gr; Theotokopoulou 20; s/d without bathroom €35/45, d with bathroom €65; ❄) On a quiet and central side street, the relaxed Mirabello has spotless though somewhat cramped rooms, with TV, phone, balconies and upgraded bathrooms. Some share single-sex bathrooms.

Hotel Rea (☎ 2810 223638; www.hotelrea.gr; Kalimeraki 1; d with/without bathroom €40/30; ⏲ Apr-Oct; 🛜) Popular with backpackers and even families, this friendly, family-run budget place, in a lane parallel with pedestrianised Handakos, offers simple rooms with fans and sinks; some have private bathrooms, while others are shared. There's a small, basic communal kitchen. Family rooms go for €60.

Hotel Lena (☎ 2810 223280; www.lena-hotel.gr; Lahana 10; s/d with bathroom €45/60, without bathroom €35/50; ⏲ year-round; ❄) On a quiet street, friendly Hotel Lena has 16 comfortable, airy rooms with phone, TV, fans and double-glazed windows. Most have private bathrooms but even shared bathrooms are pleasant and upgraded.

Kronos Hotel (☎ 2810 282240; www.kronoshotel.gr; Sofokli Venizelou 2; s/d €50/60; ❄ 💻) This well-maintained older waterfront hotel has comfortable rooms with double-glazed windows and balconies, phone and TV. Most are fridge-equipped; some have sea views.

MIDRANGE

Kastro Hotel (☎ 2810 284185; www.kastro-hotel.gr; Theotokopoulou 22; s incl breakfast from €50, d & tr incl breakfast €75-90; ❄ 💻) A refurbished, cheery B-class hotel in the back streets, the Kastro offers large rooms with fridge, TV, hairdryer and ISDN internet.

Irini Hotel (☎ 2810 229703; www.irini-hotel.com; Idomeneos 4; s/d incl breakfast €70/100; ❄) Close to the old harbour, this midsized (59-room) hotel has all mod cons in its airy rooms, with flowering balconies. Pay less by skipping breakfast.

Marin Hotel (☎ 2810 300018; www.marinhotel.gr; Doukos Beaufort 12; s incl breakfast €75, d incl breakfast €95-125; ❄ 💻) This refurbished hotel has front-facing rooms with great views of the harbour and fortress, some with big balconies. Rooms are attractive and well-appointed.

Atrion (☎ 2810 246000; www.atrion.gr; Hronaki 9; s/d incl breakfast €95/110; ❄ 💻) One of Iraklio's better hotels, the renovated Atrion has rooms tastefully deorated in neutral tones, the upper ones enjoying sea views and small balconies.

TOP END

Lato Hotel (☎ 2810 228103; www.lato.gr; Epimenidou 15; s/d €100/127, ste from €175; ✗ 🖙) The full boutique experience awaits at the well-designed Lato, marked by its superior service. Overlooking the fortress, and a short walk from the bus and port, it's one of Iraklio's best hotels. The rooms' chic contemporary design is complemented by spectacular views, especially in the spacious suites; ascend to the atmospheric rooftop restaurant and bar for panoramic views. The Lato also boasts a spa centre, a beauty salon, and a fine-dining restaurant, Brilliant (right), downstairs.

Megaron (☎ 2810 305300; www.gdmmegaron.gr; Doukos Beaufort 9; s/d €190/215, ste from €247; 🅿 ✗ 🖙 🏊) Iraklio's priciest place, this formerly derelict historic building, now transformed into a luxury hotel, has comfortable beds, Jacuzzis in the VIP suites and plasma-screen TVs. The rooftop restaurant and bar have fine harbour views, along with a unique glass-sided pool.

Eating

Many restaurants close on Sundays.

BUDGET

Giakoumis Taverna (☎ 2810 280277; Theodosaki 5-8; mayirefta €4-8; 🕑 closed Sun) One of the best of the tavernas clustered around the 1866 market side streets, Giakoumis is always busy, and serves both vegetarian fare and meats hot off the grill. Cretan specialities dominate.

Ippokambos Ouzerie (☎ 2810 280240; Sofokli Venizelou 3; seafood mezedhes €5-9) At the edge of the tourist-driven waterfront dining strip, this is another local favourite with house specialities and fresh fish (try the baked cuttlefish).

O Vrakas (☎ 6977893973; Plateia 18 Anglon; seafood mezedhes €5-12) This small street-side *ouzerie* (place that serves ouzo and light snacks) grills fresh fish alfresco before you. It's a humble place, but very popular with locals.

Fyllo...Sofies (☎ 2810 284774; Plateia Venizelou 33; bougatsa €2.50; 🕑 5am-late; 🖙) and the adjacent **Kipkop** (☎ 2810 242705; Plateia Venizelou 29) have always-packed tables sprawled out on the square, overlooking Morosini Fountain – the best spot for a breakfast *bougatsa* (creamy

semolina pudding wrapped in a pastry envelope and baked). There's even wi-fi.

MIDRANGE

Koupes (☎ 6977259038; Agiou Titou 22; mezedhes €3-6.50) This student-frequented place serving powerful Cretan *raki* with appetisers (a *rakadhiko*) opposite the school does great mezedhes (appetisers).

Terzakis (☎ 2810 221444; Marineli 17; mezedhes €5-10) On a small square opposite Agios Dimitrios church, this excellent *ouzerie* has numerous mezedhes, *mayirefta* (ready-cooked meals) and grills. Try the sea-urchin salad or, if feeling really adventurous, ask if the kitchen has 'unmentionables': *ameletita* (fried sheep testicles).

I Avli tou Defkaliona (☎ 2810 244215; Prevelaki 10; meat dishes €6-10; 🕑 dinner) This traditional taverna has simple decor, but is good for grills.

Parasies (☎ 2810 225009; Plateia Istorikou Mouseiou; grills €6.50-10) In the corner of the square next to the Historical Museum, this is a good lunch spot, with tasty grills.

Peri Orexeos (☎ 2810 222679; Koraï 10; mains €7-10) On the busy Koraï pedestrian strip, try excellent contemporary Greek food here, with creative takes like creamy chicken wrapped in *kataïfi* (angel-hair pastry), huge salads and solid Cretan cuisine.

TOP END

Brilliant (☎ 28103 34959; Lato Boutique Hotel, Epimenidou 15; mains €11-20) This upscale restaurant, part of the Lato Boutique Hotel, does fine Greek and international specialities, and has attentive and courteous service.

Prassein Aloga (☎ 2810 283429; Kydonias 21, cnr Handakos; mains €12-20) 'Mediterranean fusion' cuisine is served at this unassuming but inventive rustic-style cafe-restaurant. The menu constantly changes, and features unique dishes based on ancient Greek cuisine, like pork medallions with dried fruit on wild rice.

Loukoulos (☎ 2810 224435; Korai 5; mains €15-32) Loukoulos is as much about ambience as it is about food, served on fine china and accompanied by soft classical music. It does modern Greek and other Mediterranean dishes, but for the price they are not sufficiently special.

Drinking

our pick **Guernica** (☎ 2810 282988; Apokoronou Kritis 2; 🕑 10am-late) The cool combination of traditional decor and eclectic contemporary music makes this Iraklio's hippest bar-cafe. The bar space wraps around a leafy terrace garden with tables. It's popular as a beer bar with students, and gets lively after midnight.

Pagopiion (☎ 2810 346028; www.icefacktory.gr; Plateia Agiou Titou; ◷ 10am-late) Once an ice factory, this popular cafe-bar-restaurant is marked by eccentric decorations and lighting that create a sort of Christmas-forest ambience.

Café Plus (Plateia Agiou Titou; ◷ 9am-2am) This big outdoor cafe at the nexus of Iraklio's pedestrianised zones is a relaxing place for a coffee or drink at night.

Outopia (Handakos; ◷ 9am-2am) This cafe on pedestrianised Handakos is a known emporium of chocolates (and other sweets) with impressively long lists of both beers and teas.

Also recommended are the lively **Take Five** (☎ 2810 226564; Akroleondos 7; ◷ 10am-late), a classic bar on a pedestrian street by El Greco Park, and **Café Santan** (☎ 6976 285869; Korai 13), which aspires to be 'oriental', with hookahs, sofas and belly dancing from 11pm.

Entertainment

Iraklio has big dance clubs along Leoforos Ikarou, just down from Plateia Eleftherias and along Epimendou, though many close in summer. However, the revitalised waterfront west of the port houses some popular nightclubs, like Big Fish and Desire.

Vogue (☎ 6944577201; ◷ 10pm-6am) A bit more central, this is another waterfront place in an old building popular with Greeks; if you're foreign and look or act like you've stumbled out of a tacky package tour resort, you won't be let in.

Habanero (Handakos; ◷ 10pm-4am) This slick Latin music bar is fleshed out by lithe young Greek couples who actually know how to dance to this stuff.

Big Fish (☎ 2810 288011; cnr Makariou 17 & Venizelou; ◷ 10am-late) is housed in a restored old stone building. Desire is next door.

Getting There & Away

AIR

Iraklio's Nikos Kazantzakis Airport is Crete's biggest and gets many regular domestic, international and summertime charter flights. For details, see Island Hopping (p511).

Some operators:

Aegean Airlines (☎ 2810 344324; www.aegeanair.com)

Olympic Air (☎ 2810 244824; www.olympicairlines .com)

Sky Express (☎ 2810 223500; www.skyexpress.gr)

BOAT

For information on Iraklio's numerous ferry connections, see Island Hopping (p512). The portside **Iraklio Port Authority** (☎ 2810 244912) keeps ferry schedule information.

Ferry operators:

ANEK Lines Iraklio (☎ 2810 244912; www.anek.gr)

GA Ferries Iraklio (☎ 2810 222408; www.gaferries.gr)

LANE Lines (☎ 2810 346440; www.lane.gr)

Minoan Lines (☎ 2810 229624; www.minoan.gr)

BUS

Iraklio's main transport hub, **Bus Station A** (☎ 2810 246534; www.ktel-heraklio-lassithi.gr; Leoforos Nearhou), serves eastern and western Crete (including Knossos) from its waterfront location near the quay. **Bus Station B** (☎ 2810 255965), west of the city centre beyond Hania Gate, serves Phaestos, Agia Galini and Matala. See the boxed text, opposite, for more information. Most intercity (IC) services are reduced on weekends.

Airport bus 1 operates every 15 minutes between 6.30am and midnight (€0.90) and stops at Plateia Eleftherias.

Getting Around

Bus 1 serves the airport every 15 minutes between 6am and 1am. The bus terminal is near the Astoria Capsis Hotel on Plateia Eleftherias. An airport taxi costs €10 to €12; try **Ikarus Radio Taxi** (☎ 2810 211212).

Long-Distance Taxis (☎ 2810 210102) from Plateia Eleftherias, outside the Astoria Capsis Hotel and Bus Station B, are expensive but quick.

IRAKLIO'S WINE COUNTRY

Just south of Iraklio and Knossos, the fertile Peza region produces 70% of Cretan wines. The **Pezas Union of local producers** (☎ 2810 741945; www.pezaunion .gr; admission free; ◷ 9am-4pm Mon-Sat) has tastings, videos and a minimuseum. The state-of-the-art hilltop **Boutari Winery** (☎ 2810 731617; www.boutari.gr; Skalani; tour & tasting €4.50; ◷ 10am-6pm), about 8km from Iraklio, features a stunning tasting room and showroom overlooking the vineyard of the Fantaxometoho estate – and great wines.

IRAKLIO BUS SERVICES

From Bus Station A

Destination	Duration	Fare	Frequency
Agia Pelagia	45min	€3.20	3 daily
Agios Nikolaos	1½hr	€6.50	half-hourly
Arhanes	30min	€1.70	hourly
Hania	3hr	€10.50	18 daily
Hersonisos/Malia	45 min	€3.70	half-hourly
Ierapetra	2½hr	€10	8 daily
Knossos	20min	€1.30	3 hourly
Lasithi Plateau	2 hr	€4.70	1 daily
Milatos	1½hr	€4.70	2 daily
Rethymno	1¾hr	€6.30	18 daily
Sitia	3½hr	€13.10	5 daily

From Bus Station B

Destination	Duration	Fare	Frequency
Agia Galini	2 hr	€7.40	6 daily
Anogia	1 hr	€3.60	4 daily
Matala	2½ hr	€7.20	5 daily
Phaestos	1½ hr	€5.90	8 daily

Sample fares: Agios Nikolaos €60; Rethymno €70; Hania €100 to €120.

The airport has numerous car-hire companies, including **Alianthos Rent-a-Car & Bikes** (☎ 2810 390481, 6945449771; www.alianthos-group.com). Although not the cheapest, this island-wide agency commands a staggering 2500 cars and has flexible service and variety. Its other locations include Rethymno, Hania, Plakias and Agia Galini.

Some smaller local outlets:

Loggetta Cars (☎ 2810 289462; www.loggetta.gr; 25 Avgoustou 20)

Motor Club (☎ 2810 222408; www.motorclub.gr; Plateia 18 Anglon) Opposite the fortress; for motorcycles.

Sun Rise (☎ 2810 221609; 25 Avgoustou 46) Just off the pedestrian street.

CRETAQUARIUM

The massive **Cretaquarium** (☎ 2810 337788; www .cretaquarium.gr; adult/child over 4yr/under 4yr €8/6/free; ☺ 9am-9pm May–mid-Oct, 10am-5.30pm mid-Oct–Apr) at Gournes, 15km east of Iraklio, is the Eastern Mediterranean's largest aquarium. Several large tanks contain an amazing display of marine life, though really big fish are scarce. Interactive multimedia features and displays in several languages help explain things.

The north-coast buses (€1.70, 30 minutes) leaving from Iraklio's Bus Station A can drop you on the main road; from there it's a 10-minute walk. The turn-off to Kato Gouves is well signposted on the national road.

KNOSSOS ΚΝΩΣΣΟΣ

Crete's must-see historical attraction is the **Minoan Palace of Knossos** (☎ 2810 231940; admission €6; ☺ 8am-7pm Jun-Oct, 8am-3pm Nov-May), 5km south of Iraklio in Knossos (k-nos-*os*) village, and the capital of Minoan Crete.

Legendary home of King Minos' mythical Minotaur, Knossos was uncovered in the early 1900s by British archaeologist Sir Arthur Evans. Rival digger Heinrich Schliemann, discoverer of ancient Troy and Mycenae, had failed to win over the landowner, and Evans took the glory.

After 35 years and some £250,000 of his own money, Sir Arthur had excavated the site and accomplished partial reconstructions. His efforts proved controversial, with some archaeologists claiming that accuracy was sacrificed to imagination. However, for the casual visitor, the reconstructions are more than sufficient for visualising a real live Minoan palace.

History

Knossos' first palace (1900 BC) was destroyed by an earthquake around 1700 BC, and rebuilt with a grander and more

CRETE

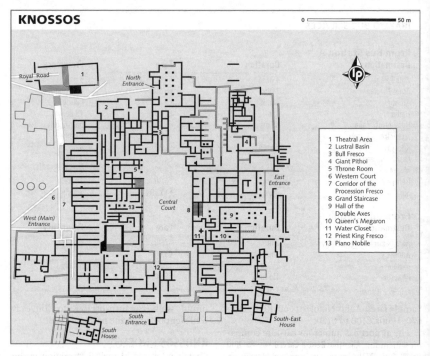

KNOSSOS

0 ———— 50 m

1 Theatral Area
2 Lustral Basin
3 Bull Fresco
4 Giant Pithoi
5 Throne Room
6 Western Court
7 Corridor of the
  Procession Fresco
8 Grand Staircase
9 Hall of the
  Double Axes
10 Queen's Megaron
11 Water Closet
12 Priest King Fresco
13 Piano Nobile

sophisticated design (Evans' reconstruction emulates the latter palace). It was partially destroyed again between 1500 and 1450 BC, then inhabited for another 50 years before finally burning down.

Knossos consisted of an immense palace, residences of officials and priests, the homes of ordinary people, and burial grounds. The palace comprised royal domestic quarters, public reception rooms, shrines, workshops, treasuries and storerooms, all built around a central court. Like all Minoan palaces, it was also the city hall, accommodating the bureaucracy.

Until 1997 visitors could enter the royal apartments, but the area was then cordoned off, before it disappeared altogether under the continual pounding of tourists' feet. Despite extensive ongoing repairs, it's unlikely to be reopened.

Exploring the Site

Evans' reconstruction brings to life the palace's most significant parts, including the reconstructed columns; painted deep brown-red with gold-trimmed black capitals, they taper gracefully at the bottom. Vibrant frescoes add another dramatic dimension to the palace. Additionally, the Minoans' highly sophisticated society is revealed by details like the advanced drainage system, the placement of light wells, and the organisation of space within rooms – meant to be cool in summer and warm in winter.

The palace complex entrance is across the **Western Court** and along the **Corridor of the Procession Fresco**, where a now-fragmentary fresco depicted a procession bearing gifts to the king. A copy, called the **Priest King Fresco**, is visible south of the Central Court.

Walking straight ahead from the Corridor of the Procession Fresco to the north entrance, you'll reach the **Theatral Area**. This series of steps may have been a theatre, or the place where important visitors arriving on the Royal Road were greeted.

The **Royal Road**, leading off to the west, was apparently Europe's first. It was flanked by workshops and ordinary residences. Sir Arthur surmised that the nearby **Lustral Basin** was where the Minoans performed ritual cleansings before religious ceremonies.

Entering the **Central Court** from the north, you pass the relief **Bull Fresco**, depicting a charging bull. Also in the palace's northern section, see the **Giant Pithoi**, large ceramic jars used for storing olive oil, wine and grain. Evans found over 100 *pithoi*, some 2m high. Ropes were required to move these heavy objects, thus warranting the raised patterns decorating the jars.

At the Central Court, once surrounded by the palace's high walls, the complex's most important rooms begin. From the northern end of the west side, steps descend to the **Throne Room**, fenced off but still visible. The centrepiece, a simple, beautifully proportioned throne, is flanked by the **Griffin Fresco** (the Minoans held these mythical beasts sacred). Possibly the room was a shrine and the throne used by a high priestess rather than a king. The Minoans worshipped their gods in small shrines, not great temples, and each palace had several.

On the 1st floor of the palace's west side is the section Evans called the **Piano Nobile** (the nobles' floor), believing that the reception and state rooms had been here. A room here displays copies of some frescoes found.

Returning to the Central Court, you'll see the impressive **Grand Staircase** leading from the palace's eastern side to the (now off-limits) royal apartments, which Evans called the **Domestic Quarter**. Within the royal apartments, the **Hall of the Double Axes** was the king's *megaron*, a spacious double room in which the ruler both slept and carried out certain court duties. There was a light well at one end and a balcony at the other to ensure air circulation. The room was named for the double axe marks on its light well, the sacred symbol of the Minoans.

A passage from here leads to the **Queen's Megaron**. Above the door is a copy of the **Dolphin Fresco**, one of the most exquisite Minoan artworks, and a blue floral design decorates the portal. Next to this room is the queen's bathroom, complete with terracotta bathtub and **water closet**, touted as the first ever to use the flush principle; water was poured down by hand.

Getting There & Away

Frequent buses from Iraklio's bus station (see p230) and from near Morosini Fountain serve Knossos. From the coastal road, occasional signs direct drivers. Since several free car parks exist close to the site, don't listen to touts advertising paid parking lots along the way.

OTHER MINOAN SITES

Besides Knossos, central Crete has other significant Minoan sites. Less reconstructed (and less flamboyant) than Knossos, they provide a somewhat different, more raw glimpse into Minoan life, without the architectural interpretations of Sir Arthur Evans. For this reason some archaeological purists prefer them to Knossos.

Malia Μάλια

Some 3km east of the package-tour sprawl of north-coast Malia, the **Minoan Palace of Malia** (☎ 28970 31597; admission €4; ☼ 8.30am-3pm Tue-Sun) is smaller than either Knossos or Phaestos. It once comprised a palace complex and a town built on this flat, fertile plain.

From the **West Court** (where the entrance is) walk to the southern end to see the eight circular pits probably used to store grain. East of these, the palace's former main entrance leads to the southern end of the **Central Court**. At the southwest corner stands the **Kernos Stone**, a disc with 34 holes around its edge; archaeologists still can't explain its original use.

The **Loggia**, north of the **Central Staircase** (at the north end of the palace's west side), was used for religious ceremonies.

The site's exhibition hall has reconstructions and interesting photos, including aerial shots. Half-hourly buses connect Malia with Iraklio (€3.70, one hour).

Phaestos Φαιστός

Conveniently, Crete's three other major archaeological sites lie near one other, forming a rough triangle 50km south of Iraklio.

Phaestos (☎ 28920 42315; adult/student €4/2, incl Agia Triada €6/3; ☼ 8am-7.30pm Jun-Oct, 8am-5pm Nov-Apr), 63km from Iraklio, was the second-most-important Minoan palace-city. Phaestos (*festos*) also enjoys the most awe-inspiring location, with panoramic views of the Mesara Plain and Mt Ida. The palace layout is identical to Knossos, with rooms arranged around a central court. And, like Knossos, most of Phaestos was built over an older palace destroyed in the late Middle Minoan period. However, unlike other Minoan sites, parts of this old palace have been excavated and its remnants are partially added on to the new palace.

CRETE

Phaestos has its own distinctive attractiveness. There's an air of mystery about the desolate, unreconstructed ruins altogether lacking at Knossos. Also in contrast to Knossos, few frescoes remain here; Phaestos' palace walls were apparently mostly covered with white gypsum.

The new palace entrance is by the 15m-wide **Grand Staircase**. The stairs access the **Central Court**. North of here lie the palace complex's best-preserved sections, the reception rooms and private apartments. While excavations continue, it's known that the entrance here was marked by an imposing portal with half columns at either side, the lower parts of which are still in situ. Unlike the Minoan freestanding columns, however, they don't taper at the base. The celebrated Phaestos disc, now in Iraklio's archaeological museum (p225), was discovered in a building north of the palace.

There are eight daily buses from Iraklio to Phaestos (€5.90, 1½ hours), also stopping at the Gortyna site. Five daily buses also connect Phaestos with Agia Galini (€2.80, 25 minutes, five daily) and Matala (€1.80, 30 minutes, five daily).

Agia Triada Αγία Τριάδα

Pronounced ah-*yee*-ah trih-*ah*-dha, **Agia Triada** (☎ 28920 91564; admission €3, incl Phaestos €6; ◷ 10am-4.30pm summer, 8.30am-3pm winter), 3km west of Phaestos, was a smaller but similarly designed palace, and possibly a royal summer villa, judging by the opulence of the objects

discovered here. North of the palace, the stoa (long, colonnaded building) of an erstwhile settlement has been unearthed. Iraklio's archaeological museum (p225) contains significant local finds, including a sarcophagus, two superlative frescoes and three vases.

The signposted right-hand turn to Agia Triada is about 500m past Phaestos on the Matala road. There's no public transport.

Gortyna Γόρτυνα

Sprawling across the road connecting Iraklio and Phaestos, on the Mesara plain, **Gortyna** (☎ 28920 31144; admission €4; ◷ 8am-7.30pm, to 5pm winter) is a vast and intriguing site. Gortyna (pronounced *gor*-tih-nah) was inhabited from Minoan to Christian times, and became capital of Rome's Cyrenaica province.

The massive stone tablets inscribed with the wide-ranging **Laws of Gortyna** (5th century BC) comprise Gortyna's most significant exhibit. Fixed remains include the 2nd-century-AD **Praetorium**, once residence of the provincial governor; a **Nymphaeum**; and the **Temple of Pythian Apollo**. Finally, see the ruined 6th-century-AD **Basilica of Agios Titos**, dedicated to this protégé of St Paul and Crete's first bishop.

The ruins are 46km southwest of Iraklio and 15km from Phaestos. There's no public transport.

ARHANES ΑΡΧΑΝΕΣ
pop 4700

Pretty Arhanes, 14km south of Iraklio, is a restored traditional village with lovely old houses and excellent tavernas set around relaxing, leafy squares. Although Arhanes once boasted a Minoan palace, only ruins remain (signposted from the main road).

The **Archaeological Museum of Arhanes** (☎ 28107 52712; admission free; ◷ 8.30am-3pm Wed-Mon) contains finds from regional archaeological excavations. The exhibits include *larnakes* (coffins) and musical instruments from Fourni, and an ornamental dagger from the Anemospilia temple.

Visit the site www.archanes.gr for online information.

Accommodation here includes **Neraidospilios** (☎ 6972720879; www.neraidospilios.gr; s/apt €40/70; ✖ ⚏) on the town outskirts. These superbly appointed, spacious studios and apartments overlook the mountains. Enquire with the owners, at Arhanes' Diahroniko cafe.

Hourly buses connect Iraklio with Arhanes (€1.70, 30 minutes).

ZAROS & AROUND ΖΑΡΟΣ
pop 2220

About 46km southwest of Iraklio, Zaros is a more rustic village, known for its spring water production. Nearby excavations indicate that this factor lured Minoans, and later Romans to settle here.

If you're driving, the Byzantine monasteries and other nearby villages are worth exploring. **Moni Agiou Nikolaou**, atop the verdant **Rouvas Gorge**, contains 14th-century paintings, while the nearby **Moni Agiou Andoniou Vrondisiou** boasts a 15th-century Venetian fountain and 14th-century frescoes.

Just outside Zaros, visit the lovely shady park at **Votomos** for its small lake, children's playground and excellent taverna-cafe, **I Limni** (☎ 28940 31338; trout per kilogram €22; ☺ 9am-late). From the lake, a path accesses both Moni Agiou Nikolaou (900m) and Rouvas Gorge (2.5km).

For overnights, try **Studios Keramos** (☎ /fax 28940 31352; Zaros; s/d incl breakfast €30/35; ☒), decorated with family heirlooms, antique beds and furniture – don't miss owner Katerina's home-cooked traditional Cretan breakfast. For eating, the main-street **Vengera** (☎ 28940 31730; Zaros; mains €4-6) serves home-cooked traditional Cretan food.

Two daily buses connect Zaros with Iraklio (€4.30, one hour).

MATALA ΜΑΤΑΛΑ
pop 100

Matala (*ma*-ta-la), on the south coast 11km southwest of Phaestos, was a groovy getaway in the early 1970s, when hippies would sleep around in the sandstone **caves** that pockmark the giant overhanging rock slab at water's edge. The caves, populated in earlier centuries, were never for particularly light sleepers – they were originally used as Roman tombs in the 1st century AD.

Matala's modern 'civilising' process of expansion has rather killed its initial escapist appeal, though it does still have its loyal returnees. It's a fairly ordinary, low-key vacation settlement nowadays, with domatia and tavernas, and a beautiful sandy **beach** below the caves. You can still clamber around freely in the caves, though they're normally

fenced off at night. There was no guard or entry charge at the time of writing. Matala also makes a convenient base for visiting Phaestos and Agia Triada.

Sleeping & Eating

Fantastic Rooms to Rent (☎ 28920 45362, s/d/tr €25/30/40, d/tr with kitchen €30/35; P ☒) Around since the hippie heydays, the Fantastic has plain but comfortable rooms, many with kitchenette, phone, kettle and fridge.

Pension Andonios (☎ 28920 45123; d/tr €30/35; P ☒) Run by the genial Antonis, this comfortable pension has attractively furnished rooms set around a lovely courtyard, many with kitchenette. The top rooms have balconies.

Hotel Zafiria (☎ 28920 45366, www.zafiria-matala .com; d incl breakfast €40; P ☒ ☒ ☒) One of Matala's bigger places, the Zafiria has comfortable rooms with all mod cons. The balconies enjoy sea views, and there's a new pool beneath the cliffs.

Gianni's Taverna (☎ 28920 45719; mains €5-7.50) This no-frills place has inexpensive grills and other simple taverna fare.

Lions (☎ 28920 45108; specials €6-10) On the beach, this old standby has above-average food, with big trays of home-style dishes inside. It gets lively in the evening, when it doubles as a watering hole.

Getting There & Away

From Iraklio, five daily buses serve Matala (€7.20, 2½ hours). Buses also run between Matala and Phaestos (€1.80, 30 minutes).

RETHYMNO ΡΕΘΥΜΝΟ
pop 27,870

Delightful Rethymno (*reth*-im-no) is Crete's third largest town, noted for its picturesque old town running down to a lively harbour overlooked by a massive Venetian fortress. Although Rethymno is showing signs of urban sprawl, travellers seem to miss it (except when looking for parking), such is the attraction of the lovely old Venetian-Turkish quarter, with its maze of narrow streets, graceful wood-balconied houses and ornate Venetian monuments; minarets add an Ottoman flourish.

Rethymno has a softer, more feminine feel than Iraklio, partly due to architecture, but also because Rethymno's University of Crete

CRETE

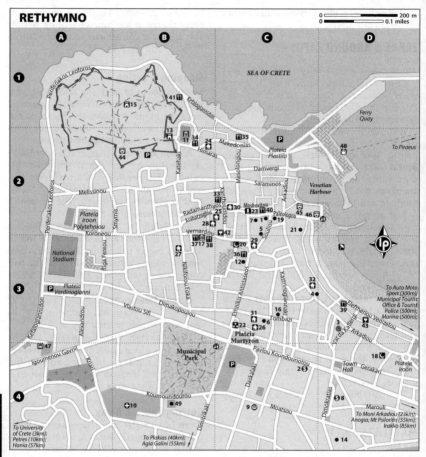

RETHYMNO

campus specialises in the humanities, which attracts more female students here than males. The full-time student population also keeps Rethymno lively in winter.

History

Rethymno's strategic position appealed to the Minoans, who settled here. The town was dubbed 'Rithymna' from the 4th century BC, when it was autonomous, issuing its own coinage. However, it waned in importance during Roman and Byzantine times.

Rethymno flourished again during Venetian rule (1210–1645), and its most important architecture dates from that period. The Ottomans ruled thereafter until 1897, when Russia became overseer of Rethymno dur-

ing the European Great Powers' occupation. The town's reputation as an artistic and intellectual centre grew from 1923, when the mandated population exchanges between Greece and Turkey brought many refugees from Constantinople.

Orientation

Rethymno's major sights and best sleeping and eating options are clustered near the harbour; a decent beach is on its eastern side.

The bus station, at the western end of Igoumenou Gavriil, is about 600m west of the Porto Guora (despite some discussions, it hadn't been relocated at the time of writing). If arriving by ferry, you'll see the old quarter opposite the quay.

Parking is very difficult around the old town in summer. Although a sign says parking isn't allowed in the giant lot by the quay, many seem to do so.

Information

BOOKSHOPS

Ilias Spondidakis bookshop (☎ 28310 54307; Souliou 43) Has English-language novels, books about Greece and Greek music.

Mediterraneo Editions (☎ 28310 50505; Paleologou 41; www.mediterraneo.gr; ☼ 8am-10pm) Friendly shop stocks foreign-language books, Lonely Planet and other guide books, and Anavasi hiking maps.

EMERGENCY

Tourist police (☎ 28310 28156; Delfini Bldg, Venizelou; ☼ 7am-2.30pm) At the municipal tourist office.

INTERNET ACCESS

Cybernet (Kallergi 44-46; per hr €3; ☼ 10am-5am)

LAUNDRY

Laundry Mat (☎ 28310 29722; Tombazi 45; wash & dry €9; ☼ 8.30am-2pm & 5.30-9pm Mon-Fri, 8.30am-2.15pm Sat) By the youth hostel.

LEFT LUGGAGE

KTEL (☎ 28310 22659; cnr Kefalogiannidon & Igoumenou Gavriil); €1.50 per day; ☼ 8am-6pm) Luggage service at the bus station.

MEDICAL SERVICES

Rethymno Hospital (☎ 28210 27491; Triandalydou 17; ☼ 24hr)

MONEY

Alpha Bank (Pavlou Koundouriotou 29)
National Bank of Greece (Dimokratias)

POST

Post office (☎ 28310 22302; Moatsou 21; ☼ 7am-7pm Mon-Fri)

TOURIST INFORMATION

Municipal Tourist Office (☎ 28310 29148; www .rethymno.gr; Delfini Bldg, Eleftheriou Venizelou; ☼ 8.30am-8.30pm Mon-Fri year-round, plus 9am-8.30pm Sat & Sun Mar-Nov)

TRAVEL AGENCIES

Alfa Odeon Holidays (☎ 28310 57610; www.odeon travel.gr; Paleologou 25) The helpful Manolis Chliaoutakis runs this full-service travel agency in the old town.
Ellotia Tours (☎ 28310 24533; www.rethymnoatcrete .com; Arkadiou 155; ☼ 9am-9pm Mar-Nov) Boat and plane tickets, currency exchange, car and bike hire and excursions can be arranged here.

Sights

Rethymno's 16th-century **fortress** (fortezza; ☎ 28310 28101; Paleokastro Hill; admission €3.10; ☼ 8am-8pm Jun-Oct) was originally an ancient acropolis. Although its massive walls once sheltered numerous buildings, only a church and a mosque survive. Nevertheless, there are many ruins to explore, and great views from the ramparts.

Once a prison, the small **archaeological museum** (☎ 28310 54668; admission €3; ☼ 8.30am-3pm Tue-Sun), near the fortress entrance, exhibits Neolithic tools, Minoan pottery excavated from nearby tombs, Mycenaean figurines and a 1st-century-AD relief of Aphrodite, plus an important coin collection.

Rethymno's **Historical & Folk Art Museum** (☎ 28310 23398; Vernardou 28-30; admission €3; ☼ 9.30am-2.30pm Mon-Sat), located in a historic Venetian building, documents traditional rural life, with its clothing, baskets, weavings and farm tools.

In the old quarter, the unmissable **Rimondi Fountain**, with its spouting lion heads and Corinthian capitals, attests to former Venetian rule, as does the 16th-century **Loggia** (now a museum shop). The well-preserved **Porto Guora** (Great Gate) is a remnant of the Venetian defensive wall.

Venetian and Turkish architecture is vividly displayed at the **Centre for Byzantine Art** (☎ 28210 50120; Ethnikis Antistaseos). This former mansion's terrace cafe offers great old-town views.

The nearby **Nerantzes Mosque**, converted from a Franciscan church in 1657, and, further east, the **Kara Musa Pasha Mosque**, with its vaulted fountain, are Rethymno's major remaining Ottoman structures. The latter now houses the **Hellenic Conservatory**, and makes an atmospheric concert venue.

Activities

The **Happy Walker** (☎ /fax 28310 52920; www.happy walker.com; Tombazi 56; ☼ 5pm-8.30pm) offers various countryside walks near Rethymno. More serious hikers should see **EOS** (Greek Mountaineering Club; ☎ 28310 57766; www.eos.rethymnon .com; Dimokratias 12) for detailed info on mountain climbing and other outdoors adventures in Rethymno prefecture.

The **Paradise Dive Centre** (☎ 28310 26317; www .diving-center.gr) runs diving activities and PADI courses for all levels. Its dive base is at Petres, 15 minutes west of Rethymno.

Festivals & Events

The annual **Renaissance Festival** (☎ 28310 51199; www.cultureguide.gr) is Rethymno's biggest event. Events primarily take place in the fortress's Erofili Theatre from July to September. The mid-July **Wine Festival** is held in the flower-filled municipal park, which is always good for a relaxing stroll. February sees fun **Winter Carnival** celebrations.

Sleeping

BUDGET

Rethymno Youth Hostel (☎ 28310 22848; www .yhrethymno.com; Tombazi 41; dm without bathroom €10, breakfast €2; 🖳 🛜) This friendly, laid-back old-town hostel stays open year-round. It enjoys an enclosed, open location, with good bathrooms and a small bar.

Sea Front (☎ 28310 51981; www.forthnet.gr/elotia; Arkadiou 159; d €35-50; 🟤) This waterfront pension has decent budget rooms with timber floors, plus studio apartments with sea views and ceiling fans further towards the beach.

Atelier (☎ 28310 24440; atelier@ret.forthnet.gr; Himaras 27; r €35-55) These clean and attractively refurbished rooms attached to Frosso Bora's pottery workshop represent great value. They're marked by Venetian architecture, like the exposed stone walls – along with flat-screen TVs, new bathrooms and kitchenettes.

Olga's Pension (☎ 28310 28665; Souliou 57; s/d/studio €40/45/65; 🟤) On touristy but colourful Souliou, Olga's has a faded charm, with eclectic decor and terraces between the basic but colourful rooms. Most include fridge, TV, fan and a basic bathroom. Rates include breakfast, served downstairs in Souliou 55.

Byzantine Hotel (☎ 28310 55609; Vosporou 26; d incl breakfast from €50; 🟤) Traditional ambience meets great value at this small hotel near the Porta Guora. The rooms in this historic structure feature carved timber furniture, and some have bathtubs. The back rooms overlook the old mosque and minaret.

Casa dei Delfini (☎ 28310 55120; kzaxa@reth.gr; Nikiforou Foka 66-68; studio €55-75, ste €80-140; 🟤) Turkish and Venetian architectural features intermingle in this elegant pension, which includes an old stone trough and hammam ceiling in one of the studio bathrooms. The traditionally decorated rooms all feature kitchenettes; most impressive is the massive maisonette, with its large private terrace.

MIDRANGE & TOP END

our pick **Hotel Veneto** (☎ 28310 56634; www.veneto.gr; Epimenidou 4; studio/ste incl breakfast €125/145; 🟤 🛜) For some of Rethymno's most beautiful aesthetic flourishes, visit the Veneto, which dates partially from the 14th century. The foyer's stunning pebble mosaic and a well-lit stone basin, where delicate flowers float, open onto a pretty back garden, where breakfast tables are set amidst verdure and a gurgling fountain. Rooms feature polished wood floors, iron beds, TV and kitchenettes. A subterranean, curving-stone chamber where monks once meditated is not the largest room, but is certainly the most striking. Out of high season, rates drop significantly.

Palazzo Rimondi (☎ 28310 51289; www.palazzo rimondi.com; cnr Xanthoulidou 21 & Trikoupi 16; d studio/ste incl breakfast €160/200; 🖳 🖳) This charming old-town Venetian mansion is a real treat, with its exquisite individually decorated studios with kitchenettes. There's a small splash pool in the breakfast courtyard.

Avli Lounge Apartments (☎ 28310 58250; www.avli .gr; cnr Xanthoudidou 22 & Radamanthyos; ste incl breakfast €210-250; 🖳) Inconspicuously spread over two beautifully restored Venetian buildings in the old town, these singular suites feature ornate iron or wooden beds, antiques, exquisite furnishings and objets d'art.

Eating

The waterfront and Venetian harbour are, unsurprisingly, occupied by touristy places; head inland for better options.

Fanari (☎ 28310 54894; Kefalogiannidon 15; mezedhes €2.50-10) West of the Venetian harbour on the waterfront, this taverna serves good mezedhes, fresh fish and Cretan cuisine. Try the *bekri mezes* (pork with wine and peppers) or *apaki*, the local smoked-pork speciality, plus the homemade wine.

Taverna Kyria Maria (☎ 28310 29078; Moshovitou 20; Cretan dishes €4-6.50) Behind the Rimondi Fountain, this taverna has great home-style Greek cooking and outdoor seating, where bird cages hang from a leafy trellis.

Souliou 55 (☎ 28310 54896; Souliou 55; mayirefta €4-7) Known informally as 'Stella's Kitchen', this little place specialising in *mayirefta* is below Olga's Pension, run by Stella herself.

Samaria (☎ 28310 24681; Eleftheriou Venizelou; mayirefta €4-7) On the waterfront but still popular with locals, Samaria does good *mayirefta*, while the soups and grills are also excellent.

Thalassografia (☎ 28310 52569; Kefalogiannidon 33; mezedhes €4-9) With a breathtaking setting overlooking the sea, under the fortress, Thalassografia is a good place to sample mezedhes at sunset, though it's perhaps overpriced. The grilled sardines are excellent, as are the creamy mushrooms.

Lemonokipos (☎ 28310 57087; Ethnikis Antistaseos 100; mains €7-9) Dine among the lemon trees in the lovely courtyard of this old-town taverna. The traditional Cretan fare includes some unique twists, such as pork and vegetables flavoured with bitter orange leaves.

Castelvecchio (☎ 28310 55163; Himaras 29; mains €8-16; 🕑 dinner Jul-Aug, dinner & lunch Sep-Jun) This welcoming family taverna on the fortress' edge is friendly and does good Cretan specialities, like the *kleftiko* (oven-baked lamb).

Avli (☎ 28310 26213; www.avli.com; cnr Xanthoudidou 22 & Radamanthyos; mains €13.50-30) This delightful former Venetian villa is the place for a special night out. The Nuevo Cretan–style food is superb, the wine list excellent and you dine in a charming courtyard bursting with pots of herbs, bougainvillea canopies, fruit trees and works of art.

Also highly recommended are **Myrogdies Mezedopoleio** (☎ 28310 26083; Vernadou 32; mezedhes €4-6) and **Ousies** (☎ 28310 56643; Vernadou 20; mezedhes €4-7), two inexpensive *mezedhopoleia* (restaurants specialising in mezedhes and *raki*) with great summertime ambience, on Vernadou.

Drinking & Entertainment

Rethymno's nightlife is concentrated in the bars, clubs and discos around Nearhou and Salaminos, near the Venetian harbour, along with the waterfront bars off Plastira Sq. The indefatigable student population keeps Rethymno lively year-round.

Figaro (☎ 28310 29431; Vernardou 21; 🕑 noon-late) Housed in an ingeniously restored old building, Figaro is an atmospheric 'art and music' all-day bar. It attracts everyone from the local intelligentsia and students to tourists drawn in by the subdued ambience and excellent music.

Living Room (☎ 28310 21386; www.livingroom-crete .gr; Venizelou 5; 🕑 9am-2am) This slick cafe-bar seems to have four waiters *per capita*, and exudes a Fashion-TV vibe in its ambient techno and eclectic modern decor. It's popular with students and other locals.

Rock Club Cafe (☎ 28310 31047; Petihaki 8; 🕑 9pm-dawn) One of Rethymno's classic hangouts, this club is popular with visitors and gets filled nightly in summer.

Fortezza Disco (Nearhou 20; 🕑 11pm-dawn) This big, flashy club gets busy late, and boasts three bars and a laser show.

Getting There & Away

BOAT
For information on ferries and high-speed boats from Rethymno, see Island Hopping (p512).

BUS
From the **bus station** (☎ 28310 22212; www.bus -service-crete-ktel.com; Igoumenou Gavriil), hourly buses

run in summer to both Hania (€6.50, one hour) and Iraklio (€6.50, 1½ hours). Four daily buses serve Preveli (€4.10, 40 to 45 minutes), while seven go to Plakias (€4.10, one hour) – including an evening bus not usually listed on schedules, which goes via Preveli. Six buses a day serve Agia Galini (€5.60, 1½ hours), three serve Moni Arkadiou (€2.50, 30 minutes), and two go to both Anogia (€4.90, 50 minutes) and Omalos (€11.90, two hours). Daily buses serve Hora Sfakion via Vryses in summer. Low-season services are greatly reduced. Four buses serve Spili (€4, one hour).

Getting Around

Auto Moto Sport (☎ 28310 24858; www.automoto sport.com.gr; Sofokli Venizelou 48) has car hire and a great variety of motorbikes and motorcycles. It's a 10-minute walk from the Venetian harbour, eastwards along the coast road (Eleftheriou Venizelou) which becomes Sofokli Venizelou.

MONI ARKADIOU ΜΟΝΗ ΑΡΚΑΔΙΟΥ

The 16th-century **Moni Arkadiou** (Arkadi; ☎ 28310 83136; admission €2; ⏰ 9am-7pm Apr-Oct) has deep significance for Cretans. This monastery, situated in the hills 23km southeast of Rethymno, was the site of an act of mass suicidal defiance that captured European public attention.

In November 1866 massive Ottoman forces arrived to crush island-wide revolts. Hundreds of Cretan men, women and children fled their villages to find shelter at Arkadiou. However, far from being a safe haven, the monastery was soon besieged by 2000 Turkish soldiers. Rather than surrender, the Cretans set light to stored gunpowder kegs, killing everyone, Turks included; one small girl miraculously survived, and lived to a ripe old age in a village nearby. A bust of this woman and one of the abbot who lit the gunpowder stand outside the monastery.

Arkadiou's most impressive building, its Venetian baroque church, has a striking facade marked by eight slender Corinthian columns and topped by an ornate triple-belled tower. Left of it is a small **museum**. The monastery's former windmill outside it has a macabre **ossuary**, containing skulls and bones of the 1866 fighters.

From Rethymno, three daily buses go to Moni Arkadiou (€2.50, 30 minutes).

ANOGIA ΑΝΩΓΕΙΑ
pop 2450

Memorable Anogia presides over the so-called 'Devil's Triangle' of macho mountain villages that occasionally get involved in armed standoffs with the police (usually, over illicit cannibis cultivation, but sometimes just due to perceived affronts to local honour), much to the excitement of the Athenian media. Perched aside **Mt Psiloritis**, 37km southwest of Iraklio, Anogia's known for its rebellious spirit and determination to express its undiluted Cretan character. Its famous 2000-guest **weddings** involve the entire village. It's also known for its stirring music and has spawned many of Crete's best known musicians.

Anogia's *kafeneia* (coffee shops) on the main square are frequented by black-shirted moustachioed men, the older ones often wearing traditional dress. The women stay home or flog the traditional blankets and other crafts that hang all over the village's shops. Indeed, Anogia is well known for its rugs and, if you know what you're looking for, you can sometimes come away with a nice one.

During WWII Anogia was a centre of resistance, and suffered heavily for it. The Nazis massacred all the local men in retaliation for their role in sheltering Allied troops and aiding in the kidnap of General Kreipe.

Anogia nowadays lives quite comfortably from its sheep-husbandry industry and tourism, the latter bolstered as much by curious Greeks as by foreign travellers in search of rustic authenticity. Don't refuse if a village man you don't even know offers to pay for your coffee – it could be considered impolite.

Anogia clings to a hillside, with the textile shops in the lower half and most accommodation and businesses above. There's an ATM-equipped bank and post office. The upper village's **Infocost** (☎ 28340 31808; per hr €3; ⏰ 5pm-late) offers internet access.

Sleeping & Eating

Hotel Aristea (☎ 28340 31459; d incl breakfast €40; P) There are good views from this upper-village location. The simple but well-outfitted rooms have bathrooms and balconies. An excellent set of new studios is next door.

Ta Skalomata (☎ 28340 31316; grills €3-7) On the upper village's eastern edge, it serves great grills and Cretan dishes at reasonable prices. Zucchini with cheese and aubergine is very tasty, and do try the home-baked bread.

Getting There & Away

Four daily buses reach Anogia from Iraklio (€3.60, one hour), while two daily buses operate from Rethymno (€4.90, 1¼ hours).

PLAKIAS ΠΛΑΚΙΑΣ
pop 180

Some things in Crete never change, and Plakias is one of them. Set beside a long southcoast beach, between two immense wind tunnels – the gorges of Selia and Kourtaliotis – this unassuming resort is livened up in summer by a curious mix of Central European package tourists and the indomitable international legions quartered at the village's extraordinary youth hostel.

Plakias has good restaurants, plenty of accommodation, and offers local walks through olive groves and along cliffs overlooking the sea, some leading to sparkling hidden beaches. It's an excellent base for regional excursions, and the local olive oil is some of Crete's best. Plakias' massive summertime wind (and distance from Iraklio) has thankfully preserved it from overdevelopment, though parents should note that small children may not enjoy the flying sand and waves at this and other southcoast beaches.

Orientation & Information

Plakias' main street runs along the beach; another runs parallel to it one block in, while two streets perpendicular to the water lead further inland. Most services are near the waterfront, including the bus stop.

There are two ATMs on the central waterfront. The **post office** (☎ 28320 31212; 7am-2pm) stands on the first perpendicular street from the water, if coming from the east. Next door, the English-speaking **Dr Manolis Alexandrakis** (☎ 28320 31770) runs a small clinic and the adjacent pharmacy. There's a well-stocked **lending library**, 250m beyond the youth hostel on the left-hand dirt track.

Waterfront cafe-bars advertise wi-fi. **Ostraco Bar** (☎ 28320 31710; per hr €4; 9am-late) on the western waterfront has wi-fi and computers; so too **Youth Hostel Plakias** (☎ 28320 32118; per hr €3.60). At the time of writing, however, the only free wi-fi was at **On The Rocks**, a cafe above the western beach, 100m beyond the Ostraco.

Sleeping

Accommodation becomes cheaper the further you go inland from the waterfront. Along

with a couple of resort-type hotels, domatia are abundant.

Youth Hostel Plakias (☎ 28320 32118; www.yhplakias.com; dm incl breakfast €9.50; Apr-Oct; P) This is a place where you come for three days and end up staying for three months, and where you make friends for life. It's one of the most unique hostels anywhere, as attested by the variety of ages and nationalities it attracts. Set around a green lawn amidst olive groves, about 500m from the waterfront, this purposefully lazy place has been led for 15 years by English manager Chris Bilson, who fosters an atmosphere of inclusiveness and good cheer, and who's constantly upgrading things. The hostel has eight-bed dorms (total capacity about 60) with fans, excellent toilets and showers (plus wash basins for clothes), while water, wine, beer and soft drinks are available.

Both roads perpendicular to the beach lead to the hostel, which is signposted in places. Book ahead if possible.

Ipokambos (☎ 28320 31525; amoutsos@otenet.gr; s/d €30/40; P) On the inland road parallel with the waterfront, this collection of spotless rooms with fridge and balconies is run by a very kind old couple. There's private parking behind.

Castello (☎ /fax 28320 31112; r/studio €35/45; P) This friendly place has cool, clean and fridge-equipped rooms, most with cooking facilities and big shady balconies. Two additional two-bedroom apartments are ideal for families (€50 to €60). Air-con costs an extra €5.

Flisvos Rooms (☎ 28320 31988; www.flisvos-plakias.gr; s/d €35/45;) On the central-eastern waterfront, the Flisvos has tasteful rooms overlooking the sea, and friendly service.

Pension Thetis (☎ 28320 31430; thetisstudios@gmail.com; studio €45-70;) A nice pick for families, these self-catering studios are set around a cool, leafy garden containing a small play park for kids. It's roughly opposite Ipokambos.

Eating

To Xehoristo (☎ 28320 31214; souvlaki €2.60) on the central-eastern waterfront is the local favourite for souvlaki (you must specify 'souvlaki *kalamaki*' when ordering, or you will be given *gyros* – the Greek version of doner kebab). The sound system plays traditional Cretan music, and the happy chefs sing along.

Nikos Souvlaki (☎ 28320 31921; mains €5-8) This bare-bones former souvlaki joint just up from the post office now serves sit-down

CRETE

meals instead, but it's still popular with the hostel crowd.

Taverna Manoussos (☎ 28320 31313; mains €5-9; ☺ 9am-1am) Cretan specialities are prepared at this friendly family-run taverna on the eastern side of the inland road parallel to the waterfront. The energetic, moustachioed owner, Manousos Christodoulakis, also rents simple rooms (double €30).

our pick **Taverna Plateia** (☎ 28320 31560; Myrthios; mains €6-9; ☺ 9am-1am) Located in Myrthios village, just above Plakias, this long-time favourite run by the gracious Fredericos Kalogerakis and family enjoys sublime views of the sea far below. Try the wonderful *myzithropitakia* (sweet cheese pies) and octopus *stifadho* (octopus in tomato and wine sauce).

Taverna Christos (☎ 28320 31472; mains €7-10) Nestled amidst the more touristy western-waterfront tavernas, Christos has a romantic tamarisk-shaded terrace and does good Cretan dishes and fresh fish.

Drinking & Entertainment

Plakias' cafes line the waterfront, while the bars – few, but lively – are clustered along the western end.

Ostraco Bar (☎ 28320 31710; ☺ 9am-late) This old favourite on the western waterfront is a small upstairs bar, where gregarious drinking and dancing to the latest pop hits takes place. There's a nice outdoor balcony facing the water.

Joe's Bar (☺ 9am-late) Officially called Nufaro, at the time of writing this was the hostel crowd's local. Despite the dark, warehouse-like interior, it plays a good selection of rock and pop and service is friendly. It's on the central waterfront.

Getting There & Away

In summer seven daily buses come from Rethymno (€4.10, one hour), including an evening one via Preveli (usually not listed on Rethymno bus station's timetables). There are no buses eastward to Frangokastello and Hora Sfakion. The bus stop has a timetable.

Getting Around

Alianthos Rent-a-Car (☎ 28320 32033; www.alianthos -group.com) has Plakias' best selection of vehicles, and island-wide service; it's a block inland on Plakias' western side.

Easy Ride (☎ 28320 20052; www.easyride.gr), close to the post office, has mountain bikes, bicy-cles, scooters and motorcycles for hire, as does nearby **Anso Travel** (☎ 28320 31712; www.ansotravel .com), which also offers guided walking tours.

AROUND PLAKIAS

Plakias is an excellent base for local activities, ranging from walks and beach adventures to traditional village exploration.

Some 2.5km west of Plakias on the coast, **Souda Beach** is an appealing sandy beach tucked within a lovely cove – often less windy than Plakias' main beach. There are umbrellas and a taverna behind, but it's more relaxed than the main one.

Also nice but more populated is **Damnoni Beach**, behind the striking stone headland that comprises Plakias Bay's eastern edge; further on, **One-Rock Beach** is an idyllic, clothing-optional sandy cove. A coastal path across the headland now allows a circular **coastal walk**, offering stunning sea views. Chris at Youth Hostel Plakias can inform about both the beach and walking trail.

The traditional villages of **Myrthios**, directly above Plakias, and the less visited **Selia**, a few kilometres further west, are two relaxing places for a stroll, with some eating, crafts shops and domatia.

Moni Preveli & Preveli Beach

Μονή Πρέβελη & Παραλία Πρεβελής

With a spectacular location high above the Libyan Sea, 14km east of Plakias and 35km from Rethymno, the well maintained and historic **Moni Preveli** (☎ 28320 31246; www.preveli .org; admission €2.50; ☺ 8am-7.30pm Jun-Oct) stands in tranquil isolation above one of Crete's most famous beaches. Like most Cretan monasteries, it was a centre of anti-Ottoman resistance, and was burned by the Turks during the 1866 onslaught.

History repeated itself after the Battle of Crete in 1941; after many Allied soldiers were sheltered here before being evacuated to Egypt, the Germans plundered the monastery. Preveli's **museum** contains a candelabra presented by grateful British soldiers after the war, along with valuable ecclesiastical objects.

Below the monastery lies the celebrated **Preveli Beach**, a highly photogenic stretch of sand also called Palm Beach (Paralia Finikodasous). It's at the mouth of the Kourtaliotis Gorge, from where the river Megalopotamos slices across it and empties into the Libyan Sea. The palm-lined riverbanks have freshwater pools good for a dip, while rugged cliffs begin where the sands end.

A steep path leads down to the beach (10 minutes) from a car park 1km before Moni Preveli. Alternatively, drive 5km down a signposted dirt road from a stone bridge just off the Moni Preveli main road. It ends at **Amoudi Beach**, from where you can walk west along a 500m track over the headland to reach Preveli.

In summer, four daily buses go from Rethymno to Preveli (€4.10, 40 to 45 minutes).

Spili Σπίλι
pop 640

A pretty mountain village with cobbled streets, rustic houses and plane trees, Spili (*spee*-lee) is 30km southeast of Rethymno, but much closer to Plakias and Preveli.

It has two ATMs and a post office, and its medical clinic also covers this part of southern Crete.

Spili's unique Venetian fountain spurts pure spring water from 19 lion heads. The village sees tourist buses during the day, but quietens down by evening. If you're looking for a bucolic inland base for operations, there are good sleeping and eating options here.

The bus stop is south of the square. Check email at Café Babis, near the fountain.

SLEEPING & EATING

Heracles Rooms (☎ /fax 28320 22411; heraclespapadakis@hotmail.com; s/d €29/40; ✂) Has spotless, nicely furnished rooms with window screens, fridge and air-con, plus great mountain views.

Costas Inn (☎ 28320 22040; d incl breakfast €35) These well kept, pleasant rooms have ceiling fans and some amenities. Some offer a fridge.

Yianni's (☎ 28320 22707; mains €4-7) Past the fountain, Yianni's has a courtyard setting and excellent traditional cooking; try the delicious rabbit in wine, mountain snails and house red.

Panorama (☎ 28320 22555) This excellent traditional taverna, run by Pantelis Vasilakis and his wife Calliope, lies on the eastern outskirts. Try the homemade bread and Cretan specialities such as kid goat with *horta* (wild greens).

GETTING THERE & AWAY

From both Preveli and Plakias (following different roads) it's a little over 20km and

a 30-minute drive from either place to Spili. There are four daily buses from Rethymno (€4, one hour).

AGIOS PAVLOS & TRIOPETRA
ΑΓΙΟΣ ΠΑΥΛΟΣ & ΤΡΙΟΠΕΤΡΑ

Idyllic, pristine and very remote, the beaches of Agios Pavlos and Triopetra have long been popular with yoga and meditation groups. However, if you're driving, they aren't particularly hard to access, via the village of Kato Saktouria (along the Spili–Agia Galini road), about 53km southeast of Rethymno. Surrounded by sand dunes and dramatic, red-rock cliffs, the coast here is certainly one of Crete's most beautiful places, ideal for escapists; the permanent local population is somewhere in the low single digits.

Agios Pavlos, the 'major' settlement, consists of a sandy cove overlooked by a few rooms, one shop, and tavernas. Better beaches are on the subsequent sandy coves, about a 10-minute walk over the western cliffs; like Plakias, strong summer winds are common.

These coves stretch west to the three giant rocks rising from the sea that give **Triopetra** its name. This junior settlement is populated by a single, though excellent, set of domatia and two tavernas above its placid sandy beach. From Agios Pavlos, it's a 3km drive along a paved road. Another 12km-long windy asphalt road from Akoumia village, west of Kato Saktouria on the Rethymno–Agia Galini road, also accesses Triopetra's westernmost beaches.

The all-encompassing silence at night and boundless starry sky, especially at Triopetra, add to the sensuous spirituality of the place, which even nonyogic visitors might appreciate. This is truly a magical spot, far from the distractions of the outside world, where you can experience southern Crete's desolate beauty at its most essential.

Sleeping & Eating

our pick **Taverna Pensione Pavlos** (☎ /fax 28310 25189, 6945998101; www.triopetra.com.gr; d/tr/q €35/37/45; P ✂) Some guests book three years in advance here. These simple rooms and terrace restaurant overlooking the sea remain the singular passion of owner Pavlos Kakogiannakis – now ably assisted by his kind, English-speaking son, Giorgos. The rooms are well maintained, with kitchenettes

CRETE

and sea-view balconies. The taverna serves local meat, home-grown organic produce, fish and lobster; since Pavlos is usually boating at dawn to check the nets, you'll only get fresher fish if you catch it yourself. It's best to 'reserve' a fish for dinner in the morning, before they're all taken. You'll encounter the taverna immediately after entering from Agios Pavlos.

Agios Pavlos Hotel & Taverna (☎ 28320 71104; www .agiospavloshotel.gr; d €40) This family-run place in Agios Pavlos is the area's main accommodation, and has a small shop selling basic supplies. The shady terrace, overlooking the beach, is bedecked with colourful hammocks and fruit drinks, creating an offbeat New-Age-meets-South-Seas kind of vibe.

The main building's simple rooms have small balconies overlooking the sea, plus rooms under the terrace below the taverna; it serves good Cretan food (*mayirefta* €5 to €8). The cafe-bar next door has internet.

Enquire at Agios Pavlos Hotel & Taverna about the large, self-contained studios on the facing cliff – the **Kavos Melissa complex** (r €45). A couple of slightly cheaper domatia exist higher above the beach, on the entry road.

AGIA GALINI ΑΓΙΑ ΓΑΛΗΝΗ
pop 1260
Further east of Agios Pavlos from the main road, the former fishing port of Agia Galini (*a-ya ga-lee-nee*) has lost much of its charm due to overdevelopment and package tourism. It's nothing like the rowdy north-coast party zones of Malia and Hersonisos; while both have large British contingents, Agia Galini is reserved more for the parents of the kids who flock to those places.

Agia Galini has a nice ambience at night, when the lights of its domatia, bars and tavernas flicker over the sea. It has a decent but crowded town beach (though boat excursions reach better beaches), and makes a convenient base for visiting Phaestos, Agia Triada, Agios Pavlos and Matala.

Orientation & Information
For information online, visit www.agia-galini.com. The bus station stands atop the entrance road, the post office is just past it. Agia Galini has ATMs and travel agencies with currency exchange, plus cafes with internet access, including **Hoi Polloi** (☎ 28320 91102; per hr €4; ☉ 9am-late).

Sleeping
Agia Galini Camping (☎ 28320 91386; camp sites per adult/tent €5/4; ☐ ☎) Next to the beach, 2.5km east of town, this well-run camping ground is shaded and has a pool, restaurant and minimarket.

Stohos Rooms & Taverna (☎ 28320 91433; www .stohos.gr; d incl breakfast €40-45; ☎ ☐) On the main beach, Stohos has self-catering apartments upstairs with big balconies, and huge studios downstairs ideal for families or groups. The excellent taverna serves *kleftiko* and other clay-oven Cretan specialities (€7 to €10).

Adonis (☎ 28320 91333; www.agia-galini.com; r €50-120; ☎ ☐ ☎) This pool-equipped hotel spread over several buildings has light and clean rooms, studios and apartments, some with sea-view balconies.

Eating
Madame Hortense (☎ 28320 91351; dishes €6-13) Agia Galini's most atmospheric and elegant restaurant stands atop the three-level Zorbas complex, enjoying great harbour views. Cuisine is primarily Greek-Mediterranean.

Kostas (☎ 28320 91323; fish €6-27) Right on the beach at the eastern end, this established fish taverna decorated in classic blue and white is always packed with locals. It has numerous mezedhes, and pricey but excellent seafood.

Faros (☎ 28320 91346; fish €7-12) Inland from the harbour, this classic *psarotaverna* (fish tavern) prepares fresh fish (from €45 per kilogram) plus grills and *mayirefta*.

Getting There & Away
In summer, six daily buses serve Iraklio (€7.40, two hours), six to Rethymno (€5.60, 1½ hours) and five to Phaestos and Matala (€3, 40 to 45 minutes).

Daily summer boats from the harbour reach the beaches of Agios Georgios, Agiofarango and Preveli Beach (€4 to €30).

WESTERN CRETE

The west is the real Crete. Proud locals will tell you so, and they certainly can make a case for the claim. Hania, the prefecture's capital, is Crete's most beautiful and historic town, with a gorgeous old Venetian quarter at its core. The father of modern Greece, Eleftherios Venizelos, hailed from there, and the general area had spawned centuries of rebels against Venetian and Turkish rule long before him.

Also in the west, the spectacular Samaria Gorge is the most famous of several enormous canyons that stretch through rugged terrain into the Libyan Sea on the southern coast, where offbeat Hora Sfakion remains Crete's spiritual capital, obstinately upholding tradition across its stony village hinterland of Sfakia. The west also boasts Crete's most stunning beaches, while you can live large without much care (or cash) in quiet coastal villages like Paleohora and Sougia.

HANIA XANIA
pop 53,370

Hania (hahn-*yah*; also spelt Chania) is Crete's most evocative city, with its pretty Venetian quarter, criss-crossed by narrow lanes, culminating at a magnificent harbour. Remnants of Venetian and Turkish architecture abound, with old townhouses now restored, transformed into atmospheric restaurants and boutique hotels.

Although all this beauty means the Old Town is deluged with tourists in summer, it's still a great place to unwind. Excellent local handicrafts mean there's good shopping, too.

Crete's second biggest city, Hania is also the major transit point for hikers doing the Samaria Gorge, and is the main transport hub for all western destinations. While a few package-tourist resorts line the beaches west of town, they're much less noticeable than the Iraklio-area resorts.

History

Minoan Kydonia occupied the hill east of Hania's harbour, and was probably both a palace site and important town (as suggested by clay tablets with Linear B script discovered here). Although Kydonia was destroyed together with most other Minoan settlements in 1450 BC, it would flourish throughout Hellenistic, Roman and Byzantine times.

In the early 13th century Crete's new Venetian rulers renamed it La Canea. The massive fortifications they constructed were impressive but couldn't keep the Turks from invading, after a two-month siege, in 1645. When Ottoman rule ended in 1898, the great powers made Hania Crete's capital; Iraklio replaced it only in 1971.

German bombers did significant damage during WWII, but much of the Old Town survives.

Orientation

Hania's bus station is on Kydonias, two blocks southwest of Plateia 1866, from where the Old Harbour is a short walk north up Halidon.

Most accommodation lies in the Old Town's western half. Hania's headland separates the Venetian port from the modern town's crowded beach, Nea Hora. Koum Kapi, in the old Turkish quarter further east, has waterfront cafes; above it, on busy Leoforos Eleftherios Venizelos, is the Halepa district, once an upscale residential and consular district where Venizelos used to live (his home is now a museum).

Boats to Hania dock 7km southeast, at Souda.

Information
BOOKSHOPS

Mediterraneo Bookstore (☎ 28210 86904; Akti Koundourioti 57) Has English-language books on Crete, novels, and indispensable Anavasi hiking maps.

Pelekanakis (☎ 28210 92512; Halidon 98) Has maps and multilingual guidebooks.

EMERGENCY

Hania Hospital (☎ 28210 22000; Mournies) Somewhat chaotic modern hospital 5km south; take public bus or taxi (€8 to €10).

Tourist police (☎ 28210 73333; Kydonias 29; ⏰ 8am-2.30pm) By the Town Hall.

INTERNET ACCESS

Triple W (☎ 28210 93478; Valadinon & Halidon; per hr €2; ⏰ 24hr)

Vranas Internet (☎ 28210 58618; Agion Deka 10; per hr €2; ⏰ 9.30am-1am)

INTERNET RESOURCES

www.chania.gr Municipality website; has general info and cultural events calendar.

www.chania-guide.gr More online information.

LAUNDRY

Old Town Laundromat (☎ 28210 59414; Karaoli Dimitriou 38; wash & dry €7; 9am-2pm & 6-9pm Mon-Sat) Also does dry cleaning.

LEFT LUGGAGE

KTEL bus station (☎ 28210 93052; Kydonias 73-77; per day €1.50)

MONEY

Most banks are in the new city, but ATMs exist in the Old Town on Halidon.

CRETE

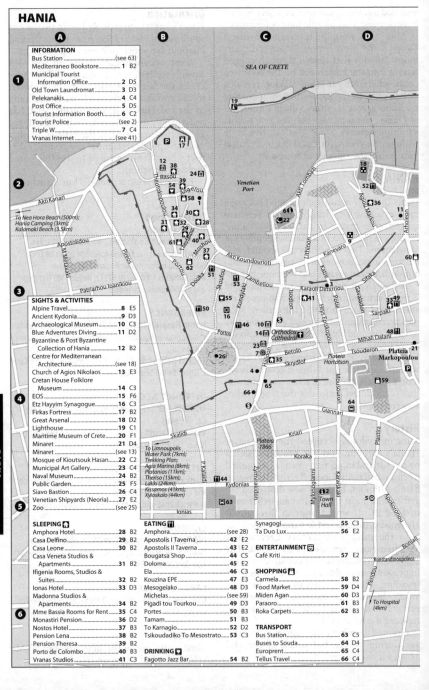

HANIA

A **B** **C** **D**

INFORMATION
Bus Station..............................(see 63)
Mediterraneo Bookstore...............1 B2
Municipal Tourist
   Information Office.......................2 D5
Old Town Laundromat...................3 D3
Pelekanakis....................................4 C4
Post Office.....................................5 D5
Tourist Information Booth.............6 C2
Tourist Police.............................(see 2)
Triple W...7 C4
Vranas Internet.........................(see 41)

SEA OF CRETE

Venetian
Port

Akti Kanari

To Nea Hora Beach (500m);
Hania Camping (3km);
Kalamaki Beach (3.5km);

Apostolidou
M. Malaxaki
Pireos

Patriarhou Ioanikiou

SIGHTS & ACTIVITIES
Alpine Travel..................................8 E5
Ancient Kydonia.............................9 D3
Archaeological Museum...............10 C3
Blue Adventures Diving................11 D2
Byzantine & Post Byzantine
   Collection of Hania...................12 B2
Centre for Mediterranean
   Architecture...........................(see 18)
Church of Agios Nikolaos.............13 E3
Cretan House Folklore
   Museum...................................14 C3
EOS..15 F6
Etz Hayyim Synagogue.................16 C3
Firkas Fortress.............................17 B2
Great Arsenal...............................18 D2
Lighthouse....................................19 C1
Maritime Museum of Crete..........20 F1
Minaret...21 D4
Minaret.....................................(see 13)
Mosque of Kioutsouk Hasan.......22 C2
Municipal Art Gallery...................23 C4
Naval Museum..............................24 C3
Public Garden...............................25 F5
Siavo Bastion...............................26 C4
Venetian Shipyards (Neoria).........27 E2
Zoo...(see 25)

SLEEPING
Amphora Hotel.............................28 B2
Casa Delfino.................................29 B2
Casa Leone...................................30 B2
Casa Veneta Studios &
   Apartments...............................31 B2
Ifigenia Rooms, Studios &
   Suites.......................................32 B2
Ionas Hotel..................................33 D3
Madonna Studios &
   Apartments...............................34 B2
Mme Bassia Rooms for Rent........35 C4
Monastiri Pension........................36 D2
Nostos Hotel................................37 B3
Pension Lena................................38 B2
Pension Theresa...........................39 B2
Porto de Colombo........................40 B3
Vranas Studios.............................41 C3

EATING
Amphora..................................(see 28)
Apostolis I Taverna.......................42 E2
Apostolis II Taverna......................43 E2
Bougatsa Shop.............................44 C5
Doloma..45 E2
Ela..46 C3
Kouzina EPE.................................47 E3
Mesogeiako..................................48 D3
Michelas...................................(see 59)
Pigadi tou Tourkou......................49 D3
Portes..50 B3
Tamam...51 B3
To Karnagio..................................52 D2
Tsikoudadiko To Mesostrato........53 C3

DRINKING
Fagotto Jazz Bar..........................54 B2

Synagogi.......................................55 C3
Ta Duo Lux...................................56 E2

ENTERTAINMENT
Café Kriti......................................57 E2

SHOPPING
Carmela..58 B2
Food Market.................................59 D4
Miden Agan..................................60 D3
Paraoro..61 B3
Roka Carpets................................62 B3

TRANSPORT
Bus Station...................................63 C5
Buses to Souda............................64 D4
Europrent.....................................65 C4
Tellus Travel.................................66 C4

To Limnoupolis
Water Park (7km);
Trekking Plan;
Agia Marina (8km);
Platanias (11km);
Theriso (15km);
Lakki (24km);
Kissamos (41km);
Xyloskalo (44km)

Plateia
1866

Plateia
Hortatson

Plateia
Markopoulou

To Hospital
(4km)

Town Hall

POST

Post office (☎ 28210 28445; Peridou 10; ⊗ 7.30am-8pm Mon-Fri, 7.30am-2pm Sat)

TOURIST INFORMATION & TRAVEL AGENCIES

Municipal Tourist Information Office (☎ 28210 36155; tourism@chania.gr; Kydonias 29; ⊗ 8am-2.30pm) Provides information and maps. The Old Harbour's information booth operates between noon and 2pm.

Tellus Travel (☎ 28210 91500; Halidon 108; www .tellustravel.gr; ⊗ 8am-11pm) Hires out cars, changes money, arranges air and boat tickets, accommodation and excursions.

Sights

MUSEUMS

Hania's **Archaeological Museum** (☎ 28210 90334; Halidon 30; admission €2, incl Byzantine collection €3; ⊗ 8.30am-3pm Tue-Sun), in the impressive 16th-century Venetian Church of San Francisco, is marked by a Turkish fountain attesting to its former incarnation as a mosque. Its collection of finds from western Crete dating from the Neolithic to the Roman era includes statues, vases, jewellery, three splendid floor mosaics and some impressive painted sarcophagi from Armeni's Late Minoan cemetery.

The **Naval Museum** (☎ 28210 91875; Akti Koundourioti; admission €3; ⊗ 9am-4pm), housed in the headland's Firkas Fortress (once a Turkish prison) exhibits model ships dating from the Bronze Age, naval instruments, paintings, photographs and Battle of Crete memorabilia. Similarly, the **Maritime Museum of Crete** (☎ 28210 91875; Akti Defkaliona; ⊗ 10am-3pm, 7-10.30pm), housed in the former Venetian shipyards, documents ancient and traditional shipbuilding.

The **Byzantine & Post Byzantine Collection of Hania** (☎ 28210 96046; Theotokopoulou; admission €2, incl Archaeological Museum €3; ⊗ 8.30am-3pm Tue-Sun), in the fortress' restored Church of San Salvatore, contains a fascinating collection of artefacts, icons, jewellery and coins, including a fine mosaic floor and a prized icon of St George slaying the dragon.

The **Cretan House Folklore Museum** (☎ 28210 90816; Halidon 46; admission €2; ⊗ 9.30am-3pm & 6-9pm) contains traditional crafts and implements, including weavings.

Some 1.5km away in the Halepa neighbourhood, the **Eleftherios Venizelos Residence & Museum** (☎ 28210 56008; Plateia Helena Venizelou; admission €2; ⊗ 10.30am-1.30pm & 6.30-9pm Mon-Fri,

CRETE

10.30am-1.30pm Sat & Sun) preserves the great statesman's home in splendid fashion, with original furnishings, maps and other information. Staff provide a guided tour. Take a public bus, or taxi (€3 to €6) to get there. Hours are reduced in winter.

OTHER ATTRACTIONS

Hania's massive **Venetian Fortifications** are impressive. Best preserved is the western wall, running from the **Firkas Fortress** to the **Siavo Bastion**. The bastion offers good views of the Old Town (enter through the Naval Museum).

The restored Venetian **lighthouse** at the entrance to the harbour is a 1.5km walk around the sea wall. On the inner harbour's eastern side, the prominent **Mosque of Kioutsouk Hasan** (also called Mosque of Janissaries) holds regular art exhibitions. Along the eastern waterfront, the hulking **Venetian Shipyards** (in Greek, 'neoria') languish, mostly unrepaired, though the easternmost portion is now the Maritime Museum. Although one can only gaze at these massive, somewhat Gothic-looking arched structures from without, their impressive size reaffirms La Serenissima's erstwhile maritime might.

The well-restored Venetian **Great Arsenal** houses the **Centre for Mediterranean Architecture**, which hosts regular events and exhibitions. Similarly, Hania's **Municipal Art Gallery** (☎ 28210 92294; www.pinakothiki-chania.gr; Halidon 98; ☯ 10am-2pm & 7-10pm Mon-Fri, 10am-2pm Sat; admission €2, Wed free) hosts exhibitions of modern Greek art.

The restored **Etz Hayyim Synagogue** (Parodos Kondylaki; ☎ 28210 86286; www.etz-hayyim-hania.org; ☯ 10am-8pm Tue-Fri, 5pm-8pm Sun, 10am-3pm & 5-8pm Mon) memorialises Hania's former Jewish population, victims of the Nazi occupation.

Just up from the eastern waterfront, the formerly Turkish **Splantzia quarter** is a relaxing spot, where the colourful, narrow streets and leafy squares now host boutique hotels, galleries, cafes and bars.

Here, on Daliani, stands one of Hania's two remaining **minarets**; the other, past a *kafeneio* on Plateia 1821, is quite memorably attached to the **Church of Agios Nikolaos** (Plateia 1821; ☯ 7am-noon & 4-7pm). Towering over the church's opposite end is a belltower. Strung along in the air across the centre of it all are flapping, intertwined flags of Greece and Byzantium, a cheery display of blues and yellows that seems to festively reassert the final victory of Orthodoxy over both former occupiers, the schismatic Venetians and the infidel Turks.

The church's foundations were laid in 1205 by Venetians, but Franciscan monks (in 1320) can probably be credited with the massive structure's curving ceiling and array of stained-glass windows, which filter a beautiful, kaleidoscopic flood of colour across the floor in late afternoon. In 1645 the Ottoman's made the church into a mosque, but the Orthodox Church recovered it in 1918.

Finally, the **Ancient Kydonia** site east of the old harbour has few remains, though excavations continue.

Activities

EOS (☎ 28210 44647; www.eoshanion.gr; Tzanakaki 90), the Greek Mountaineering Association's local branch, gives info about serious treks and climbs in the Lefka Ori, mountain refuges and the Trans-European E4 trail. It runs weekend excursions.

Friendly, English-speaking **Manolis Mesarchakis** (☎ 69769 92921; mesarchas@yahoo.gr), an alpine ski instructor and hiker, provides valuable information and can help arrange guided trips for those hungry for outdoors challenges tougher than the Samaria Gorge (see also the boxed text, p255).

Trekking Plan (☎ 28210 60861; www.cycling.gr), 8km west in Agia Marina, organises treks to the Agia Irini and Imbros gorges, climbs of Mt Gingilos, mountain-bike tours, canyoning, rappelling, rock climbing and kayaking trips. **Alpine Travel** (☎ 28210 50939; www.alpine.gr; Boniali 11-19) also organises treks.

Blue Adventures Diving (☎ 28210 40608; www .blueadventuresdiving.gr; Arholeon 11) offers a PADI certification course (€370) and daily diving trips (two dives €80), including beginner dives. Snorkelling and cruise options are offered too. Some of the popular dives take place just 6km west of Hania and include sea cave visits where unique endemic pink coral can be seen and seals occasionally visit.

Hania for Children

The **public garden**, between Tzanakaki and Dimokratias, has a playground, a shady cafe, and a small **zoo** with two *kri-kri* (endemic Cretan wild goats). The giant water park **Limnoupolis** (☎ 28210 33246; Varypetro; day pass adult/ child 6-12yr €17/12, afternoon pass €12/9; ☯ 10am-7pm) south of town is also entertaining. Buses leave regularly from the bus station (€1.70).

Tours

Boat excursions to the nearby **Agii Theodorou and Lazaretto islets**, and across the Gulf of Hania, leave from the harbour. The **M/S Irini** (☎ 28210 52001; cruises €15, sunset cruises €8, child under 7yr free) runs daily cruises on a lovely 1930s cruiser, including free snorkelling gear, and sunset cruises with complimentary fruit and *raki*. However, the advertised glass-bottomed boat tours aren't worth it.

Sleeping

Hania has evocative and memorable digs – you may linger longer than expected. However, if planning to visit out of high season, check ahead as many places may not operate year-round.

BUDGET

Hania Camping (☎ 28210 31138; camhania@otenet.gr; Agii Apostoli; caravan/camp sites per adult/child/tent €7/5/4; **P** 🅖 🌊), 3km west of town on the beach, is shaded and has a restaurant, bar and mini-market and pool. Take a Kalamaki Beach bus (every 15 minutes) from the southeast corner of Plateia 1866.

Pension Theresa (☎ /fax 28210 92798; Angelou 2; r €40-50; 🌊 🛜) Run by the kindly retired doctor Georgios Nikitas, this creaky old house with a steep spiral staircase and antique furniture oozes atmosphere. Some rooms have a view, though the best is from the rooftop terrace (which has a communal kitchen). Rooms have TV, air-con and lofts with an extra bed, though some are snug. It's small, so book ahead.

Monastiri Pension (☎ /fax 28210 41032; Agiou Markou 18 & Kanevarou; d & tr €40-65; 🌊) This older budget place has a stone arched entry and antique family furniture in the communal area. Bathrooms are a basic add-on, but rooms have fridge and some have air-con. The front rooms have sea-view balconies.

Vranas Studios (☎ 28210 58618; www.vranas.gr; Agion Deka 10; studio €40-70; 🌊 🖳) Vranas has spacious, immaculate self-catering studios with polished wooden floors, balconies, and all mod cons (plus an internet cafe attached).

Casa Veneta Studios & Apartments (☎ 28210 90007; www.casa-veneta.gr; Theotokopoulou 57; studio/apt €50/60; ☾ April-Oct; 🛜) This old-town place has new, freshly painted self-catering rooms on three levels, and friendly service. Wi-fi works in the reception area. Prices drop in low season.

Pension Lena (☎ 28210 86860; lenachania@hotmail .com; Ritsou 5; s/d €35/55; 🌊) This friendly pension in an old Turkish building has a cosy, old-world feel with scattered antiques; the front rooms are best.

Also recommended is **Mme Bassia Rooms for Rent** (☎ /fax 28210 55087; Betolo 49; d/tr €50/65; 🌊), with classy rooms in the Old Town and friendly service. Other hole-in-the-wall budget places can be found by pounding the pavement.

MIDRANGE

Ifigenia Rooms, Studios & Suites (☎ 28210 94357; www.ifigeniastudios.gr; Gamba 23 & Parodos Agelou; studio/ste €50/150; 🌊) These six refurbished Old Town houses run from simple rooms to fancy suites with kitchenettes, Jacuzzis and views. Some bathrooms are very basic and the decor's a little contrived. A new suite for couples has Jacuzzi and rooftop terrace, though opening the heavy entrance hatch while standing on the spiral staircase below requires considerable dexterity.

Ionas Hotel (☎ 28210 55090; www.ionashotel.com; Sarpaki & Sorvolou; d incl breakfast €60-80; ste incl buffet breakfast €130; 🌊 🛜) This boutique hotel in the quiet but hip Splantzia quarter has a contemporary design. Rooms have all mod cons and there's a rooftop terrace.

Madonna Studios & Apartments (☎ 28210 94747; madonnastudios@yahoo.co.uk; Gamba 33; studio €70-110; 🌊) This charming pension has five traditionally furnished studios with unique individual touches, set around a lovely flower-filled courtyard.

Nostos Hotel (☎ 28210 94743; www.nostos-hotel .com; Zambeliou 42-46; s/d/tr incl breakfast €60/80/120; 🌊) A renovated 600-year-old Venetian building, the superlative Nostos has split-level self-catering rooms; balcony rooms have harbour views.

ourpick Hotel Doma (☎ 28210 51772; www .hotel-doma.gr; Venizelos 124; s/d/tr/ste incl breakfast from €65/90/120/150; ☾ 1 Apr-31 Oct; 🌊). If ever there was a place where one could retreat to write a mystery-suspense novel, this would be it. Long a refuge for famous writers, politicos and actors, the hotel's singularity lies in the original wood floors and furnishings, scattered antiquities, flowering back garden, and even a collection of exotic Asian headdresses. Although it's a 20-minute walk from the centre, public buses serve Halepa (it's at the Attika stop), and there's street parking behind. The

CRETE

MEMORIES OF VENIZELOS

Few people can boast a family home like that of Rena and Ioanna Koutsoudakis. Built in the early 20th century as the Austro-Hungarian Empire's consulate, when Ottoman rule had just ended, it was later purchased by their family and leased to the British in August 1940, who reprised its diplomatic role. During WWII the building was reappropriated by the Germans (less subtly – a bomb in the garden blew out the windows). Then, in 1947, the Koutsoudakis' recovered it – promptly leasing it again to the British.

The Brits left in 1955, however, and the family home would become the Hotel Doma (p249), high in the Halepa district, overlooking the sea and the busy boulevard named after Eleftherios Venizelos, under whose stewardship Greece dramatically enlarged its northern and Aegean territories.

After the catastrophic Megali Idea ('Great Idea') led to the abrupt termination of 2000 years of Greek civilisation in Anatolia, Venizelos returned from a Parisian retirement to lead the Greek delegation that signed the 1923 Treaty of Lausanne, mandating the Greek-Turkish population exchanges. He later served as prime minister again, but died in Paris.

Venizelos experienced a second exile but spent many of his final years in Hania. Kyria Rena recalls Venizelos, then quite old, walking past on his morning constitutional. 'I was a little girl then,' she says, 'and my sister, who was then only two years old, would always rush to the window, at just the moment he would pass by every morning – we would wave excitedly and he would smile; he always waved back.'

She also recalls that one year, on Venizelos' name day, his political supporters promenaded past her house on the way to his home, 'carrying an enormous cake they had baked – of course, in the shape of Crete'.

Despite the partisanship that has chronically marked Greek politics, and other political factions' voluble opposition to Venizelos, when he died in 1936, at 72, there was a great outpouring of grief. In Hania, people hung black in their balconies. 'I remember that many men from the villages came in traditional dress, with knives on their belts, and my mother taking us to Agia Magdalini Church, where Venizelos was lying in state,' recalls Kyria Rena. 'When it was our turn to look in the coffin, she said to me, "Daughter, I want you to look very carefully, for this was a very great man. Look, and don't forget him!" That is a moment I have always remembered.'

---

front-facing rooms and breakfast hall enjoy sea views, while the top-floor suite has its own rooftop terrace, with kaleidoscopic views.

Porto de Colombo (☎ 28210 70945; colompo@otenet. gr; cnr Theofanous & Moshou; d/ste incl breakfast €90/115; ✖) This Venetian mansion that became the French embassy and Venizelos' office is now a charming boutique hotel with 10 well-appointed rooms; the top suites enjoy fine harbour views.

TOP END

Amphora Hotel (☎ 28210 93224; www.amphora.gr; Parodos Theotokopoulou 20; d with view €140, ste €165; ✖) This immaculately restored Venetian mansion boasts elegantly decorated rooms, the best being in the main wing, with harbour views. Rooms without a view are cheaper, though all could do with a fridge. Breakfast is €10 extra.

Casa Leone (☎ 28210 76762; www.casa-leone.com; Parodos Theotokopoulou 18; r incl breakfast €130-170; ✖) This classy former Venetian residence offers

spacious, airy rooms, with balconies overlooking the harbour.

Casa Delfino (☎ 28210 93098; www.casadelfino.com; Theofanous 7; d & apt incl breakfast €200-325; ✖) The famous Casa Delfino is Hania's most luxurious, housed in an elegant 17th-century Old Town mansion. Breakfast is in the splendid pebble-mosaic courtyard.

Eating

Avoid the mediocre, overpriced waterfront tavernas – the Old Town's back streets conceal some of Crete's finest and most atmospheric restaurants.

Bougatsa Shop (bougatsa €2; ☽ 6am-2pm) Hania's most delicious *bougatsa*, made with Crete's sweet *myzithra* cheese, has been served since 1924 at this unassuming hole in the wall, opposite the bus station.

Mesogeiako (☎ 28210 59772; Daliani 36; mezedhes €3-6) Also in Splantzia, this trendy *mezedhopoleio* (restaurant specialising in mezedhes) does excellent Cretan appetisers with a twist. Try the pork meatballs with local *raki*.

Kouzina EPE (Daskalogianni 25; mayirefta €3-7; ☾ noon-8pm) This whimsical little place (the name roughly translates as 'Limited Liability Restaurant') at the edge of the Splantzia quarter serves nourishing and tasty *mayirefta*. Much beloved by locals, it's open only for lunch and early dinners.

Tsikoudadiko To Mesostrato (☎ 28210 72783; Zambeliou 31; mezedhes €4-7) There's great atmosphere within the walls of this 400-year-old roofless Venetian structure. The Tsikoudadiko is serenaded by roving musicians, while the crickets chirp in unison as if applauding from the foliage above. Try the snail, sweet red peppers, and fried mushrooms.

Michelas (☎ 28210 90026; mains €5-8; ☾ 10am-4pm Mon-Sat) Near the meat section of the food market (p252), Michelas is an old classic serving inexpensive and authentic Cretan fare.

To Karnagio (☎ 28210 53366; Plateia Katehaki 8; mains €5-10.50) Near the Great Arsenal, this popular outdoor place does good seafood (try the grilled cuttlefish) and classic Cretan dishes.

Doloma (☎ 28210 51196; Kalergon 8; mayirefta €5.50-7; ☾ Mon-Sat) Set amidst vines and foliage on an outdoor terrace, this harbourside place has excellent traditional specialities.

Tamam (☎ 28210 96080; Zambeliou 49; mains €5.50-8.50) Housed in old Turkish baths, Tamam (meaning 'OK' in Turkish) does excellent vegetarian specialities and eastern-influenced dishes. Try the house salad and the Beyendi chicken with creamy aubergine purée.

ourpick Portes (☎ 28210 76261; Portou 48; mains €6-9) Everyone visiting Hania must dine here at least once. Set along a quiet lane in the Old Town, this excellent little place run by affable Susanna from Limerick serves Cretan treats with flair. Try the divine *gavros* (marinated anchovies) or stuffed fish baked in paper, or the tasty meatballs with leek and tomato. The homemade bread is excellent too.

Ela (☎ 28210 74128; Kondylaki 47; mains €8-18; ☾ noon-1am) This 14th-century building was a soap factory, then a school, distillery and cheese-processing plant. Now Ela serves Cretan specialities like goat with artichokes, while musicians create ambience.

Pigadi tou Tourkou (☎ 28210 54547; Sarpaki 1-3; mains €10-17; ☾ dinner, closed Mon-Tue) This former steam bath includes the well for which it is named (Well of the Turk); the tantalising dishes have similar tastes of the orient, inspired by Crete, Morocco and the Middle East.

Apostolis I & II Taverna (☎ 28210 43470; Akti Enoseos; fish per kilogram up to €65) In the quieter eastern harbour, this two-building *psarotaverna* is well known for its seafood.

Also recommended is the excellent Amphora restaurant below the hotel of the same name.

Drinking & Entertainment

Clubs lie in Platanias and Agia Marina, 11km west of Hania, though the Old Town has lively bars. Sfrantzia's small streets hide hip new emerging favourites.

Synagogi (☎ 28210 96797; Skoufou 15) In a roofless Venetian building and former synagogue, this cool place with dark stone arches is a favourite of young locals.

Fagotto Jazz Bar (☎ 28210 71877; Angelou 16; ☾ 7pm-2am Jul-May) Down inside a restored Venetian building, this cool bar plays jazz and blues. Being indoors, however, it's busiest in winter.

The arty cafe-bar **Ta Duo Lux** (☎ 28210 52519; Sarpidona 8; ☾ 10am-late) is a favourite with the youths, while the rough-and-ready **Café Kriti**

MAGICAL MYZITHRA

People come to Crete just for its distinctive sweet cheese, *myzithra* (made from sheep's or goat's milk). Often hard to find elsewhere, it's the key ingredient in restaurants' *myzithropitakia* (sweet cheese pies) – crunchy, golden-brown triangles filled with the delicious cheese.

Myzithra is also used in *kalitsounies*, soft, circular breakfast pastries, their centres filled with the cheese and flecked with cinnamon. Find them at *zaharoplasteia* (sweet shops) and bakeries.

Local specialities use *myzithra* too. In the southwestern Sfakia area, the thin *Sfakiani pita,* filled with *myzithra* and topped with honey, is a dessert; however, travel just a bit further west, to Paleohora, and you will find your *myzithropitakia* will probably be made of the sour *xynomyzithra,* according to local custom. Whatever you do, don't leave Crete without partaking in this unique and appetising treat.

HANG ON TO YOUR HATS

One of the most dangerous night-time routes in the Hania area is the 10km road between the city and the popular Platanias resort, with its bars and clubs. Haris, a young Cretan man working as a security guard in Hania Hospital's emergency room, finds the sight of so many people with terrible injuries being rushed through every day very stressful.

'Every summer, we have many cases of emergencies, involving both Greeks and tourists, who are brought here after driving motorbikes while drunk,' says Haris. 'Just the other day, four English girls were brought here after crashing their bike while returning from the disco – two had severely broken legs.' Such mishaps, often perhaps avoidable, add to the burden of the already overworked health care system of this small city.

While it would seem like common sense not to jump on a motorbike when intoxicated, in Crete's summer heat it's no surprise that many motorcyclists don't wear their helmets. You won't be stopped by police for this but a helmet here, as anywhere, might mean the difference between life and death. As Haris remarks, 'In the worst of these emergency cases, the victim might fall into a coma or even die, because they didn't wear a helmet. Those are the saddest cases of all.'

So, when preparing to hit the open road on your Cretan vacation, it's a good idea to remember your helmet. And, if you've drunk too much, it won't kill you to spend €10 on a taxi.

(☎ 28210 58661; Kalergon 22; ☺ 8pm-late) has live traditional Cretan music.

Shopping

Zambeliou and Theotokopoulou have excellent shopping, with traditional artisans often plying their trade. Skrydlof is 'leather lane', and the central market is worth perusing. Hania's magnificent covered **food market** (☺ 9am-5pm Mon & Wed, 9am-8pm Tue, Thu & Fri, 9am-2pm Sat) has an excellent assortment of traditional Cretan food and drink, herbs, meats and veg; the market should be seen, even if you aren't buying.

Carmela (☎ 28210 90487; Angelou 7) This exquisite store features original jewellery designs, plus Carmela's unique ceramics using ancient techniques. It also has jewellery and ceramics by leading Greek artists.

Paraoro (☎ 28210 88990; Theotokopoulou 16) This functioning workshop features distinctive, decorative metal boats, and some unique ceramics.

Roka Carpets (☎ 28210 74736; Zambeliou 61) Observe master weaver Mihalis Manousakis at work on his 400-year-old loom, and know you're buying genuine, handwoven rugs and other items.

Miden Agan (☎ 28210 27068; www.midenagan-shop.gr; Daskalogianni 70; ☺ 10am-3.30pm Mon & Wed, ☺ 10am-2.15pm & 6.15-10pm Tue & Thu-Sat) Unique 'house' wine and liquors, along with over 800 Greek wines, are sold at this smattering of foods shops, which also offers local gourmet delights.

Getting There & Away

AIR

Hania's airport (CHQ) is 14km east of town on the Akrotiri Peninsula. Flights only go to/from Athens and Thessaloniki. For flight details, see Island Hopping (p511).

BOAT

For information on ferries from Hania (serving Piraeus only), see Island Hopping (p512). The **port police** (☎ 28210 89240) can also provide ferry information.

Hania's main port is 7km southeast at Souda; frequent buses (€1.15) serve Hania, as do taxis (€8 to €10).

BUS

In summer, buses depart from Hania's **bus station** (KTEL; ☎ 28210 93052) during the week for numerous destinations. See the table, opposite.

Getting Around

Three daily buses serve the airport (€2.60, 20 minutes); taxis cost €18 to €20.

Local blue buses (☎ 28210 27044) meet incoming ferries at Souda port, leaving from outside Hania's food market (€1.30). Buses for western beaches leave from the main bus station.

Halidon has motorcycle-hire outlets, though Agia Marina firms offer competitive rates and can bring cars to Hania. The old town is largely pedestrianised, so find the free parking area near the Firkas Fortress (turn right off Skalidi where the big super-

BUS SERVICES FROM HANIA

Destination	Duration	Fare	Frequency
Elafonisi	2½hr	€9.60	1 daily
Falasarna	1½hr	€6.50	3 daily
Hora Sfakion	1hr 40min	€6.50	3 daily
Iraklio	2¾hr	€10.70	half-hourly
Kissamos	1hr	€4	13 daily
Moni Agias Triadas	30min	€2	2 daily
Omalos (for Samaria Gorge)	1hr	€5.90	3 daily
Paleohora	1hr 50min	€6.50	4 daily
Rethymno	1hr	€6	half-hourly
Sougia	1hr 50min	€6.10	2 daily
Stavros	30min	€1.80	3 daily

market car park is signposted, and continue to the waterfront).

You can hire cars from the following outfits:

Europrent (☎ 28210 27810; Halidon 87)

Tellus Travel (☎ 28210 91500; www.tellustravel.gr; Halidon 108) Also sells aeroplane tickets and runs excursions around the island.

AROUND HANIA

Northeast of Hania, the less visited **Akrotiri Peninsula** hosts the airport, port and a NATO base. Approximately 1500 British, Australian and New Zealand soldiers died here during the Battle of Crete; they are buried at Souda's **military cemetery**. Buses to Souda port leaving from outside the Hania food market pass this solemn place.

Near Akrotiri's northern tip, sandy **Stavros Beach** is good for a dip and famous as the dramatic backdrop for the final dancing scene in *Zorba the Greek*. From Hania, six daily buses serve Stavros beach (€2).

Straight south of Hania, the mountain village of **Theriso** was the site of a 1905 uprising against Crete's Royalist administration, through which Eleftherios Venizelos came to fame. Although the occasional taverna 'Greek night' with bussed-in package tourists can ruin the ambience, it's usually a peaceful place, and the drive passes through wonderful wooded territory. The road hugs the **Theriso Gorge**, good for hiking (check with Hania's EOS, p248).

The road from Hania to Crete's more famous Samaria Gorge (right) is truly spectacular. It heads through orange groves to Fournes, where you fork left to **Meskla**. The main road reaches **Lakki** (a total of 24km from Hania),

an unspoilt Lefka Ori (White Mountains) village with stunning views. Lakki was a centre of resistance against the Turks and later the Germans.

From Lakki, the road continues to **Omalos** and **Xyloskalo**, where the Samaria Gorge starts. Many hikers sleep in Omalos to ensure they'll get the earliest start possible. Here, the big, stone-built **Hotel Exari** (☎ 28210 67180; s/d €20/30) has well-furnished rooms with TV, bathtub and balconies. Owner Yiorgos can drive hikers to Samaria's trailhead and offers luggage delivery to Sougia for groups. Nearby, the **Hotel Gingilos** (☎ 28210 67181; s/d/tr €20/25/35) offers more sparse, but clean and large rooms (the triples are huge), with nice timber furniture and central balcony. Both hotels have tavernas.

The EOS-maintained **Kallergi Hut** (☎ 28210 33199; dm members/nonmembers €10/13), in the hills between Omalos and the Samaria Gorge, makes a good base for exploring Mt Gingilos and surrounding peaks.

SAMARIA GORGE ΦΑΡΑΓΓΙ ΤΗΣ ΣΑΜΑΡΙΑΣ

Although you'll have company (over 1000 people per day in summer), hiking the **Samaria Gorge** (☎ 28210 67179; admission €5; ⏰ 6am-3pm May–mid-Oct), remains an experience to remember. Also remember to check climatic conditions in advance – many aspiring hikers have been disappointed when park officials close Samaria on exceptionally hot days.

At 16km, the Samaria (sah-mah-rih-ah) Gorge is supposedly Europe's longest. Beginning just below the Omalos Plateau, it's carved out by the river that flows between Avlimanakou (1857m) and Volakias (2116m) peaks. Samaria's width varies from 150m to

CRETE

3m, and its containing cliffs reach 500m in height. Numerous wild flowers bloom in April and May.

Samaria also shelters endangered species like Crete's beloved wild goat, the *kri-kri*. Surviving in the wild only here, the islet of Dia, north of Iraklio, and on the eastern islet of Kri-Kri, near Agios Nikolaos, the *kri-kri* is shy and seldom seen. To save it from extinction, the gorge became a national park in 1962.

Hiking the Gorge

You can start early (before 8am) to avoid crowds, though even the first morning bus from Hania can be packed; sleeping in Omalos (p253) and getting an early lift from there allows you to get your toe on the line for the starting gun. Camping is forbidden, so time your trek (from 4½ to six hours) to finish by closing time (3pm).

Wear good hiking boots, and take sunscreen, sunglasses, hat and water bottle (springs with good water exist, though not the main stream). If it's too hard within the first hour, donkey-equipped park wardens can take you back. Look out for the elusive *kri-kri*, and for falling rocks; people have died from the latter (and from foolishly wandering off the main trail into the remote mountains).

You'll begin at **Xyloskalo**, named for the steep stone pathway flanked by wooden rails that enters the gorge, and finish at **Agia Roumeli** on the southern coast. In spring, wading through a stream is sometimes necessary; in summer, when the flow drops, the streambed rocks become stepping stones.

The gorge is wide for the first 6km, until the abandoned village of **Samaria**; its inhabitants were relocated when the gorge became a national park. Just south stands a small church dedicated to **Saint Maria of Egypt**, the gorge's namesake.

The going then narrows and becomes more dramatic until, at the 11km mark, the canyon walls shrink to only 3.5m apart – the famous **Iron Gates** (Sidiroportes). A rickety wooden pathway takes you 20m across the water to the other side. At 12.5km, the gorge ends north of almost abandoned **Old Agia Roumeli**. From here the final 2km hike to Agia Roumeli is less exciting, though most hikers will at that point just be anticipating the refreshing dip they'll take at this relaxed seaside village.

From Agia Roumeli, hikers must take a boat; most go to Sougia (and from there to

Hania by bus), though you can also reach Hora Sfakio, Loutro and Paleohora.

Agia Roumeli also has accommodation and eating, should you wish to stay over. **Farangi Restaurant** (☎ 28250 91225; mains €5-8.50) has excellent Cretan specials and rents simple but clean rooms (double/triple €30/35; air-conditioned) above, while **Gigilos Taverna & Rooms** (☎ 28250 91383; gigilos@mycosmos.gr; s/d/tr €30/35/45; ✿ ▣) on the beach has nicely furnished rooms with bathrooms, and a communal fridge. The taverna (mains €5 to €7) has a relaxing beachfront terrace.

Getting There & Away

Samaria Gorge excursions are organised by innumerable travel agencies and resorts across Crete. 'Samaria Gorge Long Way' is the regular trek from Omalos, while 'Samaria Gorge Easy Way' starts at Agia Roumeli, looping back at the Iron Gates. However, going independently, ideally from Hania or Omalos itself, is cheaper and allows more options.

Hania–Omalos buses to Xyloskalo (Omalos; €5.90, 1½ hours) leave from Hania at 6.15am, 7.30am, and 8.30am. A direct bus to Xyloskalo from Paleohora in the southwest (€5.50, 1½ hours) leaves at 6.15am.

When you finish the hike in Agia Roumeli, two daily afternoon boats to Hora Sfakion (€7.50, one hour, 3.45pm and 6pm) via Loutro (€7, 45 minutes) are timed to meet buses going back to Hania. A morning boat also runs from Paleohora to Hora Sfakion, via Agia Roumeli, if you end up sleeping over.

Alternatively, take the boat west to Paleohora (€14, 1½ hours) at 4.45pm, via Sougia (€8, 45 minutes). The **ticket office** (☎ 28250 91251) is on the port.

HORA SFAKION ΧΩΡΑ ΣΦΑΚΙΩΝ
pop 350

The more bullet holes you see in the passing road signs, the closer you are to Hora Sfakion (*ho-rah sfah-kee-*on). This eccentric, laid-back fishing port, a stopping-off point for returning Samaria Gorge hikers, is (along with Anogia) the island's most proudly 'Cretan' town. And, when surveying the barren moonscape of the surrounding territory (known as Sfakia), you do have to give the Sfakians credit; not only have they survived for time eternal in this inhospitable terrain, they also built a fighting force of extraordinary magnitude, keeping the Turks out for centuries.

EPIC ADVENTURES IN THE CRETAN WILDS

If you think Samaria is for wimps, head for the lesser-visited gorges south of Hania. They offer unparallelled opportunities for mountain treks, caving, rock climbing and even skiing in winter – though even seasoned pros will need local information and advice to ensure their safety and get the best from their experience.

The **Anavasi hiking maps**, marked with GPS coordinates, trails and other key details, are essential; most bookshops recommended in this guide sell them. Another book found mostly in Hania bookshops, *The Caves of Hania*, is recommended by local cavers.

Manolis Mesarchakis (p248), an alpine ski instructor and avid hiker from Hania, can help arrange hiking tours and cross-country ski tours (ski tours with three weeks' advance notice; €100) and advise serious outdoors adventurers. Hikers should also consult the **EOS** (p248) in Hania, which provides info, does weekend excursions and arranges stays in mountain refuges.

One of Manolis' favourite hikes is the 10-hour trek from Omalos to Sougia, via the **Trypiti Gorge**. This stunning canyon near Mt Gingilos, west of Samaria, sees few visitors – perfect for those seeking unspoilt nature. If you want to break the hike up into two days, there's a mountain hut along the way.

The sheer rock face of the **Klados Gorge**, running between and parallel to Trypiti and Samaria, 'offers exceptional rock climbing and rappelling', says Manolis. The outdoorsman also notes that 'Crete is a paradise for caving, with over 10,000 caves, including the deepest in Europe, at 1207m deep'.

Although few would expect sweltering Crete to be a ski destination, there's heavy snow in the high mountains, even until May. However, there are no resorts and no lifts, meaning you'll be doing old-school skiing on wild, unroped terrain. If you're capable of doing this stuff, you'll probably already know to bring your own equipment.

Indeed, after the rest of the island had fallen to the Ottomans, only Sfakia held out (possibly because there was nothing worth conquering in the rocky mountain region). National hero and insurrectionist Ioannis Daskalogiannis was born in the Sfakian village of Anopoli. To this day, the Sfakians cling fiercely to their local customs, culture and dialect; while most Cretans are content to simply assert that they are the best of the Greeks, Sfakia people consider themselves the best of the Cretans – and that's saying something.

Despite its small size, Hora Sfakion makes a relaxing and convenient base for western adventures, with some tasty seafood tavernas and rooms. It's also useful for catching boats further west, or south to Gavdos.

Orientation & Information

The ferry quay is at Hora Sfakion's eastern side, while water taxis leave from the western side; beyond the latter is the decent town beach.

On the eastern bluff, near the ferry ticket booth, a monument commemorates where the last British, Australian and New Zealand soldiers were evacuated after the WWII Battle of Crete. There are lovely views of the village wrapped up by its sheltering bay from here.

Buses leave from the square; if driving, park here, as vehicles aren't allowed on the waterfront promenade, where seafront tavernas and shops stretch under a long trellis that keeps the street shady. The **post office** (7am-2pm) is on the square. There are two ATMs.

Just in from the promenade's eastern side, Englishwoman Maxine Kolioveta owns a nameless, unmarked **souvenir shop** (6970414023; 9am-3pm). Among other unique gifts sold here, she does lovely, hand-etched cards, decorated with traditional Cretan motifs like violins and fishing boats.

Maxine also carries an engaging new book, *In Sfakia: Passing Time in the Wilds of Crete* (Lycabettus Press, 2008). Written by British linguist and long-time visitor Peter Trudgill, this easygoing narrative recounts the author's experiences with the proud Sfakians since the mid-1970s, and is very informative for local history. For those keen on Greek linguistics, a book consisting of about 200 pages of unique Sfakian dialect terms and phrases – some dating to Venetian, Byzantine and even Ancient Greek times – is sold here, too.

CRETE

Sleeping & Eating

Hora Sfakion has a few hotels and domatia. Its waterfront tavernas are fairly similar, and specialise in fresh fish. Be sure to try the *Sfakiani pita* (sfakian pie) – a thin, circular pie with sweet *myzithra* cheese and flecked with honey.

Rooms Stavris (☎ 28250 91220; stavris@sfakia-crete.com; s/d €25/35; ✷) On the port's western side, this place has clean, basic rooms, most of them self-catering.

our pick **Xenia Hotel** (☎ 28250 91490, 6972120547; xenia-sfakion@otenet.gr; s/d €40/45; ✷) Friendly Giorgos Lykogiannakis' runs this excellent hotel, ideally set between the harbour and the beach on Sfakia's western side. All 17 of the spacious, airy rooms have sea-view balconies, and bathrooms are modern and well kept. Stairs lead down to the hotel's pebbled sunbathing patio; for swimmers, there's a ladder on the rocks below here, leading into the sea.

Getting There & Away

BOAT

For boat tickets, see the **booths** (☎ 28250 91221) in the car park and on the eastern bluff. In summer, a daily boat serves Paleohora (€11, three hours) via Loutro, Agia Roumeli and Sougia. Four additional boats reach Agia Roumeli (€7.50, one hour) via Loutro (€4, 15 minutes). Summertime boats (€12, 1½ hours) serve Gavdos Island on Friday, Saturday and Sunday at 11.30am.

Local fishermen run **water taxis** upon request to local destinations like Sweet Water Beach and Loutro, generally from the western harbour; enquire at the taverna below the Xenia Hotel.

BUS

Four daily buses connect Hora Sfakion with Hania (€6.50, two hours), the afternoon ones at 5.30pm and 7pm timed to meet incoming boats from Agia Roumeli. Two daily buses in summer serve Rethymno via Vryses (€6.50, one hour), and two more reach Frangokastello Beach (€1.50, 25 minutes). However, no buses serve Plakias or other points further east of this beach.

AROUND HORA SFAKION

A bit beyond town, the famous **Sweet Water Beach** (in Greek, Glyka Nera) has tranquil, lapping waters. Inexpensive taxi boats go there from Hora Sfakion.

Another relaxing escape is **Loutro**, a former fishing village west of town, and southern Crete's only natural port. There's no road, but boats heading west stop there. Merely a collection of white-and-blue domatia glittering around a tiny beach set against mountains, Loutro always maintains its happily isolated feel, even when busy in high summer. For overnights, try the **Blue House** (☎ 28250 91127; bluehouseloutro@chania-cci.gr; d from €45; ✷), with its spacious, well-appointed rooms with sea-facing verandas. The downstairs taverna serves excellent *mayirefta* (€5 to €8), including local specialities.

FRANGOKASTELLO ΦΡΑΓΚΟΚΑΣΤΕΛΛΟ
pop 150

One of Crete's best beaches lies just below the equally magnificent 14th-century fortress of **Frangokastello**, 15km east of Hora Sfakion. The Venetians built it to guard against pirates and feisty Sfakians, who rebelled from the beginning of the occupation. This history has generated a ghastly legend. On 17 May 1828, during the War of Independence, many Cretan fighters were killed here by the Turks. According to legend their ghosts – the '*drosoulites*' – march along the beach each year on the battle's anniversary.

The wide, packed white-sand **beach** beneath the fortress slopes gradually into shallow warm water, making it ideal for kids. On calm days it's delightful, but when the wind's up, flying sand will chase you off quickly. There is one shaded cafe on the beach, but it's otherwise placid.

A few domatia line the main road. **Oasis** (☎ /fax 28250 92136; www.oasisrooms.com), on the western side, offers spacious self-catering rooms set in a lovely garden, and its taverna does excellent Cretan dishes (€6 to €10).

Two daily buses from Hora Sfakion reach Frangokastello (€2).

ANOPOLI & INNER SFAKIA ΑΝΟΠΟΛΗ & ΜΕΣΑ ΣΦΑΚΙΑ

A zigzagging asphalt road winding northwest from Hora Sfakion leads, after 14km, to historic Anopoli (ah-*no*-po-lee). Now a tiny, sparsely settled village in Sfakia's stony interior, Anopoli was once prosperous and powerful, and the birthplace of revolutionary leader Ioannis Daskalogiannis. This dashing character, known for his bravery, even hobnobbed with Russian royalty and

CRETE

in 1770 organised the first Cretan insurrection against the Turks. However, the promised Russian reinforcements never came and Daskalogiannis surrendered himself to save his followers; he was skinned alive in Iraklio.

Today a white statue of Daskalogiannis stands conspicuously on Anopoli's square; here, the heartily recommended **Platanos** (☎ 28250 91169; www.anopolis-sfakia.com; mains €4-9) serves excellent local specialities like roast lamb, wild greens and, of course, *Sfakiani pita* (cheese pie with *myzithra* and honey). English-speaking owner Eva Kopasis, who also rents simple **rooms** (s/d €25/30; ✿) year-round, is a proud Sfakian and provides information on local activities.

One such activity is the 1½-hour (3.5km-long) hike to the sea through the **Aradena Gorge**. The trail is signposted before the bridge leading to Aradena, on the road west from town. Alternatively, you can park in Anopoli and walk 3km to the trail head. The route is moderately difficult, ending at the lovely **Marmara Beach**. You can return to Anopoli, or go to nearby Loutro and return to Hora Sfakion by boat.

Nonhikers can drive on to **Aradena**, a small, undisturbed hamlet with a rather precarious wood-and-steel bridge that ripples as you cross it. There are great views into the gorge from here. At the end of the road lies the early Byzantine **Church of Agios Ioannis**; this whitewashed structure stands serene amidst the stones of Sfakia, but is unfortunately rarely open.

From here, a hiking path leads to the sea, forking either west to Agia Roumeli (via the Byzantine Church of Agios Pavlos, with stunning views), or east to Marmara Beach and Loutro. Before attempting such hikes, however, it's best to consult local experts (see the boxed text, p255).

If arriving by public transport, take the bus from Hora Sfakion to Anopoli at 4pm (€3, 30 minutes), which originates in Hania. The morning bus from Anopoli returns to Hora Sfakion at 6.30am, and then continues directly to Hania. Alternatively, taxis between the two cost €20.

For other forays into inner Sfakia, head north from Hora Sfakion on the main road that leads to Vryses. This breathtaking tour passes through the eastern Lefka Ori, with the stunning, 8km-long **Imbros Gorge** (admission €2) running parallel to the road on the western side. You'll soon reach the village of **Imbros**, which accesses this lesser-visited gorge; the trail ends at **Komitades** village. From here, it's a 5km walk to Hora Sfakion, or take a taxi (€20).

All Hania–Hora Sfakion buses can stop in Imbros.

SOUGIA ΣΟΥΓΙΑ
pop 110

Sougia (*soo-yah*), 67km south of Hania and on the ferry route between Hora Sfakion and Paleohora, is a tiny, laid-back beach resort with a curving sand-and-pebble beach. Archaeological remains on its eastern end, which prohibit development, have happily kept Sougia quiet. This sort-of resort has a few rooms, tavernas, lazy beach bars and two beach clubs. Campers and nudists accumulate towards the beach's eastern end.

Information

The bus stop is outside the Santa Irene Hotel, and there's an ATM. **Internet Lotos** (☎ 28230 51191; per hr €3) works from 7am until late.

Sleeping

Aretousa (☎ 28230 51178; fax 28230 51178; s/d/studio €35/40/45; ✿) This lovely, modern pension on the Hania road has comfortable, well-equipped rooms, plus self-catering studios.

Captain George (☎ 28230 51133; g-gentek@otenet .gr; r/studio/tr €35/40/50; P ✿ ⬛) Attractive, good value rooms and studios in a lovely garden with a resident *kri-kri*. The owner runs taxi-boat trips to nearby Lissos and other beaches.

Arhontiko (☎ 28230 51200; r €40-50; ✿) Behind the supermarket, Arhontiko has spacious, attractive new studios and apartments – good for longer stays.

Eating

Taverna Rembetiko (☎ 28230 51510; mezedhes €3-5) This popular place has good Cretan dishes, and great atmosphere with its traditional Greek music.

Polyfimos (☎ 28230 51343; mains €5-8; ✆ dinner) Tucked off the Hania road behind the police station, ex-hippie Yianni makes his own oil, wine and *raki* and even makes dolmadhes (vine leaves stuffed with rice and sometimes meat) from the vines that cover the shady courtyard.

CRETE

Getting There & Away

A daily bus operates between Hania and Sougia (€6.10, two hours), while morning boats leave Sougia for Agia Roumeli (€6.30, 1¾ hours), Loutro (€10, 1½ hours) and Hora Sfakion (€11, 1¾ hours). An evening boat at 5.15pm heads west to Paleohora (€7, one hour).

PALEOHORA ΠΑΛΑΙΟΧΩΡΑ

pop 2210

There' still a vaguely 1972 feel about Paleohora (pal-ee-o-*hor*-a), though its former hippie days are long over. This erstwhile fishing port is still a proud Cretan town, though, and an excellent place to enjoy authentic Cretan live music in summer. It has noticeable though low-key tourism, with two good beaches and accommodation ranging from camping grounds to small hotels. On summer evenings, tavernas fill the pretty pedestrianised streets and a couple of lively bars operate.

Although Paleohora gets a few European package tourists, including some families, it's probably Crete's most ambivalent resort. You might hear elderly domatia owners chattering in the back streets, asking rhetorically when the tourists will leave and give them back their peace and quiet. In fact, this relatively large town keeps awake during the winter, and is southwest Crete's unofficial capital.

Orientation & Information

Paleohora lies on a narrow peninsula, with a long sandy beach exposed to the wind on one side, and a sheltered pebbly beach on the other. The main street, Eleftheriou Venizelou, runs north–south. Three ATMs and a laundry are on the main drag. The post office is at Pahia Ammos Beach's northern end. Boats leave from the old harbour at the beach's southern end.

Erato Internet (☎ 28230 83010; Eleftheriou Venizelou; per hr €2)

Notos Rentals (☎ 28230 42110; www.notoscar.com; Eleftheriou Venizelou; per hr €2; ☼ 8am-10pm)

Tourist information office (☎ 28230 41507; ☼ 10am-1pm & 6-9pm Wed-Mon May-Oct)

Sights & Activities

From the elevated ruins of Paleohora's 13th-century **Venetian castle** there are great views of the sea and mountains. The castle's strategic location meant it was frequently attacked over the centuries, and little remains today.

From Paleohora, the E4 **coastal path** leads to Sougia (six hours), passing remnants of

ancient **Lissos**. Hiking the Samaria and Agia Irini Gorge from Paleohora is possible either through organised tours or the public bus service, returning by ferry.

Dolphin-watching trips (€16) and excursions to **Elafonisi Beach** (€7, one hour) are offered by travel agencies, like the friendly and helpful **Selino Travel** (☎ 28230 42272; selino2@otenet.gr) and **Tsiskakis Travel** (☎ 28230 42110; www.notoscar.com; Eleftheriou Venizelou). Both offer the usual travel agency services.

Sleeping

Most accommodation closes in the low season.

Camping Paleohora (☎ 28230 41120; camp sites per adult/tent €5/3; **P**) Some 1.5km northeast of town, this is a big but basic camping ground.

Camping Grammeno (☎ 6978388542; www.grammenocamping.gr; camp sites per adult/tent €6/4; **P**) This cheery place, 4km from Paleohora on the beach, has excellent facilities including kids' playground, communal kitchen and barbecue, all backed by a cedar forest.

our pick **Homestay Anonymous** (☎ 28230 41509; www.anonymoushomestay.com; s/d/tr €19/23/28; ☒) There's excellent value at this small pension with clean, well-furnished rooms with exposed-stone wall decor. Friendly owner Manolis is a font of information on the area. Rooms can connect for families.

Oriental Bay Rooms (☎ 28230 41076; s/d/tr €30/35/38; ☒) These immaculate, beachfront rooms are well maintained and fridge-equipped. They have balconies with sea or mountain views.

Votsalo Rooms (☎ 28230 42369; votsalo@mail.gr; d/apt €35/40; ☒) Near Kyma Restaurant on Paleohora's pebble beach, it has simple but clean rooms with relaxing sea views.

Haris Studios (☎ 28230 42438; www.paleochoraholidays .com; d/apt €45/50; ☼ year-round; ☒) These studios, just around the port on the dramatic rocky seafront, are fairly basic, though the upper rooms are better and enjoy great views.

Eating

The only sad thing about eating in Paleohora and the surrounding area is that, unlike the rest of Crete, the *myzithra* cheese used here is not usually sweet – remember when ordering.

Grammeno (☎ 28230 41505; mains €4.50-11) Drive 5km west of Paleohora for no-nonsense Cretan specialities like braised rooster, various wild greens, lamb in vine leaves and tender roast goat.

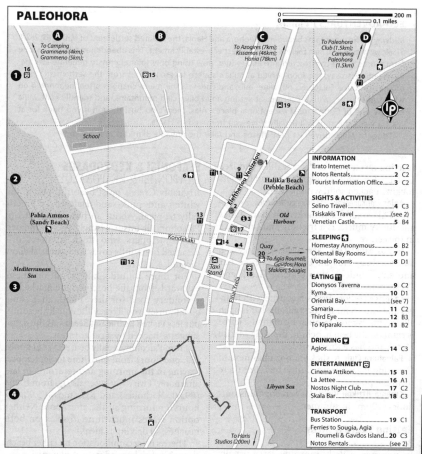

PALEOHORA

CRETE

Dionysos Taverna (☎ 28230 41243; mains €5-8) Excellent *mayirefta,* plus vegetarian dishes and grills, are served at this popular place.

Third Eye (☎ 28230 41234; mains €5-8) A local institution, the Third Eye, Crete's only vegetarian restaurant, has an eclectic menu of curries, salads, pastas and Greek and Asian dishes, plus live music weekly. Just inland from Pahia Ammos.

Oriental Bay (☎ 28230 41322; mains €5-9) This beachside taverna does good vegetarian dishes, like green beans and potatoes, plus meatier fare like 'rooster's kiss' (chicken fillet with bacon) and 'drunk cutlet' (pork chop in red wine).

ourpick Samaria (☎ 28230 41572; mains €8-10; ☽ dinner) Housed in a roofless old stone build-

ing with ambient back courtyard dining, this traditional restaurant serves *mayirefta* and specialities like lamb *tsigatiasto,* and *stamnagkathi,* a kind of greens.

To Kiparaki (☎ 28230 42281; mains €8-11) There's excellent and fresh Asian-style food at this wee Dutch-run place, with but eight tables in a back garden.

Kyma (☎ 28230 41110; top fish per kilogram €40-65) Run by a fisherman, the Kyma is one of Paleohora's more trustworthy places for fresh and fairly priced fish. It has a relaxed beach setting, with tables under the trees.

Drinking & Entertainment

Skala Bar (☎ 28230 41671; www.skalabar.gr; port; ☽ 7am-5am; ☎) A portside classic that has a

---

ECO-ADVENTURES IN MILIA

Midway in the mountains between Paleohora and Hania, the isolated settlement of **Milia** (☎ 28220 51569; www.milia.gr; d from €60) is Crete's coolest eco-establishment. This abandoned village of stone farmhouses was reconstructed into eco-lodges, now using only solar energy to generate electricity. Needless to say, the food served at Milia's superb taverna comes from the settlement's own organic produce, including oil, wine, milk and cheese. (The menu changes often, depending on what's in season.) With a spectacular setting amid olive-clad mountains, and friendly staff, Milia is really one of Crete's most exceptional places. Alas, there's no bus, though if you book for at least a week the staff will usually drive you from and to Hania.

To reach Milia, drive just past **Vlatos** and take the drivable 3km dirt road up to it.

---

relaxing terrace for coffees, waffles and free wi-fi by day, while by night the small bar gets rockin', packed solid with partiers.

Agios (cnr Kondekaki & Eleftheriou Venizelou; ⊗ 9am-3am) This small bar, marked by dark tones and funky music, is a friendly and fun place in the centre.

Nostos Night Club (btwn Eleftheriou Venizelou & the Old Harbour) Has an outdoor terrace bar and small indoor club playing Greek and Western music.

La Jettee (⊗ 9am-2am) A favourite with tourists and known for its cocktails, the bar is open all day, but is most popular by night. La Jettee is right on the beach, behind the Villa Marise Hotel, and has a lovely garden.

Paleohora Club A slick indoor club next to Camping Paleohora; a shuttle bus runs there from the port.

Cinema Attikon (tickets €5) Screens films outdoors (10pm) in summer.

Getting There & Away

BOAT

In summer, a daily morning ferry usually goes to Hora Sfakion (€14, three hours), via Sougia (€7, 50 minutes), Agia Roumeli (€11, 1½ hours) and Loutro (€13, 2½ hours). Three weekly summer boats serve Gavdos (€15, 2½ hours).

BUS

From the **bus station** (☎ 28230 41914), six daily buses serve Hania (€6.50, two hours). A special early bus leaves at 6.15am for Omalos (€5.50, two hours) and the Samaria Gorge, also stopping at the Agia Irini Gorge (€4.50).

Getting Around

Notos Rentals (☎ 28230 42110; www.notoscar.com; Eleftheriou Venizelou) has cars, motorcycles and bicycles for hire.

ELAFONISI & KEDRODASOS
ΕΛΑΦΟΝΗΣΙ & ΚΕΔΡΟΔΑΣΟΣ

Arguably Crete's most beautiful beach, the white- and pink-sand **Elafonisi** is practically tropical. About an hour's drive from Paleohora, it unsurprisingly gets inundated by day-trippers who flock to the semi-detached islets, little coves, and warm, shallow turquoise waters.

For more solitude, hike about one hour eastwards from the beach on the marked E4 secondary road (or drive) and, after some greenhouses, you'll reach the equally beautiful but less visited **Kedrodasos Beach** – as the name suggests, backed by a cedar forest.

From Paleohora a daily boat serves Elafonisi (€7, one hour) from mid-June to September, leaving in the morning and returning in late afternoon. Two daily buses also go from Hania (€9.60, 2½ hours) and Kissamos (€5.90, 1¼ hours), returning in the afternoon. Neither option leaves much time to relax on both beaches, so driving is ideal.

There's no accommodation on either beach, though snack bars operate at Elafonisi.

AZOGIRES ΑΖΟΓΙΡΕΣ
pop 40

It's not known whether the hippies who once frolicked in this mountainside hamlet were sworn to secrecy, but it is surprising that more travellers haven't been turned on to Azogires. In an island full of storied eccentricities, this tranquil village 7km north of Paleohora stands out for its wooded, rock-pool waterfalls haunted by nereids, cave churches where hermits once meditated, and overall positive vibrations. No surprise then that Azogires, set above a stunning eponymous gorge, attracts the occasional foreign yoga and meditation group. If it's solitude you're after, this is the place.

The village also offers plenty of hill walks, tasty local products like olive oil and honey, memorable characters and limited but excellent sleeping and eating options. From Azogires, B-roads also continue to several destinations including Sougia, Omalos and Hania.

Information

Entering Azogires from the south, look left for **Alfa Restaurant** (☎ 28230 41620; Azogires Sq), the centre of local life. Here, American-born local Lakkis 'Lucky' Koukoutsakis can inform you about everything from the village's history to local activities, and also leads village tours. A free village map with all the local sights is available. There are no ATMs in Azogires.

Sights & Activities

Azogires' sights are all relatively close and connected by footpaths or roads. The side of the village west of the main road contains no less than six shrines, the two most revered being the **Holy Fathers' Cave**, accessible along a winding footpath northwest of the village, and **St John the Hermit's Cave**, somewhat closer, above Alpha Rooms. These mediaeval shrines have numerous colourful legends associated with them, and are still credited with miraculous occurrences.

Just across the main road from Alpha Rooms, a short path into the woods leads to a 1m-high **waterfall**, gushing behind deep **rock pools**. Here dazzling sunlight is reflected from the water's surface through a leafy canopy where immense green dragonflies flutter; it's not hard to see why locals have, since ancient times, believed exquisitely beautiful nereids inhabit the falls and can, on certain fatal nights, steal a man's soul. The rock pools make for great swimming by day and, apparently, by night – the place was used in the early 1970s as a sort of open-air disco by the itinerant hippies.

A footpath from here through the woods leads southeast to a lovely **old bridge**; cross it to reach the **Monastery of the Holy Fathers**, with its small **museum** of local ecclesiastical items and icons. Across a narrow road further east are the **Carved Caves of Ancient Azogires**, worth a peek.

You can hike the forested **Azogires Gorge** to Paleohora on shaded but rocky trails (three hours). The hike is moderately difficult, but the trail not well maintained, so enquire locally about current conditions.

The best way to see all the local sights, with some entertaining commentary along the way, is to take a circular **village walking tour** along shaded trails. The tour lasts three to four hours; groups should be between five and 15 people; the price, whatever you feel like paying. Tours are usually led from Alpha Restaurant (below) by the knowledgeable Lakkis 'Lucky' Koukoutsakis, who traces his family roots here to the year 1712; the 26-year-old Lucky's splendidly curving, pencil-thin Cretan moustache appears to date from the same era. This wry amateur historian enlivens his tours with remarkable vignettes about events during Turkish times and WWII, plus information on local customs and traditions, and all the legends surrounding Azogires' sacred sites.

Sleeping & Eating

Alfa Hotel (☎ /fax 28230 41620; alfacafeneion@aol .com; www.alfahotelazogires.blogspot.gr; Azogires; r from €25; P ✗ ☐) Just up from the centre on the main road, the Alfa has clean, modern en suite rooms with balconies facing the far-off sea at Paleohora. Four of the eight rooms have air conditioning. There is a communal kitchen and a washing machine (€3 per load). A big hall is reserved for yoga and meditation groups; the terrace offers magnificent views of the mountains and sea. This tranquil, romantic place is ideal for alternative groups, including hill walkers and birdwatchers.

Alfa Restaurant (☎ 28230 41620; mains €4-6) Part coffee shop, part info centre, part restaurant, this place on the square does excellent local fare and makes a relaxing spot for a drink, too. Intriguing traditional implements and antiques line the walls, and local products like olive oil and honey are sold at very reasonable prices.

Getting There & Away

Azogires is about 15 minutes from Paleohora by car; taxis cost €10.

GAVDOS ISLAND ΝΙΣΙ ΓΑΥΔΟΣ

pop 100

Europe's most southerly point, Gavdos lies 65km south of Paleohora in the Libyan Sea. With but three tiny settlements and a smattering of rooms and tavernas, Gavdos is blissful, boasting several unspoilt beaches – some accessible only by boat. It attracts campers, nudists and free spirits seeking to peace out on balmy beaches under the stars.

Through the 1960s Gavdos had little water, electricity or phone lines. Water is now plentiful, but occasional power outages mean you should take a torch. When winds are too strong, boats won't risk the open-sea journey back to Crete, so always allow a little extra time just in case.

Sarakiniko Studios (☎ 28230 42182; www.gavdo studios.gr; d/tr studio incl breakfast €50/60), above Sarakiniko beach, has comfortable studios, plus new villas sleeping up to five (€80 to €100). Phone ahead for port pick-up or walk 20 minutes north from the port, Karabe.

Boat services to Gavdos vary seasonally, and can take between 1½ and five hours depending on the boat and other stops. The most direct route is from Hora Sfakion on Friday, Saturday and Sunday (€15, 1½ hours). From Paleohora, two weekly boats (increasing to three in high summer) run for €15, though they go via the other southern ports and Hora Sfakion, lengthening the trip.

Only some ferries take cars – enquire ahead if taking one.

Bike and car hire are available at Gavdos' port or in Sarakiniko, though insurance may not be included.

KISSAMOS ΚΙΣΣΑΜΟΣ
pop 3820

A sleepy tourist town sustained by agriculture, northwest-coast Kissamos is known primarily for its ferries to Kythira and the Peloponnese. However, it has a decent town beach, and fine beaches lie along the vast Kissamos Bay opposite. The superlative beaches at Falasarna and Gramvousa are also easily accessible from here.

In antiquity, Kissamos was the capital of an eponymous province. However, it later became called Kastelli, after a Venetian castle built here; the authorities intervened in 1966, ruling that confusion with Crete's other Kastelli (near Iraklio) meant the town should revert to its ancient name. Parts of the castle wall still survive.

Orientation & Information

The port is 3km west of town. In summer, a bus meets ferries; otherwise taxis cost €4 to €6. The bus station's on the main square, Plateia Tzanakaki; east lies the main commercial street, Skalidi, which has ATM-

equipped banks. The post office is on the main through-road. Most tavernas and bars line the seafront promenade.

For online info see www.kissamos.net.

Sights & Activities

Archaeological Museum of Kissamos (☎ 28220 83308; Plateia Tzanakaki; admission free; ☒ 8.30am-3pm) Housed in a Venetian-Turkish building on the square, the museum displays local artefacts, including statues, jewellery, coins and an ancient villa's mosaic floor.

Strata Walking Tours (☎ 28220 24336; www.strata tours.com) Offers easy day trips (€40 including lunch) to full-on 15-day round trips (€895) to the south coast. It also runs jeep safaris to interesting off-road destinations (€40).

Sleeping

Bikakis Family (☎ 28220 22105; www.familybikakis.gr; Iroön Polemiston 1941; s/d/studio €20/25/30; ☒ ☐) This well-run collection of self-catering rooms and studios has good views, and makes an excellent budget choice.

Thalassa (☎ 28220 31231; www.thalassa-apts. gr; Paralia Drapanias; studios €35-55; ☒ ☐ ☎) This isolated complex on the beach offers immaculate, breezy studios with all mod cons. A barbecue stands on the lawn and there's a small playground.

Eating

Kellari (☎ 28220 23883; mains €5-7) On the waterfront's eastern end, Kellari does excellent Cretan dishes, grills and fresh fish. Owned by the same family that runs Strata Walking Tours, it uses its own meat, wine, oil and other produce.

Papadakis (☎ 28220 22340; mains €6-11) One of Kissamos' oldest tavernas, this local favourite is well situated overlooking the beach and does great fish dishes.

Getting There & Away
BOAT

From Kissamos, ferries serve Kythira and Gythio; see Island Hopping (p512) for details.

BUS

From Kissamos' **bus station** (☎ 28220 22035), 14 daily buses serve Hania (€4, 40 minutes). In summer, two daily buses go to Falasarna (€3, 20 minutes), and one to Elafonisi (€5.90, 1¼ hours). One daily bus serves Paleohora (€6.50, 1¼ hours).

Getting Around

Moto Fun (☎ 28220 23440; www.motofun.info; Plateia Tzanakaki) has cars, bikes and mountain bikes for hire.

AROUND KISSAMOS

Some 16km west of Kissamos, **Falasarna** was a 4th-century-BC Greek city-state, though its mysterious place name possibly pre-dates the Greek language itself. Falasarna's long sandy beach is one of Crete's best, comprising several coves separated by rocky spits. Falasarna's end-of-the-world feel is accentuated by spectacular sunsets, when pink hues are reflected from the sand's fine coral.

Falasarna has no settlement, though a few domatia and tavernas stand behind the beach. You can drive, or else there are three buses daily from Kissamos (€3, 20 minutes), or three from Hania (€6.50, one hour).

North of Falasarna, the wild and remote **Gramvousa Peninsula** shelters the stunning **Balos Beach** on its western tip. From the idyllic sands here, you can gaze out at two islets: **Agria** (wild) and **Imeri** (tame).

A rough but drivable dirt road to Balos begins in **Kalyviani** village, and ends at a car park with a *kantina* (snack bar). A path leads down for 30 minutes to the sandy cliffs (the return takes 45 minutes).

West-bound buses from Kissamos leave you at the Kalyviani turn-off; from here it's a 2km walk to the beginning of the path, straight down Kalyviani's main street. The 3km walk to Balos is shadeless, so gear up and take water.

Summertime **boat tours** (☎ 28220 24344; www .gramvousa.com; adult/concession €25/15) go regularly from Kissamos. The morning boats stop at Imeri Gramvousa, crowned with a **Venetian castle**. The trip takes 55 minutes, departing at 10am, 10.15am and 1pm, returning at 5.45pm and 8pm.

EASTERN CRETE

If travelling east from Iraklio on the north-coast road is painful at first, close your eyes and think of England while passing the fish, chips and chlamydia of Hersonissos and Malia, the two package-tour ghettoes most infamous for foreign drunkenness and debauchery. Beyond this unfortunate stretch of road, however, Crete's less visited eastern expanse is actually quite intriguing. The fertile Lasithi Plateau, tucked into the Mt Dikti ranges, is atmospheric, offering cycling opportunities through tranquil villages to the Dikteon Cave – where Zeus himself was born. The eastern hinterland boasts the beautiful palm-forested beach of Vaï, and Minoan palace ruins at Zakros.

Eastern Crete also contains luxurious resorts around Elounda and Agios Nikolaos, frequented by the international jet set, though they also offer fun and excitement for mere mortals. Spinalonga, a former Venetian fortress with an intriguing history, lies on an islet near the former, while south-coast Ierapetra also has its own Venetian fortress and island getaway, Hrysi.

LASITHI PLATEAU ΟΡΟΠΕΔΙΟ ΛΑΣΙΘΙΟΥ

The tranquil Lasithi Plateau, 900m above sea level, contains pear and apple orchards, almond and other deciduous trees that change colour in fall. In the 17th century, some 20,000 metal windmills with white canvas sails were built here for irrigation purposes, but only 5000 still stand. Although few are still used, the windmills of Lasithi remain a distinctive and memorable sight as you arrive.

The area's relative inaccessibility allowed frequent revolts during Venetian and Turkish rule. After a 13th-century rebellion, the Venetians expelled the locals and destroyed their orchards; Lasithi lay abandoned for 200 years, until food shortages led the Venetians to cultivate this fertile area and build the irrigation trenches and wells still used today.

The largest of Lasithi's 20 villages, **Tzermiado** (population 750) is a bucolic place with two ATMs and a post office. Although tourists visiting the Dikteon Cave pass through, Tzermiado remains placid. Here **Restaurant Kourites** (☎ 28440 22054; mains €7-10) serves wood-oven specialities, like suckling pig with baked potatoes, plus vegetarian options, and offers rooms with balconies (single/double including breakfast €25/40) above the taverna. Free bicycle use is included. The same family also runs a lovely set of stone-built apartments in the abandoned upper village, **Argoulias** (☎ 28440 22754; www.argoulias.gr; d incl breakfast €60-80).

Nearby **Agios Georgios** (pronounced *aghios ye-or-gios*; population 554) is another relaxing spot; here **Hotel Maria** (☎ 28440 31774;

s/d €20/25) has nicely decorated rooms with weavings and traditional furnishings (though beds are quite narrow). Maria's nourishing **Taverna Rea** (☎ 28440 31209; mains €4.50-8) is on the main street.

Psyhro, the closest village to the **Dikteon Cave** (adult/child €4/2; ⏰ 8am-6pm Jun-Oct, 8am-2.30pm Nov-May), has tavernas and souvenir shops, but is prettier than Tzermiado. This cave was where Rhea hid the newborn Zeus from Cronos, his offspring-gobbling father. Excavated in 1900 by British archaeologist David Hogarth, the cave covers 2200 sq metres and features both stalactites and stalagmites. Numerous votives discovered here indicate cult worship; some are displayed in Iraklio's archaeological museum (p225).

Buses will drop you at Psyhro's far side; for the cave, walk 1km further uphill. It's a steep, 15-minute walk to the cave entrance. The fairly rough but shaded track on the right offers great views over the plateau; there's also a paved (but unshaded) trail next to Chalavro taverna, left of the car park. Alternatively, you can go by donkey (€10 or €15 return).

Opposite the cave, **Petros Taverna** (☎ 28440 31600; grills €6-9) has great views from the balcony. The owner also organises Mt Dikti hikes, including camping out under the stars.

Getting There & Away

From Iraklio, daily buses serve Tzermiado (€4.70, two hours), Agios Georgios (€5.10, two hours) and Psyhro. From Agios Nikolaos, buses to Lasithi only go on Sundays, though travel agencies run special cave tours.

AGIOS NIKOLAOS ΑΓΙΟΣ ΝΙΚΟΛΑΟΣ
pop 10,080

Pretty Agios Nikolaos (*ah-yee-os nih-ko-laos*), is Lasithi's capital, and enjoys a unique and photogenic setting around a curving harbour connecting to a small lake said to be once bottomless.

'Agios' has been a tourist draw since the 1960s, though infrastructure hasn't really changed since then; the narrow, one-way streets can be vexing for drivers in summer. The town, which boasts five beaches of varying sizes and reasonable nightlife, has always gone in cycles. Nowadays, Agios Nikolaos gets an intriguing mix of Western and Eastern European package tourists, plus some independents and families. With a mix of services, amenities and reasonable prices,

it is probably the north coast's best family holiday destination and serves as a good base for eastern explorations.

Orientation

The **bus station** (KTEL; ☎ 28410 22234) is 800m from the town's centre at Plateia Venizelou, though the action for tourists is centred around Voulismeni Lake. Most banks, ATMs, travel agencies and shops are on Koundourou and the parallel 28 Oktovriou.

Information

Anna Karteri Bookshop (☎ 28410 22272; Koundourou 5) Sells foreign-language maps and guidebooks.
Cafe Du Lac (☎ 28410 26837; 28 Oktovriou 17) At Du Lac Hotel. Offers free wi-fi and (pay) internet-equipped computers.
General Hospital (☎ 28410 66000; Knosou 3)
Municipal Tourist Office (☎ 28410 22357; www .agiosnikolaos.gr; ⏰ 8am-9pm Apr-Nov) Provides info, changes money and assists with accommodation.
National Bank of Greece (Nikolaou Plastira)
PK's Internet Cafe (☎ 28410 28004; Akti Koundourou 1; per hr €2; ⏰ 9am-2am)
Post office (☎ 28410 22062; 28 Oktovriou 9; ⏰ 7.30am-2pm Mon-Fri)
Tourist police (☎ 28410 91408; Erythrou Stavrou 47; ⏰ 7.30am-2.30pm Mon-Fri)

Sights & Activities

The **Archaeological Museum** (☎ 28410 24943; Paleologou Konstantinou 74; admission €4; ⏰ 8.30am-3pm Tue-Sun) has Crete's second-most-significant Minoan collection, including clay coffins, ceramic musical instruments and gold from Mohlos. The chronologically organised exhibits run from the Neolithic finds on Mt Tragistalos, north of Kato Zakros, and early Minoan finds from Agia Fotia to finds from Malia and Mohlos. The highlight, the *Goddess of Myrtos* (2500 BC), is a clay jug found near Myrtos.

The **folk museum** (☎ 28410 25093; Paleologou Konstantinou 4; admission €3; ⏰ 10am-2pm Tue-Sun), besides the tourist office, exhibits traditional handicrafts and costumes.

Within town, **Ammos Beach** and **Kytroplatia Beach** are small and crowded, though convenient for a quick dip. **Almyros Beach** (1km south), is also busy but much longer, with better sands. A taxi here costs €6, or walk (20 to 30 minutes) via a coastal path starting at Kitroplateia, passing the marina and then the stadium.

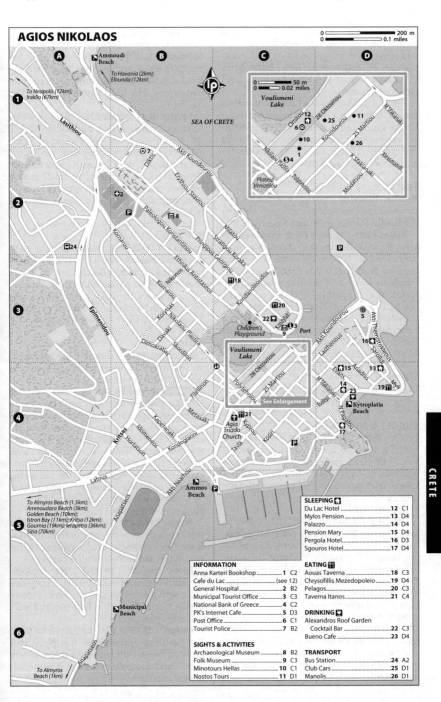

AGIOS NIKOLAOS

CRETE

INFORMATION
Anna Karteri Bookshop................1 C2
Cafe du Lac ....(see 12)
General Hospital............................2 B2
Municipal Tourist Office 3 C3
National Bank of Greece 4 C2
PK's Internet Cafe..........................5 D3
Post Office 6 C1
Tourist Police 7 B2

SIGHTS & ACTIVITIES
Archaeological Museum..............8 B2
Folk Museum 9 C3
Minotours Hellas 10 C1
Nostos Tours 11 D1

SLEEPING
Du Lac Hotel 12 C1
Mylos Pension 13 D4
Palazzo......................................14 D4
Pension Mary..............................15 D4
Pergola Hotel..............................16 D3
Sgouros Hotel..............................17 D4

EATING
Aouas Taverna 18 C3
Chrysofillis Mezedopoleio 19 D4
Pelagos......................................20 C3
Taverna Itanos............................21 C4

DRINKING
Alexandros Roof Garden
   Cocktail Bar 22 C3
Bueno Cafe 23 D4

TRANSPORT
Bus Station..................................24 A2
Club Cars....................................25 D1
Manolis......................................26 D1

Ammoudara Beach, 1.5km further south on the road towards Ierapetra, has tavernas and overpriced accommodation, but nothing else. Further towards Sitia, **Golden Beach** (Voulisma Beach) and **Istron Bay** boast long stretches of sand.

Agios Nikolaos' **Summer Cultural Festival** has almost daily events ranging from traditional Cretan music and theatre to literary readings, art exhibits and rock concerts. Some hotels and cafes have programs, while events are also advertised throughout town.

Tours

Minotours Hellas (☎ 28410 23222; www.minotours.gr; 28 Oktovriou 6) runs numerous tours, including to the Lasithi Plateau (€40) and Knossos (€40).

Nostos Tours (☎ 28410 22819; nostos@agn.forth net.gr; Roussou Koundourou 30; ◷ 8am-noon & 5-9pm) specialises in boat excursions, one being the four-hour boat trip to Spinalonga (€20), which includes a 30-minute swim on the Kolokytha Peninsula, and an on-board bar and restaurant. Nostos' full-day trip to Spinalonga (€25) includes a barbecue and two hours for swimming and sunbathing. Nostos also does full-day fishing trips in the Gulf of Mirabello (adult/child €30/20).

Sleeping

Depending on how locals think the season is going, bargaining is sometimes possible.

BUDGET & MIDRANGE

Pension Mary (☎ 28410 23760; Evans 13; s/d/tr €20/25/30; ✷) This friendly budget place has basic but clean rooms, most with private bathrooms, fridge and balconies with sea views. The upper room is cramped, though it has a terrace with barbecue. There's also a communal kitchen.

Pergola Hotel (☎ /fax 28410 28152; Sarolidi 20; r with view €35-40; ✷) This little place has simple, comfortable rooms with fridges. The pleasant veranda is good for a relaxed breakfast. Front rooms have balconies and sea views. The kindly old owners can do bus-station pick-ups and, though they're not sure what exactly it is, plan to have internet soon.

Mylos Pension (☎ 28410 23783; Sarolidi 24; d €40; ✷) This quaint pension is an extension of the friendly elderly owner's home. The small but clean rooms are basic, though the front ones have nice water views. All have fridge and TV. Air conditioning is €2 extra.

Du Lac Hotel (☎ 28410 22711; www.dulachotel.gr; 28 Oktovriou 17; s/d/studio €40/60/80; ✷ ⊚) Well positioned beside the lake, this nice place has standard rooms and spacious, fully fitted-out studios, both with stylish furnishings and nice bathrooms. The hotel's popular cafe offers free wi-fi.

Sgouros Hotel (☎ 28410 28931; N Pagalou 3; www .sgourosgrouphotels.com; s/d/tr incl breakfast €50/68/75; ✷ ⊚) Although not Agios' cheapest hotel, the recently renovated Sgouros represents great value. Well located overlooking Kitroplateia Beach, the hotel has 22 freshly painted, clean rooms with nice bathrooms, plus one suite and four interconnected family rooms.

TOP END

Palazzo (☎ 28410 25080; www.palazzo-apartments.gr; s/d/ste incl breakfast from €130/160/220; ✷ ⊟) Opposite Kitroplateia Beach, these 10 snazzy apartments have mosaic-tiled floors and marble bathrooms, the front rooms with lovely balconies. But, considering the price, it would benefit from a more highbrow location.

Eating

Lakeside restaurants, and most on Kitroplateia, are touristy and overpriced. Locals prefer the small backstreet places.

our pick **Chrysofillis Mezedopoleio** (☎ 28410 22705; Kitroplateia; mezedhes €4-7) Reserving ahead at this excellent and fairly priced *mezedhopoleio* is not a bad idea. A newspaperlike menu explains Cretan terminology and outlines the specials: fresh mussels, barley pasta with prawns, fried rabbit, excellent *myzithropitakia*, and lively, light salads are just some. The balcony water view is complemented by a stylish interior; the classic old framed photos are for sale (€22 to €40).

Taverna Itanos (☎ 28410 25340; Kyprou 1; mayirefta €4-9) Locals frequent this no-nonsense taverna, known for its home-cooked *mayirefta*, such as goat with artichokes or lamb fricassee.

Aouas Taverna (☎ 28410 23231; Paleologou Konstantinou 44; mezedhes €5-9) This family-run place with a nice enclosed garden does tasty Cretan specialities such as herb pies and pickled bulbs, plus tasty grills.

Pelagos (☎ 28410 25737; Katehaki 10; fish €8-16) For fresh fish and seafood, this place, in a restored house with ambient garden, is very good – and also quite expensive. The mezedhes are excellent.

Drinking

Nightlife is quite active in summer – just follow your ears. Places popular with Greeks and tourists alike ring the lake, and extend towards the Kitroplateia.

Bueno Cafe (☎ 28410 24289; Kitroplateia; ☺ 8am-1am) One of several popular cafes right on the town beach, with a big array of cold coffees.

ourpick **Alexandros Roof Garden Cocktail Bar** (☎ 28410 24309; cnr Kondylaki & Konstantinou; ☺ 12pm-late) With its hanging plants, soft trees and funky decor, this elevated cocktail bar is part Vegas, part Tahiti. It offers excellent views of the lake and town, lit up at night. The friendly Giorgos Halkadakis has been operating the place for 30 years, and plays an eclectic mix of popular music from five decades, for a similarly mixed Greek and international crowd.

Getting There & Away

BOAT

For ferry services from Agios Nikolaos, see Island Hopping (p512).

BUS

Agios Nikolaos' **bus station** (☎ 28410 22234) serves Elounda (€1.50, 20 minutes, 16 daily), Ierapetra (€3.50, one hour, eight daily), Iraklio (€6.50, half-hourly), Kritsa (€1.40, 15 minutes, 10 daily) and Sitia (€7.30, one hour, seven daily). Direct buses to Lasithi villages are only on Sundays, though run frequently from nearby Neapoli. To reach the bus station from downtown, walk (10 to 15 minutes) or take any local bus (€0.50, half-hourly), which stops precisely on the bridge, opposite the tourist info centre.

Note that to visit Elounda, you needn't start from the bus station; just go to the small **bus stop** opposite the tourist information centre. It displays timetables too.

Getting Around

You can hire cars from **Club Cars** (☎ 28410 25868; www.clubcars.net; 28 Oktovriou 30) from €40 per day; **Manolis** (☎ 28410 24940; 25 Martiou 12) has scooters, motorcycles, quad bikes and mountain bikes.

AROUND AGIOS NIKOLAOS

Elounda Ελούντα

pop 1660

Some 11km north of Agios Nikolaos on a gorgeous road overlooking the coast, Elounda (el-*oon*-da) is Crete's playground of the rich and (sometimes, very) famous. It's arguable whether the resorts, which unsurprisingly possess helicopter pads and even occasional exotic luxuries like maple syrup, are worth the price of admission, though if you're staying here, cost is most likely not a concern.

While enjoying Elounda's resorts can offer unexpected glimpses into the poverty of the human condition, those more reticent to make the investment can also stay in the pretty waterfront town's cheaper hotels and rooms. The Elounda municipality allegedly receives more tax euros per capita than anywhere else in Greece, because of the resorts, though you wouldn't know it from the somewhat dated, faded signage on the tourist-oriented cafetavernas and shops.

Nevertheless, Elounda has a nice sandy beach with shallow, warm waters, and if you'd like to see Spinalonga, it's much cheaper to get one of the half-hourly boats from here than to go from Agios.

INFORMATION

Municipal Tourist Office (☎ 28410 42464; ☺ 8am-8pm Jun-Oct) On the square; gives general info and changes money.

SLEEPING & EATING

Hotel Aristea (☎ 28410 41300; www.aristeahotel.com; s/d/tr incl breakfast €35/45/55; ✖) This decent, central budget option has clean rooms, most with sea view, double-glazed windows and fridge.

Corali Studios (☎ /fax 28410 41712; studios from €70; ✖) About 800m from the clock tower on Elounda's northern side, these self-catering studios are set on lush lawns with a shaded patio. The affiliated Portobello Apartments (air-conditioned apartments €65 to €75) next door are also a solid bet.

Nikos (☎ 28410 41439; fish per kilogram €40-50) No-frills Nikos on the main street is a trustworthy pick for fresh fish and lobster, and good value.

Ferryman (☎ 28410 41230; fish €7-14) Featured in the TV series *Who Pays the Ferryman*, this waterfront place does excellent, though pricey fish, plus Cretan specialities.

GETTING THERE & AWAY

From Agios Nikolaos, 13 daily buses serve Elounda (€1.50, 20 minutes). Boats to Spinalonga leave every half-hour (adult/child €10/5).

CRETE

Spinalonga Island Νήσος Σπιναλόγκας

Spinalonga Island lies just north of the Kolokytha Peninsula. Its massive **fortress** (☎ 28410 41773; admission €2; ◷ 9am-6.30pm) was built in 1579 to protect Elounda Bay and the Gulf of Mirabello. The money-minded Venetians also harvested salt here, operating up to 45 saltworks at a time. From 1639 they rented the operations to locals, while maintaining monopoly control over production. The Greek state later did the same.

Remarkably, Spinalonga withstood Turkish sieges until 1715 – 46 years after Iraklio had fallen. The Turks used it for smuggling. After Crete joined Greece in 1913, the island became Europe's last leper colony; the final leper died here in 1953 and it's been uninhabited ever since. Locals still call it 'the island of the living dead'.

Spinalonga is fascinating to explore. After buying the entry ticket (€2), take the path going left through the tunnel and follow it clockwise around the outside of the structure until you've completed the circle. Various organised tours operate simultaneously, so you'll get free commentary in numerous European languages. More useful info is printed in various places, and you can purchase lovely copies of old Venetian maps of Crete and the area (€2 to €22). You'll pass numerous ruins of churches, fortress structures and residences, and the outer turrets offer spectacular views. The island has a small snack bar right of the ticket booth.

Ferries to Spinalonga depart half-hourly from Elounda (adults/children €10/5), giving you an hour to see the sights (though you can stay longer and return on a different boat). From Plaka, 5km north of Elounda, the price is half. From Agios Nikolaos, various companies offer basic tours and longer, day-trip excursions (from €20).

Kritsa & Around Κριτσά
pop 1614

Touristy Kritsa (krit-*sah*) enjoys a nice mountain setting and is renowned for its needlework and weaving. However, the overeager villagers physically pull you into their shops, and items are rather overpriced. It's 11km from Agios Nikolaos, and served by hourly buses (€1.50, 15 minutes).

One kilometre before Kritsa, the tiny, triple-aisled **Church of Panagia Kera** (☎ 28410 51525; admission €3; ◷ 8.30am-3pm) is a very signifi-cant Byzantine shrine with priceless frescoes. And 4km north of Kritsa the 7th-century-BC Dorian city of **Lato** (admission €2; ◷ 8.30am-3pm Tue-Sun) is one of Crete's few non-Minoan ancient sites. Lato (lah-*to*), once a powerful city, sprawls over two acropolises in a lonely mountain setting, overlooking the Gulf of Mirabello. Worshipped here were Artemis and Apollo, children of Zeus by the goddess Leto – the city's namesake.

When facing the gulf, you'll see stairway remains of a **theatre**. Above it was the *prytaneion*, where Lato's rulers met. The stone circle behind the (fenced-off) central well was a threshing floor; columns beside it were from the stoa, which stood in the agora. Mosaic remains lie nearby. A right-hand path accesses the **Temple of Apollo**.

Lato gets no buses. From Kritsa, follow the (signposted) right-hand turn before Kritsa. Alternatively, enjoy the 4km walk through olive groves.

Another important site, Minoan **Gournia** (☎ 28410 24943; admission €3; ◷ 8.30am-3pm Tue-Sun), pronounced goor-*nyah*, is east of Kritsa on the coast road, 19km southeast of Agios Nikolaos. Ruins here date from 1550–1450 BC, and comprise a small palace and town. They include streets, stairways and houses, with 2m-high walls. Trade, domestic and agricultural implements discovered here indicate Gournia was fairly prosperous. Any bus east from Agios Nikolaos can drop you here.

MOHLOS ΜΟΧΛΟΣ
pop 90

Tranquil Mohlos (*moh*-los), renowned for its *psarotavernes*, lies down a 5km winding road off the Sitia–Agios Nikolaos highway. Now it's a chilled-out beach getaway with a few rooms, but from 3000 to 2000 BC it was a thriving Minoan town. The eponymous island now 200m offshore was joined to it in antiquity, and archaeologists still work in both places; an information board overlooking the harbour chronicles their finds.

While notable construction is ongoing, Mohlos' remoteness prevents it from ever being overrun. The small pebble-and-grey-sand beach has good swimming, but mind the currents between the island and the village.

Mohlos accommodation includes **Hotel Sofia** (☎ /fax 28430 94554; r €35-45; ✖), above a tasty taverna. The smallish rooms have new furniture and bedding, plus fridge; the front ones boast sea-view balconies. **Kyma** (☎ 28430 94177; soik@ in.gr; studio €35; ❷), offers spotless self-contained studios on the western side. For eating, Cretans flock to **Ta Kochilia** (☎ 28430 94432; fish €4.50-10) with its excellent fresh fish. Sea-urchin salad, cuttlefish and sea bream are all great here.

Although Mohlos lacks direct buses, any Agios Nikolaos–Sitia bus can drop you at the turn-off, from where it's a 6km walk (or hitch) to Mohlos.

SITIA ΣΗΤΕΙΑ
pop 8240

Sitia (si-*tee*-ah), de facto capital of easternmost Crete, is a quiet seaside town but does boast an airport and Dodecanese-bound ferries. Here, agriculture and commerce supersede tourism, and most visitors are low-key Greeks.

Sitia's architecture, strung up a terraced hillside, mixes Venetian and newer structures. The pretty harbour-side promenade features tavernas and cafes, while a sandy beach skirts the eastern bay. Sitia is always laid back, and makes a good base for exploring nearby beaches and sights.

Orientation & Information
Plateia Iroon Polytehniou is Sitia's main square. The bus station is at the eastern end of Karamanli, behind the bay. Ferries dock 500m north of Plateia Agnostou. Several ATMs are available in the centre of town.

Akasti Travel (☎ 28430 29444; www.akasti.gr; Kornarou & Metaxaki 4) Does trips and provides info.

Java Internet Cafe (☎ 28430 22263; Kornarou 113; ❷ 9am-late).

Post office (Dimokritou; ❷ 7.30am-3pm) Heading inland, the first left off Venizelou.

Tourist office (☎ 28430 28300; Karamanli; ❷ 9.30am-2.30pm & 5-8.30pm Mon-Fri, 9.30am-2.30pm Sat) Waterfront office offers maps.

Sights
Sitia's excellent **Archaeological Museum** (☎ 28430 23917; Piskokefalou; admission €2; ❷ 8.30am-3pm Tue-Sun) exhibits local finds dating from Neolithic to Roman times. Significant Minoan items include the *Palekastro Kouros* – a statue painstakingly pieced together from fragments made of hippopotamus tusks and adorned with gold. Zakros palace finds include a wine press, a bronze saw and cult objects scorched by the conflagration that destroyed the palace. Most important are the displayed Linear A tablets documenting administrative functions.

Sitia's towering **Venetian fort** (❷ 8.30am-3pm), locally called *kazarma* (from 'casa di arma') is now only walls, and used as an open-air venue.

The **folklore museum** (☎ 28430 22861; Kapetan Sifinos 28; admission €2; ❷ 10am-1pm Mon-Fri) displays local weavings.

Sleeping
Hotel Arhontiko (☎ 28430 28172; Kondylaki 16; d/studio without bathroom €30/35), occupying an uphill neoclassical building, has old-world ambience. This spotless guesthouse has shared bathrooms and garden.

El Greco Hotel (☎ 28430 23133; info@elgreco-sitia.gr; Arkadiou 13; s/d incl breakfast €30/40; ❷) offers very clean and presentable rooms with fridge.

Apostolis (☎ 28430 28172; Kazantzaki 27; d/tr €40/47) These domatia have ceiling fans and relatively modern bathrooms. There's a communal balcony and fridge.

Hotel Flisvos (☎ 28430 27135; www.flisvos-sitia .com; Karamanli 4; s/d/tr incl breakfast €50/70/80; ❷ 🖵) Along the southern waterfront, this modern hotel offers well-appointed rooms with all mod cons.

Eating
Taverna O Mihos (☎ 28430 22416; Kornarou 117; grills €5-8) In a traditional stone house behind the waterfront, O Mihos does great charcoal-grilled meats and Cretan fare. Eat on the beachfront terrace.

Sitia Beach (☎ 28430 22104; Karamanli 28; specials €5.50-9) Unexpectedly good pizza, plus home-style specials, are served at this beachfront place.

Balcony (☎ 28430 25084; Foundalidou 19; mains €10-19) Sitia's finest dining is upstairs in this well-decorated neoclassical building. The diverse range includes Cretan, Mexican and Asian-inspired dishes.

Getting There & Away
AIR
Sitia's **airport** (☎ 28430 24666) serves national destinations, with plans for international ones too. For domestic flight info, see Island Hopping (p511).

BOAT
Sitia's ferries primarily serve the Dodecanese. For ferry info, see Island Hopping (p512).

BUS

From Sitia's **bus station** (☎ 28430 22272), six daily buses serve Ierapetra (€5.40, 1½ hours), and seven go to Iraklio (€13.10, three hours) via Agios Nikolaos (€6.90, 1½ hours). Four buses go to Vaï (€3, 30 minutes), and two serve Kato Zakros via Palekastro and Zakros (€4.50, one hour) in summer only.

AROUND SITIA
Moni Toplou Μονή Τοπλού

The defences of the imposing fortesslike **Moni Toplou** (☎ 28430 61226; admission €2.50; ☉ 9am-6pm Apr-Oct), 18km east of Sitia, were tested by all from crusading knights to the Turks. The showpiece here is an 18th-century icon by Ioannis Kornaros, with 61 ornate miniature scenes inspired by an Orthodox prayer. More excellent icons, plus engravings, books, and Resistance-era military gear are exhibited in the monastery's **museum**. Ecclesiastical souvenirs, books on Crete, and the monastery's award-winning organic olive oil and wine are sold in the shop.

To reach Toplou, walk 3km from the Sitia–Palekastro road. Buses can stop at the junction.

Vaï Βάϊ

Europe's only 'natural' palm-forest beach is that of Vaï, 24km east of Sitia. Some say the palms sprouted from date pits spread by Roman legionaries kicking back after conquering Egypt. While closely related to the date, these palms are a separate, and unique, species. The inviting white sands here get packed in summer, though you can access a more secluded beach by clambering over a rocky outcrop behind the taverna. Also, 3km north the Minoan site of **Itanos** has good swimming nearby.

In summer, five daily buses operate from Sitia (€2.50, one hour) and stop at Palekastro. The beach car park charges €3; alternatively, park for free on the roadside 500m before Vaï.

Palekastro Παλαίκαστρο
pop 1080

Barren, agricultural Palekastro (pah-*leh*-kastro) lies on the road connecting Vaï Beach and the Zakros ruins, and itself has a promising site about 1km from town: Ancient Palekastro, where a major Minoan palace is possibly buried. The celebrated *Palekastro Kouros* in Sitia's Archaeological Museum (p269) was found there, and digging continues.

The **tourist office** (☎ 28430 61546; ☉ 9am-10pm Mon-Fri, 9am-1pm & 5.30-8pm Sat & Sun May-Oct) offers information. An ATM is adjacent. Digs include **Hotel Hellas** (☎ 28430 61240; hellas_h@otenet.gr; s/d €30/45; ✖), offering simple rooms with fridge and good bathrooms; the downstairs **taverna** serves hearty, home-style cooking (mains €4 to €8).

Nearby, the nearly deserted **Kouremenos Beach** offers excellent windsurfing, while **Hiona Beach** has good *psarotavernes*. **Freak Surf Station** (☎ 28430 61116; www.freak-surf.com) on Kouremenos rents boards.

Also here, **Casa di Mare** (☎ 28430 25304; casadi mare@hotmail.com; studio €40-60; ✖ 🏊) rents spacious, comfortable studios with stone floors and rustic-style decor, sleeping up to four. There's a small pool among the olive groves.

Five daily buses from Sitia stop at Palekastro en route to Vaï. Another two buses from Sitia to Palekastro (€2.20, 45 minutes) continue to Kato Zakros (€4.50).

KATO ZAKROS & ANCIENT ZAKROS
ΚΑΤΩ ΖΑΚΡΟΣ & ΑΡΧΑΙΑ ΖΑΚΡΟΣ
pop 790

Zakros (*zah*-kros), 37km southeast of Sitia, lies 7km from the Minoan Ancient Zakros site, and the beach settlement of Kato Zakros (*kah*-to *zah*-kros). This long pebbly beach, shaded by pines, with a few laid-back tavernas, is eternally peaceful; building is highly restricted since it's an archaeological zone. Local jaunts include the easy 8km walk from Zakros through a gorge dubbed the **Valley of the Dead**, after the cliffside **cave tombs**.

The gorge lies near the Minoan site, which is also the smallest of Crete's four palace complexes. The **Palace of Zakros** (☎ 28430 26897; Kato Zakros; admission €3; ☉ 8am-7.30pm Jul-Oct, 8.30am-3pm Nov-Jun) was a major Minoan port, doing commerce with Egypt, Syria, Anatolia and Cyprus. The palace comprised royal apartments, storerooms and workshops flanking a central courtyard.

Ancient Zakros occupied a low plain near the shore; however, rising water levels since have submerged parts of the palace – now literally living under a *helonokratia* (rule of turtles). While the ruins are sparse, the wildness and remoteness of the setting make it attractive.

Sleeping & Eating

Stella's Apartments (☎ /fax 28430 23739; www.stel apts.com; studio €40-80; ✖ 🖵) Nice studios with

CRETE

handmade wood furniture, surrounded by pines, 800m along the old road to Zakros. With barbecues, hammocks and helpful owners, they're perfect for longer stays.

Athena & Coral Rooms (d €40-50; ❄) Athena has nice, stone-walled rooms, while neighbouring Coral has small but spotless rooms with a fridge and sea views from the communal balcony.

Akrogiali Taverna (☎ 28430 26893; www.ka tozakros.cretefamilyhotels.com) At this tasty taverna, Nikos Perakis arranges several good rooms, all on the beach except for Katerina Apartments (air-conditioned apartments €40 to €60). Opposite Stella's, this offers large, stone-built studios and maisonettes with superb views.

Restaurant Nikos Platanakis (☎ 28430 26887; specials €4.50-9) While Akrogiali does great fish, this friendly place offers tasty Greek staples like rabbit stew. The produce is fresh from the back garden.

Getting There & Away
Zakros has buses from Sitia via Palekastro (€4.50, one hour, two daily); in summer, these continue to Kato Zakros.

IERAPETRA ΙΕΡΑΠΕΤΡΑ
pop 11,680
Ierapetra (yeh-*rah*-pet-rah) on the south coast lives well enough from farming (as witnessed by the many bulbous greenhouses) to not particularly care about tourism. However, it was key as a Roman port for conquering Egypt, and the Venetians later built a (still standing) fortress on the harbour. Turkish quarter remnants attest to Ierapetra's Ottoman past.

This hot and dusty place offers a more authentic Cretan experience than the northeastern coast resorts. Tavernas and cafes line the waterfront, and nightlife is busy in summer. Local beaches are fairly good, and sandy, semitropical Gaïdouronisi Island (also called Hrysi) lies just opposite.

Orientation & Information
The east-side bus station is just back from the beachfront. ATMs line the main square.
City Netcafe (☎ 28420 23164; Kothri 6; per hr €3; ⏱ 9am-late)
Post office (☎ 28420 22271; Vitsentzou Kornarou 7; ⏱ 7.30am-2pm)
www.ierapetra.net Helpful website.

Sights & Activities
Ierapetra's humble **archaeological museum** (☎ 28420 28721; Adrianou (Dimokratias) 2; admission €2; ⏱ 8.30am-3pm Tue-Sun) exhibits headless classical statuary and a superb 2nd-century-AD statue of Persephone. A *larnax* (clay coffin) from around 1300 BC, decorated with 12 vividly painted panels, is another highlight.

On the waterfront, the early Venetian 'Kales' **medieval fortress** (admission free; ⏱ 8.30am-3pm Tue-Sun), was strengthened by Francesco Morosini in 1626. Although it's still closed for restoration, you can appreciate its structure from without.

Ierapetra's main **town beach** is near the harbour, while a second **beach** stretches east from Patriarhou Metaxaki. Both have coarse grey sand, but the main one is shadier.

Sleeping & Eating
Cretan Villa Hotel (☎ /fax 28420 28522; www.cretan-villa .com; Lakerda 16; d from €40; ❄) This well-maintained 18th-century house has a great atmosphere, with traditionally furnished, fridge-equipped rooms and a peaceful courtyard. It's a five-minute walk from the bus.

Portego (☎ 28420 27733; Foniadaki 8; mezedhes €3-6) Excellent and inexpensive Cretan and Greek cuisine, like lamb in a clay pot with yoghurt, are served at this historic century-old house with a lovely courtyard for summer. The attached bar and *kafeneio* are good for drinks.

Oi Kalitehnes (☎ 28420 28547; Kyprou 26; mains €4-8) This unusual backstreet place does great-value organic food. Try the Egyptian owner's spicy falafel and kebabs.

Napoleon (☎ 28420 22410; Stratigou Samouil 26; mains €4.50-12) This respected waterfront establishment on Ierapetra's south side serves excellent fish and Greek and Cretan specialities.

Also recommended:
Coral Apartments (Lambraki; apt €45-60) These fully equipped apartments across town will satisfy families and self-caterers.
Coral Hotel (☎ 28420 22846; Katzonovatsi 12; d €30) This sister establishment to Ersi, in the quieter old town, is another good accommodation bet.
Ersi (☎ 28420 23208; Plateia Eleftherias 19; d €35; ❄) This refurbished central hotel has snug rooms with fridge, TV and sea views.

Getting There & Away
Nine daily buses from Ierapetra's **bus station** (☎ 28420 28237; Lasthenous) serve Iraklio (€9.50, 2½ hours) via Agios Nikolaos (€3.30, one hour) and Gournia (about 25 minutes); seven

CRETE

go to Sitia (€5.40, 1½ hours) via Koutsounari (for camp sites); and seven to Myrtos (€1.80, 30 minutes).

AROUND IERAPETRA

Gaïdouronisi (Hrysi) Γαιδουρονήσι (Χρυσή)

The tranquil Gaïdouronisi (Donkey Island), marketed as Hrysi (Golden Island), has nice sandy beaches, a taverna, and relaxing Lebanon cedars – the only such stand in Europe.

Regular **excursion boats** (€15 return) leave Ierapetra's port in the morning and return in the afternoon. Hrysi can get very crowded, but quiet spots are always available.

Myrtos Μύρτος

pop 440

Myrtos (*myr*-tos), 17km west of Ierapetra, is a fairly authentic coastal village popular with older European travellers. It hasn't been over-developed, thus preserving character. Myrtos makes a relaxing spot, with a decent beach and good eating options.

Prima Tours (☎ 28420 51035; www.sunbudget.net; internet per hr €3.50) offers internet access.

For overnight stays, try the west-side **Big Blue** (☎ 28420 51094; www.big-blue.gr; d/studio/apt €35/60/75; ✖). You can choose between large, airy and pricey studios with sea views or cheaper ground-floor rooms. All are self-catering. **Cretan Rooms** (☎ 28420 51427; d €35), popular with independent travellers, offers traditional-styled rooms with balconies, fridges and shared kitchens.

Myrtos Taverna (☎ 28420 51227; mains €5-9), attached to an eponymous hotel, offers many mezedhes, including vegetarian dishes. The more touristy **Platanos** (☎ 28420 51363; mains €6-8), is set under a giant thatched umbrella below a plane tree.

Seven daily buses go from Ierapetra to Myrtos (€1.80, 30 minutes).

Dodecanese
Δωδεκάνησα

When the Greek Gods were doling out sandy coves, blankets of wildflowers and lofty views, the Dodecanese seem to have received more than their fair share. Add to this a rich culture heavily influenced by Italian rule, azure waters lapping at their shores, and a wealth of natural and historical sites, and it's not surprising that the Dodecanese beckon to so many.

Strung out along the coast of western Turkey and far from Athens, the Dodecanese maintain a certain air of separateness. Despite this degree of historical autonomy, outside forces have left heavy footprints across the islands' past. Here Christianity took root in Greece and the influences of consecutive invasions by the Egyptians, Crusaders, Turks and Italians are still seen in the islands' architecture and cuisine. The islands later became one of the final battlegrounds of WWII before formally becoming part of Greece in 1947. Only 26 of the 163 islands and islets are inhabited and most of these are quite literally a hop away from one another. Many are endowed with distinctive natural features like Kos' lengthy beaches, Nisyros' steaming volcano, or Karpathos' windswept coastline. Others have captivating sights, such as Rhodes' bustling old town, St John's Monastery on Patmos and countless castles, frescoed churches and archaeological ruins dotted across the map. While the bigger islands of Kos and Rhodes afford resort-style vacations, the smaller islands like Lipsi, Leros and Kalymnos offer quiet retreats and traditional island life. If you're a hiker, botanist, beachcomber, kitesurfer, archaeologist, historian or just someone longing for a sunlounge on a quiet beach, the Dodecanese won't disappoint.

HIGHLIGHTS

- **Living it Up** Exploring the stylish nightlife and cafe scene in Rhodes Town (p285)
- **Other Worldly** Climbing inside the volcano on Nisyros (p316), with the steam rising around you
- **Stepping Back in Time** Staying in Olymbos after the tours have gone home and seeing traditional lifestyle still intact (p300), on Karpathos
- **Feeling the Rush** Cliff-diving and mountain-scaling on Kalymnos (p331)
- **Picture Perfect** Stepping into the postcard-perfect harbour scene on Symi (p305)
- **Kicking Back** Lounging on the long stretches of powder-soft beach on Kos (p324)
- **Royal Vista** Playing king at Pandeli Castle (p335), on Leros, with gob-smacking sunset views
- **Slowing Down** Immersing yourself in the quiet life on Lipsi (p342)
- **Mystical** Entering the cave where St John heard the voice of God on Patmos (p341)

- **POPULATION: 193,480**
- **AREA: 2714 SQ KM**

History

The Dodecanese islands have been inhabited since pre-Minoan times, and by the Archaic period Rhodes and Kos had emerged as the dominant islands within the group. Distance from Athens gave the Dodecanese considerable autonomy and they were, for the most part, free to prosper unencumbered by subjugation to imperial Athens. Following Alexander the Great's death in 323 BC, Ptolemy I of Egypt ruled the Dodecanese.

The Dodecanese islanders were the first Greeks to become Christians. This was through the tireless efforts of St Paul, who made two journeys to the archipelago during the 1st century, and through St John, who was banished to Patmos where he had his revelation and added a chapter to the Bible.

The early Byzantine era saw the islands prosper, but by the 7th century AD they were plundered by a string of invaders. The Knights of St John of Jerusalem (Knights Hospitaller), arrived in the 14th century and eventually became rulers of almost all the Dodecanese, building mighty fortifications that were strong enough to withstand time but not sufficient to keep out the Turks in 1522.

The Turks were ousted by the Italians in 1912 during a tussle over possession of Libya. The Italians, inspired by Mussolini's vision of a vast Mediterranean empire, made Italian the official language of the Dodecanese and prohibited the practice of Orthodoxy. The Italians constructed grandiose public buildings in the Fascist style, which was the antithesis of archetypal Greek architecture. More beneficially, they excavated and restored many archaeological monuments.

After the Italian surrender of 1943, the islands (and particularly Leros) became a battleground for British and German forces, with much suffering inflicted upon the population. The Dodecanese were formally returned to Greece in 1947.

RHODES ΡΟΔΟΣ

Rhodes (ro-dos) is the jewel in the Dodecanese crown. It embraces you with its mild climate and charms you with the best of both worlds – the buzz of its beautiful, cultured capital and the tranquillity of its beaches and stunning scenery. It has worthwhile sights and quiet villages and offers plenty of places to get lost – from the labyrinthine back streets of the almost magical World Heritage–listed Old Town to the snaking mountain roads. Rhodes is also a great base for daytrips to surrounding islands and is very family-friendly. No wonder so many people make it their sole destination.

History

The Minoans and Mycenaeans were among the first to have outposts on the islands, but it wasn't until the Dorians arrived in 1100 BC that Rhodes began to exert power and influence. The Dorians settled in the cities of Kamiros, Ialysos and Lindos, and made each of them prosperous and autonomous states.

Rhodes continued to prosper until Roman times, switching alliances like a pendulum. It was allied to Athens in the Battle of Marathon (490 BC), in which the Persians were defeated, but had shifted to the Persian side by the time of the Battle of Salamis (480 BC). After the unexpected Athenian victory at Salamis, Rhodes hastily became an ally of Athens again, joining the Delian League in 477 BC. Following the disastrous Sicilian Expedition (416–412 BC), Rhodes revolted against Athens and formed an alliance with Sparta, which it aided in the Peloponnesian Wars.

In 408 BC the cities of Kamiros, Ialysos and Lindos consolidated their powers for mutual protection and expansion by co-founding the city of Rhodes. Rhodes became Athens' ally again, and together they defeated Sparta at the Battle of Knidos (394 BC). Rhodes then joined forces with Persia in a battle against Alexander the Great but, when Alexander proved invincible, quickly allied itself with him.

In 305 BC Antigonus, one of Ptolemy's rivals, sent his son, the formidable Demetrius Poliorketes (the Besieger of Cities), to conquer Rhodes. The city managed to repel Demetrius after a long siege. To celebrate this victory, the 32m-high bronze statue of Helios Apollo (Colossus of Rhodes), one of the Seven Wonders of the Ancient World, was built.

After the defeat of Demetrius, Rhodes knew no bounds. It built the biggest navy in the Aegean and its port became a principal Mediterranean trading centre. The arts also flourished. When Greece became the battleground upon which Roman generals fought for leadership of the empire, Rhodes allied

DODECANESE

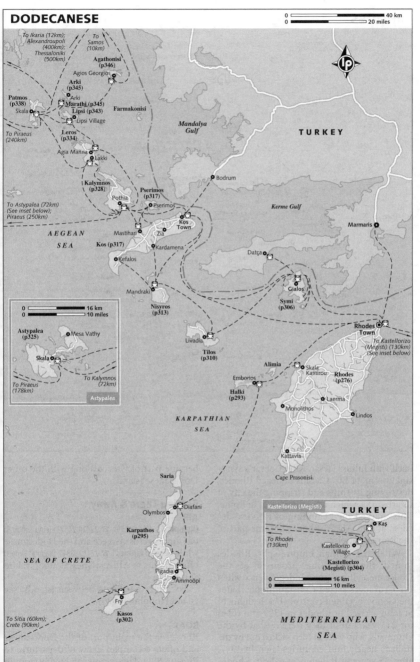

DODECANESE

0 / 40 km
0 / 20 miles

To Ikaria (12km);
Alexandroupoli
(400km);
Thessaloniki
(500km)

To
Samos
(10km)

**Agathonisi
(p346)**

Agios Georgios

**Arki
(p345)**
Arki

**Patmos
(p338)**
Skala

Marathi (p345)
Lipsi (p343)
Lipsi Village

Farmakonisi

To Piraeus
(240km)

**Leros
(p334)**
Agia Marina
Lakki

*Mandalya
Gulf*

T U R K E Y

**Kalymnos
(p328)**
Pothia

**Pserimos
(p317)**
Pserimos

Bodrum

To Astypalea (72km)
(See inset below);
Piraeus (250km)

*A E G E A N
S E A*

Mastihari
Zia
Kardamena

**Kos
Town**

Kos (p317)

Kefalos

Kerme Gulf

Marmaris

Datça

Mandraki

**Nisyros
(p313)**

Gialos
**Symi
(p306)**

**Rhodes
Town**

Livadia

**Tilos
(p310)**

Alimia
Skala
Kamirou

**Rhodes
(p276)**

Emborios
**Halki
(p293)**

Laerma

Monolithos

Lindos

0 / 16 km
0 / 10 miles

**Astypalea
(p325)**
Mesa Vathy

Skala

To Piraeus
(178km)

To Kalymnos
(72km)

Astypalea

*K A R P A T H I A N
S E A*

To Kastellorizo
(Megisti) (130km)
(See inset below)

Kattavia

Cape Prasonisi

S E A   O F   C R E T E

Saria

Olymbos
Diafani

**Karpathos
(p295)**

Pigadia
Ammoöpi

Kastellorizo (Megisti)

T U R K E Y

Kaş

To Rhodes
(130km)

Kastellorizo
Village

**Kastellorizo
(Megisti) (p304)**

0 / 16 km
0 / 10 miles

Fry

**Kasos
(p302)**

To Sitia (60km);
Crete (90km)

*M E D I T E R R A N E A N
S E A*

DODECANESE

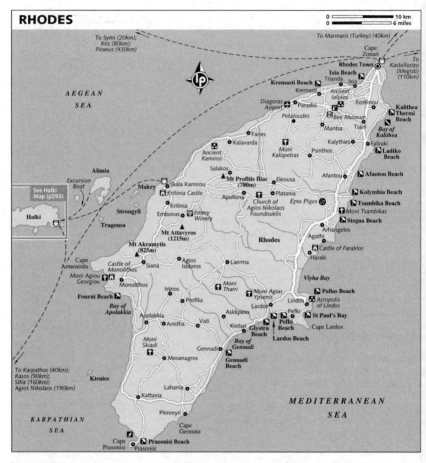

RHODES

itself with Julius Caesar. After Caesar's assassination in 44 BC, Cassius besieged Rhodes, destroying its ships and stripping the city of its artworks, which were then taken to Rome. This marked the beginning of Rhodes' decline, and in AD 70 Rhodes became part of the Roman Empire.

When the Roman Empire split, Rhodes joined the Byzantine province of the Dodecanese. It was given independence when the Crusaders seized Constantinople. Later the Genoese gained control. The Knights of St John arrived in Rhodes in 1309 and ruled for 213 years until they were ousted by the Ottomans, who were in turn kicked out by the Italians nearly four centuries later. In 1947, after 35 years of Italian occupation, Rhodes became part of Greece along with the other Dodecanese islands.

Getting There & Away

AIR

Olympic Air (Map p279; ☎ 22410 24571; Ierou Lohou 9) has flights across Greece and the Dodecanese while **Aegean Airlines** (☎ 22410 98345; Diagoras airport) offers flights to Athens, Thessaloniki, Iraklio and Rome.

For more on flights between islands, see Island Hopping (p520).

BOAT

Rhodes is the main port of the Dodecanese and offers a complex array of departures to Piraeus, Sitia, Thessaloniki and many stops in between. **Dodekanisos Seaways** (Map p280; ☎ 22410 70590; Afstralias 3) runs daily catamarans up and down the Dodecanese. Tickets are available from the kiosk at the dock. In Rhodes Town you'll also find the Sea Star ticket booth for ferries to Tilos and the ANES ticket booth for long-distance ferries to Athens.

The EOT (p278) in Rhodes Town can provide you with current schedules. Tickets are available from at Skevos' Travel Agency (p278).

Two local ferries, the *Nissos Halki* and *Nikos Express*, run daily between Halki and Skala Kamirou on Rhodes (€10, approximately 30 minutes), including a daily car-carrying caïque.

Two local ferries, the *Nissos Halki* and *Nikos Express*, run daily between Halki and Skala Kamirou on Rhodes (€10, one hour).

See also Island Hopping (p521).

International
There is a daily catamaran from Rhodes' Commercial harbour to Marmaris, Turkey (50 minutes), departing at 8am and 4.30pm from June to September. In winter, sailings twice weekly at 2pm. Tickets cost €36 one way plus €15 Turkish port tax. Same-day return tickets are only €1 more. Open return tickets cost €46 plus €29 tax. There is also a passenger and car ferry service on this same route (car/passenger €95/49 including taxes, 1¼ hours), running four or five times a week in summer and less often in winter. Book online at rhodes.marmarisinfo.com or contact Triton Holidays (p278).

Getting Around
TO/FROM THE AIRPORT
The Diagoras airport is 16km southwest of Rhodes Town, near Paradisi. Buses depart regularly between the airport and Rhodes Town's Eastern Bus Terminal (Map p279) from 6.30am to 11.15pm (€2.20, 25 minutes). On Sunday, buses stop running at around 11.45am.

BICYCLE
A range of bicycles is available for hire at **Bicycle Centre** (Map p279; ☎ 22410 28315; Griva 39; per day €5).

BOAT
There are excursion boats to Lindos and Symi (€22 return) daily in summer, leaving Mandraki Harbour at 9am and return-

ing at 6pm. An older boat heads to Diafani on Karpathos, departing at 8.30am from Mandraki Harbour and returning at 6pm. From Diafani, a bus will take you on to Olymbos. By tickets on board.

BUS
Rhodes Town has two island bus terminals, located a block away from one another, and each servicing half of the island. There is regular transport across the island all week, with fewer services on Saturday and only a few on Sunday. You can pick up schedules from the kiosks at either terminal or from the EOT office (p278). Unlimited travel tickets are available for one/two/three days (€10/15/25).

From the Eastern Bus Terminal (Map p279) there are regular services to the airport (€2.20), Kalithea Thermi (€2), Salakos (€4), Ancient Kamiros (€4.60) and Monolithos (€6). From the Western Bus Terminal (Map p279) there are services to Faliraki (€2), Tsambika Beach (€3), Stegna Beach (€3.50) and Lindos (€4.50).

CAR & MOTORCYCLE
There are numerous car- and motorcycle-hire outlets in Rhodes Town. Shop around and bargain because the competition is fierce. Agencies will usually deliver the car to you. You can also book through Triton Holidays (p278). The following agencies will deliver vehicles to you.

Drive Rent A Car (☎ 22410 68243/81011; www.driverentacar.gr; airport) Budget Rental Car outlet.
Etos Car Rental (☎ 22410 22511; www.etos.gr)
Orion Rent A Car (☎ 22410 22137)

TAXI
Rhodes Town's main taxi rank (Map p279) is east of Plateia Rimini. There are two zones on the island for taxi meters: Zone One is Rhodes Town and Zone Two (slightly higher) is everywhere else. Rates are double between midnight and 5am.

Taxis prefer to use set fare rates which are posted at the rank. Sample fares: airport €18, Lindos €43, Falaraki €15 and Kalithia €8. Ring a taxi on ☎ 22410 6800, 22410 27666 or 22410 64712 within Rhodes Town and on ☎ 22410 69600 from outside the city. For disabled-accessible taxis, call ☎ 22410 77079.

DODECANESE

RHODES TOWN
pop 56,130

The heart of Rhodes Town is the atmospheric Old Town, enclosed within massive walls and filled with winding passageways and alleys. Getting lost in this labyrinth of passages can easily be a highlight of your trip – you'll encounter quiet squares, children playing, out-of-the-way tavernas and gorgeous architecture. Visit early in the day or at dusk to see the sun reflected off the stonework and to avoid the crowds.

The New Town is mainly to the north. A few blocks are dominated by package tourism, while trendy cafes, name-brand shops, fine dining and a handful of sights take you to the more enjoyable neighbourhoods. This is also where you'll find the city's best beach.

Orientation

The Old Town is divided into three sectors: the Kollakio (Knights' Quarter), the Hora and the Jewish Quarter. The Kollakio contains most of the medieval historical sights while the Hora, often referred to as the Turkish Quarter, is primarily Rhodes Town's commercial sector with shops and restaurants. The Old Town is accessible by nine *pyles* (main gates) and two rampart-access portals and is a mesh of Byzantine, Turkish and Latin architecture. When on foot remember that, although the streets may look pedestrianised (and might not be much wider than your hips), mopeds and motorbikes zoom around the bends. If you've hired a car, don't try to drive in the Old Town – most streets are one-way and *very* narrow.

The commercial centre of the New Town lies north of the Old Town and is easily explored on foot. The Commercial Harbour (Kolona) is east of the Old Town. Excursion boats, small ferries, hydrofoils and private yachts use Mandraki Harbour, further north.

Information

INTERNET ACCESS

Mango Cafe Bar (Map p280; ☎ 22410 24877; www .mango.gr; Plateia Dorieos 3; per hr €5; ☒ 9.30am-midnight)

On The Spot Net (Map p280; ☎ 22410 34737; Perikleous 21; per hr €5; ☒ 8am-midnight) Comfortable surroundings in the Hotel Spot.

Walk Inn (Map p280; ☎ 22410 74293; Plateia Dorieos 1; per hr €2; ☒ 10am-11pm)

INTERNET RESOURCES

www.rhodesguide.com What's on, where to stay and where to hang out in Rhodes.

www.rodos.gr Upcoming events, links and background to Rhodes.

LAUNDRY

Wash House Star (Map p279; ☎ 22410 32007; Kosti Palama 4-6; per load €5; ☒ 8am-11pm, closed Sun) Have your clothes washed, dried and folded within two hours.

Washomatic (Map p280; ☎ 22410 76047; Platonos; per load €5; ☒ 8am-11pm Mon-Sat, summer only) Similar service in the Old Town.

MEDICAL SERVICES

Emergencies & ambulance (☎ 166)

General Hospital (Map p279; ☎ 22410 80000; Papalouka El Venizelou) Just northwest of the Old Town.

Krito Private Clinic (Map p279; ☎ 22410 30020; Ioannou Metaxa 3; ☒ 24hr)

MONEY

You'll find plenty of ATMs throughout Rhodes Town and at the following banks. You'll also find a handy ATM at the international ferry quay.

Alpha Credit Bank (Map p280; Plateia Kyprou)

Commercial Bank of Greece (Map p280; Plateia Symis)

National Bank of Greece New Town (Map p279; Plateia Kyprou); Old Town (Map p280; Plateia Mousiou)

POLICE

Port police (Map p279; ☎ 22410 22220; Mandrakiou)

Tourist police (Map p279; ☎ 22410 27423; ☒ 24hr) Next door to the EOT.

POST

Main post office (Map p279) On Mandraki Harbour.

TOURIST INFORMATION

EOT (Map p279; ☎ 22410 35226; www.ando.gr; cnr Makariou & Papagou; ☒ 8am-2.45pm Mon-Fri) Supplies brochures, city maps and the *Rodos News,* a free English-language newspaper.

TRAVEL AGENCIES

Charalampis Travel (Map p280; ☎ 22410 35934; ch_trav@otenet.gr; 1 Akti Saktouri) Books flights and boat tickets.

Skevos' Travel Agency (Map p279; ☎ 22410 22461; skeos@rho.forthnet.gr; 111 Amerikis) Books boat and flight tickets throughout Greece.

Triton Holidays (Map p279; ☎ 22410 21690; www.tri tondmc.gr; Plastira 9, Mandraki) Helpful staff book air and

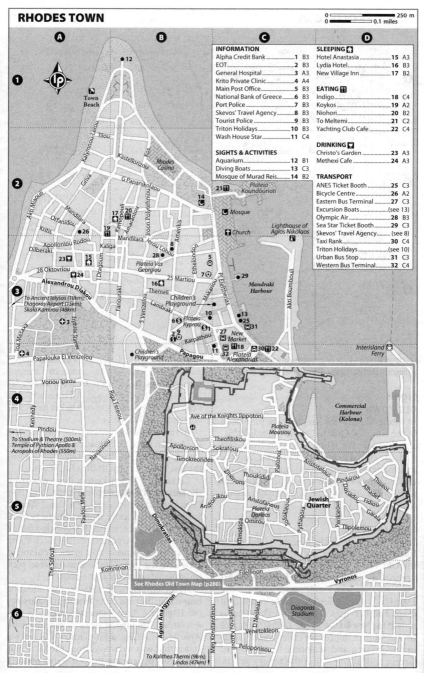

RHODES TOWN

INFORMATION	
Alpha Credit Bank	**1** B3
EOT	**2** B3
General Hospital	**3** A3
Krito Private Clinic	**4** A4
Main Post Office	**5** B3
National Bank of Greece	**6** B3
Port Police	**7** B3
Skevos' Travel Agency	**8** B3
Tourist Police	**9** B3
Triton Holidays	**10** B3
Wash House Star	**11** C4

SIGHTS & ACTIVITIES	
Aquarium	**12** B1
Diving Boats	**13** C3
Mosque of Murad Reis	**14** B2

SLEEPING	
Hotel Anastasia	**15** A3
Lydia Hotel	**16** B3
New Village Inn	**17** B2

EATING	
Indigo	**18** C4
Koykos	**19** A2
Niohori	**20** B2
To Meltemi	**21** C2
Yachting Club Cafe	**22** C4

DRINKING	
Christo's Garden	**23** A3
Methexi Cafe	**24** A3

TRANSPORT	
ANES Ticket Booth	**25** C3
Bicycle Centre	**26** A2
Eastern Bus Terminal	**27** C3
Excursion Boats	(see 13)
Olympic Air	**28** B3
Sea Star Ticket Booth	**29** C3
Skevos' Travel Agency	(see 8)
Taxi Rank	**30** C4
Triton Holidays	(see 10)
Urban Bus Stop	**31** C3
Western Bus Terminal	**32** C4

DODECANESE

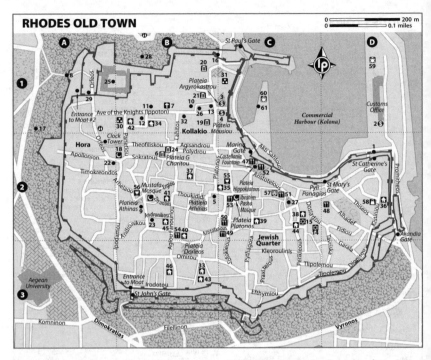

sea travel, hire cars, book accommodation and plan tours throughout the Dodecanese. They also sell tickets to Turkey.

Sights

OLD TOWN

In medieval times the Knights of St John lived in the Knights' Quarter, while other inhabitants lived in the Hora. The 12m-thick city walls are closed to the public but you can take a pleasant walk around the imposing walls of the Old Town via the wide and pedestrianised moat walk. All the Old Town sights are on Map p280.

Knights' Quarter

Begin your tour of the Knights' Quarter at **Liberty Gate**, crossing the small bridge into the Old Town. In a medieval building is the original site of the **Museum of Modern Greek Art** (☎ 22410 23766; www.mgamuseum/gr; 2 Plateia Symis; 3 sites €3; ☀ 8am-2pm Tue-Sat). Inside you'll find maps and carvings. The main exhibition is now at the **New Art Gallery** (☎ 22410 43780; Plateia G Charitou) with an impressive collection of painting, engraving and sculpture from some of Greece's most popular 20th-century artists,

including Gaitis Giannis, Vasiliou Spiros and Katraki Vaso. For the museum's temporary exhibits, head to the **Centre of Modern Art** (☎ 22410 77071; 179 Socratous St). All three galleries keep the same hours and one ticket gains you entrance to all three.

Across the pebbled street from the Museum of Modern Greek Art, take in the remains of the 3rd-century-BC **Temple of Aphrodite**, one of the few ancient ruins in the Old Town.

Continuing down Plateia Argyrokastrou, the **Museum of the Decorative Arts** (☎ 22410 72674; Plateia Argyrokastrou; admission €2; ☀ 8.30am-2.40pm Tue-Sun) houses an eclectic array of artefacts from around the Dodecanese. It's chock-a-block with instruments, pottery, carvings, clothing and spinning wheels and gives a colourful view into the past. Captions are sparse; pick up explanatory notes at the door.

In the atmospheric 15th-century knights' hospital up the road is the **Museum of Archaeology** (☎ 22410 27657; Plateia Mousiou; admission €3; ☀ 8am-4pm Tue-Sun). Its biggest draw is the exquisite *Aphrodite Bathing*, a 1st-century-BC marble statue that was recovered from the local seabed. Many believe it is the cult statue missing

INFORMATION
Charalampis Travel 1 D2
Commercial Bank ATM 2 D1
Commercial Bank of Greece 3 C1
Mango Cafe Bar (see 40)
National Bank of Greece 4 C1
On The Spot Net (see 38)
Walk Inn (see 54)
Washomatic 5 B2

SIGHTS & ACTIVITIES
Centre of Modern Art 6 B2
Chapelle Française 7 B1
D'Amboise Gate 8 A1
Hammah Turkish Baths 9 B2
Inn of France 10 B1
Inn of Provence 11 B1
Inn of Spain 12 B1
Inn of the Order of the Tongue of Italy 13 B1
Jewish Synagogue Museum 14 C2
Kahal Shalom Synagogue 15 C2
Liberty Gate 16 B1
Moat Walkway 17 A1
Mosque of Süleyman 18 B2
Museum of Archaeology 19 B1
Museum of Modern Greek Art 20 B1
Museum of the Decorative Arts 21 B1
Muslim Library 22 A2
Nelly Dimoglou Dance Company 23 B2
New Art Gallery 24 B2
Palace of the Grand Masters 25 A1
Palace of Villiers de l'sle Adam 26 B1
Plateia Evreon Martyron 27 C2
Sound & Light Show 28 B1
St Anthony's Gate 29 A1
St John of the Collachio 30 B1
Temple of Aphrodite 31 C1
Villaragut Building 32 B1

SLEEPING
Apollo Tourist House 33 B3
Avalon Boutique Hotel 34 B1
Domus Rodos Hotel 35 C2
Hotel Cava d'Oro 36 D2
Hotel Isole 37 B2
Hotel Spot 38 C2
Hotel Via Via 39 C2
Mango Rooms 40 B2
Marco Polo Mansion 41 B2
Nikos & Takis Hotel 42 B1
Pension Andreas 43 B3
Pension Eleni 44 C2
Pension Olympos 45 B2
Pink Elephant 46 B3

EATING
gelaterie.gr 47 C2
Hatzikelis 48 D2
Mandala 49 C2
Nireas 50 C2
O Meraklis 51 C2
Prince Bakery Cafe 52 C2
To Megiston 53 C2
Walk Inn 54 B2

DRINKING
Apenadi 55 C2
Rogmitou Chronou 56 B2

ENTERTAINMENT
Cafe Chantant 57 C2

SHOPPING
Byzantine Iconography 58 D2

TRANSPORT
Catamarans to Turkey 59 D1
Dodekanisos Seaways 60 C1
FB *Nisos Kalymnos* & *Dodekanisos Express* Catamaran 61 C1

from the nearby Temple of Aphrodite. The rest of the museum is filled with ancient statues and pottery found on Rhodes.

Wander up the **Avenue of the Knights** (Ippoton), once home to the knights themselves. They were divided into seven 'tongues' or languages, according to their place of origin – England, France, Germany, Italy, Aragon, Auvergne and Provence – and each was responsible for protecting a section of the bastion. The Grand Master, who was in charge, lived in the palace, and each tongue was under the auspices of a bailiff.

To this day the street exudes a noble and forbidding aura, despite modern offices now occupying most of the inns. Its lofty buildings stretch in a 600m-long unbroken wall of honey-coloured stone blocks, and its flat facade is punctuated by huge doorways and arched windows.

First on the right, if you begin at the eastern end of the Avenue of the Knights, is the 1519 **Inn of the Order of the Tongue of Italy**. Next door is the **Palace of Villiers de l'Isle Adam**; after Sultan Süleyman had taken the city, it was Villiers de l'sle who had the humiliating task of arranging the knights' departure from the island. Next along is the **Inn of France**, the most ornate and distinctive of all the inns. On the opposite side of the street is the **Villaragut Building**, a knight's home converted into an Ottoman Mansion in the 18th century. Closed for renovations at the time of writing, it now houses Byzantine antiques. Peek through the gate to see the Turkish garden.

Back on the right side is the **Chapelle Française** (Chapel of the Tongue of France), embellished with a statue of the Virgin and Child. Next door is the residence of the Chaplain of the Tongue of France. Across the alleyway is the **Inn of Provence**, with four coats of arms forming the shape of a cross, and opposite is the **Inn of Spain.**

Near the end of the avenue, **St John of the Collachio** was originally a knights' church with an underground passage linking it to the palace across the road. The Ottomans later turned it into a mosque and it was destroyed in 1856 when the gunpowder stored in the belltower exploded. Soon after, a neoclassical building was erected on the site and remains there today. Climb up to the viewing platform to also take in the ruins of the original transept and the underground gallery.

On the right is the truly magnificent 14th-century **Palace of the Grand Masters** (☎ 22410 23359; Ippoton; admission €6; 8.30am-3pm Tue-Sun), which was severely damaged by the Turkish siege and then destroyed by an explosion in the mid-1800s. The Italians rebuilt the palace

---

THE KNIGHTS OF ST JOHN

As you travel through the Dodecanese, you'll quickly realise that the Knights of St John left behind a whole lot of castles. The knights were originally formed as the Knights Hospitaller, an organisation founded in Jerusalem in 1080 to provide care for poor and sick pilgrims on their way to the Holy Land. After the loss of Jerusalem in the First Crusade, the knights relocated to Rhodes (via Cyprus) in the early 14th century and managed to oust the ruling Genoese in 1309. The Knights of St John in Rhodes were supposedly a chivalrous Christian organisation but also established themselves as purveyors of legitimate and somewhat-less legitimate commercial activities – primarily piracy, and antipiracy against Ottoman shipping and pilgrims. This irked the Ottoman Sultan Süleyman the Magnificent (not a man you'd want to irk) and he set about dislodging the knights from the stronghold. Rhodes capitulated in 1523, after which the remaining knights relocated to Malta, where they continue to meet as the Sovereign Military Hospitaller Order of St John of Jerusalem, of Rhodes and of Malta.

---

following old plans for the exterior but introducing a grandiose, lavish interior. It was intended as a holiday home for Mussolini and King Emmanuel III but is open as a museum. Only 24 of the 158 rooms can be visited; inside you'll find antique furnishing, sculptures, frescoes and mosaic floors.

From the palace, walk through **D'Amboise Gate**, the most atmospheric of the gates which takes you across the moat. When the palace is open, you can also gain access to the walkway along the top of the wall from here, affording great views into the Old Town and across to the sea. Another option is to follow the peaceful **Moat Walkway**, which you can access next to **St Anthony's Gate**. It's a green oasis with lush lawns cushioned between trees and the old walls.

Hora

Bearing many legacies of its Ottoman past is the **Hora**. During Turkish times, churches were converted to mosques and many more Muslim houses of worship were built from scratch, although most are now dilapidated. The most important is the colourful, pink-domed **Mosque of Süleyman**, at the top of Sokratous. Built in 1522 to commemorate the Ottoman victory against the knights, it was renovated in 1808. For a bird's eye view of it, follow the footpath along the side of the neighbouring (and now defunct) clock tower.

Opposite is the 18th-century **Muslim Library** (Plateia Arionos; Sokratous; admission free; 9.30am-4pm Mon-Sat). Founded in 1794 by Turkish Rhodian Ahmed Hasuf, it houses a small number of Persian and Arabic manuscripts and a collection of Korans handwritten on parchment.

Continuing through the winding pedestrian streets will bring you to the municipal **Hammam Turkish Baths** (Plateia Arionis; admission €5; 10am-5pm Mon-Fri, 8am-5pm Sat). They are open to the public, with separate male and female baths. Warm yourself on the marble stones or opt for a massage. Lockers are available.

Jewish Quarter

The **Jewish Quarter** is an almost forgotten sector of Rhodes Old Town, where life continues at an unhurried pace and local residents live seemingly oblivious to the hubbub of the Hora no more than a few blocks away. This area of quiet streets and sometimes dilapidated houses was once home to a thriving Jewish community.

Built in 1577, **Kahal Shalom Synagogue** (Polydorou 5) is Greece's oldest synagogue and the only one surviving on Rhodes. The Jewish quarter once had six synagogues and, in the 1920s, a population of 4000. Have a look in at the **Jewish Synagogue Museum** (22410 22364; www.rhodes jewishmuseum.org; Dosiadou; 10am-3pm Sun-Fri, closed winter), in the old women's prayer rooms around the corner. Exhibits include lots of early 20th-century photos, intricately decorated documents and displays about the 1673 Jews deported from Rhodes to Auschwitz in 1944. Only 151 survived.

Close by is **Plateia Evreon Martyron** (Square of the Jewish Martyrs).

NEW TOWN

The **Acropolis of Rhodes** (off Map p279), southwest of the Old Town on Monte Smith, was the site of the ancient Hellenistic city of Rhodes. The hill is named after the English admiral Sir Sydney Smith, who watched for Napoleon's fleet from here in 1802. It has superb views.

The site is not well signposted but makes for an interesting wander. The restored 2nd-century-AD tree-lined **stadium** once staged competitions in preparation for the Olympic Games. Today, locals continue to use it for jogging. The adjacent **theatre** is a reconstruction of one used for lectures by the Rhodes School of Rhetoric. Steps above here lead to the **Temple of Pythian Apollo**, with four re-erected columns. A small exhibition between the stadium and the road details the history of the site and the reconstruction. This unenclosed site can be reached on city bus 5.

North of Mandraki, at the eastern end of G Papanikolaou, is the graceful **Mosque of Murad Reis** (Map p279). In its grounds are a Turkish cemetery and the Villa Cleobolus, where Lawrence Durrell lived in the 1940s, writing *Reflections on a Marine Venus*.

To get close-up to the underwater world of the Aegean, head to Rhodes' small **Aquarium** (Map p279; ☎ 22410 27308; www.hcmr.gr; Kos 1; admission adult/child €5/free; ☼ 9am-8.30pm Apr-Oct, 9am-4.30pm Nov-Mar). The art deco building was constructed during the 1930s by the Italians as a biological research station. Walk through the sea cave to view a colourful array of molluscs, crabs, sea turtles and fish.

The town **beach** begins north of Mandraki and continues around the island's northernmost point and down the west side of the New Town. The best spots will depend on the prevailing winds but tend to be on the east side, where there's usually calmer water and more sand and facilities.

Activities

GREEK DANCING LESSONS
The **Nelly Dimoglou Dance Company** (Map p280; ☎ 22410 20157; deyappet@otenet.gr; Andronikou 7; admission per person/group €16/11; ☼ May-Oct) gives lessons and stages lively performances (9.15pm on Monday, Wednesday and Friday) in folk dance theatre.

SCUBA DIVING
A number of diving schools operate out of Mandraki, all offering a range of courses, including a 'One Day Try Dive' for €40 to €50, and PADI certification. You can get information from their **boats** at Mandraki Harbour (Map p279).

Diving Centres (☎ 22410 23780)
Diving Med College (☎ 22410 61115; www.divemed college.com)

Scuba Diving Trident School (☎ /fax 22410 29160)
Waterhoppers Diving Centre (☎ /fax 22410 38146, 6972500971; www.waterhoppers.com)

Sleeping
BUDGET
During the summer, finding an affordable bed in the Old Town is very possible, particularly if you book ahead. In winter, most budget places shut down throughout the city so you'll definitely need to call ahead. While most of the New Town's hotels are modern and characterless, there are a few exceptions.

New Village Inn (Map p279; ☎ 22410 34937, 6976475917; www.newvillageinn.gr; Konstantopedos 10; s/d €35/45) These village-style rooms in the New Town with very comfy mattresses are a home from home. All come with a ceiling fan and fridge. The tranquil interior courtyard and bar is overflowing with plants; you'd never guess that you're not near the hustle and bustle of downtown.

Hotel Isole (Map p280; ☎ 22410 20682, 6937580814; www.hotelisole.com; Evdoxou 35; s/d incl breakfast €30/50; ✖ ▢) With its entrance under a stone archway in the narrow passages of the Old Town's backstreets, these seven rooms offer great value for money. Decorated in white and blue, they're a cool, quiet retreat. Chat with the multilingual owners at the small bar.

ourpick **Hotel Anastasia** (Map p279; ☎ 22410 28007; www.anastasia-hotel.com; 28 Oktovriou 46; s/d/tr €38/52/55; ✖ ▢) Tucked away off the main drag in the New Town, this Italian mansion has big open rooms with lots of light. The tiled floors and high ceilings give it stacks of character and the lush garden is a quiet place to sip a cocktail or coffee at the outdoor bar.

Pension Olympos (Map p280; ☎ /fax 22410 33567; www.pension-olympos.com; Agiou Fanouriou 56; s/d/tr €40/55/60; ✖) These pleasant rooms have a slight granny feel about them, with traditional artwork and comfy wrought-iron beds. The very private garden is a lovely place to relax. All rooms have a small fridge.

Continue your hunt for a bed at the following places:
Pension Eleni (Map p280; ☎ 22410 73282; www.eleni rooms.gr; Dimosthenous 25; s/d €35/65) Very simple but spotlessly clean rooms in the Jewish Quarter. Some rooms have a loft to sleep four and there's a small shared patio.
Mango Rooms (Map p280; ☎ 22410 24877; www.mango.gr; Plateia Dorieos 3; s/d/tr €46/58/68; ☼ year-round; ▢) Comfortable, well-maintained but basic rooms with ceiling fans and fridges. Rooftop terrace to relax on.

DODECANESE

Pink Elephant (Map p280; ☎ 22410 22469; www.pink elephantpension.com; Timakida 9; s/d €36/60; 🛜) Simple, fan-equipped rooms. Shared fridge, small courtyard and friendly owner.

MIDRANGE

Pension Andreas (Map p280; ☎ 22410 34156; fax 22410 74285; www.hotelandreas.com; Omirou 28d; s/d €55/60; 🌙 year-round; 🍴 🖥 🛜) This small, rather ramshackle but inviting hotel has 11 individually decorated rooms. Some are airy, some bright and some have private terraces. An extra mattress can be added for a child. The terrace is very social at breakfast and offers panoramic views, while the owner is a wealth of local info. Minimum two-night stay.

Apollo Tourist House (Map p280; ☎ 22410 32003; www.apollo-touristhouse.com; Omirou 28c; s/d incl breakfast €65/70; 🖥) This small pension has tastefully furnished rooms with wooden four-poster and traditional captain's beds. Splashes of colour and lengths of muslin make it all the more homey. Enjoy the view from your room or head out to the terrace.

Hotel Via Via (Map p280; ☎ /fax 22410 77027; www .hotel-via-via.com; Lisipou 2; d €70; 🌙 year-round; 🍴 🖥) Each eclectic room here is unique – some with subtle blues and others with vibrant greens. They're not plush but comfortable and colourful. Embellished with plants, the rooftop terrace offers excellent views.

Domus Rodos Hotel (Map p280; ☎ 22410 25965; info@domusrodoshotel.gr; Platonos; d €80; 🌙 year-round; 🍴 🖥) These well-maintained, comfortable rooms are some of the few available all year-round in the Old Town. The only drawback is noise from nearby bars. Back rooms have balconies and the friendly owner has plenty of local info. Call ahead in winter.

Hotel Spot (Map p280; ☎ 22410 34737; www.spot hotelrhodes.gr; Perikleous 21; s/d/tr incl breakfast €70/90/140; 🍴 🖥 🛜) Heavy wood furniture and orange, red and golden hues give the rooms in this small boutique hotel a Rajasthan feel. It has a comfortable terrace and rooftop terrace, a small book exchange and a friendly host.

Lydia Hotel (Map p279; ☎ 22410 22871; www.lydia hotel.com; Martiou 25; s/d €80/90; 🍴 🖥 🛜) Close to the seaside, shopping and cafes and just a stroll away from the Old Town lies this classy hotel. What the comfortable rooms lack in character is more than made up for by the bar, lobby area and garden.

Hotel Cava d'Oro (Map p280; ☎ 22410 36980; www .cavadoro.com; Kisthiniou 15; d/tr incl breakfast €85/120;

🅿 🛜) Stone walls and wrought-iron furniture give you the feeling that this hotel hails from another era. Then again, the building is 800 years old. A family suite has a cool loft area and all rooms have a stylish touch. Taxis can come to the door.

Marco Polo Mansion (Map p280; ☎ 22410 25562; www .marcopolomansion.gr; Agiou Fanouriou 40-42; d incl breakfast from €90) Set in a 15th-century, carefully restored mansion and bursting with atmosphere, the rooms here have a rustic yet plush feel to them with fabric and furnishings from India and Turkey. Think warm colours, high ceilings and four-poster beds. Right in the heart of the old town, it's a cool, shady retreat.

TOP END

Nikos & Takis Hotel (Map p280; ☎ 22410 70773; www.niko stakishotel.com; Panetiou 29; d from €150; 🅿 🍴 🖥 🛜) This boutique hotel offers atmospheric, individually decorated rooms. Check out the Moroccan-themed Marokino, with its marble tub, ornately tiled floor and authentic slippers. All rooms have music piped into the bathroom and plush amenities. Breakfast is taken on a banana-tree-shaded patio.

Avalon Boutique Hotel (Map p280; ☎ 22410 31438; www.hotelavalon.gr; Charitos 9; d €300; 🍴 🖥 🛜) This peaceful oasis has stunningly luxurious rooms that ooze with character. Opt for one with a fireplace or Jacuzzi. All have flat screen TVs and individual furnishing. The lovely garden and rooftop terrace are ideal for serious relaxation.

Eating
BUDGET
Old Town

Avoid the restaurant touts along Sokratous and around Plateia Ippokratous. Hit the backstreets to find less touristy eateries.

Prince Bakery Cafe (Map p280; Plateia Ippokratous; snacks €1-5; 🌙 10am-11pm) Tucked in the corner of the square, this place has a designer feel to it. Sink into the leather seats and tuck into freshly baked breads and pastries or get something to go. There's a deli for sandwiches, an orange-juicer and a well-stocked bar. If you're more peckish, go for the sausage plate or grills.

gelaterie.gr (Map p280; ☎ 22410 38925; www .gelaterie.gr; Plateia Ippokratous 1; snacks €3-5) Organic crêpes, smoothies and mountains of ice cream will call to you from across the square. Try a rum-and-banana crêpe or spend ages perusing the smoothie options like Love Potion,

Fountain of Youth or Hangover Blaster. There are no tables but the nearby fountain makes a lovely place to slurp and watch the world go by.

O Meraklis (Map p280; Aristotelous 30; soup €4; ◷ 3am-8am) After a night out on the tiles a plate of tripe and entrails soup is what's needed – according to the Greek hangover cure. That's pretty much all it serves. An experience you *might* want to try.

Walk Inn (Map p280; ☎ 22410 74293; Plateia Dorieos 1; mains €3-7; ◷ 10am-11pm) With a good mix of tourists hanging out and locals playing chess, this low-key, backpacker-style place serves up homemade pizza, pasta and pita sandwiches.

New Town

our pick Koykos (Map p279; ☎ 22410 73022; Mandilana 20-26; mains €2-8) Popular with Rhodes younger crowds, Koykos is Greek kitsch. From the architecture to the copper-tray-swinging waiters, it would almost be tacky if it weren't so enjoyable. Crowds huddle around chess and card games while others focus on the savoury pies, seafood dishes, salads and mezes. Accompany your meal with barrel wines, ouzo or retsina. The in-house bakery makes divine sweets and breads for you to take home.

Niohori (Map p279; ☎ 22410 35116; I Kazouli 29; mains €3-8) This essentially nontouristy eatery makes little concession to appearance, but if you're a meat-lover you'll forget all about that. The owner is a butcher and serves his own country sausage and veal liver with oil and oregano.

Yachting Club Cafe (Map p279; ☎ 22410 75723; Plateia Alexandrias; snacks €3-10) Slightly pretentious but with lovely sun-filled views across the bay, this is the place to be seen. Everything is rather pricey but very good quality. Come for breakfast and try the brioche, crêpes or flaky croissants, washed down with strong coffee.

Indigo (Map p279; ☎ 6972663100; New Market 105-106; mains €5-12; ◷ dinner) Unexpectedly located in the New Market, this small restaurant has colourful tablecloths and Greek traditional dishes with creative salads. Try the house salad with croutons, rocket, walnut and garlic or the hazelnut salad with blue cheese. Handy if you're just off the bus.

MIDRANGE & TOP END
Old Town

To Megiston (Map p279; ☎ 22410 29127; Sopokelous; mains €8-15; ◷ year-round) This family-run taverna whips up amazing food, including a country-style Greek salad, swordfish and specialities from Kastellorizo. The desserts are mouth-watering and the service is exceptionally friendly.

our pick Mandala (Map p280; ☎ 22410 38119; Sofokleos 38; mains €8-15; ◷ lunch Sun & dinner daily winter; lunch & dinner daily summer) Lively and popular, the hip Mandala dishes up creative cuisine, such as chèvre-and-fig starters, salmon pasta or Moroccan chicken. The eatery offers excellent service, a well-stocked bar and frequent live music make it that much more of a treat.

Nireas (Map p280; ☎ 22410 31741; Sofokleous 45-47; mains €8-16) The fish will taste just as good whether you dine outside under a canopy of greenery or inside in the classy yellow rooms. Seared or sesame-encrusted tuna, steamed mussels with garlic and white wine – the list seems endless. Popular with families for lunch, Nireas opens onto a quiet square. To find it, just follow your nose.

Hatzikelis (Map p280; ☎ 22410 27215; Alhadef 9; mains €9-16) With a high-beamed ceiling and heavy velvet curtains, Hatzikelis is a step back in time. Popular with local families, it's well known for shellfish. Look for mussels, scallops with garlic butter and *kefalotyri* (sheep's-milk cheese), fresh clams or sea-urchin roe. The menu is in Greek only but the helpful waiters speak English.

New Town

To Meltemi (Map p279; ☎ 22410 30480; cnr Plateia Kountourioti & Rodou; mains €7-15) With traditional music and open sea views, Meltemi occupies a prime spot just north of Mandraki harbour. Grills and fish are locally revered and the creative salads are fantastic: try the Meltemi, with rocket, apple, walnut, pine nuts and dried fruit.

Drinking & Entertainment

Rhodes Town is brimming with cool places to hang out in the evening. Bars and watering holes are stylish and atmospheric – great places to mingle with the locals and unwind after a hard day of lounging on the beach.

OLD TOWN
The majority of the nightlife happens around Platonos and Ippokratous squares. Also check out Mandala (above) for live local music on Sundays and some evenings.

DODECANESE

Rogmitou Chronou (Map p280; ☎ 22410 25202; www.rogmitouxronou.gr; Plateia Arionos; ☼ 10pm-5am; ⊛) With lots of stonework and heavy wood, the Music Cafe spreads over two floors. Downstairs has a cosy, medieval feel to it and live acoustic music on Mondays, while upstairs has a hint of the '50s with red bar stools and live rock bands on Fridays. The rest of the week sees various DJs; check the on-line events listing.

Apenadi (Map p280; ☎ 22410 21055; Evripidou 13-15) Step into the set for Arabian Nights and sink into some colourful cushions, strewn beneath exquisite chandeliers. And let's not forget the funky music, mezes, cocktails and friendly service.

ourpick Cafe Chantant (Map p280; ☎ 22410 32277; Dimokratou 3; ☼ midnight-early) Locals sit at long wooden tables, drinking ouzo or beer and listening to live, traditional music. It's dark in here and you won't find snacks and nibbles, but the atmosphere is palpable and the band is lively. It's an experience you won't soon forget.

NEW TOWN

Locals hang out along the bar-lined I Dragoum, while the tourist haunts are found along Akti Miaouli, Orfanidou and Griva.

ourpick Methexi Cafe (Map p279; ☎ 22410 33440; 29 Oktovriou, cnr Griva) This colonial-style mansion is filled with black-and-white photos and stacks of magazines. The comfortable, homey feeling draws a relaxed young crowd who come for live Greek music or to drink beer on the terrace.

Christo's Garden (Map p279; Griva; ☼ 10pm-late) Prop yourself up at the grotto-style bar surrounded by lush greenery, seemingly worlds away from the city. Traditional buildings surround the inner courtyard where you can have a relaxed drink amongst the fairy lights.

Sound & Light Show (Map p280; ☎ 22410 21922; www.hellenicfestival.gr; admission €7) Squeezing many centuries of history into a show with lights, voices and music, the Sound & Light Show is something you'll either love or hate. Shows take place from Monday to Saturday next to the walls of the Old Town, off Plateia Rimini and near the D'Amboise Gate. English-language sessions are staggered, but in general begin at either 9.15pm or 11.15pm. Other languages offered are French, German and Swedish.

Shopping

You'll find lots of recognisable high-street shops in Rhodes, particularly along Lambraki (good for shoes and umbrellas) and Karpathou, a pedestrianised street with cafes and shops galore. The eastern half of 28 Oktovriou is where you'll find the posh shops and cafes.

New Market is filled with mostly tacky souvenirs. In the Old Town, look out for gold and silver jewellery, leather goods and ceramics: most shops are along Sokratous.

ourpick Byzantine Iconography (Map p280; ☎ 22410 74127; Kisthinioy 42) Visiting the studio of Basilios Per Sirimis is an experience you shouldn't miss. A teacher and accomplished artist, he follows the traditional methods of iconography, producing paintings for churches and families throughout Greece. All of his materials are natural, including gold leaf and pigments mixed with egg and vinegar. You can see paintings in various stages of production and Basilios will fascinate you with his knowledge. Paintings go for €210 to €2000.

Getting Around

Local buses leave from the **urban bus stop** (Map p279; Mandraki) on Mandraki Harbour and charge a flat €1. Bus 11 does a circuit around the coast, up past the Aquarium and on to the Acropolis. Hopping on for a loop is a good way to get your bearings. Bus 2 goes to Analipsi, bus 3 to Rodini, bus 4 to Agios Dimitrios and bus 5 to the Acropolis. Buy tickets on board.

EASTERN RHODES

The majority of Rhodes' long stretches of sandy beaches are along its east coast. Consequently, that's much more developed, with a number of villages made-over into summer resorts that tend to be filled with young package-holidaymakers and endless strips of tourist bars. If you do find yourself based in one of these resorts, you could make the most of the beach and then hire a car or hop on a bus to explore more remote beaches, the interior and the south or west coast.

From Rhodes Town, there are frequent buses to Lindos, but some of the beaches en route are a bit of a hike from the road. The obvious bonus to this is that it's still possible to find uncrowded stretches of sand even at the height of summer.

Restored to its former glory, **Kalithea Thermi** (☎ 22410 65691; Kallithea; www.kallitheasprings.gr; admission €2.50; ☺ 8am-8pm April-Oct, 8am-5pm Nov-Mar) was originally an Italian-built spa, just 9km from Rhodes Town. With grand buildings, colonnades, domed ceilings and countless archways delivering stunning sea views, it's worth a wander. Exhibitions inside show the many films made here (including scenes from *Zorba the Greek*) as well as local artwork. You'll also find a cafe and a small, sandy beach that's good for swimming. The as-yet-uncompleted, vast expanses of *hohlakia* (black-and-white pebble mosaic floors) have taken 14 years to complete so far.

Ladiko Beach, touted locally as 'Anthony Quinn Beach', is in fact two back-to-back coves with a pebbly beach on the north side and volcanic rock platforms on the south. The swimming is good, though the water is noticeably colder here.

Further down the coast, a right turn at Kolymbia takes you along a pine-fringed road to the **Epta Piges** (Seven Springs), 4km away. Head here if you're feeling parched or deprived of greenery. The springs bubble into a river, which flows into a shaded lake. You can reach the lake by following a footpath or by walking through a narrow, dark tunnel that's ankle-deep with fast flowing river water. If you're claustrophobic or tall, opt for the path. The lake itself has a magical colour and is home to turtles. It was built by the Italians who damned the river to irrigate the Kolymbia plains. There's a cafe next to the springs and a kitsch children's playground. There are no buses to Epta Piges; take a Lindos bus and get off at the turn-off.

Back on the coast, the beaches of **Kolymbia** and **Tsambika** are sandy but can get crowded in summer. On the left, a steep signposted road takes you 1.5km up to the 300 steps leading to **Moni Tsambikas**. Inside the small white chapel you'll find an 11th-century icon of Mary, found on the mountaintop by an infertile couple who soon after had a child. Since then, the site has become a place of pilgrimage for women hoping to conceive. On 18 September, the monastery's festival day, women climb up on their knees and make offerings of wax babies and silver plaques, which you'll see crowding the front of the church. The frescoes and ancient altar are worth seeing, as is the magnificent 360-degree view outside.

Further up the road is a turn-off to sandy, idyllic **Stegna Beach**. Another 4km along is a turning for Haraki from where you'll find a path up to the ruins of the 15th-century **Castle of Faraklos**. Once a prison for recalcitrant knights and the island's last stronghold to fall to the Turks, it offers great views. Nearby is the sandy cove of **Agathi**.

Lindos Λίνδος
pop 1090

Topped with an impressive acropolis and spilling down into stunning twin bays, Lindos is one of Rhodes' most picturesque villages. Following the narrow, winding alleyways will lead you through a maze of dazzling white **17th-century houses**, once the dwellings of wealthy admirals and many boasting courtyards with *hohlakia*.

Of course, the loveliness of Lindos has not gone unnoticed and it's become a bit of a tourist hotspot. Most of the day-trippers congregate between 10am and 4pm; you could visit early in the morning or spend the night to see Lindos *au naturel*. Even in the bustle of the day, head off from the teeming main thoroughfares lined with tourist shops and cafes, and you'll find quiet corners of the village to explore.

HISTORY

Lindos is the most famous of the ancient cities of the Dodecanese and was an important Doric settlement because of its excellent vantage point and good harbour. It was first established around 2000 BC and is overlaid with a conglomeration of Byzantine, Frankish and Turkish remains.

After the founding of the city of Rhodes, Lindos declined in commercial significance, but remained an important place of worship. The ubiquitous St Paul landed here en route to Rome. Later, the Byzantine fortress was strengthened by the knights, and also used by the Turks. The 15th-century Church of Agios Ioannis, within the Acropolis, is festooned with 18th-century frescoes.

ORIENTATION & INFORMATION

The village is totally pedestrianised. All vehicular traffic terminates on the central square of Plateia Eleftherias, from where the main drag, Acropolis, begins. The donkey terminus for rides up to the Acropolis itself is a little way along here. Turn right at the donkey terminus to reach the post office, after 50m.

DODECANESE

THE CAPTAIN'S HOUSE   *Korina Miller*

During the 17th century, ship captains from Lindos grew increasingly prosperous. Many of them poured their new-found wealth into building lofty homes that towered over the traditional village houses.

I'm standing inside the oldest of these captain's houses. It was built 400 years ago and is small but very grand. The whitewashed walls stretch upward to a soaring resin ceiling, intricately painted with elaborate, colourful patterns and still scorched in the corner above where the original family cooked. You might be tricked into believing that the captain's family has just stepped out – except for the rather incongruous flat-screen TV and the stylish sofas and coffee tables. Savvas Kornaros is here doing a little repainting and tells me the story of the building.

'This house has been in my wife's family for 150 years. Her great-great grandfather bought it in the 19th century. Her father turned it into a bar 33 years ago, for local people and tourists. He lived here with his family at first, with the bar in the courtyard. But everyone wanted to come inside and see the ceiling and so after a couple of years he moved into the building next door and made the house part of the bar.

The bed is a traditional *penga* (raised wooden sleeping platform) where the whole family slept. The bed and the cupboards on either side, as well as the decor, are pretty much as they were when the captain lived here. Captains' houses didn't need to be large as they spent so much time at sea. The windows in these houses are up very high. This was to let the heat out in summer and also so that the captain's wife could watch the sea for the arrival of her husband's ship. The stone doorway is hand carved and each picture or symbol has meaning. Corn means good harvest, birds mean peace, the cross brings safety and the sunflowers sunlight. The number of ropes carved around the perimeter of the door shows how many ships the captain had. You'll see these symbols on lots of doorways around Lindos.'

We go outside into the courtyard with its intricately laid stone floor. 'This *hohlakia* (black-and-white pebble mosaic) floor is from 1911. It takes a lot of work to make. First the masons have to find enough stones of a similar shape and size. They create the pattern and then use a little bit of cement to put down the black stones and then fit the white ones around them. This kind of floor is expensive; I think the very best price you'd get is €200 for a square metre. That would be a very good deal. But all of the houses and courtyards in Lindos have these floors. They look good and they're long lasting. It's tradition.'

He has just finished cleaning the floor for the summer season. 'In the summer we get very busy here; everyone wants to see inside the house. If you do come in July or August, Sundays and Mondays are probably the quietest days. But the best times to visit Lindos are May and October when the weather is good. In the winter I only open if a cruise ship comes in. Otherwise I fix the place up. I do all of the maintenance myself.'

Savvas heads behind the courtyard bar to pour drinks for some locals who have wandered in. I ask him how tourism has changed Lindos over the years. 'I don't know what you mean. It hasn't. We've had the same people coming here for the past 25 years.'

By the donkey terminus is the Commercial Bank of Greece, with an ATM. The National Bank of Greece, located on the street opposite the Church of Agia Panagia, also has an ATM.

Lindianet (☎ 22440 32142; per hr €3.60; ☒ 9.30am-9pm Mon-Sat, 4-9pm Sun) Internet access plus wi-fi. In lower village.

Lindos Library & Laundrette (☎ 22440 31333; Acropolis; per load €7.50) Laundry service and second-hand English books. Also hires out fans.

Lindos Sun Tours (☎ 22440 31333; www.lindosun tours.gr; Acropolis) Has room-letting services, hires cars

and motorcycles and can assist with airport transfers, babysitting, etc.

Medical Clinic (☎ 22440 31224) Near the church.

Municipal Tourist Office (☎ 22440 31900; Plateia Eleftherias; ☒ 7.30am-9pm) Helpful, although too few staff, too many tourists. You may have to wait a while.

www.lindos-holiday.com A handy private website with a number of alternative villa accommodation options.

SIGHTS & ACTIVITIES
Acropolis of Lindos

Spectacularly perched atop a 116m-high rock is the **Acropolis** (☎ 22440 31258; admission €6;

8.30am-2.40pm Tue-Sun Sep-May, until 6pm Tue-Sun Jun-Aug). Once inside, a flight of steps leads to a large square. On the left (facing the next flight of steps) is a trireme, hewn out of the rock by the sculptor Pythocretes; a statue of Hagesandros, priest of Poseidon, originally stood on the deck of the ship. The steps ahead lead to the Acropolis via a vaulted corridor. A sharp left leads through an enclosed room to a row of storerooms on the right, while the stairway on the right leads to the remains of a 20-columned **Hellenistic stoa** (200 BC). The Byzantine **Church of Agios Ioannis**, with its ancient frescoes, is to the right of this stairway. The wide stairway behind the stoa leads to a 5th-century-BC propylaeum, beyond which is the 4th-century **Temple to Athena**, the site's most important ancient ruin. Athena was worshipped on Lindos as early as the 10th century BC and this temple has replaced earlier ones on the site. From its far side there are splendid views of Lindos village and its beach.

Donkey rides to the Acropolis cost €5 one way – be aware that the poor creatures should not be carrying anyone over 50kg (112lbs), though this stipulation is rarely enforced. To get here on your own steam, head straight into the village from the main square, turn left at the church and follow the signs. The last stretch is a strenuous 10-minute climb up slippery steps. There's no shade at the top; pack a hat and some water.

Beaches
The **Main Beach** is to the east of the Acropolis and is sandy with warm water. You can follow a path north to the western tip of the bay to the smaller **Pallas Beach** where there are some tavernas and a jetty. Avoid swimming near the jetty as it's home to black stinging anemones. On the western side of the Acropolis is the sheltered **St Paul's Bay** with its warm, turquoise water. It's a bit more of a trek to get to but often quieter than the main beach.

SLEEPING
Accommodation can be expensive, hard to find or already reserved. Be sure to call ahead.

Anastasia Studio (☎ 22440 31751; www.lindos -studios.gr; d/tr €45/60; P ⚡) On the eastern side of town, these modern apartments are spacious and comfortable, with fantastic flower be-decked verandas affording sea views. Each has a well equipped kitchen and separate bedroom and there's a minimarket across the road.

Electra (☎ 22440 31266; s/d €45/55; ⚡) Thankfully, Lindos' true budget option is brilliant. Electra has an expansive and popular roof terrace with superb views and a beautiful shady garden of lemon trees. The 11 rooms are airy and spacious. Each has a fridge and there's a communal kitchen. Follow the donkey route to find it.

Filoxenia Guest House (☎ 22440 31266; www.lindos -filoxenia.com; d/ste incl breakfast €90/140; ⚡ 🖥) Inside a traditional home, these simple rooms are embellished with wrought-iron bed frames, antique furnishing, tiled floors or raised sleeping platforms. Family rooms are also available. All rooms have fridge and kitchenette.

our pick **Melenos** (☎ 22440 32222; www.melenoslin dos.com; ste incl breakfast €385; ⚡ 🖥 📶) The kind of place most of us dream of staying, Melenos is pure luxury. Built in 17th-century style, almost everything has been handmade, hand-carved or hand-stitched – from the sandstone motifs to the mosaic floors, painted ceiling, woven fabrics and cedar sleeping platforms. Artefacts embellish the already gorgeous rooms while the verandas offer privacy, more comfort and stunning views. Head up to the rooftop bar for your evening aperitif.

EATING
Valanda's Crepes (☎ 22440 31673; crêpes €3-5) You'll smell your way to this crêperie en route to the Acropolis. Watch the crêpes flipped in front of you within the cool blue interior. Choose from sweet and savoury fillings.

Captain's House (☎ 22440 31235; snacks €3-6) This atmospheric, shaded courtyard is an oasis after a trip up to the Acropolis. Sit on sofas in the shaded courtyard or head inside the traditional captain's house. Refresh with iced coffees, beer on tap, cocktails and juice or munch on baguettes or toasted sandwiches. Follow signs left from the Acropolis.

Eklekto (☎ 22440 31286; mains €3-6) Popular with locals and expats, this leafy courtyard and comfortable cafe has sandwiches, tortillas and salads – try Cleopatra's with dried figs, rocket and pine nuts. It's just east off the main drag.

Kalypso (☎ 22440 32135; mains €6-12) Set in one of Lindos' historic buildings, this is a family-run restaurant that's stood the test of time. Ignore the touristy outdoor appearance; inside you'll find traditional decor and a warm atmosphere. Dine on the rooftop on feta flutes, fresh tuna, sausages in mustard, or rabbit stew in red

DODECANESE

wine. The menu is enormous, with vegetarian and children's options. Take the second right off the main drag to find it.

DRINKING

Lindos has plenty of trendy bars and clubs, many of which come and go in fashion with each summer season. Just follow the throngs.

WESTERN RHODES & THE INTERIOR

Greener and more forested than the east coast, Western Rhodes makes for a great road trip with a number of worthwhile sights. It's also windier so the sea tends to be rough and the beaches are mostly pebble. The east–west roads that cross the interior have great scenery and very little traffic. If you have transport, they're well worth exploring. It's also good cycling territory if you have a suitably geared bicycle.

Ancient Ialysos Αρχαία Ιαλυσός

The Doric city of **Ialysos** (adult €3; ☼ 8.30am-3pm Tue-Sun) was built on Filerimos Hill, an excellent vantage point, and attracted successive invaders over the years. Over time, it became a hotchpotch of Doric, Byzantine and medieval remains. As you enter, stairs lead to the ancient remains of a 3rd-century-BC temple and the restored 14th-century **Chapel of Agios Georgios** and **Monastery of Our Lady**. All that's left of the temple are the foundations but the chapel is a peaceful retreat.

Take the path left from the entrance to a 12th-century **chapel** (looking like a bunker) filled with frescoes. They're not well preserved but worth a look. To the right of the entrance lies a ruined and no longer accessible **fortress** used by Süleyman the Magnificent during his siege of Rhodes Town.

There is a sign requesting that visitors dress 'properly'. Although there's no elaboration, out of respect, shoulders should be covered and women should wear long skirts or trousers. Outside the entrance you'll find a small kiosk, a whole lot of peacocks and a popular tree-lined path with the **Stations of the Cross**. There are also ruins of a **Byzantine church** below the car park. Ialysos is 10km from Rhodes, with buses running every half hour.

Ialysos to Petaloudes

Heading south from Ialysos, you'll come to the small but interesting **Bee Museum** (☎ 22410

48200; www.mel.gr; admission €2; ☼ 8.30am-3pm), with lots of English explanations. You'll learn about the process of honey-making and collecting, equipment from past and present, and the history of beekeeping on Rhodes. See bees at work, dress up in beekeepers outfits and watch demonstrations of making honey. The gift shop is a great place to stock up on souvenirs: honey rum, honey soap, honey sweets and just plain honey. To reach the museum, join the super-smooth Tsairi–Airport motorway towards Kalithies; it's on the right, just past Pastida.

From here it's a short trip to **Marista** from where the scenic road takes you up over pine forested hills to **Psinthos**, where you'll find a lively square lined with lunch spots. **To Stolidi Tis Psinthoy** (☎ 22410 59998; mains €7-9) has a country feel to it with wooden beams, checked tablecloths and family photos on the walls. Try spicy pork, dolmadhes and freshly baked country bread.

Petaloudes Πεταλούδες

Northwest of Psinthos, **Petaloudes** (adult €3; ☼ 8.30am-4.30pm) is better known as the Valley of the Butterflies. Visit in June, July or August when these colourful creatures mature, and you'll quickly see why. They're actually moths (*Callimorpha quadripunctarea*) drawn to this gorge by the scent of the resin exuded by the storax trees. In summer, this is a very popular sight frequented by tour buses. Come out of season and you'll miss the winged critters but you'll have the gorgeous forest path, rustic footbridges, streams and pools to yourself.

While the moths have undoubtedly benefited from having a reserve of their own, their numbers are under threat due to noise disturbance. You're therefore asked not to clap your hands or make any other disruptive noise.

Ancient Kamiros Αρχαία Κάμειρο

The extensive **ruins** of the Doric city of Kamiros stand on a hillside above the west coast, 34km south of Rhodes Town. The ancient city, known for its figs, oil and wine, reached the height of its powers in the 6th century BC. By the 4th century BC it had been superseded by Rhodes. Most of the city was destroyed by earthquakes in 226 and 142 BC, leaving only a discernible layout. Ruins include a **Doric temple**, with one column still standing, **Hellenistic houses**, a **Temple to Athena** and a 3rd-century **great stoa**. It was built on top of a huge 6th-century cistern that supplied the houses with rainwater through an advanced drainage system.

At the time of research, the entire site was closed due to destruction by forest fires. Check with EOT (p278) to see if it has reopened.

Ancient Kamiros to Monolithos
Αρχαία Κάμειρος προς Μονόλιθο
Skala Kamirou, 13.5km south of ancient Kamiros, serves as the access port for travellers heading to and from the island of Halki (p292). The small harbour itself is north of town and very picturesque. Even if you're not waiting for a ferry, it's worth stopping for lunch at **O Loukas** (☎ 22460 31271; mains €7-12). With big, sea views, appropriately nautical decor and a relaxed atmosphere, it serves up very fresh fish, seafood and homemade burgers.

Just south of the harbour, before the town of Skala, is a turning for Kritinia. This will lead you to the ruined 16th-century **Kritinia Castle** with awe-inspiring views along the coast and across to Halki. It's a magical setting where you expect to come across Romeo or Rapunzel.

The road south from here to Monolithos has some stunning scenery. From Skala Kamirou the road winds uphill, with a turning left for the wine-making area of Embonas (below) about 5km further on. The main road continues for another 9km to **Siana**, a picturesque village below Mt Akramytis (825m), famed for its honey and *souma* – a spirit made from seasonal fruit.

The village of Monolithos, 5km beyond Siana, has the spectacularly sited 15th-century **Castle of Monolithos** perched on a sheer 240m-high rock and reached via a dirt track. To enter, climb through the hole in the wall. Continuing along this track, bear right at the fork for **Moni Agiou Georgiou**, or left for the very pleasant shingled **Fourni Beach**.

Wine Country
From Salakos, head inland to **Embonas** on the slopes of Mt Attavyros (1215m), the island's highest mountain. Embonas is the wine capital of Rhodes and produces some of the island's best tipples. The red Cava Emery or Zacosta and white Villare are good choices. Taste and buy them at **Emery Winery** (☎ 22410 41208; www.emery.gr; Embonas; admission free; ⊙ 9.30am-4.30pm April-Oct), which offers tours of its cottage production. You'll find it on the eastern edge of town.

Embonas is no great shakes itself, despite being touted by the tourism authorities as a 'traditional village'. Detour around Mt Attavyros to **Agios Isidoros**, 14km south of Embonas, a prettier and still unspoilt wine-producing village en route to Siana.

SOUTHERN RHODES
South of Lindos, the island is lush and less developed. As you head further south, it takes on a windswept appearance and the villages seem to have a slower pace. It's well worth exploring – strike out along a quiet country road and you're sure to stumble upon lovely views, quiet villages and family tavernas pleased to whip you up a hearty meal.

Just 2km south of Lindos, sandy **Pefki Beach** is deservedly popular. If it's too crowded, try **Glystra Beach**, just down the road and a great spot for swimming.

The flourishing village of **Laerma** is 12km northwest of Lardos. From here it's another 5km through hilly, green countryside to the beautifully sited 9th-century **Moni Tharri** (entrance by donation), the island's first monastery, which has been re-established as a monastic community. It's a bit of a trek but worth the drive if you're into frescoes. Every inch of the chapel's interior is covered in ornate 13th-century paintings which are very well preserved. The monastery is generally left unlocked during the day.

Further down the coast is the turning for **Asklipieio**, with the ruins of a castle and the 11th-century **Church of Kimisis Theotokou**, with more Byzantine wall paintings.

Gennadi Γεννάδι
pop 655
A patchwork of narrow streets and white-washed houses set several hundred metres back from the beach, Gennadi (ye-*nah*-dhi) is a quiet village with enough facilities to make it a decent southern base. You'll find a fruit market, bakery, cafes, supermarket, internet access, car hire and a couple of cocktail bars to keep you going.

Effie's Dreams Apartments (☎ 22440 43410; www.effiesdreams.com; d/tr €54/58; ⊠ ▯) is next to an enormous 800-year-old mulberry tree and has simple, clean studios with small kitchenettes and lovely rural and sea vistas from the communal balcony. You'll also find a cafe and

DODECANESE

bar serving drinks and filling snacks, such as country-style sausage with onions and peppers. The beach is a 10-minute walk away.

Mama's Kitchen (☎ 22440 43547; pasta €5-6) looks pretty average but makes fresh pizza in front of you. Try one with feta, olives and swordfish. There are also pasta and grills.

Gennadi to Prasonisi Γεννάδι προς Πρασονήσι

From Gennadi an almost uninterrupted beach of pebbles, shingle and sand dunes extends down to **Plimmyri**, 11km south.

Watch for a signposted turning to **Lahania**, 2km off the main highway. The top road of Lahania is less than special, but head downhill into the old town (the first left if you're coming from the coast) to find a village of winding alleyways and traditional buildings that makes it onto very few tourist itineraries. Surrounded by lemon trees and flowers, **Agios Georgios** is a pretty church in the main square with a star-strewn ceiling and a plethora of chandeliers.

If a rural holiday takes your fancy but you want to do it in comfort, stay at the **Four Elements** (☎ 6939450014; studio/apt per week €515/550; 🕿 🖳 🖭) with its exceptionally homey and spacious apartments. Some have sea views and one has a traditional open fireplace. All have full kitchens and there's a divine pool, kid's pool, outdoor grill and garden. One of the apartments is wheelchair accessible.

While in Lahania, stop for lunch at **Taverna Platanos** (☎ 22440 46027; mains €3-5), a relaxed taverna tucked behind the church in the main square. With traditional decor and a flower-filled patio, it's a great place to take a break.

The main coastal road continues south past countless chapels to **Kattavia**, Rhodes' most southerly village. It's a friendly place that doesn't see a lot of tourist traffic. Stop in at **Penelope's** (☎ 6944794342; mains €5-12) in the main square for fresh fish, handmade chips and Greek salad made with lots of local greens.

From Kattavia, a 10km road snakes south across windswept terrain to remote and gorgeous **Cape Prasonisi**, the island's southernmost point. Once joined to Rhodes by a narrow sandy isthmus, it's now split by encroaching seas. If you're looking for lunch or a bed, there's a resort here that caters to windsurfers and has surfer-dude-style restaurants and hostels. Outside of the summer season it's totally shut.

Kattavia to Monolithos Κατταβία προς Μονόλιθος

Lonely and exposed, Rhodes' southwest coast doesn't see many visitors. Forest fires in recent years have devastated many of the west-facing hillsides but it's nevertheless a beautiful place to visit with an edge-of-the-earth feeling. The beaches along here are prone to strong winds and currents. About 10km north of Kattavia, a turn-off to the right leads to the serene 18th-century **Moni Skiadi**, with terrific views down to the coast.

HALKI ΧΑΛΚΗ

pop 310

Tiny Halki (*hal-ki*) rests in relative obscurity, just a stone's throw from Rhodes. Rocky and bare, it draws those who come for its relaxation value. Visitors park themselves for weeks at a time in restored stone villas that once belonged to sea captains, and spend their days doing little more than chilling out and socialising with the growing, seasonal expat community.

In the days of antiquity, before water had to be carted over from Rhodes, the island's wells supported a population of 7000 who produced wheat and copper (from which the island's name is derived). In later years, sponge-fishing became the main industry and its demise led to waves of emigration. The largest group departed for Florida in 1911, where they established a strong Greek community that continues to support the island. Halki existed in almost forgotten silence until the vacation boom of the 1970s and 1980s saw its fortunes rise once more.

Despite its barren appearance, Halki is humming with more life than you might think. With 14 types of butterflies, over 40 kinds of birds, fields or oregano and marjoram, countless bee boxes and around 6000 goats, it's a wonder there's room for the sun loungers at all. Visit in spring to see the island blanketed in wild flowers.

Getting There & Away

There is a daily boat from Skala Kamirou on Rhodes with a connecting bus to Rhodes Town every day but Sunday. Walk 150m from the Skala Kamirou ferry quay to the main road to find the bus stop.

Ferries also connect Halki with Sitia on Crete, Karpathos, Santorini and

DODECANESE

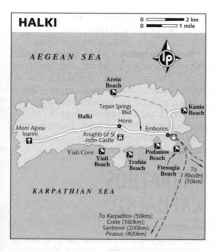

HALKI

AEGEAN SEA

Areta Beach

Tarpon Springs Blvd
Halki
Horio
Kania Beach
Moni Agiou Ioanni
Knights of St John Castle
Emborios
Yiali Cove
Yiali Beach
Podamos Beach
Trahia Beach
Ftenagia Beach
To Rhodes (10km)

KARPATHIAN SEA

To Karpathos (50km);
Crete (160km);
Santorini (200km);
Piraeus (400km)

0 — 2 km
0 — 1 mile

Piraeus. Tickets are available from Chalki Tours and Zifos Travel in Emborios (see below). For more information, see Island Hopping (p513).

Getting Around

The majority of people get around the island on foot. In summer, a minibus runs hourly between Emborios and Moni Agiou Ioanni (€2). The island also has a lone taxi usually found parked near the post office. Prices and telephone numbers are posted at kiosks. There's also a water taxi that serves the main beaches and you can find excursion boats to the uninhabited island of Alimia (€30), with fields of wild herbs. There are no hire cars or motorcycles on Halki.

EMBORIOS ΕΜΠΟΡΕΙΟΣ
pop 50

The picturesque port village of Emborios is draped around a narrow horseshoe bay of crystal-blue waters. The mansions surrounding it were once the homes of sea captains who took inspiration for the large Venetian-style shuttered windows from their travels across the Mediterranean. Cars are banned from the harbour once the ferries have come and gone, so the waterside enjoys a relaxing, vehicle-free setting.

Orientation & Information

Boats arrive at the centre of Emborios' harbour and most services and accommodation are within easy walking distance. The free quarterly *Halki Visitor* is a good source of local information.

There's a DodecNet ATM at the information booth on the harbour although there's no bank on the island.

Chalki Tours (☎ 22460 45281; fax 22460 45219) For assistance on accommodation, travel, excursions and currency exchange.

Clinic (☎ 22460 45206; ⏰ 9am-noon & 6-8pm Mon-Fri) Weekend numbers posted at clinic for emergencies.

Information Hut (quay) Local info posted.

Police and Port Police (☎ 22460 45220) On the harbour.

Post office (⏰ 9am-1.30pm Mon-Fri) On the harbour.

www.chalki.gr A useful (though slightly dated) reference point.

www.halki-travel-guide.com Packed with lots of local info.

Zifos Travel (☎ 22460 45082; zifostravel.gr) Helps with accommodation, travel, excursions and currency exchange.

Sights

The old **mansions** that festoon the harbour are a visual feast. Many have been, or are being, restored to their former glory, while others rest in a complete state of disrepair. Together they give Halki a picturesque look and make wandering around the harbour a popular pastime.

The impressive stone **clock tower** at the southern side of the harbour is a gift from the Halki community in Florida. The tower looks resolutely impressive but don't rely on it for the time.

The **Church of Agios Nikolaos** has the tallest belfry in the Dodecanese and boasts an impressive pebbled courtyard on the east side. A small upstairs **museum** (adult €2; ⏰ 6-7pm Mon & Fri, 11am-noon Sun) houses ancient bibles, icons and other ecclesiastical displays.

Sleeping

Most accommodation is prebooked months in advance by foreign tour companies, so booking ahead is best. Both travel agents in town can help you find a room.

Captain's House (☎ 22460 45201; capt50@otenet .gr; d €40) This snug 19th-century house has slightly dated decor and period furniture in comfortable rooms. The tranquil tree-shaded garden is a lovely place to relax. Bookings are always recommended.

Mouthouria (☎ 22460 72755; www.halkimouthau ria.com; house €90) Once the home of a Turkish Governor, this house is decorated in deep reds and yellows, with an intricately painted ceiling. With two bedrooms, it can accommodate up to six people and its fully equipped kitchen, garden and view-filled balcony make it ideal for longer stays.

Villa Fiona (☎ 44 01363 83343; www.villafiona.com; house per week €375) This charming restored home will make you want to stay forever. Sleeping up to six, its two bedrooms and lounge are simple and airy. The separate, bright kitchen will inspire you to whip up home-cooked meals. Relaxation is enhanced with books, games, music and sea views from the balcony. It's a minute's walk to a ladder descending into the clear harbour water.

Eating

Mavri Thalassa (☎ 22460 45021; mains €4-6) Found on the south side of the harbour, this place specialises in seafood and is popular with locals and visitors. Try the whole grilled calamari or local, minuscule Halki shrimps – eaten whole.

Maria's Taverna (☎ 22460 45300; mains €4-7) Under the shade of trees, fill up on pasta and local home-cooked specialities like Halki lamb stew. Its central location makes it a popular lunch spot.

Avra (☎ 6945148196; mains €4-7) With a long, tempting menu, Avra's Georgian owners serve excellent chicken and seafood dishes downed with draught white wine.

Remezzo (☎ 22460 45010; mains €5-7) Is your tummy feeling homesick? Give it a break from Greek salad and treat it to pizza, pasta, Mexican salad and apple dessert.

AROUND HALKI

In the next bay south, sandy **Podamos Beach** is the nearest and best beach. Only 1km from Emborios in the direction of Horio, it has shallow water that's ideal for kids. You'll find a basic taverna and loungers and umbrellas for hire. Pebbly **Ftenagia Beach**, past the headland and 500m to the south of Emborios, is excellent for rock swimming and snorkelling. The **Ftenagia Beach Taverna** (☎ 6945998333; mains €5-7; ☑ lunch & dinner) is a cosy waterside eatery.

Horio, a 30-minute walk (3km) along Tarpon Springs Blvd from Emborios, was once a thriving community of 3000 people, but it's now almost completely derelict. The **church** contains beautiful frescoes but is only unlocked for festivals. On 14 August the entire island climbs up here for a ceremony devoted to the Virgin Mary, the church's icon. A barely perceptible path leads from Horio's churchyard up to the **Knights of St John Castle**. It's a steep 15-minute walk with spectacular views.

Moni Agiou Ioanni is a two-hour, unshaded 8km walk along a broad concrete road from Horio. The church and courtyard, protected by the shade of an enormous cypress tree, is a quiet, tranquil place that comes alive each year on 28 and 29 August during the feast of the church's patron, St John. You can sometimes stay in simple rooms in exchange for a donation to the church.

KARPATHOS
ΚΑΡΠΑΘΟΣ

pop 6080

Despite its soaring mountains, colourful harbours and sandy beaches, Karpathos (kar-pa-thos) has long sat in the shadow of its northern neighbours, giving it an off-the-beaten-track quality that's now drawing tourists. The island's windswept coastline has become a magnet for surfers and hits the spotlight each summer when it hosts an international kitesurfing competition. Be prepared for gusts and gales at any time of year.

Over the years, many of the islands' inhabitants have migrated to the USA, from where they slowly trickle back to invest their overseas earnings. The consequence is a vibrant mix of contemporary and traditional culture. In the north of the island lies Olymbos, a small community that was isolated for years from the south by rugged mountains. Today it's still home to a unique culture that has survived the onslaught of modernity and offers a window into the past.

Getting There & Away

Karpathos has an airport with regular links to Athens, Kasis, Sitia and Rhodes. **Olympic Air** (☎ 22450 22057; www.olympicairlines.com; cnr Apodimon Karpathion & 25 Martiou St, Pigadia) is on the central square in Pigadia.

Scheduled ferries service Rhodes, Piraeus, Kasos, Sitia, Agios Nikolaos, Milos and Santorini. Tickets can be bought from Possi Travel (p296) in Pigadia. A small local caïque also runs three times weekly between Finiki (Karpathos) and Fry (Kasos).

For more information, see Island Hopping (p515).

KARPATHOS

Getting Around
TO/FROM THE AIRPORT
There is no airport bus. Hop in a taxi to Pigadia (€15) and beyond.

BOAT
From May to September there are daily excursion boats from Pigadia to Diafani with a bus transfer to Olymbos (€23). Boats depart Pigadia at 8.30am. Tickets are available from Possi Travel (p296). There are also frequent boats to the beaches of Kyra Panagia and Apella (€10). Tickets can be bought at the quay.

From Diafani, excursion boats go to nearby beaches and occasionally to the uninhabited islet of Saria, where there are some Byzantine remains. See p299 for details.

BUS
Pigadia is the transport hub of the island; a schedule is posted at the **bus terminus** (☎ 22450 22338; M Mattheou) and the tourist info kiosk (p296). Buses (€2; July and August only, daily except Sunday) serve most of the settlements in southern Karpathos, including the west-coast beaches. There is no bus between Pigadia and Olymbos or Diafani.

CAR, MOTORCYCLE & BICYCLE
On the eastern side of Pigadia, **Rent A Car Circle** (☎ 22450 22690/911; 28 Oktovriou) hires cars and motorcycles. Possi Travel (p296) also arranges car hire.

The precipitous, and at times hairy, 19.5km stretch of road from Spoa to Olymbos is being slowly graded and will one day be sealed. You can drive it with care; do not tackle this road by motorcycle or scooter. If you hire a vehicle and plan to drive to Olymbos, opt for a small jeep and fill up your tank before you leave.

TAXI
Pigadia's **taxi rank** (☎ 22450 22705; Dimokratias) is close to the centre of town where you'll find current rates posted. A taxi to Ammoöpi costs €8, the airport €15, Arkasa and Pyles €16, and Kyra Panagia €20.

PIGADIA ΠΗΓΑΔΙΑ
pop 1690
While it may feel a little forsaken by the rest of the Dodecanese, Pigadia (pi-*gha*-dhi-ya) is laden with restaurants, hotels and bars. Small and compact, it spills down to the edge

DODECANESE

of Vrondi Bay, where boats bob in a small harbour. The architecture is nothing special (mostly cement blocks erected in the 1960s and '70s) but, with its lively atmosphere and sandy beach, it's a pleasant spot to base yourself.

Orientation & Information

The ferry quay is at the northeastern end of the wide harbour. It's a short walk to the centre of Pigadia, which is punctuated by the main street, Apodimon Karpathion. This in turn leads west to the central square of Plateia 5 Oktovriou. For the sandy beach, head west 300m to Pigadia Bay.

Avra Tourist Shop (☎ 22450 22388; fax 22450 23486; 28 Oktovriou 50) Sells maps for driving and hiking.

Cyber Games (☎ 22450 22110; seafront; per hr €2; ✆ 9am-1am) Get online amongst gaming teenagers.

National Bank of Greece (Apodimon Karpathion) Has an ATM.

Police (☎ 22450 22224) Near the hospital at the western end of town.

Possi Travel (☎ 22450 22235; possitvl@hotmail.com; Apodimon Karpathion) The main travel agency for ferry and air tickets.

Post office (Ethnikis Andistasis) Near the hospital.

Pot Pourri (☎ 22450 29073; Apodimon Karpathion; per hr €3; ✆ 7am-1am) Internet access amidst a comfortable cafe.

Tourist information office (☎ 22450 23835; ✆ Jul-Aug) In a kiosk in the middle of the seafront.

www.inkarpathos.com Locally maintained with articles, news and info.

Sights

Looking down over the town from a small seaside bluff, the **Archaeological Museum of Karpathos** (admission free; ✆ 9am-1pm & 6-8.30pm Tue, Thu & Sat, 8.30am-3pm Wed, Fri & Sun) houses local artefacts including coins, an early baptismal font, and ceramics.

Follow the coast southwest from town to find a sandy stretch of beach and, after 2km, the ruins of the early Christian **Basilica of Agia Fotini** resting on the seashore. If you head east along the coast and past the ferry quay, you'll come to a peaceful **chapel** high on the hill with stunning views back to town and across the sea.

Sleeping

Pigadia's accommodation is plentiful, with lots of budget options. A few enterprising owners meet the boats.

Hotel Karpathos (☎ 22450 22347; fax 22450 22248; r €25; ✆) A little worn but spotlessly clean, these

rooms have a fridge and well-scrubbed bathrooms. They're small but you can escape onto the balcony. The top floors have sea views.

Rose's Studios (☎ 22450 22284, 6974725427; www.rosesstudios.com; r €30; ✆) Slightly characterless but very well maintained rooms have kitchenettes and great balconies with views to the sea. Rooms facing the back are a little cheaper. The lovely owners live downstairs and are a wealth of local info.

Elias Rooms (☎ 22450 22446, 6978587924; www.eliasrooms.com; s/d €30/35, s/d apt €35/40; ✆) As you climb the rather steep stairs to this hotel, you can console yourself knowing that the view is well worth it. The three rooms are small and plain while the apartments have more character, tiled floors and, in one, a traditional raised sleeping area. The friendly owner has lots of info to dole out.

Amarylis Hotel (☎ /fax 22450 22375; www.amarylis.gr; s/d €30/40; ✆) These very dated but amazingly spacious rooms are great for families. Many sleep up to four and all have kitchenettes and big balconies.

Hotel Titania (☎ 22450 22144; www.titaniakarpathos.gr; s/d €40/55; ✆) With bedspreads so dated they're almost back in style, these rooms are cramped and overpriced. However, in winter they may be all that's open. Ask for a sea view or a room facing the courtyard, or put up with the noisy road outside.

Lemon Tree Apartments (☎ 22450 22081; www.inkarpathos.com/lemontree; s/d €50/60; ✆) Newly refurbished rooms aren't huge but they've got excellent kitchenettes and big balconies, some with sea views. Doubles have queen-sized beds!

Eating

Amongst the plethora of indistinguishable waterfront establishments are a few gems. Watch for the local speciality, *makarounes* (homemade pasta cooked with cheese and onions). For self-catering, head to the large supermarket across from the taxi rank.

Pastry Shop (☎ 22450 22530; Dimokratias; sweets €1-4) With towering stacks of local sweets, Karpathian baklava, ice cream and waffles, this is the place to indulge with the locals, all washed down with fresh juice or coffee. You can also pick up savoury pies for a seaside picnic.

To Helliniko (☎ 22450 23932; Apodimon Karpathion; mains €4-9; ✆ year-round) Popular with locals, To Helliniko offers a fantastic dining experience.

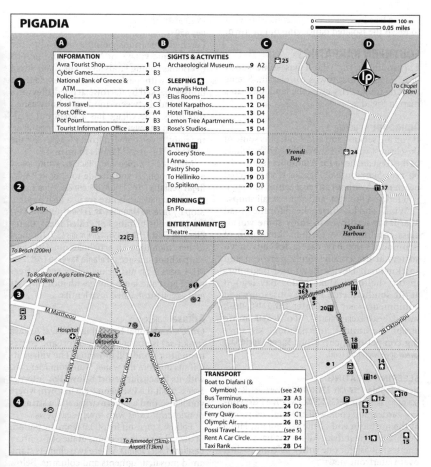

PIGADIA

INFORMATION	
Avra Tourist Shop	**1** D4
Cyber Games	**2** B3
National Bank of Greece & ATM	**3** C3
Police	**4** A3
Possi Travel	**5** C3
Post Office	**6** A4
Pot Pourri	**7** B3
Tourist Information Office	**8** B3

SIGHTS & ACTIVITIES	
Archaeological Museum	**9** A2

SLEEPING	
Amarylis Hotel	**10** D4
Elias Rooms	**11** D4
Hotel Karpathos	**12** D4
Hotel Titania	**13** D4
Lemon Tree Apartments	**14** D4
Rose's Studios	**15** D4

EATING	
Grocery Store	**16** D4
I Anna	**17** D2
Pastry Shop	**18** D3
To Helliniko	**19** D3
To Spitikon	**20** D3

DRINKING	
En Plo	**21** C3

ENTERTAINMENT	
Theatre	**22** B2

TRANSPORT	
Boat to Diafani (& Olymbos)	(see 24)
Bus Terminus	**23** A3
Excursion Boats	**24** D2
Ferry Quay	**25** C1
Olympic Air	**26** B3
Possi Travel	(see 5)
Rent A Car Circle	**27** B4
Taxi Rank	**28** D4

Map labels: To Chapel (30m); Vrondi Bay; Pigadia Harbour; Jetty; To Beach (200m); To Basilica of Agia Fotini (2km); Aperi (8km); 25 Martiou; M Mattheou; Hospital; Plateia 5 Oktovriou; Ethnikis Andistasis; Georgiou Lambraki; Mitropolitou Apostolou; Apodimon Karpathion; Dimokratias; 28 Oktovriou; To Ammoopi (5km); Airport (13km)

With lots of seating but a cosy atmosphere, you'll be served smoked sardines, Karpathian cheese, stuffed artichokes and goat cooked in tomato purée. Be sure to check out the specials board.

I Anna (☎ 22450 22820; Apodimon Karpathion; mains €5-9) You'll quickly forget about the slightly tacky decor as you dig into Pigadia's freshest fish, caught daily off the owner's own boats. Try the fisherman's macaroni with octopus, shrimps and mussels, or the Karpathian sardines in oil.

To Spitikon (☎ 22450 23675; Dimokratias; mains €7-10) A rustic, family atmosphere and attentive service makes this a popular stop. Traditional dishes are served alongside more unusual options like potatoes stuffed with peppermint

and sour cream, spring rolls with crabmeat and bacon, balsamic chicken and *kalamari* (squid) stuffed with dill and feta. The pizza is slightly greasy but satisfying and can be ordered for takeaway.

Drinking & Entertainment

Beneath the museum you'll find a new, open-air **theatre** where music and cultural events are often hosted in summer. For an evening drink, head to the seaside, which is lined with bars and cafes, particularly west of the info kiosk. Try **En Plo** (cocktails €6; ☺ 8am-late), just below the National Bank, for a huge list of cocktails and coffees in a funky, friendly atmosphere. If you're looking for somewhere to boogie, **Heaven Club** (☺ until 1am nightly, Fri & Sat only in winter)

DODECANESE

offers a free bus service to patrons who want to reach the isolated dance club out of town.

SOUTHERN KARPATHOS

The south of the island has some sandy beaches and quiet towns to relax in. Scenic walking tracks criss-cross the land; pick up a map in Pigadia.

Ammoöpi Αμμοöπή

If you are seeking sun and sand, plus some of the clearest water for snorkelling in the whole of the Aegean, head for Ammoöpi (amm-oh-oh-*pee*), 5km south of Pigadia. It's a scattered beach resort without any real centre, although you'll find a bus stop and some small shops.

Wind- and kitesurfers head for the broad **Afiartis Bay** in droves to enjoy some world-class conditions. A further 8km south of Ammoöpi, the bay caters for advanced surfers at the crazily windy northern end (nicknamed 'Devil's Bay') and beginners in the sheltered Makrygialos Bay lagoon at the southern end. For lessons, tours and equipment, visit **Pro Center** (☎ 22450 91062; www.chris-schill.com; Afiartis). To learn more about the annual international kitesurfing competition, check out **Speed World Cup** (www.speedworldcup.com).

SLEEPING & EATING

Hotel Sophia (☎ /fax 22450 81078; www.hotelsophia-karpathos.gr/sophia; d €40; ☒ ☒) With a burgeoning garden and cool, well-maintained rooms at the northern end of the settlement, Hotel Sophia is a great deal. All rooms have kitchenettes but ask for one with a balcony to dine over waterfront views.

Vardes (☎ /fax 22450 81111; www.hotelvardes.com; s/d €57/62; ☒ ☒) These simple, spacious studios are set back against the hillside among a lush olive grove and a few banana palms. Chill on the shaded balconies or at the laid-back bar. Some rooms can sleep up to five and it's an easy walk to the beach.

Ammoöpi Taverna (☎ 22450 81138; mains €4-7) At the far northern end of Ammoöpi and right on the beach, the food here is uniformly good. Look for the daily specials – the clove-laced *mousakas* (sliced aubergine and mincemeat arranged in layers and baked) is excellent.

Taverna Helios (☎ 22450 81148; mains €5-7) Just back from the main beach and handy for lunch after a swim, Helios offers Greek and international cuisine with large portions.

Menetes Μενετές
pop 450

Perched precariously atop a sheer cliff, the picturesque village of Menetes (me-ne-*tes*) overlooks rolling landscape. The main street is lined with pastel-coloured neoclassical houses, backed by narrow, stepped alleyways that wind between modest whitewashed dwellings. The village has a small but well-presented **museum** (admission free; ☒ on request) on the right as you come in from Pigadia. Ask the owner of Taverna Manolis to open it.

Menetes is a pleasant place to while away an afternoon. If you decide to stay, try **Mike Rigas Domatia** (☎ 22450 81269; d/tr €20/25), a traditional Karpathian house set in a lush garden. Stop by **Taverna Manolis** (☎ 22450 81103; mains €5-7) for generous helpings of grilled meat, or try **Dionysos Fiesta** (☎ 22450 81269; mains €5-7) for local dishes, including an artichoke omelette and Karpathian sausages. **Pelagia Taverna** (☎ 22450 81135; mains €5-8), just below town, serves free-range goat and lamb along with local cheeses and excellent mashed fava lentils.

Arkasa Αρκάσα

Once a traditional Karpathian village, Arkasa (ar-*ka*-sa) is now a low-key resort and comes to an utter standstill in winter. The village itself sits up from the water, 9km from Menetes, with its beachside resort below. For internet access, visit the Partheon Cafe in town, where you'll also find a supermarket and a string of nondescript cafes with lovely sea views.

Follow a turn-off for 500m from the bottom of the village to the remains of the 5th-century **Basilica of Agia Sophia**, where two chapels stand amid mosaic fragments and columns. Below it you can walk along the coast to an ancient **acropolis**. Just south across the headland from here is **Agios Nikolaos Beach**. About 600m off the main road, it's small and sandy and gets busy in summer with a volleyball net and clear water. Kip out on the water's edge at **Glaros Studios** (☎ 22450 61015; glaros@greekhotel.com; Agios Nikolaos; studios €65), where rooms are decorated in traditional Karpathian style. There's a relaxed adjoining restaurant.

On the road to Finiki, **Eleni Studios** (☎ /fax 22450 61248; www.elenikarpathos.gr; Arkasa; s/d €35/40; ☒) has breezy rooms with touches of colour and kitchenettes. Relax in the on-site bar or the gorgeous pool overlooking the sea. Family rooms are available here too. For something a little plusher, try **Arkasa Bay Hotel** (☎ 22450

61410; www.arkasabay.com; apt €100; ⌘ 🛜 📺) with its relatively grand rooms, cocktail bar and spectacular views. Located at the southern end of town, it caters well to families with its apartments and children's pool.

Finiki Φοινίκι

The quaint fishing village of Finiki (fi-*ni*-ki) lies 2km north of Arkasa. The best local swimming is at **Agios Georgios Beach**, between Arkasa and Finiki, while the small, sandy cove at Finiki is okay for wading in but mainly used for fishing boats. **Kamarakia Beach**, signposted before Agios Georgios, is a narrow cove with strong sea currents.

Park your bags at **Finiki View Hotel** (☎ 22450 61400; www.finikiview.gr; r €50-60, apt €60; ⌘ 🛜 📺) where you soak up the view in an outdoor pool. Rooms are simple but spacious and the pricier ones have traditional design including raised sleeping quarters. It's just above the village, overlooking the bay.

Dine on stuffed vine leaves, spicy cheese salad, chicken souvlaki and fresh fish galore at **Marina Taverna** (☎ 22450 61100; mains €4-7; ☿ year-round) where locals relax to traditional music and tables spill out along the harbour.

Nestled in a verdant garden some 9km north of Finiki are the secluded **Pine Tree Studios** (☎ 6977369948; www.pinetree-karpathos.gr; Adia; d €35, apt €45-70; ⌘). Rooms at this rural retreat are comfortable and spacious with kitchenettes and views over to Kasos. The apartments are fantastic – one with a fireplace and traditional bed and the other with stone walls and oodles of character. The on-site restaurant draws locals from around the island, serving fresh fruit and vegetables from the garden in a relaxed outdoor setting.

Walkers can head up the **Flaskia Gorge**, or as an easier option hike to the nearby **Iliondas Beach**.

Lefkos Λευκός
pop 120

You'll find Lefkos (lef-*kos*) 2km down towards the sea from the main coastal road. In summer it's a burgeoning resort centred on a series of sandy coves but in winter you'd be hard-pressed to find anyone around at all.

Archaeology buffs explore the underground remains of a **Roman cistern**, reached by heading up the approach road and looking for sign on the left to the 'catacombs'. Drive to the very

end of the rough road and then strike out along trail K16.

If you decide to stay in this neck of the woods, try **Le Grand Bleu** (☎ /fax 22450 71400; www.legrandbleu-lefkos.gr; studio/apt €50/90; 📺) for a homey, well-equipped apartment overlooking the curving Gialou Horafi middle beach in Lefkos. You'll also find an excellent, shady **Taverna** (mains €7-12) on-site with mezedhes like garlic mushrooms and *imam baïldi* (aubergine in oil with herbs), or try the Karpathian mixed platter of sausages, cheese, capers and sardines.

There are daily buses to Lefkos, and a taxi from Pigadia costs €24. **Lefkos Rent A Car** (☎ /fax 22450 71057; www.lefkosrentacar.com) is a reliable outlet that will deliver vehicles, free of charge, to anywhere in southern Karpathos.

NORTHERN KARPATHOS

As you head north, the scenery becomes more dramatic and rugged as the road ascends into the pine-forested mountains. Most people hop on a boat to reach the north; however, the somewhat treacherous road does offer spectacular coastal views as you drive along the mountains' spine. The beaches in the north are pebbly and many are good for swimming and snorkelling and there is plenty of opportunity for walking.

Diafani Διαφάνι
pop 250

Diafani is Karpathos' small northern port and a lazy kind of place in contrast to its busy sister port of Pigadia. Scheduled ferries call at the wharf and a summertime excursion boat arrives daily from Pigadia, to be met by buses that transport visitors to Olymbos. Otherwise, scheduled buses leave for Olymbos daily at 7.30am, 2.30pm and 5pm all year-round.

Most people just pass through Diafani; if you do decide to stay, you'll likely have the beaches and trails to yourself. You can exchange currency at the Travel Agency of Nikos Orfanos but there's no bank or ATM in town, so bring cash with you. There's also no post office or car hire facilities, but you will find wi-fi access in a few restaurants, check out www.diafani.com.

ACTIVITIES

Join an excursion trip on the *Captain Manolis* to the remote and otherwise inaccessible reaches of Karpathos and to the satellite island of **Saria**.

Boats leave from the stone jetty from the centre of town at around 10am, returning at 5pm. You need to take all supplies with you.

Walkers should pick up the Road Editions *1:60,000 Karpathos-Kasos* map (available in Pigadia) or visit the Environment Management office near Diafani's seafront. Walks are signposted with red or blue markers or stone cairns. Follow a half-hour coastal track for 4km north through the pines to **Vananda Beach**. You can also head south through the olive groves to the shaded **Papa Mina Bay** (one hour, around 9km). A more strenuous, two-hour walk takes you 11km northwest to the Hellenistic site of **Vroukounda**. En route you'll pass the agricultural village of **Avlona**. Take all your food and water with you as there are no facilities.

SLEEPING & EATING

You'll find quite a few small hotels in Diafani. Head to **Balaskas Hotel** (☎ 22450 51320; www.balaskashotel.com; s/d €30/40; ✗) where spic-and-span rooms overlook a pretty garden. Set back from the waterfront, all rooms have a fridge and some have small kitchenettes. At the northern end of the bay, **Thalassa Apartments** (☎ 22450 22130, 6948629267; www.karpathosbay.com; apt €60; ✗) offers comfortable rooms that are handy for a quick swim off the pebbled harbour beach.

The waterfront is lined with restaurants. **Rahati** (☎ 22450 51200; mains €4-7) uses lots of organic ingredients in local dishes like green beans in tomato sauce, octopus in red wine and fresh fish. Near the fountain is **La Gorgona** (☎ 22450 51509; mains €4-7) where the Italian owner whips up a mean pasta. Sip cappuccino or homemade *limoncello* (lemon liqueur) on the terrace or dive into her freshly baked cakes. You can also buy sandwiches and pizza picnics for the beach.

Olympbos Ολυμπος
pop 330

Clinging to the ridge of Mt Profitis Ilias (716m), Olympbos is a living museum. While it's true that the village's main income is now tourism and the hordes of visitors can give it a theme-park feel, come here out of season or stay behind after the day-trippers clamber back down the mountainside and you'll be spellbound by Olympbos' magic.

Olympbos was built high in the mountains to protect the inhabitants from pirates. Long isolated from the outside world, the locals still speak a dialect that contains traces of an ancient Dorian Greek. It's often called

'Women's Village' as men have traditionally been carted off to war or in search of work. The older women continue to wear traditional dress of bright embroidered skirts, waistcoats, headscarves and goatskin boots. The interiors of the houses are decorated with embroidered cloth and their facades feature brightly painted, ornate plaster reliefs.

Before the tourists came to town, Olympbos was an agricultural centre, at times supporting the entire island. The areas surrounding it continue to be farmed. You'll find the remains of 75 windmills in and around the village; four are still in operation, grinding flour for the local bread baked in outdoor communal ovens.

Once you're inside the village, Olympbos is only negotiable by foot, with narrow alleys and stairs. The valley rolls down its east side to Diafani while the west side drops sharply down to the crashing sea. You won't find banks or post offices here. Basic provisions are available from a couple of shops at the southern end of the village.

SLEEPING & EATING

Small hotels and restaurants are springing up at a quick tempo but if you're visiting out of season, be sure to call ahead. At the far end of Olympbos and close to the central square, **Hotel Aphrodite** (☎ 22450 51307; filippasfilipakkis@yahoo.gr; d €40) has comfortable, airy rooms with verandas looking out over the windmills to the sea. The sunset views are incredible. You'll also find simple rooms at **Mike's** (☎ 22450 51304; r €25) at the southern edge of town and more upscale versions at **Astro Hotel** (☎ 22450 51421; €40) near the centre.

Makarounes is served in most restaurants in Olympbos. You should also aim to try some of the locally made bread. Head for the atmospheric **Taverna O Mylos** (☎ 22450 51333; mains €4-8) at the northwestern end of the village. Built around a restored and working windmill, the excellent food is cooked in a wood oven and features organic meat and vegetables, including goat in red-wine sauce, artichokes and filling *pites* (pies).

Near the centre, just south of the church, is **Blue Garden** (mains €5-10), a rooftop pizzeria with stunning views. At the southern edge of the village is **Mike's Restaurant** (☎ 22450 51304; mains €3-7; ✹ year-round). With its open fire, singing birds and traditional decor, it's worth stopping here for soup, salad or daily specials made fresh by the friendly Sophia.

KASOS ΚΑΣΟΣ

pop 980
The remote outpost of Kasos (*ka*-sos) is the Dodecanese' southernmost island. Curled up close to Karpathos and not far from Crete, it sees few tourists. The slow-paced community greets those who bother to visit with a warm welcome. Don't come here for beaches, sights or nightlife. Instead, come to relax amid olive and fig trees, dry-stone walls, meandering sheep and the craggy peaks shrouded in mist. You may end up staying longer than you anticipated.

History
Despite being diminutive and remote, Kasos has an eventful history. During Turkish rule the island flourished, and by 1820 it had 11,000 inhabitants and a large mercantile fleet. (It's hard to imagine how they didn't sink the island.) Mohammad Ali, the Turkish governor of Egypt, regarded this fleet as an impediment to his plan to establish a base on Crete and on 7 June 1824 his men landed on Kasos and killed around 7000 inhabitants. This massacre is commemorated annually on the anniversary of the slaughter (known locally as Holocaust Day), and Kasiots return from around the world to participate. During the late 19th century many Kasiots emigrated to Egypt where around 5000 of them helped build the Suez Canal, and during the last century many emigrated to the USA.

Getting There & Away
There are regular flights from Kasos to Rhodes, Karpathos and Crete with **Olympic Air** (☎ 22450 41555; Kritis Airport). There are also regular boat departures to Rhodes, Piraeus, Sitia and Finiki on Karpathos.

For more details, see Island Hopping (p515).

Getting Around
The local bus serves all the island villages with a dozen or so scheduled runs; tickets are €0.60. There are two **taxis** (☎ 6977944371, 6973244371) on the island. Scooters or cars can be hired from **Oasis – Renta-a-Car & Bikes** (☎ 22450 41746) in Fry.

FRY ΦΡΥ
pop 270
Fry (*free*) is the island's capital and port. It's a pleasant, ramshackle kind of place with little tourism, though it attracts many returned Kasiot Americans. Its narrow whitewashed streets are usually busy with locals in animated discussion. The village's focal point is the cramped yet picturesque fishing harbour of Bouka. The annexe settlement of Emborio is located less than 1km east of Fry.

Orientation & Information
The large harbour complex abuts the port village right next to its main square, Plateia Iroön Kasou. Fry's main street is Kritis. The airport is 1km west along the coast road. Turn left from the harbour to get to Emborio.

A stand-alone Commercial Bank ATM is next to the port entrance, while there's a Co-operative Bank of the Dodecanese branch, with ATM, on Plateia Iroön Kasou.

ACS Internet (☎ 22450 42751; ☽ 10am-2pm & 5pm-12am) Offers wi-fi.
Farmacy (☎ 22450 41164) For all medicinal needs.
Health Centre (☎ 22450 41333) Often unattended; you may need to call ahead.
Kasos Maritime & Travel Agency (☎ 22450 41495; www.kassos-island.gr; Plateia Iroön Kasou) For all travel tickets.
Police (☎ 22450 41222) On a narrow paved street running south from Kritis.
Port police (☎ 22450 41288) Behind the Agios Spyridon Church.
Post office (☎ 22450 41255; ☽ 7.30am-2pm Mon-Fri) Diagonally opposite the Police.
www.kasos.gr An informative website in Greek and English.

Sights & Activities
Fry's minuscule **Archaeological Museum** (☎ 22450 41865; admission free; ☽ 9am-3pm, summer only) displays the islands treasures but won't turn heads. See objects pulled from ancient shipwrecks, a collection of ancient oil lamps and finds from Polis such as inscribed Hellenistic stone slabs.

The **Athina excursion boat** (☎ 22450 41047, 6977911209; return €15) travels daily in summer to the uninhabited Armathia Islet, departing Fry harbour at 3pm and returning at 7pm. The speck of an island has superb sandy beaches but you'll need to bring all of your own supplies.

Sleeping
With the exception of the days on either side of 7 June (Holocaust Memorial Day), a room can normally be found quite easily in summer. Out of season, be sure to call ahead.

Fantasis (☎ 6977905156; www.fantasishotel.gr; d €40; ☷) These six simple rooms are 300m

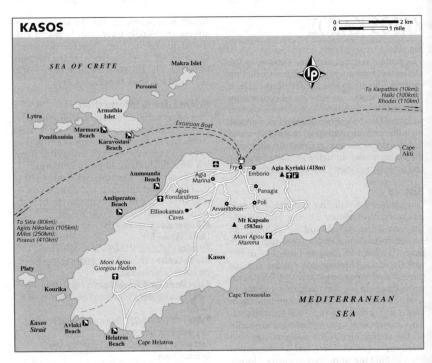

KASOS

0 ——— 2 km
0 ——— 1 mile

SEA OF CRETE

Makra Islet

Peronisi

Lytra

Armathia Islet

Marmara Beach

Pondikonisia

Karavostasi Beach

Excursion Boat

To Karpathos (10km);
Halki (100km);
Rhodes (110km)

Cape Akti

Fry

Emborio

Agia Kyriaki (418m)

Ammounda Beach

Agia Marina

Agios Konstandinos

Panagia

Andiperatos Beach

Ellinokamara Caves

Arvanitohori

Poli

To Sitia (80km);
Agios Nikolaos (105km);
Milos (250km);
Piraeus (410km)

Mt Kapsalo (583m)

Moni Agiou Mamma

Kasos

Platy

Moni Agiou Giorgiou Hadion

Kourika

MEDITERRANEAN SEA

Cape Trousoulas

Kasos Strait

Avlaki Beach

Helatros Beach

Cape Helatros

outside Fry and make for a good, quiet retreat. All have balconies, a fridge and TV. Savour home-grown figs at breakfast.

Evita Village (☎ 22450 41731, 6972703950; evitavillage@ mail.gr; s/d €45/50; ❄) Meticulously equipped studios are airy, spacious and tasteful. They sport every kitchen appliance imaginable, along with TV and DVD, and sleep up to three people.

Angelica's (☎ 22450 41268, 6992673833; www.an gelicas.gr; apt with/without sea view €65/45; ❄) With simple white walls, wrought-iron beds and beautifully hand-painted floors, these four apartments in a converted traditional home offer tranquillity and comfort. Each airy unit has a full kitchen and a courtyard; some have sea views.

Eating & Drinking

Fry is not overly endowed in the eating stakes, but there are a few decent places to dine.

O Mylos (☎ 22450 41825; Plateia Iroön Kasou; mains €3-5) A reliable eatery in a cosy corner overlooking the west side of the port. Wholesome food includes fish, meat, casserole dishes and local specials. Ask for *roïkio* – an unusual, locally produced green salad.

Apangio (☎ 22450 41880; Bouka; mezedhes €3-5; ☺ 9am until late) Enjoying a very atmospheric Bouka harbour location, the Apangio is a classy *ouzerie*-cum-cafe, serving select mezedhes and late breakfasts.

Cafe Zantana (☎ 22450 41912; Bouka) Kasiots congregate at this trendy cafe, admiring the view of Bouka harbour with a cocktail or cappuccino in hand.

AROUND KASOS

The original trading post of Kasos, tiny **Emborio** is now a satellite port of Fry used for pleasure and fishing boats. With a sandy beach and clear water, it's the nearest place to Fry for a quick dip.

The rather mediocre **Ammounda Beach**, beyond the airport near the blue-domed church of Agios Konstandinos, is the next nearest to Fry. There are slightly better beaches further along this stretch of coast, one of them being the fine-pebble **Andiperatos Beach** at the end of the road system.

The island's best beach is the isolated pebbled cove of **Helatros**, near Moni Agiou Georgiou Hadion, 11km southwest of Fry along a paved road. The beach has no facilities and you'll need your own transport to reach it. **Avlaki** is another decent yet small beach here, reached along a track from the monastery. None of Kasos' beaches offer shade.

Agia Marina, 1km southwest of Fry, is a pretty village with a gleaming white-and-blue church. On 17 July the **Festival of Agia Marina** is celebrated here. Agia Marina is also the starting point for a 3km-long hike to the former rock shelter known as **Ellinokamara**, with its odd, stone-blocked entrance. Follow the Hrysoulas signpost at the southern end of Agia Marina, proceed to the end of the road and follow a path between stone walls for about 10 minutes. Look for a track upwards and to the left to reach the cave.

From Agia Marina, the road continues to verdant **Arvanitohori**, with abundant fig and pomegranate trees. **Poli**, 3km southeast of Fry, is the former capital, built on the ancient acropolis. **Panagia**, between Fry and Poli, now has fewer than 50 inhabitants; its once-grand sea captains' and many ship owners' mansions are either standing derelict or under repair.

Monasteries

The island has two monasteries. The uninhabited **Moni Agiou Mamma**, on the south coast, is a 1½-hour walk from Fry or a 20-minute scooter ride (8km) through a dramatic, eroded landscape. A lively festival takes place here on 2 September. Detour to the chapel of **Agia Kyriaki** (no obvious sign) for eyrie-like views over Fry and the basin villages.

Similarly, there are no monks at **Moni Agiou Georgiou Hadion**, but there is a resident caretaker for most of the year. The festival at Agiou Georgiou Hadion takes place during the week after Easter.

KASTELLORIZO (MEGISTI)
ΚΑΣΤΕΛΛΟΡΙΖΟ (ΜΕΓΙΣΤΗ)

pop 430

Kastellorizo (ka-stel-o-rizo) is Greece's most far-flung island. Omitted on many maps, this speck of territory is tucked snugly beneath the underbelly of Turkey, approximately 130km east of Rhodes. Its nearest neighbour is the Turkish port of Kaş, clearly visible across a mere 5km of water. Kastellorizo was named by the Knights of St John after the island's towering red cliffs which give the impression of a medieval castle. The ruins of the Knights' own castle gaze down on the charming, well-preserved harbour with its crystal-clear water. If it all looks familiar, you may have seen the 1991 Italian movie *Mediterraneo*, which was filmed here. In recent decades Australians have arrived in large numbers in search of their parents' or grandparents' homeland. Many have reclaimed and restored homes and set up businesses, giving the island's economy a much-needed boost.

If you're not a film buff or long-lost grandchild, Kastellorizo is not an easy place to get to and doesn't have a lot of draws. But if you're curious and determined enough to get here, you'll likely enjoy uncovering the island's hidden charms. Snorkel in clear inlets, take in a few unique sights and soak up some tangible peace and quiet.

History

Kastellorizo has a tragic history. Once a thriving trade port serving Dorians, Romans, Crusaders, Egyptians, Turks and Venetians, Kastellorizo came under Ottoman control in 1552. The island was permitted to preserve its language, religion and traditions, and its cargo fleet became the largest in the Dodecanese, allowing the islanders to achieve a high degree of culture and advanced levels of education.

Kastellorizo lost all strategic and economic importance after the 1923 Greece–Turkey population exchange. In 1928 it was ceded to the Italians, who severely oppressed the islanders. Many islanders chose to emigrate to Australia, where approximately 30,000 continue to live.

During WWII Kastellorizo suffered bombardment and English commanders ordered the few remaining inhabitants to abandon the island. Most fled to Cyprus, Palestine and Egypt. When they returned they found their houses in ruins and many re-emigrated. While the island has never fully recovered from this population loss, in recent years returnees have brought a period of resurgence and resettlement. Many returning Aussies are locked in land claim battles over their family's property where locals have been squatting since the 1950s.

DODECANESE

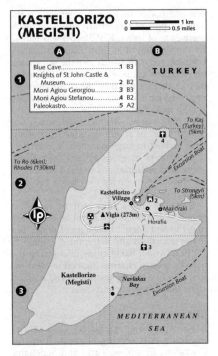

KASTELLORIZO (MEGISTI)

Blue Cave..........................1	B3
Knights of St John Castle & Museum..........................2	B2
Moni Agiou Georgiou..........3	B3
Moni Agiou Stefanou..........4	B2
Paleokastro......................5	A2

Getting There & Away

You can hop on a flight to Rhodes or wait for a ferry or catamaran, although boat services from the island are often tenuous and always infrequent. See p515 for more details. For flight and ferry tickets, visit **Papoutsis Travel** (☎ 22460 70630, 6937212530; www.kastelorizo.gr) in Kastellorizo Village.

Getting Around

To reach the airport, take the sole island **taxi** (☎ 6938739178) from the port (€5), or the local community bus (€1.50). The bus leaves the square by the port 1½ hours prior to each flight departure.

BOAT

Excursion boats go to the spectacular **Blue Cave** (Parasta), famous for its brilliant, mirror-like blue water, produced by refracted sunlight. Visitors are transferred from a larger caïque to a small motorised dingy in order to enter the very low cave entrance – claustrophobics be warned. Inside, the cave reaches up 35m and is home to pigeons and seals. Visitors are usually allowed a quick dip. The excursion

costs about €15; look for **Georgos Karagiannis** (☎ 6977855756) who runs the *Varvara* and *Agios Georgios* daily from the harbour. Boats leave at 9am and return around 1pm.

You can also take day trips to the islets of **Ro** and **Strongyli** for swims and picnics. The trips cost about €20 and boats depart around 9am from the harbour.

Join islanders on one of their frequent shopping trips to **Kaş** in Turkey. A day trip costs about €20 and is available from boats along the middle waterfront. Passports are required by the police 24 hours beforehand.

KASTELLORIZO VILLAGE
pop 275

Besides Mandraki, its satellite neighbourhood over the hill and to the east, Kastellorizo Village is the main settlement on the island. Built around a U-shaped bay, the village's waterfront is skirted by imposing, spruced-up, three-storey mansions with wooden balconies and red-tiled roofs. The labyrinthine backstreets are slowly being restored and rebuilt. The village has a strong Aussie presence, adding an upbeat energy to an otherwise subdued community.

Orientation & Information

The quay is at the southern side of the bay. The central square, Plateia Ethelondon Kastellorizou, abuts the waterfront almost halfway round the bay, next to the yachting jetty. The settlements of Horafia and Mandraki are reached by ascending the wide steps at the east side of the bay.

First Aid (☎ 22460 45206) For emergencies and basic health needs.

National Bank of Greece (☎ 22460 49054) ATM equipped.

Papoutsis Travel (☎ 22460 70630, 22460 49356; papoutsistravel@galileo.gr) For air and sea tickets.

Police station (☎ 22460 49333) On the bay's western side.

Port police (☎ 22460 49333) At eastern tip of the bay.

Post office (☎ 22460 49298) Next to the police station.

Radio Café (☎ 22460 49029; internet per hr €3) For internet access.

Sights

Follow a rickety metal staircase up to the **Knights of St John Castle** for splendid views of Turkey. Below the castle stands the **museum** (☎ 22460 49283; admission free; ⏱ 7am-2pm Tue-Sun) with a collection of archaeological finds, costumes and photos. Beyond the museum, steps lead down to a coastal pathway from where more steps go up the cliff to a rock-hewn **Lycian tomb** with an impressive Doric facade dating back as far as the 4th century BC. There are several along the Anatolian coast in Turkey, but they are very rare in Greece.

Moni Agiou Georgiou is the largest of the monasteries that dot the island. Within its church is the subterranean Chapel of Agios Haralambos, reached by steep stone steps. Greek children were given religious instruction here during Turkish times. The church is kept locked; ask around the waterfront for the whereabouts of the caretaker. To reach the monastery (approximately 1.5km), ascend the conspicuous zigzagging white stone steps behind the village.

Moni Agiou Stefanou, on the north coast, is the setting for one of the island's most important celebrations, the feast of Agios Stefanos on 1 August. The path to the little white monastery begins behind the post office. From the monastery, a path leads to a bay where you can swim.

Paleokastro was the island's ancient capital. Within the old city's Hellenistic walls is an ancient tower, a water cistern and three churches. To reach it (1km), follow the concrete steps, just beyond a soldier's sentry box on the airport road.

Sleeping

Many of Kastellorizo's hotels stay open year-round. Book ahead in high season to be sure of a bed.

Damien & Monika's (☎ 22460 49028; www.kastel lorizo.de; r €40; ✿ 🖳) These bright, comfy rooms in the centre of town have that homey touch. Each is slightly unique with traditional furnishings, a fridge and lots of windows. You'll also find a book exchange and heaps of local info.

Poseidon (☎ 22460 49257, 6945710603; www.kaste lorizo-poseidon.gr; s/d €50/60) The Poseidon's two restored houses offer large rooms with a touch of colour and character. Ground-floor rooms have private verandas; 1st-floor rooms have small balconies with big sea views. It's on the west side of the harbour, one block back from the waterfront.

Mediterraneo (☎ 22460 49007; www.mediterraneo -kastelorizo.com; r €70-85) Designed and run by an architect, these stylish waterfront rooms have rustic charm with arches, stone walls

and unique furnishings. All have garden or sea views and include breakfast. The hotel is at the far western tip of the harbour and very convenient for a quick harbour dip.

Eating

With tables perched precariously over the harbour edge, dining in Kastellorizo is both atmospheric and adventuresome – one false move and you are in for a swim.

Radio Café (☎ 22460 49029; breakfast & snacks €2-6; 🖳) Other than internet access, this cafe makes a mean coffee and dishes up filling breakfasts, light snacks and pizzas. Sunset views are thrown in for free.

Kaz Bar (☎ 22460 49067; mezedhes €3-6; 🖳) For an alternative take on mezedhes, drop by this bar-cum-bistro on the middle waterfront. Dig into pizza, chicken wings and spring rolls, as well as original salads, all washed down with Greek wine.

To Mikro Parisi (☎ 22460 49282; mains €5-7) Going strong since 1974, To Mikro Parisi still serves generous helpings of grilled fish and meat. Fish soup is the house speciality, but the rich *stifadho* (sweet stew cooked with tomato and onions) is equally satisfying.

Entertainment

It ain't no Rio, but Kastellorizo's nightlife has picked up the pace in recent years and the summer influx of Aussies certainly adds fuel. The harbour is lined with small bars and cafes that spill out onto the water's edge as the night wears on. Kaz Bar and Meltemi are staunchly popular but follow the noise and fellow revellers and you can't really go wrong.

SYMI ΣΥΜΗ

pop 2610

Arriving at the main harbour of Symi (*see-me*) is like sailing into a postcard. Restored, colourful sea captains' houses nestle the shoreline while bright boats bob in the blue-green sea. Most visitors congregate in the cafes here, alongside the growing expat community, but the island is also home to a surprisingly green interior, a sprinkling of scattered beaches and an enormous monastery that is one of the few religious sites that warrants its own ferry connection.

Symi is one of the most popular day-trip destinations from Rhodes and a popular port

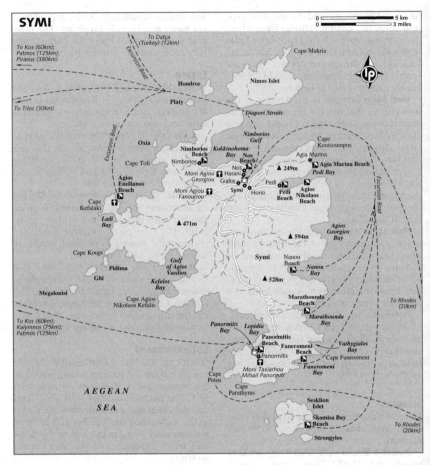

SYMI

0 ——— 5 km
0 ——— 3 miles

To Kos (60km);
Patmos (125km);
Piraeus (380km);

To Datça
(Turkey) (12km)

Cape Makria

To Tilos (30km)

Hondros

Platy

Nimos Islet

Diapori Straits

Oxia

Cape Toli

Nimborios
Gulf

Nimborios
Beach
Nimborios

Kokkinohoma
Bay

Nos
Beach
Nos

Cape
Koutsoumpos

Agia Marina

▲ 249m

Agia Marina Beach
Pedi Bay

Agios
Emilianos
Beach

Moni Agiou
Georgiou

Harani
Gialos

Moni Agiou
Fanouriou

Symi

Horio

Pedi

Pedi
Beach

Agios
Nikolaos
Beach

Cape
Kefalaki

Ladi
Bay

▲ 471m

Agios
Georgios
Bay

Cape Koupi

Pidima

Ghi

Gulf
of Agios
Vasilios

Symi

Nanou
Beach

▲ 594m

Nanou
Bay

Megalonisi

Kefalos
Bay

Cape Agios
Nikolaos Kefalis

▲ 528m

Marathounda
Beach

To Rhodes
(20km)

To Kos (60km);
Kalymnos (75km);
Patmos (125km)

Panormitis
Bay

Lopidia
Bay

Panormitis
Beach

Panormitis

Faneromeni
Beach

Vathygialos
Bay

Cape Faneromeni

Marathounda
Bay

Faneromeni
Bay

Cape
Potos

Moni Taxiarhou
Mihail Panormiti

Cape
Parathyras

AEGEAN

SEA

Sesklion
Islet

Skomisa Bay
Beach

To Rhodes
(20km)

Strongylos

of call for yachties and other sea-struck travellers. It's also an increasingly popular holiday destination in its own right.

History

Symi has a long tradition of both sponge diving and shipbuilding. During Ottoman times it was granted the right to fish for sponges in Turkish waters. In return, Symi supplied the sultan with first-class boat builders and top-quality sponges scooped straight off the ocean floor.

This exchange brought prosperity to the island. Gracious mansions were built and culture and education flourished. By the beginning of the 20th century, the population was 22,500 and the island was launching some 500

ships a year. But the Italian occupation, the introduction of the steamship and Kalymnos' rise as the Aegean's principal sponge producer put an end to Symi's prosperity.

The treaty surrendering the Dodecanese islands to the Allies was signed in Symi's Hotel (now Pension Catherinettes, p308) on 8 May 1945.

Getting There & Away

Catamarans, excursion boats and **ANES** (☎ 22460 71444; www.anek.gr) run regular boats between Symi and Rhodes, as well as to islands further north and to Kastellorizo. One service calls in at Panormitis on the south side of the island. See Island Hopping (p524) for details.

DODECANESE

Symi Tours (p308) runs Saturday excursions from Gialos to Datça in Turkey (including Turkish port taxes, €40).

Getting Around

BOAT

Several excursion boats do trips from Gialos Harbour to Moni Taxiarhou Mihail Panormiti and Sesklion Islet, where there's a shady beach. Check the boards for the best-value tickets. There are also boats to Agios Emilianos beach, on the far west side of Symi.

The small **water taxis** (☎ 22460 71423) *Konstantinos* and *Irini* go to many of the island's beaches (€10 to €15), leaving at 10.15am and 11.15am respectively.

BUS & TAXI

The bus stop and taxi rank are on the south side of the harbour in Gialos. The **grey mini-bus** (☎ 6945316284) makes hourly runs between Gialos and Pedi beach (via Horio; flat fare €1). The **blue minibus** (☎ 2246071311) departs Gialos at 10am and 3pm daily for Panormitis. Taxis depart from a rank 100m west of the bus stop.

CAR

Near the Gialos clock tower, **Glaros** (☎ 22460 71926, 6948362079; www.glarosrentacar.gr; Gialos) hires cars for around €25 and scooters for €10.

GIALOS ΓΙΑΛΟΣ

pop 2200

Gialos, Symi's port, is a visual treat. Neoclassical mansions in a medley of colours are heaped up the hills flanking its harbour of crystal-clear water. Most facilities and transport are based here, along with lots of seaside cafes where you can sip iced coffee and watch the slow bustle of the harbour.

The old town, Horio, is a steep climb from the harbour but is a great place to lose yourself for a while. Stepped alleys and zigzagging lanes take you past traditional homes, cafes, derelict buildings and churches, with gorgeous views down to the sea.

Orientation & Information

The town is divided into two parts: Gialos, the harbour; and Horio above it, crowned by the *kastro* (castle). Arriving ferries, hydrofoils and catamarans dock just to the left of the quay's clock tower; excursion boats dock a little further along. Ferries can depart from either side of the harbour so check when you buy your ticket. The harbour and the promenade running southwest from its centre are the hub of Gialos activity. Kali Strata, a broad stairway, leads from here to hilltop Horio.

There is no official tourist office in Symi Town. The *Symi Visitor* is a free English-and-Greek-language newspaper distributed by portside newspaper vendors and restaurants.

Kalodoukas Holidays (☎ 22460 71077; www.kalodoukas.gr) At the beginning of Kali Strata; rents houses and organises excursions.

National Bank of Greece (☎ 22460 72294) On the western side of the harbour with an ATM. There's a second ATM at the Co-operative Bank across the harbour.

Police (☎ 22460 71111) By the ferry quay.

Port police (☎ 22460 71205) By the ferry quay.

Post office (☎ 22460 71315) By the ferry quay.

Roloï bar (☎ 22460 71595; internet per hr €2; ⏰ 9am-3am) For internet access; a block back from the waterfront.

Symi Tours (☎ 22460 71307; fax 22460 72292; www.symitours.com) Half a block from east side of harbour. Does excursions, including to Datça in Turkey.

Symi Visitor Office (☎ 22460 72755) Small yellow building on the harbour front.

Victoria Laundry (☎ 22460 70065) At the foot of Kali Strata.

www.symivisitor.com A useful source of island information with an accommodation-booking service.

Sights

Horio is a warren of narrow streets zigzagging between brightly coloured buildings and crumbling remnants. This old town is still very much lived in, with a number of churches, a school and plenty of homes. It's a pleasant place to wander but looking for somewhere in particular is a bit like a scavenger hunt; it's a good idea to ask directions as you go.

Perched at the top of Horio is the **Knights of St John Kastro**. The *kastro* incorporates blocks from the ancient acropolis and the **Church of Megali Panagia** is within its walls. You can reach the castle through the maze of Horio's cobbled pedestrian streets or along a road that runs southeast of Gialos.

En route to the *kastro* and signposted from the stop of Kali Strata, the **Archaeological & Folklore Museum** (admission €2; ⏰ 10am-2pm Tue-Sun) has Hellenistic, Byzantine and Roman exhibits, as well as some folkloric material. The nearby **Chatziagapitos House** is a restored 18th-century mansion that you can look around when the museum is open.

Take a left from the top of Kali Strata for the ruins of **Pontiko Kastro**, a stone circle thought to

DODECANESE

date back to the Neolithic period. The site is only partially excavated and was locked at the time of research but offers great views.

Behind the **children's playground** in the port of Gialos, the **Nautical Museum** (admission €2; ⊙ 11am-4pm Tue-Sun) details Symi's shipbuilding history and has wooden models of ships and other naval memorabilia.

Activities

Symi Tours (☎ 22460 71307; fax 22460 72292) has multilingual guides who lead **guided walks** around the island, often ending with a boat ride back to Galios. The publication *Walks in Symi* by Lance Chiltern lists 20 walks on the island for novices and pros alike. Call into the **Symi Visitor Office** (☎ 22460 72755) to purchase a copy.

Sleeping

Hotel Fiona (☎ 22460 72088; www.symivisitor.com/Fiona .htm; Horio; d €50; ❄) With welcome breezes and big sea views from the balcony, Fiona's is a comfortable place to stay. Rooms are very clean with hand-painted furnishings, tiled floors and a small fridge. To reach it, turn left at the top of the stairs and walk for 50m.

Hotel Kokona (☎ 22460 71549, 6937659035; kokonafo@ otenet.gr; Gialos; d €50; ❄) One block inland from the harbour and not far from the children's playground, this hotel has comfortable, tidy rooms that are a stone's throw from the action but in a quieter corner of town. A few have balconies overlooking a small square with a church.

Pension Catherinettes (☎ 22460 71671; marina -epe@rho.forthnet.gr; Gialos; d €55; ❄ ▢) The historic Catherinettes is on the north side of the harbour. Rooms are basic but large and airy. The halls have traditional hand-painted ceilings, as do a few of the rooms. Small balconies overlook the harbour.

Hotel Pantheon (☎ 6932329202; Kali Strata, Horio; d from €80; ❄) Located halfway up Kali Strata, this restored traditional house has five plush new rooms decked out with antique wooden furniture and well-equipped kitchenettes. Rooms vary in size and layout but all are comfortable and homey. The rooftop veranda offers stellar views.

Eating

In Gialos eateries line the harbour; in Horio they tend to be clustered at the top of Kali Strata.

GIALOS

Stani (☎ 22460 71307; sweets €1-4) Tucked away on a pedestrian street, a block up from the middle harbour, this divine bakery creates local sweets, truffles, cakes and crème brûlée. The perfect stop for some gourmet picnic treats.

Mythos Restaurant (☎ 22460 71488; mezedhes €5-12) This lively harbour-side taverna serves up imaginative food. Try fisherman's risotto, calamari stuffed with pesto, or fish-fillet parcels in a saffron cream sauce. And don't miss the pears stuffed with honey and almond for pudding. Live music and dancing accompanies dinner in the evenings.

O Meraklis (☎ 22460 71003; mains €7-10) A block back from the seafront, this deservedly popular restaurant whips up some amazing dishes. Try macaroni with pistachio and swordfish or stuffed tomatoes. Tables overflow onto the pedestrianised street.

HORIO

ourpick **Olive Tree** (☎ 22460 72681; Horio; light meals €2-5; ⊙ 8am-8pm year-round) A cool retreat where you can relax on comfy sofas while savouring excellent home baking (like yummy muffins and cookies), homemade quiche or fresh rolls made to order. There are lots of vegie options (try cheese and red-pepper chutney toasties) and the kids will be kept busy with crayons and books. It's a particularly good spot for breakfast – smoothies, yoghurt with honey and fruit salad or homemade muesli will set you up for the day. Takeaway available. It's across from Hotel Fiona.

Restaurant Syllogos (☎ 22460 72148; Kali Strata; mains €5-7) At the top of the stairs, Syllogos offers imaginative fare such as chicken with prunes, pork with leek, fish with rosemary and tomato, plus vegetarian options like artichokes in egg and lemon sauce, or *spanakopita* (spinach pie).

Giorgos (☎ 22460 71984; mains €6-9) The menu here changes regularly but has enticing oven-cooked dishes like chicken stuffed with rice, herbs and pine nuts, lamb in vine leaves, or stuffed onions.

Drinking

Akrogiali Cafe (☎ 6948191637; ⊙ year-round) Right on the water's edge on the east side of the harbour, this is a great place to sip fresh juice, coffee or something stronger from the well-stocked bar.

Eva (☎ 22460 71372) A Havana-like vibe has seeped into this cool cafe, with antique sofas, funky music and a view across the harbour. In the day, get your caffeine fix here; in the evenings, it's a great place for drinks.

Jean and Tonic Bar (☎ 22460 71819; Kali Strata; ☺ 9pm-late) Feeling homesick for the 80s? Join Barry White, Tina Turner and the expat crowd for a G&T or two.

AROUND SYMI

Pedi is a little fishing village and busy mini-holiday resort in a fertile valley 2km downhill from Horio. It has some sandy stretches on its narrow beach and there are private rooms and studios to rent, as well as hotels and tavernas. The **Pedi Beach Hotel** (☎ 22460 71981; www .blueseahotel.gr; Pedi; d €90; ❄) has simple rooms decorated in white and dark wood that open on to the beach. Walking tracks down both sides of Pedi Bay lead to **Agia Marina** beach on the north side and **Agios Nikolaos** beach on the south side. Both are sandy, gently shelving beaches, suitable for children.

Nos is the closest beach to Gialos. It's a 500m walk north of the clock tower at Panormitis Bay. There you'll find a taverna, bar and sun beds. **Nimborios** is a long, pebbled beach 3km west of Gialos. It has some natural shade, as well as sun beds and umbrellas. You can walk there from Gialos along a scenic path – take the road by the east side of the central square and continue straight ahead; the way is fairly obvious, just bear left after the church and follow the stone trail. Over this way you can stay at **Niriides Apartments** (☎ 22460 71784; www.niriideshotel.com; apt €70-80). The rooms are fairly standard but the views are excellent and you're just steps from the beach.

Moni Taxiarhou Mihail Panormiti
Μονή Ταξιάρχου Μιχαήλ Πανορμίτη
A winding sealed road leads south across the island, through scented pine forests, before dipping in spectacular zigzag fashion to the large, protected Panormitis Bay. This is the site of Symi's biggest attraction – the large **Moni Taxiarhou Mihail Panormiti** (Monastery of Archangel Michael of Panormitis; admission free; ☺ dawn-sunset). The large monastery complex occupies most of the foreshore of the bay.

A monastery was first built here in the 5th or 6th century, however the present building dates from the 18th century. The principal church contains an intricately carved wooden iconostasis, frescoes, and an icon of St Michael that supposedly appeared miraculously where the monastery now stands. St Michael is the patron saint of Symi, and protector of sailors. When pilgrims and worshippers ask the saint for a favour, it's tradition to leave an offering; you'll see piles of these, plus prayers in bottles that have been dropped off boats and found their own way into the harbour.

The large monastery complex comprises a **Byzantine museum** and **folkloric museum**, a bakery with excellent bread and apple pies and a basic restaurant-cafe to the north side. Accommodation is available at the fairly basic **guest house** (☎ 22460 72414; s/d €20/32), where bookings in July and August are mandatory.

The monastery is a magnet for day-trippers, who commonly arrive at around 10.30am on excursion boats; it's a good idea to visit early or after they have left. Some ferries call in to the monastery and there is a minibus from Gialos. A taxi from Gialos costs €45. Dress modestly to enter the monastery.

TILOS ΤΗΛΟΣ

pop 530
Basking in relative obscurity, tiny Tilos (*tee*-loss) sees more migratory birds arriving on its shores than tourists. In fact, with rare species like the Eleonora's falcon, the Mediterranean shag and the Bonelli's eagle nesting here, many tourists who do arrive are avid birdwatchers. Others are drawn by the many walking trails that take you across serene mountains, valleys and meadows to small, isolated beaches surrounded by majestic limestone cliffs. Recognised as a Special Protected Area by the EU, and home to countless rare orchids and mammals such as sea turtles and the Mediterranean monk seal, Tilos is beginning to embrace a greener way of life and open its doors to ecotourism.

Often quietly ignored by the major transport companies, Tilos tends to be overshadowed by its more illustrious neighbours. Known in earlier years for its agricultural prowess rather than for its maritime eminence, it sometimes feels as if it has fallen off the map. If you're looking for a green adventure on a lost island, this is the place for you.

History
Mastodon bones – midget elephants that became extinct around 4600 BC – were found in a cave on the island in 1974. The **Harkadio Cave**

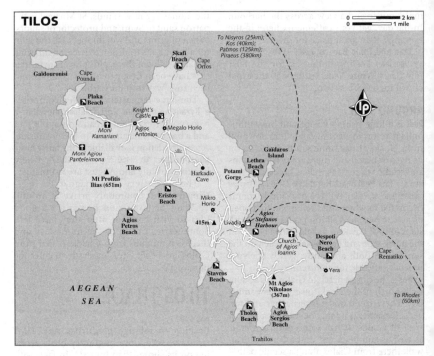

TILOS

0 — 2 km
0 — 1 mile

To Nisyros (25km);
Kos (40km);
Patmos (125km);
Piraeus (380km)

Skafi Beach
Cape Orios
Gaïdouronisi
Cape Pounda
Plaka Beach
Knight's Castle
Moni Kamariani
Agios Antonios
Megalo Horio
Moni Agiou Panteleimona
Tilos
Mt Profitis Ilias (651m)
Gaïdaros Island
Lethra Beach
Harkadio Cave
Potami Gorge
Eristos Beach
Mikro Horio
415m
Livadia
Agios Stefanos Harbour
Church of Agios Ioannis
Despoti Nero Beach
Cape Rematiko
Agios Petros Beach
Yera
To Rhodes (60km)
Stavros Beach
Mt Agios Nikolaos (367m)
AEGEAN SEA
Tholos Beach
Agios Sergios Beach
Trahilos

(closed indefinitely) is signposted from the Livadia–Megalo Horio road and is brilliantly illuminated at night. Erinna, one of the least known of ancient Greece's female poets, lived on Tilos in the 4th century BC. Elephants and poetry aside, Tilos' history shares the same catalogue of invasions and occupations as the rest of the archipelago.

In more recent times, locals have fought for a ban on hunting, which brought over 200 hunters each autumn. This ban was put in place in 1987, renewed in 2001 and is being proposed as a permanent sanction.

Getting There & Away

The Tilos-owned **Sea Star** (☎ 22460 44000; fax 22460 44044) connects the island with Rhodes. Mainland ferries erratically link Tilos to Piraeus, Rhodes and nearby islands in the Dodecanese. See Island Hopping (p525) for more details. Tickets are sold at Stefanakis Travel (opposite) in Livadia.

Getting Around

A bus ploughs up and down the island's main road seven times daily, with the first departure from Livadia at 8.20am and the last return from Megal Horio at 10.15pm. The timetable is posted at the bus stop in the square in Livadia. Stops include Megalo Horio (€1), Eristos Beach (€1.20) and Agios Andonis (€1.50). On Sunday there is a special excursion bus to Moni Agiou Panteleimona (€4 return), leaving Livadia at 11am with one hour at the monastery. For taxis ring ☎ 6944981727 or ☎ 6945200436.

During summer there are various excursions offered from Livadia to isolated beaches. Look for posters around Livadia for more information.

LIVADIA ΛΙΒΑΔΕΙΑ
pop 470

The main village and port, Livadia is a sleepy, pleasant place. It's got no wow factor with architecture or sights but knows how to relax. The waterfront walkway is great for strolling, with the sea lapping at your feet and a handful of cafes and restaurants lining the shore. In the village you will find most services and shops, as well as most of the island's accommodation.

Orientation & Information

All arrivals are at Livadia. The small port is 300m southeast of the village centre. Tilos has no official tourist bureau. The Bank of the Dodecanese has a branch and an ATM in Livadia. The post office is on the central square.

Clinic (☎ 22460 44171; noon–5pm) Behind the church.

Kosmos (☎ 22460 44074; www.tilos-kosmos.com; internet per hr €5; 9.30am–1pm & 7–11.30pm) A gift shop with internet access. Its website is a useful source of information on Tilos. It also has a book exchange and new books for sale.

Police (☎ 22460 44222) In the white Italianate building at the quay.

Port police (☎ 22460 44350) On the harbour.

Remetzo (☎ 22460 44214; internet per hr €2) Next to the ferry dock. Play pool or nibble at the deli while waiting for one of two computers.

Sea Star (☎ 22460 44000; sea-star@otenet.gr) Sells tickets for the Sea Star catamaran.

Stefanakis Travel (☎ 22460 44310) Between the port and Livadia village; has ferry tickets and car hire.

Tilos Park Association (☎ 22460 70880; www .tilos-park.org.gr) An umbrella group promoting ecological conservation on Tilos. Has a summertime kiosk on the waterfront.

Tilos Travel (☎ 22460 44294; www.tilostravel.co.uk) At the port; has helpful staff but open in summer only. Credit card withdrawals and currency exchange are available, as well as book exchange and car and mountain-bike hire.

Sights & Activities

MIKRO HORIO

Not far from Livadia, Tilos' original settlement was built inland as protection from pirates. The last inhabitants left in the 1960s, mainly due to water scarcity. Wandering around is fascinating, with houses in various states of abandonment. A couple have even been restored, with owners hoping to return.

WALKS

Due to its agricultural past, Tilos is riddled with terraced landscapes and trails once used by farmers to reach distant crops. Today many of these trails are used by those wanting to stretch their legs.

A 3km walk heads north of Livadia to **Lethra Beach**, an undeveloped pebble-and-sand cove with limited shade. The trail starts at the far north side of the port; follow the tarmac behind Ilidi Rock Hotel to the start of the footpath. The path is well maintained, fairly easy and very scenic; even if you don't make it as far as the beach, it's a worthwhile jaunt. Returning via the very picturesque **Potami Gorge** brings you to the main island highway.

A second walk is a longer return track to the small abandoned settlement of **Yera** and its accompanying beach at **Despoti Nero**. From Livadia, follow the road south around Agios Stefanos Bay, past the Church of Agios Ioannis on the east side of the bay, and keep walking. Allow half a day for this 6km-long hike.

Tilos Trails (☎ 22460 44128, 6946054593; www.tilos trails.com; per person €25) are licensed guides who conduct a number of walks of various levels around the island.

Sleeping

Kosmos Studios (☎ 22460 44164; www.tilos-kosmos .com; apt €45) Set in a garden close to the beach, these four self-catering units are spacious and private. Each has a sunny front balcony and a shaded veranda at the back. Call into Kosmos gift shop in town to enquire.

Olympus Apartments (☎ 22460 44324; www.tilos island.com; d/tr €50/60;) All rooms have amazingly well-equipped kitchens, good sea views and balconies. Village-style rooms have added character with built-in beds and traditional decor. There's also a family room with loft, but no views.

Anna's Studios (☎ 22460 44334; www.annas-studios .com; d €55) Just above the ferry dock on the north side of the bay, Anna's rooms are very homey and spacious. Gorgeous views and big balconies, kitchenettes and hand-painted wood furnishings make it a perfect home away from home. Family rooms have a second bedroom.

Hotel Irini (☎ 22460 44293; www.tilosholidays.gr; s/d incl breakfast €50/65;) Set back a little from the waterfront, this hotel is ensconced in a citrus garden with a palm-fringed pool. Rooms are comfortable though simple, all with balconies and some with sea views. The lobby and lounging areas are bright and cheerful. The hotel has a cafe, serving fresh juice, homemade cakes and sandwiches.

Livadia Beach Apartments (☎ 22460 44397; www .tilosisland.com; apt €70–85;) Right on the seafront and set around a colourful garden, these spacious, modern rooms are extremely comfortable with tiled balconies, plush sofas and great kitchens. There's also an alfresco cafe.

DODECANESE

Eating

For picnics and self-catering, there are three grocery stores in Livadia with lots of fresh local produce.

Spitico (☎ 22460 44340; snacks €2-3) Overlooking the square, this cafe makes great coffee, cheese pies and local sweets. Sit on the big veranda and watch the world go by.

our pick **To Mikro Kare** (snacks €2-5; mains €3-12; ☽ 6.30pm-late Mon-Fri, 4pm-late Sat & Sun) A recently renovated traditional stone house, this seaside eatery oozes atmosphere. Wooden rafters, portholes and nautical embellishments make it very cosy. Have sandwiches and salads while playing board games in the bar or head up to the dining room for fresh seafood.

Armenon (☎ 22460 44134; mains €3.50-7) On a lively seaside veranda, dine on shrimp baked with feta and tomato or pork with rosemary, thyme and honey. All produce is local, including Armenon's own honey and olive oil.

Taverna Trata (☎ 22460 44364; mains €8-12) The friendly proprietors serve up fresh fish, *kalamari*, goat in tomato sauce and shrimp. Dine on the tree-canopied veranda amidst pretty lanterns and watch them prepare your meal on the outdoor grill. Follow your nose up from the seafront, 100m past the square.

Drinking

Cafe Bar Georges (☎ 22460 44257) This stone building located on the square is very much a working-men's hangout – the kind of place you can lounge in for hours. It might take you that long to take in the random collection of orchids, Chinese New Year ornaments and nautical paraphernalia found here. Drink at handmade wooden tables and join in the local banter.

Paralia Cafe Bar (☎ 22460 44442) With a glass wall providing a huge view of the lapping waves, this stylish bar serves cocktails, coffees and an excellent selection of teas. Relax on big cushions and comfy sofas while listening to Greek pop music or playing monopoly.

Shopping

A number of shops in Livadia have come up aces with local goods to sell. Head to **Nefeli** (☎ 22460 44246) on the square for honey, preserves (like aubergine or cherry) and dried spices all produced locally.

MEGALO HORIO ΜΕΓΑΛΟ ΧΩΡΙΟ
pop 50

Megalo Horio, the island's tiny capital, is a quiet whitewashed village with winding alleyways. If you're looking for a taste of rural life, it can make a good alternative base during the summer season. The little **museum** (admission free; ☽ 8.30am-2.30pm, summer only) on the main street houses mastodon bones from Harkadio Cave. From Megalo Horio, you can also visit the **Knight's Castle**, a taxing 40-minute upwards walk along a track from the north end of the village. Along the way you will pass the **ancient settlement** of Tilos, which once stood precariously on rocky ledges overlooking Megalo Horio.

Miliou Studios (☎ 22460 44204; d €40) has rooms in a tree-shaded garden. Each has a balcony looking towards the sea. Dine at the **Castle** (☎ 22460 44232; mains €5-6.50), on the village's south side, with beautiful views of the bay. The menu features charcoal-grilled meats, including organic goat, locally raised pork and fresh fish. There's also a small grocery store in town.

On the road to Livadia or a short footpath away from Megalo Horio is the splendid **Joanna's Resto-Bar** (☎ 22460 44145; mains €8-12; ☽ 7pm-late, May-Sep). Set in a lush, peaceful garden, Joanna's serve authentic Italian antipasto, stone-baked pizza and homemade cakes and puddings.

Megalo Horio's bus station is at the bottom of town.

AROUND MEGALO HORIO

Just before Megalo Horio, a turn-off to the left leads 2.5km to the tamarisk-shaded **Eristos Beach**, a mixture of gritty sand and shingle. You'll find a payphone, seasonal kiosk and volleyball net that sees action in the summer. In winter, the beach has its share of rubbish but it's cleaned up for the summer. Buses don't stop here on Sundays or out of season unless you ask the driver.

Just off the beach is **Eristos Beach Hotel** (☎ /fax 22460 44025; d €32; ☒ ☒), surrounded by orange, lemon and palm trees. Decent-sized balconies look out to sea; airy studios with kitchenettes sleep up to four. There is also an on-site restaurant, a bar and a lovely pool.

Nafsika Cafe (☎ 22460 44306; mains €4-8) has big windows, lots of light and tables in the flower-filled garden. The menu is standard but all home cooked, the coffee is great and the atmosphere is tranquil. **Tropicana Taverna**

(☎ 22460 44020; mains €3.60-5.50), on the road up from the beach, serves traditional food with fresh vegies from its farm. Try the scrumptious *revythokeftedhes* (chickpea rissoles).

A signposted turn-off to the right from the junction leads to the quiet settlement of **Agios Antonios**. A further 3km west is the undeveloped, pretty **Plaka Beach**. It's situated in a cove where the water is slightly warmer and has natural shade in the afternoon. Once you wade in a little, the rock shelves are good for snorkelling.

The 18th-century, uninhabited **Moni Agiou Panteleimona** is 5km beyond here, along a scenic, winding road. It's uninhabited but fairly well maintained. Inside, the frescoes have mostly disappeared but the wooden altar is intricately carved and painted and the masonry is quite compelling. There are picnic benches and a stream-fed spout, ready for the lively three-day **festival** that takes place from 25 July. Outside of that, you probably won't find anyone here; in fact they may just leave the key in the door. On summer Sundays the island's minibus driver runs excursions here.

NISYROS ΝΙΣΥΡΟΣ

pop 950

Nisyros (*ni*-see-ross) tumbles down to the sea from its central volcano. Nearly round and built of pumice and rock, the island's volcanic soil makes it phenomenally fertile, drawing botanists and gardeners from around the world to see its unique flora. You don't come to Nisyros for its beaches (which aren't great). You come to stand in the centre of its hissing volcano, to explore its less touristy villages, to hike along its lush slopes and to dine on amazing local produce. Most visitors only make it for a day trip. Spend a couple of days to truly appreciate its beauty.

Getting There & Away

Nisyros is linked by regular ferries to Rhodes, Kos and Piraeus. The *Dodekanisos Pride* catamaran calls in with connections to neighbouring Dodecanese islands. Two small local ferries link Mandraki with Kardamena on Kos and Kos Town. See Island Hopping (p519) for more details.

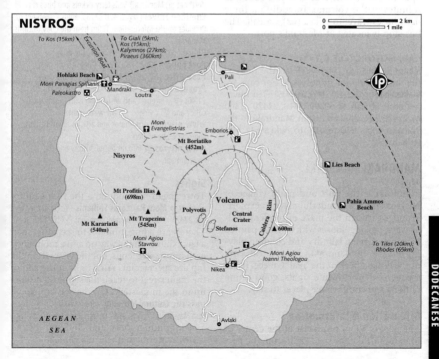

DODECANESE

UNSPRUNG

With a steaming volcano set in the middle of the Aegean Sea, it seems only natural that Nisyros would also be home to hot springs. In fact, since the time of Hippocrates, folks have been visiting the springs at Pali for their supposed medicinal properties. The Egyptians loved the springs so much, they built a luxurious palace around them for regular bathing in the early 1800s. When the owner of the palace died, his son emptied the palace of its bling and hit the sea, leaving the building to turn to rubble.

Generations later, the springs called again and a great-grandson returned to rebuild in the 1980s. He planned a luxury hotel and got as far as erecting the outer structure, which continues to dominate Pali's coastline. Unfortunately, for reasons unverified he packed up and left, leaving an empty, half-built hotel and no access to the springs. If you listen carefully, you might still hear the springs' muted call from beneath the concrete, but you'll have to be satisfied with steaming yourself at the volcano's caldera instead.

Getting Around

BOAT
In July and August there are excursion boats (return €10) to the pumice-stone islet of Giali, where there's a relaxing, sandy beach.

BUS
In summer, bus companies run up to 10 excursion buses daily between 9.30am and 3pm (€7.50 return) that give you about 40 minutes at the volcano. In addition, three daily buses travel to Nikea (€2) via Pali. The bus stop is located at Madraki's port.

CAR, MOTORCYCLE & TAXI
Manos Rentals (☎ 22420 31029) on the quay is the most handy for motorbikes. For cars, try **Diakomihalis** (☎ 22420 31459, 6977735229) in town.

For a cab call ☎ 6989969810, 22420 31460 or 22420 22420. A taxi from Mandraki to the volcano costs €20 return, to Nikea €11 and to Pali €5.

MANDRAKI ΜΑΝΔΡΑΚΙ
pop 660
Mandraki is the port and main village of Nisyros and is a wonderful place to explore. Wander through the maze of residential alleyways, passing houses with brightly painted balconies, drying laundry and children playing outside. In Mandraki you get a real sense of sneaking a peak at the 'real' Greece. It has a couple of worthwhile sights, good eating options and comfortable places to stay.

Orientation & Information
The port is 500m northeast of the centre of Mandraki. Take the road right from the port and you will hit the town centre. A couple of blocks up, you'll come to a Y-junction. Head left to reach the tree-shaded Plateia Ilikiomenis, Mandraki's focal point. Head right along the main drag for signs for the monastery and castle.

The Co-operative Bank of the Dodecanese has an ATM at the harbour and a branch in Mandraki.

Diakomihalis (☎ 22420 31015; diakomihalis@kos .forthnet.gr; Mandraki) Sells ferry tickets and hires cars.

Enetikon Travel (☎ 22420 31180; agiosnis@otenet.gr) Provides tourist information; 100m from the quay towards Mandraki.

Police (☎ 22420 31201) Opposite the quay.

Port police (☎ 22420 31222) Opposite the quay.

Post office (☎ 22420 31249) Opposite the quay.

Proveza Internet Cafe (☎ 22420 31618; per 30min €1.40; 🛜) Internet and wi-fi along with freshly ground coffee and MTV videos. On the waterfront.

www.nisyros.com Photos and articles about Nisyros, contributed by readers.

www.nisyros.gr Info on sights, history and the environment.

Sights
Towering over Mandraki is the 14th-century cliff-top **Moni Panagias Spilianis** (Virgin of the Cave; ☎ 22420 31125; admission by donation; 🕙 10.30am-3pm) There's not a huge amount to see, other than a few exhibits on the way up and a room lined with impressive icons, but the views from the top are spectacular. Turn right at the end of the main street to reach the signposted stairs up to the monastery. On the way up, you'll pass the **Cultural Museum** (admission €0.50; 🕙 10am-3pm May-Sep), which has traditional objects like a bed, grinding tools, and clothing. It's not earth-shattering but worth a gander.

Nearby, near the seafront and beneath the original cave of the monastery, lies the **Church Museum** (admission €0.50; 🕙 10am-3pm May-Sep). It's small but impressive with glittering ecclesiastic objects from churches and homes around the island. Altars, cups, fonts and objects dating back as far as the 1st century are crammed in here.

In town, the brand new **Archaeological Museum** was due to open at the time of research. If a sneak peek was anything to go by, it's definitely worth a visit.

Above Mandraki, the impressive Mycenaean-era acropolis, **Paleokastro** (Old Kastro) has restored 4th-century Cyclopean walls built from massive blocks of volcanic rock that you can perch atop for breathtaking views. There are good explanatory notes in English throughout the site. Follow the route signposted 'kastro', heading southwest from the monastery steps. This eventually leads up some stairs and becomes a path through beautiful, lush scenery. At the road, turn right and the kastro is on the left. You can drive here too.

Hohlaki is a black-stone beach and can usually be relied upon for swimming unless the wind is up, when the water can get rough. It's on the western side of Moni Panagias Spilianis and is reached by a paved footpath around the headland. Don't attempt this walk in bad weather as you can get washed right off the path. The small sandy **Mandraki beach**, halfway between the port and the village centre, is popular and OK for swimming but sometimes covered in seaweed.

Sleeping

Mandraki has fairly limited accommodation options. Book ahead to be assured of a bed in July and August.

Three Brothers Hotel (☎ 22420 31344; iiibrothers@ kos.forthnet.gr; s/d/studio €30/40/60; 😵) This welcoming, family-run hotel has smallish but well-maintained rooms with balconies and a few spacious, high-ceilinged studios with kitchenettes and verandas. All rooms have a small fridge and most have sea views. Next to the port, it's very handy for ferries.

Hotel Xenon (☎ 22420 31011; d incl breakfast €50; 😵 😩) These spotless, standard rooms are nothing special but are positioned right over the water. The hotel has a seaside pool.

Hotel Porfyris (☎ 22420 31376; diethnes@otenet.gr; d incl breakfast €55; 😵 😩) Near Plateia Ilikiomenis, this hotel was once grand but has now relaxed

into a comfortable state. Standard rooms with new bathrooms are none too big but have balconies with views of the sea or the mountain. Breakfast on the veranda and swim in the refreshing pool.

Ta Liotridia (☎ 22420 31580; www.nisyros-taliotridia .gr; apt €100; 😵) Along the waterfront, this stone building used to house oil presses. They're now luxurious rooms decorated in traditional style with raised beds, stone archways and classic furnishings. Expect fantastic sea views from the balcony. Apartments sleep four and have full kitchens.

Eating

Ask for the island speciality, pitties (chickpea and onion patties) and wash them down with a refreshing soumada, a nonalcoholic local beverage made from almond extract.

Bakery Pali (☎ 22420 31448; snacks €1-3) A block up from the waterfront, this is the place to come for traditional Nisirian breads and cakes, pastries and pies. Pack them along for a picnic or, if you can't wait that long, polish them off sitting by the fountain outside.

Taverna Panorama (☎ 22420 31185; grills €3-5) Just off Plateia Ilikiomenis, heading towards Hotel Porfyris, this little family-run joint dishes up traditional fare. Try the seftelies (Cypriot-style herb-laced sausages).

Restaurant Irini (☎ 22420 31365; Plateia Ilikiomenis; mains €3-6) Ignore the big tourist boards outside; dining here may make you wonder if you've entered Irini's own dining room. You'll be treated like family with big dishes of great home cooking. Try the excellent dolmadhes, aubergine salad, grilled meat and fish dishes and leave room for the amazing puddings.

Kleanthes Taverna (☎ 22420 31484; mains €6-12) On the seafront with views of the monastery and Kos, this restaurant is popular with locals for its fresh fish soup, mussels with rice, grilled beefburgers and baked feta.

Drinking

Plateia Ilikiomenis is lined with cafes and bars, as is the waterfront. Ta Liotridia (above) has an atmospheric music bar for an evening drink and Three Brothers Hotel (left) has a relaxed, hip cafe-bar with big windows out to sea. In Plateia Ilikiomenis, try **Beggou** (☎ 22420 03158) where a chill-out lounge is hidden behind a nondescript exterior, complete with white leather sofas and big orange cushions. It has a well-stocked bar and lots of teas, too.

DODECANESE

AROUND NISYROS
The Volcano Το Ηφαίστειο

Nisyros is on a volcanic line that passes through the islands of Aegina, Paros, Milos, Santorini, Nisyros, Giali and Kos. The island originally culminated in a mountain of 850m, but the centre collapsed 30,000 to 40,000 years ago after three violent eruptions. Their legacy are the white-and-orange pumice stones that can still be seen on the northern, eastern and southern flanks of the island, and the large lava flow that covers the whole southwest, around Nikea village.

Another violent eruption occurred in 1422 on the western side of the caldera depression (called Lakki); this, like all other eruptions since, emitted steam, gases and mud, but no lava. The islanders call the volcano Polyvotis because, during the Great War between the gods and the Titans, the Titan Polyvotis annoyed Poseidon so much that the god tore off a chunk of Kos and threw it at him. This rock pinned Polyvotis under it and became the island of Nisyros. The hapless Polyvotis from that day forth has been groaning and sighing while trying to escape.

Descending into the **caldera** (admission €2.50; 9am-8pm) is other-worldly. Cows graze near the crater's edge, amidst red, green and orange rocks. A not-so-obvious and unsignposted path descends into the largest of the five craters, **Stefanos**, where you can examine the multicoloured fumaroles, listen to their hissing and smell their sulphurous vapours. The surface is soft and hot, making sturdy footwear essential. Don't stray too far out as the ground is unstable and can collapse. Also be careful not to step into a fumarole as the gases are 100°C and corrosive. Another unsignposted but more obvious track leads to **Polyvotis**, which is smaller and wilder looking, but doesn't allow access to the caldera itself. The fumaroles are around the edge here so be very careful.

You can reach the volcano by bus, car or along a 3km-long trail from Nikia. Get there before 11am and you may have the place entirely to yourself.

Emborios & Nikea Εμπορειός & Νίκαια

Emborios and Nikea perch on the volcano's rim. From each, there are stunning views down into the caldera. Only a handful of inhabitants linger on in Emborios. You may encounter a few elderly women sitting on their doorsteps crocheting, their husbands at the *kafeneio* (coffee house).

our pick Ainria Taverna (☎ 22420 31377; Embrosios; mains €3-12), located behind the church, is the big draw in Embrosiois. It's impossible to go wrong with this menu: the country salad, meatballs, stuffed peppers, baked cheese, tomato and aubergine, and seafood are all truly gourmet. The bright decor of the traditional wooden building makes it a comfortable place to linger over a scrumptious meal.

In contrast to Emborios, picturesque Nikea, with 35 inhabitants, buzzes with life. It has dazzling white houses with vibrant gardens and a lovely mosaic-tiled central square. The bus terminates on Plateia Nikolaou Hartofyli from where Nikea's main street links the two squares. At the edge of town is the **Volcanological Museum** (☎ 22420 31400; 11am-3pm May-Sep) detailing the history of the volcano and its effects on the island. In the village's main square, **Cafe Porta Pangiotis** (☎ 22420 31285) is a cheerful, homey place to get coffee or a cool drink.

The steep path down to the volcano begins from Plateia Nikolaou Hartofyli. It takes about 40 minutes to walk it one way. Near the beginning you can detour to the signposted **Moni Agiou Ioanni Theologou**, where there is an annual **feast** on 25 to 26 September.

Pali Πάλοι

Pali is a small harbour with fishing boats and yacht anchorage. While its own beach is not very good, it's en route to **Lies**, Nisyros' most usable beach, about 5.5km around the coast. The first narrow stretch of Lies is the sandiest, with black, volcanic sand. You can also walk an extra kilometre from the end of the road along an occasionally precarious coastal track to **Pahia Ammos**, a broad expanse of gravelly volcanic sand. Bring your own shade.

If you decide to stick around Pali, head for one of the 12 comfy self-contained studios at **Mammis' Apartments** (☎ 22420 31453; www.mammis.com; d €50; year-round;), on the road to Mandraki. Set back from the sea in lush gardens, they each have a private entrance and balcony with views.

For dining in Pali, head for **Captain's House** (☎ 22420 31016; mains €4-8), where you can watch the fishermen unravel their nets as you breakfast on eggs, local sausage or yoghurt and honey. Later in the day, come here for *mousakas* and fresh fish.

KOS ΚΩΣ

pop 17,890

With some of the Dodecanese' very best beaches, impressive archaeological sites and a lush interior, it's hardly surprising that Kos (*koss*) is such a popular destination. Kos Town has a wonderful vibe and is an excellent base, catering to everyone from upmarket tourists to backpackers after a party. When you tire of the crowds, there are plenty of places to spread out – long, sandy beaches, hilltop villages and remote coves. You won't have the island to yourself, but some things are worth sharing.

History

Kos' fertile land attracted settlers from the earliest days. So many people lived here by Mycenaean times that it sent 30 ships to the Trojan War. During the 7th and 6th centuries BC, Kos prospered as an ally of the powerful Rhodian cities of Ialysos, Kamiros and Lindos. In 477 BC, after suffering an earthquake and subjugation to the Persians, it joined the Delian League and again flourished.

Hippocrates (460–377 BC), the Ancient Greek physician known as the founder of medicine, was born and lived on the island. After Hippocrates' death, the Sanctuary of Asclepius and a medical school were built, which perpetuated his teachings and made Kos famous throughout the Greek world.

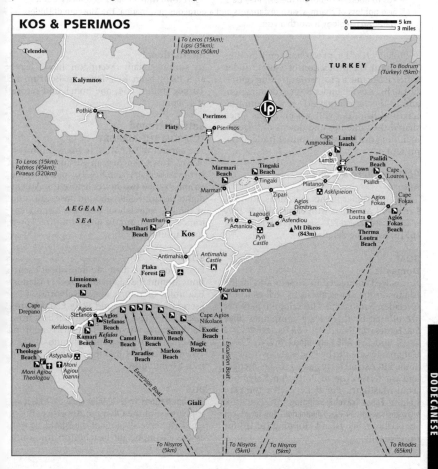

KOS & PSERIMOS

0 — 5 km
0 — 3 miles

Telendos
Kalymnos
Pothia
To Leros (15km);
Lipsi (35km);
Patmos (50km)
Pserimos
Platy
Pserimos
TURKEY
To Bodrum (Turkey) (5km)
To Leros (15km);
Patmos (45km);
Piraeus (320km)
Cape Ammoudia
Lambi Beach
Marmari Beach
Tingaki Beach
Lambi
Psalidi Beach
Kos Town
Cape Louros
Marmari
Tingaki
Platanos
Psalidi
AEGEAN SEA
Zipari
Asklipieion
Agios Fokas
Cape Fokas
Mastihari
Mastihari Beach
Pyli
Amaniou
Lagoudi
Zia
Agios Dimitrios
Asfendiou
Therma Loutra
Agios Fokas Beach
Kos
Pyli Castle
Mt Dikeos (843m)
Therma Loutra Beach
Antimahia
Antimahia Castle
Plaka Forest
Kardamena
Limnionas Beach
Cape Drepano
Agios Stefanos
Agios Stefanos Beach
Cape Agios Nikolaos
Kefalos
Kamari Beach
Kefalos Bay
Camel Beach
Banana Beach
Sunny Beach
Magic Beach
Exotic Beach
Agios Theologos Beach
Astypalia
Paradise Beach
Markos Beach
Excursion Boat
Moni Agiou Theologou
Moni Agiou Ioanni
Giali
Excursion Boat
To Nisyros (5km)
To Nisyros (5km)
To Nisyros (5km)
To Rhodes (65km)

DODECANESE

DROPPING IN ON THE NEIGHBOURS

From most of the Dodecanese Islands, Turkey looms large on the horizon. At times it appears so close, you feel like you can reach out and touch it. And you can. Day and overnight excursions run from a number of ports, making it easy to get a glimpse into the rich culture next door. Here are a few of the options.

- Rhodes to Marmaris – A tourist hotspot, Marmaris (p277) has a bustling harbour and bazaar, a buzzing nightlife and is the yachty capital of Turkey. Not far away is an unspoilt, azure coast-line backed by pine-covered mountains.

- Kastellorizo to Kaş – Kaş (p304) is a mellow town where you can relax in shady tea gardens, watch fishermen bring in their catch or wander through the shops and boutiques. There are some nearby ruins and an increasing array of adventure activities to keep you busy. Paraglid-ing anyone?

- Symi to Datça – With small sandy beaches and a pretty harbour, Datça (p307) appeals to European tourists and trendy Istanbulis and is a family-friendly destination. With no sights, it's a good place to just kick back and absorb Turkish culture.

- Kos to Bodrum – Bodrum (below) may be a big resort town with an influx of tourists, but it's also got lots of charm, stylish restaurants and a gorgeous new marina. The Museum of Under-water Archaeology is worth a visit.

Ptolemy II of Egypt was born on Kos, thus securing it the protection of Egypt, under which it became a prosperous trading centre. In 130 BC Kos fell under Roman domination, and in the 1st century AD it was adminis-tered by Rhodes, with whom it has since shared the same ups and downs of fortune, including the influential tourist trade of the present day.

Getting There & Away
AIR

There are regular flights to Athens, Rhodes, Leros and Astypalea with **Olympic Air** (☎ 22420 28330; Vasileos Pavlou 22). See Island Hopping (p516) for more details.

BOAT
Domestic

Kos is well connected to Piraeus and all the islands in the Dodecanese, as well as to the Cyclades, Samos and Thessaloniki. Services are offered by three ferry companies: **Blue Star Ferries** (☎ 22420 28914), **G&A Ferries** (☎ 22420 28545) and the **ANE Kalymnou** (☎ 22420 29900). Catamarans are run by Dodekanisos Seaways at the interisland ferry quay. Local passenger and car ferries run to Pothia on Kalymnos from Mastihari. For tickets, visit the very helpful **Fanos Travel & Shipping** (☎ 22420 20035; www.kostravel.gr; 11 Akti Kountourioti, Kos Town) on the harbour. See Island Hopping (p516) for more details.

International

In summer daily excursion boats leave at 8.30am from Kos Town to Bodrum in Turkey (return €34, one hour), and return at 4.30pm.

Getting Around
TO/FROM THE AIRPORT

The **airport** (☎ 22420 51229) is 24km southwest of Kos Town. An Aegean Airlines bus (€4) ferries passengers from Kos Town, leaving the airline's office two hours before the Athens flights depart. Kefalos-bound buses also stop at the big roundabout near the airport en-trance. A taxi from the airport to Kos Town costs around €22.

BOAT

From Kos Town there are many boat excur-sions around the island and to other islands. Examples of return fares: Kalymnos €10; Pserimos, Kalymnos and Platy €20; Nisyros €20. There is also a daily excursion boat from Kardamena to Nisyros (€14 return) and from Mastihari to Pserimos and Kalymnos. In Kos Town these boats line the southern arm of Akti Koundourioti.

BUS

The **bus station** (☎ 22420 22292; Kleopatras 7, Kos Town) is just west of the Olympic Air office. Buses regularly serve all parts of the island, as well as the all-important beaches on the south side of Kos. A bus to the beaches will cost around €3.60.

CAR, MOTORCYCLE & BICYCLE

There are numerous car, motorcycle and moped-hire outlets; always ask at your hotel as many have special deals with hire companies. Cycling is very popular in Kos and you'll be tripping over bicycles for hire; prices range from €5 per day for a boneshaker to €10 for a half-decent mountain bike. In Kos Town try **George's Bikes** (☎ 22420 24157; Spetson 48; per day €3) for decent bikes at reasonable prices.

KOS TOWN
pop 14,750

Palm-fringed and colourful, with the Castle of the Knights picturesquely perched at its centre, Kos Town's harbour hints at the lush, vibrant town that spreads beyond it. Located on the northeast coast, Kos Town is the island's capital and main port. With an abundance of palms, pines, oleander and hibiscus, its lively squares and shopping streets are balanced with impressive Hellenistic and Roman ruins seemingly strewn everywhere. Much of the Old Town was destroyed by an earthquake in 1933 but that which still exists is a wonderful place to wander around, with trendy shops, fantastic restaurants and bars. Even though you probably came to Kos for the beaches rather than the town, you'll be easily charmed by the capital.

Orientation

The ferry quay is north of the castle and Akti Koundourioti is the street edging the harbour. The central square of Plateia Eleftherias is south of here along Vasileos Pavlou. What's left of Kos' Old Town is centred around the pedestrianised Apellou Ifestou.

Southeast of the castle, the waterfront is called Akti Miaouli. It continues as Vasileos Georgiou and then Georgiou Papandreou, which leads to the beaches of Psalidi, Agios Fokas and Therma Loutra.

Information
BOOKSHOPS

News Stand (☎ 22420 30110; Riga Fereou 2) Sells foreign-language newspapers and publications, as well as guides to Kos.

EMERGENCY

Police (☎ 22420 22222) Shares the Municipality Building with the tourist police.

Port police (cnr Akti Koundourioti & Megalou Alexandrou)
Tourist police (☎ 22420 22444)

INTERNET ACCESS

Del Mare (☎ 22420 24200; Megalou Alexandrou 4; per hr €2; ⏰ 9am-1am; 📶) A popular bar with a few computers and wi-fi access.
e-global (☎ 22420 27911; cnr Artemisias & Korai; per hr €1.70-2; ⏰ 24hr) Countless computers with rates that vary depending on the time of day.
G-gates (☎ 22420 26257; cnr Irodotou & Omirou; per hr €2; ⏰ 9am-midnight) A very comfortable cafe where you can play Scrabble or drink at the bar between email sessions.
inSpot (☎ 22420 25262; Ioanou Tehologou, Old Town; per hr €1.20-2.40; ⏰ 24hr) Oodles of computers with cheap rates after midnight.

INTERNET RESOURCES

www.travel-to-kos.com Comprehensive guide to most of Kos' attractions.

LAUNDRY

Rose Laundries (Zervanou; wash & dry €6) Clean clothes in a day!

MEDICAL SERVICES

Hospital (☎ 22420 22300; Ippokratous 32) In the centre of town.

MONEY

Alpha Bank (El Venizelou) Has a 24-hour ATM.
National Bank of Greece (Riga Fereou) With ATM.

POST

Post office (Vasileos Pavlou)

TOURIST INFORMATION

Municipal Tourist Office (☎ 22420 24460; www .kosinfo.gr; Akti Kountouriotou; ⏰ 8am-2.30pm & 3-10pm Mon-Fri, 9am-2pm Sat May-Oct) General information on Kos in the office and on-line.

Sights & Activities
ARCHAEOLOGICAL MUSEUM

Cool and calm, the **archaeological museum** (☎ 22420 28326; Plateia Eleftherias; admission €3; ⏰ 8am-2.30pm Tue-Sun) is a pleasant place to take in local sculptures from the Hellenistic to Late Roman era. The most renowned statue is that of Hippocrates; there's a 3rd-century-AD mosaic in the vestibule that's worth seeing.

CASTLE OF THE KNIGHTS

You can now reach the once impregnable **Castle of the Knights** (☎ 22420 27927; Leoforos Finikon;

KOS TOWN

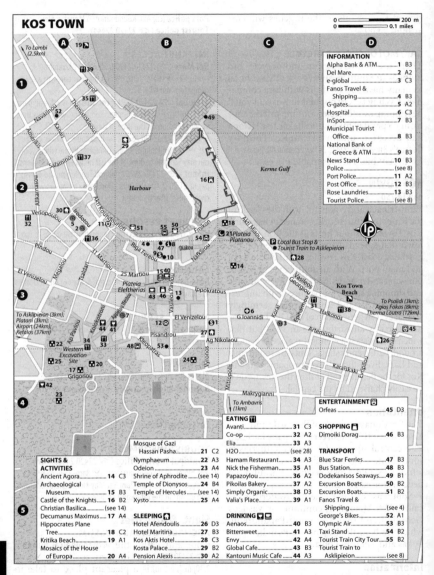

0 .... 200 m
0 .... 0.1 miles

admission €4; 🕑 8am-2.30pm Tue-Sun) by crossing a bridge over Finikon from Plateia Platanou. The castle, which had massive outer walls and an inner keep, was built in the 14th century and separated from the town by a moat (now Finikon). Damaged by an earthquake in 1495 and restored in the 16th century, it was the knights' most stalwart defence against the encroaching Ottomans. These days you'll find six resident tortoises as well as performances of Hippocrates' works in the summer.

ARCHAEOLOGICAL SITES

The **ancient agora** (admission free; 🕑 8am-2pm) is an open site south of the castle. A massive 3rd-century-BC stoa, with some reconstructed columns, stands on its western side. On the north side are the ruins of a **Shrine of Aphrodite**, **Temple of Hercules** and a 5th-century **Christian basilica**.

North of the agora is the lovely cobblestone Plateia Platanou, where you can sit in a cafe while paying respects to the once magnificent **Hippocrates Plane Tree**, under which Hippocrates is said to have taught his pupils. Plane trees don't usually live for more than 200 years; this ancient one is held up with scaffolding. Beneath it is an old sarcophagus converted by the Turks into a fountain. Opposite the tree is the 18th-century, boarded-up **Mosque of Gazi Hassan Pasha**.

On the other side of town is the **western excavation site**. Two wooden shelters at the back of the site protect the 3rd-century **mosaics of the House of Europa**. The best-preserved mosaic depicts Europa's abduction by Zeus in the guise of a bull. In front of here is an exposed section of the **Decumanus Maximus** (the Roman city's main thoroughfare), which runs parallel to the modern road then turns right towards the **nymphaeum**, which consisted of once-lavish latrines, and the **xysto**, a large Hellenistic gymnasium with restored columns. A short distance to the east, the **Temple of Dionysos** is overgrown but has a few ruins that can be viewed from above.

On the opposite side of Grigoriou is the impressive 2nd-century **odeion**. It was initially a venue for the senate and musical competitions and was restored during the Italian occupation when it was discovered, filled with sculptures (many now in the Archaeological Museum).

BEACHES

On the east side of town, **Kos Town Beach** has a thin strip of sand and deep water for swimming. It tends to be dominated by the restaurants and hotels along this stretch. West of town, **Kritika Beach** is a long sandy stretch that's polka-dotted with umbrellas in the summer. It gets crowded but is within easy walking distance from the town centre.

Sleeping

Pension Alexis (☎ 22420 28798; fax 22420 25797; Irodotou 9; d €40-50; ✹) Going since the 1970s and with little redecoration since, these big, airy rooms have bold, mismatched wallpaper and a very homey feel. All have lovely balconies; room 4 has the best harbour view. The owner is keen to dole out local info and lets you use her kitchen. The only drawbacks are thin walls and shared bathrooms.

Hotel Afendoulis (☎ 22420 25321; www.afendoulis hotel.com; Evripilou 1; s/d €30/50; ✹ ▢ ⩙) The owners of this very relaxed, family-style hotel will make you feel at home. Rooms are a little dated and on the small side but comfortable and quiet. If you opt for breakfast, expect niceties like homemade fig and apricot marmalade, fresh bread and omelettes.

Kosta Palace (☎ 22420 22855; www.kosta-palace .com; cnr Akti Kountourioti & Averof; d €70; ☾ year-round; ✹ ▢ ⩙) Easily spotted on the harbour's northern side, these rooms don't have a lot of character but are spacious and impeccably clean. Some have spectacular harbour views and there's a cafe and rooftop pool. Very friendly staff; the beach is just a short walk away.

Hotel Maritina (☎ 22420 23511-3; www.maritina .gr; Vyronos 19; ☾ year-round; s/d incl breakfast €50/75; ✹ ▢) The halls may feel a little down-at-heel but the rooms are very comfortable – stylish if anonymous – with lots of amenities and a small balcony. There's a huge breakfast and very friendly service. Substantial discounts are available out of season.

Kos Aktis Hotel (☎ 22420 47200; www.kosaktis .gr; Vasileos Georgiou 7; s/d from €140/178; ✹ ▢ ⩙) You'll fall asleep to the sound of lapping waves at this boutique hotel, set on a small beach yet close to the town centre. Very plush and very stylish, with flat-screen TVs, amazing tubs with sea views and glass balconies; you'll be well pampered. Expect big discounts out of season.

Eating

our pick **Valia's Place** (☎ 22420 27877; www.valiasplace .gr; Averof 38; mains €3-6) Hidden behind a giant tree, this place has an old jazz club feel to it, complete with lots of wood, worn leather and old photographs. With a patio on the beach, it's a popular haunt with locals and often hosts live local folkstyle music. Fill up on drunk chicken, aubergine *boureki* (pies), salads and sandwiches.

our pick **Elia** (☎ 22420 22133; Appelou Ifestou 27; mains €4-8) With their images painted beneath the wooden rafters, you will certainly feel like you're dining with the gods here. Start with chunky bread and olive pâté and then try the pumpkin balls, grilled vegies with haloumi, pork with mustard and capers or the Byzantine chicken with leek and spices. With local music, bright preserves lining the walls and a decent house wine, this stone building packs in as much atmosphere as flavour and is amazing value for money.

Nick the Fisherman (☎ 22420 23098; Averof 21; mains €5-12) This lively open-air restaurant is frequented by locals and is a relaxed place to try fresh seafood with a gourmet twist. Dishes like squid stuffed with cheese, seafood spaghetti and mussels with red sauce keep customers coming back.

Avanti (☎ 22420 20040; Vasileos Georgiou 4; mains €8-14) Ignore the hotel lobby atmosphere, this vaguely classy restaurant serves top-notch Italian-style pizza and pasta. Watch the chefs flip and cook it in the open stone oven. You can also get takeaway.

Hamam Restaurant (☎ 22420 21444; Diagora; mains €10-20; ☺ dinner) Once a traditional Turkish bath, this 16th-century building has become a distinctive dining experience. It's filled with lots of deep pinks, incense, candles and cushions, a garden lit with twinkly lights and wafting chill-out music. The menu is equally creative with swordfish souvlaki, pork with orange sauce and lots of salads and pastas.

H2O (☎ 22420 47200; Vasileos Georgiou 7; mains €15-20, snacks €5-10) Away from the hubbub of town, this is where stylish locals come to dine before huge sea views. Exceptionally stylish and ultracool, the food lives up to the decor. Try the linguine with shrimp, peppers and ouzo, or garlic lamb with rosemary and local cheese. Or just opt for an aperitif and classy snacks on the patio.

If you're self-catering, head to the well-stocked **Co-op** (Verroiopoulou). For something more organic, including fresh bread and produce, try **Papazoylou** (☎ 22420 24668; cnr Megalou Alexandrou & 31 Martiou). At the other end of town, **Simply Organic** (☎ 22420 20554; Vasileos Georgiou) has bulk snacks and baby food. For bread, sweets and tempting cakes, visit **Pikoilas Bakery** (☎ 22420 26200; cnr Salaminos & Kanari).

Drinking & Entertainment

On weekends locals congregate at Plateia Eleftherias from morning till night to drink coffee and gossip in the many cafes. Kos' nightlife geared for partying tourists is centred a block south of the harbour, along Diakou. There's also a plethora of similar bars along the waterfront on Kritika Beach. Along this stretch is Valia's Place (p321) where you can drink and listen to live music with the locals until the sun comes up. If you're looking for clubs, they pass in and out of favour so just follow the crowds.

Aenaos (☎ 22420 26044; Plateia Eleftherias) Built into the side of a mosque, this tiny place has red velvet sofas inside and a huge sea of tables beneath a tree outside. Sit for hours with coffees and fresh juices or something a little stronger in the evening.

Envy (☎ 22420 00827; Grigoriou) Denlike, with cool blue cube lighting, red chandeliers and velvet sofas, local DJs pump Greek and English music out of this traditional stone building until the wee hours.

Kantouni Music Cafe (☎ 22420 22862; Apellou 12) Popular with locals, this little place has a well-stocked bar and plays Greek pop music. Revellers squeeze inside or sit at the roadside tables.

Bittersweet (☎ 22420 26003; Apellou Ifestou) Disguised as a simple crêperie from the outside, inside you'll find a lounge-like affair with moody lighting, sofas, a fantastic garden and almost anything you can dream of drinking. Not surprisingly, the music is lounge.

Global Cafe (☎ 22420 26044; Ioannidi) Painted like a Tibetan monastery but belting out less than peaceful music, this backpacker-style cafe serves cocktails, coffees and teas. Relax on the small patio beneath palm and banana trees.

Orfeas (☎ 22420 25036; www.cine-orfeas.gr; Plateia Eleftherias; tickets adult/child €7/5) If you're suffering movie withdrawal, this cinema shows English films with Greek subtitles along with some local flicks.

Shopping

For high street-style-shops head to the eastern end of Ioannidi and the pedestrian streets south of Ippokratous. For more boutique options, visit the western end of Ioannidi, just north of the Old Town. **Dimoiki Dorag** (Plateia Eleftherias) is a market with local honey, preserves, spices and herbs that make great souvenirs.

Getting Around
BUS
Urban buses depart from Akti Miaouli and have two ticket prices: Zone A (€0.80) and Zone B (€1). Tickets from vending machines are slightly cheaper than those bought on board. You'll find one in front of the Blue Star Ferries office on the harbour. For schedules, check the Local Bus Office.

TAXI
Taxis congregate at a stand on the south side of the port.

TOURIST TRAIN

In summer, a good way to get your bearings is to hop on the city's vehicular Tourist Train's city tour (€4, 20 minutes), which runs from 10am to 2pm and 6pm to 10pm, starting from the bus station on Akti Kountouriotou. You can also take a train to the Asklipieion and back (€3.50), departing on the hour from 10am to 5pm Tuesday to Sunday, from the bus stop on Akti Miaouli.

AROUND KOS

Kos' main road runs southwest from Kos Town, with turn-offs for the mountain villages and the resorts of Tingaki and Marmari. Between the main road and the coast is a quiet road, ideal for cycling, which winds through flat agricultural land as far as Marmari.

The nearest decent beach to Kos Town is the crowded **Lambi Beach**, 4km to the northwest and an extension of Kritika Beach. Further round the coast is a long, pale-sand stretch of beach, divided into **Tingaki**, 10km from Kos Town, and **Marmari Beach**, 14km west and slightly less crowded. Windsurfing is popular at all three beaches. In summer there are boats from Marmari to the island of Pserimos.

Vasileos Georgiou in Kos Town leads to the three busy beaches of **Psalidi**, 3km from Kos Town, **Agios Fokas** (8km) and **Therma Loutra** (12km). The latter has hot mineral springs that warm the sea.

Asklipieion Ασκληπιείον

The island's most important ancient site is the **Asklipieion** (☎ 22420 28763; Platani; adult/student €4/3; ⏰ 8am-7.30pm Tue-Sun), built on a pine-covered hill 3km southwest of Kos Town, with lovely views of the town and Turkey. The Asklipieion consisted of a religious sanctuary devoted to Asclepius (the god of healing), a healing centre and a school of medicine, where training followed the teachings of Hippocrates. Until AD 554, when an earthquake destroyed the Asklipieion, people came from far and wide for treatment.

The ruins occupy three levels. The **propylaea** (approach to the main gate), Roman-era public **baths** and remains of guest rooms are on the 1st level. On the 2nd level is a 4th-century-BC **altar of Kyparissios Apollo**. West of this is the **first Temple of Asclepius**, built in the 4th century BC. To the east is the 1st-century-BC **Temple to Apollo**. On the 3rd level are the remains of the once-magnificent 2nd-century-BC **Temple of Asclepius**.

The hourly bus 3 and the Tourist Train (left) go to the site. It's also a pleasant cycle or walk.

Mastihari Μαστιχάρι

Known for its party scene but also gaining popularity with families, little Mastihari caters to independent travellers after a beach holiday and is a popular alternative to Kos Town. With a wide, sandy beach that gets a summer breeze, the village itself feels somewhat like a seasonal resort and is *very* quite outside summer. If the scene gets too much for you, excursion boats run to the island of Pserimos, where you can escape for a day to its protected sandy beach and convenient tavernas. Just 30km from Kos Town, Mastihari is also an arrival/departure point for ferries to Pothia on Kalymnos.

You'll find plenty of places to stay a block back from the seafront. **Athina Studios** (☎ 22420 59030; www.athinas-studios.gr; d €35) offers bougainvillea-strewn apartments that are airy, immaculate and feel like new, with full kitchen facilities. On the same street, **To Kyma** (☎ 22420 59045; www.kyma.kosweb.com; s/d €30/35) is a family-run hotel with smallish, simple rooms right next to the beach. Half enjoy sea views.

The beachfront is lined with restaurants and cafes, many offering children's menus. Right on the harbour, the busy **Kali Kardia Restaurant** (☎ 22420 59289; fish €6-12) is popular with locals. With fresh seafood, decent pasta and a sea breeze, you can see why.

Chill-Out Cafe (☎ 22420 59192) offers a bit of an escape in the day and is a cool place to hang out in the evening. Look for greeting-card-style swirly decor, a well-stocked bar and comfy chairs.

Mountain Villages

The villages scattered on the northern green slopes of the Dikeos mountain range are a great place for exploring. At **Zipari**, 10km from the capital, a road to the southeast leads to **Asfendiou**. En route, 3km past Zipari, stop in at **Taverna Panorama** (☎ 22420 69367; mains €6-10; ⏰ lunch & dinner) for coastal views, traditional cuisine and good mezedhes served to a primarily Greek clientele.

From Asfendiou, a turn-off to the right leads to the village of **Zia**, which pulls in coachloads of tourists for its sunset views. The main square of Zia is chock-a-block with restaurants. Head to **Niotis Jazz Cafe** (☎ 6947412440; mains €3-7) for friendly service and great music; the food here is simple (salads, pasta, crêpes and burgers). If you find Zia too packed, the **Village Tavern** (☎ 22420 69918; mains €2-6) offers sausages, *gyros* (meat slivers cooked on a vertical rotisserie; usually eaten with pitta bread), zucchini balls and grilled feta that you can take away to find your own roadside view. At the top of the village, follow the rough staircase to **Kefalovrysi** (☎ 22420 69605; mains €5-8) for well-priced, first-class traditional dishes in leafy surroundings with a great vista.

Returning north from Zia, take a left and follow signs for **Pyli**. Just before the village, a left turn leads to the extensive ruins of the medieval village of **Old Pyli** where a well-marked trail leads past the remains of houses and up to the castle. A number of the chapels on the site are currently being restored and many of the Byzantine gates and archways are still largely intact. Watch out for tortoises, too! Good footwear and a little stamina are a must. It's a great place to picnic; stock up in the grocery stores and bakeries of Pyli.

Kamari & Kefalos Bay Καμάρι & Κέφαλος

South from Mastihari, join the main road at Antimahia and continue southwest to the huge Kefalos Bay, fringed by a 12km stretch of incredible sand. Don't be put off by the tacky strip of tourist shops, restaurants and hotels behind on the main road. These divine beaches are idyllic, backed by green hills and lapped by warm water. The stretch is roughly divided into seven, each signposted from the main road. The most popular is **Paradise Beach**, while the most undeveloped is **Exotic Beach**; **Banana Beach** (also known as Langada Beach) is a good compromise.

Agios Stefanos Beach, at the far western end, is reached along a short turn-off from the main road and worth a visit to see the island of **Agios Stefanos**. Within swimming distance, this tiny island is home to the ruins of two 5th-century basilicas and to another lovely, sandy beach.

Further down the road, you'll reach **Kamari Beach,** an elongated holiday resort strip packed with restaurants, accommodation and shops that have spread to the main road with English brekkies and Yorkshire puddings. The bay itself is filled with bobbing fishing boats and the beach is most accessible east of the resort.

You'll find a small Tourism Office next to the beachside bus stop and an ATM on the top road. Excursion boats leave from here for Nisyros (€16) two or three times weekly. There are also daily boats to Paradise Beach in the summer, departing at 10.30am and returning at 5.30pm

About 150m north of the Kamari seafront bus stop you'll find accommodation at **Anthoula Studios** (☎ 22420 71904; studios €40), a spotless set of airy, roomy studios surrounded by a vegetable garden.

For something a little more authentic, head up to **Kefalos**, a traditional village perched high above the beach that indulges little in tourism. Have a coffee with the locals, dine in time-honoured tavernas and wander about to catch a glimpse of village life. For a surreal experience, visit **Cafe Neo** (snacks €1-3). Entering this blue stone building, you'll feel like you've wandered into someone's home. With a couple of benches, a wood stove, walls filled with photos and an owner who makes a mean coffee, marmalade and lace, this is a popular haunt with neighbours. You'll find it behind the church. The central square, where the bus from Kos Town terminates, has a post office and bank with an ATM.

The southern peninsula has the island's wildest and most rugged scenery. **Agios Theologos Beach** is at the end of a winding road that's dotted with tiny churches. The beach is surf-battered and the waters tempestuous but it's a beautiful setting and worlds away from resort-land. On the beach is the seasonal **Restaurant Agios Theologos** (☎ 6974503556; mains €6-15), which enjoys the best sunsets in Kos. The huge menu is filled with food from the owner's land, including homemade feta, olives, bread and goat. The rest is sourced locally – honey, seafood, burgers and vegies.

ASTYPALEA
ΑΣΤΥΠΑΛΑΙΑ

pop 1240

Flung so far west you'd be forgiven for thinking it was part of the Cycladic Islands, Astypalea (ah-stih-*pah*-lia) appeals to those after an alternative holiday experience. Outside of the bustling port of Skala and cubist hill-top town of Hora, the land is bare and rocky with nary a tree in sight. The beaches are scattered, but most are lovely; the rough terrain offers off-road thrills to adventurers; and the fresh fish and lobster thrill gastronomes. Mass foreign tourism has not yet arrived here, but in July and August Athenians descend in force.

Getting There & Away

There are regular flights from Astypalea to Athens, Leros, Kos and Rhodes. Astypalea Tours (p326) in Skala is the agent for Olympic Air.

Astypalea has ferry services to Piraeus and Rhodes with various stops along the way. They dock at the rather isolated small port of Agios Andreas, 6.5km north of Skala. A bus is scheduled to meet all arriving ferries, but don't bank on it. The Kalymnos-based ferry F/B *Nissos Kalymnos* links the island with Kalymnos and islands further north in the Dodecanese, and docks at Skala. Ferry tickets are available from **Paradisos Ferries Agency** (☎ 22430 61224; fax 22430 61450) or from Astypalea Tours, both in Skala. For more transport info, see Island Hopping (p509).

Getting Around

The airport is 8km northeast of Skala. Flights from Athens and Rhodes are usually met by the local bus, though a pick-up is a more reliable option.

In summer, buses run half-hourly from Skala to Hora and Livadi (€1), and hourly from Hora and Skala to Analipsi (Maltezana; €1.50) via Marmari Beach. Services are scaled back the rest of the year. There are only three taxis on the island and as many car- and scooter-hire agencies. **Vergoulis** (☎ 22430 61351) in Skala is a reputable agency.

From June to August, you can hop on **Thalassopouli** (☎ 6974436338) for boat excursions to the remote western beaches of Agios Ioannis, Kaminakia and Vatses, or to the islets of Koutsomytis or Kounoupa. When the weather is good, longer round-island excursions are offered. Tickets (€10 to €15) can be bought on the boat.

SKALA & HORA ΣΚΑΛΑ & ΧΩΡΑ

The main settlement of Astypalea consists of the port of Skala (known officially as Pera Yialos) and the picturesque hill-top village of

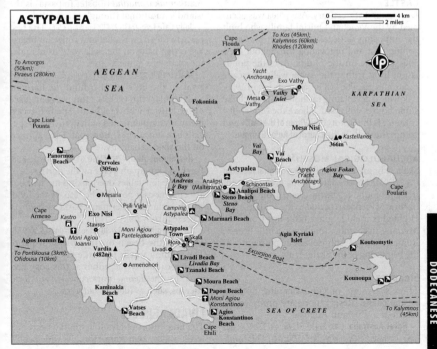

ASTYPALEA

0 —— 4 km
0 —— 2 miles

AEGEAN SEA

To Amorgos (50km); Piraeus (280km)

Cape Flouda

To Kos (45km); Kalymnos (60km); Rhodes (120km)

Yacht Anchorage

Exo Vathy

Mesa Vathy

Vathy Inlet

KARPATHIAN SEA

Fokonisia

Mesa Nisi

Cape Liani Pounta

Kastellanos 366m

Vaï Bay

Vaï Beach

Panormos Beach

Pervoles (305m)

Astypalea

Agrelio (Yacht Anchorage)

Agios Fokas Bay

Cape Poularis

Agios Andreas Bay

Analipsi (Maltezana)

Schinontas

Analipsi Beach

Steno Beach

Mesaria

Steno Bay

Cape Armeno

Psili Vigla

Kastro

Exo Nisi

Stavros

Camping Astypalea

Marmari Beach

Agia Kyriaki Islet

Koutsomytis

Agios Ioannis

Moni Agiou Ioannou

Moni Agiou Panteleïmonos

Astypalea Town

Hora

Skala

To Pontikousa (3km); Ofidousa (10km)

Vardia (482m)

Livadi

Excursion Boat

Armenohori

Livadi Beach

Livadia Bay

Tzanaki Beach

Kounoupa

Kaminakia Beach

Moura Beach

Papon Beach

Moni Agiou Konstantinou

SEA OF CRETE

To Kalymnos (45km)

Vatses Beach

Agios Konstantinos Beach

Cape Ehili

DODECANESE

Hora, crowned by an imposing 15th-century castle. Skala has a fairly popular sand-and-pebble beach but most visitors head uphill to the cooler Hora for stunning views of the port and surrounds. The main square in Hora is backed by several restored windmills. Leading upwards from here to the castle is a series of narrow streets with dazzling-white cubic houses sporting brightly painted balconies.

Information

Astypalea Tours (☎ 22430 61571; Skala) For air tickets.

Commercial Bank (☎ 22430 61402; Skala) Has an ATM on the waterfront.

Municipal Tourist Office (☎ 22430 61412; ☾ 10am-noon & 6-9pm; Hora) In a restored windmill.

Police (☎ 22430 61207; Skala) In a Italianate building on the waterfront.

Port police (☎ 22430 61208; Skala) Shares premises with the police.

Post office (☎ 22430 61223; Hora) At the top of the Skala–Hora road.

www.astypalaia.com For history, pictures, facilities and sights.

Sights

CASTLE

During the 14th-century, Astypalea was occupied by the Venetian Quirini family who built the imposing **castle** (admission free; ☾ dawn-dusk), adding to it and renovating throughout their 300-year rule. In the Middle Ages the population lived within the castle walls to escape pirate attacks. The last inhabitants left in 1953, following a devastating earthquake in which the stone houses collapsed. Above the tunnel-like entrance is the **Church of The Virgin of the Castle** and within the walls is the **Church of Agios Georgios**.

ARCHAEOLOGICAL MUSEUM

Skala is home to a small **archaeological museum** (☎ 22430 61206; admission free; ☾ 11am-1pm Tue-Sun) with treasures found across the island, from the prehistoric Mycenaean period to the Middle Ages. Highlights include grave offerings from two Mycenaean chamber tombs and a little bronze Roman statue of Aphrodite. The museum is at the beginning of the Skala–Hora road.

Sleeping

There's a range of good sleeping options on the island. Reservations are pretty much essential in July and August.

Hotel Australia (☎ 22430 61275, 6973224996; aus tralia_roomsstudios@yahoo.gr; d/tr €45/50; ✖) This long-popular hotel has simple, well-kept rooms with balcony views to the sea and castle. Each room has a fridge and the beach is only 50m away. You'll find it tucked away on the north side of Skala harbour.

Avra Studios (☎ 22430 61363, 6972134971; d €50; ✖) Right on the beach, these older, quaint rooms have kitchenettes and balconies. You can literally fall out of bed onto the sand.

Akti Rooms (☎ 22430 61114; www.aktirooms.gr; d/studio incl breakfast €80/85; ✖) Beautiful wooden furnishings, traditional touches and balconies make these rooms restful. Studios have kitchenettes; mountain-view rooms are somewhat cheaper. Swim from the private platform and enjoy the resortlike facilities. It's on the northeast side of the harbour.

Studio Kilindra (☎ 22430 61131; www.astipalea.com. gr; d/apt €150/170; ✖ 🖳 🖳) This boutique hotel sits just below the castle in Hora, providing amazing sea views. Rooms are luxurious with character added through traditional splashes. And the pool is divine.

Eating

There aren't many eating options in Astypalea. *Astakomakaronadha* (lobster in pasta) is the island's traditional (though pricey) dish.

Jolly Café (☎ 22430 22430; breakfast €5-6) The best place to fill up on waffles and coffee for breakfast is slap-bang on the Skala waterfront under the shade of a tamarisk tree.

Maïstrali (☎ 22430 61691; mains €5-8) Tucked away in the little street behind the harbour and popular with yachties, this is a good place to try lobster with spaghetti. The fish-based menu is complemented with oven-baked specials like succulent lemon goat. Dine alfresco on the shaded balcony.

Restaurant Akti (☎ 22430 61114; mains €5-8.50) Perched high up on a cliff on the north side of Skala, the few tables overlooking the harbour are enormously popular. So, too, is the food, which includes fisherman's pasta or *poungia* (cheese turnovers).

To Akrogiali (☎ 22430 61863; mains €5.50-9.50) Dine on the beach or on a pleasant patio. The yummy smells from the kitchen hint at the good-quality mezedhes at this cosy taverna. Try the *tigania* (pork cubes) or soft local cheeses, such as *hlori* or *ladotyri*.

LIVADI ΛΕΙΒΑΔΙ

The little resort of Livadi lies in the heart of a fertile valley, 2km from Hora. Its wide pebble beach is one of the best on the island and can get fairly crowded in summer. On the seafront, **Hotel Manganas** (22430 61468, 697657853; astyroom@otenet.gr; studios €50-60;) offers comfortable, simple rooms with kitchenette, shaded balconies and mini-washing machines to extract all of that sand. For a plusher option, head to **Fildisi Hotel** (22430 62060; www.fildisi.net; studios from €130;) with posh, spacious rooms that combine modern and traditional touches. Feel at home with your own kitchenette and home theatre.

The handful of places to eat at Livadi are strung out along the tree-shaded waterfront. **Trapezakia Exo** (22430 61083; mains €4-7) is at the western end and serves sandwiches and daily fish specials, while **Astropelos** (22430 61473; mains €6-9) has a small but imaginative range of seafood dishes.

WEST OF SKALA

Heading west of Skala you hit the big Astypalea outback – gnarled, bare and rolling hills with scarcely a sealed road to speak of. It's just about driveable; you'll need a solid 4WD. The road eventually leads to the **Kastro** ruins and **Moni Agiou Ioanni**, situated next to each other above the coast. From here, the strictly fit may venture downwards on foot to **Agios Ioannis beach**. An equally rough road leads to **Panormos Beach** which you'll likely have to yourself.

On the south coast, an *extremely* rough track winds downwards to **Kaminakia beach**, where there is a good seasonal restaurant, **Sti Linda** (6932610050; mains €4-7; Jul-Sep), serving hearty fish soups, oven-baked goat and home-made bread. If your nerves aren't shattered, detour to the pretty, tree-shaded **Agios Konstantinos beach** on the south side of Livadi Bay.

EAST OF SKALA

Marmari, 2km northeast of Skala, has three bays with pebble and sand beaches and is home to **Camping Astypalea** (22430 61900; camp sites per adult/ tent €6/4; Jun-Sep). This tamarisk tree-shaded and bamboo-protected camping ground is right next to the beach and has good facilities like 24-hour hot water, a kitchen, cafe and minimarket. **Steno Beach**, 2km further along, is one of the better but least frequented beaches on the island. It's sandy, shady and well protected. The island is just 2km wide here.

Analipsi (also known as Maltezana) is 7km up the road in a fertile valley on the isthmus. A former Maltese pirates' lair, it's a scattered, pleasantly laid-back settlement. On its outskirts are remains of the **Tallaras Roman baths** with mosaics. **Analipsi Beach** is southeast of town and is long, with sand, pebbles, shade and clean, shallow water.

For accommodation in Analipsi, head to **Villa Varvara** (/fax 22430 61448; studios €55;), which has comfortable blue-and-white studios overlooking a vegetable garden, just 100m from the beach; all have a kitchenette and balcony. The large **Hotel Maltezana Beach** (22430 61558; www.maltezanabeach.gr; s/d incl break-fast €80/115;) has lovely rooms in a complex kitted out with countless amenities like a spa, pool bar, playground and family rooms. There aren't many dining options in Maltezana, with the usual seaview tavernas serving traditional fare.

Continuing east, remote **Mesa Vathy** hamlet is an indolent yacht harbour in a sheltered bay. The swimming isn't good, but you can fish for your lunch or dine at the laid-back **Galini Café** (22430 61201; mains €3-5; Jun-Oct), which offers meat and fish grills and oven-baked specials.

KALYMNOS ΚΑΛΥΜΝΟΣ

pop 16,440

Once renowned for its sponge-fishing, Kalymnos (*kah*-lim-nos) still sees a daily catch of sponges sorted through at the harbour's edge. Today the island is working hard to reinvent itself as a tourist destination and with a lively main town, beautiful beaches, and perpendicular cliffs where climbers flock to test their mettle, the island has lots to offer. The island's resorts cater mainly to individuals, and walkers will find a network of ready-to-walk trails and paths that criss-cross the landscape.

Getting There & Away

AIR

Kalymnos is linked to Athens and neighbouring islands by Olympic Air, represented by **Kapellas Travel** (22430 29265; kapellastravel@gal lileo.gr; Patriarhou Maximou 12, Pothia). The airport is 3.5km northwest of Pothia and the seaplane terminal is 1.5km east. See Island Hopping (p514) for more information.

BOAT

Kalymnos is linked to Rhodes, Piraeus and islands in between via car-ferries, hydrofoils

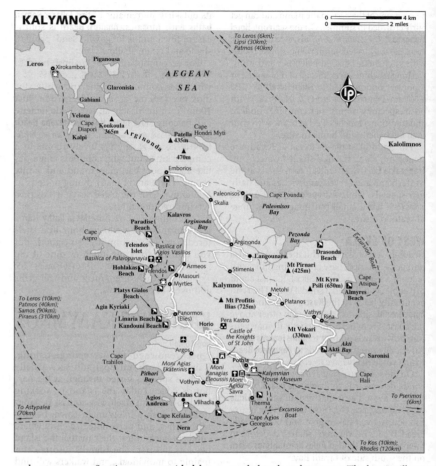

KALYMNOS

and catamarans. Services are provided by local boats and **Blue Star Ferries** (☎ 22430 26000), **G&A Ferries** (☎ 22430 23700), **Dodecanese Seaways** (☎ 22430 28777; Pothia quay) and **ANE Kalymnou** (☎ 22430 29612), and tickets can be bought from Magos Travel (opposite). For more details, see Island Hopping (p514).

Getting Around
BOAT
In summer there is a daily excursion boat from Myrties to Emborios (€8), leaving at 10am and returning at 4pm. Day trips to **Kefalas Cave** (€20), impressive for its 103m corridor filled with stalactites and stalagmites, run from both Pothia and Myrties. There are also regular boats from Pothia to Pserimos, with its big,

sandy beach and tavernas. The large sailboat **Katerina** (☎ 6938325612) does regular excursions around Kalymnos.

BUS
There are 10 departures daily from Pothia to Elies, Kandouni, Myrties and Masouri, the first leaving at 6.50am and the last returning at 9.40pm. There are also four daily return trips to Vathys at 6.30am, 7.45am, 2.10pm and 5pm. Buy tickets from the Municipality of Kalymnos ticket office by the bus stop in Pothia.

CAR & MOTORCYCLE
There are plenty of vehicle-hire companies on the island, mainly concentrated in Pothia. Try

Rent-a-Bike (☎ 6937980591) or **Automarket Rental** (☎ 22430 51780, 6927834628).

TAXI

Shared taxi services cost a little more than buses and run from the Pothia **taxi stand** (☎ 22430 50300; Plateia Kyprou) to Masouri. The taxis can also be flagged down en route. A regular taxi costs €10 to Myrties and €15 to Vathys.

POTHIA ΠΟΘΙΑ
pop 10,500

Pothia (*poth*-ya), the port and capital of Kalymnos, is a fairly large town by Dodecanese standards. Built amphitheatrically around the slopes of the surrounding valley, it's a visually arresting melange of colourful mansions and houses draped over the hills and spilling down to an equally colourful harbour. Pothia is not, however, a languid island town. It's a bustling, lively commercial centre with plenty of shops and restaurants that are filled with locals going about their busy lives, seemingly oblivious to the tourist trade. With an excellent museum, good hotels, great seafood and lots of energy, it'll keep you on your toes.

Orientation & Information

Pothia's quay is located at the southern side of the port. Most activity, however, is centred on the waterfront square, Plateia Eleftherias. The main commercial centre is on Venizelou. Stay constantly alert while walking around Pothia; traffic hurtles up and down its narrow footpath-less roads.

The Commercial, National and Ionian Banks, all with ATMs, are close to the waterfront.

Heaven @ Cafe (☎ 22430 50444; internet per hr €3; ☷ 9am-late) Small but handily located on the waterfront.

Kapellas Travel (☎ 22430 29265; fax 22430 51800; Patriarhou Maximou 12) For air tickets.

Magos Travel (☎ 22430 28777; www.magostours.gr) Hydrofoil and catamaran tickets, including a 24-hour ticket machine outside.

Main post office A 10-minute walk northwest of Plateia Eleftherias. There is a more convenient agency south of Plateia Ethinikis Andistasis.

Neon Internet C@fe (☎ 22430 59120; per hr €3; ☷ 9.30am-midnight) Popular teen hangout with internet, gaming and bowling!

Police (☎ 22430 29301; Venizelou)

Port police (☎ 22430 29304; 25 Martiou)

Tourist Information (☎ 22430 59056; 25 Martiou)

www.kalymnos-isl.gr Informative site hosted by the Municipality of Kalymnos.

Sights

The brand new **Archaeological Museum** (☎ 22430 23113; adult/student €5/3; ☷ 8.30am-2.30pm Tue-Sun) is stunningly impressive and packed with a vast array of artefacts dating back as far as 2500 BC and found as recently as 2001. One of the most striking pieces is a large, arresting bronze statue of a woman in a detailed chiton from the 2nd-century BC, found off the coast of Kalymnos. Behind the main building is the **mansion of Nickolas Vouvalis**, a wealthy 19th-century sponge trader who was the island benefactor. Inside, rooms appear as they did when he lived here.

In the centre of the waterfront is the **Nautical & Folklore Museum** (☎ 22430 51361; admission €2; ☷ 8am-1.30pm Mon-Fri, 10am-12.30pm Sat & Sun, May-Sep), with displays on traditional regional dress and the history of sponge diving. For an even bigger eyeful of sponge, visit the exporting factory of **NS Papachatzis** (☎ 22430 28501), overflowing with sponges of every conceivable shape and size. You can also see sponges hauled in every afternoon in the main square.

Sleeping

Greek House (☎ 22430 23752, 6972747494; s/d/studios/apt €25/35/40/55) Inland from the port, this pleasant budget option has four cosy wood-panelled rooms with kitchen facilities. More expensive and better-equipped studios are also available, as is a self-contained, large apartment in town.

Arhodeko Hotel (☎ 22430 24051; fax 22430 24149; s/d €30/40; ☷ year-round; ❀) Conveniently located on the harbour, this hotel has a long history. Built in the 19th-century and a bakery from 1909 until the 1980s, it has a well-preserved exterior and interior stone archways. Room 21 has the original wood-burning oven. Rooms are basic with a fridge and views over the harbour.

Hotel Panorama (☎ 22430 23138; smiksis2003@ yahoo.gr; s/d incl breakfast €30/45; ☷ year-round; ❀) Set on a hill on the south side of town, this simply but homey hotel has amazing views from the rooms' small balconies and the communal veranda. The friendly owner has lots of local info.

Evanik Hotel (☎ 22430 22057; d incl breakfast €55; ❀) Newly renovated and plush for the price, rooms here aren't full of character but are

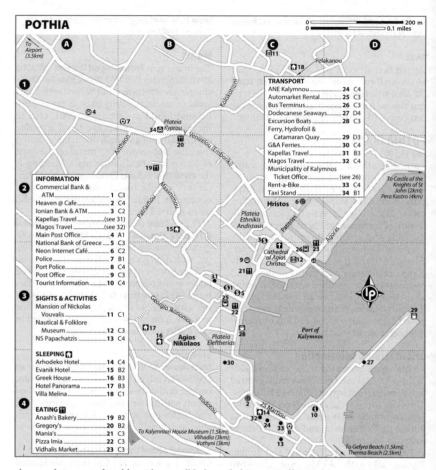

POTHIA

clean and very comfortable with a small balcony. Service is attentive and there's a stylish bar. Ask for a quieter room at the back. It's located a few blocks inland.

Villa Melina (☎ 22430 22682; antoniosantonoglu@yahoo.de; d incl breakfast €55;) With a lobby that speaks of faded glamour, this pink mansion on the hill is a unique place to stay. The doubles in the main house are individually decorated, with the quirky layout that older houses afford. The veranda overlooks the harbour and a deep pool is set in a lush garden. Surrounding the garden are plainer studios with kitchenettes.

Eating

Gregory's (☎ 22430 51888; snacks €2-4) It's true, it's part of a chain, but Gregory's deli and its co-habitant, Coffee Right, are a great stop for a quick bite. Near busy Plateia Kyprou, it's bright, popular and offers good value sandwiches, salads, smoothies, coffees, croissants and *spanakopita*.

Mania's (☎ 22430 29014; mains €5-10) One of the more atmospheric seafood restaurants along the waterfront, this colourful, comfortable place serves fresh fish, ouzo octopus, grilled calamari and *saganaki* (fried cheese). Traditional instruments hang on the walls and are played some evenings.

Pizza Imia (☎ 22430 24809; pizza €7-12) Ignore the tacky pictures of burgers and tourist food outside – come to Pizza Imia for the pizza! Loaded and thin-crusted, the pizzas are cooked in a wood oven and are delicious.

OUTDOOR ADVENTURE

In recent years Kalymnos has become something of a mecca for **rock climbers**. Spectacular limestone walls attract legions of climbers looking for seriously challenging extreme sport. There are over 20 documented climbs awaiting the adventurous, pulling in visitors from March onwards. The best place for the low-down is the **Climber's Nest** (☎ 6938173383; www.climbers-nest.com; Armeos). You'll find equipment, maps, guidebooks, guides and a notice board.

The annual **Diving Festival** held in mid-August offers participants the chance to compete in underwater target shooting, cliff diving, scuba-diving through wrecks and even hunting for lost treasure. See the **Municipality's website** (www.kalymnos-isl.gr) for further details.

Hiking has become enthusiastically organised on Kalymnos. There are 10 established hiking routes scattered all over the island and detailed on the excellent 1:25,000 *Kalymnos Hiking Map* published by **Anavasi** (☎ 21032 18104; www.mountains.gr; Stoa Arsakiou 6a, Athens). A popular hike is the Vathys-Pothia B1 4.25km 'Italian Road', a stone pathway built by the Italians at the beginning of the 20th century. A more arduous hike is the 9km circuit Patella Castle loop (C3 and C4), along the mountain ridge backing Emborios.

The house red is rather port-esque but the service is friendly.

If you're self-catering, head for **Vidhalis Market** (☎ 22430 59230), a well-stocked supermarket on the waterfront, and to **Anash's Bakery** (☎ 22430 29426) at the back of town for baked goods like olive bread and local treats.

Drinking

Pothia's harbour is hopping in the evening. The bars that line the waterfront, particularly around Plateia Eleftherias, are stylish hangouts with tables taking over the square. To the west you'll find more old-boy haunts where you can mingle with the locals over fishing stories.

AROUND POTHIA

South of Pothia, the road to Moni Agiou Savra takes you past **Kalymnian House Museum** (☎ 33420 51635; admission €2; ⏰ 9am-2pm & 4-8pm May-Sep), a small traditional home where you'll learn about local customs through guided tours in English.

Running northwards from the port is a busy valley with a series of settlements. The ruined **Castle of the Knights of St John** (Kastro Hrysoherias) looms to the left of the Pothia–Horio road with a small **church** inside its battlements.

On the east side of the valley, **Pera Kastro** was a pirate-proof village inhabited until the 18th century. Within the crumbling walls are the ruins of stone houses and six tiny, 15th-century churches. Check out the few remaining frescoes in the Church of Transfiguration. Steps lead up to Pera Kastro from the end of the main road in **Horio**; it's an unshaded climb with incredible views.

A tree-lined road continues from Horio to **Panormos**, a pretty village 5km from Pothia. Its original name of Elies (olive trees) was replaced following the destruction of the trees during WWII. A postwar mayor planted countless trees and flowers to create beautiful 'panoramas' from which its present-day name is derived. The beaches of **Kandouni** and **Linaria** are a stone's throw from one another and within walking distance of Panormos. Kandouni is a particularly pretty cove surrounded by mountains, with cafes, bars and hotels overlooking the water and a small sandy beach. You can also rock climb from here and there is an annual cliff-diving competition (see above).

For dining and sleeping, Linaria is slightly quieter. **Giorgio's Family Restaurant** (☎ 22430 47809; mains €6-12), at the northern end of Linaria beach, has creative salads, fresh fish and seafood. Try the chilli feta, *saganaki* shrimp or 'god's fish' with garlic sauce alongside a glass of local wine. Rest your head at **Sevasti Studio** (☎ 22430 48779; d/apt €40/50; ⚡). A block up the road and away from the party scene, it has cheerful, spacious rooms and a veranda with gorgeous sea views. Apartments have kitchenettes.

Up the road, **Platys Gialos** is a bit more of a trek from Panormos. The beach here is less developed and pebbly.

MYRTIES, MASOURI & ARMEOS
ΜΥΡΤΙΕΣ, ΜΑΣΟΥΡΙ & ΑΡΜΕΟΣ

From Panormos the road continues to the west coast, with stunning views of Telendos Islet perched like a giant castle in the sea. **Myrties**

DODECANESE

(myr-*tyez*), **Masouri** (mah-*soo*-ri) and **Armeos** (ar-me-*os*) are busy resort centres and essentially one long street, packed head to tail with restaurants, bars, souvenir shops and minimarkets. With lots of trees and a pretty outlook, they're much more relaxed and attractive than the average Greek resort strip. The beach here is divided into two sections by an extinct volcano plug – Myrties beach with Melitsahas harbour, and the marginally better Masouri and Armeos beaches to the north. The beaches have dark sand but aren't so great.

Spread throughout all three centres there are currency-exchange bureaus, a Dodecanet ATM and car- and motorcycle-hire outlets like the reliable **Avis Rental** (☎ 22430 47145; Myrties). To get on-line, visit **Babis Bar** (☎ 22430 47864; per hr €2).

Of the three towns, Myrties is the quietest place to stay. The comfy, spacious studios of **Villa Myrtia** (☎ 22430 47046, 6937942404; www.villamyrtia .gr; d/tr €35/60; ❄) have waves lapping at their large shaded verandas and are set amidst a gorgeous flowering garden. Next door, **Acroyali** (☎ 22430 47521; www.acroyali-Kalymnos.com; d/tr €50/55; ❄) has large traditional, village-style studios with colourful touches and wide private balconies.

Take the first turning to the left to find the seafront **To Psirri** (☎ 6932808049; mains €4-12), a long-favoured family restaurant that serves sausages, grilled burgers, fisherman spaghetti and specialities like fresh sea urchins.

From Myrties there are regular small boats to Telendos Islet (€2).

TELENDOS ISLET ΝΗΣΟΣ ΤΕΛΕΝΔΟΣ

The tranquil, traffic-free islet of Telendos is a bit of a creative outpost and an excellent escape from the busy resort strip opposite. Once part of Kalymnos, it was separated by an earthquake in AD 554.

The islet's only settlement surrounds the colourful quay. Head right for the ruins of the early Christian **basilica** of Agios Vasilios. From here you can also follow a footpath to the **basilica** of Palaiopanayia. Further along the coast, there are several small pebble-and-sand beaches including **Paradise Beach** (sometimes popular with nudists). Heading left from the quay and turning right just before Zorba's will bring you to the larger, fine-pebbled **Hohlakas Beach**. It's windswept and wild.

Telendos is a popular climbing destination; pop into Cafe Naytikos for oodles of info. The small **Katerina** (☎ 6944919073) taxis climb-

ers from Myties to sites on Telendos (€20), departing at 7am and returning at 2pm.

Hotels, rooms and restaurants are spread alongside the quay and on the eastern side of the island. Head right from the quay for the homey **On the Rocks Rooms** (☎ 22430 48260; www .otr.telendos.com; d €45; 💻) that sleep up to four and have a balcony, fridge, mossie nets and fan. You can also hire kayaks and dine at the popular cafe which has traditional fare and a gigantic cocktail menu.

A little further along the coast is **Hotel Porto Potha** (☎ 22430 47321; portopotha@klm.forthnet .gr; d incl breakfast €45, apt €45; ❄ 💻), with comfortable rooms, gorgeous views and a very friendly owner.

To fill your belly, head for **Zorba's** (☎ 22430 48660; mains €3-8). Done up like a quirky sea shanty, you'll enjoy the decor as much as the local seafood soup, fresh salads and tasty feta-stuffed squid. There are also simple rooms for rent upstairs (double €30).

ourpick **Cafe Naytikos** (☉ year-round) offers coffee (or something a little stronger). With hanging paper boats and other local artwork, eclectic music and very comfy seats, you could relax here all day.

For self-caterers, there's a small minimarket opposite the quay but you'd be wise to bring any essentials with you.

Caïques for Telendos depart regularly from the Myrties quay between 8am and 1am (one way €2).

EMBORIOS ΕΜΠΟΡΕΙΟΣ

The scenic west-coast road winds a further 11.5km from Masouri to tiny Emborios, where there's a shaded sand-and-pebble beach. The beachside **Artistico Café** (☎ 22430 40115; mains €4-8) offers dinner and regular live music.

ourpick **Harry's Paradise** (☎ 22430 40062; www .harrys-paradise.gr; mains €5-9; ❄ 💻) is found at the end of what feels like a secret garden. Incredibly lush and secluded, it's a lovely place to dine. The creative menu changes regularly; past delights have included grilled, stuffed mushrooms, filo with smoked cheese, and pork in wine and garlic. The olive oil, eggs, butter, marmalade and edible flowers are all from Emborios. The rooms here (double €45) are extremely cosy and each is individually decorated with artistic flair. All have kitchenettes and balconies overlooking the garden and (from the 1st floor) the sea beyond. Book ahead!

VATHYS & RINA ΒΑΘΥΣ & ΡΙΝΑ

Vathys, set in a long fertile valley on the east coast of Kalymnos, is one of the most beautiful and peaceful parts of the island. Vathys, meaning 'deep', refers to the slender fjord that cuts through high cliffs. Narrow roads wind between citrus orchards, bordered by high stone walls called *koumoula*.

Rina is Vathys' harbour and is a friendly little town, although there's not much to see or do. There's no beach here but if you're careful of fishing boats, you can swim off the jetty at the south side of the harbour. **Water taxis** (☎ 22430 31316, 6947082912) take tourists to quiet coves, such as nearby **Almyres** and **Drasonda** bays. There are a number of churches you can hike to from Pina, including **Hosti** with 11th-century frescoes, found on the western slope of the harbour. An annual cliff-diving competition also takes place at Vathys as part of the International Diving Festival (see p331).

The small, colourful harbour is lined with restaurants. Stop for lunch at **Harbor Taverna** (☎ 22430 31206; mains €4-9) where they've been dishing up scrumptious meals since 1916. Try the calamari with garlic, butter and wine, the fried chicken or the swordfish souvlaki.

Vathys is 13km northeast of Pothia. From here, a new road winds through the mountains from Emborios, making it a speedier way of reaching the north than via the west coast.

LEROS ΛΕΡΟΣ

pop 8210

Laid-back Leros (*leh*-ros) feels both remote and happening. With a beautiful port town, cool cafes, some great dining and lovely vistas, it's a popular spot with domestic travellers but doesn't see many foreign guests. The island is crowned with a stunning medieval castle, one of a number of worthwhile sights, and its small, sandy beaches offer good swimming. If you're after relaxation in comfort, Leros is a very good choice.

Getting There & Away

There are regular flights to Athens, Rhodes, Kos and Astypalea. **Olympic Air** (☎ 22470 22844) is in Platanos, before the turn-off for Pandeli.

Leros is on the main north-south route for ferries between Rhodes and Piraeus, with daily departures from Lakki. Buy tickets at **Blue Star Ferries** (☎ 222470 26000; Lakki) or **Leros Travel** (☎ in Lakki 22470 24000, in Agia Marina 22470 22154). In summer, hydrofoils and catamarans depart daily from Agia Marina on their trip through the Dodecanese, with tickets available on the quay. The **Anna Express** departs from Agia Marina for Kalymnos, Lipsi, Arki, Marathi and Agathonisi. A caïque also services Myrties on Kalymnos.

See Island Hopping (p517) for more transport details.

Getting Around

The **airport** (☎ 22470 22777) is near Partheni in the north. There is no airport bus and the local bus does not accommodate arriving or departing flights. A taxi from the airport to Alinda will cost €8.

The hub for Leros' buses is Platanos. There are three buses daily to Partheni via Alinda and four buses to Xirokambos via Lakki (€1 flat fare).

Car-, motorcycle- and bicycle-hire outlets are mainly on the Alinda tourist strip. **Motoland** (☎ 22470 24584) offers bikes and scooters. For a taxi, ring ☎ 22470 23340, 22470 23070 or 22470 22550.

PLATANOS & AGIA MARINA ΠΛΑΤΑΝΟΣ & ΑΓΙΑ ΜΑΡΙΝΑ

pop 3500

Platanos (*plah*-ta-nos), the capital of Leros, is a bustling village spilling over a narrow hill to the picturesque, colourful port of Agia Marina (ay-*i*-a ma-*ri*-na) to the north. With waterside cafes and good restaurants, the busy port has a strong social vibe and is a great place to unwind, surrounded by relaxed locals and bobbing fishing boats. While there's nowhere to stay right in Agia Marina, Kritonia, Alinda and Paneli offer good accommodation nearby.

Orientation & Information

The focal point of Platanos is the central square, Plateia N Roussou. From this square, Harami leads down to Agia Marina. The Platanos bus station and taxi rank are both about 50m in the other direction, along the Platanos–Lakki road. In Agia Marina, taxis wait at the quay.

The National Bank of Greece is on Platanos' central square. There are two ATMs

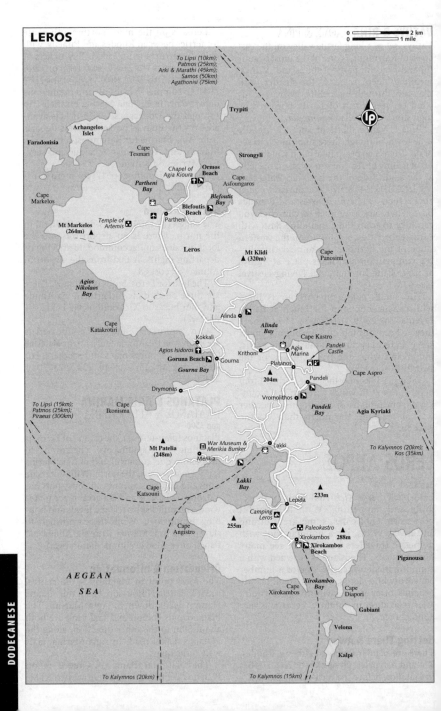

at Agia Marina, including a handy one at the port itself.

Enallaktiko Café (☎ 22470 25746; internet per hr €2; ☺ 10am-midnight) Opposite the quay, a very cool place to get on-line with a cocktail in hand.

Laskarina Tours (☎ 22470 24550; fax 22470 24551) In Platanos; ferry tickets and island cruises.

Police (☎ 22470 22222) In Agia Marina.

Post Office (☎ 22470 22929) West of the quay in Agia Marina.

Tourist Information Kiosk (☎ 22470 222244) On the quay in Agia Marina.

www.leros.org.uk Info on local history and facilities.

XTreme Net (☎ 22470 24041; internet per hr €3) Lots of computers in an office-like setting.

Sights

Perched high on the hill and overlooking the harbour, **Pandeli Castle** (☎ 22470 23211; admission castle €2, castle & museum €3; ☺ 8am-12.30pm & 4-8pm) is worth visiting for its breathtaking 360-degree views from the ramparts. The castle walls are largely intact and the ornate church inside has impressive, colourful frescoes and icons. Running south from the castle is a picturesque string of recently renovated **windmills**. To reach the castle, you can drive from Platanos or walk east of the main square and follow the arrows to the lengthy, scenic staircase.

The **Archaeological Museum** (☎ 22470 24775; admission free; ☺ 8am-2.30pm Tue-Sun May-Sep) is in a restored 19th-century building and has artefacts collected on and around Leros. You'll pass it on the edge of Agia Marina, en route up the hill to Platanos.

Eating

To Iponradiko (Agia Marina; mains €7-12; ☺ year-round) Across from the harbour, on the corner of Harami, this popular restaurant has a touch of elegance with a high ceiling, white furnishings and fancy chandeliers. Fill up on smoked mackerel, grilled salmon or shellfish – it's all fresh.

Taverna Mylos (☎ 22470 24894; Agia Marina; mains €6-15; ☺ year-round) With a home-grown, artsy feel to it, this restaurant is built right over the sea with the watermill just beyond. The creative take on local dishes makes for some tempting dining. Try pasta with smoked salmon, cream and broccoli, calamari with pesto, or chicken with mushroom sauce.

our pick To Paradosiakon (☎ 22470 25500; sweets €0.50-3) Housed in the big yellow building on the harbour, this family bakery sells

outrageously good desserts, using local ingredients like honey and walnuts. Try the almond bites.

For self-caterers, there is a small supermarket in Agia Marina as well as a fresh fish market near the harbour. Head up to Platanos for fresh fruit and veg sold in the main square.

Drinking

The cafes along the quay are very comfortable places to await the ferry or just to sit and relax next to the water. Enallaktiko Cafe (left) is a hip place for a drink and a game of pool, while **Meltemi Bar** (Agios Marina; ☺ 6pm-late) is a tiny, popular bar with a nautical theme. You may even feel it sway after a few drinks.

PANDELI ΠΑΝΤΕΛΙ

Head south from Platanos and you'll quickly reach Pandeli, a little fishing village with a sand and shingle beach. The main draw is for a pillow under your head and a full belly.

On the east side of the bay, the blue-and-white **Rooms to Rent Kavos** (☎ 22470 25020, 6972154102; d €35) has large unfussy rooms with balconies, fan and fridge. Grab a front room for a harbour view.

Pension Happiness (☎ 22470 23498; www.studios-happiness-leros.com; d/studio/apt €45/55/70; ✱) has two brand-new apartments that sleep three. More like large studios, they are spacious and very comfortable with full kitchens and verandas overlooking the sea and castle. Rooms and studios here are older but well-maintained.

Taverna Psaropoula (☎ 22470 25200; mains €5-8) is one of many restaurants right on the beach. Its popular menu includes fresh crayfish, big bowls of shellfish and prawn souvlaki.

VROMOLITHOS ΒΡΩΜΟΛΙΘΟΣ

Continue around the headland and you'll stumble upon Vromolithos, with a narrow shingly beach and some shade.

Up on the hill is the always popular **Pension Rodon** (☎ 22470 22075; d €30; ☺ year-round), a reliable and welcoming choice with comfortable rooms and big sea views. Next door, **Bald Dimitris** (☎ 22470 25626; mezedhes €3-7) offers innovative dishes under a canopy of trees. The hallmark chicken in retsina or pork in wine sauce both satisfy solidly.

our pick Cafe Del Mar (☎ 22470 24766; www.leros cafedelmar.com; snacks €3-8) sits in a hidden corner of the bay, at the eastern end of the beach. The stylish, glassed-in dining room affords

DODECANESE

phenomenal views. This ranks as Leros' coolest place to chill, with big comfy deck chairs and an amazing bar. In the day, grab a smoked trout sandwich or pancakes and stay till evening when the DJs spin.

LAKKI ΛΑΚΚΙ
pop 2370

Arriving at Lakki (lah-*kee*) by boat is akin to stepping into a long-abandoned Federico Fellini film set. Grandiose buildings and wide tree-lined boulevards attest to its creation during the Italian occupation. Few linger in Lakki, though chances are you'll end up passing through. The port has internet access at the quayside **Kinezos Café** (☎ 22470 2259; per hr €3) and there's a number of ATMs throughout the town. The island's largest grocery store is on the road to Platanos.

Even if you're not a history buff, it's worth detouring to the engrossing **War Museum** (☎ 22470 25520; admission €3; ☯ 9.30am-1.30pm), a short drive west towards Merikia. Who knew that such a decisive WWII battle took place on this wee island? While the Germans captured Leros from the Italians and British in 1943, locals hid in these bunkers which are now home to countless war-time objects.

If you have an early morning ferry from Lakki, consider staying at **Hotel Miramare** (☎ 22470 22052; georvirv@otenet.gr; d €45; ☒). An old-fashioned family place, the hotel has clean, comfortable rooms with some sea views. You'll find the place one block back from the waterfront.

Plenty of restaurants line the harbour but if you're after something fresh and affordable, grab a bite with the locals at **To Polntimo** (☎ 22470 23323; sandwiches €2-4). Choose your sandwich fillings from the well-stocked deli, have it toasted and wash it down with fruit smoothies and coffee.

XIROKAMBOS ΞΗΡΟΚΑΜΠΟΣ

Southern Xirokambos Bay has a somewhat isolated feel to it. It's a resort in as much as it has a handful of hotels and a restaurant alongside a few village homes. The beach is pebble and sand with some good spots for snorkelling. En route to Xirokambos a signposted path leads up to the ruined fortress of **Paleokastro** for pretty views.

Xirokambos is home to Leros' only camping ground, **Camping Leros** (☎ 22470 23372; 944238490; camp sites adult/tent €6.50/4; ☯ Jun-Sep). Shaded sites

are in an olive grove, 500m from the beach with a restaurant and basic facilities. Look for it on the right, 3km from Lakki. It's also home to **Panos Diving Club** (☎ 22470 23372; divingleros@hotmail.com; ☐), offering a series of wreck dives and training courses.

Just up from the beach, **Villa Alexandros** (☎ 22470 22202, 6972914552; d €55; ☒) has comfortable, self-contained studios with kitchenettes, overlooking a flower garden. Right on the beach, **To Aloni** (☎ 22470 26048; mains €4-8) is a pleasant fish taverna that draws clientele from around the island.

KRITHONI & ALINDA
ΚΡΙΘΩΝΙ & ΑΛΙΝΤΑ

Within easy reach of Agia Marina, Krithoni and Alinda sit next to each other on Alinda Bay and attract the lion's share of visitors in summer. That said, they remain small and very relaxed. Most of the action is at Alinda while, just down the road, Krithoni offers a quieter area to stay.

Leros' best beach is at Alinda – although narrow, it's long, shaded and sandy with clean, shallow water and, in summer, the occasional lifeguard on duty. **Alinta Seasport** (☎ 22470 24584) hires out row boats, canoes and motor boats. On the bay, the **Historic & Folklore Museum** (admission €3; ☯ 9am-12.30pm & 6.30-9pm Tue-Sun) is in what was once a stately home. Displays take you through the social history of Leros.

On Krithoni's waterfront there is a poignant **war cemetery**. After the Italians surrendered in WWII, Leros saw fierce fighting between German and British forces; the cemetery contains the graves of 179 British, two Canadian and two South African soldiers. You'll find various articles kept in the register box beside the gate.

Hotel Alinda (☎ 22470 23266; fax 22470 23383; Alinda; s/d €30/40; ☒) is right on the beachfront with a shaded bar out front and a pleasant taverna. It has a bit of that holiday-camp feel but has great value, comfortable rooms with lovely views.

With the reception in a neoclassical mansion next to the road, **Boulafendis Bungalows** (☎ 22470 23290; www.boulafendis.gr; Alinda; studio/apt €68/100; ☒ ☐ ☒) offer standard rooms around a gorgeous, palm-fringed pool and garden.

ourpick **Nefeli Hotel** (☎ 22470 24611; www.nefelihotels.com; studio €80, apt €100-130; ℗ ☒) has spacious, comfy rooms. Village-style architecture with kitchens and peaceful balconies is made all the more homier with elegant bohemian touches like local art and textiles. Top-floor rooms have sea views.

Set amid a lush garden of flowers, shrubs and shady trees and backed by a small vineyard, the old-style mansion **To Arhontiko tou Angelou** (☎ 22470 22749; www.hotel-angelou-leros.com; Alinda; s/d incl breakfast €90/155; ✷) has beautiful rooms with antique furnishings, wrought-iron bed and wooden floors.

Alinda is lined with lots of stylish cafes and restaurants. Where the bay bends east, **Osteria Del Buon Mangiare** (Alinda; mains €5-10) is a cheerful restaurant serving authentic Italian meals. A few doors south, **Ionos** (☎ 6977781874; mains €6-12) has a homey, old-fashioned feel with an open fire, traditional tiled floors and lots of photos on the walls. Play chess while you wait for your rabbit with fresh tomato sauce, skewered swordfish, or pork with mango sauce.

Alinda has a number of bars lining the waterfront. Head toward Krithoni for **Nemesis** (☎ 22470 22070), a lounge-style bar with sangria, cocktails and coffee and plenty of comfy sofas.

NORTHERN LEROS

The north of the island is quiet and dotted with small fishing communities, beehives and rugged, windswept terrain. Just west of the airport, the **Temple of Artemis** is from the 4th century BC but is yet to be excavated. On the site are the remains of a newer church where the altar is still used to make offerings.

East of here, **Blefoutis Beach** is a narrow stretch of sand and pebble on an enclosed bay. The setting is pretty and it's very quiet, with a seasonal taverna as the only facility.

PATMOS ΠΑΤΜΟΣ

pop 3040

Shrouded in spiritual mystery, Patmos has an atmosphere unlike any of the other Dodecanese. It's as if the island itself knows it's special. Even the light here is unusual, bathing the landscape in warm hues, and the islanders are a mix of proud locals and long-term expats drawn by the lure of harmony. It was here that St John the Divine ensconced himself in a cave and wrote the

Apocalypse (see the boxed text, p577). Since then, it has become a place of pilgrimage for both Orthodox and Western Christians and is, without doubt, the best place to experience Orthodox Easter. Beyond the tolling bells of the chapels, it's easy to locate dazzling beaches, great nosh and relaxing places to lay your head. The hard part is leaving.

History

In AD 95 St John the Divine was banished to Patmos from Ephesus by the pagan Roman Emperor Domitian. While residing in a cave on the island, St John wrote the Book of Revelations. In 1088 the Blessed Christodoulos, an abbot who came from Asia Minor to Patmos, obtained permission from the Byzantine Emperor Alexis I Komninos to build a monastery to commemorate St John. Pirate raids necessitated powerful fortifications, so the monastery looks like a mighty castle.

Under the Duke of Naxos, Patmos became a semi-autonomous monastic state, and achieved such wealth and influence that it was able to resist Turkish oppression. In the early 18th century a school of theology and philosophy was founded by Makarios and it flourished until the 19th century.

Gradually the island's wealth became polarised into secular and monastic entities. The secular wealth was acquired through shipbuilding, an industry that diminished with the arrival of the steamship.

Getting There & Away

Patmos is connected with Piraeus, Rhodes and a number of islands in between through mainline services with Blue Star Ferries and G&A Ferries. The F/B *Nissos Kalymnos* and *Anna Express* provide additional links to neighbouring islands. The local **Patmos Star** (☎ 6977601633) serves Lipsi and Leros while the **Delfini** (☎ 22470 31995) and *Lambi II* go to Marathi and Arki. Hydrofoils and catamarans also link Patmos with Samos and the rest of the Dodecanese. Boat tickets are sold by Apollon Travel (p339) in Skala. See Island Hopping (p519) for more details.

Getting Around

BOAT

Excursion boats go to Psili Ammos Beach from Skala, departing around 10am and returning about 4pm.

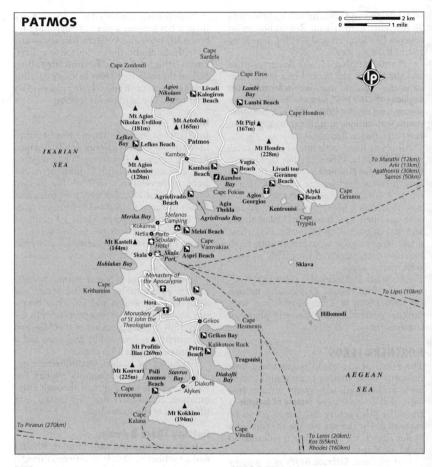

PATMOS

BUS

From Skala, there are six return buses daily to Hora and four to Grikos and Kambos. Fares are a standard €1.

CAR & MOTORCYCLE

There are several car- and motorcycle-hire outlets in Skala. Competition is fierce, so shop around. Some have headquarters in the pedestrian street behind Skala's main harbour, including **Moto Rent Express** (☎ 22470 32088), **Avis** (☎ 22470 33025) and **Theo & Girogio** (☎ 22470 32066).

TAXI

You can catch a **taxi** (☎ 22470 31225) from Skala's taxi rank opposite the police station.

SKALA ΣΚΑΛΑ

You may find Patmos' port town of Skala (*ska*-la), draped around a curving bay, slightly more glitzy than expected. Large cruise ships are often anchored offshore, while yachts anchor at the new marina. Skala certainly sees its fair share of tourists, resulting in lots of excellent accommodation and restaurants. Despite its bustle, the people here seem to be in perpetual holiday mode and relaxing is easy.

Orientation & Information

All transport arrives at the centre of the long quay, smack bang in the middle of Skala. To the right the road leads to a narrow, sandy beach, the yacht port and on to the north of

ST JOHN THE DIVINE & THE APOCALYPSE

The island of Patmos is home to the Cave of the Apocalypse where St John the Divine was allegedly visited by God and instructed to write the tell-all Book of Revelations, also known as the Book of the Apocalypse. He is often believed to be John the Apostle of Jesus or John the Evangelist, though many would dispute this due to his exile in AD 95 to Patmos by the pagan Roman Emperor Domitian. (John the Apostle would have been very, very old by then.) In the Book of Revelations, John wrote about two apocalyptic visions he had received.

The first (1:11-3:22) describes 'one like unto the Son of man, clothed with a garment down to the foot, and girt about the paps with a golden girdle', speaking with 'a great voice, as of a trumpet'. The second vision comprises the remainder of the book (4-22) and begins with 'a door…opened in the sky'. It goes on to describe the end of the world – involving the final rebellion by Satan at Armageddon, God's final defeat of Satan, and the restoration of peace to the world.

'Revelation' is considered to be open to interpretation at best and is not afforded the serious scholarly study that it would seem to merit – perhaps because of the obscure and essentially hard-to-interpret symbolism of the work. Some critics have even suggested that it was the work of a deranged man. Whatever you choose to believe, it's worth visiting the cave where it all supposedly took place. Who knows – you may even have a bit of a revelation yourself.

the island. To the left the road leads to the south side of the island. From a roundabout near the ferry terminal, a road heads inland and up to Hora. The bus terminal and taxi rank are at the quay and all main services are within 100m.

There are three ATM-equipped banks in Skala: the National Bank of Greece, the Emporiki Bank and the Commercial Bank.

AB Food Market (☎ 22470 34023) A well-stocked grocery store 100m along the Hora road in Skala.

Apollon Travel (☎ 22470 31324; apollontravel@ stratas.gr) Ticketing for flights and ferries.

Apyos News Agent (☎ 22470 32431) Selling international papers, paperbacks, maps and traditional Greek music.

Dodoni Gelateria (☎ 22470 32202; internet per hr €4; ⏱ 9am-9pm) Get online while scoffing ice cream.

Hospital (☎ 22470 31211) Two kilometres along the road to Hora.

Just like Home Laundry (☎ 22470 33170; wash & dry per load €10) Behind the new marina. A high cost for cleanliness.

Meltemi (☎ 22470 31839; internet per hr €4) Speedy computers next to the beach.

Municipal Tourist Office (☎ 22470 31666; ⏱ summer) Shares the same building as the post office and police station.

Oxerolas Bookshop (☎ 22470 32251) Secondhand books in English, French, Dutch and German.

Police (☎ 22470 31303) On the main waterfront.

Port police (☎ 22470 31231) Behind the quay's passenger-transit building.

www.patmos-island.com Lots of local listings and info.

www.patmosweb.gr A slightly flashier site with history, listings and photos.

Sights & Activities

Skala has a couple of religious sites, including the place where St John first baptised the locals in 96 AD, just north of the beach. To find out more and to see religious objects from across the island, visit the **Orthodox Culture & Information Centre** (☎ 22470 33316; ⏱ 9am-1pm Thu-Tue & 6-9pm Mon, Tue, Thu & Fri) in the harbour-side church.

If you feel like a workout, climb up to the remains of an ancient **acropolis** on the hillside to the west of town. The route is not well signposted; head for the prominent chapel then follow the dirt trail across the fields full of wildflowers and lizards. The views from the top are stunning.

Sleeping

At the port you'll find a small **info bureau** (☎ 22470 32899) with details on private rooms, studios and apartments for rent. Hotel and studio owners often meet boats at the port, but it's best to call ahead and arrange a pick-up.

Pension Maria Pascalidis (☎ 22470 32152; s/d €25/35) This longstanding traveller-friendly budget option is on the road leading to Hora. Simple but presentable rooms are part of a family home and set amid a fragrant citrus-tree garden.

Casteli Hotel (☎ 22470 31361; fax 22470 51656; s/d incl breakfast €50/70; P ⏹ ⏹) With '70s retro telephones and funky tiles in the bathroom, this place is dated but well loved. Rooms aren't huge but have great views of the harbour and Hora and there's a rooftop pool.

Hotel Chris (☎ 22470 31001; www.patmoschrishotel.gr; d back/sea view €50/80; 🅿) This hotel's age shows in the slightly down-at-heel lobby and halls but the renovated rooms have tiled floors and lovely wooden furniture. Some have four-poster double beds and sea-view rooms have balconies. A little pricy but well situated next to the beach with a popular cafe out front.

Captain's House (☎ 22470 31793; www.captains -house.gr; s/d incl breakfast €55/75; 🅿 🅿) This welcoming hotel next to the port has small but comfortable rooms with fridges and a lovely pool to cool off in. The front rooms have sea views, but can get street noise.

Studios Siroco (☎ 22470 33262; fax 22470 34090; d €80; 🅿) Next to the beach on Hohlakas Bay, these big, new studios are very comfortable with separate kitchens, brick and tiled floors and spacious verandas. You'll fall asleep to the pounding surf.

Kalderimi Apartments (☎ 22470 33008; www .kalderimi.com; apt incl breakfast from €110; 🅿) At the foot of the path up to the monastery and secluded by trees, these gorgeous apartments have traditional design with wooden beams and stone walls, along with lots of swish extras. A full kitchen, shaded balcony and lots of privacy make them a perfect retreat for longer-term stays.

Blue Bay Hotel (☎ 22470 31165; www.bluebay.50g .com; s/d/tr incl breakfast €78/116/144; 🅿 🅿 🅿) Just south of town, this hotel has an airy veranda and breakfast room. Rooms don't have much character but are spacious, well maintained and have lovely sea views from the balconies.

Eating

Meltemi (☎ 22470 31839; full breakfast €5; 🕑 9am-late; 🅿) Start your morning off right, filling up on a home-cooked breakfasts at tables on the sand. Later in the day, come here for milk-shakes, quiche and coffee while the waves lap at your toes.

Tzivaeri (☎ 22470 31170; mains €4-7; 🕑 dinner) All old-fashioned elegance with china, a record player and black-and-white photos, this beachside restaurant serves traditional dishes. The service is fast and courteous and the upstairs looks out over the harbour.

Kiliomothi (☎ 22470 34808; mains €5-9; 🕑 dinner) A block up the road to Hora, this quaint res-

taurant has a less touristy feeling than many of its neighbours. Try aubergine or octopus pancakes or fresh fish with garlic sauce.

Ostria (☎ 22470 30501; mains €7-12) Easily recognisable by the boat on its roof, this place doesn't look that special but packs in seafood connoisseurs all day long. Stuffed *kalamari*, shrimp with tomato and feta, and swordfish souvlaki are just a few of the tempting dishes.

Vegghera (☎ 22470 32988; mains €17-28) High-society diners head for this swish restaurant opposite the yacht marina. The cuisine is a melange of French and Greek with dishes like mushroom risotto, spaghetti with smoked turkey or shrimp on halva. And don't miss the chocolate soufflé.

Drinking

George's Juice Place (drinks €4-5; 🕑 8am-8pm) George whips up smoothies and fresh juice from pears, pomegranates, mangoes, carrots – you name it. Have it with milk, coconut milk or yoghurt and add a dash of booze for an extra kick. Follow the road off the main square to the back of town.

Koukoumavia (☎ 22470 32325) Sip your cocktail on the mosaic bar of this very funky drinking hole. A great selection of music, friendly staff and unique artistic creations will keep you lingering. You'll find it a block north of the turn-off for Hora.

Arion (☎ 22470 31595) Right on the harbour, this popular spot has high-beamed ceilings, polished wood tables and looks more Cuban than Greek. Join a good mix of locals and tourists at any time of day, swinging your cocktail, beer or coffee to an eclectic mix of music.

Anemos (☎ 22470 33008; 🕑 9pm-late Thu-Sun) Just outside Skala on the hill heading up to Kambos, this trendy beer house and music bar in an old stone house draws crowds on the weekends.

Shopping

There's a creative streak running through Patmos, which leads to some interesting shopping. **Koukoumavla** (☎ 22470 32325; www .patmos-island.com/koukoumavia) has funky hand-made clothing and accessories; on the harbour, **Selene** (☎ 22470 31742) has work by 40 artists from around Greece. Browse through Byzantine effigies, wooden carvings, games, pottery and jewellery. Behind the main square, **Jewel Kalogero** (☎ 22470 32453) sells locally made silver jewellery with unique designs.

On a more practical note, **Blue Fin** (☎ 22470 85500; New Marina) can equip you with everything you need for diving and fishing, including oxygen refilling and live bait.

HORA ΧΩΡΑ

High on the hill, huddled around the Monastery of St John, are the immaculate whitewashed houses of Hora, a legacy of the island's great wealth in the 17th and 18th centuries. A stroll through the mazelike streets evokes a timeless atmosphere.

The immense **Monastery of St John the Theologian** (☎ 22470 31398; admission free; ☉ 8am-1.30pm daily, plus 4-6pm Tue, Thu & Sun) crowns the island of Patmos. Attending a service here, with plumes of incense, religious chants and devoted worshippers, is like no other experience you'll have in Greece. Outside of services, you'll get a chance to see the intricate decor. To reach it, many people walk up the Byzantine path which starts from a signposted spot along the Skala–Hora road.

Some 200m along this path, a dirt trail to the left leads through pine trees to the **Monastery of the Apocalypse** (☎ 22470 31234; admission free, treasury €6; ☉ 8am-1.30pm daily, plus 4-6pm Tue, Thu & Sun), built around the cave where St John received his divine revelation. Inside you can see the rock that the saint used as a pillow, and the triple fissure in the roof from where the voice of God issued. The finest frescoes of this monastery are those in the outer narthex. It's also worth taking a peak at the icons and ecclesiastical ornaments found in the treasury.

A five-minute walk west of St John's Monastery, the **Holy Monastery of Zoodohos Pigi** (admission free; ☉ 8am-noon & 5-7pm Sun-Fri) is a women's convent with incredibly impressive frescoes. On Good Friday, a beautiful candle-lit ceremony takes place here.

Just east of St John's Monastery, **Andreas Kalatzis** (☎ 22470 31129) is a Byzantine icon artist who lives and works in a 1740s traditional home. Inside, you'll find an interesting mix of pottery, jewellery and paintings by local artists.

our pick **Archontariki** (☎ 22470 29368; www.arch ontariki-patmos.gr; ste €200-400) will do the trick if you're in need of a little luxury. Inside a 400-year-old building, four gorgeous suites are equipped with every convenience, traditional furnishings and plush touches. Relaxing under the fruit trees in the cool and quiet garden, you'll wonder why the hotel isn't named Paradise.

Loza (☎ 22470 32405; starters €3-8, mains €10-19) is hard to miss as you enter Hora. With stunning views over Skala, it serves up reasonably priced salads and starters, along with some interesting mains like sweet and sour feta in filo and ouzo prawns with basmati rice. Up the stairs and left from here is the tiny **Pantheon** (☎ 22470 31226; mains €5-12) with views of the harbour. Dolmadhes, aubergine with garlic and fish are all well prepared and great value.

Dine in the square or in the secluded garden at **Vangelis Taverna** (☎ 22470 31967; mains €6-10), with its traditional food and family ambience. For a drink, head to **Stoa Cafe** (☎ 22470 32226; ☎), a hip oasis across the square.

NORTH OF SKALA

The narrow, tree-shaded **Meloï Beach** is just 2km northeast of Skala. If you've brought your tent, head for **Stefanos Camping** (☎ 22470 31821; camp sites per person/tent €7/2; ☉ May-Oct). It's clean and well equipped with bamboo-enclosed and tree-shaded sites, a minimarket, cafe-bar and motorcycle-hire facilities. The beach itself has a taverna as well.

Just north of Skala, on the road to Kambos, is the plush **Porto Scoutari Hotel** (☎ 22470 33123; www.portoscoutari.com; d incl breakfast €80-180; P ✗ 🖥 🌊). While the reception is overflowing with impressive but stuffy antiques, the rooms are tastefully decorated and the pool is divine. You pay more for a room with gob-smacking views.

Further up the road is the inland village of Kambos, from where the road descends to the relatively wide and sandy **Kambos Beach**, perhaps the most popular and easily accessible beach on the island. Situated on a fairly enclosed bay, it's great for swimming and you can hire kayaks and sun beds.

our pick **George's Place** (☎ 22470 31881; snacks €3-7) is a fantastic beachside spot for lunch with a big selection of gourmet salads and snacks. The mint iced tea is very satisfying. Kick back and play backgammon, listen to the tunes and watch the waves roll in.

The main road soon forks left to **Lambi**, 9km from Skala, where you wind down to an impressive beach of multicoloured pebbles. High above the beach on the approach road, the warm and welcoming **Leonidas** (☎ 22470 33232; mains €4.50-8) rustles up a wide range of home-cooked dishes like Greek sausage, pork

DODECANESE

souvlaki and fresh fish. The view of the green hills rolling into the sea is very peaceful. On the beach itself, the popular **Lambi Fish Tavern** (☎ 22470 31490; mains €5-14) serves stuffed vine leaves and zucchini flowers, chicken souvlaki, octopus cooked in wine and daily platters of seasonal greens. Oh, and fish too.

Under the protected lee of the north arm of the island are several more beaches, including **Vagia Beach**. Overlooking the beach is **Cafe Vagia** (☎ 22470 31658; mains €3-5; �9am-7pm) with its amazing vegie pies, hearty omelettes and local desserts, all served in a lush garden. It's especially popular with families.

Further west is the shaded **Livadi tou Geranou Beach**, with a small church-crowned island opposite. The road here is narrow and slightly treacherous but stunning. For lunch, stop at the cute **Livadi Geranou Taverna** (☎ 22470 32046; mains €3-5) overlooking the sea from a shaded garden.

SOUTH OF SKALA

Small, tree-filled valleys and picturesque beaches fill the south of Patmos. Closest to Skala is the tiny settlement of **Sapsila**, ideal for those wanting peace and quiet. **Mathios Studios** (☎ /fax 22470 32583; www.mathiosapartments .gr; d €40-65; ☒ ▯) has studios set in a beautiful garden. Relaxed and very comfortable, they have a homey quality and are just 200m from the beach. Dine at **Benetos** (☎ 22470 33089; Sapsila; mains €7-14; ☼dinner Tue-Sun), just up the road. It's a working boutique farmhouse and specialises in Mediterranean fusion dishes with an occasional Japanese kick. Try zucchini blossoms stuffed with mushrooms and cheese, or the herb-crusted, pan-seared tuna. Finish up with a fresh, vodka-laced *sgroppino*, a lemon sorbet drink.

Grikos, 1km further along over the hill, is a relaxed low-key resort with a long, sandy beach and warm shallow water. The bay is lined with tavernas and popular with yachties; be aware that the southern section of the beach doubles as a road. In Grikos is the chapel of **Agios Ioannis Theologos**, built upon ancient public baths where many believe St John baptised islanders. At the southern end of the bay is **Ktima Petra** (☎ 22470 33207; mains €4-7), with organic, homegrown produce. The stuffed and wood-oven-baked goat melts in your mouth and the organic cheese and vegetables are scrumptious.

Just south, **Petra Beach** is very peaceful with sand, pebbles and lots of shade. A spit leads out to the startling **Kalikatsos Rock**. A rough coastal track leads from here to **Diakofti**, the last settlement in the south. (You can also get here by a longer sealed road from Hora.) From here you can follow a half-hour walking track to the long, sandy, tree-shaded **Psili Ammos Beach** where there's a seasonal taverna. You can also get here by excursion boat (p337).

LIPSI ΛΕΙΨΟΙ

pop 700

Blink on the deck of your ferry and you might miss Lipsi (lip-*see*). Long ago discovered by Italians and latterly by French travellers, who treat it as a well-kept secret, this tiny island's drawcard is its relative anonymity, its fine beaches, its lack of demands on visitors – no clubs, pubs or sights to speak of – and a sense that you have the island to yourself, apart from two or three days in August when pilgrims and revellers descend upon Lipsi for its main religious festival. Everything moves more slowly here.

Getting There & Away

Sea connections with Lipsi are tenuous, although it is linked with Piraeus through long-haul ferries and neighbouring islands via the catamaran, a Kalymnos-based ferry, the local **Anna Express** (☎ 22479 41215) and the larger *Patmos Star*. See Island Hopping (p518) for more details.

Getting Around

Stretching only 8km end to end, Lipsi is small – really small – and you can reach most places on foot. In summer, a minibus departs Lipsi Village hourly to the beaches of Platys Gialos, Katsadia and Hohlakoura (each €1) between 10.30am and 6pm. Two **taxis** (☎ 6942409677, 6942409679) operate on the island; you'll find them roaming around Lipsi Village. You can also hire **motorcycles** (☎ 22479 41358) in Lipsi Village.

LIPSI VILLAGE

pop 600

Hugging the deep harbour, Lipsi Village is a cosy community with a small, atmospheric old town and blue-shuttered homes. This tiny town's scattering of restaurants and hotels is the hub of Lipsi's action.

Orientation & Information

All boats dock at Lipsi Port, where there are two quays. Ferries, hydrofoils and catamarans all dock at the larger, outer jetty, while excursion boats dock at a smaller jetty nearer the centre of Lipsi Village. The *Anna Express* docks close to the large main church in the inner port.

The post office is opposite the church on the upper, central square in the old town. The lower, harbour-side square is home to a **tourist office** (summer only), which opens for most ferry arrivals, along with a shaded children's playground. The Co-operative Bank of the Dodecanese on the port changes money and has an ATM.

Cave (☎ 22470 44328; internet per hr €4) Internet access near the outer jetty.

Leski Internet (Old Town; per hr €4) A few computers in someone's front room, near the church.

Lipsos Travel (☎ 22470 44125) Issues tickets for the *Anna Express* and organises excursions.

Police (☎ 22470 41222) In the port.

Port police (☎ 22470 41133) In the port.

Ticket office (☎ 22470 41250; 30min prior to departures) A small office on the outer jetty issuing boat tickets.

www.lipsi-island.gr A useful resource about the island.

Activities

Liendou Beach is on the edge of the village so, naturally, is the most popular beach. With a narrow strip of sand and pebbles and shallow, calm water, it's good for swimming. It's just north of the ferry port over a small headland.

Rena and Margarita offer **boat trips** (day trip per person €20) to Lipsi's offshore islands for a sail, picnic and swim. Both excursion boats can be found at Lipsi's smaller jetty and depart at around 10am daily.

Festivals & Events

The annual religious festival of **Panagia tou Harou** takes place near the end of August when the island fills up with visitors. Following a procession, expect all-night revelry in the lower village square.

An annual **wine festival** takes place for three days during August with dancing and free wine. Check locally for the exact dates.

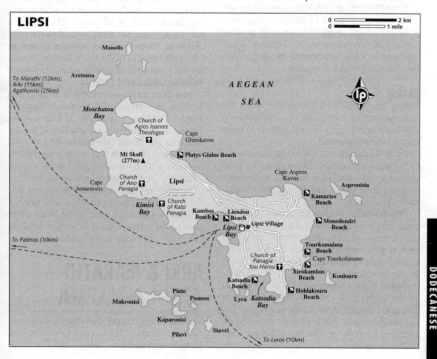

Sleeping

Panorama Studios (☎ 22470 41235; studios/apt from €50/80; ⚡) The studios here are clean with great sea vistas, while the apartments have balconies on which you could happily spend your whole holiday.

Apartments Galini (☎ 22470 41212, 6932037511; matsouri@yahoo.gr; d €55) Right on the harbour, these simple, immaculate rooms have kitchenettes, proper double beds and small balconies with great views.

Apartments Poseidon (☎ 22470 41130; www.lipsi-poseidon.gr; d incl breakfast €65; ⚡) Spacious new apartments sleeping up to four, with lovely trimmings like local pottery. Each has a full kitchen and a big balcony with an uninterrupted sea view. It's between the two quays.

Rizos Studios (☎ 6976244125; fax 22470 44225; www.annaexpress-lipsi.services.officelive.com/rizos.aspx; d €65) Like cosy cottages, these studios have lots of personal touches such as local art, fabric and plenty of cushions. Kitchens are amazingly well stocked, stone-paved floors stay cool and the spacious balconies have a view over Liendou Bay. Phone ahead for a lift from the port.

Aphroditi Hotel (☎ 22470 41000; www.hotel-aphroditi.com; s/d/apt €50/70/125; ⚡) This sprawling place is set just behind Liendou Beach, with spotless and slightly grandiose rooms. Studios have a kitchenette while apartments are huge with two balconies and full kitchen.

Eating

Bakery Shop (☎ 22470 41150; sweets €1-3) Sit on the balcony with the locals, sipping coffee, licking ice cream or indulging in baked goods. It's just next to the playground.

Porto Grill House (☎ 22470 41130; mezedhes €2-6) Between the quays. The kebabs in pita, grilled meats, stuffed tomatoes and salads here are great value. Enjoy from the shaded, view-filled patio.

Cafe de Moulin (mains €3-6) It doesn't have the most inspiring menu, but the fresh yoghurt, omelettes and skewered meats go down well at this friendly place in the old town's main square. Exchange books and meet fellow travellers.

Pefko (☎ 22470 41404; mains €4.50-8) The newest of the harbour tavernas, Pefko has perhaps the most imaginative menu selection. Try the *ambelourgou* (lamb in yoghurt wrapped in vine leaves), or the oven-baked beef with aubergine.

Manolis Tastes (☎ 22470 41065; mains €4-10) With mouth-watering dishes like seafood risotto, lamb in lemon sauce and traditional Lipsi pork chops, you'd do well to nab one of the handful of outdoor tables at this tiny restaurant. Find it in a small square in the Old Town and consider the takeaway window for your picnic lunch.

Tholari (☎ 22470 41060; mains €6-12) With stone walls and traditional sofas, this lovely harbourside restaurant does homestyle meals like sharkfish with garlic dip, beef casserole and baked chicken.

AROUND THE ISLAND

Lipsi has quite a few beaches, most of which are small and without any facilities. Getting to them makes for pleasant walks through countryside dotted with olive groves, cypress trees and endless views. The minibus services the main beaches.

Just 1km beyond Lipsi Village, **Kambos Beach** offers some shade and is narrower but sandier than its neighbour Liendou. The water is also deeper and rockier underfoot.

From here, a further 2.5km brings you to **Platys Gialos**, a small sandy beach whose only drawback is a lack of shade. The water is turquoise-coloured, shallow and perfect for children. Above the beach is **Kostas Restaurant** (☎ 6944963303; grills €4.50-6.50; ⌚ 8am-6pm Jul-Aug), for fish and grill dishes. It stays open later on Wednesday and Saturday.

Just 2km south from Lipsi Village at the bottom of a large hill, the sandy **Katsadia Beach** is wilder, especially if it's windy. Tamarisk trees offer some shade and on the beach is the **Dilaila Cafe Restaurant** (☎ 22470 41041; mains €5-8; ⌚ Jun-Sep), with a beach-bar feel and a lovely shaded garden. Try spicy 'mad feta' or the fried-rice specials.

Beaches on the east coast are more difficult to reach. Due to rough roads, neither taxis nor buses come here. Some locals claim they're the island's most beautiful beaches but many are rocky and shadeless.

ARKI & MARATHI
ΑΡΚΟΙ & ΜΑΡΑΘΙ

Serious solace seekers chill out on these two satellite islands just north of Patmos and Lipsi where yachties, artists and the occasional backpacker mingle. There are neither cars nor motorbikes – just calmness. Pack your bathers, books and iPod and leave the rest behind.

Getting There & Away

In summer there are frequent excursion boats and caïques from Lipsi and Patmos. A boat also stops regularly en route between Patmos and Samos. For more details see Island Hopping (p509).

ARKI ΑΡΚΟΙ
pop 50

Only 5km north of Lipsi, tiny Arki has rolling hills and secluded, sandy beaches. Its only settlement is the little west-coast port, also called Arki. Away from the village, the island seems almost mystical in its peace and stillness. The island sustains itself with fishing and tourism.

There is no post office or police on the island, but there is one cardphone. The **Church of Metamorfosis** stands on a hill behind the settlement with superb sea views. To visit, ask a local for the key and follow the cement road between Taverna Trypas and Taverna Nikolaos to the footpath. Several **sandy coves** can be reached along a path skirting the north side of the bay.

Tiganakia Bay, on the southeast coast, has a good sandy beach. To walk there from Arki village, follow the road heading south and then the network of goat tracks down to the water. You'll recognise it by the incredibly bright turquoise water and offshore islets.

Arki has a few tavernas with comfortable, well-maintained rooms; bookings are necessary in July and August. To the right of the quay, **O Trypas Taverna & Rooms** (☎ 22470 32230; tripas@12net.gr; d €35, mains €5-7) has simple rooms and serves excellent *fasolia mavromatika* (black-eyed beans) and *pastos tou Trypa* (salted fish). Nearby, **Taverna Nikolaos Rooms** (☎ 22470 32477; d €35, mains €5-8) dishes up potatoes au gratin, stuffed peppers with cheese, or the local goat cheese called *sfina*, which is like a mild form of feta. Rooms have sunset views.

MARATHI ΜΑΡΑΘΙ

Marathi is the largest of Arki's satellite islets, with a superb sandy beach. Before WWII it had a dozen or so inhabitants, but now has only two families. The old settlement, with

an immaculate little church, stands on a hill above the harbour. There are two tavernas on the island, both of which rent rooms. **Taverna Mihalis** (☎ 22470 31580; d €30, mains €4-6) is the more laid-back and cheaper of the two, while **Taverna Pandelis** (☎ 22470 32609; d €40, mains €4-6) at the top end of the beach is a tad plusher.

AGATHONISI
ΑΓΑΘΟΝΗΣΙ
pop 160

Agathonisi (agh-atho-*ni*-see) shows up on few travellers' radar and remains a quiet little getaway isle. Like its neighbours, it's rocky and dry, has few settlements and little organised entertainment. Accommodation is fine yet simple, food is unfussy but good quality, and there's little to do other than reflect, read and get ready for the next swim.

Getting There & Away

Agathonisi has regular ferry links with Samos and Patmos. A hydrofoil also links the island with Samos and destinations further south. Ferry agent **Savvas Kamitsis** (☎ 22470 29003) sells tickets at the harbour prior to departures. For more information see Island Hopping (p507).

Getting Around

There is no local transport, and it's a steep and sweaty 1.5km uphill walk from Agios Georgios to the main settlement of Megalo

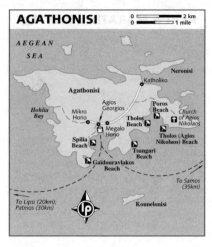

AGATHONISI

0 — 2 km
0 — 1 mile

AEGEAN SEA

Neronisi
Katholiko
Agathonisi
Agios Georgios
Poros Beach
Church of Agios Nikolaos
Hohlia Bay
Mikro Horio
Tholos Beach
Megalo Horio
Tholos (Agios Nikolaos) Beach
Spilia Beach
Tsangari Beach
Gaïdouravlakos Beach
To Samos (35km)
To Lipsi (20km); Patmos (30km)
Kounelonisi

Horio; somewhat less to Mikro Horio. From Megalo Horio, the island's eastern beaches are all within a 3km walk.

AGIOS GEORGIOS ΑΓΙΟΣ ΓΕΩΡΓΙΟΣ

The village of Agios Georgios (*agh*-ios ye-*or*-yi-os) is a languid settlement at the end of a protected fjord-like bay, with a curved, pebble beach. **Spilia Beach**, 900m southwest around the headland, is quieter and better for swimming; a track around the far side of the bay will take you there. A further 1km walk will bring you to **Gaïdouravlakos**, a small bay and beach where water from one of the island's few springs meets the sea.

Orientation & Information

Boats dock at Agios Georgios, from where roads ascend right to Megalo Horio and left to Mikro Horio. There is no tourist information, post office, bank or ATM.

The police are in a prominently marked white building at the beginning of the Megalo Horio road.

Sleeping & Eating

In the middle of the waterfront, **Pension Maria Kamitsi** (☎ 22470 29003; fax 22470 29101; d €35) has comfortable rooms that are easy to find. Above and behind Glaros Restaurant, **Domatia Giannis** (☎ 22470 29062; d/tr €40/50; ✂ ▢) has airy, modern rooms with harbour views.

There's a handful of harbour-side eateries. **Glaros Restaurant** (☎ 22470 29062; mains €4.50-7) serves *markakia* (feta in vine leaves), grills and fish dishes, all made from predominantly organic produce.

AROUND AGATHONISI

Megalo Horio is the only village of any size on the island. Sleepy and unhurried for most of the year, it comes to life with the annual religious festivals of **Agiou Panteleimonos** (26 July), **Sotiros** (6 August) and **Panagias** (22 August), when the village celebrates with abundant food, music and dancing.

To the east of Megalo Horio there's a series of accessible beaches: **Tsangari Beach**, **Tholos Beach**, **Poros Beach** and **Tholos (Agios Nikolaos) Beach**, close to the eponymous church. All are within easy walking distance although Poros Beach is the only sandy option.

If you're after a very quiet stay, **Studios Ageliki** (☎ 22470 29085; s/d €30/35) in Megalo Horio has four basic but comfortable studios with kitchenettes and stunning views over a small vineyard and down to the port. Eating in the village is limited to the reliable **Restaurant I Irini** (☎ 22470 29054; mains €5-6) on the central square, or the **Kafeneio Ta 13 Adelfia** (mains €3-4) on the square's south side, serving budget snacks and meals.

Northeastern Aegean Islands Τα Νησιά του Βορειοανατολικού Αιγαίου

These richly varied islands offer some of Greece's most unique and intriguing sights. Less visited than other island groups, their singular identities cultivate a strong and memorable sense of place. And, since they're somewhat off the beaten track, intrepid travellers can escape the crowds here, while experiencing old-fashioned island cuisine, culture and celebrations.

Eccentric Ikaria, marked by dramatic and diverse landscapes, pristine beaches and a laid-back, leftist population, is one of Greece's most remarkable islands, as is Chios, an ecotourism paradise full of flowers and fruit trees and the only place on the planet where gum is produced from mastic trees. The islands range from sprawling Lesvos, Greece's third-largest island and producer of half the world's ouzo, to midsize islands like sultry Samos and breezy Limnos, to specks in the sea like Inousses and Psara – islands which, however tiny, loom large in the illustrious histories of Greek maritime commerce and naval greatness. Other small islands stand out too, like Samothraki, with its ancient Thracian Sanctuary of the Great Gods and lush mountain waterfalls, and the serene archipelago of Fourni, renowned for its fresh seafood.

This group is less compact than other Greek island chains. Thasos and Samothraki are only accessible from Northern Greece ports, while Ikaria is just a skip across the water from Mykonos. The southernmost islands also neighbour on the Dodecanese, while Lesvos, Chios and Samos offer easy connections to Turkey's coastal resorts and historical sites.

HIGHLIGHTS

■ **Dive In** Swimming in the clear waters of Ikaria's remote, white-pebble Seychelles Beach (p354)

■ **Get Spiritual** Gazing out over Lesvos from the elevated Byzantine monastery of Moni Ypsilou (p386), home of priceless medieval manuscripts and ecclesiastical treasures

■ **Lose Yourself** Wandering the winding stone alleyways of Mesta (p372) in southern Chios

■ **Total Immersion** Wading through the river to wooded waterfalls in northwest Samos, followed by swimming and a drink on chilled-out Potami Beach (p365)

■ **Sunset Solitude** Watching from high above as the gentle folds of the Fourni archipelago fade into dusk (p356)

■ **Hot Pursuit** Careening through old-growth forests in lush Thasos' annual international mountain bike race (p402)

■ **Seafood Symphony** Watching the fishermen untangle their colourful nets, and then dining on the day's catch in the seafood tavernas of Myrina (p392) in Limnos

★ Thasos

★ Myrina

Moni Ypsilou ★

Mesta ★

Seychelles Beach ★

★ Potami Beach

★ Fourni Archipelago

■ POPULATION: 204,160

■ AREA: 3842 SQ KM

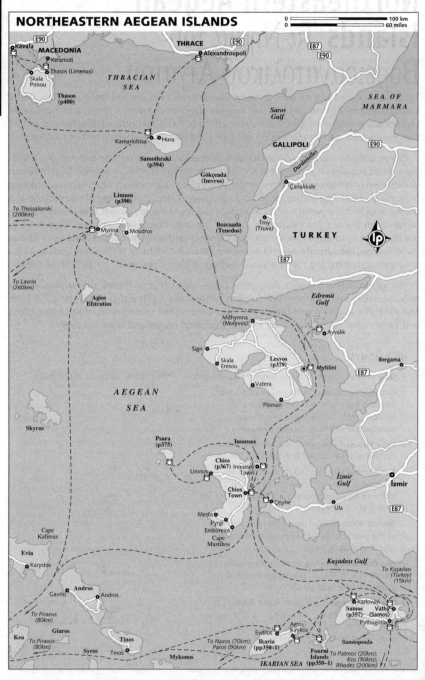

NORTHEASTERN AEGEAN ISLANDS

0 — 100 km
0 — 60 miles

THRACE

E90 Kavala
MACEDONIA
Keramoti
Thasos (Limenas)
Skala
Prinou
Thasos
(p400)

*THRACIAN
SEA*

E90 Alexandroupoli

*Saros
Gulf*

GALLIPOLI E90

Dardanelles

Kamariotissa Hora
Samothraki
(p394)

Gökçeada
(Imvros)

Çanakkale

*SEA OF
MARMARA*

E87
E90

Limnos
(p390)

To Thessaloniki
(200km)

Myrina Moudros

Bozcaada
(Tenedos)

Troy
(Truva)

T U R K E Y

E87

To Lavrio
(260km)

Agios
Efstratios

*Edremit
Gulf*

Mithymna
(Molyvos)

Ayvalik

Sigri

Skala
Eresou

Lesvos
(p379)

Mytilini

E87

Bergama

Vatera

*AEGEAN
SEA*

Plomari

Skyros

Psara
(p375)

Inousses

Chios
(p367) Inousses
Town
Limnos

Chios
Town

*İzmir
Gulf*

İzmir

Çeşme

Mesta
Pyrgi
Emborios
Cape
Mastihos

Ula

E87

Cape
Kafireas

Evia
Karystos

Kuşadası Gulf

To Kuşadası
(Turkey)
(15km)

Gavrio
Andros
Andros

To Piraeus
(80km)

Giaros

Kea To Piraeus
(80km)

Tinos

Syros Tinos

Mykonos

Evdilos

Agios
Kirykos

Ikaria
(pp350-1)

To Naxos (70km);
Paros (90km)

Samiopoula

Karlovasi
Samos
(p357) Vathy
(Samos)

Pythagorio

IKARIAN SEA

Fourni
Islands
(pp350-1)

To Patmos (20km);
Kos (90km);
Rhodes (200km)

IKARIA & THE FOURNI ISLANDS ΙΚΑΡΙΑ & ΟΙ ΦΟΥΡΝΟΙ

area 255 sq km

Ikaria and the Fourni archipelago are arguably the most magical of the northeastern Aegean Islands. Ikaria's dramatic and varied terrain comprises deep, forested gorges, rocky moonscapes and hidden beaches where aquamarine waters gently lap, while the bare, sloping hills of Fourni's little islets overlap across the horizon, running elliptically into a lobster-rich sea.

These islands have eclectic, even mythical histories. As a former hideout for nefarious pirates and other scallywags, Fourni proved a constant vexation for Byzantine and subsequently Ottoman rulers. More recently, Ikaria (ih-kah-*ree*-ah) became a dumping ground for Communist sympathisers during Greece's 1946–49 Civil War – the KKE (Greek Communist Party) remains popular on the island today. Intriguingly, Ikaria is named for Icarus, son of Daedalus, the legendary architect of King Minos' Cretan labyrinth. When the two tried to escape from Minos' prison on wings of wax, Icarus ignored his father's warning, flew too close to the sun and crashed into the sea, creating Ikaria – a rocky reminder of the dangers of overweening ambition.

Greek myth also honours Ikaria as the birthplace of Dionysos, god of wine; indeed, Homer attested that the Ikarians were the world's first wine-makers. Today travellers can enjoy the signature local red here, along with fresh and authentic local dishes in a serene environment far from the crowds; the same is doubly true for Fourni, renowned for its seafood and dotted by isolated sandy coves.

Along with the total tranquillity these islands provide, plenty of activities will keep you busy. Hiking, swimming and cycling are all excellent, while Ikaria's light-hearted summertime *panigyria* (festivals; annual celebrations of saints' days) are truly festive events, involving much food, drink, traditional dance and song – a fun-loving commingling of Orthodox Christianity and Ikaria's deeper Dionysian roots.

Being somewhat small and remote, Ikaria and the Fourni islands are fairly sleepy out of high season, with most, if not all, accommodation options likely to be closed.

Getting There & Away

AIR

For flight schedules from Ikaria, see Island Hopping (p514). **Olympic Air** (☎ 22750 22214; www.olympicairlines.com) in Agios Kirykos, and **Nas Travel** (☎ 22750 31947) in Evdilos sell tickets. There's now an airport bus, serving only Agios Kirykos and Faros. Otherwise, use airport taxis (to/from Agios Kirykos, €10).

BOAT

A caïque leaves Agios Kirykos at 1pm on Monday, Wednesday and Friday for Fourni (€4), stopping at Fourni Korseon, the capital, plus Hrysomilia or Thymena. Day-trip excursion boats to Fourni also go from Agios Kirykos and Evdilos (€20).

For ferry and hydrofoil information from Ikaria, see Island Hopping (p514). Get tickets in Agios Kirykos at **Icariada Holidays** (☎ 22750 23322; depy@ikariada.gr), **G&A Ferries** (☎ 22750 22426), or **Dolihi Tours Travel Agency** (☎ 22750 23230).

Getting Around

BOAT

Water taxis are helpful for nondrivers, or anyone desiring a good boat ride. Summer daily water taxis go from Agios Kirykos to Therma (€2 return). Heading the other way, there's a summertime caïque every Monday, Wednesday and Friday from Agios Kirykos to Karkinagri, a southwest-coast fishing village, stopping first at Maganitis and the idyllic Seychelles Beach. During high season, this boat sometimes goes daily, and represents the only realistic way for nondrivers to reach this remote corner of Ikaria.

BUS & TAXI

Theoretically, buses operate on Ikaria, though the system exists more for transporting schoolchildren than tourists. A twice-daily bus from Agios Kirykos to Hrisos Rahes, via Evdilos and Armenistis, operates (€7). If you don't hire a car, share a taxi; from Agios Kirykos to Evdilos costs around €40, though drivers may use their meter instead.

IKARIA & THE FOURNI ISLANDS

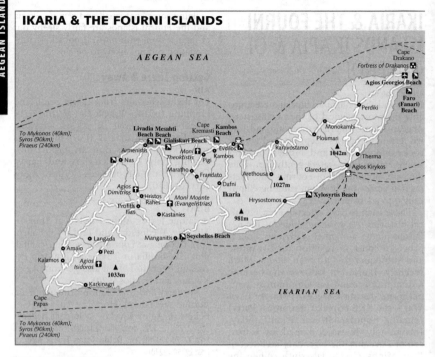

CAR & MOTORCYCLE

It can be a good idea to hire a car or scooter for travel beyond the main towns (though hitchhiking is still accepted by locals). Try **Dolihi Tours Travel Agency** (☎ 22750 23230) in Agios Kirykos, and **Aventura Car & Bike Rental** (aventura@otenet.gr) in Evdilos (p352) and Armenistis (p355).

AGIOS KIRYKOS ΑΓΙΟΣ ΚΗΡΥΚΟΣ
pop 1880

Ikaria's capital is a dated but dependable Greek port, with clustered old streets, tasty restaurants, hotels and domatia with the necessary services. It has elementary nightlife and radioactive hot springs, while Xylosyrtis Beach (4km southwest) is the best of Agios Kirykos' pebble beaches.

Orientation

The ferry quay is 150m south of the town centre; for the *plateia* (square), turn right onto the main road. Leaving the quay, turn left on the square for the bus stop, just west. Excursion boats and hydrofoils dock near Dolihi Tours Travel Agency.

Information

ATM-equipped banks line the *plateia*. The post office is left of it. Useful online resources include www.island-ikaria.com and www .ikaria.gr.
Dolihi Tours Travel Agency (☎ 22750 23230) Helpful agency can arrange accommodation; located below the police station.
Icariada Travel (☎ 22750 23322; depy@ikariada .gr) Waterfront agency sells ferry and plane tickets, and arranges accommodation.
Police (☎ 22750 22222) Above Dolihi Tours.
Port police (☎ 22750 22207)
Tourist police (☎ 22750 22222)

Sights & Activities

Opposite the police station, Ikaria's **radioactive springs** (admission €5; ⏱ 7am-2.30pm & 5-9pm Jun-Oct) are famed for their salutary effects, which include curing arthritis and infertility.

Agios Kirykos' small **archaeological museum** (☎ 22750 31300; admission free; ⏱ 10am-3pm Tue-Wed & Fri-Sun Jul-Aug) boasts local finds, highlighting the large, well-preserved *stele* (500 BC) depicting a seated mother and family. Although the (signposted) museum is near the hospital, at the

time of writing a new museum was planned for a different location – the old *gymnasio* (high school).

The **Icarus Festival for Dialogue between Cultures** (☎ 22940 76745; www.icarus-festival.ikaria.gr; per event €10; ☺ performances from 9.30pm Jul & Aug) is a summer-long, island-wide series of concerts, dramatic works and other cultural events held since 2005. The festival highlights individuals and groups who espouse multicultural values and cooperation; among them are some quite prominent Greek and international artists. Buses are organised for festival-goers.

A quirky, appropriately Ikarian event held for over 30 years is the Ikaria International Chess Tournament, organised by local chess aficionado **Savas Kyriakou** (☎ 6932478386; www .chess.gr/ikaros), If you're game, this battle of wits is held each July – the winner walks off with €1000, and special cash prices are allotted for 'ladies and veterans' as well.

Sleeping

Pension Maria-Elena (☎ 22750 22835; www.island-ikaria .com/hotels/mariaelena.asp; s/d €35/45; ❄ ☎ ☺) Some 500m from the port near the hospital, this small pension enjoys a garden setting and offers 16 simple but clean rooms with balconies overlooking the sea, plus a few suites. It's open year-round.

Hotel Akti (☎ 22750 23905; s/d €35/50; ❄) A budget choice on the rocks overlooking sea and port, Akti has small but attractive rooms with fridge, TV and mosquito netting, plus friendly, English-speaking owners. Follow the steps just right of Alpha Bank.

Hotel Kastro (☎ 22750 23480; www.island-ikaria.com/ hotels/kastro.asp; d €50; ❄ ☺) This well-appointed hotel has handsome rooms with balconies and all mod cons. There's a bar, and even a rooftop pool. From atop the stairs leading from Dolihi Tours, it's 20m to the left.

Eating & Drinking

Filoti (☎ 22750 23088; mains €4-7) This tasty eatery 30m from the square offers Agios Kirykos' best-value meals (including decent pizzas).

Taverna Klimataria (☎ 22750 22686; mains €6-9) A back-street taverna, strong on grilled meats, with a lovely summer courtyard.

Restaurant Dedalos (☎ 22750 22473; mains €7-12) Beside the square, this busy eatery serves tasty, if pricey, fresh fish.

AROUND AGIOS KIRYKOS

The **hot springs of Lefkada** (☎ 6977147014; admission €5; ☺ 7am-2.30pm & 5-9pm Jun-Oct), 2km north of Agios Kirykos, are therapeutic and relaxing, and reportedly cure many ailments. Ikaria's eastern tip boasts the 2km-long **Faro Beach**, 10km north along the coast road, and the 3rd-century BC **fortress of Drakanos**, which sponsored religious rites dedicated to Eilythia, a fertility deity. Although still not fully excavated, it's worth seeing. A path from a small chapel here leads to the sandy **Agios Georgios Beach**.

While a few tavernas hug this beach, it's more tranquil than the major northwest-coast beaches. Just up from it on the main road, the friendly Greek-Australian Evon Plakidas at **Rooms Evon** (☎ 22750 32580, 6977139208; evon.plakidas@ gmail.com; www.evonsrooms.com; ste €50-110; ☐) rents clean, high-quality suites, some with spiral stairs, all with kitchenettes. The studios hold up to six people. The adjoining cafe, where breakfast is served, has internet access.

EVDILOS ΕΥΔΗΛΟΣ
pop 460

Evdilos, Ikaria's second port, is 41km northwest of Agios Kirykos; they're connected by

Ikaria's main road. If you haven't a car, take a taxi (€40). The memorable trip takes in high mountain ridges, striking sea views and slate-roof villages. Evdilos itself is sleepy, though its streets are narrow and poorly planned for the summer influx, as attested by the chronic vehicle congestion. It features stately old houses on winding streets (follow Kalliopis Katsouli, the cobbled street leading uphill from the waterfront square). For the local beach, walk 100m uphill from the *plateia*, then take the path down past the last house on the left.

Information

The waterfront has ATMs, and the ticket agencies for **NEL Lines** (☎ 22750 31572) and

Hellas Ferries (☎ 22750 31990). **Aventura** (☎ 22750 31140), in a side street off the central waterfront, has car and bike hire, sells tickets and offers information.

Sleeping

Hotel Atheras (☎ 22750 31434; www.atheras-kerame.gr; s/d €50/60; 🟦 🟦) The almost Cycladic feel to the Atheras derives from its bright white decor contrasting with the blue Aegean beyond. The friendly, modern hotel has a pool bar. It's in the backstreets, 200m from the port.

Kerame Studios (☎ 22750 31434; www.atheras-kerame.gr; studio/apt from €70; 🟦 🟦) These diverse studios, apartments and rooms 1km before Evdilos have beach access nearby. Prices are as variable as the quarters, which include simple

---

REVEALED: THE SECRETS OF IKARIAN LONGEVITY

In 2009 Greek and foreign media announced that Ikarians enjoy the longest average lifespan in Europe. To what can be attributed this mark of distinction?

To be sure, the time-honoured, laid-back lifestyle of remote Ikaria, untroubled by mass tourism or the stresses of modern life, is a factor. But to really get the story on the secrets of Ikarian longevity, it's best to go, as reporters say, straight to the source.

Take Ioannis Tzantas: born on 9 February 1910 in the village of Akamanatra, this contented chap sitting outside the local *kafeneio* (coffee house) happily recounts his island life, and all the little things that have gone into extending it far longer than the average person's.

By the age of 14, the bespectacled centenarian recalls, he was looking after his whole household, as his father's health problems left him incapable. 'I sold goats, and worked for my family every day and night,' recounts Ioannis. 'In those days, we would walk everywhere, all day long, following the sheep – walking is very good for you, you know.'

Ioannis was married at 26, and recalls the vibrant life of a village that has since become sleepy due to emigration. 'We had many festivals, with lots of singing and dancing,' he says, 'And I would drink some wine, but I never got drunk, not once!'

Indeed, Ioannis is firm about steering clear of vices. Although he was a pipe smoker for 18 years, he never touched cigarettes. 'Life is very good, even though there are always problems that can't be avoided,' he says, 'But other potential problems can be avoided – like drunkenness and drugs. It makes me very sad when I see people with these problems.'

Instead, Ioannis prescribes two glasses of wine a day, 'but without getting drunk, of course. And no smoking!' With a twinkle in his eye, he adds, 'and be sure to have lots of sex.' (At this, Ioannis' septuagenarian sons erupt with laughter from the corner.)

It takes a hardy and disciplined diet to keep up a man's vitality, of course. Ioannis advises eating lots of eggs, cheese and milk. 'I once even had 32 eggs in one day!' (More laughter.)

For a man of his years, Ioannis has a sharp memory. As his life lessons meander into tangents, he recalls a sometimes harrowing childhood in wild Ikaria, and a facet of life that perhaps helps explain its Communist tendencies. 'In those days, the pirates attacked our island very often,' he says. 'That's why nobody wanted to have lots of things – the pirates would steal them anyway!' He also recalls WWII, when he was stationed in the north, near Albania. Although precisely 225 of his comrades were killed, 'thanks to God, I escaped every time!'

Indeed, having outlived five wars, Ioannis knows something about conflict management. Personal strife, however, endangers one's lifespan most, he believes. The village elder saves this, perhaps his most important lesson, for the end. 'It's very bad for one's health to be jealous of other people's happiness. When others have success, we should also feel joy... *afta* [That's all].'

RELIGIOUS REVELRY ON THE ISLAND OF WINE

Pagan god Dionysos may no longer reign over Ikaria's vineyards, but his legacy lives on in Christianised form in the summertime *panigyria* (festivals; all-night celebrations held on saints' days across the island). There's no better way to dive headfirst into Greek island culture than drinking, dancing and feasting while honouring a village's patron saint. Bring your wallet, however: *panigyria* are important fundraisers for the local community. Use this fact to explain away any overindulgences as well-intended philanthropy.

Western Ikaria *panigyria* occur on the following dates:

Kambos 5 May
Agios Isidoros 14 May
Armenistis 40 days after Orthodox Easter
Pezi 14 May
Agios Kirykos & Ikarian Independence Day 17 July
Hristos Rahes & Dafne 6 August
Langada 15 August
Evdilos 14–17 August
Agios Sofia 17 September

---

but well-maintained studios and apartments for four people, with separate kitchen. Rooms have spacious decks with views; the restaurant is built into a windmill.

Hotel Evdoxia (☎ 22750 31502; www.evdoxia.gr; d €70; ✿) Although it's a bit of a climb, this B-class hotel has attractive modern rooms and many facilities, like a minimarket, laundry service, currency exchange and traditional restaurant. Advance, multiday reservations get you free pick-up from the ferry.

Eating

Tsakonitis (☎ 22750 31684; Plateia Evdilou; mezedhes €4-7) This *ouzerie* (place that serves ouzo and appetisers) on the waterfront is a local favourite known for its homemade Greek yoghurt.

To Steki (☎ 22750 31723; Plateia Evdilou; mains €5-9) This harbour-side dining 'hang-out' (as its name implies in Greek) is a dependable year-round option for taverna fare, like cheese pies and *soufiko* (an Ikarian speciality, like a Greek ratatouille).

WEST OF EVDILOS

Kambos Κάμπος
pop 94
Little Kambos, 3km west of Evdilos, was once mighty Oinoe (derived from the Greek word for wine), Ikaria's capital. Traces of this ancient glory don't remain, though the village does boast a ruined Byzantine palace, Ikaria's oldest church and a small museum. Kambos' other main attractions are its sand-and-pebble beach and scenic hill walks.

INFORMATION
Kambos is fairly self-explanatory but for insider info, track down long-time local tourism provider Vasilis Kambouris. If he's not at his village shop (on the right when arriving from Evdilos, and also site of Kambos' post box and telephone), Vasilis can be found catering to guests at his Rooms Dionysos (below). Vasilis can also help organise taxis, car hire and ferry tickets.

SIGHTS & ACTIVITIES
On the right-hand side when entering Kambos from Evdilos stand the modest ruins of a **Byzantine palace**. Kambos' small **museum** (☎ 22750 31300; admission free) displays Neolithic tools, geometric vases, classical sculpture fragments, figurines and ivory trinkets. If it's closed, ask Vasilis Kambouris to open it. Adjacent stands Ikaria's oldest surviving Byzantine church, **Agia Irini Church** (12th century). Built on the site of a 4th-century basilica, it contains some columns from this original. Alas, Agia Irini's frescoes remain covered with whitewash because of no funds to pay for its removal.

SLEEPING & EATING
our pick **Rooms Dionysos** (☎ 22750 31300; dionisos@ hol.gr; www.ikaria-dionysosrooms.com; roof-terrace beds/ d/tr €10/40/50; ✿ ✿) The many happy guests who return every year attest to the magical atmosphere of this pension run by the charismatic Vasilis 'Dionysos' Kambouris, his Australian wife Demetra and brother Yiannis.

MOUNTAIN WALKS & MONKS SKULLS

With its solitude and wild nature, Ikaria's perfect for mountain walks. One that's invigorating, but not too hard on the bones, is the one-day circular walk along dirt roads from **Kambos** south through **Dafni**, the remains of the 10th-century **Byzantine Castle of Koskinas**, and picturesque **Frandato** and **Maratho** villages.

When you reach **Pigi**, look for the Frandato sign; continue past it for the unusual little **Byzantine Chapel of Theoskepasti**, tucked into overhanging granite. You must clamber upwards to get to it, and duck to get inside. Provided the row of old monks' skulls don't creep you out, the chapel makes for a wonderfully peaceful visit and is near **Moni Theoktistis**, with frescoes dating from 1686. The nearby *kafeneio* (coffee house) is good for a relaxed coffee or juice with Maria, the kindly owner.

Rooms are simple but well maintained, with private bathrooms, while the rooftop terrace beds are a steal at €10. The lovely shaded patio overlooking nearby Kambos Beach is where Vasilis serves his trademark big breakfasts, and where guests can enjoy the relaxed conviviality of the place over an evening drink. There's even a book exchange. To find it, ask at Vasilis' village shop or look for the blue-painted trees.

Balcony (☎ 22750 31604; d/tr €40/60) There are fantastic views from the six apartments at family-run Balcony, a bit of a hike to reach. Classic wrought-iron furniture distinguishes the studios, which have a kitchen and loft-sleeping area with twin mattresses. French-style doors lead to a private sitting area with coastal views.

Partheni (☎ 22750 31995; mains €6-8) On Kambos Beach, the Partheni serves simple but tasty Greek food, and great *kalamari* (fried squid). It also does nourishing *mayirefta* (ready-cooked meals), and makes a relaxing place to eat after a swim.

Pashalia (☎ 22750 31346; mains €6-10) A family-run taverna with tradition, the Pashalia offers tasty homemade mezedhes (appetisers), like wild mushrooms, fresh wild asparagus and goat's cheese, and is frequented by the locals.

Kambos to the Southwest Coast

From Kambos, two roads head west: the main road, which hugs the northern coast until the Armenistis resort, and then becomes a secondary road continuing down the north-western coast; and another secondary road, mostly dirt but doable with a good car, which ribbons slightly southwest through the stunning moonscapes of central Ikaria to remote Karkinagri on the southern coast. The latter is ideal for those seeking off-the-beaten-track adventures, while the former is the obvious choice for beach lovers.

The southern coast road through central Ikaria accesses **Moni Theoktistis** and the tiny **Chapel of Theoskepasti** (see boxed text, above), just northwest of Pigi. From Pigi, continue south to Maratho, then west for the impressive **Moni Mounte**, also called Moni Evangelistrias. Some 500m beyond it lies a kid-friendly duck pond with giant goldfish and croaking frogs.

After this, the road forks northwest and southwest: follow the signs and either will arrive at **Hristos Rahes**, an eclectic hillside village and good hiking base, once known for its late-night shopping. Along with various traditional products, there's a useful walking map, *The Round of Rahes on Foot* (€4), sold at most shops; proceeds go to maintaining the trails.

After Hristos Rahes, follow the road south through rustic **Profitis Ilias**. Head south when the road forks; after 1km take the left towards **Pezi**. The landscape now becomes even more rugged and extreme, with wind-whipped thick green trees clinging to bleak boulders, and rows of old agriculturalists' stone walls snaking across the terrain. The bouncy, dusty ride opens onto stunning views of the badlands interior and, after you turn left at Kalamos, of the sea far below. The road finally terminates at tiny **Karkinagri**, which has a few tavernas, rooms and a nearby beach.

In summer this fishing village also has a thrice-weekly boat service to Agios Kirykos (see p349). This highly recommended voyage follows Ikaria's rugged and partially inaccessible southern coast. The boat calls in at **Manganitis** village; nearby is a gorgeous, secluded stretch of white pebbles and crystal-clear waters – the appropriately named **Seychelles Beach** tucked within a protected cove and flanked by a cave.

Alternatively, if coming to Seychelles Beach by car along the coastal road connecting Manganitis with Evdilos and Agios Kirykos, you'll see an unmarked parking area on the right-hand side, after a tunnel; park here and clamber down the boulder-strewn path (a 20-minute walk) to the beach.

SLEEPING & EATING

Hotel Raches (☎ 22750 91222; Hristos Rahes; s/d €25/40) Simple but clean and inexpensive domatia have balconies with views, a communal area and friendly owners – book ahead in high season.

Kaza Papas (☎ 22750 91222; Karkinagri; d/apt €45/55; ✗) These simple but new Karkinagri domatia and apartments have great sea views. Facing the water, turn right behind the tavernas and walk 100m along the waterfront to reach them, though it's better to reserve ahead.

O Karakas (☎ 22750 91214; Karkinagri; mains €6-9) On a bamboo-roofed seafront patio, this excellent family-run taverna does good fresh fish and salads. Try Ikaria's tasty vegetable stew speciality, *soufiko*.

Armenistis to Nas Αρμενιστής Προς Να

Armenistis, 15km west of Evdilos, is Ikaria's humble version of a resort. It boasts two long, sandy beaches separated by a narrow headland, a fishing harbour and a web of hilly streets to explore, but nothing traditional. Cafes line the beach. Moderate nightlife livens up Armenistis in summer, but it's far more subdued than the typical Greek island resort.

Dolihi Tours (☎ 22750 71480), by the sea, organises walking tours and jeep safaris. **Aventura** (☎ 22750 71117), by the patisserie before the bridge, offers car hire and ticket sales.

Just 500m east of Armenistis is **Livadi Beach**, where currents are strong enough to warrant a lifeguard service and waves are sometimes big enough for surfing. Beyond Livadi are two other popular beaches, **Mesahti** and **Gialiskari**.

Westward 3.5km from Armenistis lies the pebbled beach of **Nas**, located far below the road and a few tavernas. This nudist-friendly beach has an impressive location at the mouth of a forested river, behind the ruins of an ancient **Temple of Artemis**.

Nas has become slightly upscale and preserving the equilibrium has prompted the Greek police to dismantle the impromptu beach hovels made by the hapless hippies the place attracts. They usually retreat into the river forest to camp, and are generally benign.

SLEEPING

Rooms Fotinos (☎ 22750 71235; www.island-ikaria.com/hotels/PensionFotinos.asp; Armenistis; d from €40; ✗ May-Oct; ✗) This family-run Armenistis pension, 150m above the curving beach, has seven rooms, all clean and modern, with a lovely, relaxing garden. The owners are friendly and helpful.

Gallini (☎ 22750 71293; www.galinipension.gr; Armenistis; d €60; ✗ May-Oct) These 12 domatia also hover above Armenistis. They're small but beautifully furnished, with walls of inset stone and big windows. Studios are larger, with slanting, loft-style ceilings and kitchenettes. All enjoy great sea views.

Atsachas Rooms (☎ /fax 22750 71226; www.atsachas .gr; Livadia Beach; d €60) Right on Livadia Beach, the Atsachas has clean, well-furnished rooms, some with sophisticated kitchens. Most have breezy, sea-view balconies. The cafe spills down to the lovely garden, and the restaurant has also won plaudits.

Villa Dimitri (☎ /fax 22750 71310; www.villa-dimitri .de; Armenistis; 2-person studios & apt with private patio €50-70; ✗ Mar-Oct; ✗ 💻) This assortment of separate, secluded apartments set on a cliff amid colourful flowers has a Cycladic feel. It's 800m west of Armenistis and requires advance bookings and a minimum of one week.

Panorama (☎ 22750 71177; www.ikaria-panorama .com; Nas; studios €80; 🅿) This collection of five self-catering studios is located up a steep driveway before the village. Rooms fit up to four people and feature handsome combinations of wood and marble, all with new fixtures and sea views.

EATING

Pashalia Taverna (☎ 22750 71302; Armenistis; mains from €5; ✗ Jun-Nov) Meat dishes like *katsikaki* (kid goat) or veal in a clay pot are specialities at this, the first taverna along the Armenistis harbour road.

Taverna Nas (☎ 22750 71486; Nas; mains €6-10) This simple taverna on the high bluff over Nas beach has superb views of the western sea at sunset. Although a bit touristy, it serves hearty portions of Greek standbys and fresh fish.

Kelari (☎ 22750 71227; Gialiskari; mains €6-13) Taking the fish straight off the boat, Kelari serves the best seafood available at this laid-back beach east of Armenistis.

THE FOURNI ISLANDS ΟΙ ΦΟΥΡΝΟΙ
pop 1470

The Fourni archipelago is one of Greece's great unknown island gems. Its low-lying vegetation clings to gracefully rounded hills that overlap, forming intricate bays that conceal sandy beaches and little ports where caïques bob on a placid sea. A sort of Outer Hebrides in the Mediterranean, this former pirates' lair is especially beautiful at dusk, when the setting sun suffuses its multifaceted terrain into shades of pink, violet and black – the effect is especially dramatic when viewed from an elevated point.

In centuries past, Fourni's remoteness and quietude attracted pirates seeking refuge, though today those seeking refuge – and some of the Mediterranean's best seafood – are inevitably travellers seeking a peaceful respite from the outside world. Nevertheless, Fourni's swashbuckling past is still evoked in the very appellation of the archipelago's capital, Fourni Korseon; the Corsairs were French privateers with a reputation for audacity, and their name became applied generically to all pirates and scallywags then roaming the Eastern Aegean.

Nowadays, Fourni Korseon offers most of the accommodation and services, plus several beaches. Other settlements include the much smaller Hrysomilia and Kamari to the north, plus another fishing hamlet opposite, on the island of Thymena. In the main island's very south, the monastery of Agios Ioannis Prodromos stands serene over several enticing beaches.

Orientation & Information

Fourni Korseon's waterfront, where ferries dock, is lined with tavernas and some accommodation options. Perpendicular to the central waterfront, the main street runs inland to the *plateia*; this nameless thoroughfare hosts a National Bank of Greece with ATM, travel agencies, a post office and the village **pharmacy** (☎ 22750 51188). Adjacent to it is an **internet cafe** (per hr €3; ☉ 11am-midnight). There's also a free wi-fi connection at the terrace cafe-restaurant of the Archipelagos Hotel.

Fourni Korseon also has a **doctor** (☎ 22750 51202), **police** (☎ 22750 51222) and **port police** (☎ 22750 51207).

For further information online, see www .fourni.com.

Sights & Activities

Although Fourni is ideal for relaxing, the active-minded can enjoy hiking in the island's rolling hills and swimming at its pristine beaches. The nearest to town, **Psili Ammos Beach**, is a five-minute walk 600m north on the coast road. It has umbrellas and a summer beach bar that also operates at night.

Further from town, a string of popular beaches line the coast road south. **Kampi Beach**, after 3km, is excellent. Further along, **Elidaki Beach** has two sandy stretches and one pebble beach. Beyond is the pebbled **Petrokopeio Beach**.

Near Fourni's southernmost tip, near the **Church of Agios Ioannis Prodromos**, the fine, sandy **Vlyhada Beach** lies before the more secluded **Kasidi Beach**.

Fourni's other main settlements, **Hrysomilia** and **Kamari**, are 17km and 10km from Fourni Korseon respectively (approximately a 30-minute drive on winding but freshly paved uplands roads). Both are placid fishing settlements with limited services, though they offer tranquil settings and beaches. The trip is spectacular, opening onto myriad views of Fourni's sloping hills and hidden coves.

Finally, along with the tiny hamlet of Kampi, Fourni has another inhabited island, **Thymena**, which hosts an eponymous fishing hamlet and enticing **Kermaidou Beach**.

Sleeping

Most Fourni accommodation is in Fourni Korseon, though sleeping in the smaller settlements is possible, as is free beach camping.

Nectaria's Studios (☎ 22750 51365; Fourni Korseon; d/tr €35/45) on the harbour's far side, offers clean, simple rooms.

To Akrogiali (☎ 22750 51168, 6947403019; Kamari village; self-catering apt from €50) In Kamari village, Maria Markaki's two self-catering apartments overlooking the sea are fully-equipped studios with double beds. In high season, book ahead.

our pick **Archipelagos Hotel** (☎ 22750 51250; www.archipelagoshotel.gr; Fourni Korseon; s/d/tr €45/54/72; P ☒ ☞) This elegant new hotel on the harbour's northern edge comprises Fourni's most sophisticated lodgings. From the patio restaurant, set under flowering stone arches, to the well-appointed rooms painted with soft tones complemented by matching marbled baths, the Archipelagos combines traditional yet imaginative Greek architecture with modern luxuries like wireless internet and all-natural Athenian designer soaps. Staff are friendly and helpful.

Eating

Fourni is famous for seafood – and especially, *astakomakaronadha* (lobster with pasta).

Ta Delfinakia (☎ 22750 51064; mains €3-7) When the other waterfront tavernas are taking their afternoon siesta, this is the only place to grab a bite.

Taverna Almyra (☎ 6979141653; Kamari village; fish €5-9) Up in Kamari, this relaxing fish taverna on the waterfront has subtle charm and, locals attest, the island's best fresh fish and *astakomakaronadha*.

Taverna Kali Kardia (☎ 22750 51217; mains €6-9) Hearty Kali Karida on the *plateia* does excellent grilled meats, and is enlivened by animated old locals.

Psarotaverna O Miltos (☎ 22750 51407; Fourni Korseon; mains €7-10) Excellent lobster and fresh fish are expertly prepared at this iconic waterfront taverna.

Archipelagos Hotel Restaurant (☎ 22750 51250; www.archipelagoshotel.gr; Fourni Korseon; mains €7-12) Fourni's foremost hotel offers a refined, romantic dining experience on its patio overlooking the harbour. Come after sunset for an artfully prepared dinner of fresh seafood and a glass of Greek wine.

Getting There & Away

Fourni is connected to Ikaria (Agios Kyrikos) and Samos by ferry and hydrofoil services.

For more information see Island Hopping (p513). **Fourni Island Tours** (☎ 22750 51546; Fourni Korseon; www.fourniisland.ssn.gr) provides information and sells tickets.

Getting Around

Gleaming new asphalt roads connect Fourni Korseon with Hrysomilia and Kamari; however, enjoying these Fourni freeways requires befriending a local, renting a motorbike, hitching or taking the island's lone **taxi** (☎ 22750 51223, 6977370471), commandeered by the ebullient Manolis Papaioannou.

At the time of writing, car hire was being planned; until then, hire a scooter at **Escape Rent a Motorbike** (☎ 22750 51514; gbikes@hotmail.com) on the waterfront.

Alternatively, go by **boat**. Two weekly caïques serve Hrysomilia, while another three go to Thymena year-round, departing at 7.30am.

SAMOS ΣΑΜΟΣ

pop 32,820 / area 477 sq km

Lying seductively just off the Turkish coast, semitropical Samos is one of the northeastern Aegean Islands' best-known destinations. Yet beyond the low-key resorts and the lively capital, Vathy (also called Samos), there are numerous off-the-beaten-track beaches and quiet spots in the cool, forested inland mountains, where traditional life continues more or less unchanged.

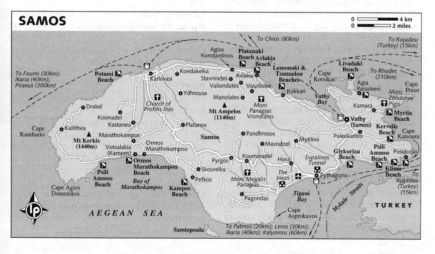

SAMOS

TURKISH CONNECTIONS

Visiting the main resorts and historical sites of Turkey's Aegean coast from Samos, Chios and Lesvos is easy. While boat itineraries, prices and even companies change often, the following explains how things generally work.

From Samos (p357), boats leave twice daily from Vathy (Samos) for **Kuşadası**, a fun resort near **ancient Ephesus**. The *Samos Star* leaves at 8.30am, and a Turkish-flagged vessel departs at 5pm. Additionally, from Pythagorio, a once-weekly boat serves Kuşadası. In low season, two ferries go weekly from Vathy. Tickets cost around €45 open return and €35 one way (plus €10 port taxes). Daily excursions run from May through October; the Sunday trip includes a visit to Ephesus (€25 extra). For tickets and more information, try **ITSA Travel** (☎ 22730 23605; www .itsatravelsamos.gr; Themistokleous Sofouli), opposite Vathy's ferry terminal. The ticket office takes your passport in advance for port formalities, though Turkish visas, where required, are issued in Turkey. Visas aren't necessary for day trips.

From Chios, boats depart year-round from Chios Town (p368) for **Çeşme**, a port near bustling **İzmir**, though they're most frequent in summer. From May to October, daily ferries to Çeşme leave Chios at 8.30am, returning at 6.30pm; on Sunday, however, they return at 5pm. Tickets cost €20 one way and €30 return. Get information and tickets from **Hatzelenis Tours** (☎ 22710 20002; mano2@otenet.gr; Leoforos Aigaiou 2) or **Sunrise Tours** (☎ 22710 41390; Kanari 28), which usually does a combination boat–bus day trip to İzmir via Çeşme (€40 return). Turkish visas, where required, are issued in Çeşme.

From Lesvos, boats leave Mytilini Town (p380) for **Dikeli** port, which serves **Ayvalik**. A Turkish company, Costar, leaves Mytilini Town to Dikeli every Tuesday, Thursday and Saturday at 9am (€20 return), returning at 6pm. The Thursday boat also offers onward buses to Ayvalik (€6), while the Tuesday and Saturday trips include a free bus to **ancient Pergamum**. Another Turkish company, Turyol, serves **Fokias** port near **İzmir** each Wednesday, leaving at 8.30am and returning at 6pm (€35).

Most Mytilini Town travel agencies sell Turkish tours; try **Olive Groove Travel** (☎ 22510 37533; www.olive-groove.gr; 11 P Kountourioti; ⏰ 7.30am-10pm).

Famous for its sweet local wine, Samos is also historically significant. It was the legendary birthplace of Hera, and the sprawling ruins of her ancient sanctuary, the Ireon – where archaeological excavations continue – are impressive. Both the great mathematician Pythagoras and the hedonistic father of atomic theory, the 4th-century BC philosopher Epicurus, were born here. Samos' scientific genius is also attested by the astonishing Evpalinos Tunnel (524 BC), a spectacular feat of ancient engineering that stretches for 1034m deep underground.

Samos is a convenient ferry hub for the Eastern Aegean, with connections extending to the northern isles, the Dodecanese in the south and the Cyclades to the west; it's also the jumping-off point for Turkey's coastal resort of Kuşadası, and the nearby ruins of ancient Ephesus.

Samos' proximity to Turkey and slightly larger size make it somewhat lively in winter, though even then only a few hotels remain open, in Vathy.

Getting There & Away

For air and boat services from Samos, see Island Hopping (p521).

AIR

Samos' airport is 4km west of Pythagorio. **Olympic Air** (www.olympicairlines.com) Vathy (☎ 22730 27237; cnr Kanari & Smyrnis); Pythagorio (☎ 22730 61213; Lykourgou Logotheti) sells tickets in both major towns, as do travel agencies.

BOAT

For information on trips to Turkey, see the boxed text, above.

The exceptionally helpful **ITSA Travel** (☎ 22730 23605; www.itsatravelsamos.gr; Themistokleous Sofouli), directly opposite the ferry terminal in Vathy (Samos), provides detailed information, offers free luggage storage (without a catch) and sells tickets, including to Turkey. Considering that the boss, Dimitris Sarlas, owns four ferries operating from Samos, it's no surprise that ITSA has the most up-to-date information on schedule changes.

In Pythagorio, double-check ferry and hydrofoil schedules with the **tourist office** (☎ 22730 61389) or the **port police** (☎ 22730 61225).

Getting Around
TO/FROM THE AIRPORT
There's no airport shuttle bus; taxis from the airport cost €12 to Vathy (Samos) or €5 to Pythagorio, from where there are local buses to other parts of the island.

BOAT
Summer excursion boats travel four times weekly from Pythagorio to Patmos (return €45), leaving at 8am. Daily excursion boats go from Pythagorio to Samiopoula islet (including lunch, €30), while a round-island boat tour begins from Pythagorio's harbour twice weekly (€50).

BUS
From Vathy (Samos) **bus station** (☎ 22730 27262; Ioannou Lekati) seven daily buses serve Kokkari (€1.40, 20 minutes). Twelve serve Pythagorio (€1.50, 25 minutes) while six go to Agios Konstantinos (€2, 40 minutes) and Karlovasi (€3.50, one hour). Five serve the Ireon (€2.10, 25 minutes) and Mytilini (€1.40, 20 minutes).

Additionally, from Pythagorio itself, five daily buses reach the Ireon (€1.40, 15 minutes) while four serve Mytilini (€1.70, 20 minutes). Buy tickets inside. Services are reduced on weekends.

CAR & MOTORCYCLE
Pegasus Rent a Car (☎ 22730 24470, 6972017092; pegasus samos@hotmail.com; Themistoklis Sofouli 5), opposite the port entrance and next to ITSA Travel in Vathy (Samos), offers the best rates on car, jeep and motorcycle hire. International car-hire outlets include **Hertz** (☎ 22730 61730; Lykourgou Logotheti 77) and **Europcar** (☎ 22730 61522; Lykourgou Logotheti 65).

If in Pythagorio, try **John's Rentals** (☎ 22730 61405; www.johns-rent-a-car.gr; Lykourgou Logotheti).

TAXI
The **taxi rank** (☎ 22730 28404) in Vathy (Samos) is by the National Bank of Greece. In Pythagorio the **taxi rank** (☎ 22730 61450) is on the waterfront at Lykourgou Logotheti.

VATHY (SAMOS) ΒΑΘΥ (ΣΑΜΟΣ)
pop 2025
Vathy (also called Samos) is the island's capital, and enjoys a striking setting within the fold of a deep bay. As in most Greek port towns, the curving waterfront is lined with bars, cafes and restaurants. However, the historic quarter of Ano Vathy, filled with steep, narrow streets and curious old folk features red-tiled 19th-century hillside houses and some atmospheric tavernas. The town centre boasts two engaging museums and a striking century-old church.

Vathy (Samos) also has two pebble beaches, the best being Gagou Beach (about 1km north of the centre); along the way there, you'll pass a string of cool night bars clinging to the town's northeastern cliff side, just before the Pythagoras Hotel, more refined and aesthetically pleasing than the cacophonous waterfront cafes.

Orientation
Facing inland from the ferry terminal, turn right for Plateia Pythagorou on the waterfront, recognisable by its four palm trees and lion statue; this square is partly a wi-fi zone. A little further along, and a block inland, are the leafy municipal gardens. The waterfront road is named after the most illustrious modern Samian, Themistoklis Sofoulis, a pioneering archaeologist and Greek prime minister during the 1946–49 civil war. The bus station is on Ioannou Lekati.

Information
ATM-equipped banks line Plateia Pythagorou and the waterfront. Pythagoras Hotel (p361) has computers and wi-fi internet access (€3 per hour).
Diavlos NetCafe (☎ 22730 22469; Themistokeous Sofouli 160; per hr €4; ☻ 8.30am-11.30pm) Internet access.
Municipal tourist office (☎ 22730 28582) Summer-only office north of Plateia Pythagorou; can find accommodation.
Port police (☎ 22730 27890)
Post office (Smyrnis)
Samos General Hospital (☎ 22730 27407) Well-supplied, efficient hospital, opposite Pythagoras Hotel.
Tourist police (☎ 22730 27980; Themistokleous Sofouli 129)

Sights
Along with the **Ano Vathy** old quarter, the relaxing **municipal gardens** and **Roditzes and Gagou Beaches**, the town's main attraction is its **archaeological museum** (☎ 22730 27469; adult/ student €3/2, Sun free; ☻ 8.30am-3pm Tue-Sun, last entry

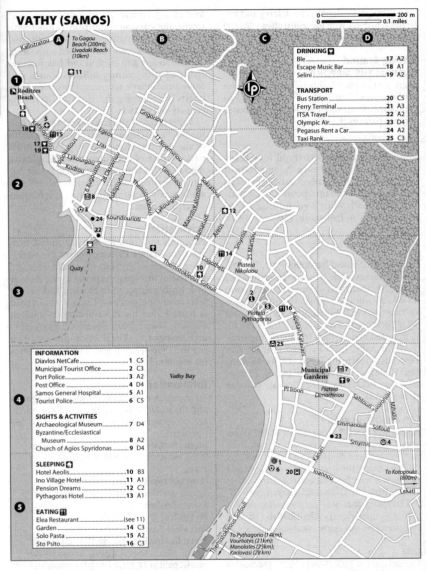

VATHY (SAMOS)

2.45pm). One of the best in the islands, it contains finds starting from the rule of Polycrates (6th century BC), the most famous being the gargantuan (5.5m) *kouros* (male statue of the Archaic period), plucked from the Ireon (Sanctuary of Hera; p364) near Pythagorio – the largest standing *kouros* known. Many other statues, most also from the Ireon, as well as bronze sculptures, *stelae* and pottery, are also exhibited.

Vathy's **Ecclesiastical Museum** (Byzantine Museum; 28 Oktovriou; adult/student €3/2, Sun free; ☺ 8.30am-3pm Tue-Sun, last entry 2.45pm) houses rare manuscripts, liturgical objects of silver and gold, as well as exceptional painted icons dating from the 13th to 19th centuries.

Samos owes some of this holy loot to its status as a bishopric (administering also Ikaria and Fourni) and thus also has some splendid churches, like the **Church of Agios Spyridonas** (Plateia Dimarheiou; ☾ 7.30-11am & 6.30-7.30pm), near Plateia Dimarheiou. Built in 1909, the ornate church has icons, impressive pillars hewn of marble from Izmir and, unusually, a silver candelabra from India and decorative columns on the iconostasis, inspired by ancient Greek and Byzantine motifs.

Sleeping

Pension Dreams (☎ 22730 24350; Areos 9; d with/ without balcony €35/30; 🕸) This small but central pension overlooks the harbour from a hill-top, and boasts an expansive rooftop studio; if that's taken, grab a balcony room with garden views. The friendly owner speaks several languages.

our pick **Pythagoras Hotel** (☎ 22730 28422, 69445 18690; www.pythagorashotel.com; Kallistratou 12; s/d/tr incl breakfast €20/35/45; ☾ Feb-Nov; 🖥 🛜) The Pythagoras, just up from the port, is perfect for independent travellers and attracts a younger crowd than most Vathy hotels. The great kindness and hospitality of Stelios Mihalakis and family is only part of what makes this budget hotel special. Many rooms have breezy, sea-facing balconies (at the time of writing, air conditioning was being planned). There's also a well-stocked shop, wi-fi connection plus computers, and a pebble beach below the shaded breakfast patio. For free pick-up from the ferry or bus station, ring Stelios, or enquire at ITSA Travel.

Hotel Aeolis (☎ 22730 28377; www.aeolis.gr; Themistokleous Sofouli 33; s/d incl breakfast €50/70; 🕸 🛜) This grandiose and very central waterfront hotel attracts a slick Greek crowd and some foreigners, drawn by its two pools, Jacuzzi, taverna and bar. Rooms are ample and modern, though with less of a personal touch than at the smaller places in town. Light sleepers should factor in the nocturnal street noise from the cafe strip below.

Ino Village Hotel (☎ 22730 23241; www.inovillage.gr; Kalami; s/d/tr incl breakfast from €65/80/100; 🅿 🕸 🖥 🛜) With its courtyard pool flanked by ivy-clad, balconied white buildings, Ino Village is a citadel of subdued elegance high above Vathy. While this miniresort is sometimes booked by tour groups, it never endangers the stylish quietude of the hotel, which also boasts a fine restaurant.

Eating

Sto Psito (☎ 22730 80800; Plateia Pythagorou; souvlaki €3) Hearty portions of souvlaki and other light grills are served at this very popular place sprawling across the square.

Kotopoula (☎ 22730 28415; Vlamaris; mains €6-8) This local favourite known for its spit-roasted chicken is 800m inland along Ioannou Lekati, in the shade of a plane tree.

Garden (☎ 22730 24033; Manolis Kalomiris; mains €6-9) Greek specialities stand out at this soothing spot off Lykourgou Logotheti, on a tree-filled outdoor terrace within a garden.

Solo Pasta (☎ 22730 23699; Kefalopoulou 13; mains €7-12) With a spic-and-span interior and brisk service, this Italian joint opposite the hillside bars does inventive salads, good bruschettas and various fancy pasta dishes.

our pick **Elea Restaurant** (☎ 22730 23241; Kalami; mains €8-12) Ino Village Hotel's patio restaurant has contemplative views over Vathy and its harbour below, and serves invigorated Greek cuisine and international dishes, while doing fine renditions of classics like swordfish souvlaki (cubes of meat on skewers). Samian wines are well represented. Beware charismatic barman Dimitrios when he tries to whip you up one of his patented shots of tequila with lemon and ground coffee.

Drinking

Vathy's nightlife is more Hellenic than in Pythagorio's blonder, Northern European–frequented bars. While most cafes and bars cling to the waterfront, the coolest ones overlook the water along Kefalopoulou. They include **Escape Music Bar**, **Ble**, and **Selini**. All play modern Greek and Western pop, plus more ambient music matching their outside lighting, which shines on the gently rippling water below to dazzling, hypnotic effect.

AROUND VATHY (SAMOS)

For something different, head 4km northeast to Arkoudolakas and the **Panouris Ranch** (☎ 6942704955; www.samostour.dk; Arkoudolakas village; ☾ 9am-noon & 6-9pm) for horse-riding expeditions in nearby forests (€10 per hour). Since the horses are well trained and docile, it's suitable for beginners. The ranch offers free pony rides for kids, and free drinks.

Beaches

The beaches east of Vathy are some of Samos' best and least crowded. Follow the north-coast road out of town for 10km and look for a signposted dirt road left leading to **Livadaki Beach**. Here, tropical azure waters lap against soft sand in a long sheltered cove with facing islets. Only Greeks in the know come to Livadaki, which has a beach bar with colourful and comfy soft chairs, and music day and night. The water is warm and very shallow for a long way out, and Livadaki's hedonistic yet mellow summer beach parties easily spill into it. Free kayaking and palm-frond umbrellas are available.

Back at the turn-off for Livadaki Beach, continue east 5km to the fishing hamlet of **Agia Paraskevi**, which has a shady pebble beach and multicoloured boats moored offshore. This beach, popular with Greek families, has a meat-and-seafood taverna, **Restaurant Aquarius** (☎ 22730 28282; Agia Paraskevi; mains €5-8).

Several other small beaches line the coast road south; for these a 4WD is advisable.

PYTHAGORIO ΠΥΘΑΓΟΡΕΙΟ
pop 1330

Down on the southeastern coast opposite Turkey, pretty Pythagorio has a yacht-lined harbour, and Samos' main archaeological sites. The waterfront is lined with touristy restaurants and, when crowded with Scandinavian package tourists, does give one the feeling of a Viking invasion. Since it's not far from Vathy (Samos), you can day-trip it from there for the fine nearby beaches and archaeological sites, though there's accommodation should you prefer to stay.

All boats travelling south of Samos dock at Pythagorio, from where day trips also depart to Samiopoula islet.

Orientation
From the ferry quay, turn right and follow the waterfront to the main street, Lykourgou Logotheti, a turn-off to the left. Most services are here. The central square (Plateia Irinis) is further along the waterfront. The bus stop is on Lykourgou Logotheti's south side.

Information
Commercial Bank (Lykourgou Logotheti) Has ATM.
Digital World (☎ 22730 62722; Pythagora; internet per hr €4; ⏱ 11am-10.30pm) Has internet access.

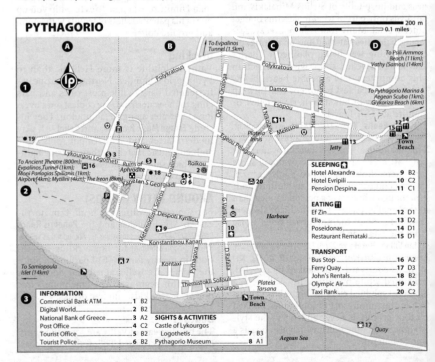

PYTHAGORIO

To Evpalinos Tunnel (1.5km)
To Psili Armmos Beach (11km); Vathy (Samos) (14km)
To Pythagorio Marina (1km); Aegean Scuba (2km); Glykoriza Beach (6km)
To Ancient Theatre (800m); Evpalinos Tunnel (1km); Moni Panagias Spilianis (1km); Airport (4km); Mytilini (4km); The Ireon (8km)
To Samiopoula Islet (14km)
Harbour
Aegean Sea

SLEEPING
Hotel Alexandra 9 B2
Hotel Evripili 10 C2
Pension Despina 11 C1

EATING
Ef Zin 12 D1
Elia 13 D2
Poseidonas 14 D1
Restaurant Remataki 15 D1

TRANSPORT
Bus Stop 16 A2
Ferry Quay 17 D3
John's Rentals 18 B2
Olympic Air 19 A2
Taxi Rank 20 C2

INFORMATION
Commercial Bank ATM 1 B2
Digital World 2 B2
National Bank of Greece ... 3 A2
Post Office 4 C2
Tourist Office 5 B2
Tourist Police 6 B2

SIGHTS & ACTIVITIES
Castle of Lykourgos
Logothetis 7 B3
Pythagorio Museum 8 A1

National Bank of Greece (Lykourgou Logotheti)
Port police (☎ 22730 61225)
Post office (Lykourgou Logotheti)
Tourist office (☎ 22730 61389; deap5@otenet.gr;
Lykourgou Logotheti; ☒ 8am-9.30pm) The friendly and
informative staff advise about historical sites and sleeping
options, provide maps, bus timetables and ferry info, and
also exchange currency.
Tourist police (☎ 22730 61100; Lykourgou Logotheti)
Left of the tourist office.

Sights & Activities

Samians took the lead locally in the 1821
War of Independence; the major relic of
that turbulent time is the **Castle of Lykourgos
Logothetis** (☒ 9am-7pm Tue-Sun), built in 1824 by
resistance leader Logothetis on a hill at the
southern end of Metamorfosis Sotiros, near
the car park. The **city walls** extend from here
to the Evpalinos Tunnel, a 25-minute walk
along this path.

The **Pythagorio Museum** (☎ 22730 61400; Town
Hall, Plateia Irinis; admission free; ☒ 8.45am-2.30pm Tue-
Sun) contains finds from the Ireon, though
the best are in the Vathy (Samos) museum.

Exiting Pythagorio northeast, traces of an
ancient theatre appear on a path to the left.
The right fork past the theatre reaches a cave
monastery, **Moni Panagias Spilianis** (Monastery of
the Virgin of the Grotto; ☎ 22730 61361; ☒ 9am-8pm) –
a welcome respite from summer heat.

EVPALINOS TUNNEL ΕΥΠΑΛΙΝΕΟ ΟΡΥΓΜΑ
Back in 524 BC, when Pythagorio (then
called Samos) was the island's capital and
a bustling metropolis of 80,000, securing
sources of drinking water became crucial.
To solve the problem, ruler Polycrates put
his dictatorial whims to good use, ordering labourers to dig into a mountainside
according to the exacting plan of his ingenious engineer, Evpalinos; many workers
died during this dangerous dig. The result
was the 1034m-long **Evpalinos Tunnel** (☎ 22730
61400; adult/student €4/2; ☒ 8.45am-2.45pm Tue-Sun),
which can be partially explored today.
In mediaeval times locals used it to hide
from pirates.

The Evpalinos Tunnel is actually two
tunnels: a service tunnel and a lower water
conduit visible from the walkway. While the
tunnel itself is wide enough, not everyone
can enter, as the entrance stairway is both
low and has very narrow walls, with no
grease provided.

The tunnel is quite cold: as sudden exposure to low temperatures on a hot day is not
healthy, wait until the sweat subsides before
entering, and perhaps pack an extra shirt to
wear while inside.

If walking, reach the tunnel from
Lykourgou Logotheti. If driving, a sign points
to the tunnel's southern mouth after entering
Pythagorio from Vathy (Samos).

DIVING

Along with swimming and sunbathing, try
scuba diving with **Aegean Scuba** (☎ /fax 22730
61194; www.aegeanscuba.gr; Pythagorio marina; ☒ year-
round). Professional instructors lead dives in
search of moray eels, sea stars, octopuses,
lobsters and other critters lurking in the
sponge-covered crevices around Pythagorio.
Snorkelling (€25) is also offered.

A dive with full equipment costs €60,
while two dives in one day costs €85.
Multiday, pay-in-advance diving gets you
discounts. Aegean Scuba also offers several
levels of beginner's courses, a scuba review
course for lapsed divers, emergency response
and rescue dive courses. For those seeking
professional PADI certification, there's a
special dive-master course.

Sleeping

Hotel Alexandra (☎ 22730 61429; Metamorfosis Sotiros
22; d €35) It has only eight rooms, but they are
lovely and some have sea views. There's also
an attractive garden.

Pension Despina (☎ 22730 61677; pansiondespina@
yahoo.gr; A Nikolaou; s/d €35/50) A clean, quiet pension on Plateia Irinis, the Despina offers
simple studios and rooms with balconies
(some have kitchenettes), plus a relaxing
back garden.

Hotel Evripili (☎ 22730 61096; Konstantinou Kanari;
s/d €50/70) This friendly and modern hotel has
well-appointed, cosy rooms off the waterfront; some have balconies.

Eating & Drinking

Poseidonas (☎ 22730 62530; mains €6-12) Next to
Restaurant Remataki, the Poseidonas specialises in seafood with an international flair.

Restaurant Remataki (☎ 22730 61104; mezedhes
€4-6, mains €7-10) Near Elia, this place has a nice
waterfront balcony and some splashy light
meals; salad with rocket leaves, Cretan *dakos*
(tomato and cheese on oil-softened rusks) and

dolmadhes (rice wrapped in vine leaves) are all recommended.

Elia (☎ 22730 61436; mains €7-12) Elia gets high marks from locals for sophisticated Greek and international fare, though it's pricey. It's located at the waterfront's far end.

Ef Zin (☎ 22730 62528; ◷ 10am-late) Also beside Remataki, this cafe-bar on a terrace has nice harbour views and an impressive wine list.

AROUND PYTHAGORIO
The Ireon Το Ηραίον
To judge merely from the scattered ruins of the **Ireon** (☎ 22730 95277; adult/student €4/3; ◷ 8.30am-3pm Tue-Sun), one couldn't imagine the former magnificence of this ancient sanctuary of Hera, located 8km west of Pythagorio. The 'Sacred Way', once flanked by thousands of marble statues, led from the city to this World Heritage–listed site, built at this goddess' legendary birthplace. However, enough survives to provide some insight into the workings of a divine sanctuary that was four times larger than the Parthenon.

Built in the 6th century BC on marshy ground, where the River Imbrasos enters the sea, the Ireon was constructed over an earlier Mycenaean temple. Plundering and earthquakes since antiquity have left only one column standing, though extensive foundations remain. There is something deeply disconcerting about the headless statues of a family, the Geneleos Group, from whose number the giant *kouros* statue in the museum at Vathy (Samos) was taken (see p359). Other remains include a stoa, more temples and a 5th-century Christian basilica. The deep trenches within the site indicate where archaeologists continue to unearth still more buried treasures.

Mytilinii Μυτιληνιοί
Skeletons of prehistoric animals, including forerunners of the giraffe and elephant, are displayed at the **palaeontology museum** (☎ 22730 52055; admission €3; ◷ 10am-2pm), in Mytilini village, northwest of Pythagorio. For more (human) skeletal relics, **Agia Triada Monastery** (☎ 22730 51339; ◷ 8am-1pm Mon-Sun) features an ossuary and a lovely rural setting. Hardy walkers can reach it from the museum.

Beaches
Glykoriza Beach, near Pythagorio, is a clean, pebble-and-sand beach with some hotels. However, sandy **Psili Ammos Beach**, 11km east, is much better. This lovely cove facing Turkey is bordered by shady trees and has shallow waters good for kids. There are tavernas and rooms, the best being **Psili Ammos Apartments** (☎ 22730 80481; s/d €38/65), above the beach's western edge. These family-friendly self-catering apartments with balconies overlooking the sea come with baby cribs and separate kids' rooms.

Buses go from Vathy (Samos) to Psili Ammos, as do excursion boats (€15) from Pythagorio. If driving, take the Pythagorio–Vathy road north and turn east where Psili Ammos is signposted. A unique pond on the left, 1km before it, is animated in spring by cheery pink flamingos.

SOUTHWESTERN SAMOS
Pythagorio to Drakei
Πυθαγόριο προς Δρακαίους
The drive west from Pythagorio traverses spectacular mountain scenery with stunning views of the south coast. This route also features many little signposted huts, where beekeepers sell the superlative but inexpensive Samian honey – stop in for a free sample and you'll walk away with a jar.

Samos' southwest coast is less touristed than the north, though the best beaches are starting to attract the inevitable resorts; however, tourism is still low-key, and secluded wild spots remain.

The drive from Pythagorio to the pebble beach at **Ormos Marathokampou** crosses mountains and the unvisited villages of **Koumaradei** and **Pyrgos**. From the beach, it's a 6km drive inland to **Marathokampos**, which has panoramic views of the immense **Ormos Marathokampou** (Bay of Marathokampos). Some 4km west of Ormos Marathokampou is **Votsalakia** (often called Kambos), with its long, sandy beach. There's an even nicer one 2km further at (the other) **Psili Ammos Beach**. Domatia are available, while beach tavernas prepare fresh fish.

Past Psili Ammos, the rugged western route skirts **Mt Kerkis**. From here until the villages of **Kallithea** and **Drakei,** where the road abruptly terminates, the coast is undeveloped and tranquil.

NORTHERN SAMOS
Vathy to Karlovasi Βαθύ προς Καρλόβασι
From Vathy (Samos), the coast road west passes many beaches and resorts. The first, **Kokkari** (10km), was once a fishing village,

---

A MATTER OF MEASUREMENTS

While the obsession with getting the 'proper pint' may seem modern, the ancient Greeks too were fixated on measuring their alcohol. Pythagoras, that great Samian mathematician (and, presumably, drinker) created an ingenious invention that ensured party hosts and publicans could not be deceived by guests aspiring to inebriation. His creation was dubbed the *dikiakoupa tou Pythagora* (Just Cup of Pythagoras). This mysterious, multiholed drinking vessel holds its contents perfectly well, unless one fills it past the engraved line – at which point the glass drains completely from the bottom, punishing the naughty drinker for gluttony.

Today faithful reproductions of the *dikiakoupa tou Pythagora*, made of colourful, glazed ceramic, are sold in Samos gift shops, tangible reminders of the Apollan Mean (the ancient Greek maxim of Apollo): 'Everything in moderation.'

---

but has become a resort. Windsurfing from its long pebble beach is good when the wind's up in summer. Rooms and tavernas are available. The popular nearby beaches of **Avlakia**, **Lemonaki** and **Tsamadou** are the most accessible for Kokkari-based walkers. The latter two are clothing-optional.

Continuing west, the landscape becomes more forested and mountainous. Take the left-hand turn-off after 5km to reach the lovely mountain village of **Vourliotes**. From here it's a 3km hike to **Moni Panagias Vrondianis**, Samos' oldest surviving monastery, built in the 1550s. Vourliotes' multicoloured, shuttered houses cluster on and above a *plateia*. Walkers can alternatively take a footpath from Kokkari.

Back on the coast road, continue west until the signposted left-hand turn-off for another enchanting village, fragrant **Manolates**, located 5km further up the lower slopes of Mt Ampelos (1140m; known as the 'Balcony of Samos'). Set amidst thick pine and deciduous forests, and boasting truly gorgeous traditional houses, Manolates is nearly encircled by mountains and offers a cool alternative to the sweltering coast. The village's upper part offers impressive views.

The mostly elderly residents of Vourliotes and Manolates are keenly aware of the tourist euro, and shops selling handmade ceramic art, icons and natural products are many. In fairness, you can find good stuff, including the Just Cup of Pythagoras (see the boxed text, above), and the taverna fare is fresh and well prepared. Despite these villages' visible popularity with tourists, they're still worth visiting for a taste of old Samos.

Back on the coast heading west, the road continues through **Agios Konstantinos**, a pretty, flower-filled village before **Karlovasi**, Samos' third port. This workaday place is useful only for

ferry connections. However, just 2km beyond it lies the sand-and-pebble **Potami Beach**, blessed with good swimming and a vaguely Rastafarian beach bar. It's complemented by nearby **forest waterfalls**; head west 50m from the beach and they're signposted on the left. Entering, you'll first encounter a small, centuries-old **chapel**, where pious Greeks light candles. Continuing through the wooded trail along the river brings you, after 10 or 15 minutes, to a deep river channel where you must wade or swim, height depending, through a forested canyon – along with the local eels – before enjoying a splash under the 2m-high waterfalls.

Sleeping

In Kokkari, **EOT** (Greek National Tourist Organisation; ☎ 22730 92217) finds accommodation. It's about 100m after the large church by the bus stop, beside the OTE (national telecom company) building.

Studio Angela (☎ 22730 94478, 21050 59708; Manolates; d €25; ✿) These five studios in Manolates, built into a hillside overlooking the sea, have modern rooms and kitchenettes.

Traditional Greek House (☎ 22730 94331; Manolates; studio €35; ✿) Phone ahead as there's only one studio available in this large old Manolates house behind the Despina Taverna. The room is quiet, romantic and tastefully furnished.

Kokkari Beach Hotel (☎ 22730 92238; Kokkari; d incl breakfast €75; ✿ ✿) This classy establishment 1km west of the bus stop, set back from the road in a pretty yellow building, has modern and comfortably furnished rooms. There's a cafe opposite.

Eating & Drinking
VOURLIOTES

Galazio Pigadi (☎ 22730 93480; Vourliotes; mains €5-7; ☉ 9am-11pm) Right after Vourliotes' *plateia*, this atmospheric place has a variety of traditional Greek mezedhes including *revythokeftedhes* (chickpea rissoles) and *bourekakia* (crunchy filo pastries filled with cheese). Try the house speciality, *kokkoras krasatos* (rooster in wine).

Pera Vrisi (☎ 22730 24181; Vourliotes; mains €5-8; ☼ 10am-12am) This old-style Samian taverna by the spring at Vourliotes' entrance offers exceptional village cuisine and homemade barrel wine.

MANOLATES

Pigi (☎ 6974984364; Manolates; mains €4-7) Opposite the parking, this outdoor place has great sea views and authentic decor; try the *pitakia* (crunchy pies with cheese and pumpkin). All the food is homemade, with ingredients from the owner's own vegetable patch.

Loukas Taverna (☎ 22730 94541; Manolates; mains €4-8) This well-signposted taverna atop Manolates offers magnificent views of mountains and sea from the outdoor balcony; the offerings, ranging from fried zucchini flowers and hearty meat portions to local muscat wine and homemade cakes, make the walk worthwhile.

Kallisti Taverna (☎ 22730 94661; Manolates; mains €5-7) This intriguing taverna on the square has numerous excellent dishes including *kleftiko* (lamb with vegetables), and desserts, like the tasty orange pie.

Despina Taverna (☎ 22730 94043; Manolates; mains €5-9) This little taverna, halfway up the village in Manolates, serves *mayirefta* and grills.

POTAMI BEACH

Hippies Beach Bar (☎ 22730 33796; Potami Beach; ☼ 9am-9pm) This appropriately exotic open cafe-bar on Potami Beach combines Greek and South Seas decor with subdued style.

CHIOS ΧΙΟΣ

---

pop 53,820 / area 859 sq km

Likeable Chios (*hee*-os) is one of Greece's bigger islands, and is significant in national history as the ancestral home of shipping barons. Since many seafaring Chians went abroad to seek their fortunes, the diaspora presence is more conspicuous here than on most Greek islands during summer. Yet Chios is a truly fascinating place even for 'unaffiliated' travellers. Its varied terrain ranges from lonesome mountain crags in the north

to the citrus-grove estates of Kampos, near the island's port capital in the centre, to the fertile Mastihohoria in the south – the only place in the world where mastic (a kind of gum) trees are productive. And the island's coasts are ringed by pristine beaches.

Chians tend to be very kind, and you'll find great hospitality here. Since Chios sees fewer visitors than better-known Greek island getaways, there's more genuine friendliness from the locals, who take great pride in their history, traditions and livelihood. For the visitor, all this translates into excellent opportunities for hands-on interaction with Chian culture, ranging from art and history to hiking and eco activities.

Chios enjoys good regular boat connections throughout the northeastern Aegean Islands, plus an airport. Between them, the ports of Chios Town in the east and Mesta in the southwest offer regular ferries to the intriguing, little-visited satellite islands of Psara and Inousses, which share Chios' legacy of maritime greatness, and to the lively Turkish coastal resorts just across the water.

Chios' large size, proximity to Turkey and shipping interests mean that a modicum of life remains in the capital, Chios Town, in winter. However, outside of high season, its dependencies of Psara and Inousses are almost completely empty.

History

As with Samos and Lesvos, geographic closeness to Turkey (the Karaburun peninsula lies just 8km away, across the Chios Strait) brought Chios both great commercial success before the 1821 revolution and great tragedy during it. Many of Greece's grand old shipping dynasties hail from Chios and its dependencies, Inousses and Psara. Under the Ottomans, Chios' monopolistic production of mastic – the sultan's favourite gum – brought Chians wealth and special privileges.

However, during the 1821–29 War of Independence, thousands of Chians were slaughtered by Ottoman troops. A century later, the Megali Idea ('Great Idea') for the liberation of Greek-majority cities in Anatolia unfolded with a naval assault from Chios – and ended, disastrously, with the Greek armies being driven back into the sea, as waves of refugees from Asia Minor flooded Chios and neighbouring islands.

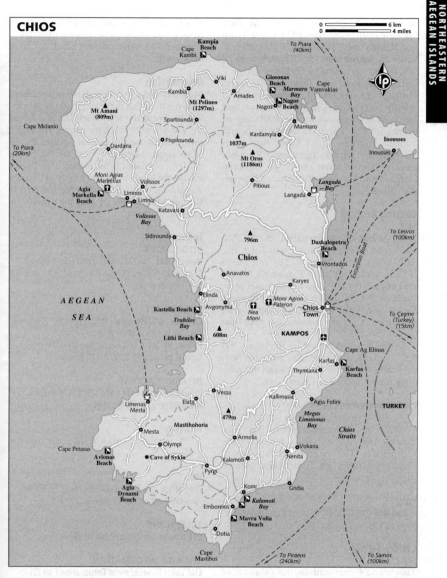

CHIOS

Getting There & Away

For information on flight and ferry access from Chios, see Island Hopping (p511).

AIR

The airport is 4km from Chios Town. There's no shuttle bus; an airport taxi to/from the town costs €6. Travel agen-

cies, like Hatzelenis Tours (p369), are in Chios Town.

BOAT

For information on trips to Turkey, see the boxed text, Turkish Connections (p358).

Buy tickets from travel agencies like Hatzelenis Tours (p369), opposite the port, or from the ferry companies, like **NEL Lines** (☎ 22710 23971; Leoforos Egeou 16) in Chios Town and **Miniotis Lines** (☎ 22710 24670; www.miniotis.gr; Neorion 23). **Sunrise Tours** (☎ 22710 41390; Kanari 28) sells tickets, including to Turkey.

The little local boat *Oinoussai III* serves Inousses (€4 one way, 1¼ hours, daily). It mainly leaves Chios in the afternoon and Inousses in the morning, necessitating an overnight stay. Purchase tickets on board. Sunrise Tours in Chios Town runs summertime day trips to Inousses (€20) twice weekly. Daily water taxis go between Langada and Inousses (€40, shared between the passengers).

Getting Around
BUS
From the **long-distance bus station** (☎ 22710 27507; www.ktelchios.gr; Leoforos Egeou) in Chios Town, five daily buses serve Pyrgi (€2.50) and Mesta (€3.50), while four serve Kardamyla (€3.00) via Langada (€1.60). Two weekly buses serve Volissos (€4.10). Buses also go to Kampia, Nagos and Lithi beaches. For up-to-date schedules, visit the website of **KTEL-Chios** (www.ktelchios.gr).

Karfas Beach is served by the blue (city) bus company, with schedules posted at both the **local bus station** (☎ 22710 22079) and the long-distance bus station in Chios Town.

CAR & MOTORCYCLE
The reliable **Chandris Rent a Car** (☎ 22710 27194, 6944972051; info@chandrisrentacar.gr; Porfyra 5) is Chios Town's best agency, with vehicles from €30 per day. The friendly and experienced Kostas Chandris gladly provides general island information.

TAXI
A **taxi rank** (☎ 22710 41111) is on Plateia Vounakiou in Chios Town.

CHIOS TOWN
pop 23,780
The island's port and capital (also called Chios) is on the central east coast, and home to almost half of the inhabitants. Like many island capitals, it features a long waterfront lined with cafes and a noisy boulevard hugging the water. Behind it, however, is a quieter, intriguing old quarter, where some lingering traditional Turkish houses stand around a Genoese castle and city walls. There's also

a fun market area, and spacious public gardens where an open-air cinema operates in summer. The nearest decent beach is Karfas, 6km south.

Orientation
Most ferries dock at the waterfront's northern end; north of this is the old Turkish quarter, Kastro. From the ferry, turn left and follow the waterfront to reach the centre. Turn right onto Kanari for the central square, Plateia Vounakiou. Northwest of it are the public gardens; southeast is the market area. Facing inland, the local bus station is right of the public gardens; the long-distance bus station is to the left. Most hotels are near the waterfront, opposite the port.

Information
BOOKSHOPS
News Stand (☎ 22710 43464; cnr Leoforos Egeou & Rodokanaki) Sells multilingual papers and books, including Lonely Planet guides.

EMERGENCY
Chios General Hospital (☎ 22710 44302; El Venizelou 7) About 2km north of the centre.
Police (☎ 22710 44427; cnr Polemidi 1 & Koundouriotou)
Tourist police (☎ 22710 44427; Neorion)

INTERNET ACCESS
InSpot Internet Café (☎ 22710 83438; Leoforos Egeou 86; per hr €2.50; ⊙ 24hr)

MONEY
ATM-equipped banks line the waterfront and *plateia*.

POST
Post office (☎ 22710 44350; Omirou 2; ⊙ 7.30am-7pm) One block behind the waterfront.

TELEPHONE
OTE (Dimokratias Roidou) Public telephone.

TOURIST INFORMATION
ENA Chios Development Corporation (☎ 22710 44830; www.chios.gr, www.enachios.gr; Agios Isodoros, Petrokokklinou, Kampos) This official tourism information unit in Kampos, financed by the prefecture of Chios, offers free tours with professional guides to Kampos, Anavatos, Olympi, Nea Moni and Chios Castle.
Municipal Tourist Office (☎ 22710 44389; infochio@ otenet.gr; Kanari 18; ⊙ 7am-10pm Apr-Oct, until 4pm Nov-Mar) Information on accommodation, car hire, bus

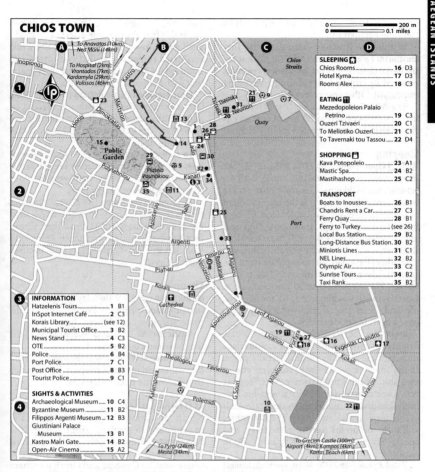

CHIOS TOWN

SLEEPING 🏠		
Chios Rooms	16	D3
Hotel Kyma	17	D3
Rooms Alex	18	C3

EATING 🍴		
Mezedopoleion Palaio Petrino	19	C3
Ouzeri Tzivaeri	20	C1
To Meliotiko Ouzeri	21	C1
To Tavernaki tou Tassou	22	D4

SHOPPING 🛍		
Kava Potopoleio	23	A1
Mastic Spa	24	B2
Mastihashop	25	C2

TRANSPORT		
Boats to Inousses	26	B1
Chandris Rent a Car	27	C3
Ferry Quay	28	B1
Ferry to Turkey	(see 26)	
Local Bus Station	29	B2
Long-Distance Bus Station	30	B2
Miniotis Lines	31	C1
NEL Lines	32	B2
Olympic Air	33	C2
Sunrise Tours	34	B2
Taxi Rank	35	B2

INFORMATION		
Hatzelenis Tours	1	B1
InSpot Internet Café	2	C3
Korais Library	(see 12)	
Municipal Tourist Office	3	B2
News Stand	4	C3
OTE	5	B2
Police	6	B4
Port Police	7	C1
Post Office	8	B3
Tourist Police	9	C1

SIGHTS & ACTIVITIES		
Archaeological Museum	10	C4
Byzantine Museum	11	B2
Filippos Argenti Museum	12	B3
Giustiniani Palace Museum	13	B1
Kastro Main Gate	14	B2
Open-Air Cinema	15	A2

and boat schedules, plus a useful free book, *Hiking Routes of Chios*.

Port Authority (☎ 22710 44432; Neorion)

Thomas Karamouslis (☎ 22710 22338, 6937786213) Affable Thomas has a vast knowledge of the history of Chios, Greece and more, and leads guided tours of important cultural monuments for the ENA Chios Development Corporation (see opposite). A man of impeccable manner and wide learning, he recounts the island's history from a refreshingly objective (and often humorous) perspective.

TRAVEL AGENCIES

Hatzelenis Tours (☎ 22710 20002; mano2@otenet .gr; Leoforos Aigaiou 2) Opposite the port, this dependable full-service travel agency sells ferry and air tickets, plans excursions, finds accommodation and offers car hire.

Sights

The **Filippos Argentis Museum** (☎ 22710 23463; Korais; admission €1.50; ⏰ 8am-2pm Mon-Fri, 5-7.30pm Fri, 8am-12.30pm Sat), located beside the impressive **Korais Library**, contains displays of embroideries, traditional costumes and portraits of the wealthy Argentis family. Born in Marseilles in 1891, Argentis devoted his life to researching Chian history, writing many significant works.

The **archaeological museum** (☎ 22710 44239; Mihalon 10; admission €2; ⏰ 8.30am-2.45pm Tue-Sun) contains sculptures, pottery and coins dating from the Neolithic period. Closed at the time of writing, the **Byzantine Museum** (☎ 22710 26866; Plateia Vounakiou) occupies a former mosque, the Medjitie Djami, and contains sculptures from the 14th- to 15th-century Genoese occupation.

Within the Kastro's main gate, the tiny **Giustiniani Palace Museum** (☎ 22710 22819; admission Tue-Sat €2, Sun €1; ⏱ 9am-3pm Tue-Sun) contains restored Byzantine wall paintings, including important 13th-century frescoes.

The **Public Gardens** make a nice spot for relaxing; in summer Hollywood hits play at an enclosed **open-air cinema** (tickets €6) nightly at 9pm.

Sleeping

ourpick Chios Rooms (☎ 22710 20198, 6972833841; www.chiosrooms.gr; Leoforos Egeou 110; s/d/tr €25/35/45) An eclectic, hostel-like neoclassical house on the waterfront, Chios Rooms is the inspiration of its owner, native New Zealander Don. Marked by vintage furnishings, traditional rugs and lofty ceilings, the place has real character. More than half of the rooms have private bathrooms (the others have bathrooms separate from the rooms). The rooftop 'penthouse' has its own terrace. Having spent over 30 years in Greece, Don has much wisdom to impart about Greek life, and life in general, and will readily do so over a beer; the dude abides.

Rooms Alex (☎ 22710 26054; Livanou 29; s/d €30/45) A bright roof garden adorned with various flags increases the visibility of this friendly place. If the interior seems dark, imagine you're in a ship's hull: kindly owner Alex Stoupas was a sea captain for 21 years, and his lovingly handmade model ships decorate each of the simple but clean rooms. The *kapetanios* will pick you up for free from the ferry, and speaks English, French and Spanish. Book ahead in summer.

Hotel Kyma (☎ 22710 44500; kyma@chi.forthnet .gr; Evgenias Handri 1; s/d/tr incl breakfast €71/90/112; 🅿 🛜) This century-old converted mansion impresses from the first sight of its central marble stairway (from 1917). The old wing's rooms live up to this promise, with stately decor, billowing curtains and sea-view balconies with red marble walls (ask for room 29). What makes the Kyma more than just another period hotel is its service; owner Theodoros Spordilis wants you to fall in love with Chios, and solves problems in English, Italian and German. Stays in the Kyma's sister hotel (opposite) in Kardamyla can be arranged.

Eating

Ouzeri Tzivaeri (☎ 22710 43559; Neoreion 13; mezedhes €3-8) The sort of food strong enough to soak up

ouzo (the Tzivaeri serves 10 kinds) is dished out at this friendly portside eatery. You might need a cast-iron gut to lay into oil-drenched sun-dried tomatoes, grilled cod strips and traditional Chios sausages – but then again, that's what a good *ouzerie* is all about.

Mezedopoleion Palaio Petrino (☎ 22710 29797; Leoforos Egeou; mezedhes €4-7) This well-decorated and friendly place offers great mezedhes, like *tyrokafteri* (spicy cheese dip) and *ktapodi krasato* (octopus in wine sauce).

To Meliotiko Ouzeri (☎ 22710 40407; Neoreion; mains €4-7) The hearty portions served at the Meliotiko, on the port, help you fill your stomach before long ferry trips.

To Tavernaki tou Tassou (☎ 22710 27542; Livanou 8; mains €6-8) This family-friendly eatery near the sea offers standard taverna fare, Chios' own Kambos lemonade and an adjoining kid's land that will help keep restless ones pacified during dinner.

Shopping

Mastihashop (☎ 22710 81600; Leoforos Egeou 36) Get mastic-based products like lotions, toothpaste, soaps and condiments here.

Mastic Spa (☎ 22710 28643; Leoforos Egeou 12) Sells mastic-based cosmetics.

Kava Potopoleio (☎ 22710 23190; Inopionos 4) Find fine wines and myriad European beers in this shop below the Public Gardens.

CENTRAL CHIOS

North of Chios Town, **Vrontados** is site of Homer's legendary stone chair, the **Daskalopetra**. Immediately south of Chios Town is **Kampos**, a lush area with citrus trees, where wealthy Genoese and Greek merchant families summered from the 14th century onwards. You can see the walled mansions, some restored, others crumbling, and elaborate gardens – especially beautiful when flowers blossom in spring. Being fairly extensive, Kampos is best toured by bicycle, moped or car.

Citrus Memories (☎ 22710 31513; www.citrus-chios .gr; Argenti 9-11, Chios Town), a museum and shop founded in 2008, aims to revive the history of citrus fruit production in Kampos over the centuries, including organised visits, and tastings, of local desserts made from citrus fruits, like marzipan, lemon and vanilla sweets. The museum's atmospheric lodgings are on an estate dating from 1742. Other dignified Kampos mansions are being transformed into atmospheric guesthouses.

The nearby resort of **Karfas** (6km south of Chios Town) has accommodation and eating, but gets hectic.

At the island's centre is **Nea Moni** (admission free; ☾ 8am-1pm & 4-8pm), a World Heritage–listed 11th-century Byzantine monastery. Since it's undergoing renovations, some buildings may be closed. Nea Moni was built to commemorate the miraculous appearance of an icon of the Virgin Mary before three shepherds. Once one of Greece's richest monasteries, Nea Moni attracted pre-eminent Byzantine artists to create the mosaics in its *katholikon* (principal church of the monastic complex).

Disastrously, during the Greek War of Independence, the Turks torched the monastery and massacred its monks. Macabre monastic skulls are lined in the ossuary at the little chapel. Another catastrophe occurred with an 1881 earthquake that demolished the *katholikon* dome, damaging mosaics. Despite this, they still rank among Greece's greatest surviving examples of Byzantine art. Nea Moni is now a nunnery.

Another solemn site lies 10km northwest, at the end of a silent road. **Anavatos**, filled with abandoned grey-stone houses, was built on a precipitous cliff over which villagers hurled themselves to avoid capture during Turkish reprisals in 1822. Note that the narrow, stepped pathways leading between the houses to the summit can be dangerous, and the route is often closed.

More happily, nearby **Avgonyma** village, distinguished by mediaeval stone architecture, is currently enjoying a revival, and offers accommodation.

The central-west-coast beaches are quiet and good for solitude seekers, though they're not Chios' most spectacular. **Lithi Beach**, the southernmost of these, is most popular.

Sleeping

Perleas Mansion (☎ 22710 32217; www.perleas.gr; Vitiadou, Kampos; s/d/tr incl breakfast €90/120/150; P ✗) One of Kampos' best restored mansion guesthouses, the Perleas offers seven well-appointed apartments. This relaxing estate, built in 1640, exemplifies high Genoese architecture. The restaurant serves traditional Greek cuisine, using homegrown organic produce.

Spitakia (☎ 22710 81200; www.spitakia.com; Avgonyma village; r from €90; P ✗) This collection of studios and cottages, spread across five locations in a striking village of mediaeval stone houses

surrounded by olive and pine forests, has fantastic ambience. Although traditional, all rooms have kitchenettes and mod cons like air conditioning, TV and central heating (in winter); some have sublime sea views.

NORTHERN CHIOS

Lonesome northern Chios, once home of shipping barons, features craggy peaks (Mt Pelineo, Mt Oros and Mt Amani), deserted villages and barren hillsides. The drive north from Chios Town along the east coast is an astonishing trip through bizarre, boulder-strewn mountains that seem from some other planet.

After the small coastal settlements of **Vrontados** and **Langada** are the main villages, **Kardamyla** and **Marmaro**, ancestral homes of many wealthy ship-owning families – though you wouldn't know it from the humble architecture. Streets are so narrow, in fact, that some buildings have lines painted on the walls so buses won't barge into them. Marmaro has an earthy sand beach, but there are better pebble beaches 5km further at **Nagos** fishing village, and at **Giosonas**, 1km beyond. The beaches have very clear water and a few tavernas, but little shade.

After Nagos, the coast road heads northwest and upwards into remote terrain, skirting craggy Mt Pelineo (1297m). **Amades** and **Viki** are two tiny villages before **Kambia**, high up on a ridge overlooking bare hillsides and the sea. Here choose between turning south on the central road through the mountains, or continuing along the coast.

The latter option passes through wild, empty hills on a jagged road, reaching the pebbly **Agia Markella Beach** and **monastery** above it, also named after Agia Markella, the island's patron saint. Some 3km southeast is **Volissos**, Homer's legendary birthplace, with its impressive Genoese fort. Volissos' port, **Limnia**, isn't striking but has a taverna. From Volissos the coastal road continues south until Elinda, then returns eastwards to Chios Town.

Sleeping

Hotel Kardamyla (☎ 22720 23353; kyma@chi.forthnet .gr; Marmaro; s/d/tr €91/114/140; P ✗) Although the 1970s architecture is somewhat dated, the simple rooms are clean and well maintained at this quiet beachfront hotel in Marmaro. Repeat visitors come for the warm hospitality of the joint Greek-Turkish Spordilis family, who invite guests for a patio lunch. This is the sister hotel of Chios Town's Hotel Kyma (p370), and stays can be arranged from there.

SOUTHERN CHIOS

Unique southern Chios is arguably the island's best destination. Here and nowhere else grows the gum-producing mastic tree, throughout a fertile, reddish territory known as the Mastihohoria (Mastic villages). This region of rolling hills, criss-crossed with elaborate stone walls running throughout olive and mastic groves, is highly atmospheric.

Ottoman rulers' penchant for mastic made the Mastihohoria wealthy for centuries. Some architectural wonders remain in the villages of Pyrgi and Mesta. The former features houses decorated in unusual colourful patterns, while the latter is a car-free, walled fortress settlement built by the Genoese in the 14th century.

Other unique southern Chios attractions include Byzantine churches, the striking Cave of Sykia with its stalactites and stalagmites, and beaches. The port of Limenas Mesta, which offers seafood tavernas, is also a convenient jumping-off point for ferries to Psara (for ferry information, see p511).

Pyrgi Πυργί
pop 1040
Located 24km southwest of Chios Town, Pyrgi (peer-*ghi*), the Mastihohoria's largest village, juxtaposes traditional and modern architecture. Its vaulted, narrow streets pass buildings with facades decorated in intricate grey and white patterns, some geometric and others based on flowers, leaves and animals. The technique used, called *xysta,* requires coating walls with a mixture of cement and black volcanic sand, painting over it with white lime and then scraping off parts of the lime with the bent prong of a fork to reveal the matt grey beneath.

Pyrgi's central square is flanked by tavernas, shops and the little 12th-century **Church of Agios Apostolos** (☎ 10am-1pm Tue-Thu & Sat). The church's 17th-century frescoes are well preserved. On the square's opposite side, the larger church's facade has Pyrgi's most impressive *xysta* designs.

On the main road, east of the square, note the house with a plaque attesting to its former occupant – one Christopher Columbus.

Although definitely worth seeing, Pyrgi is better as a drive-by than a sleepover destination. However, there are signposted domatia, and **Giannaki Rooms** (☎ 22710 25888, 6945959889; d/q €40/70; 🖭) offers regular rooms plus a house for up to eight people (€100).

Emboreios Εμπορειός
Six kilometres southeast of Pyrgi, Emboreios was the Mastihohoria's port back when the mastic producers were real high-rollers. Today it's much quieter, though it does boast **Mavra Volia Beach**, named for its black volcanic pebbles. There are domatia and, for food, the shady, atmospheric **Porto Emborios** (☎ 22710 70025; mains €5-9), decorated with fishing nets, hung chillies and garlic.

Mesta Μεστά
Mesta (mest-*aah*) is a truly memorable village, and one of Greece's most unusual. Here, appealing stone alleyways, intertwined with flowers and intricate balconies, are completely enclosed by thick defensive walls – the work of Chios' former Genoese rulers, who built this fortress town in the 14th century to keep pirates and would-be invaders out. Mesta is an ingenious example of mediaeval defensive architecture, featuring a double set of walls, four gates and a pentagonal structure. Since the rooftops are interconnected, with the right guide you can actually walk across the entire town. Dastardly locals have been known to settle scores by dumping water on an adversary's head from above.

In mediaeval times, mastic was a hot commodity, prized for its medicinal powers, meaning Mesta had to be especially well fortified. As a car-free village, it's a relaxing, romantic place where children can run around safely. Mesta also makes a good base for hill walking, exploring hidden southern beaches and caves, and participating in cultural and eco activities.

Village life converges on the central square, near the enormous church of the Taxiarhon, with small cafes and restaurants; on the tranquil, secluded laneways, rooms for rent are indistinguishably attached to the residences of bemused elders, who sit outside while the occasional cat darts past and the laughter of running children fills the air.

ORIENTATION
Buses stop outside of the village walls, on the main road; the *plateia* here is known locally as

Gyros. Facing the town from the bus shelter, turn right and then immediately left; a sign points to Mesta centre. Head down to the central square (Plateia Taxiarhon) for tourist information, rooms and eating options.

SIGHTS
There are two **churches of the Taxiarhon** (Archangels). The older and smaller one dates from Byzantine times and features a magnificent 17th-century iconostasis. The larger, 19th-century church, on the square, was built entirely from the townspeople's donations and labour. It has an ornate outer patio, huge, glittering chandeliers and very fine frescoes.

ACTIVITIES
To participate in traditional Chian farming, cooking and cultural activities, plus various outdoor activities, find Vassilis and Roula at **Masticulture Ecotourism Activities** (☎ 22710 76084, 6976113007; www.masticulture.com; Plateia Taxiarhon) by the restaurant on the square. This very kind and helpful couple provide unique ecotourism opportunities that introduce visitors to the local community, its history and culture. Some activities include mastic cultivation tours (€18), grape stomping with local winemakers (€25), cooking classes and pottery classes (€20).

Masticulture sells boat tickets, finds accommodation in Mesta, Limenas Mesta, Olympi and elsewhere, and provides general information. It's the official port agent for Limenas Mesta, and can arrange boat tickets and advance accommodation for those visiting Psara.

SLEEPING & EATING
Masticulture Ecotourism Activities can arrange rooms, or else ask in the adjacent Mesaonas restaurant for the proprietors listed below.

Anna Floradis Rooms (☎ /fax 22710 76455; floradis@ internet.gr; s/d €40/50; ✹) The friendly Anna Floradis, who speaks French and some English, has rooms, studios and self-catering suites throughout Mesta, all with TV and air-con.

Dhimitris Pipidhis Rooms (☎ 22710 76029; house €60; ✹) The friendly, English-speaking Dhimitris and Koula Pipidhis rent two traditional houses in Mesta. Each has two bedrooms, a *pounti* (the traditional small

Mesta house atrium), kitchen and washing machine. Book ahead in summer.

Mesta Medieval Castle Suites (☎ 22710 76345; www.medievalcastlesuites.com; d/tr incl breakfast €94/117; ✹ 🖳) These luxury suites for the discerning, spread throughout Mesta, seem to blend in seamlessly with the neighbouring houses. Open the door, however, and you have ultrachic rooms with all modern amenities, including flat-screen TVs and laptops; the only thing lacking, perhaps, is a bathtub. Decor is minimalist and obeys the contours of the space. The helpful staff can retrieve guests from the ferry or airport.

ourpick Mesaonas (☎ 22710 76050; Plateia Taxiarhon; mains €5-10) With tables spread across Plateia Taxiarhon, this venerable old favourite appeals to locals and tourists alike, and serves hearty portions of *mayirefta* and grills. Everything is local, right down to the *souma* (mastic-flavoured firewater). Order the mixed meat plate to share, but be sure to get the incredibly delicious beef *keftedhes* (rissoles) before they're all gone.

Limani Meston (☎ 22710 76389; Limenas Mesta; fish €6-12) For excellent and unique seafood dishes, try this waterfront fish taverna. The *astakomakaronadha* and special *atherinopita* (small fried fish with onions) are both recommended. Remarkably, it even does fresh breakfast-time *tyropita* (cheese pie) and *bougatsa* (creamy semolina pudding wrapped in a pastry envelope and baked) if you're waiting for the ferry to Psara.

GETTING AROUND
Mesta is a walking-only town; excepting the regular buses to Chios town, it can be hard to see other major sites from here. Fortunately, the friendly, English-speaking **Dimitris Kokkinos** (☎ 6972543543) provides taxi services to major destinations. Sample fares from Mesta: Limenas Mesta €6; Pyrgi €11; Olympi €20; Vessa €23; Kampos €30; Chios Town €35.

Around Mesta
Mesta's west-coast port, **Limenas Mesta** (also called Limenas Meston), is a pretty harbour of colourful fishing boats and tavernas, with nearby pebble beaches, the best being **Avlonia Beach** (7.3km west of Mesta).

Some 3km southeast of Mesta is **Olympi** – like Mesta and Pyrgi, a mastic-producing village characterised by its defensive architecture.

Continue 5km south to the splendid **Cave of Sykia** (admission incl tour €4; ☉ 10am-8pm Tue-Sun), a 150-million-year-old cavern discovered accidentally in 1985. Some 57m deep, the cave's filled with weird, multicoloured stalactites and other rock formations, shaped like giant white organs and phantasms. Selectively lit by floodlights and connected by a series of platforms with handrails, the cave is safe, though somewhat slippery. With its marvellous lighting and colours, the cave could be the set for some adventure movie: think Indiana Jones. Guided tours run every 30 minutes, the last at 7.30pm.

The good dirt road south from here passes a little-used military range, as the signs (unhelpfully, Greek-only) warn. Although there's no danger, this is not a place for random hiking; stick to the road. After 2km the road ends at a small church overlooking **Agia Dynami Beach**, a curving, sandy cove where the water is a stunning combination of blues and greens, flecked with white wavelets. The beach is completely pristine and undeveloped, and you're likely to have it to yourself.

INOUSSES ΟΙΝΟΥΣΣΕΣ

pop 1050 / area 14 sq km

Just northwest of Chios, placid Inousses is ancestral home to about one-third of Greece's shipping barons (the so-called *arhontes*), whose wealthy descendents return here annually for summer vacations from their homes in London, Paris or New York. Inousses was settled in 1750 by ship-owning families from Kardamyla in northeastern Chios, and some amassed huge fortunes during the 19th and early 20th centuries; lingering traces of this history are visible in Inousses' grand mansions and ornate family mausoleums high above the sea.

Although Inousses is little-visited by foreign tourists, it does get a bit lively in high season, with an open-air cinema, cafes and night-time beach parties. Nevertheless, it has retained its serenity and remains an escapist destination, with only one hotel and a few rooms and villas for rent.

The island's port and only town, also called Inousses, attests to its seafaring identity. Arriving by ferry, you'll see a small and green sculpted mermaid watching over the harbour – the Mother of Inoussa (Mitera Inoussiotissa), protector of mariners. And, along with the port village's white stone houses crowned by two churches, Inousses boasts a well-disciplined merchant marine academy and an eclectic museum of model ships, bequeathed by a former shipping baron. Refreshingly, the placid waterfront is lined by colourful boats where the plaintive cry of seagulls, and not domatia owners hawking rooms, greets arriving visitors.

Orientation & Information

Disembarking from the ferry, walk left along the waterfront and turn right to the *plateia*, site of the tavernas, museum and services. Further along the waterfront are cafes and, above them, a small church. A post office and National Bank of Greece stand adjacent, around the corner from the Nautical Museum. However, there's no ATM; locals explain that having one would make one of the bank's two workers redundant.

Doctor (☎ 22710 55300)

Dimarhio (Town Hall; ☎ 22710 55326) Local officials keep lists of available domatia and can phone them for you.

Police (☎ 22710 55222) Just above Hotel Thalassoporos.

Post office (☎ 22710 55398; ☉ 9.30am-2pm Mon-Fri)

Sights & Activities

Inousses has numerous hill-walking opportunities and untouched beaches. There's no tourist information, so enquire at the *dimarhio* (town hall) or the helpful Hotel Thalassoporos. **Bilali Beach**, 2km from town, is the best nearby beach, with summer night parties. Also, a summertime **open-air cinema** (tickets €4) near the central waterfront brings Hollywood hits to Inousses, nightly at 9.30pm.

The fascinating **Nautical Museum** (☎ 22710 44139; Stefanou Tsouri 20; admission €1.50; ☉ 10am-1pm Mon-Fri) celebrates Inousses' seafaring past. To create it, local shipping magnate Antonis Lemos donated his priceless collection of model ships, which include early 20th-century commercial ships, whaling ships made of ivory and whalebone, and ivory models of French prisoner-of-war vessels from the Napoleonic Wars. However, the museum is more eclectic; along with these models (accompanied by vintage maritime paintings by eminent painter Aristeides Glykas), there's a swashbuckling collection of 18th-century muskets and sabres, a WWII-era US Navy diving helmet, a hand-cranked lighthouse made in 1864, antiquarian maps of Greece and (of course) a 6th-century-BC stone scarab seal, and various Bronze Age antiquities.

In true Greek style, the museum is timed to close just before the afternoon ferry from Chios arrives and to open after the morning boat back to Chios has left. Therefore you may have to stay for two nights just to see it, unless you can get someone to open it out of hours (Eleni at Hotel Thalassoporos can sometimes help).

To experience the significance of Inousses' heritage, walk 10 minutes up the hill from the museum to the **Church of Agia Paraskevi**; in its leafy courtyard above the sea stands the **Mausoleum of Inousses** (Nekrotafion Inousson), where the island's ship-owning dynasties have endowed the tombs of their greats with huge chambers, marble sculptures and miniature churches. It's a melancholy, moving place, and speaks volumes about the worldly achievements and self-perception of the extraordinary natives of these tiny islands.

Sleeping

Ask at the *dimarhio* about private rooms.

Hotel Thalassoporos (☎ 22720 51475; s/d incl breakfast €40/50; 🛏 🖳) This recently revitalised old hotel has clean, simple rooms with TV, fridge and small balconies, plus views of Inousses town's rooftops and the waterfront. Co-owner Eleni can provide general information, and help arrange house rental elsewhere on Inousses. The hotel is a three-minute walk up a steep street on the ferry-dock side of the waterfront.

Eating & Drinking

Inomageireio To Pateroniso (☎ 22720 55586; mains €5-8) This whimsical taverna near the *plateia* serves Greek standbys and fresh fish, like the heads-and-all fry-up of *atherinia* (minnows) and onions.

Naftikos Omilos Inousson (☎ 22720 55596; 🕙 9am-3am) At the waterfront's end, the Inousses Yacht Club's long bar and outdoor patio are filled mostly with young Greeks (and their vacationing diaspora relatives), and pop music plays till late.

Getting There & Away

The little *Oinoussai III* (€4 one way, 1¼ hours, one daily) usually leaves from Inousses in the afternoon and returns in the morning (from Chios), warranting overnight stays. Purchase tickets on board,

or from **Sunrise Tours** (☎ 22710 41390; Kanari 28) in Chios Town. There are twice-weekly summertime day excursions (€20), again with Sunrise Tours.

Daily **water taxis** (☎ 6944168104) travel to/from Langada on Chios. The one-way fare is €35, split between passengers. Comparably priced water taxis serve Chios Town, too.

Getting Around

Inousses has neither buses nor car hire; ask around for its one taxi.

PSARA ΨΑΡΑ

pop 420 / area 45 sq km

Celebrated Psara (psah-*rah*), accompanied by its satellite islet of Antipsara, is one of maritime Greece's true oddities. A tiny speck in the sea two hours northwest of Chios, this island of scrub vegetation, wandering goats and weird red rock formations has one settlement (also called Psara), a remote monastery and pristine beaches. However, it's visited mostly by diaspora Greeks and thus remains something of an unknown commodity for foreign travellers. Nevertheless, it's easily accessible from Chios, and decent accommodation and eating options exist. Free camping on remote beaches is tolerated too (if you can get there).

For an island its size, Psara looms inordinately large in modern lore. The Psariot clans (once owners of around 4000 vessels) became wealthy through shipping, and participated in

the 1821–29 War of Independence. However, as in Chios, their involvement sparked a brutal Ottoman reprisal that depopulated the island in 1824 (it's still commemorated each year). Decades would pass before Psara recovered.

In the late 19th and early 20th centuries, many Psariots put their sailing and fishing skills to use on the high seas, some settling eventually in America and other foreign lands. Their descendents still return every summer, so don't be surprised if the first person you meet speaks English with a Brooklyn accent.

Orientation & Information

Psara town is tucked within a long bay on the island's southwest. When you disembark the ferry, straight on is the jagged hill from which the Psariot women and children are said to have hurled themselves during the 1824 Ottoman assault. Right of this hill, a beach with some accommodation and tavernas lies across the water. The central waterfront, stretched out across the bay, has cafes, shops and restaurants. Beyond the harbour's far side lies Katsounis Beach, with another restaurant.

Behind the waterfront, the small streets conceal houses, two churches and a monument to national hero Konstantine Kanaris (see the boxed text, below), the post office and a National Bank of Greece with ATM. There's an island **doctor** (☎ 22740 61277) and **police** (☎ 22740 61222) for emergencies, and plenty of hearty sailors. The road towards the **Moni Kimisis Theotoukou** (12km), and other beaches, is signposted.

Tourist information is scarce, and neither car nor motorbike hire existed at the time of writing (though this may change). In Chios, for general information, ferry tickets and accommodation, contact Masticulture Ecotourism Activities (p373) in Mesta, which is also the port agent for boats from Limenas Mesta to Psara. If on Psara, track down the helpful Diane Kantakouzenou at Psara Travel on the central waterfront. In any case, the presence of Greek-Americans in summer and the long foreign experience of Psariot sailors means you'll find English speakers to assist you.

Throughout town, you will notice Psara's memorable red-and-white flag waving proudly in the breeze. Emblazoned with the revolutionary slogan *Eleftheria i Thanatos* (Freedom or Death), it features a red cross at its centre, with an upturned spear jutting from one side, while on the other is an anchor apparently impaling a green snake; as if the reference to the Islamic

---

THE ADMIRABLE ADMIRAL OF PSARA

The fact that one of modern Greece's greatest heroes was born on tiny Psara might seem odd to visitors today, but it in fact speaks volumes about the bygone power and prestige of this proud, seafaring island.

One of the dominant figures of 19th-century Greek military and political affairs, **Konstantine Kanaris** (1793–1877) played a leading role in the fight to liberate Greece from the Ottoman Empire during the 1821–29 War of Independence; the heroic stature thus acquired propelled him, six times, to the position of prime minister, before his death at the age of 84.

Orphaned at an early age, Kanaris (like many of his fellow Psariots) turned to the sea. Working on an uncle's brig, he acquired sailing skills that would prove handy when Psara affirmed its readiness for revolution on 10 April 1821. The islanders turned their vast commercial sailing fleet into a veritable navy. Under leaders like Kanaris, the Psariots proved a force to be reckoned with, mounting several successful attacks on Turkish warships.

Kanaris quickly become known for a fearlessness that bordered on the suicidal. While shepherding small boats laden with explosives towards Turkish warships, he would allegedly murmur to himself, 'Konstanti, you are going to die.'

One of Kanaris' most famous operations occurred on the night of 6 June 1822. In revenge for Turkish massacres on Chios, the Psariots destroyed Turkish admiral Nasuhzade Ali Pasha's flagship while the unsuspecting enemy was holding a post-massacre celebration. Kanaris' forces detonated the powder keg of the Ottoman ship, blowing up 2000 sailors and the admiral himself. Through 1824 Kanaris led three more high-profile attacks against the Sultan that significantly affected the Turks' abilities to quell the Greek insurrection elsewhere. However, this success would come at

rule of the Turks wasn't apparent enough, there's an upside-down crescent moon and star under these items for good measure. The yellow dove of freedom flutters to one side.

Sights & Activities

The **Monastery of Kimisis Theotokou** (Monastery of the Dormition of the Virgin), 12km north of town, is Psara's main cultural attraction. Unless you find a lift, it's a two-hour walk past the rolling hills, scrubland and weird red rocks that comprise the island's topography. You may see only goats and beehives (Psara is famous for its invigorating thyme honey) on the way, so check ahead to be sure the monastery will be open.

Psara allegedly has 65 other churches (most, family-maintained chapels). In town, the **Church of Metamorfosi tou Sotiris** (Church of the Metamorphosis of the Saviour) is a five-minute walk inland from the waterfront. This grand, white-and-blue structure built around 1770 is richly decorated with icons. Since renovation work is ongoing, it's not always open. Just before it to the left is a small park containing the **Monument to Konstantine Kanaris**, where Greeks pay their respects to this national hero, who's actually buried in Athens (though his heart is apparently kept in the Naval Museum in Piraeus).

Hill walking is possible – just pick a direction, and you'll find yourself alone in nature. However, since Psara lacks trees, there's no shade.

Several pristine pebble-and-sand beaches stretch along Psara's jagged edges. The closest (except for the two town beaches) from town are the west-coast **Agios Dimitrios Beach** and **Tourlia Beach**. There's good swimming in similarly clear waters at **Kato Gialos Beach** (opposite the cliff, beneath Restaurant Ilionas Ilema) and the more secluded **Kavos Beach**, beyond the harbour's far side.

If in Psara on the last Sunday in June, attend the **religious commemoration** of the 1824 Ottoman massacre. It occurs on the jagged hill opposite the port, and is followed by folk dancing and other cultural activities in town.

Sleeping

Psara Town has domatia and even hotels; just show up, or arrange from Chios with Masticulture Ecotourism Activities (p373) in Mesta. Escapists can enjoy free camping on remote beaches (providing you can get there and can bring your own supplies).

Domatia Fotis Xaxoulis (☎ 22740 61180; studios from €40) Cheery islander Fotis rents 15 well-equipped studio apartments in town, lined by palms.

---

a heavy price for the Psariots. Determined to crush the islanders' revolt, Sultan Mahmud II was forced to entreat the powerful, semi-independent Ottoman viceroy Mohammad Ali (1769–1849) in Kavala. Together with his son, Ibrahim Pasha, Mohammad Ali commanded a personal army and navy of 100,000 men, many Egyptian. (He also enlisted French mercenary sailors left jobless after Napoleon's defeat.) To win the wily Ali's support against the Greeks, Mahmud II was forced to reward him with the very auspicious headship of Crete. It was the beginning of the end for the Ottomans' central control over their increasingly fractious empire.

The Turkish-Egyptian fleet proved just as ruthless as the Sultan had been promised. When Psara was captured on 21 June 1824 thousands who had failed to escape were butchered or sold into slavery; island lore recounts that women and children flung themselves from a craggy cliff (visible when arriving at Psara port) rather than suffer such an ignominious fate.

Despite the tragic destruction of his island, Kanaris continued to successfully harass the Turks. Still, it took the combined forces of Britain, Russia and France to completely destroy the Ottoman navy, at the Battle of Navarino off the Peloponnese on 20 October 1827.

After Greece was liberated, Konstantine Kanaris became an admiral in the new navy. Upon retiring from duty, he went into politics and was a high-ranking minister in various governments before serving briefly as prime minister in 1844, a post he held another five times. He didn't live to see Psara itself liberated (during the First Balkan War, in 1912).

The admirable admiral of Psara has been honoured frequently by the Greek Navy. Since 1941 several destroyers have been named after him. British and American naval vessels have also been transferred to Greece, and graced with Kanaris' name. The most recent reminder of this maritime legend arrived in 2002, in the form of a pretty kick-ass frigate, the FFG *Kanaris*.

Kato Gialos Apartments (☎ 22740 61178, 6945755321; s/d/apt 40/50/70) Just up from Restaurant Ilionas Ilema, Spiros Giannakis rents out clean, bright rooms and self-catering apartments overlooking Kato Gialos Beach.

Eating & Drinking

Udrohoos (☎ 22740 61182; waterfront; ◷ 8am-midnight) Right on the waterfront, this old cafe also does light breakfasts.

Kafe-Bar Baka Marianna (☎ 22740 61295; waterfront; ◷ 7am-1am) This whimsical *kafeneio* with tables just above the bobbing caïques of Psara is a relaxing place for a Greek coffee or espresso.

Restaurant Ilionas Ilema (☎ 22740 61121; mains €5-8; Kato Gialos Beach; ◷ 6am-2am) Excellent island specialities like stuffed goat and octopus with aubergines are served at this friendly restaurant with tables overlooking Kato Gialos Beach.

Spitalia (Katsounis Beach; mains €5-9; ◷ 9am-1am) Formerly an Ottoman hospital, this restaurant on Katsounis Beach, beyond the far side of the waterfront, is atmospheric and serves nourishing Greek dishes.

Ta Delfinia (☎ 22740 61352; fish €7-12; ◷ 6am-1am) With a proud 20-year tradition behind him, Manolis Thirianos offers some of Psara's best seafood at this *psarotaverna* (fish taverna) on the central waterfront.

ourpick Petrino (waterfront; ◷ 7pm-late) This handsomely restored, wood-and-stone bar on the harbour's far side has become Psara's hotspot for young people. Petrino's waterfront terrace is nice for an evening coffee, and on summer nights it gets packed with local and visiting partiers.

Getting There & Away

For ferry information, see Island Hopping (p520). Get tickets from the port agent of Limenas Mesta in Chios, Masticulture Ecotourism Activities (p373). Chios Town travel agencies can also provide tickets for boats departing from there.

Getting Around

Good luck! With neither car nor motorbike hire offered at the time of writing, you'll have to walk, unless you can enlist an islander to give you a lift. While hitchhiking is generally safe, don't count on it, as Psara's remote back roads see little traffic.

LESVOS (MYTILINI)
ΛΕΣΒΟΣ (ΜΥΤΙΛΗΝΗ)

pop 93,430 / area 1637 sq km

Greece's third-largest island, after Crete and Evia, Lesvos (Mytilini) is also one of its most breathtaking, marked by constantly changing landscapes. Long sweeps of rugged, desert-like western plains give way to sandy beaches and salt marshes in the elliptical centre, leading to thickly forested mountains and dense olive groves (some 11 million olive trees are cultivated here) further east. The island's port and capital, Mytilini Town, is a fun-loving place filled with exemplary *ouzeries*, dynamic nightlife and good accommodation, while the north-coast town of Mythimna (also called Molyvos) is an aesthetic treat, with old stone houses clustered on winding lanes overlooking the sea. Lesvos' must-see cultural attractions range from modern art museums to Byzantine monasteries.

Despite its undeniable tourist appeal, hardworking Lesvos makes its livelihood firstly from agriculture. Olive oil is a highly regarded local product, as is ouzo; indeed, the island's farmers produce around half of the aniseed-flavoured national firewater sold worldwide, and its wines are also well known.

Nature lovers will be richly rewarded here, with endless opportunities for hiking and cycling, while birdwatching is another major draw (over 279 species, ranging from raptors to waders, are seen here). Lesvos also boasts therapeutic hot springs that gush with some of the warmest mineral waters in Europe.

Lesvos' great cultural legacy stretches from the 7th-century-BC musical composer Terpander and poet Arion to 20th-century figures like Nobel Prize–winning poet Odysseus Elytis and primitive painter Theofilos. The great ancient philosophers Aristotle and Epicurus also led an exceptional philosophical academy here. Most famous, however, is Sappho, one of ancient Greece's greatest poets. Her sensuous, passionate poetry, apparently created for her female devotees, has fuelled a modern-day cult that draws lesbians from around the world to Skala Eresou, the west Lesvos beach village where she was born (c 630 BC).

The largest of the northeastern Aegean islands, Lesvos is also the one that has the most

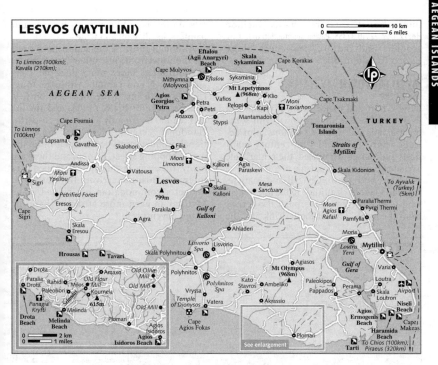

LESVOS (MYTILINI)

life year-round, chiefly thanks to its young university population, size and economic importance. It's the only island in the chain that feels somewhat lively out of high season, though this action is almost entirely to be found in the capital, Mytilini Town.

Getting There & Away
For flights and ferries from Lesvos, see Island Hopping (p517).

AIR
The airport is 8km south of Mytilini Town; a taxi costs €8.

Olympic Air (☎ 22510 28659; www.olympicairlines .com; Kavetsou 44) and **Aegean Airlines** (☎ 22510 61120; www.aegeanair.com) have offices in Mytilini Town and the airport, respectively. Mytilini Town travel agents sell tickets too.

BOAT
For information on trips to Turkey, see the boxed text, Turkish Connections (p358).

In Mytilini Town, ferry ticket offices on Pavlou Kountourioti's eastern side include Zoumboulis Tours (p381), **Samiotis Tours**

(☎ 22510 42574; Pavlou Kountourioti 43) and Olive Groove Travel (p381), which also offers Turkey excursions.

Getting Around
BUS
From Mytilini's **long-distance bus station** (☎ 22510 28873; El Venizelou), near Agias Irinis Park, three daily buses serve Skala Eresou (€8.90, 2½ hours) via Eresos; four serve Mithymna (Molyvos; €6.20, 1¾ hours) via Petra (€5.80, 1½ hours); and two reach Sigri (€9.40, 2½ hours). Five daily buses serve Plomari (€4.10, 1¼ hours), five serve Agiasos (€2.60, 45 minutes) and four end at Vatera (€5.60, 1½ hours), the latter via Polyhnitos. Travelling between these smaller places often requires changing in Kalloni, which receives four daily buses from Mytilini (€4.10, one hour). Also, five daily buses go north from Mytilini town to Moni Taxiarhon (€3.80, one hour).

CAR & MOTORCYCLE
Discover Rent-a-Car (☎ 6936057676; Venezi 3; ✹ 7:30am-1am) is a small local outfit, with good new cars and flexible service. Mytilini's

NORTHEASTERN AEGEAN ISLANDS

international car-hire chains include **Hertz** (☎ 22510 37355; Pavlou Kountourioti 87). For scooters and motorcycles, check along Pavlou Kountourioti.

MYTILINI TOWN ΜΥΤΙΛΗΝΗ
pop 27,250

Lesvos' port and major town, Mytilini, is a lively and likeable student town with some great eating and drinking options, plus eclectic churches, grand 19th-century mansions and museums; indeed, the remarkable Teriade Museum, just outside of town, boasts paintings by Picasso, Chagall and Matisse. Mytilini's laid-back attitude to life may reflect long-term leftist tendencies, but it also derives from the locals' love of food, drink and the arts, on this island known for its poets and painters, its olive oil and wine.

Although most of the action is centred on the waterfront, like other Greek ports, Mytilini offers much more than the average Greek island capital. Although tourism is significant to the local economy, it doesn't make or break things, and the locals tend to be friendly and down-to-earth. Handmade ceramics, jewellery and traditional products are sold on and around the main shopping street, Ermou, and there are many fine *ouzeries* and student-fuelled bars to enjoy. Plus, the arrival of atmospheric budget accommodation has helped make Mytilini an even more attractive base for island adventures.

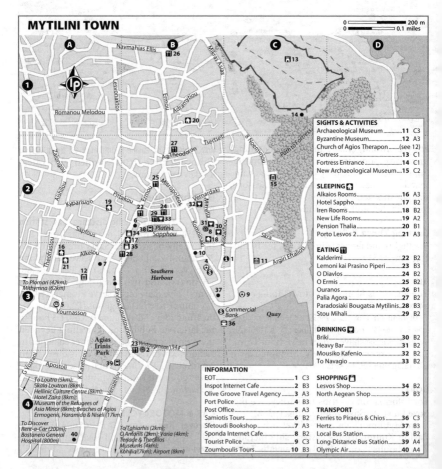

MYTILINI TOWN

0 ———— 200 m
0 ———— 0.1 miles

SIGHTS & ACTIVITIES
Archaeological Museum	**11** C3
Byzantine Museum	**12** A3
Church of Agios Therapon	(see 12)
Fortress	**13** C1
Fortress Entrance	**14** C1
New Archaeological Museum	**15** C2

SLEEPING
Alkaios Rooms	**16** A3
Hotel Sappho	**17** B2
Iren Rooms	**18** B2
New Life Rooms	**19** A2
Pension Thalia	**20** B1
Porto Lesvos 2	**21** A3

EATING
Kalderimi	**22** B2
Lemoni kai Prasino Piperi	**23** B3
O Diavlos	**24** B2
O Ermis	**25** B2
Ouranos	**26** B1
Palia Agora	**27** B2
Paradosiaki Bougatsa Mytilinis	**28** B3
Stou Mihali	**29** B2

DRINKING
Briki	**30** B2
Heavy Bar	**31** B2
Mousiko Kafenio	**32** B2
To Navagio	**33** B2

INFORMATION
EOT	**1** C3
Inspot Internet Cafe	**2** B3
Olive Groove Travel Agency	**3** A3
Port Police	**4** B3
Post Office	**5** A3
Samiotis Tours	**6** B2
Sfetoudi Bookshop	**7** A3
Sponda Internet Cafe	**8** B2
Tourist Police	**9** C3
Zoumboulis Tours	**10** B3

SHOPPING
Lesvos Shop	**34** B3
North Aegean Shop	**35** B3

TRANSPORT
Ferries to Piraeus & Chios	**36** C3
Hertz	**37** B3
Local Bus Station	**38** B2
Long-Distance Bus Station	**39** A4
Olympic Air	**40** A4

Map labels: Navmahias Ellis, Romanou Melodou, Lesvonaktos, Ermou, Adramytiou, Tsertseti, 8 Noemvriou, Ag Theodoron, Mitropoleos, Lemou, Vernardaki, Mihralia, Kioumaki, Path to Fortress, Skra, Argiri Efialtou, Komninaki, Southern Harbour, Commercial Bank, Quay, Sapfous, Alkeiou, Theofrastou, Kyparisiou, Pittakou, Kavetsou, Vournasson, Pavlou Kountourioti, Agias Irinis Park, 23 Hristougennon 1944, Apostoli, Vizantiou, Venizelou

To Plomari (42km); Mithymna (62km)
To Discover Rent-a-Car (200m); Bostaneio General Hospital (800m)
To Loutra (5km); Skala Loutron (8km); Hellinic Culture Centre (8km); Hotel Zaira (8km); Museum of the Refugees of Asia Minor (8km); Beaches of Agios Ermogenis, Haramida & Niseli (17km)
To Tahiarhis (2km); O Antonis (2km); Varia (4km); Teriade & Theofilos Museums; Kohilia (7km); Airport (8km)

Orientation

Ferries dock at the northern end of Mytilini's long and curving waterfront thoroughfare, Pavlou Kountourioti. Further along it is Plateia Sapphou (where a statue of Sappho stands), with nearby restaurants, cafes and hotels. The shopping street, Ermou, links this southern harbour with the disused, ancient northern port. East of the harbours, a large mediaeval fortress stands surrounded by pines.

The long-distance bus station is beside Agias Irinis Park and the local bus station is on Pavlou Kountourioti, near Plateia Sapphou. The airport is 8km south on the coast road.

Information

BOOKSHOPS

Sfetoudi Bookshop (☎ 22510 22287; Ermou 51) Sells good maps from Greece's leading Road Editions series and books on Lesvos.

EMERGENCY

Port police (☎ 22510 28827)
Tourist police (☎ 22510 22776) On the quay.

INTERNET ACCESS

InSpot (☎ 22510 45760; Hristougennon 1944 12; per hr €2.40)
Sponda Internet Café (☎ 22510 41007; 29-33 Komninaki; 10am-1am) Near Iren Rooms.

INTERNET RESOURCES

www.lesvos.com Online information on Lesvos.

MEDICAL SERVICES

Bostaneio General Hospital (☎ 22510 57700; E Vostani 48)

MONEY

Numerous banks equipped with ATMs line Pavlou Kountourioti.

POST

Post office (Vournasson)

TOURIST INFORMATION

EOT (☎ 22510 42512; Aristarhou 6; 9am-1pm Mon-Fri)
Port authority (☎ 22510 40827)

TRAVEL AGENCIES

Olive Groove Travel (☎ 22510 37533; www.olive-groove.gr; 11 Pavlou Kountourioti; 7.30am-10pm)

Friendly, all-purpose travel agency on the central waterfront; sells tickets for ferries and boat trips to Turkey.
Zoumboulis Tours (☎ 22510 37755; Pavlou Kountourioti 69) Sells ferry and plane tickets, runs boat trips to Turkey and rents rooms.

Sights & Activities

Mytilini's imposing early Byzantine **fortress** (adult/student €2/1; 8am-2.30pm Tue-Sun) was renovated in the 14th century by Genoese overlord Francisco Gatelouzo. The Turks enlarged it again. It's popular for a stroll and is flanked by pine forests.

The **archaeological museum** (☎ 22510 28032; adult/child €3/2; 8.30am-3pm Tue-Sun), one block north of the quay, has impressive finds from Neolithic to Roman times, including ceramic somersaulting female figurines and gold jewellery. The ticket grants entry to the **new archaeological museum** (8 Noemvriou; 8am-7.30pm), 400m away, which portrays island life from the 2nd century BC to the 3rd century AD, including spectacular floor mosaics under glass.

The bulbous dome of the **Church of Agios Therapon** crowns Mytilini's skyline. The church's ornate interior boasts a huge chandelier, an intricately carved iconostasis, a priest's throne and a frescoed dome. The **Byzantine Museum** (☎ 22510 28916; admission €2; 9am-1pm Mon-Sat) in its courtyard boasts valuable icons.

TERIADE & THEOPHILOS MUSEUMS

From Pavlou Kountourioti's northernmost section, take a local bus 4km south to **Varia**, unlikely host of the **Teriade Museum** (☎ 22510 23372; adult/student €2/1; 8.30am-2pm, 5pm-8pm Tue-Sun), with its astonishing collection of paintings by world-renowned artists like Picasso, Chagall, Miro, Le Corbusier and Matisse.

The museum honours the Lesvos-born artist and critic Stratis Eleftheriadis, who Gallicised his name to Teriade in Paris. Significantly, Teriade brought the work of primitive painter and fellow Lesvos native Theophilos to international attention.

The **Theophilos Museum** (☎ 22510 41644; admission €2; 9am-1pm & 4.30-8pm), located next door, houses works commissioned by Teriade; several prestigious Greek museums and galleries display other, more famous paintings by Theophilos, whose story followed the old pattern of many a great artist – living in abject poverty, painting coffee-house walls for his daily bread and eventually dying in the gutter.

Sleeping

BUDGET

ourpick **Alkaios Rooms** (☎ 22510 47737, 6945507089; www.alkaiosrooms.gr; Alkaiou 16 & 30; s/d/tr €30/40/50; 🔀) This collection of 30 clean, well-kept rooms nestled discreetly in several renovated traditional buildings is Mytilini's most attractive budget option. It's a two-minute walk up from Paradosiaka Bougatsa Mytilinis (below) on the waterfront.

Iren Rooms (☎ 22510 22787; cnr Komninaki & Imvrou; s/d/tr €40/50/60; 🔀) Friendly Iren has reasonably priced rooms of a good standard, though most don't have the ambience of sister establishment Alkaios Rooms. However, it's a closer walk if coming from the ferry dock, and next to an internet cafe.

New Life Rooms (☎ 22510 23400, 6947365944; Ermou 68; s/d/tr €35/50/70) New Life has bright and well-furnished rooms, a new outdoor bar and a quiet setting on a central side street. There's not always someone there, so call ahead.

MIDRANGE

Hotel Sappho (☎ 22510 22888; sappho@microchip.gr; Pavlou Kountouriotou 31; s/d/tr €45/60/70; 🔀) This perfunctory place on the central waterfront frequently fills up because of its position. Despite being dated, it has the necessary amenities and, fortunately for late-night ferry arrivals, 24-hour reception.

Porto Lesvos Hotel (☎ 22510 41771; www.porto lesvos.gr; Komninaki 21; s/d/tr incl breakfast €50/60/70; 🔀 💻) and **Porto Lesvos Hotel 2** (☎ 22510 21217; www.portlesvos.gr; Alkaiou 15; s/d/tr €50/60/70; 🔀 💻) are central sister hotels, which aspire to a slightly higher standard (as witnessed by the complimentary toiletries, bathrobe and slippers). The hotels have all mod cons, though rooms are a tad snug for the price.

Eating

Paradosiaka Bougatsa Mytilinis (22510 26918; Kountouriotou 19; bougatsa €2; ☽ Mon-Sat) Whether you're stumbling off an early-morning ferry or out for a breakfast stroll, this busy waterfront place has Mytilini's very best sweet *bougatsa*, plus various coffees.

O Diavlos (☎ 22510 22020; Ladadika 30; mezedhes €3-6) This central *ouzerie* has excellent ambience, set inside a lofty, wood-beamed building, with (purchasable) artwork lining the walls. Laid-back owner Panayiotis Molyviatis serves up unique and tasty mezedhes, like *giouslemes* (a crunchy cheese pie) and *sfongatoa* (a sort

of oven-baked cake made of zucchini, egg, onion and cheese). Also try the Turkish-flavoured beef kebabs on pitta bread with onions and *yiaourtlou kebab* (Greek yoghurt). Music ranges from relaxed to *rembetika* (Greek blues).

Ouranos (☎ 22510 47844; Navmahias Ellis; mezedhes €3-6) A popular *ouzerie* that looks across at Turkey from a breezy patio on the ancient northern port. Tempting mezedhes include *kolokythoanthi* (fried pumpkin flowers stuffed with rice), *ladotyri mytilinis* (the oil-drenched local cheese) and hefty servings of *kalamari*.

Stou Mihali (☎ 22510 43311; Ikarias 7, Plateia Sapphou; mains €3.50-5; ☽ 9am-9pm) If you're after good *mayirefta* at a good price, this is the place. Unlike many other such eateries, here you can combine half-portions and thus enjoy more variety. Try the *soutzoukakia* (tomato-soaked beef rissoles), *imam baïldi* (roast eggplant with herbs) and Greek salad.

Palia Agora (☎ 22510 91118; cnr Agion Theodoron & Ermou; mains €4-6; ☽ 8am-1am) This appealing place, usually playing old *rembetika* music, is a good and inexpensive choice for fish dishes and mezedhes. The decor is authentic, the service friendly.

ourpick **O Ermis** (☎ 22510 26232; cnr Kornarou & Ermou; mezedhes €5-8) This friendly, family-run restaurant with outdoor seating serves very tasty salads and mezedhes in portions that seem small at first, but are in the end just right. It began life in 1800 as a Turkish cafe, and the intriguing traditional decor within reveals bits and pieces of its long history since. Good Macedonian and Limnos wines are offered, and the brown bread is warm and fresh.

Lemoni kai Prasino Piperi (☎ 22510 42678; cnr Pavlou Kountourioti & Hristougennon 1944; mains €10-15; ☽ 7pm-1am) The poshest place in town, this upstairs restaurant has great waterfront views and even better food, especially the Italian dishes. Try the simple yet exquisite tomato and mozzarella salad and *tagliatelle amatriciana* (spicy tomato and bacon sauce) or *tagliatelle alfredo* (cream cheese and parmesan sauce with garlic) with salmon.

Drinking

Mytilini's loud waterfront cafes are inevitably busy, though the best watering holes are found in the backstreets.

ourpick **Mousiko Kafenio** (cnr Mitropoleos & Vernardaki; ☽ 7.30am-2am) Even if the stairs are no longer strong enough to allow you to sit upstairs in this old student favourite, the eclectic paintings, mirrors and well-worn wooden fixtures foster a relaxed, arty vibe, making it one of the most fun places in town.

To Navagio (☎ 22510 21310; Arhipelagous 23) A popular cafe-bar on Plateia Sapphou with comfy couches, perfect for a leisurely backgammon game and coffee.

Briki (cnr Hiou & Mitrelia; ☷ 8am-3am) This cool new hole-in-the-wall bar plays jazz, funk and ambient sounds, and has occasional art exhibits.

Heavy Bar (☎ 6945605383; cnr Mitrelia & Ladadika; ☷ 9pm-3am) Rock on! Mytilini's long-haired hard-rock bar is probably the only place on Lesvos where you'll find someone wearing a jean jacket in high summer. The elevated video screen means you can not only hear, but also see Axl Rose, Angus Young and Co.

Shopping

Lesvos Shop (☎ 22510 26088; Pavlou Kountourioti 33) This waterfront shop near the Hotel Sappho sells local natural products, from ouzos, olive oil and soap, to jams, handmade ceramics, wine and cheese. Proceeds benefit the municipality.

North Aegean Shop (☎ 22510 26918; Pavlou Kountourioti 21) Next to Paradosiaka Bougatsa Mytilinis, the shop sells traditional products like Greek sweets, with unusual varieties involving watermelon, olive and nuts.

Getting There & Away

Mytilini's **local bus station** (Pavlou Kountourioti), near Plateia Sapphou, serves in-town destinations and nearby Loutra, Skala Loutron and Tahiarhis. All other buses depart from the **long-distance bus station** (☎ 22510 28873; El Venizelou) near Agias Irinis Park.

SOUTH OF MYTILINI

The small, olive-groved peninsula south of Mytilini has several unique attractions. Following the coast road 7km south, opposite the airport, you'll find a long pebble beach hosting the decadent beach bar, **Kohilia** (☎ 6978773203; ☷ 8am-3am). Pulsating with house and techno music, and frequented by swimsuited students lounging on colourful couches and four-poster beds, Kohilia is a chilled-out hang-out on summer days that doubles as a night bar.

Somewhat more edifying is **Skala Loutron**, a fishing village 8km southwest of Mytilini

on the Gulf of Yera. Here the **Hellenic Culture Centre** (☎ 22510 91660, in Athens 210 523 8149; www .hcc.edu.gr; 2-week courses €650) conducts intensive summer Greek-language courses in a century-old olive-oil factory near the harbour, now restored as the **Hotel Zaira** (☎ 22510 91188; www .hotel-zaira.com; Skala Loutron; s/d €45/60), distinguished by lofty wood beams, nice stonework and home-cooked Greek food. Nonstudents can stay, too.

Also in Skala Loutron, the new **Museum of the Memorial of the Refugees of 1922** (☎ 22510 91086; admission free; ☷ 5-8pm) commemorates Anatolia's lost Greek culture, abruptly ended after 2000 years by the Greek-Turkish population exchanges of 1923. The museum features the photographs, documents, handmade clothes and silverwork of the refugees, plus large wall maps showing over 2000 villages formerly populated by Greeks – and the places in Greece where the refugees were resettled. The museum will be gladly opened outside of normal hours if you ask around.

Some 9km south, the peninsula wraps around to the popular sand-and-pebble **Agios Ermogenis Beach** and **Haramida Beach**. The eastern stretch of the latter, **Niseli Beach**, is secluded under a bluff and separated by a headland from the main beach. There's free camping provided by the municipality, with toilets and showers, under pine trees on the bluff above the beach. The camping ground is located near the lovably eccentric **Karpouzi Kantina** (☎ 6977946809), a drinks-and-snacks wagon named after its mascot – an old skiff, painted like a giant watermelon. Enthusiastic owner Fanis also oversees the camping ground.

NORTHERN LESVOS

With rolling hills garbed in pine and olive trees, peaceful beaches and the aesthetically harmonious town of Mithymna (usually called by its old name, Molyvos), northern Lesvos offers both spots for solitude and some low-key resort action. Seaside hot springs, unvisited traditional villages and intriguing Byzantine monasteries round out the region's offerings.

Moni Taxiarhon Μονί Ταξιάρχον

Some 36km north of Mytilini Town, near Mantamados village, stands one of Lesvos' most important pilgrimage sites: **Moni Taxiarhon** (Monastery of Taxiarhon; Mantamados village; admission free; ☷ 8am-8pm). An axis of Orthodoxy, myth and militarism, this grand 17th-century monastery dedicated to the Archangels is pretty full-on: note the fighter plane parked out front. It all begins to make sense when you recall that the Archangel Michael is the patron saint of the Hellenic Air Force. Indeed, you may meet the odd pious soul here who firmly attests that, even though those mischievous Turks may harass Greek airspace in their F16s on a daily basis, the saint's invisible presence prevents them from flying over the monastery itself.

While numerous reported miracles draw the faithful from around Greece, you don't have to be a believer to marvel at the monastery's magnificent architecture. Mentioned first in 1661 as a working monastery, the current church was built in 1879 as a three-aisled basilica. It's surrounded by leafy grounds (where a snack shop and toilets are conveniently located).

The voluminous interior is marked by grand columns and decorated by icons, the most venerated being an earth-toned depiction of the Archangel. Legend attests that it was created in the 10th century, after a Saracen pirate raid decimated the monastery. While the pirates were massacring the monks, the last survivor climbed to the rooftop; there the Archangel miraculously appeared, sword drawn, driving the Saracens off. To show his gratitude, the monk painted the icon, supposedly, by mixing mud with the blood of his dead comrades. In 1766, the icon was placed in a special case and the shiny faux silver markers you will see dangling before it symbolise worshippers' prayers that have been answered. There are also ornamental shoes left as sacred offerings (the alleged imprint of the Archangel's foot is in the floor near the iconostasis).

While at the monastery, visit the shop of the **Agricultural Co-op of Mandamados** (☎ 22530 61096; asmadama@otenet.gr), which sells numerous natural products from local farmers, like the unique hard cheese, *ladotyri*, made from sheep's milk.

Mithymna (Molyvos) Μήθυμνα (Μόλυβος)
pop 1500

Mithymna, more commonly called Molyvos, is a well-preserved Ottoman-era town of narrow cobbled lanes and stone houses with jutting wooden balconies, complemented by a clean pebble beach below. Drawing a mix of independent travellers and package tourists to its waterfront hotels, Molyvos is a

curious place. Yet, factoring in the intimate upper town, crowned by a grand 14th-century Byzantine castle, and good nearby beaches, Molyvos becomes a nice enough spot to spend some time while exploring northern Lesvos.

ORIENTATION
The bus stops on the main north–south road bisecting the town. Below this road is the waterfront, with a beach, several hotels and restaurants, and cafes on the northern end. Above the central road begins the upper town, consisting of narrow, winding streets, where the more atmospheric accommodation and restaurants are located. The so-called *agora* (market), clustered with tourist shops, is further up. Above this is the castle.

INFORMATION
ATM-equipped banks are centrally located.
Central Internet Café (per hr €4) On the port road.
Medical Centre (☎ 22530 71702)
Municipal tourist office (☎ 22530 71347) This small office on the left of Kastrou, between the bus stop and the fork in the central road, can provide info but has had mixed reviews regarding accommodation advice.
Post office (Kastrou)

SIGHTS & ACTIVITIES
Mithymna (Molyvos) is ideal for wandering; the upper town's small streets are lined with bright-shuttered, traditional stone houses wreathed in flowers. A 14th-century **Byzantine-Genoese castle** (☎ 22530 71803; admission €2; ⏰ 8.30am-7pm Tue-Sun) stands guard above; the steep climb is repaid by sweeping views of the town, sea and even Turkey shimmering on the horizon. Back in the 15th century, before Lesvos fell to the Turks, feisty Onetta d'Oria, wife of the Genoese governor, repulsed a Turkish onslaught after donning her husband's armour and leading the fight from here. In summer it hosts a **drama festival** (ask at the tourist office).

Beach-lovers can take an **excursion boat** at 10.30am daily for Petra, Skala Sykaminias and Eftalou (from €20). Sunset cruises and boat 'safaris' are also available. Enquire with the portside **Faonas Travel** (☎ 22530 71630; tekes@otenet.gr).

SLEEPING
Budget
Over 50 registered, good-quality domatia are available. Look for signs, or ask the municipal

tourist office. Even more expensive waterfront options sometimes give discounted rates.

Municipal Camping Mithymna (☎ 22530 71169; camp sites per adult/tent €7/3; 🕑 Jun-Sep) This publicly run camping ground occupies an excellent shady site 1.5km from town and is signposted from near the municipal tourist office. If arriving before or after high season, call ahead.

Nassos Guest House (☎ 22530 71432, 6942046279; www.nassosguesthouse.com; Arionos; s/d €20/35; 🛜) Head up to the old town's only blue house to reach one of Lesvos' most beautiful – and best-priced – sleeping spots. This refurbished Turkish mansion with a small enclosed garden features brightly painted, lovingly decorated traditional rooms with balconies overlooking the harbour. One room has a private bathroom. Friendly Dutch manager Tom provides local information, plus a book on hiking routes (€8). Check directly with him regarding availability to avoid missing out.

Captain's View (☎ 22530 71241; meltheo@otenet .gr; 2-bedroom house €90-150; 🐾) This restored old house has a well-equipped kitchen, spacious balcony and lounge. There are two bedrooms and a loft, sleeping up to six people. There are no minimum-stay requirements, but book ahead in summer.

Midrange

Molyvos Hotel (☎ 22530 71496; www.molyvos-hotels .com; waterfront; d incl breakfast €65; 🐾) Although it works with package-tour operators, this handsome waterfront hotel is also a good choice for independent travellers, with well-kept, modern rooms overlooking the sea, friendly service and a good breakfast spread. You can usually park in the narrow lane out front.

Amfitriti Hotel (☎ 22530 71741; s/d/tr incl breakfast €65/90/100; 🐾 🖳) Just 50m from the beach, this snazzy traditional stone hotel has modern, tiled rooms and a garden pool. It fills up fast and deals with package tourists, but independent travellers are welcome.

EATING & DRINKING

our pick **Alonia** (☎ 22530 72431; mains €4.50-6) Locals swear by this unpretentious place just outside of town, on the road to Eftalou Beach. Although the decor is nothing special, Alonia is the best Mithymna choice for fresh fish at good prices.

Betty's (☎ 22530 71421; 17 Noemvriou; mains €6-9) This restored Turkish pasha's residence, vis-ible under a red overhanging balcony on the upper streets, offers tasty *tyropitakia* (small cheese pies), savoury lamb souvlaki and baked eggplant with cheese. Best of all are the unusual seafood specialities, like Betty's spaghetti shrimp.

O Gatos (☎ 22530 71661; www.gatos-restaurant.gr; mains €6.50-9) Near the arch by the castle entrance, this restaurant is a bit touristy but enjoys spellbinding views over the water – good for dinner before dusk.

Sunset (☎ 22530 71093; waterfront; 🕑 8am-1am) On the waterfront, close to the Molyvos Hotel, this friendly all-day cafe has a great selection of coffees and attentive service.

Molly's Bar (☎ 22530 71209; 🕑 6pm-late) With its thickly painted walls and blue stars, beaded curtains and bottled Guinness, this whimsical British-run bar on the waterfront's far eastern side is always in shipshape condition. Molly's caters to an older, international crowd. It's flanked by another couple of watering holes that get festive in summer.

Around Mithymna (Molyvos)

Beyond Molyvos, northern Lesvos is largely unvisited; for some scenic routes, consult Tom at Nassos Guest House (left), who sells a useful hiking guide (€8).

The best-known local destination, **Petra**, is a very overrated beach village 5km south, and inexplicably a package tourism favourite. The beach itself comprises coarse sand and pebbles, while spearlike wooden poles stand ominously submerged in the water. Petra's one cultural site, situated above the giant overhanging rock for which the village was named, is the 18th-century **Panagia Glykofilousa** (Church of the Sweet-kissing Virgin), accessible on foot up 114 rock-hewn steps.

While Petra has accommodation, the village itself is barely a strip of souvenir shops and some restaurants. It's far nicer to stay in Molyvos; better yet for solitude-seekers, head a couple of kilometres northeast to **Eftalou Beach** (also called Agii Anargyri Beach). You can either park where the path heads down to the beach, or drive further to reach the Hrysi Akti Hotel and Restaurant, and further beaches beyond that.

Backed by a cliff, the narrow, pebbled Eftalou Beach has pristine waters and offers total serenity. It also boasts the **Mineral Baths of Eftalou** (old bathhouse/new bathhouse €3.50/5; 🕑 old bathhouse 6-8am & 6-10pm, new bathhouse 9am-6pm), with their clear, cathartic 46.5°C water. The old bathhouse has a pebbled floor; the new one offers private bathtubs. These springs treat rheumatism, arthritis, neuralgia, hypertension, gall stones, and gynaecological and skin problems. Or you can also just try to find the one spot on the beach in front of the bathhouse where the hot mineral water filters into the cool sea, and enjoy from there.

Beyond the baths, the beachfront **Hrysi Akti** (☎ 22530 71879; Eftalou Beach; s/d €35/45) offers simple rooms with bathrooms in an idyllic setting, right on a practically private pebbled cove. The friendly owners also own a similarly named **restaurant** (☎ 22530 71947; mains €4.50-6) just above the beach; enjoying a contemplative drink overlooking the sea here is a perfect way to wind up a Lesvos summer day.

WESTERN LESVOS

Spectacular, lonesome western Lesvos is the afterthought of massive, primeval volcanic eruptions that fossilised trees and all other living things, making it one of the world's most intriguing sites for prehistoric treasure hunters. The striking, bare landscape, broken only by craggy boulders and the occasional olive tree, is dramatically different from the rest of Lesvos.

Byzantine spiritualists in their high monastic refuges were inspired by the barren, burnt moonscapes of the west and, well before them, a certain Sappho, the 7th-century-BC poet who was dubbed 'the 10th muse' by Plato. Such was the power of her literary seduction that even the usually level-headed ancient ruler Solon despaired that he too must be taught Sappho's song, because he wanted 'to learn it and die'.

However, it is the sensuous, erotic nature of Sappho's surviving poems, and the fact that she taught them to an inner circle of female companions, that made her into a latter-day lesbian icon. Skala Eresou, her birthplace and a lesbian-frequented southwestern coastal resort, has fine beaches, seafood and sunset cocktail bars.

Kalloni to Sigri Καλλονή προς Σίγρι

After driving 34km west from Kalloni, stop for a coffee or lunch break in **Andissa**, a jovial, rustic village of narrow streets kept cool by the two enormous plane trees that stand over its *plateia*. Listen to the crickets and the banter of old-timers over a Greek coffee or frappe, while farmers hawk watermelons from the back of their trucks.

Escapists will enjoy the little-visited north-coast **Gavathas Beach**, signposted a couple of kilometres before Andissa. This long, sandy stretch lying beside a tiny fishing hamlet has warm and shallow waters ideal for children, and humble sleeping and eating options. Halfway down the main road behind the beach, look left for **O Tsolias Guest Rooms** (☎ 22530 56537; Gavathas Beach; s/d/tr €40/50/60). The kind family who runs these simple but clean rooms with bathrooms also maintains a tasty taverna below.

Some 9km west of Andissa, the Byzantine **Moni Ypsilou** (Monastery of Ypsilou; admission free; ⏰ 7.30am-10pm) stands atop a solitary peak surrounded by volcanic plains. Founded in the 8th century, this storied place includes a flowering arched courtyard, a sumptuously decorated church, and a small but spectacular museum with gold and silver reliquaries, antique liturgical vestments, centuries-old icons and Byzantine manuscripts dating back to the 10th century. From the top of the monastery stairs, you can gaze out over the fortress-like walls upon the desolate ochre plains stretched out against the sea.

Some 4km beyond the monastery a signposted left-hand road leads, after another 4.9km, to Lesvos' celebrated **petrified forest** (☎ 22530 54434; www.petrifiedforest.gr; admission €2; ⏰ 8am-4pm) – more honestly, a petrified desert. The 20-million-year-old stumps that decorate this baking, shadeless valley are few and far between, though experts insist many more lurk under the ground, waiting to be dug up.

The best specimens are in the **Natural History Museum of the Lesvos Petrified Forest** (☎ 22530 54434; admission €5; ⏰ 8am-8pm 15 Jun-18 Oct, 8.30am-4.30pm 5 Oct-5 Jun) in Sigri, a coastal village 7km west. This engaging modern museum manages to make old rocks and dusty fossils interesting, helped by interactive displays and a veritable mother lode of glittering amethyst, quartz and other semiprecious stones.

Sleepy **Sigri** is a fishing port with a sometimes operational ferry port. The village has beautiful sea views, especially at sunset, and there are idyllic, little-visited beaches just southwest. A good-quality dirt coastal road pointing south passes these beaches; it's about a 45-minute drive to Skala Eresou, western Lesvos' most popular destination.

Skala Eresou Σκάλα Ερεσού

pop 1560

All historic places are burdened by their past, but the once-quiet fishing village of Skala Eresou has learned to profit from its. This bohemian beach town, where sensuous songstress Sappho was born in 630 BC, is supposedly ground zero for the lesbian internationale – though this reputation has been overblown. In fact, with its shiatsu, fruit smoothies, healing arts and laptopped cafes, it resembles nothing so much as a New England college town (with a decidedly better climate). All in all Eresou is benign.

Skala Eresou's mainstream appeal derives from its 2km-long beach, good seafood, and low-key nightlife, while the Women Together festival each September marks the apogee of the season for lesbians.

ORIENTATION & INFORMATION

The central square of Plateia Anthis and Evristhenous abuts the waterfront; the beach extends laterally. Restaurants and bars are found here, the latter on the eastern waterfront; most cafes here offer free wi-fi internet. Behind the *plateia* is the Church of Agias Andreas. Further west along Gyrinnis are the major services and ATMs. There's also a **doctor** (☎ 22530 53947; ◷ 24hr).

The full-service **Sappho Travel** (☎ 22530 52140; www.sapphotravel.com) provides information and car hire, sells tickets, arranges accommodation and exchanges currency. It organises women-only sunset cruises and the two-week **Women Together** festival each September. The event brings lesbians from all over for workshops, music, art, therapies and socialising.

SIGHTS

Eresos' **archaeological museum** contains Greek and Roman antiquities, but was still closed at the time of writing. The nearby remains of the early Christian **Basilica of Agios Andreas** include partially intact 5th-century mosaics.

SLEEPING

Skala Eresou has reasonable domatia options, as well as (fairly pricey) hotels. Some former women-only places have gone metrosexual, though two currently remain just for women.

Domatia Maria Pantermou (☎ 22530 53267; pantermou@in.gr; s/d/tr €20/30/40; ✵) Across from the Mascot Hotel, kindly old Marianthi and Giorgios Pantermou rent these small but clean rooms with balconies.

Hotel Eressos (☎ 22530 53560; s/d €35/45; ◷ Mar-Dec; ✵) Decorated with African furnishings the owner brought from her travels, this eccentric place has well-kept, clean rooms in a quiet location, a couple of streets in from the water.

Villa La Passione (☎ 6944602080; s/d/tr €40/50/60) Self-caterers will appreciate these modern, well-outfitted studios, located near Eresou's central parking area.

Hotel Antiopi (☎ 2253053311; s/d €35/50) A women-only hotel that benefited when the Hotel Sappho went co-ed, the Antiopi has well-maintained but slightly cramped rooms that might strike one as either kitsch and cool or too cute.

Mascot Hotel (☎ 22530 52140; www.sapphotravel.com; s/d €40/60; ✵) There's no sign reading 'males forbidden', but rest assured that the Mascot is female-only. A few blocks back from the beach, it's a bohemian place with 10 snug modern rooms with balconies. Book through Sappho Travel.

Hotel Sappho (☎ 22530 53233; www.sapphohotel.com; s/d €40/60; ◷ 1 Apr-15 Oct; ✵ ☞) The Sappho was the village's first women-only hotel, but has since gone co-ed. While it has thus lost some street cred among the lesbian set, the Sappho still has a prime waterfront setting, smartly appointed rooms and free wi-fi.

EATING

Skala Eresou's restaurants and bars line the beach, the latter to the eastern side. On clear days Chios emerges on the horizon.

Eressos Palace (☎ 22530 5385; mains €6-10) A good *psarotaverna* on the western edge, it also does grills and purveys local Eressos cheese.

Soulatso (☎ 22530 52078; fish €6-13) This busy beachfront place with outdoor patio specialises in fresh fish and other seafood.

DRINKING

Skala Eresou's limited nightlife consists of a contiguous series of cafe-bars strung along the eastern waterfront, several quite pretty.

Tenth Muse (☎ 22530 53287) The first place along the main *plateia* is an old favourite of females, strong on fruit drinks, Haagen-Dazs ice cream and conviviality.

Parasol (☎ 22530 52050) With its orange lanterns further down on the waterfront, it does cocktails that match its South Seas decor.

Margaritari (☎ 22530 53042) Recognisable by its orange furnishings, it's another nice outdoor cafe with great sweets.

Breez (☎ 22530 537108) An ever-so-slick nightspot more popular with young Greeks.

Zorba the Buddha (☎ 22530 53777) The place furthest down on the eastern waterfront is a popular old standby that's full til late.

SOUTHERN LESVOS

Interspersed groves of olive and pine trees mark southern Lesvos, from the flanks of Mt Olympus (968m), the area's highest peak, right down to the sea, where the best beaches lie. This is a hot, intensely agricultural place where the vital olive-oil, wine and ouzo industries overshadow tourism. Southern Lesvos has thus retained authenticity in its villages and solitude on its beaches.

Just south of the Mytilini–Polyhtinos road, **Agiasos** is the first point of interest. On the northern side of Mt Olympus, it's a quirky, well-kept traditional hamlet where village elders sip Greek coffees in the local *kafeneia*, unmindful of time, and local artisans hawk their wares to day-trippers from Mytilini Town. Nevertheless, it's a relaxing, leafy place and boasts the exceptional **Church of the Panagia Vrefokratousa**, which hosts an icon-rich **Byzantine Museum** and **Popular Museum**. Atmospheric accommodation is also available.

Alternatively, the road south that hugs the western side of the Gulf of Gera reaches **Plomari**, the centre of Lesvos' ouzo industry and an attractive seaside village with its large, palm-lined *plateia* and waterfront tavernas. Here see the **Varvagianni Ouzo Museum** (☎ 22520 32741; ⏱ 9am-7pm Mon-Fri, by appointment Sat & Sun). The popular beach settlement of **Agios Isidoros**, 3km east, absorbs most of Plomari's summertime guests. This beach isn't bad but **Tarti**, a bit further east, is nicer and less crowded. West of Plomari, **Melinda** is a tranquil fishing village with beach, tavernas and domatia.

Melinda to Vatera Μελίντα προς Βατερά
DRIVING TOUR

From Melinda, the road less taken to the beach town of Vatera passes through tranquil mountain villages and richly forested hills, and winds between steep gorges offering breathtaking views down to the sea.

Driving north, tiny **Paleohori** is the first village, with very narrow streets and gentle elderly villagers who will peer over their thick glasses curiously at you from *kafeneia* in the hamlet's miniature *plateia*. The old church in the upper town is much grander and more ornate than Paleohori would seem to need. It's usually open and the priest can provide information (in Greek) about its history.

Continuing north from Paleohori, there are sweeping views of the sea and glimpses of even tinier villages nestled in the forested mountains opposite. Take the road west to Akrassio, and then north to **Ambeliko**; even though there's a more direct western route, it's safer to go to Ambeliko first and then, just before reaching it, turn left on the signposted, good-quality dirt road pointing downwards to **Kato Stavros**. This road lasts 9km before reverting to asphalt, and passes through serene olive and pine forests. The total driving time from Melinda to Vatera is little over an hour.

HIKING TRAILS

Hikers here can enjoy southern Lesvos' 'olive trails', which comprise paths and old local roads from Plomari and Melinda. The **Melinda–Paleohori trail** (1.2km, 30 minutes) follows the Selandas River for 200m before ascending to Paleohori, passing a spring with potable water along the way. The trail ends at one of the village's two olive presses. You can continue southwest to **Panagia Kryfti**, a cave church near a hot spring and the nearby **Drota Beach**, or take the **Paleohori–Rahidi trail** (1km, 30 minutes), paved with white stone and passing springs and vineyards. Rahidi, which got electricity only in 2001, has several charming old houses and a *kafeneio*.

Another trail heading northeast from Melinda leads to shady **Kournela** (1.8km, 40 minutes) and from there to **Milos** (800m, 20 minutes), where there's an old flour mill. Alternately, hike to Milos directly from Melinda (2km, one hour) on a trail that hugs the river and passes ruined olive mills, one spring and two bridges, as well as orange and mandarin trees. From Milos, follow the river northeast to **Amaxo** (1.75km, one hour) and be treated to refreshing mountain-spring water in plane, poplar and pine forests.

Other, more complicated hiking trails can get you directly from Melinda to Vatera; consult the **EOT** (☎ 22510 42511; Aristarhou 6; ⏱ 9am-1pm Mon-Fri) in Mytilini Town or a travel agency for precise details.

Vatera & Polyhnitos Βατερά & Πολυχνίτος

Despite its 9km-long sandy beach, Vatera (vah-ter-*ah*), remains a low-key destination, with only a few small hotels and domatia operating, and even fewer bars. Serene Vatera thus remains a perfect destination for families, couples, or anyone looking to get away from it all.

On its western edge, at Cape Agios Fokas, the sparse ruins of an ancient **Temple of Dionysos** occupy a headland overlooking the sea. In the cove between the beach and the cape, evidence has been found indicating an ancient military encampment; indeed, some historians believe this is the place Homer was referring to in the 'Iliad' as the resting point for Greek armies besieging Troy. Legend also says that nearby Vryssa village was named after a Trojan woman, Vrysseida, who died after being contested by two of the victorious Greek fighters. To this day old women and even the occasional baby girl with the name Vrysseida can be found here; the name is not given anywhere else.

Vatera's most remote history has attracted international attention. Fossils have been found here dating back 5.5 million years, including remains of a tortoise as big as a Volkswagen Bug and fossils of a gigantic horse and gazelle. A small **Museum of Natural History** (☎ 22520 61890; admission €1; ⏰ 9.30am-7.30pm), located in Vryssa'a old schoolhouse, displays these and other significant remains. Ongoing excavations mean that more exciting finds may still be made.

Agricultural **Polyhnitos**, 10km north of Vatera on the road back to Mytilini town, is known for its two nearby **hot springs**, one just to the southeast and the other 5km north, outside Lisvorio village. The former, known as the **Polyhnitos Spa** (☎ 22520 41449; admission €3; ⏰ 7am-noon & 3-8pm) is in a pretty, renovated Byzantine building, and has some of Europe's hottest baths temperatures, at 31°C (87.6°F). Rheumatism, arthritis, skin diseases and gynaecological problems are treated here.

The **Lisvorio Spa** (☎ 22530 71245; admission €3; ⏰ 8am-1pm & 3-8pm) consists of two small baths situated around a wooded stream. They're unmarked, so ask around for directions; though the buildings are run-down, bathing is unaffected. The temperature and water properties are similar to those at Polyhnitos.

Some 5km northwest of Polyhnitos, the fishing port of **Skala Polyhnitou** lies on the Gulf of Kallonis. It's a relaxing, though unremarkable place, where caïques bob at the docks and fishermen untangle their nets, and is great for low-key fresh seafood dinners with the locals.

Sleeping & Eating

Agiasos Hotel (☎ 22520 22242; Agiasos; s/d/tr €20/25/30) Next to the Church of Panagia in Agiasos, this friendly place has simple, clean rooms near the centre of the action.

Stratis Kazatzis Rooms (☎ 22520 22539; Agiasos; s/d/tr €20/25/30) Right at the entrance of Agiasos, these handsome rooms are also good value for money. Like the Agiasos Hotel, it's a small place so book ahead.

our pick **Hotel Vatera Beach** (☎ 22520 61212; www .vaterabeach.com; Vatera; s/d €65/90; P ✗ 🖳 ☑) This peaceful beachfront hotel regards its guests, many of whom return annually, as dear old friends. The congenial George and Barbara Ballis and family provide for the common needs of travellers with free multilingual newspapers and internet-equipped computers. Service is kind and courteous, while the hotel's excellent restaurant gets most of its ingredients from the owners' organic farm.

our pick **Psarotaverna O Stratos** (☎ 22520 42910; Skala Polyhnitou; fish €6-9; ⏰ 10am-1am) The best of several fish tavernas on Skala Polyhnitou's waterfront, O Stratos offers excellent and inexpensive fresh seafood, plus salads like *vlita* (wild greens) and tasty mezedhes. The small fishing boats moored right before your table add to the ambience. Service is gracious and attentive.

LIMNOS ΛΗΜΝΟΣ

pop 15,225 / area 482 sq km

Isolated Limnos, all alone in the northeastern Aegean save for neighbouring Agios Efstratios, nevertheless has much to offer to those looking for Greek island life relatively unaffected by modern tourism. Its capital, Myrina, has retained its classic Greek fishing harbour feel, while a grand Genoese castle flanked by beaches provides a dramatic backdrop. In high season, the city's chic cafes and shops are frequented by (mostly Greek) tourists but otherwise the island is quiet, especially in its tranquil inland villages.

Although it's not enormous, Limnos does offer variety. The eastern lakes are visited by spectacular flocks of flamingos and the austere

NORTHEASTERN
AEGEAN ISLANDS

central plain is filled with wildflowers in spring and autumn. Superb sandy beaches lie near the capital, as well as in more distant and intimate corners of the island. For even more isolation, you can visit Limnos' tiny island dependency of Agios Efstratios (see p393) to the south, which also boasts serene beaches and fresh fish.

Limnos is notorious for its strong summer winds, which make the island great for windsurfing; in late summer, it also suffers the curse of the northernmost Aegean islands: jellyfish. However, to Greeks it's perhaps best known as being the central command post of the Hellenic Air Force – a strategic decision, as Limnos is in an ideal position for monitoring the Straits of the Dardanelles leading into İstanbul. For this very reason the island was used as the operational base for the failed Gallipoli campaign in WWI; a moving military cemetery for fallen Commonwealth soldiers remains near Moudros, where the Allied ships were based.

Limnos, and especially its sparsely populated dependency of Agios Efstratios, are almost unvisited by tourists out of high season, though the steady population of the military

keeps Myrina more active than other small island capitals.

Getting There & Away

For flights and ferries from Limnos, see Island Hopping (p517).

AIR

The airport is 22km east of Myrina; taxis cost about €16.

Olympic Air (☎ 22540 22214; www.olympicairlines .com; Nikolaou Garoufallidou) is opposite Hotel Paris in Myrina.

BOAT

Buy ferry and hydrofoil tickets at Pravlis Travel (opposite) or Myrina Tourist & Travel Agency (opposite). The latter also sells tickets (one way/return €8/15) for day trips to Agios Efstratios on the *Aeolis* ferry, which depart every Sunday at 8am and return at 5pm.

Getting Around

BUS

Limnos' bus service has one diabolical purpose: to bring villagers to town for their morning shopping and to get them home by lunch. Going and returning by bus in the same day is only possible to four destinations, by no means the most interesting ones, either. For example, two morning buses serve Plaka, but only return the next day at 7am and 8.45am (€4.60, 1¼ hours). Similarly, two morning buses go to Skandali, only returning the next day at 7am (€4.60, 1¼ hours) and two morning buses serve Kontias, returning the next day at 7am and 9am (€2.40, 45 minutes). Two daily buses to Katalakos – a measly 25-minute trip – only return at 8.30am and 1.30pm (€1.80).

Also from Myrina, five daily buses serve Moudros, via the airport (€2.80, 30 minutes), with the last return bus leaving at 12.15pm.

Myrina's **bus station** (☎ 22540 22464; Plateia Eleftheriou Venizelou) displays schedules and has printed copies.

CAR & MOTORCYCLE
Myrina Rent-a-Car (right), near the waterfront, charges from €30 per day. Motorcycle-hire outlets are on Kyda-Karatza.

TAXI
A **taxi rank** (☎ 22540 23033) is on Myrina's central square, by the bus station.

MYRINA MYPINA
pop 5110

Backed by volcanic rock and a craggy Genoese castle, Limnos' capital is a striking place. Despite some tourism, it keeps a certain serenity, harking back to its roots as a fishing port. Here you'll see old fishermen sip Greek coffee while unfolding their nets, and colourful caïques in the harbour. Beyond the castle lies a sandy beach, and another, less windy one beyond that.

In summer Myrina comes to life, with shops selling traditional foods, handicrafts and more in its bustling *agora*. Its whitewashed stone houses, old-fashioned barber shops and *kafeneia*, crumbling neoclassical mansions and wood-balconied homes all create a relaxed feel.

The town (and Limnos in general) is mostly frequented by Greek tourists, and this has given a strongly Hellenic flavour to its nightlife, with the most popular places being stylish beachfront bars. Despite the hubbub, however, the castle's overgrown hill is inhabited by shy, fleet-footed deer who dart around at night; in winter, locals say, they even wander through the *agora* – presumably, to do their shopping.

Orientation
From the quay turn right onto Plateia Ilia Iliou. Continue past Hotel Lemnos and the town hall, turning left after the derelict Hotel Action, then immediately veer half-left onto the main thoroughfare Kyda-Karatza to reach Myrina's central square. Continue and you'll find Plateia Eleftheriou Venizelou and the bus station.

Information
ATM-equipped banks line the central square. The summertime tourist info kiosk on the quay sometimes works.

Excite-Net (☎ 22540 25525; internet per hr €1.50; ☽ 24hr) Waterfront internet cafe.

Myrina Rent-a-Car (☎ 22540 24476; Kyda-Karatza) Near the waterfront.

Myrina Tourist & Travel Agency (☎ 22540 22460; mirina@lim.forthnet.gr) Full-service agency on the waterfront.

Police station (☎ 22540 22201; Nikolaou Garoufallidou)

Port police (☎ 22540 22225)

Post office (Nikolaou Garoufallidou)

Pravlis Travel (☎ 22540 22471; pravlis@lim.forthnet .gr; Parasidi 15) For ferry tickets.

SAOS Ferries (☎ 22540 29571) Sells ferry tickets from a small compartment on the castle side of the waterfront.

Theodoros Petrides Travel Agency (☎ 22540 22039; www.petridestravel.gr; Kyda-Karatza 116) Offers sightseeing tours on the island, car hire and accommodation bookings.

Sights & Activities
Myrina's **castle** occupies a headland that divides the town from its popular beach. The sea views from here extend to Mt Athos. From the harbour, take the first side street to the left by an old Turkish fountain, where the castle is signposted. At night, sitting in front of the church on the northeastern side of the castle gives great views of the cafe lights down below and, if you're lucky, quick glimpses of bounding deer in the darkness to the left.

Myrina's beaches include the wide and sandy **Rea Maditos**, and a superior **Romeïkos Gialos**, beyond the harbour; it's accessible by taking any left from Kyda-Karatza as you're walking inland. Further on, it becomes **Riha Nera** (shallow water), named for its gently shelving, child-friendly seafloor. There's nightlife here too.

Five minutes south on the road towards Thanos Beach, **Platy Beach** is a shallow, sandy beach popular with locals, and has beach bars and restaurants.

Myrina's **archaeological museum** (admission €2; ☼ 9am-3pm Tue-Sun) occupies a neoclassical mansion overlooking Romeïkos Gialos beach, and contains finds from Limnos' three sites of Poliohni, the Sanctuary of the Kabeiroi and Hephaistia.

From June to September, Theodoros Petrides Travel Agency (p391) organises round-the-island **boat trips** (€20), with stops for swimming and lunch.

Sleeping

Hotel Filoktitis (☎ /fax 22540 23344; Ethnikis Andistasis 14; s/d €40/50; ✖) This welcoming hotel has airy, well-equipped rooms just inland of Riha Nera Beach. Follow Maroulas (the continuation of Kyda-Karatza) and then Ethnikis Andistasis; the hotel is located above the quite fine restaurant of the same name.

Hotel Lemnos (☎ 22540 22153; s/d €45/60; ✖) The harbour-side Lemnos has friendly staff and modern rooms with balconies overlooking the waterfront or castle.

Apollo Pavillion (☎ /fax 22540 23712; www.apollo pavilion.com; studios incl breakfast from €60; ✖) Tucked behind the port in a neoclassical house, the popular Apollo Pavillion offers large rooms with kitchenette and balcony. Walk along Nikolaou Garoufallidou from Kyda-Karatza and the sign is 150m along on the right.

Lemnos Village Hotel (☎ 22540 23500; www.lemnos villagehotel.com; Platy Beach; s/d/tr €50/60/70; P ✖ ☎) Just out of town on Platy Beach, this chic resort-type hotel offers many more amenities for the price than Myrina's simpler places (partly why it's popular with foreign groups).

To Arhontiko (☎ 22540 29800; cnr Sahtouri & Filellinon; s/d/tr €50/65/80; ✖) This restored mansion dating from 1814 has lovely boutique rooms with simple charm, and helpful, friendly staff. It's located on a quiet alley near the main shopping street, one street back from the beach.

Nefeli Guest Rooms (☎ 22540 22825; d/tr/q €100/120/150; P ✖ ▣) This intimate place features handsome stone rooms with great sea views high above the town. It's up the hill from the castle, next to the cafe of the same name.

Eating

ourpick Ouzeri To 11 (☎ 22540 22635; Plateia KTEL; seafood mezedhes €4.50-7) This unassuming little

ouzerie by the bus depot is the local favourite for seafood. From *kydonia* (mussels with garlic and Venus clams) to limpets, sea urchins, crayfish and more, 'To *En*-dheka' (as it's pronounced) serves all the strange stuff, along with plenty of ouzo to make you forget what you're eating.

O Platanos Taverna (☎ 22540 22070; mains €5-8) *Mayirefta* with an emphasis on meats are served at this iconic place under a giant plane tree, halfway along Kyda-Karatza.

O Sozos (☎ 22540 25085; Platy village; mains €5-8) In the mountain village of Platy, just east of Myrina, O Sozos is popular for its traditional fare. Specialities include *Kokkaras Flomaria* (rooster served with pasta).

Tzitzifies (☎ 22540 23756; fish from €7) Fresh fish and meat dishes are available at this worthwhile taverna with excellent sea views through beachfront trees.

Drinking

Myrina's summer nightlife is centred around the bars above Romeïkos Gialos beach.

Karagiozis (Romeïkos Gialos beach; ☼ 9am-5am) This popular place, on a leafy terrace near the sea, is busy until late.

Kinky Bar (☎ 6973667489; ☼ midnight-5am Wed, Fri & Sat) The island's only real club is a stylish place surrounded by trees and very popular with Greeks. It operates three days a week, from June through August only. Find it in Avlonas (3km from town) on the road towards Agios Ioannis Beach and Kaspakas.

WESTERN LIMNOS

North of Myrina, the road left after **Kaspakas** village accesses the fairly quiet **Agios Ioannis Beach**, with a few tavernas and beach houses. The beach ends with the aptly named **Rock Café**, set nicely beneath a large overhanging volcanic slab.

After Kaspakas, drive east and turn left at **Kornos**, and follow the road northwards to remote **Gomati Beach** on the north coast; a good dirt road gets there from **Katalako**.

Alternatively, drive east from Kaspakas and continue past Kornos, turning south at **Livadohori**. This road passes barren, tawny hills and modest farmlands. Further south along the coast, **Kontias** is a fairly prosaic, plastered old village now inexplicably popular among Northern European property hunters. Below Kontias the road swings southwest back to Myrina, on the way passing the sandy **Nevgatis**

Beach and **Thanos Beach**. Although they're very popular and get crowded, these beaches are truly idyllic and only a 10-minute drive from Myrina.

CENTRAL LIMNOS

Central Limnos' flat plateaus are dotted with wheat fields, small vineyards and sheep – plus the Greek Air Force's central command (large parts are thus off-limits to tourists). Limnos' second-largest town, **Moudros**, occupies the eastern side of muddy Moudros Bay, famous for its role as the principal base for the ill-fated Gallipoli campaign in February 1915.

The **East Moudros Military Cemetery**, with the graves of Commonwealth soldiers from the Gallipoli campaign, is 1km east of Moudros on the Roussopouli road. Here you can read a short history of the Gallipoli campaign. A second Commonwealth cemetery, **Portianos War Cemetery** (6km south of Livadohori on the road to Thanos Beach and Myrina) is the area's other sombre attraction.

EASTERN LIMNOS

Historical remnants and remote beaches draw visitors to eastern Limnos. Its three **archaeological sites** (admission free; ⏰ 8am-7pm) include four ancient settlements at **Poliohni** on the southeast coast, the most significant being a pre-Mycenaean city that pre-dated Troy VI (1800–1275 BC). The site is well presented, but remains are few.

The second site, the **Sanctuary of the Kabeiroi** (Ta Kaviria), lies on remote Tigani Bay. The worship of the Kabeiroi gods here actually pre-dates that which took place on Samothraki (p396). The major site, a **Hellenistic sanctuary**, has 11 columns. Nearby, the legendary **Cave of Philoctetes** is supposedly where that Trojan War hero was abandoned while his gangrenous, snake-bitten leg healed. A path from the site leads to the sea cave; there's also a narrow, unmarked entrance to the left past the main entrance.

To reach the sanctuary, take the left-hand turn-off after **Kontopouli** for 5km; from Kontopouli itself, a dirt road accesses the third site, **Hephaistia** (Ta Ifestia), once Limnos' main city. It's where Hephaestus, god of fire and metallurgy, was hurled down from Mt Olympus by Zeus. Little remains, however, other than low walls and a partially excavated theatre.

Limnos' northeastern tip has some rustic, little-visited villages, plus remote **Keros Beach**, popular with windsurfers. Flocks of flamingos sometimes strut on shallow **Lake Alyki**. From Cape Plaka, at Limnos' northeastern tip, Samothraki and Imvros (Gökçeada in Turkish) are visible. These three islands were historically considered as forming a strategic triangle for the defence of the Dardanelles, and thus İstanbul (Constantinople); this was Turkey's case for clinging to Imvros in 1923, even after Greece had won back most of its other islands a decade earlier.

AGIOS EFSTRATIOS
ΑΓΙΟΣ ΕΥΣΤΡΑΤΙΟΣ

pop 370

Little-visited Agios Efstratios lies isolated in the Aegean, south of Limnos (p389). Abbreviated by locals as 'Aï-Stratis', it attracts a few curious visitors drawn by the island's fine, remote beaches and generally escapist feel. They certainly don't come for the architecture: a 1968 earthquake destroyed Agios Efstratios' classic buildings. Nevertheless, this sparsely populated place has domatia, good seafood tavernas, relaxing hill walks and beaches (some accessible only by boat).

Agios Efstratios has had a chequered past. Even before the quake, many dissidents and suspected communists were exiled here, including the composer Mikis Theodorakis and poets Kostas Varnalis and Giannis Ritsos.

Sights & Activities

The **village beach** has dark volcanic sand and warm waters. A 90-minute walk northeast leads to **Alonitsi Beach**, a long, idyllic strand with intriguing facing islets. Take the track from the village's northeast side, starting by a small bridge; when it splits, keep right. **Lidario Beach**, on the west side, is a much tougher walk, so go by local boat to this and other hard-to-reach beaches.

Sleeping & Eating

Book rooms from Limnos with Myrina Tourist & Travel Agency (p391) or Theodoros Petrides Travel Agency (p391), or else find domatia upon arrival; only in high summer might things be crowded. The island's few tavernas offer inexpensive fare and fresh seafood.

Getting There & Away

For ferry and hydrofoil information from Agios Efstratios, see Island Hopping (p508). Buy tickets at Myrina Tourist & Travel Agency (p391) in Myrina. Bad weather can cause unpredictable cancellations and delays.

SAMOTHRAKI
ΣΑΜΟΘΡΑΚΗ

pop 2720 / area 176 sq km

Lush Samothraki sits contentedly alone in the northeastearn Aegean, halfway between the mainland port of Alexandroupoli and Limnos to the south. This thickly forested island is relatively small, with few settlements, and is rarely visited out of high season, though it does boast one of the most important archaeological sites in Greece in the ancient Thracian Sanctuary of the Great Gods. Also here stands the Aegean's loftiest peak, Mt Fengari (1611m), from where Homer recounts that Poseidon, god of the sea, watched the Trojan War unfold.

Samothraki's mountainous interior is totally unpopulated, and full of valleys bursting with massive gnarled oak and plane trees, making it ideal for hiking and mountain biking. Outdoors lovers will especially want to

seek out Samothraki's woodlands waterfalls, which plunge into deep, icy pools, providing cool relief on a hot summer's day. The island's remote beaches in the southeast are idyllic and pristine, while the west offers therapeutic hot baths at Loutra (Therma). The main port, sleepy Kamariotissa, is a whimsical fishing village, while the hilly former inland capital, Hora, is bursting with flowers and pretty traditional homes, all overlooking the distant sea.

While the famous electronic music festival seems to have been killed off due to local irritation with its spaced-out guests, the proliferation of safari hats, dreadlocks and Hindu symbols lingers, perpetuating Samothraki's exotic, jungle vibe. Although the island's remoteness and poor transport links mean that it's often forgotten by foreign island-hoppers, devotees of ancient archaeology and outdoors sorts will find this unique and laid-back island very much worth the effort it takes to get here.

Getting There & Away

For ferry and hydrofoil information from Samothraki, see Island Hopping (p522). Niki Tours (opposite) in Kamariotissa sells tickets.

Getting Around

BOAT

In summer the tour boat **Samothraki** (☎ 25510 42266) circles the island (€20), departing Loutra (Therma) at 11am and returning by 6.30pm. The boat passes sights like the Byzantine castle

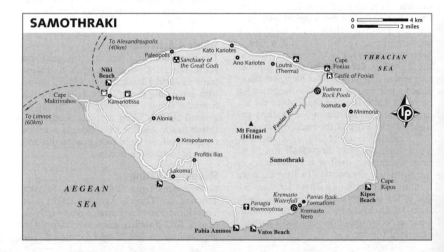

SAMOTHRAKI

0 —————— 4 km
0 —————— 2 miles

To Alexandroupolis (40km)

Paleopolis
Kato Kariotes
Sanctuary of the Great Gods
Ano Kariotes
Loutra (Therma)
Cape Fonias
Niki Beach
THRACIAN SEA
Cape Makrivrahos
Kamariotissa
Hora
Castle of Fonias
Vathres Rock Pools
To Limnos (60km)
Alonia
Isomata
Mnimoria
Fonias River
Xiropotamos
Mt Fengari (1611m)
Profitis Ilias
Samothraki
Lakoma
Cape Kipos
Kipos Beach
Kremasto Waterfall
Panias Rock Formations
Panagia Kremniotissa
Kremasto Nero
AEGEAN SEA
Pahia Ammos
Vatos Beach

of Fonias, the Panias rock formations and Kremasto Waterfall, before stopping at 1pm for four hours of swimming and sunbathing at Vatos Beach. A snack bar operates on board. For more information, ask at Petrinos Kipos Taverna in Kamariotissa or call the boat operator.

BUS

In summer 10 buses daily go from Kamariotissa **bus station** (☎ 25513 41533) to Hora (€1) and eight to Loutra (Therma; €2) via Paleopolis (€1). Some Loutra buses continue to the two camping grounds. Five daily buses serve Profitis Ilias (€2) via Alonia and Lakoma.

CAR & MOTORCYCLE

For vehicle hire, on Kamariotissa's waterfront opposite the buses, **X Rentals** (☎ 25510 42272) has cars and small jeeps, as does **Kyrkos Rent a Car** (☎ 25510 41620, 6972839231). **Rent A Motor Bike** (☎ 25510 41057), opposite the quay, offers motorcycles and scooters.

TAXI

Taxis from Kamariotissa access most destinations, including Hora (€5), Pahia Ammos (€15), Profitis Ilias (€7.50), Sanctuary of the Great Gods (€5), Loutra (Therma; €7.50), first camping ground (€8.50), second camping ground (€9.50), Fonias River (€12), and Kipos Beach (€17).

For a taxi, call the English- and German-speaking company **Petros Glinias** (☎ 6972883501) or other **taxi companies** (☎ 25510 41733, 25510 41341, 25510 41077).

KAMARIOTISSA ΚΑΜΑΡΙΩΤΙΣΣΑ

pop 960

Samothraki's port, largest town and transport hub, Kamariotissa has the island's main services and a nearby pebble beach with bars and decent swimming. While most visitors don't linger, it's a likeable enough port town filled with flowers and good fish tavernas, and roughly equidistant from Samothraki's more famous attractions.

Orientation & Information

Turn left from the ferry and you'll find a tourist information kiosk 50m along the road running along the water, on the port side. Buses wait behind this kiosk further east on the waterfront. Across the road are tavernas, travel and car- and motorcycle-hire agencies, and ATMs. Follow the waterfront further east for 100m to reach Kamariotissa's beach.

Café Action (☎ 25510 41056; internet per hr €4) At the harbour's west end.

Niki Tours (☎ 25510 41465; niki _tours@hotmail.com) A helpful, full-service travel agency, across from the buses.

Port police (☎ 25510 41305) East along the waterfront.

Tourist Information Kiosk (☎ 25510 89242) On the port.

www.samothraki.com General information about Samothraki, including boat schedules.

www.samothrace.gr Another online resource (Greek-only), with important phone numbers.

Activities

Haris Hatzigiannakoudis at Niki Tours runs a **Capoeira Camp** (a Brazilian martial art/dance) with Brazilian master Lua Rasta annually in late June, and can organise **hiking safaris** to Mt Fengari. As many of Samothraki's lush inland hiking trails are poorly marked or unmarked completely, and since the island has no official mountaineering guide, see Haris if interested in serious hiking here.

Festivals & Events

Although disapproving local authorities seem to have pulled the plug on Samothraki's natty-haired world music festival, there's always talk of a resurrection. Meanwhile, the island has somehow become a gathering point for Greek motorcyclists – a sort of Hell's Angels-meets-the-hippies juxtaposition with many intriguing possible outcomes. Check for festival news online or with Niki Tours.

Sleeping

Domatia are arranged at the port-side tourist information kiosk or Niki Tours, and are also signposted.

Niki Beach Hotel (☎ 25510 41545; s/d €45/60) This spacious hotel with large, modern rooms has a lovely garden and is fronted by poplar trees, opposite the town beach.

Hotel Aeolos (☎ 25510 41595; s/d incl breakfast €60/80; ⚄ ⚅) Up behind Niki Beach Hotel, the Aeolos stands on a hill overlooking the sea and has comfortable rooms. Front rooms face the large swimming pool and garden, while the back ones have views of Mt Fengari.

Eating

Klimitaria Restaurant (☎ 25510 41535; mains from €6) This waterfront eatery serves an unusual speciality called *gianiotiko*, an oven-baked dish of diced pork, potatoes, egg and more, as well as the usual taverna fare.

I Synantisi (☎ 25510 41308; fish €6-10) For fresh fish at good prices, head to this hard-working outdoor *ouzerie* on the central waterfront. View the daily catch, on ice inside.

HORA ΧΩΡΑ

Set within a natural fortress of two sheer cliffs, and with a commanding view of the sea, Hora (also called Samothraki) was the obvious choice for the island's capital. In the 10th century the Byzantines built a castle on its northwestern peak, though today's substantial remains mostly date from the 15th-century rule of Genoese lord Palamidi Gattilusi, who married into the last Byzantine imperial dynasty, the Palaeologi.

Marked by curving cobbled streets wreathed in flowers and colourful, crumbling traditional houses topped by terracotta roofs, Hora is perfect for ambling and enjoying a leisurely lunch or coffee. The great views and constant interplay of angles, shadows and colour make it fun for photographers, and in summer there's subdued nightlife in Hora's small streets and roof bars.

Orientation & Information

Buses and taxis stop in the square, below the village. Walk upwards along the main street, following the signs for the *kastro* (castle). Here are the OTE, Agricultural Bank and post office. The **police station** (☎ 25510 41203) is in Gattilusi's castle. Cafes and tavernas are found higher on the street and, on the right, there's a small fountain with fresh mountain spring water.

Sleeping

Hora has a few domatia. Midway up the main street, **Kyra Despina** (☎ 6974980263; s/d €45/60), who speaks some English, has fan-only, self-catering studios with sweeping views, sleeping up to four people.

Eating & Drinking

ourpick **O Lefkos Pyrgos** (☎ 25510 41601; desserts €4-6; ☺ 9am-3am Jul-Aug) The summer-only Lefkos Pyrgos is an excellent and inventive sweets shop run by master desserts inven-

tor Georgios Stergiou and wife Dafni. Only all-natural ingredients are used, without preservatives or artificial flavourings. The lemonade sweetened with honey and cinnamon is very refreshing on a hot summer's day, and some unique variations on traditional fare (like Greek yoghurt flavoured with bitter almond) are also on offer. Exotic teas, coffees and mixed drinks are also served, along with a variety of indulgent cakes and other desserts.

Café-Ouzeri 1900 (☎ 25510 41224; mains €5-9) This relaxing taverna set under a shady trellis left of the fountain offers friendly service and great views of the village's red rooftops, castle and sea. Try the *spetsofaï* (stewed green peppers, tomatoes and sausage in an earthen pot), rice with seafood, or *tzigerosarmades* (goat flavoured with onion, dill and spearmint). The large, colourful menu, printed to look like a newspaper, is a take-home memento.

Meltemi (☎ 25510 41071; ☺ 8am-late) Higher up in Hora, the side street to the left, opposite the fountain, leads to this cool bar with great views and roof garden popular by night.

SANCTUARY OF THE GREAT GODS
ΤΟ ΙΕΡΟ ΤΩΝ ΜΕΓΑΛΩΝ ΘΕΩΝ

Some 6km northeast of Kamariotissa, the **Sanctuary of the Great Gods** (admission €3, free Sun 1 Nov- 31 Mar & public holidays; ☺ 8.30am-4pm Tue-Sun), is one of Greece's most important – and mysterious – archaeological sites. The Thracians built this temple to their Great Gods around 1000 BC. By the 5th century BC, the secret rites associated with the cult had attracted many famous ancient figures. Among the initiates were Egyptian Queen Arsinou and Philip II of Macedon. Remarkably, the Sanctuary operated until paganism was forbidden in the 4th century AD.

The principal deity, the Great Mother (Alceros Cybele), was a fertility goddess; when the original Thracian religion became integrated with the state religion, she was merged with the Olympian female deities Demeter, Aphrodite and Hecate. The last of these was a mysterious goddess associated with darkness, the underworld and witchcraft. Other deities worshipped here were the Great Mother's consort, the virile young Kadmilos (god of the phallus), later integrated with the Olympian god Hermes, and the demonic Kabeiroi twins, Dardanos and Aeton, later integrated with Castor and Pollux (the Dioscuri), the twin sons of Zeus and Leda. These twins were invoked by mariners to protect them while at sea. Samothraki's Great Gods were venerated for their immense power; in comparison, the bickering Olympian gods were considered frivolous, fickle and almost comic characters.

Little is known about what actually transpired here – no surprise, since initiates who revealed the rites were punished by death. The archaeological evidence, however, points to two initiations, a lower and a higher. In the first, the Great Gods were invoked to grant the initiate a spiritual rebirth; in the second, the candidate was absolved of transgressions. Anybody who wanted could be initiated.

The site's most celebrated relic, the *Winged Victory of Samothrace* (now in the Louvre), was found by Champoiseau, the French consul, at Adrianople (present-day Edirne, Turkey) in 1863. Subsequent excavations were sporadic until just before WWII, when Karl Lehmann and Phyllis Williams Lehmann of the Institute of Fine Arts, New York University, directed an organised dig.

Exploring the Site

The site is extensive but well labelled. After entering, take the left-hand path to the rectangular **anaktoron**. At its southern end was a **sacristy**, the antechamber where white-gowned candidates assembled before going to the *anaktoron's* main room for their first (lower) initiation. One by one, each initiate would then enter the small inner temple at the structure's northern end, where a priest would explain the ceremony's symbols. Afterwards the initiates received a sort of initiation certificate in the sacristy.

Sacrifices occurred in the **arsinoein**, southwest of the *anaktoron*. Once a grand cylindrical structure, it was built in 289 BC as a gift to the Great Gods from Egyptian Queen Arsinou. Southeast stands the **sacred rock**, the site's original altar.

Following the initiations, a celebratory feast was held, probably south of the *arsinoein* in the **temenos** – a gift from Philip II. Adjacent is the prominent Doric **hieron**, the sanctuary's most photographed ruin, with five reassembled columns. Initiates received their second (higher) initiation here.

Opposite the *hieron* stand remnants of a **theatre**. Nearby, a path ascends to the **Nike monument** where once stood the magnificent

Winged Victory of Samothrace, a gift from Demetrius Poliorketes (the 'besieger of cities') to the Kabeiroi for helping him defeat Ptolemy II in battle. The ruins of a massive **stoa**, a two-aisled portico where pilgrims to the sanctuary sheltered, lie to the northwest. Initiates' names were recorded on its walls. Ruins of an unrelated **medieval fortress** lie just north.

A good **site map** is located on the path east from the Nike monument; the path continues to the southern **necropolis**, Samothraki's most important ancient cemetery, used from the Bronze Age to early Roman times. North of the cemetery once stood the sanctuary's elaborate Ionic entrance, the **propylon**, a gift from Ptolemy II.

The site ticket includes the **museum** (☎ 25510 41474; ⏱ 8.30am-3pm Tue-Sun), whose exhibits include terracotta figurines, vases, jewellery and a plaster cast of the *Winged Victory of Samothrace*.

AROUND SAMOTHRAKI
Loutra (Therma) Λουτρά (Θερμά)

Loutra (also called Therma) is 14km east of Kamariotissa and near the coast, and represents Samothraki's most popular place to stay. This relaxing village of plane and horse-chestnut trees, dense greenery and gurgling creeks comes to life at night when the young people staying in local domatia or the nearby camping grounds congregate in its laid-back outdoor cafe.

The village's synonymous names refer to its therapeutic, mineral-rich springs; the **thermal bath** (☎ 25510 98229; admission €3; ⏱ 7-10.45am & 4-7.45pm Jun-Sep) reportedly cures everything from skin problems and liver ailments to infertility. The prominent white building by the bus stop houses the official bath; however, bathing for free is possible at another indoor bath, 50m up the road to the right, and at two small outdoor baths another 20m up the hill.

SLEEPING & EATING

Samothraki's two popular camping grounds occupy the beach east of Loutra. They are both called 'Multilary Camping' (no, they don't mean 'Military') and are similar. If you come out of season, you can usually stay for free.

Multilary Camping I (Camping Plateia; ☎ 25510 41784; camp sites per adult/tent €4/3; ⏱ Jun-Aug) A shady, laid-back place on the left 2km beyond Loutra.

Multilary Camping II (☎ 25510 41491; camp sites per adult/tent €5/3; ⏱ Jun-Aug) Just past Multilary

Camping I, with a minimarket, restaurant and showers.

Studios Ktima Holovan (☎ 25510 98335, 6976695591; d/tr €70/80) Located 16km east of Kamariotissa, this relaxing place has very modern, two-room self-catering studios set on a grassy lawn 50m from the beach, and a mini-playground for kids. The price also includes a free hire car.

Mariva Bungalows (☎ 25510 98230; d incl breakfast €80; 🔀) These secluded bungalows, with breezy modern rooms, sit on a lush hillside near a waterfall. To reach them, turn from the coast road inland towards Loutra, and then take the first left. Follow the signs to the bungalows (600m further).

Kafeneio Ta Therma (☎ 25510 98325) This big open cafe near the baths is always full, whether for coffee in the morning, beer at night or homemade fruit sweets at any time.

Loutra has fast food like souvlaki, though **Paradisos Restaurant** (☎ 25510 95267; mains €5-8) and **Fengari Restaurant** (☎ 25510 98321; mains €5.50-9) have good sit-down fare; try the latter's stuffed goat or *imam tourlou* (roast eggplant stuffed with potatoes and pumpkin).

Fonias River

After Loutra on the northeast coast is the Fonias River, and the famous **Vathres rock pools** (admission €1). The walk starts at the bridge 4.7km east of Loutra, by the (summer-only) ticket booths. The first 40 minutes are easy and on a well-marked track leading to a large rock pool fed by a dramatic 12m-high waterfall. The cold water is very refreshing on a hot summer's day. The river is known as the 'Murderer', and in winter rains can transform the waters into a raging torrent. The real danger, however, is getting lost: though there are six waterfalls, marked paths only run to the first two; after that, the walk becomes dangerously confusing. For serious hiking here and in the Mt Fengari area, consult Niki Tours (p395) in Kamariotissa.

Beaches

The 800m-long **Pahia Ammos Beach** is a superb sandy beach along an 8km winding road from Lakoma on the south coast. In summer, caïques from Kamariotissa visit. The boat tour from Loutra stops around the headland at the equally superb, nudist-friendly **Vatos Beach**.

The formerly Greek-inhabited island of Imvros (Gökçeada), ceded to Turkey under the Treaty of Lausanne in 1923, is sometimes visible from Pahia Ammos.

Pebbled **Kipos Beach** on the southeast coast, accessed via the road skirting the north coast, is pretty but shadeless; like the others, it's reached in summer by caïque or excursion boat.

Other Villages

The small villages of **Profitis Ilias**, **Lakoma** and **Xiropotamos** in the southwest, and **Alonia** near Hora, are all serene and seldom visited, though they're easily accessible. The hill-side Profitis Ilias, with many trees and springs, has several tavernas; **Vrahos** (☎ 25510 95264) is particularly famous for its roast goat.

THASOS ΘΑΣΟΣ

pop 13,530

One of Greece's greenest and most gentle islands, Thasos lies 10km from mainland Kavala. While similar climate and vegetation gives the feeling that the island is but an extension of northern Greece, it boasts enviable sandy beaches and a gorgeous, forested mountain interior. It's also quite inexpensive by Greek island standards and is one of the most popular with families, as well as young people from the greater Balkan 'neighbourhood' of Bulgaria and the ex-Yugoslav republics. Frequent ferries from the mainland allow independent travellers crossing northern Greece to get here quickly, and the excellent bus network makes getting around easy.

Over its long history, Thasos has often benefited from its natural wealth. The Parians who founded the ancient city of Thasos (Limenas) in 700 BC struck gold at Mt Pangaion, creating an export trade lucrative enough to subsidise a naval fleet. While the gold is long gone, Thasos' white marble – said to be the second whitest in the world – is still being exploited, unfortunately blighting the mountainside with quarries in the process. Environmentalists have criticised this, and the (subdued) exploration for offshore oil between Thasos and Kavala.

For visitors today, however, the island's main source of wealth stems from its natural beauty and some notable historic attractions. The excellent archaeological museum in the capital, Thasos (Limenas) is complemented by the Byzantine Monastery of Arhangelou, with its stunning cliff-top setting, and the ancient Greek temple on the serene southern beach of Alyki.

While some of Thasos' best beaches have been afflicted by shabby package tourism, untouched spots remain. And, considering that the relatively short 'high season' runs essentially from mid-July to mid-August, it's possible at other times to enjoy peaceful moments on this so-called 'emerald isle'.

Living as it does largely from tourism, Thasos' shuttered domatia and hotels seem lonely out of season. Only the capital, Limenas, has a few functioning hotels in winter.

Getting There & Away

Thasos is only accessible from Kavala and Keramoti on the mainland (for details, see Island Hopping, p515). In Kavala, ferries dock on the long eastern harbour while hydrofoils wait on the dock opposite the harbour, just behind the main intercity (IC) bus station, beside the small port police kiosk.

On Thasos itself, get ferry schedules at the **ferry ticket booths** (☎ 25930 22318) in Thasos (Limenas) and the **port police** (☎ 25930 22106) at Skala Prinou. The ferry dock for Keramoti is 150m west of Thasos town centre.

Getting Around

BICYCLE

Basic bikes can be hired in Thasos (Limenas), but top-of-the-line models and detailed route information are available in Potos from local mountain biking expert, **Yiannis Raizis** (☎ 25930 52459, 6946955704; www.mtb-thassos.com).

BOAT

The **Eros 2 excursion boat** (☎ 6944945282; day trip €25) makes full-day trips around Thasos four times weekly, with stops for swimming and a barbecue. The boat departs the Old Harbour at 10am. Water taxis run regularly to Hrysi Ammoudia (Golden Beach) and Makryammos Beach from the Old Harbour. Excursion boats of varying sizes, nationalities and alcohol content also set sail regularly from the coastal resorts.

BUS

Frequent buses circle the coast in both directions and service inland villages too. Buses meet arriving ferries at Skala Prinou and Thasos (Limenas), the island's transport hub. The two port towns are connected by eight daily buses (€1.80).

Daily buses go 10 to 12 times a day from Thasos (Limenas) through west-coast villages like Skala Marion (€3.30) to Limenaria (€4), with seven continuing to Potos (€4.20). Five daily buses connect Thasos (Limenas) with Theologos (€5.30). From Thasos (Limenas) four buses daily go further south to Alyki (€3.30) and nearby Moni Arhangelou. From Potos you can follow the same route to these places on to the east coast and Paradise Beach (€3.10), Skala Potamia (€3.90) and nearby Hrysi Ammoudia (Golden Beach) for €4.20.

In summer 10 daily buses go the other way from Thasos (Limenas) to these east-coast villages, servicing Skala Potamia (€1.50) via Panagia (€1.40) and Potamia (€1.40). A full circular tour (about 100km) runs nine times daily (€9.50, 3½ hours), clockwise or anticlockwise. Helpfully, this round-the-island ticket is valid all day, meaning you can jump on and off without paying extra. The **bus station** (☎ 25930 22162) on the Thasos (Limenas) waterfront, provides timetables.

CAR & MOTORCYCLE

Avis Rent a Car Thasos (Limenas) (☎ 25930 22535); Potamia (☎ 25930 61735); Skala Prinou (☎ 25930 72075) is widespread, though smaller, local companies may be cheaper. In Thasos (Limenas), **Billy's Bikes** (☎ 25930 22490), opposite the newsagent, and **2 Wheels** (☎ 25930 23267), on the Prinos road, offer bike and motorcycle hire.

TAXI

The Thasos (Limenas) **taxi rank** (☎ 25930 22391) is on the waterfront, next to the main bus stop. In Potos, a taxi rank with listed prices is besides the main road's bus stop.

THASOS (LIMENAS) ΘΑΣΟΣ (ΛΙΜΕΝΑΣ)
pop 2610 / area 375 sq km

Thasos (also called Limenas), has the island's most services and year-round life, along with a picturesque fishing harbour, sandy beach, shopping, a few ancient ruins and an archaeological museum. Still, considering the relatively expensive accommodation rates and lacklustre restaurant offerings here, and the superior beaches, mountain forests and nightlife further on, lingering isn't necessary.

Orientation & Information

ATM-equipped banks are near the central square. The town beach, backed by waterfront tavernas and beach bars, is about 100m beyond the old harbour, a 10-minute walk from the town centre.

Billias Travel Service (☎ 25930 24003; www
.billias-travel-service.gr; Gallikis Arheologikis Scholis 2)
All-services travel agency.

Mood Café (☎ 25930 23417; cnr 18 Oktovriou & K
Dimitriadi; per hr €3; ☒ 9.30am-2am) Internet cafe with
fast connection.

Port police (☎ 25930 22106)

Tourist police (☎ 25930 23111)

www.gothassos.com Useful online resource.

Sights

Thasos' **archaeological museum** (☎ 25930 22180;
☒ 9am-3pm Tue-Sun) displays Neolithic utensils
from a mysterious central Thasos tomb, plus
Ancient Greek art, including a 5m-tall 6th-
century BC *kouros* carrying a ram.

Next door stand ruins of the **ancient agora**,
the commercial centre in ancient Greek and
Roman times. The foundations of stoas, shops
and dwellings remain. About 100m east of the
agora, the **ancient theatre** stages performances
of ancient dramas and comedies during the
Kavala Festival of Drama. The theatre is signposted from the small harbour.

From here a path leads to the **acropolis**,
where substantial remains of a medieval
fortress stand. Carved rock steps descend to
the foundations of the ancient town walls on
which the fortress was built. There are magnificent views of the coast from here as well.

Festivals & Events

In July and August plays are held in the ancient theatre during the **Kavala Festival of Drama**.
A free **Full moon concert** occurs each August,
featuring singers from all over Greece. The **EOT**
(☎ 25102 22425) in Kavala has information and
tickets, or ask Thasos' **tourist police** (☎ 25930
23111). The summertime **Thasos Festival** includes
classical drama, painting exhibitions and contemporary Greek music. Programs are available at hotels, cafes and tourist agencies.

Sleeping

BUDGET & MIDRANGE

Hotel Possidon (☎ 25930 22739; www.thassos-possidon
.com; Old Harbour; s/d €40/50; ☒ ☎) This friendly
waterfront hotel's recently renovated lobby
bar straddles both the harbour and main
shopping street of 18 Oktovriou. It's one of
the few local hotels that doesn't work with
package-tour companies. Rooms are modern
and well maintained, many with comfortable
water-view balconies.

Hotel Galini (☎ 25930 22195; Theageneou; s/d €44/50;
☒) This small, slightly worn place opposite
the Amfipolis Hotel has 16 simple but clean
rooms. Service is gruff, though a flowery back
garden restores good cheer.

Hotel Akropolis (☎ /fax 25930 22488; M Alexandrou; s/d
incl breakfast €45/55; ☒) This century-old mansion
offers a classic touch, with eclectic antiques
and a relaxing garden, though rooms are
slightly cramped.

Hotel Angelica (☎ 25930 22387; www.hotel-angelica
.gr; Old Harbour; s/d €50/60; ☒) Another waterfront
hotel, the Angelica is a dependable choice,
though not overwhelming. Bathrooms are a
bit dated but clean.

TOP END

Hotel Timoleon (☎ 25930 22177; Old Harbour; s/d €70/100;
☒) Located next to the Hotel Possidon, the
three-star Timoleon has 30 rooms (15 with
sea view) characterised by smooth fixtures
and spacious interiors; considering the price,
though, perhaps not unique enough.

Amfipolis Hotel (☎ 25930 23101; www.hotelamfipolis
.gr; cnr 18 Oktovriou & Theogenous; s/d/tr/ste incl breakfast
€95/140/165/235; ☒ Jun-Oct; ☒ ☎) Thasos'
most elegant hotel occupies this national
heritage–listed building with an imposing
blue facade. A hotel since 1938 and previous
to that a tobacco warehouse, the Amfipolis
has elegant rooms with high, wood-panelled
ceilings, and even a garden Jacuzzi.

Eating & Drinking

Simi (☎ 25930 22517; Old Harbour; mains €7-10) At
first glance, Simi looks like all the other Old

THASOS

0　　　　　6 km
0　　　　4 miles

To Kavala
(10km)
Thasos Strait
To Keramoti
(5km)

Glyfoneri Beach
Pahys Beach
Skala
Rahonis
Cape
Pahis
Cape
Vriokastro

Vasiliou Beach
Cape Prinos
Skala
Prinou
Agios
Georgiou
Thasos
(Limenas)
Makryammos

Prinos
Skala
Sotira
Rahoni
Hrysi Ammoudia
(Golden Beach)
Cape
Pyrgos

Kasaviti
(Megalos
Prinos)
Panagia
Golden Beach
Camping

Kasaviti
(Mikros
Prinos)
Potamia
Skala
Potamia

Camping
Daedalos
Thasos
Maries
Mt Ypsario
(1204m)

Skala
Kallirahis
Kallirahi
Kastro
Kinyra
Kinyra
Islet

Theologos
Paradise
Beach

Kalyvia
Skala
Marion
Limenaria
Moni
Arhangelou
Alyki
Cape
Stavros
Cape Kefalas
Pefkari
Potos

Camping
Pefkari
Astris
Livadi
Beach
Thymonia
Beach
THRACIAN
SEA

To Panagia
Islet (10m)
Cape Salonikios

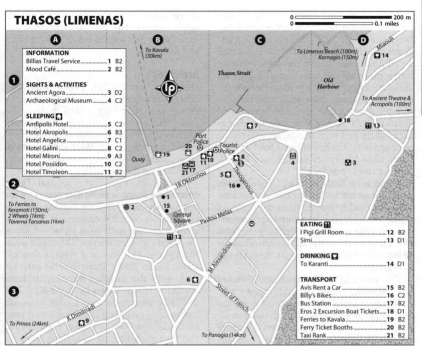

THASOS (LIMENAS)

INFORMATION
Billias Travel Service.................**1** B2
Mood Café...............................**2** B2

SIGHTS & ACTIVITIES
Ancient Agora.........................**3** D2
Archaeological Museum...........**4** C2

SLEEPING
Amfipolis Hotel.......................**5** C2
Hotel Akropolis.......................**6** B3
Hotel Angelica........................**7** C1
Hotel Galini............................**8** C2
Hotel Mironi...........................**9** A3
Hotel Possidon......................**10** C2
Hotel Timoleon......................**11** B2

EATING
I Pigi Grill Room....................**12** B2
Simi.....................................**13** D1

DRINKING
To Karanti............................**14** D1

TRANSPORT
Avis Rent a Car.....................**15** B2
Billy's Bikes..........................**16** C2
Bus Station...........................**17** B2
Eros 2 Excursion Boat Tickets....**18** D1
Ferries to Kavala...................**19** B2
Ferry Ticket Booths...............**20** B2
Taxi Rank.............................**21** B2

Harbour tavernas with touting waiters; however, locals agree that it serves Limenas' best fish. There's taverna fare, too.

I Pigi Grill Room (☎ 25930 22941; Central Square; mains €5-7.50; ☺ dinner) This friendly, central restaurant next to a spring does excellent grills; seafood mezedhes and fresh salads are good, too.

Taverna Tarsanas (☎ 25930 23933; mezedhes €4, mains €10-15) Located 1km west of Thasos, Tarsanas offers great fish and unique seafood mezedhes.

To Karanti (☎ 25930 24014; Miaouli) An outdoor *ouzerie* on the Old Harbour frequented by locals and tourists alike, To Karanti has a picturesque setting overlooking fishing boats, complemented by its traditional music and tasty mezedhes.

Karnagio (☎ 25930 23170) Stroll past the Old Harbour to the end for Karnagio, a nice open spot for a quiet sunset drink. The outdoor seating opens onto both sides of a rocky promontory lapped by waves. You can also clamber up the rocks to the small, candle-lit chapel above.

WEST COAST

Thasos' west coast has been assailed by package tourism for years, though there are still a few idyllic spots and quiet sandy beaches. Better still, the inland mountain villages preserve a traditional pace of life and some fine architecture, without much appreciable damage from the masses. There are ATMs in Skala Prinou, Limenaria and Potos, all large villages with numerous services.

Following the coast west from Thasos (Limenas), two average sandy beaches emerge, **Glyfoneri** and then **Pahys Beach**.

Continuing west, the port of **Skala Prinou** has ferries to Kavala, though little else. However, 1km south, the lovely **Vasiliou Beach** stands backed by trees, and the inland, hillside villages of **Mikros Prinos** and **Megalos Prinos** (collectively known as Kasaviti) offer a refreshingly lush break from the touristed coast, with undeniable character and a few places to stay and eat. Further southwest, two small beaches appear at **Skala Sotira** and **Skala Kallirahis**. Some 2km inland from the latter, traditional **Kallirahi** features steep narrow streets and stone houses.

However, the first real point of interest lies further south; the whimsical fishing port of **Skala Marion**. The village has been relatively unaffected by tourism – somewhat surprising, considering its long beaches on both sides (another smaller beach lies in the centre, between two jetties). Still primarily a fishing settlement, Skala Marion could be commissioned for filming some Italian romantic comedy. Its few canopied tavernas overlooking the sea are faithfully populated by village elders shuffling backgammon chips, while little children scamper about. A good choice for families and couples, Skala Marion features a few domatia, a bakery and even an internet cafe on the northern jetty. On the village's feast day (24 June), church services are followed by folk dancing and sweets for all.

Inland from Skala Marion, forested **Maries** makes for an interesting day trip. A 4km-long solid dirt road beginning from the centre of inland Maries hugs a deep, forested ravine, arriving at a manmade but still photogenic **forest lake**. Drive or enjoy the cooler upland air by **hiking** there – the road is straight, the going not too strenuous.

The coast road south passes more beaches and **Limenaria**, Thasos' second-largest town. Although it looks rather ungainly from the road, Limenaria has a nice, though small, sandy beach. Limenaria was created over a century ago for the German Speidel Metal Company; this erstwhile investor's ruined buildings, including a circular tower, still loom over the waterfront.

A few kilometres further south, the fishing-villages-turned-resorts of **Potos** and **Pefkari** have long sandy beaches, the former being especially crammed with cafes and tavernas. Although Potos has a good position for southwestern Thasos activities, including boat excursions, the kitsch and frenetic package-tour presence has scarred it irrevocably.

Although technically nowhere near the west coast, Thasos' medieval and Ottoman capital, **Theologos**, is only accessible from the main road at Potos. The turnoff is signposted, and the road leads inland for 10km before reaching Theologos, set against a rocky white peak and surrounded by forests. This tranquil hamlet of 400 souls is notable for its whitewashed, closely set traditional houses, many with slate roofs. Here see the **Church of Agios Dimitrios** (1803), distinguished by its tall, white-plastered clock tower and grand slate roof. Although buses serve Theologos, accommodation is scarce, making it a better day-trip destination.

From the Theologos-Potos corner of the main road, head southeast round the coast for views of stunning bays, some with pristine sandy beaches. The last southwestern settlement, **Astris**, has a good beach with tavernas and domatia.

Activities

Despite its touristy feel, Thasos' west coast offers worthwhile outdoors activities like scuba diving, mountain biking, birdwatching and more. The rocky, uninhabited **Panagia Islet**, southwest of Potos, is home to Greece's largest sea cormorant colony; **birdwatching boat trips** are arranged by local environmentalist Yiannis Markianos at Aldebaran Pension (below).

Also from Potos, the annual **Thasos International Mountain Biking Race** occurs on the last Sunday in April. This popular amateur event draws over 200 contestants, who race across a circular route from Potos east across the island's wooded interior. The course scales Mt Ypsario (1204m) and returns through scenic Kastro village. Incredibly, the entry fee (only €20) also includes three nights' hotel accommodation. **Yiannis Raizis** (☎ 25930 52459, 6946955704; www.mtb-thassos.com), who hires out high-quality mountain bikes year-round from his domatio in Potos, organises this event and also runs guided biking and hiking tours.

Further north, inland **Rahoni** hosts the **Pine Tree Paddock** (☎ 6945118961; ⏱ 10am-2pm & 5pm-sunset), which has mountain ponies and horses (per hour €20), and does guided trail rides (per hour €25). Advance reservations are required.

Scuba-diving lessons for beginners and excursions for the experienced are offered in Potos by Vasilis Vasiliadis of **Diving Club Vasiliadis** (☎ 6944542974; www.scuba-vas.gr), including dives at Alyki's submerged ancient marble quarry.

Sleeping

Camping Pefkari (☎ 25930 51190; camp sites per adult/tent €5/4; ⏱ Jun-Sep) This appealing camping ground on a wooded spot above Pefkari Beach is popular with families and has clean bathrooms; a minimum three-night stay is required.

Camping Daedalos (☎ /fax 25930 58251; camp sites per adult/tent €6/4) This beach-front camping ground north of Skala Sotira includes a mini-market and restaurant. Sailing, windsurfing and waterskiing lessons are offered too.

Aldebaran Pension (☎ 25930 52494, 6973209576; www.gothassos.com; Potos; d from €30; ❄) One street back from Potos beach, and set in a relaxing, leafy courtyard, this friendly, family-run pension has rooms with all mod cons and spacious balconies. Owner Yiannis Markianos, who also runs the informative Gothassos.com website, also hires out boats and does bird-watching boat trips to Panagia Islet.

Domatia Filaktaki (☎ 25930 52634, 6977413789; Skala Marion; r from €35; 🔀) These simple but air-conditioned rooms are situated above the home of the kind and helpful Maria Filaktaki and family in Skala Marion. It's the first place you'll reach when descending to the waterfront from the bus stop, above the family's restaurant, Armeno.

MTB Yiannis Raizis Domatia (☎ 25930 52459, 6946955704; www.mtb-thasos.com; Potos; d/tr/q €45/60/70; 🔀) A good option for large groups, these spacious self-catering studios run by mountain-biking enthusiast Yiannis Raizis fit up to eight people. It's 20m past the church on the Potos main road, and a five-minute walk from the beach. There are sea views from the roof garden, an adjacent pool and shaded lawn bar.

Eating

O Georgios (☎ 25930 52774; Potos; mains €4.50-7) This traditional Greek grill house set in a pebbled rose garden is a local favourite away from the tourist strip on Potos' main road, offering friendly service and big portions.

Taverna Giatrou (☎ 25930 31000; Theologos; mains €5-8) Set 800m on the right side when entering Theologos, this big taverna has great balcony views of village roofs and verdure below. Run by Kostas Giatrou ('the Doctor') and family, the place offers specialities including local roast lamb.

our pick **Armeno** (☎ 25930 51277; Skala Marion; mains €5-9) This relaxing waterfront taverna in off-beat Skala Marion has tasty fish, plus the full taverna menu. The vegetables and olive oil are organic and from the gardens of the friendly Filaktaki family, who also rent rooms and can help with local information and car hire.

Piatsa Michalis (☎ 25930 51574; Potos; mains €6-10) Potos' 50-year-old beachfront taverna started working well before mass tourism came to town, and sticks to the recipe with specialities like stewed rabbit and octopus in red-wine sauce, plus a full menu of taverna fare.

Restaurant Alphas (☎ 25930 53510; Skala Marion; mains €6-11) There's fine waterside ambience, and some good mezedhes, at this fish taverna on Skala Marion's northern pier.

Psarotaverna To Limani (☎ 25930 52790; Limenaria; mains €8-13) Limenaria's best seafood is served at this waterfront restaurant opposite the National Bank of Greece, though prices can be steep.

Kafeneio Tsiknas (☎ 25930 31202; Theologos) At the beginning of Theologos, right before the church, this charming cafe has balcony seating, coffees and snacks.

EAST COAST

Thasos' sandy east-coast beaches are packed in summer, though the tourist presence is more concentrated than on the west side – partly because the landscape features thick forests that run down from mountains to the sea. Although there are fewer organised activities here, there's a more relaxed feel, and the warm, shallow waters are excellent for families with small children.

The east coast also has photogenic (though touristy) inland villages like **Panagia** and **Potamia**, just south of Thasos (Limenas). Their characteristic architecture includes Panagia's stone-and-slate rooftops and the sumptuously decorated, blue-and-white domed **Church of the Kimisis tou Theotokou** (Church of the Dormition of the Virgin), which has a valuable icon collection. To reach this peaceful quarter, follow the sound of rushing spring water upwards along a stone path heading inland. Less-picturesque Potamia boasts the **Polygnotos Vagis Museum** (☎ 25930 61400; admission €3; 🕑 8.30am-noon & 6-8pm Tue-Sat, to noon Sun & holidays), devoted to Greek-American artist Polygnotos Vagis (born here in 1894). It's beside the main church. The Municipal Museum of Kavala (p105) also exhibits some of Vagis' work.

Potamia also makes a good jumping-off point for climbing Thasos' highest peak, **Mt Ypsario** (1204m), and for general hiking. A tractor trail west from Potamia continues to the valley's end, after which arrows and cairns point the way along a steep path upwards. The Ypsario hike is classified as being of 'moderate difficulty' and takes about three hours. You can sleep at the **Ypsario Mountain Shelter** (per bed €5), but first phone Leftheris of the Thasos Mountaineering Club in Thasos (Limenas) on ☎ 6972198032 to book and get the key. The shelter has fireplaces and spring water, but no electricity.

Both Panagia and Potamia are 4km west of the east coast's most popular beaches: sandy **Hrysi Ammoudia (Golden Beach)**, tucked inside a long, curving bay, and **Skala Potamia**, on its southern end. The latter has very warm, gentle and shallow waters, making it ideal for small children. A bus between the two (€1.30) runs every couple of hours. Both have accommodation, restaurants and some nightlife. There's one Commercial Bank ATM in Skala Potamia, rather oddly set alone on the main road, 150m west of the village turn-off.

Further south of Skala Potamia is the deservedly popular **Paradise Beach**, located down a narrow, winding dirt road 2km after tiny **Kinyra** village. Continuing around the main road's southwestern bend, peaceful **Alyki** is Thasos' best place to unwind by the beach – and get some culture, too. This escapist destination features two fine sandy coves, with small snack shops and a taverna on the western one. The beaches are separated by a little olive grove dotted with ancient ruins comprising the **archaeological site of Alyki**. This inscrutable site, deemed Thasos' second-most significant after Limenas, lies alluringly above the southeastern (and more placid) beach. A helpful English-language placard with map explaining the site stands along the stone path connecting the two beaches.

The main attraction, a former **ancient temple** where the gods were once invoked to protect sailors, is situated right above the sea and is studded by column bases. A now submerged nearby **marble quarry** operated from the 6th century BC to the 6th century AD. Clamber along the rocky path from the temple site southward around the peninsula, and you'll also see an **early Christian cave** where hermits once lived.

Continuing west from Alyki, you'll pass **Thymonia Beach** before rising upwards to the cliff-top **Moni Arhangelou** (admission free; 9am-5pm), an Athonite dependency and working nunnery, notable for its 400-year-old church and stunning views over the sea. Those improperly attired will get shawled up for entry. As at many Orthodox monasteries, pilgrims can stay overnight for free if they attend services.

Heading west from here, the road descends sharply; watch out for the small dirt road to the left, at the road's northernmost curve. It leads to a tranquil swimming spot, **Livadi Beach**. One of Thasos' most beautiful beaches, its aquamarine waters are ringed by cliffs and forests, with just a few umbrellas set in the sand.

Sleeping & Eating

Domatia and small hotels run down the coast, though most are nondescript and dated. There's less accommodation at Kinyra and Alyki than at Hrysi Ammoudia (Golden Beach) and Skala Potamia, and there's no accommodation on

Paradise Beach. Regardless of place, you can just show up and grab a room; outside of July and August, prices are often 20% cheaper.

Golden Beach Camping (25930 61472; Hrysi Ammoudia; camp sites per adult/tent €5/4; P) A party feel pervades Golden Beach Camping, with its minimarket, bar, beach volleyball, and many young people from Greece, Serbia, Bulgaria and beyond. It's a fun place on the beach's best spot.

our pick Domatia Vasso (25930 31534, 6946524706; Alyki; r €50; P) Just east of Alyki's bus stop on the main road, look for the big burst of flowers and sign pointing up the drive to this relaxing set of eight self-catering domatia run by friendly Vasso Gemetzi and daughter Aleka. There's a relaxing outdoor patio with tables and cooking space. Kids stay free. A minimum two-night stay is required.

Semeli Studios (25930 61612; www.semeli-studios .gr; Skala Potamia; d/tr €50/60; P) The Kamelia's friendly owner Eleni Stoubou also runs these larger, self-catering options just behind. From the bus stop, head towards Hryssi Ammoudia on the main road for 100m; both Hotel Kamelia and Semeli Studios are signposted on the right.

Hotel Kamelia (25930 61463; www.hotel-kamelia .gr; Skala Potamia; s/d incl breakfast €40/60; P) This beach-front hotel has an understated, arty appeal, with flowery canvases, minimalist wall sculptures and cool jazz playing in the garden bar. The spacious, fresh-smelling rooms have large balconies and all mod cons.

Thassos Inn (25930 61612; www.thassosinn.gr; Panagia; s/d €50/70) Panagia's best accommodation is ideally set near the church, with sweeping views of the village's clustered slate rooftops. It has all mod cons and good-sized rooms, though the simple floors are uninspiring. The inn is run by the welcoming Tasos Manolopoulos, who proudly shows off his vegetable patch and pool of gigantic goldfish.

Taverna Elena (25930 61709; Panagia; mains €6-9) Just next to the traditional products shop off Panagia's central square, this classic taverna has mezedhes like *bougloundi* (baked feta with tomatoes and chilli), and excellent roast lamb and goat.

Restaurant Koralli (25930 62244; Skala Potamia; mains €7-11) This big Skala Potamia taverna serves above-average mushrooms stuffed with shrimp, eggplant baked with mozzarella and parmesan, zucchinis stuffed with crab, carpaccio and 330g sirloin steaks.

Evia & the Sporades
Εύβοια & Οι Σποράδες

Evia and the four islands known as the Sporades remain largely off the beaten path, but attract more Greeks than most and consequently retain a good deal of local colour. Evia is joined to the mainland by a short drawbridge at Halkida, which spans a narrow gulf.

Only two hours from Athens, both Halkida and nearby Eretria are destinations for car loads of weekend visitors. Across the island, though, the pace slows as the landscape stretches out, dotted by hilltop monasteries, small farms and vineyards. Goats stand in the middle of the road and stare at passing cars. Small beaches await on the north, west and southeast coasts, many of them with crystal-clear bays that elsewhere would be lined with matching umbrellas. The Sporades (in Greek, 'scattered ones') seem like an extension of the forested Pelion Peninsula. In fact, in prehistoric times they were joined. Skiathos, a haven for northern Europeans, claims the sandiest beaches in the Aegean, along with several prime scuba-diving spots. Low-key Skopelos kicks back with a relaxed and postcard-worthy harbour and a good number of pristine bays, and forest meadows threaded with walking trails. Alonnisos, the most remote of the group, anchors the National Marine Park of Alonnisos – established to protect the Mediterranean monk seal – and is a model for ecological awareness throughout Greece. Skyros, the southernmost of the chain, retains a good deal of local character, and is well known for its unique cuisine, woodworking and ceramics, folk traditions that date from Byzantine times when these islands were home to rogues and pirates – something that the good-natured residents are proud to mention.

HIGHLIGHTS

- **Spa Bathing** Soaking in the therapeutic thermal waters at Loutra Edipsou (p409), on Evia
- **Dinner on the Dock** Picking out your favourite from the fresh catch at Kalamakia (p425), on Alonnisos
- **Aegean Adventure** Watching for dolphins while cruising around Greece's only national marine park at Alonnisos (p423)
- **Island Walks** Hiking through olive groves and across pristine meadows on Skopelos (p421)
- **Romantic Meditation** Catching the sunset over wine from Atsitsa Bay (p431), on Skyros
- **Midnight Music** Listening to one of Greece's best bouzouki players above the *kastro* overlooking Skopelos Town (p420)
- **Scuba Diving** Exploring an underwater reef 30m down off Tsougriaki islet, Skiathos (p416), on Skopelos

National Marine Park of Alonnisos ★

Kalamakia ★

Kastro ★

Tsougriaki ★

Atsitsa ★

Loutra Edipsou ★

- POPULATION: 228,750
- AREA: 4167 SQ KM

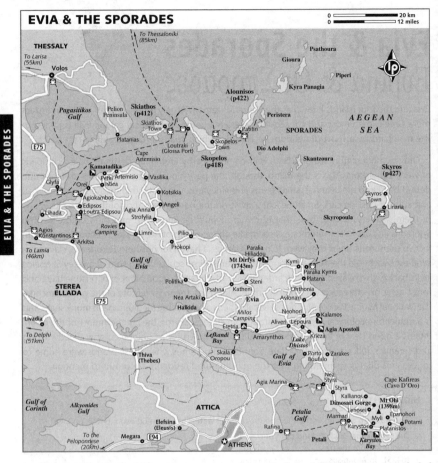

EVIA & THE SPORADES

EVIA EYBOIA

Evia (*eh*-vih-ah), Greece's second-largest island after Crete and a prime holiday destination for Greeks, remains less charted by foreign tourists. Its attractions include glorious mountain roads, challenging treks, major archaeological finds and mostly uncrowded beaches. A mountainous spine runs north–south, dividing the island's precipitous eastern cliffs from the gentler and resort-friendly west coast. Ferries link the island to the mainland, along with a short sliding drawbridge over the narrow Evripos Channel to the capital of Halkida. The current in the narrow channel reverses direction about seven times daily,

an event whose full explanation has eluded observers since Aristotle.

Getting There & Away

There are regular bus services between Halkida and Athens (€6.20, 1¼ hours, half-hourly), Ioannina (€35.50, one daily) and Thessaloniki (€36, 6 hours, twice daily). There is also a regular train service between Halkida and Athens (normal, €5, 1½/one hour, hourly/four daily), and between Halkida and Thessaloniki (normal/IC express €26/33, 5½/4½ hours, six/four daily). There are regular ferry services from Evia to Skyros, Alonnisos and Skopelos; for details see Island Hopping (p513).

Tickets may be purchased at the dock kiosk at Paralia Kymis (the port of Kymi on Evia).

CENTRAL EVIA

After crossing the bridge to Halkida, the road veers south, following the coastline to Eretria, a bustling resort and major archaeological site. Further on, a string of hamlets and fishing villages dot the route until the junction at Lepoura, where the road forks north towards Kymi. Several branch roads to the sea are worth exploring, and the sandy beach at Kalamos is exceptional. A decent dirt road leads west from Kymi above the north coastline to Paralia Hiliadou.

Young fir, pine, and olive trees are making a comeback along the coastal road south of Eretria, thanks to a joint governmental and private reforestation project, following the tragic forest fires of August 2007.

Halkida Χαλκίδα

pop 54,560

Mentioned in the 'Iliad', Halkida (aka Halkis) was a powerful city-state in the 8th and 7th centuries BC, with several colonies dotted around the Mediterranean. The name derives from the bronze manufactured here in antiquity (*halkos* means 'bronze' in Greek). Today it's a gateway to Evia, and a lively shipping and agricultural centre. As evening approaches, the waterfront promenade by the Old Bridge comes to life.

To glimpse Halkida's interesting religious history, head up Kotsou towards the *kastro* (castle) to find a striking 15th-century **mosque**, and 19th-century **synagogue**, adjacent to Plateia Tzami (Tzami Sq). Then walk south about 150m to find the Byzantine **church** of Agia Paraskevi. An **Archaeological Museum** (☎ 22210 60944; Leoforos Venizelou 13; admission €2; ⏲ 8.30am-3pm Tue-Sun) displays a fine torso of Apollo discovered at Eretria.

INFORMATION

Several ATMs cluster near the corner of Venizelou and Voudouri.

Hospital (☎ 22210 21902; cnr Gazepi & Hatzopoulou)
Kiosk (☎ 22210 76718; cnr Boudouri & Douna) International press.
Pharmacy (☎ 22210 25424; Isaiou 6)
Post office (cnr Karamourtzouni & Kriezotou; ⏲ 8am-6pm Mon-Fri)
Surf-on-Net Cafe (☎ 22210 24867; Angeli Goviou 7A; internet per hr €1.50; ⏲ 24hr)
Tourist police (☎ 22210 77777)

ACTIVITIES

Sport Apollon Scuba Diving Centre (☎ 22210 86369, 6945219619; www.sportapollon.gr; ⏲ 9am-1.30pm & 5-9pm) in Halkida organises dives off the nearby Alykes coast, led by dive team Nikos and Stavroula. A one-day dive costs about €40.

SLEEPING & EATING

Best Western Lucy Hotel (☎ 22210 23831; www.lucy-hotel.gr; Voudouri 10; s/d/tr/ste incl breakfast €70/90/137/157; P ✤ 💻 📶) Rooms at the 2009-renovated Lucy are on the modern side, with swank blond furnishings, long desks and large bathrooms. The friendly multilingual staff can also clue you in to the adjacent boardwalk cafe scene.

Ouzerie O Loukas (☎ 22210 60371; Makariou 1; mezedhes €3-6, mains €5-9) On the mainland side of the Old Bridge, this handsome *ouzerie* (place that serves ouzo and light snacks) has first-rate mains and appetisers, from grilled octopus and *horta* (wild greens) to tzatziki and mussels with rice.

Mostar Café-Bar (☎ 22210 81213; Old Bridge; drinks, snacks €3-7; ✤ 📶) You can't get any closer to the channel or the drawbridge than at this swank ultramodern bar.

GETTING THERE & AWAY

There are regular bus services between Halkida and Athens, Ioannina and Thessaloniki. Regular trains also connect Halkida with Athens and Thessaloniki.

To reach other parts of Evia, there are connections from **Halkida KTEL Bus Station** (☎ 22210 20400, cnr Styron & Arethousis), 3km east of the Old Bridge, to Eretria (€2, 25 minutes, hourly) and Kymi Town (€7.60, two hours, hourly), one of which continues to Paralia Kymis to meet the Skyros ferry. There are also buses to Steni (€2.70, one hour, twice daily), Limni (€7.10, two hours, three daily), Loutra Edipsou (€10.80, 2½ hours, once daily) and Karystos (€10.50, three hours, three daily).

For more information see also Island Hopping (p513).

Eretria Ερέτρια

pop 3160

Heading southeast from Halkida, Eretria is the first place of interest, with a small harbour and a lively boardwalk filled with mainland families who pack its fish tavernas on holiday weekends. There are late Neolithic finds around Eretria, which became a major maritime power and home to an eminent school of philosophy by the 8th century BC. The modern town was founded in the 1820s, during the War of Independence, by islanders from Psara fleeing the Turkish.

INFORMATION

For emergencies, call the Halkida **tourist police** (☎ 22210 77777). For internet access, head to **Christos Internet Cafe-Bar** (☎ 22290 61604; per hr €2; ☽ 9am-1am) on the waterfront.

SIGHTS

From the top of the **ancient acropolis** there are splendid views over to the mainland. West of the acropolis are the remains of a palace, temple and theatre with a subterranean passage once used by actors to reach the stage. Close by, the excellent **Archaeological Museum of Eretria** (☎ 22290 62206; admission €2; ☽ 8.30am-3pm Tue-Sun) contains well-displayed finds from ancient Eretria. A 200m walk will bring you to the fascinating **House of Mosaics**, and ends 50m further on at the **Sanctuary of Apollo**.

SLEEPING & EATING

Milos Camping (☎ 22290 60420; www.camping-in-evia .gr/index_en.html; camp sites per adult/tent €6.50/4) This clean, shaded camping ground on the coast 1km northwest of Eretria has a small restaurant, bar and narrow pebble beach.

Eviana Beach Hotel (☎ 22290 62113; www.eviana beach.gr; s/d/tr incl breakfast €80/105/145; P ⛶ 🖳 🎧) Tucked away 500m east of the waterfront, this 2009-renovated lodging occupies a prime beachfront spot, with spacious tile-floored rooms, plus an inviting tree-shaded beach bar.

Taverna Astra (☎ 22290 64111; Arheou Theatrou 48; mains €4-9) Just past the supermarket, this friendly waterfront taverna is known for well-priced fresh fish, along with appetisers like *taramasalata* (fish roe) and roasted sardines.

GETTING THERE & AWAY

Ferries travel daily between Eretria and Skala Oropou. For details see Island Hopping (p513).

Tickets should be purchased from the dock kiosk at the port of Eretria.

Steni Στενή
pop 1080

From Halkida, it's 31km to the lovely mountain village of Steni, with its gurgling springs and shady plane trees.

Steni is the starting point for a serious climb up **Mt Dirfys** (1743m), Evia's highest mountain. The **Dirfys Refuge** (☎ 22280 24298), at 1120m, can be reached along a 9km dirt road. From there, it's a steep 7km to the summit. Experienced hikers should allow about six hours from Steni to the summit. For refuge reservations, contact **Stamatiou** (☎ Mon-Fri 6972026862, Sat-Sun 22280 25655; per person €12). For more hiking information, contact the EOS-affiliated **Halkida Alpine Club** (☎ 22210 25230; Angeli Gouviou 22, Halkida). For tips on day hikes around Mt Dirfys, contact **Graham Beaumont** (☎ 6936523804; www.eviavillas .co.uk) in Halkida. An excellent topo map (No 5.11), *Mt Dirfys*, is published by Anavasi.

A twisting road continues from Steni to **Paralia Hiliadou** on the north coast, where a grove of maple and chestnut trees borders a fine pebble-and-sand beach, along with a few domatia and tavernas. Campers can find shelter near the big rocks at either end of the beach.

SLEEPING & EATING

Hotel Dirfys (☎ 22280 51217; s/d incl breakfast €30/40) The best of Steni's two hotels is big on knotty pine which dominates the decor, from the lobby walls to most of the furniture. The comfortable and carpeted rooms have perfect views of the forest and stream.

Taverna Kissos (Ivy Taverna; ☎ 22280 51226; mains €4-9) One of a cluster of good brookside eateries, this traditional taverna offers hearty meat grills (steaks sold by the kilo), traditional *mayirefta* (ready-cooked meals) and salads prepared from locally grown greens.

Kymi & Paralia Kymis
Κύμη & Παραλία Κύμης
pop 3040

The workaday town of Kymi is built on a cliff 250m above the sea. Things perk up at dusk when the town square comes to life. The port, Paralia Kymis, 4km downhill, is the only natural harbour on the precipitous east coast, and the departure point for ferries to Skyros.

The excellent **Folklore Museum** (☎ 22220 22011; ☽ 10am-1pm Wed & Sun, 10am-1pm & 4-6.30pm Sat), 30m downhill from the main square, has an impressive collection of local costumes and historical photos, including a display honouring Kymi-born Dr George Papanikolaou, inventor of the Pap smear test.

Kymi is home to **Figs of Kymi** (☎ 22220 31722; www.figkimi.gr; ☽ 9am-3pm Mon-Fri), an agricultural co-op dedicated to supporting local fig farmers and sustainable production in general. It's a fascinating operation to see, and you can buy dried preservative-free figs in the shop.

SLEEPING & EATING
In Paralia Kymis, the reliable **Hotel Beis** (☎ 22220 22604; www.hotel-beis.gr; s/d/tr incl breakfast €40/60; P ❄), a cavernous white block with large and spotless rooms, is opposite the ferry dock for Skyros. A string of tavernas and *ouzeries* lines the waterfront.

Just 3km south in tiny Platana, next to the seawall, try the excellent fish taverna **Koutelos** (☎ 22220 71272; mains €5-9), where Alexandra and Konstantinos will interpret the menu with dramatic pleasure. Up the hill in Kymi, little **Taverna Mouria** (☎ 22220 22629; mains €4-9), 150m north of the square, is great for shrimp grills, *mayirefta* dishes and family-sized Greek salads (€4.50).

NORTHERN EVIA
From Halkida a road heads north to **Psahna**, the gateway to the highly scenic mountainous interior of northern Evia. A good road climbs and twists through pine forests to the woodsy village of **Prokopi**, home of the pilgrimage church of **St John the Russian**. At Strofylia, 14km beyond Prokopi, a road heads southwest to picturesque Limni, then north to quaint Loutra Edipsou, the ferry port at **Agiokambos**, and **Pefki**, a small seaside resort.

Loutra Edipsou Λουτρά Αιδηψού
pop 3600
The classic spa resort of Loutra Edipsou has therapeutic sulphur waters, which have been celebrated since antiquity. Famous skinny dippers have included Aristotle, Plutarch and Sylla. The town's gradual expansion over the years has been tied to the improving technology required to carry the water further and further away from its thermal source. Today the town has Greece's most up-to-date hydrotherapy and physiotherapy centres. The town beach (Paralia Loutron) heats up year-round thanks to the thermal waters which spill into the sea.

INFORMATION
You'll find internet service at **Lan Arena** (☎ 22260 22597; per hr €2.50; ☼ 10am-1am), opposite the ferry port. For medical needs, contact

English-speaking **Dr Symeonides** (☎ 22260 23220; Omirou 17).

ACTIVITIES
Most of the hotels offer various **spa treatments**, from simple hot baths (€6) to four-hand massages (€160).

The more relaxing (and affordable) of the resort's two big spas is the **EOT Hydrotherapy-Physiotherapy Centre** (☎ 22260 23501; 25 March St 37; ☼ 7am-1pm & 5-7pm 1 Jun-31 Oct), speckled with palm trees and with a large outdoor pool that mixes mineral and sea water, and terrace overlooking the sea. Hydro-massage bath treatments start at a modest €8.

The ultraposh **Thermae Sylla Hotel & Spa** (☎ 22260 60100; www.thermaesylla.gr; Posidonos 2), with a somewhat late-Roman ambience befitting its name, offers an assortment of health and beauty treatments, from thermal mud baths to seaweed body wraps, from around €60.

Modern spa treatments (including Thai massage) are also available from the **Knossos CitySpa Hotel** (☎ 22260 22460; www.knossos-spa.com; Vyzantinon 19).

SLEEPING & EATING
Hotel Istiaia (☎ 22260 22309; 28th October 2; www.istiaia hotel.com; s/d/tr incl breakfast from €34/50/70; ❄ ▯ ☎) The Istiaia is a handsome vintage hotel with high-ceiling rooms and an old world feel, aside from the smallish bathrooms. A cafe-wine bar faces out to the seawall.

Hotel Kentrikon (☎ /fax 22260 22502; www .kentrikonhotel.com; 25th Martiou 14; s/d/tr €42/60/70; ❄ ▯ ☎ ⌨) This friendly hotel-spa, managed by a Greek-Irish couple, is equal parts kitsch and charm. An inviting thermal pool awaits, along with a massage therapist, Vicky Kavartziki (☎ 6945146374).

Thermae Sylla Hotel & Spa (☎ 22260 60100; www .thermaesylla.gr; Posidonos 2; s/d/ste from €210/250/500; P ❄ ▯ ☎ ⌨) This posh in-your-mud-masked-face spa offers luxury accommodation along with countless beauty treatments. Day visitors can sample the outdoor pool for €27.

Dina's Amfilirion Restaurant (☎ 22260 60420; 28th October 26; mains €5-10) Beautifully prepared offerings change daily here. A generous plate of grilled cod with oven potatoes, a juicy tomato-cucumber salad and a worthy house wine costs about €12. Look for the small wooden sign with green letters in Greek, 20m north of the ferry dock.

Also recommended:

Captain Cook Self-Service Restaurant (☎ 22260 23852; mains €3-7) A bit of everything, tasty and cheap.

Taverna Sbanios (☎ 22260 23111; mains €4-8) Quality grills, breakfast omelettes.

GETTING THERE & AWAY

Boat

Regular ferries run between Loutra Edipsou and mainland Arkitsa, and also between nearby Agiokambos and mainland Glyfa. For details see Island Hopping (p513).

Tickets should be purchased from the dock kiosk at the port of Loutra Edipsou.

Bus

From the **KTEL bus station** (☎ 22260 22250; Thermopotamou), 200m from the port, buses run to Halkida (€13, four hours, once daily at 5.30am), Athens (€12.30, 3½ hours, three daily via Arkitsa) and Thessaloniki (€22, five hours, daily at 10am via Glyfa). For more information on services to/from Athens and Thessaloniki, see Island Hopping (p506).

Limni Λίμνη
pop 2070

One of Evia's most picturesque ports, little Limni faces seaward, its maze of whitewashed houses and narrow lanes spilling onto a busy waterfront of cafes and tavernas. The town's cultural **museum** (☎ 22270 31900; admission €2; ⏰ 9am-1pm Mon-Sat, 10.30am-1pm Sun), just 50m up from the waterfront, features local archaeological finds along with antique looms, costumes and old coins. Seldom visited, Limni is well worth a stopover.

With your own transport, you can visit the splendid 16th-century **Convent of Galataki**, (⏰ 9am-noon & 5-8pm) 9km southeast of Limni on a hillside above a coastal road, and home to a coterie of six nuns. The fine mosaics and frescoes in its *katholikon* (main church) merit a look, especially the *Entry of the Righteous into Paradise*.

SLEEPING & EATING

Rovies Camping (☎ 22270 71120; www.campingevia .com/evia-holidays.html; camp sites per adult/tent €6.50/free) Attractive and shaded Rovies sits just above a pebble beach, 12km northwest of Limni.

Ostria Apartments (☎ /fax 22270 32248; www.os tria-apartments.gr; apt incl breakfast from €90; P ⏹ 🔲 🍴) Olive trees and bougainvillea surround 10 handsome self-catering apartments across the road from a long beach, 1km northwest of Limni.

Taverna Arga (☎ 22270 31479; mains €4-12) Pick an outside table at this waterfront taverna and enjoy the passing parade of villagers and visitors, along with well-prepared grilled octopus, *gavros* (anchovies) and *yemista* (stuffed peppers and tomatoes).

Other village options:

Zaniakos Domatia (☎ 6977936698; r €25; ⏹)

Agrabeli Apts (☎ 22270 32312; www.agrabeli.eu; r €70; P ⏹ 🔲 🛜 🍴)

Ouzerie Fiki (☎ 22270 32411; mezedhes €2-5)

SOUTHERN EVIA

Continuing east from Eretria, the road branches at Lepoura: the left fork leads north to Kymi, the right south to Karystos. A turnoff at Krieza, 3km from the junction, leads to Lake Dhistos, a shallow lake bed favoured by egrets and other wetland birds. Continuing south, you'll pass high-tech windmills and catch views of both coasts as the island narrows until it reaches the sea at Karystos Bay, near the base of Mt Ohi (1398m).

Karystos Κάρυστος
pop 4960

Set on the wide Karystos Bay below Mt Ohi, and flanked by two sandy beaches, this remote but charming coastal resort is the starting point for treks to Mt Ohi and the Dimosari Gorge. The town's lively Plateia Amalias (Amalias Sq), faces the bay and boat harbour.

INFORMATION

You'll find an Alpha Bank **ATM** on the main square, and **Polihoros Internet & Sports Cafe** (☎ 22240 24421; Kriezotou 132; per hr €3; ⏰ 9am-1am) next to the Galaxy Hotel.

SIGHTS

Karystos, mentioned in Homer's 'Iliad', was a powerful city-state during the Peloponnesian Wars. The **Karystos Museum** (☎ 22240 25661; admission €2; ⏰ 8.30am-3pm Tue-Sun) documents the town's archaeological heritage, including tiny Neolithic clay lamps, a stone plaque written in the Halkidian alphabet, 5th-century-BC grave stelae depicting Zeus and Athena, and an exhibit of the 6th-century *drakospita* (dragon houses) of Mt Ohi and Styra. The museum sits opposite a 14th-century Venetian castle, the **Bourtzi** (admission free; ⏰ year-round).

TOURS

South Evia Tours (☎ 22240 25700; fax 22240 29091; www .eviatravel.gr; Plateia Amalias) offers a range of booking services including mainland ferry tickets, excursions in the foothills of Mt Ohi, trips to the 6th-century-BC Roman-built *drakospita* near Styra, and a cruise around the Petali Islands (€35 with lunch). The resourceful owner, Nikos, can also arrange necessary taxi pickup or drop-off for serious hikes to the summit of Mt Ohi and back, or four-hour guided walks through Dimosari Gorge (€25).

FESTIVALS & EVENTS

Karystos hosts a summer **Wine & Cultural Festival** from early July until the last weekend in August. Weekend happenings include theatre performances and traditional dancing to the tune of local musicians, along with exhibits by local artists. The summer merrymaking concludes with the Wine Festival, featuring every local wine imaginable, free for the tasting. Festival schedules are available at the Karystos Museum (opposite)

SLEEPING & EATING

Hotel Karystion (☎ 22240 22391; www.karystion.gr; Kriezotou 3; s/d incl breakfast €45/55; P X ☎) The Karystion is the pick of town lodgings, with modern, well-appointed rooms, along with sea-view balconies and helpful multilingual staff. A small stairway off the courtyard leads to a sandy beach below, great for swimming.

our pick **Cavo d'Oro** (☎ 22240 22326; mains €4-7.50) Join the locals in this cheery alleyway restaurant, one block west of the main square, where tasty mains include goat with pasta (€7.50) and mackerel with rice (€6.50), along with homemade *mousakas* (layers of eggplant or zucchini, minced meat and potatoes, topped with cheese sauce and baked; €6) and salads featuring only local produce and olive oil. The genial owner, Kyriakos, is a regular at the summer wine festival, bouzouki in hand.

Other options:

Hotel Galaxy (☎ 22270 71120; cnr Kriezotou & Odysseos; s/d incl breakfast €45/65; X ☐ ☎) On the waterfront.

Taverna Mesa-Exo (In-Out Taverna; ☎ 22240 23997; mains €5-12) At the western end of the waterfront.

DRINKING

Check out the late-night scene around the *plateia* (square).

Bar Alea (☎ 22240 23085; ☐ ☎) On the *plateia*; delivers decent drinks and sounds.

Club Kohili (☎ 22240 24350) This swank-casual place is on the beach by the Apollon Suite Hotel.

GETTING THERE & AWAY

Boat

There is a regular ferry service between Marmari (10km west of Karystos) and Rafina, and from Nea Styra (35km north of Karystos) to Agia Marina. For details see Island Hopping (p513).

Tickets may be purchased from either the dock ticket kiosk at the port of Mamari, or in advance at **South Evia Tours** (☎ 22240 25700; fax 22240 29091; www.eviatravel.gr) in Karystos.

Bus

From the **Karystos KTEL bus station** (☎ 22240 26303), opposite Agios Nikolaos church, buses run to Halkida (€10.50, three hours, Sunday to Friday) and to Athens (€8.30, three hours, four daily), and Marmari (€1.70, 20 minutes, Monday to Saturday). A taxi to Marmari is about €12.

Around Karystos

The ruins of **Castello Rosso** (Red Castle), a 13th-century Frankish fortress, are a short walk from **Myli**, a delightful, well-watered village 4km inland from Karystos. A little beyond Myli there is an **ancient quarry** scattered with green and black fragments of the once-prized Karystian *cippolino* marble.

With your own transport, or taxi, you can get to the base of **Mt Ohi** where a 1½-hour hike to the summit will bring you to the ancient *drakospita* (dragon house), the finest example of a group of Stonehengelike dwellings or temples, dating from the 7th century BC, and hewn from rocks weighing up to several tons and joined without mortar. Smaller examples near **Styra** (30km north of Karystos) are nearly as fascinating.

Hikers can also head north to the **Dimosari Gorge** where a beautiful and well-maintained 10km trail can be covered in four to five hours (including time for a swim).

With a local map from South Evia Tours (left), you can easily explore the villages and chestnut forests nestling in the foothills between Mt Ohi and the coast.

SKIATHOS ΣΚΙΑΘΟΣ

pop 6160

Blessed with some of the Aegean's most beautiful beaches, it's little wonder that in July and August the island can fill up with sun-starved Europeans, as prices soar and rooms dwindle. At the island's small airport, the arrival board lists mostly incoming charter flights from northern Europe. Despite its popularity, Skiathos remains one of Greece's premier resorts.

Skiathos Town, the island's major settlement and port, lies on the southeast coast. The rest of the south coast is interspersed with walled-in holiday villas and pine-fringed sandy beaches. The north coast is precipitous and less accessible; in the 14th century the Kastro Peninsula served as a natural fortress against invaders. Aside from the ample sun and nightlife, the curious will find striking monasteries, hilltop tavernas and even secluded beaches.

Getting There & Away

See Island Hopping (p523) for details of air and sea connections to other islands and the mainland.

AIR

Along with numerous charter flights from northern Europe, during summer there is one flight daily to/from Athens (€49). **Olympic Air** (☎ 24270 22200) has an office at the airport, not in town.

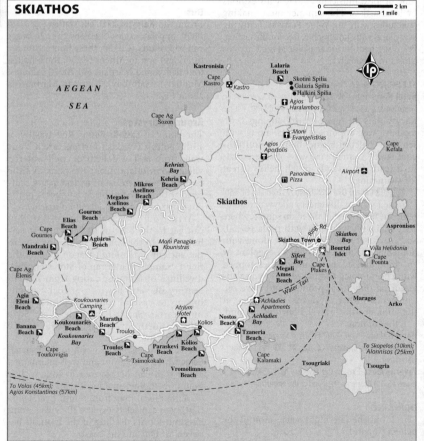

SKIATHOS

0 —————— 2 km
0 —————— 1 mile

AEGEAN SEA

Kastronisia
Cape Kastro
Kastro
Lalaria Beach
Skotini Spilia
Galazia Spilia
Halkini Spilia
Agios Haralambos
Cape Ag Sozon
Moni Evangelistrias
Agios Apostolis
Cape Kefala
Kehrias Bay
Kehria Beach
Panorama Pizza
Airport
Mikros Aselinos Beach
Megalos Aselinos Beach
Skiathos
Gournes Beach
Elias Beach
Cape Gournes
Agistros Beach
Moni Panagias Kounistras
Aspronisos
Mandraki Beach
Skiathos Town
Skiathos Bay
Bourtzi Islet
Villa Helidonia
Cape Pounta
Cape Ag Elenis
Route Rd
Siferi Bay
Megali Amos Beach
Cape Plakes
Agia Eleni Beach
Koukounaries Camping
Atrium Hotel
Achladies Apartments
Maragos
Arko
Banana Beach
Koukounaries Beach
Maratha Beach
Kolios
Nostos Beach
Achladies Bay
Troulos
Koukounaries Bay
Paraskevi Beach
Kolios Beach
Tzaneria Beach
Troulos Beach
Cape Tsimokokalo
Cape Kalamaki
Water Taxi
To Skopelos (10km); Alonnisos (25km)
Vromolimnos Beach
Tsougriaki
Tsougria
Cape Tourkovigia
To Volos (45km); Agios Konstantinos (57km)

BOAT

Skiathos' main port is Skiathos Town, with links to mainland Volos and Agios Konstantinos, and to Skopelos and Alonnisos.

Tickets can be purchased from either **Hellenic Seaways** (☎ 24270 22209; fax 24270 22750) at the bottom of Papadiamantis, or from **GA Ferries** (☎ 24270 22204; fax 24270 22979), next to Alpha Bank.

Getting Around

BOAT

Water taxis depart from the old port for Tzaneria and Kanapitsa beaches (€3, 20 minutes, hourly) and Achladies Bay (€2, 15 minutes, hourly).

BUS

Crowded buses leave Skiathos Town for Koukounaries Beach (€1.20 to €1.50, 30 minutes, every half-hour between 7.30am and 11pm). The buses stop at 26 numbered access points to the beaches along the south coast.

CAR & MOTORCYCLE

Reliable motorbike and car-hire outlets in Skiathos Town include **Europcar/Creator Tours** (☎ 24270 22385) and **Heliotropio Tourism & Travel** (☎ 24270 22430) on the new port.

TAXI

The **taxi stand** (☎ 24270 21460) is opposite the ferry dock. A taxi to/from the airport costs €5.

SKIATHOS TOWN

Skiathos Town, with its red-roofed, white-washed houses, is built on two low hills. Opposite the waterfront lies tiny and inviting **Bourtzi Islet** between the two small harbours and reached by a short causeway. The town is a major tourist centre, with hotels, souvenir shops, galleries, travel agents, tavernas and bars dominating the waterfront and the narrow main thoroughfare, Papadiamanti.

Orientation

The quay (wharf) is in the middle of the waterfront, just north of Bourtzi Islet. To the right (as you face inland) is the newer small boat harbour; to the left is the curving old harbour used by local fishing and excursion boats. Papadiamanti strikes inland from opposite the quay. Plateia Tris Ierarches (Tris Ierarches Sq) is above the old harbour. The

bus terminus is at the northern end of the new harbour.

Information

EMERGENCY

Port police (☎ 24270 22017; quay)
Tourist police (☎ 24270 23172; ⏱ 8am-9pm; Ring Rd)

INTERNET ACCESS

Creator Tours (☎ 24270 21384; waterfront; per 30min €1; ⏱ 9am-9pm) Inside Europcar office.
Internet Zone Café (☎ 24270 22767; Evangelistrias 28; per hr €2; ⏱ 10am-3am)

MEDICAL SERVICES

Health Centre Hospital (☎ 24270 22222) Above the old port.
Pharmacy Papantoniou (☎ 24270 24515; Papadiamanti 18)

MONEY

Numerous ATMs are on Papadiamanti and the waterfront.

POST

Post office (upper Papadiamanti; ⏱ 7.30am-2pm)

TRAVEL AGENCIES

For reliable information about Skiathos, or onward travel, try the following:
Creator Tours (☎ 24270 21384; www.creatortours .com; waterfront)
Heliotropio Tourism & Travel (☎ 24270 22430; www.heliotropio.gr; waterfront)
Mathinos Travel (☎ 24270 23351; Papadiamanti 18)

Sights

Skiathos was the birthplace of famous 19th-century Greek novelist and short story writer Alexandros Papadiamanti, whose writings draw upon the hard lives of the islanders he grew up with. Papadiamanti's humble 1860-vintage house is now a charming **museum** (☎ 24270 23843; Plateia Papadiamanti; admission €1; ⏱ 9.30am-1.30pm & 5-8.30pm Tue-Sun) with books, paintings and old photos documenting his life on Skiathos.

Tours

Excursion boats make half- and full-day trips around the island (€10 to €25, approximately four to six hours), and usually visit Cape Kastro, Lalaria Beach and the three *spilies* (caves) of Halkini, Skotini and Galazia, which are only accessible by boat. A few boats also visit the nearby islets of Tsougria and Tsougriaki for swimming and snorkelling; you can take one boat over and return on another. At the old harbour, check out the signboards in front of each boat for a tour and schedule to your liking.

Sleeping

Book early for July and August, when prices quoted here are nearly double those of the low season. There's also a quayside kiosk with prices and room pictures. For last-minute accommodation in high season, try the resourceful agents, **Sotos & Maria** (☎ 24270 23219, 6974716408; sotos-2@otenet.gr).

Lena's Rooms (24270 22009; Bouboulinas St; r €55; ✖) These six double rooms over the owner's flower shop are airy and spotless, each with fridge and balcony, plus a well-equipped common kitchen and shady, flower-filled veranda.

Villa Orsa (☎ 24270 22430; fax 24270 21952; s/d/f incl breakfast from €70/80/110; ✖ 🖵 🛜) Perched well above the old harbour, this classic cliff-side mansion features very comfortable, traditionally styled rooms with balcony views overlooking a secluded bay. A generous breakfast is served on the garden terrace.

ourpick Villa Helidonia (Swallows Villa; ☎ 24270 21370; 6945686542; apt €75-95; P ✖ 🖵) This unusually comfortable and secluded lodging sits above the Punta (point), only minutes from town, but a world away otherwise. There are just two apartments (minimum four-night stay), each with full kitchen, satellite TV and overhead fans, along with a fig tree within picking distance. Close by, a hidden snorkelling bay awaits.

Hotel Bourtzi (☎ 24270 21304; Moraitou 8; www .hotelbourtzi.gr; s/d/tr incl breakfast from €90/130/150; P ✖ 🖵 🛜 🐾) On upper Papadiamanti, the swank Bourtzi escapes much of the town noise, and features austere-modern rooms, an inviting garden and two small pools, one just for kids.

Also recommended:

Hotel Meltemi (☎ 24270 22493; meltemi@skiathos.gr; s/d/f €55/65/95; ✖ 🖵 🛜) Old-fashioned charmer.

Alkyon Hotel (☎ 24270 22981; www.alkyon.gr; s/d/tr incl breakfast from €63/84/105; P ✖ 🖵 🛜 🐾) Large waterfront lodging.

Eating

Skiathos has more than its share of overpriced and touristy eateries with so-so (*etsi-ketsi* in Greek) food. Explore the narrow lanes west of Papadiamanti to find exceptions like these:

Taverna-Ouzeri Kabourelia (☎ 24270 21112; mains €4-9) Poke your nose in the kitchen to glimpse the day's catch at the only year-round eatery at the old port. The cheerful owner-cooks prepare great fish grills and seafood mezedhes at moderate prices.

Taverna Alexandros (☎ 24270 22341; Mavrogiali; mains €4-9) Excellent lamb grills, traditional oven-roasted chicken and potatoes, and live acoustic Greek music await at this friendly alleyway eatery under a canopy of mulberry trees.

Taverna Bakaliko (☎ 24270 24024; Club St; mains €4.50-9) You can't get much closer to the bay than at this popular eatery, known for well-prepared and well-priced standards like stuffed cabbage leaves, tomato and parsley salad and fish soup.

Taverna Mesogia (☎ 24270 21440; mains €5-10) Another back street gem, with open kitchen, and summer seating in the narrow lane. Owner Pandelis boasts of his 'simple and traditional' cuisine; his grandfather first opened in 1923.

Medousa Pizza (☎ 24270 23923; Club St; mains €6-8) Just barfing distance from the drink-till-you-drop waterfront clubs, Medousa's wood-oven pizza is worth a trip at any hour, and they deliver.

Taverna Anemos (Wind; ☎ 24270 21003; mains €6-14) Locals know this fine fish taverna up the old harbour steps for its generous portions of fresh cod, lobster and mussels. Best of all, Vassili the cook has probably spent the morning at his other job – fishing and diving for your dinner.

ourpick Maria's Pizza (☎ 24270 22292; mains €8-15) The pizza is just the beginning at this flower-filled gem above the old port. If you don't walk inside to see Maria and crew in action, you've missed the point. Highlights include stuffed garlic bread, tagliatelle pasta with prosciutto and asparagus (€12) and salads galore, each a meal in itself.

Other fine options:

Igloo (☎ 24270 24076; Papadiamanti; drinks-snacks €1.50-4; 🕒 6am-10pm) Cold drinks, breakfast.

No Name Fast Food (☎ 6974426707; Simionos; mains €2) Not that fast, and his name is Aris. Best *gyros* (meat slivers cooked on a vertical rotisserie; usually eaten with pitta bread).

Main Street (☎ 24270 21743; Papadiamanti; breakfasts €2-4) Breakfast, wraps, burgers.

Taverna O Batis (☎ 24270 22288; mains €6-12) Fresh fish, charming service.

Drinking

our pick **Kentavros Bar** (☎ 24270 22980) The long-established and handsome Kentavros, off Plateia Papadiamanti, promises rock, soul, jazz and blues, and gets the thumbs-up from locals and expats alike for its mellow ambience, artwork and good drinks.

Rooftop Bar (☎ 6949096465) A popular place to chill above the old port, with the best happy hour on the waterfront, plus live music Saturday nights.

Rock & Roll Bar (☎ 24270 22944) Huge beanbags have replaced many of the pillows outside this trendy bar by the old port, resulting in fewer customers rolling off. Heaven for frozen strawberry-daiquiri lovers.

Bar Destiny (☎ 24270 24172; Polytechniou) Look for the soft blue light coming from this hip side-street bar with music videos, draught beer and a bit of dancing when the mood hits.

The dancing and drinking scene heats up after midnight along the club strip past the new harbour. Best DJs are at **BBC** (☎ 24270 21190), followed by **Kahlua Bar** (☎ 24270 23205) and **Club Pure** (☎ 6979773854), open till dawn.

Entertainment

Cinema Attikon (☎ 24270 22352; Papadiamanti; admission €7) Catch current English-language movies at this open-air cinema, sip a beer (beer and snacks €2 to €4) and practise speed-reading your Greek subtitles at the same time. (Greece is one of the few countries in Europe to show films in the original language, not dubbed.)

Shopping

Glittery open-air shops fill Papadiamanti. But branch off one of the ever-disappearing side streets to explore another side of Skiathos.

Loupos & his Dolphins (☎ 24270 23777; Plateia Papadiamanti; 🕙 10am-1.30pm & 6-11.30pm) Look for delicate hand-painted icons, fine Greek ceramics, along with gold and silver jewellery at this high-end gallery shop, next to Papadiamanti Museum.

Galerie Varsakis (☎ 24270 22255; Plateia Trion Ierarhon; 🕙 10am-2pm & 6-11pm) Browse for unusual antiques like 19th-century spinning sticks made by grooms for their intended brides, plus unusual Greek and African textiles. The collection rivals the best folklore museums in Greece.

Archipelagos Gallery (☎ 24270 22585; Plateia Papadiamanti; 🕙 11am-1pm & 8-10pm) Work by con-temporary Greek and visiting artists stands out at this intimate shop.

AROUND SKIATHOS
Sights & Activities
BEACHES

With some 65 beaches to choose from, beach-hopping on Skiathos can become a full-time occupation. Buses ply the south coast, stopping at 26 numbered beach access points. **Megali Amos** is only 2km from town, but fills up quickly. The first long stretch of sand worth getting off the bus for is the pine-fringed **Vromolimnos Beach**. Further along, **Kolios Beach** and **Troulos Beach** are also good but both, alas, very popular. The bus continues to **Koukounaries Beach**, backed by pine trees and touted as the best beach in Greece. But nowadays its crowded summer scene is best viewed at a distance, from where the 1200m long sweep of pale gold sand does indeed sparkle.

Big Banana Beach, known for its curving shape and soft white sand, lies at the other side of a narrow headland. Skinny-dippers tend to abscond to laid-back **Little Banana Beach** (also popular with gay and lesbian sunbathers) around the rocky corner.

West of Koukounaries, **Agia Eleni Beach** is a favourite with windsurfers. Sandy **Mandraki Beach**, a 1.5km walk along a pine-shaded path, is just far enough to keep it clear of the masses. The northwest coast's beaches are less crowded but are subject to the strong summer *meltemi* (northeasterly winds). From here a right fork continues 2km to **Mikros Aselinos Beach** and 5km further on to secluded **Kehria Beach**.

Lalaria Beach is a tranquil strand of pale-grey, egg-shaped pebbles on the northern coast. It is much featured in tourist brochures, but only reached by excursion boat from Skiathos Town (see Tours, p413).

KASTRO ΚΑΣΤΡΟ

Kastro, perched dramatically on a rocky headland above the north coast, was the fortified pirate-proof capital of the island from 1540 to 1829; an old cannon remains at the northern end. Four of the crumbling town's old churches have been restored, and the views are magnificent. Excursion boats come to the beach below Kastro, from where it's an easy clamber up to the ruins.

MONI EVANGELISTRIAS ΜΟΝΗ ΕΥΑΓΓΕΛΙΣΤΡΙΑΣ
The most famous of the island's monasteries is the 18th-century **Moni Evangelistrias** (Monastery of the Annunciation; ☎ 24270 22012; ⏱ 9.30am-1.30pm & 5-7pm), poised 450m above sea level and surrounded by pine and cypress trees. It was a refuge for freedom fighters during the War of Independence and the Greek flag was first raised here, in 1807. Today, two monks do the chores, which include wine-making. You can sample, and buy, the tasty results of their efforts in the **museum** (admission €1) shop. An adjacent shed of old olive and wine presses and vintage barrels recalls an earlier era, long before the satellite dish was installed above the courtyard.

MONI PANAGIAS KOUNISTRAS ΜΟΝΗ ΠΑΝΑΓΙΑΣ ΚΟΥΝΙΣΤΡΑΣ
From Troulos (bus stop 20), a road heads north to the 17th-century **Moni Panagias Kounistras** (Monastery of the Holy Virgin; ⏱ morning-dusk), which is worth a visit for the fine frescoes adorning its *katholikon*. It's 4km inland from Troulos.

DIVING
The small islets off the south shore of Skiathos make for great diving. Rates average €40-50 for half-day dives, equipment included.

Dive instructor team Theofanis and Eva of **Octopus Diving Centre** (☎ 24270 24549, 6944168958; www.odc-skiathos.com; new harbour) lead dives around Tsougria and Tsougriaki islets for beginners and experts alike. Call or enquire at their boat.

Skiathos Diving Centre (☎ 24270 24424; www.skiathosdivingcenter.gr; Papadiamanti), and **Dolphin Diving** (☎ 24270 21599, 6944999181; www.ddiving.gr; Nostos Beach) are also popular for first-time divers, with dives off Tsougriaki Islet exploring locations 30m deep.

HIKING
A 6km-long hiking route begins at Moni Evangelistrias, eventually reaching **Cape Kastro**, before circling back through Agios Apostolis. Kastro is a spring mecca for birdwatchers, who may spot long-necked Mediterranean shags and singing blue-rock thrushes on the nearby rocky islets.

THE GREEN BEEKEEPER OF SKIATHOS *Michael Clark*

Bouncing along a dirt road in his old car, Skiathos beekeeper Yiannis talked non-stop about his life before bees and since. 'I had once work with stock markets, and I can't sleep the night. But Hippocrates say, "Give milk and honey"', referring to the 5th-century-BC father of medicine. 'It's clean now, inside me.' Then, laughing, he corrected himself, 'It's a dirty job, but is something good to the land.'

At the bee field, Yiannis, who's in his early 30s, has scattered about 100 blue boxes, each with 7000 to 10,000 bees. 'I'm first one in Skiathos. Hard to find the young person to do this.' With that, he takes out a small 'smoke can', stuffs a handful of green weeds into it, then lights it with a match. Smoke pours out as he waves it around a bee box. 'Smoke to scare the bees. Communicate to queen 'fire danger!' Then queen, she makes more eggs!'

He talks about the honey (in Greek, *meli*) and about different blossoms and trees – *elatos* (fir) and *pefko* (pine) are favourites. 'Bees, the inside, make love the flower'. I wave off some bees who are getting a little too friendly. We are both wearing protective head nets, but our arms and hands are exposed. Yiannis shows little concern: 'The bees, they know me.' As for me, I just mutter, 'I'm with him'.

Opening another box, Yiannis' face lights up: 'Look, is the queen! You must have good queen. She live four years. One good queen, young, make lot of honey'. He reads my mind: 'Fifteen euros to buy new queen. We have Greek queen, Italian queen'.

But a new queen must be accepted by the bee colony. 'Different smell, so bees must accept her.' This entails putting the new and hungry queen in a tiny box with a door made of food. By the time she nibbles her way out 24 hours later, she is usually accepted. 'But if not understand, the bees, they kill her.'

Without partners or assistants, Yiannis works alone, but confides, 'The bees, they help!' His modest goal is to double his production from 100 to 200 boxes. 'We have best honey in all the world.' His pride is contagious, but I'm impressed that he never loses sight of the larger picture: 'The land and the sky have energy. The bee feel this. We need the honey, for the planet. To be careful, the green planet!'

Sleeping & Eating

Koukounaries Camping (☎ /fax 24270 49250; camp sites per adult/tent €10/4; **P**) Shaded by fig and mulberry trees, this family-managed site near the eastern end of Koukounaries Beach features spotless bathroom and cooking facilities, a minimarket and taverna.

Achladies Apartments (☎ 24270 22486; http://achladies.apartments.googlepages.com; Achladies Bay; d/tr/f incl breakfast €45/60/75; **P**) Look for the hand-painted yellow sign to find this welcoming gem, 5km from Skiathos Town. Along with self-catering rooms (two-night minimum stay) and ceiling fans, it features an eco-friendly tortoise sanctuary and a succulent garden winding down to a taverna and sandy beach.

our pick **Atrium Hotel** (☎ 24270 49345; www.atriumhotel.gr; Paraskevi Beach; s/d/ste incl breakfast from €100/130/200; **P** ✕ ✕ ☐ ☎ ✿) Traditional architecture and modern touches make this hillside perch the best in its class. Rooms are low-key elegant, with basin sinks and large balconies. A lavish breakfast buffet starts the day, and amenities include sauna, children's pool, billiards and ping-pong.

Panorama Pizza (☎ 6944192066; pizzas €7-10; ✆ noon-4pm, 7pm-late) Escape to this hilltop retreat, off the ring road, for pizza and panoramic views.

SKOPELOS ΣΚΟΠΕΛΟΣ

pop 4700

Skopelos is a beautiful island of pine forests, vineyards, olive groves and orchards of plums and almonds, which find their way into many local dishes.

Like Skiathos, the high cliffs of the northwest coast are exposed, while the sheltered southeast coast harbours several sand-and-pebble beaches. There are two large settlements: the capital and main port of Skopelos Town on the east coast; and the unspoilt west coast village of Glossa, 3km north of Loutraki, the island's second port.

In ancient times the island was an important Minoan outpost ruled by Stafylos (meaning 'grape'), the son of Ariadne and Dionysos in Greek mythology, and who is said to have introduced wine-making here. The island endured more recent fame as a filming location for the 2008 movie *Mama Mia!*

Getting There & Away

BOAT

Skopelos has two ports, Skopelos Town and Glossa, both with links to mainland Volos and Agios Konstantinos, and to the other Sporades islands of Skiathos, Skopelos, Alonnisos and Skyros. For details see Island Hopping (p523).

Tickets are available from **Hellenic Seaways** (☎ 24240 22767; fax 24240 23608) opposite the new quay; and **Lemonis Agency** (☎ 24240 22363) in Pension Lemonis towards the end of the new quay. In Glossa, **Hellenic Seaways** (☎ 24240 33435, 6932913748) is opposite the port.

Getting Around

BOAT

A regular water taxi departs late morning for Glysteri Beach (€5 one way), and returns around 5pm.

BUS

There are seven or eight buses per day in summer from Skopelos Town to Glossa/Loutraki (€4.30, one hour) and Elios (€3, 45 minutes), three that go only as far as Panormos (€2.20, 25 minutes) and Milia (€2.60, 35 minutes), and another two that go only to Agnontas (€1.40, 15 minutes) and Stafylos (€1.40, 15 minutes).

CAR & MOTORCYCLE

Several car- and motorcycle-hire outlets line the harbour in Skopelos Town, mostly located at the eastern end of the waterfront, including the friendly and efficient **Motor Tours** (☎ 24240 22986; fax 24240 22602) next to Hotel Eleni, and **Avis** (☎ 24240 23170).

TAXI

Taxis wait by the bus stop. A taxi to Stafylos is €7, to Limnonari €12, to Glossa €25.

SKOPELOS TOWN

Skopelos Town is one of the most captivating ports in the Sporades. It skirts a semicircular bay and clambers in tiers up a hillside, culminating in an old fortress and a cluster of four churches. Dozens of other churches are interspersed among dazzling white houses with brightly shuttered windows and flower-adorned balconies.

Orientation

The town's waterfront is flanked by two quays. The old quay is at the western end of

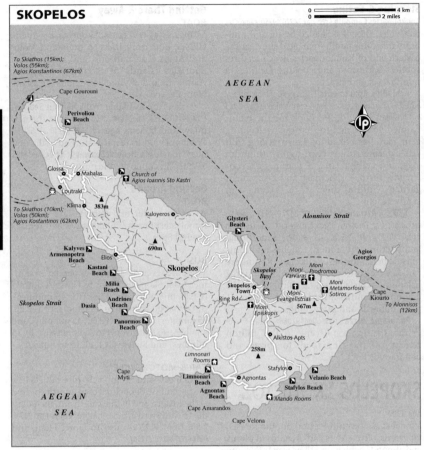

SKOPELOS

the harbour and the new quay is at the eastern end, used by all ferries and hydrofoils. From the dock, turn right to reach the bustling waterfront lined with cafes, souvenir shops and travel agencies; turn left (20m) for the bus stop. Less than 50m away is Plateia Platanos, better known as Souvlaki Sq.

Information

BOOKSHOPS

International newsstand (☎ 24240 22236; ⏱ 8am-10pm) Opposite the bus stop.

EMERGENCY

Health Centre (☎ 24240 22222) On the ring road, next to the fire station.

Police (☎ 24240 22235) Above the National Bank.
Port police (☎ 24240 22180)

INTERNET ACCESS

Blue Sea Internet Café (☎ 24240 23010; per hr €3; ⏱ 8am-2am) Beneath the *kastro* steps.
Orange Net Café (☎ 24240 23093; per hr €3; ⏱ 9am-midnight) Next to the post office.

LAUNDRY

Blue Star Washing (☎ 24240 22844) Next to the OTE office.

MONEY

There are three ATMs along the waterfront.

POST

Post office (Platanos Sq; ⏱ 7.30am-2pm)

TRAVEL AGENCIES

Madro Travel (☎ 24240 22300; www.madrotravel
.com) At the end of the new port, Madro can provide help
with booking accommodation and ticketing, and arrange
walking trips, island excursions, cooking lessons, even
marriages (partners extra).

Thalpos Holidays (☎ 24240 29036; www.holiday
islands.com) The helpful staff at this waterfront agency
offer a range of standard services including apartment and
villa accommodation and tours around the island.

Sights

Strolling around town and sitting at the
waterside cafes might be your chief occupations in Skopelos, but there are also two
small folk museums. The handsome **Folk Art
Museum** (☎ 24240 23494; Hatzistamati; admission €2;
🕑 10am-10pm) features a Skopelean wedding
room, complete with traditional costumes
and bridal bed. At the 2009-opened **Bakratsa
Museum** (☎ 24240 22940; admission €3; 🕑 11am-1pm
& 6-10pm), find out how young women and
men, married and unmarried, dressed in
days gone by new.

Tours

Day-long cruise boats (€25 to €50) depart
from the new quay by 10am, and usually take
in the Marine Park of Alonnisos (p423), pausing en route for lunch and a swim. There's a
good chance of spotting dolphins along the
way. For bookings, contact Thalpos Holidays
or Madro Travel on the waterfront.

Sleeping

Hotel prices quoted are for the July-to-August
high season, but are often reduced by 30%
to 50% at other times. An energetic kiosk
('Rooms') next to the ferry dock can help
with accommodation. Also enquire at Madro
Travel or Thalpos Holidays.

BUDGET

ourpick Sotos Pension (☎ 24240 22549; www.skopelos
.net/sotos; s/d €35/50; 🔛 🖳 🛜) The pine-floored
rooms at this charming waterfront pension
are each a bit different; an old brick oven
serves as a handy shelf in one. There's an
interior courtyard, whitewashed terrace and
communal kitchen, all neatly managed by the
welcoming Alexandra (Alex, for short).

MIDRANGE

Hotel Agnanti (☎ /fax 24240 22722; www.skopelos.net/
agnanti; s/d/tr incl breakfast from €45/65/90; P 🔛 🖳)

Theo and Eleni run the show at this inviting
12-room oasis on the far bay, with ceiling
fans, period furniture, ceramic decorations,
plus a paperback lending library in the
rustic lobby.

Alkistis Studio Apartments (☎ 24240 23006;
www.skopelosweb.gr/alkistis; d/apt from €90/120;
P 🔛 🖳 🛜 🖳) Located between Skopelos
Town and Stafylos Beach, this beautifully land-
scaped and family-friendly complex features
huge studio and apartment units with modern
bathrooms, comfy beds and satellite TV.

Hotel Dionyssos (☎ 24240 23210; www.dionyssos
hotel.com; s/d/tr incl breakfast €100/120/130; P 🔛 🛜 🖳)
The low-key Dionyssos occupies a quiet street
between the ring road and the waterfront,
and has a spacious and woodsy lobby. The
upper rooms offer balcony views of the harbour. The hotel pool bar is popular with
town residents.

Also recommended:

Hotel Regina (☎ 24240 22138; www.skopelosweb.gr/
regina; s/d incl breakfast €40/55; 🔛) Vaguely Victorian.

Ionia Hotel (☎ 24240 22568; www.ioniahotel.gr; s/d/
tr/f incl breakfast €76/95/114/137; P 🔛 🖳 🛜 🖳)
Stylish and quiet.

Eating

Just 100m up from the dock, Souvlaki Sq is
perfect for a quick bite of *gyros* or, not surprisingly, souvlaki. Skopelos is known for a variety of plum-based recipes, and most tavernas
will have one or two on the menu.

Taverna Ta Kimata (☎ 24240 22381; mains €5-9) The
oldest taverna on the island (and better known
by the owner's name, Angelos) sits at the end
of the old quay. Step inside to look over the
day's *mayirefta* dishes, such as *briam* (mixed
vegies) and octopus with pasta or lamb *stifadho* (meat cooked with onions in a tomato
purée) – both €8.50.

Taverna Englezos (☎ 24240 22230; mains €7-11)
When we asked for a menu at this waterfront prize, the owner-waiter laughed, saying
'I am the menu!' Great grills at good prices –
half a chicken on the spit for €7. Summer
meals often end with fresh fruit, on the
house.

ourpick To Perivoli Restaurant (☎ 24240 23758;
mains €7-12) Just beyond Souvlaki Sq, Perivoli
promises excellent Greek cuisine in an elegant
courtyard setting. Specialities include grilled
lamb with yoghurt and coriander, and rolled
pork with *koromila* (local plums) in wine
sauce, plus excellent Greek wines.

Anna's Restaurant (☎ 24240 24734; Gifthorema; mains €7-19) Look for the palm tree to find this handsome alleyway bistro, serving authentic Skopelos dishes like sautéed veal with plums, or black risotto with cuttlefish.

Other popular spots:

DIA Discount Supermarket (☎ 24240 24340; ☺ 8.30am-9.30pm)

Michalis (☎ 24240 23591; snacks & cakes €2-5; ☺ 9am-11pm) Great *tyropita* (cheese pie).

Nastas Ouzerie (☎ 24240 23441; mezedhes €2.50-5, mains €6-10) Opposite Hotel Eleni.

Finikas Restaurant (☎ 24240 23247; mains €5-10) Behind Sunrise Villa.

Drinking

Platanos Jazz Bar (☎ 24240 23661) Near the end of the old quay, this leafy courtyard cafe-bar is open for morning coffee and late-night drinks.

Oionos Blue Bar (☎ 6942406136) Cosy and cool, little Oionos serves up blues and soul along with over 20 brands of beer and single malt whiskies at last count.

Mercurios Music Café-Bar (☎ 24240 24593; ☺) This snappy veranda bar above the waterfront mixes music, mojitos and margaritas.

For excellent coffees, juices and free wi-fi access, grab a soft chair at either **Anemos Espresso Bar** (☎ 24240 23564; ☺) or its waterfront neighbour, **En Plo Café-Bar** (☎ 24240 23405; ☺).

Shopping

Gray Gallery (☎ 24240 24266, 6974641597) Works by island and visiting artists are featured in this hole-in-the-wall fine-arts gallery.

Ploumisti Shop (☎ 24240 22059) Browse this attractive shop for excellent ceramics, handmade jewellery, icons, silk scarves, small paintings and Greek music.

Entertainment

Ouzerie Anatoli (☎ 24240 22851; ☺ 8pm-2am, summer only) For mezedhes and traditional music, head to this breezy outdoor *ouzerie*, high above the *kastro*. From 11pm onwards you will hear traditional *rembetika* music sung by Skopelos' own exponent of the Greek blues and master of the bouzouki, Georgos Xindaris.

GLOSSA & LOUTRAKI
ΓΛΩΣΣΑ & ΛΟΥΤΡΑΚΙ

Glossa, Skopelos' other settlement, is a white-washed delight, and the upper square is a good place to get a feel for the entire village.

From the bus stop by the large church, a road winds down 3km to the low-key ferry port of Loutraki, with several tavernas and domatia; a smaller lane leads nearby to the business district, with a bank ATM, pharmacy, excellent bakery and a few eateries. A considerably shorter *kalderimi* (cobblestone path) connects both villages as well. Fans of the movie *Mama Mia!* (with Meryl Streep) can start their pilgrimage in Glossa to reach the film's little church, **O Yiannis sto Kastri** (St John of the Castle).

Loutraki means 'small bath' and you can find the remains of ancient **Roman baths**, with details in English, at the 'archaeological kiosk' on the port.

Sleeping & Eating

Hotel Selenunda (☎ 24240 34073; www.skopelosweb.gr/selenunda; Loutraki; d/tr from €40/55; P ☒ ☺) Perched well above the port, these self-catering rooms are large and airy. A family apartment sleeps four, and the genial hosts, Karen and Babbis, can suggest ways to explore the area.

Flisvos Taverna (☎ 24240 33856; Loutraki; mains €3-7) Perched above the seawall 50m north of the car park, this friendly family taverna offers fresh fish at decent prices, fresh chips, home-made *mousakas*, and perfect appetisers like *taramasalata* (a thick purée of fish roe, potato, oil and lemon juice) and tzatziki.

Taverna To Steki Mastora (☎ 24240 33563; Glossa; mains €4-7) Look for a small animal roasting on a big spit outside this popular *psistaria* (restaurant serving grilled food), between the church and bakery.

Agnanti Taverna & Bar (☎ 24240 33076; Glossa; mains €8-12) Enjoy the views of Evia from swank Agnanti's rooftop terrace, along with superb Greek fusion dishes like grilled sardines on pita with sea fennel and sun-dried tomatoes.

AROUND SKOPELOS
Sights & Activities
MONASTERIES

Skopelos has several monasteries that can be visited on a beautiful scenic drive or day-long trek from Skopelos Town. Begin by following the road (Monastery Rd), which skirts the bay and then climbs inland. Continue beyond the signposted Hotel Aegeon until the road forks. Take the left fork, which ends at the 18th-century **Moni Evangelistrias**, now a convent. The monastery's prize, aside from the superb views, is a gilded iconostasis containing an 11th-century icon of the Virgin Mary.

The right fork leads to the uninhabited 16th-century **Moni Metamorfosis Sotiros**, the island's oldest monastery. From here a decent dirt road continues to the 17th-century **Moni Varvaras** with a view to the sea, and to the 18th-century **Moni Prodromou** (now a convent), 8km from Skopelos Town.

Moni Episkopis rests within the Venetian compound of a private Skopelian family, about 250m beyond the ring road. Ring **Apostolis** (☎ 6974120450) for details and an invitation. The small chapel within is a wonder of light and Byzantine icons.

BEACHES

Skopelos' best beaches are on the sheltered southwest and west coasts. The first beach you come to is the sand-and-pebble **Stafylos Beach**, 4km southeast of Skopelos Town. From the eastern end of the beach a path leads over a small headland to the quieter **Velanio Beach**, the island's official nudist beach and coincidentally a great snorkelling spot. **Agnontas**, 3km west of Stafylos, has a small pebble-and-sand beach and from here caïques sail to the superior and sandy **Limnonari Beach**, in a sheltered bay flanked by rocky outcrops. Limnonari is also a 1.5km walk or drive from Agnontas.

From Agnontas the road cuts inland through pine forests before re-emerging at pretty **Panormos Beach**, with a few tavernas and domatia. Enquire at **Panormos Travel** (☎ 24240 23380) for accommodation bookings. One kilometre further, little **Andrines Beach** is sandy and less crowded. The next two beach bays, **Milia** and **Kastani**, are excellent for swimming.

Tours

If you can't tell a twin-tailed pascha butterfly from a double leopard orchid, join one of island resident Heather Parson's **guided walks** (☎ 6945249328; www.skopelos-walks.com; tours €15-25). She fights to maintain Skopelos' natural beauty, and her four-hour Panormos walk follows an old path across the island, ending at a beach taverna, with wonderful views to Alonnisos and Evia along the way. Her book, *Skopelos Trails* (€10.25), contains graded trail descriptions and a pull-out illustrated map, and is available in waterfront stores.

Sleeping & Eating

There are small hotels, domatia, tavernas and beach canteens at Stafylos, Agnontas, Limnonari, Panormos, Andrines and Milia.

Limnonari Rooms & Taverna (☎ 24240 23046; www.skopelos.net/limnonarirooms; Limnonari Beach; d/tr/ste €65/80/120; P ⚛) Set back on a beautiful and sandy bay, this well-managed domatio features a well-equipped communal kitchen and terrace, just 30m from the water. The garden taverna serves a perfect vegetarian *mousakas* (€7), along with owner Kostas' homemade olives and feta.

our pick **Mando Rooms** (☎ 24240 23917; www .skopelos.net/mando; s/d/tr/f €80/90/110/150; P ⚛) Having its own cove on the bay at Stafylos is a good start at this family-oriented and welcoming pension. Other extras include free coffee, a communal kitchen, satellite TV, and a platform over the rocks to enter the water.

ALONNISOS
ΑΛΟΝΝΗΣΟΣ

pop 2700

Alonnisos rises from the sea like a mountain of greenery with thick stands of pine and oak, along with mastic and arbutus bushes, and fruit trees. The west coast is mostly precipitous cliffs but the east coast is speckled with small bays and pebbly beaches and remains of a 5th-century-BC shipwreck. The water around Alonnisos has been declared a national marine park, and is the cleanest in the Aegean.

But lovely Alonnisos has had its share of bad luck. In 1952 a thriving cottage wine industry came to a halt, when vines imported from California were struck with the disease phylloxera. Robbed of their livelihood, many islanders moved away. Then, in 1965, an earthquake destroyed the hilltop capital of Alonnisos Town (now known as Old Alonnisos or Hora). The inhabitants were subsequently rehoused in hastily assembled dwellings at Patitiri.

Getting There & Away

Alonnisos' main port is Patitiri, which has links to mainland Volos and Agios Konstantinos, and to the other Sporades isles of Skiathos, Skopelos and Skyros. For details see Island Hopping (p508).

Tickets can be purchased from **Alkyon Travel** (☎ 24240 65220), or **Alonnisos Travel** (☎ 24240 65188; book@alonnisostravel.gr), both in Patitiri.

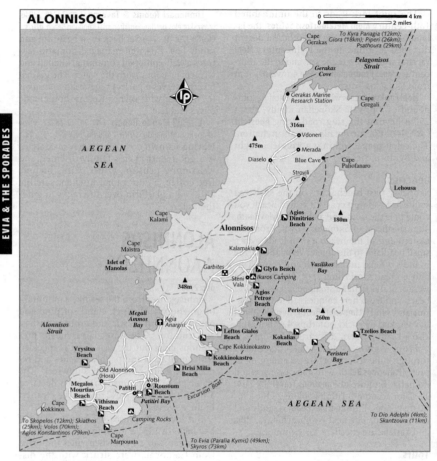

Getting Around

BOAT

Alonnisos Travel (☎ 24240 65188) hires out four-person 15hp to 25hp motorboats. The cost ranges from €48 to €60 per day in summer.

BUS

In summer, one bus plies the route between Patitiri (from opposite the quay) and Old Alonnisos (€1.20, hourly, 9am to about 3pm). There is also a service to Steni Vala from Old Alonnisos (€1.30).

CAR & MOTORCYCLE

Several motorcycle-hire outlets can be found on Pelasgon, in Patitiri, including reliable **I'm Bike** (☎ 24240 65010). Be wary when riding down

to the beaches, as some of the sand-and-shale tracks are steep and slippery. For cars, try **Albedo Travel** (☎ 24240 65804), or **Nefeli Bakery & Rent-A-Car** (☎ 24240 66497), both in Patitiri.

TAXI

The four taxis on the island (Georgos, Periklis, Theodoros and Spyros) tend to congregate opposite the quay. It's about €5 to Old Alonnisos, €8 to Megalos Mourtias and €12 to Steni Vala.

PATITIRI ΠΑΤΗΤΗΡΙ

Patitiri ('wine press' in Greek) sits between two sandstone cliffs at the southern end of the east coast. Despite its hasty origins following the devastating 1965 earthquake that levelled the old hilltop capital (Palia Alonnisos), Patitiri is gradually improving its homely looks. The town is small and relaxed, and makes a convenient base for exploring Alonnisos.

Orientation

Finding your way around Patitiri is easy. The quay is in the centre of the waterfront and two roads lead inland. With your back to the sea, turn left for Pelasgon, or right for Ikion Dolopon. In truth, there are no road signs and most people refer to them as the left-hand road and right-hand road (or main road).

Information

National Bank of Greece ATM (main road)
Play Café (☎ 24240 66119; internet per hr €3; 🕙 9am-2pm & 6-9pm) Opposite the bank.
Police (☎ 24240 65205) Top of main road.
Port police (☎ 24240 65595; quay)
Post office (main road; 🕙 7.30am-2pm)
Techno Plus (☎ 24240 29100; internet per hr €3; 🕙 9am-2pm & 5-9pm) Top of main road.

Sights

FOLKLORE MUSEUM OF THE NORTHERN SPORADES

Largely a labour of love by Kostas and Angela Mavrikis, the **Folklore Museum of the Northern Sporades** (☎ 24240 66250, 6974027465; www.alonissosmuseum.com; admission adult/child €4/free; 🕙 10am-9pm) includes an extensive and well-signed display of pirates' weapons and tools, a blacksmith's and antique nautical maps. A small cafe with displays by local artists sits atop the museum with views of the harbour, and a gift shop is open to the public. Take the stone stairway at the far west end of the harbour.

NATIONAL MARINE PARK OF ALONNISOS

In a country not noted for ecological long-sightedness, the National Marine Park of Alonnisos is a welcome innovation. Started in 1992, its prime aim has been the protection of the endangered Mediterranean monk seal (*Monachus monachus*). See the boxed text (below).

The park is divided into two zones. The carefully restricted Zone A comprises a cluster of islets to the northeast, including Kyra Panagia. Zone B is home to Alonnisos itself and Peristera.

In summer, licensed boats from Alonnisos and Skopelos conduct excursions through the marine park. Though it's unlikely you'll find the shy monk seal, your chances of spotting dolphins (striped, bottlenose and common) are fairly good.

MOM Information Centre (☎ 24240 66350; www .mom.gr; Patitiri; 🕙 10am-8pm) Don't miss this excellent info centre, all about the protected Mediterranean monk seal, with attractive displays, videos in English and helpful multilingual staff on hand.

Activities

WALKING

Walking opportunities abound on Alonnisos, and the best ones are waymarked. At the bus stop in Old Alonnisos a blue noticeboard details several walks. From Patitiri, a 2km donkey track winds up through shrubbery and orchards before bringing you to Old Alonnisos.

Consider a **guided walk** (☎ 6974080039; www .alonnisoswalks.co.uk; walks €15-30) with island resident Chris Browne. A half-day walk above Patitiri winds through pine forest trails, past

---

THE MONK SEAL

Once populating hundreds of colonies in the Black Sea and the Mediterranean, as well as along the Atlantic coast of Africa, the Mediterranean monk seal has been reduced to about 400 individuals today. Half of these live in waters between Greece and Turkey.

One of the earth's rarest mammals, this seal is on the list of the 20 most endangered species worldwide. Major threats include deliberate killings by fishermen – who see the seal as a pest that tears holes in their nets and robs their catch – incidental capture in fishing gear, decreasing food supply as fisheries decline, habitat destruction and pollution.

Recognising that this seal may become extinct if not protected, Greece established the National Marine Park of Alonnisos (above) in 1992, both to protect the seal and to promote recovery of fish stocks.

For more information, visit the website of **MOM** (Hellenic Society for the Study and Protection of the Monk Seal; www.mom.gr).

churches and olive groves overlooking the sea. His book, *Alonnisos through the souls of your feet* (€15), contains detailed forest and coastal trail descriptions, plus prime snorkelling sites. Also available at waterfront shops is the informative *Alonnisos on Foot: A Walking & Swimming Guide* (€14), by Bente Keller and Elias Tsoukanas.

CYCLING

The best mountain-bike riding is over on the southwest coast around the bay of Megali Ammos. There are several bicycle- and motorcycle-hire outlets on Ikion Dolopon.

Courses

Kali Thea (☎ 24240 65513; www.kalithea.org) offers yoga classes and massage on the outskirts of Old Alonnisos.

Tours

Three professional travel agencies on the waterfront provide maps and arrange popular marine park excursions. Enquire at **Ikos Travel** (☎ 24240 65320; www.ikostravel.com) for popular round-the-island guided excursions aboard the *Gorgona* (a classic Greek boat captained by island native, Pakis Athanasiou), which visit the **Blue Cave** on the northeast coast, and the islets of **Kyra Panagia** and **Peristera** in the marine park, with swimming breaks along the way. **Albedo Travel** (☎ 24240 65804; www.albedotravel.com) runs regular snorkelling and swimming excursions aboard the *Odyssey* to Skantzoura and nearby islands, and even arranges island weddings. **Alonnisos Travel** (☎ 24240 65188; www.alonnisostravel.gr) also runs marine park excursions, aboard the *Planitis*.

Sleeping

Prices here are for the higher July and August season; expect discounts of 25% at other times. A helpful quayside kiosk opens in July and August.

Camping Rocks (☎ 24240 65410; camp sites per adult/tent €6/3) Follow the signposts in town to this basic, clean and shaded coastal spot 1km south of Patitiri.

Pension Pleiades (☎ 24240 65235; www.pleiadeshotel.gr; s/d/tr from €25/35/50; ✖ ▣ 🖘) Take the stairway behind the newsstand to find this bright and welcoming budget option with views over Patitiri Bay.

Ilias Rent Rooms (☎ 24240 65451; fax 24240 65972; Pelasgon 27; d €45, 2-/3-bed studios €50/55; ✖) Owners Ilias and Magdalini give their spotless and bright blue-and-white domatia a warm and welcoming touch. Rooms and studios share a communal kitchen.

our pick **Liadromia Hotel** (☎ 24240 65521; www.liadromia.gr; d/tr/ste incl breakfast from €50/70/95; ℗ ✖ ▣ 🖘) This welcoming and impeccably maintained hotel overlooking the harbour was Patitiri's first. All the rooms have character to spare, from hand-embroidered curtains and antique lamps to stone floors and period wood furnishings. The gracious owner, Maria, takes obvious delight in making it all work.

Paradise Hotel (☎ 24240 65213; www.paradise-hotel.gr; s/d/incl breakfast €65/80/100; ℗ ✖ ☙) Wood ceilings and stone-tiled floors give a rustic feel to the balconied rooms, which overlook both bay and harbour. Beyond the pool bar, a small stairway leads down to the bay for swimming.

Eating

Ouzerie Archipelagos (☎ 24240 65031; mains €4-8) If you want to get the feel of this very Greek establishment, pick a table toward the back, where locals gather to order round after round of excellent mezedhes, grilled fish and ouzo (or local favourite *tsipouro*, another distilled spirit) as the night rolls on.

Anais Restaurant & Pizzeria (☎ 24240 65243; mains €5-12; ☙ breakfast, lunch & dinner) Patitiri's first restaurant, opposite the hydrofoil dock, is still going strong, with snappy service and a big menu including souvlakia, pasta, hefty Greek salads and house favourite *kleftiko* (slow-oven-baked lamb, €10).

Also recommended:

Café Flisvos (☎ 24240 65307; mains €5-8) Best *mousakas*.

To Kamaki Ouzerie (☎ 24240 65245; mains €5-15) Father-and-son eatery.

OLD ALONNISOS ΠΑΛΙΑ ΑΛΟΝΝΙΣΟΣ

Old Alonnisos (also known as Palia Alonnisos, Hora, Palio Horio or Old Town), with its winding stepped alleys, is a tranquil, picturesque place with panoramic views. From the main road just outside the village an old donkey path leads down to pebbled Megalos Mourtias Beach and other paths lead south to Vithisma and Marpounta Beaches.

Sleeping

Pension Hiliadromia (☎ /fax 24240 65814; Plateia Hristou; d/2-bed studio €35/55; ✖) Several of the pine-and-stone-floor rooms at the Hiliadromia come with balcony views, and the studios have well-equipped kitchens.

our pick **Konstantina Studios** (☎ 24240 66165, 6932271540; www.konstantinastudios.gr; s/d incl breakfast €60/80; P ⏹ 🛈) Among the nicest accommodation on Alonnisos, these handsome and quiet self-catering studios with traditional styling come with balcony views of the southwest coast. The owner, Konstantina, happily fetches her guests from the dock and offers loads of tips for navigating the island.

Eating & Drinking

our pick **Hayati** (☎ 24240 66244; Old Alonnisos; snacks €2-4; 🕙 9am-2am) Hayati is a sweets shop (*glyko-poleiou*) by day and a piano bar by night, with knock-out views of the island any time of day. Morning fare includes made-to-order Alonnisos *tyropita*. Later, you'll find home-made pastas and juicy souvlaki, handmade desserts, custards and cakes, along with the gracious hospitality of owner-cooks Meni and Angela. It's a five-minute walk from the village square.

Hayati Mezedhopoleio (☎ 24240 65885; Old Alonnisos; mezedhes €2.50-7) The same Hayati whose sweets shop is so good recently opened an excellent little mezedhes-style taverna, 50m up from the square. Menu highlights include fried prawns, *skordalia* (garlic and potato dip), *kritamos* (rock samphire salad) and grilled octopus.

Taverna Megalos Mourtias (☎ 24240 65737; mains €4-8; 🕙 breakfast, lunch & dinner) A stone's throw from the surf, this laid-back taverna and beach bar 2km down the hill from the Hora prepares fine salads, *gavros*, fish soup, and several vegie dishes.

Astrofengia (☎ 24240 65182; mains €5-12) Patitiri residents think nothing of driving up to the Hora, just to sample the evening whims of chef Demi. Shrimp with saffron and garlic in filo dough stands out, along with an excellent vegie *mousakas*. For dessert, squeeze in a slice of *galaktoboureko* (homemade custard pie), whether you have room or not.

Aerides Café-Bar (☎ 6936522583; Old Alonnisos; 🕙 9am-5pm & 7pm-2am) Maria makes the drinks, picks the music and scoops the ice cream in summer at this snappy little bar on the square.

AROUND ALONNISOS

Alonnisos' main road reaches the northern tip of the island at Gerakas (19km), home to

an EU-funded marine research station. Six kilometres north of Patitiri, another sealed road branches off to the small fishing port and yacht harbour of Steni Vala, and follows the shore past Kalamakia for 5km. A third road takes you from Patitiri to Megalos Mourtias.

Maria's Votsi Pension (☎ 24240 65510; www .pension-votsi.gr; Votsi; d/tr from €30/55; ⏹ 🖥 🛈) occupies a perfect little corner of Votsi, just 100m from the bay. Rooms are immaculate and comfortable, and owner Maria's hospitality is everywhere. Nearby, **Milia Bay Hotel Apartments** (☎ 24240 66036; www.milia-bay.gr; d/apt from €85/160; P ⏹ 🛈 🐕) spread out over the hillside with large, well-appointed and self-catering studio apartments.

The island's east coast is home to several small bays and beaches. The first one of note, tiny **Rousoum**, is tucked between Patitiri and Votsi and very popular with local families. Next is the sandy and gently sloping **Hrysi Milia Beach**, another kid-friendly beach. Two kilometres on, **Cape Kokkinokastro** is the site of the ancient city of Ikos, with remains of city walls under the sea. Continuing north, the road branches off 4km to **Leftos Gialos**, with a lovely pebble beach and the superb **Taverna Eleonas** (☎ 24240 66066; mains €5-10) with outstanding versions of traditional *pites* (pies), vegie dolmas (dolmadhes) and excellent wine made by owner Nikos.

Steni Vala, a small fishing village and deep-water yacht port with a permanent population of no more than 30, has two small but decent beaches; pebbly **Glyfa** just above the village and sandy **Agios Petros** just below. There are 50-odd rooms in domatia, a few villas, as well as modest **Ikaros Camping** (☎ 24240 65772; camp sites per adult/tent €5/5), decently shaded by olive trees. Try **Ikaros Café & Market** (☎ 24240 65390) for reliable lodging information and more. The owner, Kostas, also runs the splendid museum in Patitiri. Four tavernas overlook the small marina, with **Taverna Kalimnia** (☎ 24240 65748; mains €4-8) claiming the best views of the harbour.

Kalamakia, 2km further north, is the last village of note, and has a few domatia and tavernas. The fishing boats usually tie up directly in front of **Margarita's Taverna** (☎ 24240 65738; mains €6-15), where the morning catch of fish and lobster seems to jump from boat to plate. Simple and spotless rooms are available at **Pension Niki** (☎ 24240 65989; s/d €30/50; ⏹).

Beyond Kalamakia, the sealed road continues 3km to a wetland marsh and **Agios**

THE ORIGINAL CHEESE PIE

Tyropita (cheese pie) is almost deified in its birthplace, the northern Sporades. The popular pie is made with goat cheese which is rolled in delicate filo dough, coiled up, then fried quickly and served hot – a method that evolved in the wood-oven kitchens of Alonnisos.

However, the pie's origins are open to debate. Alonnisos residents claim their delicacy was appropriated by Skopelos in the 1950s, following the collapse of the cottage wine industry. Struggling Alonnisos farmers went to work on neighbouring Skopelos, picking plums. Their salty cheese pie lasted all day in the fields. Not surprisingly, it also made its way into the country kitchens of Skopelos, where residents claim that the treat was a motherly invention. This version has it that, when *spanakopita* (spinach pies) were slowly baking, resourceful mums quieted fussy children by tearing off a piece of filo, throwing in a handful of cheese, and frying it quickly with a reprimand, 'Here, stop your screaming'.

In the 1990s a popular daytime TV host touted the pie, but credited Skopelos with its origin. Predictably, frozen 'Skopelos Cheese Pie' soon showed up on mainland supermarket shelves. Today you can even buy it in the Athens' airport departure lounge, 'the deterioration of an imitation', according to a long-time Alonnisos resident, Pakis. Don't count on the frozen pie resembling the original and superior version.

On both Alonnisos and Skopelos there are now breakfast versions with sugar and cinnamon, and others using wild greens or lamb, especially popular in winter with red wine. But stunned Alonnisos folk still can't get over what's happened to their simple and delicious recipe. As one Skopelos businesswoman, Mahi, confided, 'Basically, we stole it!'

Dimitrios Beach, with a canteen and domatia opposite a graceful stretch of white pebbles. Beyond this, the road narrows to a footpath heading inland.

ISLETS AROUND ALONNISOS

Alonnisos is surrounded by eight uninhabited islets, all of which are rich in flora and fauna. **Piperi**, the furthest island northeast of Alonnisos, is a refuge for the monk seal and is strictly off-limits. **Gioura**, also off-limits, is home to an unusual species of wild goat known for the crucifix-shaped marking on its spine. Excursion boats can visit an old monastery and olive press on **Kyra Panagia**. The most remote of the group, **Psathoura**, boasts the submerged remains of an ancient city and the brightest lighthouse in the Aegean.

Peristera, just off Alonnisos' east coast, has several sandy beaches and the remains of a castle. Nearby **Lehousa** is known for its stalactite-filled sea caves. **Skantzoura**, to the southeast of Alonnisos, is the habitat of the Eleanora's falcon and the rare Audouin's seagull. The eighth island in the group, situated between Peristera and Skantzoura, is known as **Dio Adelphi** (Two Brothers); each 'brother' is actually a small island, both home to vipers, according to local fishermen who refuse to step foot on either.

SKYROS ΣΚΥΡΟΣ

pop 2600

Skyros is the largest of the Sporades group, though it can seem like two islands – the small bays, rolling farmland and pine forests of the north, and the arid hills and rocky shoreline of the south.

In Byzantine times, rogues and criminals exiled here from the mainland entered into a mutually lucrative collaboration with invading pirates. The exiles became the elite of Skyrian society, decorating their houses with pirate booty looted from merchant ships: hand-carved furniture, ceramic plates and copper ornaments from Europe, the Middle East and East Asia. Today, similar items adorn almost every Skyrian house.

In Greek mythology, Skyros was the hiding place of young Achilles. See the boxed text, p429, for more information about the Skyros Lenten Carnival and its traditions, which allude to Achilles' heroic feats.

Skyros was also the last port of call for the English poet Rupert Brooke (1887–1915), who died of septicaemia on a French hospital ship off the coast of Skyros en route to the Battle of Gallipoli. Today a number of expats, particularly English and Dutch, have made Skyros their home.

Getting There & Away

AIR

Skyros airport has flights to/from Athens and Thessaloniki and occasional charter flights from Oslo and Amsterdam. Winter flights operate between Skyros and Thessaloniki three times per week (Tuesday, Wednesday and Saturday). Also in winter, there are flights to Athens twice weekly (Tuesday and Saturday).

For tickets, contact **Olympic Air** (☎ 210 966 6666; www.olympicairlines.com) or visit **Skyros Travel Agency** (☎ 22220 91600; www.skyrostravel.com; Agoras St). For flight details, see Island Hopping (p523).

BOAT

Skyros' main port is Linaria, with ferry links to Evia (Paralia Kymis) and to Alonnisos and Skopelos in summer. For details see Island Hopping (p523).

You can buy tickets from **Achileas ticket office** (☎ 22220 91790; fax 22220 91792; Agoras; 🕙 9am-1pm & 7-10pm) on Agoras in Skyros Town. There is also a ferry ticket kiosk at the dock in Linaria, and another at the dock in Paralia Kymis (Evia).

Getting Around

BUS & TAXI

In high season there are daily buses departing from Skyros Town to Linaria (€1.30) and to Molos (via Magazia). Buses for both Skyros Town and Molos meet the ferry at Linaria. However, outside of high season there are only one or two buses to Linaria (to coincide with the ferry arrivals) and none to Molos. A

SKYROS

taxi from Skyros Town to Linaria is €13; to the airport it's €20.

CAR & MOTORCYCLE

Cars, motorbikes and mountain bikes can all be hired from **Martina's Rentals** (☎ 22220 92022; 6974752380) near the police station in town. The reasonable **Vayos Motorbikes** (☎ 22220 92957) is near the bus stop, and **Angelis Cars** (☎ 22220 91888) is 200m before the bus stop.

SKYROS TOWN

Skyros' capital is a striking, dazzlingly white town of flat-roofed Cycladic-style houses draped over a high rocky bluff. It's topped by a 13th-century fortress and the monastery of Agios Georgios, and is laced with labyrinthine, smooth cobblestone streets that invite wandering.

Orientation

The bus stop is at the southern end of town on the main thoroughfare (Agoras) – a lively jumble of people, tavernas, bars and grocery stores and flanked by narrow winding alleyways. The central *plateia* is another 100m beyond the bus stop, From there, the road narrows dramatically, marking the beginning of the town's pedestrian zone. Motorbikes still manage to squeeze through, but cars must park in the nearby car park.

About 100m beyond the *plateia*, the main drag of Agoras forks. The right fork leads up to the fortress and Moni Agiou Georgiou, with its fine frescoes and sweeping views. The left fork zigzags to two small museums adjacent to Plateia Rupert Brooke, where a simple bronze statue of a nude Rupert Brooke faces the sea. The frankness of the statue caused an outcry among the local islanders when it was first installed in the 1930s.

From Plateia Rupert Brooke the cobbled steps descend 1km to Magazia Beach.

Information

Mano.com (☎ 22220 92473; Agoras; internet per hr €3; ⓨ 9am-2pm & 6.30-11.30pm)
National Bank of Greece ATM (Agoras)
Police (☎ 22220 91274) Behind Skyros Travel Agency.
Post office (Agoras; ⓨ 7.30am-2pm)
Skyros Travel Agency (☎ 22220 91600, 6944884588; www.skyrostravel.com; Agoras St; ⓨ 9am-2.30pm & 6.30-11pm) This is a full-service agency that can arrange room bookings, travel reservations, car and motorbike hire, diving and excursions around Skyros.

Sights & Activities

Skyros Town has two museums. The not-to-be-missed **Manos Faltaïts Folk Museum** (☎ 22220 91232; www.faltaits.gr; Plateia Rupert Brooke; admission €2; ⓨ 10am-2pm & 6-9pm) is a one-of-a-kind private museum housing the outstanding collection of a Skyrian ethnologist, Manos Faltaïts, and detailing the mythology and folklore of Skyros. The 19th-century mansion is a labyrinth of Skyrian costumes and embroidery, antique fur-

---

WIND FARM DEBATE

Gauging which way the wind is blowing is becoming trickier on Skyros, where a running controversy continues between concerned residents and a monastery, Moni Megistis Lavras, which owns the land, and which quietly began private negotiations in 2005 with a mainland contractor, Enteka, and the government's Regulatory Authority for Energy. At stake: whether to establish a massive wind farm (at an estimated cost of €500 million) on the southern half of the island to meet the EU's requirement that Greece utilise renewable energy to provide 20% of its energy needs within the decade. Although Greece is anxious to participate in the EU's effort to mitigate climate change, not everyone is thrilled about the location.

If the plan is approved, little Skyros would be home to the largest wind farm in Europe, effectively putting the island's delicate breeding grounds for the rare and endangered Skyrian pony and the Eleonora's falcon at the mercy of 150m-high wind turbines. The proposal comes with the developer's promise to dedicate a portion of the 'wind park' to the delicate ecology in question, and to be called 'Natura 2000'.

The island municipality, together with the Union of Citizens of Skyros, have joined in opposing the proposal, and the issue has already moved to the Council of State, a Greek court that often hears environmental disputes. Of course, no one on Skyros is opposed to sustainable solutions to Greece's energy needs. As one Skyros resident said, 'It's a matter of scale'. It seems that with so much money at stake, there's not much faith in the wind these days.

SKYROS CARNIVAL

In this wild pre-Lenten festival, which takes place on the last four weekends before Clean Monday (Kathara Deftera, or Shrove Monday – the first Monday in Lent, 40 days before Easter), young men portray their elders' vigour as they don goat masks, hairy jackets and dozens of copper goat bells, often weighing up to 30kg. They then proceed to clank and dance with intricate steps through the town, each with a male partner ('korela'), dressed up as a Skyrian bride but also wearing a goat mask. During these revelries there is singing and dancing, performances of plays, recitations of satirical poems and much drinking and feasting. Women and children join in, wearing fancy dress as well. These strange goings-on are overtly pagan, with elements of Dionysian festivals, including goat worship. In ancient times, as today, Skyros was renowned for its goat's meat and milk.

The transvestism evident in the carnival seems to derive from the cult of Achilles associated with Skyros in Greek mythology. According to legend, the island was the childhood hiding place for the boy Achilles, whose mother, Thetis, feared a prophecy requiring her son's skills in the Trojan War. The boy was given to the care of King Lykomides of Skyros, who raised him disguised as one of his own daughters. Young Achilles was outwitted, however, by Odysseus, who arrived with jewels and finery for the girls, along with a sword and shield. When Achilles alone showed interest in the weapons, Odysseus discovered his secret, then persuaded him to go to Troy where he distinguished himself in battle. This annual festival is the subject of Joy Koulentianou's book *The Goat Dance of Skyros*.

niture and ceramics, daggers and cooking pots, vintage photographs and a small gift shop.

The adjacent **Archaeological Museum** (☎ 22220 91327; Plateia Rupert Brooke; admission €2; ☑ 8.30am-3pm Tue-Sun) features excellent examples of Mycenaean pottery found near Magazia and, best of all, a traditional Skyrian house interior, transported in its entirety from the benefactor's home.

Every year around mid-September, Skyros is host to a **half-marathon** (☎ 22220 92789), which starts in Atsitsa and ends at the town square in Skyros Town, with drummers welcoming the first runners across the finish line. A mini-marathon for the children sets the tone, followed by music and dancing.

Courses

Reiki courses are offered by long-time island resident and reiki master **Janet Smith** (☎ 22220 93510; Skyros Town; www.simplelifeskyros.com). It's on the south edge of Skyros Town.

Skyros is home to the British-based holistic holiday centre retreat, the **Skyros Centre** (☎ 22220 92842; www.skyros.com), with facilities both in town and Atsitsa. One- and two-week residential courses feature ever-changing themes ranging from yoga and Greek cooking to sailing and the art of flirting.

Tours

feel ingreece (☎ 22220 93100; www.feelingreece.com; Agora St) is a new endeavour by hard-working local owner Chrysanthi Zygogianni, dedicated to helping sustain the best of Skyrian culture. The focus is on the local arts and the island environment. The office arranges hiking excursions to glimpse wild Skyrian ponies. Boat trips and diving courses, pottery, woodcarving and cooking lessons, scuba diving and Greek dancing are among the offerings. Says Chrysanthi, 'I think tourism should be healthy and supporting something authentic for the community.' Prices start from around €30.

A day-long boat excursion (€35) to the Gerania sea caves on the southeast coast or nearby Sarakino Islet includes lunch and a swim. Contact Skyros Travel for details.

Contact the resourceful **Niko Sekkes** (☎ 22220 92707), manager of the Argo museum shop on upper Agoras, for details on his impromptu tours of the island and the Faltaïts Museum.

Sleeping

BUDGET & MIDRANGE

Hotel Elena (☎ /fax 22220 91738; s/d/tr €30/45/55; P ⊠ 및) A rooftop bar doubles as a breakfast spot on summer mornings here. Rooms are big and comfy, and it's just 100m past the square, easy to find after a night on the town.

our pick **Atherinis Rooms** (☎ 22220 93510, 6979292976; www.simplelifeskyros.com; d/apt from €45/60; P ⊠) Welcoming owners Dimitris Atherinis

TOP FIVE SKYRIAN POTTERY STUDIOS

Skyros is unique for its centuries-old collections of fine and unusual ceramics, dating from the days when passing pirates collaborated with rogue residents, whose houses became virtual galleries for pirate booty, ceramics included. To see the evolution of this island art, make a tour of these favourites:

- Yiannis Komboyiannis (p432)
- Stamatis Ftoulis (opposite)
- Stathis Katsarelias (opposite)
- Ioanna Asnmenou Ceramics (right)
- Efrossini Varsamou-Nikolaou (opposite)

and English transplant Janet Smith are constantly attending to detail at these self-catering apartments (300m below the bus stop). Spacious double rooms feature hand-tiled baths and overlook a well-tended garden. Breakfast (€5) includes fresh juice and homemade bread.

Pension Nikolas (☎ 22220 91778; fax 22220 93400; s/d/tr €50/60/70; P ✖) Set back on a small, quiet road, this comfortable and friendly pension is only a five-minute walk to busy Agoras. The upper rooms have air conditioning and balconies; the lower rooms have fans and open onto a shady garden.

TOP END

Hotel Nefeli & Dimitrios Studios (☎ 22220 91964; www .skyros-nefeli.gr; d/studios/ste incl breakfast €125/190/300; P ✖ ▯ ☎ ➤) This smart hotel on the edge of town has an easy minimalist-meets-Skyrian feel to it, with vintage photographs, handsome furnishings and swank bathrooms. The adjacent family-size studios are part of a remodelled Skyrian house. Both properties share a saltwater swimming pool and bar.

Eating

Skyros welcomes a steady number of visiting Athenians, with the pleasant result that island cooks do not cater to touristy tongues.

Taverna Lambros (☎ 22220 92498; mains €5-8.50) Family-run and roadside Lambros is just 3km south of Skyros Town in Aspous. Generous-sized dishes include lamb and pork grills, fresh fish gumbo and Skyrian cheese bread.

ourpick Maryetis Restaurant (☎ 22220 91311; Agoras; mains €6-9) The local favourite, by far, for grilled fish and octopus *stifadho*, Skyrian goat in lemon sauce, along with hearty soups and mezedhes such as black-eyed beans and bean dip.

O Pappous kai Ego (☎ 22220 93200; Agoras; mains €6-9) The name of this small taverna means 'my grandfather and me', and it's easy to see how one generation of family recipes followed another. Mezedhes are excellent, especially broad-bean dip and Skyrian dolmadhes made with a touch of goat's milk.

Drinking

Nightlife in Skyros Town centres mostly around the bars on Agoras; the further north you go away from the *plateia*, the more mellow the sounds.

Kalypso (☎ 22220 92160; Agoras; ▯) Classy Kalypso plays lots of jazz and blues, and owner-bartender Hristos makes a killer margarita, along with homemade sangria. A side room sports an internet connection.

Rodon (☎ 22220 92168; Agoras) This smart and comfortable late-night hang-out is a mellow spot to end the evening. Bonus points for big drinks and fresh juices.

Agora Café-Bar (☎ 22220 92535; Agoras; ☎) Next to the post office at the back of the main square, this cosy bar offers free wi-fi and a welcoming atmosphere.

Shopping

Argo (☎ 22220 92158; Agoras) Argo specialises in high-quality copies of ceramics from the Faltaïts Museum.

Andreou Woodcarving (☎ 22220 92926; Agoras) Get a close look at the intricate designs that distinguish traditional Skyrian furniture at this handsome shop on upper Agoras.

Leyteris Avgoklouris (☎ 22220 91106) Equally interesting is this open workshop in the nearby village of Aspous.

Ioanna Asnmenou Ceramics (☎ 22220 92723; Agoras) An oasis of fine work near the busy main square.

MAGAZIA & MOLOS
ΜΑΓΑΖΙΑ & ΜΩΛΟΣ

The resort of Magazia, a compact and attractive place of winding alleys, is at the southern end of a splendid, long sandy beach, situated a short distance north of Skyros Town. Skinny-dippers can leave it all behind at **Papa Houma** near the southern end of Magazia.

At the northern end of the beach, once-sleepy Molos now has its own share of decent tavernas and rooms. Its landmark windmill and adjacent rock-hewn Church of Agios Nikolaos are easy to spot.

Activities
Several potters spin their wheels in Magazia without bothering to put a sign out, but they are happy to see visitors, and some of their exceptional work is for sale. **Stathis Katsarelias** (☎ 22220 92918) runs a studio on the small lane between the main road and Taverna Stefanos; he also offers drop-in pottery workshops for adults, kids and whoever wants to get their hands muddy. The studios of **Efrossini Varsamou-Nikolaou** (☎ 22220 91142) are in the Deidamia Hotel. Just down from Taverna Stefanos, you'll find the workshop of **Stamatis Ftoulis** (☎ 22220 91559).

Sleeping
Georgia Tsakamis Rooms (☎ 22220 91357; gtsakamis @yahoo.gr; Magazia; d/tr €45/50; 🅿) You can't get much closer to the sand and sea than at these geranium-adorned domatia 20m from the beach, opposite a handy car park.

Deidamia Hotel (☎ 22220 92008; www.deidamia .com; d/tr/f from €45/50/70; 🅿 🖭 🖳 🛜) The spacious and tidy Deidamia is on the road entering Magazia, opposite a small market. Look for the bougainvillea garden and rooftop solar panels.

Ariadne Apartments (☎ 22220 91113; www. ariadnestudios.gr; d/apt from €65/95; 🖭 🛜) Just 50m from the beach at Magazia, these inviting studios and two-room apartments enclose a small courtyard and breakfast cafe (with great pastries). Handsome rooms have fully equipped kitchens and are decorated with original artwork.

ourpick Perigiali Studios (☎ 22220 92075; www. perigiali.com; d/tr/apt incl breakfast from €75/90/180; 🖭 🛜 🖳) Perigiali feels secluded despite being only 50m from the beach. One part of the compound features Skyrian-style rooms overlooking a garden with pear, apple and apricot trees, while a new upscale wing sports a pool with swank view apartments. English-speaking owner Amalia is full of ideas for travellers.

Eating & Drinking
Juicy Beach Bar (☎ 22220 93337; snacks €2-5; Magazia) Escape the midday sun or chill under the

stars at busy Juicy's, with breakfast throughout the day.

Stefanos Taverna (☎ 22220 91272; mains €4.50-8) Sit on the terrace of this traditional eatery overlooking Magazia Beach, and choose from a range of point-and-eat dishes, wild greens, souvlakia and fresh fish by the kilo. Breakfast omelettes start at €3.50.

Oi Istories Tou Barba (My Uncle's Stories; ☎ 22220 91453; Molos; mains €4-10) Look for the light blue railing above the beach in Molos to find this excellent cafe and *tsipouradhiko* with well-prepared prawn and octopus mezedhes.

Thalassa Beach Bar (Sea; ☎ 22220 92044; Molos) This thoroughly modern beach bar somehow blends in with easy-going Molos. Maybe it's the mojitos and full-moon parties.

AROUND SKYROS
Linaria Λιναριά
Linaria, the port of Skyros, is tucked into a small bay filled with bobbing fishing boats and a few low-key tavernas and *ouzeries*. Things perk up briefly whenever the *Achileas* ferry comes in, its surreal arrival announced with the booming sound of Richard Strauss' *Also Sprach Zarathustra* blasting from the speakers at a hillside bar above the port; the acoustics would make any audio engineer proud.

You can practically stumble off the ferry and into **King Lykomides Rooms to Let** (☎ 22220 93249, 6972694434; soula@skyrosnet.gr; r incl breakfast €45-60; 🅿 🖭 🖳), an efficient domatio managed by the hospitable Soula Pappas. It has well-maintained rooms, each with balcony.

Join the port regulars under the big plane tree at the friendly **Taverna O Platanos** (☎ 22220 91995; mains €5-7), which has well-prepared grilled octopus and fried *gavros*, plus oven-ready chicken and potatoes, and generous Greek salads.

For drinks at sunset there's **Kavos Bar** (☎ 22220 93213; drinks & snacks €2-5). This swank open-air bar, perched on the hill overlooking the port, pulls in Skyrians from across the island.

Atsitsa Ατσίτσα
The picturesque port village of Atsitsa on the island's west coast occupies a woodsy setting, shaded by pines that approach the shore, where **Taverna Antonis** (☎ 22220 92990; mains €4-8) sits opposite a small pier where the family's fishing boat ties up.

ourpick **Sunset Café** (☎ 22220 91331; Atsitsa; drinks & snacks €1.50-4) overlooks the bay. This snappy all-organic cafe is a treat. Choose from Greek coffee, wines from Corinth, fresh juices, ice creams, *karidhopita* (walnut cake) and delicate salads, all compliments of Mariana and family. Look for the family's adopted pelican, Poseidon, while you're there.

Nearby, just a few metres from the beach, is the ceramics workshop of **Yiannis Komboyiannis** (☎ 22220 91064; www.artinskyros.gr; Kira Panagia). This ceramics master goes about his work methodically, visitors or no visitors. The yard facing the beach is filled with rope, random sculptures, fishing nets, an old boat pulled ashore and his most recent handiwork drying in the sun. Look for workshops and gallery openings in the summer.

Beaches

Beaches on the northwest coast are subject to strong winter currents and summer *meltemi* winds.

Atsitsa has a small pebble beach shaded by pines, good for freelance camping, but too rocky for swimming. Just to the north (1.5km) is the superior swimming beach of **Kyra Panagia**, named for the monastery on the hill above. Just 1.5km to the south, the tiny and protected north-facing bay at **Cape Petritsa** is also good for swimming.

A beautiful horseshoe-shaped beach graces **Pefkos Bay**, 10km southeast of Atsitsa. Nearby, the beach at **Aherounes** has a gentle sandy bottom, very nice for children, along with two tavernas and domatia.

To the north and near the airport, **Palamari** is a graceful stretch of sandy beach that does not get crowded. Palamari is also the site of a well-marked **archaeological excavation** (www.skyros .gr/ancient-palamari-skyros.html) of a walled Bronze Age town dating from 2500 BC. At the airport junction, the popular roadside **Taverna To Perasma** (☎ 22220 92911; mains €4.50-7) serves excellent *mayirefta* dishes (goat in lemon sauce €6).

Rupert Brooke's Grave

Rupert Brooke's well-tended marble grave is in a quiet olive grove just inland from Tris Boukes Bay in the south of the island, and marked with a wooden sign in Greek on the roadside. The gravestone is inscribed with some of Brooke's verses, beginning with the following apt epitaph:

> If I should die think only this of me:
> That there's some corner of a foreign field
> That is forever England.

From coastal Kalamitsa, just east of Linaria, a road south passes the village of Nyfi, and brings you to Brooke's simple tomb. No buses come here, and travel is restricted beyond this southernmost corner of the island, which is dominated by the Greek Naval station on Tris Boukes Bay.

Ionian Islands
Τα Ιόνια Νησιά

The Ionian Sea is where 'the blue begins', in Lawrence Durrell's haunting phrase, and the Ionian Islands are certainly where Greece begins to seduce with its heat, its intensity of colour and its dazzling light. This is where the grey north relents entirely. The main islands of Corfu, Paxi, Lefkada, Ithaki, Kefallonia and Zakynthos lie scattered down the west coast of mainland Greece like fragments of a mosaic. With their olive groves, cypress trees, starkly beautiful mountains, and countless beaches fringing iridescent waters, they offer something for adventure seekers, culture vultures and beach bums alike. Devastating earthquakes and the formative hands of such occupiers as the Venetians, French and British, have shaped the architecture of the islands while Italy, especially, has inspired a unique Ionian cuisine. In Corfu Town you can admire British neoclassical palaces, drink beneath Parisian-style arcades and wander through Venetian alleyways. Yet, on all the islands, the seductive spirit of Old Greece survives, in Byzantine churches and in village *plateies* (squares) shaded by bougainvilleas and plane trees, or beneath a taverna's vine-covered canopy amid the scent of jasmine.

The islands are, of course, overwhelmed by conspicuous tourism in countless beach resorts, but it is still possible to get off the beaten track to isolated swimming coves, to wander across rugged mountains, or to seek out the dreamy silence of lonely hamlets. Cultural adventurers can explore fortresses, ancient churches and Homeric sites and can visit numerous museums and art galleries of great quality. Outdoor addicts can hike, cycle, windsurf and scuba dive and everyone can enjoy some of the finest food and drink in Greece amid the reassuring spirit of Ionian *filoxenia* (hospitality) and friendliness.

IONIAN ISLANDS

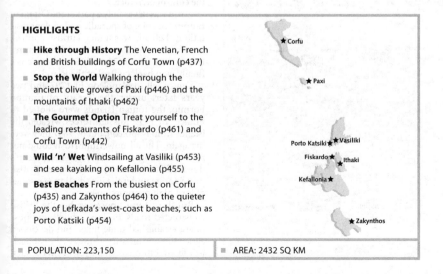

HIGHLIGHTS

- **Hike through History** The Venetian, French and British buildings of Corfu Town (p437)
- **Stop the World** Walking through the ancient olive groves of Paxi (p446) and the mountains of Ithaki (p462)
- **The Gourmet Option** Treat yourself to the leading restaurants of Fiskardo (p461) and Corfu Town (p442)
- **Wild 'n' Wet** Windsailing at Vasiliki (p453) and sea kayaking on Kefallonia (p455)
- **Best Beaches** From the busiest on Corfu (p435) and Zakynthos (p464) to the quieter joys of Lefkada's west-coast beaches, such as Porto Katsiki (p454)

★ Corfu

★ Paxi

Porto Katsiki ★ ★ Vasiliki

Fiskardo ★ ★ Ithaki

Kefallonia ★

★ Zakynthos

- POPULATION: 223,150
- AREA: 2432 SQ KM

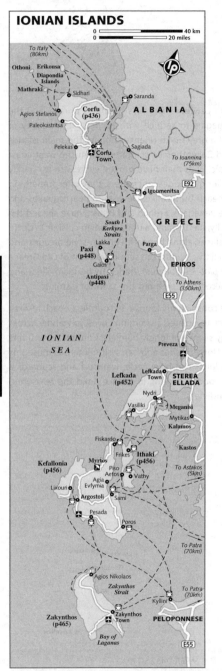

IONIAN ISLANDS

History

The origin of the name 'Ionian' is obscure, but it's thought to derive from the goddess Io. As yet another of Zeus' paramours, Io fled the wrath of a jealous Hera (in the shape of a heifer), and happened to pass through the waters now known as the Ionian Sea.

If we are to believe Homer, the islands were important during Mycenaean times; however, no traces of palaces or even modest villages from that period have been revealed, though Mycenaean tombs have been unearthed. Ancient history lies buried beneath tonnes of earthquake rubble – seismic activity has been constant on all Ionian islands.

By the 8th century BC, the Ionian Islands were in the clutches of the mighty city-state of Corinth, which regarded them as stepping stones on the route to Sicily and Italy. A century later, Corfu staged a successful revolt against Corinth, which was allied to Sparta, and became an ally of Sparta's arch enemy, Athens. This alliance provoked Sparta into challenging Athens, thus precipitating the Peloponnesian Wars (431–404 BC). The wars left Corfu depleted and it became little more than a staging post for whoever happened to be holding sway in Greece. By the end of the 3rd century BC, the Romans ruled the Ionian Islands. Following the decline of the Roman Empire, the islands saw the usual waves of invaders fastening on Greece. After the fall of Constantinople, the Ionian Islands fell under the control of Venice.

Corfu was never fully a part of the Ottoman Empire, in spite of sporadic and violent visitations. Lefkada was under Turkish control, however, except for occasional Venetian retrenchment, from 1479 until 1684 when Venice finally won back control of the island.

Venice fell to Napoleon in 1797 and two years later, under the Treaty of Campo Formio, the Ionian Islands were allotted to France. In 1799 Russian forces wrested the islands from Napoleon, but by 1807 they were his again. The all-powerful British could not resist meddling, and in 1815, after Napoleon's downfall, the Ionian Islands became a British protectorate under the jurisdiction of a series of lord high commissioners.

British rule was oppressive but the British constructed roads, bridges, schools and hospitals, established trade links, and developed agriculture and industry. However, the nationalistic fervour throughout the rest of Greece soon reached the Ionian Islands and by 1864 Britain had finally relinquished the islands to Greece.

During WWII the Italians invaded Corfu in pursuit of Mussolini's imperialistic ambitions. Italy surrendered to the Allies in September 1943 and, in revenge, the Germans massacred thousands of Italians who had occupied the Ionian Islands. They also bombed Corfu Town and sent 1795 of Corfu's 2000 Jews to be murdered at Auschwitz-Birkenau. On the way to the death camps many died in dreadful conditions that included being transported by sea to Athens in open barges. There is a striking memorial statue to Corfu's Jews in Plateia Solomou, near the Old Port in the area still known as Evraiki, the Jewish Quarter.

The islands saw a great deal of emigration after WWII, and again following the devastating earthquakes of 1948 and 1953. By the 1960s foreign holidaymakers were visiting in increasing numbers and package tourism especially became a feature. Today, tourism is a major influence in the Ionian Islands and future challenges include managing the more negative aspects of the industry in the face of often rapidly changing global trends.

CORFU KEPKYPA

pop 122,670

Corfu – or Kerkyra (*ker*-kih-rah) in Greek – is the second largest and the greenest Ionian island. It is also the best known. This was Homer's 'beautiful and rich land', Shakespeare reputedly used it as a background for *The Tempest* and in the 20th century, the writers Lawrence and Gerald Durrell – among others – extolled its virtues. The island's capital, Corfu Town is one of the loveliest towns in Greece.

WWW.PLANNING YOUR TRIP.COM

There are countless websites devoted to the Ionians – here are some of the better ones:

Corfu www.allcorfu.com, www.kerkyra.net
Kefallonia www.kefalonia.gr, www.kefalonia.net.gr
Lefkada www.lefkada.gr, www.lefkas.net
Ionian Islands www.greeka.com/ionian
Ithaki www.ithacagreek.com
Paxi www.paxos-greece.com, www.paxos.tk
Zakynthos www.zakynthos-net.gr, www.zanteweb.gr

Corfu is mountainous in its northern half where the east and west coastlines can be steep and dramatic and where the island's interior is a rolling expanse of peaceful countryside where stately cypresses rise from a pelt of shimmering olive trees. South of Corfu Town, the island narrows appreciably and becomes very flat. Beaches and resorts punctuate the entire coastline, intensively so north of Corfu Town and along the north coast, but less so in the west and south.

Getting There & Away
AIR
Domestic
Corfu has several flights to/from Athens each day. There are at least three flights a week to/from Thessaloniki, Preveza and Kefallonia. **Olympic Air** (☎ 26610 22962; www.olympicairlines.com) is based at the airport. For details see Island Hopping (p511).

International
The budget airline easyJet has daily direct flights between London and Corfu (May to October).

From May to September, many charter flights come from northern Europe and the UK to Corfu.

BOAT
Domestic
Hourly ferries travel daily between Corfu and Igoumenitsa and hydrofoils and car ferries go between Corfu and Paxi and Paxi and Igoumenitsa daily in high season

There are six ferries daily between Lefkimmi, at the southern tip of Corfu, and Igoumenitsa.

Petrakis Lines (Map p438; ☎ 26610 31649; Ethnikis Antistasis 4) operates passenger-only hydrofoils between Corfu and Paxi from May until mid-October. Be sure to book one day prior; places fill quickly.

For details of all domestic boat connections from Corfu see Island Hopping (p511).

Shipping agencies selling tickets are found in Corfu Town near the new port, along Xenofondos Stratigou and Ethnikis Antistasis. **Mancan Travel & Shipping** (p440; ☎ 26610 32664; Eleftheriou Venizelou 38) and **Agoudimos Lines/GLD Travel** (Map p438; ☎ 26610 80030; tickets@gld.gr; Ethnikis Antistasis 1) have helpful staff.

International
Corfu has regular connections with three ports in Italy (Brindisi, Bari and Venice), operated by

IONIAN ISLANDS

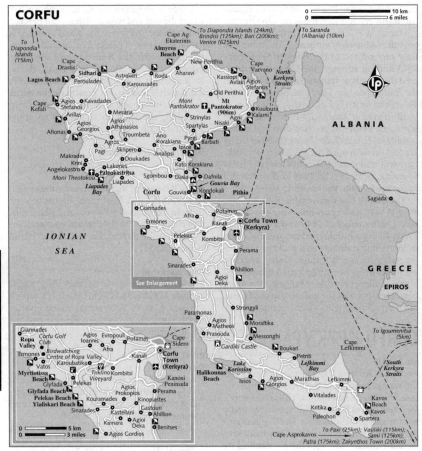

CORFU

IONIAN ISLANDS

a handful of ferry companies sailing between Italy and Igoumenitsa and/or Patra. (Travellers can also sail between Ancona and Igoumenitsa, then transfer to a local ferry.) Crossings are most frequent in July and August, but there are year-round services at least weekly between Corfu and Brindisi, Bari and Venice.

From Corfu it's possible to cross to Albania, or to visit on a day trip. **Petrakis Lines** (Map p438; ☎ 26610 31649; Ethnikis Antistasis 4) operates hydrofoil services connecting Corfu and Albania. Daily sailings go to/from the Albanian town of Saranda. As well as the ticket price, travellers also pay €10 to obtain a temporary visa for Albania.

Note: the only ferry companies that accept Eurail and Inter-rail passes are Bluestar, Superfast and Agoudimos. All international ferry companies also have special offers and concessions for seniors, families and last-minute tickets.

BUS

KTEL (☎ 26610 28898) runs buses three times daily (and on Monday, Wednesday and Friday via Lefkimmi in the island's south) between Corfu Town and Athens (€39.50, 8½ hours). There's also a daily service to/from Thessaloniki (€37.70, eight hours); for both destinations budget another €7.50 for the ferry between Corfu and the mainland. Long-distance tickets should be purchased in advance from Corfu Town's **long-distance bus station** (Map p438; ☎ 26610 28927/30627; I Theotoki), between Plateia San Rocco and the new port.

INTERNATIONAL FERRIES FROM CORFU TOWN			
Destination	Duration	Fare	Frequency
Ancona (Italy)	15¼hr	€73	1 weekly
Bari (Italy)	8hr	€30	17 weekly
Brindisi (Italy)	5½-6¼hr	€38	12 weekly
Saranda (Albania)	25min	€19	1 daily
Venice (Italy)	25hr	€73	4 weekly

Getting Around
TO/FROM THE AIRPORT

There is no bus service between Corfu Town and the airport. Buses 6 and 10 from Plateia San Rocco in Corfu Town stop on the main road 800m from the airport (en route to Benitses and Ahillion). A taxi between the airport and Corfu Town costs around €12.

BUS
Long-Distance (Green) Buses from Corfu Town

Long-distance KTEL buses (known as green buses) travel from Corfu Town's **long-distance bus station** (Map p438; ☎ 26610 28927/30627; I Theotoki).

Fares cost €1.40 to €3.40. Printed timetables are available at the ticket kiosk. Sunday and holiday services are reduced considerably, or don't run at all.

Destination	Duration	Frequency
Agios Gordios	45min	7 daily
Agios Stefanos	1½hr	5 daily
Aharavi (via Roda)	1¼hr	6 daily
Arillas (via Afionas)	1¼hr	2 daily
Barbati	45min	4 daily
Ermones	30min	4 daily
Glyfada	30min	7 daily
Kassiopi	45min	6 daily
Kavos	1½hr	10 daily
Messonghi	45min	5 daily
Paleokastritsa	45min	6 daily
Pyrgi	30min	7 daily
Sidhari	1¼hr	8 daily
Spartera	45min	2 daily

Local (Blue) Buses in Corfu Town

Local buses (blue buses) depart from the **local bus station** (Map p440; ☎ 26610 28927; Plateia San Rocco) in Corfu Old Town.

Tickets are either €0.90 or €1.30 depending on the length of journey, and can be purchased from the booth on Plateia San Rocco (although tickets for Ahillion, Benitses and Kouramades are bought on the bus). All trips are under 30 minutes.

Destination	Via	Bus No	Frequency
Agios Ioannis	Afra	8	14 daily
Ahillion		10	7 daily
Benitses		22	12 daily
Evropouli	Potamas	4	11 daily
Kanoni		2	half-hourly
Kombitsi	Kanali	14	4 daily
Kondokali & Dasia	Gouvia	7	half-hourly
Kouramades	Kinopiastes	5	14 daily
Pelekas		11	8 daily

CAR & MOTORCYCLE

Car- and motorbike-hire outlets are plentiful in Corfu Town and most of the resort towns on the island. Prices start at around €45 per day (less for longer-term hire). Most international car-hire companies are represented in Corfu Town and at the airport. Most local companies have offices along the northern waterfront.

Recommended agencies:

Budget (Map p438; ☎ 26610 22062; Ioannou Theotoki 132)

Easy Rider (Map p438; ☎ 26610 43026) Opposite the new port; rents out scooters and motorbikes.

International Rent-a-Car (Map p440; ☎ 26610 33411/37710; 20a Kapodistriou) Reliable, long-established company with an office on the Spianada (doubles as the Irish Consulate).

Sunrise (Map p438; ☎ 26610 26511/44325; www .corfusunrise.com; Ethnikis Antistasis 6) A reliable choice along the waterfront near the new port.

CORFU TOWN
pop 28,200

Corfu Town takes hold of you and never lets go. Pastel-hued Venetian-era mansions grace the old town, the Campiello. The seafront is a majestic esplanade, known as the Spianada. It is lined with handsome buildings and an arcaded promenade, the Liston, built by the French as a nostalgic nod to Paris's Rue de Rivoli. Today, the Liston, with its swath of packed cafes, is the town's social focus. At the Spianada's northern end stands the Palace of St Michael and St George, a grand neoclassical gesture that was built as the residence for a succession of British high commissioners. To seaward, across a narrow 'moat', the Contrafossa, lies the famous Palaio Frourio (Old Fortress) originating in the 6th century and massively extended by the Venetians. Inland, from all of this historic glory,

IONIAN ISLANDS

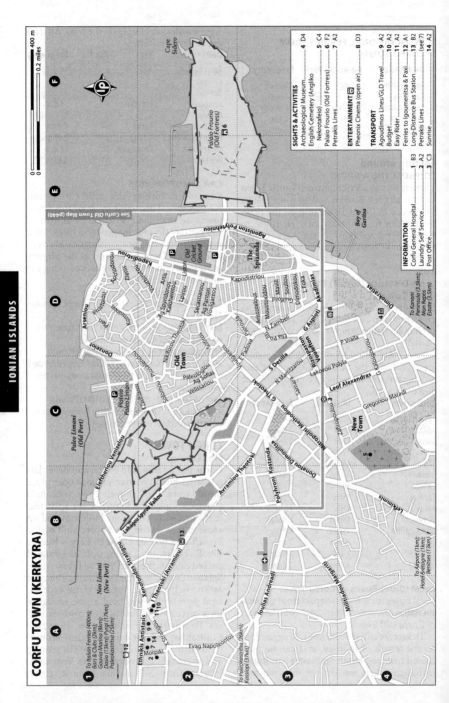

CORFU TOWN (KERKYRA)

IONIAN ISLANDS

INFORMATION	
Corfu General Hospital	1 B3
Laundry Self Service	2 A2
Post Office	3 C3

SIGHTS & ACTIVITIES	
Archaeological Museum	4 D4
English Cemetery (Angliko Nekrotafeio)	5 C4
Palaio Frourio (Old Fortress)	6 F2
Petrakis Lines	7 A2

ENTERTAINMENT	
Pheonix Cinema (open air)	8 D3

TRANSPORT	
Agoudimos Lines/GLD Travel	9 A2
Budget	10 A2
Easy Rider	11 A2
Ferries to Igoumenitsa & Paxi	12 A1
Long-Distance Bus Station	13 B2
Petrakis Lines	(see 7)
Sunrise	14 A2

marble-paved streets lined with shops lead to the bustling modern town. Corfu Town is known also as Kerkyra.

Orientation

The older districts of Corfu Town lie in the northern section between the Spianada and the Neo Frourio, the monolithic 'New Fortress' begun in the 16th century. The southern section is more modern and is crammed with most services and shops. Its main focus is the brash and busy Plateia San Rocco, also known as Plateia G Theotoki Ioannou.

The Paleo Limani (Old Port) of Kerkyra lies on the northern waterfront. At the time of writing a new yacht marina was being built. The Neo Limani (New Port) with all ferry departures, lies west of the Paleo Limani with the hulking Neo Frourio between them. The local (blue) bus station is on Plateia San Rocco and the long-distance (green) bus station is on I Theotoki (formerly known as Avramiou) between Plateia San Rocco and the new port. The airport is just under 2km southeast of the Spianada.

Information

BOOKSHOPS

Tourmoussoglou (Map p440; ☎ 26610 38451; Nikiforou Theotoki 47) For international newspapers, and a range of guidebooks and paperbacks in Greek, English and German.

EMERGENCY

Tourist police (Map p440; ☎ 26610 30265; 3rd fl, Samartzi 4) Off Plateia San Rocco. There is a manned kiosk outside the entrance.

INTERNET ACCESS

The going rate for internet access is around €3 per hour.

Bits & Bytes (Map p440 ; ☎ 26610 36812; cnr Mantzarou & Rizospaston Voulefton) Convenient, but popular with games players.

Netoikos (Map p440; ☎ 26610 47479; Kaloheretou14) Near the Church of Agios Spyridon; with bar.

LAUNDRY

Laundry Service (Map p438; ☎ 26610 34857; Morpiki; per load €12; �8.30am-2pm Mon-Sat, plus 6-8pm Wed-Fri) Around the corner from Petrakis Lines.

MEDICAL SERVICES

Corfu General Hospital (Map p438; ☎ 26610 88200; Ioulias Andreadi)

MONEY

There are banks and ATMs around Plateia San Rocco, on Georgiou Theotoki and by Paleo and Neo Limanis.

Alpha Bank (Map p440; Kapodistriou) Behind the Liston.

National Bank of Greece (Map p440; Voulgareos)

POST

Post office (Map p438; ☎ 26610 25544; 26 Leoforos Alexandras)

TELEPHONE

Public telephones can be found on most major streets and squares. Prepaid telephone cards (from €4) are available from kiosks. The scratch card type is hugely better value than the slot-in type.

TOURIST INFORMATION

There is no national tourist office in Corfu Town. During high season, a municipal **tourist kiosk** (Map p440 ; Plateia San Rocco; �9am-4pm) may operate in Plateia San Rocco, though not on Sundays from April to October. This is the least effective location and the future of even this service may not be certain. A similar kiosk may operate at the ferry arrival port in high season. English-speaking staff at **All Ways Travel** (Map p440; ☎ 26610 33955; www.corfuallwaystravel. com; Plateia San Rocco) are very helpful. Many hotels stock free Corfu maps. The *Corfiot* (€2), an English-language monthly newspaper with listings, is available from kiosks and from shops that sell newspapers.

Sights & Activities

The **Archaeological Museum** (Map p438; ☎ 26610 30680; P Vraïla 5; adult/concession €4/2, Sun free; �8.30am-3pm Tue-Sun) gives top billing to the massive Gorgon Medusa pediment, one of the best-preserved pieces of Archaic sculpture found in Greece. It was part of the west pediment of the 6th-century-BC Temple of Artemis, a Doric temple that stood on the nearby Kanoni Peninsula. The splendid Lion of Menekrates from the 7th century BC is another plus, as is a fragment of pediment featuring Dionysos and a naked youth.

The **Palace of St Michael & St George** (Map p440), at the north end of the Spianada, houses the fascinating **Museum of Asian Art** (Map p440; ☎ 26610 30443; adult/concession €4/2; �8.30am-7pm Tue-Sun May-Oct, 8.30am-3pm Tue-Sun Nov-Apr) containing 10,000 objects, including prehistoric bronzes, porcelain plates, jade figurines, coins

CORFU OLD TOWN

0 ——————— 200 m
0 ——————— 0.1 miles

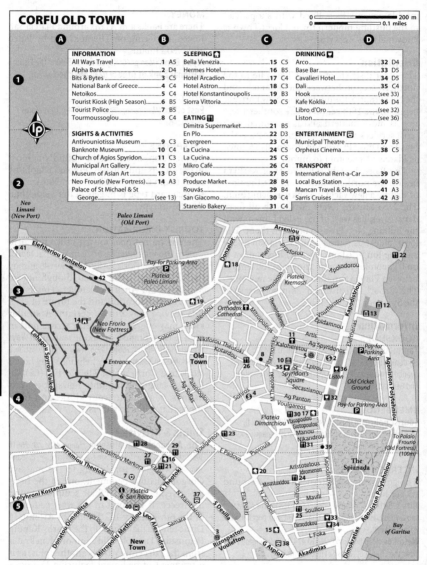

INFORMATION
All Ways Travel	1 A5
Alpha Bank	2 D4
Bits & Bytes	3 C5
National Bank of Greece	4 C4
Netoikos	5 C4
Tourist Kiosk (High Season)	6 B5
Tourist Police	7 B5
Tourmoussoglou	8 C4

SIGHTS & ACTIVITIES
Antivouniotissa Museum	9 C3
Banknote Museum	10 C4
Church of Agios Spyridon	11 C3
Municipal Art Gallery	12 D3
Museum of Asian Art	13 D3
Neo Frourio (New Fortress)	14 A3
Palace of St Michael & St George	(see 13)

SLEEPING
Bella Venezia	15 C5
Hermes Hotel	16 B5
Hotel Arcadion	17 C4
Hotel Astron	18 C3
Hotel Konstantinoupolis	19 B3
Siorra Vittoria	20 C5

EATING
Dimitra Supermarket	21 B5
En Plo	22 D3
Evergreen	23 C4
La Cucina	24 C5
La Cucina	25 C5
Mikro Café	26 C4
Pogoniou	27 B5
Produce Market	28 B4
Rouvás	29 B4
San Giacomo	30 C4
Starenio Bakery	31 C4

DRINKING
Arco	32 D4
Base Bar	33 D5
Cavalieri Hotel	34 D5
Dali	35 C4
Hook	(see 33)
Kafe Koklia	36 D4
Libro d'Oro	(see 32)
Liston	(see 36)

ENTERTAINMENT
Municipal Theatre	37 B5
Orpheus Cinema	38 C5

TRANSPORT
International Rent-a-Car	39 D4
Local Bus Station	40 B5
Mancan Travel & Shipping	41 A3
Sarris Cruises	42 A3

and artefacts in onyx, ivory and enamel, collected from China, Japan, India, Tibet, Nepal, Korea and Thailand. Apart from the museum, the palace's throne room and rotunda have impressive period furnishings and art work.

Behind the eastern side of the palace is the **Municipal Art Gallery** (Map p440; admission €2; 9am-5pm Tue-Sun). This fine collection features the work of leading Corfiot painters, a highlight being *The Assassination of Capodistrias* by Charalambos Pachis. There's also a collection of splendid icons. An annexe, showing changing exhibitions, is located in the front east wing of the palace.

Inside the 15th-century Church of Our Lady of Antivouniotissa is the **Antivouniotissa**

Museum (Byzantine Museum; Map p440; ☎ 26610 38313; admission €2; ⏰ 8am-7pm Tue-Sun Apr-Oct, 8.30am-2.30pm Tue-Sun Nov-Mar). This exquisite aisle-less and timber-roofed basilica, located off Arseniou, has an outstanding collection of Byzantine and post-Byzantine icons and artefacts dating from the 13th to the 17th centuries.

It's worth visiting the two fortresses, Corfu Town's most dominant landmarks. The **Palaio Frourio** (Old Fortress; Map p438; ☎ 26610 48310; adult/concession €4/2; ⏰ 8.30am-3pm Nov-Mar, 8.30am-7pm May-Oct) was constructed by the Venetians on the remains of a 12th-century Byzantine castle. The British made further alterations. The gatehouse area houses a Byzantine museum and exhibition space. The summit of the inner outcrop is crowned by a lighthouse and can be reached by a steep climb for superb views. The **Neo Frourio** (New Fortress; Map p440; admission €3; ⏰ 9am-9pm May-Oct) is a gaunt piece of military architecture reached by a steep climb. Again, there are fine views and the interior is an eerie mass of tunnels, rooms and staircases.

The sacred relic of Corfu's beloved patron saint, St Spyridon, lies in an elaborate silver casket in the 16th-century **Church of Agios Spyridon** (Map p440; Agiou Spyridonos). Nearby is the intriguing **Banknote Museum** (Map p440; ☎ 26610 41552; St Spyridon's Sq; admission €2; ⏰ 9am-2pm & 5.30-8.30pm Wed & Fri, 8.30am-3pm Thu, Sat, Sun Apr-Sep, 8am-3pm Wed-Sun Oct-Mar), part of the Ionian Bank. It has a collection of banknotes, including a sixpenny note from the British period.

A haunting survival of British rule is the peaceful garden-like **English Cemetery** (Angliko Nekrotafeio; Map p438; Kolokotroni) off Mitropoliti Methodiou and also known as the British Cemetery, on the southwestern outskirts of town. It has been lovingly tended by its caretaker over many years and contains the graves of soldiers and civilians of the 19th and 20th centuries.

On the southern outskirts of Corfu on the Kanoni Peninsula is the **Mon Repos Estate** (off Map p438; ⏰ 8am-7pm May-Oct, 8am-5pm Nov-Apr), an extensive wooded park surrounding an elegant neoclassical villa. The estate and villa were created in the 1830s by the second British commissioner of the Ionians, Sir Frederick Adam, as a tribute to his Corfiot wife. The British handed over Mon Repos to King George I of Greece in 1864. It was the birthplace, in 1921, of King George's grandson, the UK's current Duke of Edinburgh (Queen Elizabeth II's husband).

Eighteen months later the Duke's parents – and the baby Duke – fled the island on board a British warship when the new Greek Republic banished its then monarch, and Philip's uncle, King Constantine. For many years ownership of Mon Repos was in dispute between the Greek government and Constantine until the Municipality of Corfu took over the estate and turned it into a rather splendid public amenity. Today, the villa houses the excellent **Museum of Palaeopolis** (☎ 26610 41369; adult/concession €3/2; ⏰ 8am-7.30pm Tue-Sun May-Oct), with entertaining displays of archaeological finds and the history of Corfu Town. Rooms on the first floor are furnished in the early-19th-century Regency style of the British era. Tracks and paths lead through the wooded grounds to the ruins of two Doric temples; the first is vestigial, but the southerly one is still quite impressive.

Parking outside the gates of Mon Repos is limited.

Tours

Petrakis Lines (Map p438; ☎ 26610 31649; Ethnikis Antistasis 4) and **Sarris Cruises** (☎ 26610 25317; Eleftheriou Venizelou 13) both organise day trips from Corfu Town, including an excursion to ancient ruins (Butrinti) in Albania for €59; and a boat trip taking in Paxi (and the Blue Caves) and Antipaxi for €40. Transfers are included and Petrakis Lines offers a 15% discount if you book direct. Passports are required for trips to Albania.

Sleeping

Hotels in Corfu Town are not cheap, with 'budget' being relative to the general high prices. The nearest camping ground is Dionysus Camping Village (p444), 8km away. Book ahead for all options in high season. The hotels mentioned are open all year.

BUDGET

Hermes Hotel (Map p440; ☎ 26610 39268; www.hermes-hotel.gr; Markora 12; s/d/tr €50/60/75; ⌗) Located in a busy part of the new town, just up from Plateia San Rocco and near the market, the Hermes has had a complete makeover in recent years and has pleasant, well-appointed rooms with double glazing. Breakfast is €7.

Hotel Bretagne (off Map p438; ☎ 26610 30724; www.corfuhotelbretagne.com; K Georgaki 27; s/d/tr €50/60/80; ⌗) Close to the airport and about 1.5km from the town centre, but a good budget option with trim, well-maintained rooms; those at the back face onto a small grassy garden.

MIDRANGE

Hotel Astron (Map p440; ☎ 26610 39505; hotel_astron@hol.gr; Donzelot 15; s €75-105, d €80-110, tr €95-125; ☒ ☐) Overlooking Plateia Palaio Limani (Old Port Sq), and patiently waiting for the Old Port marina to be completed, the Astron is steadily updating its airy, good-sized rooms and installing a gym and a spa. It may rename itself the City Marina. Breakfast is €10.

Hotel Konstantinoupolis (Map p440; ☎ 26610 48716; www.konstantinoupolis.com.gr; K Zavitsianou 11; s/d/tr incl breakfast €88/98/118; ☒ ☐) Bright decor enhances the refurbished rooms at this atmospheric old Corfiot hotel overlooking Plateia Palaio Limani.

TOP END

Prices quoted here represent high season rates (reduced at other times) and include breakfast.

Hotel Arcadion (Map p440; ☎ 26610 37670; www.arcadionhotel.com; Vlasopoulou 2; s/d/tr €110/150/170; ☒ ☐) Right on the Liston's busiest corner, the Arcadion has been updated in recent years and its prices likewise.

Bella Venezia (Map p440; ☎ 26610 46500; www.bellaveneziahotel.com; N Zambeli 4; d €170; ☒ ☒ ☐) Housed in what was once a girls' school, the Venezia has comfy rooms and a stylish ambience. The gazebo breakfast room in the garden is delightful.

Siorra Vittoria (Map p440; ☎ 26610 36300; www.siorravittoria.com; Stefanou Padova 36; s €170-235 d €235-315; ☒ ☐) Expect luxury and style at this 19th-century mansion where traditional architecture and modern facilities meet. It's in a quiet location and rooms are well appointed. There's a peaceful garden for breakfasting, beneath an ancient magnolia tree.

Eating

An enduring Corfu experience is people watching and gossiping at the Liston's many cafes, although you'll pay around €3.50 to €5 for a coffee or fresh juice here. Corfiot cuisine has been influenced by many cultures, particularly Italian.

Starenio Bakery (Map p440; ☎ 26610 47370; Guilford 59; snacks under €3) This bakery has a huge selection of homemade gourmet pies, breads and the *best* of best cakes.

Evergreen (Map p440; ☎ 26610 28000; Voulgareos 86; snacks €3-7; ☽ 24hr) A useful pit stop, this street-side place does decent fast food.

Mikro Café (Map p440; ☎ 26610 31009; cnr N Theotoki 42 & Kotardhou; snacks €3.50-6) A little cafe-bar at the heart of the old town, Mikro has a leafy raised terrace and seating that clambers up a narrow lane. There's live entertainment at times and you may catch anything from acoustic riffs to very accomplished slackliners walking the wobbly walk on a shaky line slung between buildings.

En Plo (Map p440; ☎ 26610 81813; Faliraki; mains €5.50-12) A stylish place in a blissful waterside location looking across to Palaio Frourio, En Plo is reached down a slip road at the northern end of Kapodistriou, beyond the Palace of St Michael and St George. They do a fine seafood risotto, and mezedhes plates of meat or fish as well as pizzas and daytime snacks.

ourpick La Cucina Guilford (Map p440; ☎ 26610 45029; Guilford 17; mains €5.50-22); Moustoxidou (Map p440; ☎ 26610 45799; cnr Guilford & Moustoxidou) A long-established restaurant, La Cucina shines for its well-run ethos and its creative cuisine, with hand-rolled pasta dishes to the fore – cajun shrimp with cherry tomatoes, spring onions and mascarpone sauce is delicious. There's a range of creative mezedhes, fresh salads and pizzas, with excellent wines to go with it all. The good news is that a second branch, run by the same owner, has opened a few metres down Guilford at the attractive crossing with Moustoxidou.

Rouvás (Map p440; ☎ 26610 31182; S Desilla 13; mains €8-14; ☽ lunch) Resilient traditional cooking makes this a favourite lunch stop for many locals. It's just down from the market and has even caught the eye of UK celebrity chef Rick Stein for a TV cooking program.

San Giacomo (Map p440; ☎ 26610 30146; Plateia Dimarchiou; mains €8-22) Located in Town Hall Sq, this fine restaurant has such creative starters as octopus in a vinegar and herb sauce and mains of baked lamb with potatoes, paprika, onions, garlic and feta. The wine list is unassumingly good, as is the house wine.

SELF-CATERING

North of Plateia San Rocco is the bustling **produce market** (Map p440; ☽ Mon-Sat), open morning to early afternoon and selling fresh fruit, vegetables and fish. A brand new market on the site was still under construction at the time of writing. For groceries try **Dimitra supermarket**

(Map p440; G Markora). Right opposite the supermarket is the traditional food shop **Pogoniou** (☎ 26610 31320; G Markora 17) which is crammed with cheeses, cold meats, spices, olive oil and much more.

Drinking

The bars along the Liston are top places for preening. They include (all on Map p440): Libro d' Oro, Arco, Liston and Kafe Koklia. Clustered near the Cavalieri are small, intimate music bars such as Hook (p440) and Base Bar (p440).

Dali (p440; N Theotoki) There are other great bars of character deeper into town such as this one with comfy indoor seating and mainstream music.

Cavalieri Hotel (p440; Kapadistriou) The rooftop garden bar of this hotel at the southern end of Kapadistriou is a long-time favourite, if you want to rise in the world.

Entertainment

For bigger dance venues, after 11pm, head to Corfu's disco strip, 2km northwest of the new port, along Ethnikis Antistasis (off Map p438; take a taxi – it's a very busy unlit road without walkways). Recommended are the fashionable and mainstream Privilege, the enduring Au Bar (Ω in Greek) for sharper house, R'n'B and Greek music and the biggest of all, Cristal, the ex-Hippodrome, with several bars. There's usually a €10 admission fee that includes one drink.

For visual entertainment, Corfu Town's **Orpheus Cinema** (Map p440; ☎ 26610 39768; G Aspioti) screens English-language films with Greek subtitles. Just across the road is the summertime open air **Pheonix Cinema** (Map p438; ☎ 69366 91419; G Aspioti) run on the same lines, but you can order pizzas from your seat. Tickets for both are about €7.50.

The **Municipal Theatre** (Map p440; ☎ 26610 33598; Mantzarou) is Corfu's cultural power house and stages various classical music, opera, dance and drama performances, some of which are also staged at the theatre next to the Mon Repos Estate (p441).

Shopping

Numerous sweet shops and tourist haunts cram the streets of the tourist-oriented old town. Some reasonable fashion shops – for shoes, swimwear and dress items – are located in the new town, especially along G Theotoki.

NORTH & NORTHWEST OF CORFU TOWN

Much of the coast just north of Corfu Town is overwhelmed with beach resorts such as **Gouvia**, **Dasia** and the linked resorts of **Ipsos** and **Pyrgi**, all with close-quarters humanity and narrow beaches, but with everything for a fun-time holiday for all the family. To explore fully all regions of the island outside Corfu Town your own transport is advised. Beyond Pyrgi the tawny slopes of **Mt Pantokrator** (906m), the island's highest peak, crowd down to the sea and reclaim the coast at some lovely scenic stretches along a winding road.

Just beyond Pyrgi, you can detour to Mt Pantokrator. Initially, the road corkscrews upward through about 25 hairpin bends and later passes through the picturesque villages of **Spartylas** and **Strinylas**. The road then climbs through stark terrain that is transformed by wildflowers in spring to the mountain's summit and to where the monastery, **Moni Pantokrator**, is now dominated by a massive telecommunications tower sprouting from its courtyard. There's a seasonal cafe and there are superb all-round views as far as the mountains of Albania and the Greek mainland, though it's sometimes hazy. There is very little parking at the top and turning can be awkward. At busy times, park before the steeply twisting final stretch and get some exercise.

Hugging the coast north from Pyrgi, the first decent place is **Barbati** where there's a shingle beach and a water-sports centre. Further on is **Agni** renowned for its three competing tavernas – **Taverna Toula** (☎ 26630 91350), **Taverna Nikolas** (☎ 26630 91243) and **Taverna Agni** (☎ 26630 91142), all of which serve excellent food. The bay-side village of **Kalami** is famous for the picturesque White House, perched above the water. For a time it was home to Lawrence and Nancy Durrell. The Durrell family are famously associated with Corfu and lived on the island for many years prior to WWII. Lawrence became an outstanding writer and one of his nonfiction books was *Prospero's Cell*, a lyrical evocation of Corfu. His brother Gerald's equally splendid book, *My Family and Other Animals*, was based on the Durrell family's eccentric and idyllic life on the island during the 1930s. There are tavernas and rooms at Kalami. North again is **Agios Stefanos** another attractive fishing village and resort nestled in a sheltered bay and with a shingle beach.

IONIAN ISLANDS

Avlaki lies beyond a wooded headland north of Agios Stefanos and has a substantial beach with very little development and only a couple of tavernas, including the friendly **Cavo Barbaro** (☎ 26630 81905; mains €5.50-15). It can catch the wind and is popular for windsurfing.

Kassiopi is a likeable, though very busy place, its streets crammed with shops, tavernas and bars. It's noted for fine embroidery and several shops sell pieces. The town's infrastructure was refurbished in 2009 with the harbour area getting an attractive facelift. Kassiopi's strategic headland was an outpost of Corinth and saw Roman and Venetian settlement. Nero is said to have holidayed outrageously here, while today, British politicians have been guests at the Rothschild estate that lies south of Kassiopi behind the best constructed walls in Corfu, while the mega 'yacht' of Russian oligarch Oleg Deripaska has been known to drop anchor offshore. Nero would have been beside himself with excitement.

In Kassiopi's main street, opposite the church of the Blessed Virgin, steps climb to the ruins of the **Venetian castle**, which was being renovated at the time of writing. You can also walk over the headland to the nearby Battaria and Kanoni Beaches. Beyond Kassiopi, the main road heads west along Corfu's north coast past the hugely popular and custommade resorts of **Aharavi**, **Roda** and **Sidhari**, all served by a succession of beaches. At **New Perithia** halfway between Kassiopi and Aharavi is the **Art of Olive Wood** (☎ 26630 51596; www.olive-wood.gr) a showroom full of authentic artefacts by craftsman Costas Avlonitis. His main workshop is in a lovely setting at Kavadades near Arillas and Agios Georgios (see opposite).

Corfu's other **Agios Stefanos** is on the island's northwest coast and has a large sandy beach. From the nearby fishing harbour regular excursion boats head for the **Diapondia Islands**, a cluster of little-known satellite islands. For excursion details contact **San Stefano Travel** (☎ 26630 51910; www.san-stefano.gr).

Sleeping & Eating

Dionysus Camping Village (☎ 26610 91417; www.dionysuscamping.gr; camp sites per adult/child/car/tent €5.80/3.50/3.50/4, huts per person €11.50; 🛜 🖳) The closest camping ground to Corfu Town, signposted between Tzavros and Dasia and well served by bus 7, has good facilities. Tents can also be hired for €9 per person, or you can opt for simple pine-clad huts with straw roofs

our pick **Casa Lucia** (☎ 26610 91419; www.casa-lucia-corfu.com; Sgombou; studios & cottages €70-120; 🕙 year-round; 🅿 🖳) A garden complex of lovely studios and cottages, Casa Lucia has a strong artistic and alternative ethos and a warm ambience. There are yoga, t'ai chi and Pilates sessions, art, music and other cultural events. Winter lets are very reasonable. It's on the road to Paleokastritsa and is an ideal base for the entire north of Corfu.

Manessis Apartments (☎ 26610 34990; diana@otenet.gr; Kassiopi; 4-person apt €100; 🖳 🛜) It's hard to pick what's more pleasant – the friendly Greek-Irish owner, or her homely bougainvillea and vine-covered two-bedroom apartments. The location, at the end of Kassiopi's picturesque harbour, makes a lovely base. Top-floor apartments have air-conditioning; others have fans.

Little Italy (☎ 26630 81749; Kassiopi; mains €4.50-18) A longstanding Kassiopi favourite, this restaurant sources its ingredients well. The fresh pasta is the real thing and other pleasures include breast of duck with caramelised oranges and green peppers.

Also recommended:

Taverna Galini (☎ 26630 81492 Agios Stefanos; mains €5-12) Fresh local fish are displayed front of house at this efficient restaurant that does a fine seafood pasta and some creative salads and hefty steaks.

Piedra del Mar (☎ 26630 91566; Barbati; mains €7-22) Beachfront chic goes with terrific Mediterranean and international cuisine at this expensive restaurant.

SOUTH OF CORFU TOWN

The coast road continues south from Corfu Town with a turn-off to well-signposted **Ahillion Palace** (☎ 26610 56245; adult/concession €7/5; 🕙 8.30am-3pm Nov-Mar, 8am-7pm Apr-Oct) near the village of Gastouri. The Ahillion was built in the 1890s by the Empress Elizabeth of Austria, known as Sisi, as a retreat from the world and in tribute to her hero, Achilles. (Poor Sisi was later assassinated on the shores of Lake Geneva by a deranged anarchist.) Kaiser Wilhelm II bought the palace in 1908, extending the themes of both imperialism and self-aggrandisement by adding to the gardens a ferocious statue of Achilles Triumphant, before leaving Corfu for something less than triumph in 1914. The palace is a major coach tour destination. Get there early for a fascinating journey through heavily accented neoclassicism, fabulous furnishings and bold statuary, along a very thin line between style and kitsch.

South of the Ahillion is the resort of **Benitses**, enhanced by its pleasant old village, from where tracks and paths lead into the steep, wooded slopes above. The taverna **O Paxinos** (☎ 2661072339; Benitses) is noted for its mezedhes and fish dishes (by the kilo). Further south again are the popular beach resorts of **Moraitika** and **Messonghi**, from where the winding coastal road leads south to the tranquil **Boukari** with its little harbour and waterside tavernas, including the good *psarotaverna* (fish restaurant) **Spiros Karidis** (☎ 26620 51205; Boukari). You can stay at the pleasant **Golden Sunset Hotel** (☎ 26620 51853; Boukari; d incl breakfast €60-65, tr incl breakfast €70). A restaurant is attached.

Lefkimmi, just over 10km from Boukari in the southern part of the island, is one of Corfu's most authentic towns, and still gets on with everyday life. Fascinating churches are dotted throughout the older section, and it's divided by a rather quaint, but sometimes odorous, canal. Eat at the **River Restaurant (To Potami)** (☎ 69725 42153; mains €5-15), which has been blessed by UK celebrity chef Rick Stein for his Mediterranean Escapes TV show. They have decent, if slightly old-fashioned, rooms and apartments from €40 to €60.

WEST COAST

Some of Corfu's prettiest countryside, villages and beaches are situated on the west coast. The scenic and very popular resort of **Paleokastritsa**, 26km from Corfu Town, rambles for nearly 3km down a valley to a series of small, picturesque coves hidden between tall cliffs. Craggy mountains swathed in cypresses and olive trees tower above. You can venture to nearby grottoes or one of the dozen or so local beaches by small excursion boat (per person €8.20, 30 minutes), or water taxis can drop you off at a beach of your choice. There's a range of water-boat activities available. Cool sun-seekers can hang out at cafe-bar **La Grotta** (☎ 26630 41006; Paleokastritsa), which is set in a stunning rocky cove with cafe, sunbeds and diving board. It's reached down steps opposite the driveway up to Hotel Paleokastritsa.

Perched on the rocky promontory at the end of Paleokastritsa is the icon-filled **Moni Theotokou** (admission free; ☼ 7am-1pm & 3-8pm), a monastery founded in the 13th century (although the present building dates from the 18th century). Just off the monastery's garden – with ivy, vines, roses and pot plants – is a small **museum** (admission free; ☼ 9am-1pm & 3-6pm

Apr-Oct). Most interesting is the olive mill exhibition under the museum, with a small shop selling oils and herbs.

From Paleokastritsa a path ascends to the unspoilt village of **Lakones**, 5km inland by road. Be sure to check out the town's only *kafeneio* (coffee house) – Kafeneio Olympia – and the village's growing **photographic archive** (☎ 26630 41771-3) where local man Vassilis Michalas has assembled a remarkable archive of photographs that form a vivid record of island life. Lakones' not-for-profit photographic archive is housed in the Lakones' choral group's practice room in the village's municipal building. Interested visitors can phone ahead.

Quaint **Doukades** has a historic square and pleasant tavernas. The 6km road north from Paleokastritsa to **Krini** and **Makrades** climbs steeply to spectacular views; many restaurant owners have capitalised on the vistas. A left turn towards the coast leads through Krini's miniature town square and on down to **Angelokastro**, the ruins of a Byzantine castle and the most western bastion on Corfu.

Further north, via the village of **Pagi**, are the pleasant beach resorts of **Agios Georgios** and **Arillas** with between them the knuckly headland of **Cape Arillas** with the little village of **Afionas** straggling up its spine.

South of Paleokastritsa, the pebbly beach at **Ermones** is dominated by heavy development, but clings to its claim of being the beach on which Odysseus was washed ashore and where Nausicaa, daughter of King Alcinous, just happening to be sunning herself. Hilltop **Pelekas**, 4km south, is perched above wooded cliffs and one-time hippy beaches. This likeable village still attracts independent travellers.

The **Triklino Vineyard** (☎ 26610 58184, 69458 90285; www.triklinovineyard.gr; adult/under 6yr €7/free; ☼ noon-5pm Tue-Sun) 6km near Corfu Town on the Pelekas road near Karoubatika blends culture with viniculture at its delightful complex where some enticing wines are produced from local vines such as Kakotrygis. There's a tour of an olive-oil mill and winery, and wine tasting and Corfiot mezedhes. They also run a series of cultural activities and performances.

Near Pelekas village are two sandy beaches, **Glyfada** and **Pelekas** (marked on some maps as Kontogialos, and also a resort in its own right), with water sports and sunbeds galore. These beaches are quite developed and are backed by large hotels and accommodation options.

IONIAN ISLANDS

A free bus service runs from Pelekas village to these beaches. Further north is the popular, but dwindling (due to erosion) **Myrtiotissa** beach; the former unofficial nudist 'colony' has more or less merged with the happy families section, save for some giant boulders in between. It's a long slog down a steep, partly surfaced road before you see a bottom of any kind (drivers should park in the parking area on the hilltop). The taverna and bar, Elia, part way down, makes a welcome break.

Agios Gordios is a popular resort south of Glyfada where a long sandy beach can cope with the crowds.

Just along the turn off from the main road to Halikounas Beach is the Byzantine **Gardiki Castle**, which has a picturesque entranceway, but is entirely empty inside. Just south of the castle is the vast **Lake Korission**, separated from the sea by a narrow spit that is fronted by a long sandy beach where you can usually escape from the crowds.

Sleeping

Paleokastritsa has many hotels, studios and a few domatia (rooms, usually in private homes) spread along the road. Further south, in the Pelekas area, there are also plenty of sleeping options.

Paleokastritsa Camping (☎ 26630 41204; www .paleokastritsaholidays.com; Paleokastritsa; camp sites per adult/child/car/tent €5/3.10/3.10/3.50) On the right of the main approach road to town is this shady and well-organised camping ground on historic olive terraces.

Hotel Zefiros (☎ 26630 41244/41088; www.hotel -zefiros.gr; Paleokastritsa; d incl breakfast €60-80, tr incl breakfast €75-105, q incl breakfast €90-130; ⚿ 🛜) On the roadside near the seafront, but a delight and with immaculate, stylish rooms, some with a massive terrace. The downstairs cafe is a bright oasis.

Rolling Stone (☎ 26610 94942; www.pelekasbeach .com; Pelekas Beach; r €30-40, apt €98) The clean and colourful apartments and double rooms surround a big sun terrace with funky trappings at this laid-back place. There's even a resident 'wellness' practitioner (relaxation treatments €10 to €30).

Jimmy's Restaurant & Rooms (☎ 26610 94284; info@jimmyspelekas.com; Pelekas; d/tr €40/50; ⚿) These decent rooms with rooftop views are above a popular restaurant (mains €6 to €12), a short distance uphill from the centre and on the road to the Kaiser's Throne.

Yialiskari Beach Studios (☎ 26610 54901; d studio €65; Yialiskari Beach; ⚿) Studios with great vistas are perfect for those who want seclusion away from neighbouring Pelekas Beach. The studios are run by the owner of Yialiskari Beach's taverna.

There are two budget options in the Pelekas area, both on the backpackers' circuit and both piled high with facilities and activities; the **Pink Palace** (☎ 26610 53103; www.thepinkpalace .com; Agios Gordios Beach; dm per person incl breakfast & dinner €18-25, r incl breakfast & dinner €22-30; 🖳) south of Sinarades and **Sunrock** (☎ 26610 94637; www .sunrockcorfu.com; Pelekas Beach; r per person incl breakfast & dinner €18-24; 🖳 ⚿). The experience at both is relative to how young you feel.

Eating

There are also a few eating places at Afionas to the north of Paleokastritsa.

Das Blaue (The Blue House; ☎ 26630 52046; Afionas; dishes €4.50-8) Superb balcony views enhance the food at this bright place where the salads are especially good and the desserts heavenly.

Limani (☎ 26630 42080; Paleokastritsa Harbour; mains €4.50-11) Located down by Paleo's harbour, the well-run Limani, with its rose-bedecked terrace, does local dishes with a sure hand. Fish is by the kilo but a generous fish plate for two costs about €38.

Nereids (☎ 26630 41013; Paleokastritsa; mains €6.50-11) Halfway down the winding road to Paleokastritsa beach is this smart place, below road level and with a huge leafy courtyard. Specialities such as pork in a mustard sauce with oregano, lemon, peppers, garlic and cheese are hard to beat.

PAXI ΠΑΞΟΙ

pop 2440

Paxi packs a great deal into a bite-size island. At only 10km by 4km it's the smallest of the Ionian's main holiday islands and has hung on to a reputation for serenity and overall loveliness – a fine escape clause to Corfu's more metropolitan, quicker-paced pleasures. There are three colourful harbour towns – Gaïos, Loggos and Lakka. All have pretty waterfronts with Venetian-style pink-and-cream buildings set against lush green hills. Idyllic coves can be reached by motorboat, if not by car or on foot. The dispersed inland villages sit within centuries-old olive groves, accented

---

CORFU ACTIVITIES

Corfu brims with great outdoor action. Dinghy sailing and windsurfing buffs will find **Greek Sailing Holidays** (☎ 26630 81877; www.corfu-sailing-events.com) at Avlaki, while for chartering try **Corfu Sea School** (www.corfuseaschool.com) or **Sailing Holidays Ltd** (www.sailingholidays.com), both at Gouvia marina.

For **diving** in crystal-clear waters you'll find operators at Kassiopi, Agios Gordios, Agios Georgios, Ipsos, Gouvia and Paleokastritsa.

Corfu has some excellent walking. The **Corfu Trail** (www.corfutrail.org), developed by the devoted islander Hilary Whitton Paipeti, traverses the island north to south and takes between eight and 12 days to complete. For help with accommodation along the trail, contact **Aperghi Travel** (☎ 26610 48713; www.travelling.gr/aperghi). The book *In the Footsteps of Lawrence Durrell and Gerald Durrell in Corfu* (Hilary Whitton Paipeti, 1999) is an excellent buy.

For mountain-biking, especially off-road, the **Corfu Mountainbike Shop** (☎ 26610 93344; www .mountainbikecorfu.gr) is based in Dasia and rents out bikes for independent exploration, as well as organising day trips and cycling holidays. Horse riding through olive groves and on quiet trails is another excellent option with **Trailriders** (☎ 26630 23090), based in the village of Ano Korakiana. Not far from Ermones on the island's west coast is the **Corfu Golf Club** (☎ 26610 94220; www.corfu golfclub.com), one of the few such courses in Greece. Birdwatchers should check the **Birdwatching Centre of Ropa Valley** (☎ 26610 94221), who meet regularly at the Corfu Golf Club.

---

by winding stone walls, ancient windmills and olive presses. On the less accessible west coast, sheer limestone cliffs plunge hundreds of metres into the azure sea and are punctuated by caves and grottoes. The old mule trails are a walker's delight. An obligatory purchase is the *Bleasdale Walking Map of Paxos* (€10 to €15), available from the island's travel agencies.

Getting There & Away
BOAT
Ferries dock at Gaïos' new port, 1km east of the central square. Excursion boats dock along the waterfront.

Domestic
Busy passenger-only hydrofoils link Corfu and Paxi (and occasionally Igoumenitsa) from May until mid-October. For information contact **Arvanitakis Travel** (☎ 26620 32007; Gaïos), or Petrakis Lines (p441) in Corfu.

Two car ferries operate daily services between Paxi and Igoumenitsa on the mainland, and Corfu. There's also a **ferry information office** (☎ 26650 26280) in Igoumenitsa.

For details on all domestic connections see Island Hopping (p520).

Sea taxis can be a fast and effective way to travel, especially if there are other people on board. The going rate between Corfu and Paxi is around €180 per boat, shared among the passengers. Try **Nikos** (☎ 26620 32444, 69322 32072; Gaïos), or www.paxosseataxi.com.

International
You can reach Corfu and Igoumenitsa from the major ports in Italy, then transfer to a local ferry for Paxi. For details on international connections to Corfu see p435, to Igoumenitsa (from Italy) see p495.

BUS
There's a twice-weekly direct bus service between Athens and Paxi (€47, plus €7.50 for ferry ticket between Paxi and Igoumenitsa, seven hours). On Paxi, tickets are available from **Bouas Tours** (☎ 26620 32401; Gaïos). The bus leaves from Plateia Karaiskaki in Athens (note: the terminal changes so always check with Bouas beforehand).

Getting Around
The island's bus links Gaïos and Lakka via Loggos up to four times daily in either direction (€2). Taxis between Gaïos and Lakka or Loggos cost around €12. The taxi rank in Gaïos is located by the car park and bus stop inland from the waterfront.

Daily car hire ranges between €42 and €115 in high season. Reliable agencies are **ArvanitakisTravel** (☎ 26620 32007) and **Alfa Hire** (☎ 26620 32505) in Gaïos. **Rent a Scooter Vassilis** (☎ 26620 32598), opposite the bus stop in Gaïos, has a good range of scooters and mopeds. Hire is about €20 to €25 in high season. Many travel agencies rent out small boats – this is a great way to access beach coves. Rental for a day

IONIAN ISLANDS

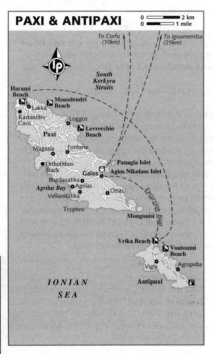

PAXI & ANTIPAXI

0 — 2 km
0 — 1 mile

To Corfu (10km)

To Igoumenitsa (25km)

South Kerkyra Straits

Harami Beach

Monodendri Beach

Lakka

Kastanitha Cave

Loggos

Paxi

Levrecchio Beach

Magazia

Fontana

Orthofithos Stack

Gaïos

Panagia Islet

Agios Nikolaos Islet

Bogdanatika

Agrilas Bay

Agrilas

Ozias

Vellianitatika

Excursion Boat

Trypitos

Mongonisi

Vrika Beach

Voutoumi Beach

Vigla

Agrapidia

IONIAN SEA

Antipaxi

IONIAN ISLANDS

ranges from €40 to €90 depending on engine capacity. Don't overestimate your needs.

GAÏOS ΓΑΪΟΣ
pop 560

Gaïos hardly needs to try for the 'picturesque' label. It's the island's main town and its pink, cream and whitewashed buildings line the water's edge of a sizeable bay to either side of the main Venetian square. The town is protected from too much open water by the wooded islet of Agios Nikolaos, named after its eponymous monastery. It lies so close to the shore that it creates the illusion of Gaïos being a pretty riverside town. The waterfront is lined with cafes and tavernas and can get crowded mid afternoon when excursion boats arrive.

The main street (Panagioti Kanga) runs inland from the main square towards the back of town, where you'll find the bus stop, taxi rank and car park. Banks and ATMs are near the square and there's an internet room at the waterfront **Bar Pío Pío** (☎ 26620 32662; per hr €5). There isn't a tourist office, but the helpful and efficient staff at **Paxos Magic Holidays** (☎ 26620

32269; www.paxosmagic.com) will happily direct you. They organise island excursions, including boating trips and walks. They can also arrange villa accommodation in advance.

The charming **Cultural Museum** (admission €2; ☺ 10am-2pm & 7-11pm), in a former school on the southern waterfront, has an eclectic collection of fossils, farming and domestic artefacts, pottery, guns, coins and clothing. Brace yourself for the 17th-century wedding night 'facilitator' that might just be described as quaint. A room is devoted to the paintings of the Paxiot priest Christodoulos Aronis.

At the far southern end of the harbour is a striking statue of Georgios Anemogiannis, a local sea captain who died heroically in 1821, aged 23, during the Greek War of Independence. The sea has 'greened' Georgios rather vividly.

Sleeping

San Giorgio Apartments (☎ 26620 32223; s/d/tr €40/70/90) Pink, blue and white are the colours of these airy and clean studios with basic cooking facilities. Head towards town from the port by the lower (pedestrian) harbour road, and follow the signposted steps.

Thekli Studios (Clara Studios; ☎ 26620 32313; d €75; P ⊠ ⊠) Thekli, a local fisher-diver and energetic personality about town, runs these immaculate and well-equipped studios. She will meet you at the port if you call ahead. Otherwise, go up the alleyway to the left of the museum, turn left and then, in 50m, turn right and up some steps for another 50m.

Paxos Beach Hotel (☎ 26620 32211; www.paxos beachhotel.gr; s/d/tr/q incl breakfast from €88/117/146/165, ste €168-380; ⊠) In a prime location 1.5km south of Gaïos these bungalow-style rooms step down to the sea and have a range of rooms from standard to superior. There's a private jetty, tennis court, beach, bar and restaurant.

Eating

Capriccio Café Creperie (☎ 26620 32687; crêpes €3-6) For a cheap and filling sweet or savoury experience, head past the museum to this waterfront crêperie. They do breakfast for €3 to €7.80 and sandwiches for €3 to €4.

Taverna Vasilis (☎ 26620 32596; mains €6.50-14) The owner of this eatery is a former butcher, and knows the best meat for tasty spit-roasts and other meaty servings. It's just back from the mid waterfront.

Karkaletzos (☎ 26620 32729; mains €7-10) Walk up an appetite to this grill house, the locals' choice, 1km behind the town. The meat dishes are balanced by some creative fish cuisine.

Taka Taka (☎ 26620 32329; mains €6-22) For upmarket seafood (€40 to €75 per kilogram) in attractive surroundings, this popular place is behind the main square. Go left from the left-hand inner corner of the square, then, after 30m, turn right.

The supermarket is west of the central square. Two excellent bakeries, one on the waterfront, the other near the main square, serve Paxiot delights. Gloria's, at the north end of the waterfront, tempts with some deeply sinful ice-cream flavours.

LOGGOS ΛΟΓΓΟΣ

Loggos is 5km northwest of Gaïos and is a mini-gem of a place with a pretty waterfront curled round a small bay. Bars and restaurants overlook the water and wooded slopes climb steeply above. There are coves and pebble beaches nearby. **Café Bar Four Seasons** (☎ 26620 31829; per hr €6) has internet facilities.

You can hire boats and scooters from **Julia's Boat & Bike** (☎ 26620 31330) at Arthur House (see below); boats are €60 to €70 per day and scooters about €25.

Sleeping & Eating

Studio (☎ 26620 31397, 26620 31030; d €55) A pleasantly bohemian – and bougainvillea – choice, this studio sits above the gift shop Marbou, just in from the waterfront. It's best to book in advance.

Arthur House (☎ 26620 31330; studio €75, apt €110) The modest and spotless studios at Arthur House are above the owner's house, a two-minute walk from the waterfront. Julia's Boat & Bike (above) hire is part of the family deal.

O Gios (☎ 26620 31735/30062; mains €6-16) A step back from the waterfront is this unvarnished place with good value seafood and grill dishes.

Vasilis (☎ 26620 31587; mains €8-14) An unexpected treat, this well run, stylish place features a clever menu card in the shape of a facsimile newspaper of the 1970s. Specialities include octopus in red wine sauce and lamb casserole, along with pasta and risotto dishes.

Drinking

There are several cafes and bars in Loggos with favourites for cocktails and music being the waterside To Taxidi and Roxy Bar.

Kafeneio Burnaos (Magazia) Don't blink or you'll miss this wonderful 60-year-old *kafeneio*, located in Magazia, several kilometres southwest of Loggos. There are no set hours, but locals gather here to play cards and backgammon (there's even a set from 1957).

Erimitis Bar (☎ 689777 53499; Magazia) A growing reputation has made this out-of-the-way place increasingly popular, especially for sunset viewing. It's down lanes and tracks towards the west coast from Magazia and you need transport.

LAKKA ΛΑΚΚΑ

The picturesque, tranquil and unspoiled harbour of Lakka lies at the end of a protective bay on the north coast. It's a popular yacht anchorage, and there are plenty of facilities as well as bars and restaurants. Small, but reasonable beaches lie round the bay's headland, including Harami Beach, and there are pleasant walks nearby.

Routsis Holidays (☎ 26620 31807/31129; www.routsis-holidays.com) is tucked away inland and **Planos Holidays** (☎ 26620 31744; www.planos-holidays.gr) is on the waterfront. Both are helpful agencies responsible for well-appointed apartments and villas for all budgets.

Paxos Blue Waves (☎ 26620 31162) on the waterfront rents boats for €35 to €65 and scooters for €18 to €20.

For a Bali experience in Corfu, visit the colourful **Il Pareo** (☎ 69721 64089) for a great collection of Indonesian Batik and other items.

For accommodation try the immaculate and comfy **Yorgos Studios** (☎ 26620 31807/31129; www.routsis-holidays.com; s/d €50/65; ❄) next door to the Routsis Holidays office and run by the company. The owners of Il Pareo also have an away-from-it-all **garden studio** (☎ 69721 64089; ste €70).

Unfussy food and drink and internet (€3 per half hour) can be had at the waterside **Arriva Taverna** (☎ 26620 30153; mains €8-13.80). A popular local place is **Diogenis** (☎ 26620 31442; mains €4.20-9.80) in the square at the back of the village. Cuttlefish with spinach and lamb in lemon sauce are well done classics. For something special head along the shore on the right-hand side of the bay to a little beach and to the Italian-influenced **La Bocca** (☎ 26620 31991;

mains €8-18) for proper *caprese* or spaghetti with fresh tuna, amid colourful decor.

ANTIPAXI ΑΝΤΙΠΑΞΟΙ
pop 25

The stunning and diminutive island of Antipaxi, 2km south of Paxi, is covered with grape vines, olives and with the occasional small hamlet here and there. Caïques and tourist boats run daily from Gaïos and Lakka, and pull in at two beach coves, the small, sandy **Vrika Beach** and the pretty, pebbly **Voutoumi Beach**. Floating in the water here – with its dazzling clarity – is a sensational experience.

An inland path links the two beaches (a 30-minute walk), or if you are more of an energetic person you can walk up to the village of **Vigla**, or as far as the lighthouse at the southernmost tip. Take plenty of water and allow 1½ hours minimum each way. Voutoumi Beach has two eateries – Bella Vista and a taverna on the beach. Vrika Beach also has two good competing tavernas – Spiros and Vrika. Main meals at both cost between €7 and €15 and fish dishes can be very pricey.

Accommodation is available through one or two of the beach tavernas. Boats to Antipaxi (from €6 return) leave Gaïos at 10am and return around 5.30pm – there are more services in high season.

LEFKADA ΛΕΥΚΑΔΑ

pop 22,500

Lefkada (or Lefkas), the fourth-largest island of the Ionians, is an absorbing destination, mountainous and in places remote. Yet it has its fair share of holiday resorts and tourism facilities and seems less insular than most, not least because it was once attached to nearby mainland Greece by a narrow isthmus until occupying Corinthians breached the land bridge with a canal in the 8th century BC. A causeway now spans the 25m strait, yet Lefkada remains steadfastly traditional and island-like in the best of ways. In remoter villages you often see older women in traditional dress and the main town of Lefkas has a splendid mid-20th-century period appeal.

Lefkada's mountains rise to over 1000m, and olive groves, vineyards, and pine forests cover huge areas of the landscape. There are 10 satellite islets off the heavily developed east coast, and the less populated west coast boasts spectacular beaches.

Getting There & Away

AIR

Lefkada has no airport, but the airport near Preveza (Aktion) on the mainland, with flights to Athens and Corfu, is about 20km away. For details see Island Hopping (p520).

Also, from May to September there are charter flights from northern Europe and the UK to Preveza.

BOAT

Four Islands Ferries (☎ 210 412 2530) runs a daily ferry service that sails to an ever-changing schedule (and with ever-changing prices) between Nydri and Frikes on Ithaki (€6.40, one hour 30 minutes), Vasiliki on Lefkada and Frikes (€8, two hours) and Vasiliki and Fiskardo on Kefallonia (€6.90, one hour). You can bring a car across to either port on Lefkada – it costs €30 from Fiskardo and €28 from Frikes. For more information on departing from Lefkada, see Island Hopping (p517).

Information and tickets can be obtained from **Borsalino Travel** (☎ 26450 92528; borsalin@ otenet.gr) in Nydri and from **Samba Tours** (☎ 26450 31520; www.sambatours.gr) in Vasiliki.

BUS

Lefkada Town's new **KTEL bus station** (☎ 26450 22364; Ant Tzeveleki) is located about 1km from the centre opposite the new marina complex. Head down Golemi to the busy road junction and go left for 750m. Buses head to Athens (€30.50, 5½ hours, four or five daily), Patra (€14.50, three hours, two to three weekly), Thessaloniki (€39.10, eight hours, one to two weekly and more in high season), Preveza (€2.70, 30 minutes, six to seven daily) and Igoumenitsa (€11, two hours, daily).

Getting Around

There's no reliable bus connection between Lefkada and Preveza's Aktion airport. Taxis are relatively expensive (around €35); a cheaper option is to take a taxi to Preveza and then a bus to Lefkada

From Lefkada Town, frequent buses ply the east coast, with up to 20 services daily to Nydri (€1.40, 30 minutes) and Vlyho (€1.60, 40 minutes) in high season, and four daily to Vasiliki (€3, one hour). There are regular buses to Agios Nikitas (€1.40, 30 minutes). Around six daily services head to the inland village of Karya (€1.40, 30 minutes). One or two buses serve other villages daily. Sunday services are reduced.

Car hire starts at €40 per day, depending on season and model. Cars can be hired from reliable **Europcar** (☎ 26450 23581; Panagou 16, Lefkada Town) or next door at **Budget** (☎ 26450 25274; Lefkada Town). Rent a bike or moped, starting at €15 per day, from **Santas** (☎ 26450 25250; Lefkada Town), next to the Ionian Star Hotel. There are countless car-and bike-hire companies in Nydri and several in Vasiliki.

LEFKADA TOWN
pop 6900

The island's engaging main town is built on a promontory at the southeastern corner of a salty lagoon. Earthquakes are a constant threat here and the town was devastated by one in 1948 (but unaffected in 1953), only to be rebuilt in a distinctively quake-proof and attractive style with the upper storey facades of some buildings in brightly painted corrugated iron.

The town has a relaxed feel, with a vibrant main thoroughfare, a pleasant plaza and handsome churches with separate ironwork bell towers, like small oil rigs, to withstand seismic activity.

Orientation & Information

The town's vibrant main pedestrian strip, Dorpfeld, starts south of the causeway. The street is named after 19th-century archaeologist Wilhelm Dorpfeld, who postulated that Lefkada, not Ithaki, was the home of Odysseus. Dorpfeld leads to Plateia Agiou Spyridonos, the main square, and continues as Ioannou Mela, which is lined with modern shops and cafes. ATMs and the post office are on Ioannou Mela. There's no tourist office. The bus station is on the southern waterfront.

There's an **Internet Café** (Koutroubi; per hr €1.50), just off 8th Merarchias.

Sights

Housed in the modern cultural centre at the western end of Agelou Sikelianou is the **Archaeological Museum** (☎ 26450 21635; adult/concession €2/1; ☯ 8.30am-3pm Tue-Sun). It contains island artefacts spanning the Palaeolithic Age to the late Roman periods. The prize exhibit is a 6th-century-BC terracotta figurine of a flute player with nymphs.

Works by icon painters from the Ionian school and Russia dating back to 1500 are displayed in an impressive **collection of post-Byzantine icons** (☎ 26450 22502; Rontogianni; admission free; ☯ 8.30am-1.30pm Tue-Sat, 6-8.15pm Tue & Thu). It's in a classical building and also houses the **public library** off Ioannou Mela.

The 14th-century Venetian **Fortress of Agia Mavra** (☯ 9am-1.30pm Mon, 8.30am-1pm Tue-Sun) is immediately across the causeway. It was first established by the crusaders but the remains mainly date from the Venetian and Turkish occupations of the island. **Moni Faneromenis**, 3km west of town, was founded in 1634, destroyed by fire in 1886 and later rebuilt. It houses a **museum** (☯ 9am-1pm, 6-8pm Mon-Sat) with ecclesiastical art from around the island. The views of the lagoon and town are also worth the ascent.

Sleeping

Hotel Santa Maura (☎ 26450 21308; fax 26450 26253; Dorpfeld; s/d/tr incl breakfast €55/70/86; ☒) A decent hotel with a mix of rooms, all in pleasantly pale decor. The rooms onto Dorpfeld overlook a busy evening scene.

Pension Pirofani (☎ 26450 25844; fax 26450 24084; Dorpfeld; d/tr €85/100; ☒) There's a colourful character to this small hotel and its stylish rooms, all in lush colours and with sparkling facilities. There's even tea- and coffee-making kit.

Ionian Star Hotel (☎ 26450 24762; www.ionion-star .gr; s/d/tr incl breakfast €100/115/130; ☒ ☒ ☐ ☒) Comfortable, light and spacious rooms mark out this business-class hotel that overlooks an attractive open area just in from the waterfront. The breakfasts are filling and there's a bar and big lounge.

Eating & Drinking

Faei Kairos (☎ 26450 24045; Golemi; mains €4.50-11) Unashamed nostalgia for the good old days of cinema defines this excellent eatery on Lefkada Town's waterfront. The eye-catching motifs go well with such treats as *spetsofai*, local sausage in a tomato sauce, or *rigamato*, pork in cream and oregano sauce or fish plates for one or two.

Ey Zhn (☎ 69746 41169; Filarmonikis 8; mains €9-13) 'Live Well' is the name here. Backstreet rather than scenic, but with an attractive interior, the food is excellent, from the filling starters such as mushroom risotto to a seafood paella

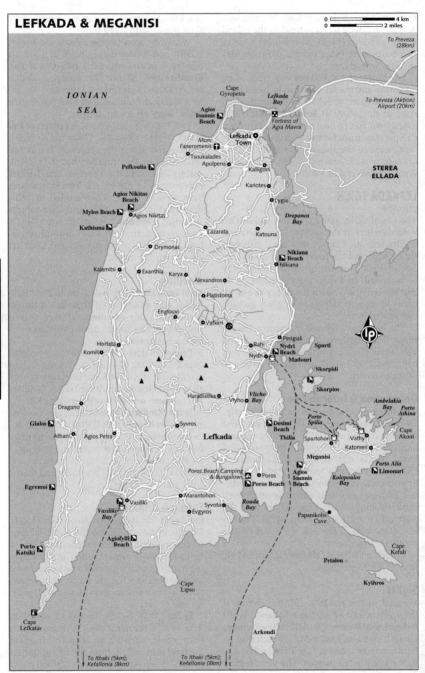

LEFKADA & MEGANISI

| 0 | 4 km |
| 0 | 2 miles |

IONIAN ISLANDS

IONIAN SEA

To Preveza (28km)

To Preveza (Aktion) Airport (20km)

Cape Gyropetra

Lefkada Bay

Agios Ioannis Beach

Fortress of Agia Mavra

Lefkada Town

Moni Faneromenis

Tsoukalades

Apolpena

Kalligoni

Pefkoulia

Kariotes

Lygia

STEREA ELLADA

Agios Nikitas Beach

Drepanos Bay

Mylos Beach

Agios Nikitas

Kathisma

Lazarata

Katouna

Kalamitsi

Drymonas

Nikiana Beach

Nikiana

Exanthia

Karya

Alexandros

Platistoma

Englouvi

Vafkeri

Rahi

Periglai

Nydri Beach

Sparti

Hortata

Komili

Nydri

Madouri

Skorpidi

Skorpios

Haradiatika

Vlyho

Vlicho Bay

Ambelakia Bay

Porto Athina

Dragano

Gialos

Athani

Agios Petra

Syvros

Lefkada

Desimi Beach

Thilia

Porto Spilia

Spartohori

Meganisi

Vathy

Cape Akoni

Katomeri

Porto Alia

Limonari

Egremni

Poros Beach Camping & Bungalows

Poros

Poros Beach

Agios Ioannis Beach

Kolopoulos Bay

Marantohori

Syvota

Rouda Bay

Vasiliki

Vasiliki Bay

Evgyros

Papanikolis Cave

Agiofylli Beach

Cape Kefali

Porto Katsiki

Cape Lefkatas

Cape Lipso

Petalou

Kythros

To Ithaki (5km); Kefallonia (8km)

To Ithaki (5km); Kefallonia (8km)

Arkoudi

for two at €18, or shrimps in garlic sauce. Evenings only.

Also recommended on the Golemi strip and with similar prices are the *ouzeries* **Frini Sto Molo** (☎ 26450 24879) and **Burano** (☎ 26450 26025), both offering well-prepared Greek classics.

Stylish bars and cafes line the western side of the waterfront; **Karma** (Dorpfeld), at the start of Dorpfeld, is the place to be seen. Plateia Agiou Spyridonos is crammed with cafes and crowds.

Self-caterers can pick up supplies from the **supermarket** (Golemi) next to the bus station or from the well-stocked **bakery** (Ioannou Mela 182).

EAST COAST & SURROUNDS

Lefkada's east coast has seen heavy tourist development over the years with the main focus at Nydri, once a fishing village but now a crowded strip of tourist shops and with not much of a beach. You can escape inland, however, to another world of scattered villages, local tavernas and pleasant walks. From Nydri itself there is another escape seaward on cruises to the islets of **Madouri**, **Sparti**, **Skorpidi** and **Skorpios**, plus **Meganisi**. Numerous excursions go to Meganisi and stop for a swim near Skorpios (€15 to €25), and some visit Ithaki and Kefallonia as well (€20). Helpful **Borsalino Travel** (☎ 26450 92528; borsalin@otenet .gr; Nydri) on the main street can organise just about everything.

Amblers might enjoy the lovely walk to **waterfalls** 3km out of Nydri (and another 400m past the taverna). The walk follows a path through a ravine; be careful of the slippery rocks.

The small harbour of **Syvota**, 15km south of Nydri, has a relaxed airy appeal. It's popular with yachts and the local fishing fleet is still active. There's no beach to speak of and you need your own transport to get the best of it.

Sleeping & Eating

Poros Beach Camping & Bungalows (☎ 26450 95452; www.porosbeach.com.gr; Poros Beach; camp sites per adult/car/ tent 9/5/5, studio €60-90; P 🅿 🖳 🖭) Twelve kilometres south of Nydri is this unpretentious complex overlooking pretty Poros Beach. It has studio apartments and a shaded camping area, plus restaurant, minimarket, bar and swimming pool.

Ionian Paradise (☎ 26450 92268; www.ionianparadise .gr; Nydri; r €75; 🅿) Nicely located off the main drag, the recently refurbished Ionian still has

an old-fashioned welcome and its rooms are pleasantly functional. Breakfast is €5. It's down a side street diagonally opposite the Avis car-hire office.

Apartments Sivota (☎ 26450 31347; fax 26450 31151; Syvota; r €45, 2-person studio €100, 3-person apt €110; 🅿) In Syvota, these very pleasant apartments are set slightly back from the waterfront, but have balconies and good views. Steps lead up from the waterfront road.

Spiridoula (☎ 26450 31989; Syvota; mains €5.50-15) The first of the harbourside tavernas in Syvota has ice storage drawers from which you can choose fish from local landings. Meat dishes feature also, but the fish soup is a rewarding choice.

Pinewood (☎ 26450 92075; Nydri; mains €6-16.50) Popular with locals and offering some subtle classics such as lamb in a red wine and herb sauce, this well-run place is at the quiet northern end of Nydri's main street.

VASILIKI ΒΑΣΙΛΙΚΗ

Vasiliki has a stony beach, but is a hot spot for the tanned and toned, mainly because it's one of the best water-sports venues in the Mediterranean. This is due to the configuration of the resort's square-cut bay where soft breezes in the morning make it ideal for instructing beginners. In the afternoon, winds whip down the flanking mountains for some serious action by aficionados. It's not all fast sailing though; the winding waterfront, with eucalyptus and canopy-covered eateries is a pleasant place in which to relax. Caïques take visitors to the island's better beaches and coves including **Agiofylli Beach**, south of Vasiliki.

Along the beach, water-sports outfits have staked their claims with flags, equipment and with their own hotels for their guests. **Wildwind** (www.wildwind.co.uk) is a main operator of all-inclusive one- and two-week action holidays ranging from €563 to €921 depending on season. **Healthy Options** (www.healthy-option.co.uk) is a linked program offering a swath of activities including yoga and Pilates, dance and fitness as well as water sports and eco-walking trips. Contact both of the above for possible short-term options.

Club Vassiliki Windsurfing (☎ 26450 31588; www .clubvass.com) organises windsurfing sessions for €25. For diving try **Nautilus Diving Club** (☎ 69361 81775; www.underwater.gr), which has a range of options, including a snorkelling safari for €30, a discover scuba diving course for €50 and an open-water course for €360. It also has sea kayaking half days for €30.

All the activities have beach stations.

Helpful **Samba Tours** (☎ 26450 31520; www .sambatours.gr) in the main street can organise car and bike hire, and answer most queries regarding the region. Other car-hire places are **Christo's Alex's** (☎ 26450 31580) near the bus stop.

Sleeping, Eating & Drinking

Vassiliki Beach Camping (26450 31308; campkingk@ otenet.gr; camp sites per person/tent/car €8/5/6) A well-run and compact camping option with easy access to the beach.

Pension Holidays (☎ 26450 31426; nicol60@ windowslive.com; s/d €60/65; ☷ year-round; ✷) Friendly Spiros and family offer Greek hospitality, breakfast (€5) on the balcony with views of the bay and harbour, and simply furnished but well-equipped rooms. Above the ferry dock; prices vary according to length of stays.

Vasiliki Bay Hotel (☎ 26450 31077; www.hotelvassiliki bay.gr; s/d incl breakfast €60/70; ✷ ☎) A few blocks inland from the waterfront is this well-appointed hotel behind Alexander Restaurant. Prices drop substantially outside August. The same family has lovely villas outside the village. Phone for details.

Delfini (Dolphin; ☎ 26450 31430; mains €6.50-13) The best of the harbour haul, the food at this traditional place is freshly cooked to order and is popular locally.

Zeus (☎ 26450 31560) Current hot club on Vasiliki's main drag, Zeus is revved up by the young water-sports crowd. You can always spill over into the next door **Yacht Café** (☎ 26450 31890).

WEST COAST & AROUND

Serious beach fanciers should head straight for Lefkada's west coast where the sea lives up to the brochure clichés; it's an incredible turquoise blue and most beaches are sandy. The best beaches include remote **Egremni** and breathtaking **Porto Katsiki** in the south. You'll pass by local stalls selling olive oil, honey and wine. The long stretches of **Pefkoulia** and **Kathisma** in the north are also lovely (the latter beach is becoming more developed and there are a few studios for rent here).

Word is out about the picturesque town of **Agios Nikitas**, and people flock here to enjoy the holiday village's pleasant atmosphere, plus the lovely **Mylos Beach** just around the headland (to walk, take the path by Taverna Poseidon. It's about 15 minutes up and over the peninsula, or for €3 you can take a water taxi from tiny Agios Nikitas beach). The town's accommodation options are plentiful, and include **Camping Kathisma** (☎ 26450 97015; www.camping-kathisma.gr; camp sites per person/tent/car €7/5/6), 1.5km south of town. Or try the modest, Greek-Canadian-run **Olive Tree Hotel** (☎ 26450 97453; www.olivetree -lefkada.com; Agios Nikitas; s/d incl breakfast €70/90) – ask a local for directions. Right on the beach is the excellent **Sapfo** (☎ 26450 97497; Agios Nikitas; fish per kilogram €40-60), Agios Nikitas' established fish taverna.

CENTRAL LEFKADA

The spectacular central spine of Lefkada, with its traditional farming villages, lush green peaks, fragrant pine trees, olive groves and vines – plus occasional views of the islets – is well worth seeing if you have time and transport. The small village of **Karya** is a bit of a tourist haunt but it boasts a pretty square with plane trees, around which are tavernas and snack bars. There's a car park just as you approach the village. Karya is famous for its special embroidery, introduced in the 19th century by a remarkable one-handed local woman, Maria Koutsochero. Visit the **Museum Maria Koutsochero** (admission €2.50; ☷ 9am-9pm) for an interesting display of embroidery paraphernalia and local artefacts all laid out in a quite haunting way throughout a traditional house. There's a cafe at the museum, though note that hours may vary. You can walk up steeply from the village or turn up a sign-posted road just before the village entrance coming from Lefkada Town.

For food, **Taverna Karaboulias** (☎ 26450 41301; Karya plateia; mains €5-13.50) is recommended for its traditional dishes, including *yemista*, tomatoes and peppers stuffed with rice and herbs and a marvellous bread-based salad. For accommodation options ask British Brenda Sherry at **Café Pierros** (☎ 26450 41760; Karya) who can arrange all (as well as a cup of tea and signature toasted sandwich).

The island's highest village, **Englouvi**, is renowned for its honey and lentil production and is only a few kilometres south of Karya.

MEGANISI ΜΕΓΑΝΗΣΙ
pop 1090

Meganisi, with its verdant landscape and deep bays of turquoise water, fringed by pebbled beaches, is the escape clause for too much of Nydri. It can fit into a day visit or a longer, more relaxed stay. There are three settlements; **Spartohori**, with narrow lanes and pretty, bougainvillea-bedecked houses, all perched on a plateau above Porto Spilia (where the ferry docks; follow the steep road or steps behind). Pretty **Vathy** is the island's second harbour, and 800m behind it is the village of **Katomeri**. With time to spare you can visit remote beaches such as **Limonari**.

Helpful **Asteria Holidays** (☎ 26450 51107), at Porto Spilia, is in the know for all things relating to the island.

Sleeping & Eating

Hotel Meganisi (☎ 26450 51240; Katomeri; d incl breakfast €100; ⊠ ⊠) Bright rooms with sea and country views from their balconies are enhanced by this pleasant hotel's generous-sized pool and terrace. It also has a good restaurant. Follow signs once you get to Katomeri.

Decent dining options include **Taverna Porto Vathy** (☎ 26450 51125; Vathy; mains €7-14), the undisputed favourite fish taverna (fish by the kilo) cast out on a small quay in Vathy; **Tropicana** (☎ 26450 51486; Spartohori), which serves excellent pizzas in Spartohori; or **Laki's** (☎ 26450 51228; Spartohori; mains €5.50-9.50), a classic taverna, also in Spartohori.

Getting There & Away

The Meganisi ferry boat runs about six times daily between Nydri and Meganisi (per person/car €2/13, 25 to 40 minutes). It calls at Porto Spilia before Vathy (the first ferry of the day stops at Vathy, then Porto Spilia).

A local bus runs five to seven times per day between Spartohori and Vathy (via Katomeri) but it's worth bringing your own transport on the car ferry.

KEFALLONIA
ΚΕΦΑΛΛΟΝΙΑ

pop 39,500
Kefallonia is the largest of the Ionian Islands and is big hearted with it. It boasts rugged mountain ranges, rich vineyards, soaring coastal cliffs, golden beaches, caves and grottoes, monasteries and antiquities. The 1953 earthquake devastated many of the island's settlements and much of the island's archi-

tecture is relatively modern in style. Enough untouched traditional villages and individual buildings survive, however, to make exploration worthwhile. Kefallonia also has a reputation for fine cuisine and great wines.

The capital is Argostoli and the main port is Sami. Other high points include the picturesque village of Fiskardo in the north of the island.

Getting There & Away

AIR
There are daily flights between Kefallonia and Athens and connections to Zakynthos and Corfu. For details see Island Hopping (p516). **Olympic Air** (☎ 26710 41511) is based at the airport.

From May to September, many charter flights come from northern Europe and the UK to Kefallonia.

BOAT
Domestic
There are frequent ferry services to Kyllini in the Peloponnese from Poros and Argostoli. One ferry links Sami with Astakos via Piso Aetos on Ithaki. In August there are direct ferries from Sami to Astakos on alternate days.

Strintzis Lines (www.ferries.gr/strintzis) has two ferries daily connecting Sami with Patra and Vathy or Piso Aetos.

There are ferries between Fiskardo and Frikes on Ithaki and between Fiskardo and Vasiliki on Lefkada. Information and tickets for these routes can be obtained from **Nautilus Travel** (☎ 26740 41440; Fiskardo), on the Fiskardo waterfront.

From the remote port of Pesada in the south there are two daily high-season services to Agios Nikolaos on the northern tip of Zakynthos (an alternative is to sail from Argostoli to Kyllini in the Peloponnese, and from there to Zakynthos Town). Getting to and from Pesada and Agios Nikolaos without your own transport can be difficult (and costly if you rely on taxis). To get to the ferry point in Pesada from Argostoli, you can catch one of two daily buses (in high season only and except Sundays). On Zakynthos, there are two buses per week to and from Agios Nikolaos to Zakynthos Town (via villages).

One ferry a day runs between Argostoli and Kyllini (three hours, €14) and up to five run between Poros and Kyllini (1½ hours, €9.90). One

KEFALLONIA & ITHAKI

ferry a day runs between Fiskardo and Frikes (55 minutes, €3.80) and between Fiskardo and Vasiliki (one hour, €6.90). Sami has two daily connections with Vathy (45 minutes, €5.60), Patra (2¾ hours, €16.90) and Piso Aetos (30 minutes, €2.80) and one daily with Astakos (three hours, €10). In summer there are two ferries a day between Pesada and Agios Nikolaos (1½ hours, €7).

For more information, see Island Hopping (p516).

International
In high season there are regular ferries between Sami and Bari (€45, 12 hours) in Italy. To get to other ports in Italy, take the ferry first from Sami to Patra.

Tickets and information can be obtained from **Vassilatos Shipping** (☎ 26710 22618; Antoni Tristi 54, Argostoli), opposite the port authority, and from **Blue Sea Travel** (☎ 26740 23007; Sami), on Sami's waterfront.

BUS
Four daily buses connect Kefallonia with Athens (€37.10, seven hours), via Patra (€21, four hours) using the various ferry services (to/from Argostoli, Sami and Poros) to the mainland.

For information contact the **KTEL bus station** (☎ 26710 22276/81; kefaloniakteltours@yahoo.gr; A Tristi 5, Argostoli) on the southern waterfront in Argostoli. The office produces an excellent printed schedule.

IONIAN ON THE VINE

The Ionian Islands would not be the same without wine and Kefallonia especially has a reputation for outstanding vintages, most notably from the unique Robola grape. High in the mountains southeast of Argostoli, at the heart of verdant Omala Valley, is the winery of the **Cooperative of Robola Producers of Kefallonia** (☎ 26710 86301; www.robola.gr; Omala; ☼ 9am-8.30pm Mon-Fri Apr-Oct, 7am-3pm Mon-Fri Nov-Mar) Here, grapes from about 300 individual growers are transformed into the yellow-green Robola, a dry white wine of subtle yet lively flavours. The Robola is said to have been introduced by the Venetians and its wine was a favourite of The Doge. It grows exuberantly on high ground and the light soils, wet winters and arid summers of Kefallonia are ideal for its cultivation. Other varieties of grape enhance the viniculture on Kefallonia. A visit to the cooperative includes wine tasting.

A smaller and very distinguished winery is **Gentilini** (☎ 6932718730; ☼ tastings 10.30am-2.30pm & 5.30-8.30pm Mon-Sat Jul-Aug, tours & tastings 5.30-8.30pm Tue, Thu, Sat Jun–mid-Sep). Here, in a charming setting, a range of superb wines, including the scintillating Classico, is produced. The winery is 2km south of Argostoli on the airport road and you can also arrange visits by appointment.

Getting Around
TO/FROM THE AIRPORT
The airport is 9km south of Argostoli. There's no airport bus service; a taxi costs around €15.

BOAT
Car ferries run hourly (more frequently in high season) from 7.30am to 10.30pm between Argostoli and Lixouri, on the island's western peninsula. The journey takes 30 minutes, and tickets cost €1.80/4.50/1.20 per person/car/motorbike.

BUS
From Argostoli's **KTEL bus station** (☎ 26710 22281, 26710 25222) on the southern waterfront there are 11 buses daily heading to the Lassi Peninsula (€1.40), with four buses to Sami (€4), two to Poros (€4.50), two to Skala (€4.50) and two to Fiskardo (€5). There's a daily east-coast service linking Katelios with Skala, Poros, Sami, Agia Evfymia and Fiskardo. No buses operate on Sunday.

CAR & MOTORCYCLE
The major resorts have plenty of car- and bike-hire companies. A very reliable local company is **Greekstones Rent a Car** (☎ 26710 44201; www.greekstones-rentacar.com) They deliver to the airport and within a 15km radius of their base at Svoronata (7km from Argostoli, near the airport). **Europcar** (☎ 26710 42020) has an office at the airport.

ARGOSTOLI ΑΡΓΟΣΤΟΛΙ
pop 8900
Argostoli is a hugely likeable and lively town. It suffered enormous damage during the 1953 earthquake and was not rebuilt in its former Venetian splendour. Today, its style is one of broad boulevards and pedestrianised shopping streets lined with the chunky, light-coloured buildings typical of Mediterranean urban architecture of the later 20th century. The central focus is an attractive, if overlarge, square, Plateia Valianou, that has drawn some life away from the long waterfront.

Orientation & Information
The main ferry quay is at the northern end of the waterfront and the bus station is at its southern end. Plateia Valianou, the large palm-treed central square, is a few blocks in from the waterfront off 21 Maïou, and its nearby surrounds. Other hubs are pedestrianised Lithostrotou, lined with smart shops, and the waterfront Antoni Tristi. There are banks with ATMs along the northern waterfront and on Lithostrotou.

Bookmark (☎ 26710 27616; 4 Lithostrotou) A bibliophile's corner, just off busy Lithostrotou, Bookmark has a menu of new and used English-language books, for sale or, indeed, for rent.

EOT (Greek National Tourist Organisation; ☎ 26710 22248; ☼ 8am-8pm Mon-Fri, 9am-3pm Sat Jul-Aug, 8am-2.30pm Mon-Fri Sep-Jun) The tourist office is on the northern waterfront beside the port police.

Excelixis (☎ 26710 25530; cnr Minoos & Asklipiou; per hr €3) Well-run internet, including wi-fi, is available upstairs at this computer shop.

Post office (Lithostrotou)

Sights & Activities
The **Korgialenio History & Folklore Museum** (☎ 26710 28835; Ilia Zervou 12; admission €4; ☼ 9am-2pm Mon-Sat)

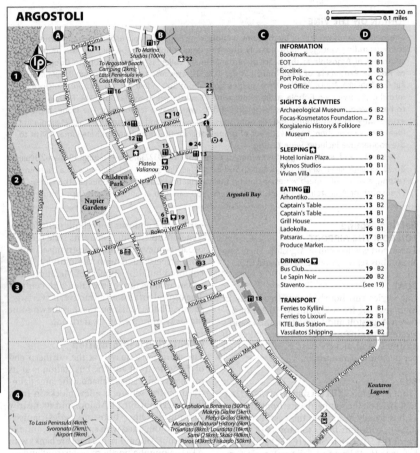

ARGOSTOLI

0   200 m
0   0.1 miles

INFORMATION
Bookmark.................................**1** B3
EOT...**2** B1
Excelixis....................................**3** B3
Port Police...............................**4** C2
Post Office................................**5** B3

SIGHTS & ACTIVITIES
Archaeological Museum............**6** B2
Focas-Kosmetatos Foundation ..**7** B2
Korgialenio History & Folklore
   Museum...............................**8** B3

SLEEPING
Hotel Ionian Plaza.....................**9** B2
Kyknos Studios........................**10** B1
Vivian Villa..............................**11** A1

EATING
Arhontiko................................**12** B2
Captain's Table........................**13** B2
Captain's Table........................**14** B1
Grill House...............................**15** B2
Ladokolla.................................**16** B1
Patsaras...................................**17** B1
Produce Market........................**18** C3

DRINKING
Bus Club..................................**19** B2
Le Sapin Noir...........................**20** B2
Stavento..............................(see 19)

TRANSPORT
Ferries to Kyllini......................**21** B1
Ferries to Lixouri.....................**22** B1
KTEL Bus Station......................**23** D4
Vassilatos Shipping..................**24** B2

---

and **Focas-Kosmetatos Foundation** (☎ 26710 26595; Vallianou; admission €3; ☽ 9.30am-1pm & 7-10pm Mon-Sat) provide interesting insights into Argostoli's cultural and political history. The Focas-Kosmetatos Foundation museum also manages the **Cephalonia Botanica** (☎ 26710 26595; ☽ 8.30am-2.30pm Tue-Sat), a lovely garden, about 2km from the centre of town, full of native flora and shrubs. The Cephalonia Botanica carries out much research into resources and climate change. Entrance to the gardens is included in the Focas-Kosmetatos Foundation ticket and you can get a leaflet with directions at the foundation's museum. Argostoli's **Archaeological Museum** (☎ 26710 28300; Rokou Vergoti; admission €3; ☽ 8.30am-3pm Tue-Sun) has a collection of island relics, including Mycenaean finds.

Six kilometres from Argostoli in Davgata is the **Museum of Natural History** (☎ 26710 84400; admission €2.50; ☽ 9am-3pm), with fascinating exhibits on the geological and natural phenomena of the island, and an excellent topographical model of the island in relief.

The town's closest and largest sandy beaches are **Makrys Gialos** and **Platys Gialos**, 5km south. Regular buses serve the area.

Lourdata, 16km from Argostoli on the Argostoli–Poros road, has an attractive long beach set against a mountainous green backdrop.

To get closer to Kefallonia's coast and sea contact **Monte Nero Activities** (☎ 69340 10400, 69329 04360; www.monte-nero-activities.com) for well-organised sea kayaking. Day tours are €55 with lunch and snorkelling gear and there are multi-day options and instructional courses. They also organise cycling and hiking tours in the island's coastal regions. At the time of writing the company was planning a name change to Sea Kayaking Kefalonia.

Tours

KTEL Tours (☎ 26710 23364) runs excellent-value tours of Kefallonia (€18) on Wednesdays and Sundays, visiting several towns and villages around the island. It also takes tours to Ithaki every Friday (€35). Bookings can be made at the KTEL bus station building.

Sleeping

Argostoli has a fair number of standard hotels, although there are several places with character. **KTEL Tours** (☎ 26710 23364) has a selection of apartments and hotel options available and will organise these via email.

Argostoli Beach Camping (☎ 26710 23487; www .argostolibeach.gr; camp sites per adult/car/tent €7.50/3.50/4.50) This pleasant and quiet camping spot is near the lighthouse on the northernmost point of the peninsula.

Kyknos Studios (☎ 26710 23398; p-krousos@otenet.gr; M Geroulanou 4; d/tr €55/60) An old well in a quirky little garden sits in front of these seven attractive, if a little faded, studios, each with a small verandah and in a quiet part of town

Marina Studios (☎ 26710 26455; maristel@hol.gr; Agnis Metaxa 1; r €55, studio €65-75; ⌨) Located in a quiet street right at the northern end of the waterfront and just across from the Naval College, the rooms here are spacious and comfy and the studios have lovely beamed angle ceilings. Subtle prints and paintings enhance the mood.

Vivian Villa (☎ 26710 23396; www.kefalonia-vivianvilla .gr; Deladetsima 9; s/d/tr €55/70/85, apt €120; ⌨) Highly recommended for its big, bright rooms and friendly owners. There are tea-making facilities in each room, and some have kitchens. The top-floor apartment is excellent. Prices are discounted for longer stays. There's a lift to upper floors.

Hotel Ionian Plaza (☎ 26710 25581; www.ionianplaza .gr; Plateia Valianou; s/d/tr €96/125/169; ⌨ 🛜) Argostoli's smartest hotel has a marble-decorated lobby, stylish public areas and well-appointed rooms with balconies.

Eating

There are numerous cafes around the edges of Plateia Valianou and along Lithostrotou.

Ladokolla (☎ 26710 25522; Xarokopou 13; dishes €1.90-7; ⏲ 1pm-1am) Forget table-top conventions, this is the 'Table Top' in every sense, where piping hot chicken, pork, lamb, kebabs, pittas and souvlaki are delivered without plates and onto very clean disposable covers. They'll bring a plate for anything saucy, but this is cracking down-to-earth noshing, hugely popular locally and with lively service.

Grill House (gyros €2.20) Cheap and cheerful fast food among the pricier cafes on Plateia Valianou, next to Hotel Aeon.

Patsuras (☎ 26710 22779; Antoni Tristi 32; mains €5.50-12) A local favourite on the waterfront road, with a great range of authentic Greek dishes and plentiful helpings.

Captain's Table waterfront (☎ 26710 27170; 1 Metaxa; mains €5.50-24.90) plateia (3 Risospaston) The seafront arm of this popular eatery offers reasonable traditional dishes. The more upmarket arm is just along from the central square.

ourpick Arhontiko (☎ 26710 27213; 5 Risospaston; mains €6.50-8.80; lunch & dinner) Top Kefallonian cuisine is on offer here, with starters such as a soufflé of spinach, cheese and cream, or shrimps and *saganaki* (fried cheese). For mains try *exohiko*, pork stuffed with tomatoes, onions, peppers and feta cheese. Even the house wine matches a good bottled vintage.

You can pick up a range of self-catering supplies from the waterfront produce market and from bakeries and supermarkets nearby.

Drinking

The Plateia Valianou area has several breezy music bars and cafes that fairly bounce by late evening. Popular venues are Le Sapin Noir, Bus Club and Stavento.

SAMI & SURROUNDS ΣΑΜΗ

pop 2200

Sami, 25km northeast of Argostoli and the main port of Kefallonia, was also flattened by the 1953 earthquake. Its exposed long strip is made up of tourist-oriented cafes, but beyond this it's an attractive place, nestled in a bay and flanked by steep hills. There are several monasteries, ancient castle ruins, caves, walks and nearby beaches that reflect the region's rich history. All facilities, including a post office and banks, are in town. Buses for Argostoli usually meet ferries, and car hire is available through **Karavomilos** (☎ 26740 23769). Sami's **tourist office** (⏲ 9am-7pm May-Sep) is at the northern end of town. An informative website is www.sami.gr.

IONIAN ISLANDS

Sights & Activities

The Municipality of Sami has published a simple brochure called *Walking Trail*, which outlines enjoyable walks through the local area. The brochures are available from the tourist office.

Antisamos Beach, 4km northeast of Sami, is a long, stony beach in a lovely green setting backed by hills. The drive here is also a highlight, offering dramatic views from cliff edges.

The rather overrated **Melissani Cave** (admission incl boat trip adult/child €7/4; ☉ 8am-8pm May-Oct), a subterranean sea-water lake that turns a distinctive blue in sunlight, is only worth visiting when the sun is overhead between noon and 2pm. It's 2.5km west of Sami. The **Drogarati Cave** (☎ 26740 22950; adult/child €5/3; ☉ 8am-8pm Jul-Aug) is a massive (natural) chamber with stalactites. Its fragile infrastructure seems to be suffering erosion from too much human pressure.

About 7km from Argostoli, on the road to Sami, a side road leads south into the heart of Robola grape country where a visit to the Cooperative of Robola Producers (see p457) is worthwhile. Near the winery is the **Moni Agiou Gerasimou** dedicated to Kefallonia's patron saint. The monastery is cared for by nuns. There's a pile of wraps outside the chapel and, out of respect, bare arms and shoulders, at least, should be covered before entering. Inside the chapel is a famous cave where Gerasimos escaped from the rigours of monastic life to even greater self-abnegation. Descent, *with great care*, is via a steep metal ladder into a small chamber 6m below. From this chamber a narrow squeeze leads to another tiny chamber. There are lights, but it's not for the claustrophobic – or the unsaintly.

Sleeping

Karavomilos Beach Camping (☎ 26740 22480; www .camping-karavomilos.gr; Sami; camp sites per adult/car/tent €7.50/3.50/6; 🖳 🛜) This is a large, award-winning camping ground in a great beachfront location, with plenty of facilities.

Hotel Melissani (☎ 26740 22464; Sami; d/tr €65/78) Unashamed retro style welcomes you at this very tall, very slim building some way in from the waterfront. Even the bar goes all out with swivelling vinyl bar stools, marble floors and groovy tiles. The smallish rooms have balconies with views of either mountains or sea.

Hotel Kastro (☎ 26740 22656; www.kastrohotel .com; Sami; s/d/tr €70/95/120) At the heart of town,

the Kastro is essentially resort modern, but a reasonable option.

Eating

Sami's waterfront is lined with fairly standard eateries.

Dolphins (☎ 26740 22008; mains €5-20) The best of the waterfront line-up, Dolphins adds value very cleverly by staging lively Greek music nights. The food is excellent Kefallonian traditional with favourites such as baked rabbit, while fish lovers can dig into a sizable seafood platter.

Paradise Beach (☎ 26740 61392; mains €6.50-13, fish per kilogram €48-52; Agia Evfymia) Bear right past the harbourfront tavernas at Agia Evfymia and keep going until the road ends at the famous Paradise, where the cast of an equally famous movie used to eat every night. Penny and Nick may be long gone, but the dolmadhes and Kefallonia meat pie are still fantastic, as is the salted cod in garlic sauce, while the welcome is unfailingly upbeat and the views outstanding.

ASSOS ΑΣΟΣ

Tiny Assos is an upmarket gem of whitewashed and pastel houses, straddling the isthmus of a peninsula on which stands a Venetian fortress. The fortress is a pleasant place to hike to and around, with superlative views and a great historical ambience.

For accommodation, try the **Pension Gerania** (☎ 26740 51526; www.pensiongerania.gr; d incl breakfast €85; ❄). It does what it says on the label at this pension with its lush garden full of geraniums, while the light and appealing rooms have pleasant views. Follow the *pension* (and parking) sign at the top of the hill as you enter town.

Cosi's Inn (☎ 26740 51420, 69367 54330; www .cosisinn.gr; 2-/3-person studio €113/129; ❄) is not typically 'Greek' but has the marks of the young and hip interior designer owner: iron beds and sofas, frosted lights and white decor feature strongly.

For eating, **Platanos** (☎ 69446 71804; mains €5.50-13) is in an attractive shady setting near the waterfront. Strong on meat dishes, there are also fish and vegetarian options such as a tasty eggplant, feta and parmesan pie.

AROUND ASSOS

One of Greece's most breathtaking and picture-perfect beaches is **Myrtos**, 8km south of

IONIAN ISLANDS

MEMORIES WITHOUT MANDOLINS

Down at the Paradise Beach taverna, the irrepressible Stavros Dendrinos still does exuberance when it comes to memories. As a youngster during WWII, Stavros longed to escape from the strictures of island life. 'Every time I saw a distant sail, my heart leapt with excitement,' he says with a smile.

Then, aged 12, during WWII, Stavros joined his uncle in running a tiny sailing motor boat to and from Kefallonia and Piraeus. They carried passengers and small amounts of local produce within strict limits imposed by the German occupiers. Under curfew rules, they had to pull ashore wherever they could, as soon as darkness fell. Years of worldwide seagoing followed and then Stavros settled in Athens until memories of Kefallonia and the bright sea of his childhood drew him back to become one of the island's best known taverna owners.

Oh… did someone mention *Captain Corelli's Mandolin* and Penelope Cruz (who is said to have dined at the Paradise taverna every night while on location)? 'Lovely lady,' says Stavros, graciously, but with his eyes on the sea and distant sails.

Assos along an exciting stretch of the west coast road. From a roadside viewing area, you can admire and photograph the white sand and shimmering blue water set between tall limestone cliffs far below and you can reach the beach from sea level at Anomeria. Be aware that the beach drops off quickly and sharply, but once you are in the water it's a heavenly experience. Think clichéd turquoise and aqua water.

FISKARDO ΦΙΣΚΑΡΔΟ
pop 230

Fiskardo, 50km north of Argostoli, was the only Kefallonian village not devastated by the 1953 earthquake. Framed by cypress-mantled hills and with fine Venetian buildings, it has an authentic picturesque appeal and is popular with well-keeled yachting fans. It has some outstanding restaurants. There's a car park above the harbour at the south end of the village.

Nautilus Travel (☎ 26740 41440) towards the ferry quay end of the waterfront is an efficient agency that can help with all your needs. **Pama Travel** (☎ 26740 41033; www.pamatravel.com) on the harbour front has foreign exchange facilities and can help with travel services including car and boat hire. It also has internet access (15 minutes €2).

Sleeping

Fiscardo has quite a fair mix of sleeping options and some seriously top-level restaurants.

Regina's Rooms (☎ 26740 41125; d/tr €50/60) Friendly Regina runs a popular place that has colourful rooms dotted with plastic flowers. Some rooms have kitchenettes and/or balconies enjoying views over the water. It's alongside the main car park at the south end of the village.

Villa Romantza (☎ 26740 41322; www.villa-romantza .gr; r/studio €50/70, apt €80-110; ✖) An excellent budget choice with simple and clean rooms. It's found next door to Regina's rooms on the car park. Cheaper out of season.

Stella Apartments (☎ 26740 41211; www.stella -apartments.gr; d €105, apt €210; ✖) Located on the quiet southern outskirts of the village about 800m from the main car park. these apartments have immaculate, spacious studios with kitchens and balconies. There's a communal dining area.

Emelisse Hotel (☎ 26740 41200; www.arthotel.gr; d €480-630, ste €510-1800, apt €770-800; ❂ year-round; ✖ ❑) In a superb position overlooking the unspoiled Emplisis Bay, this stylish and luxurious hotel has every facility for the pampered holiday. The rooms are beautifully appointed, leafy terraces surround the lavish swimming pool and there's even a gym and tennis court. Breakfast is included.

Eating & Drinking

Café Tselenti (☎ 26740 41344; mains €7.50-23) Housed in a lovely 19th-century building, owned by the Tselenti family since 1893, with a romantic outdoor terrace at the heart of the village, the cuisine at this noted restaurant is outstanding. Starters of cheese and mushroom patties and aubergine rolls are superb, as are such mains as linguine with prawns, mussels and crawfish in a tomato sauce or the pork fillet with sundried apricots, dates and fresh pineapple.

Tassia (☎ 26740 41205; mains €10-25) A complete refurbishment in 2009 has added even more lustre to this Fiskardo institution run by Tassia Dendrinou, celebrated chef and writer on Greek cuisine. Everything is a delight, but specialities include *kolokythokeftedhes*, baby marrow croquettes and a fisherman's pasta incorporating finely chopped squid, octopus, mussels and prawns in a magic mix that even includes a dash of cognac. Meat dishes are equally splendid and Tassia's desserts are famous.

Gaeta Art Bar (☎ 69322 57027) At the heart of waterfront Fiskardo, the Gaeta is the place for watching the world go by over coffee by day and for cocktails, drinks and good company at night.

Getting There & Away

You can get to/from Fiskardo by ferry to/from Lefkada and Ithaki (for details see Island Hopping, p516) or by bus to/from Argostoli. The ferry is at one end of the waterfront; ask the bus to drop you at the turn-off, or it's a 10-minute walk from the car park to the ferry.

ITHAKI ΙΘΑΚΗ

pop 3700

Sheltered Ithaki dreams happily in its lake-like setting between Kefallonia and mainland Greece. The island is celebrated as being the mythical home of Homer's Odysseus, where loyal wife Penelope waited patiently, while besieged by unsavoury suitors, for Odysseus's much delayed homecoming. This tranquil island is made up of two large peninsulas that are joined by a narrow isthmus. Sheer cliffs, precipitous mountains and vast swaths of olive groves and cypresses gild this Ionian gem. Attractive villages (much rebuilt after the 1953 earthquake) and hidden coves with pebbly beaches add to the charm, while monasteries and churches offer Byzantine delights and splendid views.

Getting There & Away

Strintzis Lines (www.ferries.gr/strintzis-ferries) has two ferries daily connecting Vathy or Piso Aetos with Patra via Sami on Kefallonia. The ferry *Ionian Pelagos* runs daily (sometimes twice a day) in high season between Piso Aetos, Sami and Astakos on the mainland.

Other ferries run to ever-changing schedules from Vasiliki and Nydri (Lefkada) to Frikes (Ithaki) and Fiskardo (Kefallonia). For details see Island Hopping (p514).

Information and tickets for the routes can be obtained from Delas Tours (below) on the main square in Vathy.

One ferry a day runs from Frikes to Fiskardo (€3.80, 55 minutes) and from Frikes to Nydri (€7, 1½ hours). Two ferries a day run from Vathy to Patra (€17.60, 3¾ hours) and two ferries a day run from Piso Aetos to Patra (€17.60, three hours).

Getting Around

Piso Aetos, on Ithaki's west coast, has no settlement; taxis often meet boats, as does the municipal bus in high season only. The island's one bus runs twice daily (weekdays only, more often in high season) between Kioni and Vathy via Stavros and Frikes (€3.90), and its limited schedule is not well suited to day-trippers. Taxis are relatively expensive (about €30 for the Vathy–Frikes trip), so your best bet is to hire a moped or car (or a motorboat) to get around. In Vathy, **Rent a Scooter** (☎ 26740 32840) is down the lane opposite the port authority. For cars, try Happy Cars – contact Polyctor Tours (below) or **Alpha Bike & Car Hire** (☎ 26740 33243) behind Alpha Bank.

VATHY ΒΑΘΥ

pop 1820

Ithaki's pretty main town sprawls along its elongated and square-cut waterfront and has a central square, lined with cafes and restaurants, as the social hub. Narrow lanes wriggle inland from the waterfront.

The ferry quay is on the western side of the bay. To reach the central square (Plateia Efstathiou Drakouli), turn left and follow the waterfront.

Ithaki has no tourist office. **Delas Tours** (☎ 26740 32104; www.ithaca.com.gr) and **Polyctor Tours** (☎ 26740 33120; www.ithakiholidays.com), both on the main square, can help with tourist information. The main square also has banks with ATMs; the post office; and internet access – try **Net** (per hr €4).

Sights & Activities

Behind Hotel Mentor is an interesting **archaeological museum** (☎ 26740 32200; admission

---

HOT HIKES AFTER HOMER

Ithaki's compact size ensures dramatic scenery changes over short distances on walks that can reveal 360-degree views of the ocean and surrounding islands. Thanks to the efforts of islander Denis Sikiotis and his band of helpers, several cleared and marked trails exist around the island. Mr Sikiotis has prepared brief notes and maps that should be available from the town hall in Vathy. Enjoyable guided walks, including the popular Homer's Walk on Wednesdays, explore little seen parts of the island and are organised through **Island Walks** (☎ 69449 90458; www.xs4all.nl/~rienz/iwalks). Routes are from 5km to 13km and cost €15 to €25.

---

free; 8.30am-3pm Tue-Sun) with some notable ancient coins depicting Odysseus. The equally entertaining and informative **nautical & folklore museum** (admission €1.50; 10am-2pm & 5-9pm Tue-Sat) is housed in an old generating station one block behind the square.

Boat excursions on the **Albatross** (☎ 69769 01643) leave from Vathy harbour in the summer months and include day trips around Ithaki and to Fiskardo (€30); Lefkada (€35); and 'unknown islands' that include Atokos and Kalamos (€35). There's also a water taxi to **Gidaki Beach**. Note: the only way to access this beach on foot is to follow the walking track from Skinari Beach.

Sleeping

Grivas Gerasimos Rooms (☎ 26740 33328; d/tr €75/88) Spacious studios with pot plants, small balconies and a seaside vista are a good bet at this pleasant place. Turn right at the Century Club on the waterfront and then go first left at the road parallel to the sea. The studios are 50m on your right. There may be a discount, depending on the length of stay.

Odyssey Apartments (☎ 26740 33400; www.ithaki -odyssey.com; apt €110-170;) You need to head right along the waterfront then turn up right, signed Skinos and Odyssey Apartments, for another 500m to this excellent option. There are light, breezy studios and apartments with balconies, and a magical view of the yacht harbour and beyond.

Hotel Perantzada (☎ 26740 33496; www.arthotel.gr/ perantzada; Odissea Androutsou; s €200, d €316-388, ste €459-707;) Part of the Emelisse group,

this stylish boutique hotel is in a transformed neoclassical building of 19th-century vintage. It all glows with modernist chic and the vibrant designs of such names as Philip Stark and Ingo Mauer. A new extension is even more dazzling and includes an infinity pool. Breakfasts are every bit as svelte.

Eating & Drinking

Vathy's waterfront eateries are fairly standard and with identical menus, although there are exceptions.

For a sweet experience, try *rovani*, the local speciality made with rice, honey and cloves, at one of the patisseries on or near the main square.

Café Karamela (☎ 26740 33580; snacks €2.50-6) The western quay is home to this welcoming place, where you have a genuine picturesque view of the bay through a massive window. Board games, books and TV, plus home-made snacks cakes and pastries make it all even more pleasant.

Dracoulis (☎ 26740 33453; snacks €5-9) Housed in a dignified old seafront villa, this bar-cafe has drinks, sandwiches, mixed plates and music. Note the little mooring pool in front of the mansion and ponder on sea level rise. The below-road channel was once navigable by small boats. You'd need a mini-sub now.

Gregory's Taverna/Paliocaravo (☎ 26740 32573; mains €5.50-19) This long-standing family concern serves fish and tasty specialities such as *savoro*, fish marinated in vinegar and raisins. It's 1km north along Vathy's waterfront and overlooks the yacht marina.

Drosia (☎ 26740 32959; mains €6-15) This well-known taverna serves authentic Greek dishes and throws in a touch of Venezuelan influence as well. Popular for its charcoal grill dishes you may also catch some impromptu dancing to the playing of bouzoukis. It's 1km up the narrow road to Filiatro from the inner corner of the harbour.

AROUND ITHAKI

Ithaki proudly claims several sites associated with Homer's tale, the 'Odyssey'. Finding the hyped-up locations can be an epic journey – signage is a bit scant. Many seem to be myths themselves, so vague are their locations, but there's no questioning the classical spirit of this island. The **Fountain of Arethousa**, in the island's south, is where Odysseus' swineherd, Eumaeus, is believed to have brought his pigs to

IONIAN ISLANDS

drink. The exposed and isolated hike – through unspoilt landscape with great sea views – takes 1½ to two hours (return) from the turn-off; this excludes the hilly 5km trudge up the road to the sign itself. Take a hat and water.

The location of Odysseus' palace has been much disputed and archaeologists have been unable to find conclusive evidence; some present-day archaeologists speculate it was on **Pelikata Hill** near Stavros, while German archaeologist Heinrich Schliemann believed it to be at **Alalkomenes**, near Piso Aetos. Also in Stavros visit the small **archaeological museum** (☎ 26740 31305; admission free; ⊗ 9am-2.30pm Tue-Sun).

Take a break from Homeric myth and head north from Vathy along a fabulously scenic mountain road to sleepy **Anogi**, the old capital. Its restored church of **Agia Panagia** (claimed to be from the 12th century) has incredible Byzantine frescoes and a Venetian bell tower. You can obtain the keys from the neighbouring *kafeneio*. About 200m uphill are the small but evocative ruins of Old Anogi within a rock-studded landscape.

Further north again is the little village of **Stavros** above the Bay of Polis, also reached along the west coast road. Heading northeast from Stavros takes you to the tiny, understated seafront village of **Frikes** clasped between windswept cliffs and with a swath of waterfront restaurants, busy bars and a relaxed ambience. It's the ferry departure point for Lefkada. From Frikes a twisting road hugs the beautiful coastline to end at **Kioni**, another small seafront village that spills down a verdant hillside to a miniature harbour where yachts overnight and tavernas and bars eagerly await them.

Sleeping & Eating

Mrs Vasilopoulos' Rooms (☎ 26740 31027; Stavros; s/d/apt €40/50/65) These homely studios, with overhead fans, are reached by going up the leftmost lane to the left of Café To Kentro from the main square in Stavros. The pretty garden overlooks olive and cypress groves.

Captain's Apartments (☎ 26740 31481; www.captains-apartments.gr; Kioni; d €65, 4-person apt €90; ⊗ year-round; P ⊠) Well-run and definitely ship-shape are these well-maintained studios and apartments that are signposted half-way down the twisting road to the harbour at Kioni.

Fatouros Taverna (☎ 26740 31385; Stavros; mains €5-12) A pleasant unvarnished place behind its red-brick facade, this popular eatery exults in spit-roast meat dishes and Greek standards.

Yiannis (☎ 26740 31363; Stavros; mains €5-12) Friendly Yiannis does a good line in pizzas and sturdy mezedhes as well as Greek main dishes. Breakfasts are about €5.

Rementzo (☎ 26740 31719; Frikes; mains €6.80-11.60) Among the usual swathe of waterside tavernas in Frikes, Rementzo does good value Greek standards.

ZAKYNTHOS
ΖΑΚΥΝΘΟΣ

pop 38,600

Zakynthos (*zahk*-in-thos), also known by its Italian name Zante, is a fascinating island, unfairly known perhaps for conspicuous and heavy package tourism along its eastern and southeast coasts, but essentially a beautiful island whose western and central regions are mountainous, green and inspiring. The Venetians called it the Flower of the Orient. Its people are welcoming and its cuisine a delight. Too much tourism is, however, endangering more than the aesthetics of island life. The loggerhead turtle (see At Loggerheads, p469) struggles in the face of commercial development.

Getting There & Away
AIR

There are at least one or two daily flights between Zakynthos and Athens and connections to other Ionian Islands including Kefallonia and Corfu. **Olympic Air** (☎ 26950 28322; Zakynthos Airport; ☎ 8am-10pm Mon-Fri) can help with information and bookings. For details see Island Hopping (p525).

From May to September, many charter flights come from northern Europe and the UK to Zakynthos.

BOAT
Domestic

Depending on the season, between five and seven ferries operate daily between Zakynthos Town and Kyllini in the Peloponnese. Tickets can be obtained from the **Zakynthos Shipping Cooperative** (☎ 26950 22083/49500; Lombardou 40) in Zakynthos Town.

ZAKYNTHOS

IONIAN SEA

Zakynthos Strait

Vassilikos Peninsula

Bay of Laganas

From the northern port of Agios Nikolaos a ferry service shuttles across to Pesada in southern Kefallonia twice daily from May to October. In high season, there are only two buses a week from Zakynthos Town to Agios Nikolaos and two buses daily from Pesada (Kefallonia) to Argostoli (Kefallonia) making crossing without your own transport difficult. An alternative is to cross to Kyllini and catch another ferry to Kefallonia.

For ferry details see Island Hopping (p525).

International
Hellenic Mediterranean Lines (www.hmlferry.com) has July and August services once or twice a week between Brindisi and Zakynthos (€69, 15½ hours).

BUS
The smart new **KTEL bus station** (☎ 26950 22255) has recently opened on the bypass to the west of Zakynthos Town. On Monday to Friday, from early morning until 3pm, a mini-bus runs every hour or so to the new bus station from the site of the **old bus station** (42 Filita St).

KTEL operates four buses daily between Zakynthos Town and Patra (€6.80, 3½ hours), and four daily connections to/from Athens (€23.20, six hours) via the Corinth Canal road (€16.60, five hours). There's also a twice-weekly service to Thessaloniki (€44.30).

Budget an additional €8.20 for the ferry fare between Zakynthos and Kyllini.

Getting Around

There's no bus service between Zakynthos Town and the airport, 6km to the southwest. A taxi costs around €10. Frequent buses go from Zakynthos Town's **KTEL bus station** (☎ 26950 22255) to the developed resorts of Alikes (€1.50), Tsilivi, Argasi, Laganas and Kalamaki (all €1.40). Bus services to other villages are infrequent. Several useful local buses take the upper or lower main roads to Katastari and Volimes. Ask at the bus station.

Car- and moped-hire places are plentiful in the larger resorts. In Zakynthos Town a good option is **Motor Club Rentals** (☎ 26950 53095)

whose rentals can also be arranged through the Zante Voyage office (see opposite). Also reliable is **Europcar** (☎ 26950 41541; Plateia Agiou Louka), which also has a branch at the airport.

ZAKYNTHOS TOWN

pop 11,200

Zakynthos Town is the capital and port of the island and straggles round an enormous bay. The town was devastated by the 1953 earthquake, but was reconstructed to its former layout with arcaded streets, imposing squares and gracious neoclassical public buildings. A Venetian fortress on a hill provides an attractive backdrop. The town has a strong Greek feel and is patently more of a vibrant commercial centre than a tourist one. It still

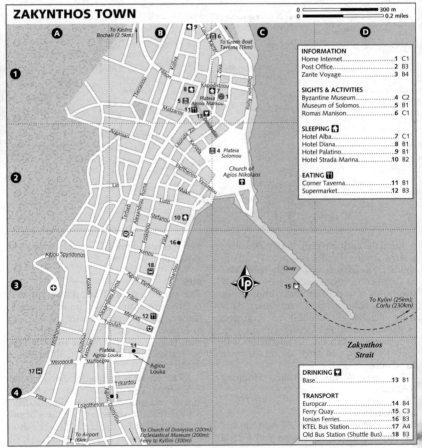

ZAKYNTHOS TOWN

0 — 300 m
0 — 0.2 miles

INFORMATION	
Home Internet	1 C1
Post Office	2 B3
Zante Voyage	3 B4

SIGHTS & ACTIVITIES	
Byzantine Museum	4 C2
Museum of Solomos	5 B1
Romas Manison	6 C1

SLEEPING	
Hotel Alba	7 C1
Hotel Diana	8 B1
Hotel Palatino	9 B1
Hotel Strada Marina	10 B2

EATING	
Corner Taverna	11 B1
Supermarket	12 B3

DRINKING	
Base	13 B1

TRANSPORT	
Europcar	14 B4
Ferry Quay	15 C3
Ionian Ferries	16 B3
KTEL Bus Station	17 A4
Old Bus Station (Shuttle Bus)	18 B3

has some outstanding cultural attractions, however, while the northern area (around Plateia Agiou Markou) has plenty of cafes, bars, and restaurants.

Orientation & Information

Plateia Solomou is at the northern end of the waterfront road of Lombardou, opposite the ferry quay. Plateia Agiou Markou is behind it. The bus station is out on the western bypass. The main thoroughfare is Alexandrou Roma, running several blocks inland, parallel to the waterfront.

Zakynthos Town has no tourist office. The helpful **Zante Voyage** (☎ 26950 25360; 12 Ágiou Dionysou) promises 'travel solutions' and does a good job of delivering on queries, accommodation, car hire and tours.

There are banks with ATMs along Lombardou and just west of Plateia Solomou. The **post office** (☎ 26950 44875; Tertseti 27; ◷ 7am-2pm) is one block west of Alexandrou Roma. **Home Internet** (12 L Ziva; per hr €3; ◷ 10am-1am) has reasonable connection.

Sights & Activities

The **Byzantine museum** (☎ 26950 42714; Plateia Solomou; admission €3; ◷ 8.30am-3pm Tue-Sun) houses two levels of fabulous ecclesiastical art, rescued from churches razed by the earthquake. It's all displayed in a beautiful setting overlooking the main plaza. Inside, the 16th-century St Andreas Monastery has been artfully 'replicated' to house its restored frescoes. The nearby **Museum of Solomos** (☎ 26950 28982; Plateia Agiou Markou; admission €4; ◷ 9am-2pm) is dedicated to Dionysios Solomos (1798–1857), who was born on Zakynthos and is regarded as the father of modern Greek poetry. His work *Hymn to Liberty* became the Greek national anthem. The museum houses his memorabilia and archives. Just north of Plateia Agiou Markou is the fascinating **Romas Mansion** (☎ 26950 28343; 19 Louka Karrer; admission €5; ◷ 10am-2pm Mon-Sat Apr-Oct). Built in the 17th century by an English merchant, the house was British-owned (Gladstone addressed the locals from its balcony) until bought by the Romas family during the 1880s. The house suffered badly in the 1953 earthquake but was partly rebuilt a few years later. Its period furnishings and decor are splendidly intact and the library has an astonishing 10,000 volumes.

The **Church of Dionysios**, the patron saint of the island, in Zakynthos Town's south has some amazing gilt work and notable frescoes. Behind the church is an **ecclesiastical museum** (admission €2; ◷ 9am-1pm & 5-9pm). It contains intriguing icons from the Monastery of Strofades, home to Dionysios, plus speech scrolls from the 13th and 14th centuries and a 12th-century book in Ancient Greek.

The peaceful, shady and pine tree-filled **Kastro** (☎ 26950 48099; admission €3; ◷ 8.30am-2.30pm Tue-Sun), a ruined Venetian fortress high above Zakynthos Town, makes for a pleasant outing. It's 2.5km from town in the viewpoint village of Bochali (take Dionysiou Roma north and turn left at Kapodistriou; it's signed from here). There's a big car park as you enter Bochali and a one-way system thereafter. You are strongly advised not to try driving up to the castle, which is 300m above Bochali's main square. There's a walkway. Bochali has several cafes and tavernas with glorious views over Zakynthos Town.

Sleeping

Tour groups tend to monopolise many out-of-town hotels, but the following are safe bets for independent travellers and all are open throughout the year.

Hotel Alba (☎ 26950 26641; www.albahotel.gr; L Ziva 38; s/d/tr incl breakfast €48/68/96; 🛏) A reasonable, if slightly dull, hotel but convenient for the centre of town. Rooms are slowly being refurbished and you pay a general €6 to €14 more for renovated ones.

Hotel Strada Marina (☎ 26950 42761; hotel@strada marina.gr; Lombardou 14; s/d incl breakfast €60/90; 🛏 🍽) A good location on the main harbourfront road makes this business standard hotel a good option. Rooms are well equipped and the upper balconies have a great view of the bay. The rooftop area has a small pool.

Hotel Diana (☎ 26950 28547; Plateia Agiou Markou; s/d/tr incl breakfast €70/90/100; 🛏 🖥 🛜) Slightly ponderous decor does not mar this comfortable and well-appointed hotel in a good, central location.

Hotel Palatino (☎ 26950 27780; www.palatino hotel.gr; Kolokotroni 10; s/d/tr €75/110/125; 🛏 🖥 🛜) Business style is the measure of this well-appointed hotel with its comfortable rooms and smooth decor.

Eating & Drinking

There are plenty of tavernas and restaurants around Plateia Agiou Markou, but they tend to be overpriced and not entirely inspiring. There are decent options here, all the same, and elsewhere in town.

Green Boat Taverna (☎ 26950 22957; Krionerou 50; mains €4-15) It's a bit of a hike of about 1km north along the waterfront but the Green Boat is worth it for its fish and excellent Greek dishes such as *melitzanes*, eggplant in tomato sauce with feta cheese. Grilled king prawns are €12 and a plate of small fish is €10.

Corner Taverna (☎ 26950 42654; Plateia Agiou Markou; mains €6-19.80) Bang at the heart of the action and very proactive in catching custom, this busy place does offer reasonable grills and pastas.

Base (☎ 26950 42409; Plateia Agiou Markou; cappuccino €3.50) In a perfect location, Base commands the flow through Plateia Agiou Markou dispensing coffees, drinks and music to a very relaxed, sometimes posey, people-watching, gossipy local crowd.

There's also a well-stocked **supermarket** (cnr Filioti & Lombardou).

AROUND ZAKYNTHOS

Transport of your own is really the way to unlock the charms of Zakynthos.

A major feature of the island are the loggerhead turtles (see At Loggerheads, opposite) that come ashore to lay their eggs on the golden-sand beaches of the huge Bay of Laganas, a national marine park on Zakynthos' south coast. Unfortunately, the turtles share the bay with holidaymakers, who are often unaware of the situation concerning turtle breeding while protective legislation covering the loggerheads is often flouted by local tourism interests.

The **Vasilikos Peninsula** is the pretty green region southeast of Zakynthos Town, and fringing Laganas Bay. It's being heavily developed and has several settlements off the main road, all with tavernas and accommodation. **Banana Beach**, a long and narrow strip of golden sand on the peninsula's northern side, has plenty of action: crowds, water sports and umbrellas. Zakynthos' best beach is the long, sandy and much-coveted **Gerakas**. It's on the other side of the peninsula, facing into Laganas Bay. This is one of the main turtle-nesting beaches, and access to the beach is forbidden between dusk and dawn during May and October. On the northeastern side of Vasilikos Peninsula is the reasonable beach of **Kaminia**.

With transport, you can reach the far southwest of the island where, beyond the

very traditional village of **Keri**, a road leads past a taverna boasting the allegedly biggest Greek flag and flagpole in the country to **Cape Keri** and its lighthouse above sheer cliffs, where some care should be taken on paths that descend to the very abrupt cliff edge.

Fascinating and sometimes happily confusing roads lead north from here through beautiful wooded hill country where the welcoming locals sell honey and other seasonal products. The way leads to appealing west coast coves, such as **Limnionas** or **Kambi** and to such inland gems as **Kiliomeno** whose church of **St Nikolaos** features an unusual roofless campanile. The bell tower of the church of **Agios Leon** was formerly a windmill. **Louka** is a lovely village that seems more northern European, with its surrounding woodland and lush greenery. The hamlet of **Exo Hora** has a collection of dry wells and what is reputed to be the oldest olive tree on the island. **Volimes** is the unashamed sales centre for all traditional products.

North of Zakynthos Town the east coast is lined with resorts but the further north you go, the more remote and lovely the island becomes until the road begins to run out at the ferry point and small resort of **Agios Nikolaos**, where development is slight. Carry on beyond and you reach the breezy Cape Skinari from where boats leave for the coastal **Blue Caves**, sea-level caverns that pierce the limestone coastal cliffs. The boats enter the caves, where the water is a translucent blue. The boats also go to the famous **Shipwreck Beach**, whose photos grace virtually every tourist brochure about Zakynthos, in Navagio Bay, about 3km west of Volimes at the northwest tip of the island. It's overhyped, inevitably, and definitely over patronised by excursion boats. There's a precariously perched lookout platform (signposted between Anafonitria and Volimes). **Potamitis Trips** (☎ 26950 31132; www.potamitisbros.gr) offers worthwhile trips in glass-bottomed boats from Cape Skinari (Blue Caves only €7.50, Shipwreck Beach and Blue Caves €15).

Sleeping

Earth Sea & Sky can arrange short- or long-term stays in villas and cottages around the Vasilikos Peninsula – book through **Ionian Eco Villagers** (☎ UK 0871 711 5065; www.relaxing-holidays .com). Alternatively, you could try your luck for a spontaneous booking with the same company at its wildlife information kiosk in Gerakas.

AT LOGGERHEADS

The Ionian Islands are home to the Mediterranean's loggerhead turtle *(Caretta caretta)*, one of Europe's most endangered marine species. The turtles bury their eggs on large tracts of clean, flat sand, unfortunately the favoured habitat of basking tourists. The implications are obvious.

Zakynthos hosts the largest density of turtle nests in the Ionian – an estimated 1100 along the 5km Bay of Laganas. During hatching time (July to October), surviving hatchlings emerge after a 60-day incubation period in the sand. Bizarrely, wooden frames with warning notes attached are placed by conservation agencies over the buried hatching sites, often alongside the sunbeds and windbreaks of tourists. Many of the nests are destroyed by sun brollies and bikes. Young turtles often don't make it to the water – they are often disoriented by sunbeds, noise and lights.

Conservation lobbyists have clashed with local authorities, tourist operators and the government. In 1999, following pressure from the EU, the Greek government declared the Bay of Laganas area a national marine park. Strict regulations were put in force regarding building, boating, mooring, fishing and water sports in designated zones.

All designated nesting beaches are completely off-limits between dusk and dawn during the breeding season (May to October). Despite this, dozens of illegal bars and tavernas operate in the area, illegal umbrellas and sunbeds are rented out to tourists, and sightseeing boats 'guarantee' turtle sightings and inevitably get too close to the creatures, an intrusion that causes stress at a crucial point in the turtles' breeding cycle.

In July 2009 savage wildfires around Laganas Bay, several allegedly started by human action, were feared to have damaged some sections of breeding areas, especially in the Daphni Beach area where dozens of holidaymakers had to be rescued. Daphni is one of the turtle beaches where protective legislation continues to be flouted.

The Greek government has been condemned by the European Court of Justice for failing to implement EU nature protection legislation. Meanwhile, WWF (Worldwide Fund for Nature), Archelon (the Sea Turtle Protection Society of Greece) and Medasset (Mediterranean Association to Save the Sea Turtles) continue their lobbying efforts. Volunteers from **Archelon** (www.archelon.gr) and the national marine park provide informal beach wardens and run excellent education and volunteer programs. For further information, visit the wildlife information centre at Gerakas Beach.

Visitors can also be aware of the following and make their judgements accordingly:

■ Avoid using umbrellas on dry sand (use the wet part of the beach).

■ Do not enter nesting beaches between dusk and dawn, and avoid visiting Daphni Beach.

■ Be aware of boating trips – where they go and what's on offer.

■ Seek information on the area's sea turtle conservation efforts and protective regulations.

Tartaruga Camping (☎ 26950 51967; www.tartaruga-camping.com; camp sites per adult/car/tent €5/3/3.60, r per person €20-50; P ✗ 🔲) A great place for happy campers – amid terraced olive groves, pines and plane trees that sprawl as far as the sea. It has a small store and a taverna (mains €4-8), and rooms for rent. It's well-signed on the road from Laganas to Keri.

Panorama Studios (☎ 26950 31013; panorama-apts@ath.forthnet.gr; Agios Nikolaos; s/d/tr €40/45/55) The English-speaking hosts at this place in Agios Nikolaos offer excellent studio accommodation on the main road 600m uphill from the port, but set back in a lovely garden area.

Revera Villas (☎ 26950 27524, 69748 75171; www.revera-zante.com; d €70, studio €80, 4-/6-person villa €150/200; P ✗ 🔲 🐾) This complex of Italian-feel villas is located 4km southwest of Limni Keriou village (and 500m southwest of Keri village), just off the road to the lighthouse. The buildings and individually decorated, luxury rooms incorporate exposed stonework. Mountain bikes are available free of charge.

Anna's Villas (☎ 69772 36243, 69772 36243; apt €90; Limni Keriou; P ✗) Two good-value studio apartments, in a garden setting and with kitchen facilities. They're set a block or so back from Limni Keriou's waterfront.

Windmill (☎ 26950 31132; Cape Skinari; www.potami tisbros.gr; 2-/4-person windmills €90/120; 🕮) There are two converted windmills at Cape Skinari in a fantastic cliff-top location. The bigger one has cooking facilities, and an adjoining cafe-bar, with excellent rooms (€70) and an apartment (€120) above, all with stunning views. Steps lead down to a lovely swimming area and one of the departure points for boat trips to the Blue Caves and Shipwreck Beach (p468).

Louha's Coffee Shop (☎ 26950 48426; mains €4-7; Louka; 🕮 lunch & dinner) Head along the lane to the Church of St John the Theologian, who would have enjoyed eating under Louha's vine-shaded terrace opposite the church. Very traditional and good local wine goes with soothing views of cypress and pine-tree dotted hills.

To Litrouvio (☎ 26950 55081; mains €6.50-16; Lithakia; 🕮 lunch & dinner) An olive-oil stone presser and various traditional artefacts add to the experience at this popular place, where good local dishes come in plentiful helpings.

KYTHIRA & ANTIKYTHIRA

KYTHIRA ΚΥΘΗΡΑ
pop 3334

The island of Kythira (kee-thih-rah), 12km south of Neapoli, is perfect for people who want to experience a genuine, functioning and unspoilt island.

Some 30km long and 18km wide, Kythira dangles off the tip of the Peloponnese's Lakonian peninsula, between the Aegean and Ionian Seas. The largely barren landscape is dominated by a rocky plateau that covers most of the island, and the population is spread among more than 40 villages that capitalise on small pockets of agriculturally viable land. The villages are linked by narrow, winding lanes, often flanked by ancient dry-stone walls.

Although Kythira is (officially) part of the Ionian Islands, some of the houses, especially those in the island's main town, Hora, are more Cycladic in looks, with whitewashed walls and blue shutters. (And, although Ionian, we've included it in this chapter because most people visit the island from the Peloponnese.) Mythology suggests that Aphrodite was born in Kythira. She's meant to have risen from the foam where Zeus had thrown Cronos'

sex organ after castrating him. The goddess of love then re-emerged near Pafos in Cyprus, so both islands haggle over her birthplace.

Tourism remains very low-key on Kythira for most of the year, until July and August, when the island goes mad. Descending visitors include the Kythiran diaspora returning from abroad (especially Australia) to visit family and friends (who themselves have returned after leaving the island several decades ago). Accommodation is virtually impossible to find during this time, and restaurants are flat out catering for the crowds. For the remaining 10 months of the year, Kythira is a wonderfully peaceful island with some fine, uncrowded beaches. The best times to visit Kythira are in late spring and around September/October.

Few people venture to the tiny island of Antikythira, the most remote island in the Ionians, 38km southeast of Kythira; it has become a bit of a forgotten outpost, although some ferries stop there on the way to/from Crete.

For information on Kythira, refer to the commercial websites: www.kythira.gr, www.kithera .gr, www.kythira.info and www.visitkythera .gr. Definitely pick up a copy of the informative community newspaper Kythera, published in English and available in travel agencies, hotels and some shops. Keen walkers should seek out a copy of Kythira on Foot: 32 Carefully Selected Walking Routes (€10) by Frank van Weerde (a long-time resident of Kythira).

GETTING THERE & AWAY
Air
In high season there are daily flights between Kythira and Athens (€52 to €70, 40 minutes). The airport is 10km east of Potamos, and **Olympic Air** (☎ 27360 33362) is on the central square in Potamos. Book also at **Kythira Travel** (☎ 27360 31390) in Hora.

Boat
The island's main connection is between Diakofti and Neapoli in the Peloponnese. Tickets are sold at the port just before departure, or at **Kythira Travel** (☎ in Hora 27360 31390, in Potamos 27360 31848) in Hora and Potamos.

LANE Lines calls at the southern port of Diakofti on its weekly schedule between Piraeus, Kythira, Antikythira, Crete and Gythio (Peloponnese). Information and tickets are available from the helpful staff at

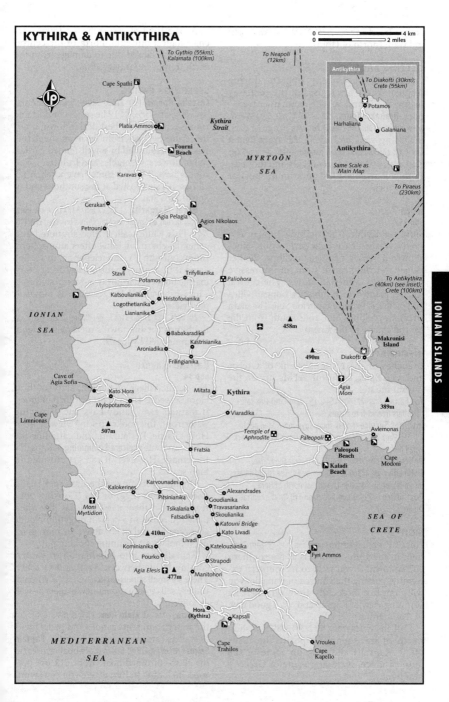

KYTHIRA & ANTIKYTHIRA

0 _____ 4 km
0 _____ 2 miles

To Gythio (55km);
Kalamata (100km)

To Neapoli
(12km)

Cape Spathi

Platia Ammos

Fourni
Beach

*Kythira
Strait*

*MYRTOÖN
SEA*

Antikythira

To Diakofti (30km);
Crete (55km)

Potamos

Harhaliana

Galaniana

Antikythira

*Same Scale as
Main Map*

Karavas

Gerakari

Agia Pelagia

Agios Nikolaos

Petrouni

To Piraeus
(230km)

Stavli

Trifyllianika

Paliohora

Potamos

Katsoulianika

Hristoforianika

Logothetianika

Lianianika

*IONIAN

SEA*

Babakaradika

Kastrisianika

Aroniadika

Frilingianika

458m

490m

To Antikythira
(40km) (see inset);
Crete (100km)

**Makronisi
Island**

Diakofti

Cave of
Agia Sofia

Kato Hora

Mylopotamos

Mitata

Kythira

*Agia
Moni*

389m

Cape
Limnionas

507m

Viaradika

Avlemonas

*Temple of
Aphrodite*

Paleopoli

Cape
Modoni

Fratsia

**Paleopoli
Beach**

**Kaladi
Beach**

Kalokerines

Karvounades

Alexandrades

Pitsinianika

Goudianika

Travasarianika

Tsikalaria

Skoulianika

*SEA OF

CRETE*

Fatsadika

Katouni Bridge

*Moni
Myrtidion*

Kato Livadi

410m

Kominianika

Livadi

Katelouzianika

Pourko

Fyri Ammos

Agia Elesis

477m

Strapodi

Manitohori

Kalamos

Hora
(Kythira)

Kapsali

*MEDITERRANEAN

SEA*

Cape
Trahilos

Vroulea

Cape
Kapello

Porfyra Travel (☎ /fax 27360 31888; www.kythira.info) in Livadi (north of Hora).

GETTING AROUND

Occasional buses may operate during August. There are taxis, but the best way to see the island is with your own transport. **Drakakis Tours** (☎ 27360 31160, 6944840497; www.drakakistours.gr; Livadi) rents a range of cars, including vans and 4WD. **Panayotis Rent A Car** (☎ 27360 31600; www.panayotis-rent-a-car.gr) on Kapsali's waterfront rents cars and mopeds. Both will arrange pick-up from the port or the airport.

Hora Χώρα
pop 267

Hora (or Kythira), the island's capital, is a pretty village of Cycladic-style white, blue-shuttered houses, perched on a long, slender ridge stretching north from an impressive 13th-century Venetian *kastro*. The central square, planted with hibiscus, bougainvillea and palms, is Plateia Dimitriou Staï. The main street, Spyridonos Staï, runs south from the central square to the *kastro*.

INFORMATION

Branches of the National Bank of Greece and ATE Bank, both with ATMs, are on the central square.

Fos Fanari (☎ 27360 31644; ☼ 8am-late) This cafe-bar offers free wi-fi to clients.

Internet Service (Kodak shop, Spyridonos Staï; per hr €5; ☼ 9am-2pm & 6-9pm Mon-Sat) Travellers can check email here.

Police station (☎ 27360 31206) Near the *kastro*.

Polyredo (☎ 27360 39000; per hr €4) The island's best internet place is based in Livadi, just north of Hora.

Post office (☼ 7.30am-2pm Mon-Fri) On the central square.

SIGHTS

Hora's Venetian **kastro** (admission free; ☼ 8am-7pm), built in the 13th century, is at the southern end of town. If you walk to its southern extremity, passing the Church of Panagia, you will come to a sheer cliff – from here there's a stunning view of Kapsali and, on a good day, of Antikythira.

Call in to **Stavros** (☎ 27360 31857), a shop north of the square (opposite the turn-off to Kapsali) and pick up some of the local produce, including some of Greece's best honey.

At the time of research, the town's archaeological museum, north of the central square, was closed due to damage from the earth tremor in January 2006.

SLEEPING& EATING

Castello Rooms (☎ 27360 31069; www.castelloapts -kythera.gr; d/tr €45/55; ⚡) The seven comfortable rooms represent the best deal in town, if not the island. Set back from the main street, this place is surrounded by a well-tended garden full of flowers, vegetables and fruit trees. The rooms have TV and some have kitchen facilities. It's signposted at the southern end of Spiridonos Staï.

Hotel Margarita (☎ 27360 31711; www.hotel -margarita.com; off Spyridonos Staï; s/d incl breakfast €70/110; ⚡) This white-walled, blue-shuttered and generally charming hotel offers atmospheric rooms (all with TV and telephone) in a renovated 19th-century mansion, featuring B&W marble floors and a quirky old spiral staircase. The whitewashed terrace affords fantastic port views.

Zorba's (☎ 27360 31655; ☼ dinner) The pick of the bunch for the town's meals, and highly recommended by locals.

Kapsali Καψάλι
pop 34

The scenic village of Kapsali, 2km south of Hora, served as Hora's port in Venetian times. It features twin sandy bays and a curving waterfront; this looks striking viewed from Hora's castle. Restaurants and cafes line the beach, and safe **sheltered swimming** is Kapsali's trademark. However, it can get crowded in high season.

Offshore you can see the stark rock island known as **Avgo** (Egg) or **Itra** (Cooking pot), rearing above the water. Locals say that when the wind blows in a certain direction clouds always gather and sit just above the rock, making it look like a steaming cooking pot.

Kapsali goes into hibernation in winter, coming to life between April and October. There's a small supermarket, and the Kytherian Gallery sells international newspapers as well as souvenirs.

Panayotis at **Moto Rent** (☎ 27360 31600), on the waterfront, rents canoes and pedal boats as well as cars, mopeds and bicycles. **Kaptain Spiros** (☎ 6974022079) takes daily boat cruises on his glass-bottomed boat (from €12 per person), including to Itra, where you can swim.

SLEEPING & EATING

Aphrodite Apartments (☎ 27360 31328; afrodite@aias.gr; d/tr/q €70/75/90) These no-nonsense, no-frills but perfectly pleasant apartments on the road and facing the sea, are run by a friendly, English-speaking local. Great value, and prices plummet outside August.

Spitia Vassilis (☎ 27360 31125; www.kythira bungalowsvasili.gr; d/tr/q €80/95/100) This attractive green-and-white complex of studios has the perfect setting – away from the hordes and overlooking Kapsali Beach. The spacious rooms feature that rustic-painted-timber-floor look and good bay views. It is on the right as you approach Kapsali from Hora. No English spoken.

El Sol Hotel (☎ 27360 31766; www.elsolhotels.gr; d/tr/ studio incl breakfast €120/140/150 **P** **X** **R**) Signposted off the Hora–Kapsali road is this luxurious resort-style, Cycladic-looking option, with a view of Kapsali and Hora's *kastro*. Management's promo line is 'If Zeus went on holidays, you'd surely have him as a room mate'. If they could throw him in, too, we'd say it's great value; at this stage, save your pennies (and energy) until the cheaper rates outside high season.

Hydragogio (☎ 27360 31065; mains €5-12, fish per kilogram €20-70) Occupying a great spot overlooking the beach at the far end by the rocks, and specialising in fresh fish and traditional Greek fare (with a good vegetarian range), this is the place to go for a good feed, and to feel you're really on holiday.

Potamos Ποταμός
pop 680

Potamos, 10km southwest of Agia Pelagia, is the island's commercial hub. The National Bank of Greece (with ATM) is on the central square and the **post office** (🕑 7.30am-2pm Mon-Fri) is just north of the central square.

Its Sunday morning **flea market** seems to attract just about everyone on the island.

There are a couple of decent places to look out for. Popular with locals, **Taverna Panaretos** (☎ 27360 34290; mains €7-14; 🕑 lunch & dinner year-round) is a natural – it uses home-grown everything, from oil to vegies and cheese. Want to try wild goat with olive oil and oregano (€9.50) or eggplant on coals (€4)? Naturally.

The island's hip and happenin' place, **Kafe Astikon** (☎ 27360 33141; 🕑 7am-late; 🛜), offers a mix of retro designer mixed with 1930s French. Add in great music – from tradi-

tional Greek to Latin and rock, plus wireless connection, and you'll not care what you're there for. Except that it's got great drinks of the top-shelf variety and all manner of snacks.

Mylopotamos Μυλοπόταμος
pop 70

Mylopotamos is a quaint village nestled in a small valley, 12km southwest of Potamos. Its central square is flanked by a charming church and the authentically traditional **Kafeneio O Platanos** (☎ 27360 33397), which in summer becomes a restaurant with an outdoor setting in the square. It's worth a stroll to the **Neraïda** (water nymph) waterfall, with luxuriant greenery and mature, shady trees. As you reach the church, take the right fork and follow the signs to an unpaved road leading down to the falls. (Alternatively, you can head there on foot – follow the signs after the church.)

To reach the abandoned **kastro** of Mylopotamos, take the left fork after the *kafeneio* and follow the old faded sign for **Kato Hora** (Lower Village) and then the modern signs for the Cave of Agia Sofia. The road leads to the centre of Kato Hora, from where a portal leads into the spooky *kastro*, with derelict houses and well-preserved little churches (locked).

Several fabulous walks start in Mylopotamos – refer to *Kythira on Foot: 32 Carefully Selected Walking Routes* (see p470). The most picturesque and challenging walk heads along a gorge where there are the ruins of former flour mills. You pass waterfalls and swimming holes along the way.

The staff at Kafeneio O Platanos (above) is happy to help you with sleeping options.

Agia Pelagia Αγία Πελαγία
pop 280

Kythira's northern port of Agia Pelagia is a simple, friendly waterfront village, although sadly, this is on the verge of being ruined by modern buildings, as are the sand-and-pebble beaches either side of the quay. Nevertheless, it's pleasant for relaxing, and **Red Beach**, south of the headland, is a good swimming spot.

A good sleeping option is the **Hotel Pelagia Aphrodite** (☎ 27360 33926/7; www.pelagia-aphrodite.com; s/d/tr €75/90/120; 🕑 Apr-Oct; **P** **X**). This Greek-Australian-run hotel is modern and spotless with large, airy rooms, most with balconies overlooking the sea. Its perfect location is on a small headland on the southern edge of the village. Breakfast is €7.

Kaleris (☎ 27360 33461; mains €5.50-12; ☯ dinner) might inspire you to ask what is a place like this doing in a place like this? Agia Pelagia is all the better for it. Owner-chef Yiannis pushes the culinary boundaries, giving Greek cuisine a refreshing new twist. Thankfully, he hasn't lost sight of his roots – he uses the best of local products. So fresh, in fact, that his delectable parcels of feta cheese drizzled with local thyme-infused honey (€6), *vrechtoladea* (traditional rusks; €5) and homemade beef tortellini (€8) simply walk out the door. See also Stirring Traditions, below.

Around Kythira

If you have transport, a spin round the island is rewarding. The monasteries of **Agia Moni** and **Agia Elesis** are mountain refuges with superb views. **Moni Myrtidion** is a beautiful monastery surrounded by trees. From Hora, drive northeast to **Avlemonas**, via **Paleopoli** with its wide, pebbled beach. Archaeologists spent years searching for evidence of a temple at Aphrodite's birthplace at Avlemonas. Here, you must stay on the ball: see if you can spot the blink-or-you'll-miss **kofinidia** – two small rock protrusions – these are the mythological (or otherwise) sex organs of Cronos, after Zeus had tossed them into the sea foam. Don't bypass the spectacularly situated ruins of the Byzantine capital of **Paliohora**, in the island's northeast, fun for exploring.

In **Kato Livadi**, don't miss the small but stunning collection of artworks of Kythira in the **Museum of Byzantine and post-Byzantine art on Kythira** (☎ 27360 31731; ☯ 8.30am-2.30pm; adult/concession €2/1; closed Mon). Just north of Kato Livadi make a detour to see the architecturally anomalous **Katouni Bridge**, a British-built legacy of Kythira's time as part of the British Protectorate

---

STIRRING TRADITIONS

Yiannis Prineas, 31, left Athens and returned to Agia Pelagia, on the island of Kythira to run his family restaurant, Kaleris (above), started by his grandfather in 1956. Yiannis is pushing the boundaries of traditional Greek cuisine, producing fine Greek dishes with a gourmet twist (think *mousakas* – usually baked layers of eggplant or zucchini – with mushrooms, and feta in cheese parcels drizzled with thyme-infused honey and sesame seeds). The result has convinced the most hardened of traditional taverna-goers – locals and visitors – that there's more to Greek food than Mama-style home cooking (as good as this may be) and a full stomach.

What is your aim? My basic vision is Greek and traditional Greek-Mediterranean but I'm trying to make modern dishes with local products. I want to make my experiences (working in five-star hotels in gourmet restaurants in Athens) into something a bit more modern with how people view traditional cuisine.

Most of the Greeks love food because it's an enjoying time [sic]…but many of the Greeks, they are not so focussed. They don't understand the flavours – they eat with beers and cigarettes. Many are hard workers – builders and farmers – and food is to fill their stomach. They do not take a menu and review it.

A lot of our food is 'Mama's food'. Mama's food is lovely, but…

Have you succeeded in changing people's views about traditional Greek food? I have changed some people and I have seen people change on their own. When they find the difference, they start to appreciate it and their minds start to work: food is not only to fill the stomach! Even if they don't like my dishes, I like this, because [at least] they have an opinion.

What is your secret? Every day is a new day. Every day is a new space for creativity. You have to be 'inside' of the food. If you are inside you do not do mistakes… You can make the best food even with not so many things [ingredients]. It's the process: how you prepare and how you cook. I change the menu every week. Here in Kythira we are in the heart of the Mediterranean with excellent cheese, vegetables, meats (sheep, goats and chickens) – our materials [ingredients] are good.

in the 19th century. In the far north of the island the village of **Karavas** is verdant, very attractive and close to both Agia Pelagia and the reasonable beach at **Platia Ammos**. Beachcombers should seek out **Kaladi Beach**, near Paleopoli. **Fyri Ammos**, closer to Hora, is another good beach – but hard to access.

EATING

Skandia (☎ 27360 33700; Paleopolis; mains €7-10; ☺ lunch & dinner Apr-Oct, Fri-Sun Nov-Mar) Among one of the most pleasant places to eat on the island, mainly because of its setting: away from the madding crowds, under shady elm trees, in a homey environment. Its fish is priced per kilogram; lobster with spaghetti is a fave (but watch the wallet – lobster weighs in at a hefty €85 per kilogram).

Varkoula (☎ 27360 34224; Platia Ammos; mains €7-12, fish per kilogram €40-75; ☺ lunch & dinner daily May-Oct, Fri & Sat Nov-Mar) At this *varkoula* ('little boat') you can enjoy freshly cooked fish to the tunes of the bouzouki-strumming owner and his cardiologist guitar-playing friend. Athena's famous fried bread with cheese is a real heart stopper. It's a beat away from Karavas, in the island's north. As it's a decent drive north, ring ahead first to confirm opening hours – these can be irregular.

Estiatorion Pierros (☎ 27360 31014; Livadi; mains €10-12, fish per kilogram €35-60; ☺ lunch & dinner) Since 1933 this family-run and long-standing favourite has served no-nonsense Greek staples. Visit the kitchen to view the daily offerings – there's no menu. On the main road through Livadi.

Sotiris (☎ 27360 33722; Avlemonas; fish per kilogram €30-75; ☺ lunch & dinner daily Apr-Oct, Fri-Sun Nov-Mar) This popular fish taverna in pretty Avlemonas has good lobster and fish soup (fish and lobster are priced per kilogram).

Psarotaverna H Manolis (☎ 27360 33748; Diakofti; fish & lobster per kilogram €45-70; ☺ lunch & dinner) A star among Diakofti's uninspiring port setting. Locals head here for the excellent fresh fish and seasonal offerings.

ANTIKYTHIRA ΑΝΤΙΚΥΘΗΡΑ
pop 20

The tiny island of Antikythira, 38km southeast of Kythira, is the most remote island in the Ionians. It has only one settlement (Potamos), one doctor, one police officer, one telephone and a monastery. It has no post office or bank. The only accommodation option is 10 basic rooms in two purpose-built blocks, open in summer only. Potamos has a *kafeneio*-cum-taverna.

Getting There & Away

The ferry company **ANEN Lines** (www.anen.gr) calls at Antikythira on its route between Kythira and Kissamos on Crete. This is not an island for tourists on a tight schedule and will probably only appeal to those who really like isolation. For information and tickets, contact **Porfyra Travel** (☎ /fax 27360 31888; porfyra@otenet.gr) in Livadi on Kythira.

IONIAN ISLANDS

Directory

CONTENTS

ACCOMMODATION

The Greek islands boast accommodation to suit every taste and budget. All places to stay are subject to strict price controls set by the tourist police. By law, a notice must be displayed in every room that states the category of the room and the maximum price that can be charged. The price includes a 4.5% community tax and 8% VAT.

Accommodation owners may add a 10% surcharge for a stay of less than three nights, but this is not mandatory. A mandatory charge of 20% is levied if an extra bed is put into a room (although this often doesn't happen if the extra bed is for a child). During July and August, accommodation owners will charge the maximum price, but in spring and autumn, prices can drop by 20% and then drop even further in winter.

Rip-offs rarely occur, but if you do suspect that you have been exploited by an accommodation owner, make sure you report it to either the tourist police or to the regular police, and they will act swiftly.

Throughout this book we have divided accommodation into budget (up to €80 in Athens; up to €60 elsewhere), midrange (€80 to €150 in Athens; €60 to €150 elsewhere) and top end (€150+) categories.

This is based on a rate for a double room in high season (July and August). Unless otherwise stated, all rooms have private bathroom facilities. It's difficult to generalise about accommodation prices in Greece as rates depend entirely on the season and location. Don't expect to pay the same price for a double on one of the islands as you would in Athens.

Camping

Camping is a good option, especially in summer. There are almost 200 camping grounds dotted around the islands, many in picturesque locations. Standard facilities include hot showers, kitchens, restaurants and mini-markets – and often a swimming pool.

Most camping grounds are open only between April and October. The **Panhellenic Camping Association** (Map p78; ☎ /fax 210 362 1560; www.panhellenic-camping-union.gr; Solonos 102, Exarhia, Athens) publishes an annual booklet listing all its camping grounds, their facilities and months of operation.

Camping fees are highest from 15 June through to the end of August. Most camping grounds charge from €5 to €7 per adult and €3 to €4 for children aged four to 12. There's no charge for children aged under four. Tent sites cost from €4 per night for small tents and from €5 per night for large tents. Caravan sites start at around €6; car costs are typically €4 to €5.

If camping in the height of summer, bring a silver fly sheet to reflect the heat off your tent. Otherwise, dark tents that are all the rage in colder countries become sweat houses. Between May and mid-September the weather is warm enough to sleep out under the stars. Many camping grounds have covered areas where tourists who don't have tents can sleep in summer; you can get by with a lightweight sleeping bag. It's a good idea to have a foam pad to lie on and a waterproof cover for your sleeping bag.

Domatia

Domatia (literally 'rooms') are the Greek equivalent of the British bed and breakfast, minus the breakfast. Once upon a time, domatia comprised little more than spare rooms in the family home that could be rented out to travellers in summer; nowadays, many are purpose-built appendages to the family house. Some come complete with fully equipped kitchens. Standards of cleanliness are generally high.

Domatia remain a popular option for budget travellers. They are classified A, B or C class. Expect to pay from €25 to €50 for a single, and €35 to €65 for a double, depending on the class, whether bathrooms are shared or private, the season and how long you plan to stay. Domatia are found throughout the mainland (except in large cities) and on almost every island that has a permanent population. Many are open only between April and October.

From June to September domatia owners are out in force, touting for customers. They meet buses and boats, shouting 'Room, room!' and often carrying photographs of their rooms. In peak season, it can prove to be a mistake not to take up an offer – but be wary of owners who are vague about the location of their accommodation.

Hostels

Most youth hostels in Greece are run by the **Greek Youth Hostel Organisation** (Map p78; ☎ 210 751 9530; www.athens-yhostel.com; Damareos 75, Pangrati, Athens). There are affiliated hostels in Athens, Olympia, Patra and Thessaloniki on the mainland, and on the islands of Crete and Santorini.

Hostel rates vary from around €10 to €20 and you don't have to be a member to stay in any of them. Few have curfews.

Hotels

Hotels in Greece are divided into six categories: deluxe, A, B, C, D and E. Hotels are categorised according to the size of the room, whether or not they have a bar, and the ratio of bathrooms to beds, rather than standards of cleanliness, comfort of the beds and friendliness of staff – all elements that may be of greater relevance to guests.

As one would expect, deluxe, A- and B-class hotels have many amenities, private bathrooms and constant hot water. C-class hotels have a snack bar, rooms have private bathrooms, but hot water may only be available at certain times of the day. D-class hotels may or may not have snack bars, most rooms will share bathrooms, but there may be some with private bathrooms, and they may have solar-heated water, which means hot water is not guaranteed. E classes do not have a snack bar, bathrooms are shared and you may have to pay extra for hot water – if it exists at all.

Prices are controlled by the tourist police and the maximum rate that can be charged for a room must be displayed on a board behind the door of each room. The classification is not often much of a guide to price. Rates in D- and E-class hotels are generally compa-

---

PRACTICALITIES

■ Greece is two hours ahead of GMT/UTC and three hours ahead during daylight saving time.

■ Use the metric system for weights and measures.

■ Plug your electrical appliances into a two-pin adaptor before plugging into the electricity supply (220V AC, 50Hz).

■ Keep up with Greek current affairs by reading the daily English-language edition of *Kathimerini* that comes with the *International Herald Tribune*.

■ Channel hop through a choice of nine free-to-air TV channels and an assortment of pay TV channels.

■ Be aware that Greece is region code 2 when you buy DVDs to watch back home.

DIRECTORY

GREEN STAYS

Park your bags in the countryside and bunk down in luxurious digs that also happen to be sustainable. Top green stays:

- **Achladies Apartments** (Achladies Bay, Skiathos; p417)
- **Harry's Paradise** (Kalymnos, Dodecanese; p332)
- **Milia** (Kissamos, Crete; p260)
- **Pine Tree Studios** (Karpathos, Dodecanese; p299)
- **Red Tractor Farm** (Korissia, Cyclades; p217)

For more ideas, visit www.guestinn.com and agrotravel.gr. Both sites have oodles of traditional rural accommodation options, listed by interests like farm stays, walking holidays or vineyard routes.

---

rable with domatia. You can pay from €35 to €60 for a single in high season in C class and €45 to €80 for a double. Prices in B class range from €50 to €85 for singles, and from €90 to €150 for doubles. A-class prices are not always much higher.

Mountain Refuges

Mountain refuges range from small huts with outdoor toilets and no cooking facilities to very comfortable modern lodges. They are run by the country's various mountaineering and skiing clubs and found on the islands of Crete and Evia. Prices start at around €7 per person, depending on the facilities. The EOT (Greek National Tourist Organisation) publication *Greece: Mountain Refuges & Ski Centres* has details about each refuge; copies are available at all EOT branches. See p487 for more information on EOT.

Pensions

Pensions in Greece are virtually indistinguishable from hotels. They are classed A, B or C. An A-class pension is equivalent in amenities and price to a B-class hotel, a B-class pension is equivalent to a C-class hotel and a C-class pension is equivalent to a D- or E-class hotel.

Villas & Apartments

A really practical way to save on money and maximise comfort is to rent a furnished apartment or villa. Prices vary considerably according to the season and the amenities offered. Many are purpose-built for tourists while others – villas in particular – may be owners' homes that they are not using. The main advantage is that you can accommodate a larger number of people under one roof and can also save money by self-catering. This option is best for a stay of more than three days. In fact some owners may insist on a minimum week's stay. A good site to spot prospective villas is www.greekislands.com.

If you're looking for long-term accommodation, it's worth checking the classified section of the *Athens News* – although most of the places are in Athens. In rural areas and islands, local websites are a good place to start your search.

ACTIVITIES

For details on popular activities throughout the Greek islands, see Greek Islands Outdoors (p71).

BUSINESS HOURS

Banks are open from 8am to 2pm Monday to Thursday, and from 8am to 2.30pm Friday. Some banks in large towns and cities also open between 3.30pm and 6.30pm on weekdays and 8am to 2pm Saturday.

Post offices are open from 7.30am to 2pm Monday to Friday. In the major cities they stay open until 8pm, and open from 7.30am to 2pm Saturday.

In summer, the usual opening hours for shops are from 8am to 2.30pm and from 5pm to 8.30pm on Tuesday, Thursday and Friday, and from 8am to 3pm on Monday, Wednesday and Saturday. Shops open 30 minutes later during winter. These times are not always strictly adhered to. Many shops in tourist resorts are open seven days a week and keep later hours.

Department stores and supermarkets are open from 8am to 8pm Monday to Friday, from 8am to at least 3pm on Saturday and are closed on Sunday.

Periptera (street kiosks) are open from early morning until late at night. They sell everything from bus tickets and cigarettes to razor blades and shaving cream.

Restaurant hours vary enormously. Most places are normally open for lunch from 11am to 3pm, and for dinner between 7pm and 1am, while restaurants in tourist areas remain open all day. Cafes normally open at about 10am and stay open until midnight.

Bars open from about 8pm until late, while discos and nightclubs don't usually open until at least 10pm; it's rare to find much of a crowd before midnight. They close at about 4am, later on Friday and Saturday.

CHILDREN

Greece is a safe and easy place to travel with children. Greeks will generally make a fuss over your children, who will find themselves on the receiving end of many small gifts and treats. Teaching your children a few words in Greek will ingratiate them further.

Matt Barrett's website (www.greektravel .com) has lots of useful tips for parents, while daughter Amarandi has put together some tips for kids (www.greece4kids.com).

Practicalities

Travelling is especially easy if you're staying at a resort hotel by the beach, where everything is set up for families with children. As well as facilities like paddling pools and playgrounds, they also have cots and highchairs.

Elsewhere, it's rare to find cots and highchairs, although most hotels and restaurants will do their best to help. The fast service in most restaurants is good news when it comes to feeding hungry kids. Ordering lots of small dishes to share gives your kids the chance to try the local cuisine and you can almost always find omelettes, chips or spaghetti on the menu. Many hotels let small children stay for free and will squeeze an extra bed in the room.

Unless you head straight for the beach, a holiday in Greece can necessitate a lot of walking. If your kids aren't old enough to walk on their own for long, consider a sturdy carrying backpack; pushchairs are a struggle in towns and villages with slippery cobbles and tall pavements. Nevertheless, if the pushchair is a sturdy, off-road style, you should be okay.

Fresh milk is available in large towns and tourist areas, but harder to find on smaller islands. Supermarkets are the best place to look. Formula is available almost everywhere, as is condensed and heat-treated milk. Disposable nappies are also available everywhere.

Travel on ferries, buses and trains is free for children under four. They pay half-fare up to the age of 10 (ferries) or 12 (buses and trains). Full fares apply otherwise. On domestic flights, you'll pay 10% of the adult fare to have a child under two sitting on your knee. Kids aged two to 12 pay half-fare. If you plan to rent a car, it's wise to bring your own car or booster seat as many of the smaller, local agencies won't have these.

Sights & Activities

Most towns will have at least a small playground, while larger cities often have fantastic, modern play parks. These offer a great opportunity for your children to play with local kids. Children seem to have an innate ability to overcome language barriers through play. Children also enjoy climbing and exploring at the many ancient sights; young imaginations go into overdrive when let loose somewhere like the 'labyrinth' at Knossos.

The **Hellenic Children's Museum** (Map p82; ☎ 210 331 2995; Kydathineon 14, Plaka, Athens; admission free; ☺ 10am-2pm Tue-Fri, 10am-3pm Sat & Sun) is an excellent diversion, where your kids can join Greek cooking and craft classes.

CLIMATE CHARTS

Greece has a mild Mediterranean climate but can be very hot during summer – in July and August the mercury can soar to 40°C (over 100°F) in the shade, just about anywhere in the country. Crete stays warm the longest of all the islands – you can swim off its southern coast from mid-April to November.

Summer is also the time of year when the *meltemi*, a strong northerly wind that sweeps the Aegean (particularly the Cyclades), is at its strongest. The *meltemi* starts off as a mild wind in May and June, and strengthens as the weather hots up – often blowing from a clear blue sky. In July, August and September it can blow at gale force for days on end. The wind is a mixed blessing: it reduces humidity, but plays havoc with ferry schedules.

The Ionian Islands escape the *meltemi*, but here the main summer wind is the *maïstros*,

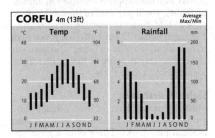

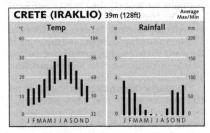

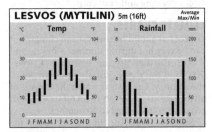

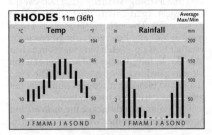

a light to moderate northwesterly that rises in the afternoon – it usually dies away at sunset.

November to February are the wettest months, and it can also get surprisingly cold. Snow is common on the mainland and in the mountains of Evia and Crete.

For tips on the best times to visit the Greek islands, see When to Go (p19) and the climate charts (left).

COURSES
Cooking
It is possible to do cooking courses on Santorini, Kea, Ikaria and Crete. See p63 for more information on cooking courses.

Dance
The **Dora Stratou Dance Theatre** (Map p78; ☎ 210 921 4650; www.grdance.org; Filopappou Hill; adult/concession €15/10; ☑ performances 9.30pm Tue-Sat, 8.15pm Sun May-Sep) runs one-week courses for visitors at its headquarters in Plaka, Athens, during July and August. On Rhodes, the Nelly Dimoglou Dance Company (p283) run courses in traditional Greek dance for foreigners.

Language
If you are serious about learning the Greek language, an intensive course at the start of your stay is a good way to go about it. Most of the courses are based in Athens, but there are also special courses on the islands in summer.

Athens Centre (Map p78; ☎ 210 701 2268; www.athenscentre.gr; Arhimidous 48, Mets, Athens) is located in the suburb of Mets, and also runs courses on the island of Spetses in June and July. The three-week courses cost €1190, and involve 66 hours of classwork.

Hellenic Culture Centre (☎ 22750 61139/40; www.hcc.gr; ☑ May-Oct), in the village of Arethousa, 7km from Evdilos, offers courses in Greek language, culture and literature. All levels of language proficiency are catered for.

CUSTOMS REGULATIONS
There are no longer duty-free restrictions within the EU. Upon entering the country from outside the EU, customs inspection is usually cursory for foreign tourists and a verbal declaration is usually all that is required. Random searches are still occasionally made for drugs.

Those arriving into the country from outside the EU may bring the following into

Greece duty-free: 200 cigarettes or 50 cigars; 1L of spirits or 2L of wine; 50ml of perfume; 250ml of eau de cologne; one camera (still or video) and film; a pair of binoculars; a portable musical instrument; a portable radio or tape recorder; a laptop computer; sports equipment; and dogs and cats (with a veterinary certificate). Restrictions apply to the importation of sailboards into Greece (see p73).

Importation of works of art and antiquities into Greece is free, but they must be declared on entry, so that they can be re-exported. Import regulations for medicines are strict; if you are taking medication, make sure you get a statement from your doctor before you leave home. It is illegal, for instance, to take codeine into Greece without an accompanying doctor's certificate.

An unlimited amount of foreign currency and travellers cheques may be brought into Greece. If you intend to leave the country with foreign banknotes in excess of US$1000, you must declare the sum upon entry.

It is strictly forbidden to export antiquities (anything over 100 years old) without an export permit. This crime is second only to drug smuggling in the penalties imposed. It is an offence to remove even the smallest article from an archaeological site.

The place to apply for an export permit is at the Antique Dealers and Private Collections section of the **Athens Archaeological Service** (Map p82; Polygnotou 13, Plaka, Athens).

Vehicles

Cars can be brought into Greece for six months without a carnet; only a green card (international third-party insurance) is required. Your only proof of entry into the country will be your ferry ticket stub (if arriving from Italy), so don't lose it. From other countries, a passport stamp will be ample evidence.

DANGERS & ANNOYANCES
Adulterated & Spiked Drinks

Adulterated drinks (known as *bombes*) are served in some bars and clubs in Athens and resorts known for partying. These drinks are usually diluted with cheap illegal imports that may leave you feeling worse for wear the next day.

Many of the party resorts catering to large budget tour groups are also unfortunately the scene of drunk and disorderly behaviour – some of it just purely annoying and some of it frighteningly violent. Spiked drinks are not uncommon; keep your hand over the top of your glass. More times than not, the perpetrators are foreign tourists rather than locals.

Bar Scams

Bar scams continue to be an unfortunate fact of life in Athens, particularly in the Syntagma area of Athens. The basic scam is some variation on a solo male traveller being lured into a bar where charming girls appear and ask for what turns out to be ludicrously overpriced drinks, leaving the traveller footing an enormous bill. See p77 for the full run-down on this scam.

Theft

Crime, especially theft, is traditionally low in Greece, but unfortunately it is on the rise. The worst area is around Omonia in central Athens – keep track of your valuables here, especially on the metro and at the Sunday flea market.

The vast majority of thefts from tourists are still committed by other tourists; the biggest danger of theft is probably in dormitory rooms in hostels and at camping grounds. Be sure not to leave valuables unattended in such places. If you are staying in a hotel room and the windows and door do not lock securely, ask for your valuables to be locked in the hotel safe – hotel proprietors are happy to do this.

DISCOUNT CARDS
Senior Cards

Card-carrying EU pensioners can claim a range of benefits, such as reduced admission at ancient sites and museums, and discounts on bus and train fares.

Student & Youth Cards

The most widely recognised form of student ID is the International Student Identity Card (ISIC). These cards can qualify the holder to half-price admission to museums and ancient sites and for discounts at some budget hotels and hostels. In some cases, only Greek student cards will be accepted but it's always worth flashing your international student card just in case. The Euro26 card is available for anyone up to the age of 30 and can get you

DIRECTORY

discounts of up to 20% at sights, shops and for some transport.

Some travel agencies in Athens are licensed to issue ISIC and Euro26 cards. For ISIC cards you must show documents proving you are a student, provide a passport photo and cough up €10. For Euro26 you just need proof of age, a photo and €14. Visit www.isic.org and www.euro26.org for more details.

Aegean Airlines offers student discounts on some domestic flights, but there are none to be had on buses, ferries or trains. Students can often find good deals on international air fares.

EMBASSIES & CONSULATES

All foreign embassies in Greece are in Athens and its suburbs, with a few consulates in Thessaloniki.

Albania (Map p78; ☎ 210 687 6200; Vekiareli 7, Athens)

Australia (Off Map p78; ☎ 210 870 4000; cnr Leoforos Alexandras & Leoforos Kifisias, Ambelokipi, Athens)

Bulgaria (☎ 210 674 8105; Stratigou Kalari 33a, Psyhiko, Athens)

Canada (Map p78; ☎ 210 727 3400; Genadiou 4, Athens)

Cyprus (Map p82; ☎ 210 723 7883; Irodotou 16, Athens)

France (Map p82; ☎ 210 361 1663; Leoforos Vasilissis Sofias 7, Athens)

Germany (Map p78; ☎ 210 728 5111; Dimitriou 3, cnr Karaoli, Kolonaki, Athens)

Ireland (Map p82; ☎ 210 723 2771; Leoforos Vasileos Konstantinou 5-7, Athens)

Italy (Map p82; ☎ 210 361 7260; Sekeri 2, Athens)

Japan (Off Map p78; ☎ 210 775 8101; Athens Tower, Mesogion 2-4, Athens)

Netherlands (Map p82; ☎ 210 723 9701; Leoforos Vasileos Konstantinou 5-7, Athens)

New Zealand (Off Map p78; ☎ 210 687 4701; Kifisias 268, Halandri, Athens)

Turkey Athens (Map p82; ☎ 210 724 5915; Leoforos Vasileos Georgiou 8, Athens); Thessaloniki (Map pp96-7; ☎ 23102 48452; Agiou Dimitriou 151, Thessaloniki)

UK Athens (Map p78; ☎ 210 723 6211; Ploutarhou 1, Athens); Thessaloniki (Map pp96-7; ☎ 23102 78006; Tsimiski 43, Thessaloniki)

USA Athens (Map p78; ☎ 210 721 2951; Leoforos Vasilissis Sofias 91, Athens); Thessaloniki (Map pp96-7; ☎ 23102 42905; Tsimiski 43, Thessaloniki)

It's important to know what your embassy – the embassy of the country of which you are a citizen – can and can't do to help if you get into trouble. Generally, it won't be much help in emergencies if the trouble you are in is remotely your own fault. Remember that you are bound by the laws of the country you are in. Your embassy will not be sympathetic if you commit a crime locally, even if such actions are legal in your own country.

In genuine emergencies you might get some assistance, but only if other channels have been exhausted. For example, if you need to get home urgently, a free ticket home is exceedingly unlikely. If you have all your money and documents stolen, it will usually assist with getting a new passport, but a loan for onward travel is very unlikely.

Some embassies used to keep letters for travellers, but these days the mail-holding service has usually been stopped.

FESTIVALS & EVENTS

Please see the Events Calendar (p23) for the top festivals and events throughout Greece.

FOOD

For large cities and towns, restaurant listings in this book are given in the following order: budget (under €15), midrange (€15 to €40) and top end (over €40), and within each section the restaurants are listed in budget order. Prices refer to a main dish for one person unless otherwise noted in the review.

For information on Greek cuisine, see p56.

GAY & LESBIAN TRAVELLERS

In a country where the church still plays a prominent role in shaping society's views on issues such as sexuality, it should come as no surprise that homosexuality is generally frowned upon by many locals – especially outside the major cities. While there is no legislation against homosexual activity, it pays to be discreet.

Some areas of Greece are, however, extremely popular destinations for gay and lesbian travellers. Athens has a busy gay scene – but most gay and lesbian travellers head for the islands. Mykonos has long been famous for its bars, beaches and general hedonism, while Skiathos also has its share of gay hang-outs. The island of Lesvos, birthplace of the lesbian poet Sappho, has become something of a place of pilgrimage for lesbians.

Information

The *Spartacus International Gay Guide*, published by Bruno Gmünder (Berlin), is widely regarded as the leading authority on the gay travel scene. The Greek section contains a wealth of information on gay venues everywhere from Alexandroupoli to Xanthi.

There is also stacks of information on the internet. **Roz Mov** (www.geocities.com /WestHollywood/2225/) has info on gay health, press, organisations, events and legal issues – and links to lots more sites. Also check out **Gayscape** (www.gayscape.com/gayscape/menugreece .html).

HOLIDAYS
Public Holidays

All banks and shops and most museums and ancient sites close on public holidays. The following are national public holidays in Greece:

New Year's Day 1 January
Epiphany 6 January
First Sunday in Lent February
Greek Independence Day 25 March
Good Friday March/April
(Orthodox) Easter Sunday April/May; Orthodox Easter Sunday falls on 4 April in 2010, 24 April in 2011 and 15 April 2012.
May Day (Protomagia) 1 May
Whit Monday (Agiou Pnevmatos) May/June; 50 days after Easter Sunday. Schools and offices close, but museums and shops usually stay open.
Feast of the Assumption 15 August
Ohi Day 28 October
Christmas Day 25 December
St Stephen's Day 26 December

School Holidays

The Greek school year is divided into three terms. The main school holidays are in July and August.

INSURANCE

A travel insurance policy to cover theft, loss and medical problems is a good idea. Some policies offer lower and higher medical-expense options; the higher ones are chiefly for countries such as the USA, which have extremely high medical costs. There is a wide variety of policies available, so check the small print.

Some policies specifically exclude 'dangerous activities', which can include scuba diving, motorcycling and even hiking. A locally acquired motorcycle licence is not valid under some policies.

You may prefer a policy that pays doctors or hospitals directly rather than you having to pay on the spot and claim later. If you have to claim later, make sure you keep all documentation. Some policies ask you to call back (reverse charges) to a centre in your home country where an immediate assessment of your problem is made. For more information on health insurance, see p526.

Paying for your ticket with a credit card sometimes provides limited travel insurance, and you may be able to reclaim the payment if the operator doesn't deliver. In the UK, for instance, credit card providers are required by law to reimburse consumers if a company goes into liquidation and the amount in contention is more than UK£100.

Buy travel insurance as early as possible. If you buy it just before you fly, you may find you're not covered for such problems as delays caused by industrial action. Worldwide travel insurance is available at www.lonelyplanet .com/travel_service. You can buy, extend and claim online anytime – even if you're already on the road.

INTERNET ACCESS

Greece has long since embraced the convenience of the internet. There has been a huge increase in the number of hotels and businesses using the internet, and where available, websites are listed throughout this book.

Internet cafes are everywhere, and are listed under the Information section for cities and islands where available. Many hotels also offer internet and wi-fi access, although hot spots are often located in lobbies rather than in your room. You'll also find many cafes offering wi-fi.

LEGAL MATTERS
Arrests

It is a good idea to have your passport with you at all times in case you are stopped by the police and questioned. Greek citizens are presumed to always have identification on them; foreign visitors are similarly presumed to by the police. If you are arrested by police, insist on an interpreter (*the*-lo dhi-ermi-*nea*) and/or a lawyer (*the*-lo dhi-ki-*go*-ro).

Travellers should note that they can be prosecuted under the law of their home country regarding age of consent, even when abroad.

Drugs

Drug laws in Greece are the strictest in Europe. Greek courts make no distinction between the possession of drugs and dealing them. Possession of even a small amount of marijuana is likely to land you in jail. See also p480 for a warning regarding codeine.

MAPS

Unless you are going to hike or drive, the free maps given out by the EOT will probably suffice, although they are not 100% accurate. On islands where there is no EOT office, there are usually tourist maps for sale for around €1.50 but, again, these are not very accurate, particularly maps of towns and villages.

The best overall maps for coverage are published by the Greek company **Road Editions** (Map p82; ☎ 210 345 5575; www.road.gr; Kozanis 21, cnr Amfipoleos, Votanikos, Athens), whose maps are produced with the assistance of the Hellenic Army Geographical Service. There is a wide range of maps to suit various needs, starting with a 1:500,000 map of Greece. Motorists should check out the company's 1:250,000 series covering the Peloponnese and Crete. Even the smallest roads and villages are clearly marked, and the distance indicators are spot-on – important when negotiating your way around the backblocks. The company also produces a Greek island series and a Greek mountain series, which is essential for any serious hiking.

Hikers should also consider the *Topo* series published by **Anavasi** (Map p82; ☎ 210 321 8104; www.mountains.gr; Stoa Arsakiou 6a, Athens), with durable plasticised paper and detailed walking trails for many of the Aegean islands. **Emvelia** (☎ 210 771 7616; www.emvelia.gr; Navarinou 12, Athens) publishes detailed maps, including some excellent plans of regional main towns, each with a handy index booklet. All maps can be bought online or at major bookshops in Greece.

MONEY

Greece has been using the euro since the beginning of 2002. There are eight euro coins, in denominations of one and two euros, then one, two, five, 10, 20 and 50 cents, and six notes in denominations of €5, €10, €20, €50, €100 and €200.

See the inside front cover for currency exchange rates, and see p19 for information on costs in Greece.

ATMs

Automated Teller Machines (ATMs) are to be found in every town large enough to support a bank and in almost all the tourist areas. If you've got MasterCard or Visa cards, there are plenty of places to withdraw money. Cirrus and Maestro users can make withdrawals in all major towns and tourist areas. Be warned that many card companies can put an automatic block on your card after your first withdrawal abroad as an anti-fraud mechanism. To avoid this happening, inform your bank of your travel plans. Also be aware that many ATMs on the islands can lose their connection for a day or two at a time, making it impossible for anyone (locals included) to withdraw money. It's useful to have a backup source of money.

Automated foreign exchange machines are common in major tourist areas. They take all the major European currencies, Australian and US dollars and Japanese yen, and are useful in an emergency, although they charge a hefty commission.

Cash

Nothing beats cash for convenience – or for risk. If you lose cash, it's gone for good and very few travel insurers will come to your rescue. Those that will, normally limit the amount to approximately US$300. It's best to carry no more cash than you need for the next few days. It's also a good idea to set aside a small amount of cash, say US$100, as an emergency stash.

Note that Greek shopkeepers and small business owners have a perennial problem with having any small change. If buying small items, it is better to tender coin or small denomination notes as the seller will inevitably never have any change.

Credit Cards

The great advantage of credit cards is that they allow you to pay for major items without carrying around great wads of cash. Credit cards are now an accepted part of the commercial scene in Greece, although they're often not accepted on many of the smaller islands or in small villages. In larger places, credit cards can be used to pay for accommodation in top-end hotels, restaurants and shops. Some C-class hotels will accept credit cards, but D- and E-class hotels rarely do.

The main credit cards are MasterCard and Visa, all of which are widely accepted in Greece. They can also be used as cash cards to draw cash from the ATMs of affiliated Greek banks in the same way as at home. Daily withdrawal limits are set by the issuing bank and are given in local currency only. American Express and Diners Club are accepted in tourist areas but unheard of elsewhere.

Tipping

In restaurants a service charge is normally included in the bill and while a tip is not expected (as it is in North America), it is always appreciated and should be left if the service has been good. Taxi drivers normally expect you to round up the fare, while bellhops who help you with your luggage to your hotel room or stewards on ferries who take you to your cabin normally expect a small gratuity of between €1 and €3.

Travellers Cheques

The main reason to carry travellers cheques rather than cash is the protection they offer against theft. They are, however, losing popularity as more and more travellers opt to put their money in a bank at home and withdraw it at ATMs as they go.

American Express, Visa and Thomas Cook cheques are available in euros and are all widely accepted and have efficient replacement policies. Maintaining a record of the cheque numbers and recording when you use them is vital when it comes to replacing lost cheques – keep this separate from the cheques themselves.

PHOTOGRAPHY & VIDEO

Digital photography has taken over in a big way in Greece and a range of memory cards can now be bought from camera stores. Film is still widely available, although it can be expensive in smaller towns. You'll find all the gear you need in the photography shops of Athens and major cities.

In Greece, it is possible to obtain video cassettes in larger towns and cities, but be sure to buy the correct format. It is usually worth buying at least a few cassettes duty-free to start off your trip.

Restrictions & Etiquette

Never photograph a military installation or anything else that has a sign forbidding photography. Flash photography is not allowed inside churches, and it's considered taboo to photograph the main altar.

Greeks usually love having their photos taken, but always ask permission first. The same goes for video cameras, probably even more annoying and offensive for locals than a still camera.

At archaeological sites you will be stopped from using a tripod as it marks you as a 'professional'.

POST

Tahydromia (post offices) are easily identifiable by the yellow signs outside. Regular post boxes are also yellow and may be labelled *esoteriko* for domestic and *exoteriko* for overseas. The red boxes are for express mail only.

Postal Rates

The postal rate for postcards and airmail letters up to 20g is €0.60 to Europe and €0.80 to North America and Australasia. Post within Europe takes between three and seven days, and five to 12 days to the USA, Australia and New Zealand. Express service (*katepiogonda*) costs about €3 and shaves a couple of days off. Some tourist shops and kiosks also sell stamps, but with a 10% surcharge.

Parcels can often only be sent from main towns and cities. In Athens, take your parcel to the Parcel post office (p77), and elsewhere to the parcel counter of a regular post office. You must leave the box open for inspection; bring your own tape to shut it as it's not usually sold at post offices.

Receiving Mail

You can receive mail poste restante (general delivery) at any main post office. The service is free, but you are required to show your passport. Ask senders to write your family name in capital letters and underline it, and also to mark the envelope 'poste restante'. It is a good idea to ask the post office clerk to check under your first name as well if letters you are expecting cannot be located. After one month, uncollected mail is returned to the sender. If you are about to leave a town and expected mail hasn't arrived, ask at the post office to have it forwarded to your next destination, c/o poste restante. Both Athens Central post

DIRECTORY

office (p77) and Syntagma Post Office (p77), also in Athens, hold poste restante mail.

Parcels are not delivered in Greece; they must be collected from the parcel counter of a post office.

SHOPPING

Shopping is big business in Greece. At times a tourist town can look like one big shop with all kinds of goods and trinkets on display. Shops and kiosks in major tourist centres are often overpriced and it's sometimes better to find out where the locals shop. That said, Athens' flea markets (p88) have a bewildering array of items on sale and you can find some good bargains. Throughout Greece, shoes and clothes can be excellent buys, especially in the postseasonal sales, and if you have room in your suitcase or backpack there are some really excellent quality artisanal works to be picked up from small boutiques and galleries, including pottery, jewellery and metalworked *objets*.

Bargaining

Getting a bit extra off the deal through bargaining is sadly a thing of the past in Greece. You might be offered a 'special deal', but the art and sport of bargaining per se has gone the way of the drachma. Instead, know your goods and decide for yourself if the price you are being offered is worth it before accepting the deal.

SMOKING

In July 2009, Greece brought in antismoking laws similar to those found throughout most of Europe. Smoking is now banned from inside public places, with the penalty being fines placed on the business owners. Home to some of the heaviest smokers in Europe, it will be a challenge for these laws to be enforced and many believe they will be imposed in only a nominal way in remote locations.

SOLO TRAVELLERS

Greece is a great destination for solo travellers, especially in summer when the Greek islands become an international meeting point. Hostels and other backpacker-friendly accommodation are good places to meet up with other solo travellers. Dining solo in restaurants is not an issue with restaurant owners and there are no real disadvantages to travelling solo – other than that you are unlikely to stay solo for long.

TELEPHONE

The Greek telephone service is modern and reasonably well maintained. There are public telephones just about everywhere, including in some unbelievably isolated spots. The phones are easy to operate and can be used for local, long distance and international calls. The 'i' at the top left of the push-button dialling panel brings up the operating instructions in English.

Note that in Greece the area code must always be dialled when making a call (ie all Greek phone numbers have 10 digits).

Mobile Phones

The number of mobile phones in Greece now exceeds the number of landline phones. If you have a compatible GSM mobile phone from a country with an overseas global roaming arrangement with Greece, you will be able to use your phone in Greece. You may need to inform your mobile phone service provider before you depart in order to have global roaming activated. USA and Canadian mobile phone users won't be able to use their mobile phones, unless their handset is equipped with a dual or tri-band system.

There are several mobile-phone service providers in Greece – among which Panafon, CosmOTE and Wind are the best known. All offer 2G connectivity. Of these three, CosmOTE tends to have the best coverage in remote areas, so try retuning your phone to CosmOTE if you find mobile coverage is patchy. All three companies offer pay-as-you-talk services by which you can buy a rechargeable SIM card and have your own Greek mobile number. The Panafon system is called 'à la Carte', the Wind system 'F2G' and CosmOTE is 'Cosmokarta'.

Note: the use of a mobile phone while driving in Greece is prohibited, but the use of a Bluetooth headset is allowed.

Phonecards

All public phones use the OTE phonecards, known as *telekarta*, not coins. These cards (€3, €5 and €9) are widely available at *periptera*, corner shops and tourist shops. A local call costs €0.30 for three minutes.

It's also possible to use these phones using a growing range of discount-card schemes, which involve dialling an access code and then punching in your card number. The OTE version of this card is known as 'Hronokarta'. The cards come with instructions in Greek and English. The talk time is enormous compared to the standard phone card rates.

TIME

Greece maintains one time zone throughout the whole country and is two hours ahead of GMT/UTC and three hours ahead on daylight saving time, which begins on the last Sunday in March, when clocks are put forward one hour. Daylight saving time ends on the last Sunday in October.

TOILETS

Most places in Greece have Western-style toilets, especially hotels and restaurants that cater for tourists. You'll occasionally come across squat toilets in older houses, *kafeneia* (coffee houses) and public toilets.

Public toilets are a rarity, except at airports and bus and train stations. Cafes are the best option if you get caught short, but you'll be expected to buy something for the privilege.

One peculiarity of the Greek plumbing system is that it can't handle toilet paper; apparently the pipes are too narrow. Whatever the reason, anything larger than a postage stamp seems to cause a problem; flushing away tampons and sanitary napkins is guaranteed to block the system. Toilet paper etc should be placed in the small bin provided next to every toilet.

TOURIST INFORMATION

Tourist information is handled by the Greek National Tourist Organisation, known by the initials GNTO abroad and EOT within Greece. The quality of service from office to office varies dramatically.

Local Tourist Offices

The EOT in Athens dispenses information including a very useful timetable of the week's ferry departures from Piraeus, and details about public transport prices and schedules from Athens. Its free map of Athens is urgently in need of an update, although most places of interest are clearly marked. The office is about 500m from Ambelokipi metro station.

EOT (www.gnto.gr) offices can be found in major tourist areas, though they are increasingly being supplemented or even replaced by local municipality tourist offices. Regional EOT's include:

Athens (Map p82; ☎ 210 331 0392; Leoforos Vasilissis Amalias 26a, Syntagma; ☒ 9am-7pm Mon-Fri, 10am-4pm Sat & Sun)

Crete (Map p224; ☎ 28102 46299; Xanthoudidou, Iraklio; ☒ 8.30am-8.30pm Apr-Oct, 8.30am-3pm Nov-Mar)

Dodecanese (Map p279; ☎ 22410 35226; cnr Makariou & Papagou, Rhodes Town; ☒ 8am-2.45pm Mon-Fri)

Ionian Islands (Map p458; ☎ 26710 22248; Argostoli, Kefallonia; ☒ 8am-8pm Mon-Fri, 9am-3pm Sat Jul & Aug, 8am-2.30pm Mon-Fri rest of year)

Macedonia (Office of Tourism Directorate; Map pp96–7; ☎ 2310 221 1000; Tsimiski 136, Thessaloniki; ☒ 8am-8pm Mon-Fri, 8am-2pm Sat)

Northeastern Aegean Islands (Map p380; ☎ 22510 42511; Aristarhou 6, Mytilini Town, Lesvos; ☒ 9am-1pm Mon-Fri)

Tourist Police

The tourist police work in cooperation with the regular Greek police and the EOT. Each tourist police office has at least one member of staff who speaks English. Hotels, restaurants, travel agencies, tourist shops, tourist guides, waiters, taxi drivers and bus drivers all come under the jurisdiction of the tourist police. If you think that you have been ripped off by any of these, report it to the tourist police and they will investigate. If you need to report a theft or loss of passport, go to the tourist police first and they will act as interpreters between you and the regular police. The tourist police also fulfil the same functions as the EOT and municipal tourist offices, dispensing maps and brochures, and giving information on transport. They can often help to find accommodation.

TRAVELLERS WITH DISABILITIES

Access for travellers with disabilities has improved somewhat in recent years, largely thanks to the Olympics. Improvements are mostly restricted to Athens, where there are more accessible sights, hotels and restaurants. Much of the rest of Greece remains inaccessible to wheelchairs and the abundance of stones, marble, slippery cobbles and stepped alleys, the terrain and towns creates a further challenge. Visually or hearing impaired people are also rarely catered to.

Careful planning before you go can make the world of difference. The British-based **Royal Association for Disability & Rehabilitation** (Radar; ☎ 020 7250 3222; www.radar.org.uk; 12 City Forum, 250 City Rd, London EC1V 8AF) publishes a useful guide called *Holidays & Travel Abroad: A Guide for Disabled People*, which gives a good overview of facilities available to disabled travellers in Europe. Also check out www.greecetravel .com/handicapped for links to local articles, resorts and tour groups catering to physically disabled tourists. Some options:

Christianakis Travel (www.greecetravel.com/handi capped/christianakis/index.htm) Creates tailor-made itineraries and can organise transportation, hotels and guides.

Sailing Holidays (www.charterayachtingreece.com/DR Yachting/index.html) Two-days to two-week sailing trips around the Greek islands in fully accessible yachts.

Sirens Resort (www.hotelsofgreece.com/central/loutraki /sirens-wheelchair-accessable-resort/index.html; Loutraki, Skaloma, Central Greece) Family-friendly resort with accessible apartments, tours and ramps into the sea.

VISAS

The list of countries whose nationals can stay in Greece for up to three months without a visa includes Australia, Canada, all EU countries, Iceland, Israel, Japan, New Zealand, Norway, Switzerland and the USA. Other countries included are the European principalities of Monaco and San Marino and most South American countries. The list changes – contact Greek embassies for the full list. Those not included can expect to pay about US$20 for a three-month visa.

Visa Extensions

If you wish to stay in Greece for longer than three months, apply at a consulate abroad or at least 20 days in advance to the **Aliens Bureau** (Map p78; ☎ 210 770 5711; Leoforos Alexandras 173, Ambelokipi, Athens; ☒ 8am-1pm Mon-Fri) in the Athens Central Police Station. Take your passport and four passport photographs along. You may be asked for proof that you can support yourself financially, so keep all your bank exchange slips (or the equivalent from a post office). These slips are not always automatically given – you may have to ask for them. Elsewhere in Greece apply to the local police authority. You will be given a permit that will authorise you to stay in the country for a period of up to six months.

Many travellers get around the need for an extension by visiting Bulgaria or Turkey briefly and then re-entering Greece. If you overstay your visa, you will be slapped with a huge fine upon leaving the country.

WOMEN TRAVELLERS

Many women travel alone in Greece. The crime rate remains relatively low and solo travel is probably safer than in most European countries. This does not mean that you should be lulled into complacency; bag snatching and

rapes do occur, particularly at party resorts on the islands.

The biggest nuisance to foreign women travelling alone are the guys the Greeks have nicknamed *kamaki*. The word means 'fishing trident' and refers to the *kamaki's* favourite pastime: 'fishing' for foreign women. You'll find them everywhere there are lots of tourists; young (for the most part), smooth-talking guys who aren't in the least bashful about sidling up to women in the street. They can be very persistent, but they are usually a hassle rather than a threat. The majority of Greek men treat foreign women with respect, and are genuinely helpful.

WORK

EU nationals don't need a work permit, but they need a residency permit and a Greek tax file number if they intend to stay longer than three months. Nationals of other countries are supposed to have a work permit.

Bar & Hostel Work

The bars of the Greek islands could not survive without foreign workers and there are thousands of summer jobs up for grabs every year. The pay is not fantastic, but you get to spend a summer in the islands. April and May are the times to go looking. Hostels and travellers hotels are other places that regularly employ foreign workers.

English Tutoring

If you are looking for a permanent job, the most widely available option is to teach English. A Teaching English as a Foreign Language (TEFL) certificate or a university degree is an advantage but is not essential. In the UK, look through the *Times* educational supplement or Tuesday's edition of the *Guardian* newspaper for opportunities – in other countries, contact the Greek embassy.

Another possibility is to find a job teaching English once you are in Greece. You will see language schools everywhere. Strictly speaking, you need a licence to teach in these schools, but many will employ teachers without one. The best time to look around for such a job is late summer.

The notice board at the **Compendium** (Map p82; ☎ 210 322 1248; Navarhou Nikodimou 5, cnr Nikis, Plaka) bookshop in Athens sometimes has advertisements looking for private English lessons.

Street Performers

The richest pickings are to be found on the islands, particularly Mykonos, Paros and Santorini. Plaka is the place to go in Athens; the area outside the church on Kydathineon is the most popular spot.

Volunteer Work

There are lots of opportunities to volunteer in Greece. Here are a few of the options:

Earth Sea & Sky (www.earthseasky) Conservation and research based in the Ionian Islands.

Hellenic Society for the Study & Protection of the Monk Seal (Map p78; ☎ 210 522 2888; fax 210 522 2450; Solomou 53, Exarhia, Athens) Volunteers used for monitoring programs on the Ionian Islands.

Hellenic Wildlife Hospital (Elliniko Kentro Perithalpsis Agrion Zoön; ☎ 22970 28367; www.ekpaz.gr, in Greek; ⏲ 11am-1pm) Welcomes volunteers in Aegina, particularly during the winter months. For more information, see p122.

Sea Turtle Protection Society of Greece (Map p78; ☎/fax 210 523 1342; www.archelon.gr; Solomou 57, Exarhia, Athens) Monitor turtles on the Peloponnese.

WWOOF (World Wide Opportunities on Organic Farms; www.wwoof.org/independents.asp) Volunteer at one of around 35 farms in Greece.

Other Work

There are often jobs advertised in the classifieds of English-language newspapers, or you can place an advertisement yourself if you wish. EU nationals can also make use of the Organismos Apasholiseos Ergatikou Dynamikou (OAED), which is the Greek National Employment Service, in their search for employment. The OAED has offices throughout the country.

Seasonal harvest work is handled by migrant workers from Albania and other Balkan nations, and is no longer a viable option for travellers.

Transport

CONTENTS

GETTING THERE & AWAY

Flights, tours and rail tickets can be booked online at www.lonelyplanet.com/travel_services.

ENTERING THE REGION

Visitors to Greece with EU passports are rarely afforded more than a cursory glance, although customs and police may be interested in what you are carrying. EU citizens may enter Greece on a national identity card.

Passports

Visitors from outside the EU may require a visa; this must be checked with consular authorities before you arrive. For visas requirements, see p488.

AIR

Flying tends to be the fastest and cheapest (if not the most environmentally-friendly) means of arriving in Greece. Visitors then hop on a ferry or an internal flight to the islands.

Airports & Airlines

Greece has four main international airports that take both chartered and scheduled flights.

Athens (Eleftherios Venizelos International Airport; code ATH; ☎ 210 353 0000; www.aia.gr)

Iraklio (Nikos Kazantzakis International Airport, Crete; code HER; ☎ 28102 28401)

Rhodes (Diagoras Airport, Dodecanese; code RHO; ☎ 22410 83222)

Thessaloniki (Macedonia International Airport, Northern Greece; code SKG; ☎ 2310 473 700)

Many of Greece's other international airports, including Corfu, Crete and Mykonos, have begun taking scheduled international flights with easyJet. Kos and Araxos also take direct flights from Germany. Other international airports across the country include Santorini, Karpathos, Samos, Skiathos, Hrysoupoli, Aktion, Kefallonia and Zakynthos. These airports are most often used for charter flights from the UK, Germany and Scandinavia.

AIRLINES FLYING TO/FROM GREECE

Olympic Air (code OA; ☎ 801 114 4444; www.olympicair lines.com) is the country's national airline, with the majority of flights to and from Athens. Olympic flies direct between Athens and destinations throughout Europe, as well as to Cairo, İstanbul, Tel Aviv, New York and Toronto. **Aegean Airlines** (code A3; ☎ 801 112 0000; www.aegeanair.com) has flights to and from destinations in Spain, Germany and Italy as well as to Paris, London, Cairo and İstanbul. The safety record of both airlines is exemplary. The contact details for local Olympic and Aegean offices are listed throughout the book.

Other airlines with offices in Athens:

Aeroflot (code SU; ☎ 210 322 0986; www.aeroflot.org)
Air Berlin (code AB; ☎ 210 353 5264; www.airberlin.com)
Air Canada (code AC; ☎ 210 617 5321; www.aircanada.ca)

THINGS CHANGE...

The information in this chapter is particularly vulnerable to change. Check directly with the airline or a travel agent to make sure you understand how a fare (and ticket you may buy) works and be aware of the security requirements for international travel. Shop carefully. The details given in this chapter should be regarded as pointers and are not a substitute for your own careful, up-to-date research.

Air France (code AF; ☎ 210 353 0380; www.airfrance
.com)
Alitalia (code AZ; ☎ 210 353 4284; www.alitalia.it)
American Airlines (code AA; ☎ 210 331 1045; www
.aa.com)
British Airways (code BA; ☎ 210 890 6666; www.british
airways.com)
Cyprus Airways (code CY; ☎ 210 372 2722; www.cyprus
air.com.cy)
Delta Airlines (code DL; ☎ 210 331 1660; www.delta
.com)
easyJet (code U2; ☎ 210 967 0000; www.easyjet.com)
EgyptAir (code MS; ☎ 210 353 1272; www.egyptair.com
.eg)
El Al (code LY; ☎ 210 353 1003; www.elal.co.il)
Emirates Airlines (code EK; ☎ 210 933 3400; www
.emirates.com)
Gulf Air (code GF; ☎ 210 322 0851; www.gulfairco.com)
Iberia (code IB; ☎ 210 323 4523; www.iberia.com)
Japan Airlines (code JL; ☎ 210 324 8211; www.jal.co.jp)
KLM (code KL; ☎ 210 353 1295; www.klm.com)
Lufthansa (code LH; ☎ 210 617 5200; www.lufthansa
.com)
Qatar Airways (code QR; ☎ 210 950 8700; www.qatar
airways.com)
SAS (code SK; ☎ 210 361 3910; www.sas.se)
Singapore Airlines (code SQ; ☎ 210 372 8000, 21035
31259; www.singaporeair.com)
Thai Airways (code TG; ☎ 210 353 1237; www.thai
airways.com)

Turkish Airlines (code TK; ☎ 210 322 1035; www
.turkishairlines.com)
Virgin Express (code TV; ☎ 210 949 0777; www.virgin
-express.com)

Tickets
Purchasing airline tickets has never been easier. Most airlines sell tickets online, offering good deals and eliminating the fear of losing your precious ticket while on holiday. Airlines will also text or email you with any changes to the flight. EasyJet offers some of the cheapest tickets between Greece and the rest of Europe and covers a huge range of destinations. If you're coming from outside Europe, consider a cheap flight to a European hub like London and then an onward ticket with easyJet. Some airlines also offer cheap deals to students. If you're planning to travel between June and September, it's wise to book ahead.

Asia
Most Asian countries offer fairly competitive deals, with Bangkok, Singapore and Hong Kong the best places to shop around for discount tickets.

Khao San Rd in Bangkok is the budget travellers' headquarters. Bangkok has a number of excellent travel agencies, but there are also some suspect ones; ask the advice of other

---

CLIMATE CHANGE & TRAVEL
Climate change is a serious threat to the ecosystems that humans rely upon, and air travel is the fastest-growing contributor to the problem. Lonely Planet regards travel, overall, as a global benefit, but believes we all have a responsibility to limit our personal impact on global warming.

Flying & Climate Change
Pretty much every form of motor travel generates CO_2 (the main cause of human-induced climate change) but planes are far and away the worst offenders, not just because of the sheer distances they allow us to travel, but because they release greenhouse gases high into the atmosphere. The statistics are frightening: two people taking a return flight between Europe and the US will contribute as much to climate change as an average household's gas and electricity consumption over a whole year.

Carbon Offset Schemes
Climatecare.org and other websites use 'carbon calculators' that allow jetsetters to offset the greenhouse gases they are responsible for with contributions to energy-saving projects and other climate-friendly initiatives in the developing world – including projects in India, Honduras, Kazakhstan and Uganda.

Lonely Planet, together with Rough Guides and other concerned partners in the travel industry, supports the carbon offset scheme run by climatecare.org. Lonely Planet offsets all of its staff and author travel.

For more information check out our website: lonelyplanet.com.

travellers. **STA Travel** (☎ 02-236 0262; www.statravel .co.th) is a good place to start.

In Singapore, **STA Travel** (☎ 6737 7188; www .statravel.com.sg) offers competitive discount fares for most destinations. Singapore, like Bangkok, has hundreds of travel agencies to choose from, so it is possible to compare prices. Chinatown Point shopping centre on New Bridge Rd has a good selection of travel agencies.

In Hong Kong, **Four Seas Tours** (☎ 2200 7760; www.fourseastravel.com) is recommended, as is **Shoestring Travel** (☎ 2723 2306; www.shoestring travel.com.hk).

Australia
STA Travel (☎ 1300 733 035; www.statravel.com.au) has its main office in Melbourne, but also has offices in all major cities and on many university campuses. Call for the location of your nearest branch. **Flight Centre** (☎ 13 16 00; www.flightcentre .com.au) has its central office in Sydney and dozens of offices throughout Australia.

Qantas no longer flies direct to Athens, but you could fly via London with a British Airways connection to Athens. Thai Airways and Singapore Airlines both have convenient connections to Athens, as do three of the Persian Gulf airlines – Emirates, Gulf and Qatar Airways. If you're planning on doing a bit of flying around Europe, it's worth looking around for special deals from the major European airlines, including KLM and Lufthansa.

Canada
Canada's national student travel agency is **Travel CUTS** (☎ 800 667 2887; www.travelcuts.com), which has offices in all major cities. **Flight Centre** (☎ 1 877 967 5302; www.flightcentre.ca) has offices in most major cities and offers discounted tickets. For online bookings go to www.expedia.ca or www.travelocity.ca.

Olympic Air has flights from Toronto to Athens via Montreal. There are no direct flights from Vancouver, but there are connecting flights via Toronto, Amsterdam, Frankfurt and London on Air Canada, KLM, Lufthansa and British Airways.

Continental Europe
Athens is linked to every major city in Europe by either Olympic Air or the flag carrier of each country. Amsterdam, Frankfurt, Berlin and Paris are all major centres for cheap airfares.

France has a network of travel agencies that can supply discount tickets to travellers of all ages. They include **OTU Voyages** (☎ 01 40 29 12 22; www.otu.fr), which has branches across the country. Other recommendations include **Voyageurs du Monde** (☎ 01 40 15 11 15; www.vdm.com) and **Nouvelles Frontières** (☎ 08 25 00 07 47; www .nouvelles- frontieres.fr).

In Germany, **STA Travel** (☎ 01805 456 422; www .statravel.de) has several offices around the country. For online fares, try **Just Travel** (☎ 089-747 33 30; www.justtravel.de) and **Expedia** (☎ 01805 006 025; www.expe dia.de).

In the Netherlands, **Airfair** (☎ 020-620 5121; www.airfair.nl) and **My Travel** (☎ 0900 10 20 300; www .mytravel.nl) are recommended.

Cyprus
Olympic Air and Cyprus Airways share the Cyprus–Greece routes. Both airlines have flights between Larnaca and Athens, as well as to Thessaloniki. Cyprus Airways also flies between Pafos and Athens once daily, while Olympic Air has two flights weekly between Larnaca and Iraklio.

Turkey
Olympic Air, Aegean Airlines and Turkish Airlines all fly between İstanbul and Athens. There are no direct flights from Ankara to Athens; all flights go via İstanbul.

UK & Ireland
Discount air travel is big business in London. Advertisements for many travel agencies appear in the travel pages of the weekend broadsheet newspapers, in *Time Out,* the *Evening Standard* and the free magazine *TNT.*

STA Travel (☎ 0871 230 0040; www.statravel.co.uk) has discounted tickets for students and travellers under 26, while **Flight Centre** (☎ 0870 499 0040; www.flightcentre.co.uk) offers competitive rates and also has deals for students. Both agencies have offices in most cities. Other recommended travel agencies in London include **Trailfinders** (☎ 020-7938 3939; www.trailfinders.co.uk), **Travel Bag** (☎ 0870 814 6614; www.travelbag.co.uk) and **ebookers** (☎ 0800 082 3000; www.ebookers.com). Online, check out www.charterflights.co.uk and www.cheapfl ights.co.uk.

The cheapest scheduled flights are with **easyJet** (☎ 0871 750 0100; www.easyjet.com), the no-frills specialist, which has flights from Luton and Gatwick to Athens. Pricing varies wildly depending on departure days and times. See the website for current rates.

USA

STA Travel (☎ 800 781 4040; www.statravel.com) has offices in most major cities that have a university. For online bookings try www.cheaptickets .com, www.expedia.com and www.orbitz .com.

New York has the widest range of options to Athens. The route to Europe is very competitive and there are new deals almost every day. Olympic Air and Delta Airlines both have direct flights, but there are numerous other connecting flights.

While there are no direct flights to Athens from the west coast, there are connecting flights to Athens from many US cities, either linking with Olympic Air in New York or flying with one of the European national airlines to its home country and then on to Athens.

LAND

Travelling by land offers you the chance to really appreciate the landscape, as well as the many experiences that go along with train or bus travel. International train travel, in particular, has become much more feasible in recent years with speedier trains and better connections. You can now travel from London to Athens by train and ferry in less than two days. By choosing to travel on the ground instead of the air, you'll also be reducing your carbon footprint. It's a win-win situation.

Border Crossings

ALBANIA

There are four crossing points between Greece and Albania. The main one at Kakavia, 60km northwest of Ioannina, can have intensely slow queues. The other crossings are at Sagiada, 28km north of Igoumenitsa; Mertziani, 17km west of Konitsa; and Krystallopigi, 14km west of Kotas on the Florina–Kastoria road.

BULGARIA

There are three Bulgarian border crossings: one located at Promahonas, 109km northeast of Thessaloniki and 41km from Serres; one at Ormenio in northeastern Thrace; and a new 448m tunnel border crossing at Exohi, 50km north of Drama. As Bulgaria is part of the EU, crossings are usually quick and hassle-free.

FORMER YUGOSLAV REPUBLIC OF MACEDONIA (FYROM)

There are three border crossings between Greece and FYROM. These are at Evzoni, 68km north of Thessaloniki; Niki, 16km north of Florina; and Doïrani, 31km north of Kilkis. A new crossing at Markova Noga, near Agios Germanos, was being discussed at the time of research.

TURKEY

The crossing points are at Kipi, 43km east of Alexandroupoli, and at Kastanies, 139km northeast of Alexandroupoli. Kipi is probably more convenient if you're heading for İstanbul, but the route through Kastanies goes via the fascinating towns of Soufli and Didymotiho in Greece, and Edirne (ancient Adrianoupolis) in Turkey.

Albania

BUS

The **Greek Railways Organisation** (OSE; www.ose .gr) operates a daily bus between Athens and Tirana via Ioannina and Gjirokastra. The bus departs Athens daily from Sidiridromou 1 near the Larisis train station, arriving in Tirana the following day.

Bulgaria

BUS

The OSE operates a bus from Athens to Sofia (15 hours, six weekly). It also operates Thessaloniki–Sofia buses (7½ hours, four daily). There is a private bus service to Plovdiv (six hours, twice weekly) and Sofia (seven hours, twice weekly) from Alexandroupoli.

TRAIN

There is a daily train to Sofia from Athens (18 hours) via Thessaloniki (nine hours). From Sofia, there are connections to Budapest and Bucharest.

Former Yugoslav Republic of Macedonia (FYROM)

TRAIN

There are two trains daily from Thessaloniki to Skopje (five hours), crossing the border between Idomeni and Gevgelija. They continue from Skopje to the Serbian capital of Belgrade (13 hours). There are no trains between Florina and FYROM, although there are one or two trains a day to Skopje from Bitola (4½ hours) on the FYROM side of the border.

TRANSPORT

Russia

TRAIN

There is a summer-only direct weekly train service from Thessaloniki to Moscow (70 hours).

Turkey

BUS

The OSE operates a bus from Athens to İstanbul (22 hours, six weekly), leaving the former Peloponnese train station in Athens in the evening and travelling via Thessaloniki (seven hours) and Alexandroupoli (13 hours). Students qualify for a 20% discount and children under 12 travel for half-price. See each city's Getting There & Away sections for information on where to buy tickets.

Buses from İstanbul to Athens leave the Anadolu Terminal (Anatolia Terminal) at the Topkapı *otogar* (bus station).

TRAIN

There are no direct trains between Athens and İstanbul. Travellers must take a train to Thessaloniki and connect with one of two daily services running to the Turkish city. The best option is the Filia–Tostluk Express service, leaving Thessaloniki in the evening (11½ hours) and arriving in İstanbul the next morning. The other service is the indirect Intercity IC90 service to Orestiada from Thessaloniki; passengers for İstanbul change at Pythio on the Greece–Turkey border.

Western Europe

If you're keen to reach Greece without taking to the air but fancy a bit more convenience and speed than offered by buses and cars, it's easily done. Train it to the western coast of Italy (there are connections throughout most of Europe) and then hop on a ferry to Greece. Not only will you be doing your bit for the earth, but you'll see some gorgeous scenery en route.

A sample itinerary from London would see you catching the Eurostar to Paris and then an overnight sleeper train to Bologna in Italy. From there, a coastal train takes you to Bari, where there's an overnight boat to Patra on the Peloponnese. From Patra, it's a 4½-hour train journey to Athens. The journey will land you in Athens within two days of leaving London.

Serious overland enthusiasts can reach Greece on a fascinating route through the Balkan Peninsula, passing through Croatia, Serbia and the Former Yugoslav Republic of Macedonia.

CAR & MOTORCYCLE

Most drivers head for an Italian port and take a ferry to Greece. The most convenient ports are Venice and Ancona. A high-speed ferry from Venice to Patra takes around 26 hours. From Patra to Athens is a further 3½ hours driving.

TRAIN

Reaching Greece by train does take some effort. You cannot buy a single ticket from Western Europe to Greece; instead you'll need multiple tickets to cover the journey. Travel agents can do this for you, or look online at www.raileurope.com.

Greece is part of the **Eurail** (www.eurail.com) network. Eurail passes can only be bought by residents of non-European countries and are supposed to be purchased before arriving in Europe. They can, however, be bought in Europe as long as your passport proves that you've been there for less than six months. In London, head for the **Rail Europe Travel Centre** (☎ 0870 584 8848; 179 Piccadilly). Check the Eurail website for full details of passes and prices.

If you are starting your European travels in Greece, you can buy your Eurail pass from the OSE office at Karolou 1-3 in Athens, and at the stations in Patra and Thessaloniki.

Greece is also part of the **Inter-Rail Pass** (www.interrailnet.com) system, available to those who have resided in Europe for six months or more. See the Inter-Rail website for details.

SEA

Albania

Corfu-based **Petrakis Lines** (☎ 26610 38690; www.ionian-cruises.com) has daily hydrofoils to the Albanian port of Saranda (25 minutes).

Cyprus & Israel

Passenger services from Greece to Cyprus and Israel have been suspended indefinitely. **Salamis Lines** (www.viamare.com/Salamis) still operates the route, but carries only vehicles and freight.

Italy

There are ferries to Greece from the Italian ports of Ancona, Bari, Brindisi and Venice. For more information about these services, see the Corfu (p435) and Kefallonia (p456) sections.

The ferries can get very crowded in summer. If you want to take a vehicle across, it's wise to make a reservation beforehand. In the UK, reservations can be made on almost all of these ferries through **Viamare Travel Ltd** (☎ 020-7431 4560; www.viamare.com).

You'll find all the latest information about ferry routes, schedules and services online at www.greekferries.gr. Main ferry companies serving Italy include Agoudimos Lines, ANEK Lines, Blue Star Ferries, Hellenic Seaways, Minoan Lines, Superfast Ferries and Ventouris Ferries. For contact details in Greece and websites, see Island Hopping (p503).

The following ferry services are for the high season (July and August), and prices are for one-way deck class. On these services, deck class means exactly that. If you want a reclining, aircraft-type seat, you'll be up for another 10% to 15% on top of the listed fares. All companies offer discounts for return travel. Prices are about 30% less in the low season.

ANCONA
In summer there are at least three daily sailings between Ancona and Patra with Superfast Ferries, Minoan Lines and ANEK (€53 to €78, 20 hours). There's also a weekly ferry between Ancona and Corfu (€73, 15 hours).

All ferry operators in Ancona have booths at the *stazione marittima* (ferry terminal) off Piazza Candy, where you can pick up timetables and price lists and make bookings. You can also buy tickets through **Morandi & Co** (☎ 071-20 20 33; Via XXIX Settembre 2/0) or at **ANEK Lines** (☎ 071-207 23 46; Via XXIX Settembre 2/0). Superfast accepts Eurail passes.

BARI
Superfast Ferries (☎ 080-52 11 416; Corso de Tullio 6) has daily sailings to Patra (€53, 14½ hours) via Corfu (€30, eight hours) and Kefallonia (€45, 14 hours). Eurail passes accepted.

Ventouris Ferries (☎ 080-52 17 609; Stazione Marittima) has daily boats to Corfu (€53, 10 hours) and Igoumenitsa (€53, 11½ hours).

BRINDISI
The trip from Brindisi was once the most popular crossing, but it now operates only between April and early October. **Hellenic Mediterranean Lines** (☎ 0831-54 80 01; Costa Morena) offers services to Patra (€53, 15 hours), calling at Igoumenitsa on the way. It also has services that call at Corfu (€38, six hours), Kefallonia

(€51, 12 hours) and Zakynthos (€69 to €99, 15 hours). Eurail passes are accepted.

VENICE
In summer there are up to 12 weekly sailings between Venice and Patra (€70 to €80, approximately 30 hours) with Minoan Lines and ANEK Lines. The boat also calls in at Corfu (€73, 25 hours).

Turkey
There are five regular ferry services between Turkey's Aegean coast and the Greek islands. Tickets for all ferries to Turkey must be bought a day in advance. You will almost certainly be asked to turn in your passport the night before the trip, but don't worry, you'll get it back the next day before you board the boat. Port tax for departures to Turkey is around €15.

See the relevant sections under individual island entries for more information about the following services. It's also possible to take a day trip over to Turkey from the Dodecanese; see p445.

CHIOS
There are daily Çeşme–Chios boats from May to October (one way/return €20/30, 1½ hours).

KOS
There are daily summertime ferries and excursion boats between Kos and Bodrum (€34, one hour). Port tax is extra.

LESVOS
In summer there are daily boats between Lesvos and Dikili (€10, one hour). There are also daily excursion boats from Greece in the summer (€20 return).

RHODES
There is a daily catamaran from Rhodes' Commercial harbour to Marmaris, Turkey (€36, 50 minutes), departing twice daily in summer. There is also a passenger and car ferry service on this same route (car/passenger €95/49 including taxes, 1¼ hours), running four or five times a week in summer. Open return tickets cost €46 plus €29 tax.

SAMOS
There are two boats daily between Kuşadası (for Ephesus) and Samos in summer (€35, 1½ hours). Port tax is extra.

TRANSPORT

GETTING AROUND

Greece is an easy place to travel around thanks to a comprehensive public transport system. Buses are the mainstay of island transport, with a network that reaches out to the smallest villages. If you're in a hurry, Greece also has an extensive domestic air network. To most visitors, though, travelling in Greece means island hopping on the multitude of ferries that crisscross the Adriatic and the Aegean. See Island Hopping (p501) for details on ferries and flights between the islands.

AIR
Airlines in Greece

See Island Hopping (p501) for details on flights between the mainland and the islands and between the islands themselves.

The vast majority of domestic mainland flights are handled by the country's national carrier, **Olympic Air** (☎ 801 114 4444; www.olympic airlines.com). Olympic has offices wherever there are flights, as well as in other major towns.

The prices listed in this book are for full-fare economy, and include domestic taxes and charges. There are discounts for return tickets for travel between Monday and Thursday, and bigger discounts for trips that include a Saturday night away. You'll find full details on Olympic's website, as well as information on timetables.

The baggage allowance on domestic flights is 15kg, or 20kg if the domestic flight is part of an international journey. Olympic Air offers a 25% student discount on domestic flights, but only if the flight is part of an international journey.

BICYCLE

Cycling is not popular among Greeks; however, it's gaining kudos with tourists. Bike lanes are rare to nonexistent and helmets are not compulsory. The island of Kos is about the most bicycle-friendly place in Greece, although Crete has gained popularity in recent years. See p73 for more details on cycling in Greece. Bicycles are carried free on ferries.

Hire

You can hire bicycles in most tourist places, but they are not as widely available as cars and motorcycles. Prices range from €5 to €12 per day, depending on the type and age of the bike.

Purchase

You can buy decent mountain or touring bikes in Greece's major towns, though you may have a problem finding a ready buyer if you wish to sell it on. Bike prices are much the same as across the rest of Europe, anywhere from €300 to €2000.

BOAT

See Island Hopping (p501) for details on getting around by boat.

BUS

All long-distance buses, on the mainland and the islands, are operated by regional collectives known as **KTEL** (Koino Tamio Eispraxeon Leoforion; www .ktel.org). The network is comprehensive. The islands of Corfu, Kefallonia and Zakynthos can also be reached directly from Athens by bus – the fares include the price of the ferry ticket. For details, see p89. The KTEL buses are safe and modern, and these days many are air-conditioned. In more-remote rural areas they tend to be older and less comfortable.

On islands where the capital is inland rather than a port, buses normally meet boats. Some of the more remote islands have not yet acquired a bus, but most have some sort of motorised transport – even if it is only a bone-shaking, three-wheeled truck. Most villages on larger islands have a daily bus service of some sort, although some may have only one or two buses a week. They operate for the benefit of people going to town to shop, rather than for tourists, and consequently leave the villages very early in the morning and return early in the afternoon.

In small towns and villages the 'bus station' may be no more than a bus stop outside a *kafeneio* (coffee house) that doubles as a booking office. In remote areas the timetable may be in Greek only, but most booking offices have timetables in both Greek and Roman script. The timetables give both the departure and return times – useful if you are making a day trip. Times are listed using the 24-hour clock system.

When you buy a ticket you may be allotted a seat number, which is noted on the ticket. The seat number is indicated on the *back* of each seat of the bus, not on the back of the seat in front. You can board a bus without a ticket and pay on board, but on a popular route or during high season this may mean that you have to stand. Keep your ticket handy for checking.

It's best to turn up at least 20 minutes before departure to make sure you get a seat, and buses have been known to leave a few minutes before their scheduled departure. Smoking is prohibited on all buses in Greece.

Costs

Fares are fixed by the government and bus travel is very reasonably priced. A journey costs approximately €5 per 100km. Some major routes include Athens–Patra (€17, three hours), Athens–Volos (€25, five hours) and Athens–Corfu (€48 including ferry, 9½ hours).

CAR & MOTORCYCLE

No one who has travelled on Greece's roads will be surprised to hear that the country's road fatality rate is the highest in Europe. More than 2000 people die on the roads every year, with overtaking listed as the greatest cause of accidents. Ever-stricter traffic laws have had little impact on the toll; Greek roads remain a good place to practise your defensive-driving techniques.

Heart-stopping moments aside, your own car is a great way to explore off the beaten track. The road network has improved enormously in recent years; many roads marked as dirt tracks on older maps have now been asphalted. It's important to get a good road map (for more information, see p484).

Almost all islands are served by car ferries, but they are expensive. Sample prices for vehicles up to 4.25m include Piraeus–Mykonos €80; Piraeus–Crete (Hania and Iraklio) €85;

TRANSPORT

CRUISING

Cruise ships aren't everyone's cup of tea but, not surprisingly, in a country with countless islands and gorgeous azure waters, they're a popular way of seeing Greece. There is something very special about sailing into the colourful harbours of the islands. The upside is you won't have to deal with the fluctuations and general havoc of ferry schedules; you don't have to prebook or hunt accommodation; and you know everything will be open as the islands take out all the stops when a cruise ship arrives in town.

There are, of course, the downsides. International cruise ships tend to be enormous floating hotels and can easily dwarf a small island. Two thousand passengers disembarking can lead to large queues and crowds. These big boats are also rarely able to dock in the small island harbours and you'll need to wait for your turn on the little boats running guests to shore.

More fitting for the Greek islands are smaller, local cruise ships. We're not talking dinghies – these boats still accommodate 500 to 800 people and have the expected amenities like spas, gyms, shops, bars and pools. They're able to dock in the island harbours and the smaller number of passengers disembarking means you're likely to have a more meaningful experience on the islands.

The most popular Greek cruise line is **Louis Cruises** (☎ 21032 14980; www.louiscruises.com), with a wide range of reasonably priced trips and various types of accommodation. A week-long cruise through the islands and to Turkey starts from €470, while a three-day cruise begins at €175. Booking through a travel agency means you may get a few days in Athens and even a discount flight from Europe tacked on. Try **Fantasy Travel** (www.fantasytravelofgreece.com), **Seafarer Cruises** (www.seafarercruises.com) or **Brendan Tours** (www.brendanvacations.com).

If you opt for the big boys, **Thomas Cook** (www.thomascook.com) has lots of cruises that include the Greek islands, including some family-friendly options. Its smallest boat, the *Calypso*, takes only 486 passengers and is an adult-only liner that visits the Aegean. Seven nights starts from €540 if you book online. **easyCruise** (www.easycruise.com) has three-day cruises from €330. Like the airline, they're cheap and cheerful.

Prices on cruises include meals, port fees and portage but there are often fuel and gratuity charges that are extra. Children often only pay port fees if they bunk in with parents. Excursions are generally additional as well and can range from €40 to €60, depending on what's included. You should be able to go to shore independent of the excursion but double-check before you book; some larger cruises dock at distant ports and the only way to reach the destination is by purchasing a place on the tour.

For information on cruising the islands by yacht, see p74.

and Piraeus–Samos €86. The charge for a large motorcycle is about the same as the price for a deck-class passenger ticket. If you're planning to island hop, you're better off hiring vehicles at each destination.

Automobile Associations

Greece's domestic automobile association is **ELPA** (Elliniki Leschi Aftokinitou kai Periigiseon; ☎ 210 606 8800; www.elpa.gr, in Greek; Leoforos Mesogion 395, Agia Paraskevi).

Bring Your Own Vehicle

EU-registered vehicles are allowed free entry into Greece, but may only stay six months without road taxes being due. A green card (international third-party insurance) is all that's required. Your only proof of the date of entry – if requested by the police – is your ferry ticket if you arrive from Italy, or your passport entry stamp if entering from elsewhere. Non-EU-registered vehicles may be logged in your passport.

Driving Licence

Drivers with an EU driving license can drive with it in Greece. If your driving license comes from outside the EU, Greece requires that you possess an International Driving Permit, which should be obtained before you leave home.

Fuel & Spare Parts

Fuel is available widely throughout the country, though service stations may be closed on weekends and public holidays. On small islands there may be only one petrol station; check where it is before you head out. Self-service pumps are not the norm in Greece, nor are credit-card pumps. Petrol in Greece is cheaper than in most other European countries, but by American or Australian standards it is expensive. Prices are generally set by the government, but can vary from region to region. Super (leaded) and *amolyvdi* (unleaded) is always available, as is *petreleo kinisis* (diesel).

Spare parts for most Japanese and European cars are available everywhere, although you may need to wait for them to be ferried to the islands.

Hire

CAR

Hire cars are available just about everywhere. All the big multinational companies are represented in Athens, and most have branches in popular tourist destinations like Rhodes, Kos and Crete. The majority of the smaller islands have at least one outlet; these are often local companies that can offer great deals. They are normally open to negotiation, especially if business is slow, with daily rates ranging from around €30 to €50, including all insurance and taxes.

High-season weekly rates with unlimited mileage start at about €280 for the smallest models, dropping to about €200 per week in winter. These prices don't include VAT. There are also optional extras such as a collision damage waiver of €12 per day (more for larger models), without which you will be liable for the first €295 of the repair bill (much more for larger models). Other costs include a theft waiver of at least €6 per day and personal accident insurance. The major companies offer much cheaper prebooked and prepaid rates.

By Greek law, hire cars have to be replaced every six years and so most vehicles you hire will be relatively new. Always check what the insurance includes; there are often rough roads or dangerous routes that you can only tackle by hiring a 4WD. If you want to take a hire car to another country or onto a ferry, you will need advance written authorisation from the hire company, as the insurance may not cover you. Unless you pay with a credit card, most hire companies will require a minimum deposit of €120 per day. See the Getting Around sections of cities and islands for details of places to hire cars.

The minimum driving age in Greece is 18 years, but most car-hire firms require you to be at least 21 – or 23 for larger vehicles.

For current rates at some of the major car-hire players in Greece, see the following websites:
Avis (☎ 210 322 4951; www.avis.gr)
Budget (☎ 210 349 8800; www.budget.gr)
Europcar (☎ 210 960 2382; www.europcar.gr)
Hertz (☎ 210 626 4000; www.hertz.gr)

MOTORCYCLE

Mopeds, motorcycles and scooters are available for hire wherever there are tourists to hire them. Most machines are newish and in good condition. Nonetheless, check the brakes at the earliest opportunity.

To hire a moped, motorcycle or scooter you must produce a licence that shows proficiency to ride the category of bike you wish to hire; this applies to everything from 50cc up. British citizens must obtain a Category A licence from the Driver and Vehicle Licensing Agency in the UK (in most other EU countries separate licences are automatically issued).

Motorcycles or scooters are a cheap way to travel around. Rates start from about €15 per day for a moped or 50cc motorcycle to €30 per day for a 250cc motorcycle. Out of season these prices drop considerably, so use your bargaining skills. Most motorcycle hirers include third-party insurance in the price, but it's wise to check this. This insurance will not include medical expenses. Helmets are compulsory and rental agencies are obliged to offer one as part of the hire deal. Police will book you if you're caught without a helmet.

Warning

Greece is not the best place to initiate yourself into motorcycling. There are still a lot of gravel roads – particularly on the islands. Novices should be very careful; dozens of tourists have accidents every year. Scooters are particularly prone to sliding on gravely bends. Try to hire a motorcycle with thinner profile tyres. If you are planning to use a motorcycle or moped, check that your travel insurance covers you for injury resulting from a motorcycle accident. Many insurance companies don't offer this cover, so read the fine print!

Insurance

Insurance is always included in any vehicle hire agreements, but you are advised to check whether it is fully comprehensive or third-party only. Otherwise you may be up for hefty costs in the event of any damage caused to your vehicle if you are at fault.

Road Conditions

Main highways in Greece have been improving steadily over the years but many still don't offer smooth sailing. Some main roads still retain the two-lane/hard shoulder format of the 1960s, which can be confusing, if not downright dangerous. Roadwork can take years and years in Greece, especially on the islands where funding often only trickles in. In other cases, excellent, new tarmac roads may have appeared that are not on any local maps.

Road Hazards

Slow drivers – many of them unsure and hesitant tourists – can cause serious traffic events on Greece's roads. Road surfaces can change rapidly when a section of road has succumbed to subsidence or weathering. Snow and ice can be a serious challenge in winter, and drivers are advised to carry snow chains. Animals in rural areas may wander onto roads, so extra vigilance is required. Roads passing through mountainous areas are often littered with fallen rocks that can cause extensive damage to a vehicle's underside or throw a bike rider.

Road Rules

In Greece, as throughout Continental Europe, you drive on the right and overtake on the left. Outside built-up areas, traffic on a main road has right of way at intersections. In towns, vehicles coming from the right have right of way. This includes roundabouts – even if you're in the roundabout, you must give way to drivers coming onto the roundabout to your right.

Seat belts must be worn in front seats, and in back seats if the car is fitted with them. Children under 12 years of age are not allowed in the front seat. It is compulsory to carry a first-aid kit, fire extinguisher and warning triangle, and it is forbidden to carry cans of petrol. Helmets are compulsory for motorcyclists if the motorcycle is 50cc or more.

Outside residential areas the speed limit is 120km/h on highways, 90km/h on other roads and 50km/h in built-up areas. The speed limit for motorcycles up to 100cc is 70km/h and for larger motorcycles 90km/h. Drivers exceeding the speed limit by 20% are liable to receive a fine of €60; exceeding it by 40% costs €150.

The police have cracked down on drink-driving laws – at last. A blood-alcohol content of 0.05% can incur a fine of €150, and over 0.08% is a criminal offence.

If you are involved in an accident and no-one is hurt, the police will not be required to write a report, but it is advisable to go to a nearby police station and explain what happened. A police report may be required for insurance purposes. If an accident involves injury, a driver who does not stop and does not inform the police may face a prison sentence.

HITCHING

Hitching is never entirely safe in any country in the world, and we don't recommend it. Travellers who decide to hitch should understand that they are taking a small but potentially serious risk. People who do choose to hitch will be safer if they travel in pairs and should let someone know where they are planning to go. In particular, it is unwise for females to hitch alone; women are better off hitching with a male companion.

Getting out of major cities tends to be hard work and Athens is notoriously difficult. Hitching is much easier in remote areas and on islands with poor public transport. On country roads it is not unknown for someone to stop and offer you a lift, even if you aren't hitching. Local hitchers don't stick a thumb up, but point a finger to the ground from an outstretched arm.

LOCAL TRANSPORT
Bus
Most Greek island towns are small enough to get around on foot. The only island towns where tourists are likely to use buses are Corfu Town, Iraklio, Kos Town and Rhodes Town. The procedure for buying tickets for local buses is covered in the Getting Around section for each city.

Metro
Athens is the only city in Greece large enough to warrant an underground system. For information, see p91. Note that only Greek student cards are valid for a student ticket on the metro.

Taxi
Taxis are widely available in Greece except on very small or remote islands. They are reasonably priced by European standards, especially if three or four people share costs.

Yellow city taxis are metered, with rates doubling between midnight and 5am. Additional costs are charged for trips from an airport or a bus, port or train station, as well as for each piece of luggage over 10kg. Island taxis do not have meters, so you should always settle on a price before you get in. In larger tourist towns, prices to popular destinations are often posted at taxi ranks.

TRAIN
None of the islands have trains. On the mainland trains are run by the **Greek Railways Organisation** (Organismos Sidirodromon Ellados; www.ose.gr), referred to as OSE. You'll find information on fares and schedules on the website. Information on domestic departures from Athens or Thessaloniki can be sought by calling ☎ 1440.

Trains are handy for getting to/from the mainland ports of Patra, Piraeus, Volos, Thessaloniki and Alexandroupoli. The network is of a good standard and is being constantly upgraded.

Classes & Costs
There are two types of service: regular (slow) trains that stop at all stations, and faster, modern intercity trains that link most major mainland cities. The slow trains represent the country's cheapest form of public transport: 2nd-class fares are absurdly cheap, and even 1st class is cheaper than bus travel. For a 2nd-class slow-train trip from Athens to Thessaloniki expect to pay €28 (six hours); and Athens to Alexandroupoli €49 (10 hours). A nonstop Athens–Thessaloniki express service costs €48 (four hours). A comfortable night service also runs between Athens and Thessaloniki, with a choice of couchettes (from €20), two-bed compartments (€31) and single compartments (€54).

Ticket prices for intercity services are subject to a distance loading charged on top of the normal fares. Seat reservations should be made as far in advance as possible, especially during summer.

Train Passes
Eurail and Inter-Rail cards are valid in Greece, but it's not worth buying one if Greece is the only place where you plan to use them. The passes can be used for 2nd-class travel on intercity services without paying the loading. There is a 30% discount on return tickets, and a 30% discount for groups of 10 people or more.

Island Hopping

CONTENTS

In Greece, getting there really is half the adventure and island hopping remains an essential part of the Greek experience. Whether you're sailing into a colourful harbour, sitting on the sun-drenched deck with the surf pounding below, or flying low over the azure waters in a propeller-driven twin-engine plane, you will undoubtedly be filled with a sense of adventure and see the islands at their most tantalising. It is still possible to board one of the slow boats chugging between the islands and to curl up on deck in your sleeping bag to save a night's accommodation, but Greece's domestic ferry scene has undergone a radical transformation in the past decade and these days you can also travel in serious comfort and at a decent speed.

The trade-off is, of course, that sea travel can be quite expensive these days. A bed for the night in a cabin from Piraeus to Rhodes can be more expensive than a discounted airline ticket. Nevertheless, deck class is still very reasonable, cabins are like hotel rooms and the experience of staying overnight on a boat is one you shouldn't pass up too quickly. The key is to choose carefully – you can still find the chug-a-lug voyages with all-night noise and insalubrious bathrooms, or you can opt for vessels more akin to the Love Boat. Try mixing your experiences – zipping over the water in a catamaran, slowly ploughing the sea aboard a slow ferry, and soaring from one island airport to the next in a tiny plane.

In the summer, lots of boats and planes connect the islands to one another and the mainland. However, travelling at peak times and between smaller islands and island groups can take some careful planning. Many local travel agents have a good handle on the transport available and can help you build an itinerary and book all necessary tickets. Out of season, planning ahead is even more essential as the number of boats and planes diminishes considerably.

Ferry and airline timetables change from year to year and season to season, and planes and boats can be subject to delays and cancellations at short notice due to bad weather and strikes. No timetable is infallible, but the comprehensive weekly list of departures from Piraeus put out by the EOT (known abroad as the GNTO, the Greek National Tourist Organisation) in Athens is as accurate as possible. The people to go to for the most up-to-date ferry information are the local *limenarhio* (port police), whose offices are usually on or near the quayside.

You'll find lots of information about ferry services on the internet and many of the larger ferry companies also have their own sites (see p503).

A couple of very useful websites:

Danae Travel (www.danae.gr) This is a good site for booking boat tickets.

Greek Travel Pages (www.gtp.gr) Has a useful search program and links for flights and ferries.

This chapter deals with domestic flight and boat connections. For international services, see p490 or the individual sections of each destination chapter.

PRACTICALITIES

THE GREEK FLEETS

With a network covering every inhabited island, the Greek ferry network is vast and varied. The slow rust-buckets that used to ply the seas are nearly a thing of the past. You'll still find slow ferries, but high-speed ferries are more popular and cover most of the long-haul routes. Local ferries, excursion boats and tiny, private fishing boats called caïques often connect neighbouring

ISLAND HOPPING

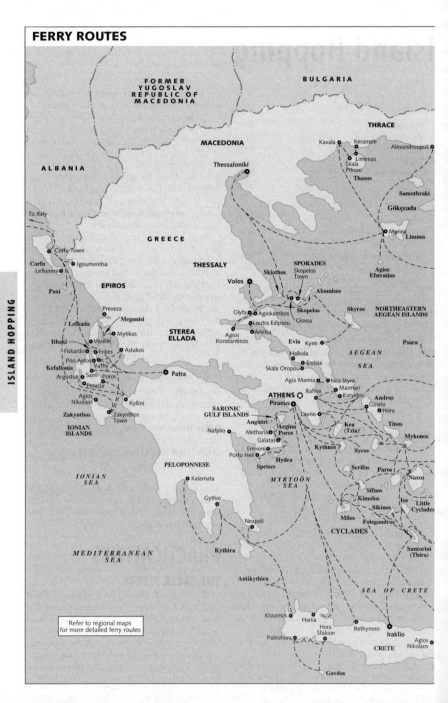

FERRY ROUTES

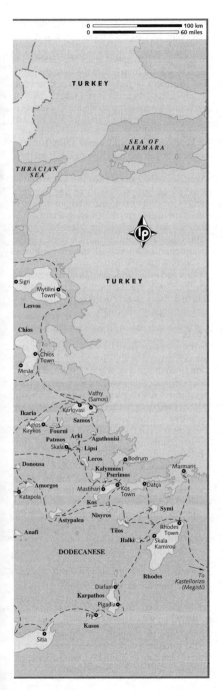

islands and islets. You'll also find water taxis that will take you to isolated beaches and coves. At the other end of the spectrum, hydrofoils and catamarans can cut travel time drastically. Hydrofoils have seen their heyday but continue to link some of the more remote islands and island groups. Catamarans have taken to the sea in a big way, offer more comfort and cope better with poor weather conditions.

While the largest and most popular islands tend to have airports, many of the smaller ones don't. Flights tend to be short and aeroplanes are small, often making for a bumpy ride. In addition to the national airlines, there are a number of smaller outfits running seaplanes or complementing the most popular routes.

For information on cruise ships, see Cruising (p497).

OPERATORS
Who's Who in the Air?
The biggest player in the sky is Olympic Air, followed closely by Aegean Airlines which often offers great discounts. Airlines often have local offices on the islands (see the relevant destination chapter for details).

Aegean Airlines (☎ 801 112 0000, 210 626 1000; www.aegeanair.com)

Athens Airways (☎ 210 669 6600; www.athensairways.com)

Olympic Air (☎ 801 114 4444; www.olympicairlines.com)

Sky Express (☎ 28102 23500; www.skyexpress.gr)

Who's Who in the Water?
Ferry companies often have local offices on many of the islands; see the relevant destination chapter for details of these as well as small, local ferries and caïques.

Aegean Flying Dolphins (☎ 210 422 1766) Hydrofoils linking Samos with Kos and islands in between.

Aegean Speed Lines (☎ 210 969 0950; www.aegeanspeedlines.gr) Superspeedy boats between Athens and the Cyclades.

Agoudimos Lines (☎ 210 414 1300; www.agoudimos-lines.com) Ferries connecting the Cyclades and mainland. Also travels to Italy via Corfu.

Alpha Ferries (☎ 210 428 4001/02; www.alphaferries.gr) Traditional ferries from Athens to the Cyclades.

ANE Kalymnou (☎ 22430 29384) Kalymnos-based hydrofoils and an old-style ferry linking some of the Dodecanese and the Cyclades.

ANEK Lines (☎ 210 419 7420; www.anek.gr) Crete-based long-haul ferries.

ANES (☎ 210 422 5625; www.anes.gr) Symi-based old-style ferries servicing the Dodecanese.

ISLAND HOPPING

Anna Express (☎ 22470 41215; www.annaexpress-lipsi
.services.officelive.com) Small, fast ferry connecting
northern Dodecanese.
Blue Star Ferries (☎ 210 891 9800; www.bluestar
ferries.com) Long-haul high-speed ferries and Seajet
catamarans between the mainland and the Cyclades.
Cyclades Fast Ferries (☎ 210 418 2005; www.fastferries
.com.gr) Comfortable ferries to the most popular Cyclades.
Dodekanisos Seaways (☎ 22410 70590; www.12ne.gr)
Runs luxurious catamarans in the Dodecanese.
Euroseas (☎ 210 413 2188; www.ferries.gr/euroseas)
Linking the Saronics with services to the mainland.
Evoikos Lines (☎ 210 413 4483; www.glyfaferries.gr,
in Greek) Comfortable short-haul ferry services between
Glyfa on the mainland and Agiokambos in northern Evia.
GA Ferries (☎ 210 419 9100; www.gaferries.gr) Old-
style, long-haul ferries serving a huge number of islands.
Hellenic Seaways (☎ 210 419 9000; www.hellenic
seaways.gr) Conventional long-haul ferries and catamarans
from the mainland to Cyclades and between the Sporades
and Saronic islands.
Ionian Ferries (☎ 210 324 9997; www.ionianferries.gr)
Large ferries serving the Ionian Islands.
LANE Lines (☎ 210 427 4011; www.ferries.gr/lane)
Long-haul ferries.
Minoan Lines (☎ 210 414 5700; www.minoan.gr)
High-speed luxury ferries between Piraeus and Iraklio, and
Patra, Igoumenitsa and Corfu.
NEL Lines (☎ 22510 26299; www.nel.gr) High-speed,
long-haul ferries.
SAOS Lines (☎ 210 625 0000; www.saos.gr) Big, slow
boats calling in at many of the islands.
Sea Jets (☎ 210 412 1001) Catamarans calling at
Athens, Crete, Santorini (Thira), Paros and many islands
in between.
Sea Star (☎ 22460 44000; www.net-club.gr/tilosseastar
.htm) High-speed catamaran connecting Tilos with Rhodes,
Halki and Nisyros.
Skyros Shipping Company (☎ 22220 92164; www
.sne.gr) Slow-boat between Skyros and Kymi on Evia.
Strintzis Ferries (☎ 26102 40000; www.strintzis
ferries.gr) Larger, older ferries in the Sporades.
Superfast Ferries (www.superfast.com) As the name
implies, speedy ferries from the mainland to Crete, Corfu
and Patra.
Ventouris Sea Lines (☎ 210 411 4911; www.ventouris
sealines.gr) Big boats from the mainland to the Cyclades.
Zante Ferries (☎ 26950 49500; www.zanteferries.gr)
Older ferries connecting the mainland with the western
Cyclades.

TICKETS
Ticket Purchase
As ferries are prone to delays and cancellations,
for short trips it's often best not to purchase a

ticket until it has been confirmed that the ferry
is leaving. During high season, or if you need
to reserve a car space, you will need to book
in advance. High-speed boats like catamarans
tend to sell out long before the slow chuggers.
For overnight ferries it's always best to book
in advance, particularly if you want a cabin or
particular type of accommodation. If a service is
cancelled you can usually transfer your ticket to
the next available service with that company.

Many ferry companies have online booking
services or you can purchase tickets from their
local offices or most travel agents in Greece.
Agencies selling tickets line the waterfront of
most ports, but rarely is there one that sells
tickets for every boat, and often an agency is
reluctant to give you information about a boat
they do not sell tickets for. Most have timetables displayed outside; check these for the
next departing boat or ask the *limenarhio*.

To find specific details on where to buy
tickets and other important local information
for the islands, see the specific island's Getting
There & Away section in the destination chapters throughout this book.

Costs
Ferry prices are fixed by the government and
are determined by the distance of the destination from the port of origin. The small differences in price you may find at ticket agencies
are the results of some agencies sacrificing
part of their designated commission to qualify
as a 'discount service'. (The discount is seldom more than €0.50.) Ticket prices include
embarkation tax, a contribution to NAT (the
seafarer's union) and 10% VAT.

High-speed ferries and hydrofoils cost about
20% more than the traditional ferries, while
catamarans are often a third to double the
price of their slower counterparts. Caïques and
water taxis are usually very reasonable while
excursion boats can be pricey but very useful to
reach out-of-the-way islands. Children under
five travel for free while those between five and
10 are usually given half-price tickets.

Almost all islands are served by car ferries but they are expensive. Sample prices for
vehicles up to 4.25m include Piraeus–
Mykonos, €80; Piraeus–Crete (Hania and
Iraklio), €90; and Piraeus–Samos, €86. The
charge for a large motorcycle is about the same
as the price for a deck-class passenger ticket. If
you're planning to island hop, you're better off
renting a vehicle at each destination.

Classes

On smaller boats, hydrofoils and catamarans, there is only one type of ticket available and these days, even on larger vessels, classes are largely a thing of the past. The public spaces on the more modern ferries are generally open to all. What does differ is the level of accommodation that you can purchase for overnight boats.

Your 'deck class' ticket typically gives you access to the deck and interior with no accommodation option. It's still a very economical option and if you're one of the first to board, you can usually find somewhere to curl up in your sleeping bag, either inside or on the deck. Next up, aeroplane-type seats give you a reserved, reclining seat in which to sleep (you hope). Then come various shades of cabin accommodation: a four-berth, three-berth or two-berth interior cabin is cheaper than an equivalent outside cabin with a porthole. On most boats, cabins are very comfortable, resembling a small hotel room with a private bathroom. While these cost the equivalent of a discount airline ticket, you also need to factor in that your ticket buys you a night's accommodation. At the other end of the spectrum are luxury cabins with a view to the front of the ship. These resemble standard cruise-ship cabins and are generally very pricey.

Unless you state otherwise, you will automatically be given deck class when purchasing a ticket. Unless otherwise indicated, prices quoted in this book are for deck-class tickets and economy flight tickets.

CONNECTIONS

Transport information is always vulnerable to change – nowhere is this truer than in Greece. It's important to remember that ferry companies and airlines can change routes and timetables faster than a catamaran can zip between the islands. Every year or two, the ferry companies may 'win' the contracts for operating different routes; thus, they can change annually. Outside of the summer season, most services are less frequent. Always check online schedules, operators or travel agencies for up-to-the-minute info.

This section first lists transport information for specific island chains, such as options for travelling from the mainland and individual islands. From p507 onwards, you'll find departure timetables for individual islands and mainland ports – listed in alphabetical order. Use these timetables to find out how to hop from where you are to your next destination, and then from there to the next destination and so on.

References to 'port' in the table headings throughout this chapter refer to the port of departure, not the destination port.

ATHENS

Most people begin their island hopping in Athens, from where it's an easy trip to the nearby ports of Piraeus, Rafina and Lavrio. Countless ferries, catamarans and hydrofoils set sail from these ports to many of the island groups. If you're beginning your journey from Athens, see p509 for the detailed tables on departures to the various islands. For general information on Athens, see p75.

CRETE

As one of Greece's major destinations, Crete is very well connected by boat and air with the rest of the country and even with some international airports/destinations. Given the size and wealth of the island, it's no surprise that some of the biggest transport companies (such as the maritime Minoan Lines and Aegean Airlines) were founded by Cretan businesspeople. Departure information from Crete is from p511 onwards. For general information on this region, see p219.

FEELING WOOZY?

Even those with the sturdiest stomachs can feel seasick when a boat hits rough weather. Here are a few tips to calm your tummy:

- Gaze at the horizon, not the sea. Don't read or stare at objects that your mind will assume are stable.

- Drink plenty and eat lightly. Many people claim ginger biscuits and ginger tea settle the stomach.

- Don't use binoculars.

- If possible stay in the fresh air – don't go below deck and avoid hydrofoils where you are trapped indoors.

- Try to keep your mind occupied.

- If you know you're prone to seasickness, consider investing in acupressure wristbands before you leave.

CYCLADES

Olympic Air provides regular flights between Athens and the Cyclades. Large high-speed boats and catamarans are a regular feature on Cyclades' routes from about mid-June to mid-September. Their travel times are usually half those of regular ferries. Ferry routes separate the Cyclades into western, northern, central and eastern subgroups. Most ferry services operating within the Cyclades connect one of these subgroups with the ports of Piraeus, Lavrio or Rafina on the mainland. The eastern Cyclades (Mykonos, Paros, Naxos, Ios and Santorini) are the most visited and have the best ferry links with the mainland, usually to Piraeus.

The small islands south of Naxos – Iraklia, Schinousa and Koufonisia – make up the main grouping known as the Little Cyclades.

For general information on this region see p134.

DODECANESE

There are regular direct flights between many of the Dodecanese and Athens, along with flights between some of the larger islands in this group. Overnight ferries between Piraeus and Rhodes stop at many of the Dodecanese en route, albeit at some fairly antisocial hours. Within the Dodecanese are a vast array of high-speed catamarans and older clunkers, calling in at the majority of the group's islands.

For general information on this region see p273.

EVIA & THE SPORADES

Skiathos and Skyros airports handle domestic flights from Athens (as well as occasional charter flights from Oslo and Amsterdam).

From Athens' Terminal B station (p89) there are buses departing to Halkida and Paralia Kymis, for Skyros; and to Agios Konstantinos, for the Sporades. From Athens' Mavromateon terminal (p89), there are frequent buses to Rafina, for Evia.

There are daily ferries to the Sporades from both Agios Konstantinos and Volos, and weekly ferries from Thessaloniki to the Sporades, as well as regular ferry routes connecting Evia to the mainland. There are frequent daily hydrofoil links from both Agios Konstantinos and Volos to the Northern Sporades (Skiathos, Skopelos and Alonnisos only). In 2009 a new service started between Skopelos, Alonnisos and Skyros (via Paralia Kymis, Evia).

For general information on this region see p405.

IONIAN ISLANDS

Corfu, Kefallonia and Zakynthos have airports; Lefkada has no airport, but Aktion airport, near Preveza on the mainland, is about 20km away. The four airports have frequent flights to/from Athens. There are interisland connections between Corfu and Preveza, Preveza and Kefallonia and between Kefallonia and Zakynthos.

KTEL long-distance buses connect each major island with Athens and Thessaloniki, and usually also with Patra or Kyllini in the Peloponnese. Buses to Corfu, Lefkada, Kefallonia, Ithaki and Zakynthos depart from Athens' Terminal A bus station.

The Peloponnese has two departure ports for the Ionian Islands: Patra for ferries to Corfu, Kefallonia and Ithaki; and Kyllini for ferries to Kefallonia and Zakynthos. Epiros has one port, Igoumenitsa, for Corfu (island) and Paxi; and Sterea Ellada has one, Astakos, for Ithaki and Kefallonia (although this service is limited to high season).

For general information on this region see p433.

NORTHEASTERN AEGEAN ISLANDS

The northeastern Aegean Islands are fairly well connected to various ports in mainland Greece and other island chains (notably the Cyclades and the Dodecanese) though not all of them have airports. However, they are not all well connected among themselves and here especially travellers will need to take a patient and flexible approach when planning trips. Budget a few extra days to be on the safe side, especially when setting sail for the smaller and more remote islands. Services out of summer can be much reduced and, when the weather is stormy, result in delays.

Just five of the northeastern Aegean Islands have airports – though none is very large. From these airports (Samos, Chios, Lesvos, Limnos and Ikaria) you can fly directly to Athens and Thessaloniki. While interisland flights are possible, most go via Athens. However, the new carrier Sky Express has several direct flights to the islands.

Although they enjoy a plethora of ferry connections, the northeastern Aegean Islands can be very vexing to circumnavigate. The northernmost of them, Thasos and

Samothraki, are currently only accessible via the northern Greece mainland, while other islands too sometimes fall victim to the grand rivalries between Greece's shipping magnates that continue to wreak havoc with ferry schedules. New lines and companies spring up, others shut down, and unscheduled 'ghost ships' set sail in the early morning hours. No surprise, therefore, that the crafty pirates of the Aegean found these islands so attractive for centuries.

The northeastern Aegean Islands are also very significant for their frequent boats to various resorts and historical sites on the Turkish coast; for details on these itineraries, see the boxed text Turkish Connections (p358). For information on other excursion boats and special short-haul lines, see the specific island sections in the Northeastern Aegean Islands chapter, p347.

NORTHERN GREECE

Getting to the islands from northern Greece is possible by flying (usually via Athens) and by boat. However, the great distances between northern ports and most of the Greek islands mean that it's a long, tiring and relatively expensive haul (with the notable exceptions of Thasos and Samothraki). However, if you need to take a vehicle from the mainland to an island, travelling by boat becomes the only option.

While ferries to Thasos and Samothraki are frequent and reliable in summer, boats to more far-flung destinations are less frequent and prone to unexpected changes, so always check well in advance.

For general information on this region see Thessaloniki, p94.

PELOPONNESE

The major ferry services in the Peloponnese run from the mainland ports of Patra (p99) and Kyllini (p102) to the Ionians; and Gythio (p98) and Neapoli (p102) to Kythira. In eastern Peloponnese, high-speed services run from Porto Heli, Ermioni and Galatas to Spetses, Hydra and Poros in the Saronic Gulf (pp123–33). Services to Italy are served by companies in Patra.

SARONIC GULF ISLANDS

The Saronic Islands have regular links to and from each other and Piraeus. At the time of writing only fast ferries ran from Piraeus to Hydra and Spetses, and Ermioni and Porto Heli on the mainland. Tickets for these ferries are often substantially more expensive than those for conventional ferries.

An alternative, cheaper way of reaching Poros, Hydra and Spetses is to travel overland through the Peloponnese and then to take local ferries to your island of choice.

For general information on this region see p117.

INDIVIDUAL ISLANDS & MAINLAND PORTS
Aegina
Saronic Gulf Islands; see also p118

BOAT SERVICES FROM AEGINA

Destination	Port	Duration	Fare	Frequency
Angistri (Skala)	Aegina Town	15min	€5	1 daily
Angistri (Skala)*	Aegina Town	10min	€6	8 daily
Methana	Aegina Town	40min	€5.70	2-3 daily
Piraeus	Aegina Town	1hr 10min	€9.50	8-10 daily
Piraeus	Agia Marina	1hr	€9.50	3-4 daily
Piraeus	Souvala	1hr 35min	€8.50	3-4 daily
Piraeus*	Aegina Town	40min	€14	hourly
Poros	Aegina Town	1hr 50min	€8.60	4 daily

*high-speed services

Agathonisi
Dodecanese; see also p345

BOAT SERVICES FROM AGATHONISI

Destination	Port	Duration	Fare	Frequency
Arki	Agios Georgios	45min	€8	2 weekly
Lipsi	Agios Georgios	1hr	€8	2 weekly
Patmos	Agios Georgios	2hr	€7	4 weekly
Rhodes*	Agios Georgios	5hr	€46	1 weekly
Samos	Agios Georgios	1hr	€5	4 weekly

*high-speed services

ISLAND HOPPING

Agios Efstratios

Northeastern Aegean Islands; see also p393

BOAT SERVICES FROM AGIOS EFSTRATIOS

Destination	Port	Duration	Fare	Frequency
Chios (Mesta)	Agios Efstratios	3½hr	€35	1 weekly
Kavala	Agios Efstratios	8hr	€19	3 weekly
Lavrio	Agios Efstratios	8½hr	€24-50	3 weekly
Lesvos (Sigri)	Agios Efstratios	3hr	€9	1 weekly
Limnos	Agios Efstratios	8½hr	€6-13	4 weekly
Psara	Agios Efstratios	3hr	€35	1 weekly

Agios Konstantinos

Central Greece (mainland port); see also p103

BOAT SERVICES FROM AGIOS KONSTANTINOS

Destination	Port	Duration	Fare	Frequency
Alonnisos*	Agios Konstantinos	3½-3¾hr	€44	1 daily
Alonnisos**	Agios Konstantinos	3hr	€44	1-2 daily
Skiathos*	Agios Konstantinos	2hr	€33	1 daily
Skiathos**	Agios Konstantinos	2hr	€33	2-3 daily
Skopelos*	Agios Konstantinos	3hr	€44	1 daily
Skopelos**	Agios Konstantinos	2½hr	€44	1-2 Mon-Fri, 2-3 Sat & Sun

*fast-ferry services
**hydrofoil services

Alexandroupoli

Northern Greece (mainland port); see also p108

AIR

Alexandroupoli's airport serves only Sitia Airport in Crete directly. Check with local travel agents or on the websites of Greek air carriers for the cumulative fares of flights from Alexandroupoli to other islands via Athens.

DOMESTIC FLIGHTS FROM ALEXANDROUPOLI

Destination	Airport	Duration	Fare	Frequency
Crete (Sitia)	Alexandroupoli	1½hr	€100	3 weekly

BOAT

Alexandroupoli is the major ferry port for Samothraki; at the time of research, the time-honoured onward service to Rhodes via the Northeast Aegean Islands and other islands in the Dodecanese had been inexplicably terminated, though it may again resume (double-check in advance). Summer hydro-foils usually serve Samothraki, but are unpredictable; check locally.

BOAT SERVICES FROM ALEXANDROUPOLI

Destination	Port	Duration	Fare	Frequency
Samothraki	Alexandroupoli	2hr	€13	2 daily

Alonnisos

Evia & the Sporades; see also p421

BOAT SERVICES FROM ALONNISOS

Destination	Port	Duration	Fare	Frequency
Agios Konstantinos*	Alonnisos	3½hr	€44	1 daily
Agios Konstantinos**	Alonnisos	4hr	€44	1 daily
Skopelos (Glossa)*	Alonnisos	1hr	€13	3 daily
Skiathos	Alonnisos	2hr	€10	4 weekly
Skiathos*	Alonnisos	1½hr	€16	3 daily
Skopelos	Alonnisos	30min	€5	4 weekly
Skopelos*	Alonnisos	20min	€9	3 daily
Volos	Alonnisos	4½hr	€23	2 weekly
Volos*	Alonnisos	3hr	€38.50	2 daily

*hydrofoil services
**fast-ferry services

Amorgos

Cyclades; see also p182

BOAT SERVICES FROM AMORGOS

Destination	Port	Duration	Fare	Frequency
Aegiali	Katapola	50min	€4.50	1-2 daily
Donousa	Katapola	2hr 20min	€6.50	1-2 daily
Folegandros*	Katapola	3hr 5min	€35	1 daily
Ios	Katapola	5hr 20min	€11.50	1 weekly
Iraklia	Katapola	1¾hr-5hr	€8.50-10.50	2-3 daily
Kos	Katapola	5hr	€22.50	2 weekly
Leros	Katapola	3hr 10min	€18	2 weekly
Milos*	Katapola	4¼hr	€39	1 daily
Naxos	Katapola	1-4hr	€7.50	1-3 daily
Paros	Katapola	3-7hr	€12.20-15	1-2 daily
Patmos	Katapola	2hr	€18	2 weekly
Piraeus	Katapola	9hr	€30	4 weekly
Piraeus*	Katapola	7hr 25min	€58	1 daily
Rhodes	Katapola	10hr	€25.50	2 weekly
Schinousa	Katapola	1hr 40min	€8-10.50	2-3 daily
Santorini (Thira)*	Katapola	1½hr	€32	1 daily
Syros	Katapola	5¼hr	€29.80	4 weekly

*high-speed services

Anafi

Cyclades; see also p201

BOAT SERVICES FROM ANAFI

Destination	Port	Duration	Fare	Frequency
Folegandros	Anafi	5hr	€21	5 weekly
Ios	Anafi	3hr	€8.80	5 weekly
Karpathos	Anafi	6hr	€16.30	5 weekly
Kea	Anafi	16hr 40min	€46.80	2 weekly
Kythnos	Anafi	15hr	€43.90	2 weekly
Naxos	Anafi	7hr 25min	€14.30	5 weekly
Paros	Anafi	7hr 25min	€17.90	3-4 weekly
Piraeus	Anafi	11hr 20min-13½hr	€29.60	3 weekly
Rhodes	Anafi	11hr 40min	€22.20	5 weekly
Santorini (Thira)	Anafi	1hr	€8	5 weekly
Sikinos	Anafi	4hr	€19.60	4 weekly
Syros	Anafi	9hr 10min	€36.30	4 weekly

Andros

Cyclades; see also p136

BOAT SERVICES FROM ANDROS

Destination	Port	Duration	Fare	Frequency
Kea	Gavrio	5hr 50min	€17.20	1 weekly
Kythnos	Gavrio	4hr 20min	€25.20	1 weekly
Mykonos	Gavrio	1¼hr	€10-13	4 daily
Naxos	Gavrio	4hr 10min	€15.70	2 weekly
Rafina	Gavrio	2½hr	€12-14	4-8 daily
Syros	Gavrio	2hr 20min	€16	7 daily
Tinos	Gavrio	1hr 35min	€8-11	4 daily

Angistri

Saronic Gulf Islands; see also p123

BOAT SERVICES FROM ANGISTRI

Destination	Port	Duration	Fare	Frequency
Aegina*	Skala	10min	€6	6 daily
Piraeus*	Skala	55min	€15	6 daily
Piraeus	Skala	1½hr	€10	1-2 daily

*high-speed services

Arki & Marathi

Dodecanese; see also p345

The F/B *Nissos Kalymnos* calls in up to four times weekly as it shuttles between Patmos and Samos on its vital milk run. The Lipsi-based, speedy *Anna Express* links Arki with Lipsi (15 minutes) twice weekly. In summer, Lipsi-based excursion boats and Patmos-based caïques do frequent day trips (return €20) to Arki and Marathi. A local caïque runs between Marathi and Arki (1¼ hours).

BOAT SERVICES FROM ARKI & MARATHI

Destination	Port	Duration	Frequency
Arki	Marathi	1¼hr	
Lipsi	Arki	15min	2 weekly
Patmos	Arki/Marathi		4 weekly
Samos	Arki/Marathi		4 weekly

Astakos

Central Greece (mainland port); see Getting There & Away under Kefallonia p455

BOAT SERVICES FROM ASTAKOS

Destination	Port	Duration	Fare	Frequency
Ithaki (Piso Aetos)	Astakos	2¼hr	€10	2 daily
Kefallonia (Sami)	Astakos	3hr	€8	1 daily

Astypalea

Dodecanese; see also p325

AIR

Olympic has three flights per week to Leros (€41, 20 minutes), Kos (€47, one hour) and Rhodes (€47, 1½ hours).

BOAT SERVICES FROM ASTYPALEA

Destination	Port	Duration	Fare	Frequency
Kalymnos	Agios Andreas	2½hr	€11	4 weekly
Kalymnos	Skala	2¾hr	€12	3 weekly
Kos	Agios Andreas	3½hr	€15	1 weekly
Naxos	Agios Andreas	3½hr	€23	4 weekly
Paros	Agios Andreas	5hr	€29	4 weekly
Piraeus	Agios Andreas	10hr	€34	4 weekly
Rhodes	Agios Andreas	9hr	€29	1 weekly

Athens

Mainland port; see also p88

AIR

Olympic Air has flights to all islands with airports, and the more popular islands are also serviced by Aegean Airlines and Athens Airways.

Aegean Airlines has eight flights daily to Rhodes, seven flights daily to Iraklio, six to Santorini (Thira), five daily to Hania, three to Lesvos (Mytilini) and Mykonos, at least two daily to Corfu and Kos and at least one daily to Chios, Kefallonia, Samos and Limnos.

ISLAND HOPPING

Athens Airways has flights to Hania, Chios, Iraklio, Kefallonia, Lesvos, Mykonos, Rhodes and Santorini.

The following table indicates starting prices (including tax).

DOMESTIC FLIGHTS FROM ATHENS

Destination	Duration	Fare	Frequency
Alexandroupoli	65min	€77	14 weekly
Astypalea	1hr	€54	5 weekly
Chios	50min	€77	20 weekly
Corfu	1hr	€77	14 weekly
Crete (Hania)	50min	€77	30 weekly
Crete (Iraklio)	50min	€77	40 weekly
Crete (Sitia)	1hr 10min	€89	4 weekly
Ikaria	55min	€60	6 weekly
Kavala	1hr	€77	13 weekly
Kefallonia	65min	€111	13 weekly
Kos	55min	€89	14 weekly
Kythira	45min	€65	7 weekly
Leros	1hr	€68	7 weekly
Lesvos (Mytilini)	50min	€89	27 weekly
Limnos	55min	€77	14 weekly
Milos	45min	€50	10 weekly
Mykonos	40min	€77	27 weekly
Naxos	45min	€80	8 weekly
Paros	40min	€79	16 weekly
Preveza	1hr	€95	3 weekly
Rhodes	1hr	€77	35 weekly
Samos	1hr	€77	27 weekly
Santorini (Thira)	50min	€77	35 weekly
Skiathos	50min	€71	7 weekly
Skyros	35min	€43	3 weekly
Syros	35min	€95	2 weekly
Thessaloniki	55min	€77	58 weekly
Zakynthos	1hr	€95	11 weekly

BOAT

Athens' main port, Piraeus, is the departure point for an overwhelming number of island destinations. The smaller east coast ports of Rafina and Lavrio service the Cyclades and Evia. See also p88.

BOAT SERVICES FROM ATHENS

to Crete

Destination	Port	Duration	Fare	Frequency
Agios Nikolaos	Piraeus	12hr	€30	2 weekly
Iraklio	Piraeus	6½hr	€33.50	3 weekly
Iraklio	Piraeus	8hr	€36-37	2 daily
Rethymno	Piraeus	10hr	€30	2 daily
Rethymno*	Piraeus	6hr	€57	1 daily
Sitia	Piraeus	14½hr	€32.10	2 weekly
Souda (Hania)	Piraeus	8½hr	€30	2 daily
Souda (Hania)*	Piraeus	4½hr	€55	1 daily

*high-speed services

to the Cyclades

Destination	Port	Duration	Fare	Frequency
Amorgos	Piraeus	9hr	€30	4 weekly
Amorgos*	Piraeus	7hr 25min	€58	1 daily
Anafi	Piraeus	11hr 20min	€29.60	3 weekly
Andros	Rafina	2hr	€12-14	4 daily
Donousa	Piraeus	7hr 10min	€30	4 weekly
Folegandros	Piraeus	3hr	€30.50	4 weekly
Folegandros*	Piraeus	4hr	€55	1-3 daily
Ios	Piraeus	7hr	€31.50	4-5 daily
Ios*	Piraeus	5½hr	€46	3 daily
Iraklia	Piraeus	7hr 20min	€30	1-2 daily
Kea (Tzia)	Lavrio	50min	€12.70	3-5 daily
Kimolos	Piraeus	9hr 20min	€24.50	5 weekly
Kimolos*	Piraeus	5¼hr	€48	3 weekly
Koufonisia	Piraeus	8hr	€30	1-2 daily
Koufonisia*	Piraeus	7hr	€58	1 daily
Kythnos	Piraeus	3hr 10min	€18	1-2 daily
Milos	Piraeus	8hr	€30.50	1-2 daily
Milos*	Piraeus	2hr 50min–3hr 55min	€49	2-3 daily
Mykonos	Piraeus	4¾hr	€30.50-39.50	2 daily
Mykonos*	Piraeus	3hr	€43	3 daily
Mykonos	Rafina	4½hr	€23	2-3 daily
Mykonos*	Rafina	2hr 10min	€41	4-5 daily
Naxos	Piraeus	4¾hr	€30	4-5 daily
Naxos*	Piraeus	3½hr	€45	3 daily
Naxos*	Rafina	3hr	€43	1 daily
Paros	Piraeus	5hr	€29-31	4 daily
Paros*	Piraeus	2½hr	€39.50	6 daily
Paros*	Rafina	2½hr	€49.50	1 daily
Santorini (Thira)	Piraeus	9hr	€33.50	4-5 daily
Santorini (Thira)*	Piraeus	5¼hr	€47-65	3 daily
Santorini (Thira)*	Rafina	4¾hr	€49	1 daily
Schinousa	Piraeus	7½hr	€30	1-2 daily
Serifos	Piraeus	5hr	€22.50	2 daily
Serifos*	Piraeus	2¼hr	€40	2 daily
Sifnos	Piraeus	5¼hr	€28	5 daily
Sifnos*	Piraeus	2hr 25min	€44	3 daily
Sikinos	Piraeus	12hr	€29.60	4 weekly
Syros	Piraeus	4hr	€26-29	4 daily
Syros*	Piraeus	2½hr	€44.50	3 daily
Syros*	Rafina	2hr 50min	€45	2 weekly
Tinos	Piraeus	4¾hr	€28	1 daily
Tinos	Rafina	4hr	€19	4 daily
Tinos*	Piraeus	3¾hr	€44	3 daily
Tinos*	Rafina	2hr	€40	4-5 daily

*high-speed services

to the Dodecanese

Destination	Port	Duration	Fare	Frequency
Astypalea	Piraeus	10hr	€34	4 weekly
Kalymnos	Piraeus	13hr	€44	3 weekly
Karpathos	Piraeus	17hr	€58	2 weekly
Kasos	Piraeus	19hr	€35	3 weekly
Kos	Piraeus	10hr	€46	4 weekly
Leros	Piraeus	8hr	€35	1 daily

ISLAND HOPPING

Lipsi	Piraeus	12hr	€42	2 weekly
Nisyros	Piraeus	18hr	€46	3 weekly
Patmos	Piraeus	7hr	€34	4 weekly
Rhodes	Piraeus	13hr	€53	1 daily
Symi*	Piraeus	15hr	€64	2 weekly
Tilos	Piraeus	19hr	€46	2 weekly

*via Rhodes

to Evia

Destination	Port	Duration	Fare	Frequency
Evia (Marmari)	Rafina	1hr	€7	4-6 daily

to the northeastern Aegean Islands

Destination	Port	Duration	Fare	Frequency
Chios	Piraeus*	6-9hr	€25-33	2 daily
Fourni	Piraeus	10hr	€30	2 weekly
Ikaria (Agios Kirykos)	Piraeus	10½hr	€35	3 weekly
Ikaria (Agios Kirykos)	Piraeus*	4¼hr	€52	2 weekly
Lesvos (Mytilini Town)	Piraeus	8½-13hr	€27-37	2 daily
Limnos	Lavrio	9½-14hr	€28.60	3 weekly
Limnos	Piraeus	21hr	€30.50	1 weekly
Samos (Vathy)	Piraeus	7-13hr	€41	1-2 daily

*high-speed services

to the Saronic Gulf Islands

Destination	Port	Duration	Fare	Frequency
Aegina	Piraeus	1hr	€8	hourly
Aegina*	Piraeus	40min	€14	hourly
Angistri*	Piraeus	55min	€15	6 daily
Angistri	Piraeus	1½hr	€10	1-2 daily
Hydra*	Piraeus	50min-1½hr	€28.40	10 daily
Poros	Piraeus	2¼hr	€13.30	4 daily
Poros*	Piraeus	1hr	€25.20	4-6 daily
Spetses*	Piraeus	2hr 10min	€39	7 daily

*high-speed services

to the Peloponnese

Destination	Port	Duration	Fare	Frequency
Ermioni*	Piraeus	2hr	€30	4 daily
Kythira	Piraeus	6½hr	€23	2 weekly
Methana	Piraeus	2hr	€12	1-3 daily
Porto Heli*	Piraeus	2hr	€29.50	4 daily

*high-speed services

Chios

Northeastern Aegean Islands; see also p367

DOMESTIC FLIGHTS FROM CHIOS

Destination	Airport	Duration	Fare	Frequency
Athens	Chios	45min	€90	7 weekly
Thessaloniki	Chios	50min	€80	5 weekly

BOAT SERVICES FROM CHIOS

Destination	Port	Duration	Fare	Frequency
Agios Efstratios	Mesta	4¼hr	€35	1 weekly
Inousses	Chios	1-1¼hr	€4-10	1 daily
Kalymnos	Chios	6¾hr	€21	1 weekly
Kos	Chios	8hr	€22	1 weekly
Lavrio	Mesta	4hr	€50	1 weekly
Lesvos (Mytilini Town)	Chios	3hr	€13-19	2 daily
Lesvos (Sigri)	Chios	3hr	€15	1 weekly
Limnos	Chios	10-12hr	€22	4 weekly
Limnos	Mesta	5hr	€40	1 weekly
Mykonos	Chios	3hr	€28.50	2 weekly
Piraeus	Chios	6-9hr	€25-33	2 daily
Psara	Chios	3½hr	€10.70	1 daily
Psara	Mesta	45min	€6-13	2 weekly
Rhodes	Chios	12hr	€34	1 weekly
Samos (Karlovasi)	Chios	2½hr	€11	2 weekly
Samos (Vathy)	Chios	3½hr	€12	2 weekly
Syros	Chios	3½hr	€30.50	5 weekly
Thessaloniki	Chios	13-20hr	€37	3 weekly

Corfu

Ionian Islands; see also p435

DOMESTIC FLIGHTS FROM CORFU

Destination	Airport	Duration	Fare	Frequency
Athens	Corfu	1hr	€60	2 daily
Kefallonia	Corfu	1hr 20min	€39	3 weekly
Preveza	Corfu	30min	€39	3 weekly
Thessaloniki	Corfu	55min	€69	3 weekly

BOAT SERVICES FROM CORFU

Destination	Port	Duration	Fare	Frequency
Igoumenitsa	Corfu	1¼hr	€7	hourly
Igoumenitsa	Lefkimmi	1hr 10min	€5.60	6 daily
Patra	Corfu	6½hr	€30	2 weekly
Paxi	Corfu	3½hr	from €8.50	3 weekly
Paxi*	Corfu	40min	€16.40	1-3 daily
Zakynthos	Corfu	8¾hr	€32	1 weekly

*high-speed services

Crete

See also p222

AIR

Nikos Kazantzakis Airport in Iraklio receives the bulk of Crete's national and international flights, though Hania is also busy. Sitia has been pegged for expansion, but remains much less used. For this reason, air tickets are sometimes cheaper from mainland Greece to Sitia, though you will want to factor in the cost of ongoing ground transport, logistics and time that will accrue if you are not planning on staying in this remote area.

To reach Crete by air from other Greek islands usually requires changing in Athens, except for some flights operated by newcomer Sky Express; the direct flight offers between Crete and other islands in the tables here are all offered by Sky Express. However, all travel agents and the online booking websites of the other individual airlines can provide actual cumulative prices that involve flying via Athens. Note, cheaper Sky Express flights restrict baggage to 12.5kg. In the high season, it's best to book somewhat in advance, as Crete is a very popular destination and tickets may sell out quickly for the dates you wish to travel.

Remarkably, international direct flights to Crete are sometimes cheaper than flying to the island from elsewhere in Greece, even from Greek carriers. Aegean Airlines has direct scheduled flights from Iraklio to Milan, Rome and other European cities, while Olympic serves even more airports abroad.

If coming from a Western European country, it may be possible to score a cheap seat on a charter flight operating for package tourists – without actually having to buy the rest of the package (accommodation, food etc). However, you'll have to check with a travel agency in such a country to see if it's feasible.

European budget airlines are also starting to serve Crete in summer months.

DOMESTIC FLIGHTS FROM CRETE

Destination	Port	Duration	Fare	Frequency
Alexandroupoli	Sitia	1½hr	€100	3 weekly
Araxos (Patra)	Iraklio	1hr	€127	2 weekly
Athens	Hania	1hr	€100	1 daily
Athens	Iraklio	1hr	€110	2 daily
Ikaria	Iraklio	55min	€127	2 weekly
Kalamata	Iraklio	1hr	€100	3 weekly
Kos	Iraklio	35min	€110	4 weekly
Lesvos (Mytilini)	Iraklio	50min	€110	2 weekly
Mykonos	Iraklio	30min	€80	12 weekly
Rhodes	Iraklio	45min	€110	11 weekly
Samos	Iraklio	50min	€110	2 weekly
Thessaloniki	Hania	1½hr	€120	1 daily
Thessaloniki	Iraklio	1½hr	€130	2 daily

BOAT

While ferry schedules to and from Crete tend to stay more stable than with other islands, you should always check ahead as routes and prices may change without much notice. Since Crete is such a large island, many visitors choose to drive while here; prices for bringing a car from Athens start at around €90.

Crete's major ferry ports are on the north coast. Iraklio is the major one, followed by Souda (for Hania), Rethymno and Sitia in the east. The small western port of Kissamos

(Kastelli) exists exclusively to service Gythio in the Peloponnese and the nearby island of Kythira. Crete also has several southern ports. From Paleohora and Hora Sfakion, it's possible to visit the most southerly point in Europe, Gavdos, two hours south in the Libyan Sea. There's also an important ferry route that hugs the coast between Paleohora and Hora Sfakion – otherwise separated by impassable mountains – making stops along the way at Sougia, Agia Roumeli and Loutro. Finally, numerous minor excursion boats and boat taxis run by local travel agencies and even fishing folk serve small coastal towns and satellite islands such as Paximadia and Gaidouronisi (Hrysi) in the south and Spinalonga in the north.

Information given here pertains only to north-coast ports. For schedules, prices and other information involving the south-coast ports and local excursion boats, see the relevant sections of the Crete chapter (see pp219–72).

BOAT SERVICES FROM CRETE

Destination	Port	Duration	Fare	Frequency
Gythio	Kissamos	7hr	€23	5 weekly
Ios	Iraklio	5¼hr	€42	2 weekly
Karpathos	Iraklio	7½hr	€19.60	2 weekly
Kasos	Iraklio	6¼hr	€17.90	2 weekly
Kythira	Kissamos	4hr	€17	5 weekly
Kythira	Rethymno	6hr	€20	1 weekly
Mykonos	Iraklio	6¾hr	€66.50	2 weekly
Paros	Iraklio	6hr	€65	2 weekly
Piraeus	Agios Nikolaos	12hr	€30	2 weekly
Piraeus	Iraklio	6½hr	€33.50	3 weekly
Piraeus	Iraklio	8hr	€36-37	2 daily
Piraeus	Rethymno	10hr	€30	2 daily
Piraeus*	Rethymno	6hr	€57	1 daily
Piraeus	Sitia	14½hr	€32.10	2 weekly
Piraeus	Souda (Hania)	8½hr	€30	2 daily
Piraeus*	Souda (Hania)	4½hr	€55	1 daily
Rhodes	Agios Nikolaos	12hr	€26.40	2 weekly
Rhodes	Iraklio	12hr	€27.50	2 weekly
Rhodes	Sitia	10hr	€26.40	2 weekly
Santorini (Thira)	Iraklio	4½hr	€16.30	4 weekly
Santorini (Thira)*	Iraklio	1¾hr	€41	1 daily
Santorini (Thira)	Rethymno	2hr 20min	€46	3 weekly

*high-speed services

Donousa

Cyclades; see also p180

BOAT SERVICES FROM DONOUSA

Destination	Port	Duration	Fare	Frequency
Amorgos	Donousa	2hr 20min	€6.50	1-2 daily
Iraklia	Donousa	2hr 20min-4hr	€7.50-14.40	1-2 daily
Naxos	Donousa	3hr-3hr 50min	€11.50-14	2-3 daily

Paros	Donousa	2½hr	€10.30-12.50	1-3 daily
Piraeus	Donousa	7hr 10min	€30	4 weekly
Schinousa	Donousa	2hr	€7.50-	1-2 daily
Syros	Donousa	4hr 20min	€15	4 weekly

Evia
Evia & the Sporades; see also p406

BOAT SERVICES FROM EVIA

Destination	Port	Duration	Fare	Frequency
Agia Marina	Evia (Nea Styra)	45min	€3.50	6-8 daily
Arkitsa	Evia (Loutra Edipsou)	40min	€3.30	10-12 daily
Glyfa	Evia (Agiokambos)	20min	€2	8-12 daily
Rafina	Evia (Marmari)	1hr	€7	4-6 daily
Skala Oropou	Evia (Eretria)	25min	€1.40	hourly
Skyros	Evia (Paralia Kymis)	1¾hr	€9	1-2 daily

Folegandros
Cyclades; see also p203

BOAT SERVICES FROM FOLEGANDROS

Destination	Port	Duration	Fare	Frequency
Amorgos*	Folegandros	3hr 20min	€35.50	1 daily
Anafi	Folegandros	4¾hr	€21.20	5 weekly
Ios	Folegandros	1hr 20min	€11.50	1-2 daily
Kea	Folegandros	11hr 25min	€38.20	2 weekly
Kimolos	Folegandros	1½hr	€7	5 weekly
Koufonisia*	Folegandros	3hr	€35	1 daily
Kythnos	Folegandros	7hr 25min	€16	2 weekly
Milos	Folegandros	2½hr	€8	5 weekly
Milos*	Folegandros	1¼hr	€16	4 weekly
Naxos	Folegandros	5hr 35min	€33.20	4 weekly
Paros	Folegandros	4-6hr	€15-16.70	5 weekly
Piraeus	Folegandros	13hr	€30.50	4 weekly
Piraeus*	Folegandros	4hr	€55	1-3 daily
Santorini (Thira)	Folegandros	2½hr	€7.50	1-3 daily
Santorini (Thira)*	Folegandros	30min	€19	1 daily
Serifos	Folegandros	7hr 40min	€16	5 weekly
Serifos*	Folegandros	1¾hr	€23	4 weekly
Sifnos	Folegandros	4½hr	€13.50	1-3 daily
Sifnos*	Folegandros	1hr	€18	4 weekly
Sikinos	Folegandros	40min	€5.50	1-3 daily
Syros	Folegandros	5hr	€23.90	4 weekly

*high-speed services

Fourni Islands
Northeastern Aegean Islands; see also p349

BOAT SERVICES FROM FOURNI

Destination	Port	Duration	Fare	Frequency
Ikaria (Agios Kirykos)	Fourni	1½hr	€5	1-3 daily
Piraeus	Fourni	10hr	€30	2 weekly
Samos (Karlovasi)	Fourni	1-3hr	€5	1-3 daily
Samos (Vathy)	Fourni	3-5hr	€8	1-2 daily*

*except Fridays

Halki
Dodecanese; see also p292

Two local ferries, the *Nissos Halki* and *Nikos Express*, run daily between Halki and Skala Kamirou on Rhodes (€10, 30 minutes).

BOAT SERVICES FROM HALKI

Destination	Port	Duration	Fare	Frequency
Karpathos	Emborios	3hr	€12	4 weekly
Piraeus	Emborios	19hr	€63	2 weekly
Rhodes	Emborios	2hr	€10	4 weekly
Rhodes*	Emborios	1¼hr	€21	2 weekly
Santorini (Thira)	Emborios	15hr	€30	2 weekly

*high-speed services

Hydra
Saronic Gulf Islands; see also p126

BOAT SERVICES FROM HYDRA

Destination	Port	Duration	Fare	Frequency
Ermioni*	Hydra	50min	€9.50	7 daily
Piraeus*	Hydra	1½hr	€28.40	7 daily
Poros*	Hydra	1hr 50min	€12.50	7 daily
Porto Heli*	Hydra	50min	€11.50	7 daily
Spetses*	Hydra	1hr	€14.50	7 daily

*high-speed services

Igoumenitsa
Northern Greece (mainland port); see also p102

BOAT

Igoumenitsa is a major port for ferries to Italy, and also has frequent boats to the Ionian islands of Corfu and Paxi, as well as Athens' port of Piraeus. Boats generally leave mornings and evenings. Hydrofoils to/from Corfu and Paxi usually run in summer; check locally.

BOAT SERVICES FROM IGOUMENITSA

Destination	Port	Duration	Fare	Frequency
Corfu	Igoumenitsa	1- 2¼hr	€7-9	15-20 daily
Patra	Igoumenitsa	5-7¾hr	from €33	2-6 daily
Paxi	Igoumenitsa	3¾hr	€8	1-2 daily
Sami	Igoumenitsa	4¾hr	€50	5 weekly

Ikaria
Northeastern Aegean Islands, p349

DOMESTIC FLIGHTS FROM IKARIA

Destination	Airport	Duration	Fare	Frequency
Athens	Ikaria	45min	€80	1 daily
Crete (Iraklio)	Ikaria	55min	€127	2 weekly

BOAT SERVICES FROM IKARIA

Destination	Port	Duration	Fare	Frequency
Chios	Agios Kirykos	4½hr	€13	1 weekly
Fourni	Agios Kirykos	1½hr	€5	1-3 daily
Kavala**	Agios Kirykos	21½hr	€37	1 weekly
Lesvos (Mytilini Town)	Agios Kirykos	8hr	€21	1 weekly
Limnos	Agios Kirykos	13¾hr	€30	1 weekly
Mykonos	Agios Kirykos	3½hr	€15	3 weekly
Piraeus	Agios Kirykos	10½hr	€35	3 weekly
Piraeus**	Agios Kirykos	4¼hr	€52	2 weekly
Samos (Karlovasi)	Agios Kirykos	2-3½hr	€13	1-2 daily*
Samos (Vathy)	Agios Kirykos	3½hr	€12	1-2 daily*

*except Friday
**high-speed services

Inousses
Northeastern Aegean Islands; see also p375

BOAT SERVICES FROM INOUSSES

Destination	Port	Duration	Fare	Frequency
Chios	Inousses	1¼hr	€4-10	1 daily

Ios
Cyclades; see also p185

BOAT SERVICES FROM IOS

Destination	Port	Duration	Fare	Frequency
Amorgos	Ios	50min	€4.50	1-2 daily
Anafi	Ios	3hr	€8.80	5 weekly
Folegandros	Ios	1hr 20min	€11.50	1-2 daily
Iraklio*	Ios	2½hr	€58	1 daily
Kera	Ios	10hr 40min	€40.40	2 weekly
Kimolos	Ios	2½hr	€20.80	5-6 weekly
Kythnos	Ios	8½hr	€16	2 weekly
Lavrio	Ios	11hr 35min	€43.30	2 weekly
Milos	Ios	3½hr	€29.50	5-6 weekly
Naxos	Ios	1hr 35min	€9.90-18.10	1-3 daily
Naxos*	Ios	50min	20.50	1-2 daily
Paros	Ios	2½-3hr 10min	€11	2 daily
Paros*	Ios	1hr	€27	1-2 daily
Piraeus	Ios	7hr	€31.50	4-5 daily
Piraeus*	Ios	5½hr	€46	3 daily
Santorini (Thira)	Ios	1¼hr	€8	5 daily
Santorini (Thira)*	Ios	40-50min	€18	3 daily
Serifos	Ios	7hr 10min	€16	4 weekly
Sifnos	Ios	6hr	€13.50	4 weekly
Sikinos	Ios	20min	€8	1-4 daily
Sikinos*	Ios	10min	€12	1 weekly
Syros	Ios	5hr 35min	€30.80	4 weekly

*high-speed services

Iraklia
Cyclades; see also p177

BOAT SERVICES FROM IRAKLIA

Destination	Port	Duration	Fare	Frequency
Amorgos	Iraklia	1¾-4hr 40min	€8.50-10.50	2-3 daily
Donousa	Iraklia	2hr 20min-4hr	€7.50-14.40	1-2 daily
Koufonisia	Iraklia	1hr	€5	2-3 daily
Naxos	Iraklia	1hr	€6.50	2-3 daily
Paros	Iraklia	2¼hr	€12.50	1-2 daily
Piraeus	Iraklia	7hr 20min	€30	1-2 daily
Schinousa	Iraklia	15min	€4.50	2-3 daily
Syros	Iraklia	3hr 35min	€22.70	4 weekly

Ithaki
Ionian Islands; see also p462

BOAT SERVICES FROM ITHAKI

Destination	Port	Duration	Fare	Frequency
Fiskardo	Frikes	55min	€3.80	1 daily
Kefallonia (Sami)	Vathy	45min	€5.60	2 daily
Kefallonia (Sami)	Piso Aetos	30min	€2.60	2 daily
Nydri	Frikes	1½hr	€7	1 daily
Patra	Piso Aetos	3hr 10min	€17.60	2 daily
Patra	Vathy	3¾hr	€17.60	2 daily

Kalymnos
Dodecanese; see also p327

AIR
Olympic has daily flights to Athens (€65, 20 minutes).

BOAT
Small, local car and passenger ferries leave three times daily from Pothia to Mastihari on Kos. The fast Lipsi-based *Anna Express* links Pothia with Leros and Lipsi three times weekly. There's also a daily caïque from Myrties to Xirokambos (€8) on Leros and Emborios (€8) in the north of Kalymnos. A caïque runs between Myrties and Telendos Islet (€2) throughout the day.

BOAT SERVICES FROM KALYMNOS

Destination	Port	Duration	Fare	Frequency
Astypalea	Pothia	3½hr	€11	3 weekly
Kos	Pothia	50min	€4	3 daily
Kos*	Pothia	35min	€15	1 daily
Leros	Pothia	1½hrs	€7	1 daily
Leros*	Pothia	50min	€20	1 daily
Lipsi*	Pothia	1hr 20min	€20	6 weekly
Patmos*	Pothia	1hr 40min	€26	6 weekly
Piraeus	Pothia	13hr	€44	3 weekly
Rhodes	Pothia	4½hr	€20	3 weekly

*high-speed services

Karpathos

Dodecanese; see also p294

AIR

Flights with Olympic Air head daily to Kasos (€21) and Sitia (€43), twice daily to Rhodes (€28) and three times per week to Athens (€69).

BOAT SERVICES FROM KARPATHOS

Destination	Port	Duration	Fare	Frequency
Halki	Diafani	2hr	€17	4 weekly
Kasos	Pigadia	1½hr	€15	2 weekly
Milos	Pigadia	16hr	€36	2 weekly
Piraeus	Pigadia	17hr	€58	2 weekly
Rhodes	Pigadia	5hr	€22	3 weekly
Santorini (Thira)	Pigadia	11hr	€25	2 weekly
Sitia	Pigadia	4hr	€18	2 weekly

Kasos

Dodecanese; see also p301

AIR

Olympic offers daily flights to Karpathos (€21, 10 minutes) and Sitia (€38, 40 minutes) and five flights per week to Rhodes (€34, one hour).

BOAT SERVICES FROM KASOS

Destination	Port	Duration	Fare	Frequency
Karpathos	Fry	1½hr	€15	2 weekly
Piraeus	Fry	19hr	€35	3 weekly
Rhodes	Fry	7hr	€24	3 weekly
Sitia	Fry	2½hr	€12	3 weekly

Kastellorizo (Megisti)

Dodecanese; see also p304

AIR

Olympic has three flights per week to Rhodes (€22, 20 minutes) from where you can get connections to Athens.

BOAT SERVICES FROM KASTELLORIZO (MEGISTI)

Destination	Port	Duration	Fare	Frequency
Piraeus	Kastellorizo	23hr	€53	1 weekly
Rhodes	Kastellorizo	4hr 40min	€17	2 weekly
Rhodes*	Kastellorizo	2½hr	€25	1 weekly

*high-speed services

Kavala/Keramoti

Northern Greece (mainland port); see also p105

AIR

From Kavala's Alexander the Great Airport, all island flights go via Thessaloniki or Athens. For cumulative fares involving these routes, check locally or with the websites of Greek air carriers.

BOAT

Kavala is one of two ports serving Thasos, and in summer has frequent ferries and hydrofoils to the island's ports of Skala Prinou and Limenas. It's also a ferry hub for the Northeast Aegean Islands. Thasos (Limenas) also has frequent connections during summer from Keramoti, 46km east of Kavala and closer to the mainland airport.

BOAT SERVICES FROM KAVALA/KERAMOTI

Destination	Port	Duration	Fare	Frequency
Agios Efstratios	Kavala	7½hr	€19	3 weekly
Chios (Chios Town)	Kavala	15hr	€31	2 weekly
Ikaria (Agios Kirykos)	Kavala	20¾hr	€37	1 weekly
Lavrio	Kavala	15½-19hr	€39	3 weekly
Lesvos (Mytilini Town)	Kavala	11hr	€26	2 weekly
Lesvos (Sigri)	Kavala	11hr	€26	1 weekly
Limnos	Kavala	5½hr	€15	5 weekly
Samos (Karlovasi)	Kavala	19hr	€37	1 weekly
Samos (Vathy)	Kavala	19hr	€37	1 weekly
Thasos (Limenas)	Keramoti	40min	€3.30	hourly
Thasos (Limenas)*	Kavala	40min	€10	4 daily
Thasos (Skala Prinou)	Kavala	1¼hr	€3.50	hourly
Thasos (Skala Prinou)*	Kavala	40min	€10	4 daily

*high-speed services

Kea (Tzia)

Cyclades; see also p217

BOAT SERVICES FROM KEA (TZIA)

Destination	Port	Duration	Fare	Frequency
Andros	Kea	5hr 50min	€17.20	1 weekly
Folegandros	Kea	7hr 40min	€16	5 weekly
Ios	Kea		€10.40-40.40	2 weekly
Kimolos	Kea	13½hr	€32	2 weekly
Kythnos	Kea	1hr	€12.80	7 weekly
Lavrio	Kea	50min	€12.70	3-5 daily
Milos	Kea	14½hr	€25.20	2 weekly
Paros	Kea	7hr 50min	€31.20	2 weekly
Naxos	Kea	8¾hr	€31.20	2 weekly
Sikinos	Kea	11hr 10min	€41.40	2 weekly
Syros	Kea	2hr 50min	€20.40	4 weekly
Tinos	Kea	4hr	€22.20	4 weekly

Kefallonia

Ionian Islands; see also p455

DOMESTIC FLIGHTS FROM KEFALLONIA

Destination	Airport	Duration	Fare	Frequency
Athens	Kefallonia	55min	€71	2 daily
Preveza	Kefallonia	30min	€34	3 weekly
Zakynthos	Kefallonia	20min	€32	3 weekly

BOAT SERVICES FROM KEFALLONIA

Destination	Port	Duration	Fare	Frequency
Astakos	Sami	3hr	€10	1 daily
Igoumenitsa	Sami	4¼hr	€13	1 weekly
Ithaki (Frikes)	Fiskardo	55min	€3.80	1 daily
Ithaki (Piso Aetos)	Sami	30min	€2.80	2 daily
Ithaki (Vathy)	Sami	45min	€5.60	2 daily
Kyllini	Argostoli	3hr	€14	1 daily
Lefkada (Vasiliki)	Fiskardo	1hr	€6.90	1 daily
Patra	Sami	2¾hr	€16.90	2 daily
Poros	Kyllini	1½hr	€9.90	3-5 daily
Zakynthos (Agios Nikolaos)	Pesada	1½hr	€7	2 daily

Kimolos

Cyclades; see also p209

BOAT SERVICES FROM KIMOLOS

Destination	Port	Duration	Fare	Frequency
Folegandros*	Kimilos	1½hr	€7	5 weekly
Ios	Kimilos	2½hr	€20.80	5-6 daily
Kea	Kimilos	13½hr	€32	2 weekly
Kythnos	Kimilos	5hr 50min	€11	2 weekly
Milos	Kimilos	35min	€5.70-9.50	8 weekly
Naxos	Kimilos	4hr 35min	€25.60	2 weekly
Paros	Kimilos	3hr 20min	€20.80	2 weekly
Piraeus*	Kimilos	5¼hr	€48	3 weekly
Piraeus	Kimilos	9hr 20min	€24.50	5 weekly
Santorini (Thira)	Kimilos	3½hr	€7.20	2 weekly
Serifos	Kimilos	4hr 10min	€8.50	5 weekly
Sifnos	Kimilos	3hr	€6	5 weekly
Syros	Kimilos	5¼hr	€25.20	5 weekly

*high-speed services

Kos

Dodecanese; see also p318

AIR

Olympic Air has two daily flights to Athens (€44, 55 minutes) and three weekly to Rhodes (€41, 20 minutes), Leros (€41, 15 minutes) and Astypalea (€47, one hour).

BOAT SERVICES FROM KOS

Destination	Port	Duration	Fare	Frequency
Kalymnos	Mastihari	1hr	€4	3 daily
Kalymnos*	Kos Town	30min	€15	1 daily
Leros	Kos Town	1hr 40min	€22	1 daily
Nisyros	Kos Town	1hr 20min	€8	4 weekly
Nisyros*	Kos Town	45min	€16	2 weekly
Patmos	Kos Town	4hr	€13	2 weekly
Patmos*	Kos Town	2½hr	€29	6 weekly
Piraeus	Kos Town	10hr	€46	4 weekly
Rhodes	Kos Town	3hr	€26	1 daily
Rhodes*	Kos Town	2½hr	€30	1 daily
Samos	Kos Town	5½hr	€19	1 daily
Symi*	Kos Town	1½hr	€22	1 daily
Thessaloniki	Kos Town	21hr	€47	1 weekly

*high-speed services

Koufonisia

Cyclades; see also p179

BOAT SERVICES FROM KOUFONISIA

Destination	Port	Duration	Fare	Frequency
Amorgos	Koufonisia	1hr 5min-1hr 40min	€7.50	3 daily
Donousa	Koufonisia	1¼hr	€5.50	1-2 daily
Folegandros*	Koufonisia	3hr	€35	1 daily
Iraklia	Koufonisia	1hr	€5	2-3 daily
Milos*	Koufonisia	3hr 40min	€39	1 daily
Naxos	Koufonisia	2hr 20min	€7.50	1-2 daily
Paros	Koufonisia	4½hr	€15.50	1-2 daily
Piraeus	Koufonisia	8hr	€30	2-3 weekly
Piraeus*	Koufonisia	7hr	€58	1 daily
Schinousa	Koufonisia	40min	€4.50	2-3 daily
Syros	Koufonisia	4½hr	€12.70	4 weekly

*high-speed services

Kythira

Ionian Islands, see also p470

BOAT SERVICES FROM KYTHIRA

Destination	Port	Duration	Fare	Frequency
Gythio	Kythira	2½	€11	2 weekly
Kalamata	Kythira	4½	€17	1 weekly
Kissamos	Kythira	4hr	€17	3 weekly (2 via Antikythira)

Neapoli	Kythira (Diakofti)	1hr	€11	1 daily
Rethymno	Kythira	6hr	€20	1 weekly

Kythnos
Cyclades, p215

BOAT SERVICES FROM KYTHNOS

Destination	Port	Duration	Fare	Frequency
Folegandros	Kea	11hr 25min	€38.20	2 weekly
Ios	Kea	2½hr	€20.80	5-6 weekly
Kea	Kea	1hr	€12.80	7 weekly
Kimolos	Kea	8½hr	€16	2 weekly
Milos	Kea	3¼hr-4hr 25min	€16-18	1-2 daily
Paros	Kea	6hr 40min	€27.40	2 weekly
Piraeus	Kea	3hr 10min	€18	1-2 daily
Santorini (Thira)	Kea	8hr	€16	2 weekly
Serifos	Kea	1hr 20min	€15	1-2 daily
Sifnos	Kea	2½hr	€13.50	1-2 daily
Syros	Kea	2hr	€9.90	4 weekly

Lefkada
Ionian Islands; see also p450

DOMESTIC FLIGHTS FROM LEFKADA

Destination	Airport	Duration	Fare	Frequency
Athens	Preveza/ Lefkada	1hr	€97	2 daily
Corfu	Preveza/ Lefkada	25min	€39	3 weekly

BOAT SERVICES FROM LEFKADA

Destination	Port	Duration	Fare	Frequency
Fiskardo via Frikes	Nydri	2½hr	€6.90	1 daily
Fiskardo	Vasiliki	1hr	€6.90	1 daily
Frikes	Nydri	1½hr	€6.40	1 daily
Frikes	Vasiliki	2hr	€8	1 daily

Leros
Dodecanese; see also p333

AIR
Olympic flies from Leros to Athens (€55, one hour) six times each week, and to Rhodes (€47, two hours), Kos (€41, 20 minutes) and Astypalea (€41, 15 minutes) three times per week.

BOAT
The Lipsi-based **Anna Express** (☎ 22479 41215) departs from Agia Marina and links Leros with Kalymnos three times per week, calling at Arki once each week. The caïque *Katerina* leaves Xirokambos each morning for Myrties on Kalymnos (€7).

BOAT SERVICES FROM LEROS

Destination	Port	Duration	Fare	Frequency
Kalymnos*	Agia Marina	50min	€20	6 weekly
Kos	Lakki	3¼hr	€11	1 daily
Kos*	Agia Marina	1hr	€22	6 weekly
Lipsi*	Agia Marina	20min	€14	6 weekly
Patmos*	Agia Marina	45min	€16	6 weekly
Piraeus	Lakki	8hr	€35	1 daily
Rhodes	Lakki	3½hr	€25	3 weekly
Rhodes*	Agia Marina	4hr	€41	6 weekly

*high-speed services

Lesvos (Mytilini)
Northeastern Aegean Islands; see also p379

DOMESTIC FLIGHTS FROM LESVOS (MYTILINI)

Destination	Airport	Duration	Fare	Frequency
Athens	Mytilini Town	55min	€110	7 weekly
Crete (Iraklio)	Mytilini Town	50min	€110	2 weekly
Thessaloniki	Mytilini Town	45min	€105	7 weekly

BOAT SERVICES FROM LESVOS (MYTILINI)

Destination	Port	Duration	Fare	Frequency
Chios	Mytilini Town	2-3¼hr	€13-20	2 daily
Karlovasi (Samos)	Mytilini Town	6½hr	€22	2 weekly
Kavala	Mytilini Town	11hr	€26	3 weekly
Limnos	Mytilini Town	6hr	€19	4 weekly
Mykonos	Mytilini Town	5½hr	€36	2 weekly
Piraeus	Mytilini Town	8½-13hr	€27-37	2 daily
Syros	Mytilini Town	6½hr	€34	5 weekly
Thessaloniki	Mytilini Town	14hr	€36	3 weekly
Vathy (Samos)	Mytilini Town	7¼hr	€17	2 weekly

Limnos
Northeastern Aegean Islands; see also p390

DOMESTIC FLIGHTS FROM LIMNOS

Destination	Airport	Duration	Fare	Frequency
Athens	Limnos	55min	€100	7 weekly
Thessaloniki	Limnos	35min	€105	6 weekly

BOAT SERVICES FROM LIMNOS

Destination	Port	Duration	Fare	Frequency
Agios Efstratios	Limnos	1½hr	€6-13	3 weekly
Alonnisos	Limnos	3hr	€37	1 weekly
Chios	Limnos	11hr	€22	3 weekly
Chios (Mesta)	Limnos	5½hr	€40	1 weekly
Ikaria (Agios Kirykos)	Limnos	15½hr	€30	1 weekly
Kavala	Limnos	5hr	€15	5 weekly
Lavrio	Limnos	9½-14hr	€28.60	3 weekly
Lesvos (Mytilini)	Limnos	6hr	€19	3 weekly
Lesvos (Sigri)	Limnos	5hr	€13	1 weekly
Piraeus	Limnos	21hr	€30.50	1 weekly
Psara	Limnos	4¼hr	€48.50	1 weekly

ISLAND HOPPING

ISLAND HOPPING

BOAT SERVICES FROM LIMNOS (CONT)

Destination	Port	Duration	Fare	Frequency
Samos (Karlovasi)	Limnos	14½hr	€30	1 weekly
Samos (Vathy)	Limnos	14hr	€28	2 weekly
Skiathos	Limnos	5hr	€39	1 weekly
Skopelos	Limnos	4hr	€38	1 weekly
Thessaloniki	Limnos	8½hr	€23	2 weekly
Volos	Limnos	7¼hr	€40	1 weekly

Lipsi

Dodecanese; see also p342

BOAT

The small local but speedy **Anna Express** (☎ 22479 41215) links Lipsi with Kalymnos and Leros three times per week, and runs to Arki twice weekly.

BOAT SERVICES FROM LIPSI

Destination	Port	Duration	Fare	Frequency
Agathonisi	Lipsi	3hr	€8	4 weekly
Agathonisi*	Lipsi	40min	€13	1 weekly
Kalymnos	Lipsi	1½hr	€8	2 weekly
Kalymnos*	Lipsi	20min	€20	1 daily
Kos*	Lipsi	5hr 50min	€29	6 weekly
Leros	Lipsi	1hr	€8	2 weekly
Leros*	Lipsi	20min	€14	6 weekly
Patmos	Lipsi	25min	€5	1 daily
Patmos*	Lipsi	10min	€13	5 weekly
Piraeus	Lipsi	12hr	€42	2 weekly
Rhodes*	Lipsi	5½hr	€45	6 weekly

*high-speed services

Milos

Cyclades; see also p207

DOMESTIC FLIGHTS FROM MILOS

Destination	Airport	Duration	Fare	Frequency
Athens	Milos	40min	€41	2 weekly

BOAT SERVICES FROM MILOS

Destination	Port	Duration	Fare	Frequency
Folegandros	Milos	2½hr	€8	5 weekly
Folegandros*	Milos	1¼hr	€16	4 weekly
Ios	Milos	3½hr	€29.50	5-6 weekly
Iraklio	Milos	7hr 25min	€21.70	3 weekly
Kea	Milos	14½hr	€25.20	2 weekly
Kimolos	Milos	35min	€9.50	8 weekly
Kythnos	Milos	3¾hr-4hr 25min	€16-18	1-2 daily
Naxos	Milos	2¼hr	€13.60	4 weekly
Paros	Milos	4hr 14min	€24.70	4 weekly
Piraeus	Milos	8hr	€30.50	1-2 daily
Piraeus*	Milos	2hr 50min-3hr 55min	€49-51	2-3 daily
Santorini (Thira)	Milos	4hr	€17	2 weekly
Santorini (Thira)*	Milos	2hr	€34	1 daily
Serifos	Milos	4hr 40min	€16	1-2 daily
Serifos*	Milos	1½hr	€16	1-3 daily
Sifnos	Milos	3hr 40min	€13.50	1-2 daily
Sifnos*	Milos	1hr	€14	1-3 daily
Syros	Milos	4hr 20min	€25.20	5 weekly

*high-speed services

Mykonos

Cyclades; see also p148

DOMESTIC FLIGHTS FROM MYKONOS

Destination	Airport	Duration	Fare	Frequency
Athens	Mykonos	50min	€52-103	3-5 daily
Santorini (Thira)	Mykonos	30min	€85	1-2 daily
Thessaloniki	Mykonos	1hr	€100	3 weekly

BOAT SERVICES FROM MYKONOS

Destination	Port	Duration	Fare	Frequency
Andros	Mykonos	2¾hr	€13	3-4 daily
Chios	Mykonos	3hr	€28.50	2 weekly
Ios*	Mykonos	1½hr	€28	2-3 daily
Iraklio*	Mykonos	1½hr	€66.50	1-2 daily
Lesvos (Mytilini)	Mykonos	5hr 35min	€35.50	2 weekly
Naxos	Mykonos	1¾hr	€12	1 weekly
Naxos*	Mykonos	40min	€18.50	2 daily
Paros*	Mykonos	1hr	€19	3 daily
Piraeus	Mykonos	4¾hr	€30.50-39.50	2 daily
Piraeus*	Mykonos	3hr	€43	3 daily
Rafina	Mykonos	4½hr	€23	2-3 daily
Rafina*	Mykonos	2hr 10min	€41	4-5 daily
Santorini (Thira)*	Mykonos	2hr 10min	€38	2-3 daily
Syros	Mykonos	1½hr	€8-11	2-3 daily
Syros*	Mykonos	30min	€13	3 daily
Tinos	Mykonos	30min	€4.50-6	5 daily
Tinos*	Mykonos	15min	€10.50	5-6 daily

*high-speed services

Naxos

Cyclades; see also p168

DOMESTIC FLIGHTS FROM NAXOS

Destination	Airport	Duration	Fare	Frequency
Athens	Naxos	45min	€62	1 daily

BOAT SERVICES FROM NAXOS

Destination	Port	Duration	Fare	Frequency
Amorgos	Naxos	3hr-3hr 50min	€11.50-14	2-3 daily
Anafi	Naxos	7hr 25min	€14.30	5 weekly
Astypalea	Naxos	5½hr	€23	5 weekly
Donousa	Naxos	1-4hr	€7.50	1-3 daily
Folegandros	Naxos	3¼hr	€14.30-20.20	5 weekly

Ios	Naxos	1hr 35min	€9.90-18.10	1-3 daily
Ios*	Naxos	50min	€20.50	1-2 daily
Iraklia	Naxos	1hr	€6.50	2-3 daily
Kalymnos	Naxos	4¾hr	€19.50	2 weekly
Kastellorizo	Naxos	16hr 20min	€38.50	2 weekly
Kea	Naxos	8¼hr	€18.70	1 weekly
Kimolos	Naxos	4hr 35min	€25.60	2 weekly
Kos	Naxos	8¼hr	€23	2 weekly
Koufonisia	Naxos	2hr-2hr 40min	€7.50-9	2 daily
Kythnos	Naxos	8hr 20min	€19.20	1 weekly
Lavrio	Naxos	10hr	€24	1 weekly
Milos	Naxos	5hr 35min	€33.20	4 weekly
Mykonos	Naxos	1¾hr	€12	1 weekly
Mykonos*	Naxos	40min	€18.50	2 daily
Paros	Naxos	1hr	€7	6 daily
Paros*	Naxos	45 min	€13	3 daily
Piraeus	Naxos	4¾hr	€30	4-5 daily
Piraeus*	Naxos	3½hr	€45	4 daily
Rafina*	Naxos	3hr	€43	1 daily
Rhodes	Naxos	14hr	€32	2 weekly
Santorini (Thira)	Naxos	3hr	€15.50	5 daily
Santorini (Thira)*	Naxos	1½hr	€27.50	2-3 daily
Schinousa	Naxos	2hr 20min	€7.50	1-2 daily
Sikinos	Naxos	2¼hr	€13.60	3-4 weekly
Syros	Naxos	3hr	€10.80	1 daily
Syros*	Naxos	1¾hr	€20	4 weekly
Tilos	Naxos	9hr 35min	€23	2 weekly
Tinos*	Naxos	4¼hr	€13	1 daily

*high-speed services

Nisyros
Dodecanese; see also p313

BOAT
The small local ferry *Agios Konstantinos* links Mandraki with Kardamena on Kos (€8, two hours, daily), while the larger *Panagia Spyliani* links Nisyros with Kos Town (€10, daily).

BOAT SERVICES FROM NISYROS
Destination	Port	Duration	Fare	Frequency
Kalymnos	Mandraki	2½hr	€7	4 weekly
Kos	Mandraki	1¼hr	€8	1 weekly
Kos*	Mandraki	45min	€16	1 weekly
Piraeus	Mandraki	18hr	€46	3 weekly
Rhodes	Mandraki	4½hr	€15	3 weekly
Rhodes*	Mandraki	2¾hr	€28	2 weekly
Symi	Mandraki	3¾hr	€11	2 weekly

*high-speed services

Paros
Cyclades; see also p159

DOMESTIC FLIGHTS FROM PAROS
Destination	Airport	Duration	Fare	Frequency
Athens	Paros	35min	€60	1 daily

BOAT SERVICES FROM PAROS
Destination	Port	Duration	Fare	Frequency
Amorgos	Paros	3-7hr	€12.20-15	1-2 daily
Anafi	Paros	7hr 25min	€17.90	3-4 weekly
Astypalea	Paros	4hr 50min	€28.50	5 weekly
Donousa	Paros	2½hr	€10.30-12.50	1-3 daily
Folegandros	Paros	4-6hr	€15-16.70	5 weekly
Ios	Paros	2½-3hr 10min	€11	2 daily
Ios*	Paros	1hr	€27	1-2 daily
Iraklia	Paros	2¼hr	€12.50	1-2 daily
Iraklio*	Paros	3hr 40min	€65	1 daily
Kalymnos	Paros	7½hr	€19.50	2 weekly
Kastellorizo	Paros	17hr 35min	€40	2 weekly
Kea	Paros	7hr 50min	31.20	2 weekly
Kimolos	Paros	3hr 20min	€20.80	2 weekly
Kos	Paros	7½hr	€23	2 weekly
Koufonisia	Paros	4½hr	€15.50	1-2 daily
Kythnos	Paros	6hr 40min	€27.40	2 weekly
Milos	Paros	4¼hr	€24.70	4 weekly
Mykonos*	Paros	1hr	€19	3 daily
Naxos	Paros	1hr	€7	5 daily
Naxos*	Paros	30min	€15	2 daily
Piraeus	Paros	4¾hr	€29-31	6 daily
Piraeus*	Paros	2½hr	€39.50	4 daily
Rafina*	Paros	2½hr	€49.50	1 daily
Rhodes	Paros	13hr 20min	€32	2 weekly
Santorini (Thira)	Paros	3-4hr	€16.50	5 daily
Santorini (Thira)*	Paros	2¼hr	€36	2-3 daily
Schinousa	Paros	2hr 20min	€10	1-2 daily
Serifos	Paros	2½hr	€10.10	2 weekly
Sifnos	Paros	2hr	€5.40	3 weekly
Sikinos	Paros	3hr 10min	€15.10	3-4 weekly
Syros*	Paros	45min	€8.20	3 daily
Tilos	Paros	10hr 50min	€23	2 weekly
Tinos*	Paros	1hr 25min	€21.50-24.50	3 daily

*high-speed services

Patmos
Dodecanese; see also p337

BOAT
The *Patmos Star* leaves Patmos daily for Lipsi and Leros (return €8) while the *Delfini* goes to Marathi daily each morning in high season and twice weekly out of season (return €15), calling twice each week at Arki. The local *Lambi II* goes to Arki, Marathi and Lipsi three times weekly. The Lipsi-based *Anna Express* connects Patmos with Lipsi and Leros three times weekly.

BOAT SERVICES FROM PATMOS
Destination	Port	Duration	Fare	Frequency
Agathonisi	Skala	55min	€8	4 weekly
Kalymnos*	Skala	1hr 40min	€26	6 weekly

ISLAND HOPPING

BOAT SERVICES FROM PATMOS *(CONT)*

Destination	Port	Duration	Fare	Frequency
Kos*	Skala	3hr	€29	6 weekly
Leros	Skala	2hr	€8	weekly
Leros*	Skala	40min	€16	6 weekly
Lipsi*	Skala	25min	€13	1 weekly
Piraeus	Skala	7hr	€34	4 weekly
Rhodes	Skala	6hr	€40	3 weekly
Rhodes*	Skala	5hr	€46	6 weekly
Samos	Skala	5hr	€9	4 weekly
Symi*	Skala	4hr	€44	5 weekly

*high-speed services

Paxi
Ionian Islands, p447

BOAT SERVICES FROM PAXI

Destination	Port	Duration	Fare	Frequency
Corfu*	Paxi	40min	€16.40	1-3 daily
Corfu	Paxi	3½hr	€8.50	3 weekly
Igoumenitsa	Paxi	2hr	€7.50	2 daily

*high-speed services

Peloponnese
See also Gythio (p98); Igoumenitsa (p102); Kyllini (p102); Neapoli (p102); Patra (p99)

BOAT
Boats between Galatas (Peloponnese) and the island of Poros run approximately every 15 minutes to 30 minutes.

BOAT SERVICES FROM THE PELOPONNESE

Destination	Port	Duration	Fare	Frequency
Corfu	Patra	6-7½hr	€30	4 weekly
Corfu	Patra	6-7½hr	€33	1 daily
Crete (Kissamos)	Gythio	7hr	€24	1 weekly (via Kythira & Antikythira)
Crete	Kalamata	7hr	€40	1 weekly (via Kythira)
Gythio	Kythira	2½hr	€11	2 weekly
Hydra	Ermioni	1hr	€9.50	4 daily
Hydra*	Ermioni	25min	€15	4 daily
Hydra*	Porto Heli	25min	€15	4 daily
Ithaki (Piso Aetos)	Patra	3¾hr	€18	1 daily
Ithaki (Vathy)	Patra	5hr	€18	1 daily
Kefallonia (Argostoli)	Kyllini	2hr	€13	1 daily
Kefallonia (Lixouri)	Kyllini	2¼hr	€14	1 daily
Kefallonia (Poros)	Kyllini	1½hr	€8	5 daily
Kefallonia (Poros)	Kyllini	1hr	€10	1 daily
Kefallonia (Poros; by bus)	Patra	3hr	€18	
Kefallonia (Sami)	Patra	2¾hr	€17	3 weekly
Kefallonia (Sami)	Patra	2¾hr	€18	2 daily

Destination	Port	Duration	Fare	Frequency
Kythira	Kalamata	4½hr	€17	1 weekly
Kythira (Diakofti)	Neapoli	1hr	€11	1 daily
Lefkada (by bus)	Patra	3hr	€14.50	2 weekly
Piraeus*	Ermioni	2hr	€29.50	4 daily
Piraeus*	Porto Heli	3hr 20min	€35.50	4 daily
Poros*	Ermioni	1hr	€15	3 daily
Poros	Methana	30min	€4.20	2-3 daily
Poros*	Porto Heli	1hr 40min	€19	2 daily
Spetses*	Ermioni	25min	€7.50	2 daily
Spetses*	Porto Heli	15min	€5.50	4 daily
Zakynthos (by bus)	Kyllini	3½hr	€15	3 on Sun
Zakynthos	Kyllini	1¼hr	€6.80	4-6 daily

*high-speed services

Preveza
Northern Greece (mainland port); see also p450

DOMESTIC FLIGHTS FROM PREVEZA

Destination	Airport	Duration	Fare	Frequency
Athens	Preveza	1hr	€95	5 weekly
Corfu	Preveza	30min	€39	3 weekly
Kefallonia	Preveza	30min	€34	3 weekly
Zakynthos	Preveza	1hr 20min	€43	3 weekly

Poros
Saronic Gulf Islands; see also p123

BOAT SERVICES FROM POROS

Destination	Port	Duration	Fare	Frequency
Aegina	Poros	1¼hr	€8.60	4 daily
Hydra*	Poros	30min	€12.50	6 daily
Methana	Poros	30min	€4.20	4 daily
Piraeus	Poros	2½hr	€13.30	8-10 daily
Piraeus*	Poros	1hr	€25.20	4 daily
Spetses*	Poros	1hr	€14.50	7 daily

*high-speed services

Psara
Northeastern Aegean Islands; see also pp375–8

BOAT SERVICES FROM PSARA

Destination	Port	Duration	Fare	Frequency
Agios Efstratios	Psara	3¼hr	€35	1 weekly
Chios	Psara	3½hr	€11	6 weekly
Lavrio	Psara	5hr	€45	1 weekly
Limnos	Psara	4hr	€48.50	1 weekly
Mesta (Chios)	Psara	45min-2hr	€6-13	2 weekly

Rhodes
Dodecanese; see also p276

AIR
Olympic Air has at least five flights daily to Athens (€58), around six per week to Karpathos (€28), three weekly to Kasos (€34), five weekly to Kastellorizo (€22), three weekly to Thessaloniki (€110), three weekly to Astypalea (€47) and two weekly to Samos

(€37). Aegean Airlines also offers daily flights to Athens (€64) and Thessaloniki (€90).

BOAT

In addition to the departures listed here, there are local ferries running daily between Skala Kamirou, on Rhodes' west coast, and Halki (€10, one hour). From Skala Kamirou services depart at 2.30pm, and from Halki at 6am. There are also excursion boats to Symi (€22 return) daily in summer, leaving Mandraki Harbour at 9am and returning at 6pm. You can buy tickets at most travel agencies, but it's better to buy them at the harbour, where you can check out the boats personally.

BOAT SERVICES FROM RHODES

Destination	Port	Duration	Fare	Frequency
Agathonisi*	Commercial Harbour (Rhodes Town)	5hr	€46	1 weekly
Alexandroupoli	Commercial Harbour (Rhodes Town)	29hr	€46	1 weekly
Astypalea	Commercial Harbour (Rhodes Town)	10hr	€30	1 weekly
Halki	Commercial Harbour (Rhodes Town)	2hr	€10	4 weekly
Halki*	Commercial Harbour (Rhodes Town)	1¼hr	€21	2 weekly
Kalymnos	Commercial Harbour (Rhodes Town)	4½hr	€20	3 weekly
Kalymnos*	Commercial Harbour (Rhodes Town)	3hr	€38	1 daily
Karpathos	Commercial Harbour (Rhodes Town)	5hr	€22	3 weekly
Kasos	Commercial Harbour (Rhodes Town)	8hr	€25	4 weekly
Kastellorizo	Commercial Harbour (Rhodes Town)	4hr 40min	€17	2 weekly
Kastellorizo*	Commercial Harbour (Rhodes Town)	2½hr	€25	1 weekly
Kos	Commercial Harbour (Rhodes Town)	3hr	€26	1 daily
Kos*	Commercial Harbour (Rhodes Town)	2½hr	€30	1 daily
Leros	Commercial Harbour (Rhodes Town)	5hr	€25	3 weekly
Leros*	Commercial Harbour (Rhodes Town)	3½hr	€41	6 weekly
Lipsi	Commercial Harbour (Rhodes Town)	8hr	€40	2 weekly
Lipsi*	Commercial Harbour (Rhodes Town)	5½hr	€45	6 weekly
Nisyros	Commercial Harbour (Rhodes Town)	4½hr	€15	3 weekly
Nisyros*	Commercial Harbour (Rhodes Town)	2¾hr	€28	2 weekly
Patmos	Commercial Harbour (Rhodes Town)	6hr	€40	3 weekly
Patmos*	Commercial Harbour (Rhodes Town)	5hr	€46	6 weekly
Piraeus	Commercial Harbour (Rhodes Town)	13hr	€53	1 daily
Sitia	Commercial Harbour (Rhodes Town)	10hr	€28	3 weekly
Symi	Mandraki	2hr	€12	1 daily
Symi*	Commercial Harbour (Rhodes Town)	50min	€15	1 daily
Thessaloniki	Commercial Harbour (Rhodes Town)	21hr	€55	1 weekly
Tilos	Commercial Harbour (Rhodes Town)	2½hr	€15	4 weekly
Tilos*	Commercial Harbour (Rhodes Town)	2hr	€25	2 weekly
Tilos*	Mandraki Harbour (Rhodes Town)	1½hr	€24	6 weekly

*high-speed services

Samos

Northeastern Aegean Islands, p357

DOMESTIC FLIGHTS FROM SAMOS

Destination	Airport	Duration	Fare	Frequency
Athens	Samos	45min	€80	7 weekly
Iraklio (Crete)	Samos	50min	€110	2 weekly
Thessaloniki	Samos	50min	€90	5 weekly

BOAT SERVICES FROM SAMOS

Destination	Port	Duration	Fare	Frequency
Chios	Karlovasi	2½hr	€11	2 weekly
Fourni	Vathy	1½-2hr	€8	1-3 daily
Ikaria (Agios Kirykos)	Vathy	2hr	€6	1-2 daily
Ikaria (Evdilos)**	Vathy	1hr	€11.50	1 daily*

ISLAND HOPPING

BOAT SERVICES FROM SAMOS (CONT)

Destination	Port	Duration	Fare	Frequency
Kalymnos	Vathy	4hr	€18	1 weekly
Kavala	Vathy	18hr	€37	1 weekly
Kos	Vathy	5¼hr	€19	1 weekly
Lesvos (Mytilini)	Karlovasi	6¼hr	€22	1 weekly
Lesvos (Sigri)	Karlovasi	6hr	€23.50	1 weekly
Limnos	Vathy	13hr	€30	1 weekly
Mykonos	Vathy	6½hr	€23	3 weekly
Naxos**	Vathy	3½hr	€29	1 daily*
Paros**	Vathy	4½hr	€30	1 daily*
Piraeus	Vathy	7-13hr	€41	1-2 daily
Rhodes	Vathy	9¼hr	€30	1 weekly
Thessaloniki	Karlovasi	15½hr	€42	1 weekly

*except Mondays
**high-speed services

Samothraki
Northern Greece; see also p394

BOAT SERVICES FROM SAMOTHRAKI

Destination	Port	Duration	Fare	Frequency
Samothraki	Alexandroupoli	2hr	€13	2 daily

Santorini (Thira)
Cyclades; see also p190

DOMESTIC FLIGHTS FROM SANTORINI (THIRA)

Destination	Port	Duration	Fare	Frequency
Athens	Santorini (Thira)	45min	€68	10 daily
Iraklio	Santorini (Thira)	30min	€85	5 weekly
Rhodes	Santorini (Thira)	1hr	€112	2 daily

BOAT SERVICES FROM SANTORINI (THIRA)

Destination	Port	Duration	Fare	Frequency
Amorgos*	Santorini (Thira)	1hr	€32	1 daily
Anafi	Santorini (Thira)	1hr	€8	5 weekly
Folegandros	Santorini (Thira)	2½hr	€7.50	1-2 daily
Folegandros*	Santorini (Thira)	30min	€19	1 daily
Iraklio	Santorini (Thira)	4½hr	€24	1 daily
Iraklio*	Santorini (Thira)	1¾hr	€42	1 daily
Karpathos	Santorini (Thira)	8hr	€25	5 weekly
Kimolos	Santorini (Thira)	3½hr	€7.20	2 weekly
Kos	Santorini (Thira)	4¼hr	€28.50	2 weekly
Kythnos	Santorini (Thira)	8hr	€16	2 weekly
Lavrio	Santorini (Thira)	16hr 20min	€50	2 weekly
Milos	Santorini (Thira)	4hr	€17	2 weekly
Milos*	Santorini (Thira)	2hr	€34	1 daily
Mykonos*	Santorini (Thira)	2hr 10min	€38	2-3 daily
Naxos	Santorini (Thira)	3hr	€15.50	5 daily
Naxos*	Santorini (Thira)	1½hr	€30	2-3 daily
Paros	Santorini (Thira)	3-4hr	€16.50	5 daily
Paros*	Santorini (Thira)	2¼hr	€36	2-3 daily
Piraeus	Santorini (Thira)	9hr	€33.50	4-5 daily
Piraeus*	Santorini (Thira)	5¼hr	€47-65	3 daily
Rafina*	Santorini (Thira)	4¾hr	€49	1 daily
Rethymno	Santorini (Thira)	2hr 20min	€46	3 weekly
Rhodes	Santorini (Thira)	13hr 10min	€27	1-2 daily
Serifos	Santorini (Thira)	9hr	€16	2 weekly
Sifnos	Santorini (Thira)	7hr 20min	€13.50	2 weekly
Sikinos	Santorini (Thira)	2¾hr	€14.10	1-4 daily
Sikinos*	Santorini (Thira)	55min	€18	1 weekly
Syros	Santorini (Thira)	5¼hr	€22	2 weekly

*high-speed services

Schinousa
Cyclades; see also Little Cyclades, p177

BOAT SERVICES FROM SCHINOUSA

Destination	Port	Duration	Fare	Frequency
Amorgos	Schinousa	1hr 40min	€8-10.50	2-3 daily
Donousa	Schinousa	2hr	€7.50	1-2 daily
Iraklia	Schinousa	15min	€4.50	2-3 daily
Koufonisia	Schinousa	40min	€4.50	2-3 daily
Naxos	Schinousa	2hr-2hr 40min	€7.50-9	1-2 daily
Paros	Schinousa	2hr 20min	€10	1-2 daily
Piraeus	Schinousa	7½hr	€30	1-2 daily
Syros	Schinousa	4hr	€22.20	4 weekly

Serifos
Cyclades; see also p212

BOAT SERVICES FROM SERIFOS

Destination	Port	Duration	Fare	Frequency
Folegandros	Serifos	7hr 40min	€16	5 weekly
Folegandros*	Serifos	1¾hr	€23	4 weekly
Ios	Serifos	7hr 10min	€16	4 weekly
Kimolos	Serifos	4hr 10min	€8.50	5 weekly
Kythnos	Serifos	1hr 20min	€15	1-2 daily
Milos	Serifos	4hr 40min	€16	1-2 daily
Milos*	Serifos	1½hr	€16	1-3 daily
Paros	Serifos	2½hr	€10.10	3 weekly
Piraeus	Serifos	5hr	€22.50	2 daily
Piraeus*	Serifos	2hr 25min	€40	3 daily
Santorini (Thira)	Serifos	9hr	€16	2 weekly
Sifnos	Serifos	50min	€11-13.50	1-2 daily
Sifnos*	Serifos	25min	€13	1-2 daily
Syros	Serifos	2hr 50min	€9.90	4 weekly

*high-speed services

Sifnos
Cyclades; see also p210

BOAT SERVICES FROM SIFNOS

Destination	Port	Duration	Fare	Frequency
Folegandros	Sifnos	4½hr	€13.50	1-3 daily
Folegandros*	Sifnos	1hr	€18	4 weekly
Ios	Sifnos	6hr	€13.50	4 weekly
Kimolos	Sifnos	3hr	€6	5 weekly
Kythnos	Sifnos	2½hr	€13.50	1-2 daily
Milos	Sifnos	3hr 40min	€13.50	1-2 daily
Milos*	Sifnos	1hr	€14	1-3 daily
Paros	Sifnos	2hr	€5.40	3 weekly
Piraeus	Sifnos	5¼hr	€28	2 daily
Piraeus*	Sifnos	2hr 40min	€44	3 daily

Santorini (Thira)	Sifnos	7hr 20min	€13.50	2 weekly
Serifos	Sifnos	50min	€11-13.50	1-2 daily
Serifos*	Sifnos	25min	€13	1-2 daily
Syros	Sifnos	4hr 10min	€17.70	5 weekly

*high-speed services

Sikinos
Cyclades; see also p201

BOAT SERVICES FROM SIKINOS
Destination	Port	Duration	Fare	Frequency
Anafi	Sikinos	4hr	€19.60	4 weekly
Folegandros	Sikinos	40min	€5.50	1-3 daily
Ios	Sikinos	20min	€8	1-4 daily
Ios*	Sikinos	10min	€12	1 weekly
Kea	Sikinos	12hr 25min	€41.40	2 weekly
Kythnos	Sikinos	11hr	€32	2 weekly
Naxos	Sikinos	2¼hr	€13.60	4 weekly
Paros*	Sikinos	4hr 10min	€50-55	1-2 daily
Piraeus	Sikinos	12hr	€29.60	4 weekly
Santorini (Thira)	Sikinos	2¾hr	€8	4 weekly
Santorini (Thira)*	Sikinos	55min	€19	1 weekly
Syros	Sikinos	5hr	€15	1-3 daily

*high-speed services

Skiathos
Evia & the Sporades; see also p412

AIR
During summer there's one flight daily to/from Athens (€49).

BOAT SERVICES FROM SKIATHOS
Destination	Port	Duration	Fare	Frequency
Agios Konstantinos	Skiathos	2hr	€32	1 daily
Agios Konstantinos*	Skiathos	2hr	€33	2 daily
Alonnisos	Skiathos	2½hr	€9.50	1 daily
Alonnisos*	Skiathos	1½hr	€16	4-5 daily
Skopelos	Skiathos	1¼hr	€9	1 daily
Skopelos (Glossa)	Skiathos	40min	€5.50	1 daily
Skopelos (Glossa)*	Skiathos	20min	€9.50	3-4 daily
Skopelos (Skopelos Town)*	Skiathos	45min	€16	4-5 daily
Thessaloniki*	Skiathos	4¼hr	€55	1 daily
Volos	Skiathos	2½hr	€18	2 daily
Volos*	Skiathos	1½hr	€30	3 daily

*hydrofoil services

Skopelos
Evia & the Sporades; see also p417

BOAT SERVICES FROM SKOPELOS
Destination	Port	Duration	Fare	Frequency
Agios Konstantinos*	Skopelos*	3½hr	€44	1 daily
Agios Konstantinos**	Skopelos**	2½hr	€44	1-3 daily
Alonnisos**	Skopelos (Glossa)	50min	€13	4-5 daily
Alonnisos	Skopelos (Skopelos Town)	30min	€5	4-5 weekly
Alonnisos**	Skopelos (Skopelos Town)	20min	€8.50	4-5 daily
Skiathos	Skopelos (Skopelos Town)	1hr	€9	1 daily
Skiathos**	Skopelos (Glossa)	20min	€9.50	4-5 daily
Skiathos*	Skopelos (Skopelos Town)	50min	€15.50	4-5 daily
Volos	Skopelos (Glossa)	3½hr	€19.50	1 daily
Volos	Skopelos (Skopelos Town)	4hr	€23	1-2 daily

*fast-ferry services
**hydrofoil services

Skyros
Evia & the Sporades; see also p427

DOMESTIC FLIGHTS FROM SKYROS
Destination	Port	Duration	Fare	Frequency
Athens	Skyros	25 minutes	€40	3 weekly
Thessaloniki	Skyros	35 minutes	€68	3 weekly

BOAT
A regular ferry service is provided by *Achileas* between the port of Kymi (Evia) and Skyros. On Friday and Sunday the ferry (usually) makes two crossings; on the remaining days, just one crossing.

BOAT SERVICES FROM SKYROS
Destination	Port	Duration	Fare	Frequency
Alonnisos	Skyros	5hr	€21	2 weekly
Evia (Paralia Kymis)	Skyros	1¾hr	€9	1-2 daily
Skopelos	Skyros	6hr	€22	2 weekly

ISLAND HOPPING

Spetses

Saronic Gulf Islands; see also p130

BOAT SERVICES FROM SPETSES

Destination	Port	Duration	Fare	Frequency
Hydra	Spetses	30min	€13	7 daily
Ermioni*	Spetses	1hr	€10	2 daily
Piraeus*	Spetses	2hr 10min	€39	7 daily
Poros	Spetses	70min	€14.50	7 daily
Porto Heli*	Spetses	10min	€7	5 daily

*high-speed services

Symi

Dodecanese; see also p306

BOAT

In summer, daily excursion boats run between Symi and Rhodes (€15). The Symi-based *Symi I* and *Symi II* usually go via Panormitis.

BOAT SERVICES FROM SYMI

Destination	Port	Duration	Fare	Frequency
Kalymnos*	Gialos	2hr	€31	1 daily
Kos*	Gialos	1½hr	€22	1 daily
Leros*	Gialos	3hr	€40	1 daily
Patmos*	Gialos	4hr	€44	1 daily
Piraeus	Gialos	15hr	€64	2 weekly
Rhodes	Gialos	2hr	€32	1 daily
Rhodes*	Gialos	1hr	€15	1 daily
Rhodes*	Gialos	50min	€21	1 daily
Tilos	Gialos	2hr	€8	2 weekly

*high-speed services

Syros

Cyclades; see also p143

DOMESTIC FLIGHTS FROM SYROS

Destination	Airport	Duration	Fare	Frequency
Athens	Syros	35min	€70	2 weekly

BOAT SERVICES FROM SYROS

Destination	Port	Duration	Fare	Frequency
Amorgos	Syros	4½hr	€19	4 weekly
Anafi	Syros	9hr	€36.30	2-3 weekly
Andros	Syros	2hr 20min	€16	4 weekly
Astypalea	Syros	6¼hr	€20.50	3 weekly
Chios	Syros	3hr 20min	€30.50	5 weekly
Donousa	Syros	4hr 20min	€15	4 weekly
Folegandros	Syros	6hr	€15.10	3 weekly
Ios	Syros	2¼hr	€42	1 daily
Iraklia	Syros	3hr 35min	€22.70	3-4 weekly
Kea	Syros	3hr	€12.30	2 weekly
Kimilos	Syros	3¾hr	€15.10	4 weekly
Kos	Syros	7hr 40min	€32	3 weekly
Koufonisia	Syros	4½hr	€12.70	4 weekly
Kythnos	Syros	2hr	€9.90	4 weekly
Lavrio	Syros	3½hr	€18.50	3 weekly
Leros	Syros	4hr 35min	€28	3 weekly
Milos	Syros	4hr 20min	€25.20	4 weekly
Mykonos	Syros	1hr 20min	€8	1 daily
Mykonos*	Syros	40min	€14.50	4 daily
Naxos	Syros	1½hr-2hr 50min	€9.20-11.50	2 daily
Paros	Syros	1¾hr	€8.50	1-3 daily
Patmos	Syros	3hr 25min	€26	3 weekly
Piraeus	Syros	4hr	€26-29	4 daily
Piraeus*	Syros	2½hr	€44.50	3 daily
Rafina*	Syros	2hr 50min	€45	2 weekly
Rhodes	Syros	9hr 25min	€38.50	3 weekly

*high-speed services

Thasos

Northeastern Aegean Islands; see also p399

BOAT SERVICES FROM THASOS

Destination	Port	Duration	Fare	Frequency
Kavala	Thasos (Skala Prinou)	1¼hr	€3.50	hourly
Kavala*	Thasos (Limenas)	40min	€10	4 daily
Kavala*	Thasos (Skala Prinou)	40min	€10	4 daily
Keramoti	Thasos (Limenas)	40min	€3.30	hourly

*high-speed services

Thessaloniki

As Greece's second city, the mainland port of Thessaloniki has plenty of air and boat connections and is an important ferry hub for the Northeast Aegean Islands. It usually has hydrofoils to the Sporades as well, but these are unpredictable, so check locally. See also pp94–8.

AIR

Some of Thessaloniki's island flights go via Athens; the following table lists direct island flights. Note that a few island flights are multistop, but don't involve change of aircraft.

DOMESTIC FLIGHTS FROM THESSALONIKI

Destination	Airport	Duration	Fare	Frequency
Chios	Thessaloniki	55min	€90	4 weekly
Corfu	Thessaloniki	50min	€75	4 weekly
Crete (Hania)	Thessaloniki	1¼hr	€100	7 weekly
Crete (Iraklio)	Thessaloniki	1¼hr	€100	2 daily
Kefallonia	Thessaloniki	1¾hr	€100	3 weekly
Kos	Thessaloniki	1¼hr	€135	2 weekly
Lesvos (Mytilini)	Thessaloniki	50min	€90	11 weekly
Limnos	Thessaloniki	30min	€75	6 weekly
Mykonos	Thessaloniki	1hr	€100	3 weekly
Rhodes	Thessaloniki	1¼hr	€100	2 daily
Samos	Thessaloniki	1hr	€90	3 weekly
Santorini (Thira)	Thessaloniki	1¼hr	€100	3 weekly

ISLAND HOPPING

BOAT SERVICES FROM THESSALONIKI

Destination	Port	Duration	Fare	Frequency
Chios	Thessaloniki	13-20hr	€35	3 weekly
Kalymnos	Thessaloniki	20hr	€46	1 weekly
Kos	Thessaloniki	19¼hr	€47	1 weekly
Lesvos (Mytilini)	Thessaloniki	15hr	€35	2 weekly
Lesvos (Sigri)	Thessaloniki	9½hr	€33	1 weekly
Limnos	Thessaloniki	8½hr	€22	2 weekly
Rhodes	Thessaloniki	25hr	€57	1 weekly
Samos (Karlovasi)	Thessaloniki	15½hr	€42	1 weekly
Samos (Vathy)	Thessaloniki	23hr	€39	1 weekly

Tilos
Dodecanese; see also p310

BOAT SERVICES FROM TILOS

Destination	Port	Duration	Fare	Frequency
Kos	Livadia	3hr	€9	2 weekly
Kos*	Livadia	1½hr	€22	2 weekly
Nisyros	Livadia	1hr	€7	6 weekly
Nisyros*	Livadia	40min	€13	2 weekly
Piraeus	Livadia	19½hr	€46	2 weekly
Rhodes	Livadia	2½hr	€15	4 weekly
Rhodes*	Livadia	1½hr	€24	6 weekly
Symi	Livadia	2hr	€8	2 weekly

*high-speed services

Tinos
Cyclades; see also p140

BOAT SERVICES FROM TINOS

Destination	Port	Duration	Fare	Frequency
Andros	Tinos	1hr 35min	€9.60	4 daily
Lavrio	Tinos	8¾hr	€16	1 weekly
Mykonos	Tinos	30-40min	€5.50-6	4 daily
Mykonos*	Tinos	15-25min	€7-10.50	5 daily
Naxos	Tinos	1hr 25min	€13	2 weekly
Paros	Tinos	1hr 25min	€21.50-24.50	3 daily
Piraeus	Tinos	4¾hr	€28	1 daily
Piraeus*	Tinos	3¾hr	€44	3 daily
Rafina	Tinos	3hr 50min	€19	5 daily
Rafina*	Tinos	2hr 10min	€40	5 daily
Syros	Tinos	2hr	€5	7 daily

*high-speed services

Volos
Central Greece (mainland port); see also p103

BOAT SERVICES FROM VOLOS

Destination	Port	Duration	Fare	Frequency
Alonnisos	Volos	5hr	€24	3 weekly
Alonnisos*	Volos	3hr	€40	2 daily
Skiathos	Volos	2½hr	€18.50	1-2 daily
Skiathos*	Volos	1½hr	€31	2 daily
Skopelos (Glossa)	Volos	3hr	€20.50	3 weekly
Skopelos (Glossa)*	Volos	2hr	€34	2 daily
Skopelos (Skopelos Town)	Volos	4hr	€24	1 daily
Skopelos (Skopelos Town)*	Volos	2½hr	€40	2 daily

*hydrofoil services

Zakynthos
Ionian Islands; see also p464

DOMESTIC FLIGHTS FROM ZAKYNTHOS

Destination	Airport	Duration	Fare	Frequency
Athens	Zakynthos	55min	€77	2 daily
Kefallonia	Zakynthos	20min	€32	3 weekly
Preveza	Zakynthos	1hr 20min	€43	3 weekly

BOAT SERVICES FROM ZAKYNTHOS

Destination	Port	Duration	Fare	Frequency
Corfu	Zakynthos Town	8¾hr	€32	2 weekly
Kefallonia (Pesada)	Agios Nikolaos	1½hr	€7	2 daily
Kyllini	Zakynthos Town	1hr	€8.20	7 daily

ISLAND HOPPING

Health

CONTENTS

BEFORE YOU GO

Prevention is the key to staying healthy while abroad. A little planning before departure, particularly for pre-existing illnesses, will save trouble later. Bring medications in their original, clearly labelled containers. A signed and dated letter from your physician describing your medical conditions and medications, including generic names, is also a good idea. For example, taking codeine into Greece is strictly prohibited unless accompanied by a doctor's certificate. See also p481.

If carrying syringes or needles, be sure to have a physician's letter documenting their medical necessity. If you are embarking on a long trip, make sure your teeth are OK and take your optical prescription with you.

INSURANCE

If you're an EU citizen, a European Health Insurance Card (EHIC; formerly the E111) covers you for most medical care but not emergency repatriation home or nonemergencies. It is available from health centres, and post offices in the UK. Citizens from other countries should find out if there is a reciprocal arrangement for free medical care between their country and Greece. If you do need health insurance, make sure you get a policy that covers you for the worst possible scenario, such as an accident requiring an emergency flight home. Find out in advance if your insurance plan will make payments directly to providers or reimburse you later for overseas health expenditures.

RECOMMENDED VACCINATIONS

No jabs are required to travel to Greece, but a yellow-fever vaccination certificate is required if you are coming from an infected area. The World Health Organization (WHO) recommends that all travellers should be covered for diphtheria, tetanus, measles, mumps, rubella and polio.

INTERNET RESOURCES

The WHO's publication *International Travel and Health* is revised annually and is available online at www.who.int/ith. Other useful websites include www.mdtravelhealth.com (travel health recommendations for every country; updated daily), www.fitfortravel.scot.nhs.uk (general travel advice for the layperson), www.ageconcern.org.uk (advice on travel for the elderly) and www.mariestopes.org.uk (information on women's health and contraception).

IN TRANSIT

DEEP VEIN THROMBOSIS (DVT)

Blood clots may form in the legs during plane flights, chiefly because of prolonged immobility (the longer the flight, the greater the risk). The chief symptom of DVT is swelling or pain of the foot, ankle, or calf, usually but not always on just one side. When a blood clot travels to the lungs, it may cause chest pain and breathing difficulties. Travellers with any of these symptoms should immediately seek medical attention. To prevent the development of DVT on long flights you should walk about the cabin, contract the leg muscles while sitting, drink plenty of fluids and avoid alcohol and tobacco.

JET LAG

To avoid jet lag drink plenty of nonalcoholic fluids and eat light meals. Upon arrival, get exposure to natural sunlight and re-adjust your schedule (for meals, sleep etc) as soon as possible.

IN GREECE

AVAILABILITY & COST OF HEALTH CARE

If you need an ambulance in Greece call ☎ 166. There is at least one doctor on every island and larger islands have hospitals. Pharmacies can dispense medicines that are available only on prescription in most European countries, so you can consult a pharmacist for minor ailments.

All this sounds fine but, although medical training is of a high standard in Greece, the public health service is badly underfunded. Hospitals can be overcrowded, hygiene is not always what it should be and relatives are expected to bring in food for the patient – which could be a problem for a tourist. Conditions and treatment are much better in private hospitals, which are expensive. All this means that a good health-insurance policy is essential.

TRAVELLER'S DIARRHOEA

If you develop diarrhoea, be sure to drink plenty of fluids, preferably in the form of an oral rehydration solution such as dioralyte. If diarrhoea is bloody, persists for more than 72 hours or is accompanied by fever, shaking, chills or severe abdominal pain you should seek medical attention.

ENVIRONMENTAL HAZARDS
Bites, Stings & Insect-Borne Diseases

Keep an eye out for sea urchins lurking around rocky beaches; if you get some of their needles embedded in your skin, olive oil should help to loosen them. If they are not removed they will become infected. You should also be wary of jellyfish, particularly during the months of September and October. Although jellyfish are not lethal in Greece, their stings can hurt. Dousing the affected area with vinegar will deactivate any stingers that have not 'fired'. Calamine lotion, antihistamines and analgesics may help reduce any reaction you experience and relieve the pain of any stings. Much more painful than either of these, but thankfully much rarer, is an encounter with the weever fish. The fish buries itself in the sand of the tidal zone with only its spines protruding, and injects a painful and powerful toxin if trodden on. Soaking your foot in very hot water (which breaks down the poison) should solve the problem but if a child is stung, medical attention should be sought. Weever-fish stings can cause permanent local paralysis in the worst case.

Greece's dangerous snakes include the adder and the less common viper and coral snakes. To minimise the possibilities of being bitten, always wear boots, socks and long trousers when walking through undergrowth where snakes may be present. Don't put your hands into holes and crevices, and be careful when collecting firewood. Snake bites do not cause instantaneous death and an antivenin is widely available. Keep the victim calm and still, wrap the bitten limb tightly, as you would for a sprained ankle, and attach a splint to immobilise it. Seek medical help, if possible with the dead snake for identification. Don't attempt to catch the snake if there is a possibility of being bitten again. Tourniquets and sucking out the poison are now comprehensively discredited.

Always check all over your body if you have been walking through a potentially tick-infested area as ticks can cause skin infections and other more serious diseases. If a tick is found attached, press down around the tick's head with tweezers, grab the head and gently pull upwards. Avoid pulling the rear of the tick's body as this may squeeze the tick's gut contents through the attached mouth parts into the skin, increasing the risk of infection and disease.

Greece is now officially rabies-free, however even if the animal is not rabid, all animal bites should be treated seriously as they can become infected or can result in tetanus.

Mosquitoes can be an annoying problem in Greece so some precautions may be needed, though there is no danger of contracting malaria. The electric plug-in mosquito repellents are usually sufficient – and more bearable than coils – to keep the insects at bay at night. Nonetheless choose accommodation that has flyscreen window-protection wherever possible. Mosquito species can vary as can your reaction to their bites. Mosquitoes in northern Greece can provoke a severe reaction. The Asian tiger mosquito (Aedes albopictus) may be encountered in mountainous areas and can be a voracious daytime biter. It is known to carry several viruses, including Eastern equine encephalitis, which can affect the central nervous system and cause severe complications and death. Use protective sprays or lotion if you suspect you are being bitten during the day.

HEALTH

Invisible bedbugs can be a major irritation if encountered. Symptoms are lots of pinprick bites that you may initially assign to mosquitoes – even if you are covered up. There is no protection other than to change to a noninfected bed. Airing the mattress thoroughly in the sun may alleviate the problem.

Heatstroke

Heatstroke occurs following excessive fluid loss with inadequate replacement of fluids and salt. Symptoms of heatstroke include headache, dizziness and tiredness. Dehydration is already happening by the time you feel thirsty – aim to drink sufficient water to produce pale, diluted urine. To treat heatstroke drink water and/or fruit juice, and cool the body with cold water and fans.

Hypothermia

Hypothermia occurs when the body loses heat faster than it can produce it. As ever, proper preparation will reduce the risks of getting it. Even on a hot day in the mountains, the weather can change rapidly so carry waterproof garments, warm layers and a hat, and inform others of your route. Hypothermia starts with shivering, loss of judgment and clumsiness. Unless rewarming occurs, the sufferer deteriorates into apathy, confusion and coma. Prevent further heat loss by seeking shelter, warm dry clothing, hot sweet drinks and shared bodily warmth.

Water

In much of Greece, tap water is drinkable and safe. However, in small villages and on some of the islands, this is not always the case. Always ask locally if the water is safe and, if in doubt, drink boiled or bought water. Even when water is safe, the substances and microbacteria in it may be different than you are used to and can cause vomiting or diarrhoea. If you suffer from either of these and think water might be the cause, stick to the bottled variety.

TRAVELLING WITH CHILDREN

Make sure children are up to date with routine vaccinations and discuss possible travel vaccines well before departure as some vaccines are not suitable for children under a year old. Lonely Planet's *Travel with Children* (Brigitte Barta et al) includes travel health advice for younger children. Children are often more susceptible to diarrhoea and dehydration, and bites and stings can have a greater impact on their smaller body mass. Keep a first-aid kit handy.

SEXUAL HEALTH

Condoms are readily available but emergency contraception may not be, so take the necessary precautions.

Language

CONTENTS

The Greek language is believed to be one of the oldest European languages, with an oral tradition of 4000 years and a written tradition of approximately 3000 years. Its evolution over the four millennia was characterised by its strength during the golden age of Athens and the Democracy (mid-5th century BC); its use as a lingua franca throughout the Middle Eastern world, spread by Alexander the Great and his successors as far as India during the Hellenistic period (330 BC to AD 100); its adaptation as the language of the new religion, Christianity; its use as the official language of the Eastern Roman Empire; and its proclamation as the language of the Byzantine Empire (380–1453).

Greek maintained its status and prestige during the rise of the European Renaissance and was employed as the linguistic perspective for all contemporary sciences and terminologies during the period of Enlightenment. Today, Greek constitutes a large part of the vocabulary of many Indo-European languages, and much of the lexicon of scientific repertoire.

The modern Greek language is a southern Greek dialect which is now used by most Greek speakers both in Greece and abroad. It is the result of the mixing of ancient vocabulary with words from Greek regional dialects, namely Cretan, Cypriot and Macedonian.

Greek is spoken throughout Greece by a population of just over 10 million, and by some 5 million Greeks living abroad.

PRONUNCIATION

All Greek words of two or more syllables have an acute accent (´), which indicates where the stress falls. For instance, άγαλμα (statue) is pronounced *aghalma*, and αγάπη (love) is pronounced *aghapi*. In our pronunciation guides, italic lettering indicates where stress falls, eg *a·ghal·ma*. Note also that **dh** is pronounced 'th' as in 'there' and **gh** is a softer, slightly guttural version of 'g'. See the box on p531 for more details.

ACCOMMODATION

I'm looking for …

Ψάχνω για …	*psa·*hno ya …
a hotel	
ένα ξενοδοχείο	*e·*na kse·no·dho·*khi·*o
a room	
ένα δωμάτιο	*e·*na dho·*ma·*ti·o
a youth hostel	
έναν ξενώνα	*e·*nan kse·*no·*na
νεότητας	ne·*o·*ti·tas

I'd like to book …

Θα ήθελα να κλείσω …	tha *i·*the·la na *kli·*so …
a bed	
ένα κρεββάτι	*e·*na kre·*va·*ti
a single room	
ένα μονόκλινο	*e·*na mo·*no·*kli·no
δωμάτιο	dho·*ma·*ti·o
a double room	
ένα δίκλινο	*e·*na *dhi·*kli·no
δωμάτιο	dho·*ma·*ti·o
a room with a double bed	
ένα δωμάτιο με	*e·*na dho·*ma·*ti·o me
δυό κρεββάτια	dhy·o kre·*va·*ti·a
a room with a bathroom	
ένα δωμάτιο με	*e·*na dho·*ma·*ti·o me
μπάνιο	*ba·*ni·o

Where's a cheap hotel?
Πού είναι ένα φτηνό ξενοδοχείο;
pou *i·*ne *e·*na fti·*no* xe·no·do·*hi·*o

What's the address?
Ποια είναι η διεύθυνση;
pya *i*·ne i dhi·*ef*·thin·si
Could you write the address, please?
Παρακαλώ, μπορείτε να γράψετε τη διεύθυνση;
pa·ra·ka·*lo* bo·*ri*·te na *ghra*·pse·te ti dhi·*ef*·thin·si
Are there any rooms available?
Υπάρχουν ελεύθερα δωμάτια;
i·*par*·chun e·*lef*·the·ra dho·*ma*·ti·a
I'd like to share a dorm.
Θα ήθελα να μοιράσω ένα κοινό δωμάτιο
με άλλα άτομα
tha *i*·the·la na mi·*ra*·so e·na ki·*no* dho·*ma*·ti·o
me *al*·la *a*·to·ma

How much is it ...? Πόσο κάνει ...; *po*·so *ka*·ni ...
per night τη βραδυά ti ·vra·*dhya*
per person το άτομο to *a*·to·mo

May I see it?
Μπορώ να το δω; bo·*ro* na to dho
Where's the bathroom?
Πού είναι το μπάνιο; pou *i*·ne to *ba*·ni·o
I'm/We're leaving today.
Φεύγω/φεύγουμε *fev*·gho/*fev*·ghou·me
σήμερα *si*·me·ra

CONVERSATION & ESSENTIALS
Hello.
Γειά σας. *ya*·sas (pol)
Γειά σου. *ya*·su (inf)
Good morning.
Καλημέρα. ka·li·*me*·ra
Good afternoon/evening.
Καλησπέρα. ka·li·*spe*·ra
Good night.
Καληνύχτα. ka·li·*nikh*·ta
Goodbye.
Αντίο. an·*di*·o
Yes.
Ναι. ne
No.
Όχι. *o*·hi
Please.
Παρακαλώ. pa·ra·ka·*lo*
Thank you.
Ευχαριστώ. ef·ha·ri·*sto*
That's fine./You're welcome.
Παρακαλώ. pa·ra·ka·*lo*
Sorry. (excuse me, forgive me)
Συγγνώμη. sigh·*no*·mi
What's your name?
Πώς σας λένε; pos sas *le*·ne
My name is ...
Με λένε ... me *le*·ne ...

Where are you from?
Από πού είστε; a·*po* pou *i*·ste
I'm from ...
Είμαι από ... *i*·me a·*po* ...
I (don't) like ...
(Δεν) μ' αρέσει ... (dhen) ma·*re*·si ...
Just a minute.
Μισό λεπτό. mi·*so* lep·*to*

DIRECTIONS
Where is ...?
Πού είναι ...; pou *i*·ne ...
Straight ahead.
Όλο ευθεία. *o*·lo ef·*thi*·a
Turn left.
Στρίψτε αριστερά. *strips*·te a·ri·ste·*ra*
Turn right.
Στρίψτε δεξιά. *strips*·te dhe·*ksia*
at the next corner
στην επόμενη γωνία stin e·*po*·me·ni gho·*ni*·a
at the traffic lights
στα φώτα sta *fo*·ta

behind	πίσω	*pi*·so
in front of	μπροστά	bro·*sta*
far/near (to)	μακριά/κοντά	ma·kri·*a*/kon·*da*
opposite	απέναντι	a·*pe*·nan·di

acropolis	ακρόπολη	a·*kro*·po·li
beach	παραλία	pa·ra·*li*·a
bridge	γέφυρα	*ye*·fi·ra
castle	κάστρο	*ka*·stro
island	νησί	ni·*si*
market	αγορά	a·gho·*ra*
museum	μουσείο	mu·*si*·o
old quarter	παλιά πόλη	pa·li·*a po*·li
ruins	αρχαία	ar·*he*·a
sea	θάλασσα	*tha*·las·sa
square	πλατεία	pla·*ti*·a
temple	ναός	na·*os*

SIGNS	
ΕΙΣΟΔΟΣ	Entry
ΕΞΟΔΟΣ	Exit
ΠΛΗΡΟΦΟΡΙΕΣ	Information
ΑΝΟΙΧΤΟ	Open
ΚΛΕΙΣΤΟ	Closed
ΑΠΑΓΟΡΕΥΕΤΑΙ	Prohibited
ΑΣΤΥΝΟΜΙΑ	Police
ΑΣΤΥΝΟΜΙΚΟΣ ΣΤΑΘΜΟΣ	Police Station
ΓΥΝΑΙΚΩΝ	Toilets (women)
ΑΝΔΡΩΝ	Toilets (men)

LANGUAGE

THE GREEK ALPHABET & PRONUNCIATION

Greek	Pronunciation Guide		Example		
Α α	a	as in 'father'	αγάπη	a·*gha*·pi	love
Β β	v	as in 'vine'	βήμα	*vi*·ma	step
Γ γ	gh	a softer, guttural 'g'	γάτα	*gha*·ta	cat
	y	as in 'yes'	για	ya	for
Δ δ	dh	as in 'there'	δέμα	*dhe*·ma	parcel
Ε ε	e	as in 'egg'	ένας	*e*·nas	one
Ζ ζ	z	as in 'zoo'	ζώο	*zo*·o	animal
Η η	i	as in 'feet'	ήταν	*i*·tan	was
Θ θ	th	as in 'throw'	θέμα	*the*·ma	theme
Ι ι	i	as in 'feet'	ίδιος	*i*·dhyos	same
Κ κ	k	as in 'kite'	καλά	ka·*la*	well
Λ λ	l	as in 'leg'	λάθος	*la*·thos	mistake
Μ μ	m	as in 'man'	μαμά	ma·*ma*	mother
Ν ν	n	as in 'net'	νερό	ne·*ro*	water
Ξ ξ	x	as in 'ox'	ξύδι	*xi*·dhi	vinegar
Ο ο	o	as in 'hot'	όλα	*o*·la	all
Π π	p	as in 'pup'	πάω	*pa*·o	I go
Ρ ρ	r	as in 'road', slightly trilled	ρέμα	*re*·ma	stream
			ρόδα	*ro*·dha	tyre
Σ σ, ς	s	as in 'sand'	σημάδι	si·*ma*·dhi	mark
Τ τ	t	as in 'tap'	τόπος	*to*·pos	site
Υ υ	i	as in 'feet'	ύστερα	*is*·te·ra	later
Φ φ	f	as in 'find'	φύλλο	*fi*·lo	leaf
Χ χ	kh	as the 'ch' in Scottish 'loch', or	χάνω	*kha*·no	I lose
	h	like a rough 'h'	χέρι	*hye*·ri	hand
Ψ ψ	ps	as in 'lapse'	ψωμί	pso·*mi*	bread
Ω ω	o	as in 'hot'	ώρα	*o*·ra	time

Combinations of Letters

The combinations of letters shown here are pronounced as follows:

Greek	Pronunciation Guide		Example		
ει	i	as in 'feet'	είδα	*i*·dha	I saw
οι	i	as in 'feet'	οικόπεδο	i·*ko*·pe·dho	land
αι	e	as in 'bet'	αίμα	*e*·ma	blood
ου	u	as in 'mood'	πού	pou	who/what/where
μπ	b	as in 'beer'	μπάλα	*ba*·la	ball
	mb	as in 'amber'	κάμπος	*kam*·bos	forest
ντ	d	as in 'dot'	ντουλάπα	dou·*la*·pa	wardrobe
	nd	as in 'bend'	πέντε	*pen*·de	five
γκ	g	as in 'green'	γκάζι	*ga*·zi	gas
γγ	ng	as in 'angle'	αγγελία	an·ge·*li*·a	announcement
γξ	ks	as in 'minks'	σφιγξ	sfinks	sphynx
τζ	dz	as in 'hands'	τζάκι	*dza*·ki	fireplace

The pairs of vowels shown above are pronounced separately if the first has an acute accent, or the second a dieresis (¨), as in the examples below:

Κάιρο	*kai*·ro	Cairo
γαϊδουράκι	gai·dhou·*ra*·ki	little donkey

Some Greek consonant sounds have no English equivalent. The υ of the groups αυ, ευ and ηυ is generally pronounced 'v'. The Greek question mark is represented with the English equivalent of a semicolon (;).

TRANSLITERATION & VARIANT SPELLINGS: AN EXPLANATION

The issue of correctly transliterating Greek into the Roman alphabet is a vexed one, fraught with inconsistencies and pitfalls. The Greeks themselves are not very consistent in this respect, though things are gradually improving. The word 'Piraeus', for example, has been variously represented by the following transliterations: *Pireas*, *Piraievs* and *Pireefs*; and when appearing as a street name (eg Piraeus St) you will also find *Pireos*!

This has been compounded by the linguistic minefield of the two forms of the Greek language. The purist form is called *Katharevousa* and the popular form is *Dimotiki* (Demotic). The *Katharevousa* form was never more than an artificiality and *Dimotiki* has always been spoken as the mainstream language, but this means there are often two Greek words for each English word. Thus, the word for 'bakery' in everyday language is *fournos*, but the shop sign will more often than not say *artopoieion*. The baker's product will be known in the street as *psomi*, but in church as *artos*.

A further complication is the issue of Anglicised vs Hellenised forms of place names: Athens vs Athina, Patra vs Patras, Thebes vs Thiva, Evia vs Euboia – the list goes on and on. The existence of both an official and everyday name for a place you see variations such as Corfu/Kerkyra, Zakynthos/Zante, and Santorini/Thira. In this guide we usually provide modern Greek equivalents for town names, with one well-known exception, Athens. For ancient sites, settlements or people from antiquity, we have tried to stick to the more familiar classical names; so we have Thucydides instead of Thoukididis, Mycenae instead of Mykines.

Problems in transliteration have particular implications for vowels, especially given that Greek has six ways of rendering the vowel sound 'ee', two ways of rendering the 'o' sound and two ways of rendering the 'e' sound. In most instances in this book, **y** has been used for the 'ee' sound when a Greek *upsilon* (υ, Υ) has been used, and **i** for Greek *ita* (η, Η) and *iota* (ι, Ι). In the case of the Greek vowel combinations that make the 'ee' sound, that is οι, ει and υι, an **i** has been used. For the two Greek 'e' sounds αι and ε, an **e** has been employed.

As far as consonants are concerned, the Greek letter *gamma* (γ, Γ) usually appears as **g** rather than **y** throughout this book. For example, *agios* (Greek for male saint) is used rather than *ayios*, and *agia* (female saint) rather than *ayia*. The letter *fi* (φ, Φ) can be transliterated as either **f** or **ph**. Here, a general rule of thumb is that classical names are spelt with a **ph** and modern names with an **f**. So Phaistos is used rather than Festos, and Folegandros is used rather than Pholegandros. The Greek *chi* (χ, Χ) has usually been represented as **h** in order to approximate the Greek pronunciation as closely as possible. Thus, we have Hania instead of Chania and Polytehniou instead of Polytechniou. Bear in mind that the **h** is to be pronounced as an aspirated 'h', much like the 'ch' in 'loch'. The letter *kapa* (κ, Κ) has been used to represent that sound, except where well-known names from antiquity have adopted by convention the letter **c**, eg Polycrates, Acropolis.

Wherever reference to a street name is made, we have omitted the Greek word *odos*, but words for avenue (*leoforos*, abbreviated *leof* on maps) and square (*plateia*) have been included.

EATING OUT

For more on food and drink, see p65.

I want to make a reservation for this evening.
Θέλω να κλείσω ένα τραπέζι για απόψε.
the·lo na kli·so e·na tra·pe·zi ya a·po·pse

A table for... please.
Ένα τραπέζι για... παρακαλώ.
e·na tra·pe·zi ya ... pa·ra·ka·lo

I'd like the menu, please.
Το μενού, παρακαλώ.
to me·nu, pa·ra·ka·lo

Do you have a menu in English?
Έχετε το μενού στα αγγλικά;
e·hye·te to me·nu sta ang·li·ka

I'd like ...
Θα ήθελα ...   *tha i·the·la ...*

Please bring the bill.
Το λογαριασμό, παρακαλώ.
to lo·ghar·ya·zmo pa·ra·ka·lo

I'm a vegetarian.
Είμαι χορτοφάγος.
i·me hor·to·fa·ghos

I don't eat meat or dairy products.
Δε τρώω κρέας ή γαλακτοκομικά προϊόντα.
dhen tro·o kre·as i gha·la·kto·ko·mi·ka pro·i·on·da

HEALTH

I'm ill.   Είμαι άρρωστος.   *i·me a·ro·stos*
It hurts here.   Πονάει εδώ.   *po·na·i e·dho*

EMERGENCIES

Help!
Βοήθεια!   vo·*i*·thya
There's been an accident.
Εγινε ατύχημα.   ey·i·ne a·*ti*·hi·ma
Go away!
Φύγε!   *fi*·ye

Call ...!   Φωνάξτε ...!   fo·*nak*·ste ...
  a doctor   ένα γιατρό   e·na yi·a·*tro*
  the police   την αστυνομία   tin a·sti·no·*mi*·a

I have ...
Εχω ...   e·ho ...
  asthma
  άσθμα   *asth*·ma
  diabetes
  ζαχαροδιαβήτη   za·ha·ro·dhi·a·*vi*·ti
  diarrhoea
  διάρροια   dhi·*a*·ri·a
  epilepsy
  επιληψία   e·pi·lip·*si*·a

I'm allergic to ...
Είμαι αλλεργικός/   *i*·me a·ler·yi·*kos*/
αλλεργική ...   a·ler·yi·*ki* ... (m/f)
  antibiotics
  στα αντιβιωτικά   sta an·di·vi·o·ti·*ka*
  aspirin
  στην ασπιρίνη   stin a·spi·*ri*·ni
  penicillin
  στην πενικιλλίνη   stin pe·ni·ki·*li*·ni
  bees
  στις μέλισσες   stis *me*·li·ses
  nuts
  στα φυστίκια   sta fi·*sti*·ki·a

contraceptive	προφυλακτικό	pro·fi·lak·ti·*ko*
medicine	φάρμακο	*farm*·a·ko
sunblock cream	κρέμα ηλίου	*kre*·ma i·*li*·u
tampons	ταμπόν	tam·*bon*

LANGUAGE DIFFICULTIES

Do you speak English?
Μιλάτε αγγλικά;   mi·*la*·te an·gli·*ka*
Does anyone speak English?
Μιλάει κανείς αγγλικά;   mi·*lai* ka·*nis* an·gli·*ka*
How do you say ... in Greek?
Πώς λέγεται ... στα   pos *le*·ghe·te ... sta
ελληνικά;   el·li·ni·*ka*
I understand.
Καταλαβαίνω.   ka·ta·la·*ve*·no

I don't understand.
Δεν καταλαβαίνω.   dhen ka·ta·la·*ve*·no
Please write it down.
Γράψτε το, παρακαλώ.   *ghrap*·ste to pa·ra·ka·*lo*
Can you show me on the map?
Μπορείτε να μου το   bo·*ri*·te na mou to
δείξετε στο χάρτη;   *dhi*·xe·te sto *har*·ti

NUMBERS

0	μηδέν	mi·*dhen*
1	ένας (m)	e·nas
	μία (f)	*mi*·a
	ένα (n)	e·na
2	δύο	*dhi*·o
3	τρεις (m&f)	tris
	τρία (n)	*tri*·a
4	τέσσερεις (m&f)	te·se·ris
	τέσσερα (n)	*te*·se·ra
5	πέντε	*pen*·de
6	έξη	e·xi
7	επτά	ep·*ta*
8	οχτώ	oh·*to*
9	εννέα	e·*ne*·a
10	δέκα	*dhe*·ka
20	είκοσι	*ik*·o·si
30	τριάντα	tri·*an*·da
40	σαράντα	sa·*ran*·da
50	πενήντα	pe·*nin*·da
60	εξήντα	e·*xin*·da
70	εβδομήντα	ev·dho·*min*·da
80	ογδόντα	ogh·*dhon*·da
90	ενενήντα	e·ne·*nin*·da
100	εκατό	e·ka·*to*
1000	χίλιοι (m)	*hi*·li·i
	χίλιες (f)	*hi*·li·ez
	χίλια (n)	*hi*·li·a
2000	δυό χιλιάδες	dhi·*o* hi·*li*·a·dhez

PAPERWORK

name
  ονοματεπώνυμο   o·no·ma·te·*po*·ni·mo
nationality
  υπηκοότητα   i·pi·ko·*o*·ti·ta
date of birth
  ημερομηνία   i·me·ro·mi·*ni*·a
  γεννήσεως   yen·*ni*·se·os
place of birth
  τόπος γεννήσεως   *to*·pos yen·*ni*·se·os
sex (gender)
  φύλον   *fi*·lon
passport
  διαβατήριο   dhia·va·*ti*·ri·o
visa
  βίζα   *vi*·za

QUESTION WORDS

Who/Which?

| Ποιος/Ποια/Ποιο; | pi·os/pi·a/pi·o (sg m/f/n) |
| Ποιοι/Ποιες/Ποια; | pi·i/pi·es/pi·a (pl m/f/n) |

Who's there?

Ποιος είναι εκεί; pi·os i·ne e·ki

Which street is this?

Ποια οδός είναι αυτή; pi·a o·dhos i·ne af·ti

What?

Τι; ti

What's this?

Τι είναι αυτό; ti i·ne af·to

Where?

Πού; pu

When?

Πότε; po·te

Why?

Γιατί; yi·a·ti

How?

Πώς; pos

How much?

Πόσο; po·so

How much does it cost?

Πόσο κάνει; po·so ka·ni

SHOPPING & SERVICES

I'd like to buy ...

Θέλω ν' αγοράσω ... the·lo na·gho·ra·so ...

How much is it?

Πόσο κάνει; po·so ka·ni

I don't like it.

Δεν μου αρέσει. dhen mu a·re·si

May I see it?

Μπορώ να το δω; bo·ro na to dho

I'm just looking.

Απλώς κοιτάζω. ap·los ki·ta·zo

It's cheap.

Είναι φτηνό. i·ne fti·no

It's too expensive.

Είναι πολύ ακριβό. i·ne po·li a·kri·vo

I'll take it.

Θα το πάρω. tha to pa·ro

Do you accept ...?	Δέχεστε ...;	dhe·he·ste ...
credit cards	πιστωτική κάρτα	pi·sto·ti·ki kar·ta
travellers cheques	ταξιδιωτικές επιταγές	tak·si·dhi·o·ti·kes e·pi·ta·ghes
more	περισσότερο	pe·ri·so·te·ro
less	λιγότερο	li·gho·te·ro
smaller	μικρότερο	mi·kro·te·ro
bigger	μεγαλύτερο	me·gha·li·te·ro

I'm looking for ...	Ψάχνω για ...	psach·no ya ...
an ATM	μια αυτόματη μηχανή	mya af·to·ma·ti mi·kha·ni
a bank	μια τράπεζα	mya tra·pe·za
the church	την εκκλησία	tin ek·kli·si·a
the city centre	το κέντρο της πόλης	to ken·dro tis po·lis
the ...	την ...	tin ...
embassy	πρεσβεία	pres·vi·a
a local internet cafe	το τοπικό καφενείο με διαδίκτυο;	to to·pi·ko ka·fe·ni·o me thi·a·thik·ti·o
the market	τη λαϊκή αγορά	ti lai·ki a·gho·ra
the museum	το μουσείο	to mu·si·o
the post office	το ταχυδρομείο	to ta·hi·dhro·mi·o
a public toilet	μια δημόσια τουαλέττα	mya dhi·mo·sia tu·a·let·ta
the tourist office	το τουριστικό γραφείο	to tu·ri·sti·ko ghra·fi·o

TIME & DATES

| **What time is it?** | Τι ώρα είναι; | ti o·ra i·ne |
| **It's (2 o'clock).** | είναι (δύο η ώρα). | i·ne (dhi·o i o·ra) |

When?	Πότε;	po·te
in the morning	το πρωί	to pro·i
in the afternoon	το απόγευμα	to a·po·yev·ma
in the evening	το βράδυ	to vra·dhi
today	σήμερα	si·me·ra
tomorrow	αύριο	av·ri·o
yesterday	χθες	hthes

Monday	Δευτέρα	dhef·te·ra
Tuesday	Τρίτη	tri·ti
Wednesday	Τετάρτη	te·tar·ti
Thursday	Πέμπτη	pemp·ti
Friday	Παρασκευή	pa·ras·ke·vi
Saturday	Σάββατο	sa·va·to
Sunday	Κυριακή	ky·ri·a·ki

January	Ιανουάριος	ia·nou·ar·i·os
February	Φεβρουάριος	fev·rou·ar·i·os
March	Μάρτιος	mar·ti·os
April	Απρίλιοςα	a·pri·li·os
May	Μάιος	mai·os
June	Ιούνιος	i·ou·ni·os
July	Ιούλιος	i·ou·li·os
August	Αύγουστος	av·ghous·tos
September	Σεπτέμβριος	sep·tem·vri·os
October	Οκτώβριος	ok·to·vri·os
November	Νοέμβριος	no·em·vri·os
December	Δεκέμβριος	dhe·kem·vri·os

TRANSPORT
Public Transport

What time does the ... leave/ arrive?	Τι ώρα φεύγει/ φτάνει το ...;	ti o·ra fev·yi/ fta·ni to ...
boat	πλοίο	pli·o
(city) bus	αστικό	a·sti·ko
(intercity) bus	λεωφορείο	le·o·fo·ri·o
plane	αεροπλάνο	ae·ro·pla·no
train	τραίνο	tre·no

I'd like (a) ...	Θα ήθελα (ένα) ...	tha i·the·la (e·na) ...
one-way ticket	απλό εισιτήριο	a·plo i·si·ti·ri·o
return ticket	εισιτήριο με επιστροφή	i·si·ti·ri·o me e·pi·stro·fi
1st class	πρώτη θέση	pro·ti the·si
2nd class	δεύτερη θέση	def·te·ri the·si

I want to go to ...
Θέλω να πάω στο/στη ...
the·lo na pao sto/sti ...

The train has been cancelled/delayed.
Το τραίνο ακυρώθηκε/καθυστέρησε
to tre·no a·ki·ro·thi·ke/ka·thi·ste·ri·se

the first
το πρώτο   to pro·to
the last
το τελευταίο   to te·lef·te·o
platform number
αριθμός αποβάθρας   a·rith·mos a·po·va·thras
ticket office
εκδοτήριο εισιτηρίων   ek·dho·ti·ri·o i·si·ti·ri·on
timetable
δρομολόγιο   dhro·mo·lo·gio
train station
σιδηροδρομικός   si·dhi·ro·dhro·mi·kos
σταθμός   stath·mos

Private Transport

I'd like to hire a ...	Θα ήθελα να νοικιάσω ...	tha i·the·la na ni·ki·a·so ...
car	ένα αυτοκίνητο	e·na af·to·ki·ni·to
4WD	ένα τέσσερα επί τέσσερα	e·na tes·se·ra e·pi tes·se·ra
(a jeep)	(ένα τζιπ)	(e·na tzip)
motorbike	μια μοτοσυκλέττα	mya mo·to·si·klet·ta
bicycle	ένα ποδήλατο	e·na po·dhi·la·to

Is this the road to ...?
Αυτός είναι ο δρόμος για ...
af·tos i·ne o dhro·mos ya ...

Where's the next service station?
Πού είναι το επόμενο βενζινάδικο;
pu i·ne to e·po·me·no ven·zi·na·dhi·ko
Please fill it up.
Γεμίστε το, παρακαλώ.
ye·mi·ste to pa·ra·ka·lo
I'd like (30) euros worth.
Θα ήθελα (30) ευρώ.
tha i·the·la (tri·an·da) ev·ro

diesel	πετρέλαιο κίνησης	pet·re·le·o ki·ni·sis
leaded petrol	σούπερ	su·per
unleaded petrol	αμόλυβδη	a·mo·liv·dhi

Can I park here?
Μπορώ να παρκάρω εδώ;
bo·ro na par·ka·ro e·dho
Where do I pay?
Πού πληρώνω;
pu pli·ro·no

The car/motorbike has broken down (at ...)
Το αυτοκίνητο/η μοτοσυκλέττα χάλασε στο ...
to af·to·ki·ni·to/i mo·to·si·klet·ta kha·la·se sto ...
The car/motorbike won't start.
Το αυτοκίνητο/η μοτοσυκλέττα δεν παίρνει μπρος.
to af·to·ki·ni·to/i mo·to·si·klet·ta dhen per·ni· bros
I have a flat tyre.
Έπαθα λάστιχο.
e·pa·tha la·sti·cho
I've run out of petrol.
Έμεινα από βενζίνη.
e·mi·na a·po ven·zi·ni
I've had an accident.
Έπαθα ατύχημα.
e·pa·tha a·ti·chi·ma

TRAVEL WITH CHILDREN
Are children allowed?
Επιτρέπονται τα παιδιά;
e·pi·tre·pon·de ta pe·dhya

Do you mind if I breastfeed here?
  Μπορώ να θηλάσω εδώ;
  bo·ro na thi·la·so e·dho

Is there a/an ...? Υπάρχει ...;   i·par·chi ...
I need a/an ...   Χρειάζομαι ...   chri·a·zo·me ...
  baby change   μέρος ν' αλλάξω   me·ros na·lak·so
    room   το μωρό   to mo·ro
  car baby seat   κάθισμα για   ka·this·ma ya
                       μωρό   mo·ro

children's menu	μενού για παιδία	me·nu ya pe·dhya
(disposable)	πάννες Pampers	pan·nez pam·pers
nappies/diapers		
(English-	μπέιμπι σίττερ	ba·bi sit·ter
speaking)	(που μιλά	(pu mi·la
babysitter	αγγλικά)	an·ghli·ka)
highchair	παιδική καρέκλα	pe·dhi·ki ka·rek·la
potty	γιογιό	yo·yo
stroller	καροτσάκι	ka·ro·tsa·ki

Also available from Lonely Planet:
Greek Phrasebook

LANGUAGE

Glossary

For culinary terms see the Food Glossary (p65), and also see Where to Eat & Drink (p58).

Achaean civilisation – see *Mycenaean civilisation*
acropolis – citadel; highest point of an ancient city
agia (f), agios (m) – saint
agora – commercial area of an ancient city; shopping precinct in modern Greece
Archaic period – also known as the *Middle Age* (800-480 BC); period in which the city-states emerged from the *'dark age'* and traded their way to wealth and power; the city-states were unified by a Greek alphabet and common cultural pursuits, engendering a sense of national identity
arhon – leading citizen of a town, often a wealthy bourgeois merchant; chief magistrate
arhontika – 17th- and 18th-century AD mansions, which belonged to *arhons*
askitiria – mini-chapels or hermitages; places of solitary worship

baglamas – small stringed instrument like a mini bouzouki
basilica – early Christian church
bouleuterion – council house
bouzouki – long-necked, stringed lutelike instrument associated with *rembetika* music
bouzoukia – any nightclub where the *bouzouki* is played and low-grade blues songs are sung
Byzantine Empire – characterised by the merging of Hellenistic culture and Christianity and named after Byzantium, the city on the Bosphorus that became the capital of the Roman Empire; when the Roman Empire was formally divided in AD 395, Rome went into decline and the eastern capital, renamed Constantinople, flourished; the Byzantine Empire (324 BC-AD 1453) dissolved after the fall of Constantinople to the Turks in 1453

caïque – small, sturdy fishing boat often used to carry passengers
Classical period – era in which the city-states reached the height of their wealth and power after the defeat of the Persians in the 5th century BC; the Classical period (480-323 BC) ended with the decline of the city-states as a result of the Peloponnesian Wars, and the expansionist aspirations of Philip II, King of Macedon (r 359-336 BC), and his son, Alexander the Great (r 336-323 BC)
Corinthian – order of Greek architecture recognisable by columns with bell-shaped capitals that have sculpted, elaborate ornaments based on acanthus leaves; see also *Doric* and *Ionic*

Cycladic civilisation – the civilisation (3000-1100 BC) that emerged following the settlement of Phoenician colonists on the Cycladic islands
cyclops (s), cyclopes (pl) – mythical one-eyed giants

dark age – period (1200-800 BC) in which Greece was under *Dorian* rule
domatio (s), domatia (pl) – room, usually in a private home; cheap accommodation option
Dorians – Hellenic warriors who invaded Greece around 1200 BC, demolishing the city-states and destroying the *Mycenaean civilisation;* heralded Greece's *'dark age'*, when the artistic and cultural advancements of the *Mycenaean* and the *Minoan civilisations* were abandoned; the Dorians later developed into land-holding aristocrats which encouraged the resurgence of independent city-states led by wealthy aristocrats
Doric – order of Greek architecture characterised by a column that has no base, a fluted shaft and a relatively plain capital, when compared with the flourishes evident on *Ionic* and *Corinthian* capitals

Ellada or Ellas – see *Hellas*
ELTA – Ellinika Tahydromia; the Greek post office organisation
EOT – Ellinikos Organismos Tourismou; main tourist office (has offices in most major towns), known abroad as *GNTO*

Filiki Eteria – Friendly Society; a group of Greeks in exile; formed during Ottoman rule to organise an uprising against the Turks
filoxenia – hospitality
frourio – fortress; sometimes also referred to as a *kastro*

Geometric period – period (1200-800 BC) characterised by pottery decorated with geometric designs; sometimes referred to as Greece's *'dark age'*
GNTO – Greek National Tourist Organisation; see also *EOT*

Hellas – the Greek name for Greece; also known as *Ellada* or *Ellas*
Hellenistic period – prosperous, influential period (323-146 BC) of Greek civilisation ushered in by Alexander the Great's empire and lasting until the Roman sacking of Corinth in 146 BC
hora – main town (usually on an island)
horio – village

IC – intercity (sometimes express) train service

Ionic – order of Greek architecture characterised by a column with truncated flutes and capitals with ornaments resembling scrolls; see also *Doric* and *Corinthian*

kastro – walled-in town; also describes a fort or castle
katholikon – principal church of a monastic complex
kore – female statue of the *Archaic period*; see also *kouros*
kouros – male statue of the *Archaic period,* characterised by a stiff body posture and enigmatic smile; see also *kore*
KTEL – Koino Tamio Eispraxeon Leoforion; national bus cooperative; runs all long-distance bus services

laïka – literally 'popular (songs)'; mainstream songs that have either been around for years or are of recent origin; also referred to as urban folk music
leoforos – avenue; commonly shortened to 'leof'
limenarhio – port police

meltemi – northeasterly wind that blows throughout much of Greece during the summer
Middle Age – see *Archaic period*
Minoan civilisation – Bronze Age (3000-1100 BC) culture of Crete named after the mythical King Minos, and characterised by pottery and metalwork of great beauty and artisanship
moni – monastery or convent
Mycenaean civilisation – the first great civilisation (1600-1100 BC) of the Greek mainland, characterised by powerful independent city-states ruled by kings; also known as the *Achaean civilisation*

nisi – island

odos – street
OSE – Organismos Sidirodromon Ellados; Greek railways organisation
OTE – Organismos Tilepikoinonion Ellados; Greece's major telecommunications carrier

Panagia – Mother of God or Virgin Mary; name frequently used for churches
panigyri (s), panigyria (p) – festival; the most common festivals celebrate annual saints' days
Pantokrator – painting or mosaic of Christ in the centre of the dome of a Byzantine church
periptero (s), periptera (pl) – street kiosk
plateia – square

rembetika – blues songs commonly associated with the underworld of the 1920s

Sarakatsani – Greek-speaking nomadic shepherd community from northern Greece
stele (s), stelae (pl) – upright stone (or pillar) decorated with inscriptions or figures
stoa – long colonnaded building, usually in an *agora;* used as a meeting place and shelter in ancient Greece

tholos – Mycenaean tomb shaped like a beehive

Vlach – traditional, seminomadic shepherds from Northern Greece who speak a Latin-based dialect

The Authors

KORINA MILLER   Coordinating Author, Dodecanese, Island Hopping

Korina first ventured to Greece as a backpacking teenager, sleeping on ferry decks and hiking in the mountains. She has since found herself drawn back to soak up the dazzling Greek sunshine, lounge on the beaches and consume vast quantities of Greek salad and strong coffee. Korina grew up on Vancouver Island and has been exploring the globe since she was 16, working, studying and travelling in 36 countries en route. She now resides in England's Sussex countryside while she plots her next adventure. Korina has been writing travel guides for Lonely Planet for the past decade with 15 titles under her belt. Korina also wrote the Destination Greek Islands, Getting Started, Events Calendar, Itineraries, Environment, Greek Islands Outdoors, Directory, Transport, Health and Glossary chapters.

MICHAEL STAMATIOS CLARK   Evia & the Sporades

Michael's Greek roots go back to the village of Karavostamo on the Aegean island of Ikaria, home of his maternal grandparents. He was born into a Greek-American community in Cambridge, Ohio, and recently became a Greek citizen. His first trip to Greece was as a deckhand aboard a Greek freighter, trading English lessons for Greek over wine and backgammon. When not travelling to Greece, Michael teaches English to international students in Berkeley, California, listens to Greek *rembetika* (blues) after midnight and searches for new ways to convert friends to the subtle pleasures of retsina.

CHRIS DELISO   Northeastern Aegean Islands, Crete

Chris Deliso was drawing maps of the Aegean by the age of five, and 20 years later he ended up in Greece while labouring away on an MPhil in Byzantine Studies at Oxford. Ever since studying Modern Greek in Thessaloniki in 1998, he has travelled frequently in Greece, including a year in Crete and a long sojourn on Mt Athos. Chris especially enjoyed stumbling upon the unexpected on remote isles like Psara, imbibing heartily in the wineries of Macedonia, gawking at the vultures ripping apart carrion in Thrace, and feasting himself on those incomparable Cretan sweet cheese pies – the *myzithropitakia*.

THE AUTHORS

THE AUTHORS

DES HANNIGAN
Saronic Gulf Islands, Cyclades, Ionian Islands

Des first surfaced (literally) in Greece many years ago in an Aegina harbour, having jumped off a boat into several feet of unexpected water. Ever since, he's been drifting around the country whenever he can, although home is on the edge of the cold Atlantic in beautiful Cornwall, England. In a previous life Des worked at sea, valuable experience for coping with the Greek ferry system. One day he'd really like to hop round the islands in a very fast yacht with all sails set, although he would happily settle for an old caïque with just one sail. Des worked on the previous editions of Lonely Planet's *Greece* and *Greek Islands* and has written guidebooks to Corfu and Rhodes for other publishers.

VICTORIA KYRIAKOPOULOS
The Culture, Food & Drink, Athens & the Mainland Ports

Victoria is a Melbourne-based journalist who morphs effortlessly into an Athenian whenever she hits the motherland. She just clocked up her 269,010th kilometre getting to Greece, has travelled widely around the country and moved there for a while (2000–04), hoping to get it out of her system. Victoria wrote Lonely Planet's first pocket *Athens* guide in 2001, did a stint as editor of *Odyssey* magazine, covered the 2004 Olympics for international media and worked on several television shows about Greece. She returns regularly for research (and pleasure), including the latest *Athens Encounter* and *Crete*. An occasional food critic back home, when not writing or making documentaries, she is working through her extensive Greek cookbook collection.

CONTRIBUTING AUTHOR

Gina Tsarouhas Born in Melbourne with Greek blood flowing through her veins, Gina packed her little suitcase at the tender age of four and took off for Greece. Gina flitted across various continents over the years until she discovered she could travel vicariously as an editor of travel guides, as well. When not editing she's co-authoring and contributing to all things Greek at Lonely Planet, including *Greece* and the *Greek Islands*; or tending to her beloved fig and olive trees in the backyard. Gina worked on the latest edition of *Greece*, and wrote the History chapter for this guidebook.

Behind the Scenes

THIS BOOK

This 6th edition of *Greek Islands* was updated by Korina Miller, Michael Stamatios Clark, Chris Deliso, Des Hannigan, Gina Tsarouhas and Victoria Kyriakopoulos. Paul Hellander, David Willett, Miriam Raphael and Andrew Stone authored previous editions. This guidebook was commissioned in Lonely Planet's London office and produced by the following:

Commissioning Editors Fiona Buchan, Sally Schafer, Joanna Potts

Coordinating Editor Gina Tsarouhas

Coordinating Cartographer Diana Duggan

Coordinating Layout Designer Jim Hsu

Managing Editor Annelies Mertens

Managing Cartographers Adrian Persoglia, Herman So

Managing Layout Designer Sally Darmody

Assisting Editors Janice Bird, Monique Choy, Kate Evans, Paul Harding, Kristin Odijk, Stephanie Pearson, Martine Power, Kirsten Rawlings, Erin Richards, Fionn Twomey

Assisting Cartographers Anita Banh, Ildiko Bogdanovits, Dennis Capparelli, Birgit Jordan, Khanh Luu, Marc Milinkovic, Peter Shields

Assisting Layout Designers Cara Smith, Wendy Wright

Cover Image research provided by lonelyplanetimages.com

Language Content Laura Crawford

Project Manager Eoin Dunlevy

Thanks to Lucy Birchley, Chris Girdler, Mark Griffiths, Laura Jane, Indra Kilfoyle, Rebecca Lalor, Trent Paton

THANKS
KORINA MILLER

A huge thank you to the countless people we met on the road for answering my unending questions and making us – and particularly my daughter – feel so very welcome. Thank you to the following people for their generosity of time and knowledge: Anastasios Pissas at GNTO, London; Mary Thymianou at EOT, Rhodes; Adriana Miska in Rhodes Town; Kalliope Karayianni at Nisyros Town Hall; Fokas Michellis in Skala, Patmos; Stavros, his parents and grandmother in Mandraki, Nisyros; and Thanasis Argyroudis in Krithoni, Leros. At Lonely Planet, a big thanks to Jo Potts and Sally Schafer for their patience and assistance, to Fiona Buchan for giving me the opportunity, and to Michala Green for an insightful brief. Thank you also to Eoin Dunlevy and his production crew and to Herman So in cartography. A big cheer to my co-authors, particularly Victoria Kyriakopoulos and Des Hannigan for their wisdom and support. And finally, love and appreciation to my husband Paul and daughter Simone for keeping up with my schedule on the road and making it a fabulous adventure.

THE LONELY PLANET STORY

Fresh from an epic journey across Europe, Asia and Australia in 1972, Tony and Maureen Wheeler sat at their kitchen table stapling together notes. The first Lonely Planet guidebook, *Across Asia on the Cheap*, was born.

Travellers snapped up the guides. Inspired by their success, the Wheelers began publishing books to Southeast Asia, India and beyond. Demand was prodigious, and the Wheelers expanded the business rapidly to keep up. Over the years, Lonely Planet extended its coverage to every country and into the virtual world via lonelyplanet.com and the Thorn Tree message board.

As Lonely Planet became a globally loved brand, Tony and Maureen received several offers for the company. But it wasn't until 2007 that they found a partner whom they trusted to remain true to the company's principles of travelling widely, treading lightly and giving sustainably. In October of that year, BBC Worldwide acquired a 75% share in the company, pledging to uphold Lonely Planet's commitment to independent travel, trustworthy advice and editorial independence.

Today, Lonely Planet has offices in Melbourne, London and Oakland, with over 500 staff members and 300 authors. Tony and Maureen are still actively involved with Lonely Planet. They're travelling more often than ever, and they're devoting their spare time to charitable projects. And the company is still driven by the philosophy of *Across Asia on the Cheap*: 'All you've got to do is decide to go and the hardest part is over. So go!'

BEHIND THE SCENES

BEHIND THE SCENES

MICHAEL STAMATIOS CLARK

Ευχαριστώ (thank you) to those who made my travels through the Greek Islands so enjoyable, among them: Keyrillos Sinioris and family (Evia); Gisela and Michael Baunach (Skiathos); Heather Parsons (Skopelos); Eirini-Georgia Kampouromyti (Alonnisos); Chrysanthi Zygogianni (Skyros). MJ Keown (Long Beach) was instrumental from the beginning. Kostas and Nana Vatsis provided invaluable help, not to mention drip-free wine. Special thanks to my fellow authors, to Korina Miller and Jo Potts, for putting it all together with grace. And to my splendiferous family – Janet, Melina and Alexander – Greek kisses on both cheeks for all.

CHRIS DELISO

Without the help of many my work would have been much less useful and interesting for the reader. Those whose assistance proved truly indispensable include George, Apostolis, Grigoris, Anastasia, Vassilis and Roula. Others deserving credit include Eri, 'Johnny Dendro' and the Zigouris clan (Epiros); Ilias, Katerina, 'Billas', Stellios Boutaris and Vangelis Gerovassiliou (Macedonia); Anna, Nikos and family (Thasos); Jenny Ballis, the Polytihniou Clinic staff, and the musclemen of Loutra (Lesvos); Vassilis and Dimitra (Ikaria); Don (Chios); Stellios and family, and the Geniko Nosokomeio Samou (Samos); Toula and Manolis (Fourni); and in Crete, Nikos Karellis, Dr Giorgos Nikitas, Kyria Rena and Anna, Yiannis, Costas, Eleftheris, Hristos, Manolis, Nikolas, Giorgos and Chris in Plakias – ya mas! I also should thank my fellow scribes, especially our ever patient coordinating author, Korina Miller, commissioning editor Jo Potts, Sally Schafer, Mark Griffiths and his merry mapmakers, and the hard-working production crew. Finally, I must thank Buba for holding down the fort, and Marco, for giving me the energy and inspiration to keep on truckin' on.

DES HANNIGAN

Warmest thanks and affection to my many friends and acquaintances in Greece who helped and advised me, as always, with characteristic good humour, wit and patience. Greatest thanks to those who know the business best of all; to John van Lerberghe and his staff on Mykonos, Lisos Zilelides on Santorini, Flavio Facciolo on Folegandros and Theresa Pirpinias-Ninou on Milos. Special thanks, as always, to Kostas Karabetsos on Mykonos for the nightlife run. Thanks, also to my fellow authors for entertaining and helpful e-conferences and to Jo Potts at Lonely Planet's London Office

and coordinating author, Korina Miller, for their help and for their stoic patience in holding it all together.

VICTORIA KYRIAKOPOULOS

Sincere thanks to Vicky Valanos for her invaluable assistance and to my dear Athens host and friend, Eleni Bertes. Athens wouldn't be as much fun without Antonis Bekiaris, Maria Zygourakis, Eleni Gialama, Mary Retiniotis and Xenia Orfanos. Thanks also to Giorgos Xylouris, Vicki Theodoropoulou, Tobias Judmaier, Athena Lambrinidou, George Hatzimanolis, Colin Dodd, Maria Rota and Ray Jones. At Lonely Planet, thanks to Sally Schafer and Jo Potts in London; and to patient coordinator Korina Miller and fellow authors for their efforts. Finally to my loving partner Chris Anastassiades for his support and encouragement, and to Rosanna De Marco for always being there.

GINA TSAROUHAS

Thank you to all who provided valuable advice. And a big nod to the Lonely Planet crew, of course, and to my co-authors, for their support. My eternal gratitude to my folks (and grandfolks, too) for inspiring my pride and deep passion for our heritage. Ευχαριστώ to George and Vicki for their love and μάκια (kisses) to Peter, Katerina and

---

SEND US YOUR FEEDBACK

We love to hear from travellers – your comments keep us on our toes and help make our books better. Our well-travelled team reads every word on what you loved or loathed about this book. Although we cannot reply individually to postal submissions, we always guarantee that your feedback goes straight to the appropriate authors, in time for the next edition. Each person who sends us information is thanked in the next edition and the most useful submissions are rewarded with a free book.

To send us your updates – and find out about Lonely Planet events, newsletters and travel news – visit our award-winning website: **lonelyplanet.com/contact**.

Note: we may edit, reproduce and incorporate your comments in Lonely Planet products such as guidebooks, websites and digital products, so let us know if you don't want your comments reproduced or your name acknowledged. For a copy of our privacy policy visit lonelyplanet.com/privacy.

Chris for being too cute. Hugs also to those darling friends and family, who are happy to argue, philosophise and even soliloquise Greek history at the dinner table – always engaging. Finally, my heart sings with thanks to Lisa Baas, for everything (όχι εσύ!).

OUR READERS

Many thanks to the travellers who used the last edition and wrote to us with helpful hints, useful advice and interesting anecdotes:

Martin Andersen, Betsy Arthur, Yannis Assimakopoulos, Kevin Baglow, Dimos Birakos, Tormod Bjørnerud, Hilde Calberson, Elliot Capp, Gilly Carr, Jen Carter, Heather Chaplow, Andriana Chronopoulos, John Connelly, Bill Cook, Anastasia Corellis, Lawrence Court, Elisabeth Cox, John Cox, Line Dalene, Robert Derash, Eydokia Despotidou, Monica Devold, Karen Deyerle, Alain Diette, Lucia Donetti, Helen Ellis, Ruth Emerson, Norman Field, Rita Frumin, Ron Gabb, Heather Gabb, Saki Galaxidis, Stephanie Giannakeas, Sara Gordon, Michael Haluschak, Brendan Haynes, Stephen Hill, Christian Hoffmann, Theresa Hollers, Mustafa Ispir, Gerbert José, Jansen Groothuis, Jos Janssen, Iris Kaeslin Grogg, Jennifer Klein, Gordon Knight, Ira Koenig, Giorgos Koutsogiannopoulos, Michael Leese, Jens Jakob Legarth, Karine Ligneau, Paula Lyons, Olli Makila, Kristin Markay, Anne Matheson, Kate McLoughlin, Fin McNicol, Clare McNicol, Raene Mewburn, Brock Millet, Dennis Mogerman Dylan Nichols, Simos Nikitas, Pelle T Nilsson, Lisa Nolan Meaghan O'Brien, Sharon Pask, Emma Peacocke, Helena Pereira, Sandy Peters, Sundiep Phanse, Megan Philpot, Julie Rand, Kasper Rassmussen, Akis Sartzetakis, Roxane Schury, Colin Scott, Rob Seal, Lloyd Sethill, Penny Smith, Nick Smith, Tom Stockman, Klaas Tjoelker, Antonis Trohalakis, Katrine Voldby, Stuart Watson, Carol Weinrich, Ken West, James Wilkinson, Rita Williams, Sean Windsor, Manuele Zunelli

ACKNOWLEDGMENTS

Many thanks to the following for the use of their content:

Globe on title page ©Mountain High Maps 1993 Digital Wisdom, Inc.

BEHIND THE SCENES

Index

INDEX

INDEX

GREENDEX

The following attractions, accommodation, shops and restaurants have been selected by Lonely Planet authors because they demonstrate a commitment to sustainability. Greece is getting greener by the day – if you find someone we've not included in our GreenDex who should be listed here, email us at http://www.lonelyplanet.com/contact. For more tips about travelling sustainably in Greece, turn to Getting Started (p20) and for further information about sustainable tourism and Lonely Planet, see www.lonelyplanet.com/responsibletravel.

INDEX

556

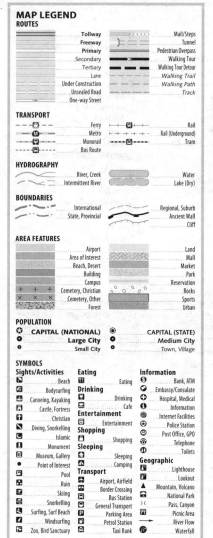

MAP LEGEND
ROUTES
Tollway
Freeway
Primary
Secondary
Tertiary
Lane
Under Construction
Unsealed Road
One-way Street
Mall/Steps
Tunnel
Pedestrian Overpass
Walking Tour
Walking Tour Detour
Walking Trail
Walking Path
Track

TRANSPORT
Ferry
Metro
Monorail
Bus Route
Rail
Rail (Underground)
Tram

HYDROGRAPHY
River, Creek
Intermittent River
Water
Lake (Dry)

BOUNDARIES
International
State, Provincial
Regional, Suburb
Ancient Wall
Cliff

AREA FEATURES
Airport
Area of Interest
Beach, Desert
Building
Campus
Cemetery, Christian
Cemetery, Other
Forest
Land
Mall
Market
Park
Reservation
Rocks
Sports
Urban

POPULATION
CAPITAL (NATIONAL)
Large City
Small City
CAPITAL (STATE)
Medium City
Town, Village

SYMBOLS
Sights/Activities
Beach
Bodysurfing
Canoeing, Kayaking
Castle, Fortress
Christian
Diving, Snorkelling
Islamic
Monument
Museum, Gallery
Point of Interest
Pool
Ruin
Skiing
Snorkelling
Surfing, Surf Beach
Windsurfing
Zoo, Bird Sanctuary

Eating
Eating
Drinking
Drinking
Cafe
Entertainment
Entertainment
Shopping
Shopping
Sleeping
Sleeping
Camping
Transport
Airport, Airfield
Border Crossing
Bus Station
General Transport
Parking Area
Petrol Station
Taxi Rank

Information
Bank, ATM
Embassy/Consulate
Hospital, Medical
Information
Internet Facilities
Police Station
Post Office, GPO
Telephone
Toilets
Geographic
Lighthouse
Lookout
Mountain, Volcano
National Park
Pass, Canyon
Picnic Area
River Flow
Waterfall

LONELY PLANET OFFICES

Australia (Head Office)
Locked Bag 1, Footscray, Victoria 3011
☎ 03 8379 8000, fax 03 8379 8111
talk2us@lonelyplanet.com.au

USA
150 Linden St, Oakland, CA 94607
☎ 510 250 6400, toll free 800 275 8555
fax 510 893 8572
info@lonelyplanet.com

UK
2nd fl, 186 City Rd,
London EC1V 2NT
☎ 020 7106 2100, fax 020 7106 2101
go@lonelyplanet.co.uk

Published by Lonely Planet Publications Pty Ltd
ABN 36 005 607 983

© Lonely Planet 2010

© photographers as indicated 2010

Cover photograph: Oia village, Santorini (Thira), Cyclades, Greece, Marco Simoni/Getty Images. Many of the images in this guide are available for licensing from Lonely Planet Images: lonelyplanetimages.com.

Printed through Colorcraft Ltd, Hong Kong
Printed in China

MIX
Paper from
responsible sources
FSC
www.fsc.org
FSC™ C021741

Although the authors and Lonely Planet have taken all reasonable care in preparing this book, we make no warranty about the accuracy or completeness of its content and, to the maximum extent permitted, disclaim all liability arising from its use.